WX £2.50

SCOTT
POETICAL WORKS

Oxford University Press, Ely House, London W. 1

GLASGOW NEW YORK TORONTO MELBOURNE WELLINGTON
CAPE TOWN SALISBURY IBADAN NAIROBI DAR ES SALAAM LUSAKA ADDIS ABABA
BOMBAY CALCUTTA MADRAS KARACHI LAHORE DACCA
KUALA LUMPUR SINGAPORE HONG KONG TOKYO

SCOTT
POETICAL WORKS

With the
Author's Introduction
and Notes

Edited by
J. Logie Robertson, M.A.

LONDON
OXFORD UNIVERSITY PRESS
NEW YORK   TORONTO

SIR WALTER SCOTT

Born, Edinburgh   .   .   15 August 1771
Died, Abbotsford   .   .   21 September 1832

This edition of Scott's Poetical Works was first published in 1904, and reprinted in 1906, 1908, 1909, 1910, 1913, 1916, 1917, 1921, 1926, 1931, 1940, 1944, 1947, 1951, 1957 1960, 1964, 1967, and 1971

ISBN 0 19 254142 0

PRINTED IN GREAT BRITAIN
O.S.A.

Preface

—◆◆—

THIS Edition of the Poetical Works of Sir Walter Scott is believed to contain every known poem and fragment of verse that
he wrote.

In its preparation the standard text of Lockhart's Editions of
1833 and 1841 has been followed, but not without independent
study of the author's meaning, and not without collation with the
text as recently edited by careful scholars. The result has been
the detection of a few obvious misprints in the longer poems,
such as 'torch' for 'touch,' 'rights' for 'rites,' &c. ; and the
discovery of several mis-references, and a good many omissions
and mistakes of minor but not uninteresting note, in the shorter
pieces, more especially in the poetry from the Waverley Novels.

There is no denying that the mottoes and lyrical fragments of
the Novels are of all Scott's work the most difficult part to edit.
His manner of procedure in supplying his chapters with mottoes
was indeed calculated, if not designed, to puzzle the critical
reader. He had at last the frankness to avow that they were
'sometimes quoted from reading, or from memory, but in the
general case were pure invention.' It was a simple deception
when he attributed those fabrications to 'Old Play' or 'New Play,'
or some anonymous son of the Muses ; but the artifice was bolder
when he advanced to the invention of verse for Dr. Isaac Watts,
and Sir David Lyndsay. Even here his invention did not end :
he found at least a score of titles for non-existent poems from
which he pretended to quote, and there is some suspicion that he
also created a poet or two upon whom to father his fabrications.

But, while the difficulty is allowed, the mistakes and omissions in the authoritative edition of 1841 are so numerous and apparent as to suggest that Lockhart, when he came to deal with that part of his subject, must have abandoned his editorial duties to an underling. For not only are there misprints, and false references to the chapters of the Novels, but lines are included which belong rightfully to Webster, Beaumont and Fletcher, Bunyan, Collins and other well-known writers, and lines are omitted which are undeniably the composition of Scott.

Without claiming for this edition absolute accuracy and completeness, I can only say that it corrects several faults in previous editions, and is as complete and accurate as I have been able to make it.

In elucidation of the text I have added, but only where it seemed necessary, a few brief notes supplementary to those of Scott and Lockhart.

J. LOGIE ROBERTSON.

1904

Contents

—◆—

Contents.

Contents.

The Lay of the Last Minstrel.

THE Poem is intended to illustrate the customs and manners which anciently prevailed on the Borders of England and Scotland. The inhabitants, living in a state partly pastoral and partly warlike, and combining habits of constant depredation with the influence of a rude spirit of chivalry, were often engaged in scenes highly susceptible of poetical ornament. As the description of scenery and manners was more the object of the author than a combined and regular narrative, the plan of the Ancient Metrical Romance was adopted, which allows greater latitude in this respect than would be consistent with the dignity of a regular Poem. The same model offered other facilities, as it permits an occasional alteration of measure, which, in some degree, authorises the change of rhythm in the text. The machinery, also, adopted from popular belief, would have seemed puerile in a poem which did not partake of the rudeness of the old Ballad, or Metrical Romance.

For these reasons the poem was put into the mouth of an ancient Minstrel, the last of the race, who, as he is supposed to have survived the Revolution, might have caught somewhat of the refinement of modern poetry, without losing the simplicity of his original model. The date of the tale itself is about the middle of the sixteenth century, when most of the personages actually flourished. The time occupied by the action is Three Nights and Three Days.

INTRODUCTION.

THE way was long, the wind was cold,
The Minstrel was infirm and old;
His wither'd cheek, and tresses gray,
Seem'd to have known a better day;
The harp, his sole remaining joy,
Was carried by an orphan boy.
The last of all the Bards was he,
Who sung of Border chivalry;
For, welladay! their date was fled,
His tuneful brethren all were dead;
And he, neglected and oppress'd,
Wish'd to be with them, and at rest.
No more on prancing palfrey borne,
He caroll'd, light as lark at morn;
No longer courted and caress'd,
High placed in hall, a welcome guest,
He pour'd to lord and lady gay
The unpremeditated lay:
Old times were changed, old manners
        gone;
A stranger fill'd the Stuarts' throne;

The bigots of the iron time
Had call'd his harmless art a crime.
A wandering Harper, scorn'd and poor,
He begg'd his bread from door to door,
And tuned, to please a peasant's ear,
The harp a king had loved to hear.

He pass'd where Newark's stately
    tower
Looks out from Yarrow's birchen
    bower :
The Minstrel gazed with wishful eye—
No humbler resting-place was nigh ;
With hesitating step at last
The embattled portal arch he pass'd,
Whose ponderous grate and massy bar
Had oft roll'd back the tide of war,
But never closed the iron door
Against the desolate and poor.
The Duchess mark'd his weary pace,
His timid mien, and reverend face,
And bade her page the menials tell
That they should tend the old man
    well :
For she had known adversity,
Though born in such a high degree ;
In pride of power, in beauty's bloom,
Had wept o'er Monmouth's bloody
    tomb !

When kindness had his wants sup-
    plied,
And the old man was gratified,
Began to rise his minstrel pride .
And he began to talk anon
Of good Earl Francis, dead and gone,
And of Earl Walter, rest him, God !
A braver ne'er to battle rode ;
And how full many a tale he knew
Of the old warriors of Buccleuch :
And, would the noble Duchess deign
To listen to an old man's strain,
Though stiff his hand, his voice though
    weak,
He thought even yet, the sooth to
    speak,
That, if she loved the harp to hear,
He could make music to her ear.

The humble boon was soon obtain'd;
The aged Minstrel audience gain'd.
But, when he reach'd the room of
    state,
Where she with all her ladies sate,
Perchance he wish'd his boon denied :
For, when to tune his harp he tried,
His trembling hand had lost the ease,
Which marks security to please ;
And scenes long past, of joy and pain,
Came wildering o'er his aged brain—
He tried to tune his harp in vain !
The pitying Duchess prais'd its
    chime,
And gave him heart, and gave him
    time,
Till every string's according glee
Was blended into harmony.
And then, he said, he would full fain
He could recall an ancient strain
He never thought to sing again.
It was not framed for village churls,
But for high dames and mighty earls;
He had play'd it to King Charles the
    Good,
When he kept court in Holyrood ;
And much he wish'd, yet fear'd, to try
The long-forgotten melody.
Amid the strings his fingers stray'd,
And an uncertain warbling made,
And oft he shook his hoary head.
But when he caught the measure
    wild,
The old man rais'd his face, and
    smil'd ;
And lighten'd up his faded eye
With all a poet's ecstasy.
In varying cadence, soft or strong,
He swept the sounding chords along :
The present scene, the future lot,
His toils, his wants, were all forgot ;
Cold diffidence, and age's frost,
In the full tide of song were lost ;
Each blank, in faithless memory void,
The poet's glowing thought supplied ;
And, while his harp responsive rung,
'Twas thus the LATEST MINSTREL sung.

Canto First.

I.

THE feast was over in Branksome
  tower,
And the Ladye had gone to her secret
  bower;
Her bower that was guarded by word
  and by spell,
Deadly to hear, and deadly to tell—
Jesu Maria, shield us well!
No living wight, save the Ladye alone,
Had dared to cross the threshold
  stone.

II.

The tables were drawn, it was idlesse
  all;
  Knight, and page, and household
    squire,
Loiter'd through the lofty hall,
  Or crowded round the ample fire:
The stag-hounds, weary with the
  chase,
  Lay stretch'd upon the rushy floor,
And urg'd, in dreams, the forest race
  From Teviot-stone to Eskdale-moor.

III.

Nine and-twenty knights of fame
  Hung their shields in Branksome
    hall;
Nine-and-twenty squires of name
  Brought them their steeds to bower
    from stall;
  Nine-and-twenty yeomen tall
  Waited, duteous, on them all:
  They were all knights of mettle
    true,
  Kinsmen to the bold Buccleuch.

IV.

Ten of them were sheath'd in steel,
With belted sword, and spur on heel:
They quitted not their harness bright,
Neither by day, nor yet by night:
  They lay down to rest,
  With corslet laced,
Pillow'd on buckler cold and hard;
  They carv'd at the meal
  With gloves of steel,
And they drank the red wine through
  the helmet barr'd.

V.

Ten squires, ten yeomen, mail-clad
  men,
Waited the beck of the warders ten:
Thirty steeds, both fleet and wight,
Stood saddled in stable day and night,
Barb'd with frontlet of steel, I trow,
And with Jedwood-axe at saddlebow;
A hundred more fed free in stall:
Such was the custom of Branksome
  Hall.

VI.

Why do these steeds stand ready
  dight?
Why watch these warriors, arm'd, by
  night?
They watch to hear the blood-hound
  baying:
They watch to hear the war-horn
  braying;
To see St. George's red cross streaming,
To see the midnight beacon gleaming:
They watch against Southern force
  and guile,
  Lest Scroop, or Howard, or Percy's
    powers,
  Threaten　　Branksome's　　lordly
    towers,
From Warkworth, or Naworth, or
  merry Carlisle.

VII.

Such is the custom of Branksome Hall.
  Many a valiant knight is here;
But he, the chieftain of them all,
His sword hangs rusting on the wall,
  Beside his broken spear.
  Bards long shall tell
  How Lord Walter fell!
  When startled burghers fled, afar,
  The furies of the Border war;

When the streets of high Dunedin
　Saw lances gleam, and falchions
　　redden,
And heard the slogan's deadly yell—
Then the Chief of Branksome fell.

VIII.

Can piety the discord heal,
　Or stanch the death-feud's enmity?
Can Christian lore, can patriot zeal,
　Can love of blessed charity?
No! vainly to each holy shrine,
　In mutual pilgrimage, they drew;
Implor'd in vain the grace divine
　For chiefs their own red falchions
　　slew:
While Cessford owns the rule of Carr,
　While Ettrick boasts the line of
　　Scott,
The slaughter'd chiefs, the mortal jar,
　The havoc of the feudal war,
　　Shall never, never be forgot!

IX.

In sorrow o'er Lord Walter's bier
　The warlike foresters had bent;
And many a flower and many a tear
　Old Teviot's maids and matrons lent:
But o'er her warrior's bloody bier
The Ladye dropp'd nor flower nor
　tear!
Vengeance, deep-brooding o'er the
　slain,
　Had lock'd the source of softer woe;
And burning pride and high disdain
　Forbade the rising tear to flow;
Until, amid his sorrowing clan,
　Her son lisp'd from the nurse's
　　knee—
'And if I live to be a man,
　My father's death reveng'd shall be!'
Then fast the mother's tears did seek
To dew the infant's kindling cheek.

X.

All loose her negligent attire,
　All loose her golden hair,

Hung Margaret o'er her slaughter'd
　sire,
　And wept in wild despair.
But not alone the bitter tear
　Had filial grief supplied;
For hopeless love and anxious fear
　Had lent their mingled tide:
Nor in her mother's alter'd eye
　Dar'd she to look for sympathy.
Her lover, 'gainst her father's clan,
　With Carr in arms had stood,
When Mathouse-burn to Melrose ran
　All purple with their blood;
And well she knew, her mother dread,
Before Lord Cranstoun she should wed,
Would see her on her dying bed.

XI.

Of noble race the Ladye came;
　Her father was a clerk of fame,
　Of Bethune's line of Picardie:
He learn'd the art that none may name,
　In Padua, far beyond the sea.
Men said he changed his mortal frame
　By feat of magic mystery;
For when, in studious mood, he pac'd
　St. Andrew's cloister'd hall,
His form no darkening shadow trac'd
　Upon the sunny wall!

XII.

And of his skill, as bards avow,
　He taught that Ladye fair,
Till to her bidding she could bow
　The viewless forms of air.
And now she sits in secret bower,
In old Lord David's western tower,
And listens to a heavy sound
That moans the mossy turrets round.
Is it the roar of Teviot's tide,
That chafes against the scaur's red
　side?
Is it the wind that swings the oaks?
Is it the echo from the rocks?
What may it be, the heavy sound,
That moans old Branksome's turrets
　round?

XIII.

At the sullen, moaning sound,
  The ban-dogs bay and howl ;
And, from the turrets round,
  Loud whoops the startled owl.
In the hall, both squire and knight
  Swore that a storm was near,
And looked forth to view the night ;
  But the night was still and clear !

XIV.

From the sound of Teviot's tide,
Chafing with the mountain's side,
From the groan of the wind-swung oak,
From the sullen echo of the rock,
From the voice of the coming storm,
  The Ladye knew it well !
It was the Spirit of the Flood that
    spoke,
  And he call'd on the Spirit of the
    Fell.

XV.

RIVER SPIRIT.
'Sleep'st thou, brother ?'

MOUNTAIN SPIRIT.
        ' Brother, nay —
On my hills the moon-beams play.
From Craik-cross to Skelfhill-pen,
By every rill, in every glen,
  Merry elves their morris pacing,
  To aërial minstrelsy,
  Emerald rings on brown heath
    tracing,
  Trip it deft and merrily.
Up, and mark their nimble feet !
Up, and list their music sweet ! '

XVI.

RIVER SPIRIT.
' Tears of an imprison'd maiden
  Mix with my polluted stream ;
Margaret of Branksome, sorrow-laden,
  Mourns beneath the moon's pale
    beam.
Tell me, thou, who view'st the stars,
When shall cease these feudal jars ?

What shall be the maiden's fate ?
Who shall be the maiden's mate ? '

XVII.

MOUNTAIN SPIRIT.
' Arthur's slow wain his course doth
    roll
In utter darkness round the pole ;
The Northern Bear lowers black and
    grim ;
Orion's studded belt is dim ;
Twinkling faint, and distant far,
Shimmers through mist each planet
    star ;
  Ill may I read their high decree !
But no kind influence deign they
    shower
On Teviot's tide and Branksome's
    tower
  Till pride be quell'd and love be
    free.'

XVIII.

The unearthly voices ceast,
  And the heavy sound was still ;
It died on the river's breast,
  It died on the side of the hill.
But round Lord David's tower
  The sound still floated near ;
For it rung in the Ladye's bower
  And it rung in the Ladye's ear.
She raised her stately head,
  And her heart throbb'd high with
    pride :—
' Your mountains shall bend,
And your streams ascend,
Ere Margaret be our foeman's bride ! '

XIX.

The Ladye sought the lofty hall,
  Where many a bold retainer lay,
And, with jocund din, among them all,
  Her son pursued his infant play.
A fancied moss-trooper, the boy
  The truncheon of a spear bestrode,
And round the hall, right merrily,
  In mimic foray rode.

Even bearded knights, in arms grown
　　old,
　Share in his frolic gambols bore,
Albeit their hearts of rugged mould
　Were stubborn as the steel they
　　wore.
For the gray warriors prophesied,
　How the brave boy, in future war,
Should tame the Unicorn's pride,
　Exalt the Crescent and the Star.

XX.

The Ladye forgot her purpose high,
　One moment, and no more ;
One moment gaz'd with a mother's
　　eye,
　As she paus'd at the arched door :
Then from amid the armed train,
She call'd to her William of Deloraine.

XXI.

A stark moss-trooping Scott was he,
As e'er couch'd Border lance by knee :
Through Solway sands, through Tar-
　　ras moss,
Blindfold, he knew the paths to cross ;
By wily turns, by desperate bounds,
Had baffled Percy's best blood-hounds ;
In Eske, or Liddel, fords were none,
But he would ride them, one by one ;
Alike to him was time or tide,
December's snow, or July's pride ;
Alike to him was tide or time,
Moonless midnight, or matin prime :
Steady of heart, and stout of hand,
As ever drove prey from Cumberland ;
Five times outlawed had he been,
By England's King, and Scotland's
　　Queen.

XXII.

' Sir William of Deloraine, good at
　　need,
Mount thee on the wightest steed ;
Spare not to spur, nor stint to ride,
Until thou come to fair Tweedside ;
And in Melrose's holy pile
Seek thou the Monk of St. Mary's aisle.

Greet the Father well from me ;
　Say that the fated hour is come,
And to-night he shall watch with
　　thee,
To win the treasure of the tomb :
For this will be St. Michael's night,
And, though stars be dim, the moon
　　is bright ;
And the Cross, of bloody red,
Will point to the grave of the mighty
　　dead.

XXIII.

' What he gives thee, see thou keep ;
Stay not thou for food or sleep :
Be it scroll, or be it book,
Into it, Knight, thou must not look ;
If thou readest, thou art lorn !
Better had'st thou ne'er been born.'

XXIV.

' O swiftly can speed my dapple-grey
　　steed,
　Which drinks of the Teviot clear ;
Ere break of day,' the Warrior 'gan
　　say,
　' Again will I be here :
And safer by none may thy errand be
　　done,
　Than, noble dame, by me ;
Letter nor line know I never a one,
　Were 't my neck-verse at Hairibee.'

XXV.

Soon in his saddle sate he fast,
And soon the steep descent he past,
Soon cross'd the sounding barbican,
And soon the Teviot side he won.
Eastward the wooded path he rode,—
Green hazels o'er his basnet nod ;
He pass'd the Peel of Goldiland,
And cross'd old Borthwick's roaring
　　strand ;
Dimly he view'd the Moat-hill's
　　mound,
Where Druid shades still flitted round ;
In Hawick twinkled many a light ;
Behind him soon they set in night ;

And soon he spurr'd his courser keen
Beneath the tower of Hazeldean.

XXVI.

The clattering hoofs the watchmen
        mark :
' Stand, ho ! thou courier of the dark.'
' For Branksome, ho ! ' the knight re-
        join'd,
And left the friendly tower behind.
    He turn'd him now from Teviotside,
        And, guided by the tinkling rill,
    Northward the dark ascent did ride,
        And gained the moor at Horslie-
        hill ;
Broad on the left before him lay,
For many a mile, the Roman way.

XXVII.

A moment now he slack'd his speed,
A moment breathed his panting steed ;
Drew saddle-girth and corslet-band,
And loosen'd in the sheath his brand.
On Minto-crags the moonbeams glint,
Where Barnhill hew'd his bed of
        flint ;
Who flung his outlaw'd limbs to rest,
Where falcons hang their giddy nest,
Mid cliffs, from whence his eagle eye
For many a league his prey could spy ;
Cliffs, doubling, on their echoes borne,
The terrors of the robber's horn ;
Cliffs, which, for many a later year,
The warbling Doric reed shall hear,
When some sad swain shall teach the
        grove,
Ambition is no cure for love !

XXVIII.

Unchalleng'd, thence pass'd Delo-
        raine,
To ancient Riddel's fair domain,
    Where Aill, from mountains freed,
Down from the lakes did raving come ;
Each wave was crested with tawny
        foam,
    Like the mane of a chestnut steed.

In vain ! no torrent, deep or broad,
Might bar the bold moss-trooper's road.

XXIX.

At the first plunge the horse sunk low,
And the water broke o'er the saddle-
        bow ;
Above the foaming tide, I ween,
Scarce half the charger's neck was
        seen ;
For he was barded from counter to tail,
And the rider was arm'd complete in
        mail :
Never heavier man and horse
Stemm'd a midnight torrent's force.
The warrior's very plume, I say,
Was daggled by the dashing spray ;
Yet, through good heart, and Our
        Ladye's grace,
At length he gain'd the landing-place.

XXX.

Now Bowden Moor the march-man
        won,
    And sternly shook his plumed head,
As glanc'd his eye o'er Halidon :
    For on his soul the slaughter red
Of that unhallow'd morn arose
When first the Scott and Carr were
        foes ;
When royal James beheld the fray ;
Prize to the victor of the day ;
When Home and Douglas, in the van,
Bore down Buccleuch's retiring clan,
Till gallant Cessford's heart-blood dear
Reek'd on dark Elliot's Border spear.

XXXI.

In bitter mood he spurred fast,
And soon the hated heath was past ;
And far beneath, in lustre wan,
Old Melros' rose, and fair Tweed ran :
Like some tall rock with lichens grey,
Seem'd dimly huge the dark Abbaye.
When Hawick he pass'd, had curfew
        rung,
Now midnight lauds were in Melrose
        sung.

The sound, upon the fitful gale,
In solemn wise did rise and fail,
Like that wild harp whose magic tone
Is waken'd by the winds alone.
But when Melrose he reach'd, 'twas
    silence all :
He meetly stabled his steed in stall,
And sought the convent's lonely wall.

———

HERE paus'd the harp ; and with its
    swell
The Master's fire and courage fell ;
Dejectedly and low he bow'd,
And, gazing timid on the crowd,
He seem'd to seek in every eye
If they approv'd his minstrelsy ;
And, diffident of present praise,
Somewhat he spoke of former days,
And how old age and wand'ring long
Had done his hand and harp some
    wrong.
The Duchess and her daughters fair,
And every gentle lady there,
Each after each in due degree,
Gave praises to his melody ;
His hand was true, his voice was
    clear,
And much they long'd the rest to hear.
Encourag'd thus, the aged man,
After meet rest, again began.

—◦+◦—

Canto Second.

I.

IF thou would'st view fair Melrose
    aright,
Go visit it by the pale moonlight ;
For the gay beams of lightsome day
Gild, but to flout, the ruins grey.
When the broken arches are black in
    night,
And each shafted oriel glimmers
    white ;

When the cold light's uncertain shower
Streams on the ruin'd central tower ;
When buttress and buttress, alter-
    nately,
Seem fram'd of ebon and ivory ;
When silver edges the imagery,
And the scrolls that teach thee to live
    and die ;
When distant Tweed is heard to rave,
And the owlet to hoot o'er the dead
    man's grave,
Then go—but go alone the while—
Then view St. David's ruin'd pile ;
And, home returning, soothly swear,
Was never scene so sad and fair !

II.

Short halt did Deloraine make there ;
Little reck'd he of the scene so fair :
With dagger's hilt, on the wicket
    strong,
He struck full loud, and struck full
    long.
The porter hurried to the gate—
' Who knocks so loud, and knocks so
    late ? '
' From Branksome I,' the warrior
    cried ;
And straight the wicket open'd wide :
For Branksome's Chiefs had in battle
    stood,
    To fence the rights of fair Melrose ;
And lands and livings, many a rood,
    Had gifted the shrine for their souls'
        repose.

III.

Bold Deloraine his errand said ;
The porter bent his humble head ;
With torch in hand, and feet unshod,
And noiseless step, the path he trod :
The arched cloister, far and wide,
Rang to the warrior's clanking stride,
Till, stooping low his lofty crest,
He enter'd the cell of the ancient
    priest,
And lifted his barred aventayle,
To hail the Monk of St. Mary's aisle.

IV.

' The Ladye of Branksome greets thee
    by me ;
Says, that the fated hour is come,
And that to-night I shall watch with
    thee,
To win the treasure of the tomb.'
From sackcloth couch the Monk arose,
    With toil his stiffen'd limbs he
    rear'd ;
A hundred years had flung their snows
    On his thin locks and floating beard.

V.

And strangely on the Knight look'd he,
    And his blue eyes gleam'd wild and
    wide ;
' And dar'st thou, Warrior ! seek to
    see
    What heaven and hell alike would
    hide ?
My breast, in belt of iron pent,
    With shirt of hair and scourge of
    thorn ;
For threescore years, in penance
    spent,
    My knees those flinty stones have
    worn ;
Yet all too little to atone
For knowing what should ne'er be
    known.
    Would'st thou thy every future year
    In ceaseless prayer and penance
    drie,
    Yet wait thy latter end with fear—
    Then, daring Warrior, follow me !'

VI.

' Penance, father, will I none ;
Prayer know I hardly one ;
For mass or prayer can I rarely
    tarry,
Save to patter an Ave Mary,
When I ride on a Border foray.
Other prayer can I none ;
So speed me my errand, and let me be
    gone.'

VII.

Again on the Knight look'd the
    Churchman old,
And again he sighed heavily ;
For he had himself been a warrior
    bold,
And fought in Spain and Italy.
And he thought on the days that were
    long since by
When his limbs were strong, and his
    courage was high :
Now, slow and faint, he led the way,
Where, cloister'd round, the garden
    lay ;
The pillar'd arches were over their
    head,
And beneath their feet were the bones
    of the dead.

VIII.

Spreading herbs, and flowerets bright,
Glisten'd with the dew of night ;
Nor herb, nor floweret, glisten'd there,
But was carv'd in the cloister-arches
    as fair.
    The Monk gazed long on the lovely
    moon,
        Then into the night he looked forth ;
    And red and bright the streamers
    light
        Were dancing in the glowing
    north.
    So had he seen, in fair Castile,
        The youth in glittering squadrons
    start,
    Sudden the flying jennet wheel,
        And hurl the unexpected dart.
He knew, by the streamers that shot
    so bright,
That spirits were riding the northern
    light.

IX.

By a steel-clench'd postern door,
    They enter'd now the chancel tall ;
The darken'd roof rose high aloof
    On pillars lofty and light and small :

The key-stone, that lock'd each ribbed
        aisle,
Was a fleur-de-lys, or a quatre-feuille ;
The corbells were carv'd grotesque
        and grim ;
And the pillars, with cluster'd shafts
        so trim,
With base and with capital flourish'd
        around,
Seem'd bundles of lances which gar-
        lands had bound.

x.

Full many a scutcheon and banner
        riven,
Shook to the cold night-wind of heaven,
        Around the screened altar's pale ;
And there the dying lamps did burn,
Before thy low and lonely urn,
O gallant Chief of Otterburne !
        And thine, dark Knight of Liddes-
        dale !
O fading honours of the dead !
O high ambition, lowly laid !

xi.

The moon on the east oriel shone
Through slender shafts of shapely
        stone,
        By foliaged tracery combin'd ;
Thou would'st have thought some
        fairy's hand
'Twixt poplars straight the ozier wand,
        In many a freakish knot, had twin'd ;
Then fram'd a spell, when the work
        was done,
And chang'd the willow-wreaths to
        stone.
The silver light, so pale and faint,
Shew'd many a prophet, and many a
        saint,
        Whose image on the glass was dyed ;
Full in the midst, his Cross of Red
Triumphant Michael brandished,
        And trampled the Apostate's pride.
The moon-beam kiss'd the holy pane,
And threw on the pavement a bloody
        stain.

xii.

They sate them down on a marble
        stone
(A Scottish monarch slept below) :
Thus spoke the Monk, in solemn tone:
        ' I was not always a man of woe ;
For Paynim countries I have trod,
And fought beneath the Cross of God :
Now, strange to my eyes thine arms
        appear,
And their iron clang sounds strange
        to my ear.

xiii

' In these far climes it was my lot
To meet the wondrous Michael Scott ;
        A wizard, of such dreaded fame,
        That when, in Salamanca's cave,
        Him listed his magic wand to wave,
        The bells would ring in Notre
        Dame !
Some of his skill he taught to me ;
And, Warrior, I could say to thee
The words that cleft Eildon hills in
        three,
        And bridled the Tweed with a curb
        of stone :
But to speak them were a deadly sin ;
And for having but thought them my
        heart within,
        A treble penance must be done.

xiv.

' When Michael lay on his dying bed,
His conscience was awakened :
He bethought him of his sinful deed,
And he gave me a sign to come with
        speed.
I was in Spain when the morning rose,
But I stood by his bed ere evening
        close.
The words may not again be said,
That he spoke to me, on death-bed
        laid ;
They would rend this Abbaye's massy
        nave,
And pile it in heaps above his grave.

XV.

'I swore to bury his Mighty Book,
That never mortal might therein look;
And never to tell where it was hid,
Save at his Chief of Branksome's need:
And when that need was past and
    o'er,
Again the volume to restore.
I buried him on St. Michael's night,
When the bell toll'd one, and the
    moon was bright,
And I dug his chamber among the
    dead,
When the floor of the chancel was
    stained red,
That his patron's cross might over him
    wave,
And scare the fiends from the Wizard's
    grave.

XVI.

'It was a night of woe and dread,
When Michael in the tomb I laid!
Strange sounds along the chancel
    pass'd,
The banners wav'd without a blast'—
—Still spoke the Monk, when the
    bell toll'd one!—
I tell you, that a braver man
Than William of Deloraine, good at
    need,
Against a foe ne'er spurr'd a steed;
Yet somewhat was he chill'd with
    dread,
And his hair did bristle upon his head.

XVII.

'Lo, Warrior! now, the Cross of Red
Points to the grave of the mighty dead;
Within it burns a wondrous light,
To chase the spirits that love the
    night:
That lamp shall burn unquenchably,
Until the eternal doom shall be.'
Slow mov'd the Monk to the broad
    flag-stone,
Which the bloody cross was trac'd
    upon:

He pointed to a secret nook;
An iron bar the Warrior took;
And the Monk made a sign with his
    wither'd hand,
The grave's huge portal to expand.

XVIII.

With beating heart to the task he went;
His sinewy frame o'er the grave-stone
    bent;
With bar of iron heav'd amain,
Till the toil-drops fell from his brows,
    like rain.
It was by dint of passing strength,
That he moved the massy stone at
    length.
I would you had been there, to see
How the light broke forth so gloriously,
Stream'd upward to the chancel roof,
And through the galleries far aloof!
No earthly flame blazed e'er so bright:
It shone like heaven's own blessed
    light,
    And, issuing from the tomb,
Show'd the Monk's cowl, and visage
    pale,
Danc'd on the dark-brow'd Warrior's
    mail,
    And kiss'd his waving plume.

XIX.

Before their eyes the Wizard lay,
As if he had not been dead a day.
His hoary beard in silver roll'd,
He seem'd some seventy winters old;
    A palmer's amice wrapp'd him
        round,
    With a wrought Spanish baldric
        bound,
        Like a pilgrim from beyond the
            sea:
    His left hand held his Book of
        Might;
    A silver cross was in his right;
        The lamp was placed beside his
            knee:

High and majestic was his look,
At which the fellest fiends had shook,
And all unruffled was his face :
They trusted his soul had gotten grace.

XX.

Often had William of Deloraine
Rode through the battle's bloody
    plain,
And trampled down the warriors slain,
   And neither known remorse nor
    awe ;
Yet now remorse and awe he own'd ;
His breath came thick, his head swam
    round,
   When this strange scene of death
    he saw.
Bewilder'd and unnerv'd he stood,
And the priest pray'd fervently and
    loud :
With eyes averted prayed he ;
He might not endure the sight to see,
Of the man he had lov'd so brotherly.

XXI.

And when the priest his death-prayer
    had pray'd,
Thus unto Deloraine he said :—
' Now, speed thee what thou hast to
    do,
Or, Warrior, we may dearly rue ;
For those thou may'st not look upon
Are gathering fast round the yawning
    stone ! '
Then Deloraine, in terror, took
From the cold hand the Mighty Book,
With iron clasp'd, and with iron bound :
He thought, as he took it, the dead
    man frown'd ;
But the glare of the sepulchral light,
Perchance, had dazzled the warrior's
    sight.

XXII.

When the huge stone sunk o'er the
    tomb,
The night return'd in double gloom ;

For the moon had gone down, and the
    stars were few,
And, as the Knight and Priest with-
    drew,
With wavering steps and dizzy brain,
They hardly might the postern gain.
'Tis said, as through the aisles they
    pass'd,
They heard strange noises on the blast;
And through the cloister-galleries
    small,
Which at mid-height thread the chan-
    cel wall,
Loud sobs, and laughter louder, ran,
And voices unlike the voice of man ;
As if the fiends kept holiday,
Because these spells were brought
    to day.
I cannot tell how the truth may be ;
I say the tale as 'twas said to me.

XXIII.

' Now, hie thee hence,' the Father
    said,
' And when we are on death-bed laid,
O may our dear Ladye, and sweet
    St. John,
Forgive our souls for the deed we
    have done ! '
   The Monk return'd him to his cell,
    And many a prayer and penance
    sped ;
   When the convent met at the noon-
    tide bell—
    The Monk of St. Mary's aisle was
    dead !
Before the cross was the body laid,
With hands clasp'd fast, as if still he
    pray'd.

XXIV.

The Knight 'breath'd free in the
    morning wind,
And strove his hardihood to find :
He was glad when he pass'd the
    tombstones grey,
Which girdle round the fair Abbaye ;

For the mystic Book, to his bosom
   prest,
Felt like a load upon his breast;
And his joints, with nerves of iron
   twin'd,
Shook, like the aspen leaves in wind.
Full fain was he when the dawn of day
Began to brighten Cheviot grey;
He joy'd to see the cheerful light,
And he said Ave Mary, as well as he
   might.

XXV.

The sun had brighten'd Cheviot grey,
   The sun had brighten'd the Carter's
      side;
And soon beneath the rising day
   Smil'd Branksome towers and
      Teviot's tide.
The wild birds told their warbling tale,
   And waken'd every flower that
      blows;
And peeped forth the violet pale,
   And spread her breast the mountain
      rose.
And lovelier than the rose so red,
   Yet paler than the violet pale,
She early left her sleepless bed,
   The fairest maid of Teviotdale.

XXVI.

Why does fair Margaret so early awake,
   And don her kirtle so hastilie;
And the silken knots, which in hurry
   she would make,
   Why tremble her slender fingers to
      tie;
Why does she stop, and look often
   around,
   As she glides down the secret stair;
And why does she pat the shaggy
      blood-hound,
   As he rouses him up from his lair;
And, though she passes the postern
   alone,
Why is not the watchman's bugle
   blown?

XXVII.

The Ladye steps in doubt and dread,
Lest her watchful mother hear her
   tread;
The Ladye caresses the rough blood-
   hound,
Lest his voice should waken the castle
   round;
The watchman's bugle is not blown,
For he was her foster-father's son;
And she glides through the greenwood
   at dawn of light
To meet Baron Henry, her own true
   knight.

XXVIII.

The Knight and Ladye fair are met,
And under the hawthorn's boughs are
   set.
A fairer pair were never seen
To meet beneath the hawthorn green.
He was stately, and young, and tall;
Dreaded in battle, and lov'd in hall:
And she, when love, scarce told, scarce
   hid,
Lent to her cheek a livelier red;
When the half sigh her swelling breast
Against the silken ribbon prest;
When her blue eyes their secret told,
Though shaded by her locks of gold —
Where would you find the peerless fair,
With Margaret of Branksome might
   compare!

XXIX.

And now, fair dames, methinks I see
You listen to my minstrelsy;
Your waving locks ye backward throw,
And sidelong bend your necks of
   snow:
Ye ween to hear a melting tale,
Of two true lovers in a dale;
   And how the Knight, with tender
      fire,
      To paint his faithful passion strove;
   Swore he might at her feet expire,
      But never, never cease to love;

And how she blush'd, and how she
     sigh'd,
And, half consenting, half denied,
And said that she would die a maid ;—
Yet, might the bloody feud be stay'd,
Henry of Cranstoun, and only he,
Margaret of Branksome's choice should
     be.

XXX.

Alas! fair dames, your hopes are vain!
My harp has lost the enchanting
     strain ;
    Its lightness would my age reprove :
My hairs are grey, my limbs are old,
My heart is dead, my veins are cold :
    I may not, must not, sing of love.

XXXI.

Beneath an oak, moss'd o'er by eld,
The Baron's Dwarf his courser held,
    And held his crested helm and spear :
That Dwarf was scarce an earthly
     man,
If the tales were true that of him ran
    Through all the Border, far and
     near.
'Twas said, when the Baron a-hunting
     rode
Through Reedsdale's glens, but rarely
     trod,
    He heard a voice cry, 'Lost! lost!
     lost!'
    And, like tennis-ball by racket toss'd,
    A leap, of thirty feet and three,
Made from the gorse this elfin shape,
Distorted like some dwarfish ape,
    And lighted at Lord Cranstoun's
     knee.
Lord Cranstoun was some whit
     dismay'd ;
'Tis said that five good miles he
     rade,
    To rid him of his company ;
But where he rode one mile, the Dwarf
     ran four,
And the Dwarf was first at the castle
     door.

XXXII.

Use lessens marvel, it is said :
This elvish Dwarf with the Baron
     staid ;
Little he ate, and less he spoke,
Nor mingled with the menial flock :
And oft apart his arms he toss'd,
And often mutter'd 'Lost! lost! lost!'
    He was waspish, arch, and litherlie,
    But well Lord Cranstoun served he :
And he of his service was full fain ;
For once he had been ta'en or slain,
    An it had not been for his ministry.
All between Home and Hermitage,
Talk'd of Lord Cranstoun's Goblin-
     Page.

XXXIII.

For the Baron went on pilgrimage,
And took with him this elvish Page,
    To Mary's Chapel of the Lowes :
For there, beside our Ladye's lake,
An offering he had sworn to make,
    And he would pay his vows.
But the Ladye of Branksome gather'd
     a band
Of the best that would ride at her
     command :
    The trysting place was Newark Lee.
Wat of Harden came thither amain,
And thither came John of Thirlestane,
And thither came William of Deloraine;
    They were three hundred spears
     and three.
Through Douglas-burn, up Yarrow
     stream,
Their horses prance, their lances gleam.
They came to St. Mary's lake ere day;
But the chapel was void, and the
     Baron away.
They burn'd the chapel for very rage,
And curs'd Lord Cranstoun's Goblin-
     Page.

XXXIV.

And now, in Branksome's good green-
     wood,
As under the aged oak he stood,

The Baron's courser pricks his ears,
As if a distant noise he hears.
The Dwarf waves his long lean arm
        on high,
And signs to the lovers to part and fly;
No time was then to vow or sigh.
Fair Margaret through the hazel grove,
Flew like the startled cushat-dove :
The Dwarf the stirrup held and rein;
Vaulted the Knight on his steed amain,
And, pondering deep that morning's
        scene,
Rode eastward through the hawthorns
        green.

_____

WHILE thus he pour'd the lengthen'd
        tale,
The Minstrel's voice began to fail :
Full slyly smiled the observant page,
And gave the wither'd hand of age
A goblet, crown'd with mighty wine,
The blood of Velez' scorched vine.
He raised the silver cup on high,
And, while the big drop fill'd his eye,
Pray'd God to bless the Duchess long,
And all who cheer'd a son of song.
The attending maidens smiled to see
How long, how deep, how zealously,
The precious juice the Minstrel quaff'd;
And he, embolden'd by the draught,
Look'd gaily back to them, and laugh'd.
The cordial nectar of the bowl
Swell'd his old veins, and cheer'd his
        soul :
A lighter, livelier prelude ran,
Ere thus his tale again began.

—•+•—

Canto Third.

I.

AND said I that my limbs were old,
And said I that my blood was cold,
And that my kindly fire was fled,
And my poor wither'd heart was dead,
    And that I might not sing of love ? —

How could I to the dearest theme,
That ever warm'd a minstrel's dream,
    So foul, so false a recreant prove !
How could I name love's very name,
Nor wake my heart to notes of flame !

II.

In peace, Love tunes the shepherd's
        reed ;
In war, he mounts the warrior's steed ;
In halls, in gay attire is seen ;
In hamlets, dances on the green.
Love rules the court, the camp, the
        grove,
And men below, and saints above ;
For love is heaven, and heaven is love.

III.

So thought Lord Cranstoun, as I
        ween,
While,. pondering deep the tender
        scene,
He rode through Branksome's haw-
        thorn green.
    But the Page shouted wild and
        shrill,
        And scarce his helmet could he
        don,
    When downward from the shady
        hill
        A stately knight came pricking
        on.
That warrior's steed, so dapple-gray,
Was dark with sweat, and splashed
        with clay ;
    His armour red with many a stain ∶
He seem'd in such a weary plight,
As if he had ridden the live-long
        night ;
For it was William of Deloraine.

IV.

But no whit weary did he seem,
When, dancing in the sunny beam,
He mark'd the crane on the Baron's
        crest ;
For his ready spear was in his rest.

Few were the words, and stern and high,
  That mark'd the foemen's feudal hate ;
For question fierce, and proud reply,
  Gave signal soon of dire debate.
Their very coursers seem'd to know
That each was other's mortal foe,
And snorted fire, when wheel'd around
To give each foe his vantage-ground.

v.

In rapid round the Baron bent ;
  He sigh'd a sigh, and pray'd a prayer :
The prayer was to his patron saint,
  The sigh was to his ladye fair.
Stout Deloraine nor sigh'd nor pray'd,
Nor saint, nor ladye, call'd to aid ;
But he stoop'd his head, and couch'd his spear,
And spurred his steed to full career.
The meeting of these champions proud
Seem'd like the bursting thunder-cloud.

vi.

Stern was the dint the Borderer lent !
The stately Baron backwards bent ;
Bent backwards to his horse's tail,
And his plumes went scattering on the gale ;
The tough ash spear, so stout and true,
Into a thousand flinders flew.
But Cranstoun's lance, of more avail,
Pierc'd through, like silk, the Borderer's mail ;
Through shield, and jack, and acton, past,
Deep in his bosom broke at last.—
Still sate the warrior saddle-fast,
Till, stumbling in the mortal shock,
Down went the steed, the girthing broke,
Hurl'd on a heap lay man and horse.
The Baron onward pass'd his course ;

Nor knew—so giddy rolled his brain—
His foe lay stretch'd upon the plain.

vii.

But when he rein'd his courser round,
And saw his foeman on the ground
  Lie senseless as the bloody clay,
He bade his page to stanch the wound,
  And there beside the warrior stay,
And tend him in his doubtful state,
And lead him to Branksome-castle gate :
His noble mind was inly moved
For the kinsman of the maid he loved.
'This shalt thou do without delay :
No longer here myself may stay ;
Unless the swifter I speed away,
Short shrift will be at my dying day.'

viii.

Away in speed Lord Cranstoun rode ;
The Goblin-Page behind abode ;
His lord's command he ne'er withstood,
Though small his pleasure to do good.
As the corslet off he took,
The Dwarf espied the Mighty Book !
Much he marvell'd a knight of pride,
Like a book-bosom'd priest should ride :
He thought not to search or stanch the wound
Until the secret he had found.

ix.

The iron band, the iron clasp,
Resisted long the elfin grasp :
For when the first he had undone,
It closed as he the next begun.
Those iron clasps, that iron band,
Would not yield to unchristen'd hand,
Till he smear'd the cover o'er
With the Borderer's curdled gore ;
A moment then the volume spread,
And one short spell therein he read :
It had much of glamour might ;
Could make a ladye seem a knight ;

The cobwebs on a dungeon wall
Seem tapestry in lordly hall ;
A nut-shell seem a gilded barge,
A sheeling seem a palace large,
And youth seem age, and age seem
          youth :
All was delusion, nought was truth.

X.

He had not read another spell,
When on his cheek a buffet fell,
So fierce, it stretch'd him on the plain
Beside the wounded Deloraine.
From the ground he rose dismay'd,
And shook his huge and matted head ;
One word he mutter'd, and no more,
' Man of age, thou smitest sore ! '
No more the Elfin Page durst try
Into the wondrous Book to pry ;
The clasps, though smear'd with
          Christian gore,
Shut faster than they were before.
He hid it underneath his cloak.
Now, if you ask who gave the stroke,
I cannot tell, so mot I thrive ;
It was not given by man alive.

XI.

Unwillingly himself he address'd,
To do his master's high behest :
He lifted up the living corse,
And laid it on the weary horse ;
He led him into Branksome hall,
Before the beards of the warders all ;
And each did after swear and say
There only pass'd a wain of hay.
He took him to Lord David's tower,
Even to the Ladye's secret bower ;
And, but that stronger spells were
          spread,
And the door might not be opened,
He had laid him on her very bed.
Whate'er he did of gramarye
Was always done maliciously ;
He flung the warrior on the ground,
And the blood well'd freshly from the
          wound.

XII.

As he repass'd the outer court,
He spied the fair young child at sport :
He thought to train him to the wood ;
For, at a word be it understood,
He was always for ill, and never for
          good.
Seem'd to the boy, some comrade gay
Led him forth to the woods to play ;
On the drawbridge the warders stout
Saw a terrier and lurcher passing out.

XIII.

He led the boy o'er bank and fell,
    Until they came to a woodland
          brook ;
The running stream dissolv'd the
          spell,
    And his own elvish shape he took.
Could he have had his pleasure vilde,
He had crippled the joints of the
          noble child ;
Or, with his fingers long and lean,
Had strangled him in fiendish spleen :
But his awful mother he had in dread,
And also his power was limited ;
So he but scowl'd on the startled child,
And darted through the forest wild ;
The woodland brook he bounding
          cross'd,
And laugh'd, and shouted, ' Lost !
          lost ! lost ! '

XIV.

Full sore amaz'd at the wondrous
          change,
    And frighten'd, as a child might be,
At the wild yell and visage strange,
    And the dark words of gramarye,
The child, amidst the forest bower,
Stood rooted like a lily flower ;
    And when at length, with trembling
          pace,
        He sought to find where Brank-
          some lay,
    He fear'd to see that grisly face
        Glare from some thicket on his
          way.

Thus, starting oft, he journey'd on,
And deeper in the wood is gone,—
For aye the more he sought his way,
The farther still he went astray,—
Until he heard the mountains round
Ring to the baying of a hound.

xv.

And hark! and hark! the deep-
mouth'd bark
Comes nigher still, and nigher :
Bursts on the path a dark blood-
hound ;
His tawny muzzle track'd the ground,
And his red eye shot fire.
Soon as the wilder'd child saw he,
He flew at him right furiouslie.
I ween you would have seen with joy
The bearing of the gallant boy,
When, worthy of his noble sire,
His wet cheek glow'd 'twixt fear and
ire !
He faced the blood-hound manfully,
And held his little bat on high ;
So fierce he struck, the dog, afraid,
At cautious distance hoarsely bay'd,
But still in act to spring ;
When dash'd an archer through the
glade,
And when he saw the hound was
stay'd,
He drew his tough bow-string ;
But a rough voice cried, 'Shoot not,
hoy !
Ho ! shoot not, Edward ; 'tis a boy !'

xvi.

The speaker issued from the wood,
And check'd his fellow's surly mood,
And quell'd the ban-dog's ire :
He was an English yeoman good,
And born in Lancashire.
Well could he hit a fallow-deer
Five hundred feet him fro ;
With hand more true, and eye more
clear,
No archer bended bow.

His coal-black hair, shorn round and
close,
Set off his sun-burn'd face :
Old England's sign, St. George's cross,
His barret-cap did grace ;
His bugle-horn hung by his side,
All in a wolf-skin baldric tied ;
And his short falchion, sharp and clear,
Had pierc'd the throat of many a deer.

xvii.

His kirtle, made of forest green,
Reach'd scantly to his knee ;
And, at his belt, of arrows keen
A furbish'd sheaf bore he ;
His buckler, scarce in breadth a span,
No larger fence had he ;
He never counted him a man,
Would strike below the knee :
His slacken'd bow was in his hand,
And the leash that was his blood-
hound's band.

xviii.

He would not do the fair child harm,
But held him with his powerful arm,
That he might neither fight nor flee ;
For when the Red-Cross spied he,
The boy strove long and violently.
' Now, by St. George,' the archer cries,
' Edward, methinks we have a prize !
This boy's fair face, and courage free,
Show he is come of high degree.'

xix.

' Yes ! I am come of high degree,
For I am the heir of bold Buccleuch ;
And, if thou dost not set me free,
False Southron, thou shalt dearly
rue !
For Walter of Harden shall come with
speed,
And William of Deloraine, good at
need,
And every Scott, from Esk to Tweed ;
And, if thou dost not let me go,
Despite thy arrows and thy bow,
I'll have thee hang'd to feed the crow !'

XX.

'Gramercy for thy good-will, fair
   boy!
My mind was never set so high;
But if thou art chief of such a clan,
And art the son of such a man,
And ever comest to thy command,
   Our wardens had need to keep good
     order;
My bow of yew to a hazel wand,
   Thou 'lt make them work upon the
     Border.
Meantime, be pleased to come with
   me,
For good Lord Dacre shalt thou see;
I think our work is well begun,
When we have taken thy father's son.'

XXI.

Although the child was led away,
In Branksome still he seem'd to stay,
For so the Dwarf his part did play;
And, in the shape of that young boy,
He wrought the castle much annoy.
The comrades of the young Buccleuch
He pinch'd, and beat, and overthrew;
Nay, some of them he wellnigh slew.
He tore Dame Maudlin's silken tire,
And, as Sym Hall stood by the fire,
He lighted the match of his bandelier,
And wofully scorch'd the hackbuteer.
It may be hardly thought or said,
The mischief that the urchin made,
Till many of the castle guess'd,
That the young Baron was possess'd!

XXII.

Well I ween the charm he held
The noble Ladye had soon dispell'd;
But she was deeply busied then
To tend the wounded Deloraine.
   Much she wonder'd to find him lie
     On the stone threshold stretch'd
     along;
   She thought some spirit of the sky
     Had done the bold moss-trooper
     wrong;

Because, despite her precept dread,
Perchance he in the Book had read;
But the broken lance in his bosom
   stood,
And it was earthly steel and wood.

XXIII.

She drew the splinter from the wound,
   And with a charm she stanch'd the
     blood;
She bade the gash be cleans'd and
   bound:
   No longer by his couch she stood;
But she has ta'en the broken lance,
   And wash'd it from the clotted gore,
   And salved the splinter o'er and o'er.
William of Deloraine, in trance,
   Whene'er she turn'd it round and
     round,
     Twisted as if she gall'd his wound.
     Then to her maidens she did say
     That he should be whole man and
     sound
      Within the course of a night and
      day.
Full long she toil'd; for she did rue
Mishap to friend so stout and true.

XXIV.

So pass'd the day; the evening fell,
'Twas near the time of curfew bell;
The air was mild, the wind was calm,
The stream was smooth, the dew was
   balm;
E'en the rude watchman on the tower
Enjoy'd and bless'd the lovely hour.
Far more fair Margaret lov'd and bless'd
The hour of silence and of rest.
On the high turret sitting lone,
She waked at times the lute's soft tone;
Touch'd a wild note, and all between
Thought of the bower of hawthorns
   green.
Her golden hair stream'd free from
   band,
Her fair cheek rested on her hand,
Her blue eyes sought the west afar,
For lovers love the western star.

XXV.

Is yon the star, o'er Penchryst Pen,
That rises slowly to her ken,
And, spreading broad its wavering
     light,
Shakes its loose tresses on the night?
Is yon red glare the western star?
O, 'tis the beacon-blaze of war!
Scarce could she draw her tighten'd
     breath,
For well she knew the fire of death!

XXVI.

The Warder view'd it blazing strong,
And blew his war-note loud and long,
Till, at the high and haughty sound,
Rock, wood, and river rung around.
The blast alarm'd the festal hall,
And startled forth the warriors all;
Far downward, in the castle-yard,
Full many a torch and cresset glared;
And helms and plumes, confusedly
     toss'd,
Were in the blaze half-seen, half-lost;
And spears in wild disorder shook,
Like reeds beside a frozen brook.

XXVII.

The Seneschal, whose silver hair
Was redden'd by the torches' glare,
Stood in the midst with gesture proud,
And issued forth his mandates loud:
'On Penchryst glows a bale of fire,
And three are kindling on Priest-
     haughswire;
    Ride out, ride out,
    The foe to scout!
Mount, mount for Branksome, every
     man!
Thou, Todrig, warn the Johnstone
     clan,
    That ever are true and stout;
Ye need not send to Liddesdale,
For when they see the blazing bale,
Elliots and Armstrongs never fail.
Ride, Alton, ride, for death and life!
And warn the Warder of the strife.

Young Gilbert, let our beacon blaze,
Our kin, and clan, and friends to raise.'

XXVIII.

Fair Margaret from the turret head
Heard, far below, the coursers' tread,
    While loud the harness rung
As to their seats, with clamour dread,
    The ready horsemen sprung:
And trampling hoofs, and iron coats,
And leaders' voices mingled notes,
     And out! and out!
     In hasty route,
    The horsemen gallop'd forth;
Dispersing to the south to scout,
    And east, and west, and north,
To view their coming enemies,
And warn their vassals and allies.

XXIX.

The ready page, with hurried hand,
Awaked the need-fire's slumbering
     brand,
    And ruddy blush'd the heaven:
For a sheet of flame from the turret
     high
Wav'd like a blood-flag on the sky,
    All flaring and uneven;
And soon a score of fires, I ween,
From height, and hill, and cliff, were
     seen;
Each with warlike tidings fraught,
Each from each the signal caught;
Each after each they glanc'd to
     sight,
As stars arise upon the night.
They gleam'd on many a dusky
     tarn,
Haunted by the lonely earn;
On many a cairn's grey pyramid,
Where urns of mighty chiefs lie hid
Till high Dunedin the blazes saw
From Soltra and Dumpender Law,
And Lothian heard the Regent's
     order
That all should bowne them for the
     Border.

XXX.

The livelong night in Branksome rang
The ceaseless sound of steel ;
The castle-bell, with backward clang,
Sent forth the larum peal ;
Was frequent heard the heavy jar,
Where massy stone and iron bar
Were piled on echoing keep and
tower,
To whelm the foe with deadly shower ;
Was frequent heard the changing
guard,
And watch-word from the sleepless
ward ;
While, wearied by the endless din,
Blood-hound and ban-dog yell'd with-
in.

XXXI.

The noble Dame, amid the broil,
Shared the grey Seneschal's high toil,
And spoke of danger with a smile ;
Cheer'd the young knights, and
council sage
Held with the chiefs of riper age.
No tidings of the foe were brought,
Nor of his numbers knew they aught,
Nor what in time of truce he sought.
Some said that there were thou-
sands ten ;
And others ween'd that it was
nought
But Leven clans, or Tynedale men,
Who came to gather in black-mail ;
And Liddesdale, with small avail,
Might drive them lightly back agen.
So pass'd the anxious night away,
And welcome was the peep of day.

CEAS'D the high sound. The listening
throng
Applaud the Master of the Song ;
And marvel much, in helpless age,
So hard should be his pilgrimage.
Had he no friend, no daughter dear,
His wandering toil to share and cheer ;

No son to be his father's stay,
And guide him on the rugged way ?
'Ay, once he had—but he was dead !'
Upon the harp he stoop'd his head,
And busied himself the strings withal
To hide the tear that fain would fall.
In solemn measure, soft and slow,
Arose a father's notes of woe.

—◆◆—

Canto Fourth.

I.

SWEET Teviot ! on thy silver tide
The glaring bale-fires blaze no
more ;
No longer steel-clad warriors ride
Along thy wild and willow'd shore ;
Where'er thou wind'st, by dale or hill,
All, all is peaceful, all is still,
As if thy waves, since Time was
born,
Since first they roll'd upon the Tweed,
Had only heard the shepherd's reed,
Nor started at the bugle-horn.

II.

Unlike the tide of human time,—
Which, though it change in cease-
less flow,
Retains each grief, retains each crime
Its earliest course was doom'd to
know ;
And, darker as it downward bears,
Is stain'd with past and present tears.
Low as that tide has ebb'd with me,
It still reflects to Memory's eye
The hour my brave, my only boy
Fell by the side of great Dundee.
Why, when the volleying musket
play'd
Against the bloody Highland blade,
Why was not I beside him laid !
Enough, he died the death of fame ;
Enough, he died with conquering
Græme.

III.

Now over Border dale and fell
  Full wide and far was terror spread ;
For pathless marsh, and mountain
    cell,
  The peasant left his lowly shed.
The frighten'd flocks and herds were
    pent
Beneath the peel's rude battlement ;
And maids and matrons dropp'd the
    tear,
While ready warriors seiz'd the spear.
From Branksome's towers, the watch-
    man's eye
Dun wreaths of distant smoke can
    spy,
Which, curling in the rising sun,
Show'd southern ravage was begun.

IV.

Now loud the heedful gate-ward
    cried—
  'Prepare ye all for blows and
    blood !
Watt Tinlinn, from the Liddel-side,
  Comes wading through the flood.
Full oft the Tynedale snatchers knock
At his lone gate, and prove the lock ;
It was but last St. Barnabright
They sieg'd him a whole summer
    night,
But fled at morning ; well they knew
In vain he never twang'd the yew.
Right sharp has been the evening
    shower
That drove him from his Liddel tower ;
And, by my faith,' the gate-ward said,
' I think 'twill prove a Warden-Raid.'

V.

While thus he spoke, the bold yeoman
Enter'd the echoing barbican.
He led a small and shaggy nag,
That through a bog, from hag to hag,
Could bound like any Billhope stag.
It bore his wife and children twain ;
A half-clothed serf was all their train ;

His wife, stout, ruddy, and dark-
    brow'd,
Of silver brooch and bracelet proud,
Laugh'd to her friends among the
    crowd.
He was of stature passing tall,
But sparely form'd, and lean withal;
A batter'd morion on his brow ;
A leather jack, as fence enow,
On his broad shoulders loosely hung ;
A border axe behind was slung ;
His spear, six Scottish ells in length,
  Seem'd newly dyed with gore ;
His shafts and bow, of wondrous
    strength,
  His hardy partner bore.

VI.

Thus to the Ladye did Tinlinn show
The tidings of the English foe :
' Belted Will Howard is marching
    here,
And hot Lord Dacre, with many a
    spear,
And all the German hackbut men,
Who have long lain at Askerten :
They cross'd the Liddel at curfew
    hour,
And burn'd my little lonely tower :
The fiend receive their souls there-
    for !
It had not been burnt this year and
    more.
Barn-yard and dwelling, blazing
    bright,
Serv'd to guide me on my flight ;
But I was chas'd the livelong night.
Black John of Akeshaw and Fergus
    Græme
Fast upon my traces came,
Until I turn'd at Priesthaugh Scrogg,
And shot their horses in the bog,
Slew Fergus with my lance out-
    right ;
I had him long at high despite—
He drove my cows last Fastern's
    night.'

VII.

Now weary scouts from Liddesdale,
Fast hurrying in, confirm'd the tale ;
  As 'far as they could judge by ken,
    Three hours would bring to
      Teviot's strand
    Three thousand armed Englishmen ;
      Meanwhile, full many a warlike
        band,
From Teviot, Aill, and Ettrick shade,
Came in, their Chief's defence to aid.
    There was saddling and mounting
      in haste,
    There was pricking o'er moor and
      lea ;
  He that was last at the trysting-place
  Was but lightly held of his gay
    ladye.

VIII.

From fair St. Mary's silver wave,
  From dreary Gamescleugh's dusky
    height,
His ready lances Thirlestane brave
  Array'd beneath a banner bright.
The treasured fleur-de-luce he claims
To wreathe his shield, since royal
  James,
Encamp'd by Fala's mossy wave,
The proud distinction grateful gave,
  For faith 'mid feudal jars ;
What time, save Thirlestane alone,
Of Scotland's stubborn barons none
  Would march to southern wars ;
And hence, in fair remembrance worn,
Yon sheaf of spears his crest has
  borne ;
Hence his high motto shines reveal'd—
'Ready, aye ready' for the field.

IX.

An aged Knight, to danger steel'd,
  With many a moss-trooper came on ;
And azure in a golden field,
The stars and crescent graced his
  shield,
  Without the bend of Murdieston.

Wide lay his lands round Oakwood
  tower,
And wide round haunted Castle-
  Ower ;
High over Borthwick's mountain flood
His wood-embosom'd mansion stood ;
In the dark glen, so deep below,
The herds of plunder'd England low—
His bold retainers' daily food,
And bought with danger, blows, and
  blood.
Marauding chief! his sole delight
The moonlight raid, the morning fight ;
Not even the Flower of Yarrow's
  charms,
In youth, might tame his rage for
  arms ;
And still, in age, he spurn'd at rest,
And still his brows the helmet press'd,
Albeit the blanched locks below
Were white as Dinlay's spotless snow ;
  Five stately warriors drew the
    sword
    Before their father's band ;
  A braver knight than Harden's lord
  Ne'er belted on a brand.

X.

Scotts of Eskdale, a stalwart band,
  Came trooping down the Todshaw-
    hill ;
By the sword they won their land,
  And by the sword they hold it still.
Hearken, Ladye, to the tale,
How thy sires won fair Eskdale.

Earl Morton was lord of that valley
  fair ;
The Beattisons were his vassals there.
The Earl was gentle, and mild of
  mood ;
The vassals were warlike, and fierce,
  and rude ;
High of heart, and haughty of word,
Little they reck'd of a tame liege
  lord.
The Earl into fair Eskdale came,
Homage and seignory to claim :

B

Of Gilbert the Galliard a heriot he
sought,
Saying, 'Give thy best steed, as a
vassal ought.'
'Dear to me is my bonny white steed,
Oft has he help d me at pinch of need;
Lord and Earl though thou be, I trow
I can rein Bucksfoot better than thou.'
Word on word gave fuel to fire,
Till so highly blazed the Beattison's ire,
But that the Earl the flight had ta'en,
The vassals there their lord had slain.
Sore he plied both whip and spur,
As he urged his steed through Eskdale
muir;
And it fell down a weary weight,
Just on the threshold of Branksome
gate.

XI.

The Earl was a wrathful man to see,
Full fain avenged would he be.
In haste to Branksome s Lord he
spoke,
Saying—'Take these traitors to thy
yoke;
For a cast of hawks, and a purse of
gold,
All Eskdale I'll sell thee, to have and
hold:
Beshrew thy heart, of the Beattisons'
clan
If thou leavest on Eske a landed man;
But spare Woodkerrick's lands alone,
For he lent me his horse to escape
upon.'
A glad man then was Branksome bold,
Down he flung him the purse of gold;
To Eskdale soon he spurr d amain,
And with him five hundred riders has
ta'en.
He left his merrymen in the mist of
the hill,
And bade them hold them close and
still;
And alone he wended to the plain,
To meet with the Galliard and all his
train.

To Gilbert the Galliard thus he said:
'Know thou me for thy liege-lord
and head;
Deal not with me as with Morton
tame,
For Scotts play best at the roughest
game.
Give me in peace my heriot due,
Thy bonny white steed, or thou shalt
rue.
If my horn I three times wind,
Eskdale shall long have the sound in
mind.'

XII.

Loudly the Beattison laugh'd in
scorn;
'Little care we for thy winded
horn.
Ne'er shall it be the Galliard's lot
To yield his steed to a haughty Scott.
Wend thou to Branksome back on
foot
With rusty spur and miry boot.'
He blew his bugle so loud and hoarse
That the dun deer started at fair
Craikcross;
He blew again so loud and clear,
Through the grey mountain-mist there
did lances appear;
And the third blast rang with such a
din
That the echoes answer'd from Pen-
toun-linn,
And all his riders came lightly in.
Then had you seen a gallant shock
When saddles were emptied and
lances broke!
For each scornful word the Galliard
had said,
A Beattison on the field was laid.
His own good sword the chieftain
drew,
And he bore the Galliard through
and through;
Where the Beattisons' blood mix'd
with the rill,
The Galliard's-Haugh men call it still.

The Scotts have scatter'd the Beattison clan,
In Eskdale they left but one landed
man.
The valley of Eske, from the mouth
to the source,
Was lost and won for that bonny
white horse.—

XIII.

Whitslade the Hawk, and Headshaw
came,
And warriors more than I may name ;
From Yarrow-cleugh to Hindhaugh-
swair,
From Woodhouselie to Chester-
glen,
Troop'd man and horse, and bow and
spear ;
Their gathering word was Bellen-
den.
And better hearts o'er Border sod
To siege or rescue never rode.
The Ladye mark'd the aids come
in,
And high her heart of pride arose :
She bade her youthful son attend,
That he might know his father's
friend,
And learn to face his foes.
' The boy is ripe to look on war ;
I saw him draw a cross-bow
stiff,
And his true arrow struck afar
The raven s nest upon the cliff ;
The red cross on a southern breast
Is broader than the raven's nest :
Thou, Whitslade, shalt teach him his
weapon to wield,
And o'er him hold his father's shield.'

XIV.

Well may you think the wily page
Car'd not to face the Ladye sage.
He counterfeited childish fear,
And shriek'd, and shed full many a
tear,

And moan'd and plain'd in manner
wild.
The attendants to the Ladye told
Some fairy, sure, had chang'd the
child,
That wont to be so free and bold.
Then wrathful was the noble dame ;
She blush'd blood-red for very
shame :
' Hence ! ere the clan his faintness
view ;
Hence with the weakling to Buc-
cleuch !
Watt Tinlinn, thou shalt be his guide
To Rangleburn's lonely side.
Sure some fell fiend has cursed our
line,
That coward should e'er be son of
mine ! '

XV.

A heavy task Watt Tinlinn had,
To guide the counterfeited lad.
Soon as the palfrey felt the weight
Of that ill-omen'd elfish freight,
He bolted, sprung, and rear d amain,
Nor heeded bit, nor curb, nor rein.
It cost Watt Tinlinn mickle toil
To drive him but a Scottish mile ;
But as a shallow brook they
cross'd,
The elf, amid the running stream,
His figure chang d, like form in
dream,
And fled, and shouted, ' Lost !
lost ! lost ! '
Full fast the urchin ran and laugh'd,
But faster still a cloth-yard shaft
Whistled from startled Tinlinn's yew,
And pierc'd his shoulder through and
through.
Although the imp might not be
slain,
And though the wound soon heal'd
again,
Yet, as he ran. he yell'd for pain ;
And Wat of Tinlinn. much aghast,
Rode back to Branksome fiery fast.

XVI.

Soon on the hill's steep verge he
  stood,
That looks o'er Branksome's towers
  and wood ;
And martial murmurs, from below,
Proclaim'd the approaching southern
  foe.
Through the dark wood, in mingled
  tone,
Were Border pipes and bugles blown ;
The coursers' neighing he could ken,
A measured tread of marching men ;
While broke at times the solemn hum
The Almayn's sullen kettle-drum ;
  And banners tall of crimson sheen
    Above the copse appear ;
  And, glistening through the haw-
    thorns green,
    Shine helm, and shield, and spear.

XVII.

Light forayers, first, to view the
  ground,
Spurr'd their fleet coursers loosely
  round ;
  Behind, in close array, and fast,
    The Kendal archers all in green,
  Obedient to the bugle blast,
    Advancing from the wood were
    seen.
To back and guard the archer band,
Lord Dacre's bill-men were at hand :
A hardy race, on Irthing bred,
With kirtles white, and crosses red,
Array'd beneath the banner tall,
That stream'd o'er Acre's conquer'd
  wall ;
And minstrels, as they march'd in
  order,
Play'd 'Noble Lord Dacre, he dwells
  on the Border.'

XVIII.

Behind the English bill and bow,
The mercenaries, firm and slow,
  Moved on to fight, in dark array,

By Conrad led of Wolfenstein,
Who brought the band from distant
  Rhine,
  And sold their blood for foreign pay.
The camp their home, their law the
  sword,
They knew no country, own'd no lord :
They were not arm'd like England's
  sons,
But bore the levin-darting guns ;
Buff coats, all frounc'd and 'broider'd
  o'er,
And morsing-horns and scarfs they
  wore ;
Each better knee was bared, to aid
The warriors in the escalade ;
All as they march'd, in rugged tongue,
Songs of Teutonic feuds they sung.

XIX.

But louder still the clamour grew,
And louder still the minstrels blew,
When, from beneath the greenwood
  tree,
Rode forth Lord Howard's chivalry ;
His men-at-arms, with glaive and
  spear,
Brought up the battle's glittering rear.
There many a youthful knight, full
  keen
To gain his spurs, in arms was seen ;
With favour in his crest, or glove,
Memorial of his ladye-love.
So rode they forth in fair array,
Till full their lengthen'd lines display ;
Then call'd a halt, and made a stand,
And cried 'St. George for merry
  England !'

XX.

Now every English eye, intent
On Branksome's armed towers was
  bent ;
So near they were, that they might
  know
The straining harsh of each cross-bow;
On battlement and bartizan
Gleam'd axe, and spear, and partisan ;

Falcon and culver, on each tower,
Stood prompt their deadly hail to
    shower ;
And flashing armour frequent broke
From eddying whirls of sable smoke,
Where upon tower and turret-head,
The seething pitch and molten lead
Reek'd, like a witch's caldron red.
While yet they gaze, the bridges
    fall,
The wicket opes, and from the wall
Rides forth the hoary Seneschal.

XXI.

Armed he rode, all save the head,
His white beard o'er his breast-plate
    spread ;
Unbroke by age, erect his seat,
He rul'd his eager courser's gait ;
Forc d him, with chasten'd fire to
    prance,
And, high curvetting, slow advance ;
In sign of truce, his better hand
Display'd a peeled willow wand ;
His squire, attending in the rear,
Bore high a gauntlet on a spear.
When they espied him riding out,
Lord Howard and Lord Dacre stout
Sped to the front of their array,
To hear what this old knight should
    say.

XXII.

'Ye English warden lords, of you
Demands the Ladye of Buccleuch,
Why, 'gainst the truce of Border tide,
In hostile guise ye dare to ride,
With Kendal bow, and Gilsland
    brand,
And all yon mercenary band,
Upon the bounds of fair Scotland?
My Ladye reads you swith return ;
And, if but one poor straw you burn
Or do our towers so much molest
As scare one swallow from her nest,
St. Mary ! but we'll light a brand
Shall warm your hearths in Cumber-
    land.'

XXIII.

A wrathful man was Dacre's lord,
But calmer Howard took the word :
' May 't please thy Dame, Sir Senes-
    chal,
To seek the castle's outward wall,
Our pursuivant-at-arms shall show
Both why we came, and when we go.'
The message sped, the noble Dame
To the wall's outward circle came ;
Each chief around lean'd on his spear
To see the pursuivant appear.
All in Lord Howard's livery dress'd,
The lion argent deck'd his breast ;
He led a boy of blooming hue—
O sight to meet a mother's view !
It was the heir of great Buccleuch.
Obeisance meet the herald made,
And thus his master's will he said :

XXIV.

' It irks, high Dame, my noble Lords,
'Gainst ladye fair to draw their
    swords ;
But yet they may not tamely see,
All through the Western Wardenry,
Your law-contemning kinsmen ride,
And burn and spoil the Border-side ;
And ill beseems your rank and birth
To make your towers a flemens-firth.
We claim from thee William of
    Deloraine,
That he may suffer march-treason
    pain.
It was but last St. Cuthbert's even
He prick'd to Stapleton on Leven,
Harried the lands of Richard Mus-
    grave,
And slew his brother by dint of
    glaive.
Then, since a lone and widow'd
    Dame
These restless riders may not tame,
Either receive within thy towers
Two hundred of my master's powers,
Or straight they sound their warrison,
And storm and spoil thy garrison :

And this fair boy, to London led,
Shall good King Edward's page be
   bred.'

XXV.

He ceased—and loud the boy did cry,
And stretch'd his little arms on high ;
Implor'd for aid each well-known
   face,
And strove to seek the Dame's em-
   brace.
A moment chang'd that Ladye's cheer,
Gush'd to her eye the unbidden tear ;
She gaz'd upon the leaders round,
And dark and sad each warrior
   frown'd ;
Then, deep within her sobbing breast
She lock'd the struggling sigh to
   rest ;
Unalter'd and collected stood,
And thus replied in dauntless mood :

XXVI.

' Say to your Lords of high emprize,
Who war on women and on boys,
That either William of Deloraine
Will cleanse him by oath of march-
   treason stain,
Or else he will the combat take
'Gainst Musgrave, for his honour's
   sake.
No knight in Cumberland so good,
But William may count with him kin
   and blood.
Knighthood he took of Douglas'
   sword,
When English blood swell'd Ancram's
   ford ;
And but Lord Dacre's steed was wight,
And bare him ably in the flight,
Himself had seen him dubb'd a knight
For the young heir of Branksome's
   line,
God be his aid, and God be mine ;
Through me no friend shall meet his
   doom ;
Here, while I live, no foe finds
   room.

Then, if thy Lords their purpose
   urge,
   Take our defiance loud and high ;
Our slogan is their lyke-wake dirge,
   Our moat the grave where they
     shall lie.'

XXVII.

Proud she look'd round, applause to
   claim—
Then lighten'd Thirlestane's eye of
   flame ;
   His bugle Wat of Harden blew ;
Pensils and pennons wide were flung,
To heaven the Border slogan rung,
   ' St. Mary for the young Buc-
     cleuch !'
The English war-cry answer'd wide,
   And forward bent each southern
     spear ;
Each Kendal archer made a stride,
   And drew the bowstring to his
     ear ;
Each minstrel's war-note loud was
   blown ;
But, ere a grey-goose shaft had
   flown,
   A horseman gallop'd from the rear.

XXVIII.

' Ah ! noble Lords !' he breathless
   said,
' What treason has your march be-
   tray'd ?
What make you here, from aid so far,
Before you walls, around you war ?
Your foemen triumph in the thought
That in the toils the lion 's caught.
Already on dark Ruberslaw
   The Douglas holds his weapon-
     schaw ;
The lances, waving in his train,
Clothe the dun heath like autumn
   grain ;
And on the Liddel's northern strand,
To bar retreat to Cumberland,

Lord Maxwell ranks his merry-men
  good,
Beneath the eagle and the rood ;
  And Jedwood, Eske, and Teviot-
    dale,
  Have to proud Angus come ;
  And all the Merse and Lauderdale
  Have risen with haughty Home.
  An exile from Northumberland,
    In Liddesdale I've wander'd long ;
  But still my heart was with merry
    England,
    And cannot brook my country's
      wrong ;
And hard I've spurr'd all night, to
  show
The mustering of the coming foe.'

XXIX.

'And let them come !' fierce Dacre
  cried ;
' For soon yon crest, my father's pride,
That swept the shores of Judah's sea,
And wav'd in gales of Galilee,
From Branksome's highest towers
  display'd,
Shall mock the rescue's lingering aid !—
Level each harquebuss on row ;
Draw, merry archers, draw the bow ;
Up, bill-men, to the walls, and cry,
Dacre for England, win or die !'

XXX.

' Yet hear,' quoth Howard, ' calmly
  hear,
Nor deem my words the words of fear :
For who, in field or foray slack,
Saw the blanche lion e'er fall back ?
But thus to risk our Border flower
In strife against a kingdom's power,
Ten thousand Scots 'gainst thousands
  three,
Certes, were desperate policy.
Nay, take the terms the Ladye made,
Ere conscious of the advancing aid :
Let Musgrave meet fierce Deloraine
In single fight, and, if he gain,

He gains for us ; but if he 's cross'd,
'Tis but a single warrior lost :
The rest, retreating as they came,
Avoid defeat, and death, and shame.'

XXXI.

Ill could the haughty Dacre brook
His brother Warden's sage rebuke ;
And yet his forward step he staid,
And slow and sullenly obey'd.
But ne'er again the Border side
Did these two lords in friendship
  ride ;
And this slight discontent, men say,
Cost blood upon another day.

XXXII.

The pursuivant-at-arms again
  Before the castle took his stand ;
His trumpet call'd, with parleying
  strain,
  The leaders of the Scottish band ;
And he defied, in Musgrave's right,
Stout Deloraine to single fight ;
A gauntlet at their feet he laid,
And thus the terms of fight he said :
' If in the lists good Musgrave's sword
  Vanquish the Knight of Deloraine,
Your youthful chieftain, Branksome's
  Lord,
  Shall hostage for his clan remain :
If Deloraine foil good Musgrave,
The boy his liberty shall have.
  Howe'er it falls, the English band,
Unharming Scots, by Scots unharm'd,
In peaceful march, like men unarm'd,
  Shall straight retreat to Cumberland.'

XXXIII.

Unconscious of the near relief,
The proffer pleased each Scottish chief,
  Though much the Ladye sage gain-
    say'd ;
For though their hearts were brave
  and true,
From Jedwood's recent sack they knew
  How tardy was the Regent's aid :

And you may guess the noble Dame
  Durst not the secret prescience
    own,
Sprung from the art she might not
    name,
  By which the coming help was
    known.
Clos'd was the compact, and agreed
That lists should be enclos'd with
    speed,
  Beneath the castle, on a lawn:
They fix'd the morrow for the strife,
On foot, with Scottish axe and knife,
  At the fourth hour from peep of
    dawn ;
When Deloraine, from sickness freed,
Or else a champion in his stead,
Should for himself and chieftain stand
Against stout Musgrave, hand to hand.

XXXIV.

I know right well, that, in their lay,
Full many minstrels sing and say,
  Such combat should be made on
    horse,
On foaming steed, in full career,
With brand to aid, when as the spear
  Should shiver in the course :
But he, the jovial Harper, taught
Me, yet a youth, how it was fought,
  In guise which now I say ;
He knew each ordinance and clause
Of Black Lord Archibald's battle-laws,
  In the old Douglas' day.
He brook'd not, he, that scoffing tongue
Should tax his minstrelsy with wrong,
  Or call his song untrue :
For this, when they the goblet plied,
And such rude taunt had chaf'd his
    pride,
  The Bard of Reull he slew.
On Teviot's side, in fight they stood,
And tuneful hands were stain'd with
    blood ;
Where still the thorn's white branches
    wave,
Memorial o'er his rival's grave.

XXXV.

Why should I tell the rigid doom
That dragg'd my master to his tomb ;
  How Ousenam's maidens tore their
    hair,
Wept till their eyes were dead and
    dim,
And wrung their hands for love of
    him,
  Who died at Jedwood Air ?
He died !—his scholars, one by one,
To the cold silent grave are gone ;
And I, alas ! survive alone,
To muse o'er rivalries of yore,
And grieve that I shall hear no more
The strains, with envy heard before ;
For, with my minstrel brethren fled,
My jealousy of song is dead.

He paused : the listening dames again
Applaud the hoary Minstrel's strain.
With many a word of kindly cheer,
In pity half, and half sincere,
Marvell'd the Duchess how so well
His legendary song could tell
Of ancient deeds, so long forgot ;
Of feuds, whose memory was not ;
Of forests, now laid waste and bare ;
Of towers, which harbour now the
    hare ;
Of manners, long since chang'd and
    gone ;
Of chiefs, who under their grey stone
So long had slept, that fickle Fame
Had blotted from her rolls their name,
And twin'd round some new minion's
    head
The fading wreath for which they bled ;
In sooth, 'twas strange, this old man's
    verse
Could call them from their marble
    hearse.

  The Harper smil'd, well-pleas'd ;
    for ne'er
Was flattery lost on poet's ear :

A simple race! they waste their toil
For the vain tribute of a smile ;
E'en when in age their flame expires,
Her dulcet breath can fan its fires :
Their drooping fancy wakes at praise,
And strives to trim the short-liv'd
    blaze.

Smil'd then, well pleas'd, the aged
    man,
And thus his tale continued ran.

—◆◆—

Canto Fifth.

I.

CALL it not vain ; they do not err,
    Who say, that when the Poet dies,
Mute Nature mourns her worshipper,
    And celebrates his obsequies :
Who say, tall cliff and cavern lone
For the departed Bard make moan ;
That mountains weep in crystal rill ;
That flowers in tears of balm distil ;
Through his lov'd groves that breezes
    sigh,
And oaks, in deeper groan, reply ;
And rivers teach their rushing wave
To murmur dirges round his grave.

II.

Not that, in sooth, o'er mortal urn
Those things inanimate can mourn ;
But that the stream, the wood, the gale,
Is vocal with the plaintive wail
Of those, who, else forgotten long,
Liv'd in the poet's faithful song,
And, with the poet's parting breath,
Whose memory feels a second death.
The Maid's pale shade, who wails her
    lot,
That love, true love, should be forgot,
From rose and hawthorn shakes the
    tear
Upon the gentle Minstrel's bier :

The phantom Knight, his glory fled,
Mourns o'er the field he heap'd with
    dead ;
Mounts the wild blast that sweeps
    amain,
And shrieks along the battle-plain.
The Chief, whose antique crownlet
    long
Still sparkled in the feudal song,
Now, from the mountain's misty throne,
Sees, in the thanedom once his own,
His ashes undistinguish'd lie,
His place, his power, his memory die :
His groans the lonely caverns fill,
His tears of rage impel the rill :
All mourn the Minstrel's harp unstrung,
Their name unknown, their praise un-
    sung.

III.

Scarcely the hot assault was staid,
The terms of truce were scarcely made,
When they could spy, from Brank-
    some's towers,
The advancing march of martial powers.
Thick clouds of dust afar appear'd,
And trampling steeds were faintly
    heard ;
Bright spears, above the columns dun,
Glanced momentary to the sun ;
And feudal banners fair display'd
The bands that moved to Branksome's
    aid.

IV.

Vails not to tell each hardy clan,
    From the fair Middle Marches came ;
The Bloody Heart blaz'd in the van,
    Announcing Douglas, dreaded
        name !
Vails not to tell what steeds did spurn,
Where the Seven Spears of Wedder-
    burne
    Their men in battle-order set ;
And Swinton laid the lance in rest,
That tamed of yore the sparkling crest
    Of Clarence's Plantagenet.
Nor list I say what hundreds more,
From the rich Merse and Lammermore,

And Tweed's fair borders to the war,
Beneath the crest of Old Dunbar,
   And Hepburn's mingled banners
      come,
Down the steep mountain glittering
      far.
   And shouting still, 'A Home! a
      Home!'

V.

Now squire and knight, from Brank-
      some sent,
On many a courteous message went;
To every chief and lord they paid
Meet thanks for prompt and powerful
      aid;
And told them,—how a truce was
      made,
   And how a day of fight was ta'en
   'Twixt Musgrave and stout Delo-
      raine;
      And how the Ladye pray'd them
         dear,
   That all would stay the fight to see,
   And deign, in love and courtesy,
      To taste of Branksome cheer.
Nor, while they bade to feast each
      Scot,
Were England's noble Lords forgot.
Himself, the hoary Seneschal
Rode forth, in seemly terms to call
Those gallant foes to Branksome Hall.
Accepted Howard, than whom knight
Was never dubb'd more bold in fight;
Nor, when from war and armour free,
More fam'd for stately courtesy:
But angry Dacre rather chose
In his pavilion to repose.

VI.

Now, noble Dame, perchance you ask
   How these two hostile armies met?
Deeming it were no easy task
   To keep the truce which here was
      set;
Where martial spirits, all on fire,
Breathed only blood and mortal ire.

By mutual inroads, mutual blows,
By habit, and by nation, foes;
   They met on Teviot's strand;
They met and sate them mingled down,
Without a threat, without a frown,
   As brothers meet in foreign land:
The hands the spear that lately
      grasp'd,
Still in the mailed gauntlet clasp'd,
   Were interchang'd in greeting dear;
Visors were raised, and faces shown,
And many a friend, to friend made
      known,
   Partook of social cheer.
Some drove the jolly bowl about;
   With dice and draughts some chas'd
      the day;
And some with many a merry shout,
In riot, revelry, and rout,
   Pursued the foot-ball play.

VII.

Yet, be it known, had bugles blown,
   Or sign of war been seen,
Those bands so fair together rang'd,
Those hands, so frankly interchang'd,
   Had dyed with gore the green:
The merry shout by Teviot-side
Had sunk in war-cries wild and wide,
   And in the groan of death;
And whingers, now in friendship bare
The social meal to part and share,
   Had found a bloody sheath.
'Twixt truce and war, such sudden
      change
Was not infrequent, nor held strange,
   In the old Border-day:
But yet on Branksome's towers and
      town,
In peaceful merriment, sunk down
   The sun's declining ray.

VIII.

The blithsome signs of wassel gay
Decay'd not with the dying day:
Soon through the lattic'd windows
      tall
Of lofty Branksome's lordly hall,

Divided square by shafts of stone,
Huge flakes of ruddy lustre shone ;
Nor less the gilded rafters rang
With merry harp and beakers' clang:
  And frequent, on the darkening plain,
    Loud hollo, whoop, or whistle ran,
    As bands, their stragglers to regain,
    Give the shrill watchword of their clan ;
And revellers, o'er their bowls, proclaim
Douglas or Dacre's conquering name.

IX.

Less frequent heard, and fainter still,
  At length the various clamours died :
And you might hear, from Branksome hill,
  No sound but Teviot's rushing tide ;
Save when the changing sentinel
The challenge of his watch could tell ;
And save where, through the dark profound,
The clanging axe and hammer's sound
  Rung from the nether lawn ;
For many a busy hand toil'd there,
Strong pales to shape, and beams to square,
The lists' dread barriers to prepare
  Against the morrow's dawn.

X.

Margaret from hall did soon retreat,
  Despite the Dame's reproving eye ;
Nor mark'd she, as she left her seat,
  Full many a stifled sigh ;
For many a noble warrior strove
To win the Flower of Teviot's love,
  And many a bold ally.
With throbbing head and anxious heart,
All in her lonely bower apart,
  In broken sleep she lay :

Betimes from silken couch she rose ;
While yet the banner'd hosts repose,
  She view'd the dawning day :
Of all the hundreds sunk to rest,
First woke the loveliest and the best.

XI.

She gaz'd upon the inner court,
  Which in the tower's tall shadow lay ;
Where coursers' clang, and stamp, and snort
Had rung the livelong yesterday ;
Now still as death ; till stalking slow—
  The jingling spurs announc'd his tread—
A stately warrior pass'd below ;
  But when he rais'd his plumed head—
    Bless'd Mary ! can it be ?
Secure, as if in Ousenam bowers,
He walks through Branksome's hostile towers
  With fearless step and free.
She dar'd not sign, she dar'd not speak—
Oh ! if one page's slumbers break,
His blood the price must pay !
Not all the pearls Queen Mary wears,
Not Margaret's yet more precious tears,
  Shall buy his life a day.

XII.

Yet was his hazard small ; for well
You may bethink you of the spell
  Of that sly urchin page ;
This to his lord he did impart,
And made him seem, by glamour art,
  A knight from Hermitage.
Unchalleng'd thus, the warder's post,
The court, unchalleng'd, thus he cross'd,
  For all the vassalage :
But O ! what magic's quaint disguise
Could blind fair Margaret's azure eyes!
  She started from her seat ;

While with surprise and fear she
   strove,
And both could scarcely master
   love,
   Lord Henry's at her feet.

XIII.

Oft have I mus'd what purpose bad
That foul malicious urchin had
   To bring this meeting round ;
For happy love 's a heavenly sight,
And by a vile malignant sprite
   In such no joy is found ;
And oft I 've deem'd perchance he
   thought
Their erring passion might have
   wrought
   Sorrow, and sin, and shame ;
And death to Cranstoun's gallant
   Knight,
And to the gentle ladye bright
   Disgrace and loss of fame.
But earthly spirit could not tell
The heart of them that lov'd so well.
True love 's the gift which God has
   given
To man alone beneath the heaven :
   It is not fantasy's hot fire,
     Whose wishes, soon as granted,
     fly ;
   It liveth not in fierce desire,
     With dead desire it doth not die ;
It is the secret sympathy,
The silver link, the silken tie,
Which heart to heart, and mind to
   mind,
In body and in soul can bind.
Now leave we Margaret and her
   Knight,
To tell you of the approaching fight.

XIV.

Their warning blasts the bugles blew,
   The pipe's shrill port arous'd each
   clan ;
In haste, the deadly strife to view,
   The trooping warriors eager ran :

Thick round the lists their lances
   stood,
Like blasted pines in Ettrick wood ;
To Branksome many a look they
   threw,
The combatants' approach to view,
And bandied many a word of boast
About the knight each favour'd most.

XV.

Meantime full anxious was the Dame;
For now arose disputed claim
Of who should fight for Deloraine,
'Twixt Harden and 'twixt Thirlestaine :
They 'gan to reckon kin and rent,
And frowning brow on brow was
   bent ;
   But yet not long the strife--for, lo !
Himself, the Knight of Deloraine,
Strong, as it seem'd, and free from
   pain,
   In armour sheath'd from top to toe,
Appear'd and crav'd the combat due.
The Dame her charm successful knew,
And the fierce chiefs their claims
   withdrew.

XVI.

When for the lists they sought the
   plain,
The stately Ladye's silken rein
   Did noble Howard hold ;
Unarmed by her side he walk'd,
And much, in courteous phrase, they
   talk'd
   Of feats of arms of old.
Costly his garb ; his Flemish ruff
Fell o'er his doublet, shap'd of buff,
   With satin slash'd and lin'd ;
Tawny his boot, and gold his spur,
His cloak was all of Poland fur,
   His hose with silver twin'd ;
His Bilboa blade, by Marchmen felt,
Hung in a broad and studded belt ;
Hence, in rude phrase, the Borderers
   still
Call'd noble Howard, Belted Will.

XVII.

Behind Lord Howard and the Dame,
Fair Margaret on her palfrey came,
  Whose foot-cloth swept the
    ground :
White was her wimple, and her veil,
And her loose locks a chaplet pale
  Of whitest roses bound ;
The lordly Angus, by her side,
In courtesy to cheer her tried ;
Without his aid, her hand in vain
Had strove to guide her broider'd
    rein.
He deem'd she shudder'd at the
    sight
Of warriors met for mortal fight ;
But cause of terror, all unguess'd,
Was fluttering in her gentle breast,
When, in their chairs of crimson
    plac'd,
The Dame and she the barriers grac'd.

XVIII.

Prize of the field, the young Buc-
    cleuch,
An English knight led forth to view ;
Scarce rued the boy his present
    plight,
So much he long'd to see the fight.
Within the lists, in knightly pride,
High Home and haughty Dacre ride ;
Their leading staffs of steel they wield
As marshals of the mortal field ;
While to each knight their care
    assign'd
Like vantage of the sun and wind.
Then heralds hoarse did loud pro-
    claim,
In King and Queen and Warden's
    name,
  That none, while lasts the strife,
Should dare, by look, or sign, or word,
Aid to a champion to afford,
  On peril of his life ;
And not a breath the silence broke,
Till thus the alternate Heralds
    spoke :

XIX.

ENGLISH HERALD.

' Here standeth Richard of Musgrave,
  Good knight and true, and freely
    born,
Amends from Deloraine to crave,
  For foul despiteous scathe and
    scorn.
He sayeth that William of Deloraine
  Is traitor false by Border laws ;
This with his sword he will maintain,
  So help him God, and his good
    cause ! '

XX.

SCOTTISH HERALD.

' Here standeth William of Deloraine,
Good knight and true, of noble strain,
Who sayeth that foul treason's stain,
  Since he bore arms, ne'er soil'd his
    coat ;
  And that, so help him God above !
  He will on Musgrave's body
    prove,
  He lies most foully in his throat.'

LORD DACRE.

' Forward, brave champions, to the
    fight !
Sound trumpets ! '

LORD HOME.

          ' God defend the right ! '
Then, Teviot ! how thine echoes rang,
When bugle-sound and trumpet-clang
  Let loose the martial foes,
And in mid list, with shield pois'd
    high,
And measur'd step and wary eye,
  The combatants did close.

XXI.

Ill would it suit your gentle ear,
Ye lovely listeners, to hear
How to the axe the helms did sound,
And blood pour'd down from many a
    wound ;
For desperate was the strife and long,
And either warrior fierce and strong.

But, were each dame a listening
     knight,
I well could tell how warriors fight !
For I have seen war's lightning
     flashing,
Seen the claymore with bayonet
     clashing,
Seen through red blood the war-horse
     dashing,
And scorn'd, amid the reeling strife,
To yield a step for death or life.

XXII.

'Tis done, 'tis done ! that fatal blow
     Has stretch'd him on the bloody
     plain ;
He strives to rise—brave Musgrave,
     no !
     Thence never shalt thou rise again !
He chokes in blood ! some friendly
     hand
Undo the visor's barred band,
Unfix the gorget's iron clasp,
And give him room for life to gasp !
O, bootless aid ! haste, holy Friar,
Haste, ere the sinner shall expire !
Of all his guilt let him be shriven,
And smooth his path from earth to
     heaven !

XXIII.

In haste the holy Friar sped ;
His naked foot was dyed with red
     As through the lists he ran ;
Unmindful of the shouts on high,
That hail'd the conqueror's victory,
     He rais'd the dying man ;
Loose wav'd his silver beard and hair,
As o'er him he kneel'd down in
     prayer ;
And still the crucifix on high
He holds before his darkening eye ;
And still he bends an anxious ear
His faltering penitence to hear ;
     Still props him from the bloody sod,
Still, even when soul and body part,
Pours ghostly comfort on his heart,
     And bids him trust in God

Unheard he prays ; the death pang 's
     o'er !
Richard of Musgrave breathes no
     more.

XXIV.

As if exhausted in the fight,
Or musing o'er the piteous sight,
     The silent victor stands ;
His beaver did he not unclasp,
Mark'd not the shouts, felt not the
     grasp
     Of gratulating hands.
When lo ! strange cries of wild
     surprise,
Mingled with seeming terror, rise
     Among the Scottish bands ;
And all, amid the throng'd array,
In panic haste gave open way
To a half-naked ghastly man
Who downward from the castle
     ran :
He cross'd the barriers at a bound,
And wild and haggard look'd around,
     As dizzy, and in pain ;
And all, upon the armed ground,
     Knew William of Deloraine !
Each ladye sprung from seat with
     speed ;
Vaulted each marshal from his steed ;
     'And who art thou,' they cried,
'Who hast this battle fought and
     won ? '
His plumed helm was soon undone—
     'Cranstoun of Teviot-side !
For this fair prize I've fought and
     won ; '
And to the Ladye led her son.

XXV.

Full oft the rescued boy she kiss'd,
And often press'd him to her breast ;
For, under all her dauntless show,
Her heart had throbb'd at every blow ;
Yet not Lord Cranstoun deign'd she
     greet,
Though low he kneeled at her feet.

Me lists not tell what words were
made,
What Douglas, Home, and Howard
said—
For Howard was a generous foe—
And how the clan united pray'd
The Ladye would the feud forego,
And deign to bless the nuptial hour
Of Cranstoun's Lord and Teviot's
Flower.

XXVI.

She look'd to river, look'd to hill,
Thought on the Spirit's prophecy,
Then broke her silence stern and
still—
' Not you, but Fate, has vanquish'd
me ;
Their influence kindly stars may
shower
On Teviot's tide and Branksome's
tower,
For pride is quell'd, and love is
free.'
She took fair Margaret by the hand,
Who, breathless, trembling, scarce
might stand ;
That hand to Cranstoun's lord gave
she :
' As I am true to thee and thine,
Do thou be true to me and mine !
This clasp of love our bond shall
be ;
For this is your betrothing day,
And all these noble lords shall stay
To grace it with their company.'

XXVII.

All as they left the listed plain,
Much of the story she did gain ;
How Cranstoun fought with Delo-
raine,
And of his page, and of the Book
Which from the wounded knight he
took ;
And how he sought her castle high,
That morn, by help of gramarye ;

How, in Sir William's armour dight,
Stolen by his page, while slept the
knight,
He took on him the single fight.
But half his tale he left unsaid,
And linger'd till he join'd the maid.
Car'd not the Ladye to betray
Her mystic arts in view of day ;
But well she thought, ere midnight
came,
Of that strange page the pride to
tame,
From his foul hands the ·Book to save,
And send it back to Michael's grave.
Needs not to tell each tender word
'Twixt Margaret and 'twixt Cran-
stoun s lord ;
Nor how she told of former woes,
And how her bosom fell and rose,
While he and Musgrave bandied
blows.
Needs not these lovers' joys to tell :
One day, fair maids, you 'll know them
well.

XXVIII.

William of Deloraine some chance
Had waken'd from his deathlike
trance ;
And taught that, in the listed plain,
Another, in his arms and shield,
Against fierce Musgrave axe did
wield
Under the name of Deloraine.
Hence to the field unarm'd he ran,
And hence his presence scar'd the
clan,
Who held him for some fleeting
wraith,
And not a man of blood and breath.
Not much this new ally he lov'd,
Yet, when he saw what hap had
prov'd,
He greeted him right heartilie :
He would not waken old debate,
For he was void of rancorous hate,
Though rude, and scant of
courtesy ;

In raids he spilt but seldom blood,
Unless when men-at-arms withstood,
Or, as was meet, for deadly feud.
He ne'er bore grudge for stalwart
    blow,
Ta'en in fair fight from gallant foe:
    And so 'twas seen of him, e'en
      now,
      When on dead Musgrave he
        look'd down;
    Grief darken'd on his rugged brow,
      Though half disguised with a
        frown;
And thus, while sorrow bent his head,
His foeman's epitaph he made.

XXIX.

'Now, Richard Musgrave, liest thou
    here!
I ween, my deadly enemy;
For, if I slew thy brother dear,
    Thou slew'st a sister's son to me;
And when I lay in dungeon dark
    Of Naworth Castle, long months
      three,
Till ransom'd for a thousand mark,
    Dark Musgrave, it was 'long of
      thee.
And, Musgrave, could our fight be
    tried,
    And thou wert now alive, as I,
No mortal man should us divide,
    Till one, or both of us, did die:
Yet, rest thee God! for well I know
I ne'er shall find a nobler foe.
In all the northern counties here,
Whose word is *Snaffle, spur, and*
    spear,
Thou wert the best to follow gear!
'Twas pleasure, as we look'd behind,
To see how thou the chase could'st
    wind,
Cheer the dark blood-hound on his
    way,
And with the bugle rouse the fray!
I'd give the lands of Deloraine,
Dark Musgrave were alive again.'

XXX.

So mourn'd he, till Lord Dacre's
    band
Were bowning back to Cumberland.
They rais'd brave Musgrave from the
    field,
And laid him on his bloody shield;
On levell'd lances, four and four,
By turns, the noble burden bore.
Before, at times, upon the gale,
Was heard the Minstrel's plaintive
    wail;
Behind, four priests, in sable stole,
Sung requiem for the warrior's soul:
Around, the horsemen slowly rode;
With trailing pikes the spearmen
    trode;
And thus the gallant knight they
    bore
Through Liddesdale to Leven's shore;
Thence to Holme Coltrame's lofty
    nave,
And laid him in his father's grave.

THE harp's wild notes, though hush'd
    the song,
The mimic march of death prolong;
Now seems it far, and now a-near,
Now meets, and now eludes the ear;
Now seems some mountain side to
    sweep,
Now faintly dies in valley deep;
Seems now as if the Minstrel's wail,
Now the sad requiem, loads the
    gale;
Last, o'er the warrior's closing grave,
Rung the full choir in choral stave.

After due pause, they bade him tell,
Why he, who touch'd the harp so
    well,
Should thus, with ill-rewarded toil,
Wander a poor and thankless soil,
When the more generous Southern
    land
Would well requite his skilful hand.

The aged Harper, howsoe'er
His only friend, his harp, was dear,
Lik'd not to hear it rank'd so high
Above his flowing poesy :
Less lik'd he still that scornful jeer
Mispris'd the land he lov'd so dear;
High was the sound, as thus again
The Bard resum'd his minstrel strain.

—++—

Canto Sixth.

I.

BREATHES there the man, with soul
    so dead,
Who never to himself hath said,
  This is my own, my native land !
Whose heart hath ne er within him
    burn'd,
As home his footsteps he hath turn'd,
  From wandering on a foreign
    strand !
If such there breathe, go, mark him
    well ;
For him no Minstrel raptures swell ;
High though his titles, proud his
    name,
Boundless his wealth as wish can
    claim ;
Despite those titles, power, and pelf,
The wretch, concentred all in self,
Living, shall forfeit fair renown,
And, doubly dying, shall go down
To the vile dust, from whence he
    sprung,
Unwept, unhonour'd, and unsung.

II.

O Caledonia ! stern and wild,
Meet nurse for a poetic child !
Land of brown heath and shaggy
    wood,
Land of the mountain and the flood,
Land of my sires ! what mortal hand
Can e'er untie the filial band,
That knits me to thy rugged strand !

Still as I view each well-known scene,
Think what is now, and what hath
    been,
Seems as, to me, of all bereft,
Sole friends thy woods and streams
    were left ;
And thus I love them better still,
Even in extremity of ill.
By Yarrow's stream still let me stray,
Though none should guide my feeble
    way ;
Still feel the breeze down Ettrick
    break,
Although it chill my wither'd cheek :
Still lay my head by Teviot Stone,
Though there, forgotten and alone,
The Bard may draw his parting groan.

III.

Not scorn'd like me, to Branksome
    Hall
The Minstrels came at festive call ;
Trooping they came, from near and
    far,
The jovial priests of mirth and war ;
Alike for feast and fight prepar d,
Battle and banquet both they shar'd.
Of late, before each martial clan,
They blew their death-note in the
    van,
But now, for every merry mate,
Rose the portcullis' iron grate ;
They sound the pipe, they strike the
    string,
They dance, they revel, and they
    sing,
Till the rude turrets shake and ring.

IV.

Me lists not at this tide declare
  The splendour of the spousal rite,
How muster'd in the chapel fair
  Both maid and matron, squire and
    knight ;
Me lists not tell of owches rare,
Of mantles green, and braided hair,
And kirtles furr'd with miniver ;

What plumage wav'd the altar round,
How spurs and ringing chainlets
    sound ;
And hard it were for bard to speak
The changeful hue of Margaret's
    cheek—
That lovely hue which comes and flies
As awe and shame alternate rise !

v.

Some bards have sung the Ladye
    high
Chapel or altar came not nigh ;
Nor durst the rites of spousal grace,
So much she fear'd each holy place.
False slanders these : I trust right well
She wrought not by forbidden spell ;
For mighty words and signs have
    power
O'er sprites in planetary hour :
Yet scarce I praise their venturous
    part,
Who tamper with such dangerous art.
    But this for faithful truth I say,
    The Ladye by the altar stood ;
    Of sable velvet her array,
    And on her head a crimson hood,
With pearls embroider'd and entwin'd,
Guarded with gold, with ermine lin'd ;
A merlin sat upon her wrist
Held by a leash of silken twist.

vi.

The spousal rites were ended soon :
'Twas now the merry hour of noon,
And in the lofty arched hall
Was spread the gorgeous festival.
Steward and squire, with heedful haste,
Marshall d the rank of every guest ;
Pages, with ready blade, were there,
The mighty meal to carve and share :
O'er capon, heron-shew, and crane,
And princely peacock s gilded train,
And o'er the boar-head, garnish'd
    brave,
And cygnet from St. Mary's wave ;
O'er ptarmigan and venison
The priest had spoke his benison.

Then rose the riot and the din,
Above, beneath, without, within !
For, from the lofty balcony,
Rung trumpet, shalm, and psaltery :
Their clanging bowls old warriors
    quaff'd,
Loudly they spoke, and loudly laugh'd ;
Whisper'd young knights, in tone
    more mild,
To ladies fair, and ladies smil'd.
The hooded hawks, high perch'd on
    beam,
The clamour join'd with whistling
    scream,
And flapp'd their wings, and shook
    their bells
In concert with the stag-hounds' yells.
Round go the flasks of ruddy wine,
From Bordeaux, Orleans, or the
    Rhine ;
Their tasks the busy sewers ply,
And all is mirth and revelry.

vii.

The Goblin Page, omitting still
No opportunity of ill,
Strove now, while blood ran hot and
    high,
To rouse debate and jealousy ;
Till Conrad, Lord of Wolfenstein,
By nature fierce, and warm with
    wine,
And now in humour highly cross'd
About some steeds his band had
    lost,
High words to words succeeding still,
Smote with his gauntlet stout Hunt-
    hill—
A hot and hardy Rutherford,
Whom men called Dickon Draw-the-
    sword.
He took it on the page's saye,
Hunthill had driven these steeds
    away.
Then Howard, Home, and Douglas
    rose,
The kindling discord to compose :

Stern Rutherford right little said,
But bit his glove, and shook his head.
A fortnight thence, in Inglewood,
Stout Conrad, cold, and drench'd in
　　blood,
His bosom gor'd with many a wound,
Was by a woodman's lyme-dog found;
Unknown the manner of his death,
Gone was his brand, both sword and
　　sheath;
But ever from that time, 'twas said,
That Dickon wore a Cologne blade.

VIII.

The dwarf, who fear'd his master's eye
Might his foul treachery espie,
Now sought the castle buttery,
Where many a yeoman, bold and
　　free,
Revell'd as merrily and well
As those that sat in lordly selle.
Watt Tinlinn, there, did frankly raise
The pledge to Arthur Fire-the-Braes;
And he, as by his breeding bound,
To Howard's merry-men sent it round.
To quit them, on the English side,
Red Roland Forster loudly cried,
'A deep carouse to yon fair bride!'
At every pledge, from vat and pail,
Foam'd forth in floods the nut-brown
　　ale,
While shout the riders every one;
Such day of mirth ne'er cheer'd their
　　clan,
Since old Buccleuch the name did gain,
When in the cleuch the buck was
　　ta'en.

IX.

The wily page, with vengeful thought,
　　Remember'd him of Tinlinn's yew,
And swore it should be dearly bought
　　That ever he the arrow drew.
First, he the yeoman did molest,
With bitter gibe and taunting jest;
Told how he fled at Solway strife,
And how Hob Armstrong cheer'd his
　　wife;

Then, shunning still his powerful
　　arm,
At unawares he wrought him harm;
From trencher stole his choicest
　　cheer,
Dash'd from his lips his can of beer;
Then, to his knee sly creeping on,
With bodkin pierced him to the
　　bone:
The venom'd wound, and festering
　　joint,
Long after rued that bodkin's point.
The startled yeoman swore and
　　spurn'd,
And board and flagons overturn'd.
Riot and clamour wild began;
Back to the hall the Urchin ran;
Took in a darkling nook his post,
And grinn'd, and mutter'd, 'Lost!
　　lost! lost!'

X.

By this, the Dame, lest farther fray
Should mar the concord of the day,
Had bid the Minstrels tune their lay.
And first stept forth old Albert
　　Græme,
The Minstrel of that ancient name:
Was none who struck the harp so
　　well
Within the Land Debateable;
Well friended, too, his hardy kin,
Whoever lost, were sure to win;
They sought the beeves that made
　　their broth,
In Scotland and in England both.
In homely guise, as nature bade,
His simple song the Borderer said.

XI.

ALBERT GRÆME.

It was an English ladye bright,
　　(The sun shines fair on Carlisle
　　　wall,)
And she would marry a Scottish
　　knight,
　　For Love will still be lord of all.

Blithely they saw the rising sun,
  When he shone fair on Carlisle
    wall ;
But they were sad ere day was done,
  Though Love was still the lord of all.

Her sire gave brooch and jewel fine,
  Where the sun shines fair on Car-
    lisle wall ;
Her brother gave but a flask of wine,
  For ire that Love was lord of all.

For she had lands, both meadow and
    lea,
  Where the sun shines fair on Car-
    lisle wall ;
And he swore her death ere he would
    see
  A Scottish knight the lord of all !

XII.

That wine she had not tasted well,
  (The sun shines fair on Carlisle
    wall,)
When dead in her true love's arms
    she fell,
  For Love was still the lord of all !

He pierc'd her brother to the heart,
  Where the sun shines fair on
    Carlisle wall :
So perish all would true love part,
  That Love may still be lord of all !

And then he took the cross divine,
  (Where the sun shines fair on Car-
    lisle wall,)
And died for her sake in Palestine ;
  So Love was still the lord of all.

Now all ye lovers that faithful
    prove,
  (The sun shines fair on Carlisle
    wall,)
Pray for their souls who died for
    love,
  For Love shall still be lord of all !

XIII.

As ended Albert's simple lay,
  Arose a bard of loftier port ;
For sonnet, rhyme, and roundelay,
  Renown'd in haughty Henry's
    court :
There rung thy harp, unrivall'd long,
Fitztraver of the silver song !
  The gentle Surrey loved his lyre—
    Who has not heard of Surrey's
      fame ?
His was the hero's soul of fire,
  And his the bard's immortal
    name,
And his was love, exalted high
By all the glow of chivalry.

XIV.

They sought, together, climes afar,
  And oft, within some olive grove,
When even came with twinkling
    star,
  They sung of Surrey's absent love.
His step the Italian peasant stay'd,
  And deem'd that spirits from on
    high,
Round where some hermit saint was
    laid,
  Were breathing heavenly melody;
So sweet did harp and voice com-
    bine
To praise the name of Geraldine.

XV.

Fitztraver ! O what tongue may say
  The pangs thy faithful bosom knew,
When Surrey, of the deathless lay,
  Ungrateful Tudor's sentence slew ?
Regardless of the tyrant's frown,
His harp call'd wrath and vengeance
    down.
He left, for Naworth's iron towers,
Windsor's green glades, and courtly
    bowers,
And faithful to his patron's name,
With Howard still Fitztraver came ;
Lord William's foremost favourite he,
And chief of all his minstrelsy.

XVI.

FITZTRAVER.

'Twas All-soul's eve, and Surrey's
 heart beat high ;
 He heard the midnight bell with
  anxious start,
Which told the mystic hour,
 approaching nigh,
 When wise Cornelius promis'd,
  by his art,
To show to him the ladye of his
 heart,
 Albeit betwixt them roar'd the
  ocean grim ;
Yet so the sage had hight to play his
 part,
 That he should see her form in
  life and limb,
And mark, if still she lov'd, and still
 she thought of him.

XVII.

Dark was the vaulted room of
 gramarye,
 To which the wizard led the
  gallant Knight,
Save that before a mirror, huge and
 high,
 A hallow'd taper shed a glimmering light
On mystic implements of magic
 might ;
 On cross, and character, and
  talisman,
And almagest, and altar, nothing
 bright:
 For fitful was the lustre, pale and
  wan,
As watchlight by the bed of some
 departing man.

XVIII.

But soon, within that mirror huge
 and high,
 Was seen a self-emitted light to
  gleam ;

And forms upon its breast the Earl
 'gan spy,
 Cloudy and indistinct, as feverish
  dream ;
Till, slow arranging, and defin'd,
 they seem
  To form a lordly and a lofty
   room,
Part lighted by a lamp with silver
 beam,
 Plac'd by a couch of Agra's silken
  loom,
And part by moonshine pale, and
 part was hid in gloom.

XIX.

Fair all the pageant : but how pass-
 ing fair
  The slender form which lay on
   couch of Ind !
O'er her white bosom stray'd her
 hazel hair ;
 Pale her dear cheek, as if for love
  she pin'd ;
All in her night-robe loose she lay
 reclin'd,
 And pensive read from tablet
  eburnine
Some strain that seem'd her inmost
 soul to find :
 That favour d strain was Surrey's
  raptur'd line,
That fair and lovely form, the Lady
 Geraldine.

XX.

Slow roll'd the clouds upon the
 lovely form,
 And swept the goodly vision all
  away—
So royal envy roll'd the murky
 storm
 O'er my beloved Master's glori-
  ous day.
Thou jealous, ruthless tyrant !
 Heaven repay
 On thee, and on thy children's
  latest line,

The wild caprice of thy despotic
   sway,
  The gory bridal bed, the plunder'd
    shrine,
The murder d Surrey's blood, the tears
   of Geraldine !

XXI.

Both Scots, and Southern chiefs, pro-
   long
Applauses of Fitztraver's song ;
These hated Henry's name as death,
And those still held the ancient
   faith.
Then, from his seat, with lofty air,
Rose Harold, bard of brave St.
   Clair ;
St. Clair, who, feasting high at
   Home,
Had with that lord to battle come.
Harold was born where restless seas
Howl round the storm-swept Or-
   cades ;
Where erst St. Clairs held princely
   sway
O'er isle and islet, strait and bay ;—
Still nods their palace to its fall,
Thy pride and sorrow, fair Kirk-
   wall !
Thence oft he mark'd fierce Pent-
   land rave,
As if grim Odin rode her wave :
And watch'd the whilst, with visage,
   pale,
And throbbing heart, the struggling
   sail ;
For all of wonderful and wild
Had rapture for the lonely child.

XXII.

And much of wild and wonderful
In these rude isles might fancy cull ;
For thither came. in times afar,
Stern Lochlin's sons of roving war,
The Norsemen, train'd to spoil and
   blood,
Skill'd to prepare the raven's food ;

Kings of the main their leaders brave,
Their barks the dragons of the wave.
And there, in many a stormy vale,
The Scald had told his wondrous
   tale ;
And many a Runic column high
Had witness'd grim idolatry.
And thus had Harold in his youth
Learn'd many a Saga's rhyme un-
   couth —
Of that Sea-Snake, tremendous curl'd,
Whose monstrous circle girds the
   world ;
Of those dread Maids, whose hideous
   yell
Maddens the battle's bloody swell ;
Of Chiefs, who, guided through the
   gloom
By the pale death-lights of the tomb,
Ransack'd the graves of warriors
   old,
Their falchions wrench'd from corpses'
   hold,
Wak'd the deaf tomb with war's
   alarms,
And bade the dead arise to arms !
With war and wonder all on flame,
To Roslin's bowers young Harold
   came,
Where, by sweet glen and greenwood
   tree,
He learn d a milder minstrelsy ;
Yet something of the Northern spell
Mix'd with the softer numbers well.

XXIII.

HAROLD.

O listen, listen, ladies gay !
  No haughty feat of arms I tell ;
Soft is the note, and sad the lay,
  That mourns the lovely Rosabelle.

—'Moor, moor the barge, ye gallant
   crew !
  And, gentle ladye, deign to stay !
Rest thee in Castle Ravensheuch,
  Nor tempt the stormy firth to-day.

' The blackening wave is edg'd with
    white :
To inch and rock the sea-mews fly ;
The fishers have heard the Water-
    Sprite,
    Whose screams forebode that wreck
      is nigh.

' Last night the gifted Seer did view
    A wet shroud swathed round ladye
      gay ;
Then stay thee, Fair, in Ravensheuch :
    Why cross the gloomy firth to-
      day ? '

' 'Tis not because Lord Lindesay's heir
    To-night at Roslin leads the ball,
But that my ladye-mother there
    Sits lonely in her castle-hall.

' 'Tis not because the ring they ride,
    And Lindesay at the ring rides well,
But that my sire the wine will chide,
    If 'tis not fill d by Rosabelle.'

O'er Roslin all that dreary night
    A wondrous blaze was seen to gleam ;
'Twas broader than the watch-fire's
      light,
    And redder than the bright moon-
      beam.

It glar'd on Roslin's castled rock,
    It ruddied all the copse wood glen ;
'Twas seen from Dryden's groves of
      oak,
    And seen from cavern'd Hawthorn-
      den.

Seem'd all on fire that chapel proud,
    Where Roslin's chiefs uncoffin'd lie,
Each Baron, for a sable shroud,
    Sheath'd in his iron panoply.

Seem'd all on fire within, around,
    Deep sacristy and altar's pale ;
Shone every pillar foliage bound,
    And glimmer'd all the dead men's
      mail.

Blaz'd battlement and pinnet high,
    Blaz'd every rose-carved buttress
      fair—
So still they blaze when fate is nigh
    The lordly line of high St. Clair.

There are twenty of Roslin's barons
    bold
    Lie buried within that proud cha-
      pelle ;
Each one the holy vault doth hold—
    But the sea holds lovely Rosabelle !

And each St. Clair was buried there,
    With candle, with book, and with
      knell ;
But the sea-caves rung, and the wild
      winds sung,
    The dirge of lovely Rosabelle.

XXIV.

So sweet was Harold's piteous lay,
    Scarce mark'd the guests the darken'd
      hall,
Though, long before the sinking day,
    A wondrous shade involv'd them all :
It was not eddying mist or fog,
    Drain'd by the sun from fen or bog ;
Of no eclipse had sages told ;
    And yet, as it came on apace,
Each one could scarce his neighbour's
      face,
    Could scarce his own stretch'd
      hand behold.
A secret horror check'd the feast,
And chill'd the soul of every guest ;
Even the high Dame stood half aghast—
She knew some evil on the blast ;
The elvish page fell to the ground,
And, shuddering, mutter'd, ' Found !
      found ! found ! '

XXV.

Then sudden, through the darken'd air,
    A flash of lightning came ;
So broad, so bright, so red the glare,
    The castle seem'd on flame.
Glanc'd every rafter of the hall,
Glanc'd every shield upon the wall ;

Each trophied beam, each sculptur'd
stone,
Were instant seen, and instant gone ;
Full through the guests' bedazzled
band
Resistless flash'd the levin-brand,
And fill'd the hall with smouldering
smoke,
As on the elvish page it broke.
It broke, with thunder long and
loud,
Dismay'd the brave, appall'd the
proud,—
From sea to sea the larum rung ;
On Berwick wall, and at Carlisle
withal,
To arms the startled warders
sprung.
When ended was the dreadful roar,
The elvish dwarf was seen no more !

XXVI.

Some heard a voice in Branksome
Hall,
Some saw a sight, not seen by all ;
That dreadful voice was heard by
some,
Cry, with loud summons, ' GYLBIN,
COME ! '
And on the spot where burst the
brand,
Just where the page had flung
him down,
Some saw an arm, and some a hand,
And some the waving of a gown.
The guests in silence pray'd and shook,
And terror dimm'd each lofty look.
But none of all the astonish'd train
Was so dismay'd as Deloraine ;
His blood did freeze, his brain did
burn,
'Twas fear'd his mind would ne'er
return ;
For he was speechless, ghastly, wan,
Like him of whom the story ran,
Who spoke the spectre-hound in
Man.

At length, by fits, he darkly told,
With broken hint, and shuddering
cold,
That he had seen, right certainly,
A shape with amice wrapp'd around,
With a wrought Spanish baldric bound,
Like pilgrim from beyond the sea ;
And knew—but how it matter'd not—
It was the wizard, Michael Scott.

XXVII.

The anxious crowd, with horror pale,
All trembling heard the wondrous
tale ;
No sound was made, no word was
spoke,
Till noble Angus silence broke;
And he a solemn sacred plight
Did to St. Bride of Douglas make,
That he a pilgrimage would take
To Melrose Abbey, for the sake
Of Michael's restless sprite.
Then each, to ease his troubled breast,
To some bless'd saint his prayers ad-
dress'd :
Some to St. Modan made their vows,
Some to St. Mary of the Lowes,
Some to the Holy Rood of Lisle,
Some to our Ladye of the Isle ;
Each did his patron witness make,
That he such pilgrimage would take,
And monks should sing, and bells
should toll,
All for the weal of Michael's soul.
While vows were ta'en, and prayers
were pray'd,
'Tis said the noble dame, dismay'd,
Renounc'd, for aye, dark magic's aid.

XXVIII.

Nought of the bridal will I tell,
Which after in short space befell ;
Nor how brave sons and daughters fair
Bless'd Teviot's Flower, and Cran-
stoun's heir :
After such dreadful scene, 'twere vain
To wake the note of mirth again.

More meet it were to mark the day
  Of penitence, and prayer divine,
When pilgrim-chiefs, in sad array,
  Sought Melrose' holy shrine.

XXIX.

With naked foot, and sackcloth vest,
And arms enfolded on his breast,
  Did every pilgrim go ;
The standers-by might hear uneath,
Footstep, or voice, or high-drawn
    breath,
  Through all the lengthen'd row :
No lordly look, nor martial stride ;
Gone was their glory, sunk their pride,
  Forgotten their renown ;
Silent and slow, like ghosts they glide
To the high altar's hallow'd side,
  And there they knelt them down :
Above the suppliant chieftains wave
The banners of departed brave ;
Beneath the letter'd stones were laid
The ashes of their fathers dead ;
From many a garnish'd niche around,
Stern saints and tortur'd martyrs
    frown'd

XXX.

And slow up the dim aisle afar,
With sable cowl and scapular,
And snow-white stoles, in order due,
The holy Fathers, two and two,
  In long procession came ;
Taper and host, and book they bare,
And holy banner, flourish'd fair
  With the Redeemer's name.
Above the prostrate pilgrim band
The mitred Abbot stretch'd his hand,
  And bless'd them as they kneel'd ;
With holy cross he sign'd them all,
And pray'd they might be sage in hall,
  And fortunate in field.
Then mass was sung, and prayers
    were said,
And solemn requiem for the dead ;
And bells toll'd out their mighty peal,
For the departed spirit's weal ;
And ever in the office close
The hymn of intercession rose ;

And far the echoing aisles prolong
The awful burthen of the song,—
  Dies iræ, dies illa,
  Solvet sæclum in favilla,—
While the pealing organ rung.
  Were it meet with sacred strain
    To close my lay, so light and vain,
Thus the holy Fathers sung :

XXXI.
HYMN FOR THE DEAD.

That day of wrath, that dreadful day,
When heaven and earth shall pass
    away,
What power shall be the sinner's stay?
How shall he meet that dreadful day ?

When, shriveling like a parched scroll,
The flaming heavens together roll ;
When louder yet, and yet more dread,
Swells the high trump that wakes the
    dead :

Oh ! on that day, that wrathful day,
When man to judgment wakes from
    clay,
Be Thou the trembling sinner's stay,
Though heaven and earth shall pass
    away !

Hush'd is the harp : the Minstrel
    gone.
And did he wander forth alone ?
Alone, in indigence and age,
To linger out his pilgrimage ?
No ; close beneath proud Newark's
    tower,
Arose the Minstrel's lowly bower ;
A simple hut ; but there was seen
The little garden hedged with green,
The cheerful hearth, and lattice clean.
There shelter'd wanderers, by the blaze,
Oft heard the tale of other days ;
For much he lov'd to ope his door,
And give the aid he begg'd before.
So pass'd the winter's day ; but still,
When summer smil'd on sweet Bow
    hill,

And July's eve, with balmy breath,
Wav'd the blue-bells on Newark
　　heath;
When throstles sung in Harehead-
　　shaw,
And corn was green on Carterhaugh,
And flourish'd broad Blackandro's
　　oak,
The aged Harper's soul awoke!

Then would he sing achievements
　　high,
And circumstance of chivalry,
Till the rapt traveller would stay,
Forgetful of the closing day;
And noble youths, the strain to hear,
Forsook the hunting of the deer;
And Yarrow, as he roll'd along,
Bore burden to the Minstrel's song.

END OF THE LAY OF THE LAST MINSTREL.

Introduction and Notes to The Lay of the Last Minstrel.

INTRODUCTION TO THE EDITION OF 1830.

A POEM of nearly thirty years' standing may be supposed hardly to need an Introduction, since, without one, it has been able to keep itself afloat through the best part of a generation. Nevertheless, as, in the edition of the Waverley Novels now in course of publication [1830], I have imposed on myself the task of saying something concerning the purpose and history of each, in their turn, I am desirous that the Poems for which I first received some marks of the public favour, should also be accompanied with such scraps of their literary history as may be supposed to carry interest along with them. Even if I should be mistaken in thinking that the secret history of what was once so popular, may still attract public attention and curiosity, it seems to me not without its use to record the manner and circumstances under which the present, and other Poems on the same plan, attained for a season an extensive reputation.

I must resume the story of my literary labours at the period at which I broke off in the Essay on the Imitation of Popular Poetry [see *post*], when I had enjoyed the first gleam of public favour, by the success of the first edition of the Minstrelsy of the Scottish Border. The second edition of that work, published in 1803, proved, in the language of the trade, rather a heavy concern. The demand in Scotland had been supplied by the first edition, and the curiosity of the English was not much awakened by poems in the rude garb of antiquity, accompanied with notes referring to the obscure feuds of barbarous clans, of whose very names civilized history was ignorant. It was, on the whole, one of those books which are more praised than they are read.

At this time I stood personally in a different position from that which I occupied when I first dipt my desperate pen in ink for other purposes than those of my profession. In 1796, when I fi st published the translations from Bürger, I was an insulated individual, with only my own wants to provide for, and having, in a great measure, my own inclinations alone to consult. In 1803,

when the second edition of the Minstrelsy appeared, I had arrived at a period of life when men, however thoughtless, encounter duties and circumstances which press consideration and plans of life upon the most careless minds. I had been for some time married—was the father of a rising family, and, though fully enabled to meet the consequent demands upon me, it was my duty and desire to place myself in a situation wh.ich would enable me to make honourable provision against the various contingencies of life.

It may be readily supposed that the attempts which I had made in literature had been unfavourable to my success at the bar. The goddess Themis is, at Edinburgh, and I suppose everywhere else, of a peculiarly jealous disposition. She will not readily consent to share her authority, and sternly demands from her votaries, not only that real duty be carefully attended to and discharged, but that a certain air of business shall be observed even in the midst of total idleness. It is prudent, if not absolutely necessary, in a young barrister, to appear completely engrossed by his profession ; however destitute of employment he may in reality be, he ought to preserve, if possible, the appearance of full occupation. He should, therefore, seem perpetually engaged among his law-papers, dusting them, as it were ; and, as Ovid advises the fair,

'Si nullus erit pulvis, tamen excute nullum.

Perhaps such extremity of attention is more especially required, considering the great number of counsellors who are called to the bar, and how very small a proportion of them are finally disposed, or find encouragement, to follow the law as a profession. Hence the number of deserters is so great, that the least lingering look behind occasions a young novice to be set down as one of the intending fugitives. Certain it is, that the Scottish Themis was at this time peculiarly jealous of any flirtation with the Muses, on the part of those who had ranged themselves under her banners. This was probably owing to her consciousness of the superior attractions of her rivals. Of late, however, she has relaxed in some instances in this particular, an eminent example of which has been shown in the case of my friend, Mr. Jeffrey, who, after long conducting one of the most influential literary periodicals of the age, with unquestionable ability, has been, by the general consent of his brethren, recently elected to be their Dean of Faculty, or President,— being the highest acknowledgment of his professional talents which they had it in their power to offer. But this is an incident much beyond the ideas of a period of thirty years' distance, when a barrister who really possessed any turn for lighter literature, was at as much pains to conceal it, as if it had in reality been something to be ashamed of; and I could mention more than one instance in which literature and society have suffered much loss, that jurisprudence might be enriched.

Such, however, was not my case; for the reader will not wonder that my open interference with matters of light literature diminished my employment in the weightier matters of the law. Nor did the solicitors, upon whose choice the counsel takes rank in his profession, do me less than justice, by regarding others among my contemporaries as fitter to discharge the duty due to their clients, than a young man who was taken up with running after ballads, whether Teutonic or national. My profession and I, therefore, came to stand nearly upon the footing which honest Slender consoled himself on having established with Mistress Anne Page; 'There was no great love between us at the beginning, and it pleased Heaven to decrease it on farther acquaintance.' I became sensible that the time was come when I must either buckle myself resolutely to the 'toil by day, the lamp by night,' renouncing all the Delilahs of my imagination, or bid adieu to the profession of the law, and hold another course.

I confess my own inclination revolted from the more severe choice, which might have been deemed by many the wiser alternative. As my transgressions had been numerous, my repentance must have been signalized by unusual sacrifices. I ought to have mentioned, that since my fourteenth or fifteenth year, my health, originally delicate, had become extremely robust. From infancy I had laboured under the infirmity of a severe lameness, but, as I believe is usually the case with men of spirit who suffer under personal inconveniences of this nature, I had, since the improvement of my health, in defiance of this incapacitating circumstance, distinguished myself by the endurance of toil on foot or horse-back, having often walked thirty miles a-day, and rode upwards of a hundred, without resting. In this manner I made many pleasant journeys through parts of the country then not very accessible, gaining more amusement and instruction than I

have been able to acquire since I have travelled in a more commodious manner. I practised most silvan sports also, with some success, and with great delight. But these pleasures must have been all resigned, or used with great moderation, had I determined to regain my station at the bar. It was even doubtful whether I could, with perfect character as a jurisconsult, retain a situation in a volunteer corps of cavalry, which I then held. The threats of invasion were at this time instant and menacing; the call by Britain on her children was universal, and was answered by some, who, like myself, consulted rather their desire than their ability to bear arms. My services, however, were found useful in assisting to maintain the discipline of the corps, being the point on which their constitution rendered them most amenable to military criticism In other respects, the squadron was a fine one, consisting chiefly of handsome men, well mounted and armed at their own expense. My attention to the corps took up a good deal of time; and while it occupied many of the happiest hours of my life, it furnished an additional reason for my reluctance again to encounter the severe course of study indispensable to success in the juridical profession.

On the other hand, my father, whose feelings might have been hurt by my quitting the bar, had been for two or three years dead, so that I had no control to thwart my own inclination; and my income being equal to all the comforts, and some of the elegancies, of life, I was not pressed to an irksome labour by necessity, that most powerful of motives; consequently, I was the more easily seduced to choose the employment which was most agreeable to me. This was yet the easier, that in 1800 I had obtained the preferment of Sheriff of Selkirkshire, about £300 a-year in value, and which was the more agreeable to me, as in that county I had several friends and relations. But I did not abandon the profession to which I had been educated, without certain prudential resolutions, which, at the risk of some egotism, I will here mention; not without the hope that they may be useful to young persons who may stand in circumstances similar to those in which I then stood.

In the first place, upon considering the lives and fortunes of persons who had given themselves up to literature, or to the task of pleasing the public, it seemed to me, that the circumstances which chiefly affected their happiness and character, were those from which Horace has bestowed upon authors the epithet of the Irritable Race. It requires no depth of philosophic reflection to perceive, that the petty warfare of Pope with the Dunces of his period could not have been carried on without his suffering the most acute torture, such as a man must endure from musquittoes, by whose stings he suffers agony, although he can crush them in his grasp by myriads. Nor is it necessary to call to me ory the many humiliating instances in which men of the greatest genius have, to avenge some pitiful quarrel, made themselves ridiculous during their lives, to become the still more degraded objects of pity to future times.

Upon the whole, as I had no pretension to the genius of the distinguished persons who had fallen into such errors, I concluded there could be no occasion for imitating them in their mistakes, or what I considered as such ; and, in adopting literary pursuits as the principal occupation of my future life, I resolved, if possible, to avoid those weaknesses of temper which seemed to have most easily beset my more celebrated predecessors.

With this view, it was my first resolution to keep as far as was in my power abreast of society, continuing to maintain my place in general company, without yielding to the very natural temptation of narrowing myself to what is called literary society. By doing so, I imagined I should escape the besetting sin of listening to language, which, from one motive or other, is apt to ascribe a very undue degree of consequence to literary pursuits, as if they were, indeed, the business, rather than the amusement, of life. The opposite course can only be compared to the injudicious conduct of one who pampers himself with cordial and luscious draughts, until he is unable to endure wholesome bitters. Like Gil Blas, therefore, I resolved to stick by the society of my *commis*, instead of seeking that of a more literary cast, and to maintain my general interest in what was going on around me, reserving the man of letters for the desk and the library.

My second resolution was a corollary from the first. I determined that, without shutting my ears to the voice of true criticism, I would pay no regard to that which assumes the form of satire. I therefore resolved to arm myself with that triple brass of Horace, of which those of my profession are seldom held deficient, against all the roving warfare of satire, parody, and sarcasm ; to laugh if the jest was a good one, or, if otherwise, to let it hum and buzz itself to sleep.

It is to the observance of these rules (according to my best belief , that, after a life of thirty years engaged in literary labours of various kinds, I attribute my never having been entangled in any literary quarrel or controversy ; and, which is a still more pleasing result, that I have been distinguished by the personal friendship of my most approved contemporaries of all parties.

I adopted, at the same time, another resolution, on which it may doubtless be remarked, that it was well for me that I had it in my power to do so, and that, therefore, it is a line of conduct which, depending upon accident, can be less generally applicable in other cases. Yet I fail not to record this

part of my plan, convinced that, though it may not be in every one's power to adopt exactly the same resolution, he may nevertheless, by his own exertions, in some shape or other, attain the object on which it was founded, namely, to secure the means of subsistence, without relying exclusively on literary talents. In this respect, I determined that literature should be my staff, but not my crutch, and that the profits of my literary labour, however convenient otherwise, should not, if I could help it, become necessary to my ordinary expenses. With this purpose I resolved, if the interest of my friends could so far favour me, to retire upon any of the respectable offices of the law, in which persons of that profession are glad to take refuge, when they feel themselves, or are judged by others, incompetent to aspire to its higher honours. Upon such a post an author might hope to retreat, without any perceptible alteration of circumstances, whenever the time should arrive that the public grew weary of his endeavours to please, or he himself should tire of the pen. At this period of my life, I possessed so many friends capable of assisting me in this object of ambition, that I could hardly over-rate my own prospects of obtaining the preferment to which I limited my wishes; and, in fact, I obtained in no long period the reversion of a situation which completely met them.

Thus far all was well, and the Author had been guilty, perhaps, of no great imprudence, when he relinquished his forensic practice with the hope of making some figure in the field of literature. But an established character with the public, in my new capacity, still remained to be acquired. I have noticed, that the translations from Bürger had been unsuccessful, nor had the original poetry which appeared under the auspices of Mr. Lewis, in the 'Tales of Wonder,' in any great degree raised my reputation. It is true, I had private friends disposed to second me in my efforts to obtain popularity. But I was sportsman enough to know, that if the greyhound does not run well, the halloos of his patrons will not obtain the prize for him.

Neither was I ignorant that the practice of ballad-writing was for the present out of fashion, and that any attempt to revive it, or to found a poetical character upon it, would certainly fail of success. The ballad measure itself, which was once listened to as to an enchanting melody, had become hackneyed and sickening, from its being the accompaniment of every grinding hand-organ; and besides, a long work in quatrains, whether those of the common ballad, or such as are termed elegiac, has an effect upon the mind like that of the bed of Procrustes upon the human body; for, as it must be both awkward and difficult to carry on a long sentence from one stanza to another, it follows, that **the meaning of each period must be com-**

prehended within four lines, and equally so that it must be extended so as to fill that space. The alternate dilation and contraction thus rendered necessary is singularly unfavourable to narrative composition; and the 'Gondibert' of Sir William D'Avenant, though containing many striking passages, has never become popular, owing chiefly to its being told in this species of elegiac verse.

In the dilemma occasioned by this objection, the idea occurred to the Author of using the measured short line, which forms the structure of so much minstrel poetry, that it may be properly termed the Romantic stanza, by way of distinction; and which appears so natural to our language, that the very best of our poets have not been able to protract it into the verse properly called Heroic, without the use of epithets which are, to say the least, unnecessary. But, on the other hand, the extreme facility of the short couplet, which seems congenial to our language, and was, doubtless for that reason, so popular with our old minstrels, is, for the same reason, apt to prove a snare to the composer who uses it in more modern days, by encouraging him in a habit of slovenly composition. The necessity of occasional pauses often forces the young poet to pay more attention to sense, as the boy's kite rises highest when the train is loaded by a due counterpoise. The Author was therefore intimidated by what Byron calls the 'fatal facility' of the octosyllabic verse, which was otherwise better adapted to his purpose of imitating the more ancient poetry.

I was not less at a loss for a subject which might admit of being treated with the simplicity and wildness of the ancient ballad. But accident dictated both a theme and measure, which decided the subject, as well as the structure of the poem.

The lovely young Countess of Dalkeith, afterwards Harriet Duchess of Buccleuch, had come to the land of her husband with the desire of making herself acquainted with its traditions and customs, as well as its manners and history. All who remember this lady will agree, that the intellectual character of her extreme beauty, the amenity and courtesy of her manners, the soundness of her understanding, and her unbounded benevolence, gave more the idea of an angelic visitant, than of a being belonging to this nether world; and such a thought was but too consistent with the short space she was permitted to tarry among us. Of course, where all made it a pride and pleasure to gratify her wishes, she soon heard enough of Border lore; among others, an aged gentleman of property, near Langholm, communicated to her ladyship the story of Gilpin Horner, a tradition in which the narrator, and many more of that country, were firm believers. The young Countess, much delighted with the legend, and the gravity and full confidence with

which it was told, enjoined on me as a task to compose a ballad on the subject. Of course, to hear was to obey; and thus the goblin story, objected to by several critics as an excrescence upon the poem, was, in fact, the occasion of its being written.

A chance similar to that which dictated the subject, gave me also the hint of a new mode of treating it. We had at that time the lease of a pleasant cottage, near Lasswade, on the romantic banks of the Esk, to which we escaped when the vacations of the Court permitted me so much leisure. Here I had the pleasure to receive a visit from Mr. Stoddart (now Sir John Stoddart, Judge-Advocate at Malta), who was at that time collecting the particulars which he afterwards embodied in his Remarks on Local Scenery in Scotland. I was of some use to him in procuring the information which he desired, and guiding him to the scenes which he wished to see. In return, he made me better acquainted than I had hitherto been with the poetic effusions which have since made the Lakes of Westmoreland, and the authors by whom they have been sung, so famous wherever the English tongue is spoken.

I was already acquainted with the 'Joan of Arc,' the 'Thalaba,' and the 'Metrical Ballads' of Mr. Southey, which had found their way to Scotland, and were generally admired. But Mr. Stoddart, who had the advantage of personal friendship with the authors, and who possessed a strong memory with an excellent taste, was able to repeat to me many long specimens of their poetry, which had not yet appeared in print. Amongst others, was the striking fragment called Christabel, by Mr. Coleridge, which, from the singularly irregular structure of the stanzas, and the liberty which it allowed the author to adapt the sound to the sense, seemed to be exactly suited to such an extravaganza as I meditated on the subject of Gilpin Horner. As applied to comic and humorous poetry, this mescolanza of measures had been already used by Anthony Hall, Anstey, Dr Wolcott, and others; but it was in Christabel that I first found it used in serious poetry, and it is to Mr. Coleridge that I am bound to make the acknowledgment due from the pupil to his master. I observe that Lord Byron, in noticing my obligations to Mr. Coleridge, which I have been always most ready to acknowledge, expressed, or was understood to express, a hope, that I did not write an unfriendly review on Mr. Coleridge's productions. On this subject I have only to say, that I do not even know the review which is alluded to; and were I ever to take the unbecoming freedom of censuring a man of Mr. Coleridge's extraordinary talents, it would be on account of the caprice and indolence with which he has thrown from him, as if in mere wantonness, those unfinished scraps of poetry, which, like the Torso of antiquity, defy the skill of his poetical brethren to complete them. The charming fragments which the author abandons to their fate, are surely too valuable to be treated like the proofs of careless engravers, the sweepings of whose studios often make the fortune of some painstaking collector.

I did not immediately proceed upon my projected labour, though I was now furnished with a subject, and with a structure of verse which might have the effect of novelty to the public ear, and afford the author an opportunity of varying his measure with the variations of a romantic theme. On the contrary, it was, to the best of my recollection, more than a year after Mr. Stoddart's visit, that, by way of experiment, I composed the first two or three stanzas of 'The Lay of the Last Minstrel.' I was shortly afterwards visited by two intimate friends, one of whom still survives. They were men whose talents might have raised them to the highest station in literature, had they not preferred exerting them in their own profession of the law, in which they attained equal preferment. I was in the habit of consulting them on my attempts at composition, having equal confidence in their sound taste and friendly sincerity. In this specimen I had, in the phrase of the Highland servant, packed all that was my own *at least*, for I had also included a line of invocation, a little softened, from Coleridge—

'Mary, mother, shield us well.'

As neither of my friends said much to me on the subject of stanzas I showed them before their departure, I had no doubt that their disgust had been greater than their good-nature chose to express. Looking upon them, therefore, as a failure, I threw the manuscript into the fire, and thought as little more as I could of the matter. Some time afterwards I met one of my two counsellors, who enquired, with considerable appearance of interest, about the progress of the romance I had commenced, and was greatly surprised at learning its fate. He confessed that neither he nor our mutual friend had been at first able to give a precise opinion on a poem so much out of the common road ; but that as they walked home together to the city, they had talked much on the subject, and the result was an earnest desire that I would proceed with the composition. He also added, that some sort of prologue might be necessary, to place the mind of the hearers in the situation to understand and enjoy the poem, and recommended the adoption of such quaint mottoes as Spenser has used to announce the contents of the chapters of the Faery Queen, such as—

'Babe's bloody hands may not be cleansed.
The face of golden Mean :
Her sisters two, Extremities,
Strive her to banish clean.'

I entirely agreed with my friendly critic in the necessity of having some sort of pitch-pipe, which might make readers aware of the object, or rather the tone, of the publication. But I doubted whether, in assuming the oracular style of Spenser's mottoes, the interpreter might not be censured as the harder to be understood of the two. I therefore introduced the Old Minstrel, as an appropriate prolocutor, by whom the lay might be sung, or spoken, and the introduction of whom betwixt the cantos, might remind the reader at intervals, of the time, place, and circumstances of the recitation. This species of *cadre*, or frame, afterwards afforded the poem its name of 'The Lay of the Last Minstrel.'

The work was subsequently shown to other friends during its progress, and received the *imprimatur* of Mr. Francis Jeffrey, who had been already for some time distinguished by his critical talent.

The poem, being once licensed by the critics as fit for the market, was soon finished, proceeding at about the rate of a canto per week. There was, indeed, little occasion for pause or hesitation, when a troublesome rhyme might be accommodated by an alteration of the stanza, or where an incorrect measure might be remedied by a variation of the rhyme. It was finally published in 1805, and may be regarded as the first work in which the writer, who has been since so voluminous, laid his claim to be considered as an original author.

The book was published by Longman and Company, and Archibald Constable and Company. The principal of the latter firm was then commencing that course of bold and liberal industry which was of so much advantage to his country and might have been so to himself, but for causes which it is needless to enter into here. The work, brought out on the usual terms of division of profits between the author and publishers, was not long after purchased by them for £500, to which Messrs. Longman and Company afterwards added £100, in their own unsolicited kindness, in consequence of the uncommon success of the work. It was handsomely given to supply the loss of a fine horse, which broke down suddenly while the author was riding with one of the worthy publishers.

It would be great affectation not to own frankly, that the author expected some success from 'The Lay of the Last Minstrel.' The attempt to return to a more simple and natural style of poetry was likely to be welcomed, at a time when the public had become tired of heroic hexameters, with all the buckram and binding which belong to them of later days. But whatever might have been his expectations, whether moderate or unreasonable, the result left them far behind, for among those who smiled on the adventurous Minstrel, were numbered the great names of William Pitt and Charles

Fox. Neither was the extent of the sale inferior to the character of the judges who received the poem with approbation. Upwards of thirty thousand copies of the Lay were disposed of by the trade; and the author had to perform a task difficult to human vanity, when called upon to make the necessary deductions from his own merits,

in a calm attempt to account for his popularity.

A few additional remarks on the author's literary attempts after this period, will be found in the Introduction to the Poem of Marmion.

ABBOTSFORD, *April* 1830.

NOTES.

NOTE I.

The feast was over in Branksome tower.
—P. 3.

IN the reign of James I, Sir William Scott of Buccleuch, chief of the clan bearing that name, exchanged, with Sir Thomas Inglis of Manor, the estate of Murdiestone, in Lanarkshire, for one-half of the barony of Branksome, or Brankholm [1], lying upon the Teviot, about three miles above Hawick. He was probably induced to this transaction from the vicinity of Branksome to the extensive domain which he possessed in Ettrick Forest and in Teviotdale. In the former district he held by occupancy the estate of Buccleuch [2], and much of the forest land on the river Ettrick. In Teviotdale, he enjoyed the barony of Eckford, by a grant from Robert II to his ancestor, Walter Scott of Kirkurd, for the apprehending of Gilbert Ridderford, confirmed by Robert III 3d May 1424. Tradition imputes the exchange betwixt Scott and Inglis to a conversation, in which the latter—a man, it would appear, of a mild and forbearing nature, complained much of the injuries which he was exposed to from the English Borderers, who frequently plundered his lands of Branksome. Sir William Scott instantly offered him the estate of Murdiestone, in exchange for that which was subject to such egregious inconvenience. When the bargain was completed, he dryly remarked, that the cattle in Cumberland were as good as those of Teviotdale; and proceeded to commence a system of reprisals upon the English, which was regularly pursued by his successors. In the next reign, James II granted to Sir Walter Scott of Branksome, and to Sir David, his son, the remaining half of the barony of Branksome, to be held in blanche for the payment of a red rose. The cause assigned for the grant is, their brave and faithful

[1] Branxholm is the proper name of the barony; but Branksome has been adopted, as suitable to the pronunciation, and more proper for poetry.
[2] There are no vestiges of any building at Buccleuch, except the site of a chapel, where, according to a tradition current in the time of Scott of Satchells, many of the ancient barons of Buccleuch lie buried. There is also said to have been a mill near this solitary spot; an extraordinary circumstance, as little or no corn grows within several miles of Buccleuch. Satchells says it was used to grind corn for the hounds of the chieftain.

exertions in favour of the King against the house of Douglas, with whom James had been recently tugging for the throne of Scotland. This charter is dated the 2d February 1443; and, in the same month, part of the barony of Langholm, and many lands in Lanarkshire, were conferred upon Sir Walter and his son by the same monarch.

After the period of the exchange with Sir Thomas Inglis, Branksome became the principal seat of the Buccleuch family. The castle was enlarged and strengthened by Sir David Scott, the grandson of Sir William, its first possessor. But, in 1570-1, the vengeance of Elizabeth, provoked by the inroads of Buccleuch, and his attachment to the cause of Queen Mary, destroyed the castle, and laid waste the lands of Branksome. In the same year the castle was repaired and enlarged by Sir Walter Scott, its brave possessor; but the work was not completed until after his death, in 1574, when the widow finished the building. This appears from the following inscriptions. Around a stone, bearing the arms of Scott of Buccleuch, appears the following legend:—'Sir W. Scott of Branxheim Kngt oe of Sir William Scott of Kirkurd Kngt began ye work upon ye 24 of Marche 1571 zear quha departit at God's pleisour ye 17 April 1574.' On a similar co-partment are sculptured the arms of Douglas, with this inscription, 'DAME MARGARET DOUGLAS HIS SPOUS COMPLETIT THE FORE-SAID WORK IN OCTOBER 1576.' Over an arched door is inscribed the following moral verse :—

In varld. is. nocht. nature. hes. vrought. gat. sal. lest. ay.
Therefore. serve. God. keip. veil. ye. rod. thy fame. sal. nocht. dekay.
Sir Walter Scott of Branxholm Knight. Margaret Douglas. 1571.

Branksome Castle continued to be the principal seat of the Buccleuch family, while security was any object in their choice of a mansion. It has since been the residence of the Commissioners, or Chamberlains, of the family. From the various alterations which the building has undergone, it is not only greatly restricted in its dimensions, but retains little of the castellated form, if we except one square tower of massy thickness, the only part of the original building which now remains. The whole forms a handsome modern residence, lately inhabited by my deceased friend, Adam Ogilvy, Esq. of Hartwoodmyres, Commissioner of his Grace the Duke of Buccleuch.

The extent of the ancient edifice can still be traced by some vestiges of its foundation, and its strength is obvious from the situation, on a deep bank surrounded by the Teviot, and flanked by a deep ravine, formed by a precipitous brook. It was anciently surrounded by wood, as appears from the survey of Roxburghshire, made for Pont's Atlas, and preserved in the Advocates' Library. This wood was cut about fifty years ago, but is now replaced by the thriving plantations, which have been formed by the noble proprietor, for miles around the ancient mansion of his forefathers.

NOTE II.

Nine-and-twenty knights of fame
Hung their shields in Branksome
hall.—P. 3.

The ancient barons of Buccleuch, both from feudal splendour and from their frontier situation, retained in their household at Branksome, a number of gentlemen of their own name, who held lands from their chief, for the military service of watching and warding his castle. Satchells tells us, in his doggrel poetry,

'No baron was better served in Britain ;
The barons of Buckleugh they kept their call,
Four and twenty gentlemen in their hall,
All being of his name and kin ;
Each two had a servant to wait upon them
Before supper and dinner, most renowned,
The bells rung and the trumpets sowned ;
And more than that, I do confess,
They kept four and twenty pensioners.
Think not I lie, nor do me blame,
For the pensioners I can all name :
There 's men alive, elder than I,
They know if I speak truth, or lie.
Every pensioner a room[1] did gain,
For service done and to be done ;
This let the reader understand,
The name both of the men and land,
Which they possessed, it is of truth,
Both from the Lairds and Lords of Buckleugh.

Accordingly, dismounting from his Pegasus, Satchells gives us, in prose, the names of twenty-four gentlemen, younger brothers of ancient families, who were pensioners to the house of Buccleuch, and describes the lands which each possessed for his Border service. In time of war with England, the garrison was doubtless augmented. Satchells adds, 'These twenty-three pensioners, all of his own name of Scott, and Walter Gladstanes of Whitelaw, a near cousin of my lord's, as aforesaid, were ready on all occasions, when his honour pleased cause to advertise them.

---

[1] *Room*, portion of land.

It is known to many of the country better than it is to me, that the rent of these lands, which the Lairds and Lords of Buccleuch did freely bestow upon their friends, will amount to above twelve or fourteen thousand merks a year.'—*History of the name of Scott*, p. 45. An immense sum in those days.

NOTE III.

——with Jedwood-axe at saddlebow.—P. 3.

'Of a truth,' says Froissart, 'the Scottish cannot boast great skill with the bow, but rather bear axes, with which, in time of need, they give heavy strokes.' The Jedwood-axe was a sort of partisan, used by horsemen, as appears from the arms of Jedburgh, which bear a cavalier mounted, and armed with this weapon. It is also called a Jedwood or Jeddart staff.

NOTE IV.

They watch against Southern force and
*   guile,*
Lest Scroop, or Howard, or Percy's powers,
Threaten Branksome's lordly towers,
From Warkworth, or Naworth, or merry
*   Carlisle.—P. 3.*

Branksome Castle was continually exposed to the attacks of the English, both from its situation and the restless military disposition of its inhabitants, who were seldom on good terms with their neighbours. The following letter from the Earl of Northumberland to Henry VIII in 1533, gives an account of a successful inroad of the English, in which the country was plundered up to the gates of the castle, although the invaders failed in their principal object, which was to kill, or make prisoner, the Laird of Buccleuch. It occurs in the Cotton MS. *Calig.* b. viii. f. 222.

'Pleaseth yt your most gracious highness to be aduertised, that my comptroller, with Raynald Carnaby, desyred licence of me to invade the realme of Scotlande, for the annoysaunce of your highnes enemys, where they thought best exploit by theyme might be done, and to haue to concur withe theyme the inhabitants of Northumberland, suche as was towards me according to theyre assembly, and as by theyre discretions vpone the same they shulde thinke most convenient ; and soo they dyde meet vppone Monday, before night, being the iii day of this instant monethe, at Wawhope, upon Northe Tyne water, above Tyndaill, where they were to the number of xv c men, and soo invadet Scotland at the hour of viii of the clok at nyght, at a place called Whele Causay ; and before xi of the clok dyd send forth a forrey of Tyndaill and Ryddisdail, and laide all the resydewe in a bushment, and actyvely did set vpon a towne

C

called Branxholme, where the Lord of Buclough dwelly the, and purpesed theymeselves
with a trayne for hym lyke to his accustomed
manner, in rysynge to all frayes ; albeit, that
knyght he was not at home, and so they
brynt the said Branxholm, and other townes,
as to say Whichestre, Whichestre-helme, and
Whelley, and haid ordered theymself, soo
that sundry of the said Lord Buclough's servants, who dyd issue fourthe of his gates, was
takyn prisoners. They dyd not leve one
house, one stak of corne, nor one shyef,
without the gate of the said Lord Buclough
vnbrynt ; and thus scrymaged and frayed,
supposing the Lord of Buclough to be within
iii or iiii myles to have trayned him to the
bushment ; and soo in the breyking of the
day dyd the forrey and the bushment mete,
and reculed homeward, making theyre way
westward from theyre invasion to be over
Lyddersdaill, as intending yf the fray frome
theyre furst entry by the Scotts waiches, or
otherwyse by warnyng, shuld haue bene
gyven to Gedworth and the countrey of
Scotland theyreabouts of theyre invasion :
whiche Gedworth is from the Wheles Causay
vi miles, that thereby the Scotts shulde have
comen further vnto theyme, and more out of
ordre ; and soo upon sundry good considerations, before they entered Lyddersdaill, as
well accompting the inhabitants of the same
to be towards your highness, and to enforce
theyme the more thereby, as alsoo to put an
occasion of suspect to the Kinge of Scotts,
and his counsaill, to be taken anenst theyme,
amonges theymeselves, made proclamacions,
commanding, vpon payne of dethe, assurance
to be for the said inhabitants of Lyddersdaill,
without any prejudice or hurt to be done by
any Inglysman vnto theyme, and soo in good
ordre abowte the howre of ten of the clok
before none, vppon Tewisday, dyd pass
through the said Lyddersdail, when dyd
come diverse of the said inhabitants there to
my servauntes, under the said assurance,
offerring theymselfs with any service they
couthe make ; and thus, thanks be to Godde,
your highnes' subjects, abowte the howre of
xii of the clok at none the same daye, came
into this your highnes realme, bringing wt
theyme above xl Scottsmen prisoners, one of
theyme named Scot, of the surname and kyn
of the said Lord of Buclough, and of his
howsehold ; they brought also ccc nowte, and
above lx horse and mares, keping in savetie
frome losse or hurte all your said highnes
subjects. There was alsoo a towne, called
Newbyggins, by diverse fotmen of Tyndaill
and Ryddesdaill, takyn vp of the night, and
spoyled, when was slayne ii Scottsmen of the
said towne, and many Scotts there hurte ;
your highnes subjects was xiii myles within
the grounde of Scotlande, and is from my
house at Werkworthe, above lx miles of the
most evil passage, where great snawes doth
lye ; heretofore the same townes now brynt
haith not at any tyme in the mynd of man in

any warrs been enterprised unto nowe ; your
subjects were thereto more encouraged for
the better advancement of your highnes
service, the said Lord of Buclough beyng
always a mortall enemy to this your Graces
realme, and he dyd say, within xiii days before, he woulde see who durst lye near hym ;
wt many other cruell words, the knowledge
whereof was certainly haid to my said
servaunts, before theyre enterprice maid vpon
him ; most humbly beseeching your majesty,
that youre highnes thanks may concur vnto
theyme, whose names be here inclosed, and to
have in your most gracious memory. the payn-
full and diligent service of my pore servaunte
Wharton, and thus, as I am most bounden,
shall dispose wt them that be under me f . . .
. . . annoysaunce of your highnes enemys.'
In resentment of this foray, Buccleuch, with
other Border chiefs, assembled an army of
3000 riders, with which they penetrated into
Northumberland, and laid waste the country
as far as the banks of Bramish. They baffled,
or defeated, the English forces opposed to
them, and returned loaded with prey.—
PINKERTON'S *History*, vol. ii. p. 318.

NOTE V.

*Bards long shall tell
How Lord Walter fell.*—P. 3.

Sir Walter Scott of Buccleuch succeeded
to his grandfather, Sir David, in 1492. He
was a brave and powerful baron, and Warden
of the West Marches of Scotland. His death
was the consequence of a feud betwixt the
Scotts and Kerrs, the history of which is
necessary, to explain repeated allusions in
the romance.

In the year 1526, in the words of Pitscottie,
'the Earl of Angus, and the rest of the
Douglasses, ruled all which they liked, and
no man durst say the contrary ; wherefore
the King (James V, then a minor) was heavily
displeased, and would fain have been out of
their hands, if he might by any way : And,
to that effect, wrote a quiet and secret letter
with his own hand, and sent it to the Laird
of Buccleuch, beseeching him that he would
come with his kin and friends, and all the
force that he might be, and meet him at
Melross, at his home passing, and there to
take him out of the Douglasses hands, and
to put him to liberty, to use himself among
the lave (*rest*) of his lords, as he thinks expedient.

'This letter was quietly directed, and sent
by one of the King's own secret servants,
which was received very thankfully by the
Laird of Buccleuch, who was very glad thereof, to be put to such charges and familiarity
with his prince, and did great diligence to
perform the King's writing, and to bring the
matter to pass as the King desired : And, to
that effect, convened all his kin and friends,

and all that would do for him, to ride with him to Melross, when he knew of the King's homecoming. And so he brought with him six hundred spears, of Liddesdale, and Annandale, and countrymen, and clans thereabout, and held themselves quiet while that the King returned out of Jedburgh, and came to Melross, to remain there all that night.

'But when the Lord Hume, Cessfoord, and Fernyherst, (the chiefs of the clan of Kerr,) took their leave of the King, and returned home, then appeared the Lord of Buccleuch in sight, and his company with him in an arrayed battle, intending to have fulfilled the King's petition, and therefore came stoutly forward on the back side of Haliden hill. By that the Earl of Angus, with George Douglas, his brother, and sundry other of his friends, seeing this army coming, they marvelled what the matter meant; while at the last they knew the Laird of Buccleuch, with a certain company of the thieves of Annandale. With him they were less affeared, and made them manfully to the field contrary them, and said to the King in this manner, "Sir, yon is Buccleuch, and thieves of Annandale with him, to unbeset your Grace from the gate" (i.e. interrupt your passage). "I vow to God they shall either fight or flee; and ye shall tarry here on this know, and my brother George with you, with any other company you please; and I shall pass, and put yon thieves off the ground, and rid the gate unto your Grace, or else die for it." The King tarried still, as was devised; and George Douglas with him, and sundry other lords, such as the Earl of Lennox, and the Lord Erskine, and some of the King's own servants; but all the lave (*rest*) past with the Earl of Angus to the field against the Laird of Buccleuch, who joyned and countered cruelly both the said parties in the field of Darnelinver, either against other, with uncertain victory. But at the last, the Lord of Hume, hearing word of that matter how it stood, returned again to the King in all possible haste, with him the Lairds of Cessfoord and Fernyhirst, to the number of fourscore spears, and set freshly on the lap and wing of the Laird of Buccleuch's field, and shortly bare them backward to the ground; which caused the Laird of Buccleuch, and the rest of his friends, to go back and flee, whom they followed and chased; and especially the Lairds of Cessfoord and Fernyhirst followed furiouslie, till at the foot of a path the Laird of Cessfoord was slain by the stroke of a spear by an Elliot, who was then servant to the Laird of Buccleuch. But when the Laird of Cessfoord was slain, the chase ceased. The Earl of Angus returned again with great merriness and victory, and thanked God that he saved him from that chance, and passed with the King to Melross, where they remained all that night. On the morn they past to Edinburgh with the King, who was very sad and dolorous of the slaughter of the

Laird of Cessfoord, and many other gentlemen and yeomen slain by the Laird of Buccleuch, containing the number of fourscore and fifteen, which died in defence of the King and at the command of his writing.'

I am not the first who has attempted to celebrate in verse the renown of this ancient baron, and his hazardous attempt to procure his sovereign's freedom. In a Scottish Latin poet we find the following verses :—

VALTERIUS SCOTUS BALCLUCHIUS,

Egregio suscepto facinore, libertate Regis, ac aliis rebus gestis clarus, sub JACOBO V. Aº. Christi, 1526.

'Intentata aliis, nullique audita priorum
 Audet, nec paviduin morsve, metusve quatit,
 Libertatem aliis soliti transcribere Regis:
   Subreptam hanc Regi restituisse paras;
 Si vincis, quanta ô succedunt praemia dextrae !
   Sin victus, falsas spes jace, pone animam.
 Hostica vis nocuit : stant a.tae robora mentis
   Atque decus. Vincet, Rege probante, fides
 Insita queis animis virtus, quosque acrior ardor
   Obsidet, obscuris nox premat an tenebris ?'

Heroes ex omni Historia Scotica lectissimi, Auctore Johan Jonstonia Abredonense Scoto, 1603.

In consequence of the battle of Melrose, there ensued a deadly feud betwixt the names of Scott and Kerr, which, in spite of all means used to bring about an agreement, raged for many years upon the Borders. Buccleuch was imprisoned, and his estates forfeited, in the year 1535, for levying war against the Kerrs, and restored by act of Parliament, dated 15th March, 1542, during the regency of Mary of Lorraine. But the most signal act of violence to which this quarrel gave rise, was the murder of Sir Walter himself, who was slain by the Kerrs in the streets of Edinburgh in 1552. This is the event alluded to in stanza vii; and the poem is supposed to open shortly after it had taken place.

The feud between these two families was not reconciled in 1596, when both chieftains paraded the streets of Edinburgh with their followers, and it was expected their first meeting would decide their quarrel. But, on July 14th of the same year, Colvil, in a letter to Mr. Bacon, informs him, 'that there was great trouble upon the Borders, which would continue till order should be taken by the Queen of England and the King, by reason of the two young Scots chieftains, Cesford and Baclugh, and of the present necessity and scarcity of corn amongst the Scots Borderers and riders. That there had been a private quarrel betwixt those two lairds on the Borders, which was like to have turned to blood; but the fear of the general trouble had reconciled them, and the injuries which they thought to have committed against each other were now transferred upon England : not unlike that emulation in France between the Baron de Biron and Mons. Jeverie, who, being both ambitious of honour, undertook more hazardous enterprises against the enemy than they would have done if they had been at concord together.'—BIRCH'S *Memorials*, vol. ii. p. 67.

Note VI.

While Cessford owns the rule of Carr,
While Ettrick boasts the line of Scott,
The slaughter'd chiefs, the mortal jar,
The havoc of the feudal war,
Shall never, never be forgot!—P. 4.

Among other expedients resorted to for
stanching the feud betwixt the Scotts and the
Kerrs, there was a bond executed in 1529,
between the heads of each clan, binding themselves to perform reciprocally the four principal pilgrimages of Scotland, for the benefit
of the souls of those of the opposite name
who had fallen in the quarrel. This indenture
is printed in the *Minstrelsy of the Scottish
Border*, vol. i. But either it never took
effect, or else the feud was renewed shortly
afterwards.

Such pactions were not uncommon in feudal
times; and, as might be expected, they were
often, as in the present case, void of the effect
desired. When Sir Walter Mauny, the renowned follower of Edward III, had taken
the town of Ryol in Gascony, he remembered
to have heard that his father lay there buried,
and offered a hundred crowns to any who
could show him his grave. A very old man
appeared before Sir Walter, and informed
him of the manner of his father's death, and
the place of his sepulture. It seems the Lord
of Mauny had, at a great tournament, unhorsed and wounded to the death, a Gascon
knight, of the house of Mirepoix, whose kinsman was Bishop of Cambray. For this deed
he was held at feud by the relations of the
knight, until he agreed to undertake a
pilgrimage to the shrine of St. James of
Compostella, for the benefit of the soul of
the deceased. But as he returned through
the town of Ryol, after accomplishment of
his vow, he was beset and treacherously
slain, by the kindred of the knight whom he
had killed. Sir Walter, guided by the old
man, visited the lowly tomb of his father;
and, having read the inscription, which was
in Latin, he caused the body to be raised, and
transported to his native city of Valenciennes,
where masses were, in the days of Froissart,
duly said for the soul of the unfortunate
pilgrim.– *Chronycle of* FROISSART, vol. i.
p. 123.

Note VII.

With Carr in arms had stood.—P. 4.

The family of Ker, Kerr, or Carr, was
very powerful on the Border. Fynes Morrison remarks, in his Travels, that their
influence extended from the village of Preston
Grange, in Lothian, to the limits of England.
Cessford Castle, the ancient baronial residence of the family, is situated near the
village of Morebattle, within two or three
miles of the Cheviot Hills. It has been a

place of great strength and consequence, but
is now ruinous. Tradition affirms that it
was founded by Halbert, or Habby Kerr, a
gigantic warrior, concerning whom many
stories are current in Roxburghshire. The
Duke of Roxburghe represents Kerr of Cessford. A distinct and powerful branch of the
same name own the Marquis of Lothian as
their chief. Hence the distinction betwixt
Kerrs of Cessford and Fairnihirst.

Note VIII.

Lord Cranstoun.—P. 4.

The Cranstouns, Lord Cranstoun, are an
ancient Border family, whose chief seat was
at Crailing, in Teviotdale. They were at
this time at feud with the clan of Scott; for
it appears that the Lady of Buccleuch, in
1557, beset the Laird of Cranstoun, seeking
his life. Nevertheless, the same Cranstoun,
or perhaps his son, was married to a daughter of the same lady.

Note IX.

Of Bethune's line of Picardie.—P. 4.

The Bethunes were of French origin, and
derived their name from a small town in
Artois. There were several distinguished
families of the Bethunes in the neighbouring
province of Picardy; they numbered among
their descendants the celebrated Duc de
Sully; and the name was accounted among
the most noble in France, while aught noble
remained in that country[1]. The family of
Bethune, or Beatoun, in Fife, produced
three learned and dignified prelates; namely,
Cardinal Beaton, and two successive Archbishops of Glasgow, all of whom flourished
about the date of the romance. Of this
family was descended Dame Janet Beaton,
Lady Buccleuch, widow of Sir Walter Scott
of Branksome. She was a woman of masculine spirit, as appeared from her riding at
the head of her son's clan, after her husband's murder. She also possessed the hereditary abilities of her family in such a
degree that the superstition of the vulgar
imputed them to supernatural knowledge.
With this was mingled, by faction, the foul
accusation of her having influenced Queen
Mary to the murder of her husband. One of
the placards, preserved in Buchanan's Detection, accuses of Darnley's murder 'the Erle
of Bothwell, Mr. James Balfour, the persoun
of Fliske, Mr. David Chalmers, black Mr.
John Spens, who was principal deviser of the
murder; and the Quene, assenting thairto,
throw the persuasion of the Erle Bothwell,
and *the witchcraft of Lady Buckleuch.*'

[1] This expression and sentiment were dictated by
the situation of France, in the year 1803, when the
poem was originally written. 1821.

NOTE X.

He learn'd the art that none may name,
In Padua, far beyond the sea.—P. 4.

Padua was long supposed, by the Scottish peasants, to be the principal school of necromancy. The Earl of Gowrie, slain at Perth, in 1600, pretended, during his studies in Italy, to have acquired some knowledge of the cabala, by which, he said, he could charm snakes, and work other miracles; and, in particular, could produce children without the intercourse of the sexes.—See the examination of Wemyss of Bogie before the Privy Council, concerning Gowrie's Conspiracy.

NOTE XI.

His form no darkening shadow trac'd
Upon the sunny wall!—P. 4.

The shadow of a necromancer is independent of the sun. Glycas informs us that Simon Magus caused his shadow to go before him, making people believe it was an attendant spirit.—HEYWOOD'S *Hierarchie*, p. 475. The vulgar conceive, that when a class of students have made a certain progress in their mystic studies, they are obliged to run through a subterraneous hall, where the devil literally catches the hindmost in the race, unless he crosses the hall so speedily that the arch-enemy can only apprehend his shadow. In the latter case, the person of the sage never after throws any shade; and those, who have thus *lost their shadow*, always prove the best magicians.

NOTE XII.

The viewless forms of air.—P. 4.

The Scottish vulgar, without having any very defined notion of their attributes, believe in the existence of an intermediate class of spirits, residing in the air, or in the waters; to whose agency they ascribe floods, storms, and all such phenomena as their own philosophy cannot readily explain. They are supposed to interfere in the affairs of mortals, sometimes with a malevolent purpose, and sometimes with milder views. It is said, for example, that a gallant baron, having returned from the Holy Land to his castle of Drummelziar, found his fair lady nursing a healthy child, whose birth did not by any means correspond to the date of his departure. Such an occurrence, to the credit of the dames of the Crusaders be it spoken, was so rare, that it required a miraculous solution. The lady, therefore, was believed, when s':e av.:rred confidently, that the Spirit of the Tweed had issued from the river while she was walking upon its bank, and compelled her to submit to his embraces; and the name of Tweedie was bestowed upon the child, who afterwards became Baron of Drummelziar, the chief of a powerful clan. To those spirits were also ascribed, in Scotland, the

> 'airy tongues, that syllable men's names,
> On sands, and shores, and desert wildernesses.

When the workmen were engaged in erecting the ancient church of Old Deer, in Aberdeenshire, upon a small hill called Bissau, they were surprised to find that the work was impeded by supernatural obstacles. At length, the Spirit of the River was heard to say,

> 'It is not here, it is not here,
> That ye shall build the church of Deer;
> But on Taptillery,
> Where many a corpse shall lie.'

The site of the edifice was accordingly transferred to Taptillery, an eminence at some distance from the place where the building had been commenced. — MACFARLANE'S *MSS.* I mention these popular fables, because the introduction of the River and Mountain Spirits may not, at first sight, seem to accord with the general tone of the romance, and the superstitions of the country where the scene is laid.

NOTE XIII.

A fancied moss-trooper, &c.—P. 5.

This was the usual appellation of the marauders upon the Borders; a profession diligently pursued by the inhabitants on both sides, and by none more actively and successfully than by Buccleuch's clan. Long after the union of the crowns the moss troopers, although sunk in reputation, and no longer enjoying the pretext of national hostility, continued to pursue their calling. Fuller includes, among the wonders of Cumberland, 'The moss-troopers: so strange in the condition of their living, if considered in their *Original, Increase, Height, Decay,* and *Ruine.*

'1. *Original.* I conceive them the same called Borderers in Mr. Camden; and characterised by him to be a *wild and warlike people.* They are called *moss-troopers*, because dwelling in the mosses, and riding in troops together. They dwell in the bounds, or meeting, of the two kingdoms, but obey the laws of neither. They come to church as seldom as the 29th of February comes into the kalendar.

'2. *Increase.* When England and Scotland were united in Great Britain, they that formerly lived by hostile incursions, betook themselves to the robbing of their neighbours. Their sons are free of the trade by their fathers' copy. They are like to Job, not in piety and patience, but in sudden plenty and poverty; sometimes having flocks and herds in the morning, none at night, and perchance many again next day. They may give for their motto, *vivitur ex rapto*, stealing from

their honest neighbours what they sometimes require. They are a nest of hornets;
strike one, and stir all of them about your
ears. Indeed, if they promise safely to conduct a traveller, they will perform it with
the fidelity of a Turkish janizary; otherwise,
woe be to him that falleth into their quarters!

'3. *Height*. Amounting, forty years since,
to some thousands. These compelled the
vicinage to purchase their security, by paying a constant rent to them. When in their
greatest height, they had two great enemies,
—*the Laws of the Land*, and the *Lord
William Howard of Naworth*. He sent
many of them to Carlisle, to that place where
the officer *doth always his work by day-
light*. Yet these moss-troopers, if possibly
they could procure the pardon for a condemned person of their company, would
advance great sums out of their common
stock, who, in such a case, *cast in their lots
amongst themselves, and all have one
purse*.

'4. *Decay*. Caused by the wisdom, valour,
and diligence of the Right Honourable
Charles Lord Howard, Earl of Carlisle, who
routed these English Tories with his regiment. His severity unto them will not only
be excused, but commended, by the judicious,
who consider how our great lawyer doth
describe such persons, who are solemnly
outlawed. BRACTON, lib. viii. trac. 2. cap.
11.—" *Ex tunc gerunt caput lupinum, ita
quod sine judiciali inquisitione rite pereant,
et secum suum judicium portent; et merito
sine lege pereunt, qui secundum legem
vivere recusarunt.*"—"Thenceforward (after
that they are outlawed) they wear a wolf's
head, so that they lawfully may be destroyed,
without any judicial inquisition, as who
carry their own condemnation about them,
and deservedly die without law, because
they refused to live according to law."

'5. *Ruine*. Such was the success of this
worthy lord's severity, that he made a
thorough reformation among them; and the
ring-leaders being destroyed, the rest are
reduced to legal obedience, and so, I trust,
will continue.'—FULLER'S *Worthies of England*, p. 216.

The last public mention of moss-troopers
occurs during the civil wars of the 17th century, when many ordinances of Parliament
were directed against them.

NOTE XIV.

—— *tame the Unicorn's pride,
Exalt the Crescent and the Star.*—P. 6.

The arms of the Kerrs of Cessford were,
Vert on a cheveron, betwixt three unicorns'
heads, erased *argent*, three mullets *sable*;
crest, a unicorn's head, erased *proper*. The
Scotts of Buccleuch bore, *Or*, on a bend
azure; a star of six points betwixt two crescents of the first.

NOTE XV.

William of Deloraine.—P. 6.

The lands of Deloraine are joined to those
of Buccleuch in Ettrick Forest. They were
immemorially possessed by the Buccleuch
family, under the strong title of occupancy,
although no charter was obtained from the
crown until 1545. Like other possessions,
the lands of Deloraine were occasionally
granted by them to vassals, or kinsmen, for
Border service. Satchells mentions, among
the twenty-four gentlemen-pensioners of the
family, 'William Scott, commonly called
Cut-at-the-Black, who had the lands of Nether
Deloraine for his service.' And again, 'This
William of Deloraine, commonly called *Cut-
at-the-Black*, was a brother of the ancient
house of Haining, which house of Haining is
descended from the ancient house of Hassendean.' The lands of Deloraine now give
an earl's title to the descendant of Henry, the
second surviving son of the Duchess of Buccleuch and Monmouth. I have endeavoured
to give William of Deloraine the attributes
which characterised the Borderers of his
day; for which I can only plead Froissart's
apology, that, 'it behoveth, in a lynage,
some to be folyshe and outrageous, to mayn-
teyne and sustayne the peasable.' As a
contrast to my Marchman, I beg leave to
transcribe, from the same author, the speech
of Amergot Marcell, a captain of the Adventurous Companions, a robber, and a
pillager of the country of Auvergne, who had
been bribed to sell his strongholds, and to
assume a more honourable military life
under the banners of the Earl of Armagnac.
But 'when he remembered alle this, he was
sorrowful; his tresour he thought he wolde
not mynysshe; he was wonte dayly to serche
for newe pyllages, wherbye encresed his
profyte, and then he sawe that alle was
closed fro' hym. Then he sayde and imag-
yned, that to pyll and to robbe (all thynge
considered) was a good lyfe, and so repented
hym of his good doing. On a tyme, he said
to his old companyons, "Sirs, there is no
sporte nor glory in this worlde amonge men
of warre, but to use suche lyfe as we have
done in tyme past. What a joy was it to us
when we rode forth at adventure, and som-
tyme found by the way a riche priour or
merchaunt, or a route of mulettes of Mount-
pellyer, of Narbonne, of Lymens, of Fon-
gans, of Besyers, of Tholous, or of Carca-
sonne, laden with cloth of Brussels, or peltre
ware comynge fro the fayres, or laden
with spycery fro Bruges, fro Damas, or fro
Alysaundre; whatsoever we met, all was
ours, or els ransoumed at our pleasures:
dayly we gate new money, and the vyllaynes
of Auvergne and of Lymosyn dayly pro-
vyded and brought to our castell whete
mele, good wynes, beffes, and fatte mottons,
pullayne, and wylde foule: We were ever
furnyshed as tho we had been kings. When

we rode forthe, all the countrey trymbled for feare: all was ours goyng and comynge. How tok we Carlast, I and the Bourge of Companye, and I and Perot of Bernoys took Caluset; how dyd we scale, with lytell ayde, the strong castell of Marquell, pertayning to the Erl Dolphyn: I kept it nat past fyve days, but I receyved for it, on a feyre table, fyve thousande frankes, and forgave one thousande for the love of the Erl Dolphin's children. By my fayth, this was a fayre and a good lyfe! wherefore I repute myselfe sore deceyved, in that I have rendered up the fortresse of Aloys; for it wolde have kept fro alle the worlde, and the daye that I gave it up, it was fournyshed with vytaylles, to have been kept seven yere without any re-vytayllinge. This Erl of Armynake hath deceyved me: Olyve Barbe, and Perot le Bernoys, shewed to me how I shulde repente myselfe; certayne I sore repente myselfe of what I have done." '—FROISSART, vol. ii. p. 195.

NOTE XVI.

By wily turns, by desperate bounds,
Had baffled Percy's best blood-hounds.—P. 6.

The kings and heroes of Scotland, as well as the Border riders, were sometimes obliged to study how to evade the pursuit of bloodhounds. Barbour informs us, that Robert Bruce was repeatedly tracked by sleuth-dogs. On one occasion, he escaped by wading a bow-shot down a brook, and ascending into a tree by a branch which overhung the water; thus, leaving no trace on land of his footsteps, he baffled the scent. The pursuers came up:

'Rycht to the burn that passyt ware,
Bot the sleuth-hund made stinting thar,
And waueryt lang tyme ta and fra,
That he na certain gate couth ga;
Till at the last that John of Lorne
Perseuvit the hund the sleuth had lorne.
        The Bruce, Book vii.

A sure way of stopping the dog was to spill blood upon the track, which destroyed the discriminating fineness of his scent. A captive was sometimes sacrificed on such occasions. Henry the Minstrel tells a romantic story of Wallace, founded on this circumstance:—The hero's little band had been joined by an Irishman, named Fawdoun, or Fadzean, a dark, savage, and suspicious character. After a sharp skirmish at Black-Erne Side, Wallace was forced to retreat with only sixteen followers. The English pursued with a Border *sleuth-bratch*, or blood-hound.

' In Gelderland there was that bratchet bred,
Siker of scent, to follow them that fled;
So was he used in Eske and Lidde dail,
While (i. e. *till*) she gat blood no fleeing might avail.

In the retreat, Fawdoun, tired, or affecting to be so, would go no farther. Wallace, having in vain argued with him, in hasty anger, struck off his head, and continued the retreat. When the English came up, their hound stayed upon the dead body:—

'The sleuth stopped at Fawdon, still she stood,
Nor farther would fra time she fund the blood.'

The story concludes with a fine Gothic scene of terror. Wallace took refuge in the solitary tower of Gask. Here he was disturbed at midnight by the blast of a horn. He sent out his attendants by two and two, but no one returned with tidings. At length, when he was left alone, the sound was heard still louder. The champion descended, sword in hand; and, at the gate of the tower, was encountered by the headless spectre of Fawdoun, whom he had slain so rashly. Wallace, in great terror, fled up into the tower, tore open the boards of a window, leapt down fifteen feet in height, and continued his flight up the river. Looking back to Gask, he discovered the tower on fire, and the form of Fawdoun upon the battlements, dilated to an immense size, and holding in his hand a blazing rafter. The Minstrel concludes,

'Trust ryght wele, that all this be sooth indeed,
Supposing it to be no point of the creed.'
        The Wallace, Book v.

Mr. Ellis has extracted this tale as a sample of Henry's poetry.—*Specimens of English Poetry*, vol. i. p. 351.

NOTE XVII.

——*the Moat-hill's mound,*
Where Druid shades still flitted round.
                —P. 6.

This is a round artificial mount near Hawick, which, from its name, (ꝳMot, *Ang. Sax. Concilium, Conventus,*) was probably anciently used as a place for assembling a national council of the adjacent tribes. There are many such mounds in Scotland, and they are sometimes, but rarely, of a square form.

NOTE XVIII.

——*the tower of Hazeldean.*—P. 7.

The estate of Hazeldean, corruptly Hassendean, belonged form-rly to a family of Scotts, thus commemorated by Satchells:—

'Hassendean came without a call,
The ancientest house among them all.

NOTE XIX.

On Minto-crags the moonbeams glint.
—P. 7.

A romantic assemblage of cliffs, which rise suddenly above the vale of Teviot, in the immediate vicinity of the family-seat, from which Lord Minto takes his title. A small platform, on a projecting crag, commanding a most beautiful prospect, is termed *Barnhills' Bed.* This Barnhills is said to have been a robber, or outlaw. There are remains of a strong tower beneath the rocks, where he is supposed to have dwelt, and from which he derived his name. On the summit of the crags are the fragments of another ancient tower, in a picturesque situation. Among the houses cast down by the Earl of Hartforde, in 1545, occur the towers of Easter Barnhills, and of Minto-crag, with Minto town and place. Sir Gilbert Elliot[1], father to the present Lord Minto, was the author of a beautiful pastoral song, of which the following is a more correct copy than is usually published. The poetical mantle of Sir Gilbert Elliot has descended to his family.

' My sheep I neglected, I broke my sheep-hook.
And all the gay haunts of my youth I forsook :
No more for Amynta fresh garlands I wove ;
Ambition, I said, would soon cure me of love.
But what had my youth with ambition to do !
Why left I Amynta ! why broke I my vow !

Through regions remote in vain do I rove,
And bid the wide world secure me from love.
Ah, fool, to imagine, that aught could subdue
A love so well founded, a passion so true !
Ah, give me my sheep, and my sheep-hook restore
And I'll wander from love and Amynta no more !

Alas ! 'tis too late at thy fate to repine !
Poor shepherd, Amynta no more can be thine !
Thy tears are all fruitless, thy wishes are vain,
The moments neglected return not again.
Ah ! what had my youth with ambition to do !
Why left I Amynta ! why broke I my vow ! '

NOTE XX.

Ancient Riddel's fair domain.—P. 7.

The family of Riddell have been very long in possession of the barony called Riddell, or Ryedale, part of which still bears the latter name. Tradition carries their antiquity to a point extremely remote ; and is, in some degree, sanctioned by the discovery of two stone coffins, one containing an earthen pot filled with ashes and arms, bearing a legible date, A.D. 727 ; the other dated 936, and filled with the bones of a man of gigantic size. These coffins were discovered in the foundations of what was, but has long ceased to be, the chapel of Riddell ; and as it was argued, with plausibility, that they contained the remains of some ancestors of the family,

1 Elected M.P. for Selkirkshire in 1754.

they were deposited in the modern place of sepulture, comparatively so termed, though built in 1110. But the following curious and authentic documents warrant most conclusively the epithet of 'ancient Riddel' : 1st, A charter by David I to Walter Rydale, Sheriff of Roxburgh, confirming all the estates of Liliesclive, &c., of which his father, Gervasius de Rydale, died possessed. 2dly, A bull of Pope Adrian IV, confirming the will of Walter de Ridale, knight, in favour of his brother Anschittil de Ridale, dated 8th April, 1155. 3dly, A bull of Pope Alexander III, confirming the said will of Walter de Ridale, bequeathing to his brother Anschittil the lands of Liliesclive, Whettunes, &c., and ratifying the bargain betwixt Anschittil and Huctredus, concerning the church of Liliesclive, in consequence of the mediation of Malcolm II, and confirmed by a charter from that monarch. This bull is dated 17th June, 1160. 4thly, A bull of the same Pope, confirming the will of Sir Anschittil de Ridale, in favour of his son Walter, conveying the said lands of Liliesclive and others, dated 10th March, 1120. It is remarkable, that Liliesclive, otherwise Rydale, or Riddell, and the Whittunes, have descended, through a long train of ancestors, without ever passing into a collateral line, to the person of Sir John Buchanan Riddell, Bart. of Riddell, the lineal descendant and representative of Sir Anschittil.—These circumstances appeared worthy of notice in a Border work.

NOTE XXI.

But when Melrose he reach'd, 'twas silence all ;
He meetly stabled his steed in stall,
And sought the convent's lonely wall.
—P. 8.

The ancient and beautiful monastery of Melrose was founded by King David I. Its ruins afford the finest specimen of Gothic architecture and Gothic sculpture which Scotland can boast. The stone of which it is built, though it has resisted the weather for so many ages, retains perfect sharpness, so that even the most minute ornaments seem as entire as when newly wrought. In some of the cloisters, as is hinted in the next Canto, there are representations of flowers, vegetables, &c., carved in stone, with accuracy and precision so delicate, that we almost distrust our senses, when we consider the difficulty of subjecting so hard a substance to such intricate and exquisite modulation. This superb convent was dedicated to St. Mary, and the monks were of the Cistertian order. At the time of the Reformation, they shared the general reproach of sensuality and irregularity, thrown upon the Roman churchmen. The old words of

Galashiels, a favourite Scotch air, ran thus:—

> 'O the monks of Melrose made gude kale [1],
>   On Fridays when they fasted,
> They wanted neither beef nor ale,
>   As long as their neighbours' lasted.'

NOTE XXII.

When buttress and buttress, alternately,
Seem fram'd of ebon and ivory;
When silver edges the imagery,
And the scrolls that teach thee to live and
*   die;*

     .   .   .

Then view St. David's ruin'd pile.—P. 8.

The buttresses ranged along the sides of the ruins of Melrose Abbey, are, according to the Gothic style, richly carved and fretted, containing niches for the statues of saints, and labelled with scrolls, bearing appropriate texts of Scripture. Most of these statues have been demolished.

David I of Scotland purchased the reputation of sanctity, by founding, and liberally endowing, not only the monastery of Melrose, but those of Kelso, Jedburgh, and many others; which led to the well-known observation of his successor, that he was *a sore saint for the crown.*

NOTE XXIII.

For mass or prayer can I rarely tarry,
Save to patter an Ave Mary,
When I ride on a Border foray.—P. 9.

The Borderers were, as may be supposed, very ignorant about religious matters. Colville, in his *Paranesis*, or *Admonition*, states, that the reformed divines were so far from undertaking distant journeys to convert the Heathen, 'as I wold wis at God that ve wold only go bot to the Hielands and Borders of our own realm, to gain our awin countrey-men, who, for lack of preching and ministra-tion of the sacraments, must, with tyme, becum either infidells, or atheists.' But we learn, from Lesley, that, however deficient in real religion, they regularly told their beads, and never with more zeal than when going on a plundering expedition.

NOTE XXIV.

So had he seen, in fair Castile,
The youth in glittering squadrons start,
Sudden the flying jennet wheel,
And hurl the unexpected dart.—P. 9.

'By my faith,' sayd the Duke of Lancaster, (to a Portuguese squire,) 'of all the feates of armes that the Castellyans, and they of your

[1] *Kale*, broth.

countrey doth use, the castynge of their dertes best pleaseth me, and gladly I wolde se it: for, as I hear say, if they strike one aryghte, without he be well armed, the dart will pierce him thrughe.'—'By my fayth, sir,' sayd the squyer, 'ye say trouth; for I have seen many a grete stroke given with them, which at one time cost us derely, and was to us great disp'easure; for, at the said skyrmishe, Sir John Lawrence of Coygne was striken with a dart in such wise, that the head perced all the plates of his cote of mayle, and a sacke stopped with sylke, and passed thrughe his body, so that he fell down dead.'—FROISSART, vol. ii. ch. 44.—This mode of fighting with darts was imitated in the military game called *Jeugo de las canas*, which the Spaniards borrowed from their Moorish invaders. A Saracen champion is thus described by Froissart: 'Among the Sarazyns, there was a yonge knight called Agadinger Dolyferne; he was always wel mounted on a redy and a lyght horse; it seemed, when the horse ranne, that he did fly in the ayre. The knighte seemed to be a good man of armes by his dedes; he bare always of usage three fethered dartes, and rychte well he could handle them; and, according to their custome, he was clene armed, with a long white towell about his head. His apparell was blacke, and his own colour browne, and a good horseman. The Crysten men say, they thoughte he dyd such deeds of armes for the love of some yonge ladye of his countrey. And true it was, that he loved entirely the King of Thune's daughter, named the Lady Azala; she was inherytor to the realme of Thune, after the discease of the kyng, her father. This Agadinger was sone to the Duke of Olyferne. I can nat telle if they were married together after or nat; but it was shewed me, that this knyght, for love of the sayd ladye, during the siege, did many feates of armes. The knyghtes of France wold fayne have taken hym; but they colde never attrape nor inclose him; his horse was so swyft, and so redy to his hand, that alwaies he escaped.' —Vol. ii. ch. 71.

NOTE XXV.

And there the dying lamps did burn,
Before thy low and lonely urn,
O gallant Chief of Otterburne!—P. 10.

The famous and desperate battle of Otter-burne was fought 15th August 1388, betwixt Henry Percy, called Hotspur, and James Earl of Douglas. Both these renowned champions were at the head of a chosen body of troops, and they were rivals in military fame: so that Froissart affirms, 'Of all the battayles and encounteryngs that I have made mencion of here before in all this hystory, great or smalle, this battayle that I treat of nowe was one of the **sorest** and best foughten, without cowardes or faynte hertes : for there was neyther knyghte nor squyer but that dyde his devoyre, and foughte hande to hande. This batayle was lyke the batayle of Becherell, the which was valiauntly fought and endured.' The issue of the conflict is well known : Percy was made prisoner, and the Scots won the day, dearly purchased by the death of their gallant general, the Earl of Douglas, who was slain in the action. He was buried at Melrose, beneath the high altar. ' His obsequye was done reverently, and on his bodye layde a tombe of stone, and his baner hangyng over hym.'—FROISSART, vol. ii. p. 165.

NOTE XXVI.

—— *dark Knight of Liddesdale.*—P. 10.

William Douglas, called the Knight of Lid.lesdale, flourished during the reign of David II, and was so distinguished by his valour, that he was called the Flower of Chivalry. Nevertheless, he tarnished his renown by the cruel murder of Sir Alexander Ramsay of Dalhousie, originally his friend and brother in arms. The King had conferred upon Ramsay the sheriffdom of Teviotdale, to which Douglas pretended some claim. In revenge of this preference, the Knight of Liddesdale came down upon Ramsay, while he was administering justice at Hawick, seized and carried him off to his remote and inaccessible castle of Hermitage, where he threw his unfortunate prisoner, horse and man, into a dungeon, and left him to perish of hunger. It is said, the miserable captive prolonged his existence for several days by the corn which fell from a granary above the vault in which he was confined[1]. So weak was the royal authority, that David, although highly incensed at this atrocious murder, found himself obliged to appoint the Knight of Liddesdale successor to his victim, as

[1] There is something affecting in the manner in which the old Prior of Lochleven turns from describing the death of the gallant Ramsay, to the general sorrow which it excited :—

'To tell you there of the manere,
It is bot sorrow for til here ;
He wes the grettast menyd man
That ony cowth have thowcht of than,
Of his state, or of mare be fare :
All menyt him, bath bettyr and war ;
The ryche and pure him menyde bath,
For of his dede wes mekil skath.'

Some years ago, a person digging for stones, about the old castle of Hermitage, broke into a vault, containing a quantity of chaff, some bones, and pieces of iron ; amongst others, the curb of an ancient bridle which the author has since given to the Earl of Dalhousie, under the impression that it possibly may be a relic of his brave ancestor. The worthy clergyman of the parish has mentioned this discovery in his Statistical Account of Castletown.

Sheriff of Teviotdale. But he was soon after slain, while hunting in Ettrick Forest, by his own godson and chieftain, William, Earl of Douglas, in revenge, according to some authors, of Ramsay's murder ; although a popular tradition, preserved in a ballad quoted by Godscroft, and some parts of which are still preserved, ascribes the resentment of the Earl to jealousy. The place where the Knight of Liddesdale was killed, is called, from his name, William-Cross, upon the ridge of a hill called William-hope, betwixt Tweed and Yarrow. His body, according to Godscroft, was carried to Lindean church the first night after his death, and thence to Melrose, where he was interred with great pomp, and where his tomb is still shown.

NOTE XXVII.

The moon on the east oriel shone.—P. 10.

It is impossible to conceive a more beautiful specimen of the lightness and elegance of Gothic architecture, when in its purity, than the eastern window of Melrose Abbey. Sir James Hall of Dunglas, Bart., has, with great ingenuity and plausibility, traced the Gothic order through its various forms and seemingly eccentric ornaments, to an architectural imitation of wicker work ; of which, as we learn from some of the legends, the earliest Christian churches were co structed. In such an edifice, the original of the clustered pillars is traced to a set of round posts, begirt with slender rods of willow, whose loose summits were brought to meet from all quarters, and bound together artificially, so as to produce the framework of the roof: and the tracery of our Gothic windows is displayed in the meeting and interlacing of rods and hoops, affording an inexhaustible variety of beautiful forms of open work. This ingenious system is alluded to in the romance. Sir James Hall's Essay on Gothic Architecture is published in *The Edinburgh Philosophical Transactions.*

NOTE XXVIII.

—— *the wondrous Michael Scott.*—P. 10.

Sir Michael Scott of Balwearie flourished during the 13th century, and was one of the ambassadors sent to bring the Maid of Norway to Scotland upon the death of Alexander III. By a poetical anachronism, he is here placed in a later era. He was a man of much learning, chiefly acquired in foreign countries. He wrote a commentary upon Aristotle, printed at Venice in 1496 ; and several treatises upon natural philosophy, from which he appears to have been addicted to the abstruse studies of judicial astrology, alchymy, physiognomy, and chiromancy. Hence he passed among his contemporaries for a skilful magician. Dempster informs us, that he remembers to have heard in his youth, that the magic books of Michael Scott were still in existence, but could not be opened without danger, on account of the malignant fiends who were thereby invoked. *Dempsteri Historia Ecclesiastica*, 1627, lib. xii. p. 495. Lesly characterises Michael Scott as '*singularie philosophiae, astronomiae, ac medicinae laude prestans ; dicebatur penitissimos magiae recessus indagasse.*' Dante also mentions him as a renowned wizard :—

' Quell altro ch~~e~~ ne' fianchi è così poco,
Michele Scotto fu, che veramente
Delle magiche frode seppe il giuoco.'

Inferno, Canto xxmo.

A personage, thus spoken of by biographers and historians, loses little of his mystical fame in vulgar tradition. Accordingly, the memory of Sir Michael Scott survives in many a legend ; and in the south of Scotland, any work of great labour and antiquity, is ascribed, either to the agency of *Auld Michael*, of Sir William Wallace, or of the devil. Tradition varies concerning the place of his burial ; some contend for Home Coltrame, in Cumberland ; others for Melrose Abbey. But all agree, that his books of magic were interred in his grave, or preserved in the convent where he died. Satchells, wishing to give some authority for his account of the origin of the name of Scott, pretends that, in 1629, he chanced to be at Burgh under Bowness, in Cumberland, where a person, named Lancelot Scott, showed him an extract from Michael Scott's works, containing that story :—

'He said the book which he gave me
Was of Sir Michael Scotts historie ;
Which history was never yet read through,
Nor never will, for no man dare it do,
Young scholars have pick'd out something
From the contents, that dare not read within,
He carried me along the castle then,
And shew'd his written book hanging on an iron pin.
His writing pen did seem to me to be
Of hardened metal, like steel, or accumie ;
The volume of it did seem so large to me,
As the Book of Martyrs and Turks historie.
Then in the church he let me see
A stone where Mr. Michael Scott did lie ;
I asked at him how that could appear,
Mr. Michael had been dead above five hundred year ?
He shew'd me none durst bury under that stone,
More than he had been dead a few years agone ;
For Mr. Michael's name does terrifie each one.'

History of the Right Honourable Name of SCOTT.

NOTE XXIX.

Salamanca's cave.—P. 10.

Spain, from the relics, doubtless, of Arabian learning and superstition, was accounted a favourite residence of magicians. Pope Sylvester, who actually imported from Spain the use of the Arabian numerals, was supposed to have learned there the magic, for which he was stigmatized by the ignorance of his age.—WILLIAM *of Malmsbury*, lib. ii. cap. 10. There were public schools, where magic, or rather the sciences supposed to involve its mysteries, were regularly taught, at Toledo, Seville, and Salamanca. In the latter city, they were held in a deep cavern ; the mouth of which was walled up by Queen Isabella, wife of King Ferdinand.— D'AUTON *on Learned Incredulity*, p. 45. These Spanish schools of magic are celebrated also by the Italian poets of romance :—

' Questo città di Tolleto solea,
Tenere studio di negromanzia ;
Quivi di magica arte si leggea
Pubblicamente, e di peromanzia ;
E molti geomanti sempre avea,
Esperimenti assai d' idromanzia
E d' altre false opinion' di sciocchi
Come è fatture, o spesso batter gli occhi.'

Il Morgante Maggiore, Canto xxv. St. 259.

The celebrated magician Maugis, cousin to Rinaldo of Montalban, called by Ariosto, Malagigi, studied the black art at Toledo, as we learn from *L'Histoire de Maugis D'Aygremont*. He even held a professor's chair in the necromantic university : for so I interpret the passage, '*qu'on tous les sept arts d'enchantement, des charmes et conjurations, il n'y avoit meilleur maistre que lui ; et en tel renom qu'on le laissoit en chaise, et l'appelloit on maistre Maugis.*' This Salamancan Domdaniel is said to have been founded by Hercules. If the classic reader inquires where Hercules himself learned magic, he may consult '*Les faicts et processes du noble et vaillant Hercules,*' where he will learn, that the fable of his aiding Atlas to support the heavens, arose from the said Atlas having taught Hercules, *the noble knighterrant*, the seven liberal sciences, and in particular, that of judicial astrology. Such, according to the idea of the middle ages, were the studies, '*maximus quae docuit Atlas.*' In a romantic history of Roderic, the last Gothic King of Spain, he is said to have entered one of those enchanted caverns. It was situated beneath an ancient tower near Toledo ; and when the iron gates, which secured the entrance, were unfolded, there rushed forth so dreadful a whirlwind, that hitherto no one had dared to penetrate into its recesses. But Roderic, threatened with an invasion of the Moors, resolved to enter the cavern, where he expected to find some prophetic intimation of the event of the war. Accordingly, his train being furnished with torches, so artificially composed that the tempest could not extinguish them, the King, with great difficulty, penetrated into a square hall, inscribed all over with Arabian characters. In the midst stood a colossal statue of brass, representing a Saracen wielding a Moorish mace, with which it discharged furious blows on all sides, and seemed thus to excite the tempest which raged around. Being conjured by Roderic, it ceased from striking, until he read, inscribed on the right hand, '*Wretched Monarch, for thy evil hast thou come hither;*' on the left hand, '*Thou shalt be dispossessed by a strange people;*' on one shoulder, '*I invoke the sons of Hagar;*' on the other, '*I do mine office.*' When the King had deciphered these ominous inscriptions, the statue returned to its exercise, the tempest commenced anew, and Roderic retired, to mourn over the predicted evils which approached his throne. He caused the gates of the cavern to be locked and barricaded; but, in the course of the night, the tower fell with a tremendous noise, and under its ruins concealed for ever the entrance to the mystic cavern. The conquest of Spain by the Saracens, and the death of the unfortunate Don Roderic, fulfilled the prophecy of the brazen statue.—*Historia verdadera del Rey Don Rodrigo por el Sabio Alcayde Abulcacim, traduzeda de la lengua Arabiga por Miquel de Luna*, 1654, cap. vi.

NOTE XXX.

The bells would ring in Notre Dame.
—P. 10.

'*Tantamne rem tam negligenter?*' says Tyrwhitt, of his predecessor, Speight; who, in his commentary on Chaucer, had omitted, as trivial and fabulous, the story of Wade and his boat Guingelot, to the great prejudice of posterity, the memory of the hero and the boat being now entirely lost. That future antiquaries may lay no such omission to my charge, I have noted one or two of the most current traditions concerning Michael Scott. He was chosen, it is said, to go upon an embassy, to obtain from the King of France satisfaction for certain piracies committed by his subjects upon those of Scotland. Instead of preparing a new equipage and splendid retinue, the ambassador retreated to his study, opened his book, and evoked a fiend in the shape of a huge black horse, mounted upon his back, and forced him to fly through the air towards France. As they crossed the sea, the devil insidiously asked his rider, What it was that the old women of Scotland muttered at bed-time? A less experienced wizard might have answered that it was the Pater Noster, which would have licensed the devil to precipitate him from his back. But Michael sternly replied, 'What is that to thee?—Mount, Diabolus, and fly!' When he arrived at Paris, he tied his horse to the gate of the palace, entered, and boldly delivered his message. An ambassador, with so little of the pomp and circumstance of diplomacy, was not received with much respect, and the King was about to return a contemptuous refusal to his demand, when Michael besought him to suspend his resolution till he had seen his horse stamp three times. The first stamp shook every steeple in Paris, and caused all the bells to ring; the second threw down three of the towers of the palace; and the infernal steed had lifted his hoof to give the third stamp, when the King rather chose to dismiss Michael, with the most ample concessions, than to stand to the probable consequences. Another time, it is said, that, when residing at the Tower of Oakwood, upon the Ettrick, about three miles above Selkirk, he heard of the fame of a sorceress, called the Witch of Falsehope, who lived on the opposite side of the river. Michael went one morning to put her skill to the test, but was disappointed, by her denying positively any knowledge of the necromantic art. In the discourse with her, he laid his wand inadvertently on the table, which the hag observing, suddenly snatched it up, and struck him with it. Feeling the force of the charm, he rushed out of the house; but, as it had conferred on him the external appearance of a hare, his servant, who waited without, halloo'd upon the discomfited wizard his own greyhounds, and pursued him so close, that, in order to obtain a moment's breathing to reverse the charm, Michael, after a very fatiguing course, was fain to take refuge in his own *jawhole* (*Anglice*, common sewer). In order to revenge himself of the witch of Falsehope, Michael, one morning in the ensuing harvest, went to the hill above the house with his dogs, and sent down his servant to ask a bit of bread from the good wife for his greyhounds, with instructions what to do if he met with a denial. Accordingly, when the witch had refused the boon with contumely, the servant, as his master had directed, laid above the door a paper which he had given him, containing, amongst many cabalistical words, the well-known rhyme,—

'Maister Michael Scott's man
Sought meat, and gat nane.

Immediately the good old woman, instead of pursuing her domestic occupation, which was baking bread for the reapers, began to dance round the fire, repeating the rhyme, and continued this exercise till her husband sent the reapers to the house, one after another, to see what had delayed their provision; but the charm caught each as they entered, and, losing all idea of returning, they joined in the dance and chorus. At length the old man himself went to the house; but as his wife's frolic with Mr. Michael, whom he had seen on the hill, made him a little cautious, he contented himself with looking in at the window, and saw the reapers at their involuntary exercise, dragging his wife, now completely exhausted, sometimes round, and sometimes through, the fire, which was, as usual, in the midst of the house. Instead of entering, he saddled a horse, and rode up the hill, to humble himself before Michael, and beg a cessation of the spell;

which the good-natured warlock immediately granted, directing him to enter the house backwards, and, with his left hand, take the spell from above the door; which accordingly ended the supernatural dance.—This tale was told less particularly in former editions, and I have been censured for inaccuracy in doing so.—A similar charm occurs in *Huon de Bourdeaux*, and in the ingenious Oriental tale, called the *Caliph Vathek*.

Notwithstanding his victory over the witch of Falsehope, Michael Scott, like his predecessor, Merlin, fell at last a victim to female art. His wife, or concubine, elicited from him the secret, that his art could ward off any danger except the poisonous qualities of broth, made of the flesh of a *breme* sow. Such a mess she accordingly administered to the wizard, who died in consequence of eating it; surviving, however, long enough to put to death his treacherous confidant.

NOTE XXXI.

The words that cleft Eildon hills in three.
—P. 10.

Michael Scott was, once upon a time, much embarrassed by a spirit, for whom he was under the necessity of finding constant employment. He commanded him to build a *cauld*, or dam-head, across the Tweed at Kelso; it was accomplished in one night, and still does honour to the infernal architect. Michael next ordered, that Eildon hill, which was then a uniform cone, should be divided into three. Another night was sufficient to part its summit into the three picturesque peaks which it now bears. At length the enchanter conquered this indefatigable demon, by employing him in the hopeless and endless task of making ropes out of sea-sand.

NOTE XXXII.

That lamp shall burn unquenchably,
Until the eternal doom shall be.—P. 11

Baptista Porta, and other authors who treat of natural magic, talk much of eternal lamps, pretended to have been found burning in ancient sepulchres. Fortunius Licetus investigates the subject in a treatise, *De Lucernis Antiquorum Reconditis*, published at Venice, 1621. One of these perpetual lamps is said to have been discovered in the tomb of Tulliola, the daughter of Cicero. The wick was supposed to be composed of asbestos. Kircher enumerates three different recipes for constructing such lamps; and wisely concludes, that the thing is nevertheless impossible.—*Mundus Subterranneus*, p. 72. Delrio imputes the fabrication of such lights to magical skill.—*Disquisitiones Magicae*, p. 58. In a very rare romance, which 'treateth of the life of Virgilius, and of his

deth, and many marvayles that he dyd in his lyfe-time, by wychecrafte and nygramancye, throughe the helpe of the devyls of hell,' mention is made of a very extraordinary process, in which one of these mystical lamps was employed. It seems that Virgil, as he advanced in years, became desirous of renovating his youth by magical art. For this purpose he constructed a solitary tower, having only one narrow portal, in which he placed twenty-four copper figures, armed with iron flails, twelve on each side of the porch. These enchanted statues struck with their flails incessantly, and rendered all entrance impossible, unless when Virgil touched the spring, which stopped their motion. To this tower he repaired privately, attended by one trusty servant, to whom he communicated the secret of the entrance, and hither they conveyed all the magician's treasure. 'Then sayde Virgilius, my dere beloved frende, and he that I above alle men truste and knowe mooste of my secret;' and then he led the man into a cellar, where he made a *fayer lamp at all seasons burnynge.* And then sayd Virgilius to the man, "Se you the barrel that standeth here?" and he sayd, yea: "Therein must thou put me: fyrst ye must slee me, and hewe me smalle to pieces, and cut my hed in iiii pieces, and salte the heed under in the bottom, and then the pieces there after, and my herte in the myddel, and then set the barrel under the lampe, that nyghte and day the fat therein may droppe and leake; and ye shall ix dayes long, ones in the day, fyll the lampe, and fayle nat. And when this is all done, then shall I be reneued, and made yonge agen."' At this extraordinary proposal, the confidant was sore abashed, and made some scruple of obeying his master's commands. At length, however, he complied, and Virgil was slain, pickled, and barrelled up, in all respects according to his own direction. The servant then left the tower, taking care to put the copper thrashers in motion at his departure. He continued daily to visit the tower with the same precaution. Meanwhile, the emperor, with whom Virgil was a great favourite, missed him from the court, and demanded of his servant where he was. The domestic pretended ignorance, till the emperor threatened him with death, when at length he conveyed him to the enchanted tower. The same threat extorted a discovery of the mode of stopping the statues from wielding their flails. 'And then the emperour entered into the castle with all his folke, and sought all aboute in every corner after Virgilius; and at the laste they sought so longe, that they came into the seller, where they sawe the lampe hang over the barrell, where Virgilius lay in deed. Then asked the emperour the man, who had made hym so herdy to put his mayster Virgilius so to dethe; and the man answered no worde to the emperour. And then the emperour, with great anger, drewe out his sworde, and slewe he there Virgilius' man. And when all this was done, then sawe the emperour, and all his folke, a naked child iii tymes rennynge about the barrell, saynge these wordes, " Cursed be the tyme that ye ever came here." And with those words vanyshed the chylde awaye, and was never sene ageyn; and thus abyd Virgilius in the barrell deed.'—*Virgilius*, bl. let., printed at Antwerpe by John Doesborcke. This curious volume is in the valuable library of Mr. Douce; and is supposed to be a translation f~om the French, printed in Flanders for the English market. See *Goujet Biblioth. Franc.* ix. 225. *Catalogue de la Bibliothèque Nationale*, tom. ii. p. 5. *De Bure*, No. 3857.

Note XXXIII.

*Then Deloraine, in terror, took
From the cold hand the Mighty Book,*
.   .   .   .   .
*He thought, as he took it, the dead man
frown'd.*—P. 12.

William of Deloraine might be strengthened in this belief by the well-known story of the Cid Ruy Diaz. When the body of that famous Christian champion was sitting in state by the high altar of the cathedral church of Toledo, where it remained for ten years, a certain malicious Jew attempted to pull him by the beard; but he had no sooner touched the formidable whiskers, than the corpse started up, and half unsheathed his sword. The Israelite fled; and so permanent was the effect of his terror, that he became Christian.—Heywood's *Hierarchie*, p. 480, quoted from *Sebastian Cobarruvias Crozee.*

Note XXXIV.

The Baron's Dwarf his courser held.—P. 14.

The idea of Lord Cranstoun's Goblin Page is taken from a being called Gilpin Horner, who appeared, and made some stay, at a farm-house among the Border-mountains. A gentleman of that country has noted down the following particulars concerning his appearance:—

'The only certain, at least most probable account, that ever I heard of Gilpin Horner, was from an old man, of the name of Anderson, who was born, and lived all his life at Todshaw-hill, in Eskedale-muir, the place where Gilpin appeared and staid for some time. He said there were two men, late in the evening, when it was growing dark, employed in fastening the horses upon the uttermost part of their ground (that is, tying their forefeet together, to hinder them from travelling far in the night), when they heard a voice, at some distance, crying, " Tint! Tint! Tint! [1] " One of the men, named Moffat, called out, " What deil has tint you? Come here." Immediately a creature, of something like a human form, appeared. It was surprisingly little, distorted in features, and misshapen in limbs. As soon as the two men could see it plainly, they ran home in a great fright, imagining they had met with some goblin. By the way, Moffat fell and it ran over him, and was home at the house as soon as either of them, and staid there a long time; but I cannot say how long. It was real flesh and blood, and ate and drank, was fond of cream, and, when it could get at it, would destroy a great deal. It seemed a mischievous creature; and any of the children whom it could master, it would beat and scratch without mercy. It was once abusing a child belonging to the same Moffat, who had been so frightened by its first appearance; and he, in a passion, struck it so violent a blow upon the side of the head, that it tumbled upon the ground; but it was not stunned, for it set up its head directly, and exclaimed, " Ah, hah, Will o' Moffat, you strike sair! " (viz. *sore*). After it had staid there long, one evening, when the women were milking the cows in the loan, it was playing among the children near by them, when suddenly they heard a loud shrill voice cry three times, "*Gilpin Horner!*" It started, and said, "*That is me, I must away,*" and instantly disappeared, and was never heard of more. Old Anderson did not remember it, but said, he had often heard his father and other old men in the place, who were there at the time, speak about it; and in my younger years I have often heard it mentioned, and never met with any who had the remotest doubt as to the truth of the story; although, I must own, I cannot help thinking there must be some misrepresentation in it.'—To this account, I have to add the following particulars from the most respectable authority. Besides constantly repeating the word *tint! tint!* Gilpin Horner was often heard to call upon Peter Bertram, or Be-te-ram, as he pronounced the word; and when the shrill voice called Gilpin Horner, he immediately acknowledged it was the summons of the said Peter Bertram: who seems therefore to have been the devil who had tint, or lost, the little imp. As much as has been objected to Gilpin Horner, on account of his being supposed rather a device of the author than a popular superstition, I can only say, that no legend which I ever heard seemed to be more universally credited; and that many persons of very good rank, and considerable information, are well known to repose absolute faith in the tradition.

---

1 *Tint* signifies *lost.*

NOTE XXXV.

But the Ladye of Branksome gather'd a band
Of the best that would ride at her command.—P. 14.

'Upon 25th June, 1557, Dame Janet Beatoune Lady Buccleuch, and a great number of the name of Scott, delaitit (accused) for coming to the kirk of St. Mary of the Lowes, to the number of two hundred persons bodin in feire of weire (arrayed in armour), and breaking open the door of the said kirk, in order to apprehend the Laird of Cranstoune for his destruction.' On the 20th July, a warrant from the Queen is presented, discharging the justice to proceed against the Lady Buccleuch while new calling.—*Abridgment of Books of Adjournal, in Advocates' Library.* The following proceedings upon this case appear on the record of the Court of Justiciary. On the 25th of June, 1557, Robert Scott, in Bowhill parish, priest of the kirk of St. Mary's, accused of the convocation of the Queen's lieges, to the number of two hundred persons, in warlike array, with jacks, helmets, and other weapons, and marching to the chapel of St. Mary of the Lowes, for the slaughter of Sir Peter Cranstoun, out of ancient feud and malice prepense, and of breaking the doors of the said kirk, is repledged by the Archbishop of Glasgow. The bail given by Robert Scott of Allanhaugh, Adam Scott of Burnfute, Robert Scott in How urde, Walter Scott in Todshawhaugh, Walter Scott younger of Synton, Thomas Scott of Hayning, Robert Scott, Willia n Scott, and James Scott, brothers of the said Walter Scott, Walter Scott in the Woll, and Walter Scott, son of William Scott of Harden, and James Wemyss in Eckford, all accused of the same crime, is declared to be forfeited. On the same day, Walter Scott of Synton, and Walter Chisholme of Chisholme, and William Scott of Harden, became bound, jointly and severally, that Sir Peter Cranstoun, and his kindred and servants, should receive no injury from them in future. At the same time, Patrick Murray of Fallohill, Alexander Stuart, uncle to the Laird of Trakwhare, John Murray of Newhall, John Fairlye, residing in Selkirk, George Tait, younger of Pirn, John Pennycuke of Pennycuke, James Ramsay of Cokpen, the Laird of Fassyde, and the Laird of Henderstoune, were all severally fined for not attending as jurors; being probably either in alliance with the accused parties, or dreading their vengeance. Upon the 20th of July following, Scott of Synton, Chisholme of Chisholme, Scott of Harden, Scott of Howpaslie, Scott of Burnfute, with many others, are ordered to appear at next calling, under the pains of treason. But no farther procedure seems to have taken place. It is said, that, upon this rising, the kirk of St. Mary was burnt by the Scotts.

NOTE XXXVI.

Like a book-bosom'd priest.—P. 16.

'At Unthank, two miles N. E. from the church (of Ewes), there are the ruins of a chapel for divine service, in time of Popery. There is a tradition, that friars were wont to come from Melrose or Jedburgh, to baptize and marry in this parish; and from being in use to carry the mass-book in their bosoms, they were called by the inhabitants, *Book-a-bosomes*. There is a man yet alive, who knew old men who had been baptized by these Book-a-bosomes, and who says one of them, called Hair, used this parish for a very long time.'—*Account of Parish of Ewes, apud Macfarlane's MSS.*

NOTE XXXVII.

All was delusion, nought was truth.—P. 17.

Glamour, in the legends of Scottish superstition, means the magic power of imposing on the eyesight of the spectators, so that the appearance of an object shall be totally different from the reality. The transformation of Michael Scott by the witch of Falsehope, already mentioned, was a genuine operation of glamour. To a similar charm the ballad of Johnny Fa' imputes the fascination of the lovely Countess, who eloped with that gipsy leader:—

'Sae soon as they saw her weel-far'd face,
They cast the *glamour* o'er her.'

It was formerly used even in war. In 1381, when the Duke of Anjou lay before a strong castle, upon the coast of Naples, a necromancer offered to 'make the ayre so thycke, that they within shall thynke that there is a great bridge on the see (by which the castle was surrounded) for ten men to go a front; and whan they within the castle se this bridge, they will be so afrayde, that they shall yelde them to your mercy. The Duke demanded,—"Fayre Master, on this bridge that ye speke of, may our people assuredly go thereon to the castell, to assayle it?"—"Syr," quod the enchantour, "I dare not assure you that; for if any that passeth on the bridge make the signe of the crosse on hym, all shall go to noughte, and they that be on the bridge shall fall into the see." Then the Duke began to laugh; and a certain of young knightes, that were there present, said, "Syr, for godsake, let the mayster assey his cunning: we shall leve making of any signe of the crosse on us for that tyme." ' The Earl of Savoy, shortly after, entered the tent, and recognised in the enchanter the same person who had put the castle into the power of Sir Charles de la Payx, who then held it, by persuading the garrison of the Queen of Naples, through magical deception, that the sea was coming over the walls. The sage avowed the feat, and added, that he was the man in the world most dreaded by Sir Charles de la Payx. '"By my fayth," quod the

Earl of Savoy, "ye say well; and I will that Syr Charles de la Payx shall know that he hath gret wronge to fear you. But I shall assure hym of you ; for ye shall never do enchantment to deceyve hym, nor yet none other. I wolde nat that in tyme to come we shulde be reproached that in so high an enterprise as we be in, wherein there be so many noble knyghtes and squyres assembled, that we shulde do any thyng be enchantment, nor that we shulde wyn our enemys be suche crafte." Then he called to him a servaunt, and said, " Go, and get a hangman, and let him stryke off this mayster's heed without delay ; " and as soone as the Erle had commanded it, incontynent it was done, for his heed was stryken of before the Erle's tent.' —FROISSART, vol. i. ch. 391, 392.

The art of glamour, or other fascination, was anciently a principal part of the skill of the *jongleur*, or juggler, whose tricks formed much of the amusement of a Gothic castle. Some instances of this art may be found in the *Minstrelsy of the Scottish Border*, vol. iv. p. 106. In a strange allegorical poem, called the Houlat, written by a dependent of the house of Douglas, about 1452-3, the jay, in an assembly of birds, plays the part of the juggler. His feats of glamour are thus described :—

' He gart them see, as it semyt in samyn houre,
  Hunting at herdis in holtis so hair ;
Some sailand on the see schippis of toure,
Bernis battalland on burd brim as a bare :
He coulde carye the coup of the kingis des,
  Syne leve in the stede,
  Bot a black bunwede ;
He could of a henis hede
Make a man mes.

'He gart the Emproure trow, and trewlye behald,
  That the *corncraik*, the pundere at hand,
Had poyndit all his pris hors in a poynd fald,
Because thai ete of the corn in the kirkland.
He could wirk windaris, quhat way that he wald,
  Mak a gray gus a gold garland,
A lang spere of a bittile, for a berne bald,
Nobilis of nutschelles, and silver of sand
Thus joukit with juxters the janglane ja.
  Fair ladyes in ringis,
  Knychtis in caralyngis,
  Bayth dansis and singis,
It semyt as sa.

NOTE XXXVIII.

Now, if you ask who gave the stroke,
  I cannot tell, so mot I thrive ;
It was not given by man alive.—P. 17.

Dr. Henry More, in a letter prefixed to Glanville's *Saducismus Triumphatus*, mentions a similar phenomenon.

' I remember an old gentleman in the country, of my acquaintance, an excellent justice of peace, and a piece of a mathematician ; but what kind of a philosopher he was, you may understand from a rhyme of his own making, which he commended to me at my taking horse in his yard, which rhyme is this :—

' Ens is nothing till sense finds out :
  Sense ends in nothing, so naught goes about.

Which rhyme of his was so rapturous to himself, that, on the reciting of the second verse, the old man turned himself about upon his toe as nimbly as one may observe a dry leaf whisked round the corner of an orchard walk by some little whirlwind. With this philosopher I have had many discourses concerning the immortality of the soul and its distinction ; when I have run him quite down by reason, he would but laugh at me, and say this is logic, H. (calling me by my Christian name), to which I replied, this is reason, father L. (for so I used and some others to call him); but it seems you are for the new lights, and immediate inspiration, which I confess he was as little for as for the other ; but I said so only in the way of drollery to him in those times, but truth is, nothing but palpable experience would move him : and being a bold man, and fearing nothing, he told me he had used all the magical ceremonies of conjuration he could, to raise the devil or a spirit, and had a most earnest desire to meet with one, but never could do it. But this he told me, when he did not so much as think of it, while his servant was pulling off his boots in the hall, some invisible hand gave him such a clap upon the back, that it made all ring again ; " so," thought he now, " I am invited to the converse of my spirit," and therefore, so soon as his boots were off, and his shoes on, out he goes into the yard and next field, to find out the spirit that had given him this familiar clap on the back, but found none neither in the yard nor field next to it.

' But though he did not feel this stroke, albeit he thought it afterwards (finding nothing came of it) a mere delusion ; yet not long before his death, it had more force with him than all the philosophical arguments I could use to him, though I could wind him and nonplus him as I pleased ; but yet all my arguments, how solid soever, made no impression upon him ; wherefore, after several reasonings of this nature, whereby I would prove to him the soul's distinction from the body, and its immortality, when nothing of such subtile consideration did any more execution on his mind than some lightning is said to do, though it melts the sword, on the fuzzy consistency of the scabbard,—" Well," said I, " father L., though none of these things move you, I have something still behind, and what yourself has acknowledged to be true, that may do the business :—Do you remember the clap on your back when your servant was pulling off your boots in the hall ? Assure yourself, says I, father L., that goblin will be the first to bid you welcome into the other world." Upon that his countenance changed most sensibly, and he was more confounded with this rubbing up his memory, than with all the rational or philosophical argumentations that I could produce.'

Note XXXIX.

The running stream dissolv'd the spell.
—P. 17.

It is a firm article of popular faith, that no enchantment can subsist in a living stream. Nay, if you can interpose a brook betwixt you and witches, spectres, or even fiends, you are in perfect safety. Burns's inimitable *Tam o' Shanter* turns entirely upon such a circumstance. The belief seems to be of antiquity. Brompton informs us, that certain Irish wizards could, by spells, convert earthen clods, or stones, into fat pigs, which they sold in the market, but which always reassumed their proper form when driven by the deceived purchaser across a running stream. But Brompton is severe on the Irish for a very good reason. 'Gens ista spurcissima non solvunt decimas.'—*Chronicon Johannis Brompton apud decem Scriptores*, p. 1076.

Note XL.

He never counted him a man,
Would strike below the knee.—P. 18.

Imitated from Drayton's account of Robin Hood and his followers :—

'A hundred valiant men had this brave Robin Hood,
Still ready at his call, that bowmen were right good ;
All clad in Lincoln green, with caps of red and blue,
His fellow's winded horn not one of them but knew.
When setting to their lips their little bugles shrill,
The warbling echoes waked from every dale and hill ;
Their bauldrics set with studs athwart their shoulders cast,
To which under their arms their sheafs were buckled fast,
A short sword at their belt, a buckler scarce a span,
Who struck below the knee not counted then a man.
All made of Spanish yew, their bows were wondrous strong,
They not an arrow drew but was a cloth-yard long.
Of archery they had the very perfect craft,
With broad arrow, or but, or prick, or roving shaft.
                         Poly-Albion, Song 26.

To wound an antagonist in the thigh, or leg, was reckoned contrary to the law of arms. In a tilt betwixt Gawain Michael, an English squire, and Joachim Cathore, a Frenchman, 'they met at the speare poyntes rudely ; the French squyer justed right pleasantly ; the Englishman ran too lowe, for he strak the Frenchman depe into the thigh. Wherewith the Erle of Buckingham was right sore displeased, and so were all the other lords, and sayde how it was shamefully done.'—FROISSART, vol. i. chap. 366. Upon a similar occasion, 'the two knyghts came a fote eche against other rudely, with their speares low couched, to stryke eche other within the foure quarters. Johan of Castell-Morant strake the English squyer on the brest in such wyse, that Syr Wyllyam Fermetone stombled and bowed, for his fote a lyttel fayled him. He helde his speare lowe with both his handes, and coude nat amende it, and strake Syr Johan of the Castell-Morant in the thighe, so that the speare went clene

throughe, that the heed was sene a handfull on the other syde. And Syr Johan with the stroke reled, but he fell nat. Than the Englyshe knyghtes and squyers were ryghte sore displeased, and sayde how it was a foule stroke. Syr Wyllam Fermeton excused himselfe, and sayde how he was sorie of that adventure, and howe that yf he had knowen that it shulde have bene so, he wolde never have begon it ; sayenge how he could nat amende it, by cause of glaunsing of his fote by constraynt of the great stroke that Syr Johan of the Castell-Morant had given him.'—FROISSART, vol. i. chap. 373.

Note XLI.

She drew the splinter from the wound,
And with a charm she stanch'd the blood.
—P. 19.

See several charms for this purpose in Reginald Scott's *Discovery of Witchcraft*, p. 273.

'Tom Potts was but a serving man,
But yet he was a doctor good ;
He bound his handkerchief on the wound,
And with some kinds of words he stanched the blood.
Pieces of Ancient Popular Poetry, Lond. 1791, p. 131.

Note XLII.

But she has ta'en the broken lance,
And wash'd it from the clotted gore,
And salved the splinter o'er and o'er.
—P. 19.

Sir Kenelm Digby, in a discourse upon the cure by sympathy, pronounced at Montpelier before an assembly of nobles and learned men, translated into English by R. White, gentleman, and published in 1658, gives us the following curious surgical case :—

'Mr. James Howel (well known in France for his public works, and particularly for his *Dendrologie*, translated into French by Mons. Baudouin) coming by chance, as two of his best friends were fighting in duel, in his endeavour to part them ; and, putting himselfe between them, seized, with his left hand, upon the hilt of the sword of one of the combatants, while with his right hand, he laid hold of the blade of the other. They, being transported with fury one against the other, struggled to rid themselves of the hinderance their friend made, that they should not kill one another; and one of them roughly drawing the blade of his sword, cuts to the very bone the nerves and muscles of Mr. Howel's hand ; and then the other disengaged his hilts, and gave a crosse blow on his adversarie's head, which glanced towards his friend, who heaving up his sore hand to save the blow, he was wounded on the back of his hand as he had been before within. It seems some strange constellation reigned then against him, that he should lose so much bloud by parting two such dear friends, who, had they been themselves, would have hazarded both their lives to have preserved his; but this involuntary effusion of bloud by them, prevented that which they sholde have drawn one from the other. For they, seeing Mr. Howel's face besmeared with bloud, by heaving up his wounded hand, they both ran to embrace him; and having searched his hurts, they bound up his hand with one of his garters, to close the veins which were cut, and bled abundantly. They brought him home, and sent for a surgeon. But this being heard at court, the King sent one of his own surgeons; for his Majesty much affected the said Mr. Howel.

'It was my chance to be lodged hard by him; and four or five days after, as I was making myself ready, he came to my house, and prayed me to view his wounds; "for I understand," said he, "that you have extraordinary remedies on such occasions, and my surgeons apprehend some fear that it may grow to a gangrene, and so the hand must be cut off." In effect, his countenance discovered that he was in much pain, which he said was insuppo table, in regard of the extreme inflammation. I told him I would willingly serve him; but if haply he knew the manner how I would cure him, without touching or seeing him, it may be he would not expose himself to my manner of curing, because he would think it, peradventure, either ineffectual or superstitious. He replied, "the wonderful things which many have related unto me of your way of medicament, makes me nothing doubt at all of its efficacy; and all that I have to say unto you is comprehended in the Spanish proverb, *Hagase el milagro y hagalo Mahoma*—Let the miracle be done, though Mahomet do it."

'I asked him then for any thing that had the blood upon it; so he presently sent for his garter, wherewith his hand was first bound; and as I called for a bason of water, as if I would wash my hands, I took a handful of powder of vitriol, which I had in my study and presently dissolved it. As soon as the bloudy garter was brought me, I put it within the bason, observing, in the interim, what Mr. Howel did, who stood talking with a gentleman in a corner of my chamber, not regarding at all what I was doing; but he started suddenly, as if he had found some strange alteration in himself. I asked him what he ailed? "I know not what ailes me; but I finde that I feel no more pain. Methinks that a pleasing kinde of freshnesse, as it were a wet cold napkin, did spread over my hand, which hath taken away the inflammation that tormented me before." I replied, "Since then that you feel already so good effect of my medicament, I advise you to cast away all your playsters; only keep the wound clean, and in a moderate temper betwixt heat and cold." This was

presently reported to the Duke of Buckingham, and a little after to the King, who were both very curious to know the circumstance of the businesse, which was, that after dinner I took the garter out of the water, and put it to dry before a great fire. It was scarce dry, but Mr. Howel's servant came running, that his master felt as much burning as ever he had done, if not more; for the heat was such as if his hand were 'twixt coles of fire. I answered, although that had happened at present, yet he should find ease in a short time; for I knew the reason of this new accident, and would provide accordingly; for his master should be free from that inflammation, it may be before he could possibly return to him; but in case he found no ease, I wished him to come presently back again; if not, he might forbear coming. Thereupon he went; and at the instant I did put again the garter into the water, thereupon he found his master without any pain at all. To be brief, there was no sense of pain afterward; but within five or six dayes the wounds were cicatrized, and entirely healed.'—Page 6.

The King (James VI.) obtained from Sir Kenelm the discovery of his secret, which he pretended had been taught him by a Carmelite friar, who had learned it in Armenia, or Persia. Let not the age of animal magnetism and metallic tractors smile at the sympathetic powder of Sir Kenelm Digby. Reginald Scott mentions the same mode of cure in these terms:—'And that which is more strange . . . . . they can remedie anie stranger with that verie sword wherewith they are wounded. Yea, and that which is beyond all admiration, if they stroke the sword upward with their fingers, the partie shall feele no pain; whereas, if they draw their fingers downwards, thereupon the partie wounded shall feele intolerable pain.' I presume that the success ascribed to the sympathetic mode of treatment might arise from the pains bestowed in washing the wound, and excluding the air, thus bringing on a cure by the first intention. It is introduced by Dryden in the *Enchanted Island*, a (very unnecessary) alteration of the *Tempest:*—

> *Ariel.* Anoint the sword which pierced him with this
> Weapon-salve, and wrap it close from air,
> Till I have time to visit him again.—*A.t* v. sc. 2.

Again, in scene 4th, Miranda enters with Hippolito's sword wrapt up:—

> *Hip.* O my wound pains me.
> *Mir.* I am come to ease you. [*She unwraps the Sword.*]
> *Hip.* Alas, I feel the cold air come to me;
> My wound shoots worse than ever.
> *Mir.* Does it still grieve you? [*She wipes and anoints the Sword.*]
> *Hip.* Now, methinks, there s something laid just upon it.
> *Mir.* Do you find no ease?
> *Hip.* Yes, yes; upon the sudden all this pain
> Is leaving me. Sweet heaven, how I am eased!

Note XLIII.

On Penchryst glows a bale of fire.—P. 20.

Bale, beacon fagot. The Border beacons, from their number and position, formed a sort of telegraphic communication with Edinburgh.—The Act of Parliament 1455, c. 48, directs, that one bale or fagot shall be warning of the approach of the English in any manner; two bales that they are *coming indeed;* four bales, blazing beside each other, that the enemy are in great force. 'The same taikenings to be watched and maid at Eggerhope (Eggerstand) Castell, fra they se the fire of Hume, that t' ey fire right swa. And in like manner on Sowtra Edge, sall se the fire of Eggerhope Castell, and mak taikening in like manner: And then may all Louthaine be warned, and in special the Castell of Edinburgh; and their four fires to be made in like manner, that they in Fife, and fra Striveling east, and the east part of Louthaine, and to Dunbar, all may se them, and come to the defence of the realme.' These beacons (at least in latter times) were a 'long and strong tree set up, with a long iron pole across the head of it, and an iron brander fixed on a stalk in the middle of it, for holding a tar-barrel.'—STEVENSON'S *History*, vol. ii. p. 701.

Note XLIV.

Our kin, and clan, and friends to raise.
—P. 20.

The speed with which the Borderers collected great bodies of horse, may be judged of from the following extract, when the subject of the rising was much less important than that supposed in the romance. It is taken from Carey's *Memoirs:*—

'Upon the death of the old Lord Scroop, the Queen gave the west wardenry to his son, that had married my sister. He having received that office, came to me with great earnestness, and desired me to be his deputy, offering me that I should live with him in his house; that he would allow me half a dozen men, and as many horses, to be kept at his charge; and his fee being 1000 merks yearly, he would part it with me, and I should have the half. This his noble offer I accepted of, and went with him to Carlisle; where I was no sooner come, but I entered into my office. We had a stirring time of it; and few days past over my head but I was on horseback, either to prevent mischief, or take malefactors, and to bring the Border in better quiet than it had been in times past. One memorable thing of God's mercy shewed unto me, was such as I have good cause still to remember it.

'I had private intelligence given me, that there were two Scottishmen that had killed a churchman in Scotland, and were by one of the Græmes relieved. This Græme dwelt within five miles of Carlisle. He had a pretty house, and close by it a strong tower, for his own defence in time of need.—About two o'clock in the morning, I took horse in Carlisle, and not above twenty-five in my company, thinking to surprise the house on a sudden. Before I could surround the house, the two Scots were gotten in the strong tower, and I could see a boy riding from the house as fast as his horse could carry him; I little suspecting what it meant. But Thomas Carleton came to me presently, and told me, that if I did not presently prevent it, both myself and all my company would be either slain or taken prisoners. It was strange to me to hear this language. He then said to me, "Do you see that boy that rideth away so fast? He will be in Scotland within this half hour; and he is gone to let them know, that you are here, and to what end you are come, and the small number you have with you; and that if they will make haste, on a sudden they may surprise us, and do with us what they please." Hereupon we took advice what was best to be done. We sent notice presently to all parts to raise the country, and to come to us with all the speed they could; and withall we sent to Carlisle to raise the townsmen; for without foot we could do no good against the tower. There we staid some hours, expecting more company; and within short time after the country came in on all sides, so that we were quickly between three and four hundred horse; and, after some longer stay, the foot of Carlisle came to us, to the number of three or four hundred men; whom we presently set to work, to get to the top of the tower, and to uncover the roof; and then some twenty of them to fall down together, and by that means to win the tower—The Scots, seeing their present danger, offered to parley, and yielded themselves to my mercy. They had no sooner opened the iron gate, and yielded themselves my prisoners, but we might see 400 horse within a quarter of a mile coming to their rescue, and to surprise me and my small company; but of a sudden they stayed, and stood at gaze. Then had I more to do than ever; for all our Borderers came crying, with full mouths, "Sir, give us leave to set upon them; for these are they that have killed our fathers, our brothers, and uncles, and our cousins; and they are coming, thinking to surprise you, upon weak grass nags, such as they could get on a sudden; and God hath put them into your hands, that we may take revenge of them for much blood that they have spilt of ours." I desired they would be patient a while, and bethought myself, if I should give them their will, there would be few or none of the Scots that would escape unkilled; (there was so many deadly feuds among them;) and therefore I resolved with myself to give them a fair answer, but not to give them their desire. So I told them, that if I were not there myself, they might then do what they pleased themselves; but being present, if I should give them leave, the blood that should be spilt that day would lie very hard upon my conscience. And therefore I desired them, for my sake, to forbear; and, if the Scots did not presently make away with all the speed they could, upon my sending to them, they should then have their wills to do what they pleased. They were ill satisfied with my answer, but durst not disobey. I sent with speed to the Scots, and bade them pack away with all the speed they could; for if they stayed the messenger's return, they should have few of them return to their own home. They made no stay; but they were returned homewards before the messenger had made an end of his message. Thus, by God's mercy, I escaped a great danger; and, by my means, there were a great many men's lives saved that day.'

Note XLV.

On many a cairn's grey pyramid,
Where urns of mighty chiefs lie hid.—P. 20.

The cairns, or piles of loose stones, which crown the summit of most of our Scottish hills, and are found in other remarkable situations, seem usually, though not universally, to have been sepulchral monuments. Six flat stones are commonly found in the centre, forming a cavity of greater or smaller dimensions, in which an urn is often placed. The author is possessed of one, discovered beneath an immense cairn at Roughlee, in Liddesdale. It is of the most barbarous construction; the middle of the substance alone having been subjected to the fire, over which, when hardened, the artist had laid an inner and outer coat of unbaked clay, etched with some very rude ornaments; his skill apparently being inadequate to baking the vase, when completely finished. The contents were bones and ashes, and a quantity of beads made of coal. This seems to have been a barbarous imitation of the Roman fashion of sepulture.

Note XLVI.

For pathless marsh, and mountain cell,
The peasant left his lowly shed. P. 22.

The morasses were the usual refuge of the Border herdsmen, on the approach of an English army.—(*Minstrelsy of the Scottish Border*, vol. i. p. 303.) Caves, hewed in the most dangerous and inaccessible places, also afforded an occasional retreat. Such caverns may be seen in the precipitous banks of the Teviot at Sunlaws, upon the Ale at Ancram, upon the Jed at Hundalee, and in many other places upon the Border. The banks of the Eske, at Gorton and Hawthornden, are hollowed into similar recesses. But even these dreary dens were not always secure places of concealment. 'In the way

as we came, not far from this place, (Long Niddry,) George Ferres, a gentleman of my Lord Protector's . . . . . . happened upon a cave in the grounde, the mouth whereof was so worne with the fresh printe of steps, that he seemed to be certayne thear wear some folke within; and gone doune to trie, he was readily receyved with a hakebut or two. He left them not yet, till he had known whether thei wolde be content to yield and come out; which they fondly refusing, he went to my lord's grace, and upon utterance of the thynge, gat licence to deale with them as he coulde; and so returned to them, with a skore or two of pioners. Three ventes had their cave, that we wear ware of, whereof he first stopt up on; anoother he fil.l'd full of strawe, and set it a fyer, whereat they within cast water apace; but it was so wel maynteyned without, that the fyer prevayled, and thei within fayn to get them belyke into anoother parler. Then devysed we (for I hapt to be with him) to stop the same up, whereby we should eyther smoother them, or fynd out their ventes, if thei hadde any moe; as this was done at another issue, about xii score of, we moughte see the fume of their smoke to come out: the which continued with so great a force, and so long a while, that we could not but thinke they must needs get them out, or smoother within: and forasmuch as we found not that they dyd the tone, we thought it for certain thei wear sure of the toother.'—PATTEN's *Account of Somerset's Expedition into Scotland,* apud DALYELL's *Fragments.*

Note XLVII.

Show'd southern ravage was begun.—P. 22.

From the following fragment of a letter from the Earl of Northumberland to King Henry VIII, preserved among the Cotton MSS. Calig. B. vii. 179, the reader may estimate the nature of the dreadful war which was occasionally waged upon the Borders, sharpened by mutual cruelties, and the personal hatred of the wardens, or leaders.

Some Scottish Barons, says the Earl, had threatened to come within 'three miles of my pore house of Werkworth, where I lye, and gif me light to put on my clothes at mydnight; and alsoo the said Marke Carr said there opynly, that, seyng they had a governor on the Marches of Scotland, as well as they had in Ingland, he shulde kepe your highness instructions, gyffyn unto your ga-ryson, for making of any day-forrey; for he and his friends wolde burne enough on the nyght, lettyng your counsaill here defyne a notable acte at theyre pleasures. Upon whiche, in your highnes name, I comaundet dewe watche to be kepte on your Marchies, for comyng in of any Scotts.—Neuertheles, upon Thursday at night last, came thyrty

light horsemen into a litil village of myne,
called Whitell, having not past sex houses,
lying towards Ryddisdaill, upon Shilbotell
More, and there wold have fyred the said
howses, but ther was no fyre to get there,
and they forgate to brynge any withe theyme;
and took a wyf being great with chylde, in
the said towne, and said to hyr, Wher we
can not gyve the lard lyght, yet we shall doo
this in spyte of hym; and gyve her iii mortall
wounds upon the heid, and another in the
right side, with a dagger: whereupon the
said wyf is deede, and the childe in her bely
is loste. Beseeching your most gracious
highness to reduce unto your gracious
memory this wylful and shamefull murder,
done within this your highnes realme, notwithstanding all the inhabitants thereabout
rose unto the said fray, and gave warnynge
by becons into the countrey afore theyme,
and yet the Scottsmen dyde escape. And
uppon certeyne knowledge to my brother
Clyfforthe, and me, had by credible persons
of Scotland, this abomynable act not only
to be done by dyverse of the Mershe, but
also the afore named persons of Tyvidaill,
and consented to, as by appearance, by
the Erle of Murey, upon Friday at night
last, let slyp C of the best horsemen of
Glendaill, with a parte of your highnes subjects of Berwyke, together with George
Dowglas, whoo came into Ingland agayne,
in the dawning of the day; but afore theyre
retorne, they dyd mar the Earl of Murreis
provisions at Coldingham; for they did not
only burne the said town of Coldingham,
with all the corne thereunto belonging, which
is esteemed worthe cii marke sterling; but
alsoo burned twa townes nye adjoining
thereunto, called Branerdergest and the Black
Hill, and toke xxiii persons, lx horse, with cc
hed of cataill, which, nowe, as I am informed,
hathe not only been a staye of the said Erle
of Murreis not coming to the Bordure as yet,
but alsoo, that none inlande man will adventure theyr self uppon the Marches. And as
for the tax that shulde have been grauntyd for
finding of the said iii hundred men, is utterly
denyed. Upon which the King of Scotland
departed from Edynburgh to Stirling, and
as yet there doth remayn. And also I, by
the advice of my brother Clyfforth, have
devysed, that within this iii nyghts, Godde
willing, Kelsey, in like case, shall be brent,
with all the corn in the said town; and then
they shall have noo place to lye any garyson
in nygh unto the Borders. And as I shall
atteigne further knowledge, I shall not faill
to satisfye your highnes, according to my
most bounden dutie. And for this burnyng
of Kelsey is devysed to be done secretly,
by Tyndaill and Ryddisdale. And thus the
holy Trynite and * * * your most royal estate,
with long lyf, and as much increase of honour
as your most noble heart can desire. *At
Werkworth the* xxiid *day of October.*' (1522.)

NOTE XLVIII.

Watt Tinlinn.—P. 22.

This person was, in my younger days, the
theme of many a fireside tale. He was a
retainer of the Buccleuch family, and held
for his Border service a small tower on the
frontiers of Liddesdale. Watt was, by profession, a *sutor*, but, by inclination and
practice, an archer and warrior. Upon one
occasion, the captain of Bewcastle, military
governor of that wild district of Cumberland,
is said to have made an incursion into Scotland, in which he was defeated, and forced to
fly. Watt Tinlinn pursued him closely
through a dangerous morass; the captain,
however, gained the firm ground; and seeing
Tinlinn dismounted, and floundering in the
bog, used these words of insult:—' Sutor
Watt, ye cannot sew your boots; the heels
risp, and the seams *rive* .'—'If I cannot sew,'
retorted Tinlinn, discharging a shaft, which
nailed the captain's thigh to his saddle,—' If
I cannot sew, I can *yerk* 2.'

NOTE XLIX.

Billhope stag.—P. 22.

There is an old rhyme, which thus celebrates the places in Liddesdale remarkable
for game:

' Billhope braes for bucks and raes,
    And Carit haugh for swine,
    And Tarras for the good bull-trout,
    If he be ta'en in time.'

The bucks and roes, as well as the old
swine, are now extinct; but the good bull-
trout is still famous.

NOTE L.

Belted Will Howard.—P. 22.

Lord William Howard, third son of
Thomas, Duke of Norfolk, succeeded to
Naworth Castle, and a large domain annexed
to it, in right of his wife Elizabeth, sister of
George Lord Dacre, who died without heirs
male, in the 11th of Queen Elizabeth. By a
poetical anachronism, he is introduced into
the romance a few years earlier than he
actually flourished. He was warden of the
Western Marches: and, from the rigour with
which he repressed the Border excesses, the
name of Belted Will Howard is still famous
in our traditions. In the castle of Naworth,
his apartments, containing a bedroom, ora-
tory, and library, are still shown. They
impress us with an unpleasing idea of the life
of a lord warden of the Marches. Three or
four strong doors, separating these rooms
from the rest of the castle, indicate the appre-

---

1 *Risp*, creak.—*Rive*, tear.
2 *Yerk*, to twitch, as shoemakers do, in securing the
stitches of their work.

hensions of treachery from his garrison ; and the secret winding passages, through which he could privately descend into the guard-room, or even into the dungeons, imply the necessity of no small degree of secret super-intendence on the part of the governor. As the ancient books and furniture have remained undisturbed, the venerable appearance of these apartments, and the armour scattered around the chamber, almost lead us to expect the arrival of the warden in person. Naworth Castle is situated near Brampton, in Cumberland. Lord William Howard is ancestor of the Earls of Carlisle.

Note LI.

Lord Dacre.—P. 22.

The well-known name of Dacre is derived from the exploits of one of their ancestors at the siege of Acre, or Ptolemais, under Richard Cœur de Lion. There were two powerful branches of that name. The first family, called Lord Dacres of the South, held the castle of the same name, and are ancestors to the present Lord Dacre. The other family, descended from the same stock, were called Lord Dacres of the North, and were barons of Gilsland and Graystock. A chieftain of the latter branch was warden of the West Marches during the reign of Edward VI. He was a man of a hot and obstinate character, as appears from some particulars of Lord Surrey's letter to Henry VIII, giving an account of his behaviour at the siege and storm of Jedburgh. It is printed in the *Minstrelsy of the Scottish Border*, Appendix to the Introduction.

Note LII.

The German hackbut men.—P. 22.

In the wars with Scotland, Henry VIII and his successors employed numerous bands of mercenary troops. At the battle of Pinky, there were in the English army six hundred hackbutters on foot, and two hundred on horseback, composed chiefly of foreigners. On the 27th of September, 1549, the Duke of Somerset, Lord Protector, writes to the Lord Dacre, warden of the West Marches:—'The Almains, in number two thousand, very valiant soldiers, shall be sent to you shortly from Newcastle, together with Sir Thomas Holcroft, and with the force of your wardenry, (which we would were advanced to the most strength of horsemen that might be,) shall make the attempt to Loughmaben, being of no such strength but that it may be skailed with ladders, whereof, beforehand, we would you caused secretly some number to be provided ; or else undermined with the pyke-axe, and so taken : either to be kept for the King's Majesty, or otherwise to be defaced, and taken from the profits of the enemy. And in like manner the house of Carlaverock to be

used.' Repeated mention occurs of the Almains, in the subsequent correspondence ; and the enterprise seems finally to have been abandoned, from the difficulty of providing these strangers with the necessary ' victuals and carriages in so poor a country as Dumfries-shire.'—*History of Cumberland*, vol. i. Introd. p. lxi. From the battle pieces of the ancient Flemish painters, we learn, that the Low Country and German soldiers marched to an assault with their right knees bared. And we may also observe, in such pictures, the extravagance to which they carried the fashion of ornamenting their dress with knots of ribbon. This custom of the Germans is alluded to in the *Mirrour for Magistrates*, p. 121 :

' Their pleited garments therewith well accord,
All jagde and frounst, with divers colours deckt.

Note LIII.

'Ready, aye ready,' for the field.—P. 23.

Sir John Scott of Thirlestane flourished in the reign of James V, and possessed the estates of Thirlestane, Gamescleuch, &c., lyng upon the river of Ettrick, and extending to St. Mary's Loch, at the head of Yarrow. It appears, that when James had assembled his nobility, and their feudal followers, at Fala, with the purpose of invading England, and was, as is well known, disappointed by the obstinate refusal of his peers, this baron alone declared himself ready to follow the King wherever he should lead. In memory of his fidelity, James granted to his family a charter of arms, entitling them to bear a border of fleurs-de-luce, similar to the tressure in the royal arms, with a bundle of spears for the crest ; motto, *Ready, aye ready*. The charter itself is printed by Nisbet ; but his work being scarce, I insert the following accurate transcript from the original, in the possession of the Right Honourable Lord Napier, the representative of John of Thirlestaine.

'JAMES Rex.

'We James, by the grace of God, King of Scottis, considerand the ffaith and guid servis of of of[1] right traist friend John Scott of Thirlestane, quha cummand to our hoste at Soutra-edge, with three score and ten launcieres on horseback of his friends and followers, and beand willing to gang with ws into England, when all our nobles and others refused, he was ready to stake at all our bidding ; ffor the quhilk cause, it is our will, and we doe straitlie command and charg our lion herauld and his deputies for the time beand, to give and to graunt to the said John Scott, a e Border of fileure de lises about his coatte of armes, sik as is on our royal banner, and alsua ane bundell of

---

1 Sic in orig.

launces above his helmet, with thir words, Readdy, ay Readdy, that he and all his after-cummers may bruik the samine as a pledge and taiken of our guid will and kyndnes for his true worthines; and thir our letters seen, ye nae waes failzie to doe. Given at Ffalla Muire, under our hand and privy cashet, the xxvii day of July, m c and xxxii zeires.[1] By the King's graces speciall ordinance.

'JO. ARSKINE.'

On the back of the charter is written,

'Edin. 14 January, 1713. Registred, conform to the act of parliament made anent probative writs, per M'Kaile, pror. and produced by Alexander Borthwick, servant to Sir William Scott of Thirlestane. M. L. J.'

NOTE LIV.

An aged Knight, to danger steel'd,
With many a moss-trooper came on,
And azure in a golden field,
The stars and crescent graced his shield,
Without the bend of Murdieston.—P. 23.

The family of Harden are descended from a younger son of the Laird of Buccleuch, who flourished before the estate of Murdieston was acquired by the marriage of one of those chieftains with the heiress, in 1296. Hence they bear the cognizance of the Scotts upon the field; whereas tho e of the Buccleuch are disposed upon a bend dexter, assumed in consequence of that marriage.—See GLADSTAINE *of Whitelawe's MSS.*, and SCOTT *of Stokoe's Pedigree,* Newcastle, 1783.

Walter Scott of Harden, who flourished during the reign of Queen Mary, was a renowned Border freebooter, concerning whom tradition has preserved a variety of anecdotes, some of which have been published in the *Minstrelsy of the Scottish Border;* others in LEYDEN'S *Scenes of Infancy;* and others, more lately, in *The Mountain Bard,* a collection of Border ballads by Mr. James Hogg. The bugle-horn, said to have been used by this formidable leader, is preserved by his descendant, the present Mr. Scott of Harden. His castle was situated upon the very brink of a dark and precipitous dell, through which a scanty rivulet steals to meet the Lorthwick. In the recess of this glen he is said to have kept his spoil, which served for the daily maintenance of his retainers, until the production of a pair of clean spurs, in a covered dish, announced to the hungry band, that they must ride for a supply of provisions. He was married to Mary Scott, daughter of Philip Scott of Dryhope, and called in song the Flower of Yarrow. He possessed a very extensive estate, which was divided among his five sons. There are numerous descendants of this old marauding Baron. The following beautiful passage of

[1] So in Scott's own Note; but it was in Nov. 1542 that this motto was earned by Scott of Thirlestane.

LEYDEN'S *Scenes of Infancy,* is founded on a tradition respecting an infant captive, whom Walter of Harden carried off in a predatory incursion, and who is said to have become the author of some of our most beautiful pastoral songs:

' Where Bortha hoarse, that loads the meads with sand,
Rolls her red tide to Teviot's western strand.
Through slaty hills, whose sides are shagg'd with thorn,
Where springs, in scatter'd tufts, the dark-green corn.
Towers wood-girt Harden, far above the vale,
And clouds of ravens o'er the turrets sail.
A hardy race, who never shrunk from war,
The *Scott,* to rival realms a mighty bar,
Here fixed his mountain home ;—a wide domain,
And rich the soil, had purple heath been grain ;
But what the niggard ground of wealth denied,
From fields more bless d his fearless arm supplied.

The waning harvest-moon shone cold and bright;
The warder's horn was heard at dead of night ;
And as the massy portals wide were flung,
With stamping hoofs the rocky pavement rung.
What fair, half veil'd, leans from her latticed hall,
Where red the wavering gleams of torchlight fall?
'Tis Yarrow's fairest flower, who, through the gloom,
Looks, wistful, for her lover's dancing plume.
Amid the piles of spoil, that strew'd the ground,
Her ear, all anxious, caught a wailing sound;
With trembling haste the youthful matron flew,
And from the hurried heaps an infant drew.

Scared at the light, his little hands he flung
Around her neck, and to her bosom clung ;
While beauteous Mary soothed, in accents mild,
His fluttering soul, and clasp'd her foster child.
Of milder mood the gentle captive grew,
Nor loved the scenes that scared his infant view ;
In vales remote. from camps and castles far,
He shunn'd the fearful shuddering joy of war :
Content the love of simple swains to sing,
Or wake to fame the harp's heroic string.

His are the strains, whose wandering echoes thrill
The shepherd, lingering on the twilight hill,
When evening brings the merry folding hours,
And sun-eyed daisies close their winking flowers.
He lived o'er Yarrow's Flower to shed the tear,
To strew the holly leaves o'er Harden's bier :
But none was found above the minstrel's tomb,
Emblem of peace. to bid the daisy bloom :
He, nameless as the race from which he sprung,
Saved other names, and left his own unsung.'

NOTE LV.

Scotts of Eskdale, a stalwart band.—P. 23.

In this, and the following stanzas, some account is given of the mode in which the property in the valley of Esk was transferred from the Beattisons, its ancient possessors, to the name of Scott. It is needless to repeat the circumstances, which are given in the poem, literally as they have been preserved by tradition. Lord Maxwell, in the latter part of the sixteenth century, took upon himself the title of Earl of Morton. The descendants of Beattison of Woodkerrick, who aided the Earl to escape from his disobedient vassals, continued to hold these lands within the memory of man, and were the only Beattisons who had property in the dale. The old people give locality to the story, by showing the Galliard's Haugh, the place where Buccleuch's men were concealed, &c.

Note LVI.

Their gathering word was Bellenden.—P.25.

Bellenden is situated near the head of Borthwick water, and being in the centre of the possessions of the Scotts, was frequently used as their place of rendezvous and gathering word.—*Survey of Selkirkshire, in Macfarlane's MSS.*, Advocates' Library. Hence Satchells calls one part of his genealogical account of the families of that clan, his Bellenden.

Note LVII.

The camp their home, their law the sword,
They knew no country, own'd no lord.
—P. 26.

The mercenary adventurers, whom, in 1380, the Earl of Cambridge carried to the assistance of the King of Portugal against the Spaniards, mutinied for want of regular pay. At an assembly of their leaders, Sir John Soltier, a natural son of Edward the Black Prince, thus addressed them: '"I counsayle, let us be alle of one alliance, and of one accorde, and let us among ourselves reyse up the banner of St. George, and let us be frendes to God, and enemyes to alle the worlde; for without we make ourselfe to be feared, we gete nothynge."

'"By my fayth," quod Sir William Helmon, "ye saye right well, and so let us do." They all agreed with one voyce, and so regarded among them who shulde be their capitayne. Then they advysed in the case how they coude nat have a better capitayne than Sir John Soltier. For they sulde than have good leyser to do yvel, and they thought he was more metelyer thereto than any other. Then they raised up the penon of St. George, and cried, "A Soltier! a Soltier! the valyaunt bastarde! frendes to God, and enemies to all the worlde!"'—FROISSART, vol. i. ch. 393.

Note LVIII.

That he may suffer march-treason pain.
—P. 27.

Several species of offences, peculiar to the Border, constituted what was called march-treason. Among others, was the crime of ridin*g*, or causing to ride, against the opposite country during the time of truce. Thus, in an indenture made at the water of Eske, beside Salom, on the 25th day of March, 1334, betwixt noble lords and mighty, Sirs Henry Percy, Earl of Northumberland, and Archibald Douglas, Lord of Galloway, a truce is agreed upon until the 1st day of July; and it is expressly accorded, 'Gif ony stellis authir on the ta part, or on the tothyr, that he shall be hanget or heofdit; and gif ony company stellis any gudes within the trieux beforesayd, ane of that company sall be hanget or heofdit, and the remnant sall

restore the gudys stolen in the dubble.'—*History of Westmoreland and Cumberland*, Introd. p. xxxix.

Note LIX.

—— *Deloraine*
Will cleanse him, by oath, of march-treason stain.—P. 28.

In dubious cases, the innocence of Border criminals was occasionally referred to their own oath. The form of excusing bills, or indictments, by Border oath, ran thus: 'You shall swear by heaven above you, hell beneath you, by your part of Paradise, by all that God made in six days and seven nights, and by God himself, you are whart out sackless of art, part, way, witting, ridd, kenning, having, or recetting of any of the goods and cattels named in this bill. So help you God.'—*History of Cumberland*, Introd. p. xxv.

Note LX.

Knighthood he took of Douglas' sword.
—P. 28.

The dignity of knighthood, according to the original institution, had this peculiarity, that it did not flow from the monarch, but could be conferred by one who himself possessed it, upon any squire who, after due probation, was found to merit the honour of chivalry. Latterly, this power was confined to generals, who were wont to create knights bannerets after or before an engagement. Even so late as the reign of Queen Elizabeth, Essex highly offended his jealous sovereign by the indiscriminate exertion of this privilege. Among others, he knighted the witty Sir John Harrington, whose favour at court was by no means enhanced by his new honours.—See the *Nugae Antiquae*, edited by Mr. Park. But probably the latest instance of knighthood, conferred by a subject, was in the case of Thomas Ker, knighted by the Earl of Huntly, after the defeat of the Earl of Argyle in the battle of Belrinnes. The fact is attested, both by a poetical and prose account of the engagement, contained in an ancient MS. in the Advocates' Library, and edited by Mr. Dalyell, in *Godly Sangs and Ballets*, Edin. 1802.

Note LXI.

When English blood swell'd Ancram's ford.—P. 28.

The battle of Ancram Moor, or Penielheuch, was fought A. D. 1545. The English, commanded by Sir Ralph Evers, and Sir Brian Latoun, were totally routed, and both their leaders slain in the action. The Scottish army was commanded by Archibald Douglas, Earl of Angus, assisted by the Laird of Buccleuch and Norman Lesley.

NOTE LXII.

For who, in field or foray slack,
Saw the blanche lion e'er fall back ?—P. 29.

This was the cognizance of the noble house of Howard in all its branches. The crest, or bearing, of a warrior, was often used as a *nomme de guerre.* Thus Richard III acquired his well-known epithet, *The Boar of York.* In the violent satire on Cardinal Wolsey, written by Roy, commonly, but erroneously, imputed to Dr. Bull, the Duke of Buckingham is called the *Beautiful Swan*, and the Duke of Norfolk, or Earl of Surrey, the *White Lion.* As the book is extremely rare, and the whole passage relates to the emblematical interpretation of heraldry, it shall be here given at length.

' The Description of the Armes.
'Of the proud Cardinal this is the shelde,
Borne up betweene two angels of Sathan ;
The six bloudy axes in a bare felde,
Sheweth the cruelte of the red man,
Which hath devoured the Beautiful Swan,
Mortal enemy unto the Whyte Lion,
Carter of Yorke, the vyle butcher's sonne,
The six bulles heddes in a felde blacke,
Betokeneth his stordy furiousness,
Wherefore, the godly lyght to put abacke,
He bryngeth in his dyvlish darcness ;
The bandog in the middes doth expresse
The mastiff curre bred in Ypswich towne,
Gnawynge with his teth a kinges crowne.
The cloubbe signifieth playne his tiranny,
Covered over with a Cardinall's hatt,
Wherein shall be ulfilled the prophecy,
Aryse up, Jacke, and put on thy salatt,
For the tyme is come of bagge and walatt.
The temporall chevalry thus thrown doune,
Wherefor, prest, take hede, and beware thy crowne.'

There were two copies of this very scarce satire in the library of the late John, Duke of Roxburghe. See an account of it also in Sir Egerton Brydges' curious miscellany, the *Censura Literaria.*

NOTE LXIII.

Let Musgrave meet fierce Deloraine
In single fight.—P. 29.

It may easily be supposed, that trial by single combat, so peculiar to the feudal system, was common on the Borders. In 1558, the well-known Kirkaldy of Grange fought a duel with Ralph Evre, brother to the then Lord Evre, in consequence of a dispute about a prisoner said to have been ill treated by the Lord Evre. Pitscottie gives the following account of the affair :—'The Lord of Ivers his brother provoked William Kircaldy of Grange to fight with him, in singular combat, on horseback, with spears ; who, keeping the appointment, accompanied with Monsieur d'Ossel, lieutenant to the French King, and the garrison of Haymouth, and Mr. Ivers, accompanied with the governor and garrison of Berwick, it was discharged, under the pain of treason, that any man should come near the champions within a flight-shot, except one man for either of them, to bear their spears, two trumpets, and two lords to be judges. When

they were in readiness, the trumpets sounded, the heraulds cried, and the judges, let them go. They then encountered very fiercely ; but Grange struck his spear through his adversary's shoulder, and bare him off his horse, being sore wounded : But whether he died, or not, it is uncertain.'—P. 202.

The following indenture will show at how late a period the trial by combat was resorted to on the Border, as a proof of guilt or innocence :—

'It is agreed between Thomas Musgrave and Launcelot Carleton, for the true trial of such controversies as are betwixt them, to have it openly tried by way of combat, before God and the face of the world, to try it in Canonbyholme, before England and Scotland, upon Thursday in Easter-week, being the eighth day of April next ensuing, A. D. 1602, betwixt nine of the clock, and one of the same day, to fight on foot, to be armed with jack, steel cap, plaite sleeves, plaite breaches, plaite sockes, two basleard swords, the blades to be one yard and half a quarter in length, two Scotch daggers, or dorks, at their girdles, and either of them to provide armour and weapons for themselves, according to this indenture. Two gentlemen to be appointed, on the field, to view both the parties, to see that they both be equal in arms and weapons, according to this indenture ; and being so viewed by the gentlemen, the gentlemen to ride to the rest of the company, and to leave them but two boys, viewed by the gentlemen, to be under sixteen years of age, to hold their horses. In testimony of this our agreement, we have both set our hands to this indenture, of intent all matters shall be made so plain, as there shall be no question to stick upon that day. Which indenture, as a witness, shall be delivered to two gentlemen. And for that it is convenient the world should be privy to every particular of the grounds of the quarrel, we have agreed to set it down in this indenture betwixt us, that, knowing the quarrel, their eyes may be witness of the trial.

'THE GROUNDS OF THE QUARREL.

' 1. Lancelot Carleton did charge Thomas Musgrave before the Lords of her Majesty's Privy Council, that Lancelot Carleton was told by a gentleman, one of her Majesty's sworn servants, that Thomas Musgrave had offered to deliver her Majesty's Castle of Bewcastle to the King of Scots ; and to witness the same, Lancelot Carleton had a letter under the gentleman's own hand for his discharge.

' 2. He chargeth him, that whereas her Majesty doth yearly bestow a great fee upon him, as captain of Bewcastle, to aid and defend her Majesty's subjects therein : Thomas Musgrave hath neglected his duty, for that her Majesty's Castle of Bewcastle was by him made a den of thieves, and an harbour and receipt for murderers, felons, and all sorts of misdemeanors. The precedent was Quintin Whitehead and Runion Blackburne.

'3. He chargeth him, that his office of Bewcastle is open for the Scotch to ride in and through, and small resistance made by him to the contrary.

'Thomas Musgrave doth deny all this charge; and saith, that he will prove that Lancelot Carleton doth falsely bely him, and will prove the same by way of combat, according to this indenture. Lancelot Carleton hath entertained the challenge; and so, by God's permission, will prove it true as before, and hath set his hand to the same.

　(Signed)　'THOMAS MUSGRAVE.
　　　　　　　'LANCELOT CARLETON.'

NOTE LXIV.
He, the jovial harper.—P. 30.

The person here alluded to, is one of our ancient Border minstrels, called Rattling Roaring Willie. This *soubriquet* was probably derived from his bullying disposition; being, it would seem, such a roaring boy, as is frequently mentioned in old plays. While drinking at Newmill, upon Teviot, about five miles above Hawick, Willie chanced to quarrel with one of his own profession, who was usually distinguished by the odd name of Sweet Milk, from a place on Rule Water so called. They retired to a meadow on the opposite side of the Teviot, to decide the contest with their swords, and Sweet Milk was killed on the spot. A thorn-tree marks the scene of the murder, which is still called Sweet Milk Thorn. Willie was taken and executed at Jedburgh, bequeathing his name to the beautiful Scotch air, called 'Rattling Roaring Willie.' Ramsay, who set no value on traditionary lore, published a few verses of this song in the *Tea Table Miscellany*, carefully suppressing all which had any connexion with the history of the author and origin of the piece. In this case, however, honest Allan is in some degree justified, by the extreme worthlessness of the poetry. A verse or two may be taken, as illustrative of the history of Roaring Willie, alluded to in the text:—

'Now Willie's gane to Jeddart,
　And he's for the *rood-day* [1];
But Stobs and young Falnash [2]
　They follow'd him a' the way;
They follow'd him a' the way,
　They sought him up and down,
In the links of Ousenam water
　They fand him sleeping sound.

Stobs light aff his horse,
　And never a word he spak,
Till he tied Willie's hands
　Fu' fast behind ais back;
Fu' fast behind his back,
　And down beneath his knee,
And drink will be dear to Willie,
　When sweet milk [3] gars him die.

[1] The day of the Rood-fair at Jedburgh.
[2] Sir Gilbert Elliot of Stobs, and Scott of Falnash.
[3] A wretched pun on his antagonist's name.

Ah wae light on ye, Stobs!
　An ill death mot ye die;
Ye're the first and foremost man
　That e'er laid hands on me;
That e'er laid hands on me,
　And took my mare me frae:
Wae to you, Sir Gilbert Elliot!
　Ye are my mortal fae!

The lasses of Ousenam water
　Are rugging and riving their hair,
And a' for the sake of Willie,
　His beauty was so fair:
His beauty was so fair,
　And comely for to see,
And drink will be dear to Willie,
　When sweet milk gars him die.

NOTE LXV.
He knew each ordinance and clause
Of Black Lord Archibald's battle-laws,
In the Old Douglas' day.—P. 30.

The title to the most ancient collection of Border regulations runs thus:—'Be it remembered, that, on the 18th day of December 1468, Earl *William Douglas* assembled the whole lords, freeholders, and eldest Borderers, that best knowledge had, at the college of *Linclouden*; and there he caused these lords and Borderers bodily to be sworn, the Holy Gospel touched, that they, justly and truly, after their cunning, should decrete, decern, deliver, and put in order and writing, the statutes, ordinances, and uses of marche, that were ordained in *Black Archibald of Douglas's* days, and Archibald his son's days, in time of warfare; and they came again to him advisedly with these statutes and ordinances which were in time of warfare before. The said Earl *William*, seeing the statutes in writing decreed and delivered by the said lords and Borderers, thought them right speedful and profitable to the Borders; the which statutes, ordinances, and points of warfare, he took, and the whole lords and Borderers he caused bodily to be sworn, that they should maintain and supply him at their goodly power, to do the law upon those that should break the statutes underwritten. Also, the said Earl *William*, and lords, and eldest Borderers, made certain points to be treason in time of warfare to be used, which were no treason before his time, but to be treason in his time, and in all time coming.'

NOTE LXVI.
The Bloody Heart blaz'd in the van,
Announcing Douglas, dreaded name.
—P. 31.

The chief of this potent race of heroes, about the date of the poem, was Archibald Douglas, seventh Earl of Angus, a man of great courage and activity. The Bloody Heart was the well-known cognizance of the House of Douglas, assumed from the time of good Lord James, to whose care Robert Bruce committed his heart, to be carried to the Holy Land.

Note LXVII.

And Swinton laid the lance in rest,
That tamed of yore the sparkling crest
Of Clarence's Plantagenet.—P. 31.

At the battle of Beaugé, in France, Thomas, Duke of Clarence, brother to Henry V, was unhorsed by Sir John Swinton of Swinton, who distinguished him by a coronet set with precious stones, which he wore around his helmet. The family of Swinton is one of the most ancient in Scotland, and produced many celebrated warriors.

Note LXVIII.

And shouting still ' A Home! a Home!'
—P. 32.

The Earls of Home, as descendants of the Dunbars, ancient Earls of March, carried a lion rampant, argent; but, as a difference, changed the colour of the shield from gules to vert, in allusion to Greenlaw, their ancient possession. The slogan, or war-cry, of this powerful family was 'A Home! a Home!' It was anciently placed in an escrol above the crest. The helmet is armed with a lion's head erased gules, with a cap of state gules, turned up ermine.

The Hepburns, a powerful family in East Lothian, were usually in close alliance with the Homes. The chief of this clan was Hepburn, Lord of Hailes; a family which terminated in the too famous Earl of Bothwell.

Note LXIX.

And some, with many a merry shout,
In riot, revelry, and rout,
Pursued the foot-ball play.—P. 32.

The foot-ball was anciently a very favourite sport all through Scotland, but especially upon the Borders. Sir John Carmichael of Carmichael, Warden of the Middle Marches, was killed in 1600 by a band of the Armstrongs, returning from a foot-ball match. Sir Robert Carey, in his Memoirs, mentions a great meeting, appointed by the Scotch riders, to be held at Kelso for the purpose of playing at foot ball, but which terminated in an incursion upon England. At present, the foot-ball is often played by the inhabitants of adjacent parishes, or of the opposite banks of a stream. The victory is contested with the utmost fury, and very serious accidents have sometimes taken place in the struggle.

Note LXX.

'Twixt truce and war, such sudden change
Was not infrequent, nor held strange,
In the old Border-day.—P. 32.

Notwithstanding the constant wars upon the Borders, and the occasional cruelties which marked the mutual inroads the in-

habitants on either side do not appear to have regarded each other with that violent and personal animosity, which might have been expected. On the contrary, like the outposts of hostile armies, they often carried on something resembling friendly intercourse, even in the middle of hostilities; and it is evident, from various ordinances against trade and intermarriages, between English and Scottish Borderers, that the governments of both countries were jealous of their cherishing too intimate a connexion. Froissart says of both nations, that 'Englyshmen on the one party, and Scottes on the other party, are good men of warre; for when they meet there is a harde fight without sparynge. There is no hoo [*truce*] between them, as long as spears, swords, axes, or daggers, will endure, but lay on eche upon uther; and whan they be well beaten, and that the one party hath obtained the victory, they then glorifye so in theyre dedes of armes, and are so joyfull, that such as be taken they shall be ransomed, or that they go out of the felde; so that shortly eche of them is so content with other, that, at their departynge, curtyslye they will say, God thank you.'—BERNERS'S *Froissart*, vol. ii. p. 153. The Border meetings, of truce, which although places of merchandise and merriment, often witnessed the most bloody scenes, may serve to illustrate the description in the text. They are vividly portrayed in the old ballad of the Reidsquair. [See Minstrelsy, vol. ii. p. 15.] Both parties came armed to a meeting of the wardens, yet they intermixed fearlessly and peaceably with each other in mutual sports and familiar intercourse, until a casual fray arose :—

'Then was there nought but bow and spear,
   And every man pulled out a brand.'

In the 29th stanza of this canto, there is an attempt to express some of the mixed feelings, with which the Borderers on each side were led to regard their neighbours.

Note LXXI.

—— on the darkening plain,
Loud hollo, whoop, or whistle ran,
As bands, their s ragglers to regain,
Give the shrill watchword of their clan.
—P. 33.

Patten remarks, with bitter censure, the disorderly conduct of the English Borderers, who attended the Protector Somerset on his expedition against Scotland. 'As we wear then a setling, and the tents a setting up, among all things els commendable in our hole journey, one thing seemed to me an intollerable disorder and abuse : that whereas always, both in all tounes of war, and in all campes of armies, quietness and stilnes, without nois, is, principally in the night, after the watch is set, observed, (I need not reason why,) our northern prikers, the Borderers notwithstandyng, with great enormitie, (as thought me,) and not unlike (to be playn) unto a masterles hounde howlyng in a hie way when he hath lost him he waited upon, sum hoopynge, sum whistlyng, and most with crying 'A Berwyke, a Berwyke! A Fenwyke, a Fenwyke! A Bulmer, a Bulmer! or so ootherwise as theyr captains names wear, never lin'de these troublous and dangerous noyses all the nyghte longe. They said, they did it to find their captain and fellows; but if the souldiers of our oother countreys and sheres had used the same maner, in that case we should have oft times had the state of our campe more like the outrage of a dissolute huntyng, than the quiet of a well ordered armye. It is a feat of war, in mine opinion, that might right well be left. I could reherse causes (but yf I take it, they are better unspoken than uttred, unless the faut wear sure to be amended) that might shew thei move alweis more peral to our armie, but in their one nyght's so doynge, then they shew good service (as some sey) in a hoole vyage.'—*Apud* DALZELL'S *Fragments*, p. 75.

NOTE LXXII.

To see how thou the chase could'st wind,
Cheer the dark blood-hound on his way,
And with the bugle rouse the fray!—P. 38.

The pursuit of Border marauders was followed by the injured party and his friends with blood-hounds and bugle-horn, and was called the *hot-trod*. He was entitled, if his dog could trace the scent, to follow the invaders into the opposite kingdom; a privilege which often occasioned bloodshed. In addition to what has been said of the blood-hound, I may add, that the breed was kept up by the Buccleuch family on their Border estates till within the 18th century. A person was alive in the memory of man, who remembered a blood-hound being kept at Eldinhope, in Ettrick Forest, for whose maintenance the tenant had an allowance of meal. At that time the sheep were always watched at night. Upon one occasion, when the duty had fallen on the narrator, then a lad, he became exhausted with fatigue, and fell asleep upon a bank, near sun-rising. Suddenly he was awakened by the tread of horses, and saw five men, well mounted and armed, ride briskly over the edge of the hill. They stopped and looked at the flock; but the day was too far broken to admit the chance of their carrying any of them off. One of them, in spite, leaped from his horse, and coming to the shepherd, seized him by the belt he wore round his waist; and, setting his foot upon his body, pulled it till it broke, and carried it away with him. They rode off at the gallop; and, the shepherd giving the alarm, the blood-hound was turned loose,

and the people in the neighbourhood alarmed. The marauders, however, escaped, notwithstanding a sharp pursuit. This circumstance serves to show how very long the license of the Borderers continued in some degree to manifest itself.

NOTE LXXIII.

She wrought not by forbidden spell.—P. 40.

Popular belief, though contrary to the doctrines of the Church, made a favourable distinction betwixt magicians, and necromancers, or wizards; the former were supposed to command the evil spirits, and the latter to serve, or at least to be in league and compact with, those enemies of mankind. The arts of subjecting the demons were manifold; sometimes the fiends were actually swindled by the magicians, as in the case of the bargain betwixt one of their number and the poet Virgil. The classical reader will doubtless be curious to peruse this anecdote:—

'Virgilius was at scole at Tolenton, where he stodyed dylygently, for he was of great understandynge. Upon a tyme, the scolers had lycense to go to play and sporte them in the fyldes, after the usance of the old tyme. And there was also Virgilius therbye, also walkynge among the hylles alle about. It fortuned he spyed a great hole in the syde of a great hyll, wherein he went so depe, that he culd not see no more lyght; and than he went a lytell farther therein, and than he saw some lyght egayne, and than he went fourth streyghte, and within a lytell wyle after he harde a voyce that called "Virgilius! Virgilius!" and looked aboute, and he colde nat see no body. Than sayd he, (i. e. the *voice*,) "Virgilius, see ye not the lytyll borde lying besyde you there marked with that word?" Than answered Virgilius, "I see that borde well anough." The voice said, "Doo awaye that borde, and lette me out there atte." Than answered Virgilius to the voice that was under the lytell borde, and sayd, "Who art thou that callest me so?" Than answered the devyll, "I am a devyll conjured out of the bodye of a certeyne man, and banysshed here tyll the day of judgmend, without that I be delyvered by the handes of men. Thus, Virgilius, I pray the, delyver me out of this payn, and I shall shewe unto the many bokes of negromancye, and how thou shalt come by it lyghtly, and know the practyse therein, that no man in the scyence of negromancye shall passe the. And moreover, I shall shewe and enforme the so, that thou shalt have alle thy de yre, whereby methinke it is a great gyfte for so lytyll a doyng. For ye may also thus all your power frendyshelpe, and make ryched your enemyes." Thorough that great promyse was Virgilius tempted; he badde the fynd show the bokes to hym, that he might have and occupy them at his wyll; and so the fynde shewed him. And than Virgilius pulled open a borde, and there was a lytell hole, and thereat wrang the devyll out like a yell, and cam and stode before Virgilius lyke a bygge man; whereof Virgilius was astonied and marveyled greatly thereof, that so great a man myght come out at so lytyll a hole. Than sayd Virgilius, "Shulde ye well passe into the hole that ye cam out of?"—"Yea, I shall well," said the devyl.—"I holde the best plegge that I have, that ye shall not do it."—"Well," sayd the devyll, "thereto I consent." And than the devyll wrange himselfe into the lytyll hole agene; and as he was therein, Virgilius kyvered the hole ageyne with the borde close, and so was the devyll begyled, and myght nat there come out agen, but abydeth shytte styll therein. Than called the devyll dredefully to Virgilius, and said, "What have ye done, Virgilius?"—Virgilius answered, "Abyde there styll to your day appoynted;" and fro thens forth abydeth he there. And so Virgilius became very connynge in the practyse of the black scyence.'

This story may remind the reader of the Arabian tale of the Fisherman and the imprisoned Genie; and it is more than probable, that many of the marvels narrated in the life of Virgil, are of Oriental extraction. Among such I am disposed to reckon the following whimsical account of the foundation of Naples, containing a curious theory concerning the origin of the earthquakes with which it is afflicted. Virgil, who was a person of gallantry, had, it seems, carried off the daughter of a certain Soldan, and was anxious to secure his prize.

'Than he thought in his mynde how he myghte marye hyr, and thought in his mynde to founde in the middes of the see a fayer towne, with great landes belongynge to it; and so he did by his cunnynge, and called it Napells. And the fandacyon of it was of egges, and in that town of Napells he made a tower with iiii corners, and in the toppe he set an apell upon an yron yarde, and no man culde pull away that apell without he brake it; and thoroughe that yren set he a bolte, and in that bolte set he a egge. And he henge the apell by the stauke upon a cheyne, and so hangeth it still. And when the egge styrreth, so shulde the towne of Napells quake; and whan the egge brake, then shulde the towne sinke. Whan he had made an ende, he lette call it Napells.' This appears to have been an article of current belief during the middle ages, as appears from the statutes of the order *Du Saint Esprit au droit désir*, instituted in 1352. A chapter of the knights is appointed to be held annually at the Castle of the Enchanted Egg, near the grotto of Virgil.—MONTFAUCON, vol. ii. p. 329.

Note LXXIV.

A merlin sat upon her wrist,
Held by a leash of silken twist.—P. 40.

A merlin, or sparrow-hawk, was actually carried by ladies of rank, as a falcon was, in time of peace, the constant attendant of a knight or baron. See LATHAM *on Falconry*.—Godscroft relates, that when Mary of Lorraine was regent, she pressed the Earl of Angus to admit a royal garrison into his Castle of Tantallon. To this he returned no direct answer; but, as if apostrophizing a goss-hawk, which sat on his wrist, and which he was feeding during the Queen's speech, he exclaimed, 'The devil's in this greedy glede, she will never be full.'—HUME'S *History of the House of Douglas*, 1743, vol. ii. p. 131. Barclay complains of the common and indecent practice of bringing hawks and hounds into churches.

Note LXXV.

And princely peacock's gilded train,
And o'er the boar-head, garnish'd brave.
—P. 40.

The peacock, it is well known, was considered, during the times of chivalry, not merely as an exquisite delicacy, but as a dish of peculiar solemnity. After being roasted, it was again decorated with its plumage, and a sponge, dipped in lighted spirits of wine, was placed in its bill. When it was introduced on days of grand festival, it was the signal for the adventurous knights to take upon them vows to do some deed of chivalry, 'before the peacock and the ladies.'

The boar's head was also a usual dish of feudal splendour. In Scotland it was sometimes surrounded with little banners, displaying the colours and achievements of the baron at whose board it was served.—PINKERTON'S *History*, vol. i. p. 432.

Note LXXVI.

Smote with his gauntlet stout Hunthill.
—P. 40.

The Rutherfords of Hunthill were an ancient race of Border Lairds, whose names occur in history, sometimes as defending the frontier against the English, sometimes as disturbing the peace of their own country. Dickon Draw-the-sword was son to the ancient warrior, called in tradition the Cock of Hunthill, remarkable for leading into battle nine sons, gallant warriors, all sons of the aged champion. Mr. Rutherford, late of New York, in a letter to the editor, soon after these songs were first published, quoted, when upwards of eighty years old, a ballad apparently the same with the Raid of Reidsquare, but which apparently is lost, except the following lines:—

'Bauld Rutherfurd he was fu' stout,
With all his nine sons him about,
He brought the lads of Jedbrught out,
And bauldly fought that day.'

NOTE LXXVII.

*—— bit his glove.—*P. 41.

To bite the thumb, or the glove, seems not to have been considered, upon the Border, as a gesture of contempt, though so used by Shakspeare, but as a pledge of mortal revenge. It is yet remembered, that a young gentleman of Teviotdale, on the morning after a hard drinking bout, observed that he had bitten his glove. He instantly demanded of his companion, with whom he had quarrelled? And, learning that he had had words with one of the party, insisted on instant satisfaction, asserting, that though he remembered nothing of the dispute, yet he was sure he never would have bit his glove unless he had received some unpardonable insult. He fell in the duel, which was fought near Selkirk, in 1721.

NOTE LXXVIII.

Since old Buccleuch the name did gain,
When in the cleuch the buck was ta'en.
*—*P. 41.

A tradition preserved by Scott of Satchells, who published, in 1688, *A true History of the Right Honourable name of Scott*, gives the following romantic origin of that name. Two brethren, natives of Galloway, having been banished from that country for a riot, or insurrection, came to Rankleburn, in Ettrick Forest, where the keeper, whose name was Brydone, received them joyfully, on account of their skill in winding the horn, and in the other mysteries of the chase. Kenneth MacAlpin, then King of Scotland, came soon after to hunt in the royal forest, and pursued a buck from Ettrick heugh to the glen now called Buckcleuch, about two miles above the junction of Rankleburn with the river Ettrick. Here the stag stood at bay; and the King and his attendants, who followed on horseback, were thrown out by the steepness of the hill and the morass. John, one of the brethren from Galloway, had followed the chase on foot; and, now coming in, seized the buck by the horns, and, being a man of great strength and activity, threw him on his back, and ran with his burden about a mile up the steep hill, to a place called Cracra Cross, where Kenneth had halted, and laid the buck at the sovereign's feet [1].

[1] Froissart relates, that a knight of the household of the Comte de Foix exhibited a similar feat of strength. The hall-fire had waxed low, and wood was wanted to mend it. The knight went down to the court-yard, where stood an ass laden with faggots, seized on the animal and burden, and, carrying him up to the hall on his shoulders, tumbled him into the chimney with his heels uppermost: a humane pleasantry, much applauded by the Count and all the spectators.

'The deer being cureed in that place,
  At his Majesty's demand,
Then John of Galloway ran apace,
  And fetched water to his hand.
The King did wash into a dish,
  And Galloway John he wot;
He said, "Thy name now after this
  Shall ever be called John Scott.

The forest and the deer therein,
  We commit to thy hand;
For thou shalt sure the ranger be,
  If thou obey command;
And for the buck thou stoutly brought
  To us up that steep heuch,
The designation ever shall
  Be John Scott in Buckscleuch."

* * * * *

In Scotland no Buckcleuch was then,
Before the buck in the cleuch was slain;
Night's men at first they did appear,
Because moon and stars to their arms they bear.
Their crest, supporters, and hunting-horn,
Show their beginning from hunting came;
Their name, and style, the book doth say,
John gained them both into one day.'
                        WATT'S *Bellenden.*

The Buccleuch arms have been altered, and now allude less pointedly to this hunting, whether real or fabulous. The family now bear *Or*, upon a bend azure, a mullet betwixt two crescents of the field; in addition to which, they formerly bore in the field a hunting-horn. The supporters, now two ladies, were formerly a hound and buck, or, according to the old terms, a *hart of leash* and a *hart of greece*. The family of Scott of Howpasley and Thirlestaine long retained the bugle horn; they also carried a bent bow and arrow in the sinister cantle, perhaps as a difference. It is said the motto was—*Best riding by moonlight*, in allusion to the crescents on the shield, and perhaps to the habits of those who bore it. The motto now given is *Amo*,—applying to the female supporters.

NOTE LXXIX.

—— old Albert Græme,
*The Minstrel of that ancient name.—*P. 41.

'John Græme, second son of *Malice*, Earl of *Monteith*, commonly sirnamed *John with the Bright Sword*, upon some displeasure risen against him at court, retired with many of his clan and kindred into the English Borders, in the reign of King Henry the Fourth, where they seated themselves; and many of their posterity have continued there ever since. Mr. Sandford, speaking of them, says, (which indeed was applicable to most of the Borderers on both sides,) "They were all stark moss-troopers, and arrant thieves: Both to England and Scotland outlawed; yet sometimes connived at, because they gave intelligence forth of Scotland, and would raise 400 horse at any time upon a raid of the English into Scotland. A saying is recorded of a mother to her son, (which is now become proverbial,) *Ride, Rowley,* hough's i' the pot: that is, the last piece of beef was in the pot, and therefore it was high time for him to go and fetch more."—*Introduction to the History of Cumberland.*

The residence of the Græmes being chiefly in the Debateable Land, so called because it was claimed by both kingdoms, their depredations extended both to England and Scotland, with impunity; for as both wardens accounted them the proper subjects of their own prince, neither inclined to demand reparation for their excesses from the opposite officers, which would have been an acknowledgment of his jurisdiction over them.— See a long correspondence on this subject betwixt Lord Dacre and the English Privy Council, in Introduction to *History of Cumberland.* The Debateable Land was finally divided betwixt England and Scotland, by commissioners appointed by both nations.

NOTE LXXX.

The sun shines fair on Carlisle wall.
—P. 41.

This burden is adopted, with some alteration, from an old Scottish song, beginning thus:—

' She lean'd her back against a thorn,
  The sun shines fair on Carlisle wa' :
And there she has her young babe born,
  And the lyon shall be lord of a'.'

NOTE LXXXI.

Who has not heard of Surrey's fame?
—P. 42.

The gallant and unfortunate Henry Howard, Earl of Surrey, was unquestionably the most accomplished cavalier of his time; and his sonnets display beauties which would do honour to a more polished age. He was beheaded on Tower-hill in 1546; a victim to the mean jealousy of Henry VIII, who could not bear so brilliant a character near his throne.

The song of the supposed bard is founded on an incident said to have happened to the Earl in his travels. Cornelius Agrippa, the celebrated alchemist, showed him, in a looking-glass, the lovely Geraldine, to whose service he had devoted his pen and his sword. The vision represented her as indisposed, and reclining upon a couch, reading her lover's verses by the light of a waxen taper.

NOTE LXXXII.

—— *the storm-swept Orcades ;*
Where erst St. Clairs held princely sway
O'er isle and islet, strait and bay.—P. 44.

The St. Clairs are of Norman extraction, being descended from William de St. Clair, second son of Walderne Compte de St. Clair, and Margaret, daughter to Richard Duke of Normandy. He was called, for his fair deportment, the Seemly St. Clair; and, settling in Scotland during the reign of Malcolm Caenmore, obtained large grants of land in Mid-Lothian.—These domains were increased by the liberality of succeeding monarchs to the descendants of the family, and comprehended the baronies of Rosline, Pentland, Cowsland, Cardaine, and several others. It is said a large addition was obtained from Robert Bruce, on the following occasion:— The King, in following the chase upon Pentland-hills, had often started a ' white faunch deer,' which had always escaped from his hounds ; and he asked the nobles, who were assembled around him, whether any of them had dogs, which they thought might be more successful. No courtier would affirm that his hounds were fleeter than those of the King, until Sir William St. Clair of Rosline unceremoniously said, he would wager his head that his two favourite dogs, *Help* and *Hold*, would kill the deer before she could cross the March-burn. The King instantly caught at his unwary offer, and betted the forest of Pentland-moor against the life of Sir William St. Clair. All the hounds were tied up, except a few ratches, or slow-hounds, to put up the deer ; while Sir William St. Clair, posting himself in the best situation for slipping his dogs, prayed devoutly to Christ, the blessed Virgin, and St. Katherine. The deer was shortly after roused, and the hounds slipped ; Sir William following on a gallant steed, to cheer his dogs. The hind, however, reached the middle of the brook ; upon which the hunter threw himself from his horse in despair. At this critical moment, however, Hold stopped her in the brook ; and Help, coming up, turned her back, and killed her on Sir William's side. The King descended from the hill, embraced Sir William, and bestowed on him the lands of Kirkton, Loganhouse, Earncraig, &c., in free forestrie. Sir William, in acknowledgment of St Katherine's intercession, built the chapel of St. Katherine in the Hopes, the churchyard of which is still to be seen. The hill, from which Robert Bruce beheld this memorable chase, is still called the King's Hill ; and the place where Sir William hunted, is called the Knight's Field.—*MS. History of the Family of St. Clair, by* RICHARD AUGUSTIN HAY, *Canon of St. Genevieve.*

This adventurous huntsman married Elizabeth, daughter of Malice Spar, Earl of Orkney and Stratherne, in whose right their son Henry was, in 1379, created Earl of Orkney, by Haco, King of Norway. His title was recognized by the Kings of Scotland, and remained with his successors until it was annexed to the crown, in 1471, by Act of Parliament. In exchange for this earldom, the castle and domains of Ravenscraig, or Ravensheuch, were conferred on William Saintclair, Earl of Caithness.

Note LXXXIII.

Still nods their palace to its fall,
Thy pride and sorrow, fair Kirkwall!
—P. 44.

The Castle of Kirkwall was built by the St. Clairs, while Earls of Orkney. It was dismantled by the Earl of Caithness about 1615, having been garrisoned against the Government by Robert Stewart, natural son to the Earl of Orkney.

Its ruins afforded a sad subject of contemplation to John, Master of St. Clair, who, flying from his native country, on account of his share in the insurrection 1715, made some stay at Kirkwall.

'I had occasion to entertain myself at Kirkwall with the melancholy prospect of the ruins of an old castle, the seat of the old Earls of Orkney, my ancestors; and of a more melancholy reflection, of so great and noble an estate as the Orkney and Shetland Isles being taken from one of them by James the Third, for faultrie, after his brother Alexander, Duke of Albany, had married a daughter of my family, and for protecting and defending the said Alexander against the King, who wished to kill him, as he had done his youngest brother, the Earl of Mar; and for which, after the forfaultrie, he *grat:fully* divorced my forfaulted ancestor's sister; though I cannot persuade myself that he had any misalliance to plead against a familie in whose veins the blood of Robert Bruce ran as fresh as in his own; for their title to the crowne was by a daughter of David Bruce, son to Robert; and our alliance was by marrying a grandchild of the same Robert Bruce, and daughter to the sister of the same David, out of the familie of Douglass, which at that time did not much sullie the blood, more than my ancestor's having not long before had the honour of marrying a daughter of the King of Denmark's, who was named Florentine, and has left in the town of Kirkwall a noble monument of the grandeur of the times, the finest church ever I saw entire in Scotland. I then had no small reason to think, in that unhappy state, on the many not inconsiderable services rendered since to the royal familie, for these many years bygone, on all occasions, when they stood most in need of friends, which they have thought themselves very often obliged to acknowledge by letters yet extant, and in a style more like friends than souveraigns; our attachment to them, without any other thanks, having brought upon us considerable losses, and among others, that of our all in Cromwell's time; and left in that condition without the least relief except what we found in our own virtue. My father was the only man of the Scots nation who had courage enough to protest in Parliament against K.ng William's title to the throne, which was lost, God knows how; and this at a time when the losses in the cause of the royall familie,

and their usual gratitude, had scarce left him bread to maintain a numerous familie of eleven children, who had soon after sprung up on him, in spite of all which, he had honourably persisted in his principle. I say, these things considered, and after being treated as I was, and in that unlucky state, when objects appear to men in their true light, as at the hour of death, could I be blamed for making some bitter reflections to myself, and laughing at the extravagance and unaccountable humour of men, and the singularitie of my own case, (an exile for the cause of the Stuart family,) when I ought to have known, that the greatest crime I, or my family, could have committed, was persevering, to my own destruction, in serving the royal family faithfully, though obstinately, after so great a share of depression, and after they had been pleased to doom me and my familie to starve.—*MS. Memoirs of John, Master of St. Clair.*

Note LXXXIV.

Of that Sea-Snake, tremendous curl'd,
Whose monstrous circle girds the world.
—P. 44.

The *jormungandr,* or Snake of the Ocean, whose folds surround the earth, is one of the wildest fictions of the Edda. It was very nearly caught by the god Thor, who went to fish for it with a hook baited with a bull's head. In the battle betwixt the evil demons and the divinities of Odin, which is to precede the *Ragnarockr,* or Twilight of the Gods, this Snake is to act a conspicuous part.

Note LXXXV.

Of those dread Maids, whose hideous yell.
—P. 44.

These were the *Valcyriur,* or Selectors of the Slain, despatched by Odin from Valhalla, to choose those who were to die, and to distribute the contest. They were well known to the English reader as Gray's Fatal Sisters.

Note LXXXVI.

Of Chiefs, who, guided through the gloom
By the pale death lights of the tomb,
Ransack'd the graves of warriors old,
Their falchions wrench'd from corpses'
hold.—P. 44.

The northern warriors were usually entombed with their arms, and their other treasures. Thus, Angantyr, before commencing the duel in which he was slain, stipulated, that if he fell, his sword Tyrfing should be buried with him. His daughter, Hervor, afterwards took it from his tomb. The dialogue which passed betwixt her and Angantyr's spirit on this occasion has been often translated. The whole history may be found in the Hervarar-Saga. Indeed, the ghosts of the northern warriors were not wont tamely to suffer their tombs to be plundered; and hence the mortal heroes had an additional temptation to attempt such adventures; for they held nothing more worthy of their valour than to encounter supernatural beings.—BARTHOLINUS. *De causis contemptae a Danis mortis,* lib. i. cap. 2, 9, 10, 13.

NOTE LXXXVII.

Castle Ravensheuch.—P. 44.

A large and strong castle, now ruinous, situated betwixt Kirkaldy and Dysart, on a steep crag, washed by the Frith of Forth. It was conferred on Sir William St. Clair as a slight compensation for the earldom of Orkney, by a charter of King James III. dated in 1471, and is now the property of Sir James St. Clair Erskine, (now Earl of Rosslyn,) representative of the family. It was long a principal residence of the Barons of Roslin.

NOTE LXXXVIII.

Seem'd all on fire within, around,
Deep sacristy and altar's pale ;
Shone every pillar foliage-bound ;
And glimmer'd all the dead men's mail.
—P. 45.

The beautiful chapel of Roslin is still in tolerable preservation. It was founded in 1446, by William St. Clair, Prince of Orkney, Duke of Oldenburgh, Earl of Caithness and Stratherne, Lord St. Clair, Lord Niddesdale, Lord Admiral of the Scottish Seas, Lord Chief Justice of Scotland, Lord Warden of the three Marches, Baron of Roslin, Pentland, Pentlandmoor, &c., Knight of the Cockle, and of the Garter, (as is affirmed,) High Chancellor, Chamberlain, and Lieutenant of Scotland. This lofty person, whose titles, says Godscroft, might weary a Spaniard, built the castle of Roslin, where he resided in princely splendour, and founded the chapel, which is in the most rich and florid style of Gothic architecture. Among the profuse carving on the pillars and buttresses, the rose is frequently introduced, in allusion to the name, with which, however, the flower has no connection; the etymology being Rosslinnhe, the promontory of the linn, or water fall. The chapel is said to appear on fire previous to the death of any of his descendants. This superstition, noticed by Slezer, in his *Theatrum Scotiae,* and alluded to in the text, is probably of Norwegian derivation, and may have been imported by the Earls of Orkney into their Lothian dominions. The tomb-fires of the north are mentioned in most of the Sagas.

The Barons of Roslin were buried in a vault beneath the chapel floor. The manner of their interment is thus described by Father Hay, in the MS. history already quoted.

'Sir William Sinclair, the father, was a lewd man. He kept a miller's daughter, with whom, it is alleged, he went to Ireland; yet I think the cause of his retreat was rather occasioned by the Presbyterians, who vexed him sadly, because of his religion being Roman Catholic. His son, Sir William, died during the troubles, and was interred in the chapel of Roslin the very same day that the battle of Dunbar was fought. When my good-father was buried, his (i.e. Sir William's) corpse seemed to be entire at the opening of the cave; but when they came to touch his body, it fell into dust. He was laying in his armour, with a red velvet cap on his head, on a flat stone; nothing was spoiled except a piece of the white furring that went round the cap, and answered to the hinder part of the head. All his predecessors were buried after the same manner, in their armour: late Rosline, my good father, was the first that was buried in a coffin, against the sentiments of King James the Seventh, who was then in Scotland, and several other persons well versed in antiquity, to whom my mother would not hearken, thinking it beggarly to be buried after that manner. The great expenses she was at in burying her husband, occasioned the sumptuary acts which were made in the following parliament.'

NOTE LXXXIX.

For he was speechless, ghastly, wan,
Like him of whom the story ran,
Who spoke the spectre-hound in Man.—P. 46.

The ancient castle of Peel town, in the Isle of Man, is surrounded by four churches, now ruinous. Throuh one of these chapels there was formerly a passage from the guard-room of the garrison. This was closed, it is said, upon the following occasion: 'They say, that an apparition, called, in the Mankish language, the *Mauthe Doog,* in the shape of a large black spaniel, with curled shaggy hair, was used to haunt Peel-castle; and has been frequently seen in every room, but particularly in the guard-chamber, where, as soon as candles were lighted, it came and lay down before the fire, in presence of all the soldiers, who, at length, by being so much accustomed to the sight of it, lost great part of the terror they were seized with at its first appearance. They still, however, retained a certain awe, as believing it was an evil spirit, which only waited permission to do them hurt; and, for that reason, forebore swearing, and all profane discourse, while in its company. But though they endured the shock of such a guest when altogether in a body, none cared to be left alone with it. It being the custom, therefore, for one of the soldiers to lock the gates of the castle at a certain hour, and carry the keys to the captain,

D

to whose apartment, as I said before, the way
led through the church, they agreed among
themselves, that whoever was to succeed the
ensuing night his fellow in this errand, should
accompany him that went first, and by this
means no man would be exposed singly to
the danger; for I forgot to mention, that the
Mauthe Doog was always seen to come out
from that passage at the close of the day,
and return to it again as soon as the morning
dawned; which made them look on this place
as its peculiar residence.

'One night a fellow being drunk, and by
the strength of his liquor rendered more
daring than ordinarily, laughed at the simplicity of his companions, and, though it was
not his turn to go with the keys, would needs
take that office upon him, to testify his courage. All the soldiers endeavoured to dissuade him; but the more they said, the more
resolute he seemed, and swore that he desired nothing more than that the *Mauthe
Doog* would follow him, as it had done the
others; for he would try if it were dog or
devil. After having talked in a very repro-
bate manner for some time, he snatched up
the keys, and went out of the guard room. In
some time after his departure, a great noise
was heard, but nobody had the boldness to
see what occasioned it, till the adventurer
returning, they demanded the knowledge of
him; but as loud and noisy as he had been
at leaving them, he was now become sober
and silent enough; for he was never heard to
speak more; and though all the time he lived,
which was three days, he was entreated by
all who came near him, either to speak, or, if

he could not do that, to make some signs, by
which they might understand what had happened to him, yet nothing intelligible could
be got from him, only that, by the distortion
of his limbs and features, it might be guessed
that he died in agonies more than is common
in a natural death.

'The *Mauthe Doog* was, however, never
after seen in the castle, nor would any one
attempt to go through that passage; for
which reason it was closed up, and another
way made. This accident happened about
three score years since; and I heard it attested by several, but especially by an old
soldier, who assured me he had seen it oftener
than he had then hairs on his head.'—WAL-
DRON'S *Description of the Isle of Man*,
p. 107.

NOTE XC.
St. Bride of Douglas.—P. 46.

This was a favourite saint of the house of
Douglas, and of the Earl of Angus in particular, as we learn from the following passage:—'The Queen-regent had proposed to
raise a rival noble to the ducal dignity; and
discoursing of her purpose with Angus, he
answered, "Why not, madam? we are happy
that have such a princess, that can know and
will acknowledge men's services, and is willing to recompense it, but, by the might of
God," (this was his oath when he was serious
and in anger; at other times, it was by St.
Bryde of Douglas,) "if he be a Duke, I will be
a Drake!"—So she desisted from prosecuting
of that purpose.'—GODSCROFT. vol. ii. p. 131.

Marmion.

—◆◆—

INTRODUCTION TO CANTO FIRST.

———

TO

WILLIAM STEWART ROSE, ESQ.

Ashestiel, Ettrick Forest.

NOVEMBER's sky is chill and drear,
November's leaf is red and sear:
Late, gazing down the steepy linn,
That hems our little garden in,
Low in its dark and narrow glen
You scarce the rivulet might ken,
So thick the tangled greenwood grew,
So feeble trill'd the streamlet through :
Now, murmuring hoarse, and frequent seen
Through bush and brier, no longer green,
An angry brook, it sweeps the glade,
Brawls over rock and wild cascade,
And, foaming brown with doubled speed,
Hurries its waters to the Tweed.

No longer Autumn's glowing red
Upon our Forest hills is shed ;
No more beneath the evening beam
Fair Tweed reflects their purple gleam ;
Away hath pass'd the heather-bell
That bloom'd so rich on Needpath-fell ;
Sallow his brow ; and russet bare
Are now the sister-heights of Yair.

The sheep, before the pinching heaven,
To shelter'd dale and down are driven,
Where yet some faded herbage pines,
And yet a watery sunbeam shines :
In meek despondency they eye
The wither'd sward and wintry sky,
And far beneath their summer hill,
Stray sadly by Glenkinnon's rill :
The shepherd shifts his mantle's fold,
And wraps him closer from the cold ;
His dogs no merry circles wheel,
But shivering follow at his heel ;
A cowering glance they often cast,
As deeper moans the gathering blast.

My imps, though hardy, bold, and wild,
As best befits the mountain child,
Feel the sad influence of the hour,
And wail the daisy's vanished flower ;
Their summer gambols tell, and mourn,
And anxious ask,—Will spring return,
And birds and lambs again be gay,
And blossoms clothe the hawthorn spray ?

Yes, prattlers, yes ; the daisy's flower
Again shall paint your summer bower ;
Again the hawthorn shall supply
The garlands you delight to tie ;
The lambs upon the lea shall bound,
The wild birds carol to the round,
And, while you frolic light as they,
Too short shall seem the summer day.

To mute and to material things
New life revolving summer brings ;

The genial call dead Nature hears,
And in her glory reappears.
But oh ! my country's wintry state
What second spring shall renovate ?
What powerful call shall bid arise
The buried warlike and the wise ;
The mind that thought for Britain's
  weal,
The hand that grasp'd the victor steel ?
The vernal sun new life bestows
Even on the meanest flower that blows ;
But vainly, vainly may he shine
Where glory weeps o'er NELSON's
  shrine ;
And vainly pierce the solemn gloom,
That shrouds, O PITT, thy hallowed
  tomb !

Deep grav'd in every British heart,
O never let those names depart !
Say to your sons,—Lo, here his grave,
Who victor died on Gadite wave.
To him, as to the burning levin,
Short, bright, resistless course was
  given.
Where'er his country's foes were
  found,
Was heard the fated thunder's sound,
Till burst the bolt on yonder shore,
Roll'd, blaz'd, destroy'd,—and was
  no more.

Nor mourn ye less his perish'd
  worth
Who bade the conqueror go forth,
And launch'd that thunderbolt of war
On Egypt, Hafnia, Trafalgar ;
Who, born to guide such high emprize,
For Britain's weal was early wise ;
Alas ! to whom the Almighty gave,
For Britain's sins, an early grave !
His worth who, in his mightiest hour,
A bauble held the pride of power,
Spurn'd at the sordid lust of pelf,
And serv'd his Albion for herself ;
Who, when the frantic crowd amain
Strain'd at subjection's bursting rein,

O'er their wild mood full conquest
  gain'd,
The pride, he would not crush, restrain'd,
Show'd their fierce zeal a worthier
  cause,
And brought the freeman's arm to aid
  the freeman's laws.

Had'st thou but liv'd, though stripp'd
  of power,
A watchman on the lonely tower,
Thy thrilling trump had rous'd the
  land,
When fraud or danger were at hand ;
By thee, as by the beacon-light,
Our pilots had kept course aright ;
As some proud column, though alone,
Thy strength had propp'd the tottering
  throne :
Now is the stately column broke,
The beacon-light is quench'd in smoke,
The trumpet's silver sound is still,
The warder silent on the hill !

Oh think, how to his latest day,
When Death, just hovering, claim'd his
  prey,
With Palinure's unalter'd mood,
Firm at his dangerous post he stood ;
Each call for needful rest repell'd,
With dying hand the rudder held,
Till, in his fall, with fateful sway,
The steerage of the realm gave way !
Then, while on Britain's thousand
  plains,
One unpolluted church remains,
Whose peaceful bells ne'er sent around
The bloody tocsin's maddening sound,
But still, upon the hallow'd day,
Convoke the swains to praise and pray ;
While faith and civil peace are dear,
Grace this cold marble with a tear,—
He, who preserved them, PITT, lies
  here !

Nor yet suppress the generous sigh,
Because his rival slumbers nigh ;

Nor be thy *requiescat* dumb,
Lest it be said o'er Fox's tomb.
For talents mourn, untimely lost,
When best employ'd, and wanted
    most ;
Mourn genius high, and lore profound,
And wit that lov'd to play, not
    wound ;
And all the reasoning powers divine,
To penetrate, resolve, combine ;
And feelings keen, and fancy's
    glow,—
They sleep with him who sleeps
    below :
And, if thou mourn'st they could not
    save
From error him who owns this grave,
Be every harsher thought suppress'd,
And sacred be the last long rest.
Here, where the end of earthly things
Lays heroes, patriots, bards, and
    kings ;
Where stiff the hand, and still the
    tongue,
Of those who fought, and spoke, and
    sung ;
Here, where the fretted aisles prolong
The distant notes of holy song,
As if some angel spoke agen,
'All peace on earth, good-will to
    men ;'
If ever from an English heart,
O, *here* let prejudice depart,
And, partial feeling cast aside,
Record, that Fox a Briton died !
When Europe crouch'd to France's
    yoke,
And Austria bent, and Prussia broke,
And the firm Russian's purpose brave,
Was barter'd by a timorous slave,
Even then dishonour's peace he
    spurn'd,
The sullied olive-branch return'd,
Stood for his country's glory fast,
And nail'd her colours to the mast !
Heaven, to reward his firmness, gave
A portion in this honour'd grave,

And ne'er held marble in its trust
Of two such wondrous men the dust.

With more than mortal powers en-
    dow'd,
How high they soar'd above the
    crowd !
Theirs was no common party race,
Jostling by dark intrigue for place ;
Like fabled Gods, their mighty war
Shook realms and nations in its jar ;
Beneath each banner proud to stand,
Look'd up the noblest of the land,
Till through the British world were
    known
The names of Pitt and Fox alone.
Spells of such force no wizard grave
E'er fram'd in dark Thessalian cave,
Though his could drain the ocean dry,
And force the planets from the sky.
These spells are spent, and, spent with
    these,
The wine of life is on the lees ;
Genius, and taste, and talent gone,
For ever tomb'd beneath the stone,
Where—taming thought to human
    pride !—
The mighty chiefs sleep side by side.
Drop upon Fox's grave the tear,
'Twill trickle to his rival's bier ;
O'er Pitt's the mournful requiem
    sound,
And Fox's shall the notes rebound.
The solemn echo seems to cry,
'Here let their discord with them die.
Speak not for those a separate doom,
Whom Fate made Brothers in the
    tomb ;
But search the land of living men,
Where wilt thou find their like agen ?'

Rest, ardent Spirits ! till the cries
Of dying Nature bid you rise ;
Not even your Britain's groans can
    pierce
The leaden silence of your hearse ;
Then, O, how impotent and vain
This grateful tributary strain !

Though not unmark'd, from northern
    clime,
Ye heard the Border Minstrel's rhyme :
His Gothic harp has o'er you rung ;
The Bard you deign'd to praise, your
    deathless names has sung.

    Stay yet, illusion, stay a while,
My wilder'd fancy still beguile !
From this high theme how can I part,
Ere half unloaded is my heart !
For all the tears e'er sorrow drew
And all the raptures fancy knew,
And all the keener rush of blood,
That throbs through bard in bard-like
    mood,
Were here a tribute mean and low,
Though all their mingled streams
    could flow—
Woe, wonder, and sensation high,
In one spring-tide of ecstasy !
It will not be, it may not last,
The vision of enchantment 's past :
Like frostwork in the morning ray,
The fancied fabric melts away ;
Each Gothic arch, memorial-stone,
And long, dim, lofty aisle, are gone ;
And, lingering last, deception dear,
The choir's high sounds die on my
    ear.
Now slow return the lonely down,
The silent pastures bleak and brown,
The farm begirt with copsewood wild,
The gambols of each frolic child,
Mixing their shrill cries with the
    tone
Of Tweed's dark waters rushing on.

    Prompt on unequal tasks to run,
Thus Nature disciplines her son :
Meeter, she says, for me to stray,
And waste the solitary day,
In plucking from yon fen the reed,
And watch it floating down the
    Tweed ;
Or idly list the shrilling lay,
With which the milkmaid cheers her
    way,

Marking its cadence rise and fail,
As from the field, beneath her pail,
She trips it down the uneven dale :
Meeter for me, by yonder cairn,
The ancient shepherd's tale to learn
Though oft he stop in rustic fear,
Lest his old legends tire the ear
Of one, who, in his simple mind,
May boast of book-learn'd taste
    refin'd.

    But thou, my friend, can'st fitly tell,
(For few have read romance so well,)
How still the legendary lay
O'er poet's bosom holds its sway ;
How on the ancient minstrel strain
Time lays his palsied hand in vain ;
And how our hearts at doughty deeds,
By warriors wrought in steely weeds,
Still throb for fear and pity's sake ;
As when the Champion of the Lake
Enters Morgana's fated house,
Or, in the Chapel Perilous
Despising spells and demons' force,
Holds converse with the unburied
    corse ;
Or when, Dame Ganore's grace to
    move,
(Alas, that lawless was their love !)
He sought proud Tarquin in his den,
And freed full sixty knights ; or when,
A sinful man, and unconfess'd,
He took the Sangreal's holy quest,
And, slumbering. saw the vision high,
He might not view with waking eye.

    The mightiest chiefs of British song
Scorn'd not such legends to prolong :
They gleam through Spenser's elfin
    dream,
And mix in Milton's heavenly theme ;
And Dryden, in immortal strain,
Had raised the Table Round again,
But that a ribald King and Court
Bade him toil on, to make them sport;
Demanded for their niggard pay,
Fit for their souls, a looser lay,
Licentious satire, song, and play ;

The world defrauded of the high
    design,
Profan'd the God-given strength, and
    marr'd the lofty line.

Warm'd by such names, well may
    we then,
Though dwindled sons of little men,
Essay to break a feeble lance
In the fair fields of old romance;
Or seek the moated castle's cell,
Where long through talisman and spell,
While tyrants rul'd, and damsels wept,
Thy Genius, Chivalry, hath slept:
There sound the harpings of the North,
Till he awake and sally forth,
On venturous quest to prick again,
In all his arms, with all his train,
Shield, lance, and brand, and plume,
    and scarf,
Fay, giant, dragon, squire, and dwarf,
And wizard with his wand of might,
And errant maid on palfrey white.
Around the Genius weave their spells,
Pure Love, who scarce his passion tells;
Mystery, half veil'd and half reveal'd;
And Honour, with his spotless shield;
Attention, with fix'd eye; and Fear,
That loves the tale she shrinks to hear;
And gentle Courtesy; and Faith,
Unchanged by sufferings, time, or
    death;
And Valour, lion-mettled lord,
Leaning upon his own good sword.

Well has thy fair achievement shown,
A worthy meed may thus be won;
Ytene's oaks—beneath whose shade
Their theme the merry minstrels made,
Of Ascapart, and Bevis bold,
And that Red King, who, while of old,
Through Boldrewood the chase he led,
By his loved huntsman's arrow bled—
Ytene's oaks have heard again
Renew'd such legendary strain;
For thou hast sung, how He of Gaul,
That Amadis so famed in hall,

For Oriana, foil'd in fight
The Necromancer's felon might;
And well in modern verse hast wove
Partenopex's mystic love:
Hear, then, attentive to my lay,
A knightly tale of Albion's elder day.

—⊷—

Canto First.

The Castle.

I.

DAY set on Norham's castled steep,
And Tweed's fair river, broad and
    deep,
    And Cheviot's mountains lone:
The battled towers, the donjon keep,
The loophole grates, where captives
    weep,
The flanking walls that round it sweep,
    In yellow lustre shone.
The warriors on the turrets high,
Moving athwart the evening sky,
    Seem'd forms of giant height:
Their armour, as it caught the rays,
Flash'd back again the western blaze,
    In lines of dazzling light.

II.

St. George's banner, broad and gay,
Now faded, as the fading ray
    Less bright, and less, was flung;
The evening gale had scarce the power
To wave it on the Donjon Tower,
    So heavily it hung.
The scouts had parted on their search,
    The Castle gates were barr'd;
Above the gloomy portal arch,
Timing his footsteps to a march,
    The Warder kept his guard;
Low humming, as he paced along,
Some ancient Border gathering song.

III.

A distant trampling sound he hears;
He looks abroad, and soon appears

O'er Horncliff-hill a plump of spears
  Beneath a pennon gay;
A horseman, darting from the crowd,
Like lightning from a summer cloud,
Spurs on his mettled courser proud,
  Before the dark array.
Beneath the sable palisade,
That clos'd the Castle barricade,
  His bugle horn he blew;
The warder hasted from the wall,
And warn'd the Captain in the hall,
  For well the blast he knew;
And joyfully that knight did call,
To sewer, squire, and seneschal.

IV.

' Now broach ye a pipe of Malvoisie,
  Bring pasties of the doe,
And quickly make the entrance free,
And bid my heralds ready be,
And every minstrel sound his glee,
  And all our trumpets blow;
And, from the platform, spare ye not
To fire a noble salvo-shot;
  Lord MARMION waits below!'
Then to the Castle's lower ward
Sped forty yeomen tall,
The iron-studded gates unbarr'd,
Rais'd the portcullis' ponderous
    guard,
The lofty palisade unsparr'd
  And let the drawbridge fall.

V.

Along the bridge Lord Marmion rode,
Proudly his red-roan charger trode,
His helm hung at the saddlebow;
Well by his visage you might know
He was a stalworth knight, and keen,
And had in many a battle been;
The scar on his brown cheek reveal'd
A token true of Bosworth field;
His eyebrow dark, and eye of fire,
Show'd spirit proud, and prompt to
    ire;
Yet lines of thought upon his cheek
Did deep design and counsel speak·

His forehead, by his casque worn bare,
His thick mustache, and curly hair,
Coal-black, and grizzled here and
    there,
  But more through toil than age;
His square-turn'd joints, and strength
    of limb,
Show'd him no carpet knight so trim,
But in close fight a champion grim,
  In camps a leader sage.

VI.

Well was he arm'd from head to heel,
In mail and plate of Milan steel;
But his strong helm, of mighty cost,
Was all with burnish'd gold emboss'd;
Amid the plumage of the crest,
A falcon hover'd on her nest,
With wings outspread, and forward
    breast;
E'en such a falcon, on his shield,
Soar'd sable in an azure field:
The golden legend bore aright,
𝔚𝔥𝔬 𝔠𝔥𝔢𝔠𝔨𝔰 𝔞𝔱 𝔪𝔢, 𝔱𝔬 𝔡𝔢𝔞𝔱𝔥 𝔦𝔰 𝔡𝔦𝔤𝔥𝔱.
Blue was the charger's broider'd rein;
Blue ribbons deck'd his arching mane;
The knightly housing's ample fold
Was velvet blue, and trapp'd with gold.

VII.

Behind him rode two gallant squires,
Of noble name, and knightly sires;
They burn'd the gilded spurs to claim;
For well could each a war-horse tame,
Could draw the bow, the sword could
    sway,
And lightly bear the ring away;
Nor less with courteous precepts
    stor'd,
Could dance in hall, and carve at
    board,
And frame love-ditties passing rare,
And sing them to a lady fair.

VIII.

Four men-at-arms came at their backs,
With halbert, bill, and battle-axe:

They bore Lord Marmion's lance so
 strong,
And led his sumpter-mules along,
And ambling palfrey, when at need
Him listed ease his battle-steed.
The last and trustiest of the four,
On high his forky pennon bore;
Like swallow's tail, in shape and hue,
Flutter'd the streamer glossy blue,
Where, blazon'd sable, as before,
The towering falcon seem'd to soar.
Last, twenty yeomen, two and two,
In hosen black, and jerkins blue,
With falcons broider'd on each breast,
Attended on their lord's behest.
Each, chosen for an archer good,
Knew hunting-craft by lake or wood;
Each one a six-foot bow could bend,
And far a cloth-yard shaft could send;
Each held a boar-spear tough and
 strong,
And at their belts their quivers rung.
Their dusty palfreys and array
Show'd they had march'd a weary way.

IX.

'Tis meet that I should tell you now,
How fairly arm'd, and order'd how,
 The soldiers of the guard,
With musket, pike, and morion,
To welcome noble Marmion,
 Stood in the Castle-yard:
Minstrels and trumpeters were there;
The gunner held his linstock yare,
 For welcome-shot prepar'd:
Enter'd the train, and such a clang,
As then through all his turrets rang,
 Old Norham never heard.

X.

The guards their morrice-pikes ad-
 vanc'd,
The trumpets flourish'd brave,
The cannon from the ramparts glanc'd,
 And thundering welcome gave.
A blithe salute, in martial sort,
 The minstrels well might sound,

For, as Lord Marmion cross'd the court,
 He scatter'd angels round.
'Welcome to Norham, Marmion!
 Stout heart, and open hand!
Well dost thou brook thy gallant roan,
 Thou flower of English land!'

XI.

Two pursuivants, whom tabarts deck,
With silver scutcheon round their
 neck,
 Stood on the steps of stone
By which you reach the donjon gate,
And there, with herald pomp and state,
 They hail'd Lord Marmion:
They hail'd him Lord of Fontenaye,
Of Lutterward, and Scrivelbaye,
 Of Tamworth tower and town;
And he, their courtesy to requite,
Gave them a chain of twelve marks'
 weight,
 All as he lighted down.
'Now, largesse, largesse, Lord Mar-
 mion,
 Knight of the crest of gold!
A blazon'd shield, in battle won,
 Ne'er guarded heart so bold.'

XII.

They marshall'd him to the Castle-hall,
 Where the guests stood all aside,
And loudly flourish'd the trumpet-call,
 And the heralds loudly cried,
'Room, lordings, room for Lord Mar-
 mion
 With the crest and helm of gold!
Full well we know the trophies won
 In the lists at Cottiswold:
There, vainly Ralph de Wilton strove
 'Gainst Marmion's force to stand;
To him he lost his lady-love,
 And to the King his land.
Ourselves beheld the listed field,
 A sight both sad and fair;
We saw Lord Marmion pierce his
 shield,
 And saw his saddle bare;

We saw the victor win the crest
   He wears with worthy pride ;
And on the gibbet-tree, revers'd,
   His foeman's scutcheon tied.
Place, nobles, for the Falcon-Knight !
   Room, room, ye gentles gay,
For him who conquer'd in the right,
   Marmion of Fontenaye !'

XIII.

Then stepp'd to meet that noble Lord,
   Sir Hugh the Heron bold,
Baron of Twisell, and of Ford,
   And Captain of the Hold.
He led Lord Marmion to the deas,
   Rais'd o'er the pavement high,
And plac'd him in the upper place :
   They feasted full and high :
The whiles a Northern harper rude
Chanted a rhyme of deadly feud,
   'How the fierce Thirwalls, and Rid-
      leys all,
      Stout Willimondswick,
      And Hardriding Dick,
   And Hughie of Hawdon, and Will o'
      the Wall,
   Have set on Sir Albany Featherston-
      haugh,
   And taken his life at the Deadman's-
      shaw.'
Scantly Lord Marmion's ear could
      brook
   The harper's barbarous lay ;
Yet much he prais'd the pains he took,
   And well those pains did pay :
For lady's suit, and minstrel's strain,
By knight should ne'er be heard in
      vain.

XIV.

'Now, good Lord Marmion,' Heron
      says,
   ' Of your fair courtesy,
I pray you bide some little space
   In this poor tower with me.
Here you may keep your arms from
      rust,
   May breathe your war-horse well ;

Seldom hath pass'd a week but giust
   Or feat of arms befell :
The Scots can rein a mettled steed,
   And love to couch a spear ;
Saint George ! a stirring life they lead,
   That have such neighbours near.
Then stay with us a little space,
   Our northern wars to learn ;
I pray you, for your lady's grace !'
   Lord Marmion's brow grew stern.

XV.

The Captain mark'd his alter'd look,
   And gave a squire the sign ;
A mighty wassail-bowl he took,
   And crown'd it high with wine.
'Now pledge me here, Lord Marmion :
   But first I pray thee fair,
Where hast thou left that page of thine,
That us'd to serve thy cup of wine,
   Whose beauty was so rare ?
When last in Raby towers we met,
   The boy I closely eyed,
And often mark'd his cheeks were wet,
   With tears he fain would hide :
His was no rugged horse-boy's hand,
To burnish shield or sharpen brand,
   Or saddle battle-steed ;
But meeter seem'd for lady fair,
To fan her cheek, or curl her hair,
Or through embroidery, rich and rare,
   The slender silk to lead :
His skin was fair, his ringlets gold,
   His bosom—when he sigh'd,
The russet doublet's rugged fold
   Could scarce repel its pride !
Say, hast thou given that lovely youth
   To serve in lady's bower ?
Or was the gentle page, in sooth,
   A gentle paramour ? '

XVI.

Lord Marmion ill could brook such
      jest ;
   He roll'd his kindling eye,
With pain his rising wrath suppress'd,
   Yet made a calm reply :

'That boy thou thought'st so goodly
          fair,
He might not brook the northern air.
More of his fate if thou wouldst learn,
I left him sick in Lindisfarn:
Enough of him. But, Heron, say,
Why does thy lovely lady gay
Disdain to grace the hall to-day?
Or has that dame, so fair and sage,
Gone on some pious pilgrimage?'
He spoke in covert scorn, for fame
Whisper'd light tales of Heron's dame.

XVII.

Unmark'd, at least unreck'd, the taunt,
     Careless the Knight replied,
'No bird, whose feathers gaily flaunt,
     Delights in cage to bide:
Norham is grim and grated close,
Hemm'd in by battlement and fosse,
     And many a darksome tower;
And better loves my lady bright
To sit in liberty and light,
     In fair Queen Margaret's bower.
We hold our greyhound in our hand,
     Our falcon on our glove;
But where shall we find leash or
          band
     For dame that loves to rove?
Let the wild falcon soar her swing,
She'll stoop when she has tir'd her
          wing.'

XVIII.

'Nay, if with Royal James's bride
The lovely Lady Heron bide,
Behold me here a messenger,
Your tender greetings prompt to bear;
For, to the Scottish court address'd,
I journey at our King's behest,
And pray you, of your grace, provide
For me, and mine, a trusty guide.
I have not ridden in Scotland since
James back'd the cause of that mock
          prince,
Warbeck, that Flemish counterfeit,
Who on the gibbet paid the cheat.

Then did I march with Surrey's
          power,
What time we raz'd old Ayton
          tower.'

XIX.

'For such-like need, my lord, I trow,
Norham can find you guides enow;
For here be some have prick'd as far,
On Scottish ground, as to Dunbar;
Have drunk the monks of St. Bothan's
          ale,
And driven the beeves of Lauderdale;
Harried the wives of Greenlaw's goods,
And given them light to set their
          hoods.'

XX.

'Now, in good sooth,' Lord Marmion
          cried,
'Were I in warlike wise to ride,
A better guard I would not lack,
Than your stout forayers at my back;
But, as in form of peace I go,
A friendly messenger, to know
Why through all Scotland, near and
          far,
Their King is mustering troops for
          war,
The sight of plundering Border spears
Might justify suspicious fears,
And deadly feud, or thirst of spoil,
Break out in some unseemly broil:
A herald were my fitting place;
Or friar, sworn in peace to bide;
Or pardoner, or travelling priest,
Or strolling pilgrim, at the least'

XXI.

The Captain mus'd a little space,
And pass'd his hand across his face:
'Fain would I find the guide you want,
But ill may spare a pursuivant,
The only men that safe can ride
Mine errands on the Scottish side:
And though a bishop built this fort,
Few holy brethren here resort;
Even our good chaplain, as I ween,
Since our last siege, we have not seen:

The mass he might not sing or say
Upon one stinted meal a·day ;
So, safe he sat in Durham aisle,
And pray'd for our success the while.
Our Norham vicar, woe betide,
Is all too well in case to ride ;
The priest of Shoreswood—he could
    rein
The wildest war-horse in your train ;
But then, no spearman in the hall
Will sooner swear, or stab, or brawl.
Friar John of Tillmouth were the man :
A blithesome brother at the can,
A welcome guest in hall and bower,
He knows each castle, town, and tower,
In which the wine and ale is good,
'Twixt Newcastle and Holy-Rood.
But that good man, as ill befalls,
Hath seldom left our castle walls,
Since, on the vigil of St. Bede,
In evil hour, he cross'd the Tweed,
To teach Dame Alison her creed.
Old Bughtrig found him with his wife ;
And John, an enemy to strife,
Sans frock and hood, fled for his life.
The jealous churl hath deeply swore
That, if again he venture o'er,
He shall shrieve penitent no more.
Little he loves such risks, I know ;
Yet, in your guard, perchance will go.

XXII.

Young Selby, at the fair hall-board,
Carv'd to his uncle and that lord,
And reverently took up the word :
' Kind uncle, woe were we each one,
If harm should hap to brother John.
He is a man of mirthful speech,
Can many a game and gambol teach ;
Full well at tables can he play,
And sweep at bowls the stake away.
None can a lustier carol bawl,
The needfullest among us all,
When time hangs heavy in the hall,
And snow comes thick at Christmastide,
And we can neither hunt, nor ride
A foray on the Scottish side.

The vow'd revenge of Bughtrig rude,
May end in worse than loss of hood.
Let Friar John, in safety, still
In chimney-corner snore his fill,
Roast hissing crabs, or flagons swill :
Last night, to Norham there came one,
Will better guide Lord Marmion.'
' Nephew,' quoth Heron, ' by my fay,
Well hast thou spoke ; say forth thy
    say.'

XXIII.

' Here is a holy Palmer come,
From Salem first, and last from Rome ;
One that hath kiss'd the blessed tomb,
And visited each holy shrine
In Araby and Palestine ;
On hills of Armenie hath been,
Where Noah's ark may yet be seen ;
By that Red Sea, too, hath he trod,
Which parted at the prophet's rod ;
In Sinai's wilderness he saw
The Mount, where Israel heard the
    law,
'Mid thunder-dint, and flashing levin,
And shadows, mists, and darkness,
    given.
He shows Saint James's cockle-shell ;
Of fair Montserrat, too, can tell ;
    And of that Grot where olives nod,
Where, darling of each heart and eye,
From all the youth of Sicily
    Saint Rosalie retired to God.

XXIV.

' To stout Saint George of Norwich
    merry,
Saint Thomas, too, of Canterbury,
Cuthbert of Durham and Saint Bede,
For his sins' pardon hath he pray'd.
He knows the passes of the North,
And seeks far shrines beyond the
    Forth ;
Little he eats, and long will wake,
And drinks but of the stream or lake.
This were a guide o'er moor and dale ;
But, when our John hath quaff'd his
    ale,

As little as the wind that blows,
And warms itself against his nose,
Kens he, or cares, which way he
    goes.'

XXV.

'Gramercy!' quoth Lord Marmion,
'Full loth were I, that Friar John,
That venerable man, for me,
Were placed in fear or jeopardy.
If this same Palmer will me lead
    From hence to Holy-Rood,
Like his good saint, I'll pay his meed,
Instead of cockle-shell, or bead,
    With angels fair and good.
I love such holy ramblers; still
They know to charm a weary hill,
    With song, romance, or lay:
Some jovial tale, or glee, or jest,
Some lying legend, at the least,
    They bring to cheer the way.'

XXVI.

'Ah! noble sir,' young Selby said,
And finger on his lip he laid,
'This man knows much, perchance
    e'en more
Than he could learn by holy lore.
Still to himself he's muttering,
And shrinks as at some unseen thing.
Last night we listen'd at his cell;
Strange sounds we heard, and, sooth
    to tell,
He murmur'd on till morn, howe'er
No living mortal could be near.
Sometimes I thought I heard it plain,
As other voices spoke again.
I cannot tell; I like it not;
Friar John hath told us it is wrote
No conscience clear and void of wrong
Can rest awake and pray so long.
Himself still sleeps before his beads
Have mark'd ten aves, and two
    creeds.'

XXVII.

'Let pass,' quoth Marmion; 'by my
    fay,
This man shall guide me on my way,

Although the great arch-fiend and he
Had sworn themselves of company.
So please you, gentle youth, to call
This Palmer to the Castle-hall.'
The summon'd Palmer came in place;
His sable cowl o'erhung his face;
In his black mantle was he clad,
With Peter's keys, in cloth of red,
    On his broad shoulders wrought;
The scallop shell his cap did deck;
The crucifix around his neck
    Was from Loretto brought;
His sandals were with travel tore;
Staff, budget, bottle, scrip, he wore;
The faded palm-branch in his hand
Show'd pilgrim from the Holy Land.

XXVIII.

Whenas the Palmer came in hall,
Nor lord, nor knight, was there more
    tall,
Or had a statelier step withal,
    Or look'd more high and keen;
For no saluting did he wait,
But strode across the hall of state.
And fronted Marmion where he sate,
    As he his peer had been.
But his gaunt frame was worn with
    toil;
His cheek was sunk, alas the while!
And when he struggled at a smile,
    His eye look'd haggard wild:
Poor wretch! the mother that him
    bare,
If she had been in presence there,
In his wan face, and sun-burn'd hair,
    She had not known her child.
Danger, long travel, want, or woe,
Soon change the form that best we
    know;
For deadly fear can time outgo,
    And blanch at once the hair;
Hard toil can roughen form and face,
And want can quench the eye's bright
    grace,
Nor does old age a wrinkle trace
    More deeply than despair.

Happy whom none of these befall,
But this poor Palmer knew them all.

XXIX.

Lord Marmion then his boon did ask ;
The Palmer took on him the task,
So he would march with morning tide,
To Scottish court to be his guide.
' But I have solemn vows to pay,
And may not linger by the way,
   To fair St. Andrews bound,
Within the ocean-cave to pray,
Where good Saint Rule his holy lay,
From midnight to the dawn of day,
   Sung to the billows' sound ;
Thence to Saint Fillan's blessed well,
Whose spring can frenzied dreams
   dispel,
   And the craz'd brain restore :
Saint Mary grant that cave or spring
Could back to peace my bosom bring,
   Or bid it throb no more ! '

XXX.

And now the midnight draught of
   sleep,
Where wine and spices richly steep,
In massive bowl of silver deep,
   The page presents on knee.
Lord Marmion drank a fair good rest,
The Captain pledg'd his noble guest,
The cup went through among the rest,
   Who drain'd it merrily ;
Alone the Palmer pass'd it by,
Though Selby press'd him courteously.
This was a sign the feast was o'er ;
It hush'd the merry wassail roar,
   The minstrels ceas'd to sound.
Soon in the castle nought was heard,
But the slow footstep of the guard,
   Pacing his sober round.

XXXI.

With early dawn Lord Marmion rose :
And first the chapel doors unclose ;
Then, after morning rites were done
(A hasty mass from Friar John)

And knight and squire had broke their
   fast
On rich substantial repast,
Lord Marmion's bugles blew to horse ;
Then came the stirrup-cup in course :
Between the Baron and his host
No point of courtesy was lost ;
High thanks were by Lord Marmion
   paid,
Solemn excuse the Captain made,
Till, filing from the gate, had pass'd
That noble train, their Lord the last.
Then loudly rung the trumpet call ;
Thunder'd the cannon from the wall,
   And shook the Scottish shore ;
Around the castle eddied slow,
Volumes of smoke as white as snow,
   And hid its turrets hoar ;
Till they roll'd forth upon the air,
And met the river breezes there,
Which gave again the prospect fair.

—++—

INTRODUCTION TO CANTO SECOND.

TO THE

REV. JOHN MARRIOTT, A.M.

Ashestiel, Ettrick Forest.

THE scenes are desert now, and bare,
Where flourish'd once a forest fair,
When these waste glens with copse
   were lin'd,
And peopled with the hart and hind.
Yon Thorn—perchance whose prickly
   spears
Have fenc'd him for three hundred
   years,
While fell around his green com-
   peers—
Yon lonely Thorn, would he could tell
The changes of his parent dell,
Since he, so grey and stubborn now,
Wav'd in each breeze a sapling bough;

Would he could tell how deep the shade
A thousand mingled branches made;
How broad the shadows of the oak,
How clung the rowan to the rock,
And through the foliage show'd his
    head,
With narrow leaves and berries red;
What pines on every mountain sprung,
O'er every dell what birches hung,
In every breeze what aspens shook,
What alders shaded every brook!

' Here, in my shade,' methinks he 'd
    say,
'The mighty stag at noontide lay:
The wolf I 've seen, a fiercer game,
(The neighbouring dingle bears his
    name,)
With lurching step around me prowl,
And stop, against the moon to howl;
The mountain-boar, on battle set,
His tusks upon my stem would whet;
While doe, and roe, and red-deer good,
Have bounded by, through gay green-
    wood.
Then oft, from Newark's riven tower,
Sallied a Scottish monarch's power:
A thousand vassals muster'd round
With horse, and hawk, and horn, and
    hound;
And I might see the youth intent
Guard every pass with crossbow bent;
And through the brake the rangers
    stalk,
And falc'ners hold the ready hawk;
And foresters, in greenwood trim,
Lead in the leash the gazehounds grim,
Attentive, as the bratchet's bay
From the dark covert drove the prey,
To slip them as he broke away.
The startled quarry bounds amain,
As fast the gallant greyhounds strain;
Whistles the arrow from the bow,
Answers the harquebuss below;
While all the rocking hills reply
To hoof-clang, hound, and hunters' cry,
And bugles ringing lightsomely.'

Of such proud huntings, many tales
Yet linger in our lonely dales,
Up pathless Ettrick and on Yarrow,
Where erst the outlaw drew his arrow.
But not more blithe that silvan court,
Than we have been at humbler sport;
Though small our pomp, and mean
    our game,
Our mirth, dear Marriott, was the same.
Remember'st thou my greyhounds
    true?
O'er holt or hill there never flew,
From slip or leash there never sprang,
More fleet of foot, or sure of fang.
Nor dull, between each merry chase,
Pass'd by the intermitted space;
For we had fair resource in store,
In Classic and in Gothic lore:
We mark'd each memorable scene,
And held poetic talk between;
Nor hill nor brook we pac'd along,
But had its legend or its song.
All silent now—for now are still
Thy bowers, untenanted Bowhill!
No longer, from thy mountains dun,
The yeoman hears the well-known
    gun,
And while his honest heart glows
    warm,
At thought of his paternal farm,
Round to his mates a brimmer fills,
And drinks 'The Chieftain of the
    Hills!'
No fairy forms, in Yarrow's bowers,
Trip o'er the walks, or tend the flowers,
Fair as the elves whom Janet saw
By moonlight dance on Carterhaugh;
No youthful Baron 's left to grace
The Forest-Sheriff's lonely chase,
And ape, in manly step and tone,
The majesty of Oberon:
And she is gone, whose lovely face
Is but her least and lowest grace;
Though, if to Sylphid Queen 'twere
    given
To show our earth the charms of
    Heaven,

She could not glide along the air
With form more light, or face more fair.
No more the widow's deafen'd ear
Grows quick that lady's step to hear:
At noontide she expects her not,
Nor busies her to trim the cot;
Pensive she turns her humming wheel,
Or pensive cooks her orphans' meal;
Yet blesses. ere she deals their bread,
The gentle hand by which they're fed.

From Yair—which hills so closely
    bind,
Scarce can the Tweed his passage find,
Though much he fret and chafe and
    toil
Till all his eddying currents boil,—
Her long-descended lord has gone,
And left us by the stream alone.
And much I miss those sportive boys,
Companions of my mountain joys,
Just at the age 'twixt boy and youth,
When thought is speech, and speech
    is truth.
Close to my side, with what delight
They press'd to hear of Wallace wight,
When, pointing to his airy mound,
I call'd his ramparts holy ground!
Kindled their brows to hear me speak;
And I have smiled, to feel my cheek,
Despite the difference of our years,
Return again the glow of theirs,
Ah, happy boys! such feelings pure,
They will not, cannot, long endure;
Condemn'd to stem the world's rude
    tide,
You may not linger by the side;
For Fate shall thrust you from the
    shore,
And Passion ply the sail and oar.
Yet cherish the remembrance still,
Of the lone mountain, and the rill;
For trust, dear boys, the time will
    come,
When fiercer transport shall be dumb,
And you will think right frequently,
But, well I hope, without a sigh,

On the free hours that we have spent
Together on the brown hill's bent.

When, musing on companions gone,
We doubly feel ourselves alone,
Something, my friend, we yet may gain;
There is a pleasure in this pain:
It soothes the love of lonely rest,
Deep in each gentler heart impress'd.
'Tis silent amid worldly toils,
And stifled soon by mental broils;
But, in a bosom thus prepar'd,
Its still small voice is often heard,
Whispering a mingled sentiment,
'Twixt resignation and content.
Oft in my mind such thoughts awake,
By lone Saint Mary's silent lake;
Thou know'st it well,—nor fen, nor
    sedge,
Pollute the pure lake's crystal edge;
Abrupt and sheer, the mountains sink
At once upon the level brink;
And just a trace of silver sand
Marks where the water meets the land.
Far in the mirror, bright and blue,
Each hill's huge outline you may view;
Shaggy with heath, but lonely bare,
Nor tree, nor bush, nor brake, is there,
Save where, of land, yon slender line
Bears thwart the lake the scatter'd pine.
Yet even this nakedness has power,
And aids the feeling of the hour:
Nor thicket, dell, nor copse you spy,
Where living thing conceal'd might lie;
Nor point, retiring, hides a dell,
Where swain, or woodman lone,
    might dwell;
There's nothing left to fancy's guess,
You see that all is loneliness:
And silence aids—though the steep
    hills
Send to the lake a thousand rills;
In summer tide, so soft they weep,
The sound but lulls the ear asleep;
Your horse's hoof-tread sounds too
    rude,
So stilly is the solitude.

Nought living meets the eye or ear,
But well I ween the dead are near;
For though, in feudal strife, a foe
Hath laid Our Lady's chapel low,
Yet still, beneath the hallow'd soil,
The peasant rests him from his toil,
And, dying, bids his bones be laid,
Where erst his simple fathers pray'd.

If age had tamed the passions' strife,
And fate had cut my ties to life,
Here, have I thought, 'twere sweet to
    dwell,
And rear again the chaplain's cell,
Like that same peaceful hermitage,
Where Milton long'd to spend his age.
'Twere sweet to mark the setting day
On Bourhope's lonely top decay;
And, as it faint and feeble died
On the broad lake, and mountain's
    side,
To say 'Thus pleasures fade away;
Youth, talents, beauty, thus decay,
And leave us dark, forlorn, and grey;'
Then gaze on Dryhope's ruin'd tower,
And think on Yarrow's faded Flower:
And when that mountain-sound I
    heard,
Which bids us be for storm prepar'd,
The distant rustling of his wings,
As up his force the Tempest brings,
'Twere sweet, ere yet his terrors rave,
To sit upon the Wizard's grave,
That Wizard Priest's, whose bones
    are thrust
From company of holy dust,
On which no sunbeam ever shines
(So superstition's creed divines),
Thence view the lake with sullen roar
Heave her broad billows to the shore;
And mark the wild-swans mount the
    gale,
Spread wide through mist their snowy
    sail,
And ever stoop again to lave
Their bosoms on the surging wave:
Then, when against the driving hail
No longer might my plaid avail,

Back to my lonely home retire,
And light my lamp, and trim my fire;
There ponder o'er some mystic lay,
Till the wild tale had all its sway,
And, in the bittern's distant shriek,
I heard unearthly voices speak,
And thought the Wizard Priest was
    come,
To claim again his ancient home!
And bade my busy fancy range,
To frame him fitting shape and strange,
Till from the task my brow I clear'd,
And smil'd to think that I had fear'd.

But chief 'twere sweet to think
    such life
(Though but escape from fortune's
    strife)
Something most matchless, good and
    wise,
A great and grateful sacrifice;
And deem each hour to musing given,
A step upon the road to heaven.

Yet him, whose heart is ill at ease,
Such peaceful solitudes displease:
He loves to drown his bosom's jar
Amid the elemental war:
And my black Palmer's choice had been
Some ruder and more savage scene,
Like that which frowns round dark
    Loch-skene.
There eagles scream from isle to shore;
Down all the rocks the torrents roar;
O'er the black waves incessant driven,
Dark mists infect the summer heaven;
Through the rude barriers of the lake,
Away its hurrying waters break,
Faster and whiter dash and curl,
Till down yon dark abyss they hurl.
Rises the fog-smoke white as snow,
Thunders the viewless stream below,
Diving, as if condemn'd to lave
Some demon's subterranean cave,
Who, prison'd by enchanter's spell,
Shakes the dark rock with groan and
    yell.

And well that Palmer's form and mien
Had suited with the stormy scene,
Just on the edge, straining his ken
To view the bottom of the den,
Where, deep deep down, and far
     within,
Toils with the rocks the roaring linn ;
Then, issuing forth one foamy wave,
And wheeling round the Giant's Grave,
White as the snowy charger's tail,
Drives down the pass of Moffatdale.

Marriott, thy harp, on Isis strung,
To many a Border theme has rung :
Then list to me, and thou shalt know
Of this mysterious man of woe.

Canto Second

The Convent.

I.

THE breeze, which swept away the
     smoke
     Round Norham Castle roll'd,
When all the loud artillery spoke,
With lightning-flash, and thunder-
     stroke,
     As Marmion left the Hold,—
It curl'd not Tweed alone, that breeze,
For, far upon Northumbrian seas,
     It freshly blew, and strong,
Where, from high Whitby's cloister'd
     pile,
Bound to Saint Cuthbert's Holy Isle,
     It bore a bark along.
Upon the gale she stoop'd her side,
And bounded o'er the swelling tide,
     As she were dancing home :
The merry seamen laugh'd to see
Their gallant ship so lustily
     Furrow the green sea-foam.
Much joy'd they in their honour'd
     freight ;
For, on the deck, in chair of state,

The Abbess of Saint Hilda plac'd,
With five fair nuns, the galley grac'd.

II.

'Twas sweet to see these holy maids,
Like birds escaped to greenwood
     shades,
     Their first flight from the cage,
How timid, and how curious too,
For all to them was strange and new,
And all the common sights they view
     Their wonderment engage.
One eyed the shrouds and swelling sail,
     With many a benedicite ;
One at the rippling surge grew pale,
     And would for terror pray ;
Then shriek'd, because the sea-dog,
     nigh,
His round black head, and sparkling
     eye,
     Rear'd o'er the foaming spray ;
And one would still adjust her veil,
Disorder'd by the summer gale,
Perchance lest some more worldly eye
Her dedicated charms might spy ;
Perchance, because such action grac'd
Her fair-turn'd arm and slender waist.
Light was each simple bosom there,
Save two, who ill might pleasure share,
The Abbess and the Novice Clare.

III.

The Abbess was of noble blood,
But early took the veil and hood,
Ere upon life she cast a look,
Or knew the world that she forsook.
Fair too she was, and kind had been
As she was fair, but ne'er had seen
For her a timid lover sigh,
Nor knew the influence of her eye.
Love, to her ear, was but a name,
Combined with vanity and shame ;
Her hopes, her fears, her joys, were all
Bounded within the cloister wall :
The deadliest sin her mind could reach,
Was of monastic rule the breach ;
And her ambition's highest aim
To emulate Saint Hilda's fame.

For this she gave her ample dower,
To raise the convent's eastern tower ;
For this, with carving rare and quaint,
She deck'd the chapel of the saint,
And gave the relic-shrine of cost,
With ivory and gems emboss'd.
The poor her Convent's bounty blest,
The pilgrim in its halls found rest.

IV.

Black was her garb, her rigid rule
Reform'd on Benedictine school ;
Her cheek was pale, her form was
　　spare ;
Vigils, and penitence austere,
Had early quench'd the light of youth,
But gentle was the dame, in sooth ;
Though, vain of her religious sway,
She loved to see her maids obey,
Yet nothing stern was she in cell,
And the nuns loved their Abbess well.
Sad was this voyage to the dame :
Summon'd to Lindisfarne, she came,
There, with Saint Cuthbert's Abbot old,
And Tynemouth's Prioress, to hold
A chapter of Saint Benedict
For inquisition stern and strict
On two apostates from the faith,
And, if need were, to doom to death.

V.

Nought say I here of Sister Clare,
Save this, that she was young and fair ;
As yet a novice unprofess'd,
Lovely and gentle, but distress'd.
She was betroth'd to one now dead,
Or worse, who had dishonour'd fled.
Her kinsmen bade her give her hand
To one, who lov'd her for her land :
Herself, almost heart-broken now,
Was bent to take the vestal vow,
And shroud, within Saint Hilda's
　　gloom,
Her blasted hopes and wither'd bloom.

VI.

She sate upon the galley's prow,
And seem'd to mark the waves below ;
Nay, seem'd, so fix'd her look and eye,
To count them as they glided by.
She saw them not—'twas seeming
　　all ;
Far other scene her thoughts recall,—
A sun-scorch'd desert, waste and bare,
Nor waves, nor breezes, murmur'd
　　there ;
There saw she where some careless
　　hand
O'er a dead corpse had heap'd the
　　sand
To hide it—till the jackals come
To tear it from the scanty tomb.
See what a woful look was given
As she raised up her eyes to heaven !

VII.

Lovely, and gentle, and distress'd—
These charms might tame the fiercest
　　breast :
Harpers have sung, and poets told,
That he, in fury uncontroll'd,
The shaggy monarch of the wood,
Before a virgin, fair and good,
Hath pacified his savage mood.
But passions in the human frame
Oft put the lion's rage to shame :
And jealousy, by dark intrigue,
With sordid avarice in league,
Had practis'd with their bowl and
　　knife
Against the mourner's harmless life.
This crime was charg'd 'gainst those
　　who lay
Prison'd in Cuthbert's islet grey.

VIII.

And now the vessel skirts the strand
Of mountainous Northumberland ;
Towns, towers, and halls, successive
　　rise,
And catch the nuns' delighted eyes.
Monk-Wearmouth soon behind them
　　lay,
And Tynemouth's priory and bay ;
They mark'd, amid her trees, the hall
Of lofty Seaton-Delaval ;

They saw the Blythe and Wansbeck
    floods
Rush to the sea through sounding
    woods;
They pass'd the tower of Widdering-
    ton,
Mother of many a valiant son;
At Coquet-isle their beads they tell
To the good Saint who own'd the cell;
Then did the Alne attention claim,
And Warkworth, proud of Percy's
    name;
And next, they cross'd themselves, to
    hear
The whitening breakers sound so near,
Where, boiling through the rocks,
    they roar,
On Dunstanborough's cavern'd shore;
Thy tower, proud Bamborough, mark'd
    they there,
King Ida's castle, huge and square,
From its tall rock look grimly down,
And on the swelling ocean frown;
Then from the coast they bore away,
And reach'd the Holy Island's bay.

IX.

The tide did now its flood-mark gain,
And girdled in the Saint's domain:
For, with the flow and ebb, its style
Varies from continent to isle;
Dry shod, o'er sands, twice every day,
The pilgrims to the shrine find way;
Twice every day, the waves efface
Of staves and sandall'd feet the trace.
As to the port the galley flew,
Higher and higher rose to view
The Castle with its battled walls,
The ancient Monastery's halls,
A solemn, huge, and dark-red pile,
Plac'd on the margin of the isle.

X.

In Saxon strength that Abbey frown'd,
With massive arches broad and round,
    That rose alternate, row and row,
    On ponderous columns, short and
      low,

    Built ere the art was known,
    By pointed aisle, and shafted stalk,
    The arcades of an alley'd walk
      To emulate in stone.
On the deep walls, the heathen Dane
Had pour'd his impious rage in vain;
And needful was such strength to these
Expos'd to the tempestuous seas,
Scourg'd by the winds' eternal sway,
Open to rovers fierce as they,
Which could twelve hundred years
    withstand
Winds, waves, and northern pirates'
    hand.
Not but that portions of the pile,
Rebuilded in a later style,
Show'd where the spoiler's hand had
    been;
Not but the wasting sea-breeze keen
Had worn the pillar's carving quaint,
And moulder'd in his niche the saint,
And rounded, with consuming power,
The pointed angles of each tower;
Yet still entire the Abbey stood,
Like veteran, worn, but unsubdu'd.

XI.

Soon as they near'd his turrets strong,
The maidens rais'd Saint Hilda's song,
    And with the sea-wave and the wind,
    Their voices, sweetly shrill, com-
      bin'd,
    And made harmonious close;
    Then, answering from the sandy
      shore,
    Half-drown'd amid the breakers'
      roar,
    According chorus rose:
Down to the haven of the Isle,
The monks and nuns in order file,
    From Cuthbert's cloisters grim;
Banner, and cross, and relics there,
To meet Saint Hilda's maids, they bare;
And, as they caught the sounds on air,
    They echo'd back the hymn.
The islanders, in joyous mood,
Rush'd emulously through the flood,

To hale the bark to land;
Conspicuous by her veil and hood,
Signing the cross, the Abbess stood,
And bless'd them with her hand.

XII.

Suppose we now the welcome said,
Suppose the Convent banquet made :
All through the holy dome,
Through cloister, aisle, and gallery,
Wherever vestal maid might pry,
Nor risk to meet unhallow'd eye,
The stranger sisters roam,—
Till fell the evening damp with dew,
And the sharp sea-breeze coldly blew,
For there, even summer night is chill.
Then, having stray'd and gaz'd their
fill,
They clos'd around the fire ;
And all, in turn, essay'd to paint
The rival merits of their saint,
A theme that ne'er can tire
A holy maid ; for, be it known,
That their saint's honour is their own.

XIII.

Then Whitby's nuns exulting told,
How to their house three Barons bold
Must menial service do ;
While horns blow out a note of shame,
And monks cry ' Fye upon your name !
In wrath, for loss of silvan game,
Saint Hilda's priest ye slew.'—
'This, on Ascension-day, each year,
While labouring on our harbour-pier,
Must Herbert, Bruce, and Percy
hear.'
They told how in their convent-cell
A Saxon princess once did dwell,
The lovely Edelfled ;
And how, of thousand snakes, each one
Was chang'd into a coil of stone,
When holy Hilda pray'd ;
Themselves, within their holy bound,
Their stony folds had often found.
They told how sea-fowls' pinions fail,
As over Whitby's towers they sail,

And, sinking down, with flutterings
faint,
They do their homage to the saint.

XIV.

Nor did Saint Cuthbert's daughters fail
To vie with these in holy tale ;
His body's resting-place, of old,
How oft their patron chang'd, they
told ;
How, when the rude Dane burn'd
their pile,
The monks fled forth from Holy Isle ;
O'er northern mountain, marsh, and
moor,
From sea to sea, from shore to shore,
Seven years Saint Cuthbert's corpse
they bore.
They rested them in fair Melrose;
But though, alive, he lov'd it
well,
Not there his relics might repose ;
For, wondrous tale to tell !
In his stone-coffin forth he rides,
A ponderous bark for river tides,
Yet light as gossamer it glides,
Downward to Tilmouth cell.
Nor long was his abiding there,
For southward did the saint repair ;
Chester-le-Street, and Rippon, saw
His holy corpse, ere Wardilaw
Hail'd him with joy and fear ;
And, after many wanderings past,
He chose his lordly seat at last,
Where his cathedral, huge and vast,
Looks down upon the Wear :
There, deep in Durham's Gothic shade,
His relics are in secret laid ;
But none may know the place,
Save of his holiest servants three,
Deep sworn to solemn secrecy,
Who share that wondrous grace.

XV.

Who may his miracles declare !
Even Scotland's dauntless king, and
heir,

(Although with them they led
Galwegians, wild as ocean's gale,
And Lodon's knights, all sheath'd in
  mail,
And the bold men of Teviotdale,)
  Before his standard fled.
'Twas he, to vindicate his reign,
Edg'd Alfred's falchion on the Dane,
And turn'd the Conqueror back again,
When, with his Norman bowyer band,
He came to waste Northumberland.

XVI.

But fain Saint Hilda's nuns would learn
If, on a rock, by Lindisfarne,
Saint Cuthbert sits, and toils to frame
The sea-born beads that bear his name:
Such tales had Whitby's fishers told,
And said they might his shape behold,
  And hear his anvil sound;
A deaden'd clang, a huge dim form,
Seen but, and heard, when gathering
  storm
  And night were closing round.
But this, as tale of idle fame,
The nuns of Lindisfarne disclaim.

XVII.

While round the fire such legends go,
Far different was the scene of woe,
Where, in a secret aisle beneath,
Council was held of life and death.
  It was more dark and lone that vault,
    Than the worst dungeon cell:
    Old Colwulf built it, for his fault,
    In penitence to dwell,
When he, for cowl and beads, laid down
The Saxon battle-axe and crown.
This den, which, chilling every sense
Of feeling, hearing, sight,
Was call'd the Vault of Penitence,
  Excluding air and light,
Was, by the prelate Sexhelm, made
A place of burial for such dead,
As, having died in mortal sin,
Might not be laid the church within.
'Twas now a place of punishment;
Whence if so loud a shriek were sent

As reach'd the upper air,
The hearers bless'd themselves, and
  said
The spirits of the sinful dead
  Bemoan'd their torments there.

XVIII.

But though, in the monastic pile,
Did of this penitential aisle
  Some vague tradition go,
Few only, save the Abbot, knew
Where the place lay; and still more few
Were those who had from him the clew
  To that dread vault to go.
Victim and executioner
Were blindfold when transported
  there.
In low dark rounds the arches hung.
From the rude rock the side-walls
  sprung;
The grave-stones, rudely sculptur'd
  o'er,
Half sunk in earth, by time half wore,
Were all the pavement of the floor;
The mildew-drops fell one by one,
With tinkling plash, upon the stone.
A cresset, in an iron chain,
Which served to light this drear
  domain,
With damp and darkness seem'd to
  strive,
As if it scarce might keep alive;
And yet it dimly serv'd to show
The awful conclave met below.

XIX.

There, met to doom in secrecy,
Were plac'd the heads of convents
  three—
All servants of Saint Benedict,
The statutes of whose order strict
  On iron table lay;
In long black dress, on seats of stone,
Behind were these three judges shown
  By the pale cresset's ray:
The Abbess of Saint Hilda's, there,
Sat for a space with visage bare,

Until, to hide her bosom's swell,
And tear-drops that for pity fell,
    She closely drew her veil :
Yon shrouded figure, as I guess,
By her proud mien and flowing dress,
Is Tynemouth's haughty Prioress,
    And she with awe looks pale :
And he, that Ancient Man, whose sight
Has long been quench'd by age's night,
Upon whose wrinkled brow alone,
Nor ruth, nor mercy's trace, is shown,
    Whose look is hard and stern,—
Saint Cuthbert's Abbot is his style ;
For sanctity call'd, through the isle,
    The Saint of Lindisfarne.

XX.

Before them stood a guilty pair ;
But, though an equal fate they share,
Yet one alone deserves our care.
Her sex a page's dress belied ;
The cloak and doublet, loosely tied,
Obscur'd her charms, but could not
    hide.
    Her cap down o'er her face she drew ;
    And, on her doublet breast,
    She tried to hide the badge of blue,
    Lord Marmion's falcon crest.
But, at the Prioress' command,
A Monk undid the silken band
That tied her tresses fair,
And rais'd the bonnet from her head,
And down her slender form they
    spread,
    In ringlets rich and rare.
Constance de Beverley they know,
Sister profess'd of Fontevraud,
Whom the Church number'd with the
    dead,
For broken vows, and convent fled.

XXI.

When thus her face was given to view,
(Although, so pallid was her hue,
It did a ghastly contrast bear
To those bright ringlets glistering fair,)
Her look compos'd, and steady eye,
Bespoke a matchless constancy ;

And there she stood so calm and pale,
That, but her breathing did not fail,
And motion slight of eye and head,
And of her bosom, warranted
That neither sense nor pulse she lacks,
You might have thought a form of wax,
Wrought to the very life, was there :
So still she was, so pale, so fair.

XXII.

Her comrade was a sordid soul,
    Such as does murder for a meed ;
Who, but of fear, knows no control,
Because his conscience, sear'd and foul,
    Feels not the import of his deed ;
One whose brute-feeling ne'er aspires
Beyond his own more brute desires.
Such tools the Tempter ever needs,
To do the savagest of deeds ;
For them no vision'd terrors daunt,
Their nights no fancied spectres haunt,
One fear with them, of all most base,
The fear of death, alone finds place.
This wretch was clad in frock and cowl,
And sham'd not loud to moan and howl,
His body on the floor to dash,
And crouch, like hound beneath the
    lash ;
While his mute partner, standing near,
Waited her doom without a tear.

XXIII.

Yet well the luckless wretch might
    shriek,
Well might her paleness terror speak !
For there were seen in that dark wall,
Two niches, narrow, deep and tall :
Who enters at such grisly door,
Shall ne'er, I ween, find exit more.
In each a slender meal was laid,
Of roots, of water, and of bread :
By each, in Benedictine dress,
Two haggard monks stood motionless ;
Who, holding high a blazing torch,
Show'd the grim entrance of the porch :
Reflecting back the smoky beam,
The dark-red walls and arches gleam.

Hewn stones and cement were dis-
　　play'd,
And building tools in order laid.

XXIV.

These executioners were chose,
As men who were with mankind foes,
And, with despite and envy fir'd,
Into the cloister had retir'd;
　Or who, in desperate doubt of grace,
　Strove, by deep penance, to efface
　　Of some foul crime the stain;
　For, as the vassals of her will,
　Such men the Church selected still,
　As either joy'd in doing ill,
　Or thought more grace to gain,
If, in her cause, they wrestled down
Feelings their nature strove to own.
By strange device were they brought
　　there,
They knew not how, nor knew not
　　where.

XXV.

And now that blind old Abbot rose,
　To speak the Chapter's doom,
On those the wall was to enclose,
　Alive, within the tomb;
But stopp'd, because that woful Maid,
Gathering her powers, to speak essay'd.
Twice she essay'd, and twice in vain;
Her accents might no utterance gain;
Nought but imperfect murmurs slip
From her convuls'd and quivering lip;
　'Twixt each attempt all was so still,
　You seem'd to hear a distant rill;
　　'Twas ocean's swells and falls;
　For though this vault of sin and fear
　Was to the sounding surge so near,
　A tempest there you scarce could
　　hear,
　　So massive were the walls.

XXVI.

At length, an effort sent apart
The blood that curdled to her heart,
　And light came to her eye,

And colour dawn'd upon her cheek,
A hectic and a flutter'd streak,
Like that left on the Cheviot peak,
　By Autumn's stormy sky;
And when her silence broke at length,
Still as she spoke she gather'd strength,
　And arm'd herself to bear.
It was a fearful sight to see
Such high resolve and constancy
　In form so soft and fair.

XXVII.

'I speak not to implore your grace,—
Well know I, for one minute's space
　Successless might I sue:
Nor do I speak your prayers to gain;
For if a death of lingering pain,
To cleanse my sins, be penance vain,
　Vain are your masses too.
I listen'd to a traitor's tale,
I left the convent and the veil;
For three long years I bow'd my
　　pride,
A horse-boy in his train to ride;
And well my folly's meed he gave,
Who forfeited, to be his slave,
All here, and all beyond the grave.
He saw young Clara's face more fair,
He knew her of broad lands the
　　heir,
Forgot his vows, his faith forswore,
And Constance was belov'd no more.
'Tis an old tale. and often told;
　But did my fate and wish agree,
　Ne'er had been read, in story old,
　Of maiden true betray'd for gold,
　That lov'd, or was aveng'd, like
　　me!

XXVIII.

'The King approv'd his favourite's
　　aim;
In vain a rival barr'd his claim,
　Whose fate with Clare's was plight,
For he attaints that rival's fame
With treason's charge—and on they
　　came,
　In mortal lists to fight.

Their oaths are said,
　Their prayers are pray'd,
Their lances in the rest are laid,
They meet in mortal shock;
And, hark! the throng, with thun-
　dering cry,
Shout "Marmion, Marmion! to the sky,
De Wilton to the block!"
Say ye, who preach Heaven shall
　decide
When in the lists two champions ride,
　Say, was Heaven's justice here?
When, loyal in his love and faith,
Wilton found overthrow or death
　Beneath a traitor's spear?
How false the charge, how true he fell,
This guilty packet best can tell.'
Then drew a packet from her breast,
Paus'd, gather'd voice, and spoke the
　rest.

XXIX.

'Still was false Marmion's bridal staid;
To Whitby's convent fled the maid,
　The hated match to shun.
" Ho! shifts she thus?" King Henry
　cried;
" Sir Marmion, she shall be thy bride
If she were sworn a nun."
One way remain'd—the King's com-
　mand
Sent Marmion to the Scottish land:
I linger'd here, and rescue plann'd
　For Clara and for me:
This caitiff Monk, for gold, did swear
He would to Whitby's shrine repair,
And, by his drugs, my rival fair
　A saint in heaven should be.
But ill the dastard kept his oath,
Whose cowardice has undone us both.

XXX.

'And now my tongue the secret tells
Not that remorse my bosom swells,
But to assure my soul that none
Shall ever wed with Marmion.
Had fortune my last hope betray'd,
This packet, to the King convey'd,

Had given him to the headsman's
　stroke,
Although my heart that instant broke.
Now, men of death, work forth your
　will,
For I can suffer, and be still;
And come he slow, or come he fast,
It is but Death who comes at last.

XXXI.

'Yet dread me, from my living tomb,
Ye vassal slaves of bloody Rome!
If Marmion's late remorse should
　wake,
Full soon such vengeance will he take,
That you should wish the fiery Dane
Had rather been your guest again.
Behind, a darker hour ascends!
The altars quake, the crosier bends,
The ire of a despotic King
Rides forth upon destruction's wing;
Then shall these vaults, so strong and
　deep
Burst open to the sea-winds' sweep;
Some traveller then shall find my
　bones
Whitening amid disjointed stones,
And, ignorant of priests' cruelty,
Marvel such relics here should be.'

XXXII.

Fix'd was her look, and stern her air:
Back from her shoulders stream'd her
　hair;
The locks, that wont her brow to
　shade,
Star'd up erectly from her head;
Her figure seem'd to rise more high;
Her voice, despair's wild energy
Had given a tone of prophecy.
Appall'd the astonish'd conclave sate;
With stupid eyes, the men of fate
Gaz'd on the light inspired form,
And listen'd for the avenging storm;
The judges felt the victim's dread;
No hand was mov'd, no word was
　said,

Till thus the Abbot's doom was given,
Raising his sightless balls to heaven :—
' Sister, let thy sorrows cease ;
Sinful brother, part in peace ! '
   From that dire dungeon, place of
     doom,
  Of execution too, and tomb,
   Pac'd forth the judges three ;
Sorrow it were, and shame, to tell
The butcher-work that there befell,
When they had glided from the cell
   Of sin and misery.

XXXIII.

An hundred winding steps convey
That conclave to the upper day ;
But, ere they breath'd the fresher air,
They heard the shriekings of despair,
  And many a stifled groan :
With speed their upward way they
   take,
(Such speed as age and fear can make,)
And cross'd themselves for terror's
   sake,
  As hurrying, tottering on :
Even in the vesper's heavenly tone,
They seem'd to hear a dying groan,
And bade the passing knell to toll
For welfare of a parting soul.
Slow o'er the midnight wave it swung,
Northumbrian rocks in answer rung ;
To Warkworth cell the echoes roll'd,
His beads the wakeful hermit told,
The Bamborough peasant rais'd his
   head,
But slept ere half a prayer he said ;
So far was heard the mighty knell,
The stag sprung up on Cheviot Fell,
Spread his broad nostril to the wind,
Listed before, aside, behind,
Then couch'd him down beside the
   hind,
And quak'd among the mountain fern,
To hear that sound so dull and stern.

—+—

INTRODUCTION TO CANTO THIRD.

TO

WILLIAM ERSKINE, ESQ.

Ashestiel, Ettrick Forest.

LIKE April morning clouds, that pass,
With varying shadow, o'er the grass,
And imitate, on field and furrow,
Life's chequer'd scene of joy and
   sorrow ;
Like streamlet of the mountain north,
Now in a torrent racing forth,
Now winding slow its silver train,
And almost slumbering on the plain ;
Like breezes of the autumn day,
Whose voice inconstant dies away,
And ever swells again as fast,
When the ear deems its murmur past ;
Thus various, my romantic theme
Flits, winds, or sinks, a morning dream.
Yet pleas'd, our eye pursues the trace
Of Light and Shade's inconstant race ;
Pleas'd, views the rivulet afar,
Weaving its maze irregular ;
And pleas'd, we listen as the breeze
Heaves its wild sigh through Autumn
   trees ;
Then, wild as cloud, or stream, or gale,
Flow on, flow unconfin'd, my Tale !

Need I to thee, dear Erskine, tell
I love the license all too well,
In sounds now lowly, and now strong,
To raise the desultory song ?
Oft, when 'mid such capricious chime,
Some transient fit of lofty rhyme
To thy kind judgment seem'd excuse
For many an error of the muse,
Oft hast thou said, ' If, still misspent,
Thine hours to poetry are lent,
Go, and to tame thy wandering course,
Quaff from the fountain at the source ;

Approach those masters, o'er whose
tomb
Immortal laurels ever bloom :
Instructive of the feebler bard,
Still from the grave their voice is
heard ;
From them, and from the paths they
show'd,
Choose honour'd guide and practis'd
road ;
Nor ramble on through brake and
maze,
With harpers rude of barbarous days.

' Or deem'st thou not our later time
Yields topic meet for classic rhyme ?
Hast thou no elegiac verse
For Brunswick's venerable hearse ?
What ! not a line, a tear, a sigh,
When valour bleeds for liberty ?
Oh, hero of that glorious time,
When, with unrivall'd light sublime,—
Though martial Austria, and though
all
The might of Russia, and the Gaul,
Though banded Europe stood her
foes—
The star of Brandenburgh arose !
Thou couldst not live to see her beam
For ever quench'd in Jena's stream.
Lamented Chief ! it was not given
To thee to change the doom of
Heaven,
And crush that dragon in its birth,
Predestin'd scourge of guilty earth.
Lamented Chief !—not thine the power,
To save in that presumptuous hour,
When Prussia hurried to the field,
And snatch d the spear, but left the
shield !
Valour and skill 'twas thine to try,
And, tried in vain, 'twas thine to die.
Ill had it seem'd thy silver hair
The last, the bitterest pang to share,
For princedoms reft, and scutcheons
riven,
And birthrights to usurpers given ;

Thy land's, thy children's wrongs to
feel,
And witness woes thou couldst not
heal !
On thee relenting Heaven bestows
For honour'd life an honour'd close ;
And when revolves, in time's sure
change,
The hour of Germany's revenge,
When, breathing fury for her sake,
Some new Arminius shall awake,
Her champion, ere he strike, shall come
To whet his sword on BRUNSWICK'S
tomb.

' Or of the Red-Cross hero teach,
Dauntless in dungeon as on breach :
Alike to him the sea, the shore,
The brand, the bridle, or the oar :
Alike to him the war that calls
Its votaries to the shatter'd walls,
Which the grim Turk, besmear'd
with blood,
Against the Invincible made good ;
Or that, whose thundering voice could
wake
The silence of the polar lake,
When stubborn Russ, and metal'd
Swede,
On the warp'd wave their death-game
play'd ;
Or that, where Vengeance and Affright
Howl'd round the father of the fight,
Who snatch'd, on Alexandria's sand,
The conqueror's wreath with dying
hand.

' Or, if to touch such chord be thine,
Restore the ancient tragic line,
And emulate the notes that wrung
From the wild harp, which silent hung
By silver Avon's holy shore,
Till twice an hundred years roll'd
o'er ;
When she, the bold Enchantress, came
With fearless hand and heart on
flame !

From the pale willow snatch'd the
    treasure,
And swept it with a kindred measure,
Till Avon's swans, while rung the
    grove
With Montfort's hate and Basil's love,
Awakening at the inspired strain,
Deem'd their own Shakspeare liv'd
    again.'

The friendship thus thy judgment
    wronging
With praises not to me belonging,
In task more meet for mightiest
    powers
Wouldst thou engage my thriftless
    hours.
But say, my Erskine, hast thou weigh'd
That secret power by all obey'd,
Which warps not less the passive mind,
Its source conceal'd or undefin'd ;
Whether an impulse, that has birth
Soon as the infant wakes on earth,
One with our feelings and our powers,
And rather part of us than ours ;
Or whether fitlier term'd the sway
Of habit, form'd in early day ?
Howe'er deriv'd, its force confest
Rules with despotic sway the breast,
And drags us on by viewless chain,
While taste and reason plead in vain.
Look east, and ask the Belgian why,
Beneath Batavia's sultry sky,
He seeks not eager to inhale
The freshness of the mountain gale,
Content to rear his whiten'd wall
Beside the dank and dull canal?
He'll say, from youth he loved to see
The white sail gliding by the tree.
Or see yon weatherbeaten hind,
Whose sluggish herds before him wind,
Whose tatter'd plaid and rugged cheek
His northern clime and kindred speak;
Through England's laughing meads he
    goes
And England's wealth around him
    flows ;

Ask, if it would content him well,
At ease in those gay plains to dwell,
Where hedge-rows spread a verdant
    screen,
And spires and forests intervene,
And the neat cottage peeps between ?
No ! not for these will he exchange
His dark Lochaber's boundless range;
Not for fair Devon's meads forsake
Ben Nevis grey, and Garry's lake.

Thus while I ape the measure wild
Of tales that charm'd me yet a child,
Rude though they be, still with the
    chime
Return the thoughts of early time ;
And feelings, rous'd in life's first day,
Glow in the line, and prompt the lay.
Then rise those crags, that mountain
    tower
Which charm'd my fancy's wakening
    hour.
Though no broad river swept along,
To claim, perchance, heroic song :
Though sigh'd no groves in summer
    gale,
To prompt of love a softer tale ;
Though scarce a puny streamlet's speed
Claim'd homage from a shepherd's
    reed ;
Yet was poetic impulse given,
By the green hill and clear blue heaven.
It was a barren scene, and wild,
Where naked cliffs were rudely pil'd ;
But ever and anon between
Lay velvet tufts of loveliest green ;
And well the lonely infant knew
Recesses where the wall-flower grew,
And honey-suckle lov'd to crawl
Up the low crag and ruin'd wall.
I deem'd such nooks the sweetest shade
The sun in all its round survey'd ;
And still I thought that shatter'd tower
The mightiest work of human power;
And marvell'd as the aged hind
With some strange tale bewitch'd my
    mind,

Of forayers, who, with headlong force,
Down from that strength had spurr'd
   their horse,
Their southern rapine to renew,
Far in the distant Cheviots blue,
And, home returning, fill'd the hall
With revel, wassel-rout, and brawl.
Methought that still with trump and
   clang
The gateway's broken arches rang;
Methought grim features, seam'd with
   scars,
Glar'd through the window's rusty
   bars,
And ever, by the winter hearth,
Old tales I heard of woe or mirth,
Of lovers' slights, of ladies' charms,
Of witches' spells, of warriors' arms;
Of patriot battles, won of old
By Wallace wight and Bruce the bold;
Of later fields of feud and fight,
When, pouring from their Highland
   height,
The Scottish clans, in headlong sway,
Had swept the scarlet ranks away.
While stretch'd at length upon the
   floor,
Again I fought each combat o'er,
Pebbles and shells, in order laid,
The mimic ranks of war display'd;
And onward still the Scottish Lion bore,
And still the scatter'd Southron fled
   before.

Still, with vain fondness, could I
   trace,
Anew, each kind familiar face,
That brighten'd at our evening fire!
From the thatch'd mansion's grey-
   hair'd Sire,
Wise without learning, plain and good,
And sprung of Scotland's gentler
   blood;
Whose eye, in age, quick, clear, and
   keen,
Show'd what in youth its glance had
   been;

Whose doom discording neighbours
   sought,
Content with equity unbought;
To him the venerable Priest,
Our frequent and familiar guest,
Whose life and manners well could
   paint
Alike the student and the saint;
Alas! whose speech too oft I broke
With gambol rude and timeless joke:
For I was wayward, bold, and wild,
A self-will'd imp, a grandame's child;
But half a plague, and half a jest,
Was still endur'd, belov'd, caress'd.

For me, thus nurtur'd, dost thou ask,
The classic poet's well-conn'd task?
Nay, Erskine, nay; on the wild hill
Let the wild heath-bell flourish still;
Cherish the tulip, prune the vine,
But freely let the woodbine twine,
And leave untrimm'd the eglantine:
Nay, my friend, nay; since oft thy
   praise
Hath given fresh vigour to my lays;
Since oft thy judgment could refine
My flatten'd thought, or cumbrous line;
Still kind, as is thy wont, attend,
And in the minstrel spare the friend.
Though wild as cloud, as stream, as gale,
Flow forth, flow unrestrain'd, my Tale!

Canto Third.

The Hostel, or Inn.

I.

The livelong day Lord Marmion rode:
The mountain path the Palmer show'd,
By glen and streamlet winded still,
Where stunted birches hid the rill.
They might not choose the lowland
   road,
For the Merse forayers were abroad,

Who, fir'd with hate and thirst of
　　prey,
Had scarcely fail'd to bar their way.
Oft on the trampling band, from crown
Of some tall cliff, the deer look'd
　　down;
On wing of jet, from his repose
In the deep heath, the black-cock
　　rose;
Sprung from the gorse the timid roe,
Nor waited for the bending bow;
And when the stony path began,
By which the naked peak they wan,
Up flew the snowy ptarmigan.
The noon had long been pass'd before
They gain'd the height of Lammer-
　　moor;
Thence winding down the northern
　　way,
Before them, at the close of day,
Old Gifford's towers and hamlet lay.

II.

No summons calls them to the tower,
To spend the hospitable hour.
To Scotland's camp the Lord was gone:
His cautious dame, in bower alone,
Dreaded her castle to unclose,
So late, to unknown friends or foes.
　　On through the hamlet as they pac'd,
　　Before a porch, whose front was
　　　grac'd
　　With bush and flagon trimly plac'd,
　　　Lord Marmion drew his rein;
　　The village inn seem'd large, though
　　　rude;
　　Its cheerful fire and hearty food
　　　Might well relieve his train.
Down from their seats the horsemen
　　sprung,
With jingling spurs the court-yard
　　rung;
They bind their horses to the stall,
For forage, food, and firing call,
And various clamour fills the hall:
Weighing the labour with the cost,
Toils everywhere the bustling host.

III.

Soon, by the chimney's merry blaze,
Through the rude hostel might you
　　gaze;
Might see, where, in dark nook aloof,
The rafters of the sooty roof
　　Bore wealth of winter cheer;
Of sea-fowl dried, and solands store,
And gammons of the tusky boar,
　　And savoury haunch of deer.
The chimney arch projected wide;
Above, around it, and beside,
　　Were tools for housewives' hand;
Nor wanted, in that martial day,
The implements of Scottish fray,
　　The buckler, lance, and brand.
Beneath its shade, the place of state,
On oaken settle Marmion sate,
And view'd around the blazing hearth.
His followers mix in noisy mirth;
Whom with brown ale, in jolly tide,
From ancient vessels ranged aside,
Full actively their host supplied.

IV.

Theirs was the glee of martial breast,
And laughter theirs at little jest;
And oft Lord Marmion deign'd to aid,
And mingle in the mirth they made;
For though, with men of high degree,
The proudest of the proud was he,
Yet, train'd in camps, he knew the art
To win the soldier's hardy heart.
They love a captain to obey,
Boisterous as March, yet fresh as May;
With open hand, and brow as free,
Lover of wine and minstrelsy;
Ever the first to scale a tower,
As venturous in a lady's bower:
Such buxom chief shall lead his host
From India's fires to Zembla's frost.

V.

Resting upon his pilgrim staff,
　　Right opposite the Palmer stood;
His thin dark visage seen but half,
　　Half hidden by his hood.

Still fix'd on Marmion was his look,
Which he, who ill such gaze could
　　brook,
　　Strove by a frown to quell;
But not for that, though more than
　　once
Full met their stern encountering
　　glance,
　　The Palmer's visage fell.

VI.

By fits less frequent from the crowd
Was heard the burst of laughter loud;
For still, as squire and archer star'd
On that dark face and matted beard,
　　Their glee and game declin'd.
All gaz'd at length in silence drear,
Unbroke, save when in comrade's ear
Some yeoman, wondering in his fear,
　　Thus whisper'd forth his mind:—
'Saint Mary! saw'st thou e'er such
　　sight?
How pale his cheek, his eye how
　　bright,
Whene'er the firebrand's fickle light
　　Glances beneath his cowl!
Full on our Lord he sets his eye;
For his best palfrey, would not I
　　Endure that sullen scowl.'

VII.

But Marmion, as to chase the awe
Which thus had quell'd their hearts
　　who saw
The ever-varying fire-light show
That figure stern and face of woe,
　　Now call'd upon a squire:
'Fitz-Eustace, know'st thou not some
　　lay,
To speed the lingering night away?
　　We slumber by the fire.'

VIII.

'So please you,' thus the youth rejoin'd,
'Our choicest minstrel's left behind.
Ill may we hope to please your ear,
Accustom'd Constant's strains to hear.

The harp full deftly can he strike,
And wake the lover's lute alike;
To dear Saint Valentine, no thrush
Sings livelier from a spring-tide bush,
No nightingale her love-lorn tune
More sweetly warbles to the moon.
Woe to the cause, whate'er it be,
Detains from us his melody,
Lavish'd on rocks, and billows stern,
Or duller monks of Lindisfarne.
Now must I venture, as I may,
To sing his favourite roundelay.'

IX.

A mellow voice Fitz-Eustace had,
The air he chose was wild and sad;
Such have I heard, in Scottish land,
Rise from the busy harvest band,
When falls before the mountaineer,
On Lowland plains, the ripen'd ear.
Now one shrill voice the notes prolong,
Now a wild chorus swells the song:
Oft have I listen'd, and stood still,
As it came soften'd up the hill,
And deem'd it the lament of men
Who languish'd for their native glen;
And thought how sad would be such
　　sound
On Susquehana's swampy ground,
Kentucky's wood-encumber'd brake,
Or wild Ontario's boundless lake,
Where heart-sick exiles, in the strain,
Recall'd fair Scotland's hills again!

X.

SONG.

Where shall the lover rest,
　　Whom the fates sever
From his true maiden's breast,
　　Parted for ever?
Where, through groves deep and high,
　　Sounds the far billow,
Where early violets die,
　　Under the willow.

Chorus.

Eleu loro, &c.　　Soft shall be his pillow.

There, through the summer day,
  Cool streams are laving;
There, while the tempests sway,
  Scarce are boughs waving;
There, thy rest shalt thou take,
  Parted for ever,
Never again to wake,
  Never, O never!

Chorus.

Eleu loro, &c.   Never, O never!

XI.

Where shall the traitor rest,
  He, the deceiver,
Who could win maiden's breast,
  Ruin, and leave her?
In the lost battle,
  Borne down by the flying,
Where mingles war's rattle
  With groans of the dying.

Chorus.

Eleu loro, &c.   There shall he be lying.

Her wing shall the eagle flap
  O'er the false-hearted;
His warm blood the wolf shall lap,
  Ere life be parted.
Shame and dishonour sit
  By his grave ever;
Blessing shall hallow it,
  Never, O never!

Chorus.

Eleu loro, &c.   Never, O never!

XII.

It ceased, the melancholy sound;
And silence sunk on all around.
The air was sad; but sadder still
  It fell on Marmion's ear,
And plain'd as if disgrace and ill,
  And shameful death, were near.
He drew his mantle past his face,
  Between it and the band,
And rested with his head a space,
  Reclining on his hand.

His thoughts I scan not; but I ween,
That, could their import have been
    seen,
The meanest groom in all the hall,
That e'er tied courser to a stall,
Would scarce have wish'd to be their
    prey,
For Lutterward and Fontenaye.

XIII.

High minds, of native pride and force,
Most deeply feel thy pangs, Remorse!
Fear, for their scourge, mean villains
    have;
Thou art the torturer of the brave
Yet fatal strength they boast to steel
Their minds to bear the wounds they
    feel,
Even while they writhe beneath the
    smart
Of civil conflict in the heart.
For soon Lord Marmion raised his head,
And, smiling, to Fitz-Eustace said—
'Is it not strange, that, as ye sung,
Seem'd in mine ear a death-peal rung,
Such as in nunneries they toll
For some departing sister's soul?
  Say, what may this portend?'
Then first the Palmer silence broke
(The livelong day he had not spoke)—
  'The death of a dear friend.'

XIV.

Marmion, whose steady heart and eye
Ne'er changed in worst extremity;
Marmion, whose soul could scantly
    brook,
Even from his King, a haughty look;
Whose accent of command controll'd,
In camps, the boldest of the bold—
Thought, look, and utterance fail'd him
    now,
Fall'n was his glance, and flush'd his
    brow:
  For either in the tone,
Or something in the Palmer's look,
So full upon his conscience strook,
  That answer he found none.

Thus oft it haps, that when within
They shrink at sense of secret sin,
   A feather daunts the brave;
A fool's wild speech confounds the wise,
And proudest princes vail their eyes
   Before their meanest slave.

XV.

Well might he falter! By his aid
Was Constance Beverley betray'd.
Not that he augur'd of the doom,
Which on the living closed the tomb;
But, tired to hear the desperate maid
Threaten by turns, beseech, upbraid;
And wroth, because in wild despair,
She practis'd on the life of Clare;
Its fugitive the Church he gave,
Though not a victim, but a slave;
And deem'd restraint in convent strange
Would hide her wrongs, and her
   revenge.
Himself, proud Henry's favourite peer,
Held Romish thunders idle fear,
Secure his pardon he might hold,
For some slight mulct of penance-gold.
Thus judging, he gave secret way,
When the stern priests surpris'd their
   prey.
His train but deem'd the favourite page
Was left behind, to spare his age;
Or other if they deem'd, none dar'd
To mutter what he thought and heard:
Woe to the vassal, who durst pry
Into Lord Marmion's privacy!

XVI.

His conscience slept—he deem'd her
   well,
And safe secured in distant cell;
But, waken'd by her favourite lay,
And that strange Palmer's boding say,
That fell so ominous and drear
Full on the object of his fear
To aid remorse's venom'd throes,
Dark tales of convent-vengeance rose;
And Constance, late betray'd and
   scorn'd,

All lovely on his soul return'd;
Lovely as when, at treacherous call,
She left her convent's peaceful wall,
Crimson'd with shame, with terror
   mute,
Dreading alike escape, pursuit,
Till love, victorious o'er alarms,
Hid fears and blushes in his arms.

XVII.

'Alas!' he thought, 'how changed
   that mien!
How changed these timid looks have
   been,
Since years of guilt, and of disguise,
Have steel'd her brow, and arm'd her
   eyes!
No more of virgin terror speaks
The blood that mantles in her cheeks;
Fierce, and unfeminine, are there,
Frenzy for joy, for grief despair;
And I the cause—for whom were given
Her peace on earth, her hopes in
   heaven!
Would,' thought he, as the picture
   grows,
'I on its stalk had left the rose!
Oh, why should man's success remove
The very charms that wake his love!
Her convent's peaceful solitude
Is now a prison harsh and rude;
And, pent within the narrow cell,
How will her spirit chafe and swell!
How brook the stern monastic laws!
The penance how—and I the cause!
Vigil and scourge—perchance even
   worse!'
And twice he rose to cry, 'To horse!'
And twice his Sovereign's mandate
   came,
Like damp upon a kindling flame;
And twice he thought, 'Gave I not
   charge
She should be safe, though not at
   large?
They durst not, for their island, shred
One golden ringlet from her head.'

E

XVIII.

While thus in Marmion's bosom strove
Repentance and reviving love,
Like whirlwinds, whose contending
   sway
I 've seen Loch Vennachar obey,
Their Host the Palmer's speech had
   heard,
And, talkative, took up the word:
'Ay, reverend Pilgrim, you, who stray
From Scotland's simple land away,
   To visit realms afar,
Full often learn the art to know
Of future weal, or future woe,
   By word, or sign, or star;
Yet might a knight his fortune hear,
If, knight-like, he despises fear,
Not far from hence;—if fathers old
Aright our hamlet legend told.'
These broken words the menials move
(For marvels still the vulgar love);
And, Marmion giving license cold,
His tale the host thus gladly told:—

XIX.

THE HOST'S TALE.

'A Clerk could tell what years have
   flown
Since Alexander fill'd our throne
(Third monarch of that warlike name),
And eke the time when here he came
To seek Sir Hugo, then our lord:
A braver never drew a sword;
A wiser never, at the hour
Of midnight, spoke the word of power:
The same, whom ancient records call
The founder of the Goblin-Hall.
I would, Sir Knight, your longer stay
Gave you that cavern to survey.
Of lofty roof, and ample size,
Beneath the castle deep it lies:
To hew the living rock profound,
The floor to pave, the arch to round,
There never toil'd a mortal arm;
It all was wrought by word and charm;
And I have heard my grandsire say,
That the wild clamour and affray

Of those dread artisans of hell,
Who labour'd under Hugo's spell,
Sounded as loud as ocean's war
Among the caverns of Dunbar.

XX.

'The King Lord Gifford's castle sought,
Deep labouring with uncertain thought;
Even then he muster'd all his host,
To meet upon the western coast:
For Norse and Danish galleys plied
Their oars within the frith of Clyde.
There floated Haco's banner trim,
Above Norweyan warriors grim,
Savage of heart, and large of limb;
Threatening both continent and isle,
Bute, Arran, Cunninghame, and Kyle.
Lord Gifford, deep beneath the ground,
Heard Alexander's bugle sound,
And tarried not his garb to change,
But, in his wizard habit strange,
Came forth,—a quaint and fearful sight:
His mantle lined with fox-skins white;
His high and wrinkled forehead bore
A pointed cap, such as of yore
Clerks say that Pharaoh's Magi wore:
His shoes were mark'd with cross and
   spell,
Upon his breast a pentacle;
His zone, of virgin parchment thin,
Or, as some tell, of dead man's skin,
Bore many a planetary sign,
Combust, and retrograde, and trine;
And in his hand he held prepar'd,
A naked sword without a guard.

XXI.

'Dire dealings with the fiendish race
Had mark'd strange lines upon his face;
Vigil and fast had worn him grim,
His eyesight dazzled seem'd and dim,
As one unus'd to upper day;
Even his own menials with dismay
Beheld, Sir Knight, the grisly Sire,
In his unwonted wild attire;
Unwonted, for traditions run,
He seldom thus beheld the sun.

"I know," he said—his voice was
        hoarse,
And broken seem'd its hollow force,—
"I know the cause, although untold,
Why the King seeks his vassal's hold:
Vainly from me my liege would know
His kingdom's future weal or woe;
But yet, if strong his arm and heart,
His courage may do more than art.

XXII.

'"Of middle air the demons proud,
Who ride upon the racking cloud,
Can read, in fix'd or wandering star,
The issue of events afar;
But still their sullen aid withhold,
Save when by mightier force con-
        troll'd.
Such late I summon'd to my hall;
And though so potent was the call
That scarce the deepest nook of hell
I deem'd a refuge from the spell,
Yet, obstinate in silence still,
The haughty demon mocks my skill.
But thou—who little know'st thy
        might,
As born upon that blessed night
When yawning graves, and dying
        groan,
Proclaim'd hell's empire overthrown—
With untaught valour shalt compel
Response denied to magic spell"
"Gramercy," quoth our Monarch free,
"Place him but front to front with me,
And, by this good and honour'd brand,
The gift of Cœur-de-Lion's hand,
Soothly I swear, that, tide what tide,
The demon shall a buffet bide."
His bearing bold the wizard view'd,
And thus, well pleas'd, his speech
        renew d:—
"There spoke the blood of Malcolm!—
        mark:
Forth pacing hence, at midnight dark,
The rampart seek, whose circling
        crown
Crests the ascent of yonder down:

A southern entrance shalt thou find;
There halt, and there thy bugle wind,
And trust thine elfin foe to see,
In guise of thy worst enemy:
Couch then thy lance, and spur thy
        steed—
Upon him! and Saint George to speed!
If he go down, thou soon shalt know
Whate'er these airy sprites can show;
If thy heart fail thee in the strife,
I am no warrant for thy life."

XXIII.

'Soon as the midnight bell did ring,
Alone, and arm'd, forth rode the King
To that old camp's deserted round:
Sir Knight, you well might mark the
        mound,
Left hand the town,—the Pictish race,
The trench, long since, in blood did
        trace;
The moor around is brown and bare,
The space within is green and fair.
The spot our village children know,
For there the earliest wild-flowers
        grow;
But woe betide the wandering wight,
That treads its circle in the night!
The breadth across, a bowshot clear,
Gives ample space for full career:
Opposed to the four points of heaven,
By four deep gaps are entrance given.
The southernmost our Monarch past,
Halted, and blew a gallant blast;
And on the north, within the ring,
Appear'd the form of England's King,
Who then, a thousand leagues afar,
In Palestine wag'd holy war:
Yet arms like England's did he wield,
Alike the leopards in the shield,
Alike his Syrian courser's frame,
The rider's length of limb the same:
Long afterwards did Scotland know,
Fell Edward was her deadliest foe.

XXIV.

'The vision made our Monarch start,
But soon he mann'd his noble heart,

And in the first career they ran,
The Elfin Knight fell, horse and
    man ;
Yet did a splinter of his lance
Through Alexander's visor glance,
And razed the skin—a puny wound.
The King, light leaping to the ground,
With naked blade his phantom foe
Compell'd the future war to show.
Of Largs he saw the glorious plain,
Where still gigantic bones remain,
    Memorial of the Danish war ;
Himself he saw, amid the field,
On high his brandish'd war-axe wield,
    And strike proud Haco from his
        car,
While all around the shadowy Kings
Denmark's grim ravens cower'd their
        wings.
'Tis said, that, in that awful night,
Remoter visions met his sight,
Foreshowing future conquests far,
When our sons' sons wage northern
        war ;
A royal city, tower and spire,
Redden'd the midnight sky with fire,
And shouting crews her navy bore,
Triumphant, to the victor shore.
Such signs may learned clerks explain,
They pass the wit of simple swain.

XXV.

'The joyful King turn'd home again,
Headed his host, and quell'd the Dane;
But yearly, when return'd the night
Of his strange combat with the sprite,
    His wound must bleed and smart ;
Lord Gifford then would gibing say,
"Bold as ye were, my liege, ye pay
    The penance of your start."
Long since, beneath Dunfermline's
    nave,
King Alexander fills his grave ;
    Our Lady give him rest !
Yet still the knightly spear and shield
The Elfin Warrior doth wield,
    Upon the brown hill's breast ;

And many a knight hath prov'd his
    chance,
In the charm'd ring to break a lance,
    But all have foully sped ;
Save two, as legends tell, and they
Were Wallace wight, and Gilbert Hay.
    Gentles, my tale is said.'

XXVI.

The quaighs were deep, the liquor
    strong,
And on the tale the yeoman-throng
Had made a comment sage and long,
    But Marmion gave a sign :
And, with their lord, the squires retire;
The rest, around the hostel fire,
    Their drowsy limbs recline ;
For pillow, underneath each head,
The quiver and the targe were laid.
Deep slumbering on the hostel floor,
Oppress'd with toil and ale, they snore:
The dying flame, in fitful change,
Threw on the group its shadows
    strange.

XXVII.

Apart, and nestling in the hay
Of a waste loft, Fitz-Eustace lay ;
Scarce, by the pale moonlight, were
    seen
The foldings of his mantle green :
Lightly he dreamt, as youth will
    dream,
Of sport by thicket, or by stream ;
Of hawk or hound, of ring or glove,
Or, lighter yet, of lady's love.
A cautious tread his slumber broke,
And, close beside him, when he woke,
In moonbeam half, and half in gloom,
Stood a tall form, with nodding plume ;
But, ere his dagger Eustace drew,
His master Marmion's voice he knew.

XXVIII.

'Fitz-Eustace ! rise, I cannot rest ;
Yon churl's wild legend haunts my
    breast,

And graver thoughts have chafed my
    mood:
The air must cool my feverish blood;
And fain would I ride forth, to see
The scene of elfin chivalry.
Arise, and saddle me my steed;
And, gentle Eustace, take good heed
Thou dost not rouse these drowsy
    slaves;
I would not, that the prating knaves
Had cause for saying, o'er their ale,
That I could credit such a tale.'—
Then softly down the steps they slid,
Eustace the stable door undid,
And, darkling, Marmion's steed
    array'd,
While, whispering, thus the Baron
    said:—

XXIX.

'Didst never, good my youth, hear
    tell,
    That on the hour when I was born,
Saint George, who graced my sire's
    chapelle,
Down from his steed of marble fell,
    A weary wight forlorn?
The flattering chaplains all agree,
The champion left his steed to me.
I would, the omen's truth to show,
That I could meet this Elfin Foe!
Blithe would I battle, for the right
To ask one question at the sprite:
Vain thought! for elves, if elves there
    be,
An empty race, by fount or sea,
To dashing waters dance and sing,
Or round the green oak wheel their
    ring.'
Thus speaking, he his steed bestrode,
And from the hostel slowly rode.

XXX.

Fitz-Eustace followed him abroad,
And mark'd him pace the village
    road,

And listen'd to his horse's tramp,
    Till, by the lessening sound,
He judg'd that of the Pictish camp
    Lord Marmion sought the round.
Wonder it seem'd, in the squire's eyes,
That one, so wary held, and wise,—
Of whom 'twas said he scarce received
For gospel what the church be-
    lieved,—
    Should, stirr'd by idle tale,
Ride forth in silence of the night,
As hoping half to meet a sprite,
    Array'd in plate and mail.
For little did Fitz-Eustace know,
That passions, in contending flow,
    Unfix the strongest mind;
Wearied from doubt to doubt to flee,
We welcome fond credulity,
    Guide confident, though blind.

XXXI.

Little for this Fitz-Eustace car'd,
But, patient, waited till he heard,
At distance, prick'd to utmost speed,
The foot-tramp of a flying steed,
    Come town-ward rushing on;
First, dead, as if on turf it trode,
Then, clattering on the village road;—
In other pace than forth he yode,
    Return'd Lord Marmion.
Down hastily he sprung from selle,
And, in his haste, wellnigh he fell;
To the squire's hand the rein he threw,
And spoke no word as he withdrew:
But yet the moonlight did betray,
The falcon-crest was soil'd with clay;
And plainly might Fitz-Eustace see,
By stains upon the charger's knee,
And his left side, that on the moor
He had not kept his footing sure.
Long musing on these wondrous signs,
At length to rest the squire reclines,
Broken and short; for still, between,
Would dreams of terror intervene.
Eustace did ne'er so blithely mark
The first notes of the morning lark.

INTRODUCTION TO CANTO FOURTH.

TO

JAMES SKENE, Esq.

Ashestiel, Ettrick Forest.

An ancient Minstrel sagely said
'Where is the life which late we led?'
That motley clown in Arden wood,
Whom humorous Jaques with envy
    view'd,
Not even that clown could amplify
On this trite text so long as I.
Eleven years we now may tell,
Since we have known each other well;
Since, riding side by side, our hand
First drew the voluntary brand;
And sure, through many a varied scene,
Unkindness never came between.
Away these winged years have flown,
To join the mass of ages gone;
And though deep mark'd; like all below,
With chequer'd shades of joy and woe;
Though thou o'er realms and seas hast
    rang'd,
Mark'd cities lost, and empires chang'd,
While here, at home, my narrower ken
Somewhat of manners saw, and men;
Though varying wishes, hopes, and
    fears,
Fever'd the progress of these years,
Yet now, days, weeks, and months, but
    seem
The recollection of a dream,—
So still we glide down to the sea
Of fathomless eternity.

    Even now it scarcely seems a day,
Since first I tuned this idle lay;
A task so often thrown aside,
When leisure graver cares denied,
That now, November's dreary gale,
Whose voice inspir'd my opening tale,
That same November gale once more
Whirls the dry leaves on Yarrow shore.

Their vex'd boughs streaming to the
    sky,
Once more our naked birches sigh,
And Blackhouse heights, and Ettrick
    Pen,
Have donn'd their wintry shrouds
    again:
And mountain dark, and flooded mead,
Bid us forsake the banks of Tweed.
Earlier than wont along the sky,
Mix'd with the rack, the snow mists
    fly;
The shepherd, who in summer sun,
Had something of our envy won,
As thou with pencil, I with pen,
The features trac'd of hill and glen;—
He who, outstretch'd the livelong day,
At ease among the heath-flowers lay,
View'd the light clouds with vacant
    look,
Or slumber'd o'er his tatter'd book,
Or idly busied him to guide
His angle o'er the lessen'd tide;—
At midnight now, the snowy plain
Finds sterner labour for the swain.

    When red hath set the beamless sun,
Through heavy vapours dark and dun;
When the tir'd ploughman, dry and
    warm,
Hears, half asleep, the rising storm
Hurling the hail, and sleeted rain,
Against the casement's tinkling pane;
The sounds that drive wild deer, and
    fox,
To shelter in the brake and rocks,
Are warnings which the shepherd ask
To dismal and to dangerous task.
Oft he looks forth, and hopes, in vain,
The blast may sink in mellowing rain;
Till, dark above, and white below,
Decided drives the flaky snow,
And forth the hardy swain must go.
Long, with dejected look and whine,
To leave the hearth his dogs repine;
Whistling and cheering them to aid,
Around his back he wreathes the plaid:

His flock he gathers, and he guides,
To open downs, and mountain-sides,
Where fiercest though the tempest
    blow,
Least deeply lies the drift below.
The blast, that whistles o'er the fells,
Stiffens his locks to icicles;
Oft he looks back, while, streaming far,
His cottage window seems a star,—
Loses its feeble gleam,—and then
Turns patient to the blast again,
And, facing to the tempest's sweep,
Drives through the gloom his lagging
    sheep.
If fails his heart, if his limbs fail,
Benumbing death is in the gale:
His paths, his landmarks, all unknown,
Close to the hut, no more his own,
Close to the aid he sought in vain,
The morn may find the stiffen'd swain:
The widow sees, at dawning pale,
His orphans raise their feeble wail;
And, close beside him, in the snow,
Poor Yarrow, partner of their woe,
Couches upon his master's breast,
And licks his cheek to break his rest.

Who envies now the shepherd's lot,
His healthy fare, his rural cot,
His summer couch by greenwood tree,
His rustic kirn's loud revelry,
His native hill-notes, tun'd on high,
To Marion of the blithesome eye;
His crook, his scrip, his oaten reed,
And all Arcadia's golden creed?

Changes not so with us, my Skene,
Of human life the varying scene?
Our youthful summer oft we see
Dance by on wings of game and glee,
While the dark storm reserves its
    rage,
Against the winter of our age:
As he, the ancient Chief of Troy,
His manhood spent in peace and joy;
But Grecian fires, and loud alarms,
Call'd ancient Priam forth to arms.

Then happy those, since each must
    drain
His share of pleasure, share of pain,—
Then happy those, beloved of Heaven,
To whom the mingled cup is given;
Whose lenient sorrows find relief,
Whose joys are chasten'd by their grief.
And such a lot, my Skene, was thine,
When thou of late wert doom'd to
    twine,
Just when thy bridal hour was by,
The cypress with the myrtle tie.
Just on thy bride her Sire had smil'd,
And bless'd the union of his child,
When love must change its joyous
    cheer,
And wipe affection's filial tear.
Nor did the actions next his end,
Speak more the father than the friend:
Scarce had lamented Forbes paid
The tribute to his Minstrel's shade;
The tale of friendship scarce was told,
Ere the narrator's heart was cold:
Far may we search before we find
A heart so manly and so kind!
But not around his honour'd urn,
Shall friends alone and kindred mourn;
The thousand eyes his care had dried,
Pour at his name a bitter tide;
And frequent falls the grateful dew,
For benefits the world ne'er knew.
If mortal charity dare claim
The Almighty's attributed name,
Inscribe above his mouldering clay
'The widow's shield, the orphan's stay.'
Nor, though it wake thy sorrow, deem
My verse intrudes on this sad theme;
For sacred was the pen that wrote,
' Thy father's friend forget thou not:'
And grateful title may I plead,
For many a kindly word and deed,
To bring my tribute to his grave:
'Tis little, but 'tis all I have.

To thee, perchance, this rambling
    strain
Recalls our summer walks again:

When, doing nought—and, to speak
        true,
Not anxious to find aught to do—
The wild unbounded hills we rang'd,
While oft our talk its topic chang'd,
And, desultory as our way,
Rang'd, unconfin'd, from grave to gay.
Even when it flagg'd, as oft will chance,
No effort made to break its trance,
We could right pleasantly pursue
Our sports in social silence too ;
Thou gravely labouring to portray
The blighted oak's fantastic spray ;
I spelling o'er, with much delight,
The legend of that antique knight,
Tirante by name, yclep'd the White.
At either's feet a trusty squire,
Pandour and Camp, with eyes of fire,
Jealous, each other's motions view'd,
And scarce suppress'd their ancient feud.
The laverock whistled from the cloud ;
The stream was lively, but not loud ;
From the white thorn the May-flower
        shed
Its dewy fragrance round our head :
Not Ariel lived more merrily
Under the blossom'd bough, than we.

And blithesome nights, too, have
        been ours,
When Winter stript the summer's
        bowers.
Careless we heard, what now I hear,
The wild blast sighing deep and drear,
When fires were bright, and lamps
        beam'd gay,
And ladies tun'd the lovely lay ;
And he was held a laggard soul,
Who shunn'd to quaff the sparkling
        bowl.
Then he, whose absence we deplore,
Who breathes the gales of Devon's shore,
The longer miss'd, bewail'd the more ;
And thou, and I, and dear-loved Rae[1],
And one whose name I may not say[2],—

For not Mimosa's tender tree
Shrinks sooner from the touch than
        he,—
In merry chorus well combin'd,
With laughter drown'd the whistling
        wind.
Mirth was within ; and Care without
Might gnaw her nails to hear our shout.
Not but amid the buxom scene
Some grave discourse might inter-
        vene—
Of the good horse that bore him best,
His shoulder, hoof, and arching crest :
For, like mad Tom's, our chiefest care,
Was horse to ride, and weapon wear.
Such nights we 've had ; and, though
        the game
Of manhood be more sober tame,
And though the field-day, or the drill,
Seem less important now—yet still
Such may we hope to share again.
The sprightly thought inspires my
        strain !
And mark, how, like a horseman true,
Lord Marmion's march I thus renew.

Canto Fourth.

The Camp.

I.

Eustace, I said, did blithely mark
The first notes of the merry lark.
The lark sang shrill, the cock he crew,
And loudly Marmion's bugles blew,
And with their light and lively call
Brought groom and yeoman to the
        stall.
    Whistling they came, and free of
        heart,
    But soon their mood was chang'd;
Complaint was heard on every part,
    Of something disarrang'd.
Some clamour'd loud for armour lost ;
Some brawl'd and wrangled with the
        host ;

---

[1] Sir William Rae of St. Catharine's, Bart., subsequently Lord Advocate of Scotland.
[2] Sir William Forbes of Pitsligo, Bart.

'By Becket's bones,' cried one, 'I fear,
That some false Scot has stolen my spear!'
Young Blount, Lord Marmion's second squire,
Found his steed wet with sweat and mire;
Although the rated horse-boy sware,
Last night he dress'd him sleek and fair.
While chaf'd the impatient squire, like thunder
Old Hubert shouts in fear and wonder—
'Help, gentle Blount! help, comrades all!
Bevis lies dying in his stall:
To Marmion who the plight dare tell,
Of the good steed he loves so well?'
Gaping for fear and ruth, they saw
The charger panting on his straw;
Till one, who would seem wisest, cried—
'What else but evil could betide,
With that cursed Palmer for our guide?
Better we had through mire and bush
Been lantern-led by Friar Rush.'

II.

Fitz-Eustace, who the cause but guess'd,
  Nor wholly understood,
His comrades' clamorous plaints suppress'd,—
  He knew Lord Marmion's mood.
Him, ere he issu'd forth, he sought,
And found deep plung'd in gloomy thought,
  And did his tale display
Simply as if he knew of nought
  To cause such disarray.
Lord Marmion gave attention cold,
Nor marvell'd at the wonders told,—
Pass'd them as accidents of course,
And bade his clarions sound to horse.

III.

Young Henry Blount, meanwhile, the cost
Had reckon'd with their Scottish host;
And, as the charge he cast and paid,
'Ill thou deserv'st thy hire,' he said;
'Dost see, thou knave, my horse's plight?
Fairies have ridden him all the night,
  And left him in a foam!
I trust that soon a conjuring band,
With English cross, and blazing brand,
Shall drive the devils from this land,
  To their infernal home:
For in this haunted den, I trow,
All night they trample to and fro.'
The laughing host look'd on the hire,—
'Gramercy, gentle southern squire,
And if thou comest among the rest,
With Scottish broadsword to be blest,
Sharp be the brand, and sure the blow,
And short the pang to undergo.'
Here stay'd their talk,—for Marmion
Gave now the signal to set on.
The Palmer showing forth the way,
They journey'd all the morning day.

IV.

The green-sward way was smooth and good,
Through Humbie's and through Saltoun's wood;
A forest glade, which, varying still,
Here gave a view of dale and hill,
There narrower clos'd, till over head
A vaulted screen the branches made.
'A pleasant path,' Fitz-Eustace said;
'Such as where errant-knights might see
Adventures of high chivalry;
Might meet some damsel flying fast,
With hair unbound, and looks aghast;
And smooth and level course were here,
In her defence to break a spear.
Here, too, are twilight nooks and dells;
And oft, in such, the story tells,
The damsel kind, from danger freed,
Did grateful pay her champion's meed.'

He spoke to cheer Lord Marmion's
mind :
Perchance to show his lore design'd ;
 For Eustace much had por'd
Upon a huge romantic tome,
In the hall window of his home,
Imprinted at the antique dome
 Of Caxton, or De Worde.
Therefore he spoke,—but spoke in vain,
For Marmion answer'd nought again.

v.

Now sudden, distant trumpets shrill,
In notes prolong'd by wood and hill,
 Were heard to echo far ;
Each ready archer grasp'd his bow,
But by the flourish soon they know,
 They breath'd no point of war.
Yet cautious, as in foeman's land,
Lord Marmion's order speeds the band,
 Some opener ground to gain ;
And scarce a furlong had they rode,
When thinner trees, receding, show'd
 A little woodland plain.
Just in that advantageous glade,
The halting troop a line had made,
As forth from the opposing shade
 Issu'd a gallant train.

vi.

First came the trumpets, at whose clang
So late the forest echoes rang ;
On prancing steeds they forward
 press'd,
With scarlet mantle, azure vest ;
Each at his trump a banner wore,
Which Scotland's royal scutcheon
 bore :
Heralds and pursuivants, by name
Bute, Islay, Marchmount, Rothsay,
 came,
In painted tabards, proudly showing
Gules, Argent, Or, and Azure glowing,
 Attendant on a King-at-arms,
Whose hand the armorial truncheon
 held,
That feudal strife had often quell'd,
 When wildest its alarms.

vii.

He was a man of middle age ;
In aspect manly, grave, and sage,
 As on King's errand come ;
But in the glances of his eye,
A penetrating, keen, and sly
 Expression found its home ;
The flash of that satiric rage,
Which, bursting on the early stage,
Branded the vices of the age,
 And broke the keys of Rome.
On milk-white palfrey forth he pac'd ;
His cap of maintenance was grac'd
 With the proud heron-plume.
From his steed's shoulder, loin, and
 breast,
Silk housings swept the ground,
With Scotland's arms, device, and
 crest,
 Embroider'd round and round.
The double tressure might you see,
 First by Achaius borne,
The thistle and the fleur-de-lis,
 And gallant unicorn.
So bright the King's armorial coat,
That scarce the dazzled eye could note,
In living colours, blazon'd brave,
The Lion, which his title gave.
A train, which well beseem'd his state,
But all unarm'd, around him wait.
 Still is thy name in high account,
 And still thy verse has charms,
Sir David Lindesay of the Mount,
 Lord Lion King-at-arms !

viii.

Down from his horse did Marmion
 spring,
Soon as he saw the Lion-King ;
For well the stately Baron knew
To him such courtesy was due,
Whom royal James himself had
 crown'd,
And on his temples plac'd the round
 Of Scotland's ancient diadem :
And wet his brow with hallow'd wine,
And on his finger given to shine
 The emblematic gem.

Their mutual greetings duly made,
The Lion thus his message said :—
' Though Scotland's King hath deeply
　　swore
Ne'er to knit faith with Henry more,
And strictly hath forbid resort
From England to his royal court ;
Yet, for he knows Lord Marmion's
　　name,
And honours much his warlike fame,
My liege hath deem'd it shame, and lack
Of courtesy, to turn him back ;
And, by his order, I, your guide,
Must lodging fit and fair provide,
Till finds King James meet time to see
The flower of English chivalry.'

IX.

Though inly chaf'd at this delay,
Lord Marmion bears it as he may.
The Palmer, his mysterious guide,
Beholding thus his place supplied,
　　Sought to take leave in vain :
Strict was the Lion-King's command,
That none, who rode in Marmion's
　　band,
　　Should sever from the train :
' England has here enow of spies
In Lady Heron's witching eyes :'
To Marchmount thus, apart, he said,
But fair pretext to Marmion made.
The right-hand path they now decline,
And trace against the stream the Tyne.

X.

At length up that wild dale they wind,
　　Where Crichtoun Castle crowns the
　　　bank ;
For there the Lion's care assign'd
　　A lodging meet for Marmion's rank.
That Castle rises on the steep
　　Of the green vale of Tyne :
And far beneath, where slow they
　　creep,
From pool to eddy, dark and deep,
Where alders moist, and willows weep,
　　You hear her streams repine.

The towers in different ages rose ;
Their various architecture shows
　　The builders' various hands ;
A mighty mass, that could oppose,
When deadliest hatred fir'd its foes,
　　The vengeful Douglas bands.

XI.

Crichtoun ! though now thy miry court
　　But pens the lazy steer and sheep,
　　Thy turrets rude, and totter'd Keep,
Have been the minstrel's lov'd resort.
Oft have I trac'd, within thy fort,
　　Of mouldering shields the mystic
　　　sense,
　　Scutcheons of honour, or pretence,
Quarter'd in old armorial sort,
　　Remains of rude magnificence ;
Nor wholly yet had time defac'd
　　Thy lordly gallery fair ;
Nor yet the stony cord unbrac'd,
Whose twisted knots, with roses lac'd,
　　Adorn thy ruin'd stair.
Still rises unimpair'd below,
The court-yard's graceful portico ;
Above its cornice, row and row
　　Of fair hewn facets richly show
　　　Their pointed diamond form,
　　Though there but houseless cattle go
　　　To shield them from the storm.
　　And, shuddering, still may we
　　　explore,
　　　Where oft whilom were captives
　　　pent,
　　The darkness of thy Massy More ;
　　　Or, from thy grass-grown battle-
　　　ment,
May trace, in undulating line,
The sluggish mazes of the Tyne.

XII.

Another aspect Crichtoun show'd,
As through its portal Marmion rode ;
But yet 'twas melancholy state
Received him at the outer gate ;
For none were in the Castle then,
But women, boys, or aged men.

With eyes scarce dried, the sorrowing
dame
To welcome noble Marmion came ;
Her son, a stripling twelve years old,
Proffer'd the Baron's rein to hold ;
For each man that could draw a
sword
Had march'd that morning with their
lord,
Earl Adam Hepburn,—he who died
On Flodden, by his sovereign's side.
Long may his Lady look in vain !
She ne'er shall see his gallant train,
Come sweeping back through Crich-
toun-Dean.
'Twas a brave race, before the name
Of hated Bothwell stain'd their fame.

XIII.

And here two days did Marmion rest,
  With every rite that honour claims
Attended as the King's own guest :—
  Such the command of Royal James,
Who marshall'd then his land's array,
Upon the Borough-moor that lay.
Perchance he would not foeman's eye
Upon his gathering host should pry,
Till full prepar'd was every band
To march against the English land.
Here while they dwelt, did Lindesay's
wit
Oft cheer the Baron's moodier fit ;
And, in his turn, he knew to prize
Lord Marmion's powerful mind, and
wise,—
Train'd in the lore of Rome and
Greece,
And policies of war and peace.

XIV.

It chanc'd, as fell the second night,
  That on the battlements they walk'd,
And, by the slowly fading light,
  Of varying topics talk'd ;
And, unaware, the Herald-bard
Said Marmion might his toil have
spar'd,
  In travelling so far ;

For that a messenger from heaven
In vain to James had counsel given
  Against the English war ;
And, closer question'd, thus he told
A tale which chronicles of old
In Scottish story have enroll'd :—

XV.

SIR DAVID LINDESAY'S TALE.

' Of all the palaces so fair,
  Built for the royal dwelling,
In Scotland, far beyond compare
  Linlithgow is excelling ;
And in its park in jovial June,
How sweet the merry linnet's tune,
  How blithe the blackbird's lay !
The wild-buck bells from ferny brake,
The coot dives merry on the lake ;
The saddest heart might pleasure take
  To see all nature gay.
But June is to our sovereign dear
The heaviest month in all the year :
Too well his cause of grief you know,
June saw his father's overthrow.
Woe to the traitors, who could bring
The princely boy against his King !
Still in his conscience burns the sting.
In offices as strict as Lent,
King James's June is ever spent.

XVI.

' When last this ruthful month was
  come
And in Linlithgow's holy dome
  The King, as wont, was praying ;
While, for his royal father's soul,
The chanters sung, the bells did toll,
  The Bishop mass was saying—
For now the year brought round again
The day the luckless king was slain—
  In Katharine's aisle the Monarch
  knelt,
  With sackcloth-shirt, and iron belt,
    And eyes with sorrow streaming ;
Around him in their stalls of state,
The Thistle's Knight-Companions
sate,
  Their banners o'er them beaming.

I too was there, and, sooth to tell,
Bedeafen'd with the jangling knell,
Was watching where the sunbeams fell,
　　Through the stain'd casement gleaming;
But, while I mark'd what next befell,
　　It seem'd as I were dreaming.
Stepp'd from the crowd a ghostly wight,
In azure gown, with cincture white;
His forehead bald, his head was bare,
Down hung at length his yellow hair.
Now, mock me not, when, good my Lord,
I pledge to you my knightly word,
That, when I saw his placid grace,
His simple majesty of face,
His solemn bearing, and his pace
　　So stately gliding on,
Seem'd to me ne'er did limner paint
So just an image of the Saint
Who propp'd the Virgin in her faint,
　　The loved Apostle John!

XVII.

'He stepp'd before the Monarch's chair,
And stood with rustic plainness there,
　　And little reverence made;
Nor head, nor body, bow'd nor bent,
But on the desk his arm he leant,
　　And words like these he said,
In a low voice, but never tone
So thrill'd through vein, and nerve, and bone:
"My mother sent me from afar,
Sir King, to warn thee not to war;
　　Woe waits on thine array;
If war thou wilt, of woman fair,
Her witching wiles and wanton snare,
James Stuart, doubly warn'd, beware:
　　God keep thee as he may!"
　　The wondering Monarch seem'd to seek
　　For answer, and found none;
　　And when he rais'd his head to speak,
　　　The monitor was gone.

The Marshal and myself had cast
To stop him as he outward pass'd;
　　But, lighter than the whirlwind's blast,
　　He vanish'd from our eyes,
Like sunbeam on the billow cast,
　　That glances but, and dies.'—

XVIII.

While Lindesay told his marvel strange,
　　The twilight was so pale,
He mark'd not Marmion's colour change,
　　While listening to the tale;
But, after a suspended pause,
The Baron spoke: 'Of Nature's laws
So strong I held the force,
That never superhuman cause
Could e'er control their course,
And, three days since, had judg'd your aim
Was but to make your guest your game.
But I have seen, since past the Tweed,
What much has chang'd my sceptic creed,
And made me credit aught.' He staid;
And seem'd to wish his words unsaid:
But, by that strong emotion press'd,
Which prompts us to unload our breast,
　　Even when discovery 's pain,
To Lindesay did at length unfold
The tale his village host had told,
　　At Gifford, to his train.
Nought of the Palmer says he there,
And nought of Constance, or of Clare;
The thoughts, which broke his sleep, he seems
To mention but as feverish dreams.

XIX.

'In vain,' said he, ' to rest I spread
My burning limbs, and couch'd my head:
　　Fantastic thoughts return'd;
And, by their wild dominion led,
　　My heart within me burn'd.

So sore was the delirious goad,
I took my steed, and forth I rode,
And, as the moon shone bright and cold,
Soon reach'd the camp upon the wold.
The southern entrance I pass'd through,
And halted, and my bugle blew.
Methought an answer met my ear;
Yet was the blast so low and drear,
So hollow, and so faintly blown,
It might be echo of my own.

XX.

'Thus judging, for a little space
I listen'd, ere I left the place;
  But scarce could trust my eyes,
Nor yet can think they serv'd me true
When sudden in the ring I view,
In form distinct of shape and hue,
  A mounted champion rise.
I've fought, Lord-Lion, many a day,
In single fight, and mix'd affray,
And ever, I myself may say,
  Have borne me as a knight;
But when this unexpected foe
Seem'd starting from the gulf below—
I care not though the truth I show—
  I trembled with affright;
And as I plac'd in rest my spear,
My hand so shook for very fear,
  I scarce could couch it right.

XXI.

'Why need my tongue the issue tell?
We ran our course,—my charger fell;
What could he 'gainst the shock of
    hell?
  I roll'd upon the plain.
High o'er my head, with threatening
    hand,
The spectre shook his naked brand;
  Yet did the worst remain:
My dazzled eyes I upward cast,—
Not opening hell itself could blast
  Their sight, like what I saw!
Full on his face the moonbeam strook,—
A face could never be mistook!
I knew the stern vindictive look,
  And held my breath for awe.

I saw the face of one who, fled
To foreign climes, has long been
    dead,—
  I well believe the last;
For ne'er, from vizor rais'd, did stare
A human warrior, with a glare
  So grimly and so ghast.
Thrice o'er my head he shook the
    blade;
But when to good Saint George I
    pray'd,
(The first time ere I ask'd his aid,)
  He plung'd it in the sheath;
And, on his courser mounting light,
He seem'd to vanish from my sight:
The moonbeam droop'd, and deepest
    night
  Sunk down upon the heath.
'Twere long to tell what cause I have
  To know his face, that met me
    there,
Call'd by his hatred from the grave,
  To cumber upper air:
Dead or alive, good cause had he
To be my mortal enemy.'

XXII.

Marvell'd Sir David of the Mount;
Then, learn'd in story, 'gan recount
  Such chance had happ'd of old,
When once, near Norham, there did
    fight,
A spectre fell of fiendish might,
In likeness of a Scottish knight,
  With Brian Bulmer bold,
And train'd him nigh to disallow
The aid of his baptismal vow.
'And such a phantom, too, 'tis said,
With Highland broadsword, targe,
    and plaid,
  And fingers, red with gore,
Is seen in Rothiemurcus glade,
Or where the sable pine-trees shade
Dark Tomantoul, and Auchnaslaid,
  Dromouchty, or Glenmore.
And yet, whate'er such legends **say**,
Of warlike demon, ghost, or **fay**,

On mountain, moor, or plain,
Spotless in faith, in bosom bold,
True son of chivalry should hold,
　These midnight terrors vain;
For seldom have such spirits power
To harm, save in the evil hour,
When guilt we meditate within,
Or harbour unrepented sin.'
Lord Marmion turn'd him half aside,
And twice to clear his voice he tried,
　Then press'd Sir David's hand,—
But nought, at length, in answer said;
And here their farther converse staid,
　Each ordering that his band
Should bowne them with the rising
　　day,
To Scotland's camp to take their
　　way.
　Such was the King's command.

XXIII.

Early they took Dun-Edin's road;
And I could trace each step they
　　trode:
Hill, brook, nor dell, nor rock, nor
　　stone,
Lies on the path to me unknown.
Much might it boast of storied lore;
But, passing such digression o'er,
Suffice it that the route was laid
Across the furzy hills of Braid.
They pass'd the glen and scanty rill,
And climb'd the opposing bank, until
They gain'd the top of Blackford Hill.

XXIV.

Blackford! on whose uncultur'd breast,
　Among the broom, and thorn, and
　　whin,
A truant-boy, I sought the nest,
Or listed, as I lay at rest,
　While rose, on breezes thin,
The murmur of the city crowd,
And, from his steeple jangling loud,
　Saint Giles's mingling din.
Now, from the summit to the plain,

Waves all the hill with yellow grain;
　And o'er the landscape as I look,
Nought do I see unchang'd remain,
　Save the rude cliffs and chiming
　　brook.
To me they make a heavy moan,
Of early friendships past and gone.

XXV.

But different far the change has been,
　Since Marmion, from the crown
Of Blackford, saw that martial scene
　Upon the bent so brown:
Thousand pavilions, white as snow,
Spread all the Borough-moor below,
　Upland, and dale, and down—
A thousand did I say? I ween,
Thousands on thousands there were
　　seen,
That chequer'd all the heath between
　The streamlet and the town;
In crossing ranks extending far,
Forming a camp irregular;
Oft giving way, where still there stood
Some relics of the old oak wood,
That darkly huge did intervene,
And tam'd the glaring white with
　　green:
In these extended lines there lay
A martial kingdom's vast array.

XXVI.

For from Hebudes, dark with rain,
To eastern Lodon's fertile plain,
And from the southern Redswire edge,
To farthest Rosse's rocky ledge;
From west to east, from south to north,
Scotland sent all her warriors forth.
Marmion might hear the mingled hum
Of myriads up the mountain come;
The horses' tramp, and tingling clank,
Where chiefs review'd their vassal rank,
　And charger's shrilling neigh;
And see the shifting lines advance,
While frequent flash'd, from shield and
　　lance,
　The sun's reflected ray.

XXVII.

Thin curling in the morning air,
The wreaths of failing smoke declare
To embers now the brands decay'd,
Where the night-watch their fires had
  made.
They saw, slow rolling on the plain,
Full many a baggage-cart and wain,
And dire artillery's clumsy car,
By sluggish oxen tugg'd to war;
And there were Borthwick's Sisters
  Seven,
And culverins which France had
  given.
Ill-omen'd gift! the guns remain
The conqueror's spoil on Flodden
  plain.

XXVIII.

Nor mark'd they less, where in the
  air
A thousand streamers flaunted fair;
  Various in shape, device, and hue,
  Green, sanguine, purple, red, and
    blue,
Broad, narrow, swallow-tail'd, and
  square,
Scroll, pennon, pensil, bandrol, there
O'er the pavilions flew.
Highest and midmost, was descried
The royal banner floating wide;
  The staff, a pine-tree, strong and
    straight,
Pitch'd deeply in a massive stone,
Which still in memory is shown,
  Yet bent beneath the standard's
    weight
    Whene'er the western wind un-
      roll'd,
    With toil, the huge and cumbrous
      fold,
And gave to view the dazzling field,
Where, in proud Scotland's royal
  shield,
  The ruddy lion ramp'd in gold.

XXIX.

Lord Marmion view'd the landscape
  bright,
He view'd it with a chief's delight,
  Until within him burn'd his heart,
  And lightning from his eye did part,
    As on the battle-day;
  Such glance did falcon never dart,
    When stooping on his prey.
'Oh! well, Lord-Lion, hast thou said,
Thy King from warfare to dissuade
  Were but a vain essay;
For, by St. George, were that host
  mine,
Not power infernal nor divine,
Should once to peace my soul incline,
Till I had dimm'd their armour's shine
  In glorious battle-fray!'
Answer'd the Bard, of milder mood:
'Fair is the sight,—and yet 'twere
  good,
  That kings would think withal,
When peace and wealth their land
  has bless'd,
'Tis better to sit still at rest,
  Than rise, perchance to fall.'

XXX.

Still on the spot Lord Marmion stay'd,
For fairer scene he ne'er survey'd.
  When sated with the martial show
  That peopled all the plain below,
  The wandering eye could o'er it go,
  And mark the distant city glow
    With gloomy splendour red;
  For on the smoke-wreaths, huge and
    slow,
  That round her sable turrets flow,
    The morning beams were shed,
  And ting'd them with a lustre proud,
  Like that which streaks a thunder-
    cloud.
Such dusky grandeur cloth'd the
  height,
Where the huge Castle holds its state,
  And all the steep slope down,

Whose ridgy back heaves to the sky,
Pil'd deep and massy, close and high,
    Mine own romantic town!
But northward far, with purer blaze,
On Ochil mountains fell the rays,
And as each heathy top they kiss'd,
    It gleam'd a purple amethyst.
Yonder the shores of Fife you saw;
Here Preston·Bay and Berwick-Law:
    And, broad between them roll'd,
The gallant Frith the eye might note,
Whose islands on its bosom float,
    Like emeralds chas'd in gold.
Fitz-Eustace' heart felt closely pent;
As if to give his rapture vent,
The spur he to his charger lent,
    And rais'd his bridle hand,
And, making demi-volte in air,
Cried 'Where's the coward that would
        not dare
    To fight for such a land!'
The Lindesay smil'd his joy to see;
Nor Marmion's frown repress'd his
    glee.

XXXI.

Thus while they look'd, a flourish
        proud,
Where mingled trump, and clarion
        loud,
    And fife, and kettle-drum,
And sackbut deep, and psaltery,
And war-pipe with discordant cry,
And cymbal clattering to the sky,
    Making wild music bold and high,
        Did up the mountain come;
The whilst the bells, with distant
        chime,
Merrily toll'd the hour of prime,
    And thus the Lindesay spoke:
'Thus clamour still the war-notes when
The king to mass his way has ta'en,
Or to St· Katharine's of Sienne,
    Or Chapel of Saint Rocque.
To you they speak of martial fame;
But me remind of peaceful game,
    When blither was their cheer,

Thrilling in Falkland-woods the air,
In signal none his steed should spare,
But strive which foremost might repair
    To the downfall of the deer.

XXXII.

'Nor less,' he said, 'when looking forth,
I view yon Empress of the North
    Sit on her hilly throne;
Her palace's imperial bowers,
Her castle, proof to hostile powers,
Her stately halls and holy towers—
    Nor less,' he said, 'I moan,
To think what woe mischance may
        bring,
And how these merry bells may ring
The death-dirge of our gallant king;
    Or with the larum call
The burghers forth to watch and
        ward,
'Gainst southern sack and fires to
        guard
    Dun-Edin's leaguer'd wall.
But not for my presaging thought
Dream conquest sure, or cheaply
        bought!
    Lord Marmion, I say nay:
God is the guider of the field,
He breaks the champion's spear and
        shield,—
    But thou thyself shalt say,
When joins yon host in deadly stowre,
That England's dames must weep in
        bower,
    Her monks the death-mass sing;
For never saw'st thou such a power
    Led on by such a King.'
And now, down-winding to the
        plain,
The barriers of the camp they gain,
    And there they made a stay.—
There stays the Minstrel, till he
        fling
His hand o'er every Border string,
And fit his harp the pomp to sing,
Of Scotland's ancient Court and King,
    In the succeeding lay.

INTRODUCTION TO CANTO
FIFTH.

TO

GEORGE ELLIS, Esq.

Edinburgh.

WHEN dark December glooms the day,
And takes our autumn joys away;
When short and scant the sunbeam
throws,
Upon the weary waste of snows,
A cold and profitless regard,
Like patron on a needy bard;
When silvan occupation 's done,
And o'er the chimney rests the gun,
And hang, in idle trophy, near,
The game-pouch, fishing-rod, and
spear;
When wiry terrier, rough and grim,
And greyhound, with his length of
limb,
And pointer, now employ'd no more,
Cumber our parlour's narrow floor;
When in his stall the impatient steed
Is long condemn'd to rest and feed;
When from our snow-encircled home
Scarce cares the hardiest step to roam,
Since path is none, save that to bring
The needful water from the spring;
When wrinkled news-page, thrice
conn'd o'er,
Beguiles the dreary hour no more,
And darkling politician, cross'd,
Inveighs against the lingering post,
And answering housewife sore com-
plains
Of carriers' snow-impeded wains;
When such the country cheer, I come,
Well pleas'd, to seek our city home;
For converse, and for books, to change
The Forest's melancholy range,
And welcome, with renew'd delight,
The busy day and social night.

Not here need my desponding rhyme
Lament the ravages of time,
As erst by Newark's riven towers,
And Ettrick stripp'd of forest bowers.
True, Caledonia's Queen is chang'd,
Since on her dusky summit rang'd,
Within its steepy limits pent,
By bulwark, line, and battlement,
And flanking towers, and laky flood,
Guarded and garrison'd she stood,
Denying entrance or resort,
Save at each tall embattled port;
Above whose arch, suspended, hung
Portcullis spiked with iron prong.
That long is gone,— but not so long,
Since, early clos'd, and opening late,
Jealous revolved the studded gate,
Whose task, from eve to morning tide,
A wicket churlishly supplied.
Stern then, and steel-girt was thy
brow,
Dun-Edin! O, how alter'd now,
When safe amid thy mountain court
Thou sit'st, like Empress at her sport,
And liberal, unconfin'd, and free,
Flinging thy white arms to the sea,
For thy dark cloud, with umber'd
lower,
That hung o'er cliff, and lake, and tower,
Thou gleam'st against the western ray
Ten thousand lines of brighter day.

Not she, the Championess of old,
In Spenser's magic tale enroll'd,
She for the charmed spear renown'd,
Which forc'd each knight to kiss the
ground,—
Not she more chang'd, when, plac'd
at rest,
What time she was Malbecco's guest,
She gave to flow her maiden vest;
When from the corslet's grasp reliev'd,
Free to the sight her bosom heav'd;
Sweet was her blue eye's modest smile,
Erst hidden by the aventayle;
And down her shoulders graceful roll'd
Her locks profuse, of paly gold.

They who whilom, in midnight fight,
Had marvell'd at her matchless might,
No less her maiden charms approv'd,
But looking lik'd, and liking lov'd.
The sight could jealous pangs beguile,
And charm Malbecco's cares a while ;
And he, the wandering Squire of
        Dames,
Forgot his Columbella's claims,
And passion, erst unknown, could gain
The breast of blunt Sir Satyrane ;
Nor durst light Paridel advance,
Bold as he was, a looser glance.
She charm'd, at once, and tamed the
        heart,
Incomparable Britomarte !

So thou, fair City ! disarray'd
Of battled wall, and rampart's aid,
As stately seem'st, but lovelier far
Than in that panoply of war.
Nor deem that from thy fenceless
        throne
Strength and security are flown ;
Still, as of yore, Queen of the North !
Still canst thou send thy children forth.
Ne'er readier at alarm-bell's call
Thy burghers rose to man thy wall,
Than now, in danger, shall be thine,
Thy dauntless voluntary line ;
For fosse and turret proud to stand,
Their breasts the bulwarks of the land.
Thy thousands, train'd to martial toil,
Full red would stain their native soil,
Ere from thy mural crown there fell
The slightest knosp, or pinnacle.
And if it come,—as come it may,
Dun-Edin ! that eventful day,—
Renown'd for hospitable deed,
That virtue much with Heaven may
        plead,
In patriarchal times whose care
Descending angels deign'd to share ;
That claim may wrestle blessings down
On those who fight for The Good Town,
Destin'd in every age to be
Refuge of injured royalty ;

Since first, when conquering York
        arose,
To Henry meek she gave repose,
Till late, with wonder, grief, and awe,
Great Bourbon's relics sad she saw [1].

Truce to these thoughts !—for, as
        they rise,
How gladly I avert mine eyes,
Bodings, or true or false, to change,
For Fiction's fair romantic range,
Or for tradition's dubious light,
That hovers 'twixt the day and night :
Dazzling alternately and dim,
Her wavering lamp I 'd rather trim,
Knights, squires, and lovely dames to
        see,
Creation of my fantasy,
Than gaze abroad on reeky fen,
And make of mists invading men.
Who loves not more the night of
        June
Than dull December's gloomy noon ?
The moonlight than the fog of frost ?
And can we say, which cheats the most ?

But who shall teach my harp to
        gain
A sound of the romantic strain,
Whose Anglo-Norman tones whilere
Could win the royal Henry's ear,
Famed Beauclerc call'd, for that he
        lov'd
The minstrel, and his lay approv'd ?
Who shall these lingering notes
        redeem,
Decaying on Oblivion's stream ;
Such notes as from the Breton tongue
Marie translated, Blondel sung ?—
O ! born, Time's ravage to repair,
And make the dying Muse thy care ;
Who, when his scythe her hoary foe
Was poising for the final blow,

---

1 In January, 1796, the exiled Count d'Artois, afterwards Charles X of France, took up his residence in
Holyrood, where he remained until August, 1799.

The weapon from his hand could
    wring,
And break his glass, and shear his wing,
And bid, reviving in his strain,
The gentle poet live again ;
Thou, who canst give to lightest lay
An unpedantic moral gay,
Nor less the dullest theme bid flit
On wings of unexpected wit ;
In letters as in life approv'd,
Example honour'd, and belov'd,—
Dear ELLIS ! to the bard impart
A lesson of thy magic art,
To win at once the head and heart,—
At once to charm, instruct, and mend,
My guide, my pattern, and my friend !

    Such minstrel lesson to bestow
Be long thy pleasing task,—but, O !
No more by thy example teach,—
What few can practise, all can
    preach,—
With even patience to endure
Lingering disease, and painful cure,
And boast affliction's pangs subdu'd
By mild and manly fortitude.
Enough, the lesson has been given :
Forbid the repetition, Heaven !

    Come listen, then ! for thou hast
    known,
And lov'd the Minstrel's varying tone,
Who, like his Border sires of old,
Wak'd a wild measure rude and bold,
Till Windsor's oaks, and Ascot plain,
With wonder heard the northern
    strain.
Come listen ! bold in thy applause,
The Bard shall scorn pedantic laws ;
And, as the ancient art could stain
Achievements on the storied pane,
Irregularly trac'd and plann'd,
But yet so glowing and so grand,—
So shall he strive, in changeful hue,
Field, feast, and combat, to renew,
And loves, and arms, and harpers' glee,
And all the pomp of chivalry.

Canto Fifth.

The Court.

I.

THE train has left the hills of Braid ;
The barrier guard have open made
(So Lindesay bade) the palisade,
    That closed the tented ground ;
Their men the warders backward drew,
And carried pikes, as they rode through
    Into its ample bound.
Fast ran the Scottish warriors there,
Upon the Southern band to stare,
And envy with their wonder rose,
To see such well-appointed foes ;
Such length of shafts, such mighty
    bows,
So huge, that many simply thought
But for a vaunt such weapons wrought ;
And little deem'd their force to feel,
Through links of mail, and plates of
    steel,
When rattling upon Flodden vale,
The cloth-yard arrows flew like hail.

II.

Nor less did Marmion's skilful view
Glance every line and squadron
    through ;
And much he marvell'd one small land
Could marshal forth such various band :
    For men-at-arms were here,
Heavily sheath'd in mail and plate,
Like iron towers for strength and
    weight,
On Flemish steeds of bone and height,
    With battle-axe and spear.
Young knights and squires, a lighter
    train,
Practis'd their chargers on the plain,
By aid of leg, of hand, and rein,
    Each warlike feat to show,
To pass, to wheel, the croupe to gain,
And high curvett, that not in vain
The sword sway might descend amain
    On foeman's casque below.

He saw the hardy burghers there
March arm'd, on foot, with faces bare,
  For vizor they wore none,
Nor waving plume, nor crest of knight;
But burnish'd were their corslets
      bright,
Their brigantines, and gorgets light,
  Like very silver shone.
Long pikes they had for standing fight,
  Two-handed swords they wore,
And many wielded mace of weight,
  And bucklers bright they bore.

III.

On foot the yeoman too, but dress'd
In his steel-jack, a swarthy vest,
  With iron quilted well;
Each at his back (a slender store)
His forty days' provision bore,
  As feudal statutes tell.
His arms were halbert, axe, or spear,
A crossbow there, a hagbut here,
  A dagger-knife, and brand.
Sober he seem'd, and sad of cheer,
As loth to leave his cottage dear,
  And march to foreign strand;
Or musing, who would guide his steer
  To till the fallow land.
Yet deem not in his thoughtful eye
Did aught of dastard terror lie;
  More dreadful far his ire,
Than theirs, who, scorning danger's
      name,
In eager mood to battle came,
Their valour like light straw on flame,
  A fierce but fading fire.

IV.

Not so the Borderer: bred to war,
He knew the battle's din afar,
  And joy'd to hear it swell.
His peaceful day was slothful ease;
Nor harp, nor pipe, his ear could please
  Like the loud slogan yell.
On active steed, with lance and blade,
The light-arm'd pricker plied his
      trade,—

Let nobles fight for fame;
Let vassals follow where they lead,
Burghers to guard their townships
      bleed,
  But war 's the Borderer's game.
Their gain, their glory, their delight,
To sleep the day, maraud the night,
  O'er mountain, moss, and moor;
Joyful to fight they took their way,
Scarce caring who might win the day,
  Their booty was secure.
These, as Lord Marmion's train pass'd
      by,
Look'd on at first with careless eye,
Nor marvell'd aught, well taught to
      know
The form and force of English bow.
But when they saw the Lord array'd
In splendid arms and rich brocade,
Each Borderer to his kinsman said,—
  'Hist, Ringan! seest thou there?
Canst guess which road they 'll home-
      ward ride?
O! could we but on Border side,
By Eusedale glen, or Liddell's tide,
  Beset a prize so fair!
That fangless Lion, too, their guide,
Might chance to lose his glistering hide;
Brown Maudlin, of that doublet pied,
  Could make a kirtle rare.'

V.

Next, Marmion mark'd the Celtic race,
Of different language, form, and face,
  A various race of man;
Just then the Chiefs their tribes array'd,
And wild and garish semblance made,
The chequer'd trews, and belted plaid,
And varying notes the war-pipes bray'd,
  To every varying clan;
Wild through their red or sable hair
Look'd out their eyes with savage stare,
  On Marmion as he pass'd;
Their legs above the knee were bare;
Their frame was sinewy, short, and
      spare,
  And harden'd to the blast;

Of taller race, the chiefs they own
Were by the eagle's plumage known.
The hunted red-deer's undress'd hide
Their hairy buskins well supplied ;
The graceful bonnet deck'd their head :
Back from their shoulders hung the
     plaid ;
A broadsword of unwieldy length,
A dagger proved for edge and strength,
     A studded targe they wore,
And quivers, bows, and shafts,—but, O!
Short was the shaft, and weak the bow,
     To that which England bore.
The Isles-men carried at their backs
The ancient Danish battle-axe.
They raised a wild and wondering cry,
As with his guide rode Marmion by.
Loud were their clamouring tongues,
     as when
The clanging sea-fowl leave the fen,
And, with their cries discordant mix'd,
Grumbled and yell'd the pipes betwixt.

VI.

Thus through the Scottish camp they
     pass'd,
And reach'd the City gate at last,
Where all around, a wakeful guard,
Arm'd burghers kept their watch and
     ward.
Well had they cause of jealous fear,
When lay encamp'd, in field so near,
The Borderer and the Mountaineer.
As through the bustling streets they
     go,
All was alive with martial show :
At every turn, with dinning clang,
The armourer's anvil clash'd and rang ;
Or toil'd the swarthy smith, to wheel
The bar that arms the charger's heel ;
Or axe, or falchion, to the side
Of jarring grindstone was applied.
Page, groom, and squire, with hurrying
     pace,
Through street, and lane, and market-
     place,
     Bore lance, or casque, or sword ;

While burghers, with important face,
     Describ'd each new-come lord,
Discuss'd his lineage, told his name,
His following, and his warlike fame.
The Lion led to lodging meet,
Which high o'erlook'd the crowded
     street :
     There must the Baron rest,
Till past the hour of vesper tide,
And then to Holy-Rood must ride,—
     Such was the King's behest.
Meanwhile the Lion's care assigns
A banquet rich, and costly wines,
     To Marmion and his train ;
And when the appointed hour suc-
     ceeds,
The Baron dons his peaceful weeds,
And following Lindesay as he leads
     The palace-halls they gain.

VII.

Old Holy-Rood rung merrily,
That night, with wassell, mirth, and
     glee :
King James within her princely
     bower,
Feasted the Chiefs of Scotland's power,
Summon'd to spend the parting hour ;
For he had charged, that his array
Should southward march by break of
     day.
Well lov'd that splendid monarch aye
     The banquet and the song,
By day the tourney, and by night
The merry dance, trac'd fast and light,
The maskers quaint, the pageant bright,
     The revel loud and long.
This feast outshone his banquets past,
It was his blithest—and his last.
The dazzling lamps, from gallery gay,
Cast on the Court a dancing ray ;
Here to the harp did minstrels sing ;
There ladies touch'd a softer string ;
With long-ear'd cap, and motley vest,
The licensed fool retail'd his jest ;
His magic tricks the juggler plied ;
At dice and draughts the gallants vied ;

While some, in close recess apart,
Courted the ladies of their heart,
　　Nor courted them in vain;
For often, in the parting hour,
Victorious Love asserts his power
　　O'er coldness and disdain;
And flinty is her heart, can view
To battle march a lover true,
Can hear, perchance, his last adieu,
　　Nor own her share of pain.

VIII.

Through this mix'd crowd of glee and
　　game,
The King to greet Lord Marmion came,
　　While, reverent, all made room.
An easy task it was, I trow,
King James's manly form to know,
Although, his courtesy to show,
He doff'd, to Marmion bending low,
　　His broider'd cap and plume.
For royal was his garb and mien,
　　His cloak, of crimson velvet pil'd,
　　Trimm'd with the fur of marten wild;
His vest of changeful satin sheen,
　　The dazzled eye beguil'd;
His gorgeous collar hung adown,
Wrought with the badge of Scotland's
　　crown,
The thistle brave, of old renown:
His trusty blade, Toledo right,
Descended from a baldric bright;
White were his buskins, on the heel
His spurs inlaid of gold and steel;
His bonnet, all of crimson fair,
Was button'd with a ruby rare:
And Marmion deem'd he ne'er had seen
A prince of such a noble mien.

IX.

The Monarch's form was middle size;
For feat of strength or exercise,
　　Shaped in proportion fair;
And hazel was his eagle eye,
And auburn of the darkest dye,
　　His short curl'd beard and hair.
Light was his footstep in the dance,
　　And firm his stirrup in the lists;

And, oh! he had that merry glance
　　That seldom lady's heart resists.
Lightly from fair to fair he flew,
And lov'd to plead, lament, and sue,
Suit lightly won, and short-liv'd pain,
For monarchs seldom sigh in vain.
　　I said he joy'd in banquet bower;
But, 'mid his mirth, 'twas often strange,
How suddenly his cheer would change,
　　His look o'ercast and lower,
If, in a sudden turn, he felt
The pressure of his iron belt,
That bound his breast in penance pain,
In memory of his father slain.
Even so 'twas strange how, evermore,
Soon as the passing pang was o'er,
Forward he rush'd, with double glee,
Into the stream of revelry;
Thus, dim-seen object of affright
Startles the courser in his flight,
And half he halts, half springs aside;
But feels the quickening spur applied,
And, straining on the tighten'd rein,
Scours doubly swift o'er hill and plain.

X.

O'er James's heart, the courtiers say,
Sir Hugh the Heron's wife held sway:
　　To Scotland's Court she came,
To be a hostage for her lord,
Who Cessford's gallant heart had
　　gor'd,
And with the King to make accord,
　　Had sent his lovely dame.
Nor to that lady free alone
Did the gay King allegiance own;
　　For the fair Queen of France
Sent him a turquois ring and glove,
And charg'd him, as her knight and
　　love,
　　For her to break a lance;
And strike three strokes with Scottish
　　brand,
And march three miles on Southron
　　land,
And bid the banners of his band
　　In English breezes dance.

And thus for France's Queen he
    drest
His manly limbs in mailed vest ;
And thus admitted English fair
His inmost counsels still to share ;
And thus, for both, he madly plann'd
The ruin of himself and land !
    And yet, the sooth to tell,
Nor England's fair, nor France's
    Queen,
Were worth one pearl-drop, bright
    and sheen,
    From Margaret's eyes that fell,—
His own Queen Margaret, who, in
    Lithgow's bower,
All lonely sat, and wept the weary
    hour.

XI.

The Queen sits lone in Lithgow pile,
    And weeps the weary day
The war against her native soil,
Her Monarch's risk in battle broil:—
And in gay Holy-Rood, the while,
Dame Heron rises with a smile
    Upon the harp to play.
Fair was her rounded arm, as o'er
    The strings her fingers flew ;
And as she touch'd and tuned them
    all,
Ever her bosom's rise and fall
    Was plainer given to view ;
For, all for heat, was laid aside
Her wimple, and her hood untied.
And first she pitch'd her voice to sing,
Then glanced her dark eye on the
    King,
And then around the silent ring ;
And laugh'd, and blush'd, and oft did
    say
Her pretty oath, by Yea, and Nay,
She could not, would not, durst not
    play !
At length, upon the harp, with glee,
Mingled with arch simplicity,
A soft, yet lively, air she rung,
While thus the wily lady sung :

XII.

LOCHINVAR.

O, young Lochinvar is come out of
    the west,
Through all the wide Border his steed
    was the best ;
And save his good broadsword he
    weapons had none,
He rode all unarm'd, and he rode all
    alone.
So faithful in love, and so dauntless
    in war,
There never was knight like the
    young Lochinvar.

He staid not for brake, and he stopp'd
    not for stone,
He swam the Eske river where ford
    there was none ;
But ere he alighted at Netherby gate,
The bride had consented, the gallant
    came late :
For a laggard in love, and a dastard
    in war,
Was to wed the fair Ellen of brave
    Lochinvar.

So boldly he enter'd the Netherby Hall,
Among bride's-men, and kinsmen, and
    brothers, and all :
Then spoke the bride's father, his
    hand on his sword,
(For the poor craven bridegroom said
    never a word,)
' O come ye in peace here, or come ye
    in war,
Or to dance at our bridal, young Lord
    Lochinvar ?'

' I long woo'd your daughter, my suit
    you denied ;—
Love swells like the Solway, but ebbs
    like its tide—
And now am I come, with this lost
    love of mine,
To lead but one measure, drink one
    cup of wine.

There are maidens in Scotland more
   lovely by far,
That would gladly be bride to the
   young Lochinvar.'

The bride kiss'd the goblet: the knight
   took it up,
He quaff'd off the wine, and he threw
   down the cup.
She look'd down to blush, and she
   look'd up to sigh,
With a smile on her lips, and a tear in
   her eye.
He took her soft hand, ere her mother
   could bar,—
'Now tread we a measure!' said
   young Lochinvar.

So stately his form, and so lovely her
   face,
That never a hall such a galliard did
   grace;
While her mother did fret, and her
   father did fume,
And the bridegroom stood dangling
   his bonnet and plume;
And the bride-maidens whisper'd,
   ''Twere better by far,
To have match'd our fair cousin with
   young Lochinvar.'

One touch to her hand, and one word
   in her ear,
When they reach'd the hall-door, and
   the charger stood near;
So light to the croupe the fair lady he
   swung,
So light to the saddle before her he
   sprung!
'She is won! we are gone, over bank,
   bush, and scaur;
They'll have fleet steeds that follow,'
   quoth young Lochinvar.

There was mounting 'mong Græmes
   of the Netherby clan;
Forsters, Fenwicks, and Musgraves,
   they rode and they ran:

There was racing and chasing on
   Cannobie Lee,
But the lost bride of Netherby ne'er
   did they see.
So daring in love, and so dauntless in
   war,
Have ye e'er heard of gallant like
   young Lochinvar?—

XIII.

The Monarch o'er the siren hung
And beat the measure as she sung;
And, pressing closer, and more near,
He whisper'd praises in her ear.
In loud applause the courtiers vied;
And ladies wink'd, and spoke aside.
  The witching dame to Marmion
    threw
    A glance, where seem'd to reign
  The pride that claims applauses due,
  And of her royal conquest too,
    A real or feign'd disdain:
Familiar was the look, and told,
Marmion and she were friends of old.
The King observ'd their meeting eyes,
With something like displeas'd sur-
   prise;
For monarchs ill can rivals brook,
Even in a word, or smile, or look.
Straight took he forth the parchment
   broad,
Which Marmion's high commission
   show'd:
'Our Borders sack'd by many a raid,
Our peaceful liege-men robb'd,' he
   said:
'On day of truce our Warden slain,
Stout Barton kill'd, his vessels ta'en—
Unworthy were we here to reign,
Should these for vengeance cry in vain;
Our full defiance, hate, and scorn,
Our herald has to Henry borne.'

XIV.

He paus'd, and led where Douglas
   stood,
And with stern eye the pageant view'd:

I mean that Douglas, sixth of yore,
Who coronet of Angus bore,
And, when his blood and heart were
  high,
Did the third James in camp defy,
And all his minions led to die
  On Lauder's dreary flat:
Princes and favourites long grew tame
And trembled at the homely name
  Of Archibald Bell-the-Cat;
The same who left the dusky vale
Of Hermitage in Liddisdale,
  Its dungeons, and its towers,
Where Bothwell's turrets brave the
  air,
And Bothwell bank is blooming fair,
  To fix his princely bowers.
Though now, in age, he had laid down
His armour for the peaceful gown,
  And for a staff his brand,
Yet often would flash forth the fire,
That could, in youth, a monarch's ire
  And minion's pride withstand;
And even that day, at council board,
  Unapt to soothe his sovereign's
    mood,
  Against the war had Angus stood,
  And chaf'd his royal lord.

xv.

His giant-form, like ruin'd tower,
Though fall'n its muscles' brawny
  vaunt,
Huge-bon'd, and tall, and grim, and
  gaunt,
  Seem'd o'er the gaudy scene to lower:
His locks and beard in silver grew;
His eyebrows kept their sable hue.
Near Douglas when the Monarch stood,
His bitter speech he thus pursued:
' Lord Marmion, since these letters say
That in the North you needs must stay
  While slightest hopes of peace
    remain,
Uncourteous speech it were, and stern,
To say—Return to Lindisfarne
  Until my herald come again.

Then rest you in Tantallon Hold;
Your host shall be the Douglas bold,—
A chief unlike his sires of old.
He wears their motto on his blade,
Their blazon o'er his towers display'd;
Yet loves his sovereign to oppose,
More than to face his country's foes.
And, I bethink me, by St. Stephen,
  But e'en this morn to me was given
A prize, the first fruits of the war,
Ta'en by a galley from Dunbar,
  A bevy of the maids of Heaven.
Under your guard, these holy maids
Shall safe return to cloister shades,
And, while they at Tantallon stay,
Requiem for Cochran's soul may say.'
And, with the slaughter'd favourite's
  name,
Across the Monarch's brow there came
A cloud of ire, remorse, and shame.

xvi.

In answer nought could Angus speak;
His proud heart swell'd wellnigh to
  break:
He turn'd aside, and down his cheek
  A burning tear there stole,
His hand the Monarch sudden took,
That sight his kind heart could not
  brook:
  ' Now, by the Bruce's soul,
Angus, my hasty speech forgive!
For sure as doth his spirit live,
As he said of the Douglas old,
  I well may say of you,
That never king did subject hold,
In speech more free, in war more bold,
  More tender and more true:
Forgive me, Douglas, once again.'—
And, while the King his hand did
  strain,
The old man's tears fell down like
  rain.
To seize the moment Marmion tried,
And whisper'd to the King aside:
' Oh! let such tears unwonted plead
For respite short from dubious deed!

A child will weep a bramble's smart,
A maid to see her sparrow part,
A stripling for a woman's heart :
But woe awaits a country, when
She sees the tears of bearded men.
Then oh ! what omen, dark and high,
When Douglas wets his manly eye !'

XVII.

Displeas'd was James, that stranger view'd
And tamper'd with his changing mood.
'Laugh those that can, weep those that may,'
Thus did the fiery Monarch say,
'Southward I march by break of day ;
And if within Tantallon strong
The good Lord Marmion tarries long,
Perchance our meeting next may fall
At Tamworth, in his castle-hall.'
The haughty Marmion felt the taunt,
And answer'd, grave, the royal vaunt :
'Much honour'd were my humble home
If in its halls King James should come ;
But Nottingham has archers good,
And Yorkshire men are stern of mood ;
Northumbrian prickers wild and rude.
On Derby Hills the paths are steep ;
In Ouse and Tyne the fords are deep ;
And many a banner will be torn,
And many a knight to earth be borne,
And many a sheaf of arrows spent,
Ere Scotland's King shall cross the Trent :
Yet pause, brave Prince, while yet you may !'
The Monarch lightly turn'd away,
And to his nobles loud did call,—
'Lords, to the dance ! a hall ! a hall !'
Himself his cloak and sword flung by,
And led Dame Heron gallantly ;
And minstrels, at the royal order,
Rung out 'Blue Bonnets o'er the Border.'

XVIII.

Leave we these revels now, to tell
What to Saint Hilda's maids befell,
Whose galley, as they sail'd again
To Whitby, by a Scot was ta'en.
Now at Dun-Edin did they bide,
Till James should of their fate decide ;
And soon, by his command,
Were gently summon'd to prepare
To journey under Marmion's care,
As escort honour'd, safe, and fair,
Again to English land.
The Abbess told her chaplet o'er,
Nor knew which saint she should implore ;
For, when she thought of Constance, sore
She fear'd Lord Marmion's mood.
And judge what Clara must have felt !
The sword that hung in Marmion's belt
Had drunk De Wilton's blood.
Unwittingly, King James had given,
As guard to Whitby's shades,
The man most dreaded under Heaven
By these defenceless maids :
Yet what petition could avail,
Or who would listen to the tale
Of woman, prisoner, and nun,
'Mid bustle of a war begun ?
They deem'd it hopeless to avoid
The convoy of their dangerous guide.

XIX.

Their lodging, so the King assign'd,
To Marmion's, as their guardian, join'd ;
And thus it fell, that, passing nigh,
The Palmer caught the Abbess' eye,
Who warn'd him by a scroll,
She had a secret to reveal,
That much concern'd the Church's weal,
And health of sinner's soul ;
And, with deep charge of secrecy,
She named a place to meet,
Within an open balcony,
That hung from dizzy pitch, and high,
Above the stately street ;
To which, as common to each home,
At night they might in secret come.

XX.

At night, in secret, there they came,
The Palmer and the holy Dame.
The moon among the clouds rose high,
And all the city hum was by.
Upon the street, where late before
Did din of war and warriors roar,
　You might have heard a pebble fall,
A beetle hum, a cricket sing,
An owlet flap his boding wing
　On Giles's steeple tall.
The antique buildings, climbing high,
Whose Gothic frontlets sought the sky,
　Were here wrapt deep in shade ;
There on their brows the moonbeam
　broke,
Through the faint wreaths of silvery
　smoke,
　And on the casements play'd.
And other light was none to see,
Save torches gliding far,
Before some chieftain of degree,
Who left the royal revelry
　To bowne him for the war.
A solemn scene the Abbess chose,
A solemn hour, her secret to disclose.

XXI.

' O holy Palmer ! ' she began,
' For sure he must be sainted man,
Whose blessed feet have trod the
　ground
Where the Redeemer's tomb is found,
For His dear Church's sake, my tale
Attend, nor deem of light avail,
Though I must speak of worldly love,
How vain to those who wed above !
De Wilton and Lord Marmion woo'd
Clara de Clare, of Gloster's blood—
(Idle it were of Whitby's dame,
To say of that same blood I came) ;
And once, when jealous rage was high,
Lord Marmion said despiteously
Wilton was traitor in his heart,
And had made league with Martin
　Swart
When he came here on Simnel's part,

And only cowardice did restrain
His rebel aid on Stokefield's plain,—
And down he threw his glove :—the
　thing
Was tried, as wont, before the King ;
Where frankly did De Wilton own,
That Swart in Gueldres he had known ;
And that between them then there
　went
Some scroll of courteous compliment.
For this he to his castle sent ;
But when his messenger return'd,
Judge how de Wilton's fury burn'd !
For in his packet there was laid
Letters that claim'd disloyal aid,
And proved King Henry's cause be-
　tray'd.
His fame, thus blighted, in the field
He strove to clear, by spear and
　shield ;—
To clear his fame in vain he strove,
For wondrous are His ways above !
Perchance some form was unobserv'd ;
Perchance in prayer, or faith, he
　swerv'd ;
Else how could guiltless champion
　quail,
Or how the blessed ordeal fail ?

XXII.

' His squire, who now De Wilton saw
As recreant doom'd to suffer law,
　Repentant, own'd in vain,
That, while he had the scrolls in care,
A stranger maiden, passing fair,
Had drench'd him with a beverage rare ;
　His words no faith could gain.
With Clare alone he credence won,
Who, rather than wed Marmion,
Did to Saint Hilda's shrine repair,
To give our house her livings fair
And die a vestal vot'ress there.
The impulse from the earth was given,
But bent her to the paths of heaven.
A purer heart, a lovelier maid,
Ne'er shelter'd her in Whitby's shade,
No, not since Saxon Edelfled ;

Only one trace of earthly strain,
　That for her lover's loss
She cherishes a sorrow vain,
　And murmurs at the cross.
And then her heritage ;—it goes
　Along the banks of Tame ;
Deep fields of grain the reaper mows,
In meadows rich the heifer lows,
The falconer and huntsman knows
　Its woodlands for the game.
Shame were it to Saint Hilda dear,
And I, her humble vot'ress here,
　Should do a deadly sin,
Her temple spoil'd before mine eyes,
If this false Marmion such a prize
　By my consent should win ;
Yet hath our boisterous monarch sworn
That Clare shall from our house be torn,
And grievous cause have I to fear,
Such mandate doth Lord Marmion
　bear.

XXIII.

' Now, prisoner, helpless, and betray'd
To evil power, I claim thine aid,
　By every step that thou hast trod
To holy shrine and grotto dim ;
By every martyr's tortur'd limb,
By angel, saint, and seraphim,
　And by the Church of God !
For mark :—When Wilton was be-
　tray'd,
And with his squire forg'd letters laid,
She was, alas ! that sinful maid,
　By whom the deed was done ;
O ! shame and horror to be said—
She was a perjur'd nun !
No clerk in all the land, like her,
Traced quaint and varying character.
Perchance you may a marvel deem,
　That Marmion's paramour
(For such vile thing she was) should
　scheme
　Her lover's nuptial hour ;
But o'er him thus she hop'd to gain,
As privy to his honour's stain,
　Illimitible power ·

For this she secretly retain'd
　Each proof that might the plot reveal,
　Instructions with his hand and seal ;
And thus Saint Hilda deign'd,
　Through sinner's perfidy impure,
　Her house's glory to secure,
And Clare's immortal weal.

XXIV.

'' Twere long, and needless, here to tell
How to my hand these papers fell ;
　With me they must not stay.
Saint Hilda keep her Abbess true !
Who knows what outrage he might do,
　While journeying by the way ?
O blessed Saint, if e'er again
I venturous leave thy calm domain,
To travel or by land or main,
　Deep penance may I pay !
Now, saintly Palmer, mark my prayer :
I give this packet to thy care,
For thee to stop they will not dare ;
　And O ! with cautious speed,
To Wolsey's hand the papers bring,
That he may show them to the King :
　And, for thy well-earn'd meed,
Thou holy man, at Whitby's shrine
A weekly mass shall still be thine,
　While priests can sing and read.
What ail'st thou ! Speak !' For as he
　took
The charge, a strong emotion shook
　His frame ; and, ere reply,
They heard a faint, yet shrilly tone,
Like distant clarion feebly blown,
　That on the breeze did die ;
And loud the Abbess shriek'd in fear,
' Saint Withold, save us ! What is here !
　Look at yon City Cross !
See on its battled tower appear
Phantoms, that scutcheons seem to rear,
　And blazon'd banners toss !'

XXV.

Dun-Edin's Cross, a pillar'd stone,
Rose on a turret octagon ;

(But now is razed that monument,
  Whence royal edict rang,
And voice of Scotland's law was sent
  In glorious trumpet-clang.
O ! be his tomb as lead to lead,
Upon its dull destroyer's head !—
A minstrel's malison is said.)
Then on its battlements they saw
A vision, passing Nature's law,
  Strange, wild, and dimly seen ;
Figures that seem'd to rise and die,
Gibber and sign, advance and fly,
While nought confirm'd could ear or
      eye
  Discern of sound or mien.
Yet darkly did it seem, as there
Heralds and Pursuivants prepare,
With trumpet sound and blazon fair,
  A summons to proclaim ;
But indistinct the pageant proud,
As fancy forms of midnight cloud,
When flings the moon upon her shroud
  A wavering tinge of flame ;
It flits, expands, and shifts, till loud,
From midmost of the spectre crowd,
  This awful summons came :—

XXVI.

'Prince, prelate, potentate, and peer,
  Whose names I now shall call,
Scottish, or foreigner, give ear ;
Subjects of him who sent me here,
  At his tribunal to appear,
    I summon one and all :
I cite you by each deadly sin,
That e'er hath soil'd your hearts within :
I cite you by each brutal lust,
That e'er defil'd your earthly dust,—
  By wrath, by pride, by fear,
By each o'ermastering passion's tone,
By the dark grave, and dying groan !
When forty days are pass'd and gone,
I cite you, at your Monarch's throne,
  To answer and appear.'
Then thunder'd forth a roll of names :
The first was thine, unhappy James !
  Then all thy nobles came.

Crawford, Glencairn, Montrose, Argyle,
Ross, Bothwell, Forbes, Lennox.
      Lyle—
Why should I tell their separate
      style ?
  Each chief of birth and fame,
Of Lowland, Highland, Border, Isle,
Foredoom'd to Flodden's carnage pile,
  Was cited there by name ;
And Marmion, Lord of Fontenaye,
Of Lutterward, and Scrivelbaye ;
De Wilton, erst of Aberley,
The self-same thundering voice did say.
  But then another spoke :
' Thy fatal summons I deny,
And thine infernal Lord defy,
Appealing me to Him on High,
  Who burst the sinner's yoke.'
At that dread accent, with a scream,
Parted the pageant like a dream,
  The summoner was gone.
Prone on her face the Abbess fell,
And fast, and fast, her beads did tell ;
Her nuns came, startled by the yell,
  And found her there alone.
She mark'd not, at the scene aghast,
What time, or how, the Palmer pass'd.

XXVII.

Shift we the scene. The camp doth
      move,
  Dun-Edin's streets are empty now,
Save when, for weal of those they
      love,
  To pray the prayer, and vow the
      vow,
The tottering child, the anxious fair,
The grey-hair'd sire, with pious care,
To chapels and to shrines repair—
Where is the Palmer now ? and where
The Abbess, Marmion, and Clare ?
Bold Douglas ! to Tantallon fair
  They journey in thy charge :
Lord Marmion rode on his right hand,
The Palmer still was with the band ;
Angus, like Lindesay, did command,
  That none should roam at large.

But in that Palmer's alter'd mien
A wondrous change might now be seen;
   Freely he spoke of war,
Of marvels wrought by single hand,
When lifted for a native land;
And still look d high, as if he plann'd
   Some desperate deed afar.
His courser would he feed and stroke,
And, tucking up his sable frocke,
Would first his mettle bold provoke,
   Then soothe or quell his pride.
Old Hubert said that never one
He saw, except Lord Marmion,
   A steed so fairly ride.

XXVIII.

Some half-hour's march behind, there
   came,
   By Eustace govern'd fair,
A troop escorting Hilda's Dame,
   With all her nuns, and Clare.
No audience had Lord Marmion sought;
   Ever he fear'd to aggravate
   Clara de Clare's suspicious hate;
And safer 'twas, he thought,
   To wait till, from the nuns remov'd,
   The influence of kinsmen lov'd,
   And suit by Henry's self approv'd,
Her slow consent had wrought.
   His was no flickering flame, that dies
   Unless when fann'd by looks and
     sighs,
   And lighted oft at lady's eyes;
   He long'd to stretch his wide com-
     mand
   O'er luckless Clara's ample land:
   Besides, when Wilton with him
     vied,
   Although the pang of humbled pride
   The place of jealousy supplied,
Yet conquest by that meanness won
He almost loath'd to think upon,
Led him, at times, to hate the cause,
Which made him burst through
   honour's laws.
If e'er he lov'd, 'twas her alone,
Who died within that vault of stone.

XXIX.

And now, when close at hand they saw
North Berwick's town, and lofty Law,
Fitz-Eustace bade them pause a while,
Before a venerable pile,
   Whose turrets view'd, afar,
The lofty Bass, the Lambie Isle,
   The ocean's peace or war.
At tolling of a bell, forth came
The convent's venerable Dame,
And pray'd Saint Hilda's Abbess rest
With her, a loved and honour'd guest,
Till Douglas should a bark prepare
To waft her back to Whitby fair.
Glad was the Abbess, you may guess,
And thank'd the Scottish Prioress;
And tedious were to tell, I ween,
The courteous speech that pass'd
   between.
   O'erjoy'd the nuns their palfreys
     leave;
But when fair Clara did intend,
Like them, from horseback to descend,
   Fitz-Eustace said—'I grieve,
Fair lady, grieve e'en from my heart,
Such gentle company to part;
   Think not discourtesy;
But lords' commands must be obey'd;
And Marmion and the Douglas said,
   That you must wend with me.
Lord Marmion hath a letter broad,
Which to the Scottish Earl he show'd,
Commanding, that, beneath his care,
Without delay, you shall repair
To your good kinsman, Lord Fitz-
   Clare.'

XXX.

The startled Abbess loud exclaim'd;
But she, at whom the blow was aim'd,
Grew pale as death, and cold as lead;
She deem'd she heard her death-doom
   read.
'Cheer thee, my child!' the Abbess said,
'They dare not tear thee from my hand,
To ride alone with armed band.'

'Nay, holy mother, nay,'
Fitz-Eustace said; 'the lovely Clare
Will be in Lady Angus' care,
    In Scotland while we stay;
And, when we move, an easy ride
Will bring us to the English side,
Female attendance to provide
    Befitting Gloster's heir:
Nor thinks nor dreams my noble lord
By slightest look or act or word
    To harass Lady Clare.
Her faithful guardian he will be,
Nor sue for slightest courtesy
    That e'en to stranger falls,
Till he shall place her, safe and free,
    Within her kinsman's halls.'
He spoke, and blush'd with earnest
        grace;
His faith was painted on his face,
    And Clare's worst fear reliev'd.
The Lady Abbess loud exclaim'd
On Henry, and the Douglas blam'd,
    Entreated, threaten'd, griev'd;
To martyr, saint, and prophet pray'd,
Against Lord Marmion inveigh'd,
    And call'd the Prioress to aid,
To curse with candle, bell, and book.
Her head the grave Cistertian shook:
'The Douglas, and the King,' she
        said,
'In their commands will be obey'd;
Grieve not, nor dream that harm can fall
The maiden in Tantallon hall.'

XXXI.

The Abbess, seeing strife was vain,
Assumed her wonted state again—
    For much of state she had—
Compos'd her veil, and rais'd her
        head,
And 'Bid,' in solemn voice she said,
    'Thy master, bold and bad,
The records of his house turn o'er,
    And, when he shall there written see,
    That one of his own ancestry
    Drove the Monks forth of Coventry,
Bid him his fate explore!

Prancing in pride of earthly trust,
His charger hurl'd him to the dust,
And, by a base plebeian thrust,
He died his band before.
    God judge 'twixt Marmion and me;
    He is a Chief of high degree,
And I a poor recluse:
    Yet oft, in holy writ, we see
    Even such weak minister as me
May the oppressor bruise:
    For thus, inspir'd, did Judith slay
        The mighty in his sin,
    And Jael thus, and Deborah'——
        Here hasty Blount broke in:
'Fitz-Eustace, we must march our
        band:
Saint Anton' fire thee! wilt thou
        stand
All day, with bonnet in thy hand,
    To hear the Lady preach?
By this good light! if thus we stay,
Lord Marmion, for our fond delay,
    Will sharper sermon teach.
Come, don thy cap, and mount thy
        horse;
The Dame must patience take per-
        force.'

XXXII.

'Submit we then to force,' said Clare,
'But let this barbarous lord despair
    His purpos'd aim to win;
Let him take living, land, and life;
But to be Marmion's wedded wife
    In me were deadly sin:
And if it be the King's decree,
That I must find no sanctuary,
    In that inviolable dome,
Where even a homicide might come,
    And safely rest his head,
Though at its open portals stood,
Thirsting to pour forth blood for blood,
    The kinsmen of the dead;
Yet one asylum is my own
    Against the dreaded hour;
A low, a silent, and a lone,
    Where kings have little power.

One victim is before me there.—
Mother, your blessing, and in prayer
Remember your unhappy Clare!'
Loud weeps the Abbess, and bestows
  Kind blessings many a one:
Weeping and wailing loud arose,
Round patient Clare, the clamorous
      woes
  Of every simple nun.
His eyes the gentle Eustace dried,
And scarce rude Blount the sight could
      bide.
  Then took the squire her rein,
And gently led away her steed,
And, by each courteous word and
      deed,
  To cheer her strove in vain.

XXXIII.

But scant three miles the band had
      rode,
When o'er a height they pass'd,
And, sudden, close before them show'd
  His towers, Tantallon vast;
Broad, massive, high, and stretching
      far,
And held impregnable in war.
On a projecting rock they rose,
And round three sides the ocean
      flows,
The fourth did battled walls enclose,
  And double mound and fosse.
By narrow drawbridge, outworks
      strong,
Through studded gates, an entrance
      long,
  To the main court they cross.
It was a wide and stately square:
Around were lodgings, fit and fair,
  And towers of various form,
Which on the court projected far,
And broke its lines quadrangular.
Here was square keep, there turret
      high,
Or pinnacle that sought the sky,
  Whence oft the Warder could descry
  The gathering ocean-storm.

XXXIV.

Here did they rest.   The princely care
Of Douglas, why should I declare,
Or say they met reception fair?
  Or why the tidings say,
Which, varying, to Tantallon came,
By hurrying posts or fleeter fame,
  With ever varying day?
And, first they heard King James had
      won
  Etall, and Wark, and Ford; and then,
  That Norham Castle strong was
      ta'en.
At that sore marvell'd Marmion;—
And Douglas hop'd his Monarch's hand
Would soon subdue Northumberland
  But whisper'd news there came,
That, while his host inactive lay,
And melted by degrees away,
King James was dallying off the day
  With Heron's wily dame.
Such acts to chronicles I yield;
  Go seek them there, and see:
Mine is a tale of Flodden Field,
  And not a history.
At length they heard the Scottish host
On that high ridge had made their
      post,
  Which frowns o'er Millfield Plain;
And that brave Surrey many a band
Had gather'd in the Southern land,
And march'd into Northumberland,
  And camp at Wooler ta'en.
Marmion, like charger in the stall,
That hears, without, the trumpet-call,
  Began to chafe, and swear—
'A sorry thing to hide my head
In castle, like a fearful maid,
  When such a field is near!
Needs must I see this battle-day:
Death to my fame if such a fray
Were fought, and Marmion away!
The Douglas, too, I wot not why,
Hath 'bated of his courtesy:
No longer in his halls I'll stay.'
Then bade his band they should array
For march against the dawning day.

F

INTRODUCTION TO CANTO
SIXTH.

TO

RICHARD HEBER, Esq.

Mertoun-House, Christmas.

HEAP on more wood!—the wind is
  chill;
But let it whistle as it will,
We 'll keep our Christmas merry still.
Each age has deem'd the new-born
  year
The fittest time for festal cheer:
Even, heathen yet, the savage Dane
At Iol more deep the mead did drain;
High on the beach his galleys drew,
And feasted all his pirate crew;
Then in his low and pine-built hall,
Where shields and axes deck'd the wall,
They gorged upon the half dress'd steer;
Caroused in seas of sable beer;
While round, in brutal jest, were
  thrown
The half-gnaw'd rib, and marrow-bone:
Or listen'd all, in grim delight,
While Scalds yell'd out the joys of fight.
Then forth, in frenzy, would they hie,
While wildly loose their red locks fly,
And dancing round the blazing pile,
They make such barbarous mirth the
  while,
As best might to the mind recall
The boisterous joys of Odin's hall.

  And well our Christian sires of old
Loved when the year its course had
  roll'd,
And brought blithe Christmas back
  again,
With all his hospitable train.
Domestic and religious rite
Gave honour to the holy night;
On Christmas eve the bells were rung;
On Christmas eve the mass was sung:

That only night in all the year,
Saw the stoled priest the chalice rear.
The damsel donn'd her kirtle sheen;
The hall was dress'd with holly green,
Forth to the wood did merry-men go,
To gather in the mistletoe.
Then open'd wide the Baron's hall
To vassal, tenant, serf, and all;
Power laid his rod of rule aside,
And Ceremony doff'd his pride.
The heir, with roses in his shoes,
That night might village partner
  choose;
The Lord, underogating, share
The vulgar game of ' post and pair.'
All hail'd, with uncontroll'd delight,
And general voice, the happy night,
That to the cottage, as the crown,
Brought tidings of salvation down.

  The fire, with well-dried logs sup-
    plied,
Went roaring up the chimney wide;
The huge hall-table's oaken face,
Scrubb'd till it shone, the day to grace,
Bore then upon its massive board
No mark to part the squire and lord.
Then was brought in the lusty brawn,
By old blue-coated serving-man;
Then the grim boar's head frown'd
  on high,
Crested with bays and rosemary.
Well can the green-garb'd ranger tell,
How, when, and where, the monster
  fell;
What dogs before his death he tore,
And all the baiting of the boar.
The wassel round, in good brown bowls,
Garnish'd with ribbons, blithely trowls.
There the huge sirloin reek'd; hard by
Plum-porridge stood, and Christmas
  pie;
Nor fail'd old Scotland to produce,
At such high tide, her savoury goose.
Then came the merry maskers in,
And carols roar'd with blithesome
  din;

If unmelodious was the song,
It was a hearty note, and strong.
Who lists may in their mumming see
Traces of ancient mystery;
White shirts supplied the masquerade,
And smutted cheeks the visors made;
But, O! what maskers, richly dight,
Can boast of bosoms half so light!
England was merry England, when
Old Christmas brought his sports again.
'Twas Christmas broach'd the mightiest
ale;
'Twas Christmas told the merriest
tale;
A Christmas gambol oft could cheer
The poor man's heart through half the
year.

Still linger, in our northern clime,
Some remnants of the good old time;
And still, within our valleys here,
We hold the kindred title dear,
Even when, perchance, its far-fetch'd
claim
To Southron ear sounds empty name;
For course of blood, our proverbs
deem,
Is warmer than the mountain-stream.
And thus, my Christmas still I hold
Where my great-grandsire came of old,
With amber beard, and flaxen hair,
And reverend apostolic air—
The feast and holy-tide to share,
And mix sobriety with wine,
And honest mirth with thoughts divine:
Small thought was his, in after time
E'er to be hitch'd into a rhyme.
The simple sire could only boast,
That he was loyal to his cost;
The banish'd race of kings rever'd,
And lost his land,—but kept his beard.

In these dear halls, where welcome
kind
Is with fair liberty combin'd;
Where cordial friendship gives the
hand,

And flies constraint the magic wand
Of the fair dame that rules the land [1],
Little we heed the tempest drear,
While music, mirth, and social cheer,
Speed on their wings the passing year.
And Mertoun's halls are fair e'en now,
When not a leaf is on the bough.
Tweed loves them well, and turns again,
As loath to leave the sweet domain,
And holds his mirror to her face,
And clips her with a close embrace:—
Gladly as he, we seek the dome,
And as reluctant turn us home.

How just that, at this time of glee,
My thoughts should, Heber, turn to
thee!
For many a merry hour we've known,
And heard the chimes of midnight's
tone.
Cease, then, my friend! a moment cease,
And leave these classic tomes in peace!
Of Roman and of Grecian lore,
Sure mortal brain can hold no more.
These ancients, as Noll Bluff might say,
'Were pretty fellows in their day;'
But time and tide o'er all prevail—
On Christmas eve a Christmas tale—
Of wonder and of war—'Profane!
What! leave the lofty Latian strain,
Her stately prose, her verse's charms,
To hear the clash of rusty arms:
In Fairy Land or Limbo lost,
To jostle conjurer and ghost,
Goblin and witch!'—Nay, Heber dear,
Before you touch my charter, hear:
Though Leyden [2] aids, alas! no more,
My cause with many-languaged lore,
This may I say:—in realms of death
Ulysses meets Alcides' *wraith*;
Aeneas, upon Thracia's shore,
The ghost of murder'd Polydore;

---

1 'A lady of noble German descent, born Countess
Harriet Bruhl of Martinskirchen, married to H Scott,
Esq. of Harden (now Lord Polwarth), the author's
relative and much valued friend almost from infancy.'—*Border Minstrelsy*.
2 John Leyden, M.D., of great service to Scott in
the preparation of the Border Minstrelsy, died at
Java in 1811, in his 36th year.

For omens, we in Livy cross,
At every turn, *locutus Bos.*
As grave and duly speaks that ox,
As if he told the price of stocks ;
Or held, in Rome republican,
The place of common-councilman.

All nations have their omens drear,
Their legends wild of woe and fear.
To Cambria look—the peasant see
Bethink him of Glendowerdy,
And shun 'the spirit's Blasted Tree.'
The Highlander, whose red claymore
The battle turn'd on Maida's shore,
Will, on a Friday morn, look pale,
If ask'd to tell a fairy tale :
He fears the vengeful Elfin King,
Who leaves that day his grassy ring :
Invisible to human ken,
He walks among the sons of men.

Did'st e'er, dear Heber, pass along
Beneath the towers of Franchémont,
Which, like an eagle's nest in air,
Hang o'er the stream and hamlet fair ?
Deep in their vaults, the peasants say,
A mighty treasure buried lay,
Amass'd through rapine and through
    wrong
By the last Lord of Franchémont.
The iron chest is bolted hard,
A huntsman sits, its constant guard ;
Around his neck his horn is hung,
His hanger in his belt is slung ;
Before his feet his blood-hounds lie ;
An 'twere not for his gloomy eye,
Whose withering glance no heart can
    brook,
As true a huntsman doth he look
As bugle e'er in brake did sound,
Or ever hollow'd to a hound.
To chase the fiend, and win the prize,
In that same dungeon ever tries
An aged necromantic priest ;
It is an hundred years at least,
Since 'twixt them first the strife begun,
And neither yet has lost nor won.

And oft the Conjurer's words will make
The stubborn Demon groan and quake ;
And oft the bands of iron break,
Or bursts one lock, that still amain,
Fast as 'tis open'd, shuts again.
That magic strife within the tomb
May last until the day of doom,
Unless the adept shall learn to tell
The very word that clench'd the spell,
When Franch'mont lock'd the treasure
    cell.
An hundred years are pass'd and gone,
And scarce three letters has he won.

Such general superstition may
Excuse for old Pitscottie say ;
Whose gossip history has given
My song the messenger from Heaven,
That warn'd, in Lithgow, Scotland's
    King,
Nor less the infernal summoning ;
May pass the Monk of Durham's tale,
Whose demon fought in Gothic mail ;
May pardon plead for Fordun grave,
Who told of Gifford's Goblin-Cave.
But why such instances to you,
Who, in an instant, can renew
Your treasured hoards of various lore,
And furnish twenty thousand more ?
Hoards, not like theirs whose volumes
    rest
Like treasures in the Franch'mont chest,
While gripple owners still refuse
To others what they cannot use ;
Give them the priest's whole century,
They shall not spell you letters three ;
Their pleasure in the books the same
The magpie takes in pilfer'd gem.
Thy volumes, open as thy heart,
Delight, amusement, science, art,
To every ear and eye impart ;
Yet who of all who thus employ them,
Can like the owner's self enjoy them ?—
But, hark ! I hear the distant drum !
The day of Flodden Field is come.—
Adieu, dear Heber ! life and health,
And store of literary wealth.

Canto Sixth.

The Battle.

I.

WHILE great events were on the gale,
And each hour brought a varying tale,
And the demeanour, changed and cold,
Of Douglas, fretted Marmion bold,
And, like the impatient steed of war,
He snuff'd the battle from afar;
And hopes were none, that back again
Herald should come from Terouenne,
Where England's King in leaguer lay,
Before decisive battle-day;
Whilst these things were, the mournful Clare
Did in the Dame's devotions share:
For the good Countess ceaseless pray'd
To Heaven and Saints, her sons to aid,
And, with short interval, did pass
From prayer to book, from book to mass,
And all in high Baronial pride,—
A life both dull and dignified;
Yet as Lord Marmion nothing press'd
Upon her intervals of rest,
Dejected Clara well could bear
The formal state, the lengthen'd prayer,
Though dearest to her wounded heart
The hours that she might spend apart.

II.

I said Tantallon's dizzy steep
Hung o'er the margin of the deep.
Many a rude tower and rampart there
Repell'd the insult of the air,
Which, when the tempest vex'd the sky,
Half breeze, half spray, came whistling by.
Above the rest, a turret square
Did o'er its Gothic entrance bear,
Of sculpture rude, a stony shield;
The Bloody Heart was in the Field,
And in the chief three mullets stood,
The cognizance of Douglas blood.

The turret held a narrow stair,
Which, mounted, gave you access where
A parapet's embattled row
Did seaward round the castle go.
Sometimes in dizzy steps descending,
Sometimes in narrow circuit bending,
Sometimes in platform broad extending,
Its varying circle did combine
Bulwark, and bartizan, and line,
And bastion, tower, and vantage-coign;
Above the booming ocean leant
The far-projecting battlement;
The billows burst, in ceaseless flow,
Upon the precipice below.
Where'er Tantallon faced the land,
Gate-works, and walls, were strongly mann'd;
No need upon the sea-girt side;
The steepy rock, and frantic tide,
Approach of human step denied;
And thus these lines and ramparts rude
Were left in deepest solitude.

III.

And, for they were so lonely, Clare
Would to these battlements repair,
And muse upon her sorrows there,
    And list the sea-bird's cry;
Or slow, like noontide ghost, would glide
Along the dark-grey bulwarks' side,
And ever on the heaving tide
    Look down with weary eye.
Oft did the cliff and swelling main
Recall the thoughts of Whitby's fane,—
A home she ne'er might see again;
    For she had laid adown,
So Douglas bade, the hood and veil,
And frontlet of the cloister pale,
    And Benedictine gown:
It were unseemly sight, he said,
A novice out of convent shade.
Now her bright locks, with sunny glow,
Again adorn'd her brow of snow;

Her mantle rich, whose borders, round,
A deep and fretted broidery bound,
In golden foldings sought the ground;
Of holy ornament, alone
Remain'd a cross with ruby stone;
  And often did she look
On that which in her hand she bore,
With velvet bound, and broider'd o'er,
  Her breviary book.
In such a place, so lone, so grim,
At dawning pale, or twilight dim,
  It fearful would have been
To meet a form so richly dress'd,
With book in hand, and cross, on breast,
  And such a woeful mien.
Fitz-Eustace, loitering with his bow,
To practise on the gull and crow,
Saw her, at distance, gliding slow,
  And did by Mary swear
Some love-lorn Fay she might have been,
Or, in Romance, some spell-bound Queen;
For ne'er, in work-day world, was seen
  A form so witching fair.

IV.

Once walking thus, at evening tide,
It chanced a gliding sail she spied,
And, sighing, thought—'The Abbess, there,
Perchance, does to her home repair;
Her peaceful rule, where Duty, free,
Walks hand in hand with Charity;
Where oft Devotion's tranced glow
Can such a glimpse of heaven bestow,
That the enraptur'd sisters see
High vision and deep mystery;
The very form of Hilda fair,
Hovering upon the sunny air,
And smiling on her votaries' prayer.
O! wherefore, to my duller eye,
Did still the Saint her form deny!
Was it, that, sear'd by sinful scorn,
My heart could neither melt nor burn?

Or lie my warm affections low,
With him, that taught them first to glow?
Yet, gentle Abbess, well I knew,
To pay thy kindness grateful due,
And well could brook the mild command,
That ruled thy simple maiden band.
How different now! condemn'd to bide
My doom from this dark tyrant's pride.
But Marmion has to learn, ere long,
That constant mind, and hate of wrong,
Descended to a feeble girl,
From Red De Clare, stout Gloster's Earl:
Of such a stem, a sapling weak
He ne'er shall bend, although he break.

V.

'But see! what makes this armour here?'—
  For in her path there lay
Targe, corslet, helm; she view'd them near.
'The breastplate pierc'd!—Ay, much I fear,
Weak fence wert thou 'gainst foeman's spear,
That hath made fatal entrance here,
  As these dark blood-gouts say.
Thus Wilton—oh! not corslet's warp,
Not truth, as diamond pure and hard,
Could be thy manly bosom's guard,
  On yon disastrous day!'
She raised her eyes in mournful mood,—
WILTON himself before her stood!
It might have seem'd his passing ghost,
For every youthful grace was lost;
And joy unwonted, and surprise,
Gave their strange wildness to his eyes.
Expect not, noble dames and lords,
That I can tell such scene in words:
What skilful limner e'er would choose
To paint the rainbow's varying hues,

Unless to mortal it were given
To dip his brush in dyes of heaven?
Far less can my weak line declare
　Each changing passion's shade;
Brightening to rapture from despair,
Sorrow, surprise, and pity there,
And joy, with her angelic air,
And hope, that paints the future fair,
　Their varying hues display'd:
Each o'er its rival's ground extending,
Alternate conquering, shifting, blend-
　　ing,
Till all, fatigued, the conflict yield,
And mighty Love retains the field.
Shortly I tell what then he said,
By many a tender word delay'd,
And modest blush, and bursting sigh,
And question kind, and fond reply:—

VI.

DE WILTON'S HISTORY.

'Forget we that disastrous day,
When senseless in the lists I lay.
　Thence dragg'd,—but how I cannot
　　know,
　For sense and recollection fled,—
I found me on a pallet low,
　Within my ancient beadsman's
　　shed.
Austin,—remember'st thou, my
　　Clare,
How thou didst blush, when the old
　　man,
When first our infant love began,
　Said we would make a matchless
　　pair?—
Menials, and friends, and kinsmen fled
From the degraded traitor's bed,—
He only held my burning head,
And tended me for many a day,
While wounds and fever held their
　　sway.
But far more needful was his care,
When sense return'd to wake despair;
　For I did tear the closing wound,
　And dash me frantic on the ground,
If e'er I heard the name of Clare.

At length, to calmer reason brought,
Much by his kind attendance wrought,
　With him I left my native strand,
And, in a palmer's weeds array'd,
My hated name and form to shade,
　I journey'd many a land;
No more a lord of rank and birth,
But mingled with the dregs of earth.
Oft Austin for my reason fear'd,
When I would sit, and deeply brood
On dark revenge, and deeds of blood,
　Or wild mad schemes uprear'd.
My friend at length fell sick, and said,
　God would remove him soon:
And, while upon his dying bed,
　He begg'd of me a boon—
If e'er my deadliest enemy
Beneath my brand should conquer'd lie,
Even then my mercy should awake,
And spare his life for Austin's sake.

VII.

'Still restless as a second Cain,
To Scotland next my route was ta'en,
　Full well the paths I knew.
Fame of my fate made various sound,
That death in pilgrimage I found,
That I had perish'd of my wound,—
　None cared which tale was true:
And living eye could never guess
De Wilton in his Palmer's dress;
For now that sable slough is shed,
And trimm'd my shaggy beard and
　　head,
I scarcely know me in the glass.
A chance most wondrous did provide,
That I should be that Baron's guide—
　I will not name his name!
Vengeance to God alone belongs;
But, when I think on all my wrongs,
　My blood is liquid flame!
And ne'er the time shall I forget,
When, in a Scottish hostel set,
　Dark looks we did exchange:
What were his thoughts I cannot tell;
But in my bosom muster'd Hell
　Its plans of dark revenge.

VIII.

'A word of vulgar augury,
That broke from me, I scarce knew
　　why,
　Brought on a village tale ;
Which wrought upon his moody sprite,
And sent him armed forth by night.
I borrow'd steed and mail,
And weapons, from his sleeping band ;
　And, passing from a postern door,
We met, and 'counter'd hand to hand,—
　He fell on Gifford moor.
For the death-stroke my brand I drew,
(O then my helmed head he knew,
　The Palmer's cowl was gone,)
Then had three inches of my blade
The heavy debt of vengeance paid ;
My hand the thought of Austin staid ;
　I left him there alone.
O good old man ! even from the grave
Thy spirit could thy master save :
If I had slain my foeman, ne'er
Had Whitby's Abbess, in her fear,
Given to my hand this packet dear,
Of power to clear my injured fame,
And vindicate De Wilton's name.
Perchance you heard the Abbess tell
Of the strange pageantry of Hell,
　That broke our secret speech—
It rose from the infernal shade,
Or featly was some juggle play'd,
　A tale of peace to teach.
Appeal to Heaven I judged was best,
When my name came among the rest.

IX.

' Now here, within Tantallon Hold,
To Douglas late my tale I told,
To whom my house was known of old.
Won by my proofs, his falchion bright
This eve anew shall dub me knight.
These were the arms that once did
　　turn
The tide of fight on Otterburne,
And Harry Hotspur forced to yield,
When the Dead Douglas won the field.

These Angus gave—his armourer's
　　care,
Ere morn shall every breach repair ;
For nought, he said, was in his halls,
But ancient armour on the walls,
And aged chargers in the stalls,
And women, priests, and grey-hair'd
　　men,
The rest were all in Twisel glen.
And now I watch my armour here,
By law of arms, till midnight 's near ;
Then, once again a belted knight,
Seek Surrey's camp with dawn of light.

X.

' There soon again we meet, my
　　Clare !
This Baron m'ans to guide thee
　　there :
Douglas reveres his King's command,
Else would he take thee from his
　　band.
And there thy kinsman, Surrey, too,
Will give De Wilton justice due.
Now meeter far for martial broil,
Firmer my limbs, and strung by toil,
Once more ' ——' O Wilton ! must we
　　then
Risk new-found happiness again,
　Trust fate of arms once more ?
And is there not an humble glen,
　Where we, content and poor,
Might build a cottage in the shade,
A shepherd thou, and I to aid
　Thy task on dale and moor ?
That reddening brow !—too well
　　I know,
Not even thy Clare can peace bestow,
　While falsehood stains thy name :
Go then to fight ! Clare bids thee go !
Clare can a warrior's feelings know,
　And weep a warrior's shame,
Can Red Earl Gilbert's spirit feel,
Buckle the spurs upon thy heel,
And belt thee with thy brand of
　　steel,
　And send thee forth to fame ! '

XI.

That night, upon the rocks and bay,
The midnight moonbeam slumbering
lay,
And pour'd its silver light, and pure,
Through loop-hole, and through em-
brazure,
Upon Tantallon tower and hall ;
But chief where arched windows wide
Illuminate the chapel's pride,
The sober glances fall.
Much was there need ; though, seam'd
with scars,
Two veterans of the Douglas' wars,
Though two grey priests were there,
And each a blazing torch held high,
You could not by their blaze descry
The chapel's carving fair.
Amid that dim and smoky light,
Chequering the silver moonshine
bright,
A bishop by the altar stood,
A noble lord of Douglas blood,
With mitre sheen, and rocquet white.
Yet show'd his meek and thoughtful
eye
But little pride of prelacy ;
More pleas'd that, in a barbarous age,
He gave rude Scotland Virgil's page,
Than that beneath his rule he held
The bishopric of fair Dunkeld.
Beside him ancient Angus stood,
Doff'd his furr'd gown, and sable hood:
O'er his huge form and visage pale,
He wore a cap and shirt of mail ;
And lean'd his large and wrinkled hand
Upon the huge and sweeping brand
Which wont of yore, in battle fray,
His foeman's limbs to shred away,
As wood-knife lops the sapling spray.
He seem'd as, from the tombs around
Rising at judgment-day,
Some giant Douglas may be found
In all his old array ;
So pale his face, so huge his limb,
So oid his arms, his look so grim.

XII.

Then at tne altar Wilton kneels,
And Clare the spurs bound on his heels;
And think what next he must have felt,
At buckling of the falchion belt !
And judge how Clara changed her
hue,
While fastening to her lover's side
A friend, which, though in danger tried,
He once had found untrue !
Then Douglas struck him with his
blade :
'Saint Michael and Saint Andrew aid,
I dub thee knight.
Arise, Sir Ralph, De Wilton's heir !
For King, for Church, for Lady fair,
See that thou fight.'—
And Bishop Gawain, as he rose,
Said—'Wilton ! grieve not for thy
woes,
Disgrace, and trouble ;
For He, who honour best bestows,
May give thee double.'—
De Wilton sobb'd, for sob he must—
'Where'er I meet a Douglas, trust
That Douglas is my brother !'—
'Nay, nay,' old Angus said, 'not so :
To Surrey's camp thou now must go,
Thy wrongs no longer smother.
I have two sons in yonder field ;
And, if thou meet'st them under shield,
Upon them bravely—do thy worst;
And foul fall him that blenches first !'

XIII.

Not far advanc'd was morning day,
When Marmion did his troop array
To Surrey's camp to ride ;
He had safe conduct for his band,
Beneath the royal seal and hand,
And Douglas gave a guide :
The ancient Earl, with stately grace,
Would Clara on her palfrey place,
And whisper'd in an under tone,
'Let the hawk stoop, his prey is
flown.'

The train from out the castle drew,
But Marmion stopp'd to bid adieu :—
  'Though something I might 'plain,'
    he said,
'Of cold respect to stranger guest,
Sent hither by your King's behest,
  While in Tantallon's towers I staid ;
Part we in friendship from your land,
And, noble Earl, receive my hand.'
But Douglas round him drew his
    cloak,
Folded his arms, and thus he spoke :
'My manors, halls, and bowers, shall
    still
Be open, at my Sovereign's will,
To each one whom he lists, howe'er
Unmeet to be the owner's peer.
My castles are my King's alone,
From turret to foundation-stone —
The hand of Douglas is his own ;
And never shall in friendly grasp
The hand of such as Marmion clasp.'

xiv.

Burn'd Marmion's swarthy cheek like
    fire,
And shook his very frame for ire,
  And 'This to me !' he said ;
'An 'twere not for thy hoary beard,
Such hand as Marmion's had not spar'd
  To cleave the Douglas' head !
And, first, I tell thee, haughty Peer,
He, who does England's message here,
Although the meanest in her state,
May well, proud Angus, be thy mate :
And, Douglas, more I tell thee here,
  Even in thy pitch of pride,
Here in thy hold, thy vassals near—
(Nay, never look upon your lord,
And lay your hands upon your sword !)
  I tell thee, thou'rt defied !
And if thou said'st I am not peer
To any lord in Scotland here,
Lowland or Highland, far or near,
  Lord Angus, thou hast lied ! '
On the Earl's cheek the flush of rage
O'ercame the ashen hue of age :

Fierce he broke forth, 'And dar'st
    thou then
To beard the lion in his den,
  The Douglas in his hall ?
And hop'st thou hence unscathed to go
No, by Saint Bride of Bothwell, no !
Up drawbridge, grooms—what, war-
    der, ho !
  Let the portcullis fall.'
Lord Marmion turn'd,—well was his
    need,
And dash'd the rowels in his steed,
Like arrow through the archway
    sprung,
The ponderous grate behind him
    rung :
To pass there was such scanty room,
The bars, descending, razed his plume.

xv.

The steed along the drawbridge flies,
Just as it trembled on the rise ;
Nor lighter does the swallow skim
Along the smooth lake's level brim :
And when Lord Marmion reach'd his
    band,
He halts, and turns with clenched hand,
And shout of loud defiance pours,
And shook his gauntlet at the towers.
'Horse ! horse !' the Douglas cried,
    'and chase !'
But soon he rein'd his fury's pace :
'A royal messenger he came,
Though most unworthy of the name.—
A letter forged ! Saint Jude to speed\
Did ever knight so foul a deed !
At first in heart it liked me ill,
When the King prais'd his clerkly skill.
Thanks to Saint Bothan, son of mine,
Save Gawain, ne'er could pen a line :
So swore I, and I swear it still,
Let my boy-bishop fret his fill.
Saint Mary mend my fiery mood !
Old age ne'er cools the Douglas blood,
I thought to slay him where he stood.
'Tis pity of him too,' he cried :
'Bold can he speak, and fairly ride,

I warrant him a warrior tried.'
With this his mandate he recalls,
And slowly seeks his castle halls.

XVI.

The day in Marmion's journey wore;
Yet, ere his passion's gust was o'er,
They cross'd the heights of Stanrig-
　　moor.
His troop more closely there he scann'd,
And miss'd the Palmer from the band.
'Palmer or not,' young Blount did say,
'He parted at the peep of day;
Good sooth, it was in strange array.'
'In what array?' said Marmion, quick.
'My Lord, I ill can spell the trick;
But all night long, with clink and bang,
Close to my couch did hammers clang;
At dawn the falling drawbridge rang,
And from a loop-hole while I peep,
Old Bell-the-Cat came from the Keep,
Wrapp'd in a gown of sables fair,
As fearful of the morning air;
Beneath, when that was blown aside,
A rusty shirt of mail I spied,
By Archibald won in bloody work,
Against the Saracen and Turk:
Last night it hung not in the hall;
I thought some marvel would befall.
And next I saw them saddled lead
Old Cheviot forth, the Earl's best steed,
A matchless horse, though something
　　old,
Prompt in his paces, cool and bold.
I heard the Sheriff Sholto say,
The Earl did much the Master pray
To use him on the battle-day;
But he preferr'd'——'Nay, Henry,
　　cease!
Thou sworn horse-courser, hold thy
　　peace.
Eustace, thou bear'st a brain—I pray,
What did Blount see at break of day?'

XVII.

'In brief, my lord we both descried
(For then I stood by Henry's side)
The Palmer mount, and outwards ride,

Upon the Earl's own favourite steed:
All sheath'd he was in armour bright,
And much resembled that same knight,
Subdu'd by you in Cotswold fight:
　　Lord Angus wish'd him speed.'
The instant that Fitz-Eustace spoke,
A sudden light on Marmion broke;—
'Ah! dastard fool, to reason lost!'
He mutter'd; ''twas nor fay nor
　　ghost
I met upon the moonlight wold,
But living man of earthly mould.
　　O dotage blind and gross!
Had I but fought as wont, one thrust
Had laid De Wilton in the dust,
　　My path no more to cross.
How stand we now?—he told his tale
To Douglas; and with some avail;
　　'Twas therefore gloom'd his rugged
　　　　brow.
Will Surrey dare to entertain,
'Gainst Marmion, charge disproved
　　and vain?
　　Small risk of that, I trow.
Yet Clare's sharp questions must
　　I shun,
Must separate Constance from the
　　Nun—
O what a tangled web we weave,
When first we practise to deceive!
A Palmer too!—no wonder why
I felt rebuk'd beneath his eye:
I might have known there was but one,
Whose look could quell Lord Marmion.'

XVIII.

Stung with these thoughts, he urg'd
　　to speed
His troop, and reach'd at eve the
　　Tweed,
Where Lennel's convent clos'd their
　　march;
(There now is left but one frail arch,
　　Yet mourn thou not its cells;
Our time a fair exchange has made;
Hard by, in hospitable shade,
　　A reverend pilgrim dwells,

Well worth the whole Bernardine
    brood,
That e'er wore sandal, frock, or hood.)
Yet did Saint Bernard's Abbot there
Give Marmion entertainment fair,
And lodging for his train and Clare.
Next morn the Baron climb'd the
    tower,
To view afar the Scottish power,
    Encamp'd on Flodden edge:
The white pavilions made a show,
Like remnants of the winter snow,
    Along the dusky ridge.
Long Marmion look'd: at length his
    eye
Unusual movement might descry
    Amid the shifting lines:
The Scottish host drawn out appears,
For, flashing on the hedge of spears
    The eastern sunbeam shines.
Their front now deepening, now
    extending;
Their flank inclining, wheeling, bend-
    ing,
Now drawing back, and now descend-
    ing,
The skilful Marmion well could know
They watch'd the motions of some foe,
Who travers'd on the plain below.

XIX.

Even so it was. From Flodden ridge
The Scots beheld the English host
    Leave Barmore-wood, their evening
    post,
    And heedful watch'd them as they
    cross'd
The Till by Twisel Bridge.
    High sight it is, and haughty, while
    They dive into the deep defile;
    Beneath the cavern'd cliff they fall,
    Beneath the castle's airy wall;
By rock, by oak, by hawthorn-tree,
    Troop after troop are disappearing;
    Troop after troop their banners rear-
    ing,
Upon the eastern bank you see;

Still pouring down the rocky den,
    Where flows the sullen Till,
And rising from the dim-wood glen,
Standards on standards, men on men,
    In slow succession still,
And, sweeping o'er the Gothic arch,
And pressing on, in ceaseless march,
    To gain the opposing hill.
That morn, to many a trumpet clang,
Twisel! thy rock's deep echo rang;
And many a chief of birth and rank,
Saint Helen! at thy fountain drank.
Thy hawthorn glade, which now we see
In spring-tide bloom so lavishly,
Had then from many an axe its doom,
To give the marching columns room.

XX.

And why stands Scotland idly now,
Dark Flodden! on thy airy brow,
Since England gains the pass the while,
And struggles through the deep defile?
What checks the fiery soul of James?
Why sits that champion of the dames
    Inactive on his steed,
And sees, between him and his land,
Between him and Tweed's southern
    strand,
    His host Lord Surrey lead?
What 'vails the vain knight-errant's
    brand?
O, Douglas, for thy leading wand!
    Fierce Randolph, for thy speed!
O for one hour of Wallace wight,
Or well-skill'd Bruce, to rule the fight,
And cry 'Saint Andrew and our
    right!'
Another sight had seen that morn,
From Fate's dark book a leaf been torn,
And Flodden had been Bannock-
    bourne!
The precious hour has pass'd in vain,
And England's host has gain'd the
    plain;
Wheeling their march, and circling
    still,
Around the base of Flodden hill.

XXI.

Ere yet the bands met Marmion's eye
Fitz-Eustace shouted loud and high,
'Hark! hark! my lord, an English
    drum!
And see ascending squadrons come
    Between Tweed's river and the hill,
Foot, horse, and cannon: hap what
    hap,
My basnet to a prentice cap,
    Lord Surrey's o'er the Till!
Yet more! yet more!—how far array'd
They file from out the hawthorn
    shade,
    And sweep so gallant by!
With all their banners bravely spread,
    And all their armour flashing high,
Saint George might waken from the
    dead,
    To see fair England's standards fly.'
'Stint in thy prate,' quoth Blount,
    'thou'dst best,
And listen to our lord's behest.'
With kindling brow Lord Marmion
    said,
'This instant be our band array'd;
The river must be quickly cross'd,
That we may join Lord Surrey's
    host.
If fight King James,—as well I trust,
That fight he will, and fight he must,—
The Lady Clare behind our lines
Shall tarry, while the battle joins.'

XXII.

Himself he swift on horseback threw,
Scarce to the Abbot bade adieu;
Far less would listen to his prayer
To leave behind the helpless Clare.
Down to the Tweed his band he
    drew,
And mutter'd as the flood they view,
'The pheasant in the falcon's claw,
He scarce will yield to please a daw:
Lord Angus may the Abbot awe,
    So Clare shall bide with me.'

Then on that dangerous ford, and deep,
Where to the Tweed Leat's eddies
    creep,
    He ventured desperately:
And not a moment will he bide,
Till squire, or groom, before him
    ride;
Headmost of all he stems the tide,
    And stems it gallantly.
Eustace held Clare upon her horse,
    Old Hubert led her rein,
Stoutly they brav'd the current's
    course,
And, though far downward driven
    per force,
    The southern bank they gain;
Behind them, straggling, came to
    shore,
    As best they might, the train:
Each o'er his head his yew-bow bore,
    A caution not in vain;
Deep need that day that every string,
By wet unharm'd, should sharply ring.
A moment then Lord Marmion staid,
And breath'd his steed, his men
    array'd,
    Then forward mov'd his band,
Until, Lord Surrey's rear-guard won,
He halted by a Cross of Stone,
That, on a hillock standing lone,
    Did all the field command.

XXIII.

Hence might they see the full array
Of either host, for deadly fray;
Their marshall'd lines stretch'd east
    and west,
    And fronted north and south,
And distant salutation pass'd
    From the loud cannon mouth;
Not in the close successive rattle,
That breathes the voice of modern
    battle,
    But slow and far between.
The hillock gain'd, Lord Marmion staid:
'Here, by this Cross,' he gently said,
    'You well may view the scene.

Here shalt thou tarry, lovely Clare :
O ! think of Marmion in thy prayer !
Thou wilt not ?—well, no less my care
Shall, watchful, for thy weal prepare.
You, Blount and Eustace, are her
　　guard,
　With ten pick'd archers of my train ;
With England if the day go hard,
　To Berwick speed amain.
But if we conquer, cruel maid,
My spoils shall at your feet be laid,
　When here we meet again.'
He waited not for answer there,
And would not mark the maid's despair,
　Nor heed the discontented look
From either squire ; but spurr'd amain,
And, dashing through the battle plain,
　His way to Surrey took.

XXIV.

' The good Lord Marmion, by my life !
　Welcome to danger's hour !
Short greeting serves in time of strife :
　Thus have I rang'd my power :
Myself will rule this central host,
　Stout Stanley fronts their right,
My sons command the vaward post,
　With Brian Tunstall, stainless
　　knight ;
　Lord Dacre, with his horsemen light,
　Shall be in rearward of the fight,
And succour those that need it most.
Now, gallant Marmion, well I know
Would gladly to the vanguard go ;
Edmund, the Admiral, Tunstall there,
With thee their charge will blithely
　share ;
There fight thine own retainers too,
Beneath De Burg, thy steward true.'
' Thanks, noble Surrey !' Marmion said,
Nor farther greeting there he paid ;
But, parting like a thunderbolt,
First in the vanguard made a halt,
　Where such a shout there rose
Of Marmion ! Marmion ! that the cry,
Up Flodden mountain shrilling high,
　Startled the Scottish foes.

XXV.

Blount and Fitz-Eustace rested still
With Lady Clare upon the hill !
On which (for far the day was spent),
The western sunbeams now were
　　bent.
The cry they heard, its meaning knew,
Could plain their distant comrades
　　view :
Sadly to Blount did Eustace say,
' Unworthy office here to stay !
No hope of gilded spurs to-day.
But see ! look up—on Flodden bent
The Scottish foe has fired his tent.'
　And sudden, as he spoke,
From the sharp ridges of the hill,
All downward to the banks of Till,
　Was wreath'd in sable smoke.
Volum'd and fast. and rolling far,
The cloud envelop'd Scotland's war,
　As down the hill they broke ;
Nor martial shout, nor minstrel tone,
Announc'd their march ; their tread
　　alone,
At times one warning trumpet blown,
　At times a stifled hum,
Told England, from his mountain-
　　throne
　King James did rushing come.
Scarce could they hear, or see their
　　foes,
　Until at weapon-point they close.
They close, in clouds of smoke and
　　dust,
With sword-sway, and with lance's
　　thrust ;
　And such a yell was there,
Of sudden and portentous birth,
As if men fought upon the earth,
　And fiends in upper air ;
O life and death were in the shout,
Recoil and rally, charge and rout,
　And triumph and despair.
Long look'd the anxious squires ; their
　　eye
Could in the darkness nought descry.

XXVI.

At length the freshening western
blast
Aside the shroud of battle cast;
And, first, the ridge of mingled spears
Above the brightening cloud appears;
And in the smoke the pennons flew,
As in the storm the white sea-mew.
Then mark'd they, dashing broad and
far,
The broken billows of the war,
And plumed crests of chieftains brave,
Floating like foam upon the wave;
    But nought distinct they see:
Wide rag'd the battle on the plain;
Spears shook, and falchions flash'd
amain;
Fell England's arrow-flight like rain;
Crests rose, and stoop'd, and rose
again,
    Wild and disorderly.
Amid the scene of tumult, high
They saw Lord Marmion's falcon fly:
And stainless Tunstall's banner white,
And Edmund Howard's lion bright,
Still bear them bravely in the fight:
    Although against them come,
Of gallant Gordons many a one,
And many a stubborn Badenoch-man,
And many a rugged Border clan,
    With Huntly, and with Home.

XXVII.

Far on the left, unseen the while,
Stanley broke Lennox and Argyle;
Though there the western mountaineer
Rush'd with bare bosom on the spear,
And flung the feeble targe aside,
And with both hands the broadsword
plied.
'Twas vain:—But Fortune, on the
right,
With fickle smile, cheer'd Scotland's
fight.
Then fell that spotless banner white,
    The Howard's lion fell;

Yet still Lord Marmion's falcon flew
With wavering flight, while fiercer
grew
    Around the battle-yell.
The Border slogan rent the sky!
A Home! a Gordon! was the cry:
    Loud were the clanging blows;
Advanc'd, forc'd back, now low, now
high,
    The pennon sunk and rose;
As bends the bark's mast in the gale,
When rent are rigging, shrouds, and
sail,
    It waver'd 'mid the foes.
No longer Blount the view could bear:
' By Heaven, and all its saints! I swear
    I will not see it lost!
Fitz-Eustace, you with Lady Clare
May bid your beads, and patter
prayer,—
    I gallop to the host.'
And to the fray he rode amain,
Follow'd by all the archer train.
The fiery youth, with desperate charge,
Made, for a space, an opening large,
    The rescued banner rose,
But darkly clos'd the war around,
Like pine-tree, rooted from the ground,
    It sunk among the foes.
Then Eustace mounted too:—yet staid
As loath to leave the helpless maid,
    When, fast as shaft can fly,
Bloodshot his eyes, his nostrils spread,
The loose rein dangling from his head,
Housing and saddle bloody red,
    Lord Marmion's steed rush'd by;
And Eustace, maddening at the sight,
A look and sign to Clara cast
To mark he would return in haste,
Then plung'd into the fight.

XXVIII.

Ask me not what the maiden feels,
    Left in that dreadful hour alone:
Perchance her reason stoops, or reels;
    Perchance a courage, not her own,
    Braces her mind to desperate tone.

The scatter'd van of England wheels ;
 She only said, as loud in air
 The tumult roar'd, 'Is Wilton there?'
They fly, or, madden'd by despair,
Fight but to die,—'Is Wilton there?'
With that, straight up the hill there rode
 Two horsemen drench'd with gore,
And in their arms, a helpless load,
 A wounded knight they bore.
His hand still strain'd the broken brand;
His arms were smear'd with blood and sand :
Dragg'd from among the horses' feet,
With dinted shield, and helmet beat,
The falcon-crest and plumage gone,
Can that be haughty Marmion !
Young Blount his armour did unlace,
And, gazing on his ghastly face,
 Said ' By Saint George, he 's gone !
That spear-wound has our master sped,
And see the deep cut on his head !
 Good-night to Marmion.'
'Unnurtur'd Blount ! thy brawling cease :
He opes his eyes,' said Eustace;
 ' peace ! '

XXIX.

When, doff'd his casque, he felt free air,
Around 'gan Marmion wildly stare :—
' Where's Harry Blount? Fitz-Eustace where ?
Linger ye here, ye hearts of hare !
Redeem my pennon,—charge again !
Cry ' Marmion to the rescue ! '—Vain !
Last of my race, on battle-plain
That shout shall ne'er be heard again !
Yet my last thought is England's ; fly,
 To Dacre bear my signet-ring :
 Tell him his squadrons up to bring.
Fitz-Eustace, to Lord Surrey hie ;
 Tunstall lies dead upon the field,
 His life-blood stains the spotless shield :
 Edmund is down :—my life is reft ;
 The Admiral alone is left.

Let Stanley charge with spur of fire,—
With Chester charge, and Lancashire,
Full upon Scotland's central host,
Or victory and England's lost.
Must I bid twice ?—hence, varlets ! fly !
Leave Marmion here alone—to die.'
They parted, and alone he lay ;
 Clare drew her from the sight away,
Till pain wrung forth a lowly moan,
And half he murmur'd, 'Is there none,
 Of all my halls have nurst,
Page, squire, or groom, one cup to bring
Of blessed water from the spring,
 To slake my dying thirst !'

XXX.

O Woman ! in our hours of ease,
Uncertain, coy, and hard to please,
And variable as the shade
By the light quivering aspen made ;
When pain and anguish wring the brow,
A ministering angel thou !
Scarce were the piteous accents said,
When, with the Baron's casque, the maid
 To the nigh streamlet ran :
Forgot were hatred, wrongs, and fears;
The plaintive voice alone she hears,
 Sees but the dying man.
She stoop'd her by the runnel's side,
 But in abhorrence backward drew;
For, oozing from the mountain's side,
Where raged the war, a dark-red tide
 Was curdling in the streamlet blue.
Where shall she turn ?—behold her mark
 A little fountain cell,
Where water, clear as diamond-spark,
 In a stone basin fell.
Above, some half-worn letters say,
Drink . weary . pilgrim . drink . and . pray.
For . the . kind . soul . of . Sybil . Grey .
Who . built . this . cross . and . well.

She fill'd the helm, and back she hied,
And with surprise and joy espied
　　A monk supporting Marmion's head:
A pious man, whom duty brought
To dubious verge of battle fought,
　　To shrieve the dying, bless the dead.

XXXI.

Deep drank Lord Marmion of the wave,
And, as she stoop'd his brow to lave—
' Is it the hand of Clare,' he said,
' Or injur'd Constance, bathes my
　　head ? '
　　Then, as remembrance rose,—
' Speak not to me of shrift or prayer !
　　I must redress her woes.
Short space, few words, are mine to
　　spare :
Forgive and listen, gentle Clare !'
' Alas !' she said, ' the while,—
O, think of your immortal weal !
In vain for Constance is your zeal ;
　　She ——— died at Holy Isle.'
Lord Marmion started from the ground,
As light as if he felt no wound ;
Though in the action burst the tide,
In torrents, from his wounded side.
' Then it was truth,' he said ; ' I knew
That the dark presage must be true.
I would the Fiend, to whom belongs
The vengeance due to all her wrongs,
　　Would spare me but a day !
For wasting fire, and dying groan,
And priests slain on the altar stone,
　　Might bribe him for delay.
It may not be ! this dizzy trance—
Curse on yon base marauder's lance,
And doubly curs'd my failing brand !
A sinful heart makes feeble hand.'
Then, fainting, down on earth he sunk,
Supported by the trembling Monk.

XXXII.

With fruitless labour, Clara bound,
And strove to stanch the gushing
　　wound :
The Monk, with unavailing cares,
Exhausted all the Church's prayers.

Ever, he said, that, close and near,
A lady's voice was in his ear,
And that the priest he could not hear ;
　　For that she ever sung,
' *In the lost battle, borne down by the
　　　flying,*
*Where mingles war's rattle with groans
　　of the dying !* '
　　So the notes rung ;—
' Avoid thee, Fiend ! with cruel hand,
Shake not the dying sinner's sand !
O, look, my son, upon yon sign
Of the Redeemer's grace divine ;
　　O, think on faith and bliss !
By many a death-bed I have been,
And many a sinner's parting seen,
　　But never aught like this.'
The war, that for a space did fail,
Now trebly thundering swell'd the
　　gale,
　　And—STANLEY ! was the cry ;
A light on Marmion's visage spread,
　　And fired his glazing eye :
With dying hand, above his head,
He shook the fragment of his blade,
　　And shouted ' Victory !
Charge, Chester, charge ! On, Stanley,
　　on !'
Were the last words of Marmion.

XXXIII.

By this though deep the evening fell,
Still rose the battle's deadly swell,
For still the Scots, around their King,
Unbroken, fought in desperate ring.
Where 's now their victor vaward
　　wing,
　　Where Huntly, and where Home ?—
O, for a blast of that dread horn,
On Fontarabian echoes borne,
　　That to King Charles did come,
When Rowland brave, and Olivier,
And every paladin and peer,
　　On Roncesvalles died !
Such blast might warn them, not in vain,
To quit the plunder of the slain,
And turn the doubtful day again,

While yet on Flodden side,
Afar, the Royal Standard flies,
And round it toils, and bleeds, and dies,
  Our Caledonian pride!
In vain the wish – for far away,
While spoil and havoc mark their way,
  Near Sybil's Cross the plunderers
    stray.
'O, Lady,' cried the Monk, 'away!'
  And plac'd her on her steed,
And led her to the chapel fair,
  Of Tilmouth upon Tweed.
There all the night they spent in prayer,
And at the dawn of morning, there
She met her kinsman, Lord Fitz-Clare.

XXXIV.

But as they left the dark'ning heath,
More desperate grew the strife of death.
The English shafts in volleys hail'd,
In headlong charge their horse assail'd;
Front, flank, and rear, the squadrons
    sweep
To break the Scottish circle deep,
  That fought around their King.
But yet, though thick the shafts as snow,
Though charging knights like whirl-
    winds go,
Though bill-men ply the ghastly blow,
  Unbroken was the ring;
The stubborn spear-men still made
    good
Their dark impenetrable wood,
Each stepping where his comrade
    stood,
  The instant that he fell.
No thought was there of dastard flight;
Link'd in the serried phalanx tight,
Groom fought like noble, squire like
    knight,
  As fearlessly and well;
Till utter darkness closed her wing
O'er their thin host and wounded King.
Then skilful Surrey's sage commands
Led back from strife his shatter'd bands;
  And from the charge they drew,
As mountain-waves, from wasted lands,
  Sweep back to ocean blue.

Then did their loss his foemen know;
Their King, their Lords, their might-
    iest low,
They melted from the field as snow,
When streams are swoln and south
    winds blow,
  Dissolves in silent dew.
Tweed's echoes heard the ceaseless
    plash,
  While many a broken band,
Disorder'd, through her currents dash,
  To gain the Scottish land;
To town and tower, to town and dale,
To tell red Flodden's dismal tale,
  And raise the universal wail.
Tradition, legend, tune, and song,
Shall many an age that wail prolong:
Still from the sire the son shall hear
Of the stern strife, and carnage drear,
  Of Flodden's fatal field,
Where shiver'd was fair Scotland's
    spear,
  And broken was her shield!

XXXV.

Day dawns upon the mountain's side:
There, Scotland! lay thy bravest pride,
Chiefs, knights, and nobles, many a one:
The sad survivors all are gone.
View not that corpse mistrustfully,
Defac'd and mangled though it be;
Nor to yon Border castle high,
Look northward with upbraiding eye;
  Nor cherish hope in vain,
That, journeying far on foreign strand,
The Royal Pilgrim to his land
  May yet return again.
He saw the wreck his rashness
    wrought;
Reckless of life, he desperate fought,
  And fell on Flodden plain:
And well in death his trusty brand,
Firm clench'd within his manly hand,
  Beseem'd the monarch slain.
But, O! how changed since yon blithe
    night!
Gladly I turn me from the sight,
  Unto my tale again.

XXXVI.

Short is my tale : Fitz-Eustace' care
A pierc'd and mangled body bare
To moated Lichfield's lofty pile ;
And there, beneath the southern aisle
A tomb, with Gothic sculpture fair,
Did long Lord Marmion's image bear.
(Now vainly for its sight you look ;
'Twas levell'd when fanatic Brook
The fair cathedral storm'd and took ;
But, thanks to Heaven and good Saint
　　Chad,
A guerdon meet the spoiler had !)
There erst was martial Marmion found,
His feet upon a couchant hound,
　　His hands to heaven uprais'd ;
And all around, on scutcheon rich,
And tablet carv'd, and fretted niche,
　　His arms and feats were blaz'd.
And yet, though all was carv'd so fair,
And priest for Marmion breath'd the
　　prayer,
The last Lord Marmion lay not there.
From Ettrick woods a peasant swain
Follow'd his lord to Flodden plain,—
One of those flowers, whom plaintive
　　lay
In Scotland mourns as 'wede away :'
Sore wounded, Sybil's Cross he spied,
And dragg'd him to its foot, and died,
Close by the noble Marmion's side.
The spoilers stripp'd and gash'd the
　　slain,
And thus their corpses were mista'en ;
And thus, in the proud Baron's tomb,
The lowly woodsman took the room.

XXXVII.

Less easy task it were, to show
Lord Marmion's nameless grave, and
　　low.
They dug his grave e'en where he lay,
　　But every mark is gone ;
Time's wasting hand has done away
The simple Cross of Sybil Grey,
　　And broke her font of stone :

But yet from out the little hill
Oozes the slender springlet still ;
　　Oft halts the stranger there,
For thence may best his curious eye
The memorable field descry ;
　　And shepherd boys repair
To seek the water-flag and rush,
And rest them by the hazel bush,
　　And plait their garlands fair ;
Nor dream they sit upon the grave,
That holds the bones of Marmion brave.
When thou shalt find the little hill,
With thy heart commune, and be still.
If ever, in temptation strong,
Thou left'st the right path for the
　　wrong ;
If every devious step, thus trod,
Still led thee farther from the road ;
Dread thou to speak presumptuous
　　doom
On noble Marmion's lowly tomb ;
But say, ' He died a gallant knight,
With sword in hand, for England's
　　right.'

XXXVIII.

I do not rhyme to that dull elf,
Who cannot image to himself,
That all through Flodden's dismal
　　night,
Wilton was foremost in the fight ;
That, when brave Surrey's steed was
　　slain,
'Twas Wilton mounted him again ;
'Twas Wilton's brand that deepest
　　hew'd,
Amid the spearmen's stubborn wood :
Unnam'd by Hollinshed or Hall,
He was the living soul of all :
That, after fight, his faith made plain,
He won his rank and lands again ;
And charg'd his old paternal shield
With bearings won on Flodden Field.
Nor sing I to that simple maid,
To whom it must in terms be said,
That King and kinsmen did agree,
To bless fair Clara's constancy ;

Who cannot, unless I relate,
Paint to her mind the bridal's state ;
That Wolsey's voice the blessing spoke,
More, Sands, and Denny, pass'd the
joke :
That bluff King Hal the curtain drew,
And Catherine's hand the stocking
threw ;
And afterwards, for many a day,
That it was held enough to say,
In blessing to a wedded pair,
'Love they like Wilton and like
Clare !'

L'ENVOY.

WHY then a final note prolong,
Or lengthen out a closing song,
Unless to bid the gentles speed,
Who long have listed to my rede ?

To Statesmen grave, if such may deign
To read the Minstrel's idle strain,
Sound head, clean hand, and piercing
wit,
And patriotic heart—as PITT !
A garland for the hero's crest,
And twin'd by her he loves the
best ;
To every lovely lady bright,
What can I wish but faithful knight ?
To every faithful lover too,
What can I wish but lady true ?
And knowledge to the studious sage ;
And pillow to the head of age.
To thee, dear schoolboy, whom my
lay
Has cheated of thy hour of play,
Light task, and merry holiday !
To all, to each, a fair good-night,
And pleasing dreams, and slumbers
light !

END OF MARMION.

Introduction and Notes to Marmion.

INTRODUCTION TO THE FIRST EDITION.

It is hardly to be expected, that an Author whom the public have honoured with some degree of applause, should not be again a trespasser on their kindness. Yet the Author of Marmion must be supposed to feel some anxiety concerning its success, since he is sensible that he hazards, by this second intrusion, any reputation which his first poem may have procured him. The present story turns upon the private adventures of a fictitious character; but is called a Tale of Flodden Field, because the hero's fate is connected with that memorable defeat, and the causes which led to it. The design of the Author was, if possible, to apprise his readers, at the outset, of the date of his story, and to prepare them for the manners of the age in which it is laid. Any historical narrative, far more an attempt at epic composition, exceeded his plan of a romantic tale; yet he may be permitted to hope, from the popularity of The Lay of the Last Minstrel, that an attempt to paint the manners of the feudal times, upon a broader scale, and in the course of a more interesting story, will not be unacceptable to the public.

The poem opens about the commencement of August, and concludes with the defeat of Flodden, 9th September, 1513.

Ashestiel, 1808.

INTRODUCTION TO THE EDITION OF 1830.

What I have to say respecting this poem may be briefly told. In the Introduction to 'The Lay of the Last Minstrel,' I have mentioned the circumstances, so far as my literary life is concerned, which induced me to resign the active pursuit of an honourable profession, for the more precarious resources of literature. My appointment to the Sheriffdom of Selkirk called for a change of residence. I left, therefore, the pleasant cottage I had upon the side of the Esk, for the 'pleasanter banks of the Tweed,' in order to comply with the law, which requires that the Sheriff shall be resident, at least during a certain number of months, within his jurisdiction. We found a delightful retirement, by my becoming the tenant of my intimate friend and cousin-german, Colonel Russell, in his mansion of Ashestiel, which was unoccupied, during his absence on military service in India. The house was adequate to our accommodation, and the exercise of a limited hospitality. The situation is uncommonly beautiful, by the side of a fine river, whose streams are there very favourable for angling, surrounded by the remains of natural woods, and by hills abounding in game. In point of society, according to the heartfelt phrase of Scripture, we dwelt 'amongst our own people;' and as the distance from the metropolis was only thirty miles, we were not out of reach of our Edinburgh friends, in which city we spent the terms of the summer and winter Sessions of the Court, that is, five or six months in the year.

An important circumstance had, about the same time, taken place in my life. Hopes had been held out to me from an influential quarter, of a nature to relieve me from the anxiety which I must have otherwise felt, as one upon the precarious tenure of whose own life rested the principal prospects of his family, and especially as one who had necessarily some dependence upon the favour of the public, which is proverbially capricious; though it is but justice to add, that, in my own case, I have not found it so. Mr. Pitt had expressed a wish to my personal friend, the Right Honourable William Dundas, now Lord Clerk Register of Scotland, that some fitting opportunity should be taken to be of service to me; and as my views and wishes pointed to a future rather than an immediate provision, an opportunity of accomplishing this was soon found. One of the Principal Clerks of Session, as they are called, (official persons who occupy an important and responsible situation, and enjoy a considerable income,) who had served upwards of thirty years, felt himself, from age, and the infirmity of deafness with which it was accompanied, desirous of retiring from his official situation. As the law then stood, such official persons were entitled to bargain with their successors, either for a sum of money, which was usually a considerable one, or for an interest in the emoluments of the office during their life. My predecessor, whose services had been unusually meritorious, stipulated for the emoluments of his office during his life, while I should enjoy the survivorship, on the condition that I discharged the duties of the office in the meantime. Mr. Pitt, however, having died in the interval, his administration was dissolved, and was succeeded by that known by the name of the Fox and Grenville Ministry. My affair was so far completed, that my commission lay in the office subscribed by his Majesty; but, from hurry or mistake, the interest of my predecessor was not expressed in it, as had been usual in such cases. Although, therefore, it only required payment of the fees, I could not in honour take out the commission in the present state, since, in the event of my dying before him, the gentleman whom I succeeded must have lost the vested interest which he had stipulated to retain. I had the honour of an interview with Earl Spencer on the subject, and he, in the most handsome manner, gave directions that the commission should issue as originally intended; adding, that the matter having received the royal assent, he regarded only as a claim of justice what he would have willingly done as an act of favour. I never saw Mr. Fox on this, or on any other occasion, and never made any application to him, conceiving that in doing so I might have been supposed to express political opinions contrary to those which I had always professed. In his private capacity, there is no man to whom I would have been more proud to owe an obligation, had I been so distinguished.

By this arrangement I obtained the survivorship of an office, the emoluments of which were fully adequate to my wishes; and as the law respecting the mode of providing for superannuated officers was, about five or six years after, altered from that which admitted the arrangement of assistant and successor, my colleague very handsomely took the opportunity of the alteration, to accept of the retiring annuity provided in such cases, and admitted me to the full benefit of the office

But although the certainty of succeeding to a considerable income, at the time I obtained it, seemed to assure me of a quiet harbour in my old age, I did not escape my share of inconvenience from the contrary tides and currents by which we are so often encountered in our journey through life. Indeed, the publication of my next poetical attempt was prematurely accelerated, from one of those unpleasant accidents which can neither be foreseen nor avoided.

I had formed the prudent resolution to endeavour to bestow a little more labour than I had yet done on my productions, and to be in no hurry again to announce myself as a candidate for literary fame. Accordingly, particular passages of a poem, which was finally called 'Marmion,' were laboured with a good deal of care, by one by whom much care was seldom bestowed. Whether the work was worth the labour or not, I am no competent judge; but I may be permitted to say, that the period of its composition was a very happy one in my life; so much so, that I remember with pleasure, at this moment, some of the spots in which particular passages were composed. It is probably owing to this, that the Introductions to the several Cantos assumed the form of familiar epistles to my intimate friends, in which I alluded, perhaps more than was necessary or graceful, to my domestic occupations and amusements—a loquacity which may be excused by those who remember that I was still young, light-headed, and happy, and that 'out of the abundance of the heart the mouth speaketh.'

The misfortunes of a near relation and friend, which happened at this time, led me to alter my prudent determination, which had been, to use great precaution in sending this poem into the world; and made it convenient at least, if not absolutely necessary, to hasten its publication. The publishers of 'The Lay of the Last Minstrel,' emboldened by the success of that poem, willingly offered a thousand pounds for 'Marmion.' The transaction being no secret, afforded Lord Byron, who was then at general war with all who blacked paper, an apology for including me in his satire, entitled 'English Bards and Scotch Reviewers.' I never could conceive how an arrangement between an author and his publishers, if satisfactory to the persons concerned, could afford matter of censure to any third party. I had taken no unusual or ungenerous means of enhancing the value of my merchandise—I had never higgled a moment about the bargain, but accepted at once what I considered the handsome offer of my publishers. These gentlemen, at least, were not of opinion that they had been taken advantage of in the transaction, which indeed was one of their own framing; on the contrary, the sale of the poem was so far beyond their expectation, as to induce them to supply the Author's cellars with what is always an acceptable present to a young Scottish housekeeper, namely, a hogshead of excellent claret.

The poem was finished in too much haste to allow me an opportunity of softening down, if not removing, some of its most prominent defects. The nature of Marmion's guilt, although similar instances were found, and might be quoted, as existing in feudal times, was nevertheless not sufficiently peculiar to be indicative of the character of the period, forgery being the crime of a commercial, rather than a proud and warlike age. This gross defect ought to have been remedied or palliated. Yet I suffered the tree to lie as it had fallen. I remember my friend, Dr. Leyden, then in the East, wrote me a furious remonstrance on the subject. I have, nevertheless, always been of opinion, that corrections, however in themselves judicious, have a bad effect—after publication. An author is never so decidedly condemned as on his own confession, and may long find apologists and partisans, until he gives up his own cause. I was not, therefore, inclined to afford matter for censure out of my own admissions;

and, by good fortune, the novelty of the subject, and, if I may say so, some force and vivacity of description, were allowed to atone for many imperfections. Thus the second experiment on the public patience, generally the most perilous,—for the public are then most apt to judge with rigour, what in the first instance they had received, perhaps, with imprudent generosity,—was in my case decidedly successful. I had the good fortune to pass this ordeal favourably, and the return of sales before me makes the copies amount to thirty-six thousand printed between 1808 and 1825, besides a considerable sale since that period. I shall here pause upon the subject of 'Marmion,' and, in a few prefatory words to 'The Lady of the Lake,' the last poem of mine which obtained eminent success, I will continue the task which I have imposed on myself respecting the origin of my productions.

ABBOTSFORD, *April*, 1830.

NOTES.

NOTE I.

As when the Champion of the Lake
Enters Morgana's fated house,
Or in the Chapel Perilous,
Despising spells and demons' force,
Holds converse with the unburied corse.
—P. 92.

THE romance of the Morte Arthur contains a sort of abridgement of the most celebrated adventures of the Round Table; and, being written in comparatively modern language, gives the general reader an excellent idea of what romances of chivalry actually were. It has also the merit of being written in pure old English; and many of the wild adventures which it contains are told with a simplicity bordering upon the sublime. Several of these are referred to in the text; and I would have illustrated them by more full extracts, but as this curious work is about to be republished, I confine myself to the tale of the Chapel Perilous, and of the quest of Sir Launcelot after the Sangreal.

'Right so Sir Launcelot departed, and when he came to the Chapell Perilous, he alighted downe, and tied his horse to a little gate. And as soon as he was within the churchyard, he saw, on the front of the chapell, many faire rich shields turned upside downe; and many of the shields Sir Launcelot had seene knights have before; with that he saw stand by him thirtie great knights, more, by a yard, than any man that ever he had seene, and all those grinned and gnashed at Sir Launcelot; and when he saw their countenance, hee dread them sore, and so

put his shield afore him, and tooke his sword in his hand, ready to doe battaile; and they were all armed in black harneis, and with their shields and swords drawn. And when Sir Launcelot would have gone through them, they scattered on every side of him, and gave him the way; and therewith he waxed all bold, and entered into the chapell, and then hee saw no light but a dimme lampe burning, and then was he ware of a corps covered with a cloath of silke; then Sir Launcelot stooped downe, and cut a piece or that cloth away, and then it fared under him as the earth had quaked a little, whereof he was afeard, and then hee saw a faire sword lye by the dead knight, and that he gat in his hand, and hied him out of the chappell. As soon as he was in the chappell-yerd, all the knights spoke to him with a grimly voice, and said, "Knight, Sir Launcelot, lay that sword from thee, or else thou shalt die."—"Whether I live or die," said Sir Launcelot, "with no great words get yee it againe, therefore fight for it and yee list." Therewith he passed through them; and, beyond the chappell-yerd, there met him a faire damosell, and said, "Sir Launcelot, leave that sword behind thee, or thou wilt die for it."—"I will not leave it," said Sir Launcelot, "for no threats."—"No?" said she; "and ye did leave that sword, Queen Guenever should ye never see."—'Then were I a fool and I would leave this sword," said Sir Launcelot. "Now, gentle knight," said the damosell, "I require thee to kisse me once."—"Nay," said Sir Launcelot, "that God forbid!"—"Well, sir," said she, "and thou haddest kissed me thy life dayes had been done: but now, alas!" said she, "I have lost all my labour; for I ordeined this chappell for thy sake, and for Sir Gawaine: and once I had Sir Gawaine within it; and at that time he fought with that knight which there lieth dead in yonder chappell, Sir Gilbert the bastard, and at that time hee smote off Sir Gilbert the bastard's left hand. And so, Sir Launcelot, now I tell thee, that I have loved thee this seaven yeare: but there may no woman have thy love but Queene Guenever; but sithen I may not rejoyce thee to have thy body alive, I had kept no more joy in this world but to have had thy dead body; and I would have balmed it and served, and so have kept it in my life daies, and daily I should have clipped thee, and kissed thee, in the despite of Queen Guenever."—"Yee say well," said Sir Launcelot; "Jesus preserve me from your subtill craft." And therewith he took his horse, and departed from her.'

NOTE II.

A sinful man, and unconfess'd,
He took the Sangreal's holy quest,
And, slumbering, saw the vision high,
He might not view with waking eye.
—P. 92.

One day, when Arthur was holding a high feast with his Knights of the Round Table, the Sangreal, or vessel out of which the last passover was eaten, (a precious relic, which had long remained concealed from human eyes, because of the sins of the land,) suddenly appeared to him and all his chivalry. The consequence of this vision was, that all the knights took on them a solemn vow to seek the Sangreal. But, alas! it could only be revealed to a knight at once accomplished in earthly chivalry, and pure and guiltless of evil conversation. All Sir Launcelot's noble accomplishments were therefore rendered vain by his guilty intrigue with Queen Guenever, or Ganore; and in his holy quest he encountered only such disgraceful disasters as that which follows:—

'But Sir Launcelot rode overthwart and endlong in a wild forest, and held no path but as wild adventure led him; and at the last, he came unto a stone crosse, which departed two wayes, in wast land; and, by the crosse, was a stone that was of marble; but it was so dark, that Sir Launcelot might not well know what it was. Then Sir Launcelot looked by him, and saw an old chappell, and there he wend to have found people. And so Sir Launcelot tied his horse to a tree, and there he put off his shield, and hung it upon a tree, and then hee went unto the chappell doore, and found it wasted and broken. And within he found a faire altar, full richly arrayed with cloth of silk, and

there stood a faire candlestick, which beare six great candles, and the candlesticke was of silver. And when Sir Launcelot saw this light, hee had a great will for to enter into the chappell, but he could find no place where hee might enter. Then was he passing heavie and dismaied. Then he returned, and came againe to his horse, and tooke off his saddle and his bridle, and let him pasture, and unlaced his helme, and ungirded his sword, and laid him downe to sleepe upon his shield, before the crosse.

'And so hee fell on sleepe; and, halfe waking and halfe sleeping, he saw come by him two palfreys, both faire and white, the which beare a litter, therein lying a sicke knight. And when he was nigh the crosse, he there abode still. All this Sir Launcelot saw and beheld, for hee slept not verily, and hee heard him say, "O sweete Lord, when shall this sorrow leave me, and when shall the holy vessell come by me, where through I shall be blessed, for I have endured thus long for little trespasse!" And thus a great while complained the knight, and allwaies Sir Launcelot heard it. With that Sir Launcelot saw the candlesticke, with the fire tapers, come before the crosse; but he could see nobody that brought it. Also there came a table of silver, and the holy vessell of the Sancgreall, the which Sir Launcelot had seen before that time in King Petchour's house. And therewithall the sicke knight set him upright, and held up both his hands, and said, "Faire sweete Lord, which is here within the holy vessell, take heede to mee, that I may bee hole of this great malady!" And therewith upon his hands, and upon his knees, he went so nigh, that he touched the holy vessell, and kissed it: And anon he was hole, and then he said, "Lord God, I thank thee, for I am healed of this malady." Soo when the holy vessell had been there a great while, it went into the chappelle againe, with the candlesticke and the light, so that Sir Launcelot wist not where it became, for he was overtaken with sinne, that hee had no power to arise against the holy vessell, wherefore afterward many men said of him shame. But he tooke repentance afterward. Then the sicke knight dressed him upright, and kissed the crosse. Then anon his squire brought him his armes, and asked his lord how he did. "Certainly," said hee, "I thanke God right heartily, for through the holy vessell I am healed: But I have right great mervaile of this sleeping knight, which hath had neither grace nor power to awake during the time that this holy vessell hath beene here present."—"I dare it right well say," said the squire, "that this same knight is defouled with some manner of deadly sinne, whereof he has never confessed."—"By my faith," said the knight, "whatsoever he be, he is unhappie; for, as I deeme, hee is of the fellowship of the Round Table, the which is entered into the quest of the Sancgreall."—"Sir," said the squire, "here I have brought you all your armes, save your helme and your sword; and, therefore, by mine assent, now may ye take this knight's helme and his sword;" and so he did. And when he was cleane armed, he took Sir Launcelot's horse, for he was better than his owne, and so they departed from the crosse.

'Then anon Sir Launcelot awaked, and set himselfe upright, and he thought him what hee had there seene, and whether it were dreames or not; right so he heard a voice that said, "Sir Launcelot, more hardy than is the stone, and more bitter than is the wood, and more naked and bare than is the liefe of the fig-tree, therefore go thou from hence, and withdraw thee from this holy place;" and when Sir Launcelot heard this, he was passing heavy, and wist not what to doe. And so he departed sore weeping, and cursed the time that he was borne; for then he deemed never to have had more worship; for the words went unto his heart, till that he knew wherefore that hee was so called.'

Note III.

And Dryden, in immortal strain,
Had raised the Table Round again.
—P. 92.

Dryden's melancholy account of his projected Epic Poem, blasted by the selfish and sordid parsimony of his patrons, is contained in an 'Essay on Satire,' addressed to the Earl of Dorset, and prefixed to the Translation of Juvenal. After mentioning a plan of supplying machinery from the guardian angels of kingdoms, mentioned in the Book of Daniel, he adds,—

'Thus, my lord, I have, as briefly as I could, given your lordship, and by you the world, a rude draught of what I have been long labouring in my imagination, and what I had intended to have put in practice; (though far unable for the attempt of such a poem;) and to have left the stage, to which my genius never much inclined me, for a work which would have taken up my life in the performance of it. This, too, I had intended chiefly for the honour of my native country, to which a poet is particularly obliged. Of two subjects, both relating to it, I was doubtful whether I should choose that of King Arthur conquering the Saxons, which, being farther distant in time, gives the greater scope to my invention; or that of Edward the Black Prince, in subduing Spain, and restoring it to the lawful prince, though a great tyrant, Don Pedro the Cruel; which, for the compass of time, including only the expedition of one year, for the greatness of the action, and its answerable event, for the magnanimity of the English hero, opposed to the ingratitude of the person whom he restored, and for the many beautiful episodes

which I had interwoven with the principal design, together with the characters of the chiefest English persons, (wherein, after Virgil and Spenser, I would have taken occasion to represent my living friends and patrons of the noblest families, and also shadowed the events of future ages in the succession of our imperial line,)—with these helps, and those of the machines which I have mentioned, I might perhaps have done as well as some of my predecessors, or at least chalked out a way for others to amend my errors in a like design; but being encouraged only with fair words by King Charles II, my little salary ill paid, and no prospect of a future subsistence, I was then discouraged in the beginning of my attempt; and now age has overtaken me, and want, a more insufferable evil, through the change of the times, has wholly disabled me.'

Note IV.

Their theme the merry minstrels made,
Of Ascapart, and Bevis bold.—P. 93.

The 'History of Bevis of Hampton' is abridged by my friend Mr. George Ellis, with that liveliness which extracts amusement even out of the most rude and unpromising of our old tales of chivalry. Ascapart, a most important personage in the romance, is thus described in an extract:—

'This geaunt was mighty and strong,
And full thirty foot was long,
He was bristled like a sow;
A foot he had between each brow;
His lips were great, and hung aside;
His eyen were hollow, his mouth was wide;
Lothly he was to look on than,
And liker a devil than a man.
His staff was a young oak,
Hard and heavy was his stroke.

Specimens of Metrical Romances, vol. ii. p. 136.

I am happy to say that the memory of Sir Bevis is still fragrant in his town of Southampton; the gate of which is sentinelled by the effigies of that doughty knighterrant and his gigantic associate.

Note V.

Day set on Norham's castled steep,
And Tweed's fair river, broad and deep,
&c. —P. 93.

The ruinous castle of Norham (anciently called Ubbanford) is situated on the southern bank of the Tweed, about six miles above Berwick, and where that river is still the boundary between England and Scotland. The extent of its ruins, as well as its historical importance, shows it to have been a place of magnificence, as well as strength. Edward I resided there when he was created umpire of the dispute concerning the Scottish succession. It was repeatedly taken and retaken during the wars between England and Scotland; and, indeed, scarce any happened, in which it had not a principal share. Norham Castle is situated on a steep bank, which overhangs the river. The repeated sieges which the castle had sustained rendered frequent repairs necessary. In 1164, it was almost rebuilt by Hugh Pudsey, Bishop of Durham, who added a huge keep, or donjon; notwithstanding which, King Henry II, in 1174, took the castle from the bishop, and committed the keeping of it to William de Neville. After this period it seems to have been chiefly garrisoned by the King, and considered as a royal fortress. The Greys of Chillingham Castle were frequently the castellans, or captains of the garrison: yet, as the castle was situated in the patrimony of St. Cuthbert, the property was in the see of Durham till the Reformation. After that period, it passed through various hands. At the union of the crowns, it was in the possession of Sir Robert Carey (afterwards Earl of Monmouth) for his own life, and that of two of his sons. After King James's accession, Carey sold Norham Castle to George Home, Earl of Dunbar, for £6,000. See his curious Memoirs, published by Mr. Constable of Edinburgh.

According to Mr. Pinkerton, there is, in the British Museum, Cal. B. 6. 216, a curious memoir of the Dacres on the state of Norham Castle in 1522, not long after the battle of Flodden. The inner ward, or keep, is represented as impregnable:—'The provisions are three great vats of salt eels, forty-four kine, three hogsheads of salted salmon, forty quarters of grain, besides many cows and four hundred sheep, lying under the castle-wall nightly; but a number of the arrows wanted feathers, and a good *Fletcher* [*i. e.* maker of arrows] was required.'—*History of Scotland*, vol. ii. p. 201, note.

The ruins of the castle are at present considerable, as well as picturesque. They consist of a large shattered tower, with many vaults, and fragments of other edifices, enclosed within an outward wall of great circuit.

Note VI.

The battled towers, the donjon keep.
—P. 93.

It is perhaps unnecessary to remind my readers, that the *donjon*, in its proper signification, means the strongest part of a feudal castle; a high square tower, with walls of tremendous thickness, situated in the centre of the other buildings, from which, however, it was usually detached. Here, in case of the outward defences being gained, the garrison retreated to make their last stand. The donjon contained the great hall, and principal rooms of state for solemn occasions,

and also the prison of the fortress; from which last circumstance we derive the modern and restricted use of the word *dungeon*. Ducange (*voce* DUNJO) conjectures plausibly, that the name is derived from these keeps being usually built upon a hill, which in Celtic is called DUN. Borlase supposes the word came from the darkness of the apartments in these towers, which were thence figuratively called Dungeons; thus deriving the ancient word from the modern application of it.

Note VII.

Well was he arm'd from head to heel,
In mail and plate of Milan steel.—P. 94.

The artists of Milan were famous in the middle ages for their skill in armoury, as appears from the following passage, in which Froissart gives an account of the preparations made by Henry, Earl of Hereford, afterwards Henry IV, and Thomas, Duke of Norfolk, Earl Marischal, for their proposed combat in the lists at Coventry:—'These two lords made ample provision of all things necessary for the combat; and the Earl of Derby sent off messengers to Lombardy, to have armour from Sir Galeas, Duke of Milan. The Duke complied with joy, and gave the knight, called Sir Francis, who had brought the message, the choice of all his armour for the Earl of Derby. When he had selected what he wished for in plated and mail armour, the Lord of Milan, out of his abundant love for the Earl, ordered four of the best armourers in Milan to accompany the knight to England, that the Earl of Derby might be more completely armed.'—JOHNES' *Froissart*, vol. iv. p. 597.

Note VIII.

Who checks at me, to death is dight.—P. 94.

The crest and motto of Marmion are borrowed from the following story:—Sir David de Lindsay, first Earl of Crauford, was, among other gentlemen of quality, attended, during a visit to London, in 1390, by Sir William Dalzell, who was, according to my authority, Bower, not only excelling in wisdom, but also of a lively wit. Chancing to be at the court, he there saw Sir Piers Courtenay, an English knight, famous for skill in tilting, and for the beauty of his person, parading the palace, arrayed in a new mantle, bearing for device an embroidered falcon, with this rhyme,—

'I bear a falcon, fairest of flight,
Whoso pinches at her, his death is dight
In graith.

The Scottish knight, being a wag, appeared next day in a dress exactly similar to that of Courtenay, but bearing a magpie instead of the falcon, with a motto ingeniously contrived to rhyme to the vaunting inscription of Sir Piers:—

'I bear a pie picking at a piece,
Whoso picks at her, I shall pick at his nese[1],
In faith.'

This affront could only be expiated by a just with sharp lances. In the course, Dalzell left his helmet unlaced, so that it gave way at the touch of his antagonist's lance, and he thus avoided the shock of the encounter. This happened twice:—in the third encounter, the handsome Courtenay lost two of his front teeth. As the Englishman complained bitterly of Dalzell's fraud in not fastening his helmet, the Scottishman agreed to run six courses more, each champion staking in the hand of the King two hundred pounds, to be forfeited, if, on entering the lists, any unequal advantage should be detected. This being agreed to, the wily Scot demanded that Sir Piers, in addition to the loss of his teeth, should consent to the extinction of one of his eyes, he himself having lost an eye in the fight of Otterburn. As Courtenay demurred to this equalization of optical powers, Dalzell demanded the forfeit; which, after much altercation, the King appointed to be paid to him, saying, he surpassed the English both in wit and valour. This must appear to the reader a singular specimen of the humour of that time. I suspect the Jockey Club would have given a different decision from Henry IV.

NOTE IX.

They hail'd Lord Marmion :
They hail'd him Lord of Fontenaye,
Of Lutterward, and Scrivelbaye,
Of Tamworth tower and town.
—P. 95.

Lord Marmion, the principal character of the present romance, is entirely a fictitious personage. In earlier times, indeed, the family of Marmion, Lords of Fontenay, in Normandy, was highly distinguished. Robert de Marmion, Lord of Fontenay, a distinguished follower of the Conqueror, obtained a grant of the castle and town of Tamworth, and also of the manor of Scrivelby, in Lincolnshire. One, or both, of these noble possessions, was held by the honourable service of being the royal champion, as the ancestors of Marmion had formerly been to the Dukes of Normandy. But after the castle and demesne of Tamworth had passed through four successive barons from Robert, the family became extinct in the person of Philip de Marmion, who died in 20th Edward I without issue male. He was succeeded in his castle of Tamworth by Alexander de

1 Nose.

Freville, who married Mazera, his granddaughter. Baldwin de Freville, Alexander's descendant, in the reign of Richard I, by the supposed tenure of his castle of Tamworth, claimed the office of royal champion, and to do the service appertaining; namely, on the day of coronation, to ride, completely armed, upon a barbed horse, into Westminster Hall, and there to challenge the combat against any who would gainsay the King's title. But this office was adjudged to Sir John Dymoke, to whom the manor of Scrivelby had descended by another of the co-heiresses of Robert de Marmion; and it remains in that family, whose representative is Hereditary Champion of England at the present day. The family and possessions of Freville have merged in the Earls of Ferrars. I have not, therefore, created a new family, but only revived the titles of an old one in an imaginary personage.

It was one of the Marmion family, who, in the reign of Edward II, performed that chivalrous feat before the very castle of Norham, which Bishop Percy has woven into his beautiful ballad, 'The Hermit of Warkworth.'—The story is thus told by Leland :—

'The Scottes cam yn to the marches of England, and destroyed the castles of Werk and Herbotel, and overran much of Northumberland marches.

'At this tyme, Thomas Gray and his friendes defended Norham from the Scottes.

'It were a wonderful processe to declare, what mischefes cam by hungre and asseges by the space of xi yeres in Northumberland; for the Scottes became so proude, after they had got Berwick, that they nothing esteemed the Englishmen.

'About this tyme there was a greate feste made yn Lincolnshir, to which came many gentlemen and ladies; and amonge them one lady brought a heaulme for a man of were, with a very riche creste of gold, to William Marmion, knight, with a letter of commandement of her lady, that he should go into the daungerest place in England, and ther to let the heaulme be seene and known as famous. So he went to Norham; whither, within 4 days of cumming, cam Philip Moubray, guardian of Berwicke, having yn his bande 40 men of armes, the very flour of men of the Scottish marches.

'Thomas Gray, capitayne of Norham, seynge this, brought his garison afore the barriers of the castel, behind whom cam William, richly arrayed, as al glittering in gold, and wearing the heaulme, his lady's present.

'Then said Thomas Gray to Marmion, "Sir Knight, ye be cum hither to fame your helmet: mount up on yowr horse, and ride lyke a valiant man to yowr foes even here at hand, and I forsake God if I rescue not thy body deade or alyve, or I myself wyl dye for it."

'Whereupon he toke his cursere, and rode

ameng the throng of ennemyes; the which layed sore stripes on him, and pulled him at the last out of his sadel to the grounde.

'Then Thomas Gray, with al the hole garrison, lette prick yn among the Scottes, and so wondid them and their horses, that they were overthrowan; and Marmion, sore beten, was horsid agayn, and, with Gray, persewed the Scottes yn chase. There were taken 50 horse of price; and the women of Norham brought them to the foote men to follow the chase.'

Note X.

— *Largesse, largesse.*—P. 95.

This was the cry with which heralds and pursuivants were wont to acknowledge the bounty received from the knights. Stewart of Lorn distinguishes a ballad, in which he satirizes the narrowness of James V and his courtiers, by the ironical burden—

> '*Lerges, lerges, lerges, hay,*
> *Lerges of this new-yeir day.*
> First lerges of the King, my chief,
> Quhilk come als quiet as a theif,
>   And in my hand slid schillingis tway,
> To put his lergnes to the prief,
> For lerges of this new-yeir day.'

The heralds, like the minstrels, were a race allowed to have great claims upon the liberality of the knights, of whose feats they kept a record, and proclaimed them aloud, as in the text, upon suitable occasions.

At Berwick, Norham, and other Border fortresses of importance, pursuivants usually resided, whose inviolable character rendered them the only persons that could, with perfect assurance of safety, be sent on necessary embassies into Scotland. This is alluded to in stanza xxi, p. 97.

Note XI.

> *Sir Hugh the Heron bold,*
> *Baron of Twisell, and of Ford,*
> *And Captain of the Hold.*—P. 96.

Were accuracy of any consequence in a fictitious narrative, this castellan's name ought to have been William; for William Heron of Ford was husband to the famous Lady Ford, whose siren charms are said to have cost our James IV so dear. Moreover, the said William Heron was, at the time supposed, a prisoner in Scotland, being surrendered by Henry VIII, on account of his share in the slaughter of Sir Robert Ker of Cessford. His wife, represented in the text as residing at the Court of Scotland, was, in fact, living in her own Castle at Ford.—See Sir RICHARD HERON's curious *Genealogy of the Heron Family.*

Note XII.

> *The whiles a Northern harper rude*
> *Chanted a rhyme of deadly feud,*
> ' *How the fierce Thirwalls, and Ridleys*
> *all,*' &c.—P. 96.

This old Northumbrian ballad was taken down from the recitation of a woman eighty years of age, mother of one of the miners of Alston-moor, by an agent for the lead mines there, who communicated it to my friend and correspondent, R. Surtees, Esquire, of Mainsforth. She had not, she said, heard it for many years; but, when she was a girl, it used to be sung at the merry-makings 'till the roof rung again.' To preserve this curious, though rude rhyme, it is here inserted. The ludicrous turn given to the slaughter, marks that wild and disorderly state of society, in which a murder was not merely a casual circumstance, but, in some cases, an exceedingly good jest. The structure of the ballad resembles the 'Fray of Suport[1],' having the same irregular stanzas and wild chorus.

I.

Hoot awa', lads, hoot awa',
Ha' ye heard how the Ridleys, and Thirwalls, and a'
Ha' set upon Albany[2] Featherstonhaugh,
And taken his life at the Deadmanshaugh?
    There was Willimoteswick,
       And Hardriding Dick,
And Hughie of Hawden, and Will of the Wa',
    I canno' tell a', I canno' tell a',
And mony a mair that the deil may knaw.

II.

The auld man went down, but Nicol, his son,
Ran away afore the fight was begun;
       And he run, and he run,
       And afore they were done,
There was many a Featherston gat sic a stun,
As never was seen since the world begun.

III.

I canno' tell a', I canno' tell a';
Some gat a skelp[3], and some gat a claw;
But they gard the Featherstons haud their jaw[4],—
       Nicol, and Alick, and a'.
Some gat a hurt, and some gat nane;
Some had harness, and some gat sta'en[5].

IV.

Ane gat a twist o' the craig[6];
Ane gat a bunch[7] o' the wame[8];
Symy Haw gat lamed of a leg,
And syne ran wallowing[9] hame.

V.

Hoot, hoot, the old man's slain outright!
Lay him now wi' his face down:—he's a sorrowful
       sight.
Janet, thou donot[10].
I'll lay my best bonnet,
Thou gets a new gude-man afore it be night.

---

[1] See *Minstrelsy of the Scottish Border*, vol. ii. p. 124.

[2] Pronounced *Awbony.*

[3] *Skelp* signifies slap, or rather is the same word which was originally spelled *schlap.*

[4] *Hold their jaw*, a vulgar expression still in use.

[5] Got stolen, or; were plundered; a very likely termination of the fray.

[6] Neck. [7] Punch. [8] Belly. [9] Bellowing.

[10] *Silly slut.* The border bard calls her so, because she was weeping for her slain husband; a loss which he seems to think might be soon repaired.

VI.

Hoo away, lads, hoo away,
We's a' be hangid if we stay.
 Tak up the dead man, and lay him ahint the biggin.
Here's the Bailey o' Haltwhistle 1,
Wi' his great bull's pizzle,
 That sup'd up the broo',—and syne——in the piggin 2.

In explanation of this ancient ditty, Mr. Surtees has furnished me with the following local memorandum :—Willimoteswick, the chief seat of the ancient family of Ridley, is situated two miles above the confluence of the Allon and Tyne. It was a house of strength, as appears from one oblong tower, still in tolerable preservation 3. It has been long in possession of the Blacket family. Hardriding Dick is not an epithet referring to horsemanship, but means Richard Ridley of Hardriding 4, the seat of another family of that name, which, in the time of Charles I, was sold on account of expenses incurred by the loyalty of the proprietor, the immediate ancestor of Sir Matthew Ridley. Will of the Wa' seems to be William Ridley of Wall-town, so called from its situation on the great Roman wall. Thirlwall Castle, whence the clan of Thirlwalls derived their name, is situated on the small river of Tippel, near the western boundary of Northumberland. It is near the wall, and takes its name from the rampart having been *thirled*, i.e. pierced, or breached, in its vicinity. Featherston Castle lies south of the Tyne, towards Alston-moor. Albany Featherstonhaugh, the chief of that ancient family, made a figure in the reign of Edward VI. A feud did certainly exist between the Ridleys and Featherstons, productive of such consequences as the ballad narrates. 24 *Oct. 22do Henrici 8vi. Inquisitio capt. apud Hautwhistle, sup. visum corpus Alexandri Featherston, Gen. apud Grensilhaugh felonice interfecti, 22 Oct. per Nicolaum Ridley de Unthanke, Gen. Hugon Ridle, Nicolaum Ridle, et alios ejusdem nominis.* Nor were the Featherstons without their revenge for 36to Henrici 8vi, we have—*Utlagatio Nicolai Fetherston, ac Thome Nyxson &c. &c. pro homicidio Will. Ridle de Morale.*

---

1 The Bailiff of Haltwhistle seems to have arrived when the fray was over. This supporter of social order is treated with characteristic irreverence by the moss-trooping poet.
2 An iron pot with two ears.
3 Willimoteswick was, in prior editions, confounded with Ridley Hall, situated two miles lower, on the same side of the Tyne, the hereditary seat of William C. Lowes, Esq.
4 Ridley, the bishop and martyr, was, according to some authorities, born at Hardriding, where a chair was preserved called the Bishop's Chair. Others, and particularly his biographer and namesake Dr. Glocester Ridley, assign the honour of the martyr's birth to Willimoteswick.

Note XIII.

James back'd the cause of that mock prince,
Warbeck, that Flemish counterfeit,
Who on the gibbet paid the cheat.
Then did I march with Surrey's power,
What time we raz'd old Ayton tower.
—P. 97.

The story of Perkin Warbeck, or Richard, Duke of York, is well known. In 1496, he was received honourably in Scotland; and James IV, after conferring upon him in marriage his own relation, the Lady Catharine Gordon, made war on England in behalf of his pretensions. To retaliate an invasion of England, Surrey advanced into Berwickshire at the head of considerable forces, but retreated, after taking the inconsiderable fortress of Ayton. Ford, in his Dramatic Chronicle of Perkin Warbeck, makes the most of this inroad:

Surrey.

' Are all our braving enemies shrunk back,
Hid in the fogges of their distemper'd climate,
Not daring to behold our colours wave
In spight of this infected ayre ? Can they
Looke on the strength of Cundrestine defac't ;
The glorie of Heydonhall devasted ; that
Of Edington cast downe ; the pile of Fulden
Orethrowne : And this, the strongest of their forts,
Old Ayton Castle, yeelded and demolished,
And yet not peepe abroad ? The Scots are bold,
Hardie in battayle, but it seems the cause
They undertake considered, appeares
Unjoynted in the frame on 't.'

Note XIV.

—— I trow,
Norham can find you guides enow ;
For here be some have prick'd as far,
On Scottish ground, as to Dunbar ;
Have drunk the monks of St. Bothan's ale,
And driven the beeves of Lauderdale ;
Harried the wives of Greenlaw's goods,
And given them light to set their hoods.
—P. 97.

The garrisons of the English castles of Wark, Norham, and Berwick, were, as may be easily supposed, very troublesome neighbours to Scotland. Sir Richard Maitland of Ledington wrote a poem, called ' The Blind Baron's Comfort,' when his barony of Blythe, in Lauderdale, was *harried* by Rowland Foster, the English captain of Wark, with his company, to the number of 300 men. They spoiled the poetical knight of 5,000 sheep, 200 nolt, 30 horses and mares; the whole furniture of his house of Blythe, worth 100 pounds Scots (£8 6s. 8d.), and everything else that was portable. ' This spoil was committed the 16th day of May, 1570 (and the said Sir Richard was threescore and fourteen years of age, and grown blind), in time of peace; when nane of that country *lippened* [expected] such a thing.'—'The Blind Baron's Comfort' consists in a string of puns on the word *Blythe*, the name of the lands thus despoiled. Like John Littlewit, he had 'a conceit left in his misery—a miserable conceit.'

The last line of the text contains a phrase, by which the Borderers jocularly intimated the burning a house. When the Maxwells, in 1685, burned the Castle of Lochwood, they said they did so to give the Lady Johnstone 'light to set her hood.' Nor was the phrase inapplicable; for, in a letter, to which I have mislaid the reference, the Earl of Northumberland writes to the King and Council, that he dressed himself at midnight, at Warkworth, by the blaze of the neighbouring villages burned by the Scottish marauders.

Note XV.

The priest of Shoreswood—he could rein The wildest war-horse in your train.
—P. 98.

This churchman seems to have been akin to Welsh, the vicar of St. Thomas of Exeter, a leader among the Cornish insurgents in 1549. 'This man,' says Hollinshed, 'had many good things in him. He was of no great stature, but well set, and mightilie compact: He was a very good wrestler; shot well, both in the long bow and also in the cross-bow; he handled his hand-gun and peece very well; he was a very good woodman, and a hardie, and such a one as would not give his head for the polling, or his beard for the washing. He was a companion in any exercise of activitie, and of a courteous and gentle behaviour. He descended of a good honest parentage, being borne at Peneverin in Cornwall; and yet, in this rebellion, an arch-captain and a principal doer.'—Vol. iv. p. 958, 4to edition. This model of clerical talents had the misfortune to be hanged upon the steeple of his own church.

Note XVI.

—— that Grot where olives nod, Where, darling of each heart and eye, From all the youth of Sicily Saint Rosalie retired to God.—P. 98.

'Sante Rosalia was of Palermo, and born of a very noble family, and, when very young, abhorred so much the vanities of this world, and avoided the converse of mankind, resolving to dedicate herself wholly to God Almighty, that she, by divine inspiration, forsook her father's house, and never was more heard of till her body was found in that cleft of a rock, on that almost inaccessible mountain, where now the chapel is built; and they

affirm she was carried up there by the hands of angels; for that place was not formerly so accessible (as now it is) in the days of the Saint; and even now it is a very bad, and steepy, and breakneck way. In this frightful place, this holy woman lived a great many years, feeding only on what she found growing on that barren mountain, and creeping into a narrow and dreadful cleft in a rock, which was always dropping wet, and was her place of retirement as well as prayer; having worn out even the rock with her knees in a certain place, which is now open'd on purpose to show it to those who come here. This chapel is very richly adorn'd; and on the spot where the Saint's dead body was discover'd, which is just beneath the hole in the rock, which is open'd on purpose, as I said, there is a very fine statue of marble, representing her in a lying posture, railed in all about with fine iron and brass work; and the altar, on which they say mass, is built just over it.'—*Voyage to Sicily and Malta*, by Mr. John Dryden (son to the poet), p. 107.

Note XVII.

Friar John . . . . . Himself still sleeps before his beads Have mark'd ten aves, and two creeds.
—P. 99.

Friar John understood the soporific virtue of his beads and breviary, as well as his namesake in Rabelais. 'But Gargantua could not sleep by any means, on which side soever he turned himself. Whereupon the monk said to him, "I never sleep soundly but when I am at sermon or prayers: Let us therefore begin, you and I, the seven penitential psalms, to try whether you shall not quickly fall asleep." The conceit pleased Gargantua very well; and beginning the first of these psalms, as soon as they came to *Beati quorum*, they fell asleep, both the one and the other.'

Note XVIII.

The summon'd Palmer came in place.
—P. 99.

A *Palmer*, opposed to a *Pilgrim*, was one who made it his sole business to visit different holy shrines; travelling incessantly, and subsisting by charity: whereas the Pilgrim retired to his usual home and occupations, when he had paid his devotions at the particular spot which was the object of his pilgrimage. The Palmers seem to have been the *Questionarii* of the ancient Scottish canons 1242 and 1296. There is in the Bannatyne MS. a burlesque account of two such persons, entitled, 'Simmy and his brother.' Their accoutrements are thus ludicrously described (I discard the ancient spelling)—

'Syne shaped them up, to loup on leas,
    Two tabards of the tartan ;
They counted nought what their clouts were
    When sew'd them on, in certain.
Syne clampit up St. Peter's keys,
    Made of an old red gartane ;
St. James's shells, on t'other side, shows
    As pretty as a partane
        Toe,
On Symmye and his brother

NOTE XIX.

To fair St. Andrews bound,
Within the ocean-cave to pray,
Where good Saint Rule his holy lay,
From midnight to the dawn of day,
Sung to the billows' sound.—P. 100.

St. Regulus (*Scottice*, St. Rule), a monk of Patrae, in Achaia, warned by a vision, is said, A.D. 370, to have sailed westward, until he landed at St. Andrews in Scotland, where he founded a chapel and tower. The latter is still standing ; and, though we may doubt the precise date of its foundation, is certainly one of the most ancient edifices in Scotland. A cave, nearly fronting the ruinous castle of the Archbishops of St. Andrews, bears the name of this religious person. It is difficult of access ; and the rock in which it is hewed is washed by the German Ocean. It is nearly round, about ten feet in diameter, and the same in height. On one side is a sort of stone altar ; on the other an aperture into an inner den, where the miserable ascetic, who inhabited this dwelling, probably slept. At full tide, egress and regress are hardly practicable. As Regulus first colonized the metropolitan see of Scotland, and converted the inhabitants in the vicinity, he has some reason to complain, that the ancient name of Killrule (*Cella Reguli*) should have been superseded, even in favour of the tutelar saint of Scotland. The reason of the change was, that St. Rule is said to have brought to Scotland the relics of St. Andrew.

NOTE XX.

—— *Saint Fillan's blessed well,*
Whose spring can frenzied dreams dispel,
And the craz'd brain restore.—P. 100.

St. Fillan was a Scottish saint of some reputation. Although Popery is, with us, matter of abomination, yet the common people still retain some of the superstitions connected with it. There are in Perthshire several wells and springs dedicated to St. Fillan, which are still places of pilgrimage and offerings, even among the Protestants. They are held powerful in cases of madness ; and, in some of very late occurrence, lunatics have been left all night bound to the holy stone, in confidence that the saint would cure and unloose them before morning.—[See various notes to the *Minstrelsy of the Scottish Border.*]

NOTE XXI.

The scenes are desert now, and bare,
Where flourish'd once a forest fair.—P. 100.

Ettrick Forest, now a range of mountainous sheep-walks, was anciently reserved for the pleasure of the royal chase. Since it was disparked, the wood has been, by degrees, almost totally destroyed, although, wherever protected from the sheep, copses soon arise without any planting. When the King hunted there, he often summoned the array of the country to meet and assist his sport. Thus, in 1528, James V 'made proclamation to all lords, barons, gentlemen, landward-men, and freeholders, that they should compear at Edinburgh, with a month's victuals, to pass with the King where he pleased, to danton the thieves of Tiviotdale, Annandale, Liddisdale, and other parts of that country ; and also warned all gentlemen that had good dogs to bring them, that he might hunt in the said country as he pleased : The whilk the Earl of Argyle, the Earl of Huntley, the Earl of Athole, and so all the rest of gentlemen of the Highland, did, and brought their hounds with them in like manner, to hunt with the King, as he pleased.

'The second day of June the King past out of Edinburgh to the hunting, with many of the nobles and gentlemen of Scotland with him, to the number of twelve thousand men ; and then past to Meggitland, and hounded and hawked all the country and bounds ; that is to say, Crammat, Pappertlaw, St. Mary-laws, Carlavrick, Chapel, Ewindoores, and Longhope. I heard say, he slew, in these bounds, eighteen score of harts .'[1]

These huntings had, of course, a military character, and attendance upon them was a part of the duty of a vassal. The act for abolishing ward or military tenures in Scotland, enumerates the services of hunting, hosting, watching, and warding, as those which were in future to be illegal.

Taylor, the water-poet, has given an account of the mode in which these huntings were conducted in the Highlands of Scotland, in the seventeenth century, having been present at Braemar upon such an occasion :—

'There did I find the truly noble and right honourable lords, John Erskine, Earl of Mar ; James Stewart, Earl of Murray ; George Gordon, Earl of Engye, son and heir to the Marquis of Huntley ; James Erskine, Earl of Buchan ; and John, Lord Erskine, son

----

[1] Pitscottie's *History of Scotland*, folio edition, p. 143.

and heir to the Earl of Mar, and their Countesses, with my much honoured, and my last assured and approved friend, Sir William Murray, knight of Abercarney, and hundreds of others, knights, esquires, and their followers; all and every man, in general, in one habit, as if Lycurgus had been there, and made laws of equality; for once in the year, which is the whole month of August, and sometimes part of September, many of the nobility and gentry of the kingdom (for their pleasure) do come into these Highland countries to hunt; where they do conform themselves to the habit of the Highlandmen, who, for the most part, speak nothing but Irish; and, in former time, were those people which were called the *Red-shanks*. Their habit is—shoes, with but one sole a-piece; stockings (which they call short hose), made of a warm stuff of diverse colours, which they call tartan; as for breeches, many of them, nor their forefathers, never wore any, but a jerkin of the same stuff that their hose is of; their garters being bands or wreaths of hay or straw; with a plaid about their shoulders; which is a mantle of diverse colours, much finer and lighter stuff than their hose; with blue flat caps on their heads; a handkerchief, knit with two knots, about their necks: and thus are they attired. Now their weapons are—long bowes and forked arrows, swords and targets, harquebusses, muskets, durks, and Lochaber axes. With these arms I found many of them armed for the hunting. As for their attire, any man, of what degree soever, that comes amongst them, must not disdain to wear it; for, if they do, then they will disdain to hunt, or willingly to bring in their dogs; but if men be kind unto them, and be in their habit, then are they conquered with kindness, and the sport will be plentiful. This was the reason that I found so many noblemen and gentlemen in those shapes. But to proceed to the hunting:—

'My good Lord of Marr having put me into that shape, I rode with him from his house, where I saw the ruins of an old castle, called the Castle of Kindroghit. It was built by King Malcolm Canmore (for a hunting-house), who reigned in Scotland, when Edward the Confessor, Harold, and Norman William, reigned in England. I speak of it, because it was the last house I saw in those parts; for I was the space of twelve days after, before I saw either house, corn-field, or habitation for any creature, but deer, wild horses, wolves, and such like creatures,—which made me doubt that I should never have seen a house again.

'Thus, the first day, we travelled eight miles, where there were small cottages, built on purpose to lodge in, which they call Lonquhards. I thank my good Lord Erskine, he commanded that I should always be lodged in his lodging: the kitchen being always on the side of a bank: many kettles and pots boiling, and many spits turning and winding, with great variety of cheer,—as venison baked; sodden, rost, and stewed beef; mutton, goats, kid, hares, fresh salmon, pigeons, hens, capons, chickens, partridges, muir-coots, heath-cocks, caperkellies, and termagants; good ale, sacke, white and claret, tent (or allegant), with most potent aquavitae.

'All these, and more than these, we had continually in superfluous abundance, caught by falconers, fowlers, fishers, and brought by my lord's tenants and purveyors to victual our camp, which consisteth of fourteen or fifteen hundred men and horses. The manner of the hunting is this: Five or six hundred men do rise early in the morning, and they do disperse themselves divers ways, and seven, eight, or ten miles compass, they do bring, or chase in, the deer in many herds (two, three, or four hundred in a herd), to such or such a place, as the noblemen shall appoint them; then, when day is come, the lords and gentlemen of their companies do ride or go to the said places, sometimes wading up to the middles, through burns and rivers; and then, they being come to the place, do lie down on the ground, till those foresaid scouts, which are called the Tinkhell, do bring down the deer; but, as the proverb says of the bad cook, so these tinkhell men do lick their own fingers; for, besides their bows and arrows, which they carry with them, we can hear, now and then, a harquebuss or a musket go off, which they do seldom discharge in vain. Then, after we had staid there three hours, or thereabouts, we might perceive the deer appear on the hills round about us (their heads making a show like a wood), which, being followed close by the tinkhell, are chased down into the valley where we lay; then all the valley, on each side, being way-laid with a hundred couple of strong Irish greyhounds, they are all let loose, as occasion serves, upon the herd of deer, that with dogs, guns, arrows, durks, and daggers, in the space of two hours, fourscore fat deer were slain; which after are disposed of, some one way, and some another, twenty and thirty miles, and more than enough left for us, to make merry withall, at our rendezvous.'

NOTE XXII.

By lone Saint Mary's silent lake.—P. 102.

This beautiful sheet of water forms the reservoir from which the Yarrow takes its source. It is connected with a smaller lake, called the Loch of the Lowes, and surrounded by mountains. In the winter, it is still frequented by flights of wild swans; hence my friend Mr. Wordsworth's lines:—

' The swan on sweet St. Mary's lake
Floats double, swan and shadow.'

Near the lower extremity of the lake are the ruins of Dryhope tower, the birth-place of Mary Scott, daughter of Philip Dryhope, and famous by the traditional name of the Flower of Yarrow. She was married to Walter Scott of Harden, no less renowned for his depredations, than his bride for her beauty. Her romantic appellation was, in later days, with equal justice, conferred on Miss Mary Lilias Scott, the last of the elder branch of the Harden family. The author well remembers the talent and spirit of the latter Flower of Yarrow, though age had then injured the charms which procured her the name. The words usually sung to the air of 'Tweedside,' beginning, 'What beauties does Flora disclose,' were composed in her honour.

Note XXIII.

—— in feudal strife, a foe
Hath laid Our Lady's chapel low.—P. 103.

The chapel of St. Mary of the Lowes (*de lacubus*) was situated on the eastern side of the lake, to which it gives name. It was injured by the clan of Scott, in a feud with the Cranstouns; but continued to be a place of worship during the seventeenth century. The vestiges of the building can now scarcely be traced; but the burial ground is still used as a cemetery. A funeral, in a spot so very retired, has an uncommonly striking effect. The vestiges of the chaplain's house are yet visible. Being in a high situation, it commanded a full view of the lake, with the opposite mountain of Bourhope, belonging, with the lake itself, to Lord Napier. On the left hand is the tower of Dryhope, mentioned in a preceding note.

Note XXIV.

—— the Wizard's grave,
That Wizard Priest's, whose bones are thrust
From company of holy dust.—P. 103.

At one corner of the burial ground of the demolished chapel, but without its precincts, is a small mound, called *Binram's Corse*, where tradition deposits the remains of a necromantic priest, the former tenant of the chaplainry. His story much resembles that of Ambrosio in 'The Monk,' and has been made the theme of a ballad, by my friend Mr. James Hogg, more poetically designed *the Ettrick Shepherd*. To his volume, entitled 'The Mountain Bard,' which contains this, and many other legendary stories and ballads of great merit, I refer the curious reader.

Note XXV.

Some ruder and more savage scene,
Like that which frowns round dark Loch-
skene.—P. 103.

Loch-skene is a mountain lake, of considerable size, at the head of the Moffat-water. The character of the scenery is uncommonly savage; and the earn, or Scottish eagle, has, for many ages, built its nest yearly upon an islet in the lake. Loch-skene discharges itself into a brook, which, after a short and precipitate course, falls from a cataract of immense height, and gloomy grandeur, called, from its appearance, the 'Grey Mare's Tail.' The 'Giant's Grave,' afterwards mentioned, is a sort of trench, which bears that name, a little way from the foot of the cataract. It has the appearance of a battery, designed to command the pass.

Note XXVI.

—— high Whitby's cloister'd pile.—P. 104.

The Abbey of Whitby, in the Archdeaconry of Cleveland, on the coast of Yorkshire, was founded A. D. 657, in consequence of a vow of Oswy, King of Northumberland. It contained both monks and nuns of the Benedictine order; but, contrary to what was usual in such establishments, the abbess was superior to the abbot. The monastery was afterwards ruined by the Danes, and rebuilt by William Percy, in the reign of the Conqueror. There were no nuns there in Henry the Eighth's time, nor long before it. The ruins of Whitby Abbey are very magnificent.

Note XXVII.

—— Saint Cuthbert's Holy Isle.—P. 104.

Lindisfarne, an isle on the coast of Northumberland, was called Holy Island, from the sanctity of its ancient monastery, and from its having been the episcopal seat of the see of Durham during the early ages of British Christianity. A succession of holy men held that office: but their merits were swallowed up in the superior fame of St. Cuthbert, who was sixth Bishop of Durham, and who bestowed the name of his 'patrimony' upon the extensive property of the see. The ruins of the monastery upon Holy Island betoken great antiquity. The arches are, in general, strictly Saxon; and the pillars which support them, short, strong, and massy. In some places, however, there are pointed windows, which indicate that the building has been repaired at a period long subsequent to the original foundation. The exterior ornaments of the building, being of a light sandy stone, have been wasted, as described in the text. Lindisfarne

G

is not properly an island, but rather, as the venerable Bede has termed it, a semi-isle; for, although surrounded by the sea at full tide, the ebb leaves the sands dry between it and the opposite coast of Northumberland, from which it is about three miles distant.

Note XXVIII.

Then Whitby's nuns exulting told,
How to their house three Barons bold
Must menial service do.—P. 107.

The popular account of this curious service, which was probably considerably exaggerated, is thus given in 'A True Account' printed and circulated at Whitby: 'In the fifth year of the reign of Henry II, after the conquest of England by William, Duke of Normandy, the Lord of Uglebarnby, then called William de Bruce; the Lord of Smeaton, called Ralph de Percy; with a gentleman and freeholder called Allatson, did, on the 16th of October, 1159, appoint to meet and hunt the wild-boar, in a certain wood, or desert place, belonging to the Abbot of Whitby: the place's name was Eskdale-side; and the abbot's name was Sedman. Then, these young gentlemen being met, with their hounds and boar-staves, in the place before mentioned, and there having found a great wild-boar, the hounds ran him well near about the chapel and hermitage of Eskdale-side, where was a monk of Whitby, who was an hermit. The boar, being very sorely pursued, and dead-run, took in at the chapel-door, there laid him down, and presently died. The hermit shut the hounds out of the chapel, and kept himself within at his meditations and prayers, the hounds standing at bay without. The gentlemen, in the thick of the wood, being just behind their game, followed the cry of their hounds, and so came to the hermitage, calling on the hermit, who opened the door and came forth; and within they found the boar lying dead: for which, the gentlemen, in a very great fury, because the hounds were put from their game, did most violently and cruelly run at the hermit with their boar-staves, whereby he soon after died. Thereupon the gentlemen, perceiving and knowing that they were in peril of death, took sanctuary at Scarborough: But at that time the abbot being in very great favour with the King, removed them out of the sanctuary; whereby they came in danger of the law, and not to be privileged, but likely to have the severity of the law, which was death for death. But the hermit, being a holy and devout man, and at the point of death, sent for the abbot, and desired him to send for the gentlemen who had wounded him. The abbot so doing, the gentlemen came; and the hermit, being very sick and weak, said unto them, "I am sure to die of those wounds you have given me."—The

abbot answered, "They shall as surely die for the same."—But the hermit answered, "Not so, for I will freely forgive them my death, if they will be content to be enjoined the penance I shall lay on them for the safeguard of their souls." The gentlemen being present, bade him save their lives. Then said the hermit, "You and yours shall hold your lands of the Abbot of Whitby, and his successors, in this manner: That, upon Ascension-day, you, or some of you, shall come to the wood of the Stray-heads, which is in Eskdale-side, the same day at sun-rising, and there shall that abbot's officer blow his horn, to the intent that you may know where to find him; and he shall deliver unto you, William de Bruce, ten stakes, eleven strout stowers, and eleven yethers, to be cut by you, or some of you, with a knife of one penny price: and you, Ralph de Percy, shall take twenty-one of each sort, to be cut in the same manner; and you, Allatson, shall take nine of each sort, to be cut as aforesaid, and to be taken on your backs and carried to the town of Whitby, and to be there before nine of the clock the same day before mentioned. At the same hour of nine of the clock, if it be full sea, your labour and service shall cease; and if low water, each of you shall set your stakes to the brim, each stake one yard from the other, and so yether them on each side with your yethers; and so stake on each side with your strout stowers, that they may stand three tides without removing by the force thereof. Each of you shall do, make, and execute the said service, at that very hour, every year, except it be full sea at that hour; but when it shall so fall out, this service shall cease. You shall faithfully do this, in remembrance that you did most cruelly slay me; and that you may the better call to God for mercy, repent unfeignedly of your sins and do good works. The officer of Eskdale-side shall blow, *Out on you! Out on you! Out on you!* for this heinous crime. If you, or your successors, shall refuse this service, so long as it shall not be full sea at the aforesaid hour, you or yours, shall forfeit your lands to the Abbot of Whitby, or his successors. This I entreat, and earnestly beg, that you may have lives and goods preserved for this service: and I request of you to promise, by your parts in Heaven, that it shall be done by you and your successors, as is aforesaid requested; and I will confirm it by the faith of an honest man."—Then the hermit said, "My soul longeth for the Lord: and I do as freely forgive these men my death as Christ forgave the thieves on the cross." And, in the presence of the abbot and the rest, he said moreover these words: "*In manus tuos, Domine, commendo spiritum meum, a vinculis enim mortis redemisti me, Domine veritatis. Amen.*"— So he yielded up the ghost the eighth day of December, anno Domini 1159, whose soul God have mercy upon. Amen.'

'This service,' it is added, 'still continues to be performed with the prescribed ceremonies, though not by the proprietors in person. Part of the lands charged therewith are now held by a gentleman of the name of Herbert.'

NOTE XXIX.

—— in their convent cell
A Saxon princess once did dwell,
The lovely Edelfled.—P. 107.

She was the daughter of King Oswy, who, in gratitude to Heaven for the great victory which he won in 655, against Penda, the Pagan King of Mercia, dedicated Edelfleda, then but a year old, to the service of God, in the monastery of Whitby, of which St. Hilda was then abbess. She afterwards adorned the place of her education with great magnificence.

NOTE XXX.

—— of thousand snakes, each one
Was changed into a coil of stone,
When holy Hilda pray'd;
They told, how sea-fowls' pinions fail,
As over Whitby's towers they sail.—P. 107.

These two miracles are much insisted upon by all ancient writers who have occasion to mention either Whitby or St. Hilda. The relics of the snakes which infested the precincts of the convent, and were, at the abbess's prayer, not only beheaded, but petrified, are still found about the rocks, and are termed by Protestant fossilists, *Ammonitæ.*

The other miracle is thus mentioned by Camden: 'It is also ascribed to the power of her sanctity, that these wild geese, which, in the winter, fly in great flocks to the lakes and rivers unfrozen in the southern parts, to the great amazement of every one, fall down suddenly upon the ground, when they are in their flight over certain neighbouring fields hereabouts: a relation I should not have made, if I had not received it from several credible men. But those who are less inclined to heed superstition, attribute it to some occult quality in the ground, and to somewhat of antipathy between it and the geese, such as they say is betwixt wolves and scyllaroots: For that such hidden tendencies and aversions, as we call sympathies and antipathies, are implanted in many things by provident Nature for the preservation of them, is a thing so evident that everybody grants it.' Mr. Charlton, in his History of Whitby, points out the true origin of the fable, from the number of sea-gulls that, when flying from a storm, often alight near Whitby; and from the woodcocks, and other birds of passage, who do the same upon their arrival on shore, after a long flight.

NOTE XXXI.

His body's resting-place, of old,
How oft their patron chang'd, they told.
—P. 107.

St. Cuthbert was, in the choice of his sepulchre, one of the most mutable and unreasonable saints in the Calendar. He died A.D. 688, in a hermitage upon the Farne Islands, having resigned the bishopric of Lindisfarne, or Holy Island, about two years before[1]. His body was brought to Lindisfarne, where it remained until a descent of the Danes, about 793, when the monastery was nearly destroyed. The monks fled to Scotland with what they deemed their chief treasure, the relics of St. Cuthbert. The Saint was, however, a most capricious fellow-traveller; which was the more intolerable, as, like Sinbad's Old Man of the Sea, he journeyed upon the shoulders of his companions. They paraded him through Scotland for several years, and came as far west as Whithern, in Galloway, whence they attempted to sail for Ireland, but were driven back by tempests. He at length made a halt at Norham; from thence he went to Melrose, where he remained stationary for a short time, and then caused himself to be launched upon the Tweed in a stone coffin, which landed him at Tilmouth, in Northumberland. This boat is finely shaped, ten feet long, three feet and a half in diameter, and only four inches thick; so that, with very little assistance, it might certainly have swam: It still lies, or at least did so a few years ago, in two pieces, beside the ruined chapel of Tilmouth. From Tilmouth, Cuthbert wandered into Yorkshire; and at length made a long stay at Chester-le-street, to which the bishop's see was transferred. At length, the Danes, continuing to infest the country, the monks removed to Ripon for a season; and it was in return from thence to Chester-le-street, that, passing through a forest called Dunholme, the Saint and his carriage became immoveable at a place named Wardlaw, or Wardilaw. Here the Saint chose his place of residence; and all who have seen Durham must admit, that, if difficult in his choice, he evinced taste in at length fixing it. It is said that the Northumbrian Catholics still keep secret the precise spot of the Saint's sepulture, which is only entrusted to three persons at a time. When one dies, the survivors associate to them, in his room, a person judged fit to be the depositary of so valuable a secret.

[The resting-place of the remains of this Saint is not now matter of uncertainty. So recently as 17th May, 1827, 1139 years after his death, their discovery and disinterment

---

[1] He resumed the bishopric of Lindisfarne, which, owing to bad health, he again relinquished within less than three months before his death.—RAINE's *St. Cuthbert.*

were effected. Under a blue stone, in the middle of the shrine of St. Cuthbert, at the eastern extremity of the choir of Durham Cathedral, there was then found a walled grave, containing the coffins of the Saint. The first, or outer one, was ascertained to be that of 1541, the second of 1041; the third, or inner one, answering in every particular to the description of that of 698, was found to contain, not indeed, as had been averred then, and even until 1539, the incorruptible body, but the entire skeleton of the Saint; the bottom of the grave being perfectly dry, free from offensive smell, and without the slightest symptom that a human body had ever undergone decomposition within its walls. The skeleton was found swathed in five silk robes of emblematical embroidery, the ornamental parts laid with gold leaf, and these again covered with a robe of linen. Beside the skeleton were also deposited several gold and silver *insignia*, and other relics of the Saint.

The Roman Catholics now allow that the coffin was that of St. Cuthbert.

The bones of the Saint were again restored to the grave in a new coffin, amid the fragments of the former ones. Those portions of the inner coffin which could be preserved, including one of its rings, with the silver altar, golden cross, stole, comb, two maniples, bracelets, girdle, gold wire of the skeleton, and fragments of the five silk robes, and some of the rings of the outer coffin made in 1541, were deposited in the library of the Dean and Chapter, where they are now preserved.

For ample details of the life of St. Cuthbert,—his coffin-journeys, an account of the opening of his tomb, and a description of the silk robes and other relics found in it,—the reader interested in such matters is referred to a work entitled 'Saint Cuthbert, by James Raine, M.A.,' (4to, Durham, 1828,) where he will find much of antiquarian history, ceremonies, and superstitions, to gratify his curiosity.]—ED.

NOTE XXXII.

Even Scotland's dauntless king, and heir, . . .
Before his standard fled.—Pp. 108-9.

Every one has heard that when David I, with his son Henry, invaded Northumberland in 1136, the English host marched against them under the holy banner of St. Cuthbert; to the efficacy of which was imputed the great victory which they obtained in the bloody battle of Northallerton, or Cutonmoor. The conquerors were at least as much indebted to the jealousy and intractability of the different tribes who composed David's army; among whom, as mentioned in the text, were the Galwegians, the Britons of Strath-Clyde, the men of Teviotdale and Lothian, with many Norman and German warriors, who asserted

the cause of the Empress Maud. See CHALMERS' *Caledonia*, vol. i. p 622; a most laborious, curious, and interesting publication, from which considerable defects of style and manner ought not to turn aside the Scottish antiquary.

NOTE XXXIII.

'Twas he, to vindicate his reign,
Edg'd Alfred's falchion on the Dane,
And turn'd the Conqueror back again.
—P. 108.

Cuthbert, we have seen, had no great reason to spare the Danes, when opportunity offered. Accordingly, I find, in Simeon of Durham, that the Saint appeared in a vision to Alfred, when lurking in the marshes of Glastonbury, and promised him assistance and victory over his heathen enemies; a consolation, which, as was reasonable, Alfred, after the victory of Ashendown, rewarded, by a royal offering at the shrine of the Saint. As to William the Conqueror, the terror spread before his army, when he marched to punish the revolt of the Northumbrians, in 1096, had forced the monks to fly once more to Holy Island with the body of the Saint. It was, however, replaced before William left the north; and, to balance accounts, the Conqueror having intimated an indiscreet curiosity to view the Saint's body, he was, while in the act of commanding the shrine to be opened, seized with heat and sickness, accompanied with such a panic terror, that, notwithstanding there was a sumptuous dinner prepared for him, he fled without eating a morsel (which the monkish historian seems to have thought no small part both of the miracle and the penance), and never drew his bridle till he got to the river Tees.

NOTE XXXIV.

Saint Cuthbert sits, and toils to frame
The sea-born beads that bear his name.
—P. 108.

Although we do not learn that Cuthbert was, during his life, such an artificer as Dunstan, his brother in sanctity, yet, since his death, he has acquired the reputation of forging those *Entrochi* which are found among the rocks of Holy Island, and pass there by the name of St. Cuthbert's Beads. While at this task, he is supposed to sit during the night upon a certain rock, and use another as his anvil. This story was perhaps credited in former days; at least the Saint's legend contains some not more probable.

Note XXXV.

Old Colwulf.—P. 108.

Ceolwulf, or Colwulf, King of Northumberland, flourished in the eighth century. He was a man of some learning; for the venerable Bede dedicates to him his 'Ecclesiastical History.' He abdicated the throne about 738, and retired to Holy Island, where he died in the odour of sanctity. Saint as Colwulf was, however, I fear the foundation of the penance vault does not correspond with his character; for it is recorded among his *memorabilia,* that, finding the air of the island raw and cold, he indulged the monks, whose rule had hitherto confined them to milk or water, with the comfortable privilege of using wine or ale. If any rigid antiquary insists on this objection, he is welcome to suppose the penance-vault was intended, by the founder, for the more genial purposes of a cellar.

These penitential vaults were the *Geisselgewölbe* of German convents. In the earlier and more rigid times of monastic discipline, they were sometimes used as a cemetery for the lay benefactors of the convent, whose unsanctified corpses were then seldom permitted to pollute the choir. They also served as places of meeting for the chapter, when measures of uncommon severity were to be adopted. But their most frequent use, as implied by the name, was as places for performing penances, or undergoing punishment.

Note XXXVI.

Tynemouth's haughty Prioress.—P. 109.

That there was an ancient priory at Tynemouth is certain. Its ruins are situated on a high rocky point; and, doubtless, many a vow was made to the shrine by the distressed mariners who drove towards the iron-bound coast of Northumberland in stormy weather. It was anciently a nunnery; for Virca, abbess of Tynemouth, presented St. Cuthbert (yet alive) with a rare winding-sheet, in emulation of a holy lady called Tuda, who had sent him a coffin. But, as in the case of Whitby, and of Holy Island, the introduction of nuns at Tynemouth in the reign of Henry VIII is an anachronism. The nunnery at Holy Island is altogether fictitious. Indeed, St. Cuthbert was unlikely to permit such an establishment; for, notwithstanding his accepting the mortuary gifts above mentioned, and his carrying on a visiting acquaintance with the Abbess of Coldingham, he certainly hated the whole female sex; and, in revenge of a slippery trick played to him by an Irish princess, he, after death, inflicted severe penances on such as presumed to approach within a certain distance of his shrine.

Note XXXVII.

On those the wall was to enclose, Alive, within the tomb.—P. 110.

It is well known, that the religious, who broke their vows of chastity, were subjected to the same penalty as the Roman vestals in a similar case. A small niche, sufficient to enclose their bodies, was made in the massive wall of the convent; a slender pittance of food and water was deposited in it, and the awful words, VADE IN PACE, were the signal for immuring the criminal. It is not likely that, in latter times, this punishment was often resorted to; but, among the ruins of the Abbey of Coldingham, were some years ago discovered the remains of a female skeleton, which, from the shape of the niche, and position of the figure, seemed to be that of an immured nun.

Note XXXVIII.

The village inn.—P. 116.

The accommodations of a Scottish hostelrie, or inn, in the sixteenth century, may be collected from Dunbar's admirable tale of 'The Friars of Berwick.' Simon Lawder, 'the gay ostlier,' seems to have lived very comfortably; and his wife decorated her person with a scarlet kirtle, and a belt of silk and silver, and rings upon her fingers; and feasted her paramour with rabbits, capons, partridges, and Bourdeaux wine. At least, if the Scottish inns were not good, it was not for want of encouragement from the legislature; who, so early as the reign of James I, not only enacted, that in all boroughs and fairs there be hostellaries, having stables and chambers, and provision for man and horse, but by another statute, ordained that no man, travelling on horse or foot, should presume to lodge anywhere except in these hostellaries; and that no person, save innkeepers, should receive such travellers, under the penalty of forty shillings, for exercising such hospitality. But, in spite of these provident enactments, the Scottish hostels are but indifferent, and strangers continue to find reception in the houses of individuals.

Note XXXIX.

The death of a dear friend.—P. 118.

Among other omens to which faithful credit is given among the Scottish peasantry, is what is called the 'dead-bell,' explained by my friend James Hogg, to be that tinkling in the ears which the country people regard as the secret intelligence of some friend's decease. He tells a story to the purpose in the 'Mountain Bard,' p. 26.

''O lady, 'tis dark, an' I heard the dead-bell! An' I darena gae yonder for gowd nor fee.'

'By the dead-bell is meant a tinkling in the ears, which our peasantry in the country regard as a secret intelligence of some friend's decease. Thus this natural occurrence strikes many with a superstitious awe. This reminds me of a trifling anecdote, which I will here relate as an instance:—Our two servant-girls agreed to go an errand of their own, one night after supper, to a considerable distance, from which I strove to persuade them, but could not prevail. So, after going to the apartment where I slept, I took a drinking-glass, and, coming close to the back of the door, made two or three sweeps round the lips of the glass with my finger, which caused a loud shrill sound. I then overheard the following dialogue:—B. "Ah, mercy! the dead-bell went through my head just now with such a knell as I never heard."—I. "I heard it too."—B. "Did you indeed? That is remarkable. I never knew of two hearing it at the same time before."—I. "We will not go to Midgehope to-night."—B. "I would not go for all the world. I shall warrant it is my poor brother Wat: who knows what these wild Irishes may have done to him?"'—HOGG'S Mountain Bard, 3rd edit., pp. 31–2.]

NOTE XL.

The Goblin-Hall.—P. 120.

A vaulted hall under the ancient castle of Gifford or Yester, (for it bears either name indifferently,) the construction of which has from a very remote period been ascribed to magic. The Statistical Account of the Parish of Garvald and Baro gives the following account of the present state of this castle and apartment:—' Upon a peninsula, formed by the water of Hopes on the east, and a large rivulet on the west, stands the ancient castle of Yester. Sir David Dalrymple, in his Annals, relates, that "Hugh Gifford de Yester died in 1267; that in his castle there was a capacious cavern, formed by magical art, and called in the country Bo-Hall, i.e. Hobgoblin Hall." A stair of twenty-four steps led down to this apartment, which is a large and spacious hall, with an arched roof; and though it hath stood for so many centuries, and been exposed to the external air for a period of fifty or sixty years, it is still as firm and entire as if it had only stood a few years. From the floor of this hall, another stair of thirty-six steps leads down to a pit which hath a communication with Hopes-water. A great part of the walls of this large and ancient castle are still standing. There is a tradition, that the castle of Yester was the last fortification, in this country, that surrendered to General Gray, sent into Scotland by Protector Somerset.' *Statistical Account*, Vol. xiii.—I have only to add, that, in 1737, the Goblin Hall was tenanted by the Marquis of Tweeddale's falconer, as I learn from a poem by Boyse, entitled ' Retirement,' written upon visiting Yester. It is now rendered inaccessible by the fall of the stair.

Sir David Dalrymple's authority for the anecdote is in Fordun, whose words are,— 'A. D. MCCLXVII. *Hugo Giffard de Yester moritur; cujus castrum, vel saltem caveam, et dongionem, arte daemonicâ antiquae relationes ferunt fabrifactum: nam ibidem habetur mirabilis specus subterraneus, opere mirifico constructus, magno terrarum spatio protelatus, qui communiter* Bo-Hall *appellatus est.*' Lib. X. cap 21.— Sir David conjectures, that Hugh de Gifford must either have been a very wise man, or a great oppressor.

NOTE XLI.

There floated Haco's banner trim,
Above Norweyan warriors grim.—P. 120.

In 1263, Haco, King of Norway, came into the Frith of Clyde with a powerful armament, and made a descent at Largs, in Ayrshire. Here he was encountered and defeated, on the 2nd October, by Alexander III. Haco retreated to Orkney, where he died soon after this disgrace to his arms. There are still existing, near the place of battle, many barrows, some of which, having been opened, were found, as usual, to contain bones and urns.

NOTE XLII.

——*wizard habit strange.*—P. 120.

'Magicians, as is well known, were very curious in the choice and form of their vestments. Their caps are oval, or like pyramids, with lappets on each side, and fur within. Their gowns are long, and furred with foxskins, under which they have a linen garment reaching to the knee. Their girdles are three inches broad, and have many cabalistical names, with crosses, trines, and circles inscribed on them. Their shoes should be of new russet leather, with a cross cut upon them. Their knives are dagger-fashion; and their swords have neither guard nor scabbard.'— See these, and many other particulars, in the Discourse concerning Devils and Spirits, annexed to REGINALD SCOTT'S *Discovery of Witchcraft*, edition 1665.

NOTE XLIII.

Upon his breast a pentacle.—P. 120.

'A pentacle is a piece of fine linen, folded with five corners, according to the five senses, and suitably inscribed with characters. This the magician extends towards the spirits which he invokes, when they are stubborn and rebellious, and refuse to be conformable unto the ceremonies and rites of magic.'—See the Discourses, &c. above mentioned, p. 66.

NOTE XLIV.

As born upon that blessed night
When yawning graves, and dying groan,
Proclaim'd hell's empire overthrown.
—P. 121.

It is a popular article of faith, that those who are born on Christmas, or Good Friday, have the power of seeing spirits, and even of commanding them. The Spaniards imputed the haggard and downcast looks of their Philip II to the disagreeable visions to which this privilege subjected him.

NOTE XLV.

Yet still the knightly spear and shield
The Elfin Warrior doth wield
Upon the brown hill's breast.—P. 122.

The following extract from the Essay upon the Fairy Superstitions, in the 'Minstrelsy of the Scottish Border,' vol. ii, will show whence many of the particulars of the combat between Alexander III and the Goblin Knight are derived :—

Gervase of Tilbury, *Otia Imperial ap. Script. rer. Brunsvic* (vol. i. p. 797), relates the following popular story concerning a fairy knight : ' Osbert, a bold and powerful baron, visited a noble family in the vicinity of Wandlebury, in the bishopric of Ely. Among other stories related in the social circle of his friends, who, according to custom, amused each other by repeating ancient tales and traditions, he was informed, that if any knight, unattended, entered an adjacent plain by moonlight, and challenged an adversary to appear, he would be immediately encountered by a spirit in the form of a knight. Osbert resolved to make the experiment, and set out, attended by a single squire, whom he ordered to remain without the limits of the plain, which was surrounded by an ancient intrenchment. On repeating the challenge, he was instantly assailed by an adversary, whom he quickly unhorsed, and seized the reins of his steed. During this operation, his ghostly opponent sprung up, and darting his spear, like a javelin, at Osbert, wounded him in the thigh. Osbert returned in triumph with the horse, which he committed to the care of his servants. The horse was of a sable colour, as well as his whole accoutrements, and apparently of great beauty and vigour. He remained with his keeper till cock-crowing, when, with eyes flashing fire, he reared, spurned the ground, and vanished. On disarming himself, Osbert perceived that he was wounded, and that one of his steel boots was full of blood.' Gervase adds, that, ' as long as he lived, the scar of his wound opened afresh on the anniversary of the eve on which he encountered the spirit.' Less fortunate was the gallant Bohemian knight, who, travelling by night with a single companion, ' came in sight of a fairy host, arrayed under displayed banners. Despising the remonstrances of his friend, the knight pricked forward to break a lance with a champion, who advanced from the ranks apparently in defiance. His companion beheld the Bohemian overthrown, horse and man, by his aërial adversary; and returning to the spot next morning, he found the mangled corpses of the knight and steed.'—*Hierarchy of Blessed Angels*, p. 554.

Besides these instances of Elfin chivalry above quoted, many others might be alleged in support of employing fairy machinery in this manner. The forest of Glenmore, in the North Highlands, is believed to be haunted by a spirit called *Lham-dearg*, in the array of an ancient warrior, having a bloody hand, from which he takes his name. He insists upon those with whom he meets doing battle with him; and the clergyman, who makes up an account of the district, extant in the Macfarlane MS. in the Advocates' Library, gravely assures us, that, in his time, *Lham-dearg* fought with three brothers whom he met in his walk, none of whom long survived the ghostly conflict. Barclay, in his ' Euphormion,' gives a singular account of an officer who had ventured, with his servant, rather to intrude upon a haunted house in a town in Flanders, than to put up with worse quarters elsewhere. After taking the usual precautions of providing fires, lights, and arms, they watched till midnight, when behold ! the severed arm of a man dropped from the ceiling ; this was followed by the legs, the other arm, the trunk, and the head of the body, all separately. The members rolled together, united themselves in the presence of the astonished soldiers, and formed a gigantic warrior, who defied them both to combat. Their blows, although they penetrated the body and amputated the limbs of their strange antagonist, had, as the reader may easily believe, little effect on an enemy who possessed such powers of self-union ; nor did his efforts make more effectual impression upon them. How the combat terminated I do not exactly remember, and have not the book by me ; but I think the spirit made to the intruders on his mansion the usual proposal, that they should renounce their redemption ; which being declined, he was obliged to retract.

The most singular tale of the kind is contained in an extract communicated to me by my friend Mr. Surtees of Mainsforth, in the Bishopric, who copied it from a MS note in a copy of Burthogge, ' On the Nature of Spirits, 8vo, 1694, which had been the property of the late Mr. Gill, attorney-general to Egerton, Bishop of Durham. ' It was not,' says my obliging correspondent, ' in Mr. Gill's own hand, but probably a hundred years older, and was said to be, *E libre Convent. Dunelm. per T. C. extract.*, whom I believe to have been Thomas Cradocke, Esq., barrister, who held several offices under the See of Durham a hundred years ago. Mr. Gill was possessed of most of his manuscripts.' The extract, which, in fact, suggested the introduction of the tale into the present poem, runs thus :—

'*Rem miram hujusmodi quae nostris temporibus evenit, teste viro nobili ac fide dignissimo, enarrare haud pigebit. Radulphus Bulmer, cum e castris, quae tunc temporis prope Norham posita erant, oblectationis causa, exiisset, ac in ulteriore Tuedae ripâ praedam cum canibus leporariis insequeretur, forte cum Scoto quodam nobili, sibi antehac, ut videbatur, familiariter cognito, congressus est; ac, ut fas erat inter inimicos, flagrante bello, brevissimâ interrogationis morâ interpositâ, alterutros invicem incitato cursu infestis animis petiere. Noster, primo occursu, equo praeacerrimo hostis impetu labante, in terram eversus pectore et capite laeso, sanguinem, mortuo similis, evomebat. Quem ut se aegre habentem comiter allocutus est alter, pollicitusque, modo auxilium non abnegaret, monitisque obtemperans ab omni rerum sacrarum cogitatione abstineret, nec Deo, Deiparae Virgini, Sanctove ullo, preces aut vota efferret vel inter sese conciperet, se brevi eum sanum validumque restituturum esse. Prae angore oblata conditio accepta est; ac veterator ille nescio quid obscaeni murmuris insusurrans, prehensa manu, dicto citius in pedes sanum ut antea sublevavit. Noster autem, maxima prae rei inauditâ novitate formidine perculsus, MI JESU! exclamat, vel quid simile; ac subito respiciens nec hostem nec ullam alium conspicit, equum solum gravissimo nuper casu afflictum, per summam pacem in rivo fluvii pascentem. Ad castra itaque mirabundus revertens, fidei dubius, rem primo occultavit, dein, confecto bello, Confessori suo totam asseruit. Delusoria procul dubio res tota, ac mala veteratoris illius aperitur fraus, qua hominem Christianum ad vetitum tale auxilium pelliceret. Nomen utcunque illius (nobilis alias ac clari) reticendum duco, cum haud dubium sit quin Diabolus, Deo permittente, formam quam libuerit, immo angeli lucis, sacro oculo Dei teste, posse assumere.*' The MS. chronicle, from which Mr. Cradocke took this curious extract, cannot now be found in the Chapter Library of Durham, or, at least, has hitherto escaped the researches of my friendly correspondent.

Lindesay is made to allude to this adventure of Ralph Bulmer, as a well-known story, in the 4th Canto, Stanza xxii. p. 132.

The northern champions of old were accustomed peculiarly to search for, and delight in, encounters with such military spectres. See a whole chapter on the subject, in BARTHOLINUS, *De Causis contemptae Mortis a Danis*, p. 253.

NOTE XLVI.

Close to the hut, no more his own,
Close to the aid he sought in vain,
The morn may find the stiffen'd swain.
—P. 125.

I cannot help here mentioning, that, on the night in which these lines were written, suggested, as they were, by a sudden fall of snow, beginning after sunset, an unfortunate man perished exactly in the manner here described, and his body was next morning found close to his own house. The accident happened within five miles of the farm of Ashestiel.

NOTE XLVII.

——*Forbes.*—P. 125.

Sir William Forbes of Pitsligo, Baronet; unequalled, perhaps, in the degree of individual affection entertained for him by his friends, as well as in the general respect and esteem of Scotland at large. His 'Life of Beattie,' whom he befriended and patronized in life, as well as celebrated after his decease, was not long published, before the benevolent and affectionate biographer was called to follow the subject of his narrative. This melancholy event very shortly succeeded the marriage of the friend, to whom this introduction is addressed, with one of Sir William's daughters.

NOTE XLVIII.

Friar Rush.—P. 127.

Alias, 'Will o' the Wisp.' This personage is a strolling demon, or *esprit follet*, who, once upon a time, got admittance into a monastery as a scullion, and played the monks many pranks. He was also a sort of Robin Goodfellow, and Jack o' Lanthern. It is in allusion to this mischievous demon that Milton's clown speaks,—

'She was pinched, and pulled, she said,
And he by *Friar's lanthern* led.

'The History of Friar Rush' is of extreme rarity, and, for some time, even the existence of such a book was doubted, although it is expressly alluded to by Reginald Scott, in his 'Discovery of Witchcraft.' I have perused a copy in the valuable library of my friend Mr. Heber; and I observe, from Mr. Beloe's 'Anecdotes of Literature,' that there is one in the excellent collection of the Marquis of Stafford.

NOTE XLIX.

Sir David Lindesay of the Mount,
Lord Lion King-at-arms.—P. 128.

The late elaborate edition of Sir David Lindesay's Works, by Mr. George Chalmers, has probably introduced him to many of my readers. It is perhaps to be regretted, that the learned Editor had not bestowed more pains in elucidating his author, even although he should have omitted, or at least reserved, his disquisitions on the origin of the language used by the poet. But, with all its faults, his work is an acceptable present to Scottish antiquaries. Sir David Lindesay was well known for his early efforts in favour of the Reformed doctrines; and, indeed, his play, coarse as it now seems, must have had a powerful effect upon the people of his age. I am uncertain if I abuse poetical licence, by introducing Sir David Lindesay in the character of Lion-Herald, sixteen years before he obtained that office. At any rate, I am not the first who has been guilty of the anachronism; for the author of 'Flodden Field' despatches *Dallamount*, which can mean nobody but Sir David de la Mont, to France, on the message of defiance from James IV to Henry VIII. It was often an office imposed on the Lion King-at-Arms, to receive foreign ambassadors; and Lindesay himself did this honour to Sir Ralph Sadler, in 1539-40. Indeed, the oath of the Lion, in its first article, bears reference to his frequent employment upon royal messages and embassies.

The office of heralds, in feudal times, being held of the utmost importance, the inauguration of the Kings-at-arms, who presided over their colleges, was proportionally solemn. In fact, it was the mimicry of a royal coronation, except that the unction was made with wine instead of oil. In Scotland, a namesake and kinsman of Sir David Lindesay, inaugurated in 1592, 'was crowned by King James with the ancient crown of Scotland, which was used before the Scottish kings assumed a close crown;' and, on occasion of the same solemnity, dined at the King's table, wearing the crown. It is probable that the coronation of his predecessor was not less solemn. So sacred was the herald's office, that, in 1515, Lord Drummond was by Parliament declared guilty of treason, and his lands forfeited, because he had struck with his fist the Lion King-at-arms, when he reproved him for his follies. Nor was he restored, but at the Lion's earnest solicitation.

NOTE L.

Crichtoun Castle.—P. 129.

A large ruinous castle on the banks of the Tyne, about ten miles from Edinburgh. As indicated in the text, it was built at different times, and with a very differing regard to splendour and accommodation. The oldest part of the building is a narrow keep, or tower, such as formed the mansion of a lesser Scottish baron; but so many additions have been made to it, that there is now a large court-yard, surrounded by buildings of different ages. The eastern front of the court

is raised above a portico, and decorated with entablatures, bearing anchors. All the stones of this front are cut into diamond facets, the angular projections of which have an uncommonly rich appearance. The inside of this part of the building appears to have contained a gallery of great length, and uncommon elegance. Access was given to it by a magnificent staircase, now quite destroyed. The soffits are ornamented with twining cordage and rosettes; and the whole seems to have been far more splendid than was usual in Scottish castles. The castle belonged originally to the Chancellor, Sir William Crichton, and probably owed to him its first enlargement, as well as its being taken by the Earl of Douglas, who imputed to Crichton's counsels the death of his predecessor, Earl William, beheaded in Edinburgh Castle, with his brother, in 1440. It is said to have been totally demolished on that occasion; but the present state of the ruin shows the contrary. In 1483, it was garrisoned by Lord Crichton, then its proprietor, against King James III, whose displeasure he had incurred by seducing his sister Margaret, in revenge, it is said, for the monarch having dishonoured his bed. From the Crichton family the castle passed to that of the Hepburns, Earls Bothwell; and when the forfeitures of Stewart, the last Earl Bothwell, were divided, the barony and castle of Crichton fell to the share of the Earl of Buccleuch. They were afterwards the property of the Pringles of Clifton, and are now that of Sir John Callander, Baronet. It were to be wished the proprietor would take a little pains to preserve these splendid remains of antiquity, which are at present used as a fold for sheep, and wintering cattle; although, perhaps, there are very few ruins in Scotland which display so well the style and beauty of ancient castle-architecture. The castle of Crichton has a dungeon vault, called the *Massy More*. The epithet, which is not uncommonly applied to the prisons of other old castles in Scotland, is of Saracenic origin. It occurs twice in the '*Epistolae Itinerariae*' of Tollius. '*Carcer subterraneus, sive, ut Mauri appellant,* MAZMORRA,' p. 147; and again, '*Coguntur omnes Captivi sub noctem in ergastula subterranea, quae Turcae Algezerani vocant* MAZMORRAS,' p. 243. The same word applies to the dungeons of the ancient Moorish castles in Spain, and serves to show from what nation the Gothic style of castle-building was originally derived.

NOTE LI.

Earl Adam Hepburn.—P. 130.

He was the second Earl of Bothwell, and fell in the field of Flodden, where, according to an ancient English poet, he distinguished himself by a furious attempt to retrieve the day:—

> 'Then on the Scottish part, right proud,
> The Earl of Bothwell then out brast,
> And stepping forth, with stomach good,
> Into the enemies' throng he thrast;
> And *Bothwell! Bothwell!* cried bold,
> To cause his souldiers to ensue,
> But there he caught a wellcome cold,
> The Englishmen straight down him threw.
> Thus Haburn through his hardy heart
> His fatal fine in conflict found,' &c.
> *Flodden Field*, a Poem; edited by
> H. Weber. Edin. 1808.

Adam was grandfather to James, Earl of Bothwell, too well known in the history of Queen Mary.

NOTE LII.

For that a messenger from heaven
In vain to James had counsel given
Against the English war.—P. 130.

This story is told by Pitscottie with characteristic simplicity:—'The King, seeing that France could get no support of him for that time, made a proclamation, full hastily, through all the realm of Scotland, both east and west, south and north, as well in the isles as in the firm land, to all manner of men between sixty and sixteen years, that they should be ready, within twenty days, to pass with him, with forty days victual, and to meet at the Burrow-muir of Edinburgh, and there to pass forward where he pleased. His proclamations were hastily obeyed, contrary the Council of Scotland's will; but every man loved his prince so well that they would on no ways disobey him; but every man caused make his proclamation so hastily, conform to the charge of the King's proclamation.

'The King came to Lithgow, where he happened to be for the time at the Council, very sad and dolorous, making his devotion to God, to send him good chance and fortune in his voyage. In this meantime there came a man, clad in a blue gown, in at the kirk door, and belted about him in a roll of linen cloth; a pair of brotikings[1] on his feet, to the great of his legs; with all other hose and clothes conform thereto: but he had nothing on his head, but syde[2] red yellow hair behind, and on his haffets[3], which wan down to his shoulders; but his forehead was bald and bare. He see med to be a man of two-and-fifty years, with a great pike-staff in his hand, and came first forward among the lords, crying and speiring[4] for the King, saying, he desired to speak with him. While, at the last, he came where the King was sitting in the desk at his prayers; but when he saw the King, he made him little reverence or salutation, but leaned down groffling on the desk before him, and said to him in this manner, as after follows. "Sir King, my mother hath sent me to you, desiring you not to pass, at this time, where thou art purposed; for if thou

does, thou wilt not fare well in thy journey, nor none that passeth with thee. Further, she bade thee mell[1] with no woman, nor use their counsel, nor let them touch thy body, nor thou theirs; for, if thou do it, thou wilt be confounded and brought to shame."

'By this man had spoken thir words unto the King's grace, the evening-song was near done, and the King paused on thir words, studying to give him an answer; but, in the meantime, before the King's eyes, and in the presence of all the lords that were about him for the time, this man vanished away, and could no ways be seen or comprehended, but vanished away as he had been a blink of the sun, or a whip of the whirlwind, and could no more be seen. I heard say, Sir David Lindesay Lyon-herauld, and John Inglis the marshal, who were, at that time, young men, and special servants to the King's grace, were standing presently beside the King, who thought to have laid hands on this man, that they might have speired further tidings at him: But all for nought; they could not touch him; for he vanished away betwixt them, and was no more seen.'

Buchanan, in more elegant, though not more impressive language, tells the same story, and quotes the personal information of our Sir David Lindesay: '*In iis*, (i. e. *qui propius astiterant*) *fuit David Lindesius, Montanus, homo spectatae fidei et probitatis, nec a literarum studiis alienus, et cujus totius vitae tenor longissime a mentiendo aberat; a quo nisi ego haec uti tradidi, pro certis accepissem, ut vulgatam vanis rumoribus fabulum, omissurus eram.*'—Lib. xiii. The King's throne, in St. Catherine's aisle, which he had constructed for himself, with twelve stalls for the Knights Companions of the Order of the Thistle, is still shown as the place where the apparition was seen. I know not by what means St. Andrew got the credit of having been the celebrated monitor of James IV; for the expression in Lindesay's narrative, 'My mother has sent me,' could only be used by St. John, the adopted son of the Virgin Mary. The whole story is so well attested, that we have only the choice between a miracle or an imposture. Mr. Pinkerton plausibly argues, from the caution against incontinence, that the Queen was privy to the scheme of those who had recourse to this expedient to deter King James from his impolitic war.

NOTE LIII.

The wild-buck bells.—P. 130.

I am glad of an opportunity to describe the cry of the deer by another word than *braying*, although the latter has been sanctified by the use of the Scottish metrical translation of the Psalms. *Bell* seems to be an abbreviation of bellow. This sylvan sound conveyed great

---

[1] Buskins. [2] Long. [3] Cheeks. [4] Asking.

[1] Meddle.

delight to our ancestors, chiefly, I suppose, from association. A gentle knight in the reign of Henry VIII, Sir Thomas Wortley, built Wantley Lodge, in Wancliffe Forest, for the pleasure (as an ancient inscription testifies) of 'listening to the hart's *bell.*'

Note LIV.

June saw his father's overthrow.—P. 130.

The rebellion against James III was signalized by the cruel circumstance of his son's presence in the hostile army. When the King saw his own banner displayed against himself, and his son in the faction of his enemies, he lost the little courage he had ever possessed, fled out of the field, fell from his horse as it started at a woman and water-pitcher, and was slain, it is not well understood by whom. James IV, after the battle, passed to Stirling, and hearing the monks of the chapel-royal deploring the death of his father, their founder, he was seized with deep remorse, which manifested itself in severe penances. See a following Note on stanza ix. of canto v. The battle of Sauchie-burn, in which James III fell, was fought 18th June, 1488.

Note LV.

The Borough-moor.—P. 133.

The Borough, or Common Moor of Edinburgh, was of very great extent, reaching from the southern walls of the city to the bottom of Braid Hills. It was anciently a forest; and, in that state, was so great a nuisance, that the inhabitants of Edinburgh had permission granted to them of building wooden galleries, projecting over the street, in order to encourage them to consume the timber, which they seem to have done very effectually. When James IV mustered the array of the kingdom there, in 1513, the Borough-moor was, according to Hawthornden, 'a field spacious and delightful by the shade of many stately and aged oaks.' Upon that, and similar occasions, the royal standard is traditionally said to have been displayed from the Hare-Stane, a high stone, now built into the wall, on the left hand of the highway leading towards Braid, not far from the head of Burntsfield Links. The Hare-Stane probably derives its name from the British word *Har*, signifying an army.

Note LVI.

Pavilions.—P. 134.

I do not exactly know the Scottish mode of encampment in 1513, but Patten gives a curious description of that which he saw after the battle of Pinkey, in 1547:—'Here now, to say somewhat of the manner of their camp. As they had no pavilions, or round houses, of any commendable compass, so wear there few other tentes with posts, as the used manner

of making is; and of these few also, none of above twenty foot length, but most far under; for the most part all very sumptuously beset (after their fashion), for the love of France with fleur-de-lys, some of blue buckeram, some of black, and some of some other colours. These white ridges, as I call them, that, as we stood on Fauxsyde Bray, did make so great muster toward us, which I did take then to be a number of tentes, when we came, we found it a linen drapery, of the coarser cambryk in dede, for it was all of canvas sheets, and wear the tenticles, or rather cabyns and couches of their soldiers; the which (much after the common building of their country beside) had they framed of four sticks, about an ell long a piece, whearof two fastened together at one end aloft, and the two endes beneath stuck in the ground, an ell asunder, standing in fashion like the bowes of a sowes yoke; over two such bowes (one, as it were, at their head, the other at their feet) they stretched a sheet down on both sides, whereby their cabin became roofed like a ridge, but skant shut at both ends, and not very close beneath on the sides, unless their sticks were the shorter, or their wives the more liberal to lend them larger napery; howbeit, when they had lined them, and stuff'd them so thick with straw, with the weather as it was not very cold, when they wear ones couched, they were as warm as they had been wrapt in horses dung.'—PATTEN'S *Account of Somerset's Expedition.*

Note LVII.

—— in proud Scotland's royal shield,
The ruddy lion ramp'd in gold.—P. 134.

The well-known arms of Scotland. If you will believe Boethius and Buchanan, the double tressure round the shield, mentioned, *counter fleur-de-lysed or lingued and armed azure*, was first assumed by Echaius, King of Scotland, contemporary of Charlemagne, and founder of the celebrated League with France; but later antiquaries make poor Eochy, or Achy, little better than a sort of King of Brentford, whom old Grig (who has also swelled into Gregorius Magnus) associated with himself in the important duty of governing some part of the north-eastern coast of Scotland.

Note LVIII.

—— Caledonia's Queen is chang'd.
—P. 136.

The Old Town of Edinburgh was secured on the north side by a lake, now drained, and on the south by a wall, which there was some attempt to make defensible even so late as 1745. The gates, and the greater part of the wall, have been pulled down, in the course of the late extensive and beautiful enlargement of the city. My ingenious and valued friend,

Mr. Thomas Campbell, proposed to celebrate Edinburgh under the epithet here borrowed. But the 'Queen of the North' has not been so fortunate as to receive from so eminent a pen the proposed distinction.

NOTE LIX.

Since first, when conquering York arose,
To Henry meek she gave repose.—P. 137.

Henry VI, with his Queen, his heir, and the chiefs of his family, fled to Scotland after the fatal battle of Towton. In this note a doubt was formerly expressed, whether Henry VI came to Edinburgh, though his Queen certainly did; Mr. Pinkerton inclining to believe that he remained at Kirkcudbright. But my noble friend, Lord Napier, has pointed out to me a grant by Henry, of an annuity of forty marks to his Lordship's ancestor, John Napier, subscribed by the King himself, *at Edinburgh*, the 28th day of August, in the thirty-ninth year of his reign, which corresponds to the year of God, 1461. This grant, Douglas, with his usual neglect of accuracy, dates in 1368. But this error being corrected from the copy in Macfarlane's MSS., pp. 119-120, removes all scepticism on the subject of Henry VI being really at Edinburgh. John Napier was son and heir of Sir Alexander Napier, and about this time was Provost of Edinburgh. The hospitable reception of the distressed monarch and his family, called forth on Scotland the encomium of Molinet, a contemporary poet. The English people, he says,—

'*Ung nouveau roy créerent,*
Par despiteux vouloir,
Le viel en deboutèrent,
Et son legitime hoir,
Qui fuytyf alla prendre,
D'Escossé le garand,
De tous siecles le mendre,
Et le plus tollerant.

—'Recollection des Avantures'

NOTE LX.

—— *the romantic strain.*
Whose Anglo-Norman tones whilere
Could win the royal Henry's ear.—P. 137.

Mr. Ellis, in his valuable Introduction to the 'Specimens of Romance,' has proved, by the concurring testimony of La Ravaillere, Tressan, but especially the Abbé de la Rue, that the courts of our Anglo-Norman Kings, rather than those of the French monarch, produced the birth of Romance literature. Marie, soon after mentioned, compiled from Armorican originals, and translated into Norman-French, or romance language, the twelve curious Lays, of which Mr. Ellis has given us a *précis* in the Appendix to his Introduction. The story of Blondel, the famous and faithful minstrel of Richard I, needs no commentary.

NOTE LXI.

The cloth-yard arrows.—P. 138.

This is no poetical exaggeration. In some of the counties of England, distinguished for archery, shafts of this extraordinary length were actually used. Thus, at the battle of Blackheath, between the troops of Henry VII and the Cornish insurgents, in 1496, the bridge of Dartford was defended by a picked band of archers from the rebel army, 'whose arrows,' says Hollinshed, 'were in length a full cloth yard.' The Scottish, according to Ascham, had a proverb, that every English archer carried under his belt twenty-four Scots, in allusion to his bundle of unerring shafts.

NOTE LXII.

To pass, to wheel, the croupe to gain,
And high curvett, that not in vain
The sword sway might descend amain
On foeman's casque below.—P. 138.

'The most useful *air*, as the Frenchmen term it, is *territerr*; the *courbettes*, *cabrioles*, or *un pas et un sault*, being fitter for horses of parade and triumph than for soldiers: yet I cannot deny but a *demivolte* with *courbettes*, so that they be not too high, may be useful in a fight or *meslee*; for, as Labroue hath it, in his Book of Horsemanship, Monsieur de Montmorency having a horse that was excellent in performing the *demivolte*, did, with his sword, strike down two adversaries from their horses in a tourney, where divers of the prime gallants of France did meet; for, taking his time, when the horse was in the height of his *courbette*, and discharging a blow then, his sword fell with such weight and force upon the two cavaliers, one after another, that he struck them from their horses to the ground.'—*Lord Herbert of Cherbury's Life*, p. 48.

NOTE LXIII.

He saw the hardy burghers there
March arm'd, on foot, with faces bare.
—P. 139.

The Scottish burgesses were, like yeomen, appointed to be armed with bows and sheaves, sword, buckler, knife, spear, or a good axe instead of a bow, if worth £100 : their armour to be of white or bright harness. They wore *white hats*, i. e. bright steel caps without crest or visor. By an act of James IV their *weapon-schawings* are appointed to be held four times a-year, under the aldermen or bailiffs.

Note LXIV.

On foot the yeoman too, . . .
Each at his back (a slender store)
His forty days' provision bore,
His arms were halbert, axe, or spear.
—P. 139.

Bows and quivers were in vain recommended to the peasantry of Scotland, by repeated statutes; spears and axes were universally to have been used instead of them. Their defensive armour was the plate-jack, hauberk, or brigantine; and their missile weapons crossbows and culverins. All wore swords of excellent temper, according to Patten; and a voluminous handkerchief round their neck, 'not for cold, but for cutting.' The mace also was much used in the Scottish army. The old poem on the battle of Flodden mentions a band—

'Who manfully did meet their foes,
With leaden mauls, and lances long.'

When the feudal array of the kingdom was called forth, each man was obliged to appear with forty days' provision. When this was expended, which took place before the battle of Flodden, the army melted away of course. Almost all the Scottish forces, except a few knights, men-at-arms, and the Border-prickers, who formed excellent light-cavalry, acted upon foot.

Note LXV.

A banquet rich, and costly wines.—P. 140.

In all transactions of great or petty importance, and among whomsoever taking place, it would seem that a present of wine was a uniform and indispensable preliminary. It was not to Sir John Falstaff alone that such an introductory preface was necessary, however well judged and acceptable on the part of Mr. Brook; for Sir Ralph Sadler, while on an embassy to Scotland in 1539-40, mentions, with complacency, 'the same night came Rothesay (the herald so called) to me again, and brought me wine from the King, both white and red.'—*Clifford's Edition*, p. 39.

Note LXVI.

——his iron belt,
That bound his breast in penance pain,
In memory of his father slain.—P. 141.

Few readers need to be reminded of this belt, to the weight of which James added certain ounces every year that he lived. Pitscottie founds his belief, that James was not slain in the battle of Flodden, because

the English never had this token of the iron belt to show to any Scottishman. The person and character of James are delineated according to our best historians. His romantic disposition, which led him highly to relish gaiety, approaching to license, was, at the same time, tinged with enthusiastic devotion. These propensities sometimes formed a strange contrast. He was wont, during his fits of devotion, to assume the dress, and conform to the rules, of the order of Franciscans; and when he had thus done penance for some time in Stirling, to plunge again into the tide of pleasure. Probably, too, with no unusual inconsistency, he sometimes laughed at the superstitious observances to which he at other times subjected himself. There is a very singular poem by Dunbar, seemingly addressed to James IV, on one of these occasions of monastic seclusion. It is a most daring and profane parody on the services of the Church of Rome, entitled,—

Dunbar's Dirige to the King
Byding ower lang in Striviling.

'We that are here, in heaven's glory,
To you that are in Purgatory,
Commend us on our hearty wise;
I mean we folks in Paradise,
In Edinburgh, with all merriness,
To you in Stirling, with distress,
Where neither pleasure nor delight is,
For pity this epistle writis,' &c.

See the whole in Sibbald's Collection, vol. i. p. 234.

Note LXVII.

Sir Hugh the Heron's wife.—P. 141.

It has been already noticed [see note to stanza xiii. of canto i, p. 178] that King James's acquaintance with Lady Heron of Ford did not commence until he marched into England. Our historians impute to the King's infatuated passion the delays which led to the fatal defeat of Flodden. The author of 'The Genealogy of the Heron Family' endeavours, with laudable anxiety, to clear the Lady Ford from this scandal; that she came and went, however, between the armies of James and Surrey, is certain. See Pinkerton's *History*, and the authorities he refers to, vol. ii. p. 99. Heron of Ford had been, in 1511, in some sort accessory to the slaughter of Sir Robert Kerr of Cessford, Warden of the Middle Marches. It was committed by his brother the bastard, Lilburn, and Starked, three Borderers. Lilburn and Heron of Ford were delivered up by Henry to James, and were imprisoned in the fortress of Fastcastle, where the former died. Part of the pretence of Lady Ford's negotiations with James was the liberty of her husband.

NOTE LXVIII.

—— *the fair Queen of France*
Sent him a turquois ring and glove,
And charg'd him, as her knight and love,
For her to break a lance.—P. 141.

'Also the Queen of France wrote a love-letter to the King of Scotland, calling him her love, showing him that she had suffered much rebuke in France for the defending of his honour. She believed surely that he would recompense her again with some of his kingly support in her necessity ; that is to say, that he would raise her an army, and come three foot of ground on English ground, for her sake. To that effect she sent him a ring off her finger, with fourteen thousand French crowns to pay his expenses.' PIT-SCOTTIE, p. 110.—A turquois ring : probably this fatal gift is, with James's sword and dagger, preserved in the College of Heralds, London.

NOTE LXIX.

Archibald Bell-the-Cat.—P. 144.

Archibald Douglas, Earl of Angus, a man remarkable for strength of body and mind, acquired the popular name of *Bell-the-Cat,* upon the following remarkable occasion:— James the Third, of whom Pitscottie complains, that he delighted more in music, and 'policies of building,' than in hunting, hawking, and other noble exercises, was so ill advised, as to make favourites of his architects and musicians, whom the same historian irreverently terms masons and fiddlers. His nobility, who did not sympathize in the King's respect for the fine arts, were extremely incensed at the honours conferred on those persons, particularly on Cochrane, a mason, who had been created Earl of Mar ; and, seizing the opportunity, when, in 1482, the King had convoked the whole array of the country to march against the English, they held a midnight council in the church of Lauder, for the purpose of forcibly removing these minions from the King's person. When all had agreed on the propriety of this measure, Lord Gray told the assembly the apologue of the Mice, who had formed a resolution, that it would be highly advantageous to their community to tie a bell round the cat's neck, that they might hear her approach at a distance ; but which public measure unfortunately miscarried, from no mouse being willing to undertake the task of fastening the bell. 'I understand the moral,' said Angus, 'and, that what we propose may not lack execution, I will *bell-the-cat.*' The rest of the strange scene is thus told by Pitscottie.

'By this was advised and spoken by their lords foresaid, Cochran, the Earl of Mar, came from the King to the council, (which council was holden in the kirk of Lauder for the time,) who was well accompanied with a band of men of war, to the number of three hundred light axes, all clad in white livery, and black bends thereon, that they might be known for Cochran the Earl of Mar's men. Himself was clad in a riding-pie of black velvet, with a great chain of gold about his neck, to the value of five hundred crowns, and four blowing horns, with both the ends of gold and silk, set with a precious stone, called a berryl, hanging in the midst. This Cochran had his heumont borne before him, overgilt with gold, and so were all the rest of his horns, and all his blowing were of fine canvas of silk, and the cords thereof fine twined silk, and the chains upon his pallions were double overgilt with gold.

'This Cochran was so proud in his conceit, that he counted no lords to be marrows to him, therefore he rushed rudely at the kirk-door. The council inquired who it was that perturbed them at that time. Sir Robert Douglas, Laird of Lochleven, was keeper of the kirk-door at that time, who inquired who that was that knocked so rudely ? and Cochran answered, "This is I, the Earl of Mar." The which news pleased well the lords, because they were ready boun to cause take him, as is before rehearsed. Then the Earl of Angus passed hastily to the door, and with him Sir Robert Douglas of Lochleven, there to receive in the Earl of Mar, and so many of his complices who were there, as they thought good. And the Earl of Angus met with the Earl of Mar, as he came in at the door, and pulled the golden chain from his craig, and said to him, a tow [1] would set him better. Sir Robert Douglas syne pulled the blowing horn from him in like manner, and said, "He had been the hunter of mischief over long." This Cochran asked, "My lords, is it mows [2], or earnest ?" They answered, and said, "It is good earnest, and so thou shalt find ; for thou and thy complices have abused our prince this long time ; of whom thou shalt have no more credence, but shalt have thy reward according to thy good service, as thou hast deserved in times bypast ; right so the rest of thy followers."

'Notwithstanding, the lords held them quiet till they caused certain armed men to pass into the King's pallion, and two or three wise men to pass with them, and give the King fair pleasant words, till they laid hands on all the King's servants, and took them and hanged them before his eyes over the bridge of Lawder. Incontinent they brought forth Cochran, and his hands bound with a tow, who desired them to take one of his own pallion tows and bind his hands, for he thought shame to have his hands bound with such tow of hemp, like a thief. The lords answered, he was a traitor, he deserved no better ; and, for despight, they took a hair tether [3], and hanged him over the bridge of Lawder, above the rest of his complices.'—PITSCOTTIE, p. 78, folio edit.

---

[1] Rope.   [2] Jest.   [3] Halter.

NOTE LXX.

Against the war had Angus stood,
And chaf'd his royal lord.—P. 144.

Angus was an old man when the war against England was resolved upon. He earnestly spoke against that measure from its commencement; and, on the eve of the battle of Flodden, remonstrated so freely upon the impolicy of fighting, that the King said to him, with scorn and indignation, 'if he was afraid he might go home.' The Earl burst into tears at this insupportable insult, and retired accordingly, leaving his sons George, Master of Angus, and Sir William of Glenbervie, to command his followers. They were both slain in the battle, with two hundred gentlemen of the name of Douglas. The aged Earl, broken-hearted at the calamities of his house and his country, retired into a religious house, where he died about a year after the field of Flodden.

NOTE LXXI.

Tantallon Hold.—P. 144.

The ruins of Tantallon Castle occupy a high rock projecting into the German Ocean, about two miles east of North Berwick. The building is not seen till a close approach, as there is rising ground betwixt it and the land. The circuit is of large extent, fenced upon three sides by the precipice which overhangs the sea, and on the fourth by a double ditch and very strong outworks. Tantallon was a principal castle of the Douglas family, and when the Earl of Angus was banished, in 1527, it continued to hold out against James V. The King went in person against it, and for its reduction, borrowed from the Castle of Dunbar, then belong ng to the Duke of Albany, two great cannons, whose names, as Pitscottie informs us with laudable minuteness, were 'Thrawn-mouth'd Meg and her Marrow'; also, 'two great botcards, and two moyan, two double falcons, and four quarter falcons'; for the safe guiding and redelivery of which, three lords were laid in pawn at Dunbar. Yet, notwithstanding all this apparatus, James was forced to raise the siege, and only afterwards obtained possession of Tantallon by treaty with the governor, Simon Panango. When the Earl of Angus returned from banishment, upon the death of James, he again obtained possession of Tantallon, and it actually afforded refuge to an English ambassador, under circumstances similar to those described in the text. This was no other than the celebrated Sir Ralph Sadler, who resided there for some time under Angus's protection, after the failure of his negotiation for matching the infant Mary with Edward VI. He says, that though this place was poorly furnished, it was of such

strength as might warrant him against the malice of his enemies, and that he now thought himself out of danger.

There is a military tradition, that the old Scottish March was meant to express the words,

'Ding down Tantallon
Mak a brig to the Bass.'

Tantallon was at length 'dung down' and ruined by the Covenanters; its lord, the Marquis of Douglas, being a favourer of the royal cause. The castle and barony were sold in the beginning of the eighteenth century to President Dalrymple of North Berwick, by the then Marquis of Douglas.

NOTE LXXII.

Their motto on his blade.—P. 144.

A very ancient sword, in possession of Lord Douglas, bears, among a great deal of flourishing, two hands pointing to a heart, which is placed betwixt them, and the date 1329, being the year in which Bruce charged the Good Lord Douglas to carry his heart to the Holy Land. The following lines (the first couplet of which is quoted by Godscroft as a popular saying in his time) are inscribed around the emblem :—

'So mony guid as of ye Dovglas beinge,
Of ane surname was ne'er in Scotland seine.

I will ye charge, efter yat I depart,
To holy grawe, and thair bury my hart;
Let it remane ever BOTHE TYME AND HOWR,
To ye last day I sie my Saviour.

I do protest in tyme of al my ringe,
Ye lyk subject had never ony keing.'

This curious and valuable relic was nearly lost during the civil war of 1745–6, being carried away from Douglas Castle by some of those in arms for Prince Charles. But great interest having been made by the Duke of Douglas among the chief partisans of the Stuart, it was at length restored. It resembles a Highland claymore, of the usual size, is of an excellent temper, and admirably poised.

NOTE LXXIII.

Martin Swart.—P. 146.

A German general, who commanded the auxiliaries sent by the Duchess of Burgundy with Lambert Simnel. He was defeated and killed at Stokefield. The name of this German general is preserved by that of the field of battle, which is called, after him, Swart-moor.—There were songs about him long current in England.—See Dissertation prefixed to RITSON'S *Ancient Songs*, 1792, p. lxi.

Note LXXIV.

Perchance some form was unobserv'd ;
Perchance in prayer, or faith, he swerv'd.
—P. 146.

It was early necessary for those who felt themselves obliged to believe in the divine judgment being enunciated in the trial by duel, to find salvos for the strange and obviously precarious chances of the combat. Various curious evasive shifts, used by those who took up an unrighteous quarrel, were supposed sufficient to convert it into a just one. Thus, in the romance of 'Amys and Amelion,' the one brother-in-arms, fighting for the other, disguised in his armour, swears that *he* did not commit the crime of which the Steward, his antagonist, truly, though maliciously, accused him whom he represented. Brantome tells a story of an Italian, who entered the lists upon an unjust quarrel, but, to make his cause good, fled from his enemy at the first onset. 'Turn, coward!' exclaimed his antagonist. 'Thou liest,' said the Italian, 'coward am I none ; and in this quarrel will I fight to the death, but my first cause of combat was unjust, and I abandon it.' '*Je vous laisse à penser,*' adds Brantome, '*s'il n'y a pas de l'abus là.*' Elsewhere he says, very sensibly, upon the confidence which those who had a righteous cause entertained of victory : '*Un autre abus y avoit-il, que ceux qui avoient un juste subjet de querelle, et qu'on les faisoit jurer avant entrer au camp, pensoient estre aussitost vainqueurs, voire s'en assuroient-t-ils du tout, mesmes que leurs confesseurs, parrains et confidants leurs en respondoient tout-à-fait, comme si Dieu leur en eust donné une patente ; et ne regardant point à d'autres fautes passées, et que Dieu en garde la punition à ce coup là pour plus grande, despiteuse, et exemplaire.*'—'Discours sur les Duels.'

Note LXXV.

The Cross.—P. 147.

The Cross of Edinburgh was an ancient and curious structure. The lower part was an octagonal tower, sixteen feet in diameter, and about fifteen feet high. At each angle there was a pillar, and between them an arch, of the Grecian shape. Above these was a projecting battlement, with a turret at each corner, and medallions, of rude but curious workmanship, between them. Above this rose the proper Cross, a column of one stone, upwards of twenty feet high, surmounted with a unicorn. This pillar is preserved in the grounds of the property of Drum, near Edinburgh. The Magistrates of Edinburgh, in 1756, with consent of the Lords of Session (*proh pudor !*) destroyed this curious monument, under a wanton pretext that it encumbered the street ; while, on the one hand, they left an ugly mass called the Luckenbooths, and, on the other, an awkward, long, and low guard-house, which were fifty times more encumbrance than the venerable and inoffensive Cross.

From the tower of the Cross, so long as it remained, the heralds published the acts of Parliament ; and its site, marked by radii, diverging from a stone centre, in the High Street, is still the place where proclamations are made.

[The pillar has been restored to its place in High St.]

Note LXXVI.

? nis awful summons came.—P. 148.

This supernatural citation is mentioned by all our Scottish historians. It was, probably, like the apparition at Linlithgow, an attempt, by those averse to the war, to impose upon the superstitious temper of James IV. The following account from Pitscottie is characteristically minute, and furnishes, besides, some curious particulars of the equipment of the army of James IV. I need only add to it, that Plotcock, or Plutock, is no other than Pluto. The Christians of the middle ages by no means misbelieved in the existence of the heathen deities ; they only considered them as devils ; and Plotcock, so far from implying anything fabulous, was a synonyme of the grand enemy of mankind. 'Yet all thir warnings, and uncouth tidings, nor no good counsel, might stop the King, at this present, from his vain purpose, and wicked enterprize, but hasted him fast to Edinburgh, and there to make his provision and furnishing, in having forth his army against the day appointed, that they should meet in the Burrowmuir of Edinburgh : That is to say, seven cannons that he had forth of the Castle of Edinburgh, which were called the Seven Sisters, casten by Robert Borthwick, the master-gunner, with other small artillery, bullet, powder, and all manner of order, as the master-gunner could devise.

'In this meantime, when they were taking forth their artillery, and the King being in the Abbey for the time, there was a cry heard at the Market-cross of Edinburgh, at the hour of midnight, proclaiming as it had been a summons, which was named and called by the proclaimer thereof, The Summons of Plotcock ; which desired all men to compear, both Earl, and Lord, and Baron, and all honest gentlemen within the town, (every man specified by his own name,) to compear, within the space of forty days, before his master, where it should happen him to appoint, and be for the time, under the pain of disobedience. But whether this summons was proclaimed by vain persons, night walkers, or drunken men, for their pastime, or if it was a spirit, I cannot tell truly; but it was shewn to me, that an indweller of the town, Mr. Richard Lawson, being evil-disposed, ganging in his gallery-stair foreanent the Cross, hearing this voice proclaiming this summons, thought marvel what it should be, cried on his servant to bring him his purse; and when he had brought him it, he took out a crown, and cast over the stair, saying, "I appeal from that summons, judgment, and sentence thereof, and takes me all whole in the mercy of God, and Christ Jesus his son." Verily, the author of this, that caused me write the manner of this summons, was a landed gentleman, who was at that time twenty years of age, and was in the town the time of the said summons; and thereafter, when the field was stricken, he swore to me, there was no man that escaped that was called in this summons, but that one man alone which made his protestation, and appealed from the said summons; but all the lave were perished in the field with the king.'

NOTE LXXVII.

— one of his own ancestry
Drove the Monks forth of Coventry.
—P. 150.

This relates to the catastrophe of a real Robert de Marmion, in the reign of King Stephen, whom William of Newbury describes with some attributes of my fictitious hero: '*Homo bellicosus, ferocia et astucia fere nullo suo tempore impar.*' This Baron, having expelled the Monks from the church of Coventry, was not long of experiencing the divine judgment, as the same monks, no doubt, termed his disaster. Having waged a feudal war with the Earl of Chester, Marmion's horse fell, as he charged in the van of his troop, against a body of the Earl's followers: the rider's thigh being broken by the fall, his head was cut off by a common footsoldier, ere he could receive any succour. The whole story is told by William of Newbury.

NOTE LXXVIII.

—— the savage Dane
At Iol more deep the mead did drain.
—P. 152.

The Iol of the heathen Danes (a word still applied to Christmas in Scotland) was solemnized with great festivity. The humour of the Danes at table displayed itself in pelting each other with bones; and Torfæus tells a long and curious story, in the History of Hrolfe Kraka, of one Hottus, an inmate of the Court of Denmark, who was

so generally assailed with these missiles, that he constructed, out of the bones with which he was overwhelmed, a very respectable intrenchment, against those who continued the raillery. The dances of the northern warriors round the great fires of pine-trees, are commemorated by Olaus Magnus, who says, they danced with such fury holding each other by the hands, that, if the grasp of any failed, he was pitched into the fire with the velocity of a sling. The sufferer, on such occasions, was instantly plucked out, and obliged to quaff off a certain measure of ale, as a penalty for 'spoiling the king's fire.'

NOTE LXXIX.

On Christmas eve.—P. 152.

In Roman Catholic countries, mass is never said at night, except on Christmas eve. Each of the frolics with which that holyday used to be celebrated, might admit of a long and curious note; but I shall content myself with the following description of Christmas, and his attributes, as personified in one of Ben Jonson's Masques for the Court.

'*Enter* CHRISTMAS, *with two or three of the Guard.* He is attired in round hose, long stockings, a close doublet, a high-crowned hat, with a brooch, a long thin beard, a truncheon, little ruffs, white shoes, his scarfs and garters tied cross, and his drum beaten before him.—*The names of his children, with their attires: Miss-Rule,* in a velvet cap, with a sprig, a short cloak, great yellow ruff, like a reveller; his torch-bearer bearing a rope, a cheese, and a basket;—*Caroll,* a long tawny coat, with a red cap, and a flute at his girdle; his torch-bearer carrying a song-book open;—*Minc'd-pie,* like a fine cook's wife, drest neat, her man carrying a pie, dish, and spoons;—*Gamboll,* like a tumbler, with a hoop and bells; his torch-bearer arm'd with cole-staff, and blinding cloth;—*Post and Pair,* with a pair-royal of aces in his hat, his garment all done over with pairs and purs; his squire carrying a box, cards, and counters;—*New-year's-Gift,* in a blue coat, serving-man like, with an orange, and a sprig of rosemary gilt on his head, his hat full of brooches, with a collar of gingerbread; his torch-bearer carrying a march-pain, with a bottle of wine on either arm;—*Mumming,* in a masquing pied suit, with a visor; his torch-bearer carrying the box, and ringing it;—*Wassal,* like a neat sempster and song-ster; her page bearing a brown bowl, drest with ribbands, and rosemary, before her;—*Offering,* in a short gown, with a porter's staff in his hand; a wyth borne before him, and a bason, by his torch-bearer;—*Baby Cocke,* drest like a boy, in a fine long coat, biggin, bib, muckender, and a little dagger; his usher bearing a great cake, with a bean and a pease.'

NOTE LXXX.

Who lists may in their mumming see
Traces of ancient mystery.—P. 153.

It seems certain, that the *Mummers* of England, who (in Northumberland at least) used to go about in disguise to the neighbouring houses, bearing the then useless ploughshare; and the *Guisards* of Scotland, not yet in total disuse, present, in some indistinct degree, a shadow of the old mysteries, which were the origin of the English drama. In Scotland, (*me ipso teste,*) we were wont, during my boyhood, to take the characters of the apostles, at least of Peter, Paul, and Judas Iscariot; the first had the keys, the second carried a sword, and the last the bag, in which the dole of our neighbours plumb-cake was deposited. One played a champion, and recited some traditional rhymes; another was

' Alexander, King of Macedon,
Who conquer'd all the world but Scotland alone :
When he came to Scotland his courage grew cold,
To see a little nation courageous and bold.'

These, and many such verses, were repeated, but by rote, and unconnectedly. There was also, occasionally, I believe, a Saint George. In all, there was a confused resemblance of the ancient mysteries, in which the characters of Scripture, the Nine Worthies, and other popular personages, were usually exhibited. It were much to be wished that the Chester Mysteries were published from the MS. in the Museum, with the annotations which a diligent investigator of popular antiquities might still supply. The late acute and valuable antiquary, Mr. Ritson, showed me several memoranda towards such a task, which are probably now dispersed or lost. See, however, his *Remarks on Shakspeare,* 1783, p. 38.

Since the first edition of Marmion appeared, this subject has received much elucidation from the learned and extensive labours of Mr. Douce; and the Chester Mysteries [edited by J. H. Markland, Esq.] have been printed in a style of great elegance and accuracy (in 1818) by Bensley and Sons, London, for the Roxburghe Club. 1830.

NOTE LXXXI.

Where my great-grandsire came of old,
With amber beard, and flaxen hair.
—P. 153.

MR. Scott of Harden, my kind and affectionate friend, and distant relation, has the original of a poetical invitation, addressed from his grandfather to my relative, from which a few lines in the text are imitated. They are dated, as the epistle in the text, from Mertoun-House, the seat of the Harden family.

' With amber beard, and flaxen hair,
And reverend apostolic air,
Free of anxiety and care,
Come hither, Christmas-day, and dine ;
We 'll mix sobriety with wine,
And easy mirth with thoughts divine.
We Christians think it holiday,
On it no sin to feast or play ;
Others, in spite, may fast and pray.
No superstition in the use
Our ancestors made of a goose ;
Why may not we, as well as they,
Be innocently blithe that day,
On goose or pie, on wine or ale,
And scorn enthusiastic zeal?—
Pray come, and welcome, or plague rott
Your friend and landlord, Walter Scott.
' *Mr. Walter Scott, Lessuden.'*

The venerable old gentleman, to whom the lines are addressed, was the younger brother of William Scott of Raeburn. Being the cadet of a cadet of the Harden family, he had very little to lose; yet he contrived to lose the small property he had, by engaging in the civil wars and intrigues of the house of Stuart. His veneration for the exiled family was so great, that he swore he would not shave his beard till they were restored: a mark of attachment, which, I suppose, had been common during Cromwell's usurpation; for, in Cowley's 'Cutter of Coleman Street,' one drunken cavalier upbraids another, that, when he was not able to afford to pay a barber, he affected to 'wear a beard for the King.' I sincerely hope this was not absolutely the original reason of my ancestor's beard; which, as appears from a portrait in the possession of Sir Henry Hay Macdougal, Bart., and another painted for the famous Dr. Pitcairn, was a beard of a most dignified and venerable appearance.

NOTE LXXXII.

The Spirit's Blasted Tree.—P. 154.

I am permitted to illustrate this passage, by inserting '*Ceubren yr Ellyll,*' or The Spirit's Blasted Tree,' a legendary tale, by the Reverend George Warrington.

The event, on which this tale is founded, is preserved by tradition in the family of the Vaughans of Hengwyrt; nor is it entirely lost, even among the common people, who still point out this oak to the passenger. The enmity between the two Welsh chieftains, Howel Sele, and Owen Glendwr, was extreme, and marked by vile treachery in the one, and ferocious cruelty in the other. The story is somewhat changed and softened, as more favourable to the character of the two chiefs, and as better answering the purpose of poetry, by admitting the passion of pity, and a greater degree of sentiment in the description. Some trace of Howel Sele's mansion was to be seen a few years ago, and

may perhaps be still visible, in the park
of Nannau, now belonging to Sir Robert
Vaughan, Baronet, in the wild and romantic
tracks of Merionethshire. The abbey mentioned passes under two names, Vener and
Cymmer. The former is retained, as more
generally used.

THE SPIRIT'S BLASTED TREE.

Ceubren yr Ellyll.

' Through Nannau's Chase, as Howel pass'd,
  A chief esteem'd both brave and kind,
Far distant borne, the stag-hounds' cry
  Came murmuring on the hollow wind.

Starting, he bent an eager ear,—
  How should the sounds return again?
His hounds lay wearied from the chase,
  And all at home his hunter train.

Then sudden anger flashed his eye,
  And deep revenge he vow'd to take,
On that bold man who dared to force
  His red-deer from the forest brake.

Unhappy Chief! would nought avail,
  No signs impress thy heart with fear,
Thy lady's dark mysterious dream,
  Thy warning from the hoary seer?

Three ravens gave the note of death,
  As through mid-air they wing'd their way;
Then o'er his head, in rapid flight,
  They croak,—they scent their destined prey.

Ill-omen'd bird! as legends say,
  Who hast the wondrous power to know,
While health fills high the throbbing veins,
  The fated hour when blood must flow.

Blinded by rage, alone he pass'd,
  Nor sought his ready vassals' aid:
But what his fate lay long unknown,
  For many an anxious year delay'd.

A peasant mark'd his angry eye;
  He saw him reach the lake's dark bourne,
He saw him near a Blasted Oak,
  But never from that hour return.

Three days pass'd o'er, no tidings came;—
  Where should the Chief his steps delay?
With wild alarm the servants ran,
  Yet knew not where to point their way.

His vassals ranged the mountain's height,
  The covert close, the wide-spread plain;
But all in vain their eager search,
  They ne'er must see their lord again.

Yet Fancy, in a thousand shapes,
  Bore to his home the Chief once more;
Some saw him on high Moal's top,
  Some saw him on the winding shore.

With wonder fraught the tale went round,
  Amazement chain'd the hearer's tongue:
Each peasant felt his own sad loss,
  Yet fondly o'er the story hung.

Oft by the moon's pale shadowy light,
  His aged nurse and steward grey
Would lean to catch the storied sounds,
  Or mark the flitting spirit stray.

Pale lights on Cader's rocks were seen,
  And midnight voices heard to moan;
'Twas even said the Blasted Oak,
  Convulsive, heaved a hollow groan:

And to this day the peasant still,
  With cautious fear, avoids the ground:
In each wild branch a spectre sees,
  And trembles at each rising sound.

Ten annual suns had held their course,
  In summer's smile, or winter storm;
The lady shed the widow'd tear,
  As oft she traced his manly form.

Yet still to hope her heart would cling,
  As o'er her mind illusions play,—
Of travel fond, perhaps her lord
  To distant lands had steer'd his way.

'Twas now November's cheerless hour,
  Which drenching rain and clouds deface;
Dreary bleak Robell's tract appear'd,
  And dull and dank each valley's space.

Loud o'er the weir the hoarse flood fell,
  And dash'd the foaming spray on high;
The west wind bent the forest tops,
  And angry frown'd the evening sky.

A stranger pass'd Llanelltid's bourne,
  His dark-grey steed with sweat besprent,
Which, wearied with the lengthen'd way,
  Could scarcely gain the hill's ascent.

The portal reach'd,—the iron bell
  Loud sounded round the outward wall;
Quick sprang the warder to the gate,
  To know what meant the clam'rous call.

"O! lead me to your lady soon;
  Say,—it is my sad lot to tell,
To clear the fate of that brave knight,
  She long has proved she loved so well."

Then, as he cross'd the spacious hall,
  The menials look surprise and fear;
Still o'er his harp old Modred hung,
  And touch'd the notes for grief's worn ear.

The lady sat amidst her train;
  A mellow'd sorrow mark'd her look:
Then, asking what his mission meant,
  The graceful stranger sigh'd and spoke:—

"O could I spread one ray of hope,
  One moment raise thy soul from woe,
Gladly my tongue would tell its tale,
  My words at ease unfetter'd flow!

"Now, lady, give attention due,
  The story claims thy full belief:
E'en in the worst events of life,
  Suspense removed is some relief.

"Though worn by care, see Madoc here,
  Great Glyndwr's friend, thy kindred's foe;
Ah, let his name no anger raise,
  For now that mighty Chief lies low.

"E'en from the day, when, chain'd by fate,
  By wizard's dream, or potent spell,
Lingering from sad Salopia's field,
  'Reft of *his* aid the Percy fell;—

"E'en from that day misfortune still,
  As if for violated faith,
Pursued him with unwearied step;
  Vindictive still for Hotspur's death.

"Vanquish'd at length, the Glyndwr fled,
  Where winds the Wye her devious flood;
To find a casual shelter there,
  In some lone cot, or desert wood.

"Clothed in a shepherd's humble guise,
  He gain'd by toil his scanty bread ;
He who had Cambria's sceptre borne,
  And her brave sons to glory led !

"To penury extreme, and grief,
  The Chieftain fell a lingering prey;
I heard his last few faltering words,
  Such as with pain I now convey.

"'To Sele's sad widow bear the tale,
  Nor let our horrid secret rest ;
Give but *his* corse to sacred earth,
  Then may my parting soul be blest.'—

"Dim wax'd the eye that fiercely shone,
  And faint the tongue that proudly spoke,
And weak that arm, still raised to me,
  Which oft had dealt the mortal stroke.

"How could I *then* his mandate bear ?
  Or how his last behest obey ?
A rebel deem'd, with him I fled ;
  With him I shunn'd the light of day.

"Proscribed by Henry's hostile rage,
  My country lost, despoil'd my land,
Desperate, I fled my native soil,
  And fought on Syria's distant strand.

"Oh, had thy long-lamented lord
  The holy cross and banner view'd,
Died in the sacred cause, who fell
  Sad victim of a private feud !

"Led by the ardour of the chase,
  Far distant from his own domain,
From where Garthmaelan spreads her shades,
  The Glyndwr sought the opening plain.

"With head aloft and antlers wide,
  A red buck roused then cross'd in view :
Stung with the sight, and wild with rage,
  Swift from the wood fierce Howel flew.

"With bitter taunt and keen reproach,
  He, all impetuous, pour'd his rage ;
Reviled the Chief, as weak in arms,
  And bade him loud the battle wage.

"Glyndwr for once restrain'd his sword,
  And, still averse, the fight delays ;
But soften'd words, like oil to fire,
  Made anger more intensely blaze.

"They fought ; and doubtful long the fray :
  The Glyndwr gave the fatal wound !
Still mournful must my tale proceed,
  And its last act all dreadful sound.

"How could we hope for wish'd retreat,
  His eager vassals ranging wide,
His bloodhounds' keen sagacious scent,
  O'er many a trackless mountain tried.

"I mark'd a broad and Blasted Oak,
  Scorch'd by the lightning's livid glare ;
Hollow its stem from branch to root,
  And all its shrivell'd arms were bare.

"Be this, I cried, his proper grave !—
  (The thought in me was deadly sin.)
Aloft we raised the hapless Chief,
  And dropp'd his bleeding corpse within."

A shriek from all the damsels burst,
  That pierced the vaulted roofs below ;
While horror-struck the Lady stood,
  A living form of sculptured woe.

With stupid stare and vacant gaze,
  Full on his face her eyes were cast,
Absorb'd !—she lost her present grief,
  And faintly thought of things long past.

Like wild-fire o'er a mossy heath,
  The rumour through the hamlet ran ;
The peasants crowd at morning dawn,
  To hear the tale—behold the man.

He led them near the Blasted Oak,
  Then, conscious, from the scene withdrew ;
The peasants work with trembling haste,
  And lay the whiten'd bones to view !—

Back they recoil'd !—the right hand still,
  Contracted, grasp'd a rusty sword ;
Which erst in many a battle gleam'd,
  And proudly deck'd their slaughter'd lord.

They bore the corse to Vener's shrine,
  With holy rites and prayers address'd ;
Nine white-robed monks the last dirge sang,
  And gave the angry spirit rest.'

Note LXXXIII.

The Highlander . . . .
Will, on a Friday morn, look pale,
If ask'd to tell a fairy tale."—P. 154.

The *Daoine shi'*, or *Men of Peace*, of the
Scottish Highlanders, rather resemble the
Scandinavian *Duergar* than the English
Fairies. Notwithstanding their name, they are,
if not absolutely malevolent, at least peevish,
discontented, and apt to do mischief on slight
provocation. The belief of their existence is
deeply impressed on the Highlanders, who
think they are particularly offended at mortals
who talk of them, who wear their favourite
colour green, or in any respect interfere with
their affairs. This is especially to be avoided on
Friday, when, whether as dedicated to Venus,
with whom, in Germany, this subterraneous
people are held nearly connected, or for a
more solemn reason, they are more active, and
possessed of greater power. Some curious
particulars concerning the popular superstitions of the Highlanders may be found in
Dr. Graham's Picturesque Sketches of Perthshire.

Note LXXXIV.

The towers of Franchémont.—P. 154.

The journal of the friend to whom the Fourth
Canto of the Poem is inscribed, furnished me
with the following account of a striking superstition.

'Passed the pretty little village of Franchémont (near Spaw), with the romantic ruins of
the old castle of the Counts of that name.
The road leads through many delightful vales
on a rising ground ; at the extremity of one

of them stands the ancient castle, now the subject of many superstitious legends. It is firmly believed by the neighbouring peasantry, that the last Baron of Franchémont deposited, in one of the vaults of the castle, a ponderous chest, containing an immense treasure in gold and silver, which, by some magic spell, was intrusted to the care of the Devil, who is constantly found sitting on the chest in the shape of a huntsman. Any one adventurous enough to touch the chest is instantly seized with the palsy. Upon one occasion, a priest of noted piety was brought to the vault: he used all the arts of exorcism to persuade his infernal majesty to vacate his seat, but in vain; the huntsman remained immovable. At last, moved by the earnestness of the priest, he told him that he would agree to resign the chest, if the exorciser would sign his name with blood. But the priest understood his meaning, and refused, as by that act he would have delivered over his soul to the Devil. Yet if anybody can discover the mystic words used by the person who deposited the treasure, and pronounce them, the fiend must instantly decamp. I had many stories of a similar nature from a peasant, who had himself seen the Devil in the shape of a great cat.'

Note LXXXV.

The very form of Hilda fair,
Hovering upon the sunny air,
And smiling on her votaries' prayer.
—P. 156.

' I shall only produce one instance more of the great veneration paid to Lady Hilda, which still prevails even in these our days : and that is, the constant opinion that she rendered, and still renders, herself visible, on some occasions, in the Abbey of Streanshalh or Whitby, where she so long resided. At a particular time of the year (viz. in the summer months), at ten or eleven in the forenoon, the sunbeams fall in the inside of the northern part of the choir; and 'tis then that the spectators, who stand on the west side of Whitby churchyard, so as just to see the most northerly part of the abbey pass the north end of Whitby church, imagine they perceive, in one of the highest windows there, the resemblance of a woman arrayed in a shroud. Though we are certain this is only a reflection caused by the splendour of the sunbeams, yet fame reports it, and it is constantly believed among the vulgar, to be an appearance of Lady Hilda in her shroud, or rather in a glorified state ; before which I make no doubt, the Papists, even in these our days, offer up their prayers with as much zeal and devotion as before any other image of their most glorified saint.'—CHARLTON'S *History of Whitby*, p. 33.

Note LXXXVI.

—— *the huge and sweeping brand*
Which wont of yore, in battle fray,
His foeman's limbs to shred away,
As wood-knife lops the sapling spray.
—P. 159.

The Earl of Angus had strength and personal activity corresponding to his courage. Spens of Kilspindie, a favourite of James IV, having spoken of him lightly, the Earl met him while hawking, and, compelling him to single combat, at one blow cut asunder his thighbone, and killed him on the spot. But ere he could obtain James's pardon for this slaughter, Angus was obliged to yield his castle of Hermitage, in exchange for that of Bothwell, which was some diminution to the family greatness. The sword with which he struck so remarkable a blow, was presented by his descendant James, Earl of Morton, afterwards Regent of Scotland, to Lord Lindesay of the Byres, when he defied Bothwell to single combat on Carberry Hill. See Introduction to the *Minstrelsy of the Scottish Border.*

Note LXXXVII.

And hop'st thou hence unscathed to go?
No! by Saint Bride of Bothwell, no!
Up drawbridge, grooms!—what, warder,
ho!
Let the portcullis fall.—P. 160.

This ebullition of violence in the potent Earl of Angus is not without its example in the real history of the house of Douglas, whose chieftains possessed the ferocity, with the heroic virtues of a savage state. The most curious instance occurred in the case of MacLellan, Tutor of Bombay, who, having refused to acknowledge the pre-eminence claimed by Douglas over the gentlemen and Barons of Galloway, was seized and imprisoned by the Earl, in his castle of the Thrieve, on the borders of Kirkcudbrightshire. Sir Patrick Gray, commander of King James the Second's guard, was uncle to the Tutor of Bombay, and obtained from the King a 'sweet letter of supplication,' praying the Earl to deliver his prisoner into Gray's hand. When Sir Patrick arrived at the castle, he was received with all the honour due to a favourite servant of the King's household; but while he was at dinner, the Earl, who suspected his errand, caused his prisoner to be led forth and beheaded. After dinner, Sir Patrick presented the King's letter to the Earl, who received it with great affectation of reverence; 'and took him by the hand, and led him forth to the green, where the gentleman was lying dead, and showed him the manner, and said, "Sir Patrick, you are come a little too late ; yonder is your sister's son lying, but he wants the head : take his body, and do with it what you will."— Sir Patrick answered again, with a sore heart, and said, "My lord, if ye have taken from him his head, dispone upon the body as ye please;" and with that called for his horse, and leaped thereon; and when he was on horseback, he said to the Earl on this manner, "My lord, if I live you shall be rewarded for your labours that you have used at this time, according to your demerits."

'At this saying the Earl was highly offended, and cried for horse. Sir Patrick, seeing the Earl's fury, spurred his horse, but he was chased near Edinburgh ere they left him; and had it not been his led horse was so tried and good, he had been taken.'—PITSCOTTIE'S *History*, p. 39.

NOTE LXXXVIII

A letter forged! Saint Jude to speed!
Did ever knight so foul a deed!—P. 160.

Lest the reader should partake of the Earl's astonishment, and consider the crime as inconsistent with the manners of the period, I have to remind him of the numerous forgeries (partly executed by a female assistant) devised by Robert of Artois, to forward his suit against the Countess Matilda; which, being detected, occasioned his flight into England, and proved the remote cause of Edward the Third's memorable wars in France. John Harding also was expressly hired by Edward VI to forge such documents as might appear to establish the claim of fealty asserted over Scotland by the English monarchs.

NOTE LXXXIX.

Lennel's convent.—P. 161.

This was a Cistertian house of religion, now almost entirely demolished. Lennel House is now the residence of my venerable friend, Patrick Brydone, Esquire, so well known in the literary world. It is situated near Coldstream, almost opposite to Cornhill, and consequently very near to Flodden Field.

NOTE XC.

Twisel Bridge.—P. 162.

On the evening previous to the memorable battle of Flodden, Surrey's head-quarters were at Barmoor Wood, and King James held an inaccessible position on the ridge of Flodden-hill, one of the last and lowest eminences detached from the ridge of Cheviot. The Till, a deep and slow river, winded between the armies. On the morning of September 9, 1513, Surrey marched in a north-westerly direction, and crossed the Till, with his van and artillery, at Twisel-bridge, nigh where that river joins the Tweed, his rear-guard column passing about a mile higher, by a ford. This movement had the double effect of placing his army between

King James and his supplies from Scotland, and of striking the Scottish monarch with surprise, as he seems to have relied on the depth of the river in his front. But as the passage, both over the bridge and through the ford, was difficult and slow, it seems possible that the English might have been attacked to great advantage while struggling with these natural obstacles. I know not if we are to impute James's forbearance to want of military skill, or to the romantic declaration which Pitscottie puts in his mouth, 'that he was determined to have his enemies before him on a plain field,' and therefore would suffer no interruption to be given, even by artillery, to their passing the river.

The ancient bridge of Twisel, by which the English crossed the Till, is still standing beneath Twisel Castle, a splendid pile of Gothic architecture, as now rebuilt by Sir Francis Blake, Bart., whose extensive plantations have so much improved the country around. The glen is romantic and delightful, with steep banks on each side, covered with copse, particularly with hawthorn. Beneath a tall rock, near the bridge, is a plentiful fountain, called St. Helen's Well.

NOTE XCI.

Hence might they see the full array,
Of either host, for deadly fray.—P. 163.

The reader cannot here expect a full account of the battle of Flodden; but, so far as is necessary to understand the romance, I beg to remind him, that, when the English army, by their skilful countermarch, were fairly placed between King James and his own country, the Scottish monarch resolved to fight; and, setting fire to his tents, descended from the ridge of Flodden to secure the neighbouring eminence of Brankstone, on which that village is built. Thus the two armies met, almost without seeing each other, when, according to the old poem of 'Flodden Field,'

'The English line stretch'd east and west,
And southward were their faces set;
The Scottish northward proudly prest,
And manfully their foes they met.'

The English army advanced in four divisions. On the right, which first engaged, were the sons of Earl Surrey, namely, Thomas Howard, the Admiral of England, and Sir Edmund, the Knight Marshal of the army. Their divisions were separated from each other; but, at the request of Sir Edmund, his brother's battalion was drawn very near to his own. The centre was commanded by Surrey in person; the left wing by Sir Edward Stanley, with the men of Lancashire, and of the palatinate of Chester. Lord Dacres, with a large body of horse, formed a reserve. When the smoke, which the wind had driven between the armies, was somewhat dispersed, they perceived the Scots, who had moved down the hill in a similar order of battle, and in deep silence. The Earls of Huntley and of Home commanded their left wing, and charged Sir Edmund Howard with such success as entirely to defeat his part of the English right wing. Sir Edmund's banner was beaten down, and he himself escaped with difficulty to his brother's division. The Admiral, however, stood firm; and Dacre advancing to his support with the reserve of cavalry, probably between the interval of the divisions commanded by the brothers Howard, appears to have kept the victors in effectual check. Home's men, chiefly Borderers, began to pillage the baggage of both armies; and their leader is branded by the Scottish historians with negligence or treachery. On the other hand, Huntley, on whom they bestow many encomiums, is said by the English historians to have left the field after the first charge. Meanwhile the Admiral, whose flank these chiefs ought to have attacked, availed himself of their inactivity, and pushed forward against another large division of the Scottish army in his front, headed by the Earls of Crawford and Montrose, both of whom were slain, and their forces routed. On the left, the success of the English was yet more decisive; for the Scottish right wing, consisting of undisciplined Highlanders, commanded by Lennox and Argyle, was unable to sustain the charge of Sir Edward Stanley, and especially the severe execution of the Lancashire archers. The King and Surrey, who commanded the respective centres of their armies, were meanwhile engaged in close and dubious conflict. James, surrounded by the flower of his kingdom, and impatient of the galling discharge of arrows, supported also by his reserve under Bothwell, charged with such fury, that the standard of Surrey was in danger. At that critical moment, Stanley, who had routed the left wing of the Scottish, pursued his career of victory, and arrived on the right flank, and in the rear of James's division, which, throwing itself into a circle, disputed the battle till night came on. Surrey then drew back his forces; for the Scottish centre not having been broken, and their left wing being victorious, he yet doubted the event of the field. The Scottish army, however, felt their loss, and abandoned the field of battle in disorder, before dawn. They lost, perhaps, from eight to ten thousand men; but that included the very prime of their nobility, gentry, and even clergy. Scarce a family of eminence but has an ancestor killed at Flodden; and there is no province in Scotland, even at this day, where the battle is mentioned without a sensation of terror and sorrow. The English lost also a great number of men, perhaps within one-third of the vanquished, but they were of inferior note.—See the only distinct detail of the Field of Flodden in PINKERTON'S *History*, Book xi; all former accounts being full of blunders and inconsistency.

The spot from which Clara views the battle must be supposed to have been on a hillock commanding the rear of the English right wing, which was defeated, and in which conflict Marmion is supposed to have fallen.

NOTE XCII.

——*Brian Tunstall, stainless knight.*
—P. 164.

Sir Brian Tunstall, called in the romantic language of the time, Tunstall the Undefiled, was one of the few Englishmen of rank slain at Flodden. He figures in the ancient English poem, to which I may safely refer my readers; as an edition, with full explanatory notes, has been published by my friend, Mr. Henry Weber. Tunstall, perhaps, derived his epithet of *undefiled* from his white armour and banner, the latter bearing a white cock, about to crow, as well as from his unstained loyalty and knightly faith. His place of residence was Thurland Castle.

NOTE XCIII.

Reckless of life, he desperate fought,
  And fell on Flodden plain :
And well in death his trusty brand,
Firm clench'd within his manly hand,
  Beseem'd the monarch slain.—P. 168.

There can be no doubt that King James fell in the battle of Flodden. He was killed, says the curious French Gazette, within a lance's length of the Earl of Surrey; and the same account adds, that none of his division were made prisoners, though many were killed; a circumstance that testifies the desperation of their resistance. The Scottish historians record many of the idle reports which passed among the vulgar of their day. Home was accused, by the popular voice, not only of failing to support the King, but even of having carried him out of the field, and murdered him. And this tale was revived in my remembrance, by an unauthenticated story of a skeleton, wrapped in a bull's hide, and surrounded with an iron chain, said to have been found in the well of Home Castle; for which, on inquiry, I could never find any better authority than the sexton of the parish having said, that, *if the well were cleaned out, he would not be surprised at such a discovery.* Home was the chamberlain of the King, and his prime favourite; he had much to lose (in fact did lose all) in consequence of James's death, and nothing earthly to gain by that event : but the retreat, or inactivity of the left wing which he commanded, after defeating Sir Edmund Howard, and even the circumstance of his returning unhurt, and loaded with spoil, from so fatal a conflict, rendered the propagation of any calumny against him easy and acceptable. Other reports gave a still more romantic turn to the King's fate, and averred that James, weary of greatness after the carnage among his nobles, had gone on a pilgrimage, to merit absolution for the death of his father, and the breach of his oath of amity to Henry. In particular, it was objected to the English, that they could never show the token of the iron belt, which, however, he was likely enough to have laid aside on the day of battle, as encumbering his personal exertions. They produce a better evidence, the monarch's sword and dagger, which are still preserved in the Heralds' College in London. Stowe has recorded a degrading story of the disgrace with which the remains of the unfortunate monarch were treated in his time. An unhewn column marks the spot where James fell, still called the King's Stone.

NOTE XCIV.

The fair cathedral storm'd and took.
—P. 169.

This storm of Lichfield cathedral, which had been garrisoned on the part of the King, took place in the Great Civil War. Lord Brook, who, with Sir John Gill, commanded the assailants, was shot with a musket-ball through the vizor of his helmet. The royalists remarked that he was killed by a shot fired from St. Chad's cathedral, and upon St. Chad's Day, and received his death-wound in the very eye with which, he had said, he hoped to see the ruin of all the cathedrals in England. The magnificent church in question suffered cruelly upon this, and other occasions; the principal spire being ruined by the fire of the besiegers.

The Lady of the Lake.

TO THE MOST NOBLE

JOHN JAMES MARQUIS OF ABERCORN

THIS POEM IS INSCRIBED BY

THE AUTHOR.

THE Scene of the following Poem is laid chiefly in the vicinity of Loch Katrine, in the Western Highlands of Perthshire. The time of Action includes Six Days, and the transactions of each Day occupy a Canto.

Canto First.

The Chase.

HARP of the North! that mouldering
 long hast hung
  On the witch-elm that shades Saint
  Fillan's spring,
And down the fitful breeze thy num-
 bers flung,
  Till envious ivy did around thee
  cling,
Muffling with verdant ringlet every
 string,—
  O minstrel Harp, still must thine
  accents sleep?
'Mid rustling leaves and fountains
 murmuring,
  Still must thy sweeter sounds their
  silence keep,
Nor bid a warrior smile, nor teach a
 maid to weep?

Not thus, in ancient days of Caledon,
  Was thy voice mute amid the festal
  crowd,
When lay of hopeless love, or glory
 won,
  Aroused the fearful, or subdued
  the proud.

At each according pause was heard
 aloud
  Thine ardent symphony sublime
  and high!
Fair dames and crested chiefs attention bow'd;
  For still the burden of thy minstrelsy
Was Knighthood's dauntless deed,
 and Beauty's matchless eye.

O wake once more! how rude soe'er
 the hand
  That ventures o'er thy magic maze
  to stray;
O wake once more! though scarce my
 skill command
  Some feeble echoing of thine earlier
  lay:
Though harsh and faint, and soon to
 die away,
  And all unworthy of thy nobler
  strain,
Yet if one heart throb higher at its
 sway,
  The wizard note has not been
  touch'd in vain.
Then silent be no more! Enchantress,
 wake again!

I.

THE stag at eve had drunk his fill,
Where danced the moon on Monan's rill,
And deep his midnight lair had made
In lone Glenartney's hazel shade;
But, when the sun his beacon red
Had kindled on Benvoirlich's head,
The deep-mouth'd bloodhound's heavy bay
Resounded up the rocky way,
And faint, from farther distance borne,
Were heard the clanging hoof and horn.

II.

As Chief, who hears his warder call,
'To arms! the foemen storm the wall,'
The antler'd monarch of the waste
Sprung from his heathery couch in haste.
But, ere his fleet career he took,
The dew-drops from his flanks he shook;
Like crested leader proud and high,
Toss'd his beam'd frontlet to the sky;
A moment gazed adown the dale,
A moment snuff'd the tainted gale,
A moment listen'd to the cry,
That thicken'd as the chase drew nigh;
Then, as the headmost foes appear'd,
With one brave bound the copse he clear'd,
And, stretching forward free and far,
Sought the wild heaths of Uam-Var.

III.

Yell'd on the view the opening pack;
Rock, glen, and cavern, paid them back;
To many a mingled sound at once
The awaken'd mountain gave response.
A hundred dogs bay'd deep and strong,
Clatter'd a hundred steeds along,
Their peal the merry horns rung out,
A hundred voices join'd the shout;
With hark and whoop and wild halloo,
No rest Benvoirlich's echoes knew.
Far from the tumult fled the roe,
Close in her covert cower'd the doe;
The falcon, from her cairn on high,
Cast on the rout a wondering eye,
Till far beyond her piercing ken
The hurricane had swept the glen.
Faint and more faint, its failing din
Return'd from cavern, cliff, and linn,
And silence settled, wide and still,
On the lone wood and mighty hill.

IV.

Less loud the sounds of silvan war
Disturb'd the heights of Uam-Var,
And roused the cavern, where, 'tis told,
A giant made his den of old;
For ere that steep ascent was won,
High in his pathway hung the sun,
And many a gallant, stay'd perforce,
Was fain to breathe his faltering horse,
And of the trackers of the deer,
Scarce half the lessening pack was near;
So shrewdly on the mountain side
Had the bold burst their mettle tried.

V.

The noble stag was pausing now
Upon the mountain's southern brow,
Where broad extended, far beneath,
The varied realms of fair Menteith.
With anxious eye he wander'd o'er
Mountain and meadow, moss and moor,
And ponder'd refuge from his toil
By far Lochard or Aberfoyle.
But nearer was the copsewood grey,
That waved and wept on Loch-Achray,
And mingled with the pine-trees blue
On the bold cliffs of Benvenue.
Fresh vigour with the hope return'd,
With flying foot the heath he spurn'd,
Held westward with unwearied race,
And left behind the panting chase.

VI.

'Twere long to tell what steeds gave
o'er,
As swept the hunt through Cambus-
more:
What reins were tighten'd in despair,
When rose Benledi's ridge in air ;
Who flagg'd upon Bochastle's heath,
Who shunn'd to stem the flooded
Teith,—
For twice that day, from shore to shore,
The gallant stag swam stoutly o'er.
Few were the stragglers, following far,
That reach'd the lake of Vennachar ;
And when the Brigg of Turk was won,
The headmost horseman rode alone.

VII.

Alone, but with unbated zeal,
That horseman plied the scourge and
steel ;
For jaded now, and spent with toil,
Emboss'd with foam, and dark with
soil,
While every gasp with sobs he drew,
The labouring stag strain'd full in view.
Two dogs of black Saint Hubert's breed,
Unmatch'd for courage, breath, and
speed,
Fast on his flying traces came,
And all but won that desperate game ;
For, scarce a spear's length from his
haunch,
Vindictive toil'd the   bloodhounds
stanch ;
Nor nearer might the dogs attain,
Nor farther might the quarry strain.
Thus up the margin of the lake,
Between the precipice and brake,
O'er stock and rock their race they take.

VIII.

The Hunter mark'd that mountain high,
The lone lake's western boundary,
And deem'd the stag must turn to bay,
Where that huge rampart barr'd the
way ;

Already glorying in the prize,
Measured his antlers with his eyes ;
For the death-wound and death-halloo,
Muster'd his breath, his whinyard
drew ;—
But thundering as he came prepared,
With ready arm and weapon bared,
The wily quarry shunn'd the shock,
And turn'd him from the opposing
rock ;
Then, dashing down a darksome glen,
Soon lost to hound and hunter's ken,
In the deep Trosachs' wildest nook
His solitary refuge took.
There, while close couch'd, the thicket
shed
Cold dews and wild-flowers on his head,
He heard the baffled dogs in vain
Rave through the hollow pass amain,
Chiding the rocks that yell'd again.

IX.

Close on the hounds the hunter came,
To cheer them on the vanish'd game ;
But, stumbling in the rugged dell,
The gallant horse exhausted fell.
The impatient rider strove in vain
To rouse him with the spur and rein,
For the good steed, his labours o'er,
Stretch'd his stiff limbs, to rise no
more ;
Then, touch'd with pity and remorse,
He sorrow'd o'er the expiring horse :
' I little thought, when first thy rein
I slack'd upon the banks of Seine,
That Highland eagle e'er should feed
On thy fleet limbs, my matchless steed !
Woe worth the chase, woe worth the
day,
That costs thy life, my gallant grey ! '

X.

Then through the dell his horn
resounds,
From vain pursuit to call the hounds.
Back limp'd, with slow and crippled
pace,
The sulky leaders of the chase ;

Close to their master's side they press'd,
With drooping tail and humbled crest;
But still the dingle's hollow throat
Prolong'd the swelling bugle-note.
The owlets started from their dream,
The eagles answer'd with their
    scream,
Round and around the sounds were
    cast,
Till echo seem'd an answering blast;
And on the hunter hied his way,
To join some comrades of the day;
Yet often paused, so strange the road,
So wondrous were the scenes it
    show'd.

XI.

The western waves of ebbing day
Roll'd o'er the glen their level way;
Each purple peak, each flinty spire,
Was bathed in floods of living fire.
But not a setting beam could glow
Within the dark ravines below,
Where twined the path in shadow hid,
Round many a rocky pyramid,
Shooting abruptly from the dell
Its thunder-splinter'd pinnacle;
Round many an insulated mass,
The native bulwarks of the pass,
Huge as the tower which builders vain
Presumptuous piled on Shinar's plain.
The rocky summits, split and rent,
Form'd turret, dome, or battlement,
Or seem'd fantastically set
With cupola or minaret,
Wild crests as pagod ever deck'd,
Or mosque of Eastern architect.
Nor were these earth-born castles bare,
Nor lack'd they many a banner fair;
For, from their shiver'd brows dis-
    play'd,
Far o'er the unfathomable glade,
All twinkling with the dewdrop sheen,
The brier-rose fell in streamers green,
And creeping shrubs, of thousand dyes,
Waved in the west-wind's summer
    sighs.

XII.

Boon nature scatter'd, free and wild,
Each plant or flower, the mountain's
    child.
Here eglantine embalm'd the air,
Hawthorn and hazel mingled there;
The primrose pale, and violet flower,
Found in each cliff a narrow bower;
Fox-glove and night-shade, side by
    side,
Emblems of punishment and pride,
Group'd their dark hues with every
    stain
The weather-beaten crags retain.
With boughs that quaked at every
    breath,
Grey birch and aspen wept beneath;
Aloft, the ash and warrior oak
Cast anchor in the rifted rock;
And, higher yet, the pine-tree hung
His shatter'd trunk, and frequent flung,
Where seem'd the cliffs to meet on
    high,
His boughs athwart the narrow'd sky.
Highest of all, where white peaks
    glanced,
Where glist'ning streamers waved and
    danced,
The wanderer's eye could barely view
The summer heaven's delicious blue;
So wondrous wild, the whole might
    seem
The scenery of a fairy dream.

XIII.

Onward, amid the copse 'gan peep
A narrow inlet, still and deep,
Affording scarce such breadth of brim
As served the wild duck's brood to
    swim.
Lost for a space, through thickets
    veering,
But broader when again appearing,
Tall rocks and tufted knolls their face
Could on the dark-blue mirror trace;
And farther as the hunter stray'd,
Still broader sweep its channels made.

The shaggy mounds no longer stood,
Emerging from entangled wood,
But, wave-encircled, seem'd to float,
Like castle girdled with its moat;
Yet broader floods extending still
Divide them from their parent hill,
Till each, retiring, claims to be
An islet in an inland sea.

XIV.

And now, to issue from the glen,
No pathway meets the wanderer's ken,
Unless he climb, with footing nice,
A far projecting precipice.
The broom's tough roots his ladder
    made,
The hazel saplings lent their aid;
And thus an airy point he won,
Where, gleaming with the setting sun,
One burnish'd sheet of living gold,
Loch Katrine lay beneath him roll'd;
In all her length far winding lay,
With promontory, creek, and bay,
And islands that, empurpled bright,
Floated amid the livelier light,
And mountains, that like giants stand,
To sentinel enchanted land.
High on the south, huge Benvenue
Down to the lake in masses threw
Crags, knolls, and mounds, confusedly
    hurl'd,
The fragments of an earlier world;
A wildering forest feather'd o'er
His ruin'd sides and summit hoar,
While on the north, through middle
    air,
Ben-an heaved high his forehead bare.

XV.

From the steep promontory gazed
The stranger, raptured and amazed.
And, 'What a scene were here,' he
    cried,
' For princely pomp, or churchman's
    pride!
On this bold brow, a lordly tower;
In that soft vale, a lady's bower;

On yonder meadow, far away,
The turrets of a cloister grey;
How blithely might the bugle-horn
Chide, on the lake, the lingering morn!
How sweet, at eve, the lover's lute
Chime, when the groves were still
    and mute!
And, when the midnight moon should
    lave
Her forehead in the silver wave,
How solemn on the ear would come
The holy matins' distant hum,
While the deep peal's commanding
    tone
Should wake, in yonder islet lone,
A sainted hermit from his cell,
To drop a bead with every knell—
And bugle, lute, and bell, and all,
Should each bewilder'd stranger call
To friendly feast, and lighted hall.

XVI.

' Blithe were it then to wander here!
But now,—beshrew yon nimble deer,—
Like that same hermit's, thin and spare,
The copse must give my evening fare;
Some mossy bank my couch must be,
Some rustling oak my canopy.
Yet pass we that; the war and chase
Give little choice of resting-place;—
A summer night, in greenwood spent,
Were but to-morrow's merriment:
But hosts may in these wilds abound,
Such as are better miss'd than found;
To meet with Highland plunderers
    here
Were worse than loss of steed or
    deer.—
I am alone;—my bugle-strain
May call some straggler of the train;
Or, fall the worst that may betide,
Ere now this falchion has been tried.'

XVII.

But scarce again his horn he wound,
When lo! forth starting at the sound,
From underneath an aged oak,
That slanted from the islet rock,

A damsel guider of its way,
A little skiff shot to the bay,
That round the promontory steep
Led its deep line in graceful sweep,
Eddying, in almost viewless wave,
The weeping willow-twig to lave,
And kiss, with whispering sound and
 slow,
The beach of pebbles bright as snow.
The boat had touch'd this silver strand,
Just as the Hunter left his stand,
And stood conceal'd amid the brake,
To view this Lady of the Lake.
The maiden paused, as if again
She thought to catch the distant strain.
With head up-raised, and look intent,
And eye and ear attentive bent,
And locks flung back, and lips apart,
Like monument of Grecian art,
In listening mood, she seem'd to stand,
The guardian Naiad of the strand.

XVIII.

And ne'er did Grecian chisel trace
A Nymph, a Naiad, or a Grace
Of finer form, or lovelier face !
What though the sun, with ardent
 frown,
Had slightly tinged her cheek with
 brown ;
The sportive toil, which, short and light,
Had dyed her glowing hue so bright,
Served too in hastier swell to show
Short glimpses of a breast of snow :
What though no rule of courtly grace
To measured mood had train'd her
 pace ;
A foot more light, a step more true,
Ne'er from the heath-flower dash'd
 the dew ;
E'en the slight harebell raised its head,
Elastic from her airy tread :
What though upon her speech there
 hung
The accents of the mountain tongue ;
Those silver sounds, so soft, so dear,
The listener held his breath to hear !

XIX.

A Chieftain's daughter seem'd the
 maid ;
Her satin snood, her silken plaid,
Her golden brooch, such birth betray'd.
And seldom was a snood amid
Such wild luxuriant ringlets hid,
Whose glossy black to shame might
 bring
The plumage of the raven's wing ;
And seldom o'er a breast so fair,
Mantled a plaid with modest care,
And never brooch the folds combin'd
Above a heart more good and kind.
Her kindness and her worth to spy,
You need but gaze on Ellen's eye ;
Not Katrine, in her mirror blue,
Gives back the shaggy banks more
 true,
Than every free-born glance confess'd
The guileless movements of her breast :
Whether joy danced in her dark eye,
Or woe or pity claim'd a sigh,
Or filial love was glowing there,
Or meek devotion pour'd a prayer,
Or tale of injury call'd forth
The indignant spirit of the North.
One only passion unreveal'd,
With maiden pride the maid conceal'd,
Yet not less purely felt the flame ;—
O need I tell that passion's name ?

XX.

Impatient of the silent horn,
Now on the gale her voice was
 borne :—
' Father ! ' she cried ; the rocks around
Loved to prolong the gentle sound.
A while she paused, no answer came ;
' Malcolm, was thine the blast ? ' the
 name
Less resolutely utter'd fell ;
The echoes could not catch the
 swell.
' A stranger I,' the Huntsman said,
Advancing from the hazel shade.

The maid, alarm'd, with hasty oar,
Push'd her light shallop from the shore,
And when a space was gain'd between,
Closer she drew her bosom's screen;
(So forth the startled swan would
    swing,
So turn to prune his ruffled wing.)
Then safe, though flutter'd and amazed,
She paused, and on the stranger gazed.
Not his the form, nor his the eye,
That youthful maidens wont to fly.

XXI.

On his bold visage middle age
Had slightly press'd its signet sage,
Yet had not quench'd the open truth
And fiery vehemence of youth;
Forward and frolic glee was there,
The will to do, the soul to dare,
The sparkling glance, soon blown to
    fire,
Of hasty love, or headlong ire.
His limbs were cast in manly mould,
For hardy sports or contest bold;
And though in peaceful garb array'd,
And weaponless, except his blade,
His stately mien as well implied
A high-born heart, a martial pride,
As if a Baron's crest he wore,
And sheathed in armour trode the
    shore.
Slighting the petty need he show'd,
He told of his benighted road;
His ready speech flow'd fair and free,
In phrase of gentlest courtesy;
Yet seem'd that tone, and gesture
    bland,
Less used to sue than to command.

XXII.

A while the maid the stranger eyed,
And, reassured, at length replied,
That Highland halls were open still
To wilder'd wanderers of the hill.
'Nor think you unexpected come
To yon lone isle, our desert home;
Before the heath had lost the dew,
This morn, a couch was pull'd for you;

On yonder mountain's purple head
Have ptarmigan and heath-cock bled,
And our broad nets have swept the
    mere,
To furnish forth your evening cheer.'
'Now, by the rood, my lovely maid,
Your courtesy has err'd,' he said;
'No right have I to claim, misplaced,
The welcome of expected guest.
A wanderer, here by fortune tost,
My way, my friends, my courser lost,
I ne'er before, believe me, fair,
Have ever drawn your mountain air,
Till on this lake's romantic strand
I found a fay in fairy land!'

XXIII.

'I well believe,' the maid replied,
As her light skiff approach'd the side,
'I well believe that ne'er before
Your foot has trod Loch Katrine's
    shore;
But yet, as far as yesternight,
Old Allan-Bane foretold your plight,—
A grey-hair'd sire, whose eye intent
Was on the vision'd future bent.
He saw your steed, a dappled grey,
Lie dead beneath the birchen way;
Painted exact your form and mien,
Your hunting suit of Lincoln green,
That tassell'd horn so gaily gilt,
That falchion's crooked blade and hilt,
That cap with heron plumage trim,
And yon two hounds so dark and grim.
He bade that all should ready be
To grace a guest of fair degree;
But light I held his prophecy,
And deem'd it was my father's horn
Whose echoes o'er the lake were
    borne.'

XXIV.

The stranger smiled: 'Since to your
    home
A destined errant-knight I come,
Announced by prophet sooth and old,
Doom'd, doubtless, for achievement
    bold,

I 'll lightly front each high emprise
For one kind glance of those bright
    eyes.
Permit me, first, the task to guide
Your fairy frigate o'er the tide.'
The maid, with smile suppress'd and
    sly,
The toil unwonted saw him try;
For seldom sure, if e'er before,
His noble hand had grasp'd an oar :
Yet with main strength his strokes
    he drew,
And o'er the lake the shallop flew ;
With heads erect, and whimpering cry,
The hounds behind their passage ply.
Nor frequent does the bright oar break
The dark'ning mirror of the lake,
Until the rocky isle they reach,
And moor their shallop on the beach.

XXV.

The stranger view'd the shore around ;
'Twas all so close with copsewood
    bound,
Nor track nor pathway might declare
That human foot frequented there,
Until the mountain-maiden show'd
A clambering unsuspected road,
That winded through the tangled
    screen,
And open'd on a narrow green,
Where weeping birch and willow
    round
With their long fibres swept the
    ground.
Here, for retreat in dangerous hour,
Some chief had framed a rustic bower.

XXVI.

It was a lodge of ample size,
But strange of structure and device ;
Of such materials, as around
The workman's hand had readiest
    found ;
Lopp'd off their boughs, their hoar
    trunks bared,
And by the hatchet rudely squared.

To give the walls their destined height
The sturdy oak and ash unite ;
While moss and clay and leaves
    combin'd
To fence each crevice from the wind.
The lighter pine-trees, over-head,
Their slender length for rafters
    spread,
And wither'd heath and rushes dry
Supplied a russet canopy.
Due westward, fronting to the green,
A rural portico was seen,
Aloft on native pillars borne,
Of mountain fir, with bark unshorn,
Where Ellen's hand had taught to
    twine
The ivy and Idaean vine,
The clematis, the favour'd flower
Which boasts the name of virgin-bower,
And every hardy plant could bear
Loch Katrine's keen and searching air.
An instant in this porch she staid,
And gaily to the stranger said,
' On heaven and on thy lady call,
And enter the enchanted hall !'

XXVII.

' My hope, my heaven, my trust must be,
My gentle guide, in following thee.'
He cross'd the threshold—and a clang
Of angry steel that instant rang.
To his bold brow his spirit rush'd,
But soon for vain alarm he blush'd
When on the floor he saw display'd,
Cause of the din, a naked blade
Dropp'd from the sheath, that careless
    flung,
Upon a stag's huge antlers swung ;
For all around, the walls to grace,
Hung trophies of the fight or chase :
A target there, a bugle here,
A battle-axe, a hunting-spear,
And broadswords, bows, and arrows
    store,
With the tusk'd trophies of the boar.
Here grins the wolf as when he died,
And there the wild-cat's brindled hide

The frontlet of the elk adorns,
Or mantles o'er the bison's horns ;
Pennons and flags defaced and stain'd,
That blackening streaks of blood
　　retain'd,
And deer-skins, dappled, dun, and white,
With otter's fur and seal's unite,
In rude and uncouth tapestry all,
To garnish forth the silvan hall.

XXVIII.

The wondering stranger round him
　　gazed,
And next the fallen weapon raised :
Few were the arms whose sinewy
　　strength
Sufficed to stretch it forth at length ;
And as the brand he poised and sway'd,
'I never knew but one,' he said,
'Whose stalwart arm might brook to
　　wield
A blade like this in battle-field.'
She sigh'd, then smiled and took the
　　word :
'You see the guardian champion's
　　sword ;
As light it trembles in his hand,
As in my grasp a hazel wand ;
My sire's tall form might grace the part
Of Ferragus or Ascabart ;
But in the absent giant's hold
Are women now, and menials old.'

XXIX.

The mistress of the mansion came,
Mature of age, a graceful dame ;
Whose easy step and stately port
Had well become a princely court ;
To whom, though more than kindred
　　knew,
Young Ellen gave a mother's due.
Meet welcome to her guest she made,
And every courteous rite was paid
That hospitality could claim,
Though all unask'd his birth and
　　name.
Such then the reverence to a guest,
That fellest foe might join the feast,

And from his deadliest foeman's door
Unquestion'd turn, the banquet o'er.
At length his rank the stranger names,
'The Knight of Snowdoun, James
　　Fitz-James ;
Lord of a barren heritage,
Which his brave sires, from age to
　　age,
By their good swords had held with
　　toil ;
His sire had fallen in such turmoil,
And he, God wot, was forced to stand
Oft for his right with blade in hand.
This morning, with Lord Moray's train,
He chased a stalwart stag in vain,
Outstripp'd his comrades, miss'd the
　　deer,
Lost his good steed, and wander'd here.'

XXX.

Fain would the Knight in turn require
The name and state of Ellen's sire.
Well show'd the elder lady's mien,
That courts and cities she had seen ;
Ellen, though more her looks display'd
The simple grace of silvan maid,
In speech and gesture, form and face,
Show'd she was come of gentle race.
'Twere strange, in ruder rank to find
Such looks, such manners, and such
　　mind.
Each hint the Knight of Snowdoun
　　gave,
Dame Margaret heard with silence
　　grave ;
Or Ellen, innocently gay,
Turn'd all inquiry light away—
' Weird women we ! by dale and down
We dwell, afar from tower and town.
We stem the flood, we ride the blast,
On wandering knights our spells we
　　cast ;
While viewless minstrels touch the
　　string,
'Tis thus our charmed rhymes we sing.'
She sung, and still a harp unseen
Fill'd up the symphony between.

H

XXXI.

SONG.

'Soldier, rest! thy warfare o'er,
  Sleep the sleep that knows not
    breaking;
Dream of battled fields no more,
  Days of danger, nights of waking.
In our isle's enchanted hall,
  Hands unseen thy couch are strew-
    ing,
Fairy strains of music fall,
  Every sense in slumber dewing.
Soldier, rest! thy warfare o'er,
Dream of fighting fields no more:
Sleep the sleep that knows not breaking,
Morn of toil, nor night of waking.

'No rude sound shall reach thine ear,
  Armour's clang, or war-steed champ-
    ing,
Trump nor pibroch summon here
  Mustering clan, or squadron tramp-
    ing.
Yet the lark's shrill fife may come
  At the day-break from the fallow,
And the bittern sound his drum,
  Booming from the sedgy shallow.
Ruder sounds shall none be near,
Guards nor warders challenge here,
Here's no war-steed's neigh and champ-
    ing,
Shouting clans, or squadrons stamping.'

XXXII.

She paused—then, blushing, led the lay
To grace the stranger of the day.
Her mellow notes awhile prolong
The cadence of the flowing song,
Till to her lips in measured frame
The minstrel verse spontaneous
    came:—

SONG CONTINUED.

'Huntsman, rest! thy chase is done;
  While our slumbrous spells assail ye,
Dream not, with the rising sun,
  Bugles here shall sound reveillé.

Sleep! the deer is in his den;
  Sleep! thy hounds are by thee lying;
Sleep! nor dream in yonder glen,
  How thy gallant steed lay dying.
Huntsman, rest! thy chase is done,
Think not of the rising sun,
For at dawning to assail ye,
Here no bugles sound reveillé.'

XXXIII.

The hall was clear'd—the stranger's
    bed
Was there of mountain heather spread,
Where oft a hundred guests had lain,
And dream'd their forest sports again.
But vainly did the heath-flower shed
Its moorland fragrance round his head;
Not Ellen's spell had lull'd to rest
The fever of his troubled breast.
In broken dreams the image rose
Of varied perils, pains, and woes:
His steed now flounders in the brake,
Now sinks his barge upon the lake;
Now leader of a broken host,
His standard falls, his honour's lost.
Then,—from my couch may heavenly
    might
Chase that worst phantom of the
    night!—
Again return'd the scenes of youth,
Of confident undoubting truth;
Again his soul he interchanged
With friends whose hearts were long
    estranged.
They come, in dim procession led,
The cold, the faithless, and the dead;
As warm each hand, each brow as gay,
As if they parted yesterday.
And doubt distracts him at the view—
O were his senses false or true?
Dream'd he of death, or broken vow,
Or is it all a vision now?

XXXIV.

At length, with Ellen in a grove
He seem'd to walk, and speak of love;
She listen'd with a blush and sigh,
His suit was warm, his hopes were high.

He sought her yielded hand to clasp,
And a cold gauntlet met his grasp:
The phantom's sex was changed and gone,
Upon its head a helmet shone;
Slowly enlarged to giant size,
With darken'd cheek and threatening eyes,
The grisly visage, stern and hoar,
To Ellen still a likeness bore.
He woke, and, panting with affright,
Recall'd the vision of the night.
The hearth's decaying brands were red,
And deep and dusky lustre shed,
Half showing, half concealing. all
The uncouth trophies of the hall.
'Mid those the stranger fix'd his eye,
Where that huge falchion hung on high,
And thoughts on thoughts, a countless throng,
Rush'd, chasing countless thoughts along,
Until, the giddy whirl to cure,
He rose, and sought the moonshine pure.

XXXV.

The wild-rose, eglantine, and broom,
Wasted around their rich perfume;
The birch-trees wept in fragrant balm,
The aspens slept beneath the calm;
The silver light, with quivering glance,
Play'd on the water's still expanse:
Wild were the heart whose passion's sway
Could rage beneath the sober ray!
He felt its calm, that warrior guest,
While thus he communed with his breast:
'Why is it, at each turn I trace
Some memory of that exiled race?
Can I not mountain-maiden spy,
But she must bear the Douglas eye?
Can I not view a Highland brand,
But it must match the Douglas hand?

Can I not frame a fever'd dream,
But still the Douglas is the theme?
I 'll dream no more; by manly mind
Not even in sleep is will resign'd.
My midnight orisons said o'er,
I 'll turn to rest, and dream no more.'
His midnight orisons he told,
A prayer with every bead of gold,
Consign'd to heaven his cares and woes,
And sunk in undisturb'd repose;
Until the heath-cock shrilly crew,
And morning dawn'd on Benvenue.

———◆◆———

Canto Second.

The Island.

I.

At morn the black-cock trims his jetty wing,
    'Tis morning prompts the linnet's blithest lay,
All Nature's children feel the matin spring
    Of life reviving with reviving day;
And while yon little bark glides down the bay,
    Wafting the stranger on his way again,
Morn's genial influence roused a minstrel grey,
    And sweetly o'er the lake was heard thy strain,
Mix'd with the sounding harp, O white-hair'd Allan-Bane!

II.

SONG.

' Not faster yonder rowers' might
    Flings from their oars the spray,
Not faster yonder rippling bright,
That tracks the shallop's course in light,
    Melts in the lake away;

Than men from memory erase
The benefits of former days;
Then, stranger, go! good speed the
    while,
Nor think again of the lonely isle.

High place to thee in royal court,
    High place in battled line,
Good hawk and hound for silvan sport,
Where beauty sees the brave resort,
    The honour'd meed be thine!
True be thy sword, thy friend sincere,
Thy lady constant, kind, and dear,
And lost in love's and friendship's smile
Be memory of the lonely isle.

III.

SONG CONTINUED.

'But if beneath yon southern sky
    A plaided stranger roam,
Whose drooping crest and stifled sigh,
And sunken cheek and heavy eye,
    Pine for his Highland home;
Then, warrior, then be thine to show
The care that soothes a wanderer's
    woe;
Remember then thy hap ere while,
A stranger in the lonely isle.

'Or if on life's uncertain main
    Mishap shall mar thy sail;
If faithful, wise, and brave in vain,
Woe, want, and exile thou sustain
    Beneath the fickle gale;
Waste not a sigh on fortune changed,
On thankless courts, or friends es-
    tranged,
But come where kindred worth shall
    smile
To greet thee in the lonely isle.'

IV.

As died the sounds upon the tide,
The shallop reach'd the mainland side,
And ere his onward way he took,
The stranger cast a lingering look,
Where easily his eye might reach
The Harper on the islet beach,

Reclined against a blighted tree,
As wasted, grey, and worn as he.
To minstrel meditation given,
His reverend brow was raised to
    heaven,
As from the rising sun to claim
A sparkle of inspiring flame.
His hand, reclined upon the wire,
Seem'd watching the awakening fire;
So still he sate, as those who wait
Till judgment speak the doom of fate;
So still, as if no breeze might dare
To lift one lock of hoary hair;
So still, as life itself were fled,
In the last sound his harp had sped.

V.

Upon a rock with lichens wild,
Beside him Ellen sate and smiled.
Smiled she to see the stately drake
Lead forth his fleet upon the lake,
While her vex'd spaniel, from the
    beach
Bay'd at the prize beyond his reach?
Yet tell me, then, the maid who knows,
Why deepen'd on her cheek the rose?
Forgive, forgive, Fidelity!
Perchance the maiden smiled to see
Yon parting lingerer wave adieu,
And stop and turn to wave anew;
And, lovely ladies, ere your ire
Condemn the heroine of my lyre,
Show me the fair would scorn to spy,
And prize such conquest of her eye!

VI.

While yet he loiter'd on the spot,
It seem'd as Ellen mark'd him not;
But when he turn'd him to the glade,
One courteous parting sign she made;
And after, oft the knight would say,
That not when prize of festal day
Was dealt him by the brightest fair
Who e'er wore jewel in her hair,
So highly did his bosom swell,
As at that simple mute farewell.
Now with a trusty mountain-guide,
And his dark stag-hounds by his side,

He parts ; the maid, unconscious still,
Watch'd him wind slowly round the
    hill ;
But when his stately form was hid,
The guardian in her bosom chid :
'Thy Malcolm ! vain and selfish maid!'
'Twas thus upbraiding conscience said :
'Not so had Malcolm idly hung
On the smooth phrase of southern
    tongue ;
Not so had Malcolm strain'd his eye,
Another step than thine to spy.'
'Wake, Allan-Bane,' aloud she cried,
To the old Minstrel by her side ;
'Arouse thee from thy moody dream !
I'll give thy harp heroic theme,
And warm thee with a noble name ;
Pour forth the glory of the Græme !'
Scarce from her lip the word had
    rush'd,
When deep the conscious maiden
    blush'd ;
For of his clan, in hall and bower,
Young Malcolm Græme was held the
    flower.

VII.

The Minstrel waked his harp ; three
    times
Arose the well-known martial chimes,
And thrice their high heroic pride
In melancholy murmurs died.
'Vainly thou bid'st, O noble maid,'
Clasping his wither'd hands, he said,
'Vainly thou bid'st me wake the
    strain,
Though all unwont to bid in vain.
Alas ! than mine a mightier hand
Has tuned my harp, my strings has
    spann'd !
I touch the chords of joy, but low
And mournful answer notes of woe ;
And the proud march, which victors
    tread,
Sinks in the wailing for the dead.
O well for me, if mine alone
That dirge's deep prophetic tone !

If, as my tuneful fathers said,
This harp, which erst Saint Modan
    sway'd,
Can thus its master's fate foretell,
Then welcome be the minstrel's knell !

VIII.

'But ah ! dear lady, thus it sigh'd
The eve thy sainted mother died ;
And such the sounds which, while
    I strove
To wake a lay of war or love,
Came marring all the festal mirth,
Appalling me who gave them birth,
And, disobedient to my call,
Wail'd loud through Bothwell's ban-
    ner'd hall,
Ere Douglases, to ruin driven,
Were exiled from their native heaven.
Oh ! if yet worse mishap and woe
My master's house must undergo,
Or aught but weal to Ellen fair
Brood in these accents of despair,
No future bard, sad Harp ! shall fling
Triumph or rapture from thy string ;
One short, one final strain shall flow,
Fraught with unutterable woe,
Then shiver'd shall thy fragments lie,
Thy master cast him down and die !'

IX.

Soothing she answer'd him, 'Assuage,
Mine honour'd friend, the fears of age ;
All melodies to thee are known,
That harp has rung, or pipe has blown,
In Lowland vale or Highland glen,
From Tweed to Spey—what marvel,
    then,
At times, unbidden notes should rise,
Confusedly bound in memory's ties,
Entangling, as they rush along,
The war-march with the funeral song ?
Small ground is now for boding fear ;
Obscure, but safe, we rest us here.
My sire, in native virtue great,
Resigning lordship, lands, and state,
Not then to fortune more resign'd,
Than yonder oak might give the wind :

The graceful foliage storms may reave,
The noble stem they cannot grieve.
For me,'—she stoop'd, and, looking
　　round,
Pluck'd a blue hare-bell from the
　　ground,—
'For me, whose memory scarce conveys
An image of more splendid days,
This little flower, that loves the lea,
May well my simple emblem be ;
It drinks heaven's dew as blithe as rose
That in the king's own garden grows ;
And when I place it in my hair,
Allan, a bard is bound to swear
He ne'er saw coronet so fair.'
Then playfully the chaplet wild
She wreath'd in her dark locks, and
　　smiled.

X.

Her smile, her speech, with winning
　　sway,
Wiled the old harper's mood away.
With such a look as hermits throw,
When angels stoop to soothe their woe,
He gazed, till fond regret and pride
Thrill'd to a tear, then thus replied :
'Loveliest and best ! thou little know'st
The rank, the honours, thou hast lost !
O might I live to see thee grace,
In Scotland's court, thy birth-right
　　place,
To see my favourite's step advance,
The lightest in the courtly dance,
The cause of every gallant's sigh,
And leading star of every eye,
And theme of every minstrel's art,
The Lady of the Bleeding Heart !'

XI.

' Fair dreams are these,' the maiden
　　cried,
(Light was her accent, yet she sigh'd ;)
'Yet is this mossy rock to me
Worth splendid chair and canopy;
Nor would my footsteps spring more
　　gay
In courtly dance than blithe strathspey,

Nor half so pleased mine ear incline
To royal minstrel's lay as thine.
And then for suitors proud and high,
To bend before my conquering eye,—
Thou, flattering bard ! thyself wilt
　　say,
That grim Sir Roderick owns its sway.
The Saxon scourge, Clan-Alpine's
　　pride,
The terror of Loch Lomond's side,
Would, at my suit, thou know'st, delay
A Lennox foray—for a day.'

XII.

The ancient bard her glee repress'd :
' Ill hast thou chosen theme for jest !
For who, through all this western wild,
Named Black Sir Roderick e'er, and
　　smiled ?
In Holy-Rood a knight he slew ;
I saw, when back the dirk he drew,
Courtiers give place before the stride
Of the undaunted homicide ;
And since, though outlaw'd, hath his
　　hand
Full sternly kept his mountain land.
Who else dared give—ah ! woe the day,
That I such hated truth should say—
The Douglas, like a stricken deer,
Disown'd by every noble peer,
Even the rude refuge we have here ?
Alas, this wild marauding Chief
Alone might hazard our relief,
And now thy maiden charms expand,
Looks for his guerdon in thy hand ;
Full soon may dispensation sought,
To back his suit, from Rome be brought.
Then, though an exile on the hill,
Thy father, as the Douglas, still
Be held in reverence and fear ;
And though to Roderick thou 'rt so
　　dear,
That thou might 'st guide with silken
　　thread,
Slave of thy will, this chieftain dread,
Yet, O loved maid, thy mirth refrain !
Thy hand is on a lion's mane.'

XIII.

'Minstrel,' the maid replied, and high
Her father's soul glanced from her
    eye,
'My debts to Roderick's house I know:
All that a mother could bestow,
To Lady Margaret's care I owe,
Since first an orphan in the wild
She sorrow'd o'er her sister's child;
To her brave chieftain son, from ire
Of Scotland's king who shrouds my sire,
A deeper, holier debt is owed;
And, could I pay it with my blood,
Allan! Sir Roderick should command
My blood, my life,—but not my hand.
Rather will Ellen Douglas dwell
A votaress in Maronnan's cell:
Rather through realms beyond the sea,
Seeking the world's cold charity,
Where ne'er was spoke a Scottish
    word,
And ne'er the name of Douglas heard,
An outcast pilgrim will she rove,
Than wed the man she cannot love.

XIV.

'Thou shakest, good friend, thy tresses
    grey,
That pleading look, what can it say
But what I own?—I grant him brave,
But wild as Bracklinn's thundering
    wave;
And generous—save vindictive mood,
Or jealous transport, chafe his blood:
I grant him true to friendly band,
As his claymore is to his hand;
But O! that very blade of steel
More mercy for a foe would feel:
I grant him liberal, to fling
Among his clan the wealth they bring,
When back by lake and glen they wind,
And in the Lowland leave behind,
Where once some pleasant hamlet
    stood,
A mass of ashes slaked with blood.
The hand that for my father fought
I honour, as his daughter ought;

But can I clasp it reeking red,
From peasants slaughter'd in their shed?
No! wildly while his virtues gleam,
They make his passions darker seem,
And flash along his spirit high,
Like lightning o'er the midnight sky.
While yet a child,—and children know,
Instinctive taught, the friend and foe,—
I shudder'd at his brow of gloom,
His shadowy plaid, and sable plume;
A maiden grown, I ill could bear
His haughty mien and lordly air:
But, if thou join'st a suitor's claim,
In serious mood, to Roderick's name,
I thrill with anguish! or, if e'er
A Douglas knew the word, with fear.
To change such odious theme were
    best;
What think'st thou of our stranger
    guest?'

XV.

'What think I of him?—woe the while
That brought such wanderer to our isle!
Thy father's battle-brand, of yore
For Tine-man forged by fairy lore,
What time he leagued, no longer foes,
His Border spears with Hotspur's
    bows,
Did, self-unscabbarded, foreshow
The footstep of a secret foe.
If courtly spy hath harbour'd here,
What may we for the Douglas fear?
What for this island, deem'd of old
Clan-Alpine's last and surest hold?
If neither spy nor foe, I pray
What yet may jealous Roderick say?
Nay, wave not thy disdainful head,
Bethink thee of the discord dread
That kindled, when at Beltane game
Thou led'st the dance with Malcolm
    Græme;
Still, though thy sire the peace renew'd,
Smoulders in Roderick's breast the
    feud.
Beware!—But hark, what sounds
    are these?
My dull ears catch no faltering breeze;

No weeping birch, nor aspens wake,
Nor breath is dimpling in the lake ;
Still is the canna's hoary beard ;
Yet, by my minstrel faith, I heard—
And hark again ! some pipe of war
Sends the bold pibroch from afar.'

XVI.

Far up the lengthen'd lake were spied
Four darkening specks upon the tide,
That, slow enlarging on the view,
Four mann'd and masted barges grew,
And, bearing downwards from Glen-
　　gyle,
Steer'd full upon the lonely isle ;
The point of Brianchoil they pass'd,
And, to the windward as they cast,
Against the sun they gave to shine
The bold Sir Roderick's banner'd
　　Pine.
Nearer and nearer as they bear,
Spears, pikes, and axes flash in air.
Now might you see the tartans brave,
And plaids and plumage dance and
　　wave :
Now see the bonnets sink and rise,
As his tough oar the rower plies ;
See, flashing at each sturdy stroke,
The wave ascending into smoke ;
See the proud pipers on the bow,
And mark the gaudy streamers flow
From their loud chanters down, and
　　sweep
The furrow'd bosom of the deep,
As, rushing through the lake amain,
They plied the ancient Highland strain.

XVII.

Ever, as on they bore, more loud
And louder rung the pibroch proud.
At first the sound, by distance tame,
Mellow'd along the waters came,
And, lingering long by cape and bay,
Wail'd every harsher note away ;
Then bursting bolder on the ear,
The clan's shrill Gathering they could
　　hear ;

Those thrilling sounds, that call the
　　might
Of old Clan-Alpine to the fight.
Thick beat the rapid notes, as when
The mustering hundreds shake the
　　glen,
And, hurrying at the signal dread,
The batter'd earth returns their tread.
Then prelude light, of livelier tone,
Express'd their merry marching on,
Ere peal of closing battle rose,
With mingled outcry, shrieks, and
　　blows ;
And mimic din of stroke and ward,
As broad sword upon target jarr'd ;
And groaning pause, ere yet again,
Condensed, the battle yell'd amain ;
The rapid charge, the rallying shout,
Retreat borne headlong into rout,
And bursts of triumph, to declare
Clan-Alpine's conquest — all were
　　there.
Nor ended thus the strain ; but slow
Sunk in a moan prolong'd and low,
And changed the conquering clarion
　　swell
For wild lament o'er those that fell.

XVIII.

The war-pipes ceased ; but lake and
　　hill
Were busy with their echoes still ;
And, when they slept, a vocal strain
Bade their hoarse chorus wake again,
While loud a hundred clansmen raise
Their voices in their Chieftain's praise.
Each boatman, bending to his oar,
With measured sweep the burden
　　bore,
In such wild cadence, as the breeze
Makes through December's leafless
　　trees.
The chorus first could Allan know,
' Roderick Vich Alpine, ho ! iro ! '
And near, and nearer as they
　　row'd,
Distinct the martial ditty flow'd.

XIX.

BOAT SONG.

'Hail to the Chief who in triumph
     advances!
  Honour'd and bless'd be the ever-
     green Pine!
Long may the tree, in his banner that
     glances,
  Flourish, the shelter and grace of
     our line!
  Heaven send it happy dew,
  Earth lend it sap anew,
Gayly to bourgeon, and broadly to
     grow,
  While every Highland glen
  Sends our shout back agen,
Roderigh Vich Alpine dhu, ho! ieroe!

'Ours is no sapling, chance-sown by
     the fountain,
  Blooming at Beltane, in winter to
     fade;
When the whirlwind has stripp'd
     every leaf on the mountain,
  The more shall Clan-Alpine exult in
     her shade.
  Moor'd in the rifted rock,
  Proof to the tempest's shock,
Firmer he roots him the ruder it
     blow;
  Menteith and Breadalbane, then,
  Echo his praise agen,
Roderigh Vich Alpine dhu, ho! ieroe!

XX.

'Proudly our pibroch has thrill'd in
     Glen Fruin,
  And Bannochar's groans to our slo-
     gan replied;
Glen Luss and Ross-dhu, they are
     smoking in ruin,
  And the best of Loch Lomond lie
     dead on her side.
  Widow and Saxon maid
  Long shall lament our raid,

Think of Clan-Alpine with fear and
     with woe;
  Lennox and Leven-glen
  Shake when they hear agen,
Roderigh Vich Alpine dhu, ho! ieroe!

'Row, vassals, row, for the pride of
     the Highlands!
  Stretch to your oars, for the ever-
     green Pine!
O! that the rose-bud that graces yon
     islands
  Were wreathed in a garland around
     him to twine!
  O that some seedling gem,
  Worthy such noble stem,
Honour'd and bless'd in their shadow
     might grow!
  Loud should Clan-Alpine then
  Ring from her deepmost glen,
Roderigh Vich Alpine dhu, ho! ieroe!'

XXI.

With all her joyful female band
Had Lady Margaret sought the strand.
Loose on the breeze their tresses flew,
And high their snowy arms they threw,
As echoing back with shrill acclaim,
And chorus wild, the Chieftain's name;
While, prompt to please, with mother's
     art,
The darling passion of his heart,
The Dame call'd Ellen to the strand,
To greet her kinsman ere he land:
'Come, loiterer, come! a Douglas thou,
And shun to wreathe a victor's brow?'
Reluctantly and slow, the maid
The unwelcome summoning obey'd,
And, when a distant bugle rung,
In the mid-path aside she sprung:
'List, Allan-Bane! From mainland
     cast,
I hear my father's signal blast.
Be ours,' she cried, 'the skiff to guide,
And waft him from the mountain side.'
Then, like a sunbeam, swift and bright,
She darted to her shallop light,

And, eagerly while Roderick scann'd,
For her dear form, his mother's band,
The islet far behind her lay,
And she had landed in the bay.

XXII.

Some feelings are to mortals given,
With less of earth in them than heaven:
And if there be a human tear
From passion's dross refined and clear,
A tear so limpid and so meek,
It would not stain an angel's cheek,
'Tis that which pious fathers shed
Upon a duteous daughter's head!
And as the Douglas to his breast
His darling Ellen closely press'd,
Such holy drops her tresses steep'd,
Though 'twas an hero's eye that
weep'd.
Nor while on Ellen's faltering tongue
Her filial welcomes crowded hung,
Mark'd she, that fear (affection's proof)
Still held a graceful youth aloof;
No! not till Douglas named his name,
Although the youth was Malcolm
Græme.

XXIII.

Allan, with wistful look the while,
Mark'd Roderick landing on the isle;
His master piteously he eyed,
Then gazed upon the Chieftain's pride.
Then dash'd, with hasty hand, away
From his dimm'd eye the gathering
spray;
And Douglas, as his hand he laid
On Malcolm's shoulder, kindly said,
'Canst thou, young friend, no meaning
spy
In my poor follower's glistening eye?
I 'll tell thee:—he recalls the day,
When in my praise he led the lay
O'er the arch'd gate of Bothwell proud,
While many a minstrel answer'd loud,
When Percy's Norman pennon, won
In bloody field, before me shone,
And twice ten knights, the least a name
As mighty as yon Chief may claim,

Gracing my pomp, behind me came.
Yet trust me, Malcolm, not so proud
Was I of all that marshall'd crowd,
Though the waned crescent own'd my
might,
And in my train troop'd lord and
knight,
Though Blantyre hymn'd her holiest
lays,
And Bothwell's bards flung back my
praise,
As when this old man's silent tear,
And this poor maid's affection dear,
A welcome give more kind and true,
Than aught my better fortunes knew.
Forgive, my friend, a father's boast,
O! it out-beggars all I lost!'

XXIV.

Delightful praise! Like summer rose,
That brighter in the dew-drop glows,
The bashful maiden's cheek appear'd,
For Douglas spoke, and Malcolm heard.
The flush of shame-faced joy to hide,
The hounds, the hawk, her cares divide;
The loved caresses of the maid
The dogs with crouch and whimper
paid;
And, at her whistle, on her hand
The falcon took his favourite stand,
Closed his dark wing, relax'd his eye,
Nor, though unhooded, sought to fly.
And, trust, while in such guise she
stood,
Like fabled Goddess of the wood,
That if a father's partial thought
O'erweigh'd her worth and beauty
aught,
Well might the lover's judgment fail
To balance with a juster scale;
For with each secret glance he stole,
The fond enthusiast sent his soul.

XXV.

Of stature tall, and slender frame,
But firmly knit, was Malcolm Græme.
The belted plaid and tartan hose
Did ne'er more graceful limbs disclose;

His flaxen hair, of sunny hue,
Curl'd closely round his bonnet blue.
Train'd to the chase, his eagle eye
The ptarmigan in snow could spy :
Each pass, by mountain, lake, and
    heath,
He knew, through Lennox and
    Menteith ;
Vain was the bound of dark-brown doe
When Malcolm bent his sounding
    bow ;
And scarce that doe, though wing'd
    with fear,
Outstripp'd in speed the mountaineer:
Right up Ben-Lomond could he press,
And not a sob his toil confess.
His form accorded with a mind
Lively and ardent, frank and kind ;
A blither heart, till Ellen came,
Did never love nor sorrow tame ;
It danced as lightsome in his breast
As play'd the feather on his crest.
Yet friends, who nearest knew the
    youth,
His scorn of wrong, his zeal for truth,
And bards who saw his features bold
When kindled by the tales of old,
Said, were that youth to manhood
    grown,
Not long should Roderick Dhu's
    renown
Be foremost voiced by mountain fame,
But quail to that of Malcolm Græme.

XXVI.

Now back they wend their watery way,
And, ' O my sire ! ' did Ellen say,
' Why urge thy chase so far astray ?
And why so late return'd ? And
    why '—
The rest was in her speaking eye.
' My child, the chase I follow far,
'Tis mimicry of noble war ;
And with that gallant pastime reft
Were all of Douglas I have left.
I met young Malcolm as I stray'd,
Far eastward, in Glenfinlas' shade.

Nor stray'd I safe ; for, all around,
Hunters and horsemen scour'd the
    ground.
This youth, though still a royal ward,
Risk'd life and land to be my guard,
And through the passes of the wood
Guided my steps, not unpursued ;
And Roderick shall his welcome make,
Despite old spleen, for Douglas' sake.
Then must he seek Strath-Endrick
    glen,
Nor peril aught for me agen.'

XXVII.

Sir Roderick, who to meet them came,
Redden'd at sight of Malcolm Græme,
Yet, not in action, word, or eye,
Fail'd aught in hospitality.
In talk and sport they whiled away
The morning of that summer day ;
But at high noon a courier light
Held secret parley with the knight,
Whose moody aspect soon declared
That evil were the news he heard.
Deep thought seem'd toiling in his
    head ;
Yet was the evening banquet made,
Ere he assembled round the flame
His mother, Douglas, and the Græme,
And Ellen too ; then cast around
His eyes, then fix'd them on the ground,
As studying phrase that might avail
Best to convey unpleasant tale.
Long with his dagger's hilt he play'd,
Then raised his haughty brow, and
    said :

XXVIII.

' Short be my speech ; nor time
    affords,
Nor my plain temper, glozing words.
Kinsman and father—if such name
Douglas vouchsafe to Roderick's claim ;
Mine honour'd mother ; Ellen—why,
My cousin, turn away thine eye ?
And Græme—in whom I hope to know
Full soon a noble friend or foe,

When age shall give thee thy com-
    mand
And leading in thy native land :
List all !—The King's vindictive pride
Boasts to have tamed the Border-side,
Where chiefs, with hound and hawk
    who came
To share their monarch's silvan game,
Themselves in bloody toils were
    snared ;
And when the banquet they prepared,
And wide their loyal portals flung,
O'er their own gateway struggling
    hung.
Loud cries their blood from Meggat's
    mead,
From Yarrow braes, and banks of
    Tweed,
Where the lone streams of Ettrick
    glide,
And from the silver Teviot's side ;
The dales, where martial clans did
    ride,
Are now one sheep-walk, waste and
    wide.
This tyrant of the Scottish throne,
So faithless and so ruthless known,
Now hither comes ; his end the same,
The same pretext of silvan game.
What grace for Highland Chiefs, judge
    ye
By fate of Border chivalry.
Yet more ; amid Glenfinlas green,
Douglas, thy stately form was seen :
This by espial sure I know.
Your counsel ! in the streight I show.'

XXIX.

Ellen and Margaret fearfully
Sought comfort in each other's eye,
Then turn'd their ghastly look, each
    one,
This to her sire, that to her son.
The hasty colour went and came
In the bold cheek of Malcolm Græme ;
But from his glance it well appear'd,
 'Twas but for Ellen that he fear'd ;

While, sorrowful, but undismay'd,
The Douglas thus his counsel said :—
' Brave Roderick, though the tempest
    roar,
It may but thunder and pass o'er ;
Nor will I here remain an hour,
To draw the lightning on thy bower ;
For well thou know'st, at this grey
    head
The royal bolt were fiercest sped.
For thee, who, at thy King's command,
Canst aid him with a gallant band,
Submission, homage, humbled pride,
Shall turn the Monarch's wrath aside.
Poor remnants of the Bleeding Heart,
Ellen and I will seek, apart,
The refuge of some forest cell,
There, like the hunted quarry, dwell,
Till on the mountain and the moor,
The stern pursuit be pass'd and o'er.'

XXX.

' No, by mine honour,' Roderick said,
' So help me heaven, and my good
    blade !
No, never ! Blasted be yon Pine,
My fathers' ancient crest and mine,
If from its shade in danger part
The lineage of the Bleeding Heart !
Hear my blunt speech : Grant me
    this maid
To wife, thy counsel to mine aid ;
To Douglas, leagued with Roderick
    Dhu,
Will friends and allies flock enow ;
Like cause of doubt, distrust, and grief,
Will bind to us each Western Chief.
When the loud pipes my bridal tell,
The Links of Forth shall hear the knell,
The guards shall start in Stirling's
    porch ;
And, when I light the nuptial torch,
A thousand villages in flames
Shall scare the slumbers of King James !
Nay, Ellen, blench not thus away,
And, mother, cease these signs, I pray ;
I meant not all my heat might say.

Small need of inroad, or of fight,
When the sage Douglas may unite
Each mountain clan in friendly band,
To guard the passes of their land,
Till the foil'd king, from pathless glen,
Shall bootless turn him home agen.'

XXXI.

There are who have, at midnight hour,
In slumber scaled a dizzy tower,
And, on the verge that beetled o'er
The ocean-tide's incessant roar,
Dream'd calmly out their dangerous
    dream,
Till waken'd by the morning beam ;
When, dazzled by the eastern glow,
Such startler cast his glance below,
And saw unmeasured depth around,
And heard unintermitted sound,
And thought the battled fence so frail,
It waved like cobweb in the gale ;—
Amid his senses' giddy wheel,
Did he not desperate impulse feel,
Headlong to plunge himself below,
And meet the worst his fears fore-
    show ?
Thus, Ellen, dizzy and astound,
As sudden ruin yawn'd around,
By crossing terrors wildly toss'd,
Still for the Douglas fearing most,
Could scarce the desperate thought
    withstand,
To buy his safety with her hand.

XXXII.

Such purpose dread could Malcolm
    spy
In Ellen's quivering lip and eye,
And eager rose to speak ; but ere
His tongue could hurry forth his fear,
Had Douglas mark'd the hectic strife,
Where death seem'd combating with
    life ;
For to her cheek, in feverish flood,
One instant rush'd the throbbing blood,
Then ebbing back, with sudden sway,
Left its domain as wan as clay.

'Roderick, enough ! enough !' he cried,
' My daughter cannot be thy bride ;
Not that the blush to wooer dear,
Nor paleness that of maiden fear.
It may not be ; forgive her, Chief,
Nor hazard aught for our relief.
Against his sovereign, Douglas ne'er
Will level a rebellious spear.
'Twas I that taught his youthful hand
To rein a steed and wield a brand ;
I see him yet, the princely boy !
Not Ellen more my pride and joy ;
I love him still, despite my wrongs,
By hasty wrath, and slanderous
    tongues.
O seek the grace you well may find,
Without a cause to mine combined.'

XXXIII.

Twice through the hall the Chieftain
    strode ;
The waving of his tartans broad,
And darken'd brow, where wounded
    pride
With ire and disappointment vied,
Seem'd, by the torch's gloomy light,
Like the ill Demon of the night,
Stooping his pinions' shadowy sway
Upon the nighted pilgrim's way :
But, unrequited Love ! thy dart
Plunged deepest its envenom'd smart,
And Roderick, with thine anguish
    stung,
At length the hand of Douglas wrung,
While eyes, that mock'd at tears before,
With bitter drops were running o'er.
The death-pangs of long-cherish'd hope
Scarce in that ample breast had scope,
But, struggling with his spirit proud,
Convulsive heaved its chequer'd
    shroud,
While every sob—so mute were all—
Was heard distinctly through the hall.
The son's despair, the mother's look,
Ill might the gentle Ellen brook ;
She rose, and to her side there came,
To aid her parting steps, the Græme.

XXXIV.

Then Roderick from the Douglas broke;
As flashes flame through sable smoke,
Kindling its wreaths, long, dark, and low,
To one broad blaze of ruddy glow,
So the deep anguish of despair
Burst, in fierce jealousy, to air.
With stalwart grasp his hand he laid
On Malcolm's breast and belted plaid:
'Back, beardless boy!' he sternly said,
'Back, minion! hold'st thou thus at naught
The lesson I so lately taught?
This roof, the Douglas, and that maid,
Thank thou for punishment delay'd.'
Eager as greyhound on his game,
Fiercely with Roderick grappled Græme.
'Perish my name, if aught afford
Its Chieftain safety save his sword!'
Thus as they strove, their desperate hand
Griped to the dagger or the brand,
And death had been—but Douglas rose,
And thrust between the struggling foes
His giant strength :—' Chieftains, forego!
I hold the first who strikes, my foe.
Madmen, forbear your frantic jar!
What! is the Douglas fall'n so far,
His daughter's hand is doom'd the spoil
Of such dishonourable broil?'
Sullen and slowly they unclasp,
As struck with shame, their desperate grasp,
And each upon his rival glared,
With foot advanced, and blade half bared.

XXXV.

Ere yet the brands aloft were flung,
Margaret on Roderick's mantle hung,
And Malcolm heard his Ellen's scream,
As falter'd through terrific dream.
Then Roderick plunged in sheath his sword,
And veil'd his wrath in scornful word.
'Rest safe till morning; pity 'twere
Such cheek should feel the midnight air!
Then mayest thou to James Stuart tell
Roderick will keep the lake and fell,
Nor lackey, with his freeborn clan,
The pageant pomp of earthly man.
More would he of Clan-Alpine know,
Thou canst our strength and passes show.
Malise, what ho!'—his henchman came;
'Give our safe-conduct to the Græme.'
Young Malcolm answer'd, calm and bold,
'Fear nothing for thy favourite hold;
The spot an angel deigned to grace
Is bless'd, though robbers haunt the place.
Thy churlish courtesy for those
Reserve, who fear to be thy foes.
As safe to me the mountain way
At midnight as in blaze of day,
Though with his boldest at his back
Even Roderick Dhu beset the track.
Brave Douglas,—lovely Ellen,—nay,
Nought here of parting will I say.
Earth does not hold a lonesome glen
So secret, but we meet agen.
Chieftain! we too shall find an hour.'
He said, and left the silvan bower.

XXXVI.

Old Allan follow'd to the strand
(Such was the Douglas's command)
And anxious told, how, on the morn,
The stern Sir Roderick deep had sworn
The Fiery Cross should circle o'er
Dale, glen, and valley, down, and moor.
Much were the peril to the Græme,
From those who to the signal came;

Far up the lake 'twere safest land,
Himself would row him to the strand.
He gave his counsel to the wind,
While Malcolm did, unheeding, bind,
Round dirk and pouch and broad-
      sword roll'd,
His ample plaid in tighten'd fold,
And stripp'd his limbs to such array
As best might suit the watery way ;

XXXVII.

Then spoke abrupt : ' Farewell to thee,
Pattern of old fidelity ! '
The   Minstrel's   hand   he   kindly
      press'd,—
' O ! could I point a place of rest !
My sovereign holds in ward my land,
My uncle leads my vassal band ;
To tame his foes, his friends to aid,
Poor Malcolm has but heart and blade.
Yet, if there be one faithful Græme
Who loves the Chieftain of his name,
Not long shall honour'd Douglas dwell,
Like hunted stag, in mountain cell ;
Nor, ere yon pride-swoll'n robber
      dare—
I may not give the rest to air !
Tell   Roderick   Dhu,   I   owed   him
      nought,
Not the poor service of a boat,
To waft me to yon mountain-side. '
Then plunged he in the flashing tide.
Bold o'er the flood his head he bore,
And stoutly steer'd him from the
      shore ;
And Allan strain'd his anxious eye,
Far 'mid the lake his form to spy,
Darkening across each puny wave,
To which the moon her silver gave.
Fast as the cormorant could skim,
The swimmer plied each active limb ;
Then landing in the moonlight dell,
Loud shouted, of his weal to tell.
The Minstrel heard the far halloo,
And joyful from the shore withdrew.

—◆—

Canto Third.

The Gathering.

I.

TIME rolls his ceaseless course.   The
      race of yore,
   Who danced our infancy upon their
      knee,
And told our marvelling boyhood
      legends store,
   Of their strange ventures happ'd by
      land or sea,
How are they blotted from the things
      that be !
   How few, all weak and wither'd of
      their force,
Wait on the verge of dark eternity,
   Like stranded wrecks, the tide
      returning hoarse,
To sweep them from our sight ! Time
      rolls his ceaseless course.

Yet live there still who can remember
      well,
   How, when a mountain chief his
      bugle blew,
Both field and forest, dingle, cliff, and
      dell,
   And solitary heath, the signal knew ;
And fast the faithful clan around him
      drew,
   What time the warning note was
      keenly wound,
What time aloft their kindred banner
      flew,
   While clamorous war-pipes yell'd
      the gathering sound,
And while the Fiery Cross glanced,
      like a meteor, round.

II.

The summer dawn's reflected hue
To purple changed Loch Katrine blue ;
Mildly and soft the western breeze
Just kiss'd the Lake, just stirr'd the
      trees,

And the pleased lake, like maiden coy,
Trembled but dimpled not for joy;
The mountain-shadows on her breast
Were neither broken nor at rest;
In bright uncertainty they lie,
Like future joys to Fancy's eye.
The water-lily to the light
Her chalice rear'd of silver bright;
The doe awoke, and to the lawn,
Begemm'd with dew-drops, led her
    fawn;
The grey mist left the mountain side,
The torrent show'd its glistening pride;
Invisible in flecked sky,
The lark sent down her revelry;
The blackbird and the speckled thrush
Good-morrow gave from brake and
    bush;
In answer coo'd the cushat dove
Her notes of peace, and rest, and love.

III.

No thought of peace, no thought of rest,
Assuaged the storm in Roderick's
    breast.
With sheathed broadsword in his hand,
Abrupt he paced the islet strand,
And eyed the rising sun, and laid
His hand on his impatient blade.
Beneath a rock, his vassals' care
Was prompt the ritual to prepare,
With deep and deathful meaning
    fraught;
For such Antiquity had taught
Was preface meet, ere yet abroad
The Cross of Fire should take its road.
The shrinking band stood oft aghast
At the impatient glance he cast;—
Such glance the mountain eagle threw,
As, from the cliffs of Benvenue,
She spread her dark sails on the wind,
And, high in middle heaven, reclined,
With her broad shadow on the lake,
Silenced the warblers of the brake.

IV.

A heap of wither'd boughs was piled,
Of juniper and rowan wild,
Mingled with shivers from the oak,
Rent by the lightning's recent stroke.
Brian, the Hermit, by it stood,
Barefooted, in his frock and hood.
His grisled beard and matted hair
Obscured a visage of despair;
His naked arms and legs, seam'd o'er,
The scars of frantic penance bore.
That monk, of savage form and face,
The impending danger of his race
Had drawn from deepest solitude,
Far in Benharrow's bosom rude.
Not his the mien of Christian priest,
But Druid's, from the grave released,
Whose harden'd heart and eye might
    brook
On human sacrifice to look;
And much, 'twas said, of heathen lore
Mix'd in the charms he mutter'd o'er.
The hallow'd creed gave only worse
And deadlier emphasis of curse;
No peasant sought that Hermit's
    prayer,
His cave the pilgrim shunn'd with care,
The eager huntsman knew his bound,
And in mid chase call'd off his hound;
Or if, in lonely glen or strath,
The desert-dweller met his path,
He pray'd, and sign'd the cross
    between,
While terror took devotion's mien.

V.

Of Brian's birth strange tales were told.
His mother watch'd a midnight fold,
Built deep within a dreary glen,
Where scatter'd lay the bones of men,
In some forgotten battle slain,
And bleach'd by drifting wind and rain.
It might have tamed a warrior's heart,
To view such mockery of his art!
The knot-grass fetter'd there the hand
Which once could burst an iron band;
Beneath the broad and ample bone,
That buckler'd heart to fear unknown,
A feeble and a timorous guest,
The field-fare framed her lowly nest;

There the slow blind-worm left his
　　slime
On the fleet limbs that mock'd at time;
And there, too, lay the leader's skull,
Still wreathed with chaplet, flush'd
　　and full,
For heath-bell with her purple bloom
Supplied the bonnet and the plume.
All night, in this sad glen, the maid
Sate, shrouded in her mantle's shade:
—She said no shepherd sought her
　　side,
No hunter's hand her snood untied;
Yet ne'er again to braid her hair
The virgin snood did Alice wear;
Gone was her maiden glee and sport,
Her maiden girdle all too short,
Nor sought she, from that fatal night,
Or holy church or blessed rite,
But lock'd her secret in her breast,
And died in travail, unconfess'd.

VI.

Alone, among his young compeers,
Was Brian from his infant years;
A moody and heart-broken boy,
Estranged from sympathy and joy,
Bearing each taunt which careless
　　tongue
On his mysterious lineage flung.
Whole nights he spent by moonlight
　　pale,
To wood and stream his hap to wail,
Till, frantic, he as truth received
What of his birth the crowd believed,
And sought, in mist and meteor fire,
To meet and know his Phantom Sire!
In vain, to soothe his wayward fate,
The cloister oped her pitying gate;
In vain, the learning of the age
Unclasp'd the sable-letter'd page;
Even in its treasures he could find
Food for the fever of his mind.
Eager he read whatever tells
Of magic, cabala, and spells,
And every dark pursuit allied
To curious and presumptuous pride;

Till with fired brain and nerves o'er-
　　strung,
And heart with mystic horrors wrung,
Desperate he sought Benharrow's
　　den,
And hid him from the haunts of men.

VII.

The desert gave him visions wild,
Such as might suit the spectre's child.
Where with black cliffs the torrents
　　toil,
He watch'd the wheeling eddies boil,
Till, from their foam, his dazzled eyes
Beheld the River Demon rise;
The mountain mist took form and limb,
Of noontide hag, or goblin grim;
The midnight wind came wild and
　　dread,
Swell'd with the voices of the dead;
Far on the future battle-heath
His eye beheld the ranks of death:
Thus the lone Seer, from mankind
　　hurl'd,
Shaped forth a disembodied world.
One lingering sympathy of mind
Still bound him to the mortal kind;
The only parent he could claim
Of ancient Alpine's lineage came.
Late had he heard, in prophet's dream,
The fatal Ben-Shie's boding scream;
Sounds, too, had come in midnight
　　blast,
Of charging steeds, careering fast
Along Benharrow's shingly side,
Where mortal horseman ne'er might
　　ride;
The thunderbolt had split the pine;
All augur'd ill to Alpine's line.
He girt his loins, and came to show
The signals of impending woe,
And now stood prompt to bless or ban,
As bade the Chieftain of his clan.

VIII.

'Twas all prepared; and from the rock.
A goat, the patriarch of the flock.

Before the kindling pile was laid,
And pierced by Roderick's ready blade.
Patient the sickening victim eyed
The life-blood ebb in crimson tide,
Down his clogg'd beard and shaggy
          limb,
Till darkness glazed his eyeballs dim.
The grisly priest, with murmuring
          prayer,
A slender crosslet form'd with care,
A cubit's length in measure due ;
The shaft and limbs were rods of yew,
Whose parents in Inch-Cailliach wave
Their shadows o'er Clan-Alpine's grave,
And, answering Lomond's breezes
          deep,
Soothe many a chieftain's endless sleep.
The Cross, thus form'd, he held on high,
With wasted hand, and haggard eye,
And strange and mingled feelings woke,
While his anathema he spoke :

IX.

'Woe to the clansman, who shall view
This symbol of sepulchral yew,
Forgetful that its branches grew
Where weep the heavens their holiest
          dew
          On Alpine's dwelling low !
Deserter of his Chieftain's trust,
He ne'er shall mingle with their dust,
But, from his sires and kindred thrust,
Each clansman's execration just
          Shall doom him wrath and woe.'
He paused ;—the word the vassals
          took,
With forward step and fiery look,
On high their naked brands they
          shook,
Their clattering targets wildly strook ;
          And first in murmur low,
Then, like the billow in his course,
That far to seaward finds his source,
And flings to shore his muster'd force,
Burst, with loud roar, their answer
          hoarse,
          'Woe to the traitor, woe !'

Ben-an's grey scalp the accents knew,
The joyous wolf from covert drew,
The exulting eagle scream'd afar,—
They knew the voice of Alpine's war.

X.

The shout was hush'd on lake and fell,
The monk resumed his mutter'd spell :
Dismal and low its accents came,
The while he scathed the Cross with
          flame ;
And the few words that reach'd the air,
Although the holiest name was there,
Had more of blasphemy than prayer.
But when he shook above the crowd
Its kindled points, he spoke aloud :

'Woe to the wretch who fails to rear
At this dread sign the ready spear !
For, as the flames this symbol sear,
His home, the refuge of his fear,
          A kindred fate shall know ;
Far o'er its roof the volumed flame
Clan-Alpine's vengeance shall pro-
          claim,
While maids and matrons on his name
Shall call down wretchedness and
          shame,
          And infamy and woe.'

Then rose the cry of females, shrill
As goss-hawk's whistle on the hill,
Denouncing misery and ill,
Mingled with childhood's babbling trill
          Of curses stammer'd slow ;
Answering, with imprecation dread,
'Sunk be his home in embers red !
And cursed be the meanest shed
That e'er shall hide the houseless head,
          We doom to want and woe !'
A sharp and shrieking echo gave,
Coir-Uriskin, thy goblin cave !
And the grey pass where birches wave
          On Beala-nam-bo.

XI.

Then deeper paused the priest anew,
And hard his labouring breath he drew,

While, with set teeth and clenched
 hand,
And eyes that glow'd like fiery brand,
He meditated curse more dread,
And deadlier, on the clansman's head,
Who, summon'd to his Chieftain's aid,
The signal saw and disobey'd.
The crosslet's points of sparkling wood,
He quenched among the bubbling
 blood,
And, as again the sign he rear'd,
Hollow and hoarse his voice was heard:
'When flits this Cross from man to
 man,
Vich-Alpine's summons to his clan,
Burst be the ear that fails to heed!
Palsied the foot that shuns to speed!
May ravens tear the careless eyes,
Wolves make the coward heart their
 prize!
As sinks that blood-stream in the earth,
So may his heart's-blood drench his
 hearth!
As dies in hissing gore the spark,
Quench thou his light, Destruction dark,
And be the grace to him denied,
Bought by this sign to all beside!'
He ceased; no echo gave agen
The murmur of the deep Amen.

XII.

Then Roderick, with impatient look,
From Brian's hand the symbol took:
'Speed, Malise, speed!' he said, and
 gave
The crosslet to his henchman brave.
'The muster-place be Lanrick mead—
Instant the time: speed, Malise, speed!'
Like heath-bird, when the hawks
 pursue,
A barge across Loch Katrine flew;
High stood the henchman on the
 prow;
So rapidly the barge-men row,
The bubbles, where they launch'd the
 boat,
Were all unbroken and afloat,

Dancing in foam and ripple still,
When it had near'd the mainland hill;
And from the silver beach's side
Still was the prow three fathom wide,
When lightly bounded to the land
The messenger of blood and brand.

XIII.

Speed, Malise, speed! the dun deer's
 hide
On fleeter foot was never tied.
Speed, Malise, speed! such cause of
 haste
Thine active sinews never braced.
Bend 'gainst the steepy hill thy
 breast,
Burst down like torrent from its crest;
With short and springing footstep pass
The trembling bog and false morass;
Across the brook like roebuck bound,
And thread the brake like questing
 hound;
The crag is high, the scaur is deep,
Yet shrink not from the desperate leap:
Parch'd are thy burning lips and brow,
Yet by the fountain pause not now;
Herald of battle, fate, and fear,
Stretch onward in thy fleet career!
The wounded hind thou track'st not
 now,
Pursuest not maid through greenwood
 bough,
Nor pliest thou now thy flying pace,
With rivals in the mountain race;
But danger, death, and warrior deed,
Are in thy course; speed, Malise,
 speed!

XIV.

Fast as the fatal symbol flies,
In arms the huts and hamlets rise;
From winding glen, from upland
 brown
They pour'd each hardy tenant down.
Nor slack'd the messenger his pace;
He show'd the sign, he named the
 place,

And, pressing forward like the wind,
Left clamour and surprise behind.
The fisherman forsook the strand,
The swarthy smith took dirk and
     brand;
With changed cheer, the mower blithe
Left in the half-cut swath the scythe;
The herds without a keeper stray'd,
The plough was in mid-furrow staid,
The falc'ner toss'd his hawk away,
The hunter left the stag at bay;
Prompt at the signal of alarms,
Each son of Alpine rush'd to arms;
So swept the tumult and affray
Along the margin of Achray.
Alas, thou lovely lake! that e'er
Thy banks should echo sounds of fear!
The rocks, the bosky thickets, sleep
So stilly on thy bosom deep,
The lark's blithe carol, from the cloud,
Seems for the scene too gaily loud.

xv.

Speed, Malise, speed! the lake is past,
Duncraggan's huts appear at last,
And peep, like moss-grown rocks, half
     seen,
Half hidden in the copse so green;
There mayest thou rest, thy labour done,
Their Lord shall speed the signal on.
As stoops the hawk upon his prey,
The henchman shot him down the way.
—What woeful accents load the gale?
The funeral yell, the female wail!
A gallant hunter's sport is o'er,
A valiant warrior fights no more.
Who, in the battle or the chase,
At Roderick's side shall fill his place!—
Within the hall, where torches' ray
Supplies the excluded beams of day,
Lies Duncan on his lowly bier,
And o'er him streams his widow's tear.
His stripling son stands mournful by,
His youngest weeps, but knows not
     why;
The village maids and matrons round
The dismal coronach resound.

xvi.

CORONACH.

'He is gone on the mountain,
   He is lost to the forest,
Like a summer-dried fountain,
   When our need was the sorest.
The font, reappearing,
   From the rain-drops shall borrow,
But to us comes no cheering,
   To Duncan no morrow!

The hand of the reaper
   Takes the ears that are hoary,
But the voice of the weeper
   Wails manhood in glory.
The autumn winds rushing
   Waft the leaves that are searest,
But our flower was in flushing,
   When blighting was nearest.

Fleet foot on the correi,
   Sage counsel in cumber,
Red hand in the foray,
   How sound is thy slumber!
Like the dew on the mountain,
   Like the foam on the river,
Like the bubble on the fountain,
   Thou art gone, and for ever!'

xvii.

See Stumah, who, the bier beside,
His master's corpse with wonder eyed,
Poor Stumah! whom his least halloo
Could send like lightning o'er the dew,
Bristles his crest, and points his ears,
As if some stranger step he hears.
'Tis not a mourner's muffled tread
Who comes to sorrow o'er the dead,
But headlong haste, or deadly fear,
Urge the precipitate career.
All stand aghast:—unheeding all,
The henchman bursts into the hall;
Before the dead man's bier he stood;
Held forth the Cross besmear'd with
     blood;
'The muster-place is Lanrick mead;
Speed forth the signal! clansmen,
     speed!'

XVIII.

Angus, the heir of Duncan's line,
Sprung forth and seized the fatal sign.
In haste the stripling to his side
His father's dirk and broadsword tied;
But when he saw his mother's eye
Watch him in speechless agony,
Back to her open'd arms he flew,
Press'd on her lips a fond adieu—
'Alas!' she sobb'd, 'and yet, be gone,
And speed thee forth, like Duncan's
    son!'
One look he cast upon the bier,
Dash'd from his eye the gathering tear,
Breathed deep to clear his labouring
    breast,
And toss'd aloft his bonnet crest,
Then, like the high-bred colt, when,
    freed,
First he essays his fire and speed,
He vanish'd, and o'er moor and moss
Sped forward with the Fiery Cross.
Suspended was the widow's tear,
While yet his footsteps she could hear;
And when she mark'd the henchman's
    eye
Wet with unwonted sympathy,
'Kinsman,' she said, 'his race is run,
That should have sped thine errand on;
The oak has fall'n,—the sapling bough
Is all Duncraggan's shelter now.
Yet trust I well, his duty done,
The orphan's God will guard my son.
And you, in many a danger true,
At Duncan's hest your blades that drew,
To arms, and guard that orphan's head!
Let babes and women wail the dead.'
Then weapon-clang, and martial call,
Resounded through the funeral hall,
While from the walls the attendant band
Snatch'd sword and targe, with hurried
    hand;
And short and flitting energy
Glanced from the mourner's sunken eye,
As if the sounds to warrior dear,
Might rouse her Duncan from his bier.

But faded soon that borrow'd force;
Grief claim'd his right, and tears their
    course.

XIX.

Benledi saw the Cross of Fire,
It glanced like lightning up Strath-Ire;
O'er dale and hill the summons flew,
Nor rest nor pause young Angus knew;
The tear that gather'd in his eye
He left the mountain breeze to dry;
Until, where Teith's young waters roll,
Betwixt him and a wooded knoll,
That graced the sable strath with green,
The chapel of St. Bride was seen.
Swoln was the stream, remote the
    bridge,
But Angus paused not on the edge;
Though the dark waves danced dizzily,
Though reel'd his sympathetic eye,
He dash'd amid the torrent's roar:
His right hand high the crosslet bore,
His left the pole-axe grasp'd, to guide
And stay his footing in the tide.
He stumbled twice—the foam splash'd
    high,
With hoarser swell the stream raced by;
And had he fall'n,—for ever there
Farewell Duncraggan's orphan heir!
But still, as if in parting life,
Firmer he grasp'd the Cross of strife,
Until the opposing bank he gain'd,
And up the chapel pathway strain'd.

XX.

A blithesome rout, that morning tide,
Had sought the chapel of St. Bride.
Her troth Tombea's Mary gave
To Norman, heir of Armandave.
And, issuing from the Gothic arch,
The bridal now resumed their march.
In rude, but glad procession, came
Bonneted sire and coif-clad dame;
And plaided youth, with jest and jeer,
Which snooded maiden would not hear;
And children, that, unwitting why,
Lent the gay shout their shrilly cry;

And minstrels, that in measures vied
Before the young and bonny bride,
Whose downcast eye and cheek dis-
    close
The tear and blush of morning rose.
With virgin step, and bashful hand,
She held the 'kerchief's snowy band;
The gallant bridegroom by her side,
Beheld his prize with victor's pride,
And the glad mother in her ear
Was closely whispering word of cheer.

XXI.

Who meets them at the churchyard
    gate?
The messenger of fear and fate!
Haste in his hurried accent lies,
And grief is swimming in his eyes.
All dripping from the recent flood,
Panting and travel-soil'd he stood,
The fatal sign of fire and sword
Held forth, and spoke the appointed
    word:
'The muster-place is Lanrick mead;
Speed forth the signal! Norman,
    speed!'
And must he change so soon the hand,
Just link'd to his by holy band,
For the fell Cross of blood and brand?
And must the day, so blithe that rose,
And promised rapture in the close,
Before its setting hour, divide
The bridegroom from the plighted
    bride?
O fatal doom! it must! it must!
Clan-Alpine's cause, her Chieftain's
    trust,
Her summons dread, brook no delay;
Stretch to the race; away! away!

XXII.

Yet slow he laid his plaid aside,
And, lingering, eyed his lovely bride,
Until he saw the starting tear
Speak woe he might not stop to cheer;
Then, trusting not a second look,
In haste he sped him up the brook,

Nor backward glanced, till on the heath
Where Lubnaig's lake supplies the
    Teith.
What in the racer's bosom stirr'd?
The sickening pang of hope deferr'd,
And memory, with a torturing train
Of all his morning visions vain.
Mingled with love's impatience, came
The manly thirst for martial fame;
The stormy joy of mountaineers,
Ere yet they rush upon the spears;
And zeal for Clan and Chieftain
    burning,
And hope, from well-fought field
    returning,
With war's red honours on his crest,
To clasp his Mary to his breast.
Stung by such thoughts, o'er bank
    and brae,
Like fire from flint he glanced away,
While high resolve, and feeling strong,
Burst into voluntary song:—

XXIII.

SONG.

'The heath this night must be my bed,
The bracken curtain for my head,
My lullaby the warder's tread,
    Far far from love and thee, Mary;
To-morrow eve, more stilly laid,
My couch may be my bloody plaid,
My vesper song, thy wail, sweet maid!
    It will not waken me, Mary!

I may not, dare not, fancy now
The grief that clouds thy lovely brow,
I dare not think upon thy vow,
    And all it promised me, Mary.
No fond regret must Norman know;
When bursts Clan-Alpine on the foe,
His heart must be like bended bow,
    His foot like arrow free, Mary.

A time will come with feeling fraught,
For, if I fall in battle fought,
Thy hapless lover's dying thought
    Shall be a thought on thee, Mary.

And if return'd from conquer'd foes,
How blithely will the evening close,
How sweet the linnet sing repose,
   To my young bride and me, Mary !'

XXIV.

Not faster o'er thy heathery braes,
Balquidder, speeds the midnight blaze,
Rushing, in conflagration strong,
Thy deep ravines and dells along,
Wrapping thy cliffs in purple glow,
And reddening the dark lakes below ;
Nor faster speeds it, nor so far,
As o'er thy heaths the voice of war.
The signal roused to martial coil
The sullen margin of Loch Voil,
Waked still Loch Doine, and to the
   source
Alarm'd, Balvaig, thy swampy course ;
Thence southward turn'd its rapid
   road
Adown Strath-Gartney's valley broad,
Till rose in arms each man might claim
A portion in Clan-Alpine's name,
From the grey sire, whose trembling
   hand
Could hardly buckle on his brand,
To the raw boy, whose shaft and bow
Were yet scarce terror to the crow.
Each valley, each sequester'd glen,
Muster'd its little horde of men,
That met as torrents from the height
In Highland dales their streams unite,
Still gathering, as they pour along,
A voice more loud, a tide more strong,
Till at the rendezvous they stood
By hundreds prompt for blows and
   blood ;
Each train'd to arms since life began,
Owning no tie but to his clan,
No oath, but by his chieftain's hand,
No law, but Roderick Dhu's command.

XXV.

That summer morn had Roderick Dhu
Survey'd the skirts of Benvenue,
And sent his scouts o'er hill and heath,
To view the frontiers of Menteith.

All backward came with news of truce ;
Still lay each martial Græme and Bruce,
In Rednoch courts no horsemen wait,
No banner waved on Cardross gate,
On Duchray's towers no beacon shone,
Nor scared the herons from Loch Con ;
All seem'd at peace.—Now, wot ye
   why
The Chieftain, with such anxious eye,
Ere to the muster he repair,
This western frontier scann'd with
   care ?—
In Benvenue's most darksome cleft,
A fair, though cruel, pledge was left ;
For Douglas, to his promise true,
That morning from the isle withdrew,
And in a deep sequester'd dell
Had sought a low and lonely cell.
By many a bard, in Celtic tongue,
Has Coir-nan-Uriskin been sung ;
A softer name the Saxons gave,
And call'd the grot the Goblin-cave.

XXVI.

It was a wild and strange retreat,
As e'er was trod by outlaw's feet.
The dell, upon the mountain's crest,
Yawn'd like a gash on warrior's breast ;
Its trench had staid full many a rock,
Hurl'd by primeval earthquake shock
From Benvenue's grey summit wild,
And here, in random ruin piled,
They frown'd incumbent o'er the spot,
And form'd the rugged silvan grot.
The oak and birch, with mingled shade,
At noontide there a twilight made,
Unless when short and sudden shone
Some straggling beam on cliff or stone,
With such a glimpse as prophet's eye
Gains on thy depth, Futurity.
No murmur waked the solemn still,
Save tinkling of a fountain rill ;
But when the wind chafed with the
   lake,
A sullen sound would upward break,
With dashing hollow voice, that spoke
The incessant war of wave and rock.

Suspended cliffs, with hideous sway,
Seem'd nodding o'er the cavern grey.
From such a den the wolf had sprung,
In such the wild-cat leaves her young ;
Yet Douglas and his daughter fair
Sought for a space their safety there.
Grey Superstition's whisper dread
Debarr'd the spot to vulgar tread ;
For there, she said, did fays resort,
And satyrs hold their silvan court,
By moonlight tread their mystic maze,
And blast the rash beholder's gaze.

XXVII.

Now eve, with western shadows long,
Floated on Katrine bright and strong,
When Roderick, with a chosen few,
Repass'd the heights of Benvenue.
Above the Goblin-cave they go,
Through the wild pass of Beal-nam-bo :
The prompt retainers speed before,
To launch the shallop from the shore,
For cross Loch Katrine lies his way
To view the passes of Achray,
And place his clansmen in array.
Yet lags the chief in musing mind,
Unwonted sight, his men behind.
A single page, to bear his sword,
Alone attended on his lord ;
The rest their way through thickets
    break,
And soon await him by the lake.
It was a fair and gallant sight,
To view them from the neighbouring
    height,
By the low-levell'd sunbeam's light !
For strength and stature, from the
    clan
Each warrior was a chosen man,
As even afar might well be seen,
By their proud step and martial mien.
Their feathers dance, their tartans
    float,
Their targets gleam, as by the boat
A wild and warlike group they stand,
That well became such mountain-
    strand.

XXVIII.

Their Chief, with step reluctant, still
Was lingering on the craggy hill,
Hard by where turn'd apart the road
To Douglas's obscure abode.
It was but with that dawning morn,
That Roderick Dhu had proudly sworn
To drown his love in war's wild roar,
Nor think of Ellen Douglas more ;
But he who stems a stream with sand,
And fetters flame with flaxen band,
Has yet a harder task to prove,
By firm resolve to conquer love !
Eve finds the Chief, like restless ghost,
Still hovering near his treasure lost ;
For though his haughty heart deny
A parting meeting to his eye,
Still fondly strains his anxious ear,
The accents of her voice to hear,
And inly did he curse the breeze
That waked to sound the rustling trees.
But hark ! what mingles in the strain ?
It is the harp of Allan-Bane,
That wakes its measure slow and high,
Attuned to sacred minstrelsy.
What melting voice attends the strings ?
'Tis Ellen, or an angel, sings.

XXIX.

HYMN TO THE VIRGIN.

'Ave Maria ! maiden mild !
    Listen to a maiden's prayer !
Thou canst hear though from the wild,
    Thou canst save amid despair.
Safe may we sleep beneath thy care,
    Though banish'd, outcast, and re-
       viled ;
Maiden ! hear a maiden's prayer—
    Mother, hear a suppliant child !
               Ave Maria !

Ave Maria ! undefiled !
    The flinty couch we now must share
Shall seem with down of eider piled,
    If thy protection hover there.

The murky cavern's heavy air
　Shall breathe of balm if thou hast
　　smiled ;
Then, Maiden ! hear a maiden's prayer;
　Mother, list a suppliant child !
　　　　　　　　　　Ave Maria !

Ave Maria ! stainless styled !
　Foul demons of the earth and air,
From this their wonted haunt exiled,
　Shall flee before thy presence fair.
We bow us to our lot of care,
　Beneath thy guidance reconciled ;
Hear for a maid a maiden's prayer,
　And for a father hear a child !
　　　　　　　　　Ave Maria ! '

xxx.

Died on the harp the closing hymn.
Unmoved in attitude and limb,
As list'ning still, Clan-Alpine's lord
Stood leaning on his heavy sword,
Until the page, with humble sign,
Twice pointed to the sun's decline.
Then while his plaid he round him cast,
'It is the last time, 'tis the last,'
He mutter'd thrice,—'the last time e'er
That angel voice shall Roderick hear !'
It was a goading thought—his stride
Hied hastier down the mountain-side ;
Sullen he flung him in the boat,
And instant 'cross the lake it shot.
They landed in that silvery bay,
And eastward held their hasty way,
Till, with the latest beams of light,
The band arrived on Lanrick height,
Where muster'd, in the vale below,
Clan-Alpine's men in martial show.

xxxi.

A various scene the clansmen made ;
Some sate, some stood, some slowly
　stray'd ;
But most, with mantles folded round,
Were couch'd to rest upon the ground,
Scarce to be known by curious eye,
From the deep heather where they lie,

So well was match'd the tartan screen
With heath-bell dark and brackens
　green ;
Unless where, here and there, a blade,
Or lance's point, a glimmer made,
Like glow-worm twinkling through
　the shade.
But when, advancing through the
　gloom,
They saw the Chieftain's eagle plume,
Their shout of welcome, shrill and wide,
Shook the steep mountain's steady side.
Thrice it arose, and lake and fell
Three times return'd the martial yell ;
It died upon Bochastle's plain,
And Silence claim'd her evening reign.

—◆—

Canto Fourth.

The Prophecy.

I.

' THE rose is fairest when 'tis budding
　new,
　And hope is brightest when it dawns
　　from fears ;
The rose is sweetest wash'd with
　morning dew,
　And love is loveliest when embalm'd
　　in tears.
O wilding rose, whom fancy thus en-
　dears,
　I bid your blossoms in my bonnet
　　wave,
Emblem of hope and love through
　future years ! '
　Thus spoke young Norman, heir of
　　Armandave,
What time the sun arose on Venna-
　char's broad wave.

II.

Such fond conceit, half said, half sung,
Love prompted to the bridegroom's
　tongue.

All while he stripp'd the wild-rose
    spray,
His axe and bow beside him lay,
For on a pass 'twixt lake and wood,
A wakeful sentinel he stood.
Hark! on the rock a footstep rung,
And instant to his arms he sprung.
' Stand, or thou diest!—What, Malise?
    soon
Art thou return'd from Braes of Doune.
By thy keen step and glance I know,
Thou bring'st us tidings of the foe.'
(For while the Fiery Cross hied on,
On distant scout had Malise gone.)
' Where sleeps the Chief?' the hench-
    man said.
' Apart, in yonder misty glade;
To his lone couch I'll be your guide;'
Then call'd a slumberer by his side,
And stirr'd him with his slacken'd
    bow—
' Up, up, Glentarkin! rouse thee, ho!
We seek the Chieftain; on the track,
Keep eagle watch till I come back.'

III.

Together up the pass they sped:
' What of the foemen?' Norman said.
' Varying reports from near and far;
This certain, that a band of war
Has for two days been ready boune,
At prompt command, to march from
    Doune;
King James the while, with princely
    powers,
Holds revelry in Stirling towers.
Soon will this dark and gathering cloud
Speak on our glens in thunder loud.
Inured to bide such bitter bout,
The warrior's plaid may bear it out;
But, Norman, how wilt thou provide
A shelter for thy bonny bride?'
' What! know ye not that Roderick's
    care
To the lone isle hath caused repair
Each maid and matron of the clan,
And every child and aged man

Unfit for arms; and given his charge,
Nor skiff nor shallop, boat nor barge,
Upon these lakes shall float at large,
But all beside the islet moor,
That such dear pledge may rest secure?'

IV.

' 'Tis well advised; the Chieftain's plan
Bespeaks the father of his clan.
But wherefore sleeps Sir Roderick Dhu
Apart from all his followers true?'
' It is, because last evening-tide
Brian an augury hath tried,
Of that dread kind which must not be
Unless in dread extremity,
The Taghairm call'd; by which, afar,
Our sires foresaw the events of war,
Duncraggan's milk-white bull they
    slew '—

MALISE.

' Ah! well the gallant brute I knew!
The choicest of the prey we had,
When swept our merry-men Gallangad.
His hide was snow, his horns were dark,
His red eye glow'd like fiery spark;
So fierce, so tameless, and so fleet,
Sore did he cumber our retreat,
And kept our stoutest kernes in awe,
Even at the pass of Beal 'maha.
But steep and flinty was the road,
And sharp the hurrying pikemen's
    goad,
And when we came to Dennan's Row,
A child might scatheless stroke his
    brow.'

V.

NORMAN.

' That bull was slain: his reeking hide
They stretch'd the cataract beside,
Whose waters their wild tumult toss
Adown the black and craggy boss
Of that huge cliff, whose ample verge
Tradition calls the Hero's Targe.
Couch'd on a shelve beneath its brink,
Close where the thundering torrents
    sink,

Rocking beneath their headlong sway,
And drizzled by the ceaseless spray,
Midst groan of rock, and roar of stream,
The wizard waits prophetic dream.
Nor distant rests the Chief ;—but hush !
See, gliding slow through mist and bush,
The hermit gains yon rock, and stands
To gaze upon our slumbering bands.
Seems he not, Malise, like a ghost,
That hovers o'er a slaughter'd host ?
Or raven on the blasted oak,
That, watching while the deer is broke,
His morsel claims with sullen croak ?'

MALISE.

'Peace ! peace ! to other than to me,
Thy words were evil augury ;
But still I hold Sir Roderick's blade
Clan-Alpine's omen and her aid,
Not aught that, glean'd from heaven or hell,
Yon fiend-begotten monk can tell.
The Chieftain joins him, see ; and now,
Together they descend the brow.'

VI.

And, as they came, with Alpine's Lord
The Hermit Monk held solemn word :
'Roderick ! it is a fearful strife,
For man endow'd with mortal life,
Whose shroud of sentient clay can still
Feel feverish pang and fainting chill,
Whose eye can stare in stony trance,
Whose hair can rouse like warrior's lance,—
'Tis hard for such to view unfurl'd
The curtain of the future world.
Yet—witness every quaking limb,
My sunken pulse, my eyeballs dim,
My soul with harrowing anguish torn—
This for my Chieftain have I borne !
The shapes that sought my fearful couch,
An human tongue may ne'er avouch ;
No mortal man, save he who, bred
Between the living and the dead,

Is gifted beyond nature's law,
Had e'er survived to say he saw.
At length the fateful answer came,
In characters of living flame !
Not spoke in word, nor blazed in scroll,
But borne and branded on my soul—
WHICH SPILLS THE FOREMOST FOEMAN'S LIFE,
THAT PARTY CONQUERS IN THE STRIFE !'

VII.

'Thanks, Brian, for thy zeal and care !
Good is thine augury, and fair.
Clan-Alpine ne'er in battle stood,
But first our broadswords tasted blood.
A surer victim still I know,
Self-offer'd to the auspicious blow :
A spy has sought my land this morn,—
No eve shall witness his return !
My followers guard each pass's mouth,
To east, to westward, and to south ;
Red Murdoch, bribed to be his guide,
Has charge to lead his steps aside,
Till, in deep path or dingle brown,
He light on those shall bring him down.
—But see who comes his news to show !
Malise ! what tidings of the foe ?'

VIII.

'At Doune, o'er many a spear and glaive
Two Barons proud their banners wave.
I saw the Moray's silver star,
And mark'd the sable pale of Mar.'
'By Alpine's soul, high tidings those !
I love to hear of worthy foes.
When move they on ?' 'To-morrow's noon
Will see them here for battle boune.'
'Then shall it see a meeting stern !
But, for the place—say, couldst thou learn
Nought of the friendly clans of Earn ?
Strengthen'd by them, we well might bide
The battle on Benledi's side.
Thou couldst not ? Well ! Clan-Alpine's men
Shall man the Trosachs' shaggy glen ;

Within Loch Katrine's gorge we 'll
    fight,
All in our maids' and matrons' sight,
Each for his hearth and household fire,
Father for child, and son for sire,
Lover for maid beloved!—But why—
Is it the breeze affects mine eye ?
Or dost thou come, ill-omen'd tear !
A messenger of doubt or fear ?
No ! sooner may the Saxon lance
Unfix Benledi from his stance,
Than doubt or terror can pierce through
The unyielding heart of Roderick Dhu !
'Tis stubborn as his trusty targe.
Each to his post—all know their charge.'
The pibroch sounds, the bands advance,
The broadswords gleam, the banners
    dance,
Obedient to the Chieftain's glance.
I turn me from the martial roar,
And seek Coir-Uriskin once more.

IX.

Where is the Douglas ?—he is gone ;
And Ellen sits on the grey stone
Fast by the cave, and makes her moan ;
While vainly Allan's words of cheer
Are pour'd on her unheeding ear :
'He will return—dear lady, trust !—
With joy return ; he will, he must.
Well was it time to seek afar
Some refuge from impending war,
When e'en Clan-Alpine's rugged
    swarm
Are cow'd by the approaching storm.
I saw their boats with many a light
Floating the live-long yesternight,
Shifting like flashes darted forth
By the red streamers of the north ;
I mark'd at morn how close they ride,
Thick moor'd by the lone islet's side,
Like wild-ducks couching in the fen,
When stoops the hawk upon the glen.
Since this rude race dare not abide
The peril on the mainland side,
Shall not thy noble father's care
Some safe retreat for thee prepare ? '

X.

ELLEN.

' No, Allan, no ! Pretext so kind
My wakeful terrors could not blind.
When in such tender tone, yet grave,
Douglas a parting blessing gave,
The tear that glisten'd in his eye
Drown'd not his purpose fix'd and high.
My soul, though feminine and weak,
Can image his ; e'en as the lake,
Itself disturb'd by slightest stroke,
Reflects the invulnerable rock.
He hears report of battle rife,
He deems himself the cause of strife,
I saw him redden, when the theme
Turn'd, Allan, on thine idle dream
Of Malcolm Græme in fetters bound,
Which I, thou saidst, about him wound.
Think'st thou he trow'd thine omen
    aught ?
Oh no ! 'twas apprehensive thought
For the kind youth,—for Roderick
    too—
(Let me be just) that friend so true ;
In danger both, and in our cause !
Minstrel, the Douglas dare not pause.
Why else that solemn warning given.
" If not on earth, we meet in heaven ! "
Why else, to Cambus-kenneth's fane,
If eve return him not again,
Am I to hie, and make me known ?
Alas ! he goes to Scotland's throne,
Buys his friend's safety with his own ;
He goes to do—what I had done,
Had Douglas' daughter been his son ! '

XI.

ALLAN.

' Nay, lovely Ellen !—dearest, nay !
If aught should his return delay,
He only named yon holy fane
As fitting place to meet again.
Be sure he 's safe ; and for the Græme,—
Heaven's blessing on his gallant name !
My vision'd sight may yet prove true,
Nor bode of ill to him or you.

When did my gifted dream beguile?
Think of the stranger at the isle,
And think upon the harpings slow,
That presaged this approaching woe!
Sooth was my prophecy of fear;
Believe it when it augurs cheer.
Would we had left this dismal spot!
Ill luck still haunts a fairy grot.
Of such a wondrous tale I know—
Dear lady, change that look of woe,
My harp was wont thy grief to cheer.'

ELLEN.

'Well, be it as thou wilt; I hear,
But cannot stop the bursting tear.'

The Minstrel tried his simple art,
But distant far was Ellen's heart:

XII.

BALLAD.

ALICE BRAND.

Merry it is in the good greenwood,
    When the mavis and merle are
        singing,
When the deer sweeps by, and the
        hounds are in cry,
    And the hunter's horn is ringing.

'O Alice Brand, my native land
    Is lost for love of you;
And we must hold by wood and wold,
    As outlaws wont to do.

'O Alice, 'twas all for thy locks so
        bright,
    And 'twas all for thine eyes so blue,
That on the night of our luckless flight
    Thy brother bold I slew.

'Now must I teach to hew the beech
    The hand that held the glaive,
For leaves to spread our lowly bed,
    And stakes to fence our cave.

'And for vest of pall, thy fingers small,
    That wont on harp to stray,
A cloak must shear from the slaughter'd
        deer,
    To keep the cold away.'

'O Richard! if my brother died,
    'Twas but a fatal chance;
For darkling was the battle tried,
    And fortune sped the lance.

'If pall and vair no more I wear,
    Nor thou the crimson sheen,
As warm, we'll say, is the russet grey,
    As gay the forest-green.

'And, Richard, if our lot be hard,
    And lost thy native land,
Still Alice has her own Richard,
    And he his Alice Brand.'

XIII.

'Tis merry, 'tis merry, in good green-
        wood,
    So blithe Lady Alice is singing;
On the beech's pride, and oak's brown
        side,
    Lord Richard's axe is ringing.

Up spoke the moody Elfin King,
    Who won'd within the hill;
Like wind in the porch of a ruin'd
        church,
    His voice was ghostly shrill.

'Why sounds yon stroke on beech
        and oak,
    Our moonlight circle's screen?
Or who comes here to chase the deer,
    Beloved of our Elfin Queen?
Or who may dare on wold to wear
    The fairies' fatal green?

'Up, Urgan, up! to yon mortal hie,
    For thou wert christen'd man;
For cross or sign thou wilt not fly,
    For mutter'd word or ban.

'Lay on him the curse of the wither'd
        heart,
    The curse of the sleepless eye;
Till he wish and pray that his life would
        part,
    Nor yet find leave to die.'

XIV.

'Tis merry, 'tis merry, in good green-
wood,
  Though the birds have still'd their
    singing;
The evening blaze doth Alice raise,
  And Richard is fagots bringing.

Up Urgan starts, that hideous dwarf,
  Before Lord Richard stands,
And, as he cross'd and bless'd himself,
'I fear not sign,' quoth the grisly elf,
  'That is made with bloody hands.'

But out then spoke she, Alice Brand,
  That woman, void of fear,—
'And if there 's blood upon his hand,
  'Tis but the blood of deer.'

'Now loud thou liest, thou bold of mood!
  It cleaves unto his hand,
The stain of thine own kindly blood,
  The blood of Ethert Brand.'

Then forward stepp'd she, Alice Brand,
  And made the holy sign,—
'And if there 's blood on Richard's hand,
  A spotless hand is mine.'

'And I conjure thee, Demon elf,
  By Him whom Demons fear,
To show us whence thou art thyself,
  And what thine errand here?'

XV.

'"Tis merry, 'tis merry, in Fairy-land,
  When fairy birds are singing,
When the court doth ride by their
    monarch's side,
  With bit and bridle ringing:

'And gaily shines the Fairy-land—
  But all is glistening show,
Like the idle gleam that December's
    beam
  Can dart on ice and snow.

'And fading, like that varied gleam,
  Is our inconstant shape,
Who now like knight and lady seem,
  And now like dwarf and ape.

'It was between the night and day,
  When the Fairy King has power,
That I sunk down in a sinful fray,
And, 'twixt life and death, was snatch'd
    away
  To the joyless Elfin bower.

'But wist I of a woman bold,
  Who thrice my brow durst sign,
I might regain my mortal mold,
  As fair a form as thine.'

She cross'd him once, she cross'd him
    twice,
  That lady was so brave;
The fouler grew his goblin hue,
  The darker grew the cave.

She cross'd him thrice, that lady bold;
  He rose beneath her hand
The fairest knight on Scottish mold,
  Her brother, Ethert Brand!

Merry it is in good greenwood,
  When the mavis and merle are sing-
    ing,
But merrier were they in Dunfermline
    grey,
  When all the bells were ringing.

XVI.

Just as the minstrel sounds were staid,
A stranger climb'd the steepy glade:
His martial step, his stately mien,
His hunting suit of Lincoln green,
His eagle glance remembrance claims:
'Tis Snowdoun's Knight, 'tis James
    Fitz-James.
Ellen beheld as in a dream,
Then, starting, scarce suppress'd a
    scream:
'O stranger! in such hour of fear,
What evil hap has brought thee here?'
'An evil hap how can it be,
That bids me look again on thee?
By promise bound, my former guide
Met me betimes this morning tide,
And marshall'd, over bank and bourne,
The happy path of my return.'

'The happy path!—what! said he
nought
Of war, of battle to be fought,
Of guarded pass?' 'No, by my faith!
Nor saw I aught could augur scathe.'
'O haste thee, Allan, to the kern,—
Yonder his tartans I discern;
Learn thou his purpose, and conjure
That he will guide the stranger sure!
What prompted thee, unhappy man?
The meanest serf in Roderick's clan
Had not been bribed by love or fear,
Unknown to him to guide thee here.'

XVII.

'Sweet Ellen, dear my life must be,
Since it is worthy care from thee;
Yet life I hold but idle breath,
When love or honour's weigh'd with
death.
Then let me profit by my chance,
And speak my purpose bold at once.
I come to bear thee from a wild,
Where ne'er before such blossom
smiled;
By this soft hand to lead thee far
From frantic scenes of feud and war.
Near Bochastle my horses wait;
They bear us soon to Stirling gate.
I'll place thee in a lovely bower,
I'll guard thee like a tender flower'—
'O! hush, Sir Knight! 'twere female art,
To say I do not read thy heart;
Too much, before, my selfish ear
Was idly soothed my praise to hear.
That fatal bait hath lured thee back,
In deathful hour, o'er dangerous track;
And how, O how, can I atone
The wreck my vanity brought on!
One way remains—I'll tell him all;
Yes! struggling bosom, forth it shall!
Thou, whose light folly bears the blame,
Buy thine own pardon with thy shame!
But first, my father is a man
Outlaw'd and exiled under ban;
The price of blood is on his head;
With me 'twere infamy to wed.

Still wouldst thou speak? then hear
the truth!
Fitz-James, there is a noble youth,
If yet he is! exposed for me
And mine to dread extremity—
Thou hast the secret of my heart;
Forgive, be generous, and depart!'

XVIII.

Fitz-James knew every wily train
A lady's fickle heart to gain;
But here he knew and felt them vain.
There shot no glance from Ellen's eye,
To give her steadfast speech the lie;
In maiden confidence she stood,
Though mantled in her cheek the blood,
And told her love with such a sigh
Of deep and hopeless agony,
As death had seal'd her Malcolm's
doom,
And she sat sorrowing on his tomb.
Hope vanish'd from Fitz-James's eye,
But not with hope fled sympathy.
He proffer'd to attend her side,
As brother would a sister guide.
'O! little know'st thou Roderick's
heart!
Safer for both we go apart.
O haste thee, and from Allan learn,
If thou may'st trust yon wily kern.'
With hand upon his forehead laid,
The conflict of his mind to shade,
A parting step or two he made;
Then, as some thought had cross'd his
brain,
He paused, and turn'd, and came again.

XIX.

'Hear, lady, yet, a parting word!
It chanced in fight that my poor sword
Preserved the life of Scotland's lord.
This ring the grateful Monarch gave,
And bade, when I had boon to crave,
To bring it back, and boldly claim
The recompense that I would name.
Ellen, I am no courtly lord,
But one who lives by lance and sword,

Whose castle is his helm and shield,
His lordship the embattled field.
What from a prince can I demand,
Who neither reck of state nor land?
Ellen, thy hand—the ring is thine;
Each guard and usher knows the sign.
Seek thou the King without delay;
This signet shall secure thy way;
And claim thy suit, whate'er it be,
As ransom of his pledge to me.'
He placed the golden circlet on,
Paused, kiss'd her hand, and then was
　　gone.
The aged Minstrel stood aghast,
So hastily Fitz-James shot past.
He join'd his guide, and wending down
The ridges of the mountain brown,
Across the stream they took their way,
That joins Loch Katrine to Achray.

XX.

All in the Trosachs' glen was still,
Noontide was sleeping on the hill:
Sudden his guide whoop'd loud and
　　high—
'Murdoch! was that a signal cry?'
He stammer'd forth, 'I shout to scare
Yon raven from his dainty fare.'
He look'd, he knew the raven's prey—
His own brave steed :—'Ah! gallant
　　grey!
For thee, for me perchance, 'twere well
We ne'er had seen the Trosachs' dell.
Murdoch, move first—but silently;
Whistle or whoop, and thou shalt die!'
Jealous and sullen, on they fared,
Each silent, each upon his guard.

XXI.

Now wound the path its dizzy ledge
Around a precipice's edge,
When lo! a wasted female form,
Blighted by wrath of sun and storm,
In tatter'd weeds and wild array,
Stood on a cliff beside the way,
And glancing round her restless eye,
Upon the wood, the rock, the sky,

Seem'd nought to mark, yet all to
　　spy.
Her brow was wreath'd with gaudy
　　broom;
With gesture wild she waved a plume
Of feathers, which the eagles fling
To crag and cliff from dusky wing;
Such spoils her desperate step had
　　sought,
Where scarce was footing for the goat.
The tartan plaid she first descried,
And shriek'd till all the rocks replied;
As loud she laugh'd when near they
　　drew,
For then the Lowland garb she knew;
And then her hands she wildly wrung,
And then she wept, and then she sung.
She sung!—the voice, in better time,
Perchance to harp or lute might chime;
And now, though strain'd and rough-
　　en'd, still
Rung wildly sweet to dale and hill:

XXII

SONG.

'They bid me sleep, they bid me pray,
　　They say my brain is warp'd and
　　　wrung;
I cannot sleep on Highland brae,
　　I cannot pray in Highland tongue.
But were I now where Allan glides,
Or heard my native Devan's tides,
So sweetly would I rest and pray
That Heaven would close my wintry
　　day!

''Twas thus my hair they bade me braid,
　　They made me to the church repair;
It was my bridal morn, they said,
　　And my true love would meet me
　　　there.
But woe betide the cruel guile,
That drown'd in blood the morning
　　smile!
And woe betide the fairy dream!
I only waked to sob and scream.'

XXIII.

'Who is this maid? what means her lay?
She hovers o'er the hollow way,
And flutters wide her mantle grey,
As the lone heron spreads his wing,
By twilight, o'er a haunted spring.'
' 'Tis Blanche of Devan,' Murdoch said,
'A crazed and captive Lowland maid,
Ta'en on the morn she was a bride,
When Roderick foray'd Devan-side.
The gay bridegroom resistance made,
And felt our Chief's unconquer'd blade;
I marvel she is now at large,
But oft she 'scapes from Maudlin's
      charge.
Hence, brain-sick fool!' He raised his
      bow:
' Now if thou strik'st her but one blow,
I'll pitch thee from the cliff as far
As ever peasant pitch'd a bar!'
'Thanks, champion, thanks!' the
      maniac cried,
And press'd her to Fitz-James's side;
' See the grey pennons I prepare
To seek my true-love through the air!
I will not lend that savage groom,
To break his fall, one downy plume!
No! deep amid disjointed stones,
The wolves shall batten on his bones,
And then shall his detested plaid,
By bush and brier in mid-air staid,
Wave forth a banner fair and free,
Meet signal for their revelry.'

XXIV.

' Hush thee, poor maiden, and be still!'
' O! thou look'st kindly, and I will.
Mine eye has dried and wasted been,
But still it loves the Lincoln green;
And, though mine ear is all unstrung,
Still, still it loves the Lowland tongue.

' For O my sweet William was
      forester true,
      He stole poor Blanche's heart
      away!

His coat it was all of the greenwood
      hue,
      And so blithely he trill'd the
      Lowland lay!

' It was not that I meant to tell . . .
But thou art wise and guessest well.'
Then, in a low and broken tone,
And hurried note, the song went on.
Still on the Clansman, fearfully,
She fix'd her apprehensive eye;
Then turn'd it on the Knight, and then
Her look glanced wildly o'er the glen.

XXV.

' The toils are pitch'd, and the stakes
      are set,
      Ever sing merrily, merrily;
The bows they bend, and the knives
      they whet,
      Hunters live so cheerily.

' It was a stag, a stag of ten,
      Bearing its branches sturdily;
He came stately down the glen,
      Ever sing hardily, hardily.

' It was there he met with a wounded
      doe,
      She was bleeding deathfully;
She warn'd him of the toils below,
      O, so faithfully, faithfully!

' He had an eye, and he could heed,
      Ever sing warily, warily;
He had a foot, and he could speed—
      Hunters watch so narrowly.'

XXVI.

Fitz-James's mind was passion-toss'd,
When Ellen's hints and fears were lost;
But   Murdoch's   shout   suspicion
      wrought,
And Blanche's song conviction brought.
Not like a stag that spies the snare,
But lion of the hunt aware,
He waved at once his blade on high,
' Disclose thy treachery, or die!'

I

Forth at full speed the Clansman flew,
But in his race his bow he drew.
The shaft just grazed Fitz-James's crest,
And thrill'd in Blanche's faded breast !
Murdoch of Alpine ! prove thy speed,
For ne'er had Alpine's son such need !
With heart of fire, and foot of wind,
The fierce avenger is behind !
Fate judges of the rapid strife—
The forfeit death—the prize is life !
Thy kindred ambush lies before,
Close couch'd upon the heathery moor ;
Them couldst thou reach !—it may
    not be—
Thine ambush'd kin thou ne'er shalt see,
The fiery Saxon gains on thee !
—Resistless speeds the deadly thrust,
As lightning strikes the pine to dust ;
With foot and hand Fitz-James must
    strain,
Ere he can win his blade again.
Bent o'er the fall'n, with falcon eye,
He grimly smiled to see him die ;
Then slower wended back his way,
Where the poor maiden bleeding lay.

XXVII.

She sate beneath the birchen-tree,
Her elbow resting on her knee ;
She had withdrawn the fatal shaft,
And gazed on it, and feebly laugh'd ;
Her wreath of broom and feathers grey,
Daggled with blood, beside her lay.
The Knight to stanch the life-stream
    tried ;
' Stranger, it is in vain !' she cried.
' This hour of death has given me more
Of reason's power than years before ;
For, as these ebbing veins decay,
My frenzied visions fade away.
A helpless injured wretch I die,
And something tells me in thine eye,
That thou wert mine avenger born.—
Seest thou this tress ?—O ! still I 've
    worn
This little tress of yellow hair,
Through danger, frenzy, and despair !

It once was bright and clear as thine,
But blood and tears have dimm'd its
    shine.
I will not tell thee when 'twas shred,
Nor from what guiltless victim's head—
My brain would turn !—but it shall
    wave
Like plumage on thy helmet brave,
Till sun and wind shall bleach the
    stain,
And thou wilt bring it me again.—
I waver still. O God ! more bright
Let reason beam her parting light !
O ! by thy knighthood's honour'd sign,
And for thy life preserved by mine,
When thou shalt see a darksome man,
Who boasts him Chief of Alpine's
    Clan,
With tartans broad, and shadowy
    plume,
And hand of blood, and brow of gloom,
Be thy heart bold, thy weapon strong,
And wreak poor Blanche of Devan's
    wrong !
They watch for thee by pass and
    fell . . .
Avoid the path . . . O God ! . . .
    farewell.'

XXVIII.

A kindly heart had brave Fitz-James ;
Fast pour'd his eyes at pity's claims ;
And now, with mingled grief and ire,
He saw the murder'd maid expire.
' God, in my need, be my relief,
As I wreak this on yonder Chief !'
A lock from Blanche's tresses fair
He blended with her bridegroom's hair ;
The mingled braid in blood he dyed,
And placed it on his bonnet-side :
' By Him whose word is truth ! I swear,
No other favour will I wear,
Till this sad token I imbrue
In the best blood of Roderick Dhu !
But hark ! what means yon faint halloo !
The chase is up ; but they shall know,
The stag at bay 's a dangerous foe.'

Barr'd from the known but guarded
    way,
Through copse and cliffs Fitz-James
    must stray,
And oft must change his desperate track,
By stream and precipice turn'd back.
Heartless, fatigued, and faint, at length,
From lack of food and loss of strength,
He couch'd him in a thicket hoar,
And thought his toils and perils o'er:
'Of all my rash adventures past,
This frantic feat must prove the last!
Who e'er so mad but might have guess'd,
That all this Highland hornet's nest
Would muster up in swarms so soon
As e'er they heard of bands at Doune?
Like bloodhounds now they search
    me out,—
Hark, to the whistle and the shout!—
If farther through the wilds I go,
I only fall upon the foe:
I'll couch me here till evening grey,
Then darkling try my dangerous way.'

XXIX.

The shades of eve come slowly down,
The woods are wrapt in deeper brown,
The owl awakens from her dell,
The fox is heard upon the fell;
Enough remains of glimmering light
To guide the wanderer's steps aright,
Yet not enough from far to show
His figure to the watchful foe.
With cautious step, and ear awake,
He climbs the crag and threads the
    brake;
And not the summer solstice, there,
Temper'd the midnight mountain air,
But every breeze, that swept the wold,
Benumb'd his drenched limbs with
    cold.
In dread, in danger, and alone,
Famish'd and chill'd, through ways
    unknown,
Tanglèd and steep, he journey'd on;
Till, as a rock's huge point he turn'd,
A watch-fire close before him burn'd.

XXX.

Beside its embers red and clear,
Bask'd in his plaid a mountaineer;
And up he sprung with sword in hand,—
'Thy name and purpose! Saxon,
    stand!'
'A stranger.' 'What dost thou re-
    quire?'
'Rest and a guide, and food and fire.
My life's beset, my path is lost,
The gale has chill'd my limbs with frost.'
'Art thou a friend to Roderick?' 'No.'
'Thou darest not call thyself a foe?'
'I dare! to him and all the band
He brings to aid his murderous hand.'
'Bold words! but, though the beast
    of game
The privilege of chase may claim,
Though space and law the stag we lend,
Ere hound we slip, or bow we bend,
Who ever reck'd, where, how, or when,
The prowling fox was trapp'd or slain?
Thus treacherous scouts,—yet sure
    they lie
Who say thou cam'st a secret spy!'
'They do, by heaven! Come Roderick
    Dhu,
And of his clan the boldest two,
And let me but till morning rest,
I write the falsehood on their crest.'
'If by the blaze I mark aright,
Thou bear'st the belt and spur of
    Knight.'
'Then by these tokens mayest thou
    know
Each proud oppressor's mortal foe.'
'Enough, enough; sit down and share
A soldier's couch, a soldier's fare.'

XXXI.

He gave him of his Highland cheer,
The harden'd flesh of mountain deer;
Dry fuel on the fire he laid,
And bade the Saxon share his plaid.
He tended him like welcome guest,
Then thus his farther speech address'd:

'Stranger, I am to Roderick Dhu
A clansman born, a kinsman true;
Each word against his honour spoke,
Demands of me avenging stroke;
Yet more,—upon thy fate, 'tis said,
A mighty augury is laid.
It rests with me to wind my horn,—
Thou art with numbers overborne;
It rests with me, here, brand to brand,
Worn as thou art, to bid thee stand:
But, not for clan, nor kindred's cause,
Will I depart from honour's laws;
To assail a wearied man were shame,
And stranger is a holy name;
Guidance and rest, and food and fire,
In vain he never must require.
Then rest thee here till dawn of day;
Myself will guide thee on the way,
O'er stock and stone, through watch
       and ward,
Till past Clan-Alpine's outmost guard,
As far as Coilantogle's ford;
From thence thy warrant is thy sword.'
'I take thy courtesy, by heaven,
As freely as 'tis nobly given!'
'Well, rest thee; for the bittern's cry
Sings us the lake's wild lullaby.'
With that he shook the gather'd heath,
And spread his plaid upon the wreath;
And the brave foemen, side by side,
Lay peaceful down, like brothers tried,
And slept until the dawning beam
Purpled the mountain and the stream.

——◆◆——

Canto Fifth.

The Combat.

I.

FAIR as the earliest beam of eastern
       light,
   When first, by the bewilder'd pil-
       grim spied,
It smiles upon the dreary brow of night,
   And silvers o'er the torrent's foaming
       tide,

And lights the fearful path on moun-
       tain side,—
   Fair as that beam, although the
       fairest far,
Giving to horror grace, to danger
       pride,
   Shine martial Faith, and Courtesy's
       bright star,
Through all the wreckful storms that
       cloud the brow of War.

II.

That early beam, so fair and sheen,
Was twinkling through the hazel
       screen,
When, rousing at its glimmer red,
The warriors left their lowly bed,
Look'd out upon the dappled sky,
Mutter'd their soldier matins by,
And then awaked their fire, to steal,
As short and rude, their soldier meal.
That o'er, the Gael around him threw
His graceful plaid of varied hue,
And, true to promise, led the way,
By thicket green and mountain grey.
A wildering path! they winded now
Along the precipice's brow,
Commanding the rich scenes beneath,
The windings of the Forth and Teith,
And all the vales beneath that lie,
Till Stirling's turrets melt in sky;
Then, sunk in copse, their farthest
       glance
Gain'd not the length of horseman's
       lance.
'Twas oft so steep, the foot was fain
Assistance from the hand to gain;
So tangled oft, that, bursting through,
Each hawthorn shed her showers of
       dew,—
That diamond dew, so pure and clear,
It rivals all but Beauty's tear.

III.

At length they came where, stern and
       steep,
The hill sinks down upon the deep

Here Vennachar in silver flows,
There, ridge on ridge, Benledi rose;
Ever the hollow path twined on,
Beneath steep bank and threatening
    stone;
An hundred men might hold the post
With hardihood against a host.
The rugged mountain's scanty cloak
Was dwarfish shrubs of birch and oak,
With shingles bare, and cliffs between,
And patches bright of bracken green,
And heather black, that waved so high,
It held the copse in rivalry.
But where the lake slept deep and still,
Dank osiers fringed the swamp and hill;
And oft both path and hill were torn,
Where wintry torrents down had
    borne,
And heap'd upon the cumber'd land
Its wreck of gravel, rocks. and sand.
So toilsome was the road to trace,
The guide, abating of his pace,
Led slowly through the pass's jaws,
And ask'd Fitz-James, by what strange
    cause
He sought these wilds, traversed by
    few,
Without a pass from Roderick Dhu.

IV.

'Brave Gael, my pass in danger tried,
Hangs in my belt, and by my side;
Yet, sooth to tell,' the Saxon said,
'I dreamt not now to claim its aid.
When here, but three days since,
    I came,
Bewilder'd in pursuit of game,
All seem'd as peaceful and as still
As the mist slumbering on yon hill;
Thy dangerous Chief was then afar,
Nor soon expected back from war.
Thus said, at least, my mountain-
    guide,
Though deep, perchance, the villain
    lied.'
'Yet why a second venture try?'
'A warrior thou, and ask me why?

Moves our free course by such fix'd
    cause
As gives the poor mechanic laws?
Enough, I sought to drive away
The lazy hours of peaceful day;
Slight cause will then suffice to guide
A Knight's free footsteps far and
    wide,—
A falcon flown, a greyhound stray'd,
The merry glance of mountain maid:
Or, if a path be dangerous known,
The danger's self is lure alone.'

v.

'Thy secret keep, I urge thee not;
Yet, ere again ye sought this spot,
Say, heard ye nought of Lowland war,
Against Clan-Alpine, raised by Mar?'
'No, by my word;—of bands prepared
To guard King James's sports I heard;
Nor doubt I aught, but, when they hear
This muster of the mountaineer,
Their pennons will abroad be flung,
Which else in Doune had peaceful
    hung.'
'Free be they flung! for we were loth
Their silken folds should feast the moth.
Free be they flung! as free shall wave
Clan-Alpine's pine in banner brave.
But, Stranger, peaceful since you came,
Bewilder'd in the mountain game,
Whence the bold boast by which you
    show
V'ch-Alpine's vow'd and mortal foe?'
'Warrior, but yester-morn, I knew
Nought of thy Chieftain, Roderick
    Dhu,
Save as an outlaw'd desperate man,
The chief of a rebellious clan,
Who, in the Regent's court and sight,
With ruffian dagger stabb'd a knight;
Yet this alone might from his part
Sever each true and loyal heart.'

VI.

Wrothful at such arraignment foul,
Dark lower'd the clansman's sable
    scowl.

A space he paused, then sternly said,
'And heard'st thou why he drew his
    blade ?
Heard'st thou that shameful word and
    blow
Brought Roderick's vengeance on his
    foe ?
What reck'd the Chieftain if he stood
On Highland heath, or Holy-Rood ?
He rights such wrong where it is given,
If it were in the court of heaven.'
'Still was it outrage ;— yet, 'tis true,
Not then claim'd sovereignty his due ;
While Albany, with feeble hand,
Held borrow'd truncheon of command,
The young King, mew'd in Stirling
    tower,
Was stranger to respect and power.
But then, thy Chieftain's robber life !
Winning mean prey by causeless strife,
Wrenching from ruin'd Lowland swain
His herds and harvest reared in vain.
Methinks a soul, like thine, should
    scorn
The spoils from such foul foray borne.'

VII.

The Gael beheld him grim the while,
And answer'd with disdainful smile,
'Saxon, from yonder mountain high,
I mark'd thee send delighted eye,
Far to the south and east, where lay,
Extended in succession gay,
Deep waving fields and pastures green,
With gentle slopes and groves be-
    tween :
These fertile plains, that soften'd vale,
Were once the birthright of the Gael ;
The stranger came with iron hand,
And from our fathers reft the land.
Where dwell we now ? See, rudely
    swell
Crag over crag, and fell o'er fell.
Ask we this savage hill we tread,
For fatten'd steer or household bread ;
Ask we for flocks these shingles dry,
And well the mountain might reply,—

"To you, as to your sires of yore,
Belong the target and claymore !
I give you shelter in my breast,
Your own good blades must win the
    rest."
Pent in this fortress of the North,
Think'st thou we will not sally forth,
To spoil the spoiler as we may,
And from the robber rend the prey ?
Ay, by my soul ! While on yon plain
The Saxon rears one shock of grain,
While of ten thousand herds there
    strays
But one along yon river's maze,
The Gael, of plain and river heir,
Shall with strong hand redeem his
    share.
Where live the mountain Chiefs who
    hold,
That plundering Lowland field and fold
Is aught but retribution true ?
Seek other cause 'gainst Roderick
    Dhu.'

VIII.

Answer'd Fitz-James, 'And, if I sought,
Think'st thou no other could be
    brought ?
What deem ye of my path waylaid ?
My life given o'er to ambuscade ?'
'As of a meed to rashness due :
Hadst thou sent warning fair and true—
I seek my hound, or falcon stray'd,
I seek, good faith, a Highland maid—
Free hadst thou been to come and go ;
But secret path marks secret foe.
Nor yet, for this, even as a spy,
Hadst thou unheard been doom'd to
    die,
Save to fulfil an augury.'
'Well, let it pass ; nor will I now
Fresh cause of enmity avow,
To chafe thy mood and cloud thy brow.
Enough, I am by promise tied
To match me with this man of pride :
Twice have I sought Clan-Alpine's glen
In peace ; but when I come agen,

I come with banner, brand, and bow,
As leader seeks his mortal foe.
For love-lorn swain, in lady's bower,
Ne'er panted for the appointed hour,
As I, until before me stand
This rebel Chieftain and his band!'

IX.

'Have, then, thy wish!' He whistled
　　shrill,
And he was answer'd from the hill;
Wild as the scream of the curlew,
From crag to crag the signal flew.
Instant, through copse and heath,
　　arose
Bonnets and spears and bended bows;
On right, on left, above, below,
Sprung up at once the lurking foe;
From shingles grey their lances start,
The bracken bush sends forth the
　　dart,
The rushes and the willow-wand
Are bristling into axe and brand,
And every tuft of broom gives life
To plaided warrior arm'd for strife.
That whistle garrison'd the glen
At once with full five hundred men,
As if the yawning hill to heaven
A subterranean host had given.
Watching their leader's beck and will,
All silent there they stood, and still.
Like the loose crags, whose threatening
　　mass
Lay tottering o'er the hollow pass,
As if an infant's touch could urge
Their headlong passage down the
　　verge,
With step and weapon forward flung,
Upon the mountain-side they hung.
The Mountaineer cast glance of pride
Along Benledi's living side,
Then fix'd his eye and sable brow
Full on Fitz-James—'How say'st thou
　　now?
These are Clan-Alpine's warriors
　　true;
And, Saxon,—I am Roderick Dhu!'

X.

Fitz-James was brave.　Though to his
　　heart
The life-blood thrill'd with sudden start,
He mann'd himself with dauntless air,
Return'd the Chief his haughty stare,
His back against a rock he bore,
And firmly placed his foot before:
'Come one, come all! this rock shall fly
From its firm base as soon as I.'
Sir Roderick mark'd, and in his eyes
Respect was mingled with surprise,
And the stern joy which warriors feel
In foemen worthy of their steel.
Short space he stood, then waved his
　　hand:
Down sunk the disappearing band;
Each warrior vanish'd where he stood,
In broom or bracken, heath or wood;
Sunk brand and spear and bended bow,
In osiers pale and copses low;
It seem'd as if their mother Earth
Had swallow'd up her warlike birth.
The wind's last breath had toss'd in air
Pennon, and plaid, and plumage fair;
The next but swept a lone hill-side,
Where heath and fern were waving
　　wide:
The sun's last glance was glinted back,
From spear and glaive, from targe and
　　jack;
The next, all unreflected, shone
On bracken green and cold grey stone.

XI.

Fitz-James look'd round, yet scarce
　　believed
The witness that his sight received;
Such apparition well might seem
Delusion of a dreadful dream.
Sir Roderick in suspense he eyed,
And to his look the Chief replied,
'Fear nought—nay, that I need not
　　say—
But doubt not aught from mine array.
Thou art my guest; I pledged my word
As far as Coilantogle ford:

Nor would I call a clansman's brand
For aid against one valiant hand,
Though on our strife lay every vale
Rent by the Saxon from the Gael.
So move we on; I only meant
To show the reed on which you leant,
Deeming this path you might pursue
Without a pass from Roderick Dhu.'
They moved. I said Fitz-James was brave
As ever knight that belted glaive,
Yet dare not say that now his blood
Kept on its wont and temper'd flood,
As, following Roderick's stride, he drew
That seeming lonesome pathway through,
Which yet, by fearful proof, was rife
With lances, that, to take his life,
Waited but signal from a guide
So late dishonour'd and defied.
Ever, by stealth, his eye sought round
The vanish'd guardians of the ground,
And still, from copse and heather deep,
Fancy saw spear and broadsword peep,
And in the plover's shrilly strain,
The signal-whistle heard again.
Nor breathed he free till far behind
The pass was left; for then they wind
Along a wide and level green,
Where neither tree nor tuft was seen,
Nor rush nor bush of broom was near,
To hide a bonnet or a spear.

XII.

The Chief in silence strode before,
And reach'd that torrent's sounding shore,
Which, daughter of three mighty lakes,
From Vennachar in silver breaks,
Sweeps through the plain, and ceaseless mines
On Bochastle the mouldering lines,
Where Rome, the Empress of the world,
Of yore her eagle wings unfurl'd.
And here his course the Chieftain staid,
Threw down his target and his plaid,
And to the Lowland warrior said:

' Bold Saxon! to his promise just,
Vich-Alpine has discharged his trust.
This murderous Chief, this ruthless man,
This head of a rebellious clan,
Hath led thee safe, through watch and ward,
Far past Clan-Alpine's outmost guard.
Now man to man, and steel to steel,
A Chieftain's vengeance thou shalt feel.
See here, all vantageless I stand,
Arm'd like thyself with single brand:
For this is Coilantogle ford,
And thou must keep thee with thy sword.'

XIII.

The Saxon paused: ' I ne'er delay'd,
When foeman bade me draw my blade;
Nay, more, brave Chief, I vow'd thy death;
Yet sure thy fair and generous faith,
And my deep debt for life preserved,
A better meed have well deserved:
Can nought but blood our feud atone?
Are there no means?' ' No, Stranger, none!
And hear, to fire thy flagging zeal, —
The Saxon cause rests on thy steel;
For thus spoke Fate, by prophet bred
Between the living and the dead:
"Who spills the foremost foeman's life
His party conquers in the strife."'
' Then, by my word,' the Saxon said,
' The riddle is already read.
Seek yonder brake beneath the cliff;
There lies Red Murdoch, stark and stiff.
Thus Fate has solved her prophecy,
Then yield to Fate, and not to me.
To James, at Stirling, let us go,
When, if thou wilt be still his foe,
Or if the King shall not agree
To grant thee grace and favour free,
I plight mine honour, oath, and word,
That, to thy native strengths restored,
With each advantage shalt thou stand,
That aids thee now, to guard thy land.'

XIV.

Dark lightning flash'd from Roderick's
    eye:
'Soars thy presumption, then, so high,
Because a wretched kern ye slew,
Homage to name to Roderick Dhu?
He yields not, he, to man nor Fate!
Thou add'st but fuel to my hate:
My clansman's blood demands revenge.
Not yet prepared? By heaven, I change
My thought, and hold thy valour light
As that of some vain carpet knight,
Who ill deserved my courteous care,
And whose best boast is but to wear
A braid of his fair lady's hair.'
'I thank thee, Roderick, for the word!
It nerves my heart, it steels my sword;
For I have sworn this braid to stain
In the best blood that warms thy vein.
Now, truce, farewell! and, ruth,
    begone!
Yet think not that by thee alone,
Proud Chief! can courtesy be shown;
Though not from copse, or heath, or
    cairn,
Start at my whistle clansmen stern,
Of this small horn one feeble blast
Would fearful odds against thee cast.
But fear not, doubt not—which thou
    wilt—
We try this quarrel hilt to hilt.'—
Then each at once his falchion drew,
Each on the ground his scabbard threw,
Each look d to sun, and stream, and
    plain,
As what he ne'er might see again;
Then foot, and point, and eye opposed,
In dubious strife they darkly closed.

XV.

Ill fared it then with Roderick Dhu,
That on the field his targe he threw,
Whose brazen studs and tough bull-
    hide
Had death so often dash'd aside;
For, train'd abroad his arms to wield,
Fitz-James's blade was sword and
    shield.

He practised every pass and ward,
To thrust, to strike, to feint, to guard;
While less expert, though stronger
    far,
The Gael maintain'd unequal war.
Three times in closing strife they stood,
And thrice the Saxon blade drank
    blood;
No stinted draught, no scanty tide,
The gushing flood the tartans dyed.
Fierce Roderick felt the fatal drain,
And shower'd his blows like wintry
    rain;
And, as firm rock, or castle-roof,
Against the winter shower is proof,
The foe, invulnerable still,
Foil'd his wild rage by steady skill;
Till, at advantage ta'en, his brand
Forced Roderick's weapon from his
    hand,
And backward borne upon the lea,
Brought the proud Chieftain to his
    knee.

XVI.

'Now, yield thee, or by Him who made
The world, thy heart's blood dyes my
    blade!'
'Thy threats, thy mercy, I defy!
Let recreant yield, who fears to die.'
Like adder darting from his coil,
Like wolf that dashes through the toil,
Like mountain-cat who guards her
    young,
Full at Fitz-James's throat he sprung;
Received, but reck'd not of a wound,
And lock'd his arms his foeman round.
Now, gallant Saxon, hold thine own!
No maiden's hand is round thee thrown!
That desperate grasp thy frame might
    feel
Through bars of brass and triple steel!
They tug, they strain! down, down
    they go,
The Gael above, Fitz-James below.
The Chieftain's gripe his throat
    compress'd,
His knee was planted in his breast;

His clotted locks he backward threw,
Across his brow his hand he drew,
From blood and mist to clear his sight,
Then gleam'd aloft his dagger bright !
But hate and fury ill supplied
The stream of life's exhausted tide,
And all too late the advantage came,
To turn the odds of deadly game ;
For, while the dagger gleam'd on high,
Reel'd soul and sense, reel'd brain
and eye.
Down came the blow—but in the heath,
The erring blade found bloodless
sheath.
The struggling foe may now unclasp
The fainting Chief's relaxing grasp ;
Unwounded from the dreadful close,
But breathless all, Fitz-James arose.

XVII.

He falter'd thanks to Heaven for life,
Redeem'd, unhoped, from desperate
strife ;
Next on his foe his look he cast,
Whose every gasp appear'd his last ;
In Roderick's gore he dipt the braid—
'Poor Blanche ! thy wrongs are dearly
paid :
Yet with thy foe must die, or live,
The praise that Faith and Valour give.'
With that he blew a bugle-note,
Undid the collar from his throat,
Unbonneted, and by the wave
Sate down his brow and hands to lave.
Then faint afar are heard the feet
Of rushing steeds in gallop fleet ;
The sounds increase, and now are seen
Four mounted squires in Lincoln green ;
Two who bear lance, and two who lead,
By loosen'd rein, a saddled steed ;
Each onward held his headlong course,
And by Fitz-James rein'd up his horse,
With wonder view'd the bloody spot—
—'Exclaim not, gallants ! question not.
You, Herbert and Luffness, alight,
And bind the wounds of yonder knight ;
Let the grey palfrey bear his weight,

We destined for a fairer freight,
And bring him on to Stirling straight ;
I will before at better speed,
To seek fresh horse and fitting weed.
The sun rides high ; I must be boune,
To see the archer-game at noon ;
But lightly Bayard clears the lea.
De Vaux and Herries, follow me.

XVIII.

'Stand, Bayard, stand !' The steed
obey'd,
With arching neck and bended head,
And glancing eye and quivering ear,
As if he loved his lord to hear.
No foot Fitz-James in stirrup staid,
No grasp upon the saddle laid,
But wreath'd his left hand in the mane,
And lightly bounded from the plain,
Turn'd on the horse his armed heel,
And stirr'd his courage with the steel
Bounded the fiery steed in air,
The rider sate erect and fair,
Then like a bolt from steel crossbow
Forth launch'd, along the plain they
go.
They dash'd that rapid torrent through,
And up Carhonie's hill they flew ;
Still at the gallop prick'd the Knight,
His merry-men follow'd as they might.
Along thy banks, swift Teith ! they
ride,
And in the race they mock thy tide ;
Torry and Lendrick now are past,
And Deanstown lies behind them cast ;
They rise, the banner'd towers of
Doune,
They sink in distant woodland soon ;
Blair-Drummond sees the hoofs strike
fire,
They sweep like breeze through
Ochtertyre ;
They mark just glance and disappear
The lofty brow of ancient Kier ;
They bathe their courser's sweltering
sides,
Dark Forth ! amid thy sluggish tides,

And on the opposing shore take ground,
With plash, with scramble, and with
    bound.
Right-hand they leave thy cliffs, Craig-
    Forth !
And soon the bulwark of the North,
Grey Stirling, with her towers and
    town,
Upon their fleet career look'd down.

XIX.

As up the flinty path they strain'd
Sudden his steed the leader rein'd ;
A signal to his squire he flung,
Who instant to his stirrup sprung :
' Seest thou, De Vaux, yon woodsman
    grey,
Who town-ward holds the rocky way,
Of stature tall and poor array ?
Mark'st thou the firm, yet active stride,
With which he scales the mountain-
    side ?
Know'st thou from whence he comes,
    or whom ? '
' No, by my word ; a burly groom
He seems, who in the field or chase
A baron's train would nobly grace.'
' Out, out, De Vaux ! can fear supply,
And jealousy, no sharper eye ?
Afar, ere to the hill he drew,
That stately form and step I knew ;
Like form in Scotland is not seen,
Treads not such step on Scottish green.
'Tis James of Douglas, by Saint Serle !
The uncle of the banish'd Earl.
Away, away to court, to show
The near approach of dreaded foe :
The King must stand upon his guard ;
Douglas and he must meet prepared.'
Then right-hand wheel'd their steeds,
    and straight
They won the castle's postern gate.

XX.

The Douglas, who had bent his way
From Cambus-Kenneth's abbey grey,
Now, as he climb'd the rocky shelf,
Held sad communion with himself :

' Yes ! all is true my fears could frame ;
A prisoner lies the noble Græme,
And fiery Roderick soon will feel
The vengeance of the royal steel.
I, only I, can ward their fate ;
God grant the ransom come not late !
The Abbess hath her promise given
My child shall be the bride of Heaven ;
Be pardon'd one repining tear !
For He who gave her knows how
    dear,
How excellent—but that is by,
And now my business is to die.
Ye towers ! within whose circuit dread
A Douglas by his sovereign bled ;
And thou, O sad and fatal mound !
That oft hast heard the death-axe sound,
As on the noblest of the land
Fell the stern headsman's bloody hand,
The dungeon, block, and nameless
    tomb
Prepare, for Douglas seeks his doom !
But hark ! what blithe and jolly peal
Makes the Franciscan steeple reel ?
And see ! upon the crowded street,
In motley groups what masquers meet!
Banner and pageant, pipe and drum,
And merry morrice-dancers come.
I guess, by all this quaint array,
The burghers hold their sports to-day.
James will be there ; he loves such
    show,
Where the good yeoman bends his bow,
And the tough wrestler foils his foe,
As well as where, in proud career,
The high-born tilter shivers spear.
I'll follow to the Castle-park,
And play my prize ; King James shall
    mark
If age has tamed these sinews stark,
Whose force so oft, in happier days,
His boyish wonder loved to praise.'

XXI.

The Castle gates were open flung,
The quivering drawbridge rock'd and
    rung,

And echo'd loud the flinty street
Beneath the coursers' clattering feet,
As slowly down the steep descent
Fair Scotland's King and nobles went,
While all along the crowded way
Was jubilee and loud huzza.
And ever James was bending low
To his white jennet's saddle-bow,
Doffing his cap to city dame,
Who smiled and blush'd for pride and
     shame.
And well the simperer might be vain;
He chose the fairest of the train.
Gravely he greets each city sire,
Commends each pageant's quaint attire,
Gives to the dancers thanks aloud,
And smiles and nods upon the crowd,
Who rend the heavens with their
     acclaims,
'Long live the Commons' King, King
     James!'
Behind the King throng'd peer and
     knight,
And noble dame and damsel bright,
Whose fiery steeds ill brook'd the stay
Of the steep street and crowded way.
But in the train you might discern
Dark lowering brow and visage stern;
There nobles mourn'd their pride re-
     strain'd,
And the mean burgher's joys disdain'd;
And chiefs, who, hostage for their clan,
Were each from home a banish'd man,
There thought upon their own grey
     tower,
Their waving woods, their feudal
     power,
And deem'd themselves a shameful part
Of pageant which they cursed in heart.

XXII.

Now, in the Castle-park, drew out
Their chequer'd bands the joyous rout.
There morricers, with bell at heel,
And blade in hand, their mazes wheel:
But chief, beside the butts, there stand
Bold Robin Hood and all his band—
Friar Tuck with quarterstaff and cowl,
Old Scathelocke with his surly scowl,
Maid Marion, fair as ivory bone,
Scarlet, and Mutch, and Little John;
Their bugles challenge all that will,
In archery to prove their skill.
The Douglas bent a bow of might;
His first shaft centered in the white,
And when in turn he shot again,
His second split the first in twain.
From the King's hand must Douglas
     take
A silver dart, the archer's stake;
Fondly he watch'd, with watery eye,
Some answering glance of sympathy;
No kind emotion made reply!
Indifferent as to archer wight,
The monarch gave the arrow bright.

XXIII.

Now, clear the ring! for, hand to
     hand,
The manly wrestlers take their stand.
Two o'er the rest superior rose,
And proud demanded mightier foes,
Nor call'd in vain; for Douglas came.
—For life is Hugh of Larbert lame;
Scarce better John of Alloa's fare,
Whom senseless home his comrades
     bear.
Prize of the wrestling match, the King
To Douglas gave a golden ring,
While coldly glanced his eye of blue,
As frozen drop of wintry dew.
Douglas would speak, but in his breast
His struggling soul his words sup-
     press'd;
Indignant then he turn'd him where
Their arms the brawny yeomen bare,
To hurl the massive bar in air.
When each his utmost strength had
     shown,
The Douglas rent an earth-fast stone
From its deep bed, then heaved it high,
And sent the fragment through the sky
A rood beyond the farthest mark.
And still in Stirling's royal park,

The grey-hair'd sires, who know the
　　past,
To strangers point the Douglas-cast,
And moralize on the decay
Of Scottish strength in modern day.

XXIV.

The vale with loud applauses rang,
The Ladies' Rock sent back the clang.
The King, with look unmoved, be-
　　stow'd
A purse well-fill'd with pieces broad.
Indignant smiled the Douglas proud,
And threw the gold among the crowd,
Who now, with anxious wonder, scan,
And sharper glance, the dark grey
　　man;
Till whispers rose among the throng,
That heart so free, and hand so strong,
Must to the Douglas blood belong;
The old men mark'd, and shook the
　　head,
To see his hair with silver spread;
And wink'd aside, and told each son,
Of feats upon the English done,
Ere Douglas of the stalwart hand
Was exiled from his native land.
The women praised his stately form,
Though wreck'd by many a winter's
　　storm;
The youth with awe and wonder saw
His strength surpassing Nature's law.
Thus judged, as is their wont, the crowd,
Till murmur rose to clamours loud.
But not a glance from that proud ring
Of peers, who circled round the King,
With Douglas held communion kind,
Or call'd the banish'd man to mind;
No, not from those who, at the chase,
Once held his side the honour'd place,
Begirt his board, and, in the field,
Found safety underneath his shield;
For he, whom royal eyes disown,
When was his form to courtiers
　　known!

XXV.

The Monarch saw the gambols flag,
And bade let loose a gallant stag,

Whose pride, the holiday to crown,
Two favourite greyhounds should pull
　　down,
That venison free, and Bourdeaux
　　wine,
Might serve the archery to dine.
But Lufra, whom from Douglas' side
Nor bribe nor threat could e'er divide,
The fleetest hound in all the North,
Brave Lufra saw, and darted forth.
She left the royal hounds mid-way,
And dashing on the antler'd prey,
Sunk her sharp muzzle in his flank,
And deep the flowing life-blood drank.
The King's stout huntsman saw the
　　sport
By strange intruder broken short,
Came up, and with his leash unbound,
In anger struck the noble hound.
The Douglas had endured, that morn,
The King's cold look, the nobles'
　　scorn,
And last, and worst to spirit proud,
Had borne the pity of the crowd;
But Lufra had been fondly bred,
To share his board, to watch his bed,
And oft would Ellen Lufra's neck
In maiden glee with garlands deck;
They were such playmates, that with
　　name
Of Lufra, Ellen's image came.
His stifled wrath is brimming high,
In darken'd brow and flashing eye;
As waves before the bark divide,
The crowd gave way before his stride;
Needs but a buffet and no more,
The groom lies senseless in his gore.
Such blow no other hand could deal,
Though gauntleted in glove of steel.

XXVI.

Then clamour'd loud the royal train,
And brandish'd swords and staves
　　amain.
But stern the Baron's warning—
　　' Back!
Back, on your lives, ye menial pack!

Beware the Douglas.   Yes! behold,
King James! the Douglas, doom'd of
   old,
And vainly sought for near and far,
A victim to atone the war,
A willing victim, now attends,
.Nor craves thy grace but for his friends.'
'Thus is my clemency repaid?
Presumptuous Lord!' the monarch
   said;
'Of thy mis-proud ambitious clan,
Thou, James of Bothwell, wert the man,
The only man, in whom a foe
My woman-mercy would not know:
But shall a Monarch's presence brook
Injurious blow, and haughty look?
What ho! the Captain of our Guard!
Give the offender fitting ward.
Break off the sports!'—for tumult rose,
And yeomen 'gan to bend their bows.
'Break off the sports!' he said, and
   frown'd,
'And bid our horsemen clear the
   ground.'

XXVII.

Then uproar wild and misarray
Marr'd the fair form of festal day.
The horsemen prick'd among the
   crowd,
Repell'd by threats and insult loud;
To earth are borne the old and weak,
The timorous fly, the women shriek;
With flint, with shaft, with staff, with
   bar,
The hardier urge tumultuous war.
At once round Douglas darkly sweep
The royal spears in circle deep,
And slowly scale the pathway steep;
While on the rear in thunder pour
The rabble with disorder'd roar.
With grief the noble Douglas saw
The Commons rise against the law,
And to the leading soldier said,
'Sir John of Hyndford! 'twas my blade
That knighthood on thy shoulder laid;
For that good deed, permit me then
A word with these misguided men.

XXVIII.

'Hear, gentle friends! ere yet for me,
Ye break the bands of fealty.
My life, my honour, and my cause,
I tender free to Scotland's laws.
Are these so weak as must require
The aid of your misguided ire?
Or, if I suffer causeless wrong,
Is then my selfish rage so strong,
My sense of public weal so low,
That, for mean vengeance on a foe,
Those cords of love I should unbind,
Which knit my country and my kind?
Oh no! Believe, in yonder tower
It will not soothe my captive hour
To know those spears our foes should
   dread
For me in kindred gore are red;
To know, in fruitless brawl begun,
For me that mother wails her son;
For me that widow's mate expires;
For me that orphans weep their sires;
That patriots mourn insulted laws,
And curse the Douglas for the cause.
O let your patience ward such ill,
And keep your right to love me still!'

XXIX.

The crowd's wild fury sunk again
In tears, as tempests melt in rain.
With lifted hands and eyes, they pray'd
For blessings on his generous head,
Who for his country felt alone,
And prized her blood beyond his own.
Old men, upon the verge of life,
Bless'd him who staid the civil strife;
And mothers held their babes on high,
The self-devoted Chief to spy,
Triumphant over wrongs and ire,
To whom the prattlers owed a sire:
Even the rough soldier's heart was
   moved;
As if behind some bier beloved,
With trailing arms and drooping head,
The Douglas up the hill he led,
And at the Castle's battled verge,
With sighs resign'd his honour'd
   charge.

XXX.

The offended Monarch rode apart,
With bitter thought and swelling heart,
And would not now vouchsafe again
Through Stirling streets to lead his
    train.
'O Lennox, who would wish to rule
This changeling crowd, this common
    fool?
Hear'st thou,' he said, 'the loud
    acclaim,
With which they shout the Douglas
    name?
With like acclaim, the vulgar throat
Strain'd for King James their morning
    note;
With like acclaim they hail'd the day
When first I broke the Douglas' sway;
And like acclaim would Douglas greet,
If he could hurl me from my seat.
Who o'er the herd would wish to reign,
Fantastic, fickle, fierce, and vain?
Vain as the leaf upon the stream,
And fickle as a changeful dream;
Fantastic as a woman's mood,
And fierce as Frenzy's fever'd blood.
Thou many-headed monster-thing,
O who would wish to be thy king!

XXXI.

'But soft! what messenger of speed
Spurs hitherward his panting steed?
I guess his cognizance afar—
What from our cousin, John of Mar?'
'He prays, my liege, your sports keep
    bound
Within the safe and guarded ground:
For some foul purpose yet unknown—
Most sure for evil to the throne—
The outlaw'd Chieftain, Roderick Dhu,
Has summon'd his rebellious crew;
'Tis said, in James of Bothwell's aid
These loose banditti stand array'd.
The Earl of Mar, this morn, from
    Doune,
To break their muster march'd, and
    soon

Your grace will hear of battle fought;
But earnestly the Earl besought,
Till for such danger he provide,
With scanty train you will not ride.'

XXXII.

'Thou warn'st me I have done amiss;
I should have earlier look'd to this:
I lost it in this bustling day.
Retrace with speed thy former way;
Spare not for spoiling of thy steed,
The best of mine shall be thy meed.
Say to our faithful Lord of Mar,
We do forbid the intended war:
Roderick, this morn, in single fight,
Was made our prisoner by a knight;
And Douglas hath himself and cause
Submitted to our kingdom's laws.
The tidings of their leaders lost
Will soon dissolve the mountain host,
Nor would we that the vulgar feel,
For their Chief's crimes, avenging steel.
Bear Mar our message, Braco: fly!'
He turn'd his steed,—'My liege, I hie,
Yet, ere I cross this lily lawn,
I fear the broadswords will be drawn.'
The turf the flying courser spurn'd,
And to his towers the King return'd.

XXXIII.

Ill with King James's mood, that day,
Suited gay feast and minstrel lay;
Soon were dismiss'd the courtly throng,
And soon cut short the festal song.
Nor less upon the sadden'd town
The evening sunk in sorrow down.
The burghers spoke of civil jar,
Of rumour'd feuds and mountain war,
Of Moray, Mar, and Roderick Dhu,
All up in arms:—the Douglas too,
They mourn'd him pent within the hold
'Where stout Earl William was of old,'
And there his word the speaker staid,
And finger on his lip he laid,
Or pointed to his dagger blade.
But jaded horsemen, from the west,
At evening to the Castle press'd;

And busy talkers said they bore
Tidings of fight on Katrine's shore;
At noon the deadly fray begun,
And lasted till the set of sun.
Thus giddy rumour shook the town,
Till closed the Night her pennons
   brown.

—◦—

Canto Sixth.

The Guard-Room.

I.

THE sun, awakening, through the
   smoky air
Of the dark city casts a sullen glance,
Rousing each caitiff to his task of care,
   Of sinful man the sad inheritance;
Summoning revellers from the lagging
   dance,
   Scaring the prowling robber to his
     den;
Gilding on battled tower the warder's
   lance,
   And warning student pale to leave
     his pen,
And yield his drowsy eyes to the
   kind nurse of men.

What various scenes, and, O! what
   scenes of woe,
   Are witness'd by that red and
     struggling beam!
The fever'd patient, from his pallet low,
   Through crowded hospital beholds
     its stream;
The ruin'd maiden trembles at its
   gleam,
   The debtor wakes to thought of
     gyve and jail,
The love-lorn wretch starts from
   tormenting dream;
   The wakeful mother, by the glim-
     mering pale,
Trims her sick infant's couch, and
   soothes his feeble wail.

II.

At dawn the towers of Stirling rang
With soldier-step and weapon-clang,
While drums, with rolling note, foretell
Relief to weary sentinel.
Through narrow loop and casement
   barr'd,
The sunbeams sought the Court of
   Guard,
And, struggling with the smoky air,
Deaden'd the torches' yellow glare.
In comfortless alliance shone
The lights through arch of blacken'd
   stone,
And show'd wild shapes in garb of war,
Faces deform'd with beard and scar,
All haggard from the midnight watch,
And fever'd with the stern debauch;
For the oak table's massive board,
Flooded with wine, with fragments
   stored,
And beakers drain'd, and cups o'er-
   thrown,
Show'd in what sport the night had
   flown.
Some, weary, snored on floor and
   bench;
Some labour'd still their thirst to
   quench;
Some, chill'd with watching, spread
   their hands
O'er the huge chimney's dying brands,
While round them, or beside them
   flung,
At every step their harness rung.

III.

These drew not for their fields the
   sword,
Like tenants of a feudal lord,
Nor own'd the patriarchal claim
Of Chieftain in their leader's name;
Adventurers they, from far who roved,
To live by battle which they loved.
There the Italian's clouded face,
The swarthy Spaniard's there you
   trace;

The mountain-loving Switzer there
More freely breathed in mountain-air;
The Fleming there despised the soil,
That paid so ill the labourer's toil;
Their rolls show'd French and Ger-
    man name;
And merry England's exiles came,
To share, with ill conceal'd disdain,
Of Scotland's pay the scanty gain.
All brave in arms, well train'd to wield
The heavy halberd, brand, and shield;
In camps licentious, wild, and bold;
In pillage fierce and uncontroll'd;
And now, by holytide and feast,
From rules of discipline released.

IV.

They held debate of bloody fray,
Fought 'twixt Loch Katrine and
    Achray.
Fierce was their speech, and, 'mid
    their words,
Their hands oft grappled to their
    swords;
Nor sunk their tone to spare the ear
Of wounded comrades groaning near,
Whose mangled limbs, and bodies
    gored,
Bore token of the mountain sword,
Though, neighbouring to the Court
    of Guard,
Their prayers and feverish wails were
    heard;
Sad burden to the ruffian joke,
And savage oath by fury spoke!
At length up-started John of Brent,
A yeoman from the banks of Trent;
A stranger to respect or fear,
In peace a chaser of the deer.
In host a hardy mutineer,
But still the boldest of the crew,
When deed of danger was to do.
He grieved, that day, their games cut
    short,
And marr'd the dicer's brawling sport,
And shouted loud, 'Renew the bowl!
And, while a merry catch I troll,

Let each the buxom chorus bear,
Like brethren of the brand and spear:—

V.

SOLDIER'S SONG.

'Our vicar still preaches that Peter
    and Poule
Laid a swinging long curse on the
    bonny brown bowl,
That there's wrath and despair in the
    jolly black-jack,
And the seven deadly sins in a flagon
    of sack;
Yet whoop, Barnaby! off with thy
    liquor,
Drink upsees out, and a fig for the
    vicar!

Our vicar he calls it damnation to sip
The ripe ruddy dew of a woman's
    dear lip,
Says, that Beelzebub lurks in her
    kerchief so sly,
And Apollyon shoots darts from her
    merry black eye;
Yet whoop, Jack! kiss Gillian the
    quicker,
Till she bloom like a rose, and a fig
    for the vicar!

Our vicar thus preaches—and why
    should he not?
For the dues of his cure are the
    placket and pot;
And 'tis right of his office poor laymen
    to lurch,
Who infringe the domains of our good
    Mother Church.
Yet whoop, bully-boys! off with your
    liquor,
Sweet Marjorie's the word, and a fig
    for the vicar!'

VI.

The warder's challenge, heard without,
Staid in mid-roar the merry shout.

A soldier to the portal went,—
'Here is old Bertram, sirs, of Ghent;
And, beat for jubilee the drum!
A maid and minstrel with him come.'
Bertram, a Fleming, grey and scarr'd,
Was entering now the Court of Guard,
A harper with him, and in plaid
All muffled close, a mountain maid,
Who backward shrunk to 'scape the
        view
Of the loose scene and boisterous crew.
'What news?' they roar'd. 'I only
        know,
From noon till eve we fought with foe,
As wild and as untameable
As the rude mountains where they
        dwell;
On both sides store of blood is lost,
Nor much success can either boast.'
'But whence thy captives, friend?
        such spoil
As theirs must needs reward thy toil.
Old dost thou wax, and wars grow
        sharp;
Thou now hast glee-maiden and harp!
Get thee an ape, and trudge the land,
The leader of a juggler band.'

VII.

'No, comrade; no such fortune mine.
After the fight these sought our line,
That aged harper and the girl,
And, having audience of the Earl,
Mar bade I should purvey them steed,
And bring them hitherward with speed.
Forbear your mirth and rude alarm,
For none shall do them shame or
        harm.'
'Hear ye his boast?' cried John of Brent,
Ever to strife and jangling bent;
'Shall he strike doe beside our lodge,
And yet the jealous niggard grudge
To pay the forester his fee?
I'll have my share, howe'er it be,
Despite of Moray, Mar, or thee.'
Bertram his forward step withstood;
And, burning in his vengeful mood,

Old Allan, though unfit for strife,
Laid hand upon his dagger-knife;
But Ellen boldly stepp'd between,
And dropp'd at once the tartan screen:
So, from his morning cloud, appears
The sun of May, through summer tears.
The savage soldiery, amazed,
As on descended angel gazed;
Even hardy Brent, abash'd and tamed,
Stood half admiring, half ashamed.

VIII.

Boldly she spoke, 'Soldiers, attend!
My father was the soldier's friend;
Cheer'd him in camps, in marches led,
And with him in the battle bled.
Not from the valiant, or the strong,
Should exile's daughter suffer wrong.'
Answer'd De Brent, most forward still
In every feat or good or ill—
'I shame me of the part I play'd:
And thou an outlaw's child, poor maid!
An outlaw I by forest laws,
And merry Needwood knows the cause.
Poor Rose—if Rose be living now'—
He wiped his iron eye and brow—
'Must bear such age, I think, as thou.
Hear ye, my mates;—I go to call
The Captain of our watch to hall:
There lies my halberd on the floor;
And he that steps my halberd o'er,
To do the maid injurious part,
My shaft shall quiver in his heart!
Beware loose speech, or jesting rough:
Ye all know John de Brent. Enough.'

IX.

Their Captain came, a gallant young,
(Of Tullibardine's house he sprung,)
Nor wore he yet the spurs of knight;
Gay was his mien, his humour light,
And, though by courtesy controll'd,
Forward his speech, his bearing bold,
The high-born maiden ill could brook
The scanning of his curious look
And dauntless eye;—and yet, in sooth,
Young Lewis was a generous youth;

But Ellen's lovely face and mien,
Ill suited to the garb and scene,
Might lightly bear construction strange,
And give loose fancy scope to range.
'Welcome to Stirling towers, fair maid!
Come ye to seek a champion's aid,
On palfrey white, with harper hoar,
Like errant damosel of yore?
Does thy high quest a knight require,
Or may the venture suit a squire?'
Her dark eye flash'd; she paused and
    sigh'd,
'O what have I to do with pride!
Through scenes of sorrow, shame, and
    strife,
A suppliant for a father's life,
I crave an audience of the King.
Behold, to back my suit, a ring,
The royal pledge of grateful claims,
Given by the Monarch to Fitz-James.

x.

The signet-ring young Lewis took,
With deep respect and alter'd look;
And said, 'This ring our duties own;
And pardon, if to worth unknown,
In semblance mean obscurely veil'd,
Lady, in aught my folly fail'd.
Soon as the day flings wide his gates,
The King shall know what suitor waits.
Please you, meanwhile, in fitting bower
Repose you till his waking hour;
Female attendance shall obey
Your hest, for service or array.
Permit I marshall you the way.'
But, ere she followed, with the grace
And open bounty of her race,
She bade her slender purse be shared
Among the soldiers of the guard.
The rest with thanks their guerdon took;
But Brent, with shy and awkward look,
On the reluctant maiden's hold
Forced bluntly back the proffer'd gold—
'Forgive a haughty English heart,
And O forget its ruder part!
The vacant purse shall be my share,
Which in my barret-cap I'll bear,

Perchance, in jeopardy of war,
Where gayer crests may keep afar.'
With thanks (twas all she could) the
    maid
His rugged courtesy repaid.

xi.

When Ellen forth with Lewis went,
Allan made suit to John of Brent:
'My lady safe, O let your grace
Give me to see my master's face!
His minstrel I; to share his doom
Bound from the cradle to the tomb;
Tenth in descent, since first my sires
Waked for his noble house their lyres;
Nor one of all the race was known
But prized its weal above their own.
With the Chief's birth begins our care;
Our harp must soothe the infant heir,
Teach the youth tales of fight, and grace
His earliest feat of field or chase;
In peace, in war, our rank we keep,
We cheer his board, we soothe his sleep,
Nor leave him till we pour our verse,
A doleful tribute! o'er his hearse.
Then let me share his captive lot;
It is my right, deny it not!'
'Little we reck,' said John of Brent,
'We Southern men, of long descent;
Nor wot we how a name, a word,
Makes clansmen vassals to a lord:
Yet kind my noble landlord's part,—
God bless the house of Beaudesert!
And, but I loved to drive the deer,
More than to guide the labouring steer,
I had not dwelt an outcast here.
Come, good old Minstrel, follow me;
Thy Lord and Chieftain shalt thou see.'

xii.

Then, from a rusted iron hook,
A bunch of ponderous keys he took,
Lighted a torch, and Allan led
Through grated arch and passage dread;
Portals they pass'd, where, deep
    within,
Spoke prisoner's moan, and fetters' din;

Through rugged vaults, where, loosely
    stored,
Lay wheel, and axe, and headsman's
    sword,
And many an hideous engine grim,
For wrenching joint, and crushing limb,
By artist form'd, who deem'd it shame
And sin to give their work a name.
They halted at a low-brow'd porch,
And Brent to Allan gave the torch,
While bolt and chain he backward
    roll'd,
And made the bar unhasp its hold.
They enter'd : 'twas a prison-room
Of stern security and gloom,
Yet not a dungeon ; for the day
Through lofty gratings found its way,
And rude and antique garniture
Deck'd the sad walls and oaken floor ;
Such as the rugged days of old
Deem'd fit for captive noble's hold.
'Here,' said De Brent, 'thou mayst
    remain
Till the leech visit him again.
Strict is his charge, the warders tell,
To tend the noble prisoner well.'
Retiring then, the bolt he drew,
And the lock's murmurs growl'd anew.
Roused at the sound, from lowly bed
A captive feebly raised his head ;
The wondering Minstrel look'd, and
    knew
Not his dear lord, but Roderick Dhu !
For, come from where Clan-Alpine
    fought,
They, erring, deem'd the Chief he
    sought.

XIII.

As the tall ship, whose lofty prore
Shall never stem the billows more,
Deserted by her gallant band,
Amid the breakers lies astrand,
So, on his couch, lay Roderick Dhu !
And oft his fever'd limbs he threw
In toss abrupt, as when her sides
Lie rocking in the advancing tides,

That shake her frame with ceaseless
    beat,
Yet cannot heave her from her seat ;
O ! how unlike her course at sea !
Or his free step on hill and lea !
Soon as the Minstrel he could scan,
' What of thy lady ? of my clan ?
My mother ? Douglas ? tell me all !
Have they been ruin'd in my fall ?
Ah, yes ! or wherefore art thou here ?
Yet speak, speak boldly, do not fear.'
(For Allan, who his mood well knew,
Was choked with grief and terror
    too.)—
' Who fought—who fled ? Old man,
    be brief ;
Some might—for they had lost their
    Chief.
Who basely live ? who bravely died ?'
' O, calm thee, Chief !' the Minstrel
    cried,
' Ellen is safe.'—' For that, thank
    Heaven ! '
' And hopes are for the Douglas given ;
The Lady Margaret, too, is well ;
And, for thy clan,—on field or fell,
Has never harp of minstrel told,
Of combat fought so true and bold.
Thy stately Pine is yet unbent,
Though many a goodly bough is rent.'

XIV.

The Chieftain rear'd his form on high,
And fever's fire was in his eye ;
But ghastly, pale, and livid streaks
Chequer'd his swarthy brow and
    cheeks.
—' Hark, Minstrel ! I have heard thee
    play,
With measure bold, on festal day,
In yon lone isle, . . . again where ne'er
Shall harper play, or warrior hear ! . . .
That stirring air that peals on high,
O'er Dermid's race our victory.
Strike it ! and then (for well thou
    canst)
Free from thy minstrel-spirit glanced,

Fling me the picture of the fight
When met my clan the Saxon might.
I 'll listen, till my fancy hears
The clang of swords, the crash of
    spears!
These grates, these walls, shall vanish
    then,
For the fair field of fighting men,
And my free spirit burst away,
As if it soar'd from battle fray.'
The trembling Bard with awe obey'd,
Slow on the harp his hand he laid;
But soon remembrance of the sight
He witness'd from the mountain's
    height,
With what old Bertram told at night,
Awaken'd the full power of song,
And bore him in career along—
As shallop launch'd on river's tide,
That slow and fearful leaves the side,
But, when it feels the middle stream,
Drives downward swift as lightning's
    beam:

XV.

BATTLE OF BEAL' AN DUINE.

' The Minstrel came once more to view
The eastern ridge of Benvenue,
For, ere he parted, he would say
Farewell to lovely Loch Achray:
Where shall he find, in foreign land,
So lone a lake, so sweet a strand!
   There is no breeze upon the fern,
     Nor ripple on the lake;
   Upon her eyry nods the erne,
     The deer has sought the brake;
   The small birds will noᵗ sing aloud,
     The springing trout lies still,
   So darkly glooms yon thunder cloud,
   That swathes, as with a purple
     shroud,
     Benledi's distant hill.
   Is it the thunder's solemn sound
     That mutters deep and dread,
   Or echoes from the groaning ground
     The warrior's measured tread?

   Is it the lightning's quivering glance
     That on the thicket streams,
   Or do they flash on spear and lance
     The sun's retiring beams?
I see the dagger-crest of Mar,
I see the Moray's silver star
Wave o'er the cloud of Saxon war,
That up the lake comes winding far!
   To hero bound for battle-strife,
     Or bard of martial lay,
   'Twere worth ten years of peaceful
     life,
     One glance at their array!

XVI.

' Their light-arm'd archers far and
    near
   Survey'd the tangled ground;
Their centre ranks, with pike and
    spear,
   A twilight forest frown'd;
Their barbed horsemen, in the rear,
   The stern battalia crown'd.
No cymbal clash'd, no clarion rang,
   Still were the pipe and drum;
Save heavy tread, and armour's
    clang,
   The sullen march was dumb.
There breathed no wind their crests
    to shake,
   Or wave their flags abroad;
Scarce the frail aspen seem'd to
    quake,
   That shadow'd o'er their road.
Their vaward scouts no tidings bring,
   Can rouse no lurking foe,
Nor spy a trace of living thing,
   Save when they stirr'd the roe;
The host moves like a deep-sea
    wave,
Where rise no rocks its pride to
    brave,
   High-swelling, dark, and slow.
The lake is pass'd, and now they gain
A narrow and a broken plain,
Before the Trosachs' rugged jaws;
And here the horse and spearmen pause,

While, to explore the dangerous glen,
Dive through the pass the archer-men.

XVII.

' At once there rose so wild a yell
Within that dark and narrow dell,
As all the fiends, from heaven that fell,
Had peal'd the banner-cry of hell !
    Forth from the pass in tumult driven,
    Like chaff before the wind of heaven,
    The archery appear ;
    For life ! for life ! their plight they
      ply—
And shriek, and shout, and battle-cry,
And plaids and bonnets waving high,
And broadswords flashing to the sky,
    Are maddening in the rear.
Onward they drive, in dreadful race,
    Pursuers and pursued ;
Before that tide of flight and chase,
How shall it keep its rooted place,
    The spearmen's twilight wood ?
" Down, down," cried Mar, "your
    lances down !
    Bear back both friend and foe!"
Like reeds before the tempest's
    frown,
That serried grove of lances brown
    At once lay levell'd low ;
And closely shouldering side to side,
The bristling ranks the onset bide.
" We 'll quell the savage moun-
    taineer,
    As their Tinchel cows the game !
They come as fleet as forest deer,
    We 'll drive them back as tame."

XVIII.

' Bearing before them, in their course,
The relics of the archer force,
Like wave with crest of sparkling foam,
Right onward did Clan-Alpine come.
    Above the tide, each broadsword
    bright
Was brandishing like beam of light,
    Each targe was dark below ;
And with the ocean's mighty swing,
When heaving to the tempest swing,
    They hurl'd them on the foe.

I heard the lance's shivering crash,
As when the whirlwind rends the ash,
I heard the broadsword's deadly clang,
As if an hundred anvils rang !
But Moray wheel'd his rearward rank
Of horsemen on Clan-Alpine's flank,
    " My banner-man, advance !
I see," he cried, "their column shake.
Now, gallants ! for your ladies' sake,
    Upon them with the lance!"
The horsemen dash'd among the
    rout,
    As deer break through the broom;
Their steeds are stout, their swords
    are out,
    They soon make lightsome room.
Clan-Alpine's best are backward
    borne !
    Where, where was Roderick
    then ?
One blast upon his bugle-horn
    Were worth a thousand men !
And refluent through the pass of fear,
    The battle's tide was pour'd ;
Vanish'd the Saxon's struggling
    spear,
    Vanish'd the mountain-sword.
As Bracklinn's chasm, so black and
    steep,
    Receives her roaring linn,
As the dark caverns of the deep
    Suck the wild whirlpool in,
So did the deep and darksome pass
Devour the battle's mingled mass :
None linger now upon the plain,
Save those who ne'er shall fight again.

XIX.

' Now westward rolls the battle's
    din,
That deep and doubling pass within.
Minstrel, away, the work of fate
Is bearing on : its issue wait,
Where the rude Trosachs' dread defile
Opens on Katrine's lake and isle.
Grey Benvenue I soon repass'd,
Loch Katrine lay beneath me cast.

The sun is set; the clouds are met,
　The lowering scowl of heaven
An inky hue of livid blue
　To the deep lake has given;
Strange gusts of wind from mountain-
　　glen
Swept o'er the lake, then sunk agen.
I heeded not the eddying surge,
Mine eye but saw the Trosachs' gorge,
Mine ear but heard the sullen sound,
Which like an earthquake shook the
　　ground,
And spoke the stern and desperate
　　strife
That parts not but with parting life,
Seeming, to minstrel ear, to toll
The dirge of many a passing soul.
Nearer it comes; the dim-wood glen
The martial flood disgorged agen,
　But not in mingled tide;
The plaided warriors of the North
High on the mountain thunder forth
　And overhang its side;
While by the lake below appears
The dark'ning cloud of Saxon spears.
At weary bay each shatter'd band,
Eyeing their foemen, sternly stand;
Their banners stream like tatter'd sail,
That flings its fragments to the gale,
And broken arms and disarray
Mark'd the fell havoc of the day.

XX.

'Viewing the mountain's ridge a-
　　skance,
The Saxon stood in sullen trance,
Till Moray pointed with his lance,
　And cried—'Behold yon isle!
See! none are left to guard its strand,
But women weak, that wring the hand:
'Tis there of yore the robber band
　Their booty wont to pile;
My purse, with bonnet-pieces store,
To him will swim a bow-shot o'er,
And loose a shallop from the shore.
Lightly we 'll tame the war-wolf then,
Lords of his mate, and brood, and den.'

Forth from the ranks a spearman
　　sprung,
On earth his casque and corslet rung,
　He plunged him in the wave:
All saw the deed, the purpose knew,
And to their clamours Benvenue
　A mingled echo gave;
The Saxons shout, their mate to cheer,
The helpless females scream for fear,
And yells for rage the mountaineer.
'Twas then, as by the outcry riven,
Pour'd down at once the lowering
　　heaven:
A whirlwind swept Loch Katrine's
　　breast,
Her billows rear'd their snowy crest.
Well for the swimmer swell'd they high,
To mar the Highland marksman's eye;
For round him shower'd, 'mid rain
　　and hail,
The vengeful arrows of the Gael.
In vain; he nears the isle, and lo!
His hand is on a shallop's bow.
Just then a flash of lightning came,
It tinged the waves and strand with
　　flame;
I mark'd Duncraggan's widow'd dame,
Behind an oak I saw her stand,
A naked dirk gleam'd in her hand:
It darken'd; but, amid the moan
Of waves, I heard a dying groan;
Another flash!—the spearman floats
A weltering corse beside the boats,
And the stern matron o'er him stood,
Her hand and dagger streaming blood.

XXI.

'"Revenge! revenge!" the Saxons
　　cried,
The Gaels' exulting shout replied.
Despite the elemental rage,
Again they hurried to engage;
But, ere they closed in desperate fight,
Bloody with spurring came a knight,
Sprung from his horse, and, from
　　a crag,
Waved 'twixt the hosts a milk-white
　　flag.

Clarion and trumpet by his side
Rung forth a truce-note high and wide,
While, in the Monarch's name, afar
An herald's voice forbade the war,
For Bothwell's lord, and Roderick bold,
Were both, he said, in captive hold.'

But here the lay made sudden stand!
The harp escaped the Minstrel's hand!
Oft had he stolen a glance, to spy
How Roderick brook'd his minstrelsy:
At first, the Chieftain, to the chime,
With lifted hand, kept feeble time;
That motion ceased, yet feeling strong
Varied his look as changed the song;
At length, no more his deafen'd ear
The minstrel melody can hear;
His face grows sharp, his hands are clench'd,
As if some pang his heart-strings wrench'd;
Set are his teeth, his fading eye
Is sternly fix'd on vacancy;
Thus, motionless, and moanless, drew
His parting breath, stout Roderick Dhu!
Old Allan-bane look'd on aghast,
While grim and still his spirit pass'd:
But when he saw that life was fled,
He pour'd his wailing o'er the dead:

XXII.

LAMENT.

' And art thou cold and lowly laid,
Thy foeman's dread, thy people's aid,
Breadalbane's boast, Clan-Alpine's shade!
For thee shall none a requiem say?
For thee, who loved the minstrel's lay,
For thee, of Bothwell's house the stay,
The shelter of her exiled line,
E'en in this prison-house of thine,
I'll wail for Alpine's honour'd Pine!

'What groans shall yonder valleys fill!
What shrieks of grief shall rend yon hill!
What tears of burning rage shall thrill,
When mourns thy tribe thy battles done,
Thy fall before the race was won,
Thy sword ungirt ere set of sun!
There breathes not clansman of thy line,
But would have given his life for thine.
O woe for Alpine's honour'd Pine!

' Sad was thy lot on mortal stage!
The captive thrush may brook the cage,
The prison'd eagle dies for rage.
Brave spirit, do not scorn my strain!
And, when its notes awake again,
Even she, so long beloved in vain,
Shall with my harp her voice combine,
And mix her woe and tears with mine,
To wail Clan-Alpine's honour'd Pine.'

XXIII.

Ellen the while with bursting heart
Remain'd in lordly bower apart,
Where play'd with many-colour'd gleams,
Through storied pane the rising beams.
In vain on gilded roof they fall,
And lighten'd up a tapestried wall,
And for her use a menial train
A rich collation spread in vain.
The banquet proud, the chamber gay,
Scarce drew one curious glance astray;
Or, if she look'd, 'twas but to say,
With better omen dawn'd the day
In that lone isle, where waved on high
The dun-deer's hide for canopy;
Where oft her noble father shared
The simple meal her care prepared,
While Lufra, crouching by her side
Her station claim'd with jealous pride,
And Douglas, bent on woodland game,
Spoke of the chase to Malcolm Græme,
Whose answer, oft at random made,
The wandering of his thoughts betray'd.
Those who such simple joys have known,
Are taught to prize them when they're gone.

But sudden, see, she lifts her head!
The window seeks with cautious tread.
What distant music has the power
To win her in this woful hour!
'Twas from a turret that o'erhung
Her latticed bower, the strain was sung:

XXIV.

LAY OF THE IMPRISONED HUNTSMAN.

' My hawk is tired of perch and hood,
My idle greyhound loathes his food,
My horse is weary of his stall,
And I am sick of captive thrall.

I wish I were, as I have been,
Hunting the hart in forest green,
With bended bow and bloodhound free,
For that's the life is meet for me.

I hate to learn the ebb of time
From yon dull steeple's drowsy chime,
Or mark it as the sunbeams crawl,
Inch after inch, along the wall.

The lark was wont my matins ring,
The sable rook my vespers sing;
These towers, although a king's they be,
Have not a hall of joy for me.

No more at dawning morn I rise,
And sun myself in Ellen's eyes,
Drive the fleet deer the forest through,
And homeward wend with evening
    dew;

A blithesome welcome blithely meet,
And lay my trophies at her feet,
While fled the eve on wing of glee:
That life is lost to love and me!'

XXV.

The heart-sick lay was hardly said,
The list'ner had not turn'd her head,
It trickled still, the starting tear,
When light a footstep struck her ear,
And Snowdoun's graceful knight was
    near.
She turn'd the hastier, lest again
The prisoner should renew his strain.

' O welcome, brave Fitz-James!' she
    said;
' How may an almost orphan maid
Pay the deep debt'—— 'O say not so!
To me no gratitude you owe.
Not mine, alas! the boon to give,
And bid thy noble father live;
I can but be thy guide, sweet maid,
With Scotland's king thy suit to aid.
No tyrant he, though ire and pride
May lay his better mood aside.
Come, Ellen, come! 'tis more than time,
He holds his court at morning prime.'
With beating heart, and bosom wrung,
As to a brother's arm she clung,
Gently he dried the falling tear,
And gently whisper'd hope and cheer;
Her faltering steps half led, half staid,
Through gallery fair, and high arcade,
Till, at his touch. its wings of pride
A portal arch unfolded wide.

XXVI.

Within 'twas brilliant all and light,
A thronging scene of figures bright;
It glow'd on Ellen's dazzled sight,
As when the setting sun has given
Ten thousand hues to summer even,
And from their tissue fancy frames
Aërial knights and fairy dames.
Still by Fitz-James her footing staid;
A few faint steps she forward made,
Then slow her drooping head she
    raised,
And fearful round the presence gazed;
For him she sought, who own'd this
    state,
The dreaded prince whose will was
    fate.
She gazed on many a princely port,
Might well have ruled a royal court;
On many a splendid garb she gazed,
Then turn'd bewilder'd and amazed,
For all stood bare; and in the room,
Fitz-James alone wore cap and plume.
To him each lady's look was lent;
On him each courtier's eye was bent;

Midst furs, and silks, and jewels sheen,
He stood, in simple Lincoln green,
The centre of the glittering ring.
And Snowdoun's Knight is Scotland's
    King!

XXVII.

As wreath of snow, on mountain-
    breast,
Slides from the rock that gave it rest,
Poor Ellen glided from her stay,
And at the Monarch's feet she lay;
No word her choking voice commands;
She show'd the ring, she clasp'd her
    hands.
O! not a moment could he brook,
The generous prince, that suppliant
    look!
Gently he raised her; and, the while,
Check'd with a glance the circle's smile;
Graceful, but grave, her brow he kiss'd,
And bade her terrors be dismiss'd:
'Yes, fair, the wandering poor Fitz-
    James
The fealty of Scotland claims.
To him thy woes, thy wishes, bring;
He will redeem his signet ring.
Ask nought for Douglas; yester even,
His prince and he have much forgiven.
Wrong hath he had from slanderous
    tongue,
I, from his rebel kinsmen, wrong.
We would not, to the vulgar crowd,
Yield what they craved with clamour
    loud;
Calmly we heard and judged his cause,
Our council aided, and our laws.
I stanch'd thy father's death-feud stern
With stout De Vaux and Grey Glen-
    cairn;
And Bothwell's Lord henceforth we
    own
The friend and bulwark of our Throne.
But, lovely infidel, how now?
What clouds thy misbelieving brow?
Lord James of Douglas, lend thine aid;
Thou must confirm this doubting maid.'

XXVIII.

Then forth the noble Douglas sprung,
And on his neck his daughter hung.
The Monarch drank, that happy hour,
The sweetest, holiest draught of Power,
When it can say, with godlike voice,
Arise, sad Virtue, and rejoice!
Yet would not James the general eye
On Nature's raptures long should pry;
He stepp'd between—'Nay, Douglas,
    nay,
Steal not my proselyte away!
The riddle 'tis my right to read,
That brought this happy chance to
    speed.
Yes, Ellen, when disguised I stray
In life's more low but happier way,
'Tis under name which veils my power,
Nor falsely veils, for Stirling's tower
Of yore the name of Snowdoun claims,
And Normans call me James Fitz-
    James.
Thus watch I o'er insulted laws,
Thus learn to right the injured cause.'
Then, in a tone apart and low,—
'Ah, little traitress! none must know
What idle dream, what lighter thought,
What vanity full dearly bought,
Join'd to thine eye's dark witchcraft,
    drew
My spell-bound steps to Benvenue,
In dangerous hour, and all but gave
Thy Monarch's life to mountain
    glaive!'—
Aloud he spoke—'Thou still dost hold
That little talisman of gold,
Pledge of my faith, Fitz-James's ring;
What seeks fair Ellen of the King?'

XXIX.

Full well the conscious maiden guess'd
He probed the weakness of her breast;
But, with that consciousness, there
    came
A lightening of her fears for Græme,
And more she deem'd the Monarch's ire
Kindled 'gainst him, who, for her sire,

Rebellious broadsword boldly drew;
And, to her generous feeling true,
She craved the grace of Roderick Dhu.
' Forbear thy suit: the King of kings
Alone can stay life's parting wings:
I know his heart, I know his hand,
Have shared his cheer, and proved his brand:
My fairest earldom would I give
To bid Clan-Alpine's Chieftain live!
Hast thou no other boon to crave?
No other captive friend to save?'
Blushing, she turn'd her from the King,
And to the Douglas gave the ring,
As if she wish'd her sire to speak
The suit that stain'd her glowing cheek.—
' Nay, then, my pledge has lost its force,
And stubborn justice holds her course.
Malcolm, come forth!' And at the word,
Down kneel'd the Græme to Scotland's Lord.
'For thee, rash youth, no suppliant sues,
From thee may Vengeance claim her dues,
Who, nurtured underneath our smile,
Hast paid our care by treacherous wile,
And sought, amid thy faithful clan,
A refuge for an outlaw'd man,
Dishonouring thus thy loyal name.
Fetters and warder for the Græme!'
His chain of gold the King unstrung,
The links o'er Malcolm's neck he flung,
Then gently drew the glittering band,
And laid the clasp on Ellen's hand.

———

Harp of the North, farewell! The hills grow dark,
  On purple peaks a deeper shade descending;
In twilight copse the glow-worm lights her spark,
  The deer, half-seen, are to the covert wending.

Resume thy wizard elm! the fountain lending,
  And the wild breeze, thy wilder minstrelsy;
Thy numbers sweet with nature's vespers blending,
  With distant echo from the fold and lea,
And herd-boy's evening pipe, and hum of housing bee.

Yet once again farewell, thou Minstrel harp!
  Yet once again forgive my feeble sway,
And little reck I of the censure sharp
  May idly cavil at an idle lay.
Much have I owed thy strains on life's long way,
  Through secret woes the world has never known,
When on the weary night dawn'd wearier day,
  And bitterer was the grief devour'd alone.
That I o'erlive such woes, Enchantress! is thine own.

Hark! as my lingering footsteps slow retire,
  Some Spirit of the Air has waked thy string!
'Tis now a seraph bold, with touch of fire,
  'Tis now the brush of Fairy's frolic wing.
Receding now, the dying numbers ring
  Fainter and fainter down the rugged dell,
And now the mountain breezes scarcely bring
  A wandering witch-note of the distant spell—
And now, 'tis silent all!—Enchantress, fare thee well!

END OF THE LADY OF THE LAKE.

INTRODUCTION TO THE EDITION OF 1830.

AFTER the success of 'Marmion,' I felt inclined to exclaim with Ulysses in the 'Odyssey'—

Οὗτος μὲν δὴ ἄεθλος ἀάατος ἐκτετέλεσται·
Νῦν αὖτε σκοπὸν ἄλλον.   Odys. χ. l. 5.

'One venturous game my hand has won to-day—
Another, gallants, yet remains to play.'

The ancient manners, the habits and customs of the aboriginal race by whom the Highlands of Scotland were inhabited, had always appeared to me peculiarly adapted to poetry. The change in their manners, too, had taken place almost within my own time, or at least I had learned many particulars concerning the ancient state of the Highlands from the old men of the last generation. I had always thought the old Scottish Gael highly adapted for poetical composition. The feuds, and political dissensions, which, half a century earlier, would have rendered the richer and wealthier part of the kingdom indisposed to countenance a poem, the scene of which was laid in the Highlands, were now sunk in the generous compassion which the English, more than any other nation, feel for the misfortunes of an honourable foe. The Poems of Ossian had, by their popularity, sufficiently shown, that if writings on Highland subjects were qualified to interest the reader, mere national prejudices were, in the present day, very unlikely to interfere with their success.

I had also read a great deal, seen much, and heard more, of that romantic country, where I was in the habit of spending some time every autumn; and the scenery of Loch Katrine was connected with the recollection of many a dear friend and merry expedition of former days. This poem, the action of which lay among scenes so beautiful, and so deeply imprinted on my recollection, was a labour of love; and it was no less so to recall the manners and incidents introduced. The frequent custom of James IV, and particularly of James V, to walk through their kingdom in disguise, afforded me the hint of an incident, which never fails to be interesting, if managed with the slightest address or dexterity.

I may now confess, however, that the employment, though attended with great pleasure, was not without its doubts and anxieties. A lady, to whom I was nearly related, and with whom I lived, during her whole life, on the most brotherly terms of affection, was residing with me at the time when the work was in progress, and used to ask me, what I could possibly do to rise so early in the morning (that happening to be the most convenient time to me for composition). At last I told her the subject of my meditations; and I can never forget the anxiety and affection expressed in her reply. 'Do not be so rash,' she said, 'my dearest cousin. You are already popular—more so, perhaps, than you yourself will believe, or than even I, or other partial friends, can fairly allow to your merit. You stand high— do not rashly attempt to climb higher, and incur the risk of a fall; for, depend upon it, a favourite will not be permitted even to stumble with impunity.' I replied to this affectionate expostulation in the words of Montrose—

'He either fears his fate too much,
    Or his deserts are small,
Who dares not put it to the touch
    To gain or lose it all.'

'If I fail,' I said, for the dialogue is strong in my recollection, 'it is a sign that I ought never to have succeeded, and I will write prose for life: you shall see no change in my temper, nor will I eat a single meal the worse. But if I succeed,

"Up with the bonnie blue bonnet,
The dirk, and the feather, and a'!"

Afterwards, I showed my affectionate and anxious critic the first canto of the poem, which reconciled her to my imprudence. Nevertheless, although I answered thus confidently, with the obstinacy often said to be proper to those who bear my surname, I acknowledge that my confidence was considerably shaken by the warning of her excellent taste and unbiassed friendship. Nor was I much comforted by her retractation of the unfavourable judgment, when I recollected how likely a natural partiality was to effect that change of opinion. In such cases, affection rises like a light on the canvas, improves any favourable tints which it formerly exhibited, and throws its defects into the shade.

I remember that about the same time a friend started in to 'heeze up my hope,' like the 'sportsman with his cutty gun' in the old song. He was bred a farmer, but a man of powerful understanding, natural good taste, and warm poetical feeling, perfectly competent to supply the wants of an imperfect or irregular education. He was a passionate admirer of field-sports, which we often pursued together.

As this friend happened to dine with me at Ashestiel one day, I took the opportunity of reading to him the first canto of 'The Lady of the Lake,' in order to ascertain the effect the poem was likely to produce upon a person who was but too favourable a representative of readers at large. It is, of course, to be supposed that I determined rather to guide my opinion by what my friend might appear to feel, than by what he might think fit to say. His reception of my recitation, or prelection, was rather singular. He placed his hand across his brow, and listened with great attention through the whole account of the stag-hunt, till the dogs threw themselves into the lake to follow their master, who embarks with Ellen Douglas. He then started up with a sudden exclamation, struck his hand on the table, and declared, in a voice of censure calculated for the occasion, that the dogs must have been totally ruined by being permitted to take the water after such a severe chase. I own I was much encouraged by the species of reverie which had possessed so zealous a follower of the sports of the ancient Nimrod, who had been completely surprised out of all doubts of the reality of the tale. Another of his remarks gave me less pleasure. He detected the identity of the King with the wandering knight, Fitz-James, when he winds his bugle to summon his attendants. He was probably thinking of the lively, but somewhat licentious, old ballad, in which the denouement of a royal intrigue takes place as follows:

'He took a bugle frae his side,
He blew both loud and shrill,
And four-and-twenty belted knights
Came skipping ower the hill;
Then he took out a little knife,
Let a' his duddies fa',
And he was the brawest gentleman
That was amang them a'.
And we'll go no more a-roving,' &c. [1]

This discovery, as Mr. Pepys says of the rent in his camlet cloak, was but a trifle, yet it troubled me; and I was at a good deal of pains to efface any marks by which I thought my secret could be traced before the conclusion, when I relied on it with the same hope of producing effect, with which the Irish postboy is said to reserve a 'trot for the avenue.'

I took uncommon pains to verify the accuracy of the local circumstances of this story. I recollect, in particular, that to ascertain whether I was telling a probable tale, I went into Perthshire, to see whether King James could actually have ridden from the banks of Loch Vennachar to Stirling Castle within the time supposed in the Poem, and had the pleasure to satisfy myself that it was quite practicable.

After a considerable delay, 'The Lady of the Lake' appeared in May 1810; and its success was certainly so extraordinary as to induce me for the moment to conclude that I had at last fixed a nail in the proverbially inconstant wheel of Fortune, whose stability in behalf of an individual who had so boldly courted her favours for three successive times, had not as yet been shaken. I had attained, perhaps, that degree of public reputation at which prudence, or certainly timidity, would have made a halt, and discontinued efforts by which I was far more likely to diminish my fame than to increase it. But, as the celebrated John Wilkes is said to have explained to his late Majesty, that he himself, amid his full tide of popularity, was never a Wilkite, so I can, with honest truth, exculpate myself from having been at any time a partisan of my own poetry, even when it was in the highest fashion with the million. It must not be supposed, that I was either so ungrateful, or so superabundantly candid, as to despise or scorn the value of those whose voice had elevated me so much higher than my own opinion told me I deserved. I felt, on the contrary, the more grateful to the public, as receiving that from partiality to me, which I could not have claimed from merit; and I endeavoured to deserve the partiality, by continuing such exertions as I was capable of for their amusement.

It may be that I did not, in this continued course of scribbling, consult either the interest

---

[1] The Jolly Beggar, attributed to King James V.—Herd's *Collection*, 1776.

of the public or my own. But the former had effectual means of defending themselves, and could, by their coldness, sufficiently check any approach to intrusion; and for myself, I had now for several years dedicated my hours so much to literary labour, that I should have felt difficulty in employing myself otherwise; and so, like Dogberry, I generously bestowed all my tediousness on the public, comforting myself with the reflection, that if posterity should think me undeserving of the favour with which I was regarded by my contemporaries, 'they could not but say I *had* the crown,' and had enjoyed for a time that popularity which is so much coveted.

I conceived, however, that I held the distinguished situation I had obtained, however unworthily, rather like the champion of pugilism, on the condition of being always ready to show proofs of my skill, than in the manner of the champion of chivalry, who performs his duties only on rare and solemn occasions. I was in any case conscious that I could not long hold a situation which the caprice, rather than the judgment, of the public, had bestowed upon me, and preferred being deprived of my precedence by some more worthy rival, to sinking into contempt for my indolence, and losing my reputation by what Scottish lawyers call the *negative proscription.* Accordingly, those who choose to look at the Introduction to Rokeby, in the present edition, will be able to trace the steps by which I declined as a poet to figure as a novelist; as the ballad says, Queen

Eleanor sunk at Charing-Cross to rise again at Queenhithe.

It only remains for me to say that, during my short pre-eminence of popularity, I faithfully observed the rules of moderation which I had resolved to follow before I began my course as a man of letters. If a man is determined to make a noise in the world, he is as sure to encounter abuse and ridicule, as he who gallops furiously through a village, must reckon on be:ng followed by the curs in full cry. Experienced persons know, that in stretching to flog the latter, the rider is very apt to catch a bad fall; nor is an attempt to chastise a malignant critic attended with less danger to the author. On this principle, I let parody, burlesque, and squibs, find their own level; and while the latter hissed most fiercely, I was cautious never to catch them up, as schoolboys do, to throw them back against the naughty boy who fired them off, wisely remembering that they are, in such cases, apt to explode in the handling. Let me add, that my reign (since Byron has so called it) was marked by some instances of good-nature as well as patience. I never refused a literary person of merit such services in smoothing his way to the public as were in my power: and I had the advantage, rather an uncommon one with our irritable race, to enjoy general favour, without incurring permanent ill-will, so far as is known to me, among any of my contemporaries.

W. S.

ABBOTSFORD, *April* 1830.

NOTES.

NOTE I.

——*the heights of Uam-Var,*
And roused the cavern, where, 'tis told,
A giant made his den of old.—P. 208.

Va-var, as the name is pronounced, or more properly *Uaighmor*, is a mountain to the north-east of the village of Callender in Menteith, deriving its name, which signifies the great den, or cavern, from a sort of retreat among the rocks on the south side, said, by tradition, to have been the abode of a giant. In latter times, it was the refuge of robbers and banditti, who have been only extirpated within these forty or fifty years. Strictly speaking, this stronghold is not a cave, as the name would imply, but a sort of small enclosure, or recess, surrounded with large rocks, and open above head. It may have been originally designed as a toil for deer, who might get in from the outside, but would find it difficult to return. This opinion prevails among the old sportsmen and deer-stalkers in the neighbourhood.

NOTE II.

Two dogs of black Saint Hubert's breed,
Unmatch'd for courage, breath, and speed.
—P. 209.

'The hounds which we call Saint Hubert's hounds, are commonly all blacke, yet neuertheless, the race is so mingled at these days, that we find them of all colours. These are the hounds which the abbots of St. Hubert haue always kept some of their race or kind, in honour or remembrance of the saint, which was a hunter with S. Eustace. Whereupon we may conceiue that (by the grace of God) all good huntsmen shall follow them into paradise. To return vnto my former purpose, this kind of dogges hath bené dispersed through the counties of Henault, Lorayne, Flanders, and Burgoyne. They are mighty of body, neuerthelesse their legges are low and short, likewise they are not swift, although they be very good of sent, hunting chaces which are farre straggled, fearing neither water nor cold, and doe more couet the chaces that smell, as foxes, bore, and such like, than other, because they find themselves neither of swiftness nor courage to hunt and kill the chaces that are lighter and swifter. The bloodhounds of this colour proue good, especially those that are cole blacke, but I made no great account to breed on them, or to keepe the kind, and yet I found a book which a hunter did dedicate to a prince of Lorayne, which seemed to loue hunting much, wherein was a blason which the same hunter gaue to his bloodhound, called Souyllard, which was white :—

> " My name came first from holy Hubert's race,
> Souyllard my sire, a hound of singular grace."

Whereupon we may presume that some of the kind proue white sometimes, but they are not of the kind of the Grefflers or Bouxes, which we haue at these dayes.'—*The noble Art of Venerie or Hunting, translated and collected for the Use of all Noblemen and Gentlemen.* Lond. 1611, 4to, p. 15.

NOTE III.

For the death-wound and death-halloo,
Muster'd his breath, his whinyard drew.
—P. 209.

When the stag turned to bay, the ancient hunter had the perilous task of going in upon, and killing or disabling the desperate animal. At certain times of the year this was held particularly dangerous, a wound received from a stag's horn being then deemed poisonous, and more dangerous than one from the tusks of a boar, as the old rhyme testifies :—

> 'If thou be hurt with hart, it brings thee to thy bier,
> But barber's hand will boar's hurt heal, therefore thou need'st not fear.'

At all times, however, the task was dangerous, and to be adventured upon wisely and warily, either by getting behind the stag while he was gazing on the hounds, or by watching an opportunity to gallop roundly in upon him, and kill him with the sword. See many directions to this purpose in the Booke of Hunting, chap. 41. Wilson the historian has recorded a providential escape which befell him in this hazardous sport, while a youth and follower of the Earl of Sussex.

'Sir Peter Lee, of Lime, in Cheshire, invited my lord one summer to hunt the stag. And having a great stagg in chase, and many gentlemen in the pursuit, the stagg took soyle. And divers, whereof I was one, alighted, and stood with swords drawne, to have a cut at him, at his coming out of the water. The staggs there being wonderfully fierce and dangerous, made us youths more eager to be at him. But he escaped us all. And it was my misfortune to be hindered of my coming nere him, the way being sliperie, by a falle; which gave occasion to some, who did not know mee, to speak as if I had

falne for feare. Which being told mee, I left the stagg, and followed the gentleman who [first] spake it. But I found him of that cold temper, that it seems his words made an escape from him; as by his denial and repentance it appeared. But this made mee more violent in the pursuit of the stagg, to recover my reputation. And I happened to be the only horseman in, when the dogs sett him up at bay; and approaching near him on horsebacke, he broke through the dogs, and run at mee, and tore my horse's side with his hornes, close by my thigh. Then I quitted my horse, and grew more cunning (for the dogs had sette him up againe), stealing behind him with my sword, and cut his hamstrings; and then got upon his back, and cut his throate; which, as I was doing, the company came in, and blamed my rashness for running such a hazard.'—PECK'S *Desiderato Curiosa*, ii. 464.

NOTE IV.

And now, to issue from the glen,
No pathway meets the wanderer's ken,
Unless he climb, with footing nice,
A far projecting precipice.—P. 211.

Until the present road was made through the romantic pass which I have presumptuously attempted to describe in the preceding stanzas, there was no mode of issuing out of the defile called the Trosachs, excepting by a sort of ladder, composed of the branches and roots of trees.

NOTE V.

To meet with Highland plunderers here,
Were worse than loss of steed or deer.
—P. 211.

The clans who inhabited the romantic regions in the neighbourhood of Loch Katrine were, even until a late period, much addicted to predatory excursions upon their Lowland neighbours. 'In former times, those parts of this district, which are situated beyond the Grampian range, were rendered almost inaccessible by strong barriers of ro ks, and mountains, and lakes. It was a border country, and, though on the very verge of the low country, it was almost totally sequestered from the world, and, as it were, insulated with respect to society. 'Tis well known that in the Highlands, it was, in former times, accounted not only lawful, but honourable, among hostile tribes, to commit depredations on one another; and these habits of the age were perhaps strengthened in this district, by the circumstances which have been mentioned. It bordered on a country, the inhabitants of which, while they were richer, were less warlike than they, and widely differenced by language and manners.' —GRAHAM'S *Sketches of Scenery in Perth-*

shire. Edin. 1806, p. 97. The reader will therefore be pleased to remember, that the scene of this poem is laid in a time,

> 'When tooming faulds, or sweeping of a glen,
> Had still been held the deed of gallant men.'

Note VI.

A grey-hair'd sire, whose eye intent
Was on the vision'd future bent.—P. 213.

If force of evidence could authorise us to believe facts inconsistent with the general laws of nature, enough might be produced in favour of the existence of the Second-sight. It is called in Gaelic *Taishitaraugh*, from *Taish*, an unreal or shadowy appearance; and those possessed of the faculty are called *Taishatrin*, which may be aptly translated visionaries. Martin, a steady believer in the second-sight, gives the following account of it :—

'The second-sight is a singular faculty, of seeing an otherwise invisible object, without any previous means used by the person that used it for that end: the vision makes such a lively impression upon the seers, that they neither see, nor think of anything else, except the vision, as long as it continues; and then they appear pensive or jovial, according to the object that was represented to them.

'At the sight of a vision, the eyelids of the person are erected, and the eyes continue staring until the object vanish. This is obvious to others who are by, when the persons happen to see a vision, and occurred more than once to my own observation, and to others that were with me.

'There is one in Skie, of whom his acquaintance observed, that when he sees a vision, the inner part of his eyelids turns so far upwards, that, after the object disappears, he must draw them down with his fingers, and sometimes employ others to d aw them down, which he finds to be the much easier way.

'This faculty of the second-sight does not lineally descend in a family, as some imagine, for I know several parents who are endowed with it, but their children not, and *vice versa;* neither is it acquired by any previous compact. And, after a strict enquiry, I could never learn that this faculty was communicable any way whatsoever.

'The seer knows neither the object, time, nor place of a vision, before it appears; and the same object is often seen by different persons living at a considerable distance from one another. The true way of judging as to the time and circumstance of an object, is by observation; for several persons of judgment, without this faculty, are more capable to judge of the design of a vision, than a novice that is a seer. If an object appear in the day or night, it will come to pass sooner or later accordingly.

'If an object is seen early in the morning (which is not frequent) it will be accomplished in a few hours afterwards. If at noon, it will commonly be accomplished that very day. If in the evening, perhaps that night; if after candles be lighted, it will be accomplished that night: the later always in accomplishment, by weeks, months, and sometimes years, according to the time of night the vision is seen.

'When a shroud is perceived about one, it is a sure prognostic of death; the time is judged according to the height of it about the person; for if it is seen above the middle, death is not to be expected for the space of a year, and perhaps some months longer; and as it is frequently seen to ascend higher towards the head, death is concluded to be at hand within a few days, if not hours, as daily experience confirms. Examples of this kind were shewn me, when the persons of whom the observations were then made, enjoyed perfect health.

'One instance was lately foretold by a seer, that was a novice, concerning the death of one of my acquaintance; this was communicated to a few only, and with great confidence; I being one of the number, did not in the least regard it, until the death of the person, about the time foretold, did confirm me of the certainty of the prediction. The novice mentioned above, is now a skilful seer, as appears from many late instances; he lives in the parish of St. Mary's, the most northern in Skie.

'If a woman is seen standing at a man's left hand, it is a presage that she will be his wife, whether they be married to others, or unmarried at the time of the apparition.

'If two or three women are seen at once near a man's left hand, she that is next him will undoubtedly be his wife first, and so on, whether all three, or the man, be single or married at the time of the vision or not; of which there are several late instances among those of my acquaintance. It is an ordinary thing for them to see a man that is to come to the house shortly after: and if he is not of the seer's acquaintance, yet he gives such a lively description of his stature, complexion, habit, &c. that upon his arrival he answers the character given him in all respects.

'If the person so appearing be one of the seer's acquaintance, he will tell his name, as well as other particulars; and he can tell by his countenance whether he comes in a good or bad humour.

'I have been seen thus myself by seers of both sexes, at some hundred miles' distance; some that saw me in this manner had never seen me personally, and it happened according to their vision, without any previous design of mine to go to those places, my coming there being purely accidental.

'It is ordinary with them to see houses, gardens, and trees, in places void of all three; and this in progress of time uses to be accomplished: as at Mogshot, in the Isle of

Skie, where there were but a few sorry cow-houses, thatched with straw, yet in a very few years after, the vision, which appeared often, was accomplished, by the building of several good houses on the very spot represented by the seers, and by the planting of orchards there.

'To see a spark of fire fall upon one's arm or breast, is a forerunner of a dead child to be seen in the arms of those persons ; of which there are several fresh instances.

'To see a seat empty at the time of one's sitting in it, is a presage of that person's death soon after.

'When a novice, or one that has lately obtained the second-sight, sees a vision in the night-time without doors, and he be near a fire, he presently falls into a swoon.

'Some find themselves as it were in a crowd of people, having a corpse which they carry along with them ; and after such visions, the seers come in sweating, and describe the people that appeared : if there be any of their acquaintance among 'em, they give an account of their names, as also of the bearers, but they know nothing concerning the corpse.

'All those who have the second-sight do not always see these visions at once, though they be together at the time. But if one who has this faculty, designedly touch his fellow-seer at the instant of a vision's appearing, then the second sees it as well as the first ; and this is sometimes discerned by those that are near them on such occasions.'—MARTIN'S *Description of the Western Islands*, 1716, 8vo, p. 300 *et seq.*

To these particulars innumerable examples might be added, all attested by grave and credible authors. But, in despite of evidence which neither Bacon, Boyle, nor Johnson were able to resist, the *Taisch*, with all its visionary properties, seems to be now universally abandoned to the use of poetry. The exquisitely beautiful poem of Lochiel will at once occur to the recollection of every reader.

NOTE VII.

Here, for retreat in dangerous hour,
Some chief had framed a rustic bower.
—P. 214.

The Celtic chieftains, whose lives were continually exposed to peril, had usually, in the most retired spot of their domains, some place of retreat for the hour of necessity, which, as circumstances would admit, was a tower, a cavern, or a rustic hut, in a strong and secluded situation. One of these last gave refuge to the unfortunate Charles Edward, in his perilous wanderings after the battle of Culloden.

'It was situated in the face of a very rough, high, and rocky mountain, called Letter-nilichk, still a part of Benalder, full of great stones and crevices, and some scattered wood

interspersed. The habitation called the Cage, in the face of that mountain, was within a small thick bush of wood. There were first some rows of trees laid down, in order to level the floor for a habitation ; and as the place was steep, this raised the lower side to an equal height with the other : and these trees, in the way of joists or planks, were levelled with earth and gravel. There were betwixt the trees, growing naturally on their own roots, some stakes fixed in the earth, which, with the trees, were interwoven with ropes, made of heath and birch twigs, up to the top of the Cage, it being of a round or rather oval shape; and the whole thatched and covered over with fog. The whole fabric hung, as it were, by a large tree, which reclined from the one end, all along the roof, to the other, and which gave it the name of the Cage ; and by chance there happened to be two stones at a small distance from one another, in the side next the precipice, resembling the pillars of a chimney, where the fire was placed. The smoke had its vent out here, all along the fall of the rock, which was so much of the same colour, that one could discover no difference in the clearest day.'—HOME'S *History of the Rebellion*, Lond. 1802, 4to, p. 381.

NOTE VIII.

My sire's tall form might grace the part
Of Ferragus or Ascabart.—P. 215.

These two sons of Anak flourished in romantic fable. The first is well known to the admirers of Ariosto, by the name of Ferrau. He was an antagonist of Orlando, and was at length slain by him in single combat. There is a romance in the Auchinleck MS., in which Ferragus is thus described :—

'On a day come tiding
  Unto Charls the King,
    Al of a doughti knight
Was comen to Navers,
Stout he was and fers,
    Vernagu he hight.
Of Babiloun the soudan
Thider him sende gan,
  With King Charls to fight.
So hard he was to fond [1]
That no dint of brond
  No greued him, aplight.
He hadde twenti men strengthe
And forti fet of lengthe,
  Thilke painim hede [2],
And four feet in the face,
Y-meten [3] in the place,
  And fifteen in brede [4].
His nose was a fot and more ;
His brow, as bristles wore [5];
  He that it seighe it sede.
He loked lotheliche,
And was swart [6] as any piche,
  Of him men might adrede.
    Romance of Charlemagne, ll. 461-484.
      Auchinleck MS., folio 265.

---

1 Found, proved.   2 Had.   3 Measured.
4 Breadth.   5 Were.   6 Black.

K

Ascapart, or Ascabart, makes a very material figure in the History of Bevis of Hampton, by whom he was conquered. His effigies may be seen guarding one side of a gate at Southampton, while the other is occupied by Sir Bevis himself. The dimensions of Ascabart were little inferior to those of Ferragus, if the following description be correct :—

> 'They metten with a geaunt,
> With a lotheliche semblaunt.
> He was wonderliche strong,
> Rome [1] thretti fote long,
> His berd was bot gret and rowe [2];
> A space of a fot betweene is [3] browe;
> His clob was, to yeue [4] a strok,
> A lite bodi of an oak [5].
>
> Beues hadde of him wonder gret,
> And askede him what a het [6],
> And yaf [7] men of his contre
> Were ase meche [6] ase was he.
> "Me name," a sede [9], "is Ascopard,
> Garci me sent hiderward,
> For to bring this quene ayen.
> And the Beues her of-slen [10].
> Incham Garci is [11] champioun,
> And was i-driue out of me [12] toun
> Al for that ich was so lite [13].
> Eueri man me wolde smite,
> Ich was so lite and so merugh [14],
> Eueri man me clepede dwerugh [15],
> And now icham in this londe,
> I wax mor [16] ich understonde,
> And stranger than other tene [17];
> And that schel on us be sene."
>
> *Sir Bevis of Hampton*, i. 2512.
> *Auchinleck MS.*, fol. 189.

Note IX.

Though all unask'd his birth and name.
—P. 215.

The Highlanders, who carried hospitality to a punctilious excess, are said to have considered it as churlish, to ask a stranger his name or lineage, before he had taken refreshment. Feuds were so frequent among them, that a contrary rule would in many cases have produced the discovery of some circumstance which might have excluded the guest from the benefit of the assistance he stood in need of.

Note X.

*—— and still a harp unseen
Fill'd up the symphony between.*
—P. 215.

'They' (meaning the Highlanders) 'delight much in musicke, but chiefly in harps and clairschoes of their own fashion. The strings of the clairschoes are made of brass wire, and the strings of the harps of sinews; which strings they strike either with their nayles, growing long, or else with an instrument appointed for that use. They take great pleasure to decke their harps and clairschoes with silver and precious stones; the poore ones that cannot attayne hereunto, decke them with christall. They sing verses prettily compound, contayning (for the most part) prayses of valiant men. There is not almost any other argument, whereof their rhymes intreat. They speak the ancient French language altered a little [1].'—'The harp and clairschoes are now only heard of in the Highlands in ancient song. At what period these instruments ceased to be used, is not on record; and tradition is silent on this head. But, as Irish harpers occasionally visited the Highlands and Western Isles till lately, the harp might have been extant so late as the middle of the last century. Thus far we know, that from remote times down to the present, harpers were received as welcome guests, particularly in the Highlands of Scotland; and so late as the latter end of the sixteenth century, as appears by the above quotation, the harp was in common use among the natives of the Western Isles. How it happened that the noisy and unharmonious bagpipe banished the soft and expressive harp, we cannot say; but certain it is, that the bagpipe is now the only instrument that obtains universally in the Highland districts.' —Campbell's *Journey through North Britain.* Lond. 1808. 4to. i. 175.

Mr. Gunn, of Edinburgh, has lately published a curious Essay upon the Harp and Harp Music of the Highlands of Scotland. That the instrument was once in common use there is most certain. Clelland numbers an acquaintance with it among the few accomplishments which his satire allows to the Highlanders:—

> 'In nothing they're accounted sharp,
> Except in bagpipe or in harp.'

Note XI.

Morn's genial influence roused a minstrel grey.—P. 217.

That Highland chieftains, to a late period, retained in their service the bard, as a family officer, admits of very easy proof. The author of the Letters from the North of Scotland, an officer of engineers, quartered at Inverness about 1720, who certainly cannot be deemed a favourable witness, gives the following account of the office, and of a bard whom he heard exercise his talent of recita-

---

[1] Fully. [2] Rough. [3] His. [4] Give. [5] The stem of a little oak-tree. [6] He hight, was called.
[7] If. [8] Great. [9] He said. [10] Slay. [11] His.
[12] My. [13] Little. [14] Lean. [15] Dwarf.
[16] Greater, taller. [17] Ten.

---

[1] *Vide* 'Certayne Matters concerning the Realme of Scotland, &c. as they were Anno Domini 1597.' Lond. 1603. 4to.

tion :—'The bard is skilled in the genealogy of all the Highland families, sometimes preceptor to the young laird, celebrates in Irish verse the original of the tribe, the famous warlike actions of the successive heads, and sings his own lyricks as an opiate to the chief when indisposed for sleep ; but poets are not equally esteemed and honoured in all countries. I happened to be a witness of the dishonour done to the muse at the house of one of the chiefs, where two of these bards were set at a good distance, at the lower end of a long table, with a parcel of Highlanders of no extraordinary appearance, over a cup of ale. Poor inspiration ! They were not asked to drink a glass of wine at our table, though the whole company consisted only of the *great man*, one of his near relations, and myself. After some little time, the chief ordered one of them to sing me a Highland song. The bard readily obeyed, and with a hoarse voice, and in a tune of few various notes, began, as I was told, one of his own lyricks ; and when he had proceeded to the fourth or fifth stanza, I perceived, by the names of several persons, glens, and mountains, which I had known or heard of before, that it was an account of some clan battle. But in his going on the chief (who piques himself upon his school-learning), at some particular passage, bid him cease, and cried out, 'There's nothing like that in Virgil or Homer.' I bowed, and told him I believed so. This you may believe was very edifying and delightful.'—*Letters*, ii. 167.

Note XII.

The Græme.—P. 219.

The ancient and powerful family of Graham (which, for metrical reasons, is here spelt after the Scottish pronunciation) held extensive possessions in the counties of Dumbarton and Stirling. Few families can boast of more historical renown, having claim to three of the most remarkable characters in the Scottish annals. Sir John the Græme, the faithful and undaunted partaker of the labours and patriotic warfare of Wallace, fell in the unfortunate field of Falkirk, in 1298. The celebrated Marquis of Montrose, in whom De Retz saw realized his abstract idea of the heroes of antiquity, was the second of these worthies. And, notwithstanding the severity of his temper, and the rigour with which he executed the oppressive mandates of the princes whom he served, I do not hesitate to name as a third, John Græme of Claverhouse, Viscount of Dundee, whose heroic death in the arms of victory may be allowed to cancel the memory of his cruelty to the Nonconformists during the reigns of Charles II and James II.

Note XIII.

This harp, which erst Saint Modan sway'd.
—P. 219.

I am not prepared to show that Saint Modan was a performer on the harp. It was, however, no unsaintly accomplishment ; for Saint Dunstan certainly did play upon that instrument, which retaining, as was natural, a portion of the sanctity attached to its master's character, announced future events by its spontaneous sounds. 'But labouring once in these mechanic arts for a devout matrone that had sett him on work, his violl, that hung by him on the wall, of its own accord, without anie man's helpe, distinctly sounded this anthime :—*Gaudent in coelis animae sanctorum qui Christi vestigia sunt secuti ; et quia pro eius amore sanguinem suum fuderunt, ideo cum Christo gaudent aeternum*. Whereat all the companie being much astonished, turned their eyes from beholding him working, to looke on that strange accident. . . . Not long after, manie of the court that hitherunto had borne a kind of fayned friendship towards him, began now greatly to envie at his progress and rising in goodnes, using manie crooked, backbiting meanes to diffame his vertues with the black maskes of hypocrisie. And the better to authorize their calumnie, they brought in this that happened in the violl, affirming it to have been done by art magick. What more ? This wicked rumour encreased dayly till the king and others of the nobilitie taking hould thereof, Dunstan grew odious in their sight. Therefore he resolued to leaue the court and go to Elphegus, surnamed the Bauld, then Bishop of Winchester, who was his cozen. Which his enemies understanding, they layd wayt for him in the way, and hauing throwne him off his horse, beate him, and dragged him in the durt in the most miserable manner, meaning to have slaine him, had not a companie of mastiue dogges that came unlookt upon them defended and redeemed him from their crueltie. When with sorrow he was ashamed to see dogges more humane than they. And giuing thankes to Almightie God, he sensibly againe perceiued that the tunes of his violl had giuen him a warning of future accidents.'—*Flower of the Lives of the most renowned Saincts of England, Scotland, and Ireland, by the R. Father Hierome Porter.* Doway, 1632, 4to, tome i. p. 438.

The same supernatural circumstance is alluded to by the anonymous author of 'Grim, the Collier of Croydon.'

'[*Dunstan's harp sounds on the wall.*]
Forest Hark, hark, my lords, the holy abbot's harp
Sounds by itself so hanging on the wall !
Dunstan. Unhallow'd man, that scorn'st the sacred rede,
Hark, how the testimony of my truth
Sounds heavenly music with an angel's hand,
To testify Dunstan's integrity
And prove thy active boast of no effect.'

NOTE XIV.

Ere Douglases, to ruin driven,
Were exiled from their native heaven.
—P. 219.

The downfall of the Douglases of the house of Angus during the reign of James V is the event alluded to in the text. The Earl of Angus, it will be remembered, had married the queen dowager, and availed himself of the right which he thus acquired, as well as of his extensive power, to retain the king in a sort of tutelage, which approached very near to captivity. Several open attempts were made to rescue James from this thraldom, with which he was well known to be deeply disgusted; but the valour of the Douglases and their allies gave them the victory in every conflict. At length the king, while residing at Falkland, contrived to escape by night out of his own court and palace, and rode full speed to Stirling Castle, where the governor, who was of the opposite faction, joyfully received him. Being thus at liberty, James speedily summoned around him such peers as he knew to be most inimical to the domination of Angus—and laid his complaint before them, says Pitscottie, 'with great lamentations; showing to them how he was holden in subjection, thir years bygone, by the Earl of Angus and his kin and friends, who oppressed the whole country and spoiled it, under the pretence of justice and his authority; and had slain many of his lieges, kinsmen, and friends, because they would have had it mended at their hands, and put him at liberty, as he ought to have been, at the counsel of his whole lords, and not have been subjected and corrected with no particular men, by the rest of his nobles. Therefore, said he, I desire, my lords, that I may be satisfied of the said earl, his kin, and friends; for I avow that Scotland shall not hold us both while [i. e. till] I be revenged on him and his.

'The lords, hearing the king's complaint and lamentation, and also the great rage, fury, and malice that he bore toward the Earl of Angus, his kin and friends, they concluded all, and thought it best that he should be summoned to underly the law; if he found no caution, nor yet compear himself, that he should be put to the horn, with all his kin and friends, so many as were contained in the letters. And farther, the lords ordained, by advice of his majesty, that his brother and friends should be summoned to find caution to underly the law within a certain day, or else be put to the horn. But the earl appeared not, nor none for him; and so he was put to the horn, with all his kin and friends: so many as were contained in the summons that compeared not were banished, and holden traitors to the king.'

NOTE XV.

In Holy-Rood a Knight he slew.—P. 220.

This was by no means an uncommon occurrence in the Court of Scotland; nay, the presence of the sovereign himself scarcely restrained the ferocious and inveterate feuds which were the perpetual source of bloodshed among the Scottish nobility. The following instance of the murder of Sir William Stuart of Ochiltree, called *The Bloody*, by the celebrated Francis, Earl of Bothwell, may be produced among many; but as the offence given in the royal court will hardly bear a vernacular translation, I shall leave the story in Johnstone's Latin, referring for further particulars to the naked simplicity of Birrell's Diary, July 30, 1588.

'*Mors improbi hominis non tam ipsa immerita, quam pessimo exemplo in publicum, faedè perpetrata. Gulielmus Stuartus Alkiltrius, Arani frater, naturâ ac moribus, cujus saepius memini, vulgo propter sitem sanguinis sanguinarius dictus, a Bothvelio, in Sanctae Crucis Regiâ exardescente irâ, mendacii probro lacessitus, obscaenum osculum liberius retorquebat; Bothvelius hanc contumeliam tacitus tulit, sed ingentum irarum molem animo concepit. Utrinque postridie Edinburgi conventum, totidem numero comitibus armatis, praesidii causa, et acriter pugnatum est; caeteris amicis et clientibus metu torpentibus, aut vi absterritis, ipse Stuartus fortissimè dimicat; tandem excusso gladio à Bothvelio, Scythicâ feritate transfoditur, sine cujusquam misericordiâ; habuit itaque quem debuit exitum. Dignus erat Stuartus qui pateretur; Bothvelius qui faceret. Vulgus sanguinem sanguine praedicabit, et horum cruore innocuorum manibus egregiè parentatum.*' — Johnstoni *Historia Rerum Britannicarum*, ab anno 1572 ad annum 1628. Amstelodami 1665, fol., p. 135.

NOTE XVI.

The Douglas, like a stricken deer,
Disown'd by every noble peer.—P. 220.

The exile state of this powerful race is not exaggerated in this and subsequent passages. The hatred of James against the race of Douglas was so inveterate, that numerous as their allies were, and disregarded as the regal authority had usually been in similar cases, their nearest friends, even in the most remote parts of Scotland, durst not entertain them, unless under the strictest and closest disguise. James Douglas, son of the banished Earl of Angus, afterwards well known by the title of Earl of Morton, lurked, during the exile of his family, in the north of Scotland, under the assumed name of James Innes, otherwise *James the Grieve* (i. e. Reve or Bailiff). 'And as he bore the name,' says Godscroft, 'so did he also execute the office of a grieve or overseer of the lands and rents, the corn and cattle of him with whom he lived.' From the habits of frugality and observation which he acquired in his humble situation, the historian traces that intimate acquaintance with popular character which enabled him to rise so high in the state, and that honourable economy by which he repaired and established the shattered estates of Angus and Morton.—*History of the House of Douglas*, Edinburgh, 1743, vol. ii. p. 160.

Note XVII.

Maronnan's cell.—P. 221.

The parish of Kilmaronock, at the eastern extremity of Loch Lomond, derives its name from a cell or chapel, dedicated to Saint Maronock, or Marnock, or Maronnan, about whose sanctity very little is now remembered. There is a fountain devoted to him in the same parish; but its virtues, like the merits of its patron, have fallen into oblivion.

Note XVIII.

Bracklinn's thundering wave.—P. 221.

This is a beautiful cascade made by a mountain stream called the Keltie, at a place called the Bridge of Bracklinn, about a mile from the village of Callender in Menteith. Above a chasm, where the brook precipitates itself from a height of at least fifty feet, there is thrown, for the convenience of the neighbourhood, a rustic footbridge, of about three feet in breadth, and without ledges, which is scarcely to be crossed by a stranger without awe and apprehension.

Note XIX.

For Tine-man forged by fairy lore.—P. 221.

Archibald, the third Earl of Douglas, was so unfortunate in all his enterprises, that he acquired the epithet of TINE-MAN, because he *tined*, or lost, his followers in every battle which he fought. He was vanquished, as every reader must remember, in the bloody battle of Homildon-hill, near Wooler, where he himself lost an eye, and was made prisoner by Hotspur. He was no less unfortunate when allied with Percy, being wounded and taken at the battle of Shrewsbury. He was so unsuccessful in an attempt to besiege

Roxburgh Castle, that it was called the *Foul Raid*, or disgraceful expedition. His ill-fortune left him indeed at the battle of Beaugé, in France; but it was only to return with double emphasis at the subsequent action of Vernoil, he last and most unlucky of his encounters, in which he fell, with the flower of the Scottish chivalry, then serving as auxiliaries in France, and about two thousand common soldiers, A.D. 1424.

Note XX.

Did, self-unscabbarded, foreshow The footstep of a secret foe.—P. 221.

The ancient warriors, whose hope and confidence rested chiefly in their blades, were accustomed to deduce omens from them, especially from such as were supposed to have been fabricated by enchanted skill, of which we have various instances in the romances and legends of the time. The wonderful sword SKOFNUNG, wielded by the celebrated Hrolf Kraka, was of this description. It was deposited in the tomb of the monarch at his death, and taken from thence by Skeggo, a celebrated pirate, who bestowed it upon his son-in-law, Kormak, with the following curious directions:—' "The manner of using it will appear strange to you. A small bag is attached to it, which take heed not to violate. Let not the rays of the sun touch the upper part of the handle, nor unsheathe it, unless thou art ready for battle. But when thou comest to the place of fight, go aside from the rest, grasp and extend the sword, and breathe upon it. Then a small worm will creep out of the handle; lower the handle, that he may more easily return into it." Kormak, after having received the sword, returned home to his mother. He showed the sword, and attempted to draw it, as unnecessarily as ineffectually, for he could not pluck it out of the sheath. His mother, Dalla, exclaimed, "Do not despise the counsel given to thee, my son." Kormak, however, repeating his efforts, pressed down the handle with his feet, and tore off the bag, when Skofnung emitted a hollow groan: but still he could not unsheathe the sword. Kormak then went out with Bessus, whom he had challenged to fight with him, and drew apart to the place of combat. He sat down upon the ground, and ungirding the sword, which he bore above his vestments, did not remember to shield the hilt from the rays of the sun. In vain he endeavoured to draw it, till he placed his foot against the hilt; then the worm issued from it. But Kormak did not rightly handle the weapon, in consequence whereof good fortune deserted it. As he unsheathed Skofnung, it emitted a hollow murmur.'—*Bartholini de Causis Contemptae a Danis adhuc Gentilibus*

Mortis, Libri Tres. Hofniae, 1689, 4to, p. 574.

To the history of this sentient and prescient weapon, I beg leave to add, from memory, the following legend, for which I cannot produce any better authority. A young nobleman, of high hopes and fortune, chanced to lose his way in the town which he inhabited, the capital, if I mistake not, of a German province. He had accidentally involved himself among the narrow and winding streets of a suburb, inhabited by the lowest order of the people, and an approaching thunder-shower determined him to ask a short refuge in the most decent habitation that was near him. He knocked at the door, which was opened by a tall man, of a grisly and ferocious aspect, and sordid dress. The stranger was readily ushered to a chamber, where swords, scourges, and machines, which seemed to be implements of torture, were suspended on the wall. One of these swords dropped from its scabbard, as the nobleman, after a moment's hesitation, crossed the threshold. His host immediately stared at him with such a marked expression, that the young man could not help demanding his name and business, and the meaning of his looking at him so fixedly. 'I am,' answered the man, 'the public executioner of this city; and the incident you have observed is a sure augury that I shall, in discharge of my duty, one day cut off your head with the weapon which has just now spontaneously unsheathed itself.' The nobleman lost no time in leaving his place of refuge; but, engaging in some of the plots of the period, was shortly after decapitated by that very man and instrument. Lord Lovat is said, by the author of the Letters from Scotland, to have affirmed, that a number of swords that hung up in the hall of the mansion-house, leaped of themselves out of the scabbard at the instant he was born. The story passed current among his clan, but, like that of the story I have just quoted, proved an unfortunate omen.—*Letters from Scotland,* vol. ii. p. 214.

NOTE XXI.

Those thrilling sounds, that call the might Of old Clan-Alpine to the fight.—P. 222.

The connoisseurs in pipe-music affect to discover in a well-composed pibroch, the imitative sounds of march, conflict, fight, pursuit, and all the 'current of a heady fight.' To this opinion Dr. Beattie has given his suffrage, in the following elegant passage:— 'A *pibroch* is a species of tune, peculiar, I think, to the Highlands and Western Isles of Scotland. It is performed on a bagpipe, and differs totally from all other music. Its rhythm is so irregular, and its notes, especially in the quick movement, so mixed and huddled together, that a stranger finds it impossible to reconcile his ear to it, so as to perceive its modulation. Some of these pibrochs, being intended to represent a battle, begin with a grave motion resembling a march; then gradually quicken into the onset; run off with noisy confusion, and turbulent rapidity, to imitate the conflict and pursuit; then swell into a few flourishes of triumphant joy; and perhaps close with the wild and slow wailings of a funeral procession.'—*Essay on Laughter and Ludicrous Composition,* chap. iii. Note.

NOTE XXII.

Roderigh Vich Alpine dhu, ho! ieroe!
—P. 223.

Besides his ordinary name and surname, which were chiefly used in the intercourse with the Lowlands, every Highland chief had an epithet expressive of his patriarchal dignity as head of the clan, and which was common to all his predecessors and successors, as Pharaoh to the kings of Egypt, or Arsaces to those of Parthia. This name was usually a patronymic, expressive of his descent from the founder of the family. Thus the Duke of Argyle is called MacCallum More, or the *son of Colin the Great.* Sometimes, however, it is derived from armorial distinctions, or the memory of some great feat; thus Lord Seaforth, as chief of the Mackenzies, or Clan Kennet, bears the epithet of Caber-fae, or *Buck's Head,* as representative of Colin Fitzgerald, founder of the family, who saved the Scottish king when endangered by a stag. But besides this title, which belonged to his office and dignity, the chieftain had usually another peculiar to himself, which distinguished him from the chieftains of the same race. This was sometimes derived from complexion, as *dhu* or *roy*; sometimes from size, as *beg* or *more*; at other times from some peculiar exploit, or from some peculiarity of habit or appearance. The line of the text therefore signifies,

'Black Roderick, the descendant of Alpine.'

The song itself is intended as an imitation of the *jorrams*, or boat songs, of the Highlanders, which were usually composed in honour of a favourite chief. They are so adapted as to keep time with the sweep of the oars, and it is easy to distinguish between those intended to be sung to the oars of a galley, where the stroke is lengthened and doubled, as it were, and those which were timed to the rowers of an ordinary boat.

NOTE XXIII.

The best of Loch Lomond lie dead on her side.
—P. 223.

The Lennox, as the district is called, which encircles the lower extremity of Loch Lomond, was peculiarly exposed to the incursions of the mountaineers, who inhabited the inaccessible fastnesses at the upper end of the lake, and the neighbouring district of Loch Katrine. These were often marked by circumstances of great ferocity, of which the noted conflict of Glen-fruin is a celebrated instance. This was a clan-battle, in which the Macgregors, headed by Allaster Macgregor, chief of the clan, encountered the sept of Colquhouns, commanded by Sir Humphry Colquhoun of Luss. It is on all hands allowed that the action was desperately fought, and that the Colquhouns were defeated with great slaughter, leaving two hundred of their name dead upon the field. But popular tradition has added other horrors to the tale. It is said, that Sir Humphry Colquhoun, who was on horseback, escaped to the castle of Benechra, or Banochar, and was next day dragged out and murdered by the victorious Macgregors in cold blood. Buchanan of Auchmar, however, speaks of his slaughter as a subsequent event, and as perpetrated by the Macfarlanes. Again, it is reported that the Macgregors murdered a number of youths, whom report of the intended battle had brought to be spectators, and whom the Colquhouns, anxious for their safety, had shut up in a barn to be out of danger. One account of the Macgregors denies this circumstance entirely: another ascribes it to the savage and bloodthirsty disposition of a single individual, the bastard brother of the Laird of Maegregor, who amused himself with this second massacre of the innocents, in express disobedience to the chief, by whom he was left their guardian during the pursuit of the Colquhouns. It is added, that Macgregor bitterly lamented this atrocious action, and prophesied the ruin which it must bring upon their ancient clan. The following account of the conflict, which is indeed drawn up by a friend of the Clan-Gregor, is altogether silent on the murder of the youths. 'In the spring of the year 1602, there happened great dissensions and troubles between the laird of Luss, chief of the Colquhouns, and Alexander, laird of Macgregor. The original of these quarrels proceeded from injuries and provocations mutually given and received, not long before. Macgregor, however, wanting to have them ended in friendly conferences, marched at the head of two hundred of his clan to Leven, which borders on Luss, his country, with a view of settling matters by the mediation of friends: but Luss had no such intentions, and projected his measures with a different view, for he privately drew together a body of 300 horse and 500 foot, composed partly of his own clan and their followers, and partly of the Buchanans, his neighbours, and resolved to cut off Macgregor and his party to a man, in case the issue of the conference did not answer his inclination. But matters fell otherwise than he expected; and though Macgregor had previous information of his insidious design, yet dissembling his resentment, he kept the appointment, and parted good friends in appearance.

'No sooner was he gone, than Luss, thinking to surprise him and his party in full security, and without any dread or apprehension of his treachery, followed with all speed, and came up with him at a place called Glenfroon. Macgregor, upon the alarm, divided his men into two parties, the greatest part whereof he commanded himself, and the other he committed to the care of his brother John, who, by his orders, led them about another way, and attacked the Colquhouns in flank. Here it was fought with great bravery on both sides for a considerable time; and, notwithstanding the vast disproportion of numbers, Macgregor, in the end, obtained an absolute victory. So great was the rout, that 200 of the Colquhouns were left dead upon the spot. most of the leading men were killed, and a multitude of prisoners taken. But what seemed most surprising and incredible in this defeat, was, that none of the Macgregors were missing, except John, the laird's brother, and one common fellow, though indeed many of them were wounded.'—Professor Ross's *History of the Family of Sutherland*, 1631.

The consequences of the battle of Glenfruin were very calamitous to the family of Macgregor, who had already been considered as an unruly clan. The widows of the slain Colquhouns, sixty, it is said, in number, appeared in doleful procession before the king at Stirling, each riding upon a white palfrey, and bearing in her hand the bloody shirt of her husband displayed upon a pike. James VI was so much moved by the complaints of this 'choir of mourning dames,' that he let loose his vengeance against the Macgregors, without either bounds or moderation. The very name of the clan was proscribed, and those by whom it had been borne were given up to sword and fire, and absolutely hunted down by bloodhounds like wild beasts. Argyle and the Campbells, on the one hand, Montrose, with the Grahames and Buchanans, on the other, are said to have been the chief instruments in suppressing this devoted clan. The Laird of Macgregor surrendered to the former, on condition that he would take him out of Scottish ground. But, to use Birrel's expression, he kept 'a Highlandman's promise'; and, although he fulfilled his word to the letter, by carrying him as far as Berwick, he afterwards brought him back to Edinburgh, where he was executed with eighteen of his clan.—BIRREL'S *Diary*, Oct. 2, 1603. The

Clan-Gregor being thus driven to utter despair, seem to have renounced the laws from the benefit of which they were excluded, and their depredations produced new acts of council, confirming the severity of their proscription, which had only the effect of rendering them still more united and desperate. It is a most extraordinary proof of the ardent and invincible spirit of clanship, that, notwithstanding the repeated proscriptions providently ordained by the legislature 'for the *timeous preventing* the disorders and oppression that may fall out by the said name and clan of Macgregors, and their followers,' they were in 1715 and 1745 a potent clan, and continue to subsist as a distinct and numerous race.

NOTE XXIV.

—— The King's vindictive pride
Boasts to have tamed the Border-side.
—P. 226.

In 1529, James V made a convention at Edinburgh for the purpose of considering the best mode of quelling the Border robbers, who, during the license of his minority, and the troubles which followed, had committed many exorbitances. Accordingly, he assembled a flying army of ten thousand men, consisting of his principal nobility and their followers, who were directed to bring their hawks and dogs with them, that the monarch might refresh himself with sport during the intervals of military execution. With this array he swept through Ettrick Forest, where he hanged over the gate of his own castle, Piers Cockburn of Henderland, who had prepared, according to tradition, a feast for his reception. He caused Adam Scott of Tushielaw also to be executed, who was distinguished by the title of King of the Border. But the most noted victim of justice, during that expedition, was John Armstrong of Gilnockie, famous in Scottish song, who, confiding in his own supposed innocence, met the King, with a retinue of thirty-six persons, all of whom were hanged at Carlenrig, near the source of the Teviot. The effect of this severity was such, that, as the vulgar expressed it, 'the rush-bush kept the cow,' and 'thereafter was great peace and rest a long time, wherethrough the King had great profit; for he had ten thousand sheep going in the Ettrick Forest in keeping by Andrew Bell, who made the King as good count of them as they had gone in the bounds of Fife.'— PITSCOTTIE'S *History*, p. 153.

NOTE XXV.

What grace for Highland Chiefs, judge ye
By fate of Border chivalry.—P. 226.

James was in fact equally attentive to restrain rapine and feudal oppression in every part of his dominions. 'The king past to the

Isles, and there held justice courts, and punished both thief and traitor according to their demerit. And also he caused great men to show their holdings, wherethrough he found many of the said lands in non-entry; the which he confiscate and brought home to his own use, and afterwards annexed them to the crown, as ye shall hear. Syne brought many of the great men of the Isles captive with him, such as Mudyart, M'Connel, M'Loyd of the Lewes, M'Neil, M'Lane, M'Intosh, John Mudyart, M'Kay, M'Kenzie, with many other that I cannot rehearse at this time. Some of them he put in ward and some in court, and some he took pledges for good rule in time coming. So he brought the Isles, both north and south, in good rule and peace; wherefore he had great profit, service, and obedience of people a long time thereafter; and as long as he had the heads of the country in subjection, they lived in great peace and rest, and there was great riches and policy by the king's justice.'— PITSCOTTIE, p. 152.

NOTE XXVI.

Rest safe till morning; pity 'twere
Such cheek should feel the midnight air.
—P. 228.

Hardihood was in every respect so essential to the character of a Highlander, that the reproach of effeminacy was the most bitter which could be thrown upon him. Yet it was sometimes hazarded on what we might presume to think slight grounds. It is reported of Old Sir Ewen Cameron of Lochiel, when upwards of seventy, that he was surprised by night on a hunting or military expedition. He wrapped him in his plaid, and lay contentedly down upon the snow, with which the ground happened to be covered. Among his attendants, who were preparing to take their rest in the same manner, he observed that one of his grandsons, for his better accommodation, had rolled a large snowball, and placed it below his head. The wrath of the ancient chief was awakened by a symptom of what he conceived to be degenerate luxury. 'Out upon thee,' said he, kicking the frozen bolster from the head which it supported; 'art thou so effeminate as to need a pillow?' The officer of engineers, whose curious letters from the Highlands have been more than once quoted, tells a similar story of Macdonald of Keppoch, and subjoins the following remarks:—' This and many other stories are romantick; but there is one thing, that at first thought might seem very romantick, of which I have been credibly assured, that when the Highlanders are constrained to lie among the hills, in cold dry windy weather, they sometimes soak the plaid in some river or burn (i. e. brook), and then, holding up a corner of it a little above their heads, they turn themselves round and round, till they are enveloped by the whole mantle. They then lay themselves down on the heath, upon the leeward side of some hill, where the wet and the warmth of their bodies make a steam like that of a boiling kettle. The wet, they say, keeps them warm by thickening the stuff, and keeping the wind from penetrating. I must confess I should have been apt to question this fact, had I not frequently seen them wet from morning to night, and even at the beginning of the rain, not so much as stir a few yards to shelter, but continue in it without necessity, till they were, as we say, wet through and through. And that is soon effected by the looseness and spunginess of the plaiding; but the bonnet is frequently taken off and wrung like a dishclout, and then put on again. They have been accustomed from their infancy to be often wet, and to take the water like spaniels, and this is become a second nature, and can scarcely be called a hardship to them, insomuch that I used to say, they seemed to be of the duck kind, and to love water as well. Though I never saw this preparation for sleep in windy weather, yet, setting out early in a morning from one of the huts, I have seen the marks of their lodging, where the ground has been free from rime or snow, which remained all round the spot where they had lain.'—*Letters from Scotland*, Lond. 1754, 8vo, ii. p. 108.

Note XXVII.

—*his henchman came.*—P. 228.

'This officer is a sort of secretary, and is to be ready, upon all occasions, to venture his life in defence of his master; and at drinking-bouts he stands behind his seat, at his haunch, from whence his title is derived, and watches the conversation, to see if any one offends his patron. An English officer being in company with a certain chieftain, and several other Highland gentlemen, near Killichumen, had an argument with the *great man*; and both being well warmed with usky, at last the dispute grew very hot. A youth who was henchman, not understanding one word of English, imagined his chief was insulted, and thereupon drew his pistol from his side, and snapped it at the officer's head: but the pistol missed fire, otherwise it is more than probable he might have suffered death from the hand of that little vermin. But it is very disagreeable to an Englishman over a bottle, with the Highlanders, to see every one of them have his gilly, that is, his servant, standing behind him all the while, let what will be the subject of conversation.'—*Letters from Scotland*, ii. 159.

Note XXVIII.

And while the Fiery Cross glanced, like a meteor, round.—P. 229.

When a chieftain designed to summon his clan upon any sudden or important emergency, he slew a goat, and making a cross of any light wood, seared its extremities in the fire, and extinguished them in the blood of the animal. This was called the *Fiery Cross*, also *Crean Tarigh*, or the *Cross of Shame*, because disobedience to what the symbol implied, inferred infamy. It was delivered to a swift and trusty messenger, who ran full speed with it to the next hamlet, where he presented it to the principal person, with a single word, implying the place of rendezvous. He who received the symbol was bound to send it forward, with equal despatch, to the next village; and thus it passed with incredible celerity through all the district which owed allegiance to the chief, and also among his allies and neighbours, if the danger was common to them. At sight of the Fiery Cross, every man, from sixteen years old to sixty, capable of bearing arms, was obliged instantly to repair, in his best arms and accoutrements, to the place of rendezvous. He who failed to appear suffered the extremities of fire and sword, which were emblematically denounced to the disobedient by the bloody and burnt marks upon this warlike signal. During the civil war of 1745-6, the Fiery Cross often made its circuit; and upon one occasion it passed through the whole district of Breadalbane, a tract of thirty-two miles, in three hours. The late Alexander Stewart, Esq., of Invernahyle, described to me his having sent round the Fiery Cross through the district of Appine, during the same commotion. The coast was threatened by a descent from two English frigates, and the flower of the young men were with the army of Prince Charles Edward, then in England; yet the summons was so effectual, that even old age and childhood obeyed it; and a force was collected in a few hours, so numerous and so enthusiastic, that all attempt at the intended diversion upon the country of the absent warriors was in prudence abandoned, as desperate.

This practice, like some others, is common to the Highlanders with the ancient Scandinavians, as will appear by the following extract from Olaus Magnus:—

'When the enemy is upon the sea-coast, or within the limits of northern kingdomes, then presently, by the command of the principal governours, with the counsel and consent of the old soldiers, who are notably skilled in such like business, a staff of three hands length, in the common sight of them all, is carried, by the speedy running of some active young man, unto that village or city, with this command,—that on the third, fourth, or eighth day, one, two, or three, or else every man in particular, from fifteen years old, shall come with his arms, and expenses for ten or twenty days, upon pain that his or their houses shall be burnt (which is intimated by the burning of the staff,) or else the master to be hanged (which is signified by the cord tied to it,) to appear speedily on such a bank, or field, or valley, to hear the cause he is called, and to hear orders from the said provincial governours what he shall do. Wherefore that messenger, swifter than any post or waggon, having done his commission, comes slowly back again, bringing a token with him that he hath done all legally, and every moment one or another runs to every village and tells those places what they must do. . . . . The messengers, therefore, of the footmen, that are to give warning to the people to meet for the battail, run fiercely and swiftly; for no snow, no rain, nor heat can stop them, nor night hold them; but they will soon run the race they undertake. The first messenger tells it to the next village, and that to the next; and so the hubbub runs all over till they all know it in that stift or territory, where, when and wherefore they must meet.'— OLAUS MAGNUS' *History of the Goths*, englished by J. S. Lond. 1658, book iv. chap. 3, 4.

NOTE XXIX.

That monk, of savage form and face.
—P. 230.

The state of religion in the middle ages afforded considerable facilities for those whose mode of life excluded them from regular worship, to secure, nevertheless, the ghostly assistance of confessors, perfectly willing to adapt the nature of their doctrine to the necessities and peculiar circumstances of their flock. Robin Hood, it is well known, had his celebrated domestic chaplain, Friar Tuck. And that same curtal friar was probably matched in manners and appearance by the ghostly fathers of the Tynedale robbers, who are thus described in an excommunication fulminated against their patrons by Richard Fox, Bishop of Durham, tempore Henrici VIII. 'We have further understood, that there are many chaplains in the said territories of Tynedale and Redesdale, who are public and open maintainers of concubinage, irregular, suspended, excommunicated, and interdicted persons, and withal so utterly ignorant of letters, that it has been found by those who objected this to them, that there were some who, having celebrated mass for ten years, were still unable to read the sacramental service. We have

also understood there are persons among them who, although not ordained, do take upon them the offices of priesthood; and, in contempt of God, celebrate the divine and sacred rites, and administer the sacraments, not only in sacred and dedicated places, but in those which are profane and interdicted, and most wretchedly ruinous; they themselves being attired in ragged, torn, and most filthy vestments, altogether unfit to be used in divine, or even in temporal offices. The which said chaplains do administer sacraments and sacramental rights to the aforesaid manifest and infamous thieves, robbers, depredators, receivers of stolen goods, and plunderers, and that without restitution, or intention to restore, as evinced by the act; and do also openly admit them to the rites of ecclesiastical sepulchre, without exacting security for restitution, although they are prohibited from doing so by the sacred canons, as well as by the institutes of the saints and fathers. All which infers the heavy peril of their own souls, and is a pernicious example to the other believers in Christ, as well as no slight, but an aggravated injury, to the numbers despoiled and plundered of their goods, gear, herds, and chattels[1].'

To this lively and picturesque description of the confessors and churchmen of predatory tribes, there may be added some curious particulars respecting the priests attached to the several septs of native Irish, during the reign of Queen Elizabeth. These friars had indeed to plead, that the incursions, which they not only pardoned, but even encouraged, were made upon those hostile to them, as well in religion as from national antipathy; but by Protestant writers they are uniformly alleged to be the chief instruments of Irish insurrection, the very well-spring of all rebellion towards the English government. Lithgow, the Scottish traveller, declares the Irish wood-kerne, or predatory tribes, to be but the hounds of their hunting priests, who directed their incursions by their pleasure, partly for sustenance, partly to gratify animosity, partly to foment general division, and always for the better security and easier domination of the friars[2]. Derrick, the liveliness and minuteness of whose descriptions may frequently apologize for his doggerel verses, after describing an Irish feast, and the encouragement given, by the songs of the bards, to its termination in an incursion upon the parts of the country more immediately under the dominion of the Eng-

---

[1] The Monition against the Robbers of Tynedale and Redesdale, with which I was favoured by my friend, Mr. Surtees of Mainsforth, may be found in the original Latin, in the Appendix to the Introduction to the Border Minstrelsy, No. VII. vol. i. p. 274.
[2] Lithgow's Travels, first edition, p. 431.

lish, records the no less powerful arguments
used by the friar to excite their animosity:—

> 'And more t' augment the flame,
>   and rancour of their harte,
> The frier, of his counsells vile,
>   to rebelles doth imparte,
> Affirming that it is
>   an almose deede to God,
> To make the English subjectes taste
>   the Irish rebells' rodde.
> To spoile, to kill, to burne,
>   this frier's counsell is ;
> And for the doing of the same,
>   he warrantes heavenlie blisse.
> He tells a holie tale ;
>   the white he tournes to black ;
> And through the pardons in his male,
>   he workes a knavishe knacke.'

The wreckful invasion of a part of the
English pale is then described with some
spirit ; the burning of houses, driving off
cattle, and all pertaining to such predatory
inroads, are illustrated by a rude cut. The
defeat of the Irish, by a party of English
soldiers from the next garrison, is then commemorated, and in like manner adorned
with an engraving, in which the frier is
exhibited mourning over the slain chieftain ;
or, as the rubric expresses it,

> 'The frier then, that treacherous knave ; with ough
>   ough-hone lament,
> To see his cousin Devil's-son to have so foul event.'

The matter is handled at great length in
the text, of which the following verses are
more than sufficient sample :

> 'The frier seyng this,
>   laments that lucklesse parte,
> And curseth to the pitte of hell
>   the death man's sturdie hearte ;
> Yet for to quight them with
>   the frier taketh paine,
> For al the synnes that ere he did
>   remission to obtaine.
> And therefore serves his booke,
>   the candell and the bell ;
> But thinke you that such apishe toies
>   bring damned souls from hell?
> It 'longs not to my parte
>   infernall things to knowe ;
> But I beleve till later daie,
>   thei rise not from belowe,
> Yet hope that friers give
>   to this rebellious rout,
> If that their souls should chaunce in hell,
>   to bringe them quicklie out,
> Doeth make them lead suche lives,
>   as neither God nor man,
> Without revenge for their desartes,
>   permitte or suffer can.
> Thus friers are the cause,
>   the fountain, and the spring,
> Of hurleburies in this lande,
>   of eche unhappie thing.
> Thei cause them to rebell
>   against their soveraigne quene,
> And through rebellion often tymes,
>   their lives do vanish clene.
> So as by friers meanes,
>   in whom all follie swimme,
> The Irishe karne doe often lose
>   the life, with hedde and limme¹.'

¹ This curious picture of Ireland was inserted by
the author in the republication of Somers' Tracts,
vol. i, in which the plates have been also inserted,
from the only impressions known to exist, belonging
to the copy in the Advocates' Library. See Somers'
Tracts, vol. i. pp. 591, 594.

As the Irish tribes and those of the
Scottish Highlands are much more intimately
allied, by language, manners, dress, and customs, than the antiquaries of either country
have been willing to admit, I flatter myself
I have here produced a strong warrant for
the character sketched in the text. The
following picture, though of a different kind,
serves to establish the existence of ascetic
religionists, to a comparatively late period, in
the Highlands and Western Isles. There
is a great deal of simplicity in the description,
for which, as for much similar information,
I am obliged to Dr. John Martin, who visited
the Hebrides at the suggestion of Sir
Robert Sibbald, a Scottish antiquarian of
eminence, and early in the eighteenth century published a description of them, which
procured him admission into the Royal
Society. He died in London about 1719.
His work is a strange mixture of learning,
observation, and gross credulity.

'I remember,' says this author, 'I have
seen an old lay-capuchin here (in the island
of Benbecula), called in their language
Brahir-bocht, that is, *Poor Brother* ; which
is literally true ; for he answers this character, having nothing but what is given
him ; he holds himself fully satisfied with
food and rayment, and lives in as great
simplicity as any of his order ; his diet is
very mean, and he drinks only fair water ;
his habit is no less mortifying than that of
his brethren elsewhere : he wears a short
coat, which comes no farther than his
middle, with narrow sleeves like a waistcoat : he wears a plad above it, girt about
the middle, which reaches to his knee : the
plad is fastened on his breast with a wooden
pin, his neck bare, and his feet often so
too ; he wears a hat for ornament, and the
string about it is a bit of a fisher's line,
made of horse-hair. This plad he wears instead of a gown worn by those of his order
in other countries. I told him he wanted
the flaxen girdle that men of his order
usually wear ; he answered me, that he
wore a leathern one, which was the same
thing. Upon the matter, if he is spoke to
when at meat, he answers again ; which is
contrary to the custom of his order. This
poor man frequently diverts himself with
angling of trouts ; he lies upon straw, and
has no bell (as others have) to call him to
his devotions, but only his conscience, as
he told me.'—MARTIN's *Description of the
Western Highlands*, p. 82.

NOTE XXX.

Of Brian's birth strange tales were told.
—P. 230.

The legend which follows is not of the
author's invention. It is possible he may
differ from modern critics, in supposing
that the records of human superstition, if

peculiar to, and characteristic of, the country in which the scene is laid, are a legitimate subject of poetry. He gives, however, a ready assent to the narrower proposition which condemns all attempts of an irregular and disordered fancy to excite terror, by accumulating a train of fantastic and incoherent horrors, whether borrowed from all countries, and patched upon a narrative belonging to one which knew them not, or derived from the author's own imagination. In the present case, therefore, I appeal to the record which I have transcribed, with the variation of a very few words, from the geographical collections made by the Laird of Macfarlane. I know not whether it be necessary to remark, that the miscellaneous concourse of youths and maidens on the night and on the spot where the miracle is said to have taken place, might, even in a credulous age, have somewhat diminished the wonder which accompanied the conception of Gilli-Doir-Magrevollich.

'There is bot two myles from Inverloghie, the church of Kilmalee, in Lochyeld. In ancient tymes there was ane church builded upon ane hill, which was above this church, which doeth now stand in this toune; and ancient men doeth say, that there was a battell foughten on ane litle hill not the tenth part of a myle from this church, be certaine men which they did not know what they were. And long tyme thereafter, certaine herds of that toune, and of the next toune, called Unnatt, both wenches and youthes, did on a tyme conveen with others on that hill; and the day being somewhat cold, did gather the bones of the dead men that were slayne long tyme before in that place, and did make a fire to warm them. At last they did all remove from the fire, except one maid or wench, which was verie cold, and she did remaine there for a space. She being quyetlie her alone, without anie other companie, took up her cloaths above her knees, or thereby, to warm her; a wind did come and caste the ashes upon her, and she was conceived of ane man-chyld. Severall tymes thereafter she was verie sick, and at last she was knowne to be with chyld. And then her parents did ask at her the matter heiroff, which the wench could not weel answer which way to satisfie them. At last she resolved them with ane answer. As fortune fell upon her concerning this marvellous miracle, the chyld being borne, his name was called *Gili-doir Maghrevollich*, that is to say, the *Black Child, Son to the Bones*. So called, his grandfather sent him to school, and so he was a good schollar, and godlie. He did build this church which doeth now stand in Lochyeld, called Kilmalie.'—MACFARLANE, *ut supra*, ii. 188.

NOTE XXXI.

Yet ne'er again to braid her hair
The virgin snood did Alice wear.
—P. 231.

The *snood*, or riband, with which a Scottish lass braided her hair, had an emblematical signification, and applied to her maiden character. It was exchanged for the *curch*, *toy*, or coif, when she passed, by marriage, into the matron state. But if the damsel was so unfortunate as to lose pretensions to the name of maiden, without gaining a right to that of matron, she was neither permitted to use the snood, nor advanced to the graver dignity of the curch. In old Scottish songs there occur many sly allusions to such misfortune; as in the old words to the popular tune of 'Ower the muir amang the heather.'

'Down amang the broom, the broom,
   Down amang the broom, my dearie,
The lassie lost her silken snood,
   That gard her greet till she was wearie.'

NOTE XXXII.

The desert gave him visions wild,
Such as might suit the spectre's child.
—P. 231.

In adopting the legend concerning the birth of the founder of the Church of Kilmalie, the author has endeavoured to trace the effects which such a belief was likely to produce, in a barbarous age, on the person to whom it related. It seems likely that he must have become a fanatic or an impostor, or that mixture of both which forms a more frequent character than either of them, as existing separately. In truth, mad persons are frequently more anxious to impress upon others a faith in their visions, than they are themselves confirmed in their reality; as, on the other hand, it is difficult for the most cool-headed impostor long to personate an enthusiast, without in some degree believing what he is so eager to have believed. It was a natural attribute of such a character as the supposed hermit, that he should credit the numerous superstitions with which the minds of ordinary Highlanders are almost always imbued. A few of these are slightly alluded to in this stanza. The River-demon, or River-horse, for it is that form which he commonly assumes, is the Kelpy of the Lowlands, an evil and malicious spirit, delighting to forbode and to witness calamity. He frequents most Highland lakes and rivers; and one of his most memorable exploits was performed upon the banks of Loch Vennachar, in the very district which forms the scene of our action: it consisted in the destruction of a funeral procession with all its attendants. The 'noontide hag,' called in Gaelic *Glaslich*, a tall, emaciated, gigantic female figure, is supposed in particular to haunt the district of Knoidart. A goblin, dressed in antique armour, and having one hand covered with blood, called from that circumstance, *Lham-dearg*, or Red-hand, is a tenant of the forests of Glenmore and Rothiemurcus. Other spirits of the desert, all frightful in shape and malignant in disposition, are believed to frequent different mountains and glens of the Highlands, where any unusual appearance, produced by mist, or the strange lights that are sometimes thrown upon particular objects, never fails to present an apparition to the imagination of the solitary and melancholy mountaineer.

Note XXXIII.

The fatal Ben-Shie's boding scream.
—P. 231.

Most great families in the Highlands were supposed to have a tutelar, or rather a domestic spirit, attached to them, who took an interest in their prosperity, and intimated, by its wailings, any approaching disaster. That of Grant of Grant was called *May Moullach*, and appeared in the form of a girl, who had her arm covered with hair. Grant of Rothiemurcus had an attendant called *Bodach-an-dun*, or the Ghost of the Hill; and many other examples might be mentioned. The Ban-Schie implies a female Fairy, whose lamentations were often supposed to precede the death of a chieftain of particular families. When she is visible, it is in the form of an old woman, with a blue mantle and streaming hair. A superstition of the same kind is, I believe, universally received by the inferior ranks of the native Irish.

The death of the head of a Highland family is also sometimes supposed to be announced by a chain of lights of different colours, called *Dr'eug*, or death of the Druid. The direction which it takes, marks the place of the funeral. [See the Essay on Fairy Superstitions in the Border Minstrelsy.]

Note XXXIV.

Sounds, too, had come in midnight blast,
Of charging steeds, careering fast
Along Benharrow's shingly side,
Where mortal horseman ne'er might ride.
—P. 231.

A presage of the kind alluded to in the text is still believed to announce death to the ancient Highland family of M'Lean of Lochbuy. The spirit of an ancestor slain in battle is heard to gallop along a stony

bank, and then to ride thrice around the family residence, ringing his fairy bridle, and thus intimating the approaching calamity. How easily the eye, as well as the ear, may be deceived upon such occasions, is evident from the stories of armies in the air, and other spectral phenomena with which history abounds. Such an apparition is said to have been witnessed upon the side of Southfell mountain, between Penrith and Keswick, upon the 23rd June 1744, by two persons, William Lancaster of Blakehills, and Daniel Stricket, his servant, whose attestation to the fact, with a full account of the apparition, dated the 21st July 1745, is printed in Clarke's Survey of the Lakes. The apparition consisted of several troops of horse moving in regular order, with a steady rapid motion, making a curved sweep around the fell, and seeming to the spectators to disappear over the ridge of the mountain. Many persons witnessed this phenomenon, and observed the last, or last but one, of the supposed troop, occasionally leave his rank, and pass at a gallop to the front, when he resumed the same steady pace. This curious appearance, making the necessary allowance for imagination, may be perhaps sufficiently accounted for by optical deception.—*Survey of the Lakes*, p. 25.

Supernatural intimations of approaching fate are not, I believe, confined to Highland families. Howel mentions having seen, at a lapidary's, in 1632, a monumental stone, prepared for four persons of the name of Oxenham, before the death of each of whom, the inscription stated a white bird to have appeared and fluttered around the bed while the patient was in the last agony.—*Familiar Letters*, edit. 1726, 247. Glanville mentions one family, the members of which received this solemn sign by music, the sound of which floated from the family residence, and seemed to die in a neighbouring wood; another, that of Captain Wood of Bampton, to whom the signal was given by knocking. But the most remarkable instance of the kind occurs in the MS. Memoirs of Lady Fanshaw, so exemplary for her conjugal affection. Her husband, Sir Richard, and she, chanced during their abode in Ireland to visit a friend, the head of a sept, who resided in his ancient baronial castle, surrounded with a moat. At midnight she was awakened by a ghastly and supernatural scream, and, looking out of bed, beheld, by the moonlight, a female face and part of the form, hovering at the window. The distance from the ground, as well as the circumstance of the moat, excluded the possibility that what she beheld was of this world. The face was that of a young and rather handsome woman, but pale; and the hair, which was reddish, was loose and dishevelled. The dress, which Lady Fanshaw's terror did not prevent her remarking accurately, was that of the ancient Irish. This apparition continued to exhibit itself for some time, and then vanished with two shrieks, similar to that which had first excited Lady Fanshaw's attention. In the morning, with infinite terror, she communicated to her host what she had witnessed, and found him prepared not only to credit but to account for the apparition. 'A near relation of my family,' said he, 'expired last night in this castle. We disguised our certain expectation of the event from you, lest it should throw a cloud over the cheerful reception which was due to you. Now, before such an event happens in this family and castle, the female spectre whom you have seen always is visible. She is believed to be the spirit of a woman of inferior rank, whom one of my ancestors degraded himself by marrying, and whom afterwards, to expiate the dishonour done his family, he caused to be drowned in the castle moat.'

NOTE XXXV.

Whose parents in Inch-Cailliach wave
Their shadows o'er Clan-Alpine's grave.
—P. 232.

Inch-Cailliach, the Isle of Nuns, or of Old Women, is a most beautiful island at the lower extremity of Loch Lomond. The church belonging to the former nunnery was long used as the place of worship for the parish of Buchanan, but scarce any vestiges of it now remain. The burial-ground continues to be used, and contains the family places of sepulture of several neighbouring clans. The monuments of the lairds of Macgregor, and of other families, claiming a descent from the old Scottish King Alpine, are most remarkable. The Highlanders are as zealous of their rights of sepulture, as may be expected from a people whose whole laws and government, if clanship can be called so, turned upon the single principle of family descent. 'May his ashes be scattered on the water,' was one of the deepest and most solemn imprecations which they used against an enemy. [See a detailed description of the funeral ceremonies of a Highland chieftain in the Fair Maid of Perth. *Waverley Novels*, vol. 43, chaps. x. and xi. Edit. 1834.]

NOTE XXXVI.

—— the dun deer's hide
On fleeter foot was never tied.—P. 233.

The present *brogue* of the Highlanders is made of half-dried leather, with holes to admit and let out the water; for walking the moors dry-shod is a matter altogether out of the question. The ancient buskin was still ruder, being made of undressed deer's hide, with the hair outwards; a circumstance which procured the Highlanders

the well-known epithet of *Red-shanks*. The process is very accurately described by one Elder (himself a Highlander) in the project for a union between England and Scotland, addressed to Henry VIII. 'We go a-hunting, and after that we have slain red-deer, we flay off the skin by-and-by, and setting of our bare-foot on the inside thereof, for want of cunning shoemakers, by your grace's pardon, we play the cobblers, compassing and measuring so much thereof as shall reach up to our ankles, pricking the upper part thereof with holes, that the water may repass where it enters, and stretching it up with a strong thong of the same above our said ankles. So, and please your noble grace, we make our shoes. Therefore, we using such manner of shoes, the rough hairy side outwards, in your grace's dominions of England, we be called *Roughfooted Scots*.'—PINKERTON'S *History*, vol. ii. p. 397.

NOTE XXXVII.

The dismal coronach.—P. 234.

The *Coronach* of the Highlanders, like the *Ululatus* of the Romans, and the *Ululoo* of the Irish, was a wild expression of lamentation, poured forth by the mourners over the body of a departed friend. When the words of it were articulate, they expressed the praises of the deceased, and the loss the clan would sustain by his death. The following is a lamentation of this kind, literally translated from the Gaelic, to some of the ideas of which the text stands indebted. The tune is so popular, that it has since become the war-march, or Gathering of the clan.

Coronach on Sir Lauchlan, Chief of Maclean.

Which of all the Senachies
Can trace thy line from the root up to Paradise
But Macvuirih, the son of Fergus?
No sooner had thine ancient stately tree
Taken firm root in Albion,
Than one of thy forefathers fell at Harlaw.—
'Twas then we lost a chief of deathless name.

Tis no base weed—no planted tree,
Nor a seedling of last Autumn;
Nor a sapling planted at Beltain[1];
Wide, wide around were spread its lofty branches—
But the topmost bough is lowly laid!
Thou hast forsaken us before Sawaine[2].

Thy dwelling is the winter house;—
Loud, sad, sad, and mighty is thy death-song!
Oh! courteous champion of Montrose!
Oh! stately warrior of the Celtic Isles!
Thou shalt buckle thy harness on no more!

The coronach has for some years past been superseded at funerals by the use of the bagpipe; and that also is, like many other Highland peculiarities, falling into disuse, unless in remote districts.

---

[1] Bell's fire, or Whitsunday.   [2] Hallowe'en.

NOTE XXXVIII.

Benledi saw the Cross of Fire,
It glanced like lightning up Strath-Ire.
—P. 235.

Inspection of the provincial map of Perthshire, or any large map of Scotland, will trace the progress of the signal through the small district of lakes and mountains, which, in exercise of my poetical privilege, I have subjected to the authority of my imaginary chieftain, and which, at the period of my romance, was really occupied by a clan who claimed a descent from Alpine; a clan the most unfortunate, and most persecuted, but neither the least distinguished, least powerful, nor least brave, of the tribes of the Gael.

> ' Slioch non rioghridh duchaisach
> Bha-shios an Dun-Staiobhinish
> Aig an roubh crun na Halba othus
> 'Stag a cheii duchas fast ris.'

The first stage of the Fiery Cross is to Duncraggan, a place near the Brigg of Turk, where a short stream divides Loch Achray from Loch Vennachar. From thence, it passes towards Callender, and then, turning to the left up the pass of Leny, is consigned to Norman at the chapel of Saint Bride, which stood on a small and romantic knoll in the middle of the valley, called Strath-Ire. Tombea and Arnandave, or Ardmandave, are names of places in the vicinity. The alarm is then supposed to pass along the lake of Lubnaig, and through the various glens in the district of Balquidder, including the neighbouring tracts of Glenfinlas and Strathgartney.

NOTE XXXIX.

Not faster o'er thy heathery braes,
Balquidder, speeds the midnight blaze.
—P. 237.

It may be necessary to inform the southern reader, that the heath on the Scottish moorlands is often set fire to, that the sheep may have the advantage of the young herbage produced, in room of the tough old heather plants. This custom (execrated by sportsmen) produces occasionally the most beautiful nocturnal appearances, similar almost to the discharge of a volcano. This simile is not new to poetry. The charge of a warrior, in the fine ballad of Hardyknute, is said to be ' like fire to heather set.'

NOTE XL.

No oath, but by his chieftain's hand,
No law, but Roderick Dhu's command.
—P. 237.

The deep and implicit respect paid by the Highland clansmen to their chief, rendered this both a common and a solemn oath. In other respects they were like most savage nations, capricious in their ideas concerning the obligatory power of oaths. One solemn mode of swearing was by kissing the *dirk*, imprecating upon themselves death by that, or a similar weapon, if they broke their vow. But for oaths in the usual form, they are said to have had little respect. As for the reverence due to the chief, it may be guessed from the following odd example of a Highland point of honour:—

'The clan whereto the above-mentioned tribe belongs, is the only one I have heard of, which is without a chief; that is, being divided into families, under several chieftains, without any particular patriarch of the whole name. And this is a great reproach, as may appear from an affair that fell out at my table, in the Highlands, between one of that name and a Cameron. The provocation given by the latter was, "Name your chief." —The return of it at once was, "You are a fool." They went out next morning, but having early notice of it, I sent a small party of soldiers after them, which, in all probability, prevented some barbarous mischief that might have ensued: for the chiefless Highlander, who is himself a petty chieftain, was going to the place appointed with a small sword and pistol, whereas the Cameron (an old man) took with him only his broadsword, according to the agreement.

'When all was over, and I had, at least seemingly, reconciled them, I was told the words, of which I seemed to think but slightly, were, to one of the clan, the greatest of all provocations.'—*Letters from Scotland*, vol. ii. p. 221.

NOTE XLI.

—— a low and lonely cell.
By many a bard, in Celtic tongue,
Has Coir-nan-Uriskin been sung.—P. 237.

This is a very steep and most romantic hollow in the mountain of Benvenue, over-hanging the south-eastern extremity of Loch Katrine. It is surrounded with stupendous rocks, and overshadowed with birch-trees, mingled with oaks, the spontaneous production of the mountain, even where its cliffs appear denuded of soil. A dale in so wild a situation, and amid a people whose genius bordered on the romantic, did not remain without appropriate deities. The name literally implies the Corri, or Den, of the Wild or Shaggy men. Perhaps this, as conjectured by Mr. Alexander Campbell[1], may have originally only implied its being the haunt of a ferocious banditti. But tradition has ascribed to the *Urisk*, who gives name to the cavern, a figure between a goat and a man; in short, however much the classical reader may be startled, precisely

---

[1] *Journey from Edinburgh.* 1802, p. 100.

that of the Grecian Satyr. The *Urisk* seems not to have inherited, with the form, the petulance of the sylvan deity of the classics: his occupation, on the contrary, resembled those of Milton's Lubbar Fiend, or of the Scottish Brownie, though he differed from both in name and appearance. 'The *Urisks*,' says Dr. Graham, 'were a set of lubberly supernaturals, who, like the Brownies, could be gained over by kind attention, to perform the drudgery of the farm, and it was believed that many of the families in the Highlands had one of the order attached to it. They were supposed to be dispersed over the Highlands, each in his own wild recess, but the solemn stated meetings of the order were regularly held in this Cave of Benvenue. This current superstition, no doubt, alludes to some circumstance in the ancient history of this country.'—*Scenery on the Southern Confines of Perthshire*, p. 19, 1806.—It must be owned that the *Coir*, or Den, does not, in its present state, meet our ideas of a subterraneous grotto, or cave, being only a small and narrow cavity, among huge fragments of rocks rudely piled together. But such a scene is liable to convulsions of nature, which a Lowlander cannot estimate, and which may have choked up what was originally a cavern. At least the name and tradition warrant the author of a fictitious tale to assert its having been such at the remote period in which this scene is laid.

Note XLII.

The wild pass of Beal-nam-bo.—P. 238.

Bealach-nam-bo, or the pass of cattle, is a most magnificent glade, overhung with aged birch-trees, a little higher up the mountain than the Coir-nan-Uriskin, treated of in a former note. The whole composes the most sublime piece of scenery that imagination can conceive.

Note XLIII.

A single page, to bear his sword,
Alone attended on his lord.—P. 238.

A Highland chief, being as absolute in his patriarchal authority as any prince, had a corresponding number of officers attached to his person. He had his body-guards, called *Luichttach*, picked from his clan for strength, activity, and entire devotion to his person. These, according to their deserts, were sure to share abundantly in the rude profusion of his hospitality. It is recorded, for example, by tradition, that Allan MacLean, chief of that clan, happened upon a time to hear one of these favourite retainers observe to his comrade, that their chief grew old. 'Whence do you infer that?' replied the other.—'When was it,' rejoined

the first, 'that a soldier of Allan's was obliged, as I am now, not only to eat the flesh from the bone, but even to tear off the inner skin, or filament?' The hint was quite sufficient, and MacLean next morning, to relieve his followers from such dire necessity, undertook an inroad on the mainland, the ravage of which altogether effaced the memory of his former expeditions for the like purpose.

Our officer of Engineers, so often quoted, has given us a distinct list of the domestic officers who, independent of *Luichttach*, or *gardes de corps*, belonged to the establishment of a Highland Chief. These are, 1. *The Henchman*. See these notes, p. 287. 2. *The Bard*. See pp. 280 1. 3. *Bladier*, or spokesman. 4. *Gillie-more*, or sword-bearer, alluded to in the text. 5. *Gillie-casflue*, who carried the chief, if on foot, over the fords. 6. *Gillie-comstraine*, who leads the chief's horse. 7. *Gillie-Trushanarinsh*, the baggage man. 8. *The piper*. 9. The piper's gillie or attendant, who carries the bagpipe[1]. Although this appeared, naturally enough, very ridiculous to an English officer, who considered the master of such a retinue as no more than an English gentleman of £500 a-year, yet in the circumstances of the chief, whose strength and importance consisted in the number and attachment of his followers, it was of the last consequence, in point of policy, to have in his gift subordinate offices, which called immediately round his person those who were most devoted to him, and, being of value in their estimation, were also the means of rewarding them.

Note XLIV.

The Taghairm call'd; by which, afar,
Our sires foresaw the events of war.
—P. 240.

The Highlanders, like all rude people, had various superstitious modes of inquiring into futurity. One of the most noted was the *Taghairm*, mentioned in the text. A person was wrapped up in the skin of a newly-slain bullock, and deposited beside a waterfall, or at the bottom of a precipice, or in some other strange, wild, and unusual situation, where the scenery around him suggested nothing but objects of horror. In this situation, he revolved in his mind the question proposed; and whatever was impressed upon him by his exalted imagination, passed for the inspiration of the disembodied spirits, who haunt the desolate recesses. In some of these Hebrides, they attributed the same oracular power to a large black stone by the sea-shore, which they approached with certain solemnities, and considered the first fancy which came into their own minds, after they did so, to be

---

[1] *Letters from Scotland*, vol. ii. p. 15.

the undoubted dictate of the tutelar deity of the stone, and, as such, to be, if possible, punctually complied with. Martin has recorded the following curious modes of Highland augury, in which the Taghairm, and its effects upon the person who was subjected to it, may serve to illustrate the text.

'It was an ordinary thing among the over-curious to consult an invisible oracle, concerning the fate of families and battles, &c. This was performed three different ways: the first was by a company of men, one of whom, being detached by lot, was afterwards carried to a river, which was the boundary between two villages; four of the company laid hold on him, and, having shut his eyes, they took him by the legs and arms, and then, tossing him to and again, struck his hips with force against the bank. One of them cried out, What is it you have got here? another answers, A log of birch-wood. The other cries again, Let his invisible friends appear from all quarters, and let them relieve him by giving an answer to our present demands: and in a few minutes after, a number of little creatures came from the sea, who answered the question, and disappeared suddenly. The man was then set at liberty, and they all returned home, to take their measures according to the prediction of their false prophets; but the poor deluded fools were abused, for their answer was still ambiguous. This was always practised in the night, and may literally be called the works of darkness.

'I had an account from the most intelligent and judicious men in the Isle of Skie, that about sixty-two years ago, the oracle was thus consulted only once, and that was in the parish of Kilmartin, on the east side, by a wicked and mischievous race of people, who are now extinguished, both root and branch.

'The second way of consulting the oracle was by a party of men, who first retired to solitary places, remote from any house, and there they singled out one of their number, and wrapt him in a big cow's hide, which they folded about him; his whole body was covered with it, except his head, and so left in this posture all night, until his invisible friends relieved him, by giving a proper answer to the question in hand; which he received, as he fancied, from several persons that he found about him all that time. His consorts returned to him at the break of day, and then he communicated his news to them; which often proved fatal to those concerned in such unwarrantable enquiries.

'There was a third way of consulting, which was a confirmation of the second above mentioned. The same company who put the man into the hide, took a live cat, and put him on a spit; one of the number was employed to turn the spit, and one of his consorts enquired of him, What are you doing? he answered, I roast this cat, until his friends answer the question; which must be the same that was proposed by the man shut up in the hide. And afterwards, a very big cat [1] comes, attended by a number of lesser cats, desiring to relieve the cat turned upon the spit, and then answers the question. If this answer proved the same that was given to the man in the hide, then it was taken as a confirmation of the other, which, in this case, was believed infallible.

'Mr. Alexander Cooper, present minister of North-Vist, told me, that one John Erach, in the Isle of Lewis, assured him, it was his fate to have been led by his curiosity with some who consulted this oracle, and that he was a night within the hide, as above mentioned; during which time he felt and heard such terrible things, that he could not express them; the impression it made on him was such as could never go off, and he said, for a thousand worlds he would never again be concerned in the like performance, for this had disordered him to a high degree. He confessed it ingenuously, and with an air of great remorse, and seemed to be very penitent under a just sense of so great a crime: he declared this about five years since, and is still living in the Lewis for any thing I know.'—*Description of the Western Isles*, p. 110. See also PENNANT'S *Scottish Tour*, vol. ii. p. 361.

NOTE XLV.

The choicest of the prey we had,
When swept our merry-men Gallangad.
—P. 240.

I know not if it be worth observing, that this passage is taken almost literally from the mouth of an old Highland Kern or Ketteran, as they were called. He used to narrate the merry doings of the good old time when he was follower of Rob Roy MacGregor. This leader, on one occasion, thought proper to make a descent upon the lower part of the Loch Lomond district, and summoned all the heritors and farmers to meet at the Kirk of Drymen, to pay him black-mail, i. e. tribute for forbearance and protection. As this invitation was supported by a band of thirty or forty stout fellows, only one gentleman—an ancestor, if I mistake not, of the present Mr. Grahame of Gartmore—ventured to decline compliance. Rob Roy instantly swept his land of all he could drive away, and among the spoil was a bull of the old Scottish wild breed, whose ferocity occasioned great plague to the Ketterans. 'But ere we had reached the Row of Dennan,' said the old man, 'a child

---

[1] The reader may have met with the story of the 'King of the Cats,' in Lord Littleton's Letters. It is well known in the Highlands as a nursery tale.

might have scratched his ears[1].' The circumstance is a minute one, but it paints the times when the poor beeve was compelled

> 'To hoof it o'er as many weary miles,
> With grinding pikemen hollowing at his heels,
> As e'er the bravest antler of the woods.'
> *Ethwald.*

NOTE XLVI.

——*that huge cliff, whose ample verge*
Tradition calls the Hero's Targe.—P. 240.

There is a rock so named in the Forest of Glenfinlas, by which a tumultuary cataract takes its course. This wild place is said in former times to have afforded refuge to an outlaw, who was supplied with provisions by a woman, who lowered them down from the brink of the precipice above. His water he procured for himself, by letting down a flagon tied to a string, into the black pool beneath the fall.

NOTE XLVII.

Or raven on the blasted oak,
That, watching while the deer is broke,
His morsel claims with sullen croak?
—P. 241.

Broke = *quartered*. Everything belonging to the chase was matter of solemnity among our ancestors; but nothing was more so than the mode of cutting up, or, as it was technically called, *breaking*, the slaughtered stag. The forester had his allotted portion; the hounds had a certain allowance; and, to make the division as general as possible, the very birds had their share also 'There is a little gristle,' says Turberville, 'which is upon the spoone of the brisket, which we call the raven's bone; and I have seen in some places a raven so wont and accustomed to it, that she would never fail to croak and cry for it all the time you were in breaking up of the deer, and would not depart till she had it.' In the very ancient metrical romance of Sir Tristrem, that peerless knight, who is said to have been the very deviser of all rules of chase, did not omit the ceremony :—

> 'The rauen he yaue his yiftes
> Sat on the fourched tre.'
> *Sir Tristrem.*

The raven might also challenge his rights by the Book of St. Albans; for thus says Dame Juliana Berners :—

> 'Slitteth anon
> The bely to the side, from the corbyn bone,
> That is corbyn's fee, at the death he will be.'

---

[1] This anecdote was, in former editions, inaccurately ascribed to Gregor Macgregor of Glengyle, called *Ghlune Dhu*, or Black-knee, a relation of Rob Roy, but, as I have been assured, not addicted to his predatory excesses.—*Note to Third Edition.*

Jonson, in 'The Sad Shepherd,' gives a more poetical account of the same ceremony :—

> '*Marian.*   He that undoes him,
> Doth cleave the brisket bone, upon the spoon
> Of which a little gristle grows—you call it—
>   *Robin Hood.*—The raven's bone.
>   *Marian.*   Now o'er head sat a raven
> On a sere bough, a grown, great bird, and hoarse,
> Who, all the while the deer was breaking up,
> So croak'd and cried for 't, as all the huntsmen,
> Especially old Scathlock, thought it ominous.'

NOTE XLVIII.

Which spills the foremost foeman's life,
That party conquers in the strife.'—P. 241.

Though this be in the text described as a response of the Taghairm, or Oracle of the Hide, it was of itself an augury frequently attended to. The fate of the battle was often anticipated in the imagination of the combatants, by observing which party first shed blood. It is said that the Highlanders under Montrose were so deeply imbued with this notion, that, on the morning of the battle of Tippermoor, they murdered a defenceless herdsman, whom they found in the fields, merely to secure an advantage of so much consequence to their party.

NOTE XLIX.

Alice Brand.—P. 243.

This little fairy tale is founded upon a very curious Danish ballad, which occurs in the *Kæmpe Viser*, a collection of heroic songs, first published in 1591, and reprinted in 1695, inscribed by Anders Sofrensen, the collector and editor, to Sophia Queen of Denmark. I have been favoured with a literal translation of the original, by my learned friend Mr. Robert Jamieson, whose deep knowledge of Scandinavian antiquities will, I hope, one day be displayed in illustration of the history of Scottish Ballad and Song, for which no man possesses more ample materials. The story will remind the readers of the Border Minstrelsy of the tale of Young Tamlane. But this is only a solitary and not very marked instance of coincidence, whereas several of the other ballads in the same collection find exact counterparts in the *Kæmpe Viser*. Which may have been the originals, will be a question for future antiquaries. Mr. Jamieson, to secure the power of literal translation, has adopted the old Scottish idiom, which approaches so near to that of the Danish, as almost to give word for word, as well as line for line, and indeed in many verses the orthography alone is altered. As *Wester Haf*, mentioned in the first stanzas of the ballad, means the *West Sea*, in opposition to the Baltic, or *East Sea*, Mr. Jamieson inclines to be of opinion, that the scene of the disenchantment is laid in one of the Orkney, or Hebride Islands. To each

verse in the original is added a burden,
having a kind of meaning of its own, but not
applicable, at least not uniformly applicable,
to the sense of the stanza to which it is subjoined : this is very common both in Danish
and Scottish song.

THE ELFIN GRAY.

TRANSLATED FROM THE DANISH KÆMPE VISER,
p. 143, AND FIRST PUBLISHED IN 1591.

Der ligger en vold i Vester Haf,
Der agter en bonde at bygge:
Hand fører did baade hôg og hund,
Og agter der om vinteren at ligge.
(DE VILDE DIUR OG DIURENE UDI SKOFVEN.)

1. There liggs a wold in Wester Haf,
   There a husbande means to bigg,
   And thither he carries baith hawk and hound,
   There meaning the winter to ligg.
   (*The wild deer and daes i' the shaw out.*)

2. He taks wi' him baith hound and cock,
   The langer he means to stay,
   The wild deer in the shaws that are
   May sairly rue the day.
   (*The wild deer, &c.*)

3. He's hew'd the beech, and he's fell'd the aik,
   Sae has he the poplar gray ;
   And grim in mood was the grewsome elf,
   That be sae bald he may.

4. He hew'd him kipples, he hew'd him bawks,
   Wi' mickle moil and haste,
   Syne speer'd the Elf i' the knock that bade,
   ' Wha 's hacking here sae fast ? '

5. Syne up and spak the weiest Elf,
   Crean'd as an immert smä :
   ' It 's here is come a Christian man ;—
   I'll fley him or he ga.'

6. It 's up syne started the firsten Elf,
   And glower'd about sae grim :
   ' It 's we'll awa' to the husbande's house,
   And hald a court on him.

7. ' Here hews he down baith skugg and shaw
   And works us skaith and scorn :
   His huswife he sall gie to me ;—
   They 's rue the day they were born !

8. The Elfen a' i' the knock that were,
   Gaed dancing in a string ;
   They nighed near the husband's house,
   Sae lang their tails did hing.

9. The hound he yowls i' the yard,
   The herd toots in his horn ;
   The earn scraighs, and the cock craws,
   As the husbande has gi'en him his corn.

10. The Elfen were five score and seven,
    Sae laidly and sae grim ;
    And they the husbande's guests maun be,
    To eat and drink wi' him.

11. The husbande, out o' Villenshaw,
    At his winnock the Elves can see :
    ' Help me, now, Jesu, Mary's son ;
    Thir Elves they mint at me ! '

12. In every nook a cross he coost,
    In his chalmer maist ava ;
    The Elfen a' were fley'd thereat,
    And flew to the wild-wood shaw.

13. And some flew east, and some flew west,
    And some to the norwart flew ;
    And some they flew to the deep dale down,
    There still they are, I trow.

14. It was then the weiest Elf,
    In at the door braids he ;
    Agast was the husbande, for that Elf
    For cross nor sign wad flee.

15. The huswife she was a canny wife,
    She set the Elf at the board ;
    She set before him baith ale and meat,
    Wi' mony a weel-waled word.

16. ' Hear thou, Gudeman o' Villenshaw,
    What now I say to thee ;
    Wha bade thee bigg within our bounds,
    Without the leave o' me ?

17. ' But, an' thou in our bounds will bigg,
    And bide, as well as may be,
    Then thou thy dearest huswife maun
    To me for a lemman gie.'

18. Up spak the luckless husbande then,
    As God the grace him gae ;
    ' Eline she is to me sae dear,
    Her thou may nae-gate hae.'

19. Till the Elf he answer'd as he couth :
    ' Let but my huswife be,
    And tak whate'er, o' gude or gear,
    Is mine, awa wi' thee.'—

20. ' Then I'll thy Eline tak and thee,
    Aneath my feet to tread ;
    And hide thy goud and white monie
    Aneath my dwalling stead.'

21. The husbande and his household a'
    In sary rede they join :
    ' Far better that she be now forfairn,
    Nor that we a' should tyne.'

22. Up, will of rede, the husbande stood,
    Wi' heart fu' sad and sair ;
    And he has gien his huswife Eline
    Wi' the young Elfe to fare.

23. Then blyth grew he, and sprang about :
    He took her in his arm :
    The rud it left her comely cheek ;
    Her heart was clem'd wi' harm.

24. A waefu' woman then she was ane,
    And the moody tears loot fa' :
    ' God rew on me, unseely wife,
    How hard a weird I fa' !

25. ' My fay I plight to the fairest wight
    That man on mold mat see ;—
    Maun I now mell wi' a laidly El,
    His light lemman to be ? '

26. He minted ance—he minted twice,
    Wae wax'd her heart that syth :
    Syne the laidliest fiend he grew that e'er
    To mortal ee did kyth.

27. When he the thirden time can mint
    To Mary's son she pray'd,
    And the laidly Elf was clean awa,
    And a fair knight in his stead.

28. This fell under a linden green,
    That again his shape he found ;
    O' wae and care was the word nae mair,
    A' were sae glad that stound.

29. ' O dearest Eline, hear thou this,
    And thou my wife sall be,
    And a' the goud in merry England
    Sae freely I'll gi'e thee !

30. ' Whan I was but a little wee bairn,
    My mither died me fra ;
    My stepmither sent me awa' fra her ;
    I turn'd till an *Elfin Gray.*

31. 'To thy husbande I a gift will gie,
    Wi' mickle state and gear,
    As mends for Eline his huswife ;—
    Thou's be my heartis dear.'—

32. 'Thou nobil knyght, we thank now God
    That has freed us frae skaith ;
    Sae wed thou thee a maiden free,
    And joy attend ye baith !

33. 'Sin' I to thee nae maik can be
    My dochter may be thine ;
    And thy gud will right to fulfill,
    Lat this be our propine.'—

34. 'I thank thee, Eline, thou wise woman;
    My praise thy worth sall ha'e ;
    And thy love gin I fail to win,
    Thou here at hame sall stay.'

35. The husbande biggit now on his öe,
    And nae ane wrought him wrang ;
    His dochter wore crown in Engeland,
    And happy lived and lang.

36. Now Eline. the husbande's huswife, has
    Cour'd a' her grief and harms ;
    She 's mither to a noble queen
    That sleeps in a kingis arms.

GLOSSARY.

Stanza 1. *Wold*, a wood ; woody fastness. *Husbande*, from the Dan. *hos*, with, and *bonde*, a villain, or bondsman, who was a cultivator of the ground, and could not quit the estate to which he was attached without the permission of his lord. This is the sense of the word in the old Scottish records. In the Scottish 'Burghe Laws,' translated from the *Reg. Majest.* (Auchinleck MS. in the Adv. Lib.) it is used indiscriminately with the Dan. and Swed. *bonde*. *Bigg*, build. *Ligg*, lie. *Daes*, does.

2. *Shaw*, wood. *Sairly*, sorely.

3. *Aik*, oak. *Grewsome*, terrible. *Bald*, bold.

4. *Kipples* (couples). beams joined at the top, for supporting a roof, in building. *Bawks*, balks ; crossbeams. *Moil*, laborious industry. *Speer'd*, asked. *Knock*, hillock.

5. *Weiest*, smallest. *Crean'd*, shrunk, diminished ; from the Gaelic, *crian*, very small. *Immert*, emmet ; ant. *Christian*, used in the Danish ballads, &c. in contradistinction to *demoniac*, as it is in England in contradistinction to *brute* ; in which sense, a person of the lower class in England would call a *Jew* or a *Turk* a *Christian*. *Fley*, frighten.

6. *Glow'r'd*, stared. *Hald*, hold.

7. *Skugg*, shade. *Skaith*, harm.

8. *Nighed*, approached.

9. *Yowls*, howls. *Toots*.—In the Dan. *tude* is applied both to the howling of a dog, and the sound of a horn. *Scraighs*, screams.

10. *Laidly*, loathly ; disgustingly *ugly*. *Grim*, fierce.

11. *Winnock*, window. *Mint*, aim at.

12. *Coost*, cast. *Chalmer*, chamber. *Maist*, most. *Ava*, of all.

13. *Norwart*, northward. *Trow*, believe.

14. *Braids*, strides quickly forward. *Wad*, would.

15. *Canny*, adroit. *Mony*, many. *Weel-waled*, well-chosen.

17. *An*, if. *Bide*, abide. *Lemman*, mistress.

18. *Nae-gate*, nowise.

19. *Couth*, could, knew how to. *Lat be*, let alone. *Gude*, goods ; property.

20. *Aneath*, beneath. *Dwalling-stead*, dwelling-place.

21. *Sary*, sorrowful. *Rede*, counsel ; consultation. *Forfairn*, forlorn ; lost ; *gone*. *Tyne* (verb neut.), be lost ; perish.

22. *Will of rede*, bewildered in thought ; in the Danish original '*vildraadage*' ; Lat. 'inops consilii' ; Gr. ἄπορων. This expression is left among the *desiderata* in the Glossary to Ritson's Romances, and has never been explained. It is obsolete in the Danish as well as in English. *Fare*, go.

23. *Rud*, red of the cheek. *Clem'd*, in the Danish *klemt* (which in the north of England is still in use, as the word *starved* is with us) ; brought to a dying state. It is used by our old comedians. *Harm*, grief ; as in the original, and in the old Teutonic, English, and Scottish poetry.

24. *Waefu'*, woeful. *Moody*, strongly and wilfully passionate. *Rew*, take ruth ; pity. *Unseely*, unhappy ; unblest. *Weird*, fate. *Fa* (Isl., Dan., and Swed.), take ; get ; acquire ; procure ; have for my lot.—This Gothic verb answers, in its direct and secondary significations, exactly to the Latin *capio* ; and Allan Ramsay was right in his definition of it. It is quite a different word from *fa'*, an abbreviation of '*fall*, or *befall* ; and is the principal root in FANGEN, to *fang*, take, or lay hold of.

25. *Fay*, faith. *Mold*, mould ; earth. *Mat*, mote ; might. *Maun*, must. *Mell*, mix. *El*, an Elf. This term, in the Welsh, signifies *what has in itself the power of motion* ; *a moving principle* ; *an intelligence* ; *a spirit* ; *an angel*. In the Hebrew it bears the same import.

26. *Min'ed*, attempted ; meant ; showed a *mind*, or intention to. The original is—

'Hand *mindte* hende forst—og anden gang ;—
Hun giordis i hiortet sa vee :
End blef hand den *lediste* deif-vel
Mand kunde med öyen see.
Der hand vilde *minde* den tredie gang,' &c.

Syth, tide, time. *Kyth*, appear.

28. *Stound*, hour ; time ; moment.

29. *Merry* (old Teut. *mere*), famous ; renowned ; answering, in its etymological meaning, exactly to the Latin *mactus*. Hence *merry-men*, as the address of a chief to his followers ; meaning, not me of mirth, but of renown. The term is found in its original sense in the Gael. *mara*, and the Welsh *mawr*, great ; and in the oldest Teut. Romances, *mar*, *mer*, and *mere*, have sometimes the same signification.

31. *Mends*, amends ; recompense.

33. *Maik*, match ; peer ; equal. *Propine*, pledge ; gift.

35. *öe*, an island of the *second* magnitude ; an island of the *first* magnitude being called a *land*, and one of the *third* magnitude a *holm*.

36. *Cour'd*, recover'd.

THE GHAIST'S WARNING.

TRANSLATED FROM THE DANISH KÆMPE VISER, p. 721.

By the permission of Mr. Jamieson, this ballad is added from the same curious Collection. It contains some passages of great pathos.

———

Svend Dyring hand rider sig op under öe,
(*Varè jeg selver ung*)
Der fæstè hand sig saa ven en möe.
(*Mig lyster udi lunden at ride,*) &c.

———

1. Child Dyring has ridden him up under öe [1],
   (*And O gin I were young !*)
   There wedded he him sae fair [2] a may.
   (*I' the greenwood it lists me to ride.*)

———

[1] '*Under öe*.'—The original expression has been preserved here and elsewhere, because no other could be found to supply it place. There is just as much meaning in it in the translation as in the original ; but it is a standard Danish phrase ; and as such, it is hoped, will be allowed to pass.

[2] '*Fair*.'—The Dan. and Swed. *ven*, *væn*, or *venne*, and the Gaël. *bàn*, in the oblique cases *bhàn* (*vàn*), is the origin of the Scottish *bonny*, which has so much puzzled all the etymologists.

2. Thegither they lived for seven lang year,
   (*And O, &c.*)
   And they seven bairns hae gotten in fere.
   (*I' the greenwood, &c.*)

3. Sae Death 's come there intill that stead,
   And that winsome lily flower is dead.

4. That swain he has ridden him up under öe,
   And syne he has married anither may.

5. He 's married a may, and he 's fessen her hame ;
   But she was a grim and a laidly dame.

6. When into the castell court drave she,
   The seven bairns stood wi' the tear in their ee.

7. The bairns they stood wi' dule and dout ;—
   She up wi' her foot, and she kick'd them out.

8. Nor ale nor mead to the bairnies she gave :
   ' But hunger and hate frae me ye's have.'

9. She took frae them the bowster blae,
   And said, ' Ye sall ligg i' the bare strae !

10. She took frae them the groff wax-light :
    Says, ' Now ye sall ligg i' the mirk a' night !

11. 'Twas lang i' the night, and the bairnies grat :
    Their mither she under the mools heard that ;

12. That heard the wife under the eard that lay :
    ' For sooth maun I to my bairnies gae !'

13. That wife can stand up at our Lord's knee,
    And ' May I gang and my bairnies see ?'

14. She prigged sae sair, and she prigged sae lang,
    That he at the last ga'e her leave to gang.

15. 'And thou sall come back when the cock does craw,
    For thou nae langer sall bide awa.'

16. Wi' her banes sae stark a bowt she gae ;
    She 's riven baith wa' and marble gray[1].

17. Whan near to the dwalling she can gang,
    The dogs they wow'd till the lift it rang.

18. When she came till the castell yett,
    Her eldest dochter stood thereat.

19. ' Why stand ye here, dear dochter mine ?
    How are sma' brithers and sisters thine ? '—

20. ' For sooth ye're a woman baith fair and fine ;
    But ye are nae dear mither of mine.'—

21. 'Och ! how should I be fine or fair ?
    My cheek it is pale, and the ground 's my lair.

22. ' My mither was white, wi' cheek sae red ;
    But thou art wan, and liker ane dead.'—

23. 'Och ! how should I be white and red,
    Sae lang as I've been cauld and dead ?'—

24. When she cam till the chalmer in,
    Down the bairns' cheeks the tears did rin.

25. She buskit the tane, and she brush'd it there
    She kem'd and plaited the tither's hair.

[1] The original of this and the following stanza is very fine.

' Hun sköd op sinè modigè been,
   Der revenedè muur og graa marmorsteen.

Der hungik igennem den by.
   De hundè de tudè saa hojt i sky.'

26. The thirden she doodl'd upon her knee,
    And the fourthen she dichted sae cannilie.

27. She 's ta'en the fifthen upon her lap,
    And sweetly suckled it at her pap.

28. Till her eldest dochter syne said she,
    ' Ye bid Child Dyring come here to me.'

29. Whan he cam till the chalmer in,
    Wi' angry mood she said to him :

30. ' I left you routh o' ale and bread :
    My bairnies quail for hunger and need.

31. ' I left ahind me braw bowsters blae ;
    My bairnies are liggin' i' the bare strae.

32. ' I left ye sae mony a groff wax-light ;
    My bairnies ligg i' the mirk a' night.

33. ' Gin aft I come back to visit thee,
    Wae, dowy, and weary thy luck shall be.'

34. Up spak little Kirstin in bed that lay :
    ' To thy bairnies I'll do the best I may.'

35. Aye when they heard the dog nirr and bell,
    Sae ga'e they the bairnies bread and ale.

36. Aye whan the dog did wow, in haste
    They cross'd and sain'd themsells frae the ghaist

37. Aye whan the little dog yowl'd, with fear
    (*And O gin I were young !*)
    They shook at the thought the dead was near.
    (*I' the greenwood it lists me to ride.*)
    or.
    (*Fair words sae mony a heart they cheer.*)

GLOSSARY.

Stanza 1. *May*, maid.   *Lists*, pleases.
2. *Bairns*, children.   *In fere*, together.
3. *Stead*, place.   *Winsome*, engaging ; giving joy (old Teut.).
4. *Syne*, then.
5. *Fessen*, fetched ; brought.
6. *Drave*, drove.
7. *Dule*, sorrow.   *Dout*, fear.
9. *Bowster*, bolster ; cushion ; bed.   *Blae*, blue. *Strae*, straw.
10. *Groff*, great ; large in girt.   *Mark*, mirk ; dark.
11. *Lang i' the night*, late.   *Grat*, wept.   *Mools*, mould ; earth.
12. *Eard*, earth.   *Gae*, go.
14. *Prigged*, entreated earnestly and perseveringly. *Gang*, go.
15. *Craw*, crow.
16. *Banes*, bones.   *Stark*, strong.   *Bowt*, bolt ; elastic spring, like that of a *bolt* or *arrow* from a bow. *Riven*, split asunder.   *Wa'*, wall.
17. *Wow'd*, howled.   *Lift*, sky, firmament ; air.
18. *Yett*, gate.
19. *Sma'*, small.
23. *Cauld*, cold.
24. *Till*, to.   *Rin*, run.
25. *Buskit*, dressed.   *Kem'd*, combed.   *Tither*, the other.
30. *Routh*, plenty.   *Quail*, are quelled ; die. *Need*, want.
31. *Ahind*, behind.   *Braw*, brave ; fine.
33. *Dowy*, sorrowful.
35. *Nirr*, snarl.   *Bell*, bark.
36. *Sain'd*, blessed ; literally, *signed* with the *sign* of the cross. Before the introduction of Christianity, *Runes* were used in *saining*, as a spell against the power of enchantment and evil genii.   *Ghaist*, ghost.

NOTE L.

——the moody Elfin King.—P. 243.

In a long dissertation upon the Fairy Superstitions, published in the Minstrelsy of the Scottish Border, the most valuable part of which was supplied by my learned and indefatigable friend, Dr. John Leyden, most of the circumstances are collected which can throw light upon the popular belief which even yet prevails respecting them in Scotland. Dr. Grahame, author of an entertaining work upon the Scenery of the Perthshire Highlands, already frequently quoted, has recorded, with great accuracy, the peculiar tenets held by the Highlanders on this topic, in the vicinity of Loch Katrine. The learned author is inclined to deduce the whole mythology from the Druidical system,—an opinion to which there are many objections.

'The *Daoine Shi*', or Men of Peace of the Highlanders, though not absolutely malevolent, are believed to be a peevish, repining race of beings, who, possessing themselves but a scanty portion of happiness, are supposed to envy mankind their more complete and substantial enjoyments. They are supposed to enjoy in their subterraneous recesses a sort of shadowy happiness,—a tinsel grandeur; which, however, they would willingly exchange for the more solid joys of mortality.

'They are believed to inhabit certain round grassy eminences, where they celebrate their nocturnal festivities by the light of the moon. About a mile beyond the source of the Forth above Lochcon, there is a place called *Coirshi'an*, or the Cove of the Men of Peace, which is still supposed to be a favourite place of their residence. In the neighbourhood are to be seen many round conical eminences; particularly one, near the head of the lake, by the skirts of which many are still afraid to pass after sunset. It is believed, that if, on Hallow-eve, any person, alone, goes round one of these hills nine times, towards the left hand (*sinistrorsum*) a door shall open, by which he will be admitted into their subterraneous abodes. Many, it is said, of mortal race, have been entertained in their secret recesses. There they have been received into the most splendid apartments, and regaled with the most sumptuous banquets, and delicious wines. Their females surpass the daughters of men in beauty. The *seemingly* happy inhabitants pass their time in festivity, and in dancing to notes of the softest music. But unhappy is the mortal who joins in their joys, or ventures to partake of their dainties. By this indulgence, he forfeits for ever the society of men, and is bound down irrevocably to the condition of *Shi'ich*, or Man of Peace.

'A woman, as is reported in the Highland tradition, was conveyed, in days of yore, into the secret recesses of the Men of Peace. There she was recognized by one who had formerly been an ordinary mortal, but who

had, by some fatality, become associated with the Shi'ichs. This acquaintance, still retaining some portion of human benevolence, warned her of her danger, and counselled her, as she valued her liberty, to abstain from eating and drinking with them for a certain space of time. She complied with the counsel of her friend; and when the period assigned was elapsed, she found herself again upon earth, restored to the society of mortals. It is added, that when she examined the viands which had been presented to her, and which had appeared so tempting to the eye, they were found, now that the enchantment was removed, to consist only of the refuse of the earth.'—Pp. 107-111.

NOTE LI.

*Why sounds yon stroke on beech and oak,
Our moonlight circle's screen?
Or who comes here to chase the deer,
Beloved of our Elfin Queen?*—P. 243.

It has been already observed, that fairies, if not positively malevolent, are capricious, and easily offended. They are, like other proprietors of forests, peculiarly jealous of their rights of *vert* and *venison*, as appears from the cause of offence taken, in the original Danish ballad. This jealousy was also an attribute of the northern *Duergar*, or dwarfs; to many of whose distinctions the fairies seem to have succeeded, if, indeed, they are not the same class of beings. In the huge metrical record of German Chivalry, entitled the Helden-Buch, Sir Hildebrand, and the other heroes of whom it treats, are engaged in one of their most desperate adventures, from a rash violation of the rose-garden of an Elfin, or Dwarf King.

There are yet traces of a belief in this worst and most malicious order of Fairies, among the Border wilds. Dr. Leyden has introduced such a dwarf into his ballad entitled the Cout of Keeldar, and has not forgot his characteristic detestation of the chase.

'The third blast that young Keeldar blew,
 Still stood the limber fern,
And a wee man, of swarthy hue,
 Upstarted by a cairn.

His russet weeds were brown as heath
 That clothes the upland fell;
And the hair of his head was frizzly red
 As the purple heather-bell.

An urchin, clad in prickles red,
 Clung cow'ring to his arm;
The hounds they howl'd, and backward fled,
 As struck by fairy charm.

" Why rises high the stag-hound's cry,
 Where stag-hound ne'er should be?
Why wakes that horn the silent morn,
 Without the leave of me?"—

"Brown dwarf, that o'er the moorland strays,
 Thy name to Keeldar tell!"—
"The Brown man of the Moors, who stays
 Beneath the heather-bell.

"'Tis sweet beneath the heather-bell
 To live in autumn brown ;
And sweet to hear the lav'rock's swell,
 Far, far from tower and town.

"But woe betide the shrilling horn,
 The chase's surly cheer !
And ever that hunter is forlorn,
 Whom first at morn I hear."'

The poetical picture here given of the Duergar corresponds exactly with the following Northumbrian legend, with which I was lately favoured by my learned and kind friend, Mr. Surtees of Mainsforth, who has bestowed indefatigable labour upon the antiquities of the English Border counties. The subject is in itself so curious, that the length of the note will, I hope, be pardoned.

'I have only one record to offer of the appearance of our Northumbrian Duergar. My narratrix is Elizabeth Cockburn, an old wife of Offerton, in this county, whose credit, in a case of this kind, will not, I hope, be much impeached, when I add, that she is, by her dull neighbours, supposed to be occasionally insane, but, by herself, to be at those times endowed with a faculty of seeing visions, and spectral appearances which shun the common ken.

'In the year before the great rebellion, two young men from Newcastle were sporting on the high moors above Elsdon, and after pursuing their game several hours, sat down to dine in a green glen, near one of the mountain streams. After their repast, the younger lad ran to the brook for water, and after stooping to drink, was surprised, on lifting his head again, by the appearance of a brown dwarf, who stood on a crag covered with brackens, across the burn. This extraordinary personage did not appear to be above half the stature of a common man, but was uncommonly stout and broad-built, having the appearance of vast strength. His dress was entirely brown, the colour of the brackens, and his head covered with frizzled red hair. His countenance was expressive of the most savage ferocity, and his eyes glared like a bull. It seems he addressed the young man first, threatening him with his vengeance, for having trespassed on his demesnes, and asking him if he knew in whose presence he stood ? The youth replied, that he now supposed him to be the lord of the moors ; that he offended through ignorance ; and offered to bring him the game he had killed. The dwarf was a little mollified by this submission, but remarked, that nothing could be more offensive to him than such an offer, as he considered the wild animals as his subjects, and never failed to avenge their destruction. He condescended further to inform him, that he was, like himself, mortal, though of years far exceeding the lot of common humanity; and (what I should not have had an idea of) that he hoped for salvation. He never, he added, fed on anything that had life, but lived in the summer on wortle-berries, and in winter on nuts and apples, of which he had great store in the woods. Finally, he invited his new acquaintance to accompany him home and partake his hospitality ; an offer which the youth was on the point of accepting, and was just going to spring across the brook (which, if he had done, says Elizabeth, the dwarf would certainly have torn him in pieces), when his foot was arrested by the voice of his companion, who thought he had tarried long ; and on looking round again, "the wee brown man was fled." The story adds, that he was imprudent enough to slight the admonition, and to sport over the moors on his way homewards ; but soon after his return, he fell into a lingering disorder, and died within the year.'

Note LII.

*Or who may dare on wold to wear
 The fairies' fatal green ?*—P. 243.

As the *Daoine Shi'*, or Men of Peace, wore green habits, they were supposed to take offence when any mortals ventured to assume their favourite colour. Indeed, from some reason which has been, perhaps, originally a general superstition, *green* is held in Scotland to be unlucky to particular tribes and counties. The Caithness men, who hold this belief, allege as a reason, that their bands wore that colour when they were cut off at the battle of Flodden ; and for the same reason they avoid crossing the Ord on a Monday, being the day of the week on which their ill-omened array set forth. Green is also disliked by those of the name of Ogilvy ; but more especially is it held fatal to the whole clan of Grahame. It is remembered of an aged gentleman of that name, that when his horse fell in a fox-chase, he accounted for it at once by observing, that the whipcord attached to his lash was of this unlucky colour.

Note LIII.

For thou wert christen'd man.—P. 243.

The elves were supposed greatly to envy the privileges acquired by Christian initiation, and they gave to those mortals who had fallen into their power a certain precedence, founded upon this advantageous distinction. Tamlane, in the old ballad, describes his own rank in the fairy procession :—

'For I ride on a milk-white steed
 And aye nearest the town ;
Because I was a christen'd knight
 They give me that renown.'

I presume that, in the Danish ballad of the *Elfin Gray* (see above, p. 297), the obstinacy of the 'Weiest Elf,' who would not flee for cross or sign, is to be derived from the circumstance of his having been 'christen'd man.'

How eager the Elves were to obtain for their offspring the prerogatives of Christianity will be proved by the following story:—'In the district called Haga, in Iceland, dwelt a nobleman called Sigward Forster, who had an intrigue with one of the subterranean females. The elf became pregnant, and exacted from her lover a firm promise that he would procure the baptism of the infant. At the appointed time, the mother came to the churchyard, on the wall of which she placed a golden cup, and a stole for the priest, agreeable to the custom of making an offering at baptism. She then stood a little apart. When the priest left the church, he enquired the meaning of what he saw, and demanded of Sigward if he avowed himself the father of the child. But Sigward, ashamed of the connection, denied the paternity. He was then interrogated if he desired that the child should be baptized ; but this also he answered in the negative, lest, by such request, he should admit himself to be the father. On which the child was left untouched and unbaptized. Whereupon the mother, in extreme wrath, snatched up the infant and the cup, and retired, leaving the priestly cope, of which fragments are still in preservation. But this female denounced and imposed upon Sigward and his posterity, to the ninth generation, a singular disease, with which many of his descendants are afflicted at this day.' Thus wrote Einar Dudmond, pastor of the parish of Garpsdale, in Iceland, a man profoundly versed in learning, from whose manuscript it was extracted by the learned Torfæus.—*Historia Hrolfi Krakii, Hafniæ,* 1715, *prefatio.*

Note LIV.

And gaily shines the Fairy-land—
But all is glistening show.—P. 244.

No fact respecting Fairy-land seems to be better ascertained than the fantastic and illusory nature of their apparent pleasure and splendour. It has been already noticed in the former quotations from Dr. Grahame's entertaining volume, and may be confirmed by the following Highland tradition : 'A woman, whose new-born child had been conveyed by them into their secret abodes, was also carried thither herself, to remain, however, only until she should suckle her infant. She one day, during this period, observed the Shi'ichs busily employed in mixing various ingredients in a boiling caldron ; and, as soon as the composition was prepared, she remarked that they all carefully anointed their eyes with it, laying the remainder aside for future use. In a moment when they were all absent, she also attempted to anoint her eyes with the precious drug, but had time to apply it to one eye only, when the *Daoine Shi'* returned. But with that eye she was henceforth enabled to see everything as it really passed in their secret abodes. She saw every object, not as she hitherto had done, in deceptive splendour and elegance, but in its genuine colours and form. The gaudy ornaments of the apartment were reduced to the walls of a gloomy cavern. Soon after, having discharged her office, she was dismissed to her own home. Still, however, she retained the faculty of seeing, with her medicated eye, everything that was done, anywhere in her presence, by the deceptive art of the order. One day, amidst a throng of people, she chanced to observe the *Shi'ich,* or man of peace, in whose possession she had left her child ; though to every other eye invisible. Prompted by maternal affection, she inadvertently accosted him, and began to enquire after the welfare of her child. The man of peace, astonished at being thus recognized by one of mortal race, demanded how she had been enabled to discover him. Awed by the terrible frown of his countenance, she acknowledged what she had done. He spat in her eye, and extinguished it for ever.'—GRAHAME'S *Sketches,* pp. 116–118. It is very remarkable that this story, translated by Dr. Grahame from popular Gaelic tradition, is to be found in the Otia Imperialia of Gervase of Tilbury. A work of great interest might be compiled upon the origin of popular fiction, and the transmission of similar tales from age to age, and from country to country. The mythology of one period would then appear to pass into the romance of the next century, and that into the nursery tale of the subsequent ages. Such an investigation, while it went greatly to diminish our ideas of the richness of human invention, would also show that these fictions, however wild and childish, possess such charms for the populace, as enable them to penetrate into countries unconnected by manners and language, and having no apparent intercourse to afford the means of transmission. It would carry me far beyond my bounds, to produce instances of this community of fable among nations who never borrowed from each other anything intrinsically worth learning. Indeed, the wide diffusion of popular fictions may be compared to the facility with which straws and feathers are dispersed abroad by the wind, while valuable metals cannot be transported without trouble and labour. There lives, I believe, only one gentleman, whose unlimited acquaintance with this subject might enable him to do it justice ; I mean my friend, Mr. Francis Douce, of the British Museum, whose usual kindness will, I hope, pardon my mentioning his name, while on a subject so closely connected with his extensive and curious researches.

Note LV.

—*I sunk down in a sinful fray,*
And, 'twixt life and death, was snatch'd
away
To the joyless Elfin bower.—P. 244.

The subjects of Fairy-land were recruited from the regions of humanity by a sort of *crimping* system, which extended to adults as well as to infants. Many of those who were in this world supposed to have discharged the debt of nature, had only become denizens of the 'Londe of Faery.' In the beautiful Fairy Romance of Orfee and Heurodiis (Orpheus and Eurydice) in the Auchinleck MS. is the following striking enumeration of persons thus abstracted from middle earth. Mr. Ritson unfortunately published this romance from a copy in which the following, and many other highly poetical passages, do not occur :—

'Then he gan biholde about al,
And seighe ful liggeand with in the wal,
Of folk that were thidder y-brought,
And thought dede and nere nought ;
Some stode withouten hadde ;
And sum non armes nade ;
And some thurch the bodi hadde wounde ;
And some lay wode y-bounde ;
And sum armed on hors sete ;
And sum astrangled as thai ete ;
And sum war in water adreynt ;
And sum with fire al forschreynt ;
Wives ther lay on childe bedde ;
Sum dede, and sum awedde ;
And wonder fele ther lay besides,
Right as thai slepe her undertides :
Eche was thus in the warl y-nome,
With fairi thider y-come.'

Note LVI.

Who ever reck'd, where, how, or when,
The prowling fox was trapp'd or slain ?
—P. 249.

St. John actually used this illustration when engaged in confuting the plea of law proposed for the unfortunate Earl of Strafford: 'It was true, we gave laws to hares and deer, because they are beasts of chase ; but it was never accounted either cruelty or foul play to knock foxes or wolves on the head as they can be found, because they are beasts of prey. In a word, the law and humanity were alike ; the one being more fallacious, and the other more barbarous, than in any age had been vented in such an authority.'—CLARENDON'S *History of the Rebellion.* Oxford, 1702, fol. vol. p. 183.

Note LVII.

—— *his Highland cheer,*
The harden'd flesh of mountain deer.
—P. 249.

The Scottish Highlanders in former times had a concise mode of cooking their venison, or rather of dispensing with cooking it, which appears greatly to have surprised the French whom chance made acquainted with it. The Vidame of Charters, when a hostage in England, during the reign of Edward VI, was permitted to travel into Scotland, and penetrated as far as to the remote Highlands (*au fin fond des Sauvages*). After a great hunting party, at which a most wonderful quantity of game was destroyed, he saw these *Scottish Savages* devour a part of their venison raw, without any farther preparation than compressing it between two batons of wood, so as to force out the blood, and render it extremely hard. This they reckoned a great delicacy ; and when the Vidame partook of it, his compliance with their taste rendered him extremely popular. This curious trait of manners was communicated by Mons. de Montmorency, a great friend of the Vidame, to Brantome, by whom it is recorded in *Vies des Hommes Illustres, Discours*, lxxxix. art. 14. The process by which the raw venison was rendered eatable is described very minutely in the romance of Perceforest, where Estonne, a Scottish knight-errant, having slain a deer, says to his companion Claudius : 'Sire, or mangerez vous et moy aussi. Voire si nous auions de feu, dit Claudius. Par l'ame de mon pere, dist Estonne, ie vous atourneray et cuiray a la maniere de nostre pays comme pour cheualier errant. Lors tira son espee, et sen vint a la branche dung arbre, et y fait vng grant trou, et puis fend la branche bien dieux piedx, et boute la cuisse du serf entredeux, et puis prent le licol de son cheval, et en lye la branche, et destraint si fort, que le sang et les humeurs de la chair saillent hors, et demeure la chair doulce et seiche. Lors prent la chair, et oste ius le cuir, et la chaire demeure aussi blanche comme si ce feust dung chappon. Dont dist a Claudius, Sire, ie la vous ay cuiste a la guise de mon pays, vous en pouez manger hardyement, car ie mangeray premier. Lors met sa main a sa selle en vng lieu quil y auoit, et tire hors sel et poudre de poiure et gingembre, mesle ensemble, et le iecte dessus, et le frote sus bien fort, puis le couppe a moytie, et en donne a Claudius l'une des pieces, et puis mort en l'autre aussi sauoureussement quil est aduis que il en feist la pouldre voller. Quant Claudius veit quil le mangeoit de tel goust, il en print grant faim, et commence a manger tresvoulentiers, et dist a Estonne : Par l'ame de moy, ie ne mangeay oncquesmais de chair atournee de telle guise : mais doresenauant ie ne me retourneroye pas hors de mon chemin pour auoir la cuite. Sire, dist Estonne, quant ie suis en desers d'Ecosse, dont ie suis seigneur, ie cheuaucheray huit iours ou quinze que ie n'entreray en chastel ne en maison, et si ne verray feu ne personne viuant fors que bestes sauuages, et de celles mangeray atournees en ceste maniere, et mieulx me plaira que la viande de l'empereur. Ainsi sen vont mangeant et cheuauchant iusques adonc quilz arriuerent sur une moult belle fontaine que estoit en vne valee. Quant Estonne la vit il dist a Claudius, allons boire a ceste fontaine.

Or beuuons, dist Estonne, du boir que le grant dieu a pourueu a toutes gens, et que ne plaist mieulx que les ceruoises d'Angleterre.'—*La TreseleganteHystoire du tresnoble Roy Perceforest.* Paris, 1531, fol. tome i. fol. lv. vers.

After all, it may be doubted whether *la chaire nostree,* for so the French called the venison thus summarily prepared, was anything more than a mere rude kind of deer-ham.

Note LVIII.

Not then claim'd sovereignty his due;
While Albany, with feeble hand,
Held borrow'd truncheon of command.
—P. 252.

There is scarcely a more disorderly period in Scottish history than that which succeeded the battle of Flodden, and occupied the minority of James V. Feuds of ancient standing broke out like old wounds, and every quarrel among the independent nobility, which occurred daily, and almost hourly, gave rise to fresh bloodshed. 'There arose,' says Pitscottie, 'great trouble and deadly feuds in many parts of Scotland, both in the north and west parts. The Master of Forbes, in the north, slew the Laird of Meldrum, under tryst:' (i e. *at an agreed and secure meeting*). 'Likewise, the Laird of Drummelzier slew the Lord Fleming at the hawking ; and likewise there was slaughter among many other great lords.'—P. 121. Nor was the matter much mended under the government of the Earl of Angus: for though he caused the King to ride through all Scotland, 'under the pretence and colour of justice, to punish thief and traitor, none were found greater than were in their own company. And none at that time durst strive with a Douglas, nor yet a Douglas's man ; for if they would, they got the worst. Therefore, none durst plainzie of no extortion, theft, reiff, nor slaughter, done to them by the Douglases, or their men ; in that cause they were not heard, so long as the Douglas had the court in guiding.'—*Ibid.* p. 133.

Note LIX.

The Gael, of plain and river heir,
Shall with strong hand redeem his share.
—P. 252.

The ancient Highlanders verified in their practice the lines of Gray :—

' An iron race the mountain cliffs maintain,
Foes to the gentler genius of the plain ;
For where unwearied sinews must be found,
With side-long plough to quell the flinty ground ;
To turn the torrent's swift descending flood ;
To tame the savage rushing from the wood ;
What wonder if, to patient valour train'd,
They guard with spirit what by strength they gain'd :
And while their rocky ramparts round they see
The rough abode of want and liberty,
(As lawless force from confidence will grow,)
Insult the plenty of the vales below ?'
Fragment on the Alliance of Education
and Government.

So far, indeed, was a *Creagh,* or foray, from being held disgraceful, that a young chief was always expected to show his talents for command so soon as he assumed it, by leading his clan on a successful enterprize of this nature, either against a neighbouring sept, for which constant feuds usually furnished an apology, or against the *Sassenach,* Saxons, or Lowlanders, for which no apology was necessary. The Gaels, great traditional historians, never forgot that the Lowlands had, at some remote period, been the property of their Celtic forefathers, which furnished an ample vindication of all the ravages that they could make on the unfortunate districts which lay within their reach. Sir James Grant of Grant is in possession of a letter of apology from Cameron of Lochiel, whose men had committed some depredation upon a farm called Moines, occupied by one of the Grants. Lochiel assures Grant, that, however the mistake had happened, his instructions were precise, that the party should foray the province of Moray (a Lowland district), where, as he coolly observes, ' all men take their prey.'

Note LX.

—— I only meant
To show the reed on which you leant,
Deeming this path you might pursue
Without a pass from Roderick Dhu.
—P. 254.

This incident, like some other passages in the poem, illustrative of the character of the ancient Gael, is not imaginary, but borrowed from fact. The Highlanders, with the inconsistency of most nations in the same state, were alternately capable of great exertions of generosity, and of cruel revenge and perfidy. The following story I can only quote from tradition, but with such an assurance from those by whom it was communicated, as permits me little doubt of its authenticity. Early in the last century, John Gunn, a noted Cateran, or Highland robber, infested Inverness-shire, and levied *black-mail* up to the walls of the provincial capital. A garrison was then maintained in the castle of that town, and their pay (country banks being unknown) was usually transmitted in specie, under the guard of a small escort. It chanced that the officer who commanded this little party was unexpectedly obliged to halt, about thirty miles from Inverness, at a miserable inn. About nightfall, a stranger, in the Highland dress, and of very prepossessing appearance, entered the same house. Separate accommodation being impossible, the Englishman offered the newly-arrived guest a part of his supper, which was accepted with reluctance. By the conversation he found his new acquaintance knew well all the passes of the country, which induced him eagerly to request his company on the ensuing morning. He neither disguised his business and charge, nor his apprehensions of that celebrated free-booter, John Gunn. The Highlander hesitated a moment, and then frankly consented to be his guide. Forth they set in the morning; and, in travelling through a solitary and dreary glen, the discourse again turned on John Gunn. 'Would you like to see him?' said the guide; and, without waiting an answer to this alarming question, he whistled, and the English officer, with his small party, were surrounded by a body of Highlanders, whose numbers put resistance out of question, and who were all well armed. 'Stranger,' resumed the guide, 'I am that very John Gunn by whom you feared to be intercepted, and not without cause: for I came to the inn last night with the express purpose of learning your route, that I and my followers might ease you of your charge by the road. But I am incapable of betraying the trust you reposed in me, and having convinced you that you were in my power, I can only dismiss you unplundered and uninjured.' He then gave the officer directions for his journey, and disappeared with his party as suddenly as they had presented themselves.

Note LXI.

On Bochastle the mouldering lines,
Where Rome, the Empress of the world,
Of yore her eagle wings unfurl'd.—P. 254.

The torrent which discharges itself from Loch Vennachar, the lowest and eastmost of the three lakes which form the scenery adjoining to the Trosachs, sweeps through a flat and extensive moor, called Bochastle. Upon a small eminence, called the *Dun* of Bochastle, and indeed on the plain itself, are some intrenchments, which have been thought Roman. There is, adjacent to Callender, a sweet villa, the residence of Captain Fairfoul, entitled the Roman Camp.

['One of the most entire and beautiful remains of a Roman encampment now to be found in Scotland, is to be seen at Ardoch, near Greenloaning, about six miles to the eastward of Dunblane. This encampment is supposed, on good grounds, to have been constructed during the fourth campaign of Agricola in Britain; it is 1060 feet in length, and 900 in breadth; it could contain 26,000 men, according to the ordinary distribution of the Roman soldiers in their encampments. There appears to have been three or four ditches, strongly fortified, surrounding the camp. The four entries crossing the lines are still to be seen distinctly. The *general's quarter* rises above the level of the camp, but is not exactly in the centre. It is a regular square of twenty yards, enclosed with a stone wall, and containing the foundations of a house, 30 feet by 20. There is a subterraneous communication with a smaller encampment at a little

distance, in which several Roman helmets, spears, &c., have been found. From this camp at Ardoch, the great Roman highway runs east to Bertha, about 14 miles distant, where the Roman army is believed to have passed over the Tay into Strathmore.'—Grahame.]

Note LXII.

See here, all vantageless I stand,
Arm'd like thyself with single brand.
—P. 254.

The duellists of former times did not always stand upon those punctilios respecting equality of arms, which are now judged essential to fair combat. It is true, that in former combats in the lists, the parties were, by the judges of the field, put as nearly as possible in the same circumstances. But in private duel it was often otherwise. In that desperate combat which was fought between Quelus, a minion of Henry III of France, and Antraguet, with two seconds on each side, from which only two persons escaped alive, Quelus complained that his antagonist had over him the advantage of a poniard which he used in parrying, while his left hand, which he was forced to employ for the same purpose, was cruelly mangled. When he charged Antraguet with this odds, 'Thou hast done wrong,' answered he, 'to forget thy dagger at home. We are here to fight, and not to settle punctilios of arms.' In a similar duel, however, a younger brother of the house of Aubanye, in Angoulesme, behaved more generously on the like occasion, and at once threw away his dagger when his enemy challenged it as an undue advantage. But at this time hardly anything can be conceived more horribly brutal and savage than the mode in which private quarrels were conducted in France. Those who were most jealous of the point of honour, and acquired the title of *Ruffinés*, did not scruple to take every advantage of strength, numbers, surprise, and arms, to accomplish their revenge. The Sieur de Brantome, to whose discourse on duels I am obliged for these particulars, gives the following account of the death and principles of his friend, the Baron de Vitaux:—

'J'ay ouï conter à un Tireur d'armes, qui apprit à Millaud à en tirer, lequel s'appelloit Seigneur le Jacques Ferron, de la ville d'Ast, qui avoit esté à moy, il fut depuis tué à Saincte-Basille en Gascogne, lors que Monsieur du Mayne l'assi[c]gea lui servant d'Ing[c]nieur; et de malheur, je l'avois addressé audit Baron quelques trois mois auparavant, pour l'exercer à tirer, bien qu'il en sçeust prou ; mais il ne'en fit compte ; et le laissant, Millaud s'en servit, et le rendit fort adroit. Ce Seigneur Jacques donc me raconta, qu'il s'estoit monté sur un noyer, assez loing, pour en voir le combat, et qu'il ne vist jamais homme y aller plus bravement, ny plus résolument, ny de grace plus asseurée ny déterminée. Il commença de marcher de cinquante pas vers son ennemy, relevant souvent ses moustaches en haut d'une main; et estant à vingt pas de son ennemy, (non plustost,) il mit la main, à l'espée qu'il tenoit en la main, non qu'il l'eust tirée encore; mais en marchant, il fit voller le fourreau en l'air, en le secouant, ce qui est le beau de cela, et qui monstroit bien une grace de combat bien asseurée et froide, et nullement téméraire, comme il y en a qui tirent leurs espées de cinq cents pas de l'ennemy, voire de mille, comme j'en ay veu aucuns. Ainsi mourut ce brave Baron, le paragon de France, qu'on nommoit tel, à bien venger ses querelles, par grandes et déterminées résolutions. Il n'estoit pas seulement estimé en France, mais en Italie, Espaigne, Allemaigne, en Boulogne et Angleterre; et desiroient fort les Etrangers, venant en France, le voir; car je l'ay veu, tant sa renommée volloit. Il estoit fort petit de corps, mais fort grand de courage. Ses ennemis disoient qu'il ne tuoit pas bien ses gens, que par advantages et supercheries. Certes, je tiens de grands capitaines, et mesme d'Italiens, qui ont estez d'autres fois les premiers vengeurs du monde, in *ogni modo*, disoient ils, qui ont tenu cette maxime, qu'une supercherie ne se devoit payer que par semblable monnoye, et n'y alloit point là de déshonneur.'—*Œuvres de Brantome,* Paris, 1787–8. Tome viii. pp. 90-92. It may be necessary to inform the reader, that this paragon of France was the most foul assassin of his time, and had committed many desperate murders, chiefly by the assistance of his hired banditti; from which it may be conceived how little the point of honour of the period deserved its name. I have chosen to give my heroes, who are indeed of an earlier period, a stronger tincture of the spirit of chivalry.

Note LXIII.

Ill fared it then with Roderick Dhu,
That on the field his targe he threw, ...
For, train'd abroad his arms to wield,
Fitz-James's blade was sword and shield.
—P. 255.

A round target of light wood, covered with strong leather, and studded with brass or iron, was a necessary part of a Highlander's equipment. In charging regular troops, they received the thrust of the bayonet in this buckler, twisted it aside, and used the broadsword against the encumbered soldier. In the civil war of 1745, most of the front rank of the clans were thus armed: and Captain Grose informs us, that, in 1747, the privates of the 42nd regiment, then in Flanders, were, for the most part, permitted to carry targets.—*Military Antiquities,* vol. i. p. 164. A person thus armed had a considerable advantage in private fray. Among verses between Swift and Sheridan, lately pub-

lished by Dr. Barret, there is an account of such an encounter, in which the circumstances, and consequently the relative superiority of the combatants, are precisely the reverse of those in the text:—

' A Highlander once fought a Frenchman at Margate,
The weapons, a rapier, a backsword, and target;
Brisk Monsieur advanced as fast as he could,
But all his fine pushes were caught in the wood,
And Sawney, with backsword, did slash him and nick him,
While t' other, enraged that he could not once prick him,
Cried, "Sirrah, you rascal, you son of a whore,
Me will fight you, be gar! if you'll come from your door."'

The use of defensive armour, and particularly of the buckler, or target, was general in Queen Elizabeth's time, although that of the single rapier seems to have been occasionally practised much earlier. Rowland Yorke, however, who betrayed the fort of Zutphen to the Spaniards, for which good service he was afterwards poisoned by them, is said to have been the first who brought the rapier fight into general use. Fuller, speaking of the swash-bucklers, or bullies, of Queen Elizabeth's time, says—'West Smithfield was formerly called Ruffians' Hall, where such men usually met, casually or otherwise, to try *masteries* with sword and buckler. More were frightened than hurt, more hurt than killed therewith, it being accounted unmanly to strike beneath the knee. But since that desperate traitor Rowland Yorke first introduced thrusting with rapiers, sword and buckler are disused.' In 'The Two Angry Women of Abingdon,' a comedy, printed in 1599, we have a pathetic complaint:—'Sword and buckler fight begins to grow out of use. I am sorry for it: I shall never see good manhood again. If it be once gone, this poking fight of rapier and dagger will come up; then a tall man, and a good sword-and-buckler man, will be spitted like a cat or rabbit.' But the rapier had upon the continent long superseded, in private duel, the use of sword and shield. The masters of the noble science of defence were chiefly Italians. They made great mystery of their art and mode of instruction, never suffered any person to be present but the scholar who was to be taught, and even examined closets, beds, and other places of possible concealment. Their lessons often gave the most treacherous advantages; for the challenger, having the right to choose his weapons, frequently selected some strange, unusual, and inconvenient kind of arms, the use of which he practised under these instructors, and thus killed at his ease his antagonist, to whom it was presented for the first time on the field of battle. See BRANTOME's *Discourse on Duels,* and the work on the same subject, '*si gentement ecrit,*' by the venerable Dr. Paris de Puteo. The Highlanders continued to use broadsword and target until disarmed after the affair of 1745-6.

NOTE LXIV.

Thy threats, thy mercy, I defy!
Let recreant yield, who fears to die.
—P. 255.

I have not ventured to render this duel so savagely desperate as that of the celebrated Sir Ewan of Lochiel, chief of the clan Cameron, called, from his sable complexion, Ewan Dhu. He was the last man in Scotland who maintained the royal cause during the great Civil War, and his constant incursions rendered him a very unpleasant neighbour to the republican garrison at Inverlochy, now Fort-William. The governor of the fort detached a party of three hundred men to lay waste Lochiel's possessions, and cut down his trees; but, in a sudden and desperate attack made upon them by the chieftain with very inferior numbers, they were almost all cut to pieces. The skirmish is detailed in a curious memoir of Sir Ewan's life, printed in the Appendix of Pennant's Scottish Tour. 'In this engagement, Lochiel himself had several wonderful escapes. In the retreat of the English, one of the strongest and bravest of the officers retired behind a bush, when he observed Lochiel pursuing, and seeing him unaccompanied with any, he leapt out, and thought him his prey. They met one another with equal fury. The combat was long and doubtful: the English gentleman had by far the advantage in strength and size; but Lochiel, exceeding him in nimbleness and agility, in the end tript the sword out of his hand: they closed and wrestled, till both fell to the ground in each other's arms. The English officer got above Lochiel, and pressed him hard, but stretching forth his neck, by attempting to disengage himself, Lochiel, who by this time had his hands at liberty, with his left hand seized him by the collar, and jumping at his extended throat, he bit it with his teeth quite through, and kept such a hold of his grasp, that he brought away his mouthful: this, he said, *was the sweetest bit he ever had in his lifetime.*'—Vol. i. p. 375.

NOTE LXV.

Ye towers! within whose circuit dread
A Douglas by his sovereign bled;
And thou, O sad and fatal mound!
That oft hast heard the death-axe sound.
—P. 257.

An eminence on the north-east of the Castle, where state criminals were executed. Stirling was often polluted with noble blood. It is thus apostrophized by J. Johnston:—

'Discordia tristis
Heu quoties procerum sanguine tinxit humum!
Hoc uno infelix, et felix cetera; nusquam
Laetior aut coeli frons geniusve soli.'

The fate of William, eighth Earl of Douglas, whom James II stabbed in Stirling Castle with his own hand, and while under his royal safe-conduct, is familiar to all who read Scottish history. Murdack Duke of Albany, Duncan Earl of Lennox, his father-in-law, and his two sons, Walter and Alexander Stuart, were executed at Stirling, in 1425. They were beheaded upon an eminence without the castle walls, but making part of the same hill, from whence they could behold their strong castle of Doune, and their extensive possessions. This 'heading hill,' as it was sometimes termed, bears commonly the less terrible name of Hurly-hacket, from its having been the scene of a courtly amusement alluded to by Sir David Lindsay, who says of the pastimes in which the young king was engaged,

'Some harled him to the Hurly-hacket;'

which consisted in sliding, in some sort of chair it may be supposed, from top to bottom of a smooth bank. The boys of Edinburgh, about twenty years ago, used to play at the hurly-hacket, on the Calton Hill, using for their seat a horse's skull.

NOTE LXVI.

The burghers hold their sports to-day.
—P. 257.

Every burgh of Scotland, of the least note, but more especially the considerable towns, had their solemn *play*, or festival, when feats of archery were exhibited, and prizes distributed to those who excelled in wrestling, hurling the bar, and the other gymnastic exercises of the period. Stirling, a usual place of royal residence, was not likely to be deficient in pomp upon such occasions, especially since James V was very partial to them. His ready participation in these popular amusements was one cause of his acquiring the title of King of the Commons, or *Rex Plebeiorum*, as Lesley has latinized it. The usual prize to the best shooter was a silver arrow. Such a one is preserved at Selkirk and at Peebles. At Dumfries, a silver gun was substituted, and the contention transferred to fire-arms. The ceremony, as there performed, is the subject of an excellent Scottish poem, by Mr. John Mayne, entitled the Siller Gun, 1808, which surpasses the efforts of Fergusson, and comes near to those of Burns.

Of James's attachment to archery, Pitscottie, the faithful, though rude recorder of the manners of that period, has given us evidence:—

'In this year there came an embassador out of England, named Lord William Howard, with a bishop with him, with many other gentlemen, to the number of threescore horse, which were all able men and waled [picked] men for all kinds of games and pastimes, shooting, louping, running, wrestling, and casting of the stone, but they were well 'sayed [essayed or tried] ere they passed out of Scotland, and that by their own provocation; but ever they tint: till at last, the Queen of Scotland, the king's mother, favoured the English-men, because she was the King of England's sister; and therefore she took an enterprise of archery upon the English-men's hands, contrary her son the king, and any six in Scotland that he would wale, either gentlemen or yeomen, that the Englishmen should shoot against them, either at pricks, revers, or buts, as the Scots pleased.

'The king, hearing this of his mother, was content, and gart her pawn a hundred crowns, and a tun of wine, upon the English-men's hands; and he incontinent laid down as much for the Scottish-men. The field and ground was chosen in St. Andrews, and three landed men and three yeomen chosen to shoot against the English-men,—to wit, David Wemyss of that ilk, David Arnot of that ilk, and Mr. John Wedderburn, vicar of Dundee; the yeomen, John Thomson, in Leith, Steven Taburner, with a piper, called Alexander Bailie; they shot very near, and warred [worsted] the English-men of the enterprise, and wan the hundred crowns and the tun of wine, which made the king very merry that his men wan the victory.'—P. 147.

Note LXVII.

Robin Hood.—P. 258.

The exhibition of this renowned outlaw and his band was a favourite frolic at such festivals as we are describing. This sporting, in which kings did not disdain to be actors, was prohibited in Scotland upon the Reformation, by a statute of the 6th Parliament of Queen Mary, c. 61, A.D. 1555, which ordered, under heavy penalties, that 'na manner of person be chosen Robert Hude, nor Little John, Abbot of Unreason, Queen of May, nor otherwise.' But in 1561, the 'rascal multitude,' says John Knox, 'were stirred up to make a Robin Hude, whilk enormity was of many years left and damned by statute and act of Parliament; yet would they not be forbidden.' Accordingly, they raised a very serious tumult, and at length made prisoners the magistrates who endeavoured to suppress it, and would not release them till they extorted a formal promise that no one should be punished for his share of the disturbance. It would seem, from the complaints of the General Assembly of the Kirk, that these profane festivities were continued down to 1592[1]. Bold Robin was, to say the least, equally successful in maintaining his ground against the reformed clergy of England: for the simple and evangelical Latimer complains of coming to a

[1] Book of the Universal Kirk, p. 414.

country church, where the people refused to hear him, because it was Robin Hood's day; and his mitre and rochet were fain to give way to the village pastime. Much curious information on this subject may be found in the Preliminary Dissertation to the late Mr. Ritson's edition of the songs respecting this memorable outlaw. The game of Robin Hood was usually acted in May; and he was associated with the morrice-dancers, on whom so much illustration has been bestowed by the commentators on Shakespeare. A very lively picture of these festivities, containing a great deal of curious information on the subject of the private life and amusements of our ancestors, was thrown, by the late ingenious Mr. Strutt, into his romance entitled Queenhoo Hall, published after his death, in 1808.

Note LXVIII.

Indifferent as to archer wight,
The monarch gave the arrow bright.—P. 258.

The Douglas of the poem is an imaginary person, a supposed uncle of the Earl of Angus. But the King's behaviour during an unexpected interview with the Laird of Kilspindie, one of the banished Douglases, under circumstances similar to those in the text, is imitated from a real story told by Hume of Godscroft. I would have availed myself more fully of the simple and affecting circumstances of the old history, had they not been already woven into a pathetic ballad by my friend Mr. Finlay[2].

'His (the king's) implacability (towards the family of Douglas) did also appear in his carriage towards Archibald of Kilspindie, whom he, when he was a child, loved singularly well for his ability of body, and was wont to call him his Grey-Steill[3]. Archibald, being banished into England, could not well comport with the humour of that nation, which he thought to be too proud, and that they had too high a conceit of themselves, joined with a contempt and despising of all others. Wherefore, being wearied of that life, and remembering the king's favour of old towards him, he determined to try the king's mercifulness and clemency. So he comes into Scotland, and taking occasion of the king's hunting in the park at Stirling, he casts himself to be in his way, as he was coming home to the castle. So soon as the king saw him afar off, ere he came near, he guessed it was he, and said to one of his courtiers, yonder is my Grey-Steill, Archibald of Kilspindie, if he be alive. The other answered, that it could not be he, and that he durst not come into the king's presence. The king approaching, he fell upon his knees

[2] See Scottish Historical and Romantic Ballads. Glasgow, 1808, vol. ii. p. 117.
[3] A champion of popular romance. See *Ellis's Romances*, vol. iii.

and craved pardon, and promised from thenceforward to abstain from meddling in public affairs, and to lead a quiet and private life. The king went by without giving him any answer, and trotted a good round pace up the hill. Kilspindie followed, and though he wore on him a secret, a shirt of mail, for his particular enemies, was as soon at the castle gate as the king. There he sat him down upon a stone without, and entreated some of the king's servants for a cup of drink, being weary and thirsty; but they, fearing the king's displeasure, durst give him none. When the king was set at his dinner, he asked what he had done, what he had said, and whither he had gone? It was told him that he had desired a cup of drink, and had gotten none. The king reproved them very sharply for their discourtesy, and told them, that if he had not taken an oath that no Douglas should ever serve him, he would have received him into his service, for he had seen him sometime a man of great ability. Then he sent him word to go to Leith, and expect his further pleasure. Then some kinsman of David Falconer, the cannonier, that was slain at Tantallon, began to quarrel with Archibald about the matter, wherewith the king showed himself not well pleased when he heard of it. Then he commanded him to go to France for a certain space, till he heard farther from him. And so he did, and died shortly after. This gave occasion to the King of England (Henry VIII) to blame his nephew, alleging the old saying, That a king's face should give grace. For this Archibald (whatsoever were Angus's or Sir George's fault) had not been principal actor of anything, nor no counsellor nor stirrer up, but only a follower of his friends, and that noways cruelly disposed.'—*Hume of Godscroft*, ii. 107.

Note LXIX.

Prize of the wrestling match, the King
To Douglas gave a golden ring.—P. 258.

The usual prize of a wrestling was a ram and a ring, but the animal would have embarrassed my story. Thus, in the Cokes Tale of Gamelyn, ascribed to Chaucer:

> 'There happed to be there beside
> Tryed a wrestling:
> And therefore there was y-setten
> A ram and als a ring.'

Again the Litil Geste of Robin Hood:

> ——' By a bridge was a wrestling,
> And there taryed was he,
> And there was all the best yemen
> Of all the west countrey.
> A full fayre game there was set up,
> A white bull up y-pight,
> A great courser with saddle and brydle,
> With gold burnished full bryght;
> A payre of gloves, a red golde ringe,
> A pipe of wyne, good fay;
> What man bereth him best, I wis,
> The prise shall bear away.'

RITSON'S *Robin Hood*, vol. i.

Note LXX.

These drew not for their fields the sword,
Like tenants of a feudal lord,
Nor own'd the patriarchal claim
Of Chieftain in their leader's name;
Adventurers they—— —P. 262.

The Scottish armies consisted chiefly of the nobility and barons, with their vassals, who held lands under them, for military service by themselves and their tenants. The patriarchal influence exercised by the heads of clans in the Highlands and Borders was of a different nature, and sometimes at variance with feudal principles. It flowed from the *Patria Potestas*, exercised by the chieftain as representing the original father of the whole name, and was often obeyed in contradiction to the feudal superior. James V seems first to have introduced, in addition to the militia furnished from these sources, the service of a small number of mercenaries, who formed a body-guard, called the Foot-Band. The satirical poet, Sir David Lindsay (or the person who wrote the prologue to his play of the 'Three Estaites,') has introduced Finlay of the Foot-Band, who, after much swaggering upon the stage, is at length put to flight by the Fool, who terrifies him by means of a sheep's skull upon a pole. I have rather chosen to give them the harsh features of the mercenary soldiers of the period, than of this Scottish Thraso. These partook of the character of the Adventurous Companions of Froissart or the Condottieri of Italy.

One of the best and liveliest traits of such manners is the last will of a leader, called Geffroy Tete Noir, who having been slightly wounded in a skirmish, his intemperance brought on a mortal disease. When he found himself dying, he summoned to his bedside the adventurers whom he commanded, and thus addressed them :—

' Fayre sirs, quod Geffray, I knowe well ye have alwayes served and honoured me as men ought to serve their soveraygne and capitayne, and I shal be the gladder if ye wyll agre to have to your capitayne one that is discended of my blode. Beholde here Aleyne Roux, my cosyn, and Peter his brother, who are men of armes and of my blode. I require you to make Aleyne your capitayne, and to swere to hym faythe, obeysaunce, love, and loyalte, here in my presence, and also to his brother : howe be it, I wyll that Aleyne have the soverayne charge. Sir, quod they, we are well content, for ye haave ryght well chosen. There all the companyons made them servyant to Aleyne Roux and to Peter his brother.'—LORD BERNERS' *Froissart*.

Note LXXI.

Thou now hast glee-maiden and harp!
Get thee an ape, and trudge the land,
The leader of a juggler band.—P. 264.

The jongleurs, or jugglers, as we learn

from the elaborate work of the late Mr. Strutt, on the sports and pastimes of the people of England, used to call in the aid of various assistants, to render these performances as captivating as possible. The glee-maiden was a necessary attendant. Her duty was tumbling and dancing; and therefore the Anglo-Saxon version of Saint Mark's Gospel states Herodias to have vaulted or tumbled before King Herod. In Scotland, these poor creatures seem, even at a late period, to have been bondswomen to their masters, as appears from a case reported by Fountainhall :—'Reid the mountebank pursues Scott of Harden and his lady, for stealing away from him a little girl, called the tumbling lassie, that danced upon his stage: and he claimed damages, and produced a contract, whereby he bought her from her mother for £30 Scots. But we have no slaves in Scotland, and mothers cannot sell their bairns; and physicians attested the employment of tumbling would kill her; and her joints were now grown stiff, and she declined to return; though she was at least a 'prentice, and so could not run away from her master: yet some cited Moses's law, that if a servant shelter himself with thee, against his master's cruelty, thou shalt surely not deliver him up. The Lords, *renitente cancellario*, assoilzied Harden, on the 27th of January (1687).'—FOUNTAIN-HALL'S *Decisions*, vol. i. p. 439[1].

The facetious qualities of the ape soon rendered him an acceptable addition to the strolling band of the jongleur. Ben Jonson, in his splenetic introduction to the comedy of 'Bartholomew Fair,' is at pains to inform the audience 'that he has ne'er a sword-and-buckler man in his Fair, nor a juggler, with a well-educated ape, to come over the chaine for the King of England, and back again for the Prince, and sit still on his haunches for the Pope and the King of Spaine.'

Note LXXII.

That stirring air that peals on high,
O'er Dermid's race our victory.
Strike it! —P. 266.

There are several instances, at least in tradition, of persons so much attached to particular tunes, as to require to hear them on their deathbed. Such an anecdote is mentioned by the late Mr. Riddel of Glenriddel, in his collection of Border tunes, respecting an air called the 'Dandling of

[1] Though less to my purpose, I cannot help noticing a circumstance respecting another of this Mr. Reid's attendants, which occurred during James II's zeal for Catholic proselytism, and is told by Fountainhall, with dry Scotch irony :—' *January 17th*, 1687.—Reid the mountebank is received into the Popish church, and one of his blackamores was persuaded to accept of baptism from the Popish priests, and to turn Christian papist; which was a great trophy: he was called James, after the king and chancellor, and the Apostle James.—*Ibid.* p. 440.

the Bairns,' for which a certain Gallovidian laird is said to have evinced this strong mark of partiality. It is popularly told of a famous freebooter, that he composed the tune known by the name of Macpherson's Rant, while under sentence of death, and played it at the gallows-tree. Some spirited words have been adapted to it by Burns. A similar story is recounted of a Welsh bard, who composed and played on his deathbed the air called *Dafyddy Garregg Wen.* But the most curious example is given by Brantome, of a maid of honour at the court of France, entitled, Mademoiselle de Limeuil. 'Durant sa maladie, dont elle trespassa, jamais elle ne cessa, ains causa tousjours; car elle estoit fort grande parleuse, brocardeuse, et très-bien et fort à propos, et très-belle avec cela. Quand l'heure de sa fin fut venue, elle fit venir a soy son valet (ainsi que le filles de la cour en ont chacune un), qui s'appelloit Julien, et scavoit très-bien joüer du violon. "Julien," luy dit elle, "prenez vostre violon, et sonnez moy tousjours jusques a ce que vous me voyez morte (car je m'y en vais) la défaite des Suisses, et le mieux que vous pourrez, et quand vous serez sur le mot, 'Tout est perdu,' sonnez le par quatre ou cinq fois le plus piteusement que vous pourrez," ce qui fit l'autre, et elle-mesme luy aidoit de la voix, et quand ce vint "tout est perdu," elle le réïtera par deux fois; et se tournant de l'autre costé du chevet, elle dit à ses compagnes: "Tout est perdu à ce coup, et à bon escient;" et ainsi décéda. Voila une morte joyeuse et plaisante. Je tiens ce conte de deux de ses compagnes, dignes de foi, qui virent jouer ce mystere.'—*Œuvres de Brantome*, iii. 507. The tune to which this fair lady chose to make her final exit, was composed on the defeat of the Swiss at Marignano. The burden is quoted by Panurge, in Rabelais, and consists of these words, imitating the jargon of the Swiss, which is a mixture of French and German:

'Tout est verlore,
La Tintelore,
Tout est verlore, bi Got!

Note LXXIII.

Battle of Beal' an Duine.—P. 267.

A skirmish actually took place at a pass thus called in the Trosachs, and closed with the remarkable incident mentioned in the text. It was greatly posterior in date to the reign of James V.

'In this roughly-wooded island[2], the country people secreted their wives and children, and their most valuable effects, from the rapacity of Cromwell's soldiers, during their inroad into this country, in the time of the republic. These invaders, not venturing to

[2] That at the eastern extremity of Loch Katrine.

ascend by the ladders, along the side of the lake, took a more circuitous road, through the heart of the Trosachs, the most frequented path at that time, which penetrates the wilderness about half way between Binean and the lake, by a tract called Yea-chilleach, or the Old Wife's Bog.

'In one of the defiles of this by-road, the men of the country at that time hung upon the rear of the invading enemy, and shot one of Cromwell's men, whose grave marks the scene of action, and gives name to that pass. In revenge of this insult, the soldiers resolved to plunder the island, to violate the women, and put the children to death. With this brutal intention, one of the party, more expert than the rest, swam towards the island, to fetch the boat to his comrades, which had carried the women to their asylum, and lay moored in one of the creeks. His companions stood on the shore of the mainland, in full view of all that was to pass, waiting anxiously for his return with the boat. But just as the swimmer had got to the nearest point of the island, and was laying hold of a black rock, to get on shore, a heroine, who stood on the very point where he meant to land, hastily snatching a dagger from below her apron, with one stroke severed his head from the body. His party seeing this disaster, and relinquishing all future hope of revenge or conquest, made the best of their way out of their perilous situation. This amazon's great-grandson lives at Bridge of Turk, who, besides others, attests the anecdote.'—*Sketch of the Scenery near Callendar*, Stirling, 1806, p. 20. I have only to add to this account, that the heroine's name was Helen Stuart.

Note LXXIV.

And Snowdoun's Knight is Scotland's King.—P. 272.

This discovery will probably remind the reader of the beautiful Arabian tale of *Il Bondocani*. Yet the incident is not borrowed from that elegant story, but from Scottish tradition. James V, of whom we are treating, was a monarch whose good and benevolent intentions often rendered his romantic freaks venial, if not respectable, since, from his anxious attention to the interests of the lower and most oppressed class of his subjects, he was, as we have seen, popularly termed the *King of the Commons.* For the purpose of seeing that justice was regularly administered, and frequently from the less justifiable motive of gallantry, he used to traverse the vicinage of his several palaces in various disguises. The two excellent comic songs, entitled, 'The Gaberlunzie man,' and 'We'll gae nae mair a roving,' are said to have been founded upon the success of his amorous adventures when travelling in the disguise of a beggar. The

latter is perhaps the best comic ballad in any language.

Another adventure, which had nearly cost James his life, is said to have taken place at the village of Cramond, near Edinburgh, where he had rendered his addresses acceptable to a pretty girl of the lower rank. Four or five persons, whether relations or lovers of his mistress is uncertain, beset the disguised monarch as he returned from his rendezvous. Naturally gallant, and an admirable master of his weapon, the king took post on the high and narrow bridge over the Almond river, and defended himself bravely with his sword. A peasant, who was threshing in a neighbouring barn, came out upon the noise, and whether moved by compassion or by natural gallantry, took the weaker side, and laid about with his flail so effectually, as to disperse the assailants, well threshed, even according to the letter. He then conducted the king into his barn, where his guest requested a basin and a towel, to remove the stains of the broil. This being procured with difficulty, James employed himself in learning what was the summit of his deliverer's earthly wishes, and found that they were bounded by the desire of possessing, in property, the farm of Braehead, upon which he laboured as a bondsman. The lands chanced to belong to the crown; and James directed him to come to the palace of Holyrood, and enquire for the Guidman (i.e. farmer) of Ballengiech, a name by which he was known in his excursions, and which answered to the *Il Bondocani* of Haroun Alraschid. He presented himself accordingly, and found, with due astonishment, that he had saved h.s monarch's life, and that he was to be gratified with a crown charter of the lands of Braehead, under the service of presenting a ewer, basin and towel, for the king to wash his hands when he shall happen to pass the Bridge of Cramond. This person was ancestor of the Howisons of Braehead, in Mid-Lothian, a respectable family, who continue to hold the lands (now passed into the female line) under the same tenure.

Another of James's frolics is thus narrated by Mr. Campbell from the Statistical Account:—'Being once benighted when out a hunting, and separated from his attendants, he happened to enter a cottage in the midst of a moor at the foot of the Ochil hills, near Alloa, where, unknown, he was kindly received. In order to regale their unexpected guest, the *gudeman* (i.e. landlord, farmer) desired the *gudewife* to fetch the hen that roosted nearest the cock, which is always the plumpest, for the stranger's supper. The king, highly pleased with his night's lodging and hospitable entertainment, told mine host at parting, that he should be glad to return his civility, and requested that the first time he came to Stirling, he would call at the castle, and enquire for the *Gudeman of Ballenguich.*

L

'Donaldson, the landlord, did not fail to call on the *Gudeman of Ballenguich*, when his astonishment at finding that the king had been his guest afforded no small amusement to the merry monarch and his courtiers; and, to carry on the pleasantry, he was thenceforth designated by James with the title of King of the Moors, which name and designation have descended from father to son ever since, and they have continued in possession of the identical spot, the property of Mr. Erskine of Mar, till very lately, when this gentleman, with reluctance, turned out the descendant and representative of the King of the Moors, on account of his majesty's invincible indolence, and great dislike to reform or innovation of any kind, although, from the spirited example of his neighbour tenants on the same estate, he is convinced similar exertion would promote his advantage.'

The author requests permission yet farther to verify the subject of his poem, by an extract from the genealogical work of Buchanan of Auchmar, upon Scottish surnames:—

'This John Buchanan of Auchmar and Arnpryor was afterwards termed King of Kippen, upon the following account. King James V, a very sociable, debonair prince, residing at Stirling, in Buchanan of Arnpryor's time, carriers were very frequently passing along the common road, being near Arnpryor's house, with necessaries for the use of the king's family: and he, having some extraordinary occasion, ordered one of these carriers to leave his load at his house, and he would pay him for it; which the carrier refused to do, telling him he was the king's carrier, and his load for his majesty's use; to which Arnpryor seemed to have small regard, compelling the carrier, in the end, to leave his load; telling him, if King James was King of Scotland, he was King of Kippen, so that it was reasonable he should share with his neighbour king in some of these loads, so frequently carried that road. The carrier representing his usage, and telling the story, as Arnpryor spoke it, to some of the king's servants, it came at length to his majesty's ears, who, shortly thereafter, with a few attendants, came to visit his neighbour king, who was in the meantime at dinner. King James, having sent a servant to demand access, was denied the same by a tall fellow with a battle-axe, who stood porter at the gate, telling, there could be no access till dinner was over. This answer not satisfying the king, he sent to demand access a second time; upon which he was desired by the porter to desist, otherwise he would find cause to repent his rudeness. His majesty finding this method would not do, desired the porter to tell his master that the Goodman of Ballageich desired to speak with the King of Kippen. The porter telling Arnpryor so much, he, in all humble manner, came and received the king, and having entertained him with much sumptuousness and jollity, became so agreeable to King James, that he allowed him to take so much of any provision he found carrying that road as he had occasion for; and seeing he made the first visit, desired Arnpryor in a few days to return him a second to Stirling, which he performed, and continued in very much favour with the king, always thereafter being termed King of Kippen while he lived.'—BUCHANAN'S *Essay upon the Family of Buchanan.* Edin. 1775, 8vo, p. 74.

The readers of Ariosto must give credit for the amiable features with which King James V is represented, since he is generally considered as the prototype of Zerbino, the most interesting hero of the Orlando Furioso.

NOTE LXXV.

—— *Stirling's tower*
Of yore the name of Snowdoun claims.
—P. 272.

William of Worcester, who wrote about the middle of the fifteenth century, calls Stirling Castle Snowdoun. Sir David Lindsay bestows the same epithet upon it in his complaint of the Papingo:

'Adieu, fair Snowdoun, with thy towers high,
Thy chaple-royal, park, and table round;
May, June, and July, would I dwell in thee,
Were I a man, to hear the birdis sound,
Whilk doth againe thy royal rock rebound.'

Mr. Chalmers, in his late excellent edition of Sir David Lindsay's works, has refuted the chimerical derivation of Snawdoun from *snedding*, or cutting. It was probably derived from the romantic legend which connected Stirling with King Arthur, to which the mention of the Round Table gives countenance. The ring within which justs were formerly practised, in the castle park, is still called the Round Table. Snawdoun is the official title of one of the Scottish heralds, whose epithets seem in all countries to have been fantastically adopted from ancient history or romance.

It appears (see Note LXXIV) that the real name by which James was actually distinguished in his private excursions, was the *Goodman of Ballenguich;* derived from a steep pass leading up to the Castle of Stirling, so called. But the epithet would not have suited poetry, and would besides at once, and prematurely, have announced the plot to many of my countrymen, among whom the traditional stories above mentioned are still current.

Rokeby.

—◆◆—

TO

JOHN B. S. MORRITT, ESQ.,

THIS POEM,

THE SCENE OF WHICH IS LAID IN HIS BEAUTIFUL DEMESNE OF ROKEBY,

IS INSCRIBED, IN TOKEN OF SINCERE FRIENDSHIP, BY

WALTER SCOTT.

—◆◆—

The Scene of this Poem is laid at Rokeby, near Greta Bridge, in Yorkshire, and shifts to the adjacent fortress of Barnard Castle, and to other places in that vicinity.

The Time occupied by the Action is a space of Five Days, Three of which are supposed to elapse between the end of the Fifth and beginning of the Sixth Canto.

The date of the supposed events is immediately subsequent to the great Battle of Marston Moor, July 3, 1644. This period of public confusion has been chosen, without any purpose of combining the Fable with the Military or Political Events of the Civil War, but only as affording a degree of probability to the Fictitious Narrative now presented to the Public.

Canto First.

I.

The Moon is in her summer glow,
But hoarse and high the breezes blow,
And, racking o'er her face, the cloud
Varies the tincture of her shroud;
On Barnard's towers, and Tees's stream,
She changes as a guilty dream,
When conscience, with remorse and fear,
Goads sleeping fancy's wild career.
Her light seems now the blush of shame,
Seems now fierce anger's darker flame,
Shifting that shade, to come and go,
Like apprehension's hurried glow;
Then sorrow's livery dims the air,
And dies in darkness, like despair.
Such varied hues the warder sees
Reflected from the woodland Tees,
Then from old Baliol's tower looks forth,
Sees the clouds mustering in the north,
Hears, upon turret-roof and wall,
By fits the plashing rain-drop fall,
Lists to the breeze's boding sound,
And wraps his shaggy mantle round.

II.

Those towers, which in the changeful gleam
Throw murky shadows on the stream,
Those towers of Barnard hold a guest,
The emotions of whose troubled breast,
In wild and strange confusion driven,
Rival the flitting rack of heaven.
Ere sleep stern Oswald's senses tied,
Oft had he changed his weary side,

Composed his limbs, and vainly sought
By effort strong to banish thought.
Sleep came at length, but with a train
Of feelings true and fancies vain,
Mingling, in wild disorder cast,
The expected future with the past.
Conscience, anticipating time,
Already rues the enacted crime,
And calls her furies forth, to shake
The sounding scourge and hissing
    snake;
While her poor victim's outward throes
Bear witness to his mental woes,
And show what lesson may be read
Beside a sinner's restless bed.

III.

Thus Oswald's labouring feelings trace
Strange changes in his sleeping face,
Rapid and ominous as these
With which the moonbeams tinge the
    Tees.
There might be seen of shame the blush,
There anger's dark and fiercer flush,
While the perturbed sleeper's hand
Seem'd grasping dagger-knife, or
    brand.
Relax'd that grasp, the heavy sigh,
The tear in the half-opening eye,
The pallid cheek and brow, confess'd
That grief was busy in his breast;
Nor paused that mood—a sudden start
Impell'd the life-blood from the heart:
Features convulsed, and mutterings
    dread,
Show terror reigns in sorrow's stead.
That pang the painful slumber broke,
And Oswald with a start awoke.

IV.

He woke, and fear'd again to close
His eyelids in such dire repose;
He woke,—to watch the lamp, and tell
From hour to hour the castle-bell,
Or listen to the owlet's cry,
Or the sad breeze that whistles by,
Or catch, by fits, the tuneless rhyme
With which the warder cheats the time,

And envying think, how, when the
    sun
Bids the poor soldier's watch be done,
Couch'd on his straw, and fancy-free,
He sleeps like careless infancy.

V.

Far town-ward sounds a distant tread,
And Oswald, starting from his bed,
Hath caught it, though no human ear,
Unsharpen'd by revenge and fear,
Could e'er distinguish horse's clank
Until it reach'd the castle bank.
Now nigh and plain the sound appears,
The warder's challenge now he hears,
Then clanking chains and levers tell
That o'er the moat the drawbridge fell,
And, in the castle court below,
Voices are heard, and torches glow,
As marshalling the stranger's way
Straight for the room where Oswald
    lay;
The cry was,—'Tidings from the host,
Of weight—a messenger comes post.'
Stifling the tumult of his breast,
His answer Oswald thus express'd—
'Bring food and wine, and trim the
    fire;
Admit the stranger, and retire.'

VI.

The stranger came with heavy stride,
The morion's plumes his visage hide,
And the buff-coat, an ample fold,
Mantles his form's gigantic mould.
Full slender answer deigned he
To Oswald's anxious courtesy,
But mark'd, by a disdainful smile,
He saw and scorn'd the petty wile,
When Oswald changed the torch's
    place,
Anxious that on the soldier's face
Its partial lustre might be thrown,
To show his looks, yet hide his own.
His guest, the while, laid low aside
The ponderous cloak of tough bull's
    hide,

And to the torch glanced broad and
    clear
The corslet of a cuirassier;
Then from his brows the casque he
    drew,
And from the dank plume dash'd the
    dew,
From gloves of mail relieved his hands,
And spread them to the kindling brands,
And, turning to the genial board,
Without a health, or pledge, or word
Of meet and social reverence said,
Deeply he drank, and fiercely fed;
As free from ceremony's sway,
As famish'd wolf that tears his prey.

VII.

With deep impatience, tinged with fear,
His host beheld him gorge his cheer,
And quaff the full carouse, that lent
His brow a fiercer hardiment.
Now Oswald stood a space aside,
Now paced the room with hasty stride,
In feverish agony to learn
Tidings of deep and dread concern,
Cursing each moment that his guest
Protracted o'er his ruffian feast.
Yet, viewing with alarm, at last,
The end of that uncouth repast,
Almost he seem'd their haste to rue,
As, at his sign, his train withdrew,
And left him with the stranger, free
To question of his mystery.
Then did his silence long proclaim
A struggle between fear and shame.

VIII.

Much in the stranger's mien appears
To justify suspicious fears.
On his dark face a scorching clime,
And toil, had done the work of time,
Roughen'd the brow, the temples bared,
And sable hairs with silver shared,
Yet left—what age alone could tame—
The lip of pride, the eye of flame;
The full-drawn lip that upward curl'd,
The eye, that seem'd to scorn the world.

That lip had terror never blench'd;
Ne'er in that eye had tear-drop
    quench'd
The flash severe of swarthy glow,
That mock'd at pain, and knew not woe.
Inured to danger's direst form,
Tornade and earthquake, flood and
    storm,
Death had he seen by sudden blow,
By wasting plague, by tortures slow,
By mine or breach, by steel or ball,
Knew all his shapes, and scorn'd them
    all.

IX.

But yet, though BERTRAM's harden'd
    look,
Unmoved, could blood and danger
    brook,
Still worse than apathy had place
On his swart brow and callous face;
For evil passions, cherish'd long,
Had plough'd them with impressions
    strong.
All that gives gloss to sin, all gay
Light folly, past with youth away,
But rooted stood, in manhood's hour,
The weeds of vice without their flower.
And yet the soil in which they grew,
Had it been tamed when life was new,
Had depth and vigour to bring forth
The hardier fruits of virtuous worth.
Not that, e'en then, his heart had
    known
The gentler feelings' kindly tone;
But lavish waste had been refined
To bounty in his chasten'd mind,
And lust of gold, that waste to feed,
Been lost in love of glory's meed,
And, frantic then no more, his pride
Had ta'en fair virtue for its guide.

X.

Even now, by conscience unrestrain'd,
Clogg'd by gross vice, by slaughter
    stain'd,
Still knew his daring soul to soar,
And mastery o'er the mind he bore;

For meaner guilt, or heart less hard,
Quail'd beneath Bertram's bold regard.
And this felt Oswald, while in vain
He strove, by many a winding train,
To lure his sullen guest to show,
Unask'd, the news he long'd to know,
While on far other subject hung
His heart, than falter'd from his tongue.
Yet nought for that his guest did deign
To note or spare his secret pain,
But still, in stern and stubborn sort,
Return'd him answer dark and short,
Or started from the theme, to range
In loose digression wild and strange,
And forced the embarrass'd host to buy,
By query close, direct reply.

XI.

A while he glozed upon the cause
Of Commons, Covenant, and Laws,
And Church Reform'd—but felt rebuke
Beneath grim Bertram's sneering look,
Then stammer'd—'Has a field been
    fought?
Has Bertram news of battle brought?
For sure a soldier, famed so far
In foreign fields for feats of war,
On eve of fight ne'er left the host
Until the field were won and lost.'
'Here, in your towers by circling Tees,
You, Oswald Wycliffe, rest at ease;
Why deem it strange that others come
To share such safe and easy home,
From fields where danger, death, and
    toil,
Are the reward of civil broil?'
'Nay, mock not, friend! since well
    we know
The near advances of the foe,
To mar our northern army's work,
Encamp'd before beleaguer'd York;
Thy horse with valiant Fairfax lay,
And must have fought; how went the
    day?'

XII.

'Wouldst hear the tale? On Marston
    heath
Met, front to front, the ranks of death;

Flourish'd the trumpets fierce, and
    now
Fired was each eye, and flush'd each
    brow;
On either side loud clamours ring,
"God and the Cause!"—"God and
    the King!"
Right English all, they rush'd to blows,
With nought to win, and all to lose.
I could have laugh'd—but lack'd the
    time—
To see, in phrenesy sublime,
How the fierce zealots fought and bled
For king or state, as humour led;
Some for a dream of public good,
Some for church-tippet, gown, and
    hood,
Draining their veins, in death to claim
A patriot's or a martyr's name.
Led Bertram Risingham the hearts,
That counter'd there on adverse parts,
No superstitious fool had I
Sought El Dorados in the sky!
Chili had heard me through her states,
And Lima oped her silver gates,
Rich Mexico I had march'd through,
And sack'd the splendours of Peru,
Till sunk Pizarro's daring name,
And, Cortez, thine, in Bertram's fame.'
'Still from the purpose wilt thou stray!
Good gentle friend, how went the day?'

XIII.

'Good am I deem'd at trumpet-sound,
And good where goblets dance the
    round,
Though gentle ne'er was join'd, till
    now,
With rugged Bertram's breast and
    brow.
But I resume.   The battle's rage
Was like the strife which currents
    wage
Where Orinoco, in his pride,
Rolls to the main no tribute tide,
But 'gainst broad ocean urges far
A rival sea of roaring war;

While, in ten thousand eddies driven,
The billows fling their foam to heaven,
And the pale pilot seeks in vain
Where rolls the river, where the main.
Even thus, upon the bloody field,
The eddying tides of conflict wheel'd
Ambiguous, till that heart of flame,
Hot Rupert, on our squadrons came,
Hurling against our spears a line
Of gallants, fiery as their wine;
Then ours, though stubborn in their
zeal,
In zeal's despite began to reel.
What wouldst thou more? In tumult
tost,
Our leaders fell, our ranks were lost.
A thousand men, who drew the sword
For both the Houses and the Word,
Preach'd forth from hamlet, grange,
and down,
To curb the crosier and the crown,
Now, stark and stiff, lie stretch'd in
gore,
And ne'er shall rail at mitre more.—
Thus fared it, when I left the fight,
With the good Cause and Commons'
right.'

XIV.

'Disastrous news!' dark Wycliffe said;
Assumed despondence bent his head,
While troubled joy was in his eye,
The well-feign'd sorrow to belie.
'Disastrous news!—when needed
most,
Told ye not that your chiefs were lost?
Complete the woful tale, and say,
Who fell upon that fatal day;
What leaders of repute and name
Bought by their death a deathless fame.
If such my direst foeman's doom,
My tears shall dew his honour'd tomb.
No answer? Friend, of all our host,
Thou know'st whom I should hate
the most,
Whom thou too, once, wert wont to
hate,
Yet leavest me doubtful of his fate.'

With look unmoved, 'Of friend or foe,
Aught,' answer'd Bertram, 'wouldst
thou know,
Demand in simple terms and plain,
A soldier's answer shalt thou gain;
For question dark, or riddle high,
I have nor judgment nor reply.'

XV.

The wrath his art and fear suppress'd
Now blazed at once in Wycliffe's breast;
And brave, from man so meanly born,
Roused his hereditary scorn.
'Wretch! hast thou paid thy bloody
debt?
PHILIP OF MORTHAM, lives he yet?
False to thy patron or thine oath,
Trait'rous or perjured, one or both,
Slave! hast thou kept thy promise
plight,
To slay thy leader in the fight?'
Then from his seat the soldier sprung,
And Wycliffe's hand he strongly
wrung;
His grasp, as hard as glove of mail,
Forced the red blood-drop from the
nail—
'A health!' he cried; and, ere he
quaff'd,
Flung from him Wycliffe's hand, and
laugh'd:
'Now, Oswald Wycliffe, speaks thy
heart!
Now play'st thou well thy genuine part!
Worthy, but for thy craven fear,
Like me to roam a bucanier.
What reck'st thou of the Cause divine,
If Mortham's wealth and lands be thine?
What carest thou for beleaguer'd York,
If this good hand have done its work!
Or what, though Fairfax and his best
Are reddening Marston's swarthy
breast,
If Philip Mortham with them lie,
Lending his life-blood to the dye?
Sit, then! and as 'mid comrades free
Carousing after victory,

When tales are told of blood and fear,
That boys and women shrink to hear,
From point to point I frankly tell
The deed of death as it befell.

XVI.

'When purposed vengeance I forego,
Term me a wretch, nor deem me foe;
And when an insult I forgive,
Then brand me as a slave, and live!
Philip of Mortham is with those
Whom Bertram Risingham calls foes;
Or whom more sure revenge attends,
If number'd with ungrateful friends.
As was his wont, ere battle glow'd,
Along the marshall'd ranks he rode,
And wore his vizor up the while.
I saw his melancholy smile,
When, full opposed in front, he knew
Where ROKEBY's kindred banner flew.
"And thus," he said, "will friends
     divide!"
I heard, and thought how, side by side,
We two had turn'd the battle's tide
In many a well-debated field,
Where Bertram's breast was Philip's
     shield.
I thought on Darien's deserts pale,
Where death bestrides the evening
     gale,
How o'er my friend my cloak I threw,
And fenceless faced the deadly dew;
I thought on Quariana's cliff,
Where, rescued from our foundering
     skiff,
Through the white breakers' wrath
     I bore
Exhausted Mortham to the shore;
And when his side an arrow found,
I suck'd the Indian's venom'd wound.
These thoughts like torrents rush'd
     along,
To sweep away my purpose strong.

XVII.

' Hearts are not flint, and flints are rent;
Hearts are not steel, and steel is bent.

When Mortham bade me, as of yore,
Be near him in the battle's roar,
I scarcely saw the spears laid low,
I scarcely heard the trumpets blow;
Lost was the war in inward strife,
Debating Mortham's death or life.
'Twas then I thought, how, lured to
     come,
As partner of his wealth and home,
Years of piratic wandering o'er,
With him I sought our native shore.
But Mortham's lord grew far estranged
From the bold heart with whom he
     ranged;
Doubts, horrors, superstitious fears,
Sadden'd and dimm'd descending
     years;
The wily priests their victim sought,
And damn'd each free-born deed and
     thought.
Then must I seek another home,
My licence shook his sober dome;
If gold he gave, in one wild day
I revell'd thrice the sum away.
An idle outcast then I stray'd,
Unfit for tillage or for trade,
Deem'd, like the steel of rusted lance,
Useless and dangerous at once.
The women fear'd my hardy look,
At my approach the peaceful shook;
The merchant saw my glance of flame,
And lock'd his hoards when Bertram
     came;
Each child of coward peace kept far
From the neglected son of war.

XVIII.

'But civil discord gave the call,
And made my trade the trade of all.
By Mortham urged, I came again
His vassals to the fight to train.
What guerdon waited on my care?
I could not cant of creed or prayer;
Sour fanatics each trust obtain'd,
And I, dishonour'd and disdain'd,
Gain'd but the high and happy lot,
In these poor arms to front the shot!

All this thou know'st, thy gestures tell;
Yet hear it o'er, and mark it well.
'Tis honour bids me now relate
Each circumstance of Mortham's fate.

XIX.

' Thoughts, from the tongue that slowly
          part,
Glance quick as lightning through the
          heart.
As my spur press'd my courser's side,
Philip of Mortham's cause was tried,
And, ere the charging squadrons mix'd,
His plea was cast, his doom was fix'd.
I watch'd him through the doubtful
          fray
That changed as March's moody day,
Till, like a stream that bursts its bank,
Fierce Rupert thunder'd on our flank.
'Twas then, midst tumult, smoke, and
          strife,
Where each man fought for death or
          life,
'Twas then I fired my petronel,
And Mortham, steed and rider, fell.
One dying look he upward cast,
Of wrath and anguish—'twas his last.
Think not that there I stopp'd to view
What of the battle should ensue ;
But ere I clear'd that bloody press,
Our northern horse ran masterless ;
Monckton and Mitton told the news,
How troops of Roundheads choked the
          Ouse,
And many a bonny Scot, aghast,
Spurring his palfrey northward, past,
Cursing the day when zeal or meed
First lured their Lesley o'er the Tweed.
Yet when I reach'd the banks of Swale,
Had rumour learn'd another tale ;
With his barb'd horse, fresh tidings say,
Stout Cromwell has redeem'd the day :
But whether false the news, or true,
Oswald, I reck as light as you.'

XX.

Not then by Wycliffe might be shown
How his pride startled at the tone

In which his 'complice, fierce and free,
Asserted guilt's equality.
In smoothest terms his speech he wove,
Of endless friendship, faith, and love;
Promised and vow'd in courteous sort,
But Bertram broke professions short.
' Wycliffe, be sure not here I stay,
No, scarcely till the rising day ;
Warn'd by the legends of my youth,
I trust not an associate's truth.
Do not my native dales prolong
Of Percy Rede the tragic song,
Train'd forward to his bloody fall,
By Girsonfield, that treacherous Hall?
Oft, by the Pringle's haunted side,
The shepherd sees his spectre glide.
And near the spot that gave me name,
The moated mound of Risingham,
Where Reed upon her margin sees
Sweet Woodburne's cottages and
          trees,
Some ancient sculptor's art has shown
An outlaw's image on the stone ;
Unmatch'd in strength, a giant he,
With quiver'd back, and kirtled knee.
Ask how he died, that hunter bold,
The tameless monarch of the wold,
And age and infancy can tell,
By brother's treachery he fell.
Thus warn'd by legends of my youth,
I trust to no associate's truth.

XXI.

' When last we reason'd of this deed,
Nought, I bethink me, was agreed,
Or by what rule, or when, or where,
The wealth of Mortham we should
          share ;
Then list, while I the portion name,
Our differing laws give each to claim.
Thou, vassal sworn to England's
          throne,
Her rules of heritage must own ;
They deal thee, as to nearest heir,
Thy kinsman's lands and livings fair,
And these I yield :—do thou revere
The statutes of the Bucanier.

Friend to the sea, and foeman sworn
To all that on her waves are borne,
When falls a mate in battle broil,
His comrade heirs his portion'd spoil;
When dies in fight a daring foe,
He claims his wealth who struck the
　　blow ;
And either rule to me assigns
Those spoils of Indian seas and mines,
Hoarded in Mortham's caverns dark;
Ingot of gold and diamond spark,
Chalice and plate from churches borne,
And gems from shrieking beauty torn,
Each string of pearl, each silver bar,
And all the wealth of western war.
I go to search, where, dark and deep,
Those Transatlantic treasures sleep.
Thou must along—for, lacking thee,
The heir will scarce find entrance free ;
And then farewell.　I haste to try
Each varied pleasure wealth can buy;
When cloy'd each wish, these wars
　　afford
Fresh work for Bertram's restless
　　sword.'

XXII.

An undecided answer hung
On Oswald's hesitating tongue.
Despite his craft, he heard with awe
This ruffian stabber fix the law ;
While his own troubled passions veer
Through hatred, joy, regret, and fear ;—
Joy'd at the soul that Bertram flies,
He grudged the murderer's mighty
　　prize,
Hated his pride's presumptuous tone,
And fear'd to wend with him alone.
At length, that middle course to steer,
To cowardice and craft so dear,
' His charge,' he said, ' would ill allow
His absence from the fortress now ;
WILFRID on Bertram should attend,
His son should journey with his friend.'

XXIII.

Contempt kept Bertram's anger down,
And wreathed to savage smile his frown.

' Wilfrid, or thou—'tis one to me,
Whichever bears the golden key.
Yet think not but I mark, and
　　smile
To mark, thy poor and selfish wile !
If injury from me you fear,
What, Oswald Wycliffe, shields thee
　　here ?
I've sprung from walls more high than
　　these,
I've swam through deeper streams
　　than Tees.
Might I not stab thee, ere one yell
Could rouse the distant sentinel ?
Start not—it is not my design,
But, if it were, weak fence were thine;
And, trust me, that, in time of need,
This hand hath done more desperate
　　deed.
Go, haste and rouse thy slumbering
　　son ;
Time calls, and I must needs be gone.'

XXIV.

Nought of his sire's ungenerous part
Polluted Wilfrid's gentle heart ;
A heart too soft from early life
To hold with fortune needful strife.
His sire, while yet a hardier race
Of numerous sons were Wycliffe's
　　grace,
On Wilfrid set contemptuous brand,
For feeble heart and forceless hand ;
But a fond mother's care and joy
Were centred in her sickly boy.
No touch of childhood's frolic mood
Show'd the elastic spring of blood ;
Hour after hour he loved to pore
On Shakespeare's rich and varied lore,
But turn'd from martial scenes and
　　light,
From Falstaff's feast and Percy's fight,
To ponder Jaques' moral strain,
And muse with Hamlet, wise in vain,
And weep himself to soft repose
O'er gentle Desdemona's woes.

XXV.

In youth he sought not pleasures found
By youth in horse, and hawk, and
      hound,
But loved the quiet joys that wake
By lonely stream and silent lake ;
In Deepdale's solitude to lie,
Where all is cliff and copse and sky ;
To climb Catcastle's dizzy peak,
Or lone Pendragon's mound to seek.
Such was his wont; and there his
      dream
Soar'd on some wild fantastic theme,
Of faithful love, or ceaseless Spring,
Till Contemplation's wearied wing
The enthusiast could no more sustain,
And sad he sunk to earth again.

XXVI.

He loved—as many a lay can tell
Preserved in Stanmore's lonely dell ;
For his was minstrel's skill, he caught
The art unteachable, untaught ;
He loved—his soul did nature frame
For love, and fancy nursed the flame ;
Vainly he loved— for seldom swain
Of such soft mould is loved again ;
Silent he loved—in every gaze
Was passion, friendship in his phrase.
So mused his life away, till died
His brethren all, their father's pride.
Wilfrid is now the only heir
Of all his stratagems and care,
And destined, darkling, to pursue
Ambition's maze by Oswald's clue.

XXVII.

Wilfrid must love and woo the bright
Matilda, heir of Rokeby's knight.
To love her was an easy hest,
The secret empress of his breast ;
To woo her was a harder task
To one that durst not hope or ask.
Yet all Matilda could, she gave
In pity to her gentle slave ;
Friendship, esteem, and fair regard,
And praise, the poet's best reward !
She read the tales his taste approved,
And sung the lays he framed or loved ;
Yet, loth to nurse the fatal flame
Of hopeless love in friendship's name,
In kind caprice she oft withdrew
The favouring glance to friendship
      due,
Then grieved to see her victim's pain,
And gave the dangerous smiles again.

XXVIII.

So did the suit of Wilfrid stand
When war's loud summons waked the
      land.
Three banners, floating o'er the Tees,
The woe-foreboding peasant sees ;
In concert oft they braved of old
The bordering Scot's incursion bold ;
Frowning defiance in their pride,
Their vassals now and lords divide.
From his fair hall on Greta banks
The Knight of Rokeby led his ranks,
To aid the valiant northern Earls
Who drew the sword for royal Charles.
Mortham, by marriage near allied,—
His sister had been Rokeby's bride,
Though long before the civil fray
In peaceful grave the lady lay,—
Philip of Mortham raised his band,
And march'd at Fairfax's command ;
While Wycliffe, bound by many a train
Of kindred art with wily Vane,
Less prompt to brave the bloody field,
Made Barnard's battlements his shield,
Secured them with his Lunedale
      powers,
And for the Commons held the towers.

XXIX.

The lovely heir of Rokeby's Knight
Waits in his halls the event of fight ;
For England's war revered the claim
Of every unprotected name,
And spared, amid its fiercest rage,
Childhood and womanhood and age.
But Wilfrid, son to Rokeby's foe,
Must the dear privilege forego,

By Greta's side, in evening grey,
To steal upon Matilda's way,
Striving, with fond hypocrisy,
For careless step and vacant eye;
Calming each anxious look and glance,
To give the meeting all to chance,
Or framing, as a fair excuse,
The book, the pencil, or the muse:
Something to give, to sing, to say,
Some modern tale, some ancient lay.
Then, while the long'd-for minutes
       last,—
Ah! minutes quickly over-past!
Recording each expression free,
Of kind or careless courtesy,
Each friendly look, each softer tone,
As food for fancy when alone.
All this is o'er—but still, unseen,
Wilfrid may lurk in Eastwood green,
To watch Matilda's wonted round,
While springs his heart at every sound.
She comes!—'tis but a passing sight,
Yet serves to cheat his weary night;
She comes not—he will wait the
       hour
When her lamp lightens in the tower;
'Tis something yet, if, as she past,
Her shade is o'er the lattice cast,
'What is my life, my hope?' he said;
'Alas! a transitory shade.'

XXX.

Thus wore his life, though reason
       strove
For mastery in vain with love,
Forcing upon his thoughts the sum
Of present woe and ills to come,
While still he turn'd impatient ear
From Truth's intrusive voice severe.
Gentle, indifferent, and subdued,
In all but this, unmoved he view'd
Each outward change of ill and good.
But Wilfrid, docile, soft, and mild,
Was Fancy's spoil'd and wayward
       child;
In her bright car she bade him ride,
With one fair form to grace his side,

Or, in some wild and lone retreat,
Flung her high spells around his seat,
Bathed in her dews his languid head,
Her fairy mantle o'er him spread,
For him her opiates gave to flow
Which he who tastes can ne'er forego,
And placed him in her circle, free
From every stern reality,
Till, to the Visionary, seem
Her day-dreams truth, and truth a
       dream.

XXXI.

Woe to the youth whom Fancy gains,
Winning from Reason's hand the reins!
Pity and woe! for such a mind
Is soft, contemplative, and kind;
And woe to those who train such youth,
And spare to press the rights of truth,
The mind to strengthen and anneal,
While on the stithy glows the steel!
O teach him, while your lessons last,
To judge the present by the past;
Remind him of each wish pursued,
How rich it glow'd with promised good;
Remind him of each wish enjoy'd,
How soon his hopes possession cloy'd!
Tell him, we play unequal game
Whene'er we shoot by Fancy's aim;
And, ere he strip him for her race,
Show the conditions of the chase.
Two sisters by the goal are set,
Cold Disappointment and Regret;
One disenchants the winner's eyes
And strips of all its worth the prize,
While one augments its gaudy show
More to enhance the loser's woe.
The victor sees his fairy gold
Transform'd, when won, to drossy
       mold;
But still the vanquish'd mourns his loss,
And rues, as gold, that glittering dross.

XXXII.

More wouldst thou know—yon tower
       survey,
Yon couch unpress'd since parting day,

Yon untrimm'd lamp, whose yellow
　　gleam
Is mingling with the cold moonbeam,
And yon thin form!—the hectic red
On his pale cheek unequal spread;
The head reclined, the loosen'd hair,
The limbs relax'd, the mournful air.
See, he looks up;—a woful smile
Lightens his woeworn cheek a while,—
'Tis Fancy wakes some idle thought
To gild the ruin she has wrought;
For, like the bat of Indian brakes,
Her pinions fan the wound she makes,
And soothing thus the dreamer's pain,
She drinks his life-blood from the vein.
Now to the lattice turn his eyes,
Vain hope! to see the sun arise.
The moon with clouds is still o'ercast,
Still howls by fits the stormy blast;
Another hour must wear away
Ere the East kindle into day.
And hark! to waste that weary hour
He tries the minstrel's magic power:

XXXIII.

SONG.

TO THE MOON.

' Hail to thy cold and clouded beam,
　　Pale pilgrim of the troubled sky!
Hail, though the mists that o'er thee
　　stream
　　Lend to thy brow their sullen dye!
How should thy pure and peaceful eye
　　Untroubled view our scenes below,
Or how a tearless beam supply
　　To light a world of war and woe!

Fair Queen! I will not blame thee now,
　　As once by Greta's fairy side;
Each little cloud that dimm'd thy brow
　　Did then an angel's beauty hide.
And of the shades I then could chide,
　　Still are the thoughts to memory
　　dear,
For, while a softer strain I tried,
　　They hid my blush, and calm'd my
　　fear.

Then did I swear thy ray serene
　　Was form'd to light some lonely dell,
By two fond lovers only seen
　　Reflected from the crystal well;
Or sleeping on their mossy cell,
　　Or quivering on the lattice bright,
Or glancing on their couch, to tell
　　How swiftly wanes the summer
　　night!'

XXXIV.

He starts; a step at this lone hour!
A voice! his father seeks the tower,
With haggard look and troubled sense,
Fresh from his dreadful conference.
'Wilfrid! what, not to sleep address'd?
Thou hast no cares to chase thy rest.
Mortham has fall'n on Marston-moor;
Bertram brings warrant to secure
His treasures, bought by spoil and
　　blood,
For the State's use and public good.
The menials will thy voice obey;
Let his commission have its way
In every point, in every word.'
Then, in a whisper—'Take thy sword!
Bertram is—what I must not tell.
I hear his hasty step, farewell!'

—◆—

Canto Second.

I.

FAR in the chambers of the west
The gale had sigh'd itself to rest;
The moon was cloudless now and clear,
But pale, and soon to disappear.
The thin grey clouds wax dimly light
On Brusleton and Houghton height;
And the rich dale, that eastward lay
Waited the wakening touch of day,
To give its woods and cultured plain,
And towers and spires, to light again.
But, westward, Stanmore's shapeless
　　swell,
And Lunedale wild, and Kelton-fell,

And rock-begirdled Gilmanscar,
And Arkingarth, lay dark afar ;
While, as a livelier twilight falls,
Emerge proud Barnard's banner'd walls.
High-crown'd he sits, in dawning pale,
The sovereign of the lovely vale.

II.

What prospects, from his watch-tower high,
Gleam gradual on the warder's eye !—
Far sweeping to the east, he sees
Down his deep woods the course of Tees,
And tracks his wanderings by the steam
Of summer vapours from the stream ;
And ere he paced his destined hour
By Brackenbury's dungeon-tower,
These silver mists shall melt away
And dew the woods with glittering spray.
Then in broad lustre shall be shown
That mighty trench of living stone,
And each huge trunk that, from the side,
Reclines him o'er the darksome tide,
Where Tees, full many a fathom low,
Wears with his rage no common foe;
For pebbly bank nor sand-bed here,
Nor clay-mound, checks his fierce career,
Condemn'd to mine a channell'd way
O'er solid sheets of marble grey.

III.

Nor Tees alone, in dawning bright,
Shall rush upon the ravish'd sight;
But many a tributary stream
Each from its own dark dell shall gleam:
Staindrop, who, from her silvan bowers,
Salutes proud Raby's battled towers;
The rural brook of Egliston,
And Balder, named from Odin's son ;
And Greta, to whose banks ere long
We lead the lovers of the song ;

And silver Lune, from Stanmore wild,
And fairy Thorsgill's murmuring child,
And last and least, but loveliest still,
Romantic Deepdale's slender rill.
Who in that dim-wood glen hath stray'd,
Yet long'd for Roslin's magic glade ?
Who, wandering there, hath sought to change
Even for that vale so stern and strange,
Where Cartland's Crags, fantastic rent,
Through her green copse like spires are sent ?
Yet, Albin, yet the praise be thine,
Thy scenes and story to combine !
Thou bid'st him, who by Roslin strays,
List to the deeds of other days ;
'Mid Cartland's Crags thou show'st the cave,
The refuge of thy champion brave ;
Giving each rock its storied tale,
Pouring a lay for every dale,
Knitting, as with a moral band,
Thy native legends with thy land,
To lend each scene the interest high
Which genius beams from Beauty's eye.

IV.

Bertram awaited not the sight
Which sun-rise shows from Barnard's height,
But from the towers, preventing day
With Wilfrid took his early way,
While misty dawn, and moonbeam pale,
Still mingled in the silent dale.
By Barnard's bridge of stately stone
The southern bank of Tees they won ;
Their winding path then eastward cast,
And Egliston's grey ruins pass'd ;
Each on his own deep visions bent,
Silent and sad they onward went.
Well may you think that Bertram's mood
To Wilfrid savage seem'd and rude;
Well may you think bold Risingham
Held Wilfrid trivial, poor, and tame;

And small the intercourse, I ween,
Such uncongenial souls between.

v.

Stern Bertram shunn'd the nearer way
Through Rokeby's park and chase that
        lay,
And, skirting high the valley's ridge,
They cross'd by Greta's ancient bridge,
Descending where her waters wind
Free for a space and unconfined,
As, 'scaped from Brignal's dark-wood
        glen,
She seeks wild Mortham's deeper den.
There, as his eye glanced o'er the
        mound
Raised by that Legion long renown'd,
Whose votive shrine asserts their
        claim
Of pious, faithful, conquering fame,
'Stern sons of war!' sad Wilfrid sigh'd,
' Behold the boast of Roman pride!
What now of all your toils are known?
A grassy trench, a broken stone ! '
This to himself ; for moral strain
To Bertram were address'd in vain.

vi.

Of different mood, a deeper sigh
Awoke when Rokeby's turrets high
Were northward in the dawning seen
To rear them o'er the thicket green.
O then, though Spenser's self had
        stray'd
Beside him through the lovely glade,
Lending his rich luxuriant glow
Of fancy, all its charms to show,
Pointing the stream rejoicing free,
As captive set at liberty,
Flashing her sparkling waves abroad,
And clamouring joyful on her road ;
Pointing where, up the sunny banks,
The trees retire in scatter'd ranks,
Save where, advanced before the rest,
On knoll or hillock rears his crest,
Lonely and huge, the giant Oak,
As champions, when their band is
        broke,

Stand forth to guard the rearward post,
The bulwark of the scatter'd host :
All this, and more, might Spenser say,
Yet waste in vain his magic lay,
While Wilfrid eyed the distant tower
Whose lattice lights Matilda's bower.

vii.

The open vale is soon passed o'er ;
Rokeby, though nigh, is seen no more ;
Sinking mid Greta's thickets deep,
A wild and darker course they keep,
A stern and lone, yet lovely road,
As e'er the foot of Minstrel trode !
Broad shadows o'er their passage fell,
Deeper and narrower grew the dell ;
It seem'd some mountain, rent and
        riven,
A channel for the stream had given,
So high the cliffs of limestone grey
Hung beetling o'er the torrent's way,
Yielding, along their rugged base,
A flinty footpath's niggard space,
Where he, who winds 'twixt rock and
        wave,
May hear the headlong torrent rave,
And like a steed in frantic fit,
That flings the froth from curb and bit,
May view her chafe her waves to spray
O'er every rock that bars her way,
Till foam-globes on her eddies ride
Thick as the schemes of human pride
That down life's current drive amain,
As frail, as frothy, and as vain !

viii.

The cliffs that rear their haughty head
High o'er the river's darksome bed
Were now all naked, wild, and grey,
Now waving all with greenwood spray ;
Here trees to every crevice clung,
And o'er the dell their branches hung ;
And there, all splinter'd and uneven,
The shiver'd rocks ascend to heaven ;
Oft, too, the ivy swath'd their breast,
And wreathed its garland round their
        crest,

Or from the spires bade loosely flare
Its tendrils in the middle air.
As pennons wont to wave of old
O'er the high feast of Baron bold,
When revell'd loud the feudal rout,
And the arch'd halls return'd their
    shout ;
Such and more wild is Greta's roar,
And such the echoes from her shore :
And so the ivied banners gleam,
Waved wildly o'er the brawling stream.

IX.

Now from the stream the rocks recede
But leave between no sunny mead—
No, nor the spot of pebbly sand,
Oft found by such a mountain strand,
Forming such warm and dry retreat
As fancy deems the lonely seat
Where hermit, wandering from his
    cell,
His rosary might love to tell.
But here, 'twixt rock and river, grew
A dismal grove of sable yew,
With whose sad tints were mingled
    seen
The blighted fir's sepulchral green.
Seem'd that the trees their shadows
    cast,
The earth that nourish'd them to blast ;
For never knew that swarthy grove
The verdant hue that fairies love ;
Nor wilding green, nor woodland
    flower,
Arose within its baleful bower :
The dank and sable earth receives
Its only carpet from the leaves,
That, from the withering branches cast,
Bestrew'd the ground with every blast.
Though now the sun was o'er the
    hill,
In this dark spot 'twas twilight still,
Save that on Greta's farther side
Some straggling beams through copse-
    wood glide ;
And wild and savage contrast made
That dingle's deep and funeral shade,

With the bright tints of early day,
Which, glimmering through the ivy
    spray,
On the opposing summit lay.

X.

The lated peasant shunn'd the dell ;
For Superstition wont to tell
Of many a grisly sound and sight,
Scaring its path at dead of night.
When Christmas logs blaze high and
    wide,
Such wonders speed the festal tide ;
While Curiosity and Fear,
Pleasure and Pain, sit crouching near,
Till childhood's cheek no longer glows,
And village maidens lose the rose.
The thrilling interest rises higher,
The circle closes nigh and nigher,
And shuddering glance is cast behind
As louder moans the wintry wind.
Believe, that fitting scene was laid
For such wild tales in Mortham glade ;
For who had seen on Greta's side,
By that dim light, fierce Bertram stride,
In such a spot, at such an hour,—
If touch'd by Superstition's power,
Might well have deem'd that Hell had
    given
A murderer's ghost to upper heaven,
While Wilfrid's form had seem'd to
    glide
Like his pale victim by his side.

XI.

Nor think to village swains alone
Are these unearthly terrors known ;
For not to rank nor sex confined
Is this vain ague of the mind :
Hearts firm as steel, as marble hard,
'Gainst faith, and love, and pity barr'd,
Have quaked like aspen leaves in May
Beneath its universal sway.
Bertram had listed many a tale
Of wonder in his native dale,
That in his secret soul retain'd
The credence they in childhood gain'd ;

Nor less his wild adventurous youth
Believed in every legend's truth ;
Learn'd when, beneath the tropic gale,
Full swell'd the vessel's steady sail,
And the broad Indian moon her light
Pour'd on the watch of middle night,
When seamen love to hear and tell
Of portent, prodigy, and spell :
What gales are sold on Lapland's shore,
How whistle rash bids tempests roar,
Of witch, of mermaid, and of sprite,
Of Erick's cap and Elmo's light ;
Or of that Phantom Ship, whose form
Shoots like a meteor through the storm ;
When the dark scud comes driving
    hard,
And lower'd is every topsail-yard,
And canvas, wove in earthly looms,
No more to brave the storm presumes !
Then, 'mid the war of sea and sky,
Top and top-gallant hoisted high,
Full spread and crowded every sail,
The Demon Frigate braves the gale ;
And well the doom'd spectators know
The harbinger of wreck and woe.

XII.

Then, too, were told, in stifled tone,
Marvels and omens all their own ;
How, by some desert isle or key,
Where Spaniards wrought their
    cruelty,
Or where the savage pirate's mood
Repaid it home in deeds of blood,
Strange nightly sounds of woe and fear
Appall'd the listening Bucanier,
Whose light-arm'd shallop anchor'd lay
In ambush by the lonely bay.
The groan of grief, the shriek of pain,
Ring from the moonlight groves of cane ;
The fierce adventurer's heart they
    scare,
Who wearies memory for a prayer,
Curses the roadstead, and with gale
Of early morning lifts the sail,
To give, in thirst of blood and prey,
A legend for another bay.

XIII.

Thus, as a man, a youth, a child,
Train'd in the mystic and the wild,
With this on Bertram's soul at times
Rush'd a dark feeling of his crimes ;
Such to his troubled soul their form
As the pale Death-ship to the storm,
And such their omen, dim and dread,
As shrieks and voices of the dead.
That pang, whose transitory force
Hover'd 'twixt horror and remorse ;
That pang, perchance, his bosom
    press'd,
As Wilfrid sudden he address'd :—
' Wilfrid, this glen is never trode
Until the sun rides high abroad ;
Yet twice have I beheld to-day
A Form that seem'd to dog our way ;
Twice from my glance it seem'd to flee,
And shroud itself by cliff or tree.
How think'st thou ?—Is our path way-
    laid ?
Or hath thy sire my trust betray'd ?
If so '—— Ere, starting from his dream,
That turn'd upon a gentler theme,
Wilfrid had roused him to reply,
Bertram sprung forward, shouting
    high,
' Whate'er thou art, thou now shalt
    stand ! '
And forth he darted, sword in hand.

XIV.

As bursts the levin in its wrath,
He shot him down the sounding path ;
Rock, wood, and stream rang wildly
    out
To his loud step and savage shout.
Seems that the object of his race
Hath scaled the cliffs ; his frantic chase
Sidelong he turns, and now 'tis bent
Right up the rock's tall battlement ;
Straining each sinew to ascend,
Foot, hand, and knee their aid must
    lend.
Wilfrid, all dizzy with dismay,
Views from beneath his dreadful way :

Now to the oak's warp'd roots he
   clings,
Now trusts his weight to ivy strings;
Now, like the wild-goat, must he dare
An unsupported leap in air;
Hid in the shrubby rain-course now,
You mark him by the crashing bough,
And by his corslet's sullen clank,
And by the stones spurn'd from the
   bank,
And by the hawk scared from her
   nest,
And ravens croaking o'er their guest,
Who deem his forfeit limbs shall pay
The tribute of his bold essay.

XV.

See, he emerges! desperate now
All farther course; yon beetling brow,
In craggy nakedness sublime,
What heart or foot shall dare to climb?
It bears no tendril for his clasp,
Presents no angle to his grasp:
Sole stay his foot may rest upon
Is yon earth-bedded jetting stone.
Balanced on such precarious prop,
He strains his grasp to reach the top.
Just as the dangerous stretch he makes,
By heaven, his faithless footstool
   shakes!
Beneath his tottering bulk it bends,
It sways, . . . it loosens, . . . it de-
   scends!
And downward holds its headlong
   way,
Crashing o'er rock and copsewood
   spray.
Loud thunders shake the echoing dell!
Fell it alone? Alone it fell
Just on the very verge of fate,
The hardy Bertram's falling weight
He trusted to his sinewy hands,
And on the top unharm'd he stands!

XVI.

Wilfrid a safer path pursued;
At intervals where, roughly hew'd,

Rude steps ascending from the dell
Render'd the cliffs accessible.
By circuit slow he thus attain'd
The height that Risingham had gain'd,
And when he issued from the wood,
Before the gate of Mortham stood.
'Twas a fair scene! the sunbeam lay
On battled tower and portal grey:
And from the grassy slope he sees
The Greta flow to meet the Tees;
Where, issuing from her darksome
   bed,
She caught the morning's eastern red,
And through the softening vale below
Roll'd her bright waves, in rosy glow,
All blushing to her bridal bed,
Like some shy maid in convent bred;
While linnet, lark, and blackbird gay,
Sing forth her nuptial roundelay.

XVII.

'Twas sweetly sung, that roundelay;
That summer morn shone blithe and
   gay;
But morning beam, and wild-bird's
   call,
Awaked not Mortham's silent hall.
No porter, by the low-brow'd gate,
Took in the wonted niche his seat;
To the paved court no peasant drew;
Waked to their toil no menial crew;
The maiden's carol was not heard,
As to her morning task she fared:
In the void offices around
Rung not a hoof, nor bay'd a hound;
Nor eager steed, with shrilling neigh,
Accused the lagging groom's delay;
Untrimm'd, undress'd, neglected now,
Was alley'd walk and orchard bough;
All spoke the master's absent care,
All spoke neglect and disrepair.
South of the gate, an arrow-flight,
Two mighty elms their limbs unite,
As if a canopy to spread
O'er the lone dwelling of the dead;
For their huge boughs in arches bent
Above a massive monument,

Carved o'er in ancient Gothic wise,
With many a scutcheon and device :
There, spent with toil and sunk in
    gloom,
Bertram stood pondering by the tomb.

XVIII.

' It vanish'd, like a flitting ghost !
Behind this tomb,' he said, ' 'twas lost—
This tomb, where oft I deem'd lies
    stored
Of Mortham's Indian wealth the hoard.
'Tis true, the aged servants said
Here his lamented wife is laid ;
But weightier reasons may be guess'd
For their lord's strict and stern behest,
That none should on his steps intrude,
Whene'er he sought this solitude.—
An ancient mariner I knew,
What time I sail'd with Morgan's
    crew,
Who oft, 'mid our carousals, spake
Of Raleigh, Frobisher, and Drake ;
Adventurous hearts ! who barter'd,
    bold,
Their English steel for Spanish gold.
Trust not, would his experience say,
Captain or comrade with your prey ;
But seek some charnel, when, at full,
The moon gilds skeleton and skull :
There dig, and tomb your precious
    heap,
And bid the dead your treasure keep ;
Sure stewards they, if fitting spell
Their service to the task compel.
Lacks there such charnel ? kill a slave,
Or prisoner, on the treasure-grave ;
And bid his discontented ghost
Stalk nightly on his lonely post.
Such was his tale. Its truth, I ween,
Is in my morning vision seen.'

XIX.

Wilfrid, who scorn'd the legend wild,
In mingled mirth and pity smiled,
Much marvelling that a breast so bold
In such fond tale belief should hold ;

But yet of Bertram sought to know
The apparition's form and show.
The power within the guilty breast,
Oft vanquish'd, never quite suppress'd,
That unsubdued and lurking lies
To take the felon by surprise,
And force him, as by magic spell,
In his despite his guilt to tell,—
That power in Bertram's breast awoke ;
Scarce conscious he was heard, he
    spoke :
' 'Twas Mortham's form, from foot to
    head !
His morion, with the plume of red,
His shape, his mien—'twas Mortham
    right,
As when I slew him in the fight.'
' Thou slay him ? thou ?'—With con-
    scious start
He heard, then mann'd his haughty
    heart :—
' I slew him ? I ! I had forgot
Thou, stripling, knew'st not of the
    plot.
But it is spoken ; nor will I
Deed done, or spoken word, deny.
I slew him ; I ! for thankless pride ;
'Twas by this hand that Mortham died !'

XX.

Wilfrid, of gentle hand and heart,
Averse to every active part,
But most averse to martial broil,
From danger shrunk, and turn'd from
    toil ;
Yet the meek lover of the lyre
Nursed one brave spark of noble fire :
Against injustice, fraud, or wrong,
His blood beat high, his hand wax'd
    strong.
Not his the nerves that could sustain,
Unshaken, danger, toil, and pain ;
But, when that spark blazed forth to
    flame,
He rose superior to his frame.
And now it came, that generous mood :
And, in full current of his blood,

On Bertram he laid desperate hand,
Placed firm his foot, and drew his brand.
'Should every fiend to whom thou 'rt
    sold
Rise in thine aid, I keep my hold.
Arouse there, ho! take spear and
    sword!
Attach the murderer of your Lord!'

XXI.

A moment, fix'd as by a spell,
Stood Bertram. It seem'd miracle
That one so feeble, soft, and tame
Set grasp on warlike Risingham.
But when he felt a feeble stroke,
The fiend within the ruffian woke!
To wrench the sword from Wilfrid's
    hand,
To dash him headlong on the sand,
Was but one moment's work,—one
    more
Had drench'd the blade in Wilfrid's
    gore;
But, in the instant it arose,
To end his life, his love, his woes,
A warlike form, that mark'd the scene,
Presents his rapier sheath'd between,
Parries the fast-descending blow,
And steps 'twixt Wilfrid and his foe;
Nor then unscabbarded his brand,
But, sternly pointing with his hand,
With monarch's voice forbade the fight,
And motion'd Bertram from his sight.
'Go, and repent,' he said, 'while time
Is given thee; add not crime to crime.'

XXII.

Mute, and uncertain, and amazed,
As on a vision Bertram gazed!
'Twas Mortham's bearing, bold and
    high,
His sinewy frame, his falcon eye,
His look and accent of command,
The martial gesture of his hand,
His stately form, spare-built and tall,
His war-bleach'd locks—'twas Mor-
    tham all.

Through Bertram's dizzy brain career
A thousand thoughts, and all of fear;
His wavering faith received not quite
The form he saw as Mortham's sprite;
But more he fear'd it, if it stood
His lord, in living flesh and blood.
What spectre can the charnel send
So dreadful as an injured friend?
Then, too, the habit of command,
Used by the leader of the band,
When Risingham, for many a day,
Had march'd and fought beneath his
    sway,
Tamed him—and, with reverted face,
Backwards he bore his sullen pace;
Oft stopp'd, and oft on Mortham stared,
And dark as rated mastiff glared;
But when the tramp of steeds was
    heard,
Plunged in the glen, and disappear'd.
Nor longer there the Warrior stood,
Retiring eastward through the wood;
But first to Wilfrid warning gives,
'Tell thou to none that Mortham lives.'

XXIII.

Still rung these words in Wilfrid's ear,
Hinting he knew not what of fear;
When nearer came the coursers'
    tread,
And, with his father at their head,
Of horsemen arm'd a gallant power
Rein'd up their steeds before the tower.
'Whence these pale looks, my son?'
    he said:
'Where 's Bertram? why that naked
    blade?'
Wilfrid ambiguously replied,
(For Mortham's charge his honour
    tied,)
'Bertram is gone—the villain's word
Avouch'd him murderer of his lord!
Even now we fought; but, when your
    tread
Announced you nigh, the felon fled.'
In Wycliffe's conscious eye appear
A guilty hope, a guilty fear;

On his pale brow the dewdrop broke,
And his lip quiver'd as he spoke:

XXIV.

'A murderer! Philip Mortham died
Amid the battle's wildest tide.
Wilfrid, or Bertram raves or you!
Yet, grant such strange confession
			true,
Pursuit were vain; let him fly far—
Justice must sleep in civil war.'
A gallant Youth rode near his side,
Brave Rokeby's page, in battle tried;
That morn, an embassy of weight
He brought to Barnard's castle gate,
And follow'd now in Wycliffe's train,
An answer for his lord to gain.
His steed, whose arch'd and sable neck
An hundred wreaths of foam bedeck,
Chafed not against the curb more high
Than he at Oswald's cold reply;
He bit his lip, implored his saint,
(His the old faith) then burst restraint.

XXV.

'Yes! I beheld his bloody fall,
By that base traitor's dastard ball,
Just when I thought to measure sword,
Presumptuous hope! with Mortham's
			lord.
And shall the murderer 'scape, who
			slew
His leader, generous, brave, and true?
Escape, while on the dew you trace
The marks of his gigantic pace?
No! ere the sun that dew shall dry,
False Risingham shall yield or die.
Ring out the castle 'larum bell!
Arouse the peasants with the knell!
Meantime disperse—ride, gallants,
			ride!
Beset the wood on every side.
But if among you one there be
That honours Mortham's memory,
Let him dismount and follow me!
Else on your crests sit fear and shame,
And foul suspicion dog your name!'

XXVI.

Instant to earth young REDMOND
			sprung;
Instant on earth the harness rung
Of twenty men of Wycliffe's band,
Who waited not their lord's command.
Redmond his spurs from buskins drew,
His mantle from his shoulders threw,
His pistols in his belt he placed,
The greenwood gain'd, the footsteps
			traced,
Shouted like huntsman to his hounds,
'To cover, hark!' and in he bounds.
Scarce heard was Oswald's anxious cry,
'Suspicion! yes, pursue him—fly;
But venture not, in useless strife,
On ruffian desperate of his life.
Whoever finds him, shoot him dead!
Five hundred nobles for his head!'

XXVII.

The horsemen gallop'd, to make good
Each path that issued from the wood.
Loud from the thickets rung the shout
Of Redmond and his eager rout;
With them was Wilfrid, stung with ire,
And envying Redmond's martial fire,
And emulous of fame.—But where
Is Oswald, noble Mortham's heir?
He, bound by honour, law, and faith,
Avenger of his kinsman's death?—
Leaning against the elmin tree,
With drooping head and slacken'd
			knee,
And clenched teeth, and close-clasp'd
			hands,
In agony of soul he stands!
His downcast eye on earth is bent,
His soul to every sound is lent;
For in each shout that cleaves the air
May ring discovery and despair.

XXVIII.

What 'vail'd it him, that brightly play'd
The morning sun on Mortham's glade?
All seems in giddy round to ride,
Like objects on a stormy tide,

Seen eddying by the moonlight dim,
Imperfectly to sink and swim.
What 'vail'd it, that the fair domain,
Its battled mansion, hill, and plain,
On which the sun so brightly shone,
Envied so long, was now his own?
The lowest dungeon, in that hour,
Of Brackenbury's dismal tower,
Had been his choice, could such a doom
Have open'd Mortham's bloody tomb !
Forced, too, to turn unwilling ear
To each surmise of hope or fear,
Murmur'd among the rustics round,
Who gather'd at the 'larum sound ;
He dared not turn his head away,
E'en to look up to heaven to pray,
Or call on hell, in bitter mood,
For one sharp death-shot from the
     wood !

XXIX.

At length, o'erpast that dreadful space,
Back straggling came the scatter'd
     chase ;
Jaded and weary, horse and man,
Return'd the troopers, one by one.
Wilfrid, the last, arrived to say,
All trace was lost of Bertram's way,
Though Redmond still, up Brignal
     wood,
The hopeless quest in vain pursued.—
O, fatal doom of human race !
What tyrant passions passions chase !
Remorse from Oswald's brow is gone,
Avarice and pride resume their throne ;
The pang of instant terror by,
They dictate thus their slave's reply :

XXX.

' Ay—let him range like hasty hound !
And if the grim wolf's lair be found,
Small is my care how goes the game
With Redmond, or with Risingham.
Nay, answer not, thou simple boy !
Thy fair Matilda, all so coy
To thee, is of another mood
To that bold youth of Erin's blood.

Thy ditties will she freely praise,
And pay thy pains with courtly phrase ;
In a rough path will oft command—
Accept at least—thy friendly hand ;
His she avoids, or, urged and pray'd,
Unwilling takes his proffer'd aid,
While conscious passion plainly speaks
In downcast look and blushing cheeks.
Whene'er he sings will she glide nigh,
And all her soul is in her eye ;
Yet doubts she still to tender free
The wonted words of courtesy.
These are strong signs ! yet wherefore
     sigh,
And wipe, effeminate, thine eye ?
Thine shall she be, if thou attend
The counsels of thy sire and friend.

XXXI.

' Scarce wert thou gone, when peep
     of light
Brought genuine news of Marston's
     fight.
Brave Cromwell turn'd the doubtful
     tide,
And conquest bless'd the rightful side ;
Three thousand cavaliers lie dead,
Rupert and that bold Marquis fled :
Nobles and knights, so proud of late,
Must fine for freedom and estate.
Of these, committed to my charge,
Is Rokeby, prisoner at large ;
Redmond, his page, arrived to say
He reaches Barnard's towers to-day.
Right heavy shall his ransom be,
Unless that maid compound with thee !
Go to her now—be bold of cheer,
While her soul floats 'twixt hope and
     fear ;
It is the very change of tide,
When best the female heart is tried—
Pride, prejudice, and modesty,
Are in the current swept to sea ;
And the bold swain, who plies his oar,
May lightly row his bark to shore.'

—*+*—

Canto Third.

I.

THE hunting tribes of air and earth
Respect the brethren of their birth ;
Nature, who loves the claim of kind,
Less cruel chase to each assign'd.
The falcon, poised on soaring wing,
Watches the wild-duck by the spring ;
The slow-hound wakes the fox's lair ;
The greyhound presses on the hare ;
The eagle pounces on the lamb ;
The wolf devours the fleecy dam ;
Even tiger fell, and sullen bear,
Their likeness and their lineage spare :
Man, only, mars kind Nature's plan,
And turns the fierce pursuit on man ;
Plying war's desultory trade,
Incursion, flight, and ambuscade,
Since Nimrod, Cush's mighty son,
At first the bloody game begun.

II.

The Indian, prowling for his prey,
Who hears the settlers track his way,
And knows in distant forest far
Camp his red brethren of the war ;
He, when each double and disguise
To baffle the pursuit he tries,
Low crouching now his head to hide,
Where swampy streams through
    rushes glide,
Now covering with the wither'd leaves
The footprints that the dew receives :
He, skill'd in every silvan guile,
Knows not, nor tries, such various wile,
As Risingham, when on the wind
Arose the loud pursuit behind.
In Redesdale his youth had heard
Each art her wily dalesmen dared,
When Rooken-edge, and Redswair
    high,
To bugle rung and bloodhound's cry,
Announcing Jedwood-axe and spear,
And Lid'sdale riders in the rear ;
And well his venturous life had proved
The lessons that his childhood loved.

III.

Oft had he shown, in climes afar,
Each attribute of roving war ;
The sharpen'd ear, the piercing eye,
The quick resolve in danger nigh ;
The speed, that in the flight or chase,
Outstripp'd the Carib's rapid race ;
The steady brain, the sinewy limb,
To leap, to climb, to dive. to swim ;
The iron frame, inured to bear
Each dire inclemency of air,
Nor less confirm'd to undergo
Fatigue's faint chill, and famine's throe.
These arts he proved, his life to save,
In peril oft by land and wave,
On Arawaca's desert shore,
Or where La Plata's billows roar,
When oft the sons of vengeful Spain
Track'd the marauder's steps in vain.
These arts, in Indian warfare tried,
Must save him now by Greta's side.

IV.

'Twas then, in hour of utmost need,
He proved his courage, art, and speed.
Now slow he stalk'd with stealthy pace,
Now started forth in rapid race,
Oft doubling back in mazy train,
To blind the trace the dews retain ;
Now clombe the rocks projecting high,
To baffle the pursuer's eye ;
Now sought the stream, whose brawl-
    ing sound
The echo of his footsteps drown'd.
But if the forest verge he nears,
There trample steeds, and glimmer
    spears ;
If deeper down the copse he drew,
He heard the rangers' loud halloo,
Beating each cover while they came,
As if to start the silvan game.
'Twas then—like tiger close beset
At every pass with toil and net,
'Counter'd, where'er he turns his glare,
By clashing arms and torches' flare,
Who meditates, with furious bound,
To burst on hunter, horse, and hound,—

'Twas then that Bertram's soul arose,
Prompting to rush upon his foes :
But as that crouching tiger, cow'd
By brandish'd steel and shouting
    crowd,
Retreats beneath the jungle's shroud,
Bertram suspends his purpose stern,
And couches in the brake and fern,
Hiding his face, lest foemen spy
The sparkle of his swarthy eye.

v.

Then Bertram might the bearing trace
Of the bold youth who led the chase ;
Who paused to list for every sound,
Climb'd every height to look around,
Then rushing on with naked sword,
Each dingle's bosky depths explored.
'Twas Redmond—by the azure eye ;
'Twas Redmond—by the locks that fly
Disorder'd from his glowing cheek ;
Mien, face, and form, young Redmond
    speak.
A form more active, light, and strong,
Ne'er shot the ranks of war along ;
The modest, yet the manly mien,
Might grace the court of maiden queen ;
A face more fair you well might find,
For Redmond's knew the sun and wind,
Nor boasted, from their tinge when
    free,
The charm of regularity ;
But every feature had the power
To aid the expression of the hour :
Whether gay wit, and humour sly,
Danced laughing in his light-blue eye ;
Or bended brow, and glance of fire,
And kindling cheek, spoke Erin's ire ;
Or soft and sadden'd glances show
Her ready sympathy with woe ;
Or in that wayward mood of mind,
When various feelings are combined,
When joy and sorrow mingle near,
And hope's bright wings are check'd
    by fear,
And rising doubts keep transport down,
And anger lends a short-lived frown ;

In that strange mood which maids
    approve,
Even when they dare not call it love ;
With every change his features play'd,
As aspens show the light and shade.

vi.

Well Risingham young Redmond
    knew :
And much he marvell'd that the crew,
Roused to revenge bold Mortham dead,
Were by that Mortham's foeman led ;
For never felt his soul the woe
That wails a generous foeman low,
Far less that sense of justice strong,
That wreaks a generous foeman's
    wrong.
But small his leisure now to pause ;
Redmond is first, whate'er the cause :
And twice that Redmond came so near
Where Bertram couch'd like hunted
    deer,
The very boughs his steps displace
Rustled against the ruffian's face,
Who, desperate, twice prepared to
    start,
And plunge his dagger in his heart !
But Redmond turn'd a different way,
And the bent boughs resumed their
    sway,
And Bertram held it wise, unseen,
Deeper to plunge in coppice green.
Thus, circled in his coil, the snake,
When roving hunters beat the brake,
Watches with red and glistening eye,
Prepared, if heedless step draw nigh,
With forked tongue and venom'd fang
Instant to dart the deadly pang ;
But if the intruders turn aside,
Away his coils unfolded glide,
And through the deep savannah wind,
Some undisturb'd retreat to find.

vii.

But Bertram, as he backward drew,
And heard the loud pursuit renew,
And Redmond's hollo on the wind,
Oft mutter'd in his savage mind—

'Redmond O'Neale! were thou and I
Alone this day's event to try,
With not a second here to see
But the grey cliff and oaken tree,—
That voice of thine, that shouts so loud,
Should ne'er repeat its summons proud!
No! nor e'er try its melting power
Again in maiden's summer bower.'
Eluded, now behind him die,
Faint and more faint, each hostile cry;
He stands in Scargill wood alone,
Nor hears he now a harsher tone
Than the hoarse cushat's plaintive cry,
Or Greta's sound that murmurs by;
And on the dale, so lone and wild,
The summer sun in quiet smiled.

VIII.

He listen'd long with anxious heart,
Ear bent to hear, and foot to start,
And, while his stretch'd attention glows,
Refused his weary frame repose.
'Twas silence all—he laid him down
Where purple heath profusely strown,
And throatwort, with its azure bell,
And moss and thyme his cushion swell.
There, spent with toil, he listless eyed
The course of Greta's playful tide;
Beneath her banks now eddying dun,
Now brightly gleaming to the sun,
As, dancing over rock and stone,
In yellow light her currents shone,
Matching in hue the favourite gem
Of Albin's mountain diadem.
Then, tired to watch the current's play,
He turn'd his weary eyes away
To where the bank opposing show'd
Its huge square cliffs through shaggy wood.
One, prominent above the rest,
Rear'd to the sun its pale grey breast;
Around its broken summit grew
The hazel rude, and sable yew;
A thousand varied lichens dyed
Its waste and weather-beaten side

And round its rugged basis lay,
By time or thunder rent away,
Fragments, that, from its frontlet torn,
Were mantled now by verdant thorn.
Such was the scene's wild majesty
That fill'd stern Bertram's gazing eye.

IX.

In sullen mood he lay reclined,
Revolving, in his stormy mind
The felon deed, the fruitless guilt,
His patron's blood by treason spilt;
A crime, it seem'd, so dire and dread,
That it had power to wake the dead.
Then, pondering on his life betray'd
By Oswald's art to Redmond's blade,
In treacherous purpose to withhold,
So seem'd it, Mortham's promised gold,
A deep and full revenge he vow'd
On Redmond, forward, fierce, and proud;
Revenge on Wilfrid—on his sire
Redoubled vengeance, swift and dire!—
If, in such mood, (as legends say,
And well believed that simple day,)
The Enemy of Man has power
To profit by the evil hour,
Here stood a wretch, prepared to change
His soul's redemption for revenge!
But though his vows, with such a fire
Of earnest and intense desire
For vengeance dark and fell, were made,
As well might reach hell's lowest shade,
No deeper clouds the grove embrown'd,
No nether thunders shook the ground:
The demon knew his vassal's heart,
And spared temptation's needless art.

X.

Oft, mingled with the direful theme,
Came Mortham's form. Was it a dream?
Or had he seen, in vision true,
That very Mortham whom he slew!

Or had in living flesh appear'd
The only man on earth he fear'd?—
To try the mystic cause intent,
His eyes, that on the cliff were bent,
'Counter'd at once a dazzling glance,
Like sunbeam flash'd from sword or lance.
At once he started as for fight,
But not a foeman was in sight;
He heard the cushat's murmur hoarse,
He heard the river's sounding course;
The solitary woodlands lay,
As slumbering in the summer ray.
He gazed, like lion roused, around,
Then sunk again upon the ground.
'Twas but, he thought, some fitful beam,
Glanced sudden from the sparkling stream;
Then plunged him in his gloomy train
Of ill-connected thoughts again,
Until a voice behind him cried,
'Bertram! well met on Greta side.'

XI.

Instant his sword was in his hand,
As instant sunk the ready brand;
Yet, dubious still, opposed he stood
To him that issued from the wood:
'Guy Denzil! is it thou?' he said;
'Do we two meet in Scargill shade?—
Stand back a space!—thy purpose show,
Whether thou comest as friend or foe.
Report hath said, that Denzil's name
From Rokeby's band was razed with shame.'—
'A shame I owe that hot O'Neale,
Who told his knight, in peevish zeal,
Of my marauding on the clowns
Of Calverley and Bradford downs.
I reck not. In a war to strive,
Where, save the leaders, none can thrive,
Suits ill my mood; and better game
Awaits us both, if thou 'rt the same
Unscrupulous, bold Risingham,

Who watch'd with me in midnight dark,
To snatch a deer from Rokeby-park.
How think'st thou?' 'Speak thy purpose out;
I love not mystery or doubt.'

XII.

'Then list. Not far there lurk a crew
Of trusty comrades, stanch and true,
Glean'd from both factions—Roundheads, freed
From cant of sermon and of creed;
And Cavaliers, whose souls, like mine,
Spurn at the bonds of discipline.
Wiser, we judge, by dale and wold,
A warfare of our own to hold,
Than breathe our last on battle-down,
For cloak or surplice, mace or crown.
Our schemes are laid, our purpose set,
A chief and leader lack we yet.
Thou art a wanderer, it is said;
For Mortham's death thy steps waylaid,
Thy head at price—so say our spies,
Who range the valley in disguise.
Join then with us:—though wild debate
And wrangling rend our infant state,
Each, to an equal loth to bow,
Will yield to chief renown'd as thou.'

XIII.

'Even now,' thought Bertram, passion-stirr'd,
'I call'd on hell, and hell has heard!
What lack I, vengeance to command,
But of stanch comrades such a band?
This Denzil, vow'd to every evil,
Might read a lesson to the devil.
Well, be it so! each knave and fool
Shall serve as my revenge's tool.'
Aloud, 'I take thy proffer, Guy,
But tell me where thy comrades lie?'
'Not far from hence,' Guy Denzil said;
'Descend, and cross the river's bed,
Where rises yonder cliff so grey.'
'Do thou,' said Bertram, 'lead the way.'

Then mutter'd, ' It is best make sure ;
Guy Denzil's faith was never pure.'
He follow'd down the steep descent,
Then through the Greta's streams they
    went ;
And, when they reach'd the farther
    shore,
They stood the lonely cliff before.

XIV.

With wonder Bertram heard within
The flinty rock a murmur'd din ;
But when Guy pull'd the wilding
    spray,
And brambles, from its base away,
He saw, appearing to the air,
A little entrance, low and square,
Like opening cell of hermit lone,
Dark, winding through the living stone.
Here enter'd Denzil, Bertram here ;
And loud and louder on their ear,
As from the bowels of the earth,
Resounded shouts of boisterous mirth.
Of old, the cavern strait and rude
In slaty rock the peasant hew'd ;
And Brignal's woods, and Scargill's
    wave,
E'en now, o'er many a sister cave,
Where, far within the darksome rift,
The wedge and lever ply their thrift.
But war had silenced rural trade,
And the deserted mine was made
The banquet-hall, and fortress too,
Of Denzil and his desperate crew.
There Guilt his anxious revel kept ;
There, on his sordid pallet, slept
Guilt-born Excess, the goblet drain'd
Still in his slumbering grasp retain'd ;
Regret was there, his eye still cast
With vain repining on the past ;
Among the feasters waited near
Sorrow, and unrepentant Fear,
And Blasphemy, to frenzy driven,
With his own crimes reproaching
    heaven ;
While Bertram show'd, amid the crew,
The Master-Fiend that Milton drew.

XV.

Hark ! the loud revel wakes again,
To greet the leader of the train.
Behold the group by the pale lamp,
That struggles with the earthy damp.
By what strange features Vice hath
    known
To single out and mark her own !
Yet some there are, whose brows retain
Less deeply stamp'd her brand and stain.
See yon pale stripling ! when a boy,
A mother's pride, a father's joy !
Now, 'gainst the vault's rude walls
    reclined,
An early image fills his mind :
The cottage, once his sire's, he sees,
Embower'd upon the banks of Tees ;
He views sweet Winston's woodland
    scene,
And shares the dance on Gainford-green.
A tear is springing—but the zest
Of some wild tale, or brutal jest,
Hath to loud laughter stirr'd the rest.
On him they call, the aptest mate
For jovial song and merry feat :
Fast flies his dream—with dauntless air,
As one victorious o'er Despair,
He bids the ruddy cup go round,
Till sense and sorrow both are drown'd ;
And soon, in merry wassail, he,
The life of all their revelry,
Peals his loud song ! The muse has
    found
Her blossoms on the wildest ground,
'Mid noxious weeds at random strew'd,
Themselves all profitless and rude.
With desperate merriment he sung,
The cavern to the chorus rung ;
Yet mingled with his reckless glee
Remorse's bitter agony.

XVI.

SONG.

O, Brignal banks are wild and fair,
    And Greta woods are green,
And you may gather garlands there
    Would grace a summer queen.

And as I rode by Dalton-hall,
  Beneath the turrets high,
A maiden on the castle wall
  Was singing merrily,—
' O, Brignal banks are fresh and fair,
  And Greta woods are green ;
I 'd rather rove with Edmund there,
  Than reign our English queen.'

' If, maiden, thou wouldst wend with
    me,
  To leave both tower and town,
Thou first must guess what life lead we,
  That dwell by dale and down.
And if thou canst that riddle read,
  As read full well you may,
Then to the greenwood shalt thou
    speed,
  As blithe as Queen of May.'
Yet sung she, ' Brignal banks are fair,
  And Greta woods are green ;
I 'd rather rove with Edmund there,
  Than reign our English queen.

XVII.

I read you, by your bugle-horn,
  And by your palfrey good,
I read you for a ranger sworn,
  To keep the king's greenwood.'
'A ranger, lady, winds his horn,
  And 'tis at peep of light ;
His blast is heard at merry morn,
  And mine at dead of night.'
Yet sung she, 'Brignal banks are
    fair,
  And Greta woods are gay ;
I would I were with Edmund there,
  To reign his Queen of May !

With burnish'd brand and musketoon,
  So gallantly you come,
I read you for a bold dragoon,
  That lists the tuck of drum.'
' I list no more the tuck of drum,
  No more the trumpet hear ;
But when the beetle sounds his hum,
  My comrades take the spear.

And O ! though Brignal banks be fair,
  And Greta woods be gay,
Yet mickle must the maiden dare,
  Would reign my Queen of May !

XVIII.

Maiden ! a nameless life I lead,
  A nameless death I 'll die ;
The fiend, whose lantern lights the
    mead,
  Were better mate than I !
And when I 'm with my comrades met
  Beneath the greenwood bough,
What once we were we all forget,
  Nor think what we are now.
Yet Brignal banks are fresh and fair,
  And Greta woods are green,
And you may gather garlands there
  Would grace a summer queen.'

When Edmund ceased his simple song,
Was silence on the sullen throng,
Till waked some ruder mate their glee
With note of coarser minstrelsy.
But, far apart, in dark divan,
Denzil and Bertram many a plan,
Of import foul and fierce, design'd,
While still on Bertram's grasping mind
The wealth of murder'd Mortham hung ;
Though half he fear'd his daring tongue,
When it should give his wishes birth,
Might raise a spectre from the earth !

XIX.

At length his wondrous tale he told :
When, scornful, smiled his comrade
    bold ;
For, train'd in license of a court,
Religion's self was Denzil's sport ;
Then judge in what contempt he held
The visionary tales of eld !
His awe for Bertram scarce repress'd
The unbeliever's sneering jest.
'Twere hard,' he said, ' for sage or seer
To spell the subject of your fear :
Nor do I boast the art renown'd,
Vision and omen to expound.

Yet, faith if I must needs afford
To spectre watching treasured hoard,
As bandog keeps his master's roof,
Bidding the plunderer stand aloof,
This doubt remains—thy goblin gaunt
Hath chosen ill his ghostly haunt;
For why his guard on Mortham hold,
When Rokeby castle hath the gold
Thy patron won on Indian soil,
By stealth, by piracy, and spoil?'

XX.

At this he paused, for angry shame
Lower'd on the brow of Risingham.
He blush'd to think that he should seem
Assertor of an airy dream,
And gave his wrath another theme.
'Denzil,' he says, ' though lowly laid,
Wrong not the memory of the dead ;
For, while he lived, at Mortham's look
Thy very soul, Guy Denzil, shook !
And when he tax'd thy breach of word
To yon fair Rose of Allenford,
I saw thee crouch like chasten'd hound,
Whose back the huntsman's lash hath found.
Nor dare to call his foreign wealth
The spoil of piracy or stealth;
He won it bravely with his brand
When Spain waged warfare with our land.
Mark, too—I brook no idle jeer,
Nor couple Bertram's name with fear ;
Mine is but half the demon's lot,
For I believe, but tremble not.—
Enough of this.—Say, why this hoard
Thou deem'st at Rokeby castle stored ;
Or think'st that Mortham would bestow
His treasure with his faction's foe ?'

XXI.

Soon quench'd was Denzil's ill-timed mirth ;
Rather he would have seen the earth
Give to ten thousand spectres birth,
Than venture to awake to flame
The deadly wrath of Risingham.
Submiss he answer'd, ' Mortham's mind,
Thou know'st, to joy was ill inclined.
In youth, 'tis said, a gallant free,
A lusty reveller was he ;
But since return'd from over sea,
A sullen and a silent mood
Hath numb'd the current of his blood.
Hence he refused each kindly call
To Rokeby's hospitable hall,
And our stout knight, at dawn of morn
Who loved to hear the bugle-horn,
Nor less, when eve his oaks embrown'd,
To see the ruddy cup go round,
Took umbrage that a friend so near
Refused to share his chase and cheer;
Thus did the kindred barons jar,
Ere they divided in the war.
Yet, trust me, friend, Matilda fair
Of Mortham's wealth is destined heir.'

XXII.

'Destined to her ! to yon slight maid !
The prize my life had wellnigh paid,
When 'gainst Laroche, by Cayo's wave,
I fought my patron's wealth to save !—
Denzil, I knew him long, yet ne'er
Knew him that joyous cavalier,
Whom youthful friends and early fame
Call'd soul of gallantry and game.
A moody man, he sought our crew,
Desperate and dark, whom no one knew ;
And rose, as men with us must rise,
By scorning life and all its ties.
On each adventure rash he roved,
As danger for itself he loved ;
On his sad brow nor mirth nor wine
Could e'er one wrinkled knot untwine;
Ill was the omen if he smiled,
For 'twas in peril stern and wild ;
But when he laugh'd, each luckless mate
Might hold our fortune desperate.
Foremost he fought in every broil,
Then scornful turn'd him from the spoil;

Nay, often strove to bar the way
Between his comrades and their prey;
Preaching, even then, to such as we,
Hot with our dear-bought victory,
Of mercy and humanity.

XXIII.

I loved him well; his fearless part,
His gallant leading, won my heart.
And after each victorious fight,
'Twas I that wrangled for his right,
Redeem'd his portion of the prey
That greedier mates had torn away:
In field and storm thrice saved his
    life,
And once amid our comrades' strife.—
Yes, I have loved thee! well hath
    proved
My toil, my danger, how I loved!
Yet will I mourn no more thy fate,
Ingrate in life, in death ingrate
Rise if thou canst!' he look'd around,
And sternly stamp'd upon the ground—
'Rise, with thy bearing proud and
    high,
Even as this morn it met mine eye,
And give me, if thou darest, the lie!'
He paused; then, calm and passion-
    freed,
Bade Denzil with his tale proceed.

XXIV.

'Bertram, to thee I need not tell,
What thou hast cause to wot so well,
How Superstition's nets were twined
Around the Lord of Mortham's mind;
But since he drove thee from his tower,
A maid he found in Greta's bower,
Whose speech, like David's harp, had
    sway,
To charm his evil fiend away.
I know not if her features moved
Remembrance of the wife he loved;
But he would gaze upon her eye,
Till his mood soften'd to a sigh.
He, whom no living mortal sought
To question of his secret thought,

Now every thought and care confess'd
To his fair niece's faithful breast;
Nor was there aught of rich and rare,
In earth, in ocean, or in air,
But it must deck Matilda's hair,
Her love still bound him unto life;
But then awoke the civil strife,
And menials bore, by his commands,
Three coffers, with their iron bands,
From Mortham's vault, at midnight
    deep,
To her lone bower in Rokeby-keep,
Ponderous with gold and plate of pride,
His gift, if he in battle died.'

XXV.

'Then Denzil, as I guess, lays train,
These iron-banded chests to gain;
Else, wherefore should he hover here,
Where many a peril waits him near,
For all his feats of war and peace,
For plunder'd boors, and harts of
    grease?
Since through the hamlets as he fared,
What hearth has Guy's marauding
    spared,
Or where the chase that hath not rung
With Denzil's bow, at midnight
    strung?'
'I hold my wont—my rangers go
Even now to track a milk-white doe.
By Rokeby-hall she takes her lair,
In Greta wood she harbours fair,
And when my huntsman marks her
    way,
What think'st thou, Bertram, of the
    prey?
Were Rokeby's daughter in our
    power,
We rate her ransom at her dower.'

XXVI.

''Tis well! there's vengeance in the
    thought!
Matilda is by Wilfrid sought;
And hot-brain'd Redmond, too, 'tis said,
Pays lover's homage to the maid.

Bertram she scorn'd—if met by chance,
She turn'd from me her shuddering
    glance,
Like a nice dame, that will not brook
On what she hates and loathes to look;
She told to Mortham she could ne'er
Behold me without secret fear,
Foreboding evil ;—she may rue
To find her prophecy fall true !
The war has weeded Rokeby's train,
Few followers in his halls remain ;
If thy scheme miss, then, brief and bold,
We are enow to storm the hold ;
Bear off the plunder, and the dame,
And leave the castle all in flame.'

XXVII.

'Still art thou Valour's venturous son !
Yet ponder first the risk to run :
The menials of the castle, true,
And stubborn to their charge, though
    few ;
The wall to scale—the moat to cross—
The wicket-grate—the inner fosse'——
—'Fool ! if we blench for toys like
    these,
On what fair guerdon can we seize ?
Our hardiest venture, to explore
Some wretched peasant's fenceless
    door,
And the best prize we bear away,
The earnings of his sordid day.'—
'.A while thy hasty taunt forbear :
In sight of road more sure and fair,
Thou wouldst not choose, in blindfold
    wrath,
Or wantonness, a desperate path ?
List, then ; for vantage or assault,
From gilded vane to dungeon-vault,
Each pass of Rokeby-house I know :
There is one postern, dark and low,
That issues at a secret spot,
By most neglected or forgot.
Now, could a spial of our train
On fair pretext admittance gain,
That sally-port might be unbarr'd :
Then, vain were battlement and ward !'

XXVIII.

'Now speak'st thou well : to me the
    same,
If force or art shall urge the game ;
Indifferent, if like fox I wind,
Or spring like tiger on the hind.
But, hark ! our merry-men so gay
Troll forth another roundelay.'

SONG.

'A weary lot is thine, fair maid,
    A weary lot is thine !
To pull the thorn thy brow to braid,
    And press the rue for wine !
A lightsome eye, a soldier's mien,
    A feather of the blue,
A doublet of the Lincoln green,—
    No more of me you knew,
                My love !
    No more of me you knew.

This morn is merry June, I trow,
    The rose is budding fain ;
But she shall bloom in winter snow,
    Ere we two meet again.'
He turn'd his charger as he spake,
    Upon the river shore,
He gave his bridle-reins a shake,
    Said, 'Adieu for evermore,
                My love !
    And adieu for evermore.'

XXIX.

'What youth is this, your band among,
The best for minstrelsy and song ?
In his wild notes seem aptly met
A strain of pleasure and regret.'—
'Edmund of Winston is his name ;
The hamlet sounded with the fame
Of early hopes his childhood gave,—
Now centred all in Brignal cave !
I watch him well—his wayward course
Shows oft a tincture of remorse.
Some early love-shaft grazed his heart,
And oft the scar will ache and smart.
Yet is he useful ;—of the rest,
By fits, the darling and the jest,

His harp, his story, and his lay,
Oft aid the idle hours away :
When unemploy'd, each fiery mate
Is ripe for mutinous debate.
He tuned his strings e'en now—again
He wakes them, with a blither strain.'

XXX.
SONG.
ALLEN-A-DALE.

Allen-a-Dale has no fagot for burning,
Allen-a-Dale has no furrow for turning,
Allen-a-Dale has no fleece for the
spinning,
Yet Allen-a-Dale has red gold for the
winning.
Come, read me my riddle! come,
hearken my tale!
And tell me the craft of bold Allen-a-
Dale.

The Baron of Ravensworth prances
in pride,
And he views his domains upon Ar-
kindale side ;
The mere for his net, and the land for
his game,
The chase for the wild, and the park
for the tame ;
Yet the fish of the lake, and the deer
of the vale,
Are less free to Lord Dacre than
Allen-a-Dale !

Allen-a-Dale was ne'er belted a knight,
Though his spur be as sharp, and his
blade be as bright ;
Allen-a-Dale is no baron or lord,
Yet twenty tall yeomen will draw at
his word ;
And the best of our nobles his bonnet
will vail,
Who at Rere-cross on Stanmore meets
Allen-a-Dale.

Allen-a-Dale to his wooing is come ;
The mother, she ask'd of his household
and home :

'Though the castle of Richmond stand
fair on the hill,
My hall,' quoth bold Allen, 'shows
gallanter still ;
'Tis the blue vault of heaven, with its
crescent so pale,
And with all its bright spangles !' said
Allen-a-Dale.

The father was steel, and the mother
was stone ;
They lifted the latch, and they bade
him be gone ;
But loud, on the morrow, their wail
and their cry :
He had laugh'd on the lass with his
bonny black eye,
And she fled to the forest to hear a love-
tale,
And the youth it was told by was
Allen-a-Dale !

XXXI.

'Thou see'st that, whether sad or gay,
Love mingles ever in his lay.
But when his boyish wayward fit
Is o'er, he hath address and wit ;
O! 'tis a brain of fire, can ape
Each dialect, each various shape.'
'Nay, then, to aid thy project, Guy—
Soft! who comes here?' 'My trusty spy.
Speak, Hamlin! hast thou lodged our
deer?'
'I have—but two fair stags are near.
I watch'd her, as she slowly stray'd
From Egliston up Thorsgill glade ;
But Wilfrid Wycliffe sought her side,
And then young Redmond, in his pride,
Shot down to meet them on their way ;
Much, as it seem'd, was theirs to say :
There's time to pitch both toil and net
Before their path be homeward set.'
A hurried and a whisper'd speech
Did Bertram's will to Denzil teach ;
Who, turning to the robber band,
Bade four, the bravest, take the brand.

Canto Fourth.

I.

WHEN Denmark's raven soar'd on high,
Triumphant through Northumbrian
        sky,
Till, hovering near, her fatal croak
Bade Reged's Britons dread the yoke,
And the broad shadow of her wing
Blacken'd each cataract and spring,
Where Tees in tumult leaves his source,
Thundering o'er Caldron and High-
        Force;
Beneath the shade the Northmen came,
Fix'd on each vale a Runic name,
Rear'd high their altar's rugged stone,
And gave their Gods the land they won.
Then, Balder, one bleak garth was
        thine,
And one sweet brooklet's silver line,
And Woden's Croft did title gain
From the stern Father of the Slain;
But to the Monarch of the Mace,
That held in fight the foremost place,
To Odin's son, and Sifia's spouse,
Near Stratforth high they paid their
        vows,
Remember'd Thor's victorious fame,
And gave the dell the Thunderer's
        name.

II.

Yet Scald or Kemper err'd, I ween,
Who gave that soft and quiet scene,
With all its varied light and shade,
And every little sunny glade,
And the blithe brook that strolls along
Its pebbled bed with summer song,
To the grim God of blood and scar,
The grisly King of Northern War.
O, better were its banks assign'd
To spirits of a gentler kind!
For where the thicket-groups recede,
And the rath primrose decks the mead,
The velvet grass seems carpet meet
For the light fairies' lively feet.

Yon tufted knoll, with daisies strown,
Might make proud Oberon a throne,
While, hidden in the thicket nigh,
Puck should brood o'er his frolic sly;
And where profuse the wood-vetch
        clings
Round ash and elm, in verdant rings,
Its pale and azure-pencill'd flower
Should canopy Titania's bower.

III.

Here rise no cliffs the vale to shade;
But, skirting every sunny glade,
In fair variety of green
The woodland lends its silvan screen.
Hoary, yet haughty, frowns the oak,
Its boughs by weight of ages broke;
And towers erect, in sable spire,
The pine-tree scathed by lightning-
        fire;
The drooping ash and birch, between,
Hang their fair tresses o'er the green,
And all beneath, at random grow
Each coppice dwarf of varied show,
Or, round the stems profusely twined,
Fling summer odours on the wind.
Such varied group Urbino's hand
Round Him of Tarsus nobly plann'd,
What time he bade proud Athens own
On Mars's Mount the God Unknown!
Then grey Philosophy stood nigh,
Though bent by age, in spirit high:
There rose the scar-seam'd Veteran's
        spear,
There Grecian Beauty bent to hear,
While Childhood at her foot was placed,
Or clung delighted to her waist.

IV.

'And rest we here,' Matilda said,
And sat her in the varying shade.
'Chance-met, we well may steal an
        hour,
To friendship due, from fortune's
        power.
Thou, Wilfrid, ever kind, must lend
Thy counsel to thy sister-friend;

M

And, Redmond, thou, at my behest,
No farther urge thy desperate 'quest.
For to my care a charge is left,
Dangerous to one of aid bereft;
Wellnigh an orphan, and alone,
Captive her sire, her house o'erthrown.'
Wilfrid, with wonted kindness graced,
Beside her on the turf she placed;
Then paused, with downcast look and
　　eye,
Nor bade young Redmond seat him
　　nigh.
Her conscious diffidence he saw,
Drew backward, as in modest awe,
And sat a little space removed,
Unmark'd to gaze on her he loved.

V.

Wreath'd in its dark-brown rings, her
　　hair
Half hid Matilda's forehead fair,
Half hid and half reveal'd to view
Her full dark eye of hazel hue.
The rose, with faint and feeble streak,
So slightly tinged the maiden's cheek,
That you had said her hue was pale;
But if she faced the summer gale,
Or spoke, or sung, or quicker moved,
Or heard the praise of those she loved,
Or when of interest was express'd
Aught that waked feeling in her breast,
The mantling blood in ready play
Rivall'd the blush of rising day.
There was a soft and pensive grace,
A cast of thought upon her face,
That suited well the forehead high,
The eyelash dark, and downcast eye;
The mild expression spoke a mind
In duty firm, composed, resign'd;
'Tis that which Roman art has given
To mark their maiden Queen of Heaven.
In hours of sport, that mood gave way
To Fancy's light and frolic play;
And when the dance, or tale, or song,
In harmless mirth sped time along,
Full oft her doating sire would call
His Maud the merriest of them all.

But days of war and civil crime
Allow'd but ill such festal time,
And her soft pensiveness of brow
Had deepen'd into sadness now.
In Marston field her father ta'en,
Her friends dispersed, brave Mortham
　　slain,
While every ill her soul foretold,
From Oswald's thirst of power and
　　gold,
And boding thoughts that she must part
With a soft vision of her heart,—
All lower'd around the lovely maid,
To darken her dejection's shade.

VI.

Who has not heard—while Erin yet
Strove 'gainst the Saxon's iron bit—
Who has not heard how brave O'Neale
In English blood imbrued his steel,
Against St. George's cross blazed high
The banners of his Tanistry,
To fiery Essex gave the foil,
And reign'd a prince on Ulster's soil?
But chief arose his victor pride,
When that brave Marshal fought and
　　died,
And Avon-Duff to ocean bore
His billows, red with Saxon gore.
'Twas first in that disastrous fight,
Rokeby and Mortham proved their
　　might.
There had they fallen 'mongst the rest,
But pity touch'd a chieftain's breast;
The Tanist he to great O'Neale;
He check'd his followers' bloody zeal,
To quarter took the kinsmen bold,
And bore them to his mountain-hold,
Gave them each silvan joy to know,
Slieve-Donard's cliffs and woods could
　　show,
Shared with them Erin's festal cheer,
Show'd them the chase of wolf and deer,
And, when a fitting time was come,
Safe and unransom'd sent them home,
Loaded with many a gift, to prove
A generous foe's respect and love.

VII.

Years speed away. On Rokeby's head
Some touch of early snow was shed;
Calm he enjoy'd, by Greta's wave,
The peace which James the Peaceful
      gave,
While Mortham, far beyond the main,
Waged his fierce wars on Indian
      Spain.—
It chanced upon a wintry night,
That whiten'd Stanmore's stormy
      height,
The chase was o'er, the stag was kill'd,
In Rokeby-hall the cups were fill'd,
And by the huge stone chimney sate
The Knight in hospitable state.
Moonless the sky, the hour was late,
When a loud summons shook the gate,
And sore for entrance and for aid
A voice of foreign accent pray'd.
The porter answer'd to the call,
And instant rush'd into the hall
A Man, whose aspect and attire
Startled the circle by the fire.

VIII.

His plaited hair in elf-locks spread
Around his bare and matted head;
On leg and thigh, close stretch'd and
      trim,
His vesture show'd the sinewy limb;
In saffron dyed, a linen vest
Was frequent folded round his breast;
A mantle long and loose he wore,
Shaggy with ice, and stain'd with gore.
He clasp'd a burden to his heart,
And, resting on a knotted dart,
The snow from hair and beard he shook,
And round him gazed with wilder'd
      look.
Then up the hall, with staggering pace,
He hasten'd by the blaze to place,
Half lifeless from the bitter air,
His load, a Boy of beauty rare.
To Rokeby, next, he louted low,
Then stood erect his tale to show,
With wild majestic port and tone,
Like envoy of some barbarous throne.
'Sir Richard, Lord of Rokeby, hear!
Turlough O'Neale salutes thee dear;
He graces thee, and to thy care
Young Redmond gives, his grandson
      fair.
He bids thee breed him as thy son,
For Turlough's days of joy are done;
And other lords have seized his land,
And faint and feeble is his hand;
And all the glory of Tyrone
Is like a morning vapour flown.
To bind the duty on thy soul,
He bids thee think on Erin's bowl!
If any wrong the young O'Neale,
He bids thee think of Erin's steel.
To Mortham first this charge was due,
But, in his absence, honours you.—
Now is my master's message by,
And Ferraught will contented die.'

IX.

His look grew fix'd, his cheek grew
      pale,
He sunk when he had told his tale;
For, hid beneath his mantle wide,
A mortal wound was in his side.
Vain was all aid—in terror wild,
And sorrow, scream'd the orphan
      child.
Poor Ferraught raised his wistful
      eyes,
And faintly strove to soothe his cries;
All reckless of his dying pain,
He blest and blest him o'er again!
And kiss'd the little hands outspread,
And kiss'd and cross'd the infant head,
And, in his native tongue and phrase,
Pray'd to each saint to watch his
      days;
Then all his strength together drew,
The charge to Rokeby to renew.
When half was falter'd from his breast,
And half by dying signs express'd,
'Bless the O'Neale!' he faintly said,
And thus the faithful spirit fled.

X.

'Twas long ere soothing might prevail
Upon the child to end the tale;
And then he said, that from his home
His grandsire had been forced to roam,
Which had not been if Redmond's hand
Had but had strength to draw the brand,
The brand of Lenaugh More the Red,
That hung beside the grey wolf's
　　head.—
'Twas from his broken phrase descried,
His foster-father was his guide,
Who, in his charge, from Ulster bore
Letters and gifts a goodly store;
But ruffians met them in the wood,
Ferraught in battle boldly stood,
Till wounded and o'erpower'd at
　　length,
And stripp'd of all, his failing strength
Just bore him here—and then the
　　child
Renew'd again his moaning wild

XI.

The tear down childhood's cheek that
　　flows
Is like the dewdrop on the rose;
When next the summer breeze comes
　　by,
And waves the bush, the flower is dry.
Won by their care, the orphan child
Soon on his new protector smiled,
With dimpled cheek and eye so fair,
Through his thick curls of flaxen hair:
But blithest laugh'd that cheek and
　　eye
When Rokeby's little maid was nigh;
'Twas his, with elder brother's pride,
Matilda's tottering steps to guide;
His native lays in Irish tongue,
To soothe her infant ear he sung,
And primrose twined with daisy fair
To form a chaplet for her hair.
By lawn, by grove, by brooklet's strand,
The children still were hand in hand,
And good Sir Richard smiling eyed
The early knot so kindly tied.

XII.

But summer months bring wilding shoot
From bud to bloom, from bloom to fruit;
And years draw on our human span,
From child to boy, from boy to man;
And soon in Rokeby's woods is seen
A gallant boy in hunter's green.
He loves to wake the felon boar
In his dark haunt on Greta's shore,
And loves, against the deer so dun,
To draw the shaft, or lift the gun:
Yet more he loves, in autumn prime,
The hazel's spreading boughs to climb,
And down its cluster'd stores to hail,
Where young Matilda holds her veil.
And she, whose veil receives the
　　shower,
Is alter'd too, and knows her power;
Assumes a monitress's pride,
Her Redmond's dangerous sports to
　　chide;
Yet listens still to hear him tell
How the grim wild-boar fought and fell,
How, at his fall the bugle rung,
Till rock and greenwood answer flung;
Then blesses her, that man can find
A pastime of such savage kind!

XIII.

But Redmond knew to weave his tale
So well with praise of wood and dale,
And knew so well each point to trace,
Gives living interest to the chase,
And knew so well o'er all to throw
His spirit's wild romantic glow,
That, while she blamed, and while
　　she fear'd,
She loved each venturous tale she
　　heard.
Oft, too, when drifted snow and rain
To bower and hall their steps restrain,
Together they explored the page
Of glowing bard or gifted sage;
Oft, placed the evening fire beside,
The minstrel art alternate tried,
While gladsome harp and lively lay
Bade winter-night flit fast away:

Thus, from their childhood, blending
   still
Their sport, their study, and their skill,
A union of the soul they prove,
But must not think that it was love.
But though they dared not, envious
   Fame
Soon dared to give that union name;
And when so often, side by side,
From year to year the pair she eyed,
She sometimes blamed the good old
   Knight,
As dull of ear and dim of sight,
Sometimes his purpose would declare,
That young O'Neale should wed his
   heir.

XIV.

The suit of Wilfrid rent disguise
And bandage from the lovers' eyes;
'Twas plain that Oswald, for his son,
Had Rokeby's favour wellnigh won.
Now must they meet with change of
   cheer,
With mutual looks of shame and fear;
Now must Matilda stray apart,
To school her disobedient heart:
And Redmond now alone must rue
The love he never can subdue.
But factions rose, and Rokeby sware,
No rebel's son should wed his heir;
And Redmond, nurtured while a child
In many a bard's traditions wild,
Now sought the lonely wood or stream,
To cherish there a happier dream,
Of maiden won by sword or lance,
As in the regions of romance;
And count the heroes of his line,
Great Nial of the Pledges Nine,
Shane-Dymas wild, and Geraldine,
And Connan-More, who vow'd his race
For ever to the fight and chase,
And cursed him, of his lineage born,
Should sheathe the sword to reap the
   corn,
Or leave the mountain and the wold,
To shroud himself in castled hold.

From such examples hope he drew,
And brighten'd as the trumpet blew.

XV.

If brides were won by heart and blade,
Redmond had both his cause to aid,
And all beside of nurture rare
That might beseem a baron's heir.
Turlough O'Neale, in Erin's strife,
On Rokeby's Lord bestow'd his life,
And well did Rokeby's generous
   knight
Young Redmond for the deed requite.
Nor was his liberal care and cost
Upon the gallant stripling lost:
Seek the North-Riding broad and wide,
Like Redmond none could steed
   bestride;
From Tynemouth search to Cumber-
   land,
Like Redmond none could wield a
   brand;
And then, of humour kind and free,
And bearing him to each degree
With frank and fearless courtesy,
There never youth was form'd to steal
Upon the heart like brave O'Neale.

XVI.

Sir Richard loved him as his son;
And when the days of peace were
   done,
And to the gales of war he gave
The banner of his sires to wave,
Redmond, distinguish'd by his care,
He chose that honour'd flag to bear,
And named his page, the next degree,
In that old time, to chivalry.
In five pitch'd fields he well maintain'd
The honour'd place his worth obtain'd,
And high was Redmond's youthful
   name
Blazed in the roll of martial fame.
Had fortune smiled on Marston fight,
The eve had seen him dubb'd a knight;
Twice, 'mid the battle's doubtful strife,
Of Rokeby's Lord he saved the life,

But when he saw him prisoner made,
He kiss'd and then resign'd his blade,
And yielded him an easy prey
To those who led the Knight away;
Resolved Matilda's sire should prove
In prison, as in fight, his love.

XVII.

When lovers meet in adverse hour,
'Tis like a sun-glimpse through a
  shower,
A wat'ry ray an instant seen
The darkly closing clouds between.
As Redmond on the turf reclined,
The past and present fill'd his mind:
'It was not thus,' Affection said,
'I dream'd of my return, dear maid!
Not thus, when, from thy trembling
  hand,
I took the banner and the brand,
When round me, as the bugles blew,
Their blades three hundred warriors
  drew,
And, while the standard I unroll'd,
Clash'd their bright arms, with clamour
  bold.
Where is that banner now?—its pride
Lies 'whelm'd in Ouse's sullen tide!
Where now these warriors?—in their
  gore,
They cumber Marston's dismal moor!
And what avails a useless brand,
Held by a captive's shackled hand,
That only would his life retain,
To aid thy sire to bear his chain!'
Thus Redmond to himself apart;
Nor lighter was his rival's heart;
For Wilfrid, while his generous soul
Disdain'd to profit by control,
By many a sign could mark too
  plain,
Save with such aid, his hopes were
  vain.—
But now Matilda's accents stole
On the dark visions of their soul,
And bade their mournful musing fly,
Like mist before the zephyr's sigh.

XVIII.

'I need not to my friends recall,
How Mortham shunn'd my father's
  hall;
A man of silence and of woe,
Yet ever anxious to bestow
On my poor self whate'er could
  prove
A kinsman's confidence and love.
My feeble aid could sometimes chase
The clouds of sorrow for a space:
But oftener, fix'd beyond my power,
I mark'd his deep despondence lower.
One dismal cause, by all unguess'd,
His fearful confidence confess'd;
And twice it was my hap to see
Examples of that agony,
Which for a season can o'erstrain
And wreck the structure of the brain.
He had the awful power to know
The approaching mental overthrow,
And while his mind had courage yet
To struggle with the dreadful fit,
The victim writhed against its throes,
Like wretch beneath a murderer's
  blows.
This malady, I well could mark,
Sprung from some direful cause and
  dark;
But still he kept its source conceal'd,
Till arming for the civil field;
Then in my charge he bade me hold
A treasure huge of gems and gold,
With this disjointed dismal scroll,
That tells the secret of his soul,
In such wild words as oft betray
A mind by anguish forced astray.'—

XIX.

MORTHAM'S HISTORY.

'Matilda! thou hast seen me start,
As if a dagger thrill'd my heart,
When it has hap'd some casual phrase
Waked memory of my former days.
Believe, that few can backward cast
Their thoughts with pleasure on the
  past;

But I!—my youth was rash and vain,
And blood and rage my manhood stain,
And my grey hairs must now descend
To my cold grave without a friend!
Even thou, Matilda, wilt disown
Thy kinsman, when his guilt is known.
And must I lift the bloody veil
That hides my dark and fatal tale?
I must—I will— Pale phantom, cease!
Leave me one little hour in peace!
Thus haunted, think'st thou I have skill
Thine own commission to fulfil?
Or, while thou point'st with gesture fierce,
Thy blighted cheek, thy bloody hearse,
How can I paint thee as thou wert,
So fair in face, so warm in heart?

XX.

'Yes, she was fair!—Matilda,' thou
Hast a soft sadness on thy brow;
But hers was like the sunny glow
That laughs on earth and all below!
We wedded secret—there was need—
Differing in country and in creed;
And, when to Mortham's tower she came,
We mention'd not her race and name,
Until thy sire, who fought afar,
Should turn him home from foreign war,
On whose kind influence we relied
To soothe her father's ire and pride.
Few months we lived retired, unknown,
To all but one dear friend alone,
One darling friend—I spare his shame,
I will not write the villain's name!
My trespasses I might forget,
And sue in vengeance for the debt
Due by a brother worm to me,
Ungrateful to God's clemency,
That spared me penitential time,
Nor cut me off amid my crime.

XXI.

'A kindly smile to all she lent,
But on her husband's friend 'twas bent
So kind, that, from its harmless glee,
The wretch misconstrued villany.
Repulsed in his presumptuous love,
A 'vengeful snare the traitor wove.
Alone we sat—the flask had flow'd,
My blood with heat unwonted glow'd,
When through the alley'd walk we spied
With hurried step my Edith glide,
Cowering beneath the verdant screen,
As one unwilling to be seen.
Words cannot paint the fiendish smile
That curl'd the traitor's cheek the while!
Fiercely I question'd of the cause;
He made a cold and artful pause,
Then pray'd it might not chafe my mood—
"There was a gallant in the wood!"
We had been shooting at the deer;
My cross-bow (evil chance!) was near:
That ready weapon of my wrath
I caught, and, hasting up the path,
In the yew grove my wife I found,
A stranger's arms her neck had bound!
I mark'd his heart—the bow I drew—
I loosed the shaft—'twas more than true!
I found my Edith's dying charms
Lock'd in her murder'd brother's arms!
He came in secret to inquire
Her state, and reconcile her sire.

XXII.

'All fled my rage—the villain first,
Whose craft my jealousy had nursed;
He sought in far and foreign clime
To 'scape the vengeance of his crime.
The manner of the slaughter done
Was known to few, my guilt to none;
Some tale my faithful steward framed—
I know not what—of shaft mis-aim'd;
And even from those the act who knew,
He hid the hand from which it flew.
Untouch'd by human laws I stood,
But God had heard the cry of blood!
There is a blank upon my mind,
A fearful vision ill-defined,

Of raving till my flesh was torn,
Of dungeon-bolts and fetters worn—
And when I waked to woe more mild,
And question'd of my infant child—
(Have I not written, that she bare
A boy, like summer morning fair?)—
With looks confused my menials tell
That armed men in Mortham dell
Beset the nurse's evening way,
And bore her, with her charge, away.
My faithless friend, and none but he,
Could profit by this villany;
Him then, I sought, with purpose dread
Of treble vengeance on his head!
He 'scaped me—but my bosom's wound
Some faint relief from wandering found;
And over distant land and sea
I bore my load of misery.

XXIII.

''Twas then that fate my footsteps led
Among a daring crew and dread,
With whom full oft my hated life
I ventured in such desperate strife,
That even my fierce associates saw
My frantic deeds with doubt and awe.
Much then I learn'd, and much can show,
Of human guilt and human woe,
Yet ne'er have, in my wanderings, known
A wretch, whose sorrows match'd my own!
It chanced, that after battle fray,
Upon the bloody field we lay;
The yellow moon her lustre shed
Upon the wounded and the dead,
While, sense in toil and wassail drown'd,
My ruffian comrades slept around,
There came a voice—its silver tone
Was soft, Matilda, as thine own—
'Ah, wretch!' it said, 'what makest thou here,
While unavenged my bloody bier,
While unprotected lives mine heir,
Without a father's name and care?'

XXIV.

'I heard—obey'd—and homeward drew;
The fiercest of our desperate crew
I brought, at time of need to aid
My purposed vengeance, long delay'd.
But, humble be my thanks to Heaven,
That better hopes and thoughts has given,
And by our Lord's dear prayer has taught,
Mercy by mercy must be bought!—
Let me in misery rejoice--
I've seen his face—I've heard his voice—
I claim'd of him my only child;
As he disown'd the theft, he smiled!
That very calm and callous look,
That fiendish sneer his visage took,
As when he said, in scornful mood,
"There is a gallant in the wood!"—
I did not slay him as he stood—
All praise be to my Maker given!
Long suffrance is one path to Heaven.'

XXV.

Thus far the woful tale was heard,
When something in the thicket stirr'd.
Up Redmond sprung; the villain Guy
(For he it was that lurk'd so nigh)
Drew back—he durst not cross his steel
A moment's space with brave O'Neale,
For all the treasured gold that rests
In Mortham's iron-banded chests.
Redmond resumed his seat;—he said,
Some roe was rustling in the shade.
Bertram laugh'd grimly when he saw
His timorous comrade backward draw:
'A trusty mate art thou, to fear
A single arm, and aid so near!
Yet have I seen thee mark a deer.
Give me thy carabine; I'll show
An art that thou wilt gladly know,
How thou mayst safely quell a foe.'

XXVI.

On hands and knees fierce Bertram drew
The spreading birch and hazels through,

Till he had Redmond full in view;
The gun he levell'd—mark like this
Was Bertram never known to miss,
When fair opposed to aim there sate
An object of his mortal hate.
That day young Redmond's death had
          seen,
But twice Matilda came between
The carabine and Redmond's breast,
Just ere the spring his finger press'd.
A deadly oath the ruffian swore,
But yet his fell design forbore:
'It ne'er,' he mutter'd, 'shall be said,
That thus I scath'd thee, haughty maid!'
Then moved to seek more open aim,
When to his side Guy Denzil came:
'Bertram, forbear! we are undone
For ever, if thou fire the gun.
By all the fiends, an armed force
Descends the dell, of foot and horse!
We perish if they hear a shot—
Madman! we have a safer plot—
Nay, friend, be ruled, and bear thee
          back!
Behold, down yonder hollow track,
The warlike leader of the band
Comes, with his broadsword in his
          hand.'
Bertram look'd up; he saw, he knew
That Denzil's fears had counsell'd true,
Then cursed his fortune and withdrew,
Threaded the woodlands undescried,
And gain'd the cave on Greta side.

XXVII.

They whom dark Bertram, in his wrath,
Doom'd to captivity or death,
Their thoughts to one sad subject lent,
Saw not nor heard the ambushment.
Heedless and unconcern'd they sate,
While on the very verge of fate;
Heedless and unconcern'd remain'd,
When Heaven the murderer's arm
          restrain'd;
As ships drift darkling down the tide,
Nor see the shelves o'er which they
          glide,

Uninterrupted thus they heard
What Mortham's closing tale declared.
He spoke of wealth as of a load,
By Fortune on a wretch bestow'd,
In bitter mockery of hate,
His cureless woes to aggravate;
But yet he pray'd Matilda's care
Might save that treasure for his heir—
His Edith's son—for still he raved
As confident his life was saved;
In frequent vision, he averr'd,
He saw his face, his voice he heard;
Then argued calm—had murder been,
The blood, the corpses, had been seen;
Some had pretended, too, to mark
On Windermere a stranger bark,
Whose crew, with jealous care, yet
          mild,
Guarded a female and a child.
While these faint proofs he told and
          press'd,
Hope seem'd to kindle in his breast;
Though inconsistent, vague, and vain,
It warp'd his judgment and his brain.

XXVIII.

These solemn words his story close:—
'Heaven witness for me, that I chose
My part in this sad civil fight,
Moved by no cause but England's right.
My country's groans have bid me draw
My sword for gospel and for law;—
These righted, I fling arms aside,
And seek my son through Europe wide.
My wealth, on which a kinsman nigh
Already casts a grasping eye,
With thee may unsuspected lie.
When of my death Matilda hears,
Let her retain her trust three years;
If none, from me, the treasure claim,
Perish'd is Mortham's race and name:
Then let it leave her generous hand,
And flow in bounty o'er the land;
Soften the wounded prisoner's lot,
Rebuild the peasant's ruin'd cot;
So spoils, acquired by fight afar,
Shall mitigate domestic war.'

XXIX.

The generous youths, who well had
        known
Of Mortham's mind the powerful tone,
To that high mind, by sorrow swerved,
Gave sympathy his woes deserved ;
But Wilfrid chief, who saw reveal'd
Why Mortham wish'd his life conceal'd,
In secret, doubtless, to pursue
The schemes his wilder'd fancy drew.
Thoughtful he heard Matilda tell,
That she would share her father's cell,
His partner of captivity,
Where'er his prison-house should be ;
Yet grieved to think that Rokeby-hall,
Dismantled, and forsook by all,
Open to rapine and to stealth,
Had now no safeguard for the wealth
Entrusted by her kinsman kind,
And for such noble use design'd.
'Was Barnard Castle then her choice,'
Wilfrid inquired with hasty voice,
'Since there the victor's laws ordain,
Her father must a space remain ? '
A flutter'd hope his accents shook,
A flutter'd joy was in his look.
Matilda hasten'd to reply,
For anger flash'd in Redmond's eye :—
'Duty,' she said, with gentle grace,
'Kind Wilfrid, has no choice of place ;
Else had I for my sire assign'd
Prison less galling to his mind,
Than that his wild-wood haunts which
        sees
And hears the murmur of the Tees,
Recalling thus, with every glance,
What captive's sorrow can enhance ;
But where those woes are highest, there
Needs Rokeby most his daughter's
        care.'

XXX.

He felt the kindly check she gave,
And stood abash'd—then answer'd
        grave :
'I sought thy purpose, noble maid,
Thy doubts to clear, thy schemes to aid.

I have beneath mine own command,
So wills my sire, a gallant band,
And well could send some horseman
        wight
To bear the treasure forth by night,
And so bestow it as you deem
In these ill days may safest seem.'—
'Thanks, gentle Wilfrid, thanks,' she
        said :
'O, be it not one day delay'd !
And, more, thy sister-friend to aid,
Be thou thyself content to hold,
In thine own keeping, Mortham's gold,
Safest with thee.'—While thus she
        spoke,
Arm'd soldiers on their converse broke,
The same of whose approach afraid,
The ruffians left their ambuscade.
Their chief to Wilfrid bended low,
Then look'd around as for a foe.
'What mean'st thou, friend,' young
        Wycliffe said,
'Why thus in arms beset the glade ? '
'That would I gladly learn from you ;
For up my squadron as I drew,
To exercise our martial game
Upon the moor of Barninghame,
A stranger told you were waylaid,
Surrounded, and to death betray'd.
He had a leader's voice, I ween,
A falcon glance, a warrior's mien.
He bade me bring you instant aid ;
I doubted not, and I obey'd.'

XXXI.

Wilfrid changed colour, and, amazed,
Turn'd short, and on the speaker gazed ;
While Redmond every thicket round
Track'd earnest as a questing hound,
And Denzil's carabine he found,
Sure evidence, by which they knew
The warning was as kind as true.
Wisest it seem'd, with cautious speed
To leave the dell.   It was agreed
That Redmond, with Matilda fair,
And fitting guard, should home repair ;
At nightfall Wilfrid should attend,
With a strong band, his sister-friend,

To bear with her from Rokeby's bowers
To Barnard Castle's lofty towers,
Secret and safe, the banded chests
In which the wealth of Mortham rests.
This hasty purpose fix'd, they part,
Each with a grieved and anxious heart.

—◆—

Canto Fifth.

I.

THE sultry summer day is done,
The western hills have hid the sun,
But mountain peak and village spire
Retain reflection of his fire.
Old Barnard's towers are purple still
To those that gaze from Toller-hill;
Distant and high, the tower of Bowes
Like steel upon the anvil glows;
And Stanmore's ridge, behind that lay,
Rich with the spoils of parting day,
In crimson and in gold array'd,
Streaks yet a while the closing shade,
Then slow resigns to darkening heaven
The tints which brighter hours had
    given.
Thus aged men, full loth and slow,
The vanities of life forego,
And count their youthful follies o'er,
Till Memory lends her light no more.

II.

The eve, that slow on upland fades,
Has darker closed on Rokeby's glades,
Where, sunk within their banks pro-
    found,
Her guardian streams to meeting
    wound.
The stately oaks, whose sombre frown
Of noontide made a twilight brown,
Impervious now to fainter light,
Of twilight make an early night.
Hoarse into middle air arose
The vespers of the roosting crows,
And with congenial murmurs seem
To wake the Genii of the stream;

For louder clamour'd Greta's tide,
And Tees in deeper voice replied,
And fitful waked the evening wind,
Fitful in sighs its breath resign'd.
Wilfrid, whose fancy-nurtured soul
Felt in the scene a soft control,
With lighter footstep press'd the
    ground,
And often paused to look around;
And, though his path was to his love,
Could not but linger in the grove
To drink the thrilling interest dear,
Of awful pleasure check'd by fear.
Such inconsistent moods have we,
Even when our passions strike the key.

III.

Now, through the wood's dark mazes
    past,
The opening lawn he reach'd at last,
Where, silver'd by the moonlight ray,
The ancient Hall before him lay.
Those martial terrors long were fled
That frown'd of old around its head:
The battlements, the turrets grey,
Seem'd half abandon'd to decay;
On barbican and keep of stone
Stern Time the foeman's work had
    done.
Where banners the invader braved,
The harebell now and wallflower
    waved;
In the rude guard-room, where of yore
Their weary hours the warders wore,
Now, while the cheerful fagots blaze,
On the paved floor the spindle plays;
The flanking guns dismounted lie,
The moat is ruinous and dry,
The grim portcullis gone—and all
The fortress turn'd to peaceful Hall.

IV.

But yet precautions, lately ta'en,
Show'd danger's day revived again;
The court-yard wall show'd marks of
    care,
The fall'n defences to repair,

Lending such strength as might with-
    stand
The insult of marauding band.
The beams once more were taught to
    bear
The trembling drawbridge into air,
And not, till question'd o'er and o'er,
For Wilfrid oped the jealous door ;
And when he enter'd, bolt and bar
Resumed their place with sullen jar ;
Then, as he cross'd the vaulted porch,
The old grey porter raised his torch,
And view'd him o'er, from foot to head,
Ere to the hall his steps he led.
That huge old hall, of knightly state,
Dismantled seem'd and desolate.
The moon through transom-shafts of
    stone,
Which cross'd the latticed oriels,
    shone,
And, by the mournful light she gave,
The Gothic vault seem'd funeral cave.
Pennon and banner waved no more
O'er beams of stag and tusks of boar,
Nor glimmering arms were marshal 'd
    seen
To glance those silvan spoils between.
Those arms, those ensigns, borne
    away,
Accomplish'd Rokeby's brave array,
But all were lost on Marston's day !
Yet here and there the moonbeams fall
Where armour yet adorns the wall,
Cumbrous of size, uncouth to sight,
And useless in the modern fight ;
Like veteran relic of the wars,
Known only by neglected scars.

v.

Matilda soon to greet him came,
And bade them light the evening flame ;
Said, all for parting was prepared,
And tarried but for Wilfrid's guard.
But then, reluctant to unfold
His father's avarice of gold,
He hinted, that lest jealous eye
Should on their precious burden pry,

He judged it best the castle gate
To enter when the night wore late ;
And therefore he had left command
With those he trusted of his band,
That they should be at Rokeby met,
What time the midnight-watch was
    set.
Now Redmond came, whose anxious
    care
Till then was busied to prepare
All needful, meetly to arrange
The mansion for its mournful change.
With Wilfrid's care and kindness
    pleased,
His cold unready hand he seized,
And press'd it, till his kindly strain
The gentle youth return'd again.
Seem'd as between them this was said,
' Awhile let jealousy be dead ;
And let our contest be, whose care
Shall best assist this helpless fair.'

vi.

There was no speech the truce to bind,
It was a compact of the mind,—
A generous thought at once impress'd
On either rival's generous breast.
Matilda well the secret took,
From sudden change of mien and look ;
And—for not small had been her fear
Of jealous ire and danger near—
Felt, even in her dejected state,
A joy beyond the reach of fate.
They closed beside the chimney's blaze,
And talk'd, and hoped for happier days,
And lent their spirits' rising glow
Awhile to gild impending woe ;
High privilege of youthful time,
Worth all the pleasures of our prime !
The bickering fagot sparkled bright,
And gave the scene of love to sight,
Bade Wilfrid's cheek more lively glow,
Play'd on Matilda's neck of snow,
Her nut-brown curls and forehead high,
And laugh'd in Redmond's azure eye.
Two lovers by the maiden sate,
Without a glance of jealous hate ;

The maid her lovers sat between,
With open brow and equal mien ;
It is a sight but rarely spied,
Thanks to man's wrath and woman's
　　　pride.

VII.

While thus in peaceful guise they sate
A knock alarm'd the outer gate,
And ere the tardy porter stirr'd
The tinkling of a harp was heard.
A manly voice, of mellow swell,
Bore burden to the music well.

SONG.

'Summer eve is gone and past,
　Summer dew is falling fast ;
　I have wander'd all the day,
　Do not bid me farther stray !
　Gentle hearts, of gentle kin,
　Take the wandering harper in !'

But the stern porter answer gave,
With 'Get thee hence, thou strolling
　　　knave !
The king wants soldiers ; war, I trow,
Were meeter trade for such as thou.'
At this unkind reproof, again
Answer'd the ready minstrel's strain.

SONG RESUMED.

'Bid not me, in battle-field,
　Buckler lift, or broadsword wield !
　All my strength and all my art
　Is to touch the gentle heart
　With the wizard notes that ring
　From the peaceful minstrel-string.'

The porter, all unmoved, replied,—
'Depart in peace, with Heaven to
　　　guide ;
If longer by the gate thou dwell,
Trust me, thou shalt not part so well.'

VIII.

With somewhat of appealing look,
The harper's part young Wilfrid took :
'These notes so wild and ready thrill,
They show no vulgar minstrel's skill ;

Hard were his task to seek a home
More distant, since the night is come ;
And for his faith I dare engage—
Your Harpool's blood is sour'd by age ;
His gate, once readily display'd
To greet the friend, the poor to aid,
Now even to me, though known of old,
Did but reluctantly unfold.'—
'O blame not, as poor Harpool's crime,
An evil of this evil time.
He deems dependent on his care
The safety of his patron's heir,
Nor judges meet to ope the tower
To guest unknown at parting hour,
Urging his duty to excess
Of rough and stubborn faithfulness.
For this poor harper, I would fain
He may relax :—Hark to his strain !'—

IX.

SONG RESUMED.

'I have song of war for knight,
　Lay of love for lady bright,
　Fairy tale to lull the heir,
　Goblin grim the maids to scare ;
　Dark the night, and long till day,
　Do not bid me farther stray !

Rokeby's lords of martial fame,
I can count them name by name ;
Legends of their line there be,
Known to few, but known to me ;
If you honour Rokeby's kin
Take the wandering harper in !

Rokeby's lords had fair regard
For the harp and for the bard ;
Baron's race throve never well
Where the curse of minstrel fell ;
If you love that noble kin
Take the weary harper in !'—

'Hark ! Harpool parleys—there is
　　　hope,'
Said Redmond, 'that the gate will ope.'
—'For all thy brag and boast, I trow,
Nought know'st thou of the Felon Sow,'

Quoth Harpool, 'nor how Greta-side
She roam'd, and Rokeby forest wide;
Nor how Ralph Rokeby gave the beast
To Richmond's friars to make a feast.
Of Gilbert Griffinson the tale
Goes, and of gallant Peter Dale,
That well could strike with sword amain,
And of the valiant son of Spain,
Friar Middleton, and blithe Sir Ralph;
There were a jest to make us laugh!
If thou canst tell it, in yon shed
Thou'st won thy supper and thy bed.'

x.

Matilda smiled; 'Cold hope,' said she,
'From Harpool's love of minstrelsy!
But, for this harper, may we dare,
Redmond, to mend his couch and fare?'
'O, ask me not! At minstrel-string
My heart from infancy would spring;
Nor can I hear its simplest strain
But it brings Erin's dream again,
When placed by Owen Lysagh's knee,
(The Filea of O'Neale was he,
A blind and bearded man, whose eld
Was sacred as a prophet's held,)
I've seen a ring of rugged kerne,
With aspects shaggy, wild, and stern,
Enchanted by the master's lay,
Linger around the livelong day,
Shift from wild rage to wilder glee,
To love, to grief, to ecstasy,
And feel each varied change of soul
Obedient to the bard's control.
Ah, Clandeboy! thy friendly floor
Slieve-Donard's oak shall light no more;
Nor Owen's harp, beside the blaze,
Tell maiden's love, or hero's praise!
The mantling brambles hide thy hearth,
Centre of hospitable mirth;
All undistinguish'd in the glade
My sires' glad home is prostrate laid,
Their vassals wander wide and far,
Serve foreign lords in distant war,

And now the stranger's sons enjoy
The lovely woods of Clandeboy!'
He spoke, and proudly turn'd aside,
The starting tear to dry and hide.

xi.

Matilda's dark and soften'd eye
Was glistening ere O'Neale's was dry.
Her hand upon his arm she laid,
'It is the will of Heaven,' she said.
'And think'st thou, Redmond, I can part
From this loved home with lightsome heart,
Leaving to wild neglect whate'er
Even from my infancy was dear?
For in this calm domestic bound
Were all Matilda's pleasures found.
That hearth, my sire was wont to grace,
Full soon may be a stranger's place;
This hall, in which a child I play'd,
Like thine, dear Redmond, lowly laid,
The bramble and the thorn may braid;
Or, pass'd for aye from me and mine,
It ne'er may shelter Rokeby's line.
Yet is this consolation given,
My Redmond—'tis the will of Heaven.'
Her word, her action, and her phrase,
Were kindly as in early days;
For cold reserve had lost its power
In sorrow's sympathetic hour.
Young Redmond dared not trust his voice;
But rather had it been his choice
To share that melancholy hour,
Than, arm'd with all a chieftain's power,
In full possession to enjoy
Slieve-Donard wide, and Clandeboy.

xii.

The blood left Wilfrid's ashen cheek;
Matilda sees, and hastes to speak—
'Happy in friendship's ready aid,
Let all my murmurs here be stay'd!
And Rokeby's maiden will not part
From Rokeby's hall with moody heart,
This night at least, for Rokeby's fame,
The hospitable hearth shall flame,

And, ere its native heir retire,
Find for the wanderer rest and fire,
While this poor harper, by the blaze,
Recounts the tale of other days.
Bid Harpool ope the door with speed,
Admit him, and relieve each need.
Meantime, kind Wycliffe, wilt thou try
Thy minstrel skill? Nay, no reply—
And look not sad! I guess thy thought,
Thy verse with laurels would be bought,
And poor Matilda, landless now,
Has not a garland for thy brow.
True, I must leave sweet Rokeby's
        glades,
Nor wander more in Greta shades;
But sure, no rigid jailer, thou
Wilt a short prison-walk allow,
Where summer flowers grow wild at
        will,
On Marwood-chase and Toller Hill;
Then holly green and lily gay
Shall twine in guerdon of thy lay.'
The mournful youth, a space aside,
To tune Matilda's harp applied;
And then a low sad descant rung,
As prelude to the lay he sung.

XIII.

THE CYPRESS WREATH.

O Lady, twine no wreath for me,
Or twine it of the cypress-tree!
Too lively glow the lilies light,
The varnish'd holly 's all too bright,
The May-flower and the eglantine
May shade a brow less sad than mine;
But, Lady, weave no wreath for me,
Or weave it of the cypress-tree!

Let dimpled Mirth his temples twine
With tendrils of the laughing vine;
The manly oak, the pensive yew,
To patriot and to sage be due;
The myrtle bough bids lovers live,
But that Matilda will not give;
Then, Lady, twine no wreath for me,
Or twine it of the cypress-tree!

Let merry England proudly rear
Her blended roses, bought so dear;
Let Albin bind her bonnet blue
With heath and harebell dipp'd in
        dew;
On favour'd Erin's crest be seen
The flower she loves of emerald
        green—
But, Lady, twine no wreath for me,
Or twine it of the cypress-tree!

Strike the wild harp, while maids
        prepare
The ivy meet for minstrel's hair;
And, while his crown of laurel-
        leaves
With bloody hand the victor weaves,
Let the loud trump his triumph tell;
But when you hear the passing-bell,
Then, Lady, twine a wreath for me,
And twine it of the cypress-tree!

Yes! twine for me the cypress-bough;
But, O Matilda, twine not now!
Stay till a few brief months are past,
And I have look'd and loved my last!
When villagers my shroud bestrew
With pansies, rosemary, and rue,—
Then, Lady, weave a wreath for me,
And weave it of the cypress tree!

XIV.

O'Neale observed the starting tear,
And spoke with kind and blithesome
        cheer—
' No, noble Wilfrid! ere the day
When mourns the land thy silent lay,
Shall many a wreath be freely wove
By hand of friendship and of love.
I would not wish that rigid Fate
Had doom'd thee to a captive's state,
Whose hands are bound by honour's
        law,
Who wears a sword he must not
        draw;
But were it so, in minstrel pride
The land together would we ride,

On prancing steeds, like harpers old,
Bound for the halls of barons bold :
Each lover of the lyre we'd seek,
From Michael's Mount to Skiddaw's
    Peak,
Survey wild Albin's mountain strand,
And roam green Erin's lovely land ;
While thou the gentler souls should
    move
With lay of pity and of love,
And I, thy mate, in rougher strain,
Would sing of war and warriors slain.
Old England's bards were vanquish'd
    then,
And Scotland's vaunted Hawthornden,
And, silenced on Iernian shore,
M'Curtin's harp should charm no more !'
In lively mood he spoke, to wile
From Wilfrid's woeworn cheek a
    smile.

xv.

'But,' said Matilda, ' ere thy name,
Good Redmond gain its destined fame,
Say, wilt thou kindly deign to call
Thy brother-minstrel to the hall ?
Bid all the household, too, attend,
Each in his rank a humble friend ;
I know their faithful hearts will grieve
When their poor mistress takes her
    leave ;
So let the horn and beaker flow
To mitigate their parting woe.'
The harper came ;— in youth's first
    prime
Himself ; in mode of olden time
His garb was fashion'd, to express
The ancient English minstrel's dress,
A seemly gown of Kendal green,
With gorget closed of silver sheen ;
His harp in silken scarf was slung,
And by his side an anlace hung.
It seem'd some masquer's quaint array
For revel or for holiday.

xvi.

He made obeisance with a free
Yet studied air of courtesy.

Each look and accent, framed to
    please,
Seem'd to affect a playful ease ;
His face was of that doubtful kind
That wins the eye, but not the mind ;
Yet harsh it seem'd to deem amiss
Of brow so young and smooth as
    this.
His was the subtle look and sly,
That, spying all, seems nought to
    spy ;
Round all the group his glances stole,
Unmark'd themselves, to mark the
    whole,
Yet sunk beneath Matilda's look,
Nor could the eye of Redmond brook.
To the suspicious, or the old,
Subtile and dangerous and bold
Had seem'd this self-invited guest ;
But young our lovers,—and the rest,
Wrapt in their sorrow and their fear
At parting of their mistress dear,
Tear-blinded to the Castle-hall
Came as to bear her funeral pall.

xvii.

All that expression base was gone
When waked the guest his minstrel
    tone ;
It fled at inspiration's call,
As erst the demon fled from Saul.
More noble glance he cast around,
More free-drawn breath inspired the
    sound,
His pulse beat bolder and more high,
In all the pride of minstrelsy !
Alas ! too soon that pride was o'er,
Sunk with the lay that bade it soar !
His soul resumed, with habit's chain,
Its vices wild and follies vain,
And gave the talent, with him born,
To be a common curse and scorn.
Such was the youth whom Rokeby's
    maid,
With condescending kindness, pray'd
Here to renew the strains she loved,
At distance heard and well approved.

XVIII.

SONG.

THE HARP.

I was a wild and wayward boy,
My childhood scorn'd each childish toy;
Retired from all, reserved and coy,
  To musing prone,
I woo'd my solitary joy,
  My Harp alone.

My youth, with bold Ambition's mood,
Despised the humble stream and wood
Where my poor father's cottage stood,
  To fame unknown;
What should my soaring views make
  good?
  My Harp alone!

Love came with all his frantic fire,
And wild romance of vain desire:
The baron's daughter heard my lyre,
  And praised the tone;—
What could presumptuous hope in-
  spire?
  My Harp alone!

At manhood's touch the bubble burst,
And manhood's pride the vision curst,
And all that had my folly nursed
  Love's sway to own;
Yet spared the spell that lull'd me first,
  My Harp alone!

Woe came with war, and want with
  woe;
And it was mine to undergo
Each outrage of the rebel foe:
  Can aught atone
My fields laid waste, my cot laid low?
  My Harp alone!

Ambition's dreams I've seen depart,
Have rued of penury the smart,
Have felt of love the venom'd dart
  When hope was flown;
Yet rests one solace to my heart,—
  My Harp alone!

Then over mountain, moor, and hill,
My faithful Harp, I'll bear thee still;
And when this life of want and ill
  Is well-nigh gone,
Thy strings mine elegy shall thrill,
  My Harp alone!

XIX.

'A pleasing lay!' Matilda said;
But Harpool shook his old grey
  head,
And took his baton and his torch
To seek his guard-room in the porch.
Edmund observed; with sudden
  change,
Among the strings his fingers range,
Until they waked a bolder glee
Of military melody;
Then paused amid the martial sound,
And look'd with well-feign'd fear
  around;
'None to this noble house belong,'
He said, 'that would a minstrel wrong
Whose fate has been, through good
  and ill,
To love his Royal Master still;
And with your honour'd leave, would
  fain
Rejoice you with a loyal strain.'
Then, as assured by sign and look,
The warlike tone again he took;
And Harpool stopp'd, and turn'd to
  hear
A ditty of the Cavalier.

XX.

SONG.

THE CAVALIER.

While the dawn on the mountain was
  misty and grey,
My true love has mounted his steed
  and away,
Over hill, over valley, o'er dale, and
  o'er down;
Heaven shield the brave Gallant that
  fights for the Crown!

He has doff'd the silk doublet the
  breastplate to bear,
He has placed the steel-cap o'er his
  long flowing hair,
From his belt to his stirrup his broadsword hangs down,—
Heaven shield the brave Gallant that
  fights for the Crown!

For the rights of fair England that
  broadsword he draws,
Her King is his leader, her Church is
  his cause;
His watchword is honour, his pay is
  renown,—
GOD strike with the Gallant that
  strikes for the Crown!

They may boast of their Fairfax, their
  Waller, and all
The roundheaded rebels of West-
  minster Hall;
But tell these bold traitors of London's
  proud town
That the spears of the North have
  encircled the Crown!

There's Derby and Cavendish, dread
  of their foes;
There's Erin's high Ormond, and
  Scotland's Montrose!
Would you match the base Skippon,
  and Massey, and Brown,
With the Barons of England that
  fight for the Crown?

Now joy to the crest of the brave
  Cavalier!
Be his banner unconquer'd, resistless
  his spear,
Till in peace and in triumph his toils
  he may drown
In a pledge to fair England, her
  Church, and her Crown!

XXI.

'Alas!' Matilda said, 'that strain,
Good harper, now is heard in vain!

The time has been, at such a sound,
When Rokeby's vassals gather'd
  round,
An hundred manly hearts would
  bound;
But now the stirring verse we hear,
Like trump in dying soldier's ear!
Listless and sad the notes we own,
The power to answer them is flown.
Yet not without his meet applause
Be he that sings the rightful cause,
Even when the crisis of its fate
To human eye seems desperate.
While Rokeby's heir such power
  retains
Let this slight guerdon pay thy
  pains:—
And lend thy harp; I fain would try
If my poor skill can aught supply,
Ere yet I leave my fathers' hall,
To mourn the cause in which we fall.'

XXII.

The harper, with a downcast look,
And trembling hand, her bounty took.
As yet, the conscious pride of art
Had steel'd him in his treacherous part;
A powerful spring, of force unguess'd,
That hath each gentler mood sup-
  press'd,
And reign'd in many a human breast;
From his that plans the red campaign,
To his that wastes the woodland reign.
The failing wing, the bloodshot eye,
The sportsman marks with apathy,
Each feeling of his victim's ill
Drown'd in his own successful skill.
The veteran, too, who now no more
Aspires to head the battle's roar,
Loves still the triumph of his art,
And traces on the pencill'd chart
Some stern invader's destined way,
Through blood and ruin, to his prey;
Patriots to death, and towns to flame,
He dooms, to raise another's name,
And shares the guilt, though not the
  fame.

What pays him for his span of time
Spent in premeditating crime?
What against pity arms his heart?—
It is the conscious pride of art.

XXIII.

But principles in Edmund's mind
Were baseless, vague, and undefined.
His soul, like bark with rudder lost,
On Passion's changeful tide was tost;
Nor Vice nor Virtue had the power
Beyond the impression of the hour;
And O! when Passion rules, how rare
The hours that fall to Virtue's share!
Yet now she roused her—for the pride,
That lack of sterner guilt supplied,
Could scarce support him when arose
The lay that mourned Matilda's woes.

SONG.

The Farewell.

'The sound of Rokeby's woods I hear,
  They mingle with the song:
Dark Greta's voice is in mine ear,
  I must not hear them long.
From every loved and native haunt
  The native heir must stray,
And, like a ghost whom sunbeams
    daunt,
  Must part before the day.

Soon from the halls my fathers rear'd,
  Their scutcheons may descend,
A line so long beloved and fear'd
  May soon obscurely end.
No longer here Matilda's tone
  Shall bid those echoes swell;
Yet shall they hear her proudly own
  The cause in which we fell.'

The Lady paused, and then again
Resumed the lay in loftier strain.

XXIV.

'Let our halls and towers decay,
  Be our name and line forgot,
Lands and manors pass away,—
  We but share our Monarch's lot.
If no more our annals show
  Battles won and banners taken,
Still in death, defeat, and woe,
  Ours be loyalty unshaken!
Constant still in danger's hour,
  Princes own'd our fathers' aid;
Lands and honours, wealth and power,
  Well their loyalty repaid.
Perish wealth, and power, and pride!
  Mortal boons by mortals given;
But let Constancy abide,—
  Constancy's the gift of Heaven.'

XXV.

While thus Matilda's lay was heard
A thousand thoughts in Edmund stirr'd.
In peasant life he might have known
As fair a face, as sweet a tone;
But village notes could ne'er supply
That rich and varied melody;
And ne'er in cottage-maid was seen
The easy dignity of mien,
Claiming respect, yet waiving state,
That marks the daughters of the great.
Yet not, perchance, had these alone
His scheme of purposed guilt o'er-
    thrown;
But while her energy of mind
Superior rose to griefs combined,
Lending its kindling to her eye,
Giving her form new majesty,—
To Edmund's thought Matilda seem'd
The very object he had dream'd;
When, long ere guilt his soul had
    known,
In Winston bowers he mused alone,
Taxing his fancy to combine
The face, the air, the voice divine,
Of princess fair, by cruel fate
Reft of her honours, power, and state,
Till to her rightful realm restored
By destined hero's conquering sword.

XXVI.

'Such was my vision! Edmund
    thought;
'And have I, then, the ruin wrought

Of such a maid, that fancy ne'er
In fairest vision form'd her peer?
Was it my hand that could unclose
The postern to her ruthless foes?
Foes, lost to honour, law, and faith,
Their kindest mercy sudden death!
Have I done this? I! who have swore,
That if the globe such angel bore,
I would have traced its circle broad
To kiss the ground on which she
    trod!—
And now—O! would that earth would
    rive,
And close upon me while alive!—
Is there no hope? Is all then lost?—
Bertram's already on his post!
Even now, beside the Hall's arch'd
    door,
I saw his shadow cross the floor!
He was to wait my signal strain—
A little respite thus we gain:
By what I heard the menials say,
Young Wycliffe's troop are on their
    way—
Alarm precipitates the crime!
My harp must wear away the time.'—
And then, in accents faint and low,
He falter'd forth a tale of woe.

XXVII.

BALLAD.

'And whither would you lead me,
    then?'
    Quoth the Friar of orders grey;
And the Ruffians twain replied again,
    'By a dying woman to pray.'

'I see,' he said, 'a lovely sight,
    A sight bodes little harm,
A lady bright as a lily bright,
    With an infant on her arm.'

'Then do thine office, Friar grey,
    And see thou shrive her free!
Else shall the sprite, that parts to-
    night,
    Fling all its guilt on thee.

'Let mass be said, and trentals read,
    When thou'rt to convent gone,
And bid the bell of St. Benedict
    Toll out its deepest tone.'

The shrift is done, the Friar is gone,
    Blindfolded as he came—
Next morning, all in Littlecot Hall
    Were weeping for their dame.

Wild Darrell is an alter'd man,
    The village crones can tell;
He looks pale as clay, and strives to
    pray,
    If he hears the convent bell.

If prince or peer cross Darrell's way,
    He'll beard him in his pride—
If he meet a Friar of orders grey,
    He droops and turns aside.

XXVIII.

'Harper! methinks thy magic lays,'
Matilda said, 'can goblins raise!
Well-nigh my fancy can discern,
Near the dark porch, a visage stern;
E'en now, in yonder shadowy nook,
I see it!—Redmond, Wilfrid, look!—
A human form distinct and clear—
God, for thy mercy!—It draws near!'
She saw too true. Stride after stride,
The centre of that chamber wide
Fierce Bertram gain'd; then made a
    stand,
And, proudly waving with his hand,
Thunder'd—'Be still, upon your
    lives!—
He bleeds who speaks, he dies who
    strives.'
Behind their chief, the robber crew
Forth from the darken'd portal drew
In silence—save that echo dread
Return'd their heavy measured tread.
The lamp's uncertain lustre gave
Their arms to gleam, their plumes to
    wave;
File after file in order pass,
Like forms on Banquo's mystic glass.

Then, halting at their leader's sign,
At once they form'd and curved their
line,
Hemming within its crescent drear
Their victims, like a herd of deer.
Another sign, and to the aim
Levell'd at once their muskets came,
As waiting but their chieftain's word
To make their fatal volley heard.

XXIX.

Back in a heap the menials drew;
Yet, even in mortal terror, true,
Their pale and startled group oppose
Between Matilda and the foes.
'O, haste thee, Wilfrid!' Redmond
cried;
'Undo that wicket by thy side!
Bear hence Matilda—gain the wood—
The pass may be a while made good—
Thy band, ere this, must sure be nigh—
O speak not—dally not—but fly!'
While yet the crowd their motions
hide,
Through the low wicket-door they
glide.
Through vaulted passages they wind,
In Gothic intricacy twined;
Wilfrid half led, and half he bore,
Matilda to the postern-door,
And safe beneath the forest tree
The Lady stands at liberty.
The moonbeams, the fresh gale's caress,
Renew'd suspended consciousness;—
'Where's Redmond?' eagerly she
cries:
'Thou answer'st not—he dies! he dies!
And thou hast left him, all bereft
Of mortal aid—with murderers left!
I know it well—he would not yield
His sword to man—his doom is seal'd!
For my scorn'd life, which thou hast
bought
At price of his, I thank thee not.'

XXX.

The unjust reproach, the angry look,
The heart of Wilfrid could not brook.

'Lady,' he said, ' my band so near,
In safety thou may'st rest thee here.
For Redmond s death thou shalt not
mourn,
If mine can buy his safe return.'
He turn'd away—his heart throbb'd
high,
The tear was bursting from his eye;
The sense of her injustice press'd
Upon the maid's distracted breast,—
'Stay, Wilfrid, stay! all aid is vain!'
He heard, but turn'd him not again;
He reaches now the postern-door,
Now enters—and is seen no more.

XXXI.

With all the agony that e'er
Was gender'd 'twixt suspense and fear,
She watch'd the line of windows tall,
Whose Gothic lattice lights the Hall,
Distinguish'd by the paly red
The lamps in dim reflection shed,
While all beside in wan moonlight
Each grated casement glimmer'd white,
No sight of harm, no sound of ill,
It is a deep and midnight still.
Who look'd upon the scene had guess'd
All in the Castle were at rest:
When sudden on the windows shone
A lightning flash, just seen and gone!
A shot is heard—Again the flame
Flash'd thick and fast—a volley came!
Then echo'd wildly, from within,
Of shout and scream the mingled din,
And weapon-clash and maddening cry,
Of those who kill, and those who die!—
As fill'd the Hall with sulphurous
smoke,
More red, more dark, the death-flash
broke;
And forms were on the lattice cast,
That struck, or struggled, as they past.

XXXII.

What sounds upon the midnight wind
Approach so rapidly behind?
It is, it is, the tramp of steeds!
Matilda hears the sound, she speeds,

Seizes upon the leader's rein—
'O, haste to aid, ere aid be vain !
Fly to the postern—gain the Hall !'
From saddle spring the troopers all ;
Their gallant steeds, at liberty,
Run wild along the moonlight lea.
But, ere they burst upon the scene,
Full stubborn had the conflict been.
When Bertram mark'd Matilda's flight
It gave the signal for the fight ;
And Rokeby's veterans, seam'd with
    scars
Of Scotland's and of Erin's wars,
Their momentary panic o'er,
Stood to the arms which then they bore ;
(For they were weapon'd, and prepared
Their mistress on her way to guard.)
Then cheer'd them to the fight O'Neale,
Then peal'd the shot, and clash'd the
    steel ;
The war-smoke soon with sable breath
Darken'd the scene of blood and death,
While on the few defenders close
The Bandits, with redoubled blows,
And, twice driven back, yet fierce
    and fell
Renew the charge with frantic yell.

XXXIII.

Wilfrid has fall'n—but o'er him stood
Young Redmond, soil'd with smoke
    and blood,
Cheering his mates with heart and hand
Still to make good their desperate
    stand.
'Up, comrades, up ! in Rokeby halls
Ne'er be it said our courage falls.
What ! faint ye for their savage cry,
Or do the smoke-wreaths daunt your
    eye ?
These rafters have return'd a shout
As loud at Rokeby's wassail rout,
As thick a smoke these hearths have
    given
At Hallow-tide or Christmas-even.
Stand to it yet ! renew the fight,
For Rokeby's and Matilda's right !

These slaves ! they dare not, hand to
    hand,
Bide buffet from a true man's brand.'
Impetuous, active, fierce, and young,
Upon the advancing foes he sprung.
Woe to the wretch at whom is bent
His brandish'd falchion's sheer descent!
Backward they scatter'd as he came,
Like wolves before the levin flame,
When, 'mid their howling conclave
    driven,
Hath glanced the thunderbolt of
    heaven.
Bertram rush'd on—but Harpool
    clasp'd
His knees, although in death he gasp'd,
His falling corpse before him flung,
And round the trammell'd ruffian clung.
Just then, the soldiers fill'd the dome,
And, shouting, charged the felons home
So fiercely, that, in panic dread,
They broke, they yielded, fell, or fled.
Bertram's stern voice they heed no
    more,
Though heard above the battle's roar ;
While, trampling down the dying man,
He strove, with volley'd threat and ban,
In scorn of odds, in fate's despite,
To rally up the desperate fight.

XXXIV.

Soon murkier clouds the Hall enfold
Than e'er from battle-thunders roll'd ;
So dense, the combatants scarce know
To aim or to avoid the blow.
Smothering and blindfold grows the
    fight—
But soon shall dawn a dismal light !
'Mid cries, and clashing arms, there
    came
The hollow sound of rushing flame ;
New horrors on the tumult dire
Arise—the Castle is on fire !
Doubtful, if chance had cast the brand,
Or frantic Bertram's desperate hand.
Matilda saw — for frequent broke
From the dim casements gusts of smoke

Yon tower, which late so clear defined
On the fair hemisphere reclined,
That, pencill'd on its azure pure,
The eye could count each embrazure,
Now, swath'd within the sweeping
    cloud,
Seems giant spectre in his shroud;
Till, from each loop-hole flashing light,
A spout of fire shines ruddy bright,
And, gathering to united glare,
Streams high into the midnight air;
A dismal beacon, far and wide,
That waken'd Greta's slumbering side.
Soon all beneath, through gallery long,
And pendant arch, the fire flash'd
    strong,
Snatching whatever could maintain,
Raise, or extend, its furious reign;
Startling, with closer cause of dread,
The females who the conflict fled,
And now rush'd forth upon the plain,
Filling the air with clamours vain.

XXXV.

But ceased not yet, the Hall within,
The shriek, the shout, the carnage-din,
Till bursting lattices give proof
The flames have caught the rafter'd roof.
What! wait they till its beams amain
Crash on the slayers and the slain?
The alarm is caught — the drawbridge
    falls,
The warriors hurry from the walls,
But, by the conflagration's light,
Upon the lawn renew the fight.
Each struggling felon down was hew'd,
Not one could gain the sheltering wood;
But forth the affrighted harper sprung,
And to Matilda's robe he clung.
Her shriek, entreaty, and command,
Stopp'd the pursuer's lifted hand.
Denzil and he alive were ta'en;
The rest, save Bertram, all are slain.

XXXVI.

And where is Bertram?—Soaring high,
The general flame ascends the sky;

In gather'd group the soldiers gaze
Upon the broad and roaring blaze,
When, like infernal demon, sent,
Red from his penal element,
To plague and to pollute the air,—
His face all gore, on fire his hair,
Forth from the central mass of smoke
The giant form of Bertram broke!
His brandish'd sword on high he rears,
Then plunged among opposing spears;
Round his left arm his mantle truss'd,
Received and foil'd three lances' thrust;
Nor these his headlong course with-
    stood,
Like reeds he snapp'd the tough ash-
    wood.
In vain his foes around him clung;
With matchless force aside he flung
Their boldest,—as the bull, at bay,
Tosses the ban-dogs from his way,
Through forty foes his path he made,
And safely gain'd the forest glade.

XXXVII.

Scarce was this final conflict o'er,
When from the postern Redmond bore
Wilfrid, who, as of life bereft,
Had in the fatal Hall been left,
Deserted there by all his train;
But Redmond saw, and turn'd again.—
Beneath an oak he laid him down,
That in the blaze gleam'd ruddy brown,
And then his mantle's clasp undid;
Matilda held his drooping head,
Till, given to breathe the freer air,
Returning life repaid their care.
He gazed on them with heavy sigh,—
'I could have wish'd even thus to
    die!'
No more he said—for now with speed
Each trooper had regain'd his steed;
The ready palfreys stood array'd
For Redmond and for Rokeby's maid;
Two Wilfrid on his horse sustain,
One leads his charger by the rein.
But oft Matilda look'd behind,
As up the Vale of Tees they wind,

Where far the mansion of her sires
Beacon'd the dale with midnight fires.
In gloomy arch above them spread,
The clouded heaven lower'd bloody
    red;
Beneath, in sombre light, the flood
Appear'd to roll in waves of blood.
Then, one by one, was heard to fall
The tower, the donjon-keep, the hall,
Each rushing down with thunder
    sound,
A space the conflagration drown'd;
Till, gathering strength, again it rose,
Announced its triumph in its close,
Shook wide its light the landscape o'er,
Then sunk—and Rokeby was no more!

—⁙—

Canto Sixth.

I.

THE summer sun, whose early power
Was wont to gild Matilda's bower,
And rouse her with his matin ray
Her duteous orisons to pay,—
That morning sun has three times seen
The flowers unfold on Rokeby green,
But sees no more the slumbers fly
From fair Matilda's hazel eye;
That morning sun has three times broke
On Rokeby's glades of elm and oak,
But, rising from their silvan screen,
Marks no grey turrets glance between.
A shapeless mass lie keep and tower,
That, hissing to the morning shower,
Can but with smouldering vapour pay
The early smile of summer day.
The peasant, to his labour bound,
Pauses to view the blacken'd mound,
Striving, amid the ruin'd space,
Each well-remember'd spot to trace.
That length of frail and fire-scorch'd
    wall
Once screen'd the hospitable hall;
When yonder broken arch was whole,
'Twas there was dealt the weekly dole;

And where yon tottering columns nod,
The chapel sent the hymn to God.—
So flits the world's uncertain span!
Nor zeal for God, nor love for man,
Gives mortal monuments a date
Beyond the power of Time and Fate.
The towers must share the builder's
    doom;
Ruin is theirs, and his a tomb:
But better boon benignant Heaven
To Faith and Charity has given,
And bids the Christian hope sublime
Transcend the bounds of Fate and
    Time.

II.

Now the third night of summer came,
Since that which witness'd Rokeby's
    flame.
On Brignal cliffs and Scargill brake
The owlet's homilies awake,
The bittern scream'd from rush and
    flag,
The raven slumber'd on his crag,
Forth from his den the otter drew,—
Grayling and trout their tyrant knew,
As between reed and sedge he peers,
With fierce round snout and sharpen'd
    ears,
Or, prowling by the moonbeam cool,
Watches the stream or swims the
    pool;—
Perch'd on his wonted eyrie high,
Sleep seal'd the tercelet's wearied
    eye,
That all the day had watch'd so well
The cushat dart across the dell.
In dubious beam reflected shone
That lofty cliff of pale grey stone,
Beside whose base the secret cave
To rapine late a refuge gave.
The crag's wild crest of copse and yew
On Greta's breast dark shadows threw:
Shadows that met or shunn'd the sight
With every change of fitful light;
As hope and fear alternate chase
Our course through life's uncertain
    race.

III.

Gliding by crag and copsewood green,
A solitary form was seen
To trace with stealthy pace the wold,
Like fox that seeks the midnight fold,
And pauses oft, and cowers dismay'd,
At every breath that stirs the shade.
He passes now the ivy bush,—
The owl has seen him, and is hush;
He passes now the dodder'd oak,—
Ye heard the startled raven croak;
Lower and lower he descends,
Rustle the leaves, the brushwood
          bends;
The otter hears him tread the shore,
And dives, and is beheld no more;
And by the cliff of pale grey stone
The midnight wanderer stands alone.
Methinks, that by the moon we trace
A well-remember'd form and face!
That stripling shape, that cheek so
          pale,
Combine to tell a rueful tale,
Of powers misused, of passion's force,
Of guilt, of grief, and of remorse!
'Tis Edmund's eye, at every sound
That flings that guilty glance around:
'Tis Edmund's trembling haste divides
The brushwood that the cavern hides;
And, when its narrow porch lies bare,
'Tis Edmund's form that enters there.

IV.

His flint and steel have sparkled bright,
A lamp hath lent the cavern light;
Fearful and quick his eye surveys
Each angle of the gloomy maze.
Since last he left that stern abode
It seem'd as none its floor had trode;
Untouch'd appear'd the various spoil,
The purchase of his comrades' toil;
Masks and disguises grim'd with mud,
Arms broken and defiled with blood,
And all the nameless tools that aid
Night-felons in their lawless trade,
Upon the gloomy walls were hung,
Or lay in nooks obscurely flung.

Still on the sordid board appear
The relics of the noontide cheer:
Flagons and emptied flasks were there,
And bench o'erthrown, and shatter'd
          chair;
And all around the semblance show'd,
As when the final revel glow'd,
When the red sun was setting fast,
And parting pledge Guy Denzil past.
'To Rokeby treasure-vaults!' they
          quaff'd,
And shouted loud and wildly laugh'd,
Pour'd maddening from the rocky door,
And parted—to return no more!
They found in Rokeby vaults their
          doom,—
A bloody death, a burning tomb!

V.

There his own peasant-dress he spies,
Doff'd to assume that quaint disguise;
And, shuddering, thought upon his
          glee,
When prank'd in garb of minstrelsy.
'O, be the fatal art accurst,'
He cried, 'that moved my folly first;
Till, bribed by bandits' base applause,
I burst through God's and Nature's
          laws!
Three summer days are scantly past
Since I have trod this cavern last,
A thoughtless wretch, and prompt to
          err—
But, O, as yet no murderer!
Even now I list my comrades' cheer,
That general laugh is in mine ear,
Which raised my pulse and steel'd my
          heart,
As I rehearsed my treacherous part—
And would that all since then could
          seem
The phantom of a fever's dream!
But fatal Memory notes too well
The horrors of the dying yell
From my despairing mates that broke,
When flash'd the fire and roll'd the
          smoke;

When the avengers shouting came,
And hemm'd us 'twixt the sword and
flame !
My frantic flight,—the lifted brand,—
That angel's interposing hand ! ---
If, for my life from slaughter freed,
I yet could pay some grateful meed !
Perchance this object of my quest
May aid'—he turn'd, nor spoke the
rest.

VI.

Due northward from the rugged hearth,
With paces five he metes the earth,
Then toil'd with mattock to explore
The entrails of the cavern floor,
Nor paused till, deep beneath the
ground,
His search a small steel casket found.
Just as he stoop'd to loose its hasp
His shoulder felt a giant grasp ;
He started, and look'd up aghast,
Then shriek'd !—'Twas Bertram held
him fast.
'Fear not !' he said ; but who could
hear
That deep stern voice, and cease to fear?
'Fear not !—By heaven, he shakes as
much
As partridge in the falcon's clutch !'—
He raised him, and unloosed his hold,
While from the opening casket roll'd
A chain and reliquaire of gold.
Bertram beheld it with surprise,
Gazed on its fashion and device,
Then, cheering Edmund as he could,
Somewhat he smooth'd his rugged
mood :
For still the youth's half-lifted eye
Quiver'd with terror's agony,
And sidelong glanced, as to explore,
In meditated flight, the door.
'Sit,' Bertram said, 'from danger free :
Thou canst not, and thou shalt not,
flee.
Chance brings me hither ; hill and plain
I 've sought for refuge-place in vain.

And tell me now, thou aguish boy,
What makest thou here ? what means
this toy ?
Denzil and thou, I mark'd, were ta'en ;
What lucky chance unbound your
chain ?
I deem'd, long since on Baliol's tower,
Your heads were warp'd with sun
and shower.
Tell me the whole—and, mark ! nought
e'er
Chafes me like falsehood, or like fear.'
Gathering his courage to his aid,
But trembling still, the youth obey'd.

VII.

'Denzil and I two nights pass'd o'er
In fetters on the dungeon floor.
A guest the third sad morrow brought ;
Our hold dark Oswald Wycliffe sought,
And eyed my comrade long askance,
With fix'd and penetrating glance.
" Guy Denzil art thou call'd ?"—"The
same."—
" At Court who served wild Bucking-
hame ;
Thence banish'd, won a keeper's place,
So Villiers will'd, in Marwood-chase ;
That lost—I need not tell thee why—
Thou madest thy wit thy wants supply,
Then fought for Rokeby :—Have I
guess'd
My prisoner right?"—"At thy be-
hest."—
He paused a while, and then went on
With low and confidential tone ;—
Me, as I judge, not then he saw,
Close nestled in my couch of straw.—
" List to me, Guy. Thou know'st the
great
Have frequent need of what they
hate ;
Hence, in their favour oft we see
Unscruped, useful men like thee.
Were I disposed to bid thee live
What pledge of faith hast thou to
give ?"

VIII.

'The ready Fiend, who never yet
Hath failed to sharpen Denzil's wit,
Prompted his lie—" His only child
Should rest his pledge."—The Baron
    smiled,
And turn'd to me—"Thou art his son?"
I bowed—our fetters were undone,
And we were led to hear apart
A dreadful lesson of his art.
Wilfrid, he said, his heir and son,
Had fair Matilda's favour won;
And long since had their union been
But for her father's bigot spleen,
Whose brute and blindfold party rage
Would, force per force, her hand
    engage
To a base kern of Irish earth,
Unknown his lineage and his birth,
Save that a dying ruffian bore
The infant brat to Rokeby door.
Gentle restraint, he said, would lead
Old Rokeby to enlarge his creed;
But fair occasion he must find
For such restraint well-meant and kind,
The Knight being render'd to his charge
But as a prisoner at large.

IX.

'He school'd us in a well-forged tale,
Of scheme the Castle walls to scale,
To which was leagued each Cavalier
That dwells upon the Tyne and Wear;
That Rokeby, his parole forgot,
Had dealt with us to aid the plot.
Such was the charge, which Denzil's
    zeal
Of hate to Rokeby and O'Neale
Proffer'd, as witness, to make good,
Even though the forfeit were their
    blood.
I scrupled, until o'er and o'er
His prisoners' safety Wycliffe swore;
And then—alas! what needs there
    more?
I knew I should not live to say
The proffer I refused that day;

Ashamed to live, yet loth to die,
I soil'd me with their infamy!'—
'Poor youth,' said Bertram, 'wavering
    still,
Unfit alike for good or ill!
But what fell next?'—'Soon as at large
Was scroll'd and sign'd our fatal charge,
There never yet, on tragic stage,
Was seen so well a painted rage
As Oswald's show'd! With loud alarm
He call'd his garrison to arm;
From tower to tower, from post to post,
He hurried as if all were lost;
Consign'd to dungeon and to chain
The good old Knight and all his train;
Warn'd each suspected Cavalier,
Within his limits, to appear
To-morrow, at the hour of noon,
In the high church of Egliston.'

X.

'Of Egliston!—Even now I pass'd,'
Said Bertram, 'as the night closed fast;
Torches and cressets gleam'd around,
I heard the saw and hammer sound,
And I could mark they toil'd to raise
A scaffold, hung with sable baize,
Which the grim headsman's scene
    display'd,
Block, axe, and sawdust ready laid.
Some evil deed will there be done,
Unless Matilda wed his son;—
She loves him not—'tis shrewdly
    guess'd
That Redmond rules the damsel's
    breast.
This is a turn of Oswald's skill;
But I may meet, and foil him still!
How camest thou to thy freedom?'—
    'There
Lies mystery more dark and rare.
In midst of Wycliffe's well-feign'd rage,
A scroll was offer'd by a page,
Who told, a muffled horseman late
Had left it at the Castle-gate.
He broke the seal—his cheek show'd
    change,
Sudden, portentous, wild, and strange;

The mimic passion of his eye
Was turn'd to actual agony;
His hand like summer sapling shook,
Terror and guilt were in his look.
Denzil he judged, in time of need,
Fit counsellor for evil deed;
And thus apart his counsel broke,
While with a ghastly smile he spoke:—

XI.

'"As in the pageants of the stage,
The dead awake in this wild age.
Mortham—whom all men deem'd decreed
In his own deadly snare to bleed,
Slain by a bravo, whom, o'er sea,
He train'd to aid in murdering me,—
Mortham has 'scaped! The coward shot
The steed, but harm'd the rider not."'
Here, with an execration fell,
Bertram leap'd up, and paced the cell:—
'Thine own grey head, or bosom dark,'
He mutter'd, ' may be surer mark!'
Then sat, and sign'd to Edmund, pale
With terror, to resume his tale.
'Wycliffe went on:—"Mark with what flights
Of wilder'd reverie he writes:—

THE LETTER.

'"Ruler of Mortham's destiny!
Though dead, thy victim lives to thee.
Once had he all that binds to life,
A lovely child, a lovelier wife;
Wealth, fame, and friendship, were his own—
Thou gavest the word, and they are flown.
Mark how he pays thee:—To thy hand
He yields his honours and his land,
One boon premised;—Restore his child!
And, from his native land exiled,
Mortham no more returns to claim
His lands, his honours, or his name;
Refuse him this, and from the slain
Thou shalt see Mortham rise again."

XII.

'This billet while the Baron read,
His faltering accents show'd his dread;
He press'd his forehead with his palm,
Then took a scornful tone and calm;
"Wild as the winds, as billows wild!
What wot I of his spouse or child?
Hither he brought a joyous dame,
Unknown her lineage or her name:
Her, in some frantic fit, he slew;
The nurse and child in fear withdrew.
Heaven be my witness! wist I where
To find this youth, my kinsman's heir,—
Unguerdon'd, I would give with joy
The father's arms to fold his boy,
And Mortham's lands and towers resign
To the just heirs of Mortham's line."
Thou know'st that scarcely e'en his fear
Suppresses Denzil's cynic sneer;—
"Then happy is thy vassal's part,"
He said, "to ease his patron's heart!
In thine own jailer's watchful care
Lies Mortham's just and rightful heir;
Thy generous wish is fully won,—
Redmond O'Neale is Mortham's son."

XIII.

' Up starting with a frenzied look,
His clenched hand the Baron shook:
"Is Hell at work? or dost thou rave,
Or darest thou palter with me, slave!
Perchance thou wot'st not, Barnard's towers
Have racks, of strange and ghastly powers."
Denzil, who well his safety knew,
Firmly rejoin'd, " I tell thee true.
Thy racks could give thee but to know
The proofs, which I, untortured, show.
It chanced upon a winter night,
When early snow made Stanmore white,

That very night, when first of all
Redmond O'Neale saw Rokeby-hall,
It was my goodly lot to gain
A reliquary and a chain,
Twisted and chased of massive gold.
—Demand not how the prize I hold!
It was not given, nor lent, nor sold.
Gilt tablets to the chain were hung,
With letters in the Irish tongue.
I hid my spoil, for there was need
That I should leave the land with
    speed;
Nor then I deem'd it safe to bear
On mine own person gems so rare.
Small heed I of the tablets took,
But since have spell'd them by the
    book,
When some sojourn in Erin's land
Of their wild speech had given com-
    mand.
But darkling was the sense; the phrase
And language those of other days,
Involved of purpose, as to foil
An interloper's prying toil.
The words, but not the sense, I knew,
Till fortune gave the guiding clew.

XIV.

' " Three days since was that clew
    reveal'd,
In Thorsgill as I lay conceal'd,
And heard at full when Rokeby's maid
Her uncle's history display'd;
And now I can interpret well
Each syllable the tablets tell.
Mark, then: Fair Edith was the joy
Of old O'Neale of Clandeboy;
But from her sire and country fled,
In secret Mortham's Lord to wed.
O'Neale, his first resentment o'er,
Despatch'd his son to Greta's shore,
Enjoining he should make him known
(Until his farther will were shown)
To Edith, but to her alone.
What of their ill-starr'd meeting fell
Lord Wycliffe knows, and none so
    well.

XV.

' " O Neale it was, who, in despair,
Robb'd Mortham of his infant heir;
He bred him in their nurture wild,
And call'd him murder'd Connel's
    child.
Soon died the nurse; the clan believed
What from their Chieftain they re-
    ceived.
His purpose was, that ne'er again
The boy should cross the Irish main;
But, like his mountain sires, enjoy
The woods and wastes of Clandeboy.
Then on the land wild troubles came,
And stronger chieftains urged a claim,
And wrested from the old man's hands
His native towers, his father's lands.
Unable then, amid the strife,
To guard young Redmond's rights or
    life,
Late and reluctant he restores
The infant to his native shores,
With goodly gifts and letters stored,
With many a deep conjuring word,
To Mortham and to Rokeby's Lord.
Nought knew the clod of Irish earth,
Who was the guide, of Redmond's
    birth;
But deem'd his Chief's commands were
    laid
On both, by both to be obey'd.
How he was wounded by the way,
I need not, and I list not say."

XVI.

' " A wondrous tale! and, grant it true,
What," Wycliffe answer'd, "might I
    do?
Heaven knows, as willingly as now
I raise the bonnet from my brow,
Would I my kinsman's manors fair
Restore to Mortham, or his heir;
But Mortham is distraught—O'Neale
Has drawn for tyranny his steel,
Malignant to our rightful cause,
And train'd in Rome's delusive laws.

Hark thee apart ! "—They whisper'd
    long,
Till Denzil's voice grew bold and
    strong :
" My proofs ! I never will," he said,
" Show mortal man where they are laid.
Nor hope discovery to foreclose,
By giving me to feed the crows ;
For I have mates at large, who know
Where I am wont such toys to stow.
Free me from peril and from band,
These tablets are at thy command ;
Nor were it hard to form some train,
To wile old Mortham o'er the main.
Then, lunatic's nor papist's hand
Should wrest from thine the goodly
    land."
—"I like thy wit," said Wycliffe, "well ;
But here in hostage shalt thou dwell.
Thy son, unless my purpose err,
May prove the trustier messenger.
A scroll to Mortham shall he bear
From me, and fetch these tokens rare.
Gold shalt thou have, and that good
    store,
And freedom, his commission o'er ;
But if his faith should chance to fail,
The gibbet frees thee from the jail."

XVII.

' Mesh'd in the net himself had twined,
What subterfuge could Denzil find ?
He told me, with reluctant sigh,
That hidden here the tokens lie ;
Conjured my swift return and aid
By all he scoff'd and disobey'd,
And look'd as if the noose were tied,
And I the priest who left his side.
This scroll for Mortham Wycliffe gave,
Whom I must seek by Greta's wave ;
Or in the hut where chief he hides,
Where Thorsgill's forester resides.
(Thence chanced it, wandering in the
    glade,
That he descried our ambuscade.)
I was dismiss'd as evening fell,
And reach'd but now this rocky cell.'—

' Give Oswald's letter.'—Bertram read,
And tore it fiercely, shred by shred :—
' All lies and villany ! to blind
His noble kinsman's generous mind,
And train him on from day to day,
Till he can take his life away.
And now, declare thy purpose, youth,
Nor dare to answer, save the truth ;
If aught I mark of Denzil's art,
I'll tear the secret from thy heart !'

XVIII.

' It needs not. I renounce,' he said,
' My tutor and his deadly trade.
Fix'd was my purpose to declare
To Mortham, Redmond is his heir ;
To tell him in what risk he stands,
And yield these tokens to his hands.
Fix'd was my purpose to atone,
Far as I may, the evil done ;
And fix'd it rests—if I survive
This night, and leave this cave alive.'—
' And Denzil ?'—' Let them ply the
    rack,
Even till his joints and sinews crack !
If Oswald tear him limb from limb,
What ruth can Denzil claim from him,
Whose thoughtless youth he led astray,
And damn'd to this unhallow'd way ?
He school'd me, faith and vows were
    vain ;
Now let my master reap his gain.'
' True,' answer'd Bertram, ' 'tis his
    meed ;
There's retribution in the deed.
But thou—thou art not for our course,
Hast fear, hast pity, hast remorse ;
And he, with us the gale who braves,
Must heave such cargo to the waves,
Or lag with overloaded prore,
While barks unburden'd reach the
    shore.'

XIX.

He paused, and, stretching him at
    length,
Seem'd to repose his bulky strength.

Communing with his secret mind,
As half he sat, and half reclined,
One ample hand his forehead press'd,
And one was dropp'd across his breast.
The shaggy eyebrows deeper came
Above his eyes of swarthy flame ;
His lip of pride awhile forbore
The haughty curve till then it wore ;
The unalter'd fierceness of his look
A shade of darken'd sadness took,—
For dark and sad a presage press'd
Resistlessly on Bertram's breast, —
And when he spoke, his wonted tone,
So fierce, abrupt, and brief, was gone.
His voice was steady, low, and deep,
Like distant waves when breezes sleep ;
And sorrow mix'd with Edmund's fear,
Its low unbroken depth to hear.

XX.

'Edmund, in thy sad tale I find
The woe that warp'd my patron's mind:
'Twould wake the fountains of the
    eye
In other men, but mine are dry.
Mortham must never see the fool
That sold himself base Wycliffe's tool ;
Yet less from thirst of sordid gain,
Than to avenge supposed disdain.
Say, Bertram rues his fault ;— a word,
Till now, from Bertram never heard :
Say, too, that Mortham's Lord he
    prays
To think but on their former days ;
On Quariana's beach and rock,
On Cayo's bursting battle-shock,
On Darien's sands and deadly dew,
And on the dart Tlatzeca threw ;—
Perchance my patron yet may hear
More that may grace his comrade's
    bier.
My soul hath felt a secret weight,
A warning of approaching fate :
A priest had said, " Return, repent ! "
As well to bid that rock be rent.
Firm as that flint I face mine end ;
My heart may burst, but cannot bend.

XXI.

The dawning of my youth, with awe,
And prophecy, the Dalesmen saw ;
For over Redesdale it came,
As bodeful as their beacon-flame.
Edmund, thy years were scarcely mine,
When, challenging the clans of Tyne
To bring their best my brand to prove,
O'er Hexham's altar hung my glove ;
But Tynedale, nor in tower nor town,
Held champion meet to take it down.
My noontide, India may declare ;
Like her fierce sun, I fired the air !
Like him, to wood and cave bade fly
Her natives, from mine angry eye.
Panama's maids shall long look pale
When Risingham inspires the tale ;
Chili's dark matrons long shall tame
The froward child with Bertram's name.
And now, my race of terror run,
Mine be the eve of tropic sun !
No pale gradations quench his ray,
No twilight dews his wrath allay ;
With disk like battle-target red,
He rushes to his burning bed,
Dyes the wide wave with bloody light,
Then sinks at once—and all is night.

XXII.

' Now to thy mission, Edmund. Fly,
Seek Mortham out, and bid him hie
To Richmond, where his troops are
    laid,
And lead his force to Redmond's aid.
Say, till he reaches Egliston,
A friend will watch to guard his son.
Now, fare-thee-well ; for night draws
    on,
And I would rest me here alone.'
Despite his ill-dissembled fear,
There swam in Edmund's eye a tear ;
A tribute to the courage high
Which stoop'd not in extremity,
But strove, irregularly great,
To triumph o'er approaching fate !
Bertram beheld the dewdrop start,
It almost touch'd his iron heart :—

'I did not think there lived,' he said,
'One who would tear for Bertram
  shed.'
He loosen'd then his baldric's hold,
A buckle broad of massive gold ;—
'Of all the spoil that paid his pains,
But this with Risingham remains ;
And this, dear Edmund, thou shalt take,
And wear it long for Bertram's sake.
Once more—to Mortham speed amain;
Farewell ! and turn thee not again.'

XXIII.

The night has yielded to the morn,
And far the hours of prime are worn.
Oswald, who, since the dawn of day,
Had cursed his messenger's delay,
Impatient question'd now his crew,
'Was Denzil's son return'd again ?'
It chanced there answer'd of the crew,
A menial, who young Edmund knew:
'No son of Denzil this,' he said ;
'A peasant boy from Winston glade,
For song and minstrelsy renown'd,
And knavish pranks, the hamlets round.'
'Not Denzil's son !—From Winston
  vale !—
Then it was false, that specious tale ;
Or, worse, he hath despatch'd the youth
To show to Mortham's Lord its truth.
Fool that I was !— but 'tis too late ;—
This is the very turn of fate !—
The tale, or true or false, relies
On Denzil's evidence !—He dies !—
Ho ! Provost Marshall ! instantly
Lead Denzil to the gallows-tree !
Allow him not a parting word ;
Short be the shrift, and sure the cord !
Then let his gory head appal
Marauders from the Castle-wall.
Lead forth thy guard, that duty done,
With best despatch to Egliston.
—Basil, tell Wilfrid he must straight
Attend me at the Castle-gate.'

XXIV.

'Alas !' the old domestic said,
And shook his venerable head,
'Alas, my Lord ! full ill to-day
May my young master brook the way !
The leech has spoke with grave alarm
Of unseen hurt, of secret harm,
Of sorrow lurking at the heart,
That mars and lets his healing art.'—
'Tush, tell not me !—Romantic boys
Pine themselves sick for airy toys.
I will find cure for Wilfrid soon ;
Bid him for Egliston be boune,
And quick !—I hear the dull death-drum
Tell Denzil's hour of fate is come.'
He paused with scornful smile, and then
Resumed his train of thought agen.
'Now comes my fortune's crisis near !
Entreaty boots not—instant fear,
Nought else, can bend Matilda's pride,
Or win her to be Wilfrid's bride.
But when she sees the scaffold placed,
With axe and block and headsman
  graced,
And when she deems, that to deny
Dooms Redmond and her sire to die,
She must give way.   Then, were the
  line
Of Rokeby once combined with mine,
I gain the weather-gage of fate !
If Mortham come, he comes too late,
While I, allied thus and prepared,
Bid him defiance to his beard.
If she prove stubborn, shall I dare
To drop the axe?—soft ! pause we there.
Mortham still lives—yon youth may tell
His tale—and Fairfax loves him well ;—
Else, wherefore should I now delay
To sweep this Redmond from my
  way ?
But she to piety perforce
Must yield.—Without there ! sound
  to horse.'

XXV.

'Twas bustle in the court below :
'Mount, and march forward !'—Forth
  they go ;
Steeds neigh and trample all around,
Steel rings, spears glimmer, trumpets
  sound.

Just then was sung his parting hymn ;
And Denzil turn'd his eyeballs dim,
And, scarcely conscious what he sees,
Follows the horsemen down the Tees;
And scarcely conscious what he hears,
The trumpets tingle in his ears.
O'er the long bridge they 're sweeping now,
The van is hid by greenwood bough ;
But ere the rearward had pass'd o'er,
Guy Denzil heard and saw no more !
One stroke, upon the Castle bell,
To Oswald rung his dying knell.

XXVI.

Oh for that pencil, erst profuse
Of chivalry's emblazon'd hues,
That traced of old, in Woodstock bower,
The pageant of the Leaf and Flower,
And bodied forth the tourney high
Held for the hand of Emily !
Then might I paint the tumult broad
That to the crowded abbey flow'd,
And pour'd, as with an ocean's sound,
Into the church's ample bound !
Then might I show each varying mien,
Exulting, woful, or serene ;
Indifference, with his idiot stare,
And Sympathy, with anxious air ;
Paint the dejected Cavalier,
Doubtful, disarm'd, and sad of cheer ;
And his proud foe, whose formal eye
Claim'd conquest now and mastery ;
And the brute crowd, whose envious zeal
Huzzas each turn of Fortune's wheel,
And loudest shouts when lowest lie
Exalted worth and station high.
Yet what may such a wish avail ?
'Tis mine to tell an onward tale,
Hurrying, as best I can, along,
The hearers and the hasty song ;—
Like traveller when approaching home,
Who sees the shades of evening come,
And must not now his course delay,
Or choose the fair but winding way ;

Nay, scarcely may his pace suspend,
Where o'er his head the wildings bend,
To bless the breeze that cools his brow,
Or snatch a blossom from the bough.

XXVII.

The reverend pile lay wild and waste,
Profaned, dishonour'd, and defaced.
Through storied lattices no more
In soften'd light the sunbeams pour,
Gilding the Gothic sculpture rich
Of shrine, and monument, and niche.
The Civil fury of the time
Made sport of sacrilegious crime ;
For dark Fanaticism rent
Altar, and screen, and ornament,
And peasant hands the tombs o'erthrew
Of Bowes, of Rokeby, and Fitz-Hugh.
And now was seen, unwonted sight,
In holy walls a scaffold dight !
Where once the priest, of grace divine
Dealt to his flock the mystic sign ;
There stood the block display'd, and there
The headsman grim his hatchet bare ,
And for the word of Hope and Faith,
Resounded loud a doom of death.
Thrice the fierce trumpet's breath was heard,
And echo'd thrice the herald's word,
Dooming, for breach of martial laws,
And treason to the Commons' cause,
The Knight of Rokeby and O'Neale
To stoop their heads to block and steel.
The trumpets flourish'd high and shrill,
Then was a silence dead and still ;
And silent prayers to heaven were cast,
And stifled sobs were bursting fast,
Till from the crowd begun to rise
Murmurs of sorrow or surprise,
And from the distant aisles there came
Deep-mutter'd threats, with Wycliffe's name.

XXVIII.

But Oswald, guarded by his band,
Powerful in evil, waved his hand,
And bade Sedition's voice be dead,
On peril of the murmurer's head.

N

Then first his glance sought Rokeby's
     Knight;
Who gazed on the tremendous sight
As calm as if he came a guest
To kindred Baron's feudal feast,
As calm as if that trumpet-call
Were summons to the banner'd hall;
Firm in his loyalty he stood,
And prompt to seal it with his blood.
With downcast look drew Oswald
     nigh,—
He durst not cope with Rokeby's
     eye!—
And said, with low and faltering breath,
'Thou know'st the terms of life and
     death.'
The Knight then turn'd, and sternly
     smiled:
'The maiden is mine only child,
Yet shall my blessing leave her head,
If with a traitor's son she wed.'
Then Redmond spoke: 'The life of one
Might thy malignity atone,
On me be flung a double guilt!
Spare Rokeby's blood, let mine be
     spilt!'
Wycliffe had listen'd to his suit,
But dread prevail'd, and he was mute.

XXIX.

And now he pours his choice of fear
In secret on Matilda's ear;
'An union form'd with me and mine
Ensures the faith of Rokeby's line.
Consent, and all this dread array,
Like morning dream, shall pass away;
Refuse, and, by my duty press'd,
I give the word—thou know'st the
     rest.'
Matilda, still and motionless,
With terror heard the dread address,
Pale as the sheeted maid who dies
To hopeless love a sacrifice;
Then wrung her hands in agony,
And round her cast bewilder'd eye,
Now on the scaffold glanced, and now
On Wycliffe's unrelenting brow.

She veil'd her face, and, with a voice
Scarce audible,—'I make my choice!
Spare but their lives!—for aught beside,
Let Wilfrid's doom my fate decide.
He once was generous!'—As she
     spoke,
Dark Wycliffe's joy in triumph broke:—
'Wilfrid, where loiter'd ye so late?
Why upon Basil rest thy weight?
Art spell-bound by enchanter's
     wand?—
Kneel, kneel, and take her yielded
     hand;
Thank her with raptures, simple boy!
Should tears and trembling speak thy
     joy?'—
'O hush, my sire! To prayer and tear
Of mine thou hast refused thine ear;
But now the awful hour draws on
When truth must speak in loftier tone.'

XXX.

He took Matilda's hand:—'Dear maid,
Couldst thou so injure me,' he said,
'Of thy poor friend so basely deem,
As blend with him this barbarous
     scheme?
Alas! my efforts, made in vain,
Might well have saved this added pain.
But now, bear witness earth and
     heaven,
That ne'er was hope to mortal given,
So twisted with the strings of life,
As this—to call Matilda wife!
I bid it now for ever part,
And with the effort bursts my heart!'
His feeble frame was worn so low
With wounds, with watching, and with
     woe,
That nature could no more sustain
The agony of mental pain.
He kneel'd—his lip her hand had
     press'd,—
Just then he felt the stern arrest;
Lower and lower sunk his head,—
They raised him,—but the life was
     fled!

Then, first alarm'd, his sire and train
Tried every aid, but tried in vain.
The soul, too soft its ills to bear,
Had left our mortal hemisphere,
And sought in better world the meed
To blameless life by Heaven decreed.

XXXI.

The wretched sire beheld, aghast,
With Wilfrid all his projects past.
All turn'd and centred on his son,
On Wilfrid all—and he was gone.
'And I am childless now,' he said;
'Childless, through that relentless
        maid!
A lifetime's arts, in vain essay'd,
Are bursting on their artist's head!
Here lies my Wilfrid dead—and there
Comes hated Mortham for his heir,
Eager to knit in happy band
With Rokeby's heiress Redmond's
        hand.
And shall their triumph soar o'er all
The schemes deep-laid to work their
        fall?
No!—deeds, which prudence might
        not dare,
Appal not vengeance and despair.
The murd'ress weeps upon his bier—
I'll change to real that feigned tear!
They all shall share destruction's
        shock;—
Ho! lead the captives to the block!'
But ill his Provost could divine
His feelings, and forbore the sign.
'Slave! to the block!—or I, or they,
Shall face the judgment-seat this day!'

XXXII.

The outmost crowd have heard a sound
Like horse's hoof on harden'd ground;
Nearer it came, and yet more near,—
The very death's-men paused to hear.
'Tis in the churchyard now—the tread
Hath waked the dwelling of the dead!
Fresh sod, and old sepulchral stone,
Return the tramp in varied tone.

All eyes upon the gateway hung,
When through the Gothic arch there
        sprung
A horseman arm'd, at headlong speed—
Sable his cloak, his plume, his steed.
Fire from the flinty floor was spurn'd,
The vaults unwonted clang return'd!—
One instant's glance around he threw,
From saddlebow his pistol drew.
Grimly determined was his look!
His charger with the spurs he strook—
All scatter'd backward as he came,
For all knew Bertram Risingham!
Three bounds that noble courser gave;
The first has reach'd the central nave,
The second clear'd the chancel wide,
The third—he was at Wycliffe's side.
Full levell'd at the Baron's head,
Rung the report—the bullet sped—
And to his long account, and last,
Without a groan dark Oswald past!
All was so quick, that it might seem
A flash of lightning, or a dream.

XXXIII.

While yet the smoke the deed conceals,
Bertram his ready charger wheels;
But flounder'd on the pavement-floor
The steed, and down the rider bore,
And, bursting in the headlong sway,
The faithless saddle-girths gave way.
'Twas while he toil'd him to be freed,
And with the rein to raise the steed,
That from amazement's iron trance
All Wycliffe's soldiers waked at once.
Sword, halberd, musket-but, their
        blows
Hail'd upon Bertram as he rose;
A score of pikes, with each a wound,
Bore down and pinn'd him to the
        ground;
But still his struggling force he rears,
'Gainst hacking brands and stabbing
        spears;
Thrice from assailants shook him free,
Once gain'd his feet, and twice his
        knee.

By tenfold odds oppress'd at length,
Despite his struggles and his strength,
He took a hundred mortal wounds
As mute as fox 'mongst mangling
    hounds;
And when he died, his parting groan
Had more of laughter than of moan!
—They gazed, as when a lion dies,
And hunters scarcely trust their eyes,
But bend their weapons on the slain
Lest the grim king should rouse again!
Then blow and insult some renew'd,
And from the trunk the head had
    hew'd,
But Basil's voice the deed forbade;
A mantle o'er the corse he laid:—
'Fell as he was in act and mind,
He left no bolder heart behind;
Then give him, for a soldier meet,
A soldier's cloak for winding-sheet.'

XXXIV.

No more of death and dying pang,
No more of trump and bugle clang,
Though through the sounding woods
    there come
Banner and bugle, trump and drum.
Arm'd with such powers as well had
    freed
Young Redmond at his utmost need,
And back'd with such a band of horse
As might less ample powers enforce;
Possess'd of every proof and sign
That gave an heir to Mortham's line,
And yielded to a father's arms
An image of his Edith's charms,—
Mortham is come, to hear and see
Of this strange morn the history.

What saw he?—not the church's floor
Cumber'd with dead and stain'd with
    gore;
What heard he?—not the clamorous
    crowd,
That shout their gratulations loud:
Redmond he saw and heard alone,
Clasp'd him, and sobb'd, 'My son! my
    son!'—

XXXV.

This chanced upon a summer morn,
When yellow waved the heavy corn;
But when brown August o'er the land
Call'd forth the reapers' busy band,
A gladsome sight the silvan road
From Egliston to Mortham show'd.
Awhile the hardy rustic leaves
The task to bind and pile the sheaves,
And maids their sickles fling aside
To gaze on bridegroom and on bride,
And childhood's wondering group
    draws near,
And from the gleaner's hands the ear
Drops, while she folds them for a prayer
And blessing on the lovely pair.
'Twas then the Maid of Rokeby gave
Her plighted troth to Redmond brave;
And Teesdale can remember yet
How Fate to Virtue paid her debt,
And, for their troubles, bade them prove
A lengthen'd life of peace and love.

Time and Tide had thus their sway,
Yielding, like an April day,
Smiling noon for sullen morrow,
Years of joy for hours of sorrow!

END OF ROKEBY.

Introduction and Notes to Rokeby.

—◦◦—

INTRODUCTION TO THE EDITION OF 1830.

BETWEEN the publication of 'The Lady of the Lake,' which was so eminently successful, and that of 'Rokeby,' in 1813, three years had intervened. I shall not, I believe, be accused of ever having attempted to usurp a superiority over many men of genius, my contemporaries; but, in point of popularity, not of actual talent, the caprice of the public had certainly given me such a temporary superiority over men, of whom, in regard to poetical fancy and feeling, I scarcely thought myself worthy to loose the shoe-latchet. On the other hand, it would be absurd affectation in me to deny that I conceived myself to understand, more perfectly than many of my contemporaries, the manner most likely to interest the great mass of mankind. Yet, even with this belief, I must truly and fairly say that I always considered myself rather as one who held the bets, in time to be paid over to the winner, than as having any pretence to keep them in my own right.

In the meantime years crept on, and not without their usual depredations on the passing generation. My sons had arrived at the age when the paternal home was no longer their best abode, as both were destined to active life. The field-sports, to which I was peculiarly attached, had now less interest, and were replaced by other amusements of a more quiet character; and the means and opportunity of pursuing these were to be sought for. I had, indeed, for some years attended to farming, a knowledge of which is, or at least was then, indispensable to the comfort of a family residing in a solitary country house; but although this was the favourite amusement of many of my friends, I have never been able to consider it as a source of pleasure. I never could think it a matter of passing importance that my cattle or crops were better or more plentiful than those of my neighbours, and nevertheless I began to feel the necessity of some more quiet out-door occupation, different from those I had hitherto pursued.

I purchased a small farm of about one hundred acres, with the purpose of planting and improving it, to which property circumstances afterwards enabled me to make considerable additions; and thus an era took place in my life, almost equal to the important one mentioned by the Vicar of Wakefield when he removed from the blue room to the brown. In point of neighbourhood, at least, the change of residence made little *more* difference. Abbotsford, to which we removed, was only six or seven miles down the Tweed, and lay on the same beautiful stream. It did not possess the romantic character of Ashestiel, my former residence; but it had a stretch of meadow-land along the river, and possessed, in the phrase of the landscape-gardener, considerable capabilities. Above all, the land was my own, like Uncle Toby's bowling-green, to do what I would with. It had been, though the gratification was long postponed, an early wish of mine to connect myself with my mother earth, and prosecute those experiments by which a species of creative power is exercised over the face of nature. I can trace, even to childhood, a pleasure derived from Dodsley's account of Shenstone's Leasowes, and I envied the poet much more for the pleasure of accomplishing the objects detailed in his friend's sketch of his grounds, than for the possession of pipe, crook, flock, and Phillis to boot. My memory, also, tenacious of quaint expressions, still retained a phrase which it had gathered from an old almanack of Charles the Second's time (when everything down to almanacks affected to be smart), in which the reader, in the month of June, is advised for health's sake to walk a mile or two every day before breakfast, and, if he can possibly so manage, to let his exercise be taken upon his own land.

With the satisfaction of having attained the fulfilment of an early and long-cherished hope, I commenced my improvements, as delightful in their progress as those of the child who first makes a dress for a new doll. The nakedness of the land was in time hidden by woodlands of considerable extent; the smallest of possible cottages was progressively expanded into a sort of dream of a mansion house, whimsical in the exterior, but convenient within. Nor did I forget what is the natural pleasure of every man who has been a reader; I mean the filling the shelves of a tolerably large library. All these objects I kept in view, to be executed as convenience should serve; and, although I knew many years must elapse before they could be attained, I was of a disposition to comfort myself with the Spanish proverb, ' Time and I against any two.'

The difficult and indispensable point of finding a permanent subject of occupation was now at length attained ; but there was annexed to it the necessity of becoming again a candidate for public favour; for, as I was turned improver on the earth of the every-day world, it was under condition that the small tenement of Parnassus, which might be accessible to my labours, should not remain uncultivated.

I meditated, at first, a poem on the subject of Bruce, in which I made some progress, but afterwards judged it advisable to lay it aside, supposing that an English story might have more novelty ; in consequence, the precedence was given to ' Rokeby.'

If subject and scenery could have influenced the fate of a poem, that of ' Rokeby' should have been eminently distinguished; for the grounds belonged to a dear friend with whom I had lived in habits of intimacy for many years, and the place itself united the romantic beauties of the wilds of Scotland with the rich and smiling aspect of the southern portion of the island. But the Cavaliers and Roundheads whom I attempted to summon up to tenant this beautiful region, had for the public neither the novelty nor the peculiar interest of the primitive Highlanders. This, perhaps, was scarcely to be expected, considering that the general mind sympathizes readily and at once with the stamp which nature herself has affixed upon the manners of a people living in a simple and patriarchal state ; whereas it has more difficulty in understanding or interesting itself in manners founded upon those peculiar habits of thinking or acting which are produced by the progress of society. We could read with pleasure the tale of the adventures of a Cossack or a Mongol Tartar, while we only wonder and stare over those of the lovers in ' The Pleasing Chinese History,' where the embarrassments turn upon difficulties arising out of unintelligible delicacies peculiar to the customs and manners of that affected people.

The cause of my failure had, however, a far deeper root. The manner, or style, which, by its novelty, attracted the public in an unusual degree, had now, after having been three times before them, exhausted the patience of the reader, and began in the fourth to lose its charms. The reviewers may be said to have apostrophized the author in the language of Parnell's Edwin—

> ' And here reverse the charm, he cries,
> And let it fairly now suffice,
> The gambol has been shown.'

The licentious combination of rhymes, in a manner not perhaps very congenial to our language, had not been confined to the author. Indeed, in most similar cases, the inventors of such novelties have their reputation destroyed by their own imitators, as Actaeon fell under the fury of his own dogs. The present author, like Bobadil, had taught his trick of fence to a hundred gentlemen (and ladies) who could fence very nearly or quite as well as himself. For this there was no remedy ; the harmony became tiresome and ordinary, and both the original inventor and his invention must have fallen into contempt if he had not found out another road to public favour. What has been said of the metre only, must be considered to apply equally to the structure of the poem and of the style. The very best passages of any popular style are not, perhaps, susceptible of imitation, but they may be approached by men of talent ; and those who are less able to copy them at least lay hold of their peculiar features so as to produce a strong burlesque. In either way, the effect of the manner is rendered cheap and common ; and, in the latter case, ridiculous to boot. The evil consequences to an author's reputation are at least as fatal as those which come upon the musical composer when his melody falls into the hands of the street ballad-singer.

Of the unfavourable species of imitation, the author's style gave room to a very large number, owing to an appearance of facility to which some of those who used the measure unquestionably leaned too far. The effect of the more favourable imitations, composed by persons of talent, was almost equally unfortunate to the original minstrel, by showing that they could overshoot him with his own bow. In short, the popularity which once attended the *School*, as it was called, was now fast decaying.

Besides all this, to have kept his ground at the crisis when 'Rokeby' appeared, its author ought to have put forth his utmost strength, and to have possessed at least all his original advantages, for a mighty and unexpected rival was advancing on the stage—a rival not in poetical powers only, but in that art of attracting popularity in which the present writer had hitherto preceded better men than himself. The reader will easily see that Byron is here meant, who, after a little velitation of no great promise, now appeared as a serious candidate, in the First Two Cantos of ' Childe Harold.' I was astonished at the power evinced by that work, which neither the Hours of Idleness' nor the ' English Bards and Scotch Reviewers ' had prepared me to expect from its author. There was a depth in his thought, an eager abundance in his diction, which argued full confidence in the inexhaustible resources of which he felt himself possessed; and there was some appearance of that labour of the file which indicates that the author is conscious of the necessity of doing every justice to his work that it may pass warrant. Lord Byron was also a traveller, a man whose ideas were fired by having seen, in distant scenes of difficulty and danger, the places whose very names are recorded in our bosoms as the shrines of ancient poetry. For his own misfortune, perhaps, but certainly to the high increase of his poetical character, nature had mixed in Lord Byron's system those passions which agitate the human heart with most violence, and which may be said to have hurried his bright career to an early close. There would have been little wisdom in measuring my force with so formidable an antagonist; and I was as likely to tire of playing the second fiddle in the concert, as my audience of hearing me. Age also was advancing. I was growing insensible to those subjects of excitation by which youth is agitated. I had around me the most pleasant but least exciting of all society, that of kind friends and an affectionate family. My circle of employments was a narrow one; it occupied me constantly, and it became daily more difficult for me to interest myself in poetical composition.

' How happily the days of Thalaba went by!

Yet, though conscious that I must be, in the opinion of good judges, inferior to the place I had for four or five years held in letters, and feeling alike that the latter was one to which I had only a temporary right, I could not brook the idea of relinquishing literary occupation, which had been so long my chief diversion. Neither was I disposed to choose the alternative of sinking into a mere editor and commentator, though that was a species of labour which I had practised, and to which I was attached. But I could not endure to think that I might not, whether known or concealed, do something of more importance. My inmost thoughts were those of the Trojan captain in the galley race—

'Non jam prima peto Mnestheus, neque vincere certo:
Quanquam O!—sed superent, quibus hoc, Neptune, dedisti.
Extremos pudeat rediisse: hoc vincite, cives,
Et prohibete nefas.'—ÆN. v. 194-197.

I had, indeed, some private reasons for my *Quanquam O!* which were not worse than those of Mnestheus. I have already hinted that the materials were collected for a poem on the subject of Bruce, and fragments of it had been shown to some of my friends, and received with applause. Notwithstanding, therefore, the eminent success of Byron, and the great chance of his taking the wind out of my sails, there was, I judged, a species of cowardice in desisting from the task which I had undertaken, and it was time enough to retreat when the battle should be more decidedly lost. The sale of 'Rokeby,' excepting as compared with that of 'The Lady of the Lake,' was in the highest degree respectable; and as it included fifteen hundred quartos, in those quarto-reading days, the trade had no reason to be dissatisfied.

WALTER SCOTT.

ABBOTSFORD, *April* 1830.

NOTES.

NOTE I.

On Barnard's towers, and Tees's stream.
—P. 313.

'BARNARD CASTLE,' saith old Leland, 'standeth stately upon Tees.' It is founded upon a very high bank, and its ruins impend over the river, including within the area a circuit of six acres and upwards. This once magnificent fortress derives its name from its founder, Barnard Baliol, the ancestor of the short and unfortunate dynasty of that name, which succeeded to the Scottish throne under the patronage of Edward I and Edward III. Baliol's Tower, afterwards mentioned in the poem, is a round tower of great size, situated at the western extremity of the building. It bears marks of great antiquity, and was remarkable for the curious construction of its vaulted roof, which has been lately greatly injured by the opera-

tions of some persons, to whom the tower has been leased for the purpose of making patent shot! The prospect from the top of Baliol's Tower commands a rich and magnificent view of the wooded valley of the Tees.

Barnard Castle often changed masters during the middle ages. Upon the forfeiture of the unfortunate John Baliol, the first king of Scotland of that family, Edward I seized this fortress among the other English estates of his refractory vassal. It was afterwards vested in the Beauchamps of Warwick, and in the Staffords of Buckingham, and was also sometimes in the possession of the Bishops of Durham, and sometimes in that of the crown. Richard III is said to have enlarged and strengthened its fortifications, and to have made it for some time his principal residence, for the purpose of bridling and suppressing the Lancastrian faction in the northern counties. From the Staffords, Barnard

Castle passed, probably by marriage, into the possession of the powerful Nevilles, Earls of Westmorelan 1, and belonged to the last representative of that family, when he engaged with the Earl of Northumberland in the ill-concerted insurrection of the twelfth of Queen Elizabeth. Upon this occasion, however, Sir George Bowes of Sheatlam, who held great possessions in the neighbourhood, anticipated the two insurgent earls, by seizing upon and garrisoning Barnard Castle, which he held out for ten days against all their forces, and then surrendered it upon honourable terms. See Sadler's State Papers, vol. ii. p. 330. In a ballad, contained in Percy's Reliques of Ancient Poetry, vol. i., the siege is thus commemorated :—

' Then Sir George Bowes he straight way rose,
    After them some spoyle to make ;
These noble erles turned back againe,
    And aye they vowed that knight to take.

That baron he to his castle fled ;
    To Barnard Castle then fled he ;
The uttermost walles were eathe to won,
    The erles have won them presentlie.

The uttermost walles were lime and brick ;
    But though they won them soon anone,
Long ere they wan the innermost walles,
    For they were cut in rock and stone.'

By the suppression of this rebellion, and the consequent forfeiture of the Earl of Westmoreland, Barnard Castle reverted to the crown, and was sold or leased out to Car, Earl of Somerset, the guilty and unhappy favourite of James I. It was afterwards granted to Sir Henry Vane the elder, and was therefore, in all probability, occupied for the Parliament, whose interest during the Civil War was so keenly espoused by the Vanes. It is now, with the other estates of that family, the property of the Right Honourable Earl of Darlington.

NOTE II.

—— *no human ear,*
Unsharpen'd by revenge and fear,
Could e'er distinguish horse's clank.
        —P. 314.

I have had occasion to remark, in real life, the effect of keen and fervent anxiety in giving acuteness to the organs of sense. My gifted friend, Miss Joanna Baillie, whose dramatic works display such intimate acquaintance with the operations of human passion, has not omitted this remarkable circumstance :—

' *De Montfort.* (*Off his guard.*) 'Tis Rezenvelt :
    I heard his well-known foot,
From the first staircase mounting step by step.
    Freb. How quick an ear thou hast for distant sound !
I heard him not.

    (*De Montfort looks embarrassed, and is silent.*)

NOTE III.

The morion's plumes his visage hide,
And the buff-coat, an ample fold,
Mantles his form's gigantic mould.
        —P. 314.

The use of complete suits of armour was fallen into disuse during the Civil War, though they were still worn by leaders of rank and importance. 'In the reign of King James I,' says our military antiquary, 'no great alterations were made in the article of defensive armour, except that the buff-coat, or jerkin, which was originally worn under the cuirass, now became frequently a substitute for it, it having been found that a good buff leather would of itself resist the stroke of a sword; this, however, only occasionally took place among the light-armed cavalry and infantry, complete suits of armour being still used among the heavy horse. Buff-coats continued to be worn by the city trained-bands till within the memory of persons now living, so that defensive armour may, in some measure, be said to have terminated in the same materials with which it began, that is, the skins of animals, or leather.'—GROSE'S *Military Antiquities.* Lond. 1801, 4to, vol. ii. p. 323.

Of the buff-coats, which were worn over the corslets, several are yet preserved ; and Captain Grose has given an engraving of one which was used in the time of Charles I by Sir Francis Rhodes, Bart. of Balbrough-Hall, Derbyshire. They were usually lined with silk or linen, secured before by buttons, or by a lace, and often richly decorated with gold or silver embroidery. From the following curious account of a dispute respecting a buff-coat between an old roundhead captain and a justice of peace, by whom his arms were seized after the Restoration, we learn, that the value and importance of this defensive garment were considerable :—'A party of horse came to my house, commanded by Mr. Peebles ; and he told me he was come for my arms, and that I must deliver them. I asked him for his order. He told me he had a better order than Oliver used to give ; and, clapping his hand upon his sword-hilt, he said, that was his order. I told him, if he had none but that, it was not sufficient to take my arms ; and then he pulled out his warrant, and I read it. It was signed by Wentworth Armitage, a general warrant to search all persons they suspected, and so left the power to the soldiers at their pleasure. They came to us at Coalley-Hall, about sun-setting ; and I caused a candle to be lighted, and conveyed Peebles into the room where my arms were. My arms were near the kitchen fire ; and there they took away my fowling-pieces, pistols, muskets, carbines, and such like, better than £20. Then Mr. Peebles asked me for my buff-coat ; and I told him they had no order to take away my apparel. He told me I was not to dispute their orders ;

but if I would not deliver it, he would carry me away prisoner, and had me out of doors. Yet he let me alone unto the next morning, that I must wait upon Sir John, at Halifax; and, coming before him, he threatened me, and said, if I did not send the coat, for it was too good for me to keep. I told him it was not in his power to demand my apparel; and he, growing into a fit, called me rebel and traitor, and said, if I did not send the coat with all speed, he would send me where I did not like well. I told him I was no rebel, and he did not well to call me so before these soldiers and gentlemen, to make me the mark for every one to shoot at. I departed the room; yet, notwithstanding all the threatenings, did not send the coat. But the next day he sent John Lyster, the son of Mr. Thomas Lyster, of Shipden Hall, for this coat, with a letter, verbatim thus:—"Mr. Hodson, I admire you will play the child so with me as you have done, in writing such an inconsiderate letter. Let me have the buff-coat sent forthwith, otherwise you shall so hear from me as will not very well please you." I was not at home when this messenger came; but I had ordered my wife not to deliver it, but, if they would take it, let them look to it: and he took it away; and one of Sir John's brethren wore it many years after. They sent Captain Butt to compound with my wife about it; but I sent word I would have my own again: but he advised me to take a price for it, and make no more ado. I said, it was hard to take my arms and apparel too; I had laid out a great deal of money for them; I hoped they did not mean to destroy me, by taking my goods illegally from me. He said he would make up the matter, if I pleased, betwixt us; and, it seems, had brought Sir John to a price for my coat. I would not have taken £10 for it; he would have given about £4; but, wanting my receipt for the money, he kept both sides, and I had never satisfaction.'—*Memoirs of Captain Hodgson.* Edin. 1806, p. 178.

NOTE IV.

On his dark face a scorching clime,
And toil, had done the work of time.

Death had he seen by sudden blow,
By wasting plague, by tortures slow.
—P. 315.

In this character, I have attempted to sketch one of those West Indian adventurers, who, during the course of the seventeenth century, were popularly known by the name of Bucaniers. The successes of the English in the predatory incursions upon Spanish America, during the reign of Elizabeth, had never been forgotten; and, from that period downward, the exploits of Drake and Raleigh were imitated, upon a smaller scale indeed, but with equally desperate valour, by small bands of pirates, gathered from all nations, but chiefly French and English. The engrossing policy of the Spaniards tended greatly to increase the number of these freebooters, from whom their commerce and colonies suffered, in the issue, dreadful calamity. The Windward Islands, which the Spaniards did not deem worthy their own occupation, had been gradually settled by adventurers of the French and English nations. But Frederic of Toledo, who was despatched in 1630 with a powerful fleet against the Dutch, had orders from the Court of Madrid to destroy these colonies, whose vicinity at once offended the pride and excited the jealous suspicions of their Spanish neighbours. This order the Spanish Admiral executed with sufficient rigour; but the only consequence was, that the planters, being rendered desperate by persecution, began, under the well-known name of Bucaniers, to commence a retaliation so horridly savage, that the perusal makes the reader shudder. When they carried on their depredations at sea, they boarded, without respect to disparity of number, every Spanish vessel that came in their way; and, demeaning themselves, both in the battle and after the conquest, more like demons than human beings, they succeeded in impressing their enemies with a sort of superstitious terror, which rendered them incapable of offering effectual resistance. From piracy at sea, they advanced to making predatory descents on the Spanish territories; in which they displayed the same furious and irresistible valour, the same thirst of spoil, and the same brutal inhumanity to their captives. The large treasures which they acquired in their adventures, they dissipated by the most unbounded licentiousness in gaming, women, wine, and debauchery of every species. When their spoils were thus wasted, they entered into some new association, and undertook new adventures. For farther particulars concerning these extraordinary banditti, the reader may consult Raynal, or the common and popular book called the History of the Bucaniers.

NOTE V.

——On Marston heath
Met, front to front, the ranks of death.
—P. 316.

The well-known and desperate battle of Long-Marston Moor, which terminated so unfortunately for the cause of Charles, commenced under very different auspices. Prince Rupert had marched with an army of 20,000 men for the relief of York, then besieged by Sir Thomas Fairfax, at the head of the Parliamentary army, and the Earl of Leven, with the Scottish auxiliary forces. In this he so completely succeeded, that he compelled the besiegers to retreat to Marston Moor, a large open plain, about eight miles distant from the city. Thither they were followed by the Prince, who had now united to his army the garrison of York, probably not less than 10,000 men strong, under the gallant Marquis (then Earl) of Newcastle. White- locke has recorded, with much impartiality, the following particulars of this eventful day: —'The right wing of the Parliament was commanded by Sir Thomas Fairfax, and consisted of all his horse, and three regiments of the Scots horse; the left wing was com- manded by the Earl of Manchester and Colonel Cromwell. One body of their foot was commanded by Lord Fairfax, and consisted of his foot, and two brigades of the Scots foot for reserve; and the main body of the rest of the foot was commanded by General Leven.

'The right wing of the Prince's army was commanded by the Earl of Newcastle; the left wing by the Prince himself; and the main body by General Goring, Sir Charles Lucas, and Major-General Porter. Thus were both sides drawn up into battalia.

'July 3rd, 1644. In this posture both armies faced each other, and about seven o'clock in the morning the fight began between them. The Prince, with his left wing, fell on the Parliament's right wing, routed them, and pursued them a great way; the like did General Goring, Lucas, and Porter, upon the Parliament's main body. The three generals, giving all for lost, hasted out of the field, and many of their soldiers fled, and threw down their arms; the King's forces too eagerly following them, the victory, now almost achieved by them, was again snatched out of their hands. For Colonel Cromwell, with the brave regiment of his countrymen, and Sir Thomas Fairfax, having rallied some of his horse, fell upon the Prince's right wing, where the Earl of Newcastle was, and routed them; and the rest of their companions rallying, they fell altogether upon the divided bodies of Rupert and Goring, and totally dispersed them, and obtained a complete victory, after three hours' fight.

'From this battle and the pursuit, some reckon were buried 7000 Englishmen; all agree that above 3000 of the Prince's men were slain in the battle, besides those in the chase, and 3000 prisoners taken, many of their chief officers, twenty-five pieces of ordnance, forty-seven colours, 10,000 arms, two wag- gons of carabins and pistols, 130 barrels of powder, and all their bag and bag- gage.'—WHITELOCKE's *Memoirs*, fol. p. 89. Lond. 1682.

Lord Clarendon informs us, that the King, previous to receiving the true account of the battle, had been informed, by an express from Oxford, 'that Prince Rupert had not only relieved York, but totally defeated the Scots, with many particulars to confirm it, all which was so much believed there, that they had made public fires of joy for the victory '

NOTE VI.

Monckton and Mitton told the news,
How troops of Roundheads choked the Ouse,
And many a bonny Scot, aghast,
Spurring his palfrey northward, past,
Cursing the day when zeal or meed
First lured their Lesley o'er the Tweed.
—P. 319.

Monckton and Mitton are villages near the river Ouse, and not very distant from the field of battle. The particulars of the action were violently disputed at the time; but the following extract, from the Manuscript History of the Baronial House of Somerville, is decisive as to the flight of the Scottish general, the Earl of Leven. The particulars are given by the author of the history on the authority of his father, then the representative of the family. This curious manuscript has been published by consent of my noble friend, the present Lord Somerville.

'The order of this great battell, wherin both armies was neer of ane equall number, consisting, to the best calculatione, neer to three score thousand men upon both sydes, I shall not take upon me to discryve; albeit, from the draughts then taken upon the place, and information I receaved from this gentle- man, who being then a volunteer, as having no command, had opportunitie and libertie to ryde from the one wing of the armie to the other, to view all ther several squadrons of horse and battallions of foot, how formed, and in what manner drawn up, with every other circumstance relating to the fight, and that both as to the King's armies and that of the Parliament's, amongst whom, untill the engadgment, he went from statione to statione to observe ther order and forme; but that the descriptione of this battell, with the various success on both sides at the beginning, with the loss of the royal armie, and the sad effects that followed that mis- fortune as to his Majestie's interest, hes been so often done already by English authors, little to our commendatione, how justly I shall not dispute, seing the truth is, as our principall generall fled that night neer fourtie mylles from the place of the fight, that part of the armie where he commanded being totallie routed; but it is as true, that much of the victorie is attributed to the good con- duct of David Lesselie, lievetennent-generall of our horse. Cromwell himself, that minione of fortune, but the rod of God's wrath, to punish eftirward three rebellious nations, disdained not to take orders from him, albeit then in the same qualitie of command for the Parliament, as being lievetennent-general to the Earl of Manchester's horse, whom, with the assistance of the Scots horse, haveing routed the Prince's right wing, as he had done that of the Parliament's. These two commanders of the horse upon that wing wisely restrained the great bodies of their horse from persuing these brocken troups, but, wheeling to the left-hand, falls in upon the naked flanks of the Prince's main battallion of foot, carying them doune with great violence; nether mett they with any great resistance untill they came to the Marques of Newcastle his battallione of White Coats, who, first peppering them soundly with ther shott, when they came to charge, stoutly bore them up with their picks that they could not enter to break them. Here the Parliament's horse of that wing receaved ther greatest losse, and a stop for sometyme putt to ther hoped-for victorie; and that only by the stout resistance of this gallant battallione, which consisted neer of four thousand foot, until at length a Scots regiment of dragouns, commanded by Collonell Frizeall, with other two, was brought to open them upon some hand, which at length they did, when all the ammunitione was spent. Having refused quarters, every man fell in the same order and ranke wherein he had foughten.

'Be this execution was done, the Prince returned from the persuite of the right wing of the Parliament's horse, which he had beatten and followed too farre, to the losse of the battell, which certanely, in all men's opinions, he might have caryed if he had not been too violent upon the pursuite; which gave his enemies upon the left-hand opportunitie to disperse and cut doune his infantrie, who, haveing cleared the field of all the standing bodies of foot, wer now, with many . . . . of their oune, standing ready to receave the charge of his allmost spent horses, if he should attempt it; which the Prince observeing, and seeing all lost, he retreated to Yorke with two thousand horse. Notwithstanding of this, ther was that night such a consternation in the Parliament armies, that it 's believed by most of those that wer there present, that if the Prince, haveing so great a body of horse inteire, had made ane onfall that night, or the ensueing morning be-tyme, he had carryed the victorie out of ther hands; for it 's certane, by the morning's light, he had rallyed a body of ten thousand men, wherof ther was neer three thousand gallant horse. These, with the assistance of the toune and garrisoune of Yorke, might have done much to have recovered the victory, for the loss of this battell in effect lost the King and his interest in the three kingdomes; his Majestie never being able eftir this to make head in the north, but lost his garrisons every day.

'As for Generall Lesselie, in the beginning of this flight haveing that part of the army quite brocken, whare he had placed himself, by the valour of the Prince, he imagined, and was confermed by the opinione of others then upon the place with him, that the battell was irrecoverably lost, seeing they wer fleeing upon all hands; theirfore they humblie intreated his excellence to reteir and wait his better fortune, which, without farder advyse-ing, he did; and never drew bridle untill he

came the lenth of Leads, having ridden all that night with a cloak of *drap de berrie* about him, belonging to this gentleman of whom I write, then in his retinue, with many other officers of good qualitie. It was neer twelve the next day befor they had the certanety who was master of the field, when at length ther arryves ane expresse, sent by David Lesselie, to acquaint the General they had obtained a most glorious victory, and that the Prince, with his brocken troupes, was fled from Yorke. This intelligence was somewhat amazeing to these gentlemen that had been eye-witnesses to the disorder of the armie before ther retearing, and had then accompanyed the General in his flight; who, being much wearyed that evening of the battell with ordering of his armie, and now quite spent with his long journey in the night, had casten himselfe doune upon a bed to rest, when this gentleman comeing quyetly into his chamber, he awoke, and hastily cryes out, "Lievetennent-collonell, what news?"— "All is safe, may it please your Excellence; the Parliament's armie hes obtained a great victory;" and then delyvers the letter. The Generall, upon the hearing of this, knocked upon his breast, and sayes, "I would to God I had died upon the place!" and then opens the letter, which, in a few lines, gave ane account of the victory, and in the close pressed his speedy returne to the armie, which he did the next day, being accompanyed some mylles back by this gentleman, who then takes his leave of him, and receaved at parting many expressions of kyndenesse, with promises that he would never be unmyndful of his care and respect towards him; and in the end he intreats him to present his service to all his friends and acquaintances in Scotland. Thereftir the Generall sets forward in his journey for the armie, as this gentleman did for . . . . , in order to his trans-portatione for Scotland, where he arryved sex dayes eftir the fight of Mestoune Muir, and gave the first true account and descriptione of that great battell, wherein the Covenanters then gloryed soe much, that they impiously boasted the Lord had now signally appeared for his cause and people; it being ordinary for them, dureing the whole time of this warre, to attribute the greatnes of their success to the goodnes and justice of ther cause, untill Divine Justice trysted them with some crosse dispensatione, and then you might have heard this language from them, "That it pleases the Lord to give his oune the heavyest end of the tree to bear, that the saints and the people of God must still be sufferers while they are here away, that the malignant party was God's rod to punish them for ther unthankfullnesse, which in the end he will cast into the fire;" with a thousand other expressions and scripture citations, prophanely and blasphemously uttered by them, to palliate ther villainie and rebellion.'
—*Memoirs of the Somervilles.* Edin. 1815.

NOTE VII.

With his barb'd horse, fresh tidings say,
Stout Cromwell has redeem'd the day.
—P. 319.

Cromwell, with his regiment of cuirassiers, had a principal share in turning the fate of the day at Marston Moor; which was equally matter of triumph to the Independents, and of grief and heart-burning to the Presbyterians and to the Scottish. Principal Baillie expresses his dissatisfaction as follows:—

'The Independents sent up one quickly to assure that all the glory of that night was theirs; and they and their Major General Cromwell had done it all there alone: but Captain Stuart afterward showed the vanity and falsehood of their disgraceful relation. God gave us that victory wonderfully. There were three generals on each side, Lesley, Fairfax, and Manchester; Rupert, Newcastle, and King. Within half an hour and less, all six took them to their heels;—this to you alone. The disadvantage of the ground, and violence of the flower of Prince Rupert's horse, carried all our right wing down; only Eglinton kept ground, to his great loss; his lieutenant-crowner, a brave man, I fear shall die, and his son Robert be mutilated of an arm. Lindsay had the greatest hazard of any; but the beginning of the victory was from David Lesly, who before was much suspected of evil designs: he, with the Scots and Cromwell's horse, having the advantage of the ground, did dissipate all before them.' —BAILLIE'S *Letters and Journals.* Edin. 1785, 8vo, ii. 36.

NOTE VIII.

Do not my native dales prolong
Of Percy Rede the tragic song,
Train'd forward to his bloody fall,
By Girsonfield, that treacherous Hall?
—P. 319.

In a poem, entitled 'The Lay of the Reedwater Minstrel,' Newcastle, 1809, this tale, with many others peculiar to the valley of the Reed, is commemorated:—'The particulars of the traditional story of Parcy Reed of Troughend, and the Halls of Girsonfield, the author had from a descendant of the family of Reed. From his account, it appears that Percival Reed, Esquire, a keeper of Reedsdale, was betrayed by the Halls (hence denominated the false-hearted Ha's) to a band of moss-troopers of the name of Crosier, who slew him at Batinghope, near the source of the Reed.

'The Halls were, after the murder of Parcy Reed, held in such universal abhorrence and contempt by the inhabitants of Reedsdale, for their cowardly and treacherous behaviour, that they were obliged to leave the country.' In another passage, we are informed that the ghost of the injured Borderer is supposed to haunt the banks of a brook called the Pringle. These Redes of Troughend were a very ancient family, as may be conjectured from their deriving their surname from the river on which they had their mansion. An epitaph on one of their tombs affirms, that the family held their lands of Troughend, which are situated on the Reed, nearly opposite to Otterburn, for the incredible space of nine hundred years.

NOTE IX.

And near the spot that gave me name,
The moated mound of Risingham,
Where Reed upon her margin sees
Sweet Woodburne's cottages and trees,
Some ancient sculptor's art has shown
An outlaw's image on the stone.—P. 319.

Risingham, upon the river Reed, near the beautiful hamlet of Woodburn, is an ancient Roman station, formerly called Habitancum. Camden says, that in his time the popular account bore, that it had been the abode of a deity, or giant, called Magon; and appeals, in support of this tradition, as well as to the etymology of Risingham, or Reisenham, which signifies, in German, the habitation of the giants, to two Roman altars taken out of the river, inscribed, DEO MOGONTI CADENORUM. About half a mile distant from Risingham, upon an eminence covered with scattered birch-trees and fragments of rock, there is cut upon a large rock, in *alto relievo,* a remarkable figure, called Robin of Risingham, or Robin of Reedsdale. It presents a hunter, with his bow raised in one hand, and in the other what seems to be a hare. There is a quiver at the back of the figure, and he is dressed in a long coat, or kirtle, coming down to the knees, and meeting close, with a girdle bound round him. Dr. Horseley, who saw all monuments of antiquity with Roman eyes, inclines to think this figure a Roman archer: and certainly the bow is rather of the ancient size than of that which was so formidable in the hand of the English archers of the middle ages. But the rudeness of the whole figure prevents our founding strongly upon mere inaccuracy of proportion. The popular tradition is, that it represents a giant, whose brother resided at Woodburn, and he himself at Risingham. It adds, that they subsisted by hunting, and that one of them, finding the game become too scarce to support them, poisoned his companion, in whose memory the monument was engraved. What strange and tragic circumstance may be concealed under this legend, or whether it is utterly apocryphal, it is now impossible to discover.

The name of Robin of Redesdale was given to one of the Umfravilles, Lords of Prudhoe, and afterwards to one Hilliard, a friend and follower of the king-making Earl of Warwick. This person commanded an army of North-

amptonshire and northern men, who seized
on and beheaded the Earl Rivers, father to
Edward the Fourth's queen, and his son,
Sir John Woodville.—See HOLINSHED, *ad
annum*, 1469.

NOTE X.

—— *do thou revere
The statutes of the Bucanier.*—P. 319.

The 'statutes of the Bucaniers' were, in
reality, more equitable than could have been
expected from the state of society under
which they had been formed. They chiefly
related, as may readily be conjectured, to
the distribution and the inheritance of their
plunder.

When the expedition was completed, the
fund of prize-money acquired was thrown
together, each party taking his oath that he
had retained or concealed no part of the
common stock. If any one transgressed in
this important particular, the punishment
was, his being set ashore on some desert key
or island, to shift for himself as he could.
The owners of the vessel had then their share
assigned for the expenses of the outfit. These
were generally old pirates, settled at Tobago,
Jamaica, St. Domingo, or some other French
or English settlement. The surgeon's and
carpenter's salaries, with the price of provisions and ammunition, were also defrayed.
Then followed the compensation due to the
maimed and wounded, rated according to
the damage they had sustained; as six
hundred pieces of eight, or six slaves, for the
loss of an arm or leg, and so in proportion.

'After this act of justice and humanity, the
remainder of the booty was divided into as
many shares as there were Bucaniers. The
commander could only lay claim to a single
share, as the rest; but they complimented
him with two or three, in proportion as he
had acquitted himself to their satisfaction.
When the vessel was not the property of the
whole company, the person who had fitted it
out, and furnished it with necessary arms
and ammunition, was entitled to a third of
all the prizes. Favour had never any influence in the division of the booty, for every
share was determined by lot. Instances of
such rigid justice as this are not easily met
with, and they extended even to the dead.
Their share was given to the man who was
known to be their companion when alive,
and therefore their heir. If the person who
had been killed had no intimate, his part was
sent to his relations, when they were known.
If there were no friends nor relations, it was
distributed in charity to the poor and to
churches, which were to pray for the person
in whose name these benefactions were given,
the fruits of inhuman, but necessary piratical
plunders.'—RAYNAL'S *History of European
Settlements in the East and West Indies,
by Justamond.* Lond. 1776, 8vo, iii. p. 41.

NOTE XI.

The course of Tees.—P. 324.

The view from Barnard Castle commands
the rich and magnificent valley of Tees.
Immediately adjacent to the river, the banks
are very thickly wooded; at a little distance
they are more open and cultivated; but,
being interspersed with hedge-rows, and with
isolated trees of great size and age, they still
retain the richness of woodland scenery. The
river itself flows in a deep trench of solid
rock, chiefly limestone and marble. The
finest view of its romantic course is from
a handsome modern-built bridge over the
Tees, by the late Mr. Morritt of Rokeby. In
Leland's time, the marble quarries seem to
have been of some value. 'Hard under the
cliff by Egliston, is found on eche side of Tese
very fair marble, wont to be taken up booth
by marbelers of Barnardes Castelle and of
Egliston, and partly to have been wrought
by them, and partly sold onwrought to
others.'—*Itinerary.* Oxford, 1768, 8vo, p. 88.

NOTE XII.

Egliston's grey ruins.—P. 324.

The ruins of this abbey, or priory, (for
Tanner calls it the former, and Leland the
latter,) are beautifully situated upon the
angle, formed by a little dell called Thorsgill,
at its junction with the Tees. A good part
of the religious house is still in some degree
habitable, but the church is in ruins. Egliston was dedicated to St. Mary and St. John
the Baptist, and is supposed to have been
founded by Ralph de Multon about the end
of Henry the Second's reign. There were
formerly the tombs of the families of Rokeby,
Bowes, and Fitz-Hugh.

NOTE XIII.

—— *the mound,
Raised by that Legion long renown'd,
Whose votive shrine asserts their claim
Of pious, faithful, conquering fame.*
—P. 325.

Close behind the George Inn at Greta
Bridge there is a well-preserved Roman
encampment, surrounded with a triple ditch,
lying between the river Greta and a brook
called the Tutta. The four entrances are
easily to be discerned. Very many Roman
altars and monuments have been found in
the vicinity, most of which are preserved at
Rokeby by my friend Mr. Morritt. Among
others is a small votive altar, with the inscription, LEG. VI. VIC. P. F. F., which has been
rendered *Legio. Sexta. Victrix. Pia. Fortis.
Fidelis.*

Note XIV.
Rokeby's turrets high.—P. 325.

This ancient manor long gave name to a family by whom it is said to have been possessed from the Conquest downward, and who are at different times distinguished in history. It was the Baron of Rokeby who finally defeated the insurrection of the Earl of Northumberland, *tempore Hen. IV*, of which Holinshed gives the following account:—'The King, advertised hereof, caused a great armie to be assembled, and came forward with the same towards his enemies; but yer the King came to Nottingham, Sir Thomas, or (as other copies haue) Sir Rafe Rokesbie, Shiriffe of Yorkeshire, assembled the forces of the countrie to resist the Earle and his power; coming to Grimbautbrigs, beside Knaresborough, there to stop them the passage; but they returning aside, got to Weatherbie, and so to Tadcaster, and finally came forward unto Bramham-moor, near to Haizlewood, where they chose their ground meet to fight upon. The Shiriffe was as readie to giue battell as the Erle to receiue it; and so with a standard of S. George spread, set fiercelie vpon the Earle, who, vnder a standard of his owne armes, encountered his aduersaries with great manhood. There was a sore incounter and cruell conflict betwixt the parties, but in the end the victorie fell to the Shiriffe. The Lord Bardolfe was taken, but sore wounded, so that he shortlie after died of the hurts. As for the Earle of Northumberland, he was slain outright; so that now the prophecy was fulfilled, which gaue an in'cling of this his heauy hap long before, namelie,

"Stirps Persitina periet confusa ruina."

For this Earle was the stocke and maine root of all th at were left aliue, called by the name of Persie; and of manie more by diuers slaughters dispatched. For whose misfortune the people were not a little sorrie, making report of the gentleman's valiantnesse, renowne, and honour, and applieing vnto him certeine lamentable verses out of Lucaine, saieng,

"Sed nos nec sanguis, nec tantum vulnera nostri
Affecere senis: quantum gestata per urbem
Ora ducis, quae transfixo deformia pilo
Vidimus."

For his head, full of siluer horie haires, being put vpon a stake, was openlie carried through London, and set vpon the bridge of the same citie: in like manner was the Lord Bardolfes.'—HOLINSHED'S *Chronicles*. Lond. 1808, 4to, iii. 45. The Rokeby, or Rokesby family, continued to be distinguished until the great Civil War, when, having embraced the cause of Charles I, they suffered severely by fines and confiscations. The estate then passed from its ancient possessors to the family of the Robinsons, from whom it was purchased by the father of my valued friend, the present proprietor.

Note XV.
A stern and lone, yet lovely road,
As e'er the foot of Minstrel trode!
—P. 325.

What follows is an attempt to describe the romantic glen, or rather ravine, through which the Greta finds a passage between Rokeby and Mortham; the former situated upon the left bank of Greta, the latter on the right bank, about half a mile nearer to its junction with the Tees. The river runs with very great rapidity over a bed of solid rock, broken by many shelving descents, down which the stream dashes with great noise and impetuosity, vindicating its etymology, which has been derived from the Gothic, *Gridan*, to clamour. The banks partake of the same wild and romantic character, being chiefly lofty cliffs of limestone rock, whose grey colour contrasts admirably with the various trees and shrubs which find root among their crevices, as well as with the hue of the ivy, which clings around them in profusion, and hangs down from their projections in long sweeping tendrils. At other points the rocks give place to precipitous banks of earth, bearing large trees intermixed with copsewood. In one spot the dell, which is elsewhere very narrow, widens for a space to leave room for a dark grove of yew trees, intermixed here and there with aged pines of uncommon size. Directly opposite to this sombre thicket, the cliffs on the other side of the Greta are tall, white, and fringed with all kinds of deciduous shrubs. The whole scenery of this spot is so much adapted to the ideas of superstition, that it has acquired the name of Blockula, from the place were the Swedish witches were supposed to hold their Sabbath. The dell, however, has superstitions of its own growth, for it is supposed to be haunted by a female spectre, called the Dobie of Mortham. The cause assigned for her appearance is a lady's having been whilom murdered in the wood, in evidence of which, her blood is shown upon the stairs of the old tower at Mortham. But whether she was slain by a jealous husband, or by savage banditti, or by an uncle who coveted her estate, or by a rejected lover, are points upon which the traditions of Rokeby do not enable us to decide.

Note XVI.
How whistle rash bids tempests roar.
—P. 327.

That this is a general superstition, is well known to all who have been on ship-board, or who have conversed with seamen. The most formidable whistler that I remember to have met with was the apparition of a certain Mrs. Leakey, who, about 1636, resided, we are told, at Mynehead, in Somerset, where her only son drove a considerable trade between that port and Waterford, and was owner of several vessels. This old gentle-woman was of a social disposition, and so acceptable to her friends, that they used to say to her and to each other, it were pity such an excellent good-natured old lady should die; to which she was wont to reply, that whatever pleasure they might find in her company just now, they would not greatly like to see or converse with her after death, which nevertheless she was apt to think might happen. Accordingly, after her death and funeral, she began to appear to various persons by night and by noonday, in her own house, in the town and fields, at sea and upon shore. So far had she departed from her former urbanity, that she is recorded to have kicked a doctor of medicine for his impolite negligence in omitting to hand her over a stile. It was also her humour to appear upon the quay, and call for a boat. But especially so soon as any of her son's ships approached the harbour, 'this ghost would appear in the same garb and likeness as when she was alive, and, standing at the mainmast, would blow with a whistle, and though it were never so great a calm, yet immediately there would arise a most dreadful storm, that would break, wreck, and drown ship and goods.' When she had thus proceeded until her son had neither credit to freight a vessel, nor could have procured men to sail in it, she began to attack the persons of his family, and actually strangled their only child in the cradle. The rest of her story, showing how the spectre looked over the shoulder of her daughter-in-law while dressing her hair at a looking-glass, and how Mrs. Leakey the younger took courage to address her, and how the beldam despatched her to an Irish prelate, famous for his crimes and misfortunes, to exhort him to repentance, and to apprize him that otherwise he would be hanged, and how the bishop was satisfied with replying, that if he was born to be hanged, he should not be drowned;—all these, with many more particulars, may be found at the end of one of John Dunton's publications, called Athenianism, London, 1710, where the tale is engrossed under the title of 'The Apparition Evidence.'

Note XVII.

Of Erick's cap and Elmo's light.
—P. 327.

'This Ericus, King of Sweden, in his time was held second to none in the magical art; and he was so familiar with the evil spirits, which he exceedingly adored, that which way soever he turned his cap, the wind would presently blow that way. From this occasion he was called Windy Cap; and many men believed that Regnerus, King of Denmark, by the conduct of this Ericus, who was his nephew, did happily extend his piracy into the most

remote parts of the earth, and conquered many countries and fenced cities by his cunning, and at last was his coadjutor ; that by the consent of the nobles, he should be chosen King of Sweden, which continued a long time with him very happily, until he died of old age.'—OLAUS, *ut supra*, p. 45.

Note XVIII.

The Demon Frigate.—P. 327.

This is an allusion to a well-known nautical superstition concerning a fantastic vessel, called by sailors the Flying Dutchman, and supposed to be seen about the latitude of the Cape of Good Hope. She is distinguished from earthly vessels by bearing a press of sail when all others are unable, from stress of weather, to show an inch of canvas. The cause of her wandering is not altogether certain ; but the general account is, that she was originally a vessel loaded with great wealth, on board of which some horrid act of murder and piracy had been committed ; that the plague broke out among the wicked crew who had perpetrated the crime, and that they sailed in vain from port to port, offering, as the price of shelter, the whole of their ill-gotten wealth ; that they were excluded from every harbour, for fear of the contagion which was devouring them ; and that, as a punishment of their crimes, the apparition of the ship still continues to haunt those seas in which the catastrophe took place, and is considered by the mariners as the worst of all possible omens.

My late lamented friend, Dr. John Leyden, has introduced this phenomenon into his 'Scenes of Infancy,' imputing, with poetical ingenuity, the dreadful judgment to the first ship which commenced the slave trade :—

'Stout was the ship, from Benin's palmy shore
That first the weight of barter'd captives bore ;
Bedimm'd with blood, the sun with shrinking beams
Beheld her bounding o'er the ocean streams ;
But, ere the moon her silver horns had rear'd,
Amid the crew the speckled plague appear'd.
Faint and despairing, on their watery bier,
To every friendly shore the sailors steer ;
Repell'd from port to port, they sue in vain,
And track with slow unsteady sail the main.
Where ne'er the bright and buoyant wave is seen
To streak with wandering foam the sea-weeds green,
Towers the tall mast, a lone and leafless tree,
Till self-impell'd amid the waveless sea ;
Where summer breezes ne'er were heard to sing,
Nor hovering snow-birds spread the downy wing,
Fix'd as a rock amid the boundless plain,
The yellow stream pollutes the stagnant main,
Till far through night the funeral flames aspire,
As the red lightning smites the ghastly pyre.
  Still doom'd by fate on weltering billows roll'd,
Along the deep their restless course to hold,
Scenting the storm, the shadowy sailors guide
The prow with sails opposed to wind and tide ;
The Spectre Ship, in livid glimpsing light,
Glares baleful on the shuddering watch at night,
Unblest of God and man !—Till time shall end,
Its view strange horror to the storm shall lend.'

Note XIX.
——by some desert isle or key.—P. 327.

What contributed much to the security of the Bucaniers about the Windward Islands, was the great number of little islets, called in that country *keys.* These are small sandy patches, appearing just above the surface of the ocean, covered only with a few bushes and weeds, but sometimes affording springs of water, and, in general, much frequented by turtle. Such little uninhabited spots afforded the pirates good harbours, either for refitting or for the purpose of ambush; they were occasionally the hiding-place of their treasure, and often afforded a shelter to themselves. As many of the atrocities which they practised on their prisoners were committed in such spots, there are some of these keys which even now have an indifferent reputation among seamen, and where they are with difficulty prevailed on to remain ashore at night, on account of the visionary terrors incident to places which have been thus contaminated.

Note XX.
Before the gate of Mortham stood.
—P. 328.

The castle of Mortham, which Leland terms 'Mr. Rokesby's Place, in *ripa citer*, scant a quarter of a mile from Greta Bridge, and not a quarter of a mile beneath into Tees,' is a picturesque tower, surrounded by buildings of different ages, now converted into a farm-house and offices. The battlements of the tower itself are singularly elegant, the architect having broken them at regular intervals into different heights; while those at the corners of the tower project into octangular turrets. They are also from space to space covered with stones laid across them, as in modern embrasures, the whole forming an uncommon and beautiful effect. The surrounding buildings are of a less happy form, being pointed into high and steep roofs. A wall, with embrasures, encloses the southern front, where a low portal arch affords an entry to what was the castle-court. At some distance is most happily placed, between the stems of two magnificent elms, the monument alluded to in the text. It is said to have been brought from the ruins of Egliston Priory, and, from the armoury with which it is richly carved, appears to have been a tomb of the Fitz-Hughs.

The situation of Mortham is eminently beautiful, occupying a high bank, at the bottom of which the Greta winds out of the dark, narrow, and romantic dell, which the text has attempted to describe, and flows onward through a more open valley to meet the Tees about a quarter of a mile from the castle. Mortham is surrounded by old trees, happily and widely grouped with Mr. Morritt's new plantations.

Note XXI.
There dig, and tomb your precious heap,
And bid the dead your treasure keep.
—P. 329.

If time did not permit the Bucaniers to lavish away their plunder in their usual debaucheries, they were wont to hide it, with many superstitious solemnities, in the desert islands and keys which they frequented, and where much treasure, whose lawless owners perished without reclaiming it, is still supposed to be concealed. The most cruel of mankind are often the most superstitious; and these pirates are said to have had recourse to a horrid ritual, in order to secure an unearthly guardian to their treasures. They killed a Negro or Spaniard, and buried him with the treasure, believing that his spirit would haunt the spot, and terrify away all intruders. I cannot produce any other authority on which this custom is ascribed to them than that of maritime tradition, which is, however, amply sufficient for the purposes of poetry.

Note XXII.
The power . . . . . .
That unsubdued and lurking lies
To take the felon by surprise,
And force him, as by magic spell,
In his despite his guilt to tell.—P. 329.

All who are conversant with the administration of criminal justice, must remember many occasions in which malefactors appear to have conducted themselves with a species of infatuation, either by making unnecessary confidences respecting their guilt, or by sudden and involuntary allusions to circumstances by which it could not fail to be exposed. A remarkable instance occurred in the celebrated case of Eugene Aram. A skeleton being found near Knaresborough, was supposed, by the persons who gathered around the spot, to be the remains of one Clarke, who had disappeared some years before, under circumstances leading to a suspicion of his having been murdered. One Houseman, who had mingled in the crowd, sudden'y said, while looking at the skeleton, and hearing the opinion which was buzzed around, 'That is no more Dan Clarke's bone than it is mine!'—a sentiment expressed so positively, and with such peculiarity of manner, as to lead all who heard him to infer that he must necessarily know where the real body had been interred. Accordingly, being apprehended, he confessed having assisted Eugene Aram to murder Clarke, and to hide his body in Saint Robert's Cave. It happened to the author himself, while conversing with a person accus·d of an atrocious crime, for the purpose of rendering him professional assistance upon his trial, to hear the prisoner, after the most solemn and reiterated protestations that he was guiltless, suddenly, and, as it were, involuntarily, in the course of his communications, make such an admission as was altogether incompatible with innocence.

Note XXIII.

Brackenbury's dismal tower.—P. 332.

This tower has been already mentioned. It is situated near the north-eastern extremity of the wall which encloses Barnard Castle, and is traditionally said to have been the prison. By an odd coincidence, it bears a name which we naturally connect with imprisonment, from its being that of Sir Robert Brackenbury, lieutenant of the Tower of London under Edward IV and Richard III. There is, indeed, some reason to conclude, that the tower may actually have derived the name from that family, for Sir Robert Brackenbury himself possessed considerable property not far from Barnard Castle.

Note XXIV.

Nobles and knights, so proud of late,
Must fine for freedom and estate.

. . . .
Right heavy shall his ransom be,
Unless that maid compound with thee!
—P. 332.

After the battle of Marston Moor, the Earl of Newcastle retired beyond sea in disgust, and many of his followers laid down their arms, and made the best composition they could with the Committees of Parliament. Fines were imposed upon them in proportion to their estates and degrees of delinquency, and these fines were often bestowed upon such persons as had deserved well of the Commons. In some circumstances it happened, that the oppressed cavaliers were fain to form family alliances with some powerful person among the triumphant party. The whole of Sir Robert Howard's excellent comedy of *The Committee* turns upon the plot of Mr. and Mrs. Day to enrich their family, by compelling Arabella, whose estate was under sequestration, to marry their son Abel, as the price by which she was to compound with Parliament for delinquency; that is, for attachment to the royal cause.

Note XXV.

The Indian, prowling for his prey,
Who hears the settlers track his way.
—P. 333.

The patience, abstinence, and ingenuity exerted by the North-American Indians, when in pursuit of plunder or vengeance, is the most distinguished feature in their character; and the activity and address which they display in their retreat is equally surprising. Adair, whose most absurd hypotheses and turgid style do not affect the general authenticity of his anecdotes, has recorded an instance which seems incredible.

'When the Chickasah nation was engaged in a former war with the Muskohge, one of their young warriors set off against them to revenge the blood of a near relation. . . . He went through the most unfrequented and thick parts of the woods, as such a dangerous enterprise required, till he arrived opposite to the great and old beloved town of refuge, Koosah, which stands high on the eastern side of a bold river, about 250 yards broad, that runs by the late dangerous Albehama-Fort, down to the black poisoning Mobille, and so into the Gulf of Mexico. There he concealed himself under cover of the top of a fallen pine-tree, in view of the ford of the old trading-path, where the enemy now and then pass the river in their light poplar canoes. All his war-store of provisions consisted of three stands of barbicued venison, till he had an opportunity to revenge blood, and return home. He waited with watchfulness and patience almost three days, when a young man, a woman, and a girl, passed a little wide of him an hour before sunset. The former he shot down, tomahawked the other two, and scalped each of them in a trice, in full view of the town. By way of bravado, he shaked the scalps before them, sounding the awful death-whoop, and set off along the trading-path, trusting to his heels, while a great many of the enemy ran to their arms and gave chase. Seven miles from thence he entered the great blue ridge of the Apalahche Mountains. About an hour before day he had run over seventy miles of that mountainous tract; then, after sleeping two hours in a sitting posture, leaning his back against a tree, he set off again with fresh speed. As he threw away the venison when he found himself pursued by the enemy, he was obliged to support nature with such herbs, roots, and nuts, as his sharp eyes, with a running glance, directed him to snatch up in his course. Though I often have rode that war-path alone, when delay might have proved dangerous, and with as fine and strong horses as any in America, it took me five days to ride from the aforesaid Koosah to this sprightly warrior's place in the Chickasah country, the distance of 300 computed miles; yet he ran it, and got home safe and well at about eleven o'clock of the third day, which was only one day and a half and two nights.'—ADAIR'S *History of the American Indians.* Lond. 1775, 4to. p. 395.

NOTE XXVI.

In Redesdale his youth had heard
Each art her wily dalesmen dared,
When Rooken-edge, and Redswair high,
To bugle rung and bloodhound's cry.
—P. 333.

'What manner of cattle-stealers they are that inhabit these valleys in the marches of both kingdoms, John Lesley, a Scotchman himself, and Bishop of Ross, will inform you. They sally out of their own borders in the night, in troops, through unfrequented by-ways and many intricate windings. All the day-time they refresh themselves and their horses in lurking holes they had pitched upon before, till they arrive in the dark in those places they have a design upon. As soon as they have seized upon the booty, they, in like manner, return home in the night, through blind ways, and fetching many a compass. The more skilful any captain is to pass through those wild deserts, crooked turnings, and deep precipices, in the thickest mists, his reputation is the greater, and he is looked upon as a man of an excellent head. And they are so very cunning, that they seldom have their booty taken from them, unless sometimes when, by the help of bloodhounds following them exactly upon the track, they may chance to fall into the hands of their adversaries. When being taken, they have so much persuasive eloquence, and so many smooth insinuating words at command, that if they do not move their judges, nay, and even their adversaries, (notwithstanding the severity of their natures,) to have mercy, yet they incite them to admiration and compassion.'—CAMDEN'S *Britannia.*

The inhabitants of the valleys of Tyne and Reed were, in ancient times, so inordinately addicted to these depredations, that in 1564, the Incorporated Merchant-adventurers of Newcastle made a law that none born in these districts should be admitted apprentice. The inhabitants are stated to be so generally addicted to rapine, that no faith should be reposed in those proceeding from 'such lewde and wicked progenitors.' This regulation continued to stand unrepealed until 1771. A beggar, in an old play, describes himself as 'born in Redesdale, in Northumberland, and come of a wight-riding surname, called the Robsons, good honest men and true, *saving a little shifting for their living,* *God help them!'*—a description which would have applied to most Borderers on both sides.

Reidswair, famed for a skirmish to which it gives name, [see Border Minstrelsy, vol. ii. p. 15,] is on the very edge of the Carter-fell, which divides England from Scotland. The Rooken is a place upon Reedwater. Bertram, being described as a native of these dales, where the habits of hostile depredation long survived the union of the crowns, may have been, in some degree, prepared by education for the exercise of a similar trade in the wars of the Bucaniers.

NOTE XXVII.

Hiding his face, lest foemen spy
The sparkle of his swarthy eye.—P. 334.

After one of the recent battles, in which the Irish rebels were defeated, one of their most active leaders was found in a bog, in which he was immersed up to the shoulders, while his head was concealed by an impending ledge of turf. Being detected and seized, notwithstanding his precaution, he became solicitous to know how his retreat had been discovered. 'I caught,' answered the Sutherland Highlander, by whom he was taken, 'the sparkle of your eye.' Those who are accustomed to mark hares upon their form usually discover them by the same circumstance.

NOTE XXVIII.

Here stood a wretch, prepared to change
His soul's redemption for revenge!
—P. 335.

It is agreed by all the writers upon magic and witchcraft, that revenge was the most common motive for the pretended compact between Satan and his vassals. The ingenuity of Reginald Scot has very happily stated how such an opinion came to root itself, not only in the minds of the public and of the judges, but even in that of the poor wretches themselves who were accused of sorcery, and were often firm believers in their own power and their own guilt.

'One sort of such as are said to be witches, are women which be commonly old, lame, blear-eyed, pale, foul, and full of wrinkles; poor, sullen, superstitious, or papists, or such as know no religion; in whose drowsie minds the devil hath gotten a fine seat; so as what mischief, mischance, calamity, or slaughter is brought to pass, they are easily perswaded the same is done by themselves, imprinting in their minds an earnest and constant imagination thereof. . . . These go from house to house, and from door to door, for a pot of milk, yest, drink, pottage, or some such relief, without the which they could hardly live; neither obtaining for their service or pains, nor yet by their art, nor yet at the devil's hands, (with whom they are said to make a perfect and visible bargain,) either beauty, money, promotion, wealth, pleasure, honour, knowledge, learning, or any other benefit whatsoever.

'It falleth out many a time, that neither their necessities nor their expectation is answered or served in those places where they beg or borrow, but rather their lewdness is by their neighbours reproved. And farther, in tract of time the witch waxeth odious and tedious to her neighbours, and they again are despised and despited of her; so as sometimes she curseth one, and sometimes another, and that from the master of the house, his wife, children, cattle, &c., to the little pig that lieth in the stie. Thus, in process of time, they have all displeased her, and she hath wished evil luck unto them all; perhaps with curses and imprecations made in form. Doubtless (at length) some of her neighbours die or fall sick, or some of their children are visited with diseases that vex them strangely, as apoplexies, epilepsies, convulsions, hot fevers, worms, &c., which, by ignorant parents, are supposed to be the vengeance of witches. . . .

'The witch, on the other side, expecting her neighbours' mischances, and seeing things sometimes come to pass according to her wishes, curses, and incantations, (for Bodin himself confesses, that not above two in a hundred of their witchings or wishings take effect,) being called before a justice, by due examination of the circumstances, is driven to see her imprecations and desires, and her neighbours' harms and losses, to concur, and, as it were, to take effect; and so confesseth that she (as a goddess) hath brought such things to pass. Wherein not only she, but the accuser, and also the justice, are foully deceived and abused, as being, through her confession, and other circumstances, persuaded (to the injury of God's glory) that she hath done, or can do, that which is proper only to God himself.'—SCOT'S *Discovery of Witchcraft.* Lond. 1655, fol. pp. 4, 5.

NOTE XXIX.

Of my marauding on the clowns
Of Calverley and Bradford downs.
—P. 336.

The troops of the King, when they first took the field, were as well disciplined as could be expected from circumstances. But as the circumstances of Charles became less favourable, and his funds for regularly paying his forces decreased, habits of military license prevailed among them in greater excess. Lacy the player, who served his master during the Civil War, brought out, after the Restoration, a piece called The Old Troop, in which he seems to have commemorated some real incidents which occurred in his military career. The names of the officers of the Troop sufficiently express their habits. We have Flea-flint Plunder-Master-General, Captain Ferret-farm, and Quarter-Master Burn-drop. The officers of the Troop are in league with these worthies, and connive at their plundering the country for a suitable share in the booty. All this was undoubtedly drawn from the life, which Lacy had an opportunity to study. The moral of the whole is comprehended in a rebuke given to the lieutenant, whose disorders in the country are said to prejudice the King's cause more than his courage in the field could recompense. The piece is by no means void of farcical humour.

NOTE XXX.

——*Brignal's woods, and Scargill's wave,*
E'en now, o'er many a sister cave.—P. 337.

The banks of the Greta, below Rutherford Bridge, abound in seams of greyish slate, which are wrought in some places to a very great depth under ground, thus forming artificial caverns, which, when the seam has been exhausted, are gradually hidden by the underwood which grows in profusion upon the romantic banks of the river. In times of public confusion, they might be well adapted to the purposes of banditti.

NOTE XXXI.

When Spain waged warfare with our land.—P. 339.

There was a short war with Spain in 1625-6, which will be found to agree pretty well with the chronology of the poem. But probably Bertram held an opinion very common among the maritime heroes of the age, that 'there was no peace beyond the Line.' The Spanish *guarda-costas* were constantly employed in aggressions upon the trade and settlements of the English and French; and, by their own severities, gave room for the system of bucaniering, at first adopted in self-defence and retaliation, and afterwards persevered in from habit and thirst of plunder.

NOTE XXXII.

——*our comrades' strife.*—P. 340.

The laws of the Bucaniers, and their successors the Pirates, however severe and equitable, were, like other laws, often set aside by the stronger party. Their quarrels about the division of the spoil fill their history, and they as frequently arose out of mere frolic, or the tyrannical humour of their chiefs. An anecdote of Teach, (called Blackbeard,) shows that their habitual indifference for human life extended to their companions, as well as their enemies and captives.

'One night, drinking in his cabin with Hands, the pilot and another man, Blackbeard, without any provocation, privately draws out a small pair of pistols, and cocks them under the table, which, being perceived by the man, he withdrew upon deck, leaving Hands, the pilot, and the captain together. When the pistols were ready, he blew out the candles, and, crossing his hands, discharged them at his company. Hands, the master, was shot through the knee, and lamed for life; the other pistol did no execution.'—JOHNSON'S *History of Pirates.* Lond. 1724, 8vo, vol. i. p. 38.

Another anecdote of this worthy may be also mentioned. 'The hero of whom we are writing was thoroughly accomplished this way, and some of his frolics of wickedness were so extravagant, as if he aimed at making his men believe he was a devil incarnate; for, being one day at sea, and a little flushed with drink, "Come," says he, "let us make a hell of our own, and try how long we can bear it." Accordingly, he, with two or three others, went down into the hold, and, closing up all the hatches, filled several pots full of brimstone and other combustible matter, and set it on fire, and so continued till they were almost suffocated, when some of the men cried out for air. At length he opened the hatches, not a little pleased that he held out the longest.'—*Ibid.* p. 90.

NOTE XXXIII.

—— *my rangers go*
Even now to track a milk-white doe.
—P. 340.

'Immediately after supper, the huntsman should go to his master's chamber, and if he serve a king, then let him go to the master of the game's chamber, to know in what quarter he determineth to hunt the day following, that he may know his own quarter; that done, he may go to bed, to the end that he may rise the earlier in the morning, according to the time and season, and according to the place where he must hunt: then when he is up and ready, let him drinke a good draught, and fetch his hound, to make him breake his fast a little: and let him not forget to fill his bottel with good wine: that done, let him take a little vinegar into the palme of his hand, and put it in the nostrils of his hound, for to make him snuffe, to the end his scent may be the perfecter, then let him go to the wood. . . . . When the huntsman perceiveth that it is time to begin to beat, let him put his hound before him, and beat the outsides of springs or thickets; and if he find an hart or deer that likes him, let him mark well whether it be fresh or not, which he may know as well by the maner of his hounds drawing, as also by the eye. . . . . When he hath well considered what maner of hart it may be, and hath marked every thing to judge by, then let him draw till he come to the couert where he is gone to; and let him harbour him if he can, still marking all his tokens, as well by the slot as by the entries, foyles, or such-like. That done, let him plash or bruse down small twigges, some aloft and some below, as the art requireth, and therewithall, whilest his hound is hote, let him beat the outsides, and make his ring-walkes, twice or thrice about the wood.'—*The Noble Art of Venerie, or Hunting.* Lond. 1611, 4to, pp. 76, 77.

NOTE XXXIV.

Adieu for evermore.—P. 341.

The last verse of this song is taken from the fragment of an old Scottish ballad, of which I only recollected two verses when the first edition of Rokeby was published. Mr. Thomas Sheridan kindly pointed out to me an entire copy of this beautiful song, which seems to express the fortunes of some follower of the Stuart family :—

> It was a' for our rightful king
> That we left fair Scotland's strand
> It was a' for our rightful king
> That we e'er saw Irish land,
>> My dear,
> That we e'er saw Irish land.
>
> Now all is done that man can do,
> And all is done in vain !
> My love ! my native land, adieu !
> For I must cross the main,
>> My dear,
> For I must cross the main.
>
> He turn'd him round and right about,
> All on the Irish shore,
> He gave his bridle-reins a shake,
> With, Adieu for evermore,
>> My dear !
> Adieu for evermore !
>
> The soldier frae the war returns,
> And the merchant frae the main,
> But I hae parted wi' my love,
> And ne'er to meet again,
>> My dear,
> And ne'er to meet again.
>
> When day is gone and night is come,
> And a' are boun' to sleep,
> I think on them that's far awa
> The lee-lang night, and weep,
>> My dear,
> The lee-lang night, and weep.

NOTE XXXV.

Rere-cross on Stanmore.—P. 342.

This is a fragment of an old cross, with its pediment, surrounded by an intrenchment, upon the very summit of the waste ridge of Stanmore, near a small house of entertainment called the Spittal. It is called Rere-cross, or Ree-cross, of which Holinshed gives us the following explanation :—

' At length a peace was concluded betwixt the two kings vnder these conditions, that Malcolme should enjoy that part of Northumberland which lieth betwixt Tweed, Cumberland, and Stainmore, and doo homage to the Kinge of England for the same. In the midst of Stainmore there shall be a crosse set up, with the Kinge of England's image on the one side, and the Kinge of Scotland's on the other, to signifie that one is march to England, and the other to Scotland. This crosse was called the Roi-crosse, that is, the crosse of the King.'—HOLINSHED. Lond. 1808, 4to, v. 280.

Holinshed's sole authority seems to have been Boethius. But it is not improbable that his account may be the true one, although the circumstance does not occur in Wintoun's Chronicle. The situation of the cross, and the pains taken to defend it, seem to indicate that it was intended for a land-mark of importance.

NOTE XXXVI.

Hast thou lodged our deer ?—P. 342.

The duty of the ranger, or pricker, was first to lodge or harbour the deer ; i. e. to discover his retreat, as described at length in Note XXXIII, and then to make his report to his prince or master :—

'Before the King I come report to make,
Then husht and peace for nobie Tristrame's sake. . .
My liege, I went this morning on my quest,
My hound did stick, and seem'd to vent some beast.
I held him short, and drawing after him,
I might behold the hart was feeding trym ;
His head was high, and large in each degree,
Well paulmed eke, and seem'd full sound to be.
Of colour browne, he beareth eight and tenne,
Of stately height, and long he seemed then.
His beam seem'd great, in good proportion led,
Well barred and round, well pearled neare his head.
He seemed fayre tweene blacke and berrie brounde,
He seeme l well fed by all the signes I found.
For when I had well marked him with eye,
I stept aside, to watch where he would lye.
And when I had so wayted full an houre,
That he might be at layre and in his boure,
I cast about to harbour him full sure ;
My hound by sent did me thereof assure. . .
Then if he ask what slot or view I found,
I say the slot or view was long on ground ;
The toes were great, the joynt bones round and short,
The shinne bones large, the dew-claws close in port :
Short ioynted was he, hollow-footed eke,
An hart to hunt as any man can seeke.'

The Art of Venerie, ut supra, p. 97.

NOTE XXXVII.

When Denmark's raven soar'd on high,
Triumphant through Northumbrian sky,
Till, hovering near, her fatal croak
Bade Reged's Britons dread the yoke.
—P. 343.

About the year of God 866, the Danes, under their celebrated leaders Inguar (more properly Agnar) and Hubba, sons, it is said, of the still more celebrated Regnar Lodbrog, invaded Northumberland, bringing with them the magical standard, so often mentioned in poetry, called REAFEN, or *Rumfan*, from its bearing the figure of a raven :—

'Wrought by the sisters of the Danish king,
Of furious Ivar in a midnight hour :
While the sick moon, at their enchanted song
Wrapt in pale tempest, la bour'd through the clouds,
The demons of destruction then, they say,
Were all abroad, and mixing with the woof
Their baleful power : The sisters ever sung,
"Shake, standard, shake this ruin on our foes."

THOMSON and MALLET'S *Alfred*.

The Danes renewed and extended their incursions, and began to colonize, establishing a kind of capital at York, from which they spread their conquests and incursions in every direction. Stanmore, which divides the mountains of Westmoreland and Cumberland, was probably the boundary of the Danish kingdom in that direction. The district to the west, known in ancient British

history by the name of Reged, had never been conquered by the Saxons, and continued to maintain a precarious independence until it was ceded to Malcolm, King of Scots, by William the Conqueror, probably on account of its similarity in language and manners to the neighbouring British kingdom of Strath-Clyde.

Upon the extent and duration of the Danish sovereignty in Northumberland, the curious may consult the various authorities quoted in the *Gesta et Vestigia Danorum extra Daniam*, tom. ii. p. 40. The most powerful of their Northumbrian leaders seems to have been Ivar, called, from the extent of his conquests, *Widfam*, that is, *The Strider*.

NOTE XXXVIII.

Beneath the shade the Northmen came,
Fix'd on each vale a Runic name. – P. 343.

The heathen Danes have left several traces of their religion in the upper part of Teesdale. Balder-garth, which derives its name from the unfortunate son of Odin, is a tract of waste land on the very ridge of Stanmore ; and a brook, which falls into the Tees near Barnard Castle, is named after the same deity. A field upon the banks of the Tees is also termed Woden-Croft, from the supreme deity of the Edda. Thorsgill, of which a description is attempted in stanza ii, is a beautiful little brook and dell, running up behind the ruins of Egliston Abbey. Thor was the Hercules of the Scandinavian mythology, a dreadful giant-queller, and in that capacity the champion of the gods, and the defender of Asgard, the northern Olympus, against the frequent attacks of the inhabitants of Jotunheim. There is an old poem in the Edda of Sœmund, called the Song of Thrym, which turns upon the loss and recovery of the Mace, or Hammer, which was Thor's principal weapon, and on which much of his power seems to have depended. It may be read to great advantage in a version equally spirited and literal, among the Miscellaneous Translations and Poems of the Honourable William Herbert.

XXXIX.

Who has not heard how brave O'Neale
In English blood imbrued his steel ?—P. 344.

The O'Neale here meant, for more than one succeeded to the chieftainship during the reign of Elizabeth, was Hugh, the grandson of Con O'Neale, called Con Bacco, or the Lame. His father, Matthew O'Kelly, was illegitimate, and, being the son of a blacksmith's wife, was usually called Matthew the Blacksmith. His father, nevertheless, destined his succession to him ; and he was created, by Elizabeth, Baron of Dungannon. Upon the death of Con Bacco, this Matthew was slain by his brother. Hugh narrowly escaped the same fate, and was protected by the English. Shane O'Neale, his uncle, called Shane Dymas, was succeeded by Turlough Lynogh O'Neale; after whose death Hugh, having assumed the chieftainship, became nearly as formidable to the English as any by whom it had been possessed. He rebelled repeatedly, and as often made submissions, of which it was usually a condition that he should not any longer assume the title of O'Neale; in lieu of which he was created Earl of Tyrone. But this condition he never observed longer than until the pressure of superior force was withdrawn. His baffling the gallant Earl of Essex in the field, and overreaching him in a treaty, was the induction to that nobleman's tragedy. Lord Mountjoy succeeded in finally subjugating O'Neale; but it was not till the succession of James, to whom he made personal submission, and was received with civility at court. Yet, according to Morrison, 'no respect to him could containe many weomen in those parts, who had lost husbands and children in the Irish warres, from flinging durt and stones at the earle as he passed, and from reuiling him with bitter words; yea, when the earle had been at court, and there obtaining his majestie's direction for his pardon and performance of all conditions promised him by the Lord Mountjoy, was about September to returne, he durst not pass by those parts without direction to the shiriffes, to convey him with troops of horse from place to place, till he was safely imbarked and put to sea for Ireland.'— *Itinerary*, p. 296.

NOTE XL.

But chief arose his victor pride,
When that brave Marshal fought and died.
—P. 344.

The chief victory which Tyrone obtained over the English was in a battle fought near Blackwater, while he besieged a fort garrisoned by the English, which commanded the passes into his country.

'This captain and his few warders did with no less courage suffer hunger, and, having eaten the few horses they had, lived vpon hearbes growing in the ditches and wals, suffering all extremities, till the lord-lieutenant, in the moneth of August, sent Sir Henry Bagnal, marshall of Ireland, with the most choice companies of foot and horse-troopes of the English army to victual this fort, and to raise the rebels siege. When the English entered the place and thicke woods beyond Armagh, on the east side, Tyrone (with all the rebels assembled to him pricked forward with rage, enuy, and settled rancour against the marshall, assayled the English, and turning his full force against the marshall's person, had the successe to kill him,

valiantly fighting among the thickest of the rebels. Whereupon the English being dismayed with his death, the rebels obtained a great victory against them. I terme it great, since the English, from their first arriual in that kingdome, neuer had received so great an ouerthrow as this, commonly called the Defeat of Blackewater; thirteene valiant captaines and 1500 common souldiers (whereof many were of the old companies which had serued in Brittany vnder General Norreys) were slain in the field. The yielding of the fort of Blackewater followed this disaster, when the assaulted guard saw no hope of relief; but especially vpon messages sent to Captain Williams from our broken forces, retired to Armagh, professing that all their safety depended vpon his yielding the fort into the hands of Tyrone, without which danger Captaine Williams professed that no want or miserie should haue induced him thereunto.'—FYNES MORYSON'S *Itinerary*. London, 1617, fol. part ii. p. 24.

Tyrone is said to have entertained a personal animosity against the knight-marshal, Sir Henry Bagnal, whom he accused of detaining the letters which he sent to Queen Elizabeth, explanatory of his conduct, and offering terms of submission. The river, called by the English, Blackwater, is termed in Irish, Avon-Duff, which has the same signification. Both names are mentioned by Spenser in his 'Marriage of the Thames and the Medway.' But I understand that his verses relate not to the Blackwater of Ulster, but to a river of the same name in the south of Ireland:—

'Swift Avon-Duff, which of the Englishmen
Is called Blackwater.'

NOTE XLI.

The Tanist he to great O'Neale.—P. 344.

'*Eudox.* What is that which you call Tanist and Tanistry? These be names and terms never heard of nor known to us.

'*Iren.* It is a custom amongst all the Irish, that presently after the death of one of their chiefe lords or captaines, they doe presently assemble themselves to a place generally appointed and knowne unto them, to choose another in his stead, where they do nominate and elect, for the most part not the eldest sonne, nor any of the children of the lord deceased, but the next to him in blood, that is, the eldest and worthiest, as commonly the next brother unto him, if he have any, or the next cousin, or so forth, as any is elder in that kindred or sept; and then next to them doe they choose the next of the blood to be Tanist, who shall next succeed him in the said captainry, if he live thereunto.

'*Eudox.* Do they not use any ceremony in this election, for all barbarous nations are commonly great observers of ceremonies and superstitious rites?

'*Iren.* They use to place him that shall be their captaine upon a stone, always reserved to that purpose, and placed commonly upon a hill. In some of which I have seen formed and engraven a foot, which they say was the measure of their first captaine's foot; whereon hee standing, receives an oath to preserve all the ancient former customes of the countrey inviolable, and to deliver up the succession peaceably to his Tanist, and then hath a wand delivered unto him by some whose proper office that is; after which, descending from the stone, he turneth himself round, thrice forwards and thrice backwards.

'*Eudox.* But how is the Tanist chosen?

'*Iren.* They say he setteth but one foot upon the stone, and receiveth the like oath that the captaine did.'—SPENSER'S *View of the State of Ireland,* apud *Works,* Lond. 1805, 8vo. vol. viii. p. 306.

The Tanist, therefore, of O'Neale, was the heir-apparent of his power. This kind of succession appears also to have regulated, in very remote times, the succession to the crown of Scotland. It would have been imprudent, if not impossible, to have asserted a minor's right of succession in those stormy days, when the principles of policy were summed up in my friend Mr. Wordsworth's lines:—

———' the good old rule
Sufficeth them ; the simple plan,
That they should take who have the power,
And they should keep who can.'

NOTE XLII.

His plaited hair in elf-locks spread, &c.
—P. 345.

There is here an attempt to describe the ancient Irish dress, of which a poet of Queen Elizabeth's day has given us the following particulars :—

' I marvailde in my mynde,
and thereupon did muse,
To see a bride of heavenlie hewe
an ouglie fere to chuse.
This bride it is the soile,
the bridegroome is the karne.
With writhed glibbes, like wicked sprits,
with visage rough and stearne ;
With sculles upon their poalles,
instead of civill cappes ;
With speares in hand, and swordes besydes.
to beare off after clappes ;
With jackettes long and large,
which shroud simplicitie,
Though spitfull darts which they do beare
importe iniquitie.
Their shirtes be very strange,
not reaching past the thie ;
With pleates on pleates thei pleated are
as thick as pleates may lye.
Whose sleaves hang trailing doune
almost unto the shoe ;
And with a mantell commonlie
the Irish karne do goe.
Now some amongst the reste
doe use another weede ;

A coate I meane, of strange devise,
which fancy first did breade.
His skirts be very shorte,
with pleates thick about,
And Irish trouzes moe to put
their strange protactours out.
DERRICK'S *Image of Ireland*, apud SOMERS'
Tracts. Edin. 1809, 4to, vol. i. p. 585.

Some curious wooden engravings accompany this poem, from which it would seem that the ancient Irish dress was (the bonnet excepted) very similar to that of the Scottish Highlanders. The want of a covering on the head was supplied by the mode of plaiting and arranging the hair, which was called the *glibbe.* These glibbes, according to Spenser, were fit marks for a thief, since, when he wished to disguise himself, he could either cut it off entirely, or so pull it over his eyes as to render it very hard to recognize him. This, however, is nothing to the reprobation with which the same poet regards that favourite part of the Irish dress, the mantle.

' It is a fit house for an outlaw, a meet bed for a rebel, and an apt cloke for a thief. First, the outlaw being for his many crimes and villanyes banished from the townes and houses of honest men, and wandring in waste places far from danger of law, maketh his mantle his house, and under it covereth himself from the wrath of heaven, from the offence of the earth, and from the sight of men. When it raineth, it is his pent-house ; when it bloweth, it is his tent ; when it freezeth, it is his tabernacle. In summer he can wear it loose, in winter he can wrap it close ; at all times he can use it ; never heavy, never cumbersome. Likewise for a rebel it is as serviceable ; for in his warre that he maketh, (if at least it deserve the name of warre,) when he still flyeth from his foe, and lurketh in the thicke woods and straite passages, waiting for advantages, it is his bed, yea, and almost his household stuff. For the wood is his house against all weathers, and his mantle is his couch to sleep in. Therein he wrappeth himself round, and coucheth himself strongly against the gnats, which in that country doe more annoy the naked rebels while they keep the woods, and doe more sharply wound them, than all their enemies swords or speares, which can seldom come nigh them : yea, and oftentimes their mantle serveth them when they are neere driven, being wrapped about their left arme, instead of a target, for it is hard to cut thorough with a sword ; besides, it is light to beare, light to throw away, and being (as they commonly are) naked, it is to them all in all. Lastly, for a thiefe it is so handsome as it may seem it was first invented for him ; for under it he may cleanly convey any fit pillage that cometh handsomely in his way, and when he goeth abroad in the night in freebooting, it is his best and surest friend ; for lying, as they often do, two or three nights together abroad to watch for their booty, with that they can prettily shroud themselves under a bush or bankside till they may conveniently do their errand; and when all is over, he can in his mantle passe through any town or company, being close hooded over his head, as he useth, from knowledge of any to whom he is indangered. Besides this, he or any man els that is disposed to mischief or villany, may, under his mantle, goe privily armed without suspicion of any, carry his head-piece, his skean, or pistol, if he please, to be always in readiness.'—SPENSER'S *View of the State of Ireland*, apud *Works*, ut supra, viii. 367.

The javelins, or darts, of the Irish, which they threw with great dexterity, appear, from one of the prints already mentioned, to have been about four feet long, with a strong steel head and thick knotted shaft.

NOTE XLIII.

With wild majestic port and tone,
Like envoy of some barbarous throne.
—P. 345.

The Irish chiefs, in their intercourse with the English, and with each other, were wont to assume the language and style of independent royalty. Morrison has preserved a summons from Tyrone to a neighbouring chieftain, which runs in the following terms:—

'O'Neale commendeth him unto you, Morish Fitz-Thomas; O'Neale requesteth you, in God's name, to take part with him, and fight for your conscience and right; and in so doing, O'Neale will spend to see you righted in all your affaires, and will help you. And if you come not at O'Neale betwixt this and to-morrow at twelve of the clocke, and take his part, O'Neale is not beholding to you, and will doe to the uttermost of his power to overthrow you, if you come not to him at furthest by Satturday at noone. From Knocke Dumayne in Calrie, the fourth of February, 1599.

'O'Neale requesteth you to come speake with him, and doth giue you his word that you shall receive no harme neither in comming nor going from him, whether you be friend or not, and bring with you to O'Neale Gerat Fitzgerald.

(Subscribed) 'O'NEALE.'

Nor did the royalty of O'Neale consist in words alone. Sir John Harrington paid him a visit at the time of his truce with Essex, and, after mentioning his 'fern table, and fern forms, spread under the stately canopy of heaven,' he notices what constitutes the real power of every monarch, the love, namely, and allegiance of his subjects. 'His guards, for the most part, were beardless boys without shirts; who in the frost wade as familiarly through rivers as water-spaniels. With what charm such a master makes them love him, I know not; but if he bid come,

they come; if go, they do go; if he say do this, they do it.'—*Nugae Antiquae.* Lond. 1784, 8vo, vol. i. p. 251.

NOTE XLIV.

His foster-father was his guide.—P. 346.

There was no tie more sacred among the Irish than that which connected the foster-father, as well as the nurse herself, with the child they brought up.

'Foster-fathers spend much more time, money, and affection on their foster-children than their own; and in return take from them clothes, money for their several professions, and arms, and, even for any vicious purposes, fortunes and cattle, not so much by a claim of right as by extortion; and they will even carry those things off as plunder. All who have been nursed by the same person preserve a greater mutual affection and confidence in each other than if they were natural brothers, whom they will even hate for the sake of these. When chid by their parents, they fly to their foster-fathers, who frequently encourage them to make open war on their parents, train them up to every excess of wickedness, and make them most abandoned miscreants; as, on the other hand, the nurses make the young women, whom they bring up for every excess. If a foster child is sick, it is incredible how soon the nurses hear of it, however distant, and with what solicitude they attend it by day and night.'—*Giraldus Cambrensis*, quoted by Camden, iv. 368.

This custom, like many other Irish usages, prevailed till of late in the Scottish Highlands, and was cherished by the chiefs as an easy mode of extending their influence and connexion; and even in the Lowlands, during the last century, the connexion between the nurse and foster-child was seldom dissolved but by the death of one party.

NOTE XLV.

Great Nial of the Pledges Nine.—P. 347.

Neal Naighvallach, or Of the Nine Hostages, is said to have been Monarch of all Ireland, during the end of the fourth or beginning of the fifth century. He exercised a predatory warfare on the coast of England and of Bretagne, or Armorica; and from the latter country brought off the celebrated Saint Patrick, a youth of sixteen, among other captives, whom he transported to Ireland. Neal derived his epithet from nine nations, or tribes, whom he held under his subjection, and from whom he took hostages. From one of Neal's sons were derived the Kineleoguin, or Race of Tyrone, which afforded monarchs both to Ireland and to Ulster. Neal (according to O'Flaherty's Ogygia) was killed by a poisoned arrow, in one of his descents on the coast of Bretagne.

Note XLVI.

Shane-Dymas wild.—P. 347.

This Shane-Dymas, or John the Wanton, held the title and power of O'Neale in the earlier part of Elizabeth's reign, against whom he rebelled repeatedly.

'This chieftain is handed down to us as the most proud and profligate man on earth. He was immoderately addicted to women and wine. He is said to have had 200 tuns of wine at once in his cellar at Dandram, but usquebaugh was his favourite liquor. He spared neither age nor condition of the fair sex. Altho' so illiterate that he could not write, he was not destitute of address; his understanding was strong, and his courage daring. He had 600 men for his guard; 4000 foot, 1000 horse for the field. He claimed superiority over all the lords of Ulster, and called himself king thereof. When commissioners were sent to treat with him, he said, "That, tho' the Queen were his sovereign lady, he never made peace with her *but at her lodging*; that she had made a wise Earl of Macartymore, but that he kept as good a man as he; that he cared not for so mean a title as Earl; that his blood and power were better than the best; that his ancestors were Kings of Ulster; and that he would give place to none." His kinsman, the Earl of Kildare, having persuaded him of the folly of contending with the crown of England, he resolved to attend the Queen, but in a style suited to his princely dignity. He appeared in London with a magnificent train of Irish Galloglasses, arrayed in the richest habiliments of their country, their heads bare, their hair flowing on their shoulders, with their long and open sleeves dyed with saffron. Thus dressed, and surcharged with military harness, and armed with battle-axes, they afforded an astonishing spectacle to the citizens, who regarded them as the intruders of some very distant part of the globe. But at Court his versatility now prevailed; his title to the sovereignty of Tyrone was pleaded from English laws and Irish institutions, and his allegations were so specious, that the Queen dismissed him with presents and assurances of favour. In England this transaction was looked on as the humiliation of a repenting rebel; in Tyrone it was considered as a treaty of peace between two potentates.'—CAMDEN'S *Britannia*, by Gough. London, 1806, fol., vol. iv. p. 442.

When reduced to extremity by the English, and forsaken by his allies, this Shane-Dymas fled to Clandeboy, then occupied by a colony of Scottish Highlanders of the family of Mac-Donell. He was at first courteously received; but by degrees they began to quarrel about the slaughter of some of their friends whom Shane-Dymas had put to death, and advancing from words to deeds, fell upon him with their broadswords, and cut him to pieces. After his death a law was made that none should presume to take the name and title of O'Neale.

Note XLVII.

Geraldine.— P. 347.

The O'Neales were closely allied with this powerful and warlike family; for Henry Owen O'Neale married the daughter of Thomas Earl of Kildare, and their son Con-More married his cousin-german, a daughter of Gerald Earl of Kildare. This Con-More cursed any of his posterity who should learn the English language, sow corn, or build houses, so as to invite the English to settle in their country. Others ascribe this anathema to his son Con-Bacco. Fearflatha O'Gnive, bard to the O'Neales of Clannaboy, complains in the same spirit of the towers and ramparts with which the strangers had *disfigured* the fair sporting fields of Erin.—See WALKER'S *Irish Bards*, p. 140.

Note XLVIII.

He chose that honour'd flag to bear.
—P. 347.

Lacy informs us, in the old play already quoted, how the cavalry raised by the country gentlemen for Charles's service were usually officered. 'You, cornet, have a name that's proper for all cornets to be called by, for they are all beardless boys in our army. The most part of our horse were raised thus:—The honest country gentleman raises the troop at his own charge; then he gets a Low-country lieutenant to fight his troop safely; then he sends for his son from school to be his cornet: and then he puts off his child's coat to put on a buff-coat: and this is the constitution of our army.'

Note XLIX.

——his page, the next degree,
In that old time, to chivalry.—P. 347.

Originally, the order of chivalry embraced three ranks—1, the Page; 2, the Squire; 3, the Knight;—a gradation which seems to have been imitated in the mystery of free-masonry. But, before the reign of Charles I, the custom of serving as a squire had fallen into disuse, though the order of the page was still, to a certain degree, in observance. This state of servitude was so far from inferring anything degrading, that it was considered as the regular school for acquiring every quality necessary for future distinction. The proper nature, and the decay of the institution, are pointed out by old Ben Jonson, with his own forcible moral colouring. The dialogue occurs between Lovell, 'a compleat gentleman, a soldier, and a scholar, known to have been page to the old Lord Beaufort, and so to have followed him in the French wars, after companion of his studies, and left guardian to his son,' and the facetious Goodstock, host of the Light Heart. Lovel had offered to take Goodstock's son for his page, which the latter, in reference to the recent abuse of the establishment, declares as 'a desperate course of life' :—

'*Lovell.* Call you that desperate, which by a line
Of institution, from our ancestors
Hath been derived down to us, and received
In a succession, for the noblest way
Of breeding up our youth, in letters, arms,
Fair mien, discourses, civil exercise,
And all the blazon of a gentleman?
Where can he learn to vault, to ride, to fence,
To move his body gracefully ; to speak
His language purer ; or to tune his mind,
Or manners, more to the harmony of nature,
Than in the nurseries of nobility?
Host. Ay, that was when the nursery's self was
noble,
And only virtue made it, not the market,
That titles were not vented at the drum,
Or common outcry. Goodness gave the greatness,
And greatness worship : every house became
An academy of honour ; and those parts
We see departed, in the practice, now,
Quite from the institution.
Lovell. Why do you say so?
Or think so enviously? Do they not still
Learn there the Centaur's skill. the art of Thrace,
To ride? or, Pollux' mystery, to fence?
The Pyrrhic gestures, both to dance and spring
In armour, to be active in the wars?
To study figures, numbers, and proportions,
May yield them great in counsels, and the arts
Grave Nestor and the wise Ulysses practised?
To make their English sweet upon their tongue,
As reverend Chaucer says?
Host. Sir, you mistake ;
To play Sir Pandarus, my copy hath it,
And carry messages to Madame Cressida ;
Instead of backing the brave steed o' mornings,
To court the chambermaid ; and for a leap
O' the vaulting horse, to ply the vaulting house :
For exercise of arms, a bale of dice,
Or two or three packs of cards to show the cheat,
And nimbleness of hand ; mistake a cloak
Upon my lord's back, and pawn it ; ease his pocket
Of a superfluous watch ; or geld a jewel
Of an odd stone or so ; twinge two or three buttons
From off my lady's gown : These are the arts
Or seven liberal deadly sciences
Of pagery, or rather paganism,
As the tides run ; to which if he apply him,
He may perhaps take a degree at Tyburn,
A year the earlier ; come to take a lecture
Upon Aquinas at St. Thomas a Watering's,
And so go forth a laureat in hemp circle !'
BEN JONSON'S *New Inn*, Act I. Scene III.

NOTE L.

Seem'd half abandon'd to decay.—P. 353.

The ancient castle of Rokeby stood exactly upon the site of the present mansion, by which a part of its walls is enclosed. It is surrounded by a profusion of fine wood, and the park in which it stands is adorned by the junction of the Greta and of the Tees. The title of Baron Rokeby of Armagh was, in 1777, conferred on the Right Reverend Richard Robinson, Primate of Ireland, descended of the Robinsons, formerly of Rokeby, in Yorkshire.

NOTE LI.

Rokeby's lords of martial fame,
I can count them name by name.—P. 355.

The following brief pedigree of this very ancient and once powerful family was kindly supplied to the author by Mr. Rokeby of Northamptonshire, descended of the ancient Barons of Rokeby :—

'*Pedigree of the House of Rokeby.*

1. Sir Alex. Rokeby, Knt. married to Sir Hump. Liftle's [1] daughter.
2. Ralph Rokeby, Esq. to Tho. Lumley's daughter.
3. Sir Tho. Rokeby, Knt. to Tho. Hubborn's daughter.
4. Sir Ralph Rokeby, Knt. to Sir Ralph Biggot's daughter.
5. Sir Thos. Rokeby, Knt. to Sir John de Melsass' daughter, of Bennet Hall, in Holderness.
6. Ralph Rokeby, Esq. to Sir Brian Stapleton's daughter, of Weighill.
7. Sir Thos. Rokeby, Knt. to Sir Ralph Ury's daughter [2].
8. Ralph Rokeby, Esq. to daughter of Mansfield, heir of Morton .
9. Sir Tho. Rokeby, Knt. to Stroode's daughter and heir.
10. Sir Ralph Rokeby, Knt. to Sir James Strangwayes' daughter.
11. Sir Thos. Rokeby, Knt. to Sir John Hotham's daughter.
12. Ralph Rokeby, Esq. to Danby of Yafforth's daughter and heir [4].
13. Tho. Rokeby, Esq. to Rob. Constable's daughter, of Cliff, serjt. at law.
14. Christopher Rokeby, Esq. to Lasscells of Brackenburgh's daughter [5].
15. Thos. Rokeby, Esq. to the daughter of Thweng.
16. Sir Thomas Rokeby, Knt. to Sir Ralph Lawson's daughter, of Brough.
17. Frans. Rokeby, Esq. to Faucett's daughter, citizen of London.
18. Thos. Rokeby, Esq. to the daughter of Wickliffe of Gales.

High Sheriffs of Yorkshire.

1337. 11 Edw. 3. Ralph Hastings and Thos. de Rokeby.

1343. 17 Edw. 3. Thos. de Rokeby, pro sept. annis.

1 Lisle. 2 Temp. Edw. 2di. 3 Temp. Edw. 3tii.
4 Temp. Henr. 7mi, and from him is the house of Skyers, of a fourth brother.
5 From him is the house of Hotham, and of the second brother that had issue.

1358. 25 Edw. 3. Sir Thomas Rokeby, Justiciary of Ireland for six years; died at the castle of Kilka.

1407. 8 Hen. 4. Thomas Rokeby Miles, defeated and slew the Duke of Northumberland at the battle of Bramham Moor.

1411. 12 Hen. 4. Thos. Rokeby Miles.

1486. . . . . Thomas Rokeby, Esq.

1539. . . . . . . Robert Holgate, Bishop of Landaff, afterwards P. of York, Ld. President of the Council for the Preservation of Peace in the North.

1564. 6 Eliz. Thomas Younge, Archbishop of Yorke, Ld. President.

30 Hen. 8. Tho. Rokeby, LL.D., one of the Council. Jn. Rokeby, LL.D., one of the Council.

1572. 15 Eliz. Henry Hastings, Earl of Huntingdon, Ld. President. Jo. Rokeby, Esq., one of the Council. Jo. Rokeby, LL.D., ditto. Ralph Rokeby, Esq., one of the Secretaries.

1574. 17 Eliz. Jo. Rokeby, Precentor of York.

7 Will. 3. Sir J. Rokeby, Knt., one of the Justices of the King's Bench.

The family of De Rokeby came over with the Conqueror.

The old motto belonging to the family is *In Bivio Dextra.*

The arms, argent, chevron sable, between three rooks proper.

'There is somewhat more to be found in our family in the Scottish history about the affairs of Dun-Bretton town, but what it is, and in what time, I know not, nor can have convenient leisure to search. But Parson Blackwood, the Scottish chaplain to the Lord of Shrewsbury, recited to me once a piece of a Scottish song, wherein was mentioned, that William Wallis, the great deliverer of the Scots from the English bondage, should, at Dun-Bretton, have been brought up under a Rokeby, captain then of the place; and as he walked on a cliff, should thrust him on a sudden into the sea, and thereby have gotten that hold, which, I think, was about the 33rd of Edward I, or before. Thus, leaving our ancestors of record, we must also with them leave the Chronicle of Malmesbury Abbey, called *Eulogium Historiarum,* out of which Mr. Leland reporteth this history, and coppy down unwritten story, the which have yet the testimony of later times, and the fresh memory of men

yet alive, for their warrant and credit, of whom I have learned it, that in K. Henry the 7th's reign, one Ralph Rokeby, Esq. was owner of Morton, and I guess that this was he that deceived the fryars of Richmond with his felon swine, on which a jargon was made.'

The above is a quotation from a manuscript written by Ralph Rokeby; when he lived is uncertain.

To what metrical Scottish tradition Parson Blackwood alluded, it would be now in vain to inquire. But in Blind Harry's History of Sir William Wallace, we find a legend of one Rukbie, whom he makes keeper of Stirling Castle under the English usurpation, and whom Wallace slays with his own hand :—

'In the great press Wallace and Rukbie met,
With his good sword a stroke upon him set;
Derfly to death the old Rukbie he drave,
But his two sons escaped among the lave.

These sons, according to the romantic Minstrel, surrendered the castle on conditions, and went back to England, but returned to Scotland in the days of Bruce, when one of them became again keeper of Stirling Castle. Immediately after this achievement follows another engagement, between Wallace and those Western Highlanders who embraced the English interest, at a pass in Glendouchart, where many were precipitated into the lake over a precipice. These circumstances may have been confused in the narrative of Parson Blackwood, or in the recollection of Mr. Rokeby.

In the old ballad of Chevy Chase, there is mentioned, among the English warriors, 'Sir Raff the ryche Rugbe,' which may apply to Sir Ralph Rokeby, the tenth baron in the pedigree. The more modern copy of the ballad runs thus :—

'Good Sir Ralph Raby ther was slain,
Whose prowess did surmount.

This would rather seem to relate to one of the Nevilles of Raby. But, as the whole ballad is romantic, accuracy is not to be looked for.

NOTE LII.

*The Felon Sow.—*P. 355.

The ancient minstrels had a comic as well as a serious strain of romance; and although the examples of the latter are by far the most numerous, they are, perhaps, the less valuable. The comic romance was a sort of parody upon the usual subjects of minstrel poetry. If the latter described deeds of heroic achievement, and the events of the battle, the tourney, and the chase, the former, as in the Tournament of Tottenham, introduced a set of clowns debating in the field, with all the assumed circumstances of chivalry; or, as in the Hunting of the Hare (see Weber's *Metrical Romances*, vol. iii), persons of the same description following the chase, with all the grievous mistakes and blunders incident to such unpractised sportsmen. The idea, therefore, of Don Quixote's frenzy, although inimitably embodied and brought out, was not, perhaps, in the abstract, altogether original. One of the very best of these mock romances, and which has no small portion of comic humour, is the Hunting of the Felon Sow of Rokeby by the Friars of Richmond. Ralph Rokeby, who (for the jest's sake apparently) bestowed this intractable animal on the convent of Richmond, seems to have flourished in the time of Henry VII, which, since we know not the date of Friar Theobald's wardenship, to which the poem refers us, may indicate that of the composition itself. Morton, the Mortham of the text, is mentioned as being this facetious baron's place of residence; accordingly, Leland notices, that 'Mr. Rokeby hath a place called Mortham, a little beneath Grentey-bridge, almost on the mouth of Grentey.' That no information may be lacking which is in my power to supply, I have to notice, that the Mistress Rokeby of the romance, who so charitably refreshed the sow after she had discomfited Friar Middleton and his auxiliaries, was, as appears from the pedigree of the Rokeby family, daughter and heir of Danby of Yaffort.

This curious poem was first published in Mr. Whitaker's History of Craven, but, from an inaccurate manuscript, not corrected very happily. It was transferred by Mr. Evans to the new edition of his Ballads, with some well-judged conjectural improvements. I have been induced to give a more authentic and full, though still an imperfect, edition of this humorsome composition, from being furnished with a copy from a manuscript in the possession of Mr. Rokeby, to whom I have acknowledged my obligations in the last note. It has three or four stanzas more than that of Mr. Whitaker, and the language seems, where they differ, to have the more ancient and genuine readings.

THE FELON SOW OF ROKEBY AND THE
FRIARS OF RICHMOND.

Ye men that will of aunters [1] winne,
That late wi.hin this land hath beene,
  Of one I will you tell;
And of a sew [2] that was sea [3] strang,
Alas! that ever she lived sae lang,
  For fell [4] folk did she whell [5].

---

[1] Both the MS. and Mr. Whitaker's copy read *ancestors*, evidently a corruption of *aunters*, adventures, as corrected by Mr. Evans.
[2] Sow, according to provincial pronunciation.
[3] So; Yorkshire dialect.   [4] Feie, many; Sax.
[5] A corruption of *quell*, to kill.

She was mare [1] than other three,
The grisliest beast that ere might be,
  Her head was great and gray:
She was bred in Rokeby wood,
There were few that thither goed [2],
  That came on live [3] away.

Her walk was endlong [4] Greta side;
There was no bren [5] that durst her bide,
  That was froe [6] heaven to hell;
Nor never man that had that might,
That ever durst come in her sight,
  Her force it was so fell.

Ralph of Rokeby, with good will,
The Fryers of Richmond gave her till [7],
  Full well to garre [8] them fare;
Fryar Middleton by his name,
He was sent to fetch her hame,
  That rued him sine [9] full sare.

With him tooke he wicht men two,
Peter Dale was one of thoe,
  That ever was brim as beare [10];
And well durst strike with sword and knife,
And fight full manly for his life,
  What time as mister ware [11].

These three men went at God's will,
This wicked sew while they came till,
  Liggan [12] under a tree;
Rugg and rusty was her haire;
She raise up with a felon fare [13],
  To fight against the three.

She was so grisely for to meete,
She rave the earth up with her feete,
  And bark came fro the tree;
When Fryar Middleton her saugh [14],
Weet ye well he might not laugh,
  Full earnestly look't hee.

These men of aunters that was so wight [15],
They bound them baukily [16] for to fight,
  And strike at her full sare:
Until a kiln they garred her flee,
Wold God send them the victory,
  The wold ask him noa mare.

The sew was in the kiln hole down,
As they were on the balke aboon [17],
  For [18] hurting of their feet;
They were so saulted [19] with this sew,
That among them was a stalworth stew,
  The kiln began to reeke.

Durst noe man neigh her with his hand,
But put a rape [20] down with his wand,
  And haltered her full meete;
They hurled her forth against her will,
Whiles they came into a hill
  A little fro the street [21].

---

[1] More, greater.   [2] Went.
[3] Alive.   [4] Along the side of Greta.
[5] Barn, child, man in general. [6] From.
[7] To.   [8] Make.   [9] Since.
[10] Fierce as a bear. Mr. Whitaker's copy reads, perhaps in consequence of mistaking the MS., 'T'other was Bryan of Bear.
[11] Need were. Mr. Whitaker reads *musters*.
[12] Lying.   [13] A fierce countenance or manner.
[14] Saw.
[15] Wight, brave. The Rokeby MS. reads *incounters*, and Mr. Whitaker *auncestors*.
[16] Boldly.   [17] On the beam above.
[18] To prevent.   [19] Assaulted.   [20] Rope.
[21] Watling Street. See the sequel.

And there she made them such a fray,
If they should live to Doomes-day,
  They tharrow [1] it ne'er forgett ;
She braded [2] upon every side,
And ran on them gaping full wide,
  For nothing would she lett [3].

She gave such brades [4] at the band
That Peter Dale had in his hand,
  He might not hold his feet.
She chafed them to and fro,
The wight men was never soe woe,
  Their measure was not so meete.

She bound her boldly to abide ;
To Peter Dale she came aside,
  With many a hideous yell ;
She gaped soe wide and cried soe hee,
The Fryar seid, ' I conjure thee [5],
  Thou art a feind of hell.

' Thou art come hither for some traine [6],
I conjure thee to go againe
  Where thou wast wont to dwell.'
He sayned [7] him with crosse and creede,
Took forth a book, began to reade
  In St. John his gospell.

The sew she would not Latin heare,
But rudely rushed at the Frear,
  That blinked all his blee [8] ;
And when she would have taken her hold,
The Fryar leaped as Jesus wold,
  And bealed him [9] with a tree.

She was as brim [10] as any beare,
For all their meete to labour there [11],
  To them it was no boote :
Upon trees and bushes that by her stood,
She ranged as she was wood [12],
  And rave them up by roote.

He sayd, ' Alas, that I was Frear !
And I shall be rugged [13] in sunder here,
  Hard is my destinie !
Wist [14] my brethren in this houre,
That I was sett in such a stoure [15],
  They would pray for me.'

This wicked beast that wrought this woe,
Tooke that rape from the other two,
  And then they fledd all three ;
They fledd away by Watling-street,
They had no succour but their feet,
  It was the more pity.

The feild it was both lost and wonne [1] ;
The sew went hame, and that full soone,
  To Morton on the Greene ;
When Ralph of R keby saw the rape [2],
He wist [3] that there had been debate,
  Whereat the sew had beene.

He bad them stand out of her way,
For she had had a sudden fray,—
  ' I saw never so keene ;
Some new things shall we heare
Of her and Middleton the Frear,
  Some battell hath there beene.

But all that served him for nought
Had they not better succour sought,
  They were served therefore loe.
Then Mistress Rokeby came anon,
And for her brought shee meate full soone,
  The sew came her unto.

She gave her meate upon the flower,
 .   .   .   .   . [4]

    [*Hiatus valde deflendus.*]

When Fryar Middleton came home,
His brethren was full fain ilkone [5],
  And thanked God of his life ;
He told them all unto the end,
How he had foughten with a fiend,
  And lived through mickle strife.

' We gave her battell half a day,
And sithin [6] was fain to fly away,
  For saving of our life · ;
And Pater Dale would never blinn [8],
But as fast as he could ryn [9],
  Till he came to his wife.'

The warden said, ' I am full of woe,
That ever ye should be torment so,
  But wee with you had beene !
Had wee been there your brethren all,
Wee should have garred the warle [10] fall
  That wrought you all this teyne [11].

Fryar Middleton said soon, 'Nay,
In faith you would have fled away,
  When most mister [12] had beene ;
You will all speake words at hame,
A man would ding [1] you every ilk ane,
  And if it be as I weine.'

He look't so griesly all that night,
The warden said, ' Yon man will fight
  If you say ought but good ;
Yon guest [14] hath grieved him so sare,
Hold your tongues and speake noe mare,
  He looks as he were woode.'

---

[1] Dare.   [2] Rushed.   [3] Leave it.   [4] Pulls.
[5] This line is wanting in Mr. Whitaker's copy,
whence it has been conjectured that something
is wanting after this stanza, which now there is no
occasion to suppose.
  [6] Evil device.   [7] Blessed. Fr.   [8] Lost his colour.
[9] Sheltered himself.   [10] Fierce.
[11] The MS. reads, *to labour weere.* The text
seems to mean, that all their labour to obtain their
intended meat was of no use to them. Mr. Whitaker
reads,

  ' She was brim as any boar,
    And gave a grisly hideous roar,
    To them it was no boot.'

Besides the want of connection between the last line
and the two former, the second has a very modern
sound, and the reading of the Rokeby MS. with the
slight alteration in the text, is much better.
  [12] Mad.   [13] Torn, pulled.   [14] Knew.
[15] Combat, perilous fight.

[1] This stanza, with the two following, and the fragment of a fourth, are not in Mr. Whitaker's edition.
[2] The rope about the sow's neck.   [3] Knew.
[4] This line is almost illegible.   [5] Each one.
[6] Since then, after that.
[7] The above lines are wanting in Mr. Whitaker's
copy.
  [8] Cease, stop.   [9] Run.
[10] Warlock, or wizard.   [11] Harm.   [12] Need.
[13] Beat. The copy in Mr. Whitaker's History of
Craven reads, perhaps better—

  ' The fiend would ding you down ilk one.'

[14] ' Yon guest, may be yon *gest*, i. e. that adventure ; or it may mean yon *ghaist*, or apparition, which in old poems is applied sometimes to
what is supernaturally hideous. The printed copy
reads, ' The beast hath,' &c.

The warden waged [1] on the morne,
Two boldest men that ever were borne,
 I weine, or ever shall be ;
The one was Gibbert Griffin s son,
Full mickle worship has he wonne,
 Both by land and sea.

The other was a bastard son of Spain,
Many a Sarazin hath he slain,
 His dint [2] hath gart them die.
These two men the battle undertooke,
Against the sew, as says the booke,
 And sealed security.

That they should boldly bide and fight,
And skomfit her in maine and might,
 Or therefore should they die.
The warden sealed to them againe,
And said, 'In feild if ye be slain,
 This condition make I :

'We shall for you pray, sing, and read
To doomesday with hearty speede,
 With all our progeny.
Then the letters well was made,
Bands bound with seales brade [3],
 As deedes of armes should be.'

These men of armes that weere so wight,
With armour and with brandes bright,
 They went this sew to see ;
She made on them slike a rerd [4],
That for her they were sare afer'd,
 And almost bound to flee.

She came roveing them egaine ;
That saw the bastard son of Spaine,
 He braded [5] out his brand ;
Full spiteously at her he strake,
For all the fence that he could make,
 She gat sword out of hand ;
And rave in sunder half his shielde,
And bare him backward in the feilde,
 He might not her gainstand.

She would have riven his privich geare,
But Gilbert with his sword of werre,
 He strake at her full strong,
On her shoulder till she held the swerd :
Then was good Gilbert sore afer d,
 When the blade brake in throng [6].

Since in his hands he hath her tane,
She tooke him by the shoulder bane [7],
 And held her hold full fast ;
She strave so stiffly in that stower [8],
That through all his rich armour
 The blood came at the last.

Then Gilbert grieved was sea sare,
That he rave off both hide and haire,
 The flesh came fro the bone ;
And with all force he felled her there,
And wann her worthily in werre,
 And band her him alone.

And lift her on a horse sea hee,
Into two paniers well-made of a tre,
 And to Richmond they did hay [9] :
When they saw her come,
They sang merrily Te Deum,
 The Fryers on that day [10].

They thanked God and St. Francis,
As they had won the best of pris [1],
 And never a man was slaine :
There did never a man more manly
Knight Marcus, nor yett Sir Gui,
 Nor Loth of Louthyane [2].

If ye will any more of this,
In the Fryers of Richmond 'tis
 In parchment good and fine ;
And how Fryar Middleton that was so kend [3],
At Greta Bridge conjured a feind
 In likeness of a swine.

It is well known to many a man,
That Fryar Theobald was warden than,
 And this fell in his time ;
And Christ them bless both farre and neare,
All that for solace list this to heare,
 And him that made the rhime. .

Ralph Rokeby with full good will,
The Fryers of Richmond he gave her till,
 This sew to mend their fare :
Fryar Middleton by his name,
Would needs bring the fat sew hame,
 That rued him since full sare.

Note LIII.

*The Filea of O'Neale was he.—*P. 356.

The Filea, or Ollamh Re Dan, was the proper bard, or, as the name literally implies, poet. Each chieftain of distinction had one or more in his service, whose office was usually hereditary. The late ingenious Mr. Cooper Walker has assembled a curious collection of particulars concerning this order of men, in his Historical Memoirs of the Irish Bards. There were itinerant bards of less elevated rank, but all were held in the highest veneration. The English, who considered them as chief supporters of the spirit of national independence, were much disposed to proscribe this race of poets, as Edward I is said to have done in Wales. Spenser, while he admits the merit of their wild poetry, as 'savouring of sweet wit and good invention, and sprinkled with some pretty flowers of their natural device,' yet rigorously condemns the whole application of their poetry, as abased to 'the gracing of wickedness and vice.' The household minstrel was admitted even to the feast of the prince whom he served, and sat at the same table. It was one of the customs of which Sir Richard Sewry, to whose charge Richard II committed the instruction of our Irish monarchs in the civilisation of the period, found it most difficult to break his royal disciples, though he had also much ado to subject them to other English rules, and particularly to reconcile them to wear breeches. 'The kyng, my souereigne lord's entent was, that in

---

[1] Hired, a Yorkshire phrase. [2] Blow.
[3] Broad, large. [4] Such like a roar.
[5] Drew out. [6] In the combat. [7] Bone.
[8] Meeting, battle. [9] Hie, hasten.
[10] The MS. reads, mistakenly, *every* day.

[1] Price.
[2] The father of Sir Gawain, in the romance of Arthur and Merlin. The MS. is thus corrupted—
 'More loth of Louth Ryme.'
[3] Either 'kind,' or 'well-known.'

maner, countenaunce, and apparel of clothyng, they sholde use according to the maner of Englande, for the kynge thought to make them all four knyghtes: they had a fayre house to lodge in, in Duvelyn, and I was charged to abyde styll with them, and not to departe; and so two or three dayes I suffered them to do as they lyst, and sayde nothyng to them, but folowed their owne appetytes: they wolde sitte at the table, and make countenance nother good nor fayre. Than I thought I shulde cause them to chaunge that maner; they wolde cause their mynstrells, their seruantes, and varlettes, to sytte with them, and to eate in their owne dyssche, and to drinke of their cuppes; and they shewed me that the usage of their cuntre was good, for they sayd in all thyngs (except their beddes) they were and lyved as comen. So the fourthe day I ordayned other tables to be couered in the hall, after the usage of Englande, and I made these four knyghtes to sytte at the hyghe table, and there mynstrels at another borde, and their seruauntes and varlettes at another byneth them, wherof by semynge they were displeased, and beheld each other, and wolde not eate, and sayde, how I wolde take fro them their good usage, wherein they had been norished. Then I answered them, smylyng, to apeace them, that it was not honourable for their estates to do as they dyde before, and that they must leave it, and use the custom of Englande, and that it was the kynge's pleasure they shulde so do, and how he was charged so to order them. When they harde that, they suffred it, bycause they had putte themselfe under the obeysance of the Kynge of England, and parceuered in the same as long as I was with them; yet they had one use which I knew was well used in their cuntre, and that was, they dyde were no breches; I caused breches of lynen clothe to be made for them. Whyle I was with them I caused them to leaue many rude thynges, as well in clothyng as in other causes. Moche ado I had at the fyrst to cause them to weare gownes of sylke, furred with myneuere and gray; for before these kynges thought themselfe well apparelled whan they had on a mantell. They rode alwayes without saddles and styropes, and with great payne I made them to ride after our usage.'— LORD BERNERS' *Froissart.* Lond. 1812, 4to, vol. ii. p. 621.

The influence of these bards upon their patrons, and their admitted title to interfere in matters of the weightiest concern, may be also proved from the behaviour of one of them at an interview between Thomas Fitzgerald, son of the Earl of Kildare, then about to renounce the English allegiance, and the Lord Chancellor Cromer, who made a long and goodly oration to dissuade him from his purpose. The young lord had come to the council 'armed and weaponed,' and attended by seven score horsemen in their

shirts of mail; and we are assured that the chancellor, having set forth his oration 'with such a lamentable action as his cheekes were all beblubbered with teares, the horsemen, namelie, such as understood not English, began to diuine what the lordchancellor meant with all this long circumstance; some of them reporting that he was preaching a sermon, others said that he stood making of some heroicall poetry in the praise of the Lord Thomas. And thus as every idiot shot his foolish bolt at the wise chancellor his discourse, who in effect had nought else but drop pretious stones before hogs, one Bard de Nolan, an Irish rithmour, and a rotten sheepe to iniect a whole flocke, was chatting of Irish verses, as though his toong had run on pattens, in commendation of the Lord Thomas, investing him with the title of Silken Thomas, bicaus his horsemens jacks were gorgeously imbroidered with silke: and in the end he told him that he lingered there ouer long; whereat the Lord Thomas being quickened,' as Holinshed expresses it, bid defiance to the chancellor, threw down contemptuously the sword of office, which, in his father's absence, he held as deputy, and rushed forth to engage in open insurrection.

NOTE LIV.

Ah, Clandeboy! thy friendly floor
Slieve-Donard's oak shall light no more.
—P. 356.

Clandeboy is a district of Ulster, formerly possessed by the sept of the O'Neales, and Slieve-Donard, a romantic mountain in the same province. The clan was ruined after Tyrone's great rebellion, and their places of abode laid desolate. The ancient Irish, wild and uncultivated in other respects, did not yield even to their descendants in practising the most free and extended hospitality; and doubtless the bards mourned the decay of the mansion of their chiefs in strains similar to the verses of the British Llywarch Hen on a similar occasion, which are affecting, even through the discouraging medium of a literal translation:—

'Silent-breathing gale, long wilt thou be heard!
There is scarcely another deserving praise,
Since Urien is no more.

Many a dog that scented well the prey, and aërial hawk,
Have been trained on this floor
Before Erlleon became polluted.

This hearth, ah, will it not be covered with nettles!
Whilst its defender lived,
More congenial to it was the foot of the needy petitioner.

This hearth, will it not be covered with green sod
In the lifetime of Owain and Elphin,
Its ample cauldron boiled the prey taken from the foe.

This hearth, will it not be covered with toad-stools !
Around the viand it prepared, more cheering was
The clattering sword of the fierce dauntless warrior.

This hearth, will it not be overgrown with spreading
    brambles !
Till now, logs of burning wood lay on it,
Accustom'd to prepare the gifts of Reged !

This hearth, will it not be covered with thorns !
More congenial on it would have been the mixed
    group
Of Owain's social friends united in harmony.

This hearth, will it not be covered with ants !
More adapted to it would have been the bright
    torches
And harmless festivities !

This hearth, will it not be covered with dock-leaves !
More congenial on its floor would have been
The mead, and the talking of wine-cheer'd warriors.

This hearth, will it not be turned up by the swine !
More congenial to it would have been the clamour
    of men,
And the circling horns of the banquet.'
        Heroic Elegies of Llywarc Hen, by OWEN.
                    Lond. 1792, 8vo, p. 41.

The hall of Cynddylan is gloomy this night,
Without fire, without bed—
I must weep a while, and then be silent !

The hall of Cynddylan is gloomy this night,
Without fire, without candle—
Except God doth, who will endue me with patience ?

The hall of Cynddylan is gloomy this night,
Without fire, without being lighted—
Be thou encircled with spreading silence !

The hall of Cynddylan, gloomy seems its roof
Since the sweet smile of humanity is no more—
Woe to him that saw it, if he neglects to do good !

The hall of Cynddylan, art thou not bereft of thy
    appearance?
Thy shield is in the grave ;
Whilst he lived there was no broken roof !

The hall of Cynddylan is without love this night,
Since he that own'd it is no more—
Ah, death : it will be but a short time he will leave
    me !

The hall of Cynddylan is not easy this night,
On the top of the rock of Hydwyth,
Without its lord, without company, without the
    circling feasts !

The hall of Cynddylan is gloomy this night,
Without fire, without songs—
Tears afflict the cheeks !

The hall of Cynddylan is gloomy this night,
Without fire, without family—
My overflowing tears gush out !

The hall of Cynddylan pierces me to see it,
Without a covering, without fire—
My general dead, and I alive myself !

The hall of Cynddylan is the seat of chill grief this
    night,
After the respect I experienced ;
Without the men, without the women, who reside
    there !

The hall of Cynddylan is silent this night,
After losing its master—
The great merciful God, what shall I do ?
                            Ibid. p. 77.

NOTE LV.

M'Curtin's harp.—P. 358.

'MacCurtin, hereditary Ollamh of North
Munster, and Filea to Donough, Earl of
Thomond, and President of Munster. This
nobleman was amongst those who were
prevailed upon to join Elizabeth's forces.
Soon as it was known that he had basely
abandoned the interests of his country, Mac-
Curtin presented an adulatory poem to
MacCarthy, chief of South Munster, and of the
Eugenian line, who, with O'Neil, O'Donnel,
Lacy, and others, were deeply engaged in
protecting their violated country. In this
poem he dwells with rapture on the courage
and patriotism of MacCarthy ; but the verse
that should (according to an established law
of the order of the bards) be introduced in
the praise of O'Brien, he turns into severe
satire :—"How am I afflicted (says he) that
the descendant of the great Brion Boiromh
cannot furnish me with a theme worthy the
honour and glory of his exalted race !" Lord
Thomond, hearing this, vowed vengeance on
the spirited bard, who fled for refuge to the
county of Cork. One day observing the
exasperated nobleman and his equipage at
a small distance, he thought it was in vain to
fly, and pretended to be suddenly seized with
the pangs of death ; directing his wife to
lament over him, and tell his lordship, that
the sight of him, by awakening the sense of
his ingratitude, had so much affected him
that he could not support it ; and desired her
at the same time to tell his lordship, that he
entreated, as a dying request, his forgiveness.
Soon as Lord Thomond arrived, the feigned
tale was related to him. That nobleman
was moved to compassion, and not only
declared that he most heartily forgave him,
but, opening his purse, presented the fair
mourner with some pieces to inter him.
This instance of his lordship's pity and
generosity gave courage to the trembling
bard ; who, suddenly springing up, recited an
extemporaneous ode in praise of Donough,
and, re-entering into his service, became once
more his favourite.'—WALKER'S *Memoirs
of the Irish Bards.* Lond. 1786, 4to, p. 141.

NOTE LVI.

The ancient English minstrel's dress.
                            —P. 358.

Among the entertainments presented to
Elizabeth at Kenilworth Castle, was the introduction of a person designed to represent
a travelling minstrel, who entertained her
with a solemn story out of the Acts of King
Arthur. Of this person's dress and appearance Mr. Laneham has given us a very accurate account, transferred by Bishop Percy to
the preliminary Dissertation on Minstrels,
prefixed to his *Reliques of Ancient Poetry,*
vol. i.

Note LVII.

Littlecot Hall.—P. 362.

The tradition from which the ballad is founded, was supplied by a friend, (the late Lord Webb Seymour,) whose account I will not do the injustice to abridge, as it contains an admirable picture of an old English hall:—
'Littlecote House stands in a low and lonely situation. On three sides it is surrounded by a park that spreads over the adjoining hill; on the fourth, by meadows which are watered by the river Kennet. Close on one side of the house is a thick grove of lofty trees, along the verge of which runs one of the principal avenues to it through the park. It is an irregular building of great antiquity, and was probably erected about the time of the termination of feudal warfare, when defence came no longer to be an object in a country mansion. Many circumstances, however, in the interior of the house, seem appropriate to feudal times. The hall is very spacious, floored with stones, and lighted by large transom windows, that are clothed with casements. Its walls are hung with old military accoutrements, that have long been left a prey to rust. At one end of the hall is a range of coats of mail and helmets, and there is on every side abundance of old-fashioned pistols and guns, many of them with matchlocks. Immediately below the cornice hangs a row of leathern jerkins, made in the form of a shirt, supposed to have been worn as armour by the vassals. A large oak table, reaching nearly from one end of the room to the other, might have feasted the whole neighbourhood, and an appendage to one end of it made it answer at other times for the old game of shuffleboard. The rest of the furniture is in a suitable style, particularly an arm-chair of cumbrous workmanship, constructed of wood, curiously turned, with a high back and triangular seat, said to have been used by Judge Popham in the reign of Elizabeth. The entrance into the hall is at one end, by a low door, communicating with a passage that leads from the outer door in the front of the house to a quadrangle[1] within; at the other, it opens upon a gloomy staircase, by which you ascend to the first floor, and, passing the doors of some bed-chambers, enter a narrow gallery, which extends along the back front of the house from one end to the other of it, and looks upon an old garden. This gallery is hung with portraits, chiefly in the Spanish dresses of the sixteenth century. In one of the bed-chambers, which you pass in going towards the gallery, is a bedstead with blue furniture, which time has now made dingy and threadbare, and in the bottom of one of the bed-curtains you are shown a place where a small

[1] I think there is a chapel on one side of it, but am not quite sure.

piece has been cut out and sewn in again,—a circumstance which serves to identify the scene of the following story:—
'It was on a dark rainy night in the month of November, that an old midwife sat musing by her cottage fireside, when on a sudden she was startled by a loud knocking at the door. On opening it she found a horseman, who told her that her assistance was required immediately by a person of rank, and that she should be handsomely rewarded; but that there were reasons for keeping the affair a strict secret, and, therefore, she must submit to be blindfolded, and to be conducted in that condition to the bedchamber of the lady. With some hesitation the midwife consented; the horseman bound her eyes, and placed her on a pillion behind him. After proceeding in silence for many miles through rough and dirty lanes, they stopped, and the midwife was led into a house, which, from the length of her walk through the apartments, as well as the sounds about her, she discovered to be the seat of wealth and power. When the bandage was removed from her eyes, she found herself in a bed-chamber, in which were the lady on whose account she had been sent for, and a man of a haughty and ferocious aspect. The lady was delivered of a fine boy. Immediately the man commanded the midwife to give him the child, and catching it from her, he hurried across the room, and threw it on the back of the fire, that was blazing in the chimney. The child, however, was strong, and, by its struggles, rolled itself upon the hearth when the ruffian again seized it with fury, and, in spite of the intercession of the midwife, and the more piteous entreaties of the mother, thrust it under the grate, and, raking the live coals upon it, soon put an end to its life. The midwife, after spending some time in affording all the relief in her power to the wretched mother, was told that she must be gone. Her former conductor appeared, who again bound her eyes, and conveyed her behind him to her own home; he then paid her handsomely, and departed. The midwife was strongly agitated by the horrors of the preceding night; and she immediately made a deposition of the facts before a magistrate. Two circumstances afforded hopes of detecting the house in which the crime had been committed; one was, that the midwife, as she sat by the bedside, had, with a view to discover the place, cut out a piece of the bed-curtain, and sewn it in again; the other was, that as she had descended the staircase she had counted the steps. Some suspicions fell upon one Darrell, at that time the proprietor of Littlecote House, and the domain around it. The house was examined, and identified by the midwife, and Darrell was tried at Salisbury for the murder. By corrupting his judge, he escaped the sentence of the law; but broke his neck, by a fall from his horse in hunting, in a few months after. The place

O

where this happened is still known by the name of Darrell's Style,—a spot to be dreaded by the peasant whom the shades of evening have overtaken on his way.

'Littlecote House is two miles from Hungerford, in Berkshire, through which the Bath road passes. The fact occurred in the reign of Elizabeth. All the important circumstances I have given exactly as they are told in the country; some trifles only are added, either to render the whole connected, or to increase the impression.'

To Lord Webb's edition of this singular story, the author can now add the following account, extracted from Aubrey's Correspondence. It occurs among other particulars respecting Sir John Popham :—

'Sir . . . Dayrell, of Littlecote, in Com. Wilts, having gott his lady's waiting woman with child, when her travell came, sent a servant with a horse for a midwife, whom he was to bring hood-winked. She was brought, and layd the woman, but as soon as the child was born, she sawe the knight take the child and murther it, and burn it in the fire in the chamber. She having done her businesse, was extraordinarily rewarded for her paines, and sent blindfolded away. This horrid action did much run in her mind, and she had a desire to discover it, but knew not where 'twas. She considered with herself the time that she was riding, and how many miles she might have rode at that rate in that time, and that it must be some great person's house, for the roome was 12 foot high; and she should know the chamber if she sawe it. She went to a Justice of Peace, and search was made. The very chamber found. The Knight was brought to his tryall; and, to be short, this judge had this noble house, parke, and manner, and (I thinke) more, for a bribe to save his life.

'Sir John Popham gave sentence according to lawe, but being a great person and a favourite, he procured a *noli prosequi*.'

With this tale of terror the author has combined some circumstances of a similar legend, which was current at Edinburgh during his childhood.

About the beginning of the eighteenth century, when the large castles of the Scottish nobles, and even the secluded hotels, like those of the French noblesse, which they possessed in Edinburgh, were sometimes the scenes of strange and mysterious transactions, a divine of singular sanctity was called up at midnight to pray with a person at the point of death. This was no unusual summons; but what followed was alarming. He was put into a sedan-chair, and after he had been transported to a remote part of the town, the bearers insisted upon his being blindfolded. The request was enforced by a cocked pistol, and submitted to; but in the course of the discussion, he conjectured, from the phrases employed by the chairmen, and from some part of their dress, not completely concealed by their cloaks, that they were greatly above the menial station they had assumed. After many turns and windings, the chair was carried up stairs into a lodging, where his eyes were uncovered, and he was introduced into a bedroom, where he found a lady, newly delivered of an infant. He was commanded by his attendants to say such prayers by her bedside as were fitting for a person not expected to survive a mortal disorder. He ventured to remonstrate, and observe, that her safe delivery warranted better hopes. But he was sternly commanded to obey the orders first given, and with difficulty recollected himself sufficiently to acquit himself of the task imposed on him. He was then again hurried into the chair; but as they conducted him down stairs, he heard the report of a pistol. He was safely conducted home; a purse of gold was forced upon him; but he was warned, at the same time, that the least allusion to this dark transaction would cost him his life. He betook himself to rest, and, after long and broken musing, fell into a deep sleep. From this he was awakened by his servant, with the dismal news that a fire of uncommon fury had broken out in the house of . . ., near the head of the Canongate, and that it was totally consumed; with the shocking addition, that the daughter of the proprietor, a young lady eminent for beauty and accomplishments, had perished in the flames. The clergyman had his suspicions, but to have made them public would have availed nothing. He was timid; the family was of the first distinction; above all, the deed was done, and could not be amended. Time wore away, however, and with it his terrors. He became unhappy at being the solitary depositary of this fearful mystery, and mentioned it to some of his brethren, through whom the anecdote acquired a sort of publicity. The divine, however, had been long dead, and the story in some degree forgotten, when a fire broke out again on the very same spot where the house of . . . . had formerly stood, and which was now occupied by buildings of an inferior description. When the flames were at their height, the tumult, which usually attends such a scene, was suddenly suspended by an unexpected apparition. A beautiful female, in a night-dress, extremely rich, but at least half a century old, appeared in the very midst of the fire, and uttered these tremendous words in her vernacular idiom : '*Anes* burned, *twice* burned; the *third* time I'll scare you all !' The belief in this story was formerly so strong, that on a fire breaking out, and seeming to approach the fatal spot, there was a good deal of anxiety testified, lest the apparition should make good her denunciation.

NOTE LVIII.

As thick a smoke these hearths have given
At Hallow-tide or Christmas-even.—P. 364.

Such an exhortation was, in similar circumstances, actually given to his followers by a Welsh chieftain :—

'Enmity did continue betweene Howell ap Rys ap Howell Vaughan and the sonnes of John ap Meredith. After the death of Evan ap Rebert, Griffith ap Gronw (cosen-german to John ap Meredith's sonnes of Gwynfryn, who had long served in France, and had charge there) comeing home to live in the countrey, it happened that a servant of his, comeing to fish in Stymllyn, his fish was taken away, and the fellow beaten by Howell ap Rys his servants, and by his commandment. Griffith ap John ap Gronw took the matter in such dudgeon that he challenged Howell ap Rys to the field, which he refusing, assembling his cosins John ap Meredith's sonnes and his friends together, assaulted Howell in his own house, after the maner he had seene in the French warres, and consumed with fire his barnes and his out-houses. Whilst he was thus assaulting the hall, which Howell ap Rys and many other people kept, being a very strong house, he was shot out of a crevice of the house, through the sight of his beaver into the head, and slayne outright, being otherwise armed at all points. Notwithstanding his death, the assault of the house was continued with great vehemence, the doores fired with great burthens of straw; besides this, the smoake of the out-houses and barnes not farre distant annoyed greatly the defendants, for that most of them lay under boordes and benches upon the floore, in the hall, the better to avoyd the smoake. During this scene of confusion onely the old man, Howell ap Rys, never stooped, but stood valiantly in the midst of the floore, armed with a gleve in his hand, and called unto them, and bid "them arise like men, for shame, for he had knowne there as great a smoake in that hall upon Christmas-even." In the end, seeing the house could noe longer defend them, being overlayed with a multitude, upon parley betweene them, Howell ap Rys was content to yeald himself prisoner to Morris ap John ap Meredith, John ap Meredith's eldest sonne, soe as he would swear unto him to bring him safe to Carnarvon Castle, to abide the triall of the law for the death of Graff' ap John ap Gronw, who was cosen-german removed to the said Howell ap Rys, and of the very same house he was of. Which Morris ap John ap Meredith undertaking, did put a guard about the said Howell of his trustiest friends and servants, who kept and defended him from the rage of his kindred, and especially of Owen ap John ap Meredith, his brother, who was very eager against him. They passed by leisure thence like a campe to Carnarvon : the whole countrie being assembled, Howell his friends posted a horseback from one place or other by the way, who brought word that he was come thither safe, for they were in great fear lest he should be murthered, and that Morris ap John ap Meredith could not be able to defend him, neither durst any of Howell's friends be there, for fear of the kindred. In the end, being delivered by Morris ap John ap Meredith to the Constable of Carnarvon Castle, and there kept safely in ward untill the assises, it fell out by law, that the burning of Howell's houses, and assaulting him in his owne house, was a more haynous offence in Morris ap John ap Meredith and the rest, than the death of Graff' ap John ap Gronw in Howell, who did it in his own defence; whereupon Morris ap John ap Meredith, with thirty-five more, were indicted of felony, as appeareth by the copie of the indictment, which I had from the records.'—SIR JOHN WYNNE's *History of the Gwydir Family.* Lond. 1770, 8vo, p. 116.

NOTE LIX.

O'er Hexham's altar hung my glove.
—P. 373.

This custom among the Redesdale and Tynedale Borderers is mentioned in the interesting Life of Bernard Gilpin, where some account is given of these wild districts, which it was the custom of that excellent man regularly to visit.

'This custom (of duels) still prevailed on the Borders, where Saxon barbarism held its latest possession. These wild Northumbrians, indeed, went beyond the ferocity of their ancestors. They were not content with a duel : each contending party used to muster what adherents he could, and commence a kind of petty war. So that a private grudge would often occasion much bloodshed.

'It happened that a quarrel of this kind was on foot when Mr. Gilpin was at Rothbury, in those parts. During the two or three first days of his preaching, the contending parties observed some decorum, and never appeared at church together. At length, however, they met. One party had been early at church, and just as Mr. Gilpin began his sermon, the other entered. They stood not long silent. Inflamed at the sight of each other, they began to clash their weapons, for they were all armed with javelins and swords, and mutually approached. Awed, however, by the sacredness of the place, the tumult in some degree ceased. Mr. Gilpin proceeded : when again the combatants began to brandish their weapons, and draw towards each other. As a fray seemed near, Mr. Gilpin stepped from the pulpit, went between them, and addressed the leaders, put an end to the quarrel for the present, but could not effect an entire reconciliation. They promised him, however, that till the sermon was over they would make no more disturbance. He then went again into the pulpit, and spent the rest of the time in endeavouring to make them ashamed of what they had done. His behaviour and discourse affected them so much, that, at his farther entreaty, they promised to forbear all acts of hostility while he continued in the country. And so much respected was he among them, that whoever was in fear of his enemy used to resort where Mr. Gilpin was, esteeming his presence the best protection.

'One Sunday morning, coming to a church in those parts, before the people were assembled, he observed a glove hanging up, and was informed by the sexton, that it was meant as a challenge to any one who should take it down. Mr. Gilpin ordered the sexton to reach it to him; but upon his utterly refusing to touch it, he took it down himself, and put it into his breast. When the people were assembled, he went into the pulpit, and, before he concluded his sermon, took occasion to rebuke them severely for these inhuman challenges. "I hear," saith he, "that one among you hath hanged up a glove, even in this sacred place, threatening to fight any one who taketh it down: see, I have taken it down;" and, pulling out the glove, he held it up to the congregation, and then showed them how unsuitable such savage practices were to the profession of Christianity, using such persuasives to mutual love as he thought would most affect them.'—*Life of Bernard Gilpin.* Lond. 1753, 8vo, p. 177.

Note LX.

A horseman arm'd, at headlong speed.
—P. 377.

This, and what follows, is taken from a real achievement of Major Robert Philipson, called from his desperate and adventurous courage, Robin the Devil; which, as being very inaccurately noticed in this note upon the first edition, shall be now given in a more authentic form. The chief place of his retreat was not Lord's Island, in Derwentwater, but Curwen's Island, in the Lake of Windermere:—

'This island formerly belonged to the Philipsons, a family of note in Westmoreland. During the Civil Wars, two of them, an elder and a younger brother, served the King. The former, who was the proprietor of it, commanded a regiment; the latter was a major.

'The major, whose name was Robert, was a man of great spirit and enterprise; and for his many feats of personal bravery had obtained, among the Oliverians of those parts, the appellation of Robin the Devil.

'After the war had subsided, and the direful effects of public opposition had ceased, revenge and malice long kept alive the animosity of individuals. Colonel Briggs, a steady friend to usurpation, resided at this time at Kendal, and, under the double character of a leading magistrate (for he was a Justice of Peace) and an active commander, held the country in awe. This person having heard that Major Philipson was at his brother's house on the island in Windermere, resolved, if possible, to seize and punish a man who had made himself so particularly obnoxious. How it was conducted, my authority[1] does not inform us—whether he got together the navigation of the lake, and blockaded the place by sea, or whether he landed and carried on his approaches in form. Neither do we learn the strength of the garrison within, nor of the works without. All we learn is, that Major Philipson endured a siege of eight months with great gallantry, till his brother, the Colonel, raised a party and relieved him.

'It was now the Major's turn to make reprisals. He put himself, therefore, at the head of a little troop of horse, and rode to Kendal. Here, being informed that Colonel Briggs was at prayers, (for it was on a Sunday morning,) he stationed his men properly in the avenues, and himself armed, rode directly into the church. It probably was not a regular church, but some large place of meeting. It is said he intended to seize the Colonel and carry him off; but as this seems to have been totally impracticable, it is rather probable that his intention was to kill him on the spot, and in the midst of the confusion to escape. Whatever his intention was, it was frustrated, for Briggs happened to be elsewhere.

'The congregation, as might be expected, was thrown into great confusion on seeing an armed man on horseback make his appearance among them; and the Major, taking advantage of their astonishment, turned his horse round, and rode quietly out. But having given an alarm, he was presently assaulted as he left the assembly, and being seized, his girths were cut, and he was unhorsed.

'At this instant his party made a furious attack on the assailants, and the Major killed with his own hand the man who had seized him, clapped the saddle, ungirthed as it was, upon his horse, and, vaulting into it, rode full speed through the streets of Kendal, calling his men to follow him; and, with his whole party, made a safe retreat to his asylum in the lake. The action marked the man. Many knew him: and they who did not, knew as well from the exploit that it could be nobody but Robin the Devil.'

[1] Dr. Burn's History of Westmoreland.

The Lord of the Isles.

The Scene of this Poem lies, at first, in the Castle of Artornish, on the coast of Argyleshire; and, afterwards, in the Islands of Skye and Arran, and upon the coast of Ayrshire. Finally it is laid near Stirling. The story opens in the spring of the year 1307, when Bruce, who had been driven out of Scotland by the English, and the Barons who adhered to that foreign interest, returned from the Island of Rachrin on the coast of Ireland, again to assert his claims to the Scottish crown. Many of the personages and incidents introduced are of historical celebrity. The authorities used are chiefly those of the venerable Lord Hailes, as well entitled to be called the restorer of Scottish history, as Bruce the restorer of Scottish Monarchy; and of Archdeacon Barbour, author of a Metrical History of Robert Bruce.

Canto First.

Autumn departs; but still his
    mantle's fold
Rests on the groves of noble
    Somerville;
Beneath a shroud of russet dropp'd
    with gold
Tweed and his tributaries mingle
    still;
Hoarser the wind, and deeper sounds
    the rill,
Yet lingering notes of silvan music
    swell,
The deep-toned cushat, and the
    redbreast shrill;
And yet some tints of summer
    splendour tell
When the broad sun sinks down on
    Ettrick's western fell.

Autumn departs; from Gala's fields
    no more
Come rural sounds our kindred banks
    to cheer;
Blent with the stream, and gale that
    wafts it o'er,
No more the distant reaper's mirth
    we hear.

The last blithe shout hath died upon
    our ear,
And harvest-home hath hush'd the
    clanging wain;
On the waste hill no forms of life
    appear,
Save where, sad laggard of the
    autumnal train,
Some age-struck wanderer gleans few
    ears of scatter'd grain.

Deem'st thou these sadden'd scenes
    have pleasure still?
Lovest thou through Autumn's fading
    realms to stray,
To see the heath-flower wither'd on
    the hill,
To listen to the wood's expiring lay,
To note the red leaf shivering on the
    spray,
To mark the last bright tints the
    mountain stain,
On the waste fields to trace the
    gleaner's way,
And moralize on mortal joy and
    pain?
O! if such scenes thou lovest, scorn
    not the minstrel strain.

No! do not scorn, although its
　　hoarser note
Scarce with the cushat's homely song
　　can vie,
Though faint its beauties as the tints
　　remote
That gleam through mist in autumn's
　　evening sky,
And few as leaves that tremble, sear
　　and dry,
When wild November hath his bugle
　　wound;
Nor mock my toil—a lonely gleaner I,
Through fields time-wasted, on sad
　　inquest bound,
Where happier bards of yore have
　　richer harvest found.

So shalt thou list, and haply not
　　unmoved,
To a wild tale of Albyn's warrior day;
In distant lands, by the rough West
　　reproved,
Still live some relics of the ancient lay.
For, when on Coolin's hills the lights
　　decay,
With such the Seer of Skye the eve
　　beguiles;
'Tis known amid the pathless wastes
　　of Reay,
In Harries known, and in Iona's
　　piles,
Where rest from mortal coil the Mighty
　　of the Isles.

I.

'Wake, Maid of Lorn!' the Minstrels
　　sung.
Thy rugged halls, Artornish! rung,
And the dark seas, thy towers that lave,
Heaved on the beach a softer wave,
As 'mid the tuneful choir to keep
The diapason of the Deep.
Lull'd were the winds on Inninmore,
And green Loch-Alline's woodland
　　shore,

As if wild woods and waves had
　　pleasure
In listing to the lovely measure.
And ne'er to symphony more sweet
Gave mountain echoes answer meet,
Since, met from mainland and from isle,
Ross, Arran, Ilay, and Argyle,
Each minstrel's tributary lay
Paid homage to the festal day.
Dull and dishonour'd were the bard,
Worthless of guerdon and regard,
Deaf to the hope of minstrel fame,
Or lady's smiles, his noblest aim,
Who on that morn's resistless call
Were silent in Artornish hall.

II.

'Wake, Maid of Lorn!' 'twas thus they
　　sung,
And yet more proud the descant rung,
'Wake, Maid of Lorn! high right is
　　ours,
To charm dull sleep from Beauty's
　　bowers;
Earth, Ocean, Air, have nought so shy
But owns the power of minstrelsy.
In Lettermore the timid deer
Will pause, the harp's wild chime to
　　hear;
Rude Heiskar's seal, through surges
　　dark,
Will long pursue the minstrel's bark;
To list his notes, the eagle proud
Will poise him on Ben-Cailliach's
　　cloud;
Then let not Maiden's ear disdain
The summons of the minstrel train,
But, while our harps wild music make,
Edith of Lorn, awake, awake!

III.

'O wake, while Dawn, with dewy
　　shine,
Wakes Nature's charms to vie with
　　thine!
She bids the mottled thrush rejoice
To mate thy melody of voice;

The dew that on the violet lies
Mocks the dark lustre of thine eyes;
But, Edith, wake, and all we see
Of sweet and fair shall yield to thee!'—
'She comes not yet,' grey Ferrand
  cried;
'Brethren, let softer spell be tried,
Those notes prolong'd, that soothing
  theme,
Which best may mix with Beauty's
  dream,
And whisper, with their silvery tone,
The hope she loves, yet fears to own.'
He spoke, and on the harp-strings died
The strains of flattery and of pride;
More soft, more low, more tender fell
The lay of love he bade them tell.

IV.

'Wake, Maid of Lorn! the moments fly,
  Which yet that maiden-name allow;
Wake, Maiden, wake! the hour is nigh,
  When Love shall claim a plighted
    vow.
By Fear, thy bosom's fluttering guest,
  By Hope, that soon shall fears
    remove,
We bid thee break the bonds of rest,
  And wake thee at the call of Love!

Wake, Edith, wake! in yonder bay
Lies many a galley gaily mann'd,
We hear the merry pibrochs play,
  We see the streamers' silken band.
What Chieftain's praise these pibrochs
  swell,
What crest is on these banners wove,
The harp, the minstrel, dare not tell—
  The riddle must be read by Love.'

V.

Retired her maiden train among,
Edith of Lorn received the song,
But tamed the minstrel's pride had been
That had her cold demeanour seen;
For not upon her cheek awoke
The glow of pride when Flattery spoke,

Nor could their tenderest numbers
  bring
One sigh responsive to the string.
As vainly had her maidens vied
In skill to deck the princely bride.
Her locks, in dark-brown length
  array'd,
Cathleen of Ulne, 'twas thine to braid;
Young Eva with meet reverence drew
On the light foot the silken shoe,
While on the ankle's slender round
Those strings of pearl fair Bertha
  wound,
That, bleach'd Lochryan's depths
  within,
Seem'd dusky still on Edith's skin.
But Einion, of experience old,
Had weightiest task—the mantle's fold
In many an artful plait she tied,
To show the form it seem'd to hide,
Till on the floor descending roll'd
Its waves of crimson blent with gold.

VI.

O! lives there now so cold a maid,
Who thus in beauty's pomp array'd,
In beauty's proudest pitch of power,
And conquest won—the bridal hour,
With every charm that wins the heart,
By Nature given, enhanced by Art,
Could yet the fair reflection view,
In the bright mirror pictured true,
And not one dimple on her cheek
A tell-tale consciousness bespeak?—
Lives still such maid?—Fair damsels,
  say,
For further vouches not my lay,
Save that such lived in Britain's isle,
When Lorn's bright Edith scorn'd to
  smile.

VII.

But Morag, to whose fostering care
Proud Lorn had given his daughter
  fair,
Morag, who saw a mother's aid
By all a daughter's love repaid,

(Strict was that bond—most kind of
    all—
Inviolate in Highland hall)
Grey Morag sate a space apart,
In Edith's eyes to read her heart.
In vain the attendants' fond appeal
To Morag's skill, to Morag's zeal ;
She mark'd her child receive their care,
Cold as the image sculptured fair
(Form of some sainted patroness)
Which cloister'd maids combine to
    dress ;
She mark'd—and knew her nursling's
    heart
In the vain pomp took little part.
Wistful a while she gaz'd—then press'd
The maiden to her anxious breast
In finish'd loveliness—and led
To where a turret's airy head,
Slender and steep, and battled round,
O'erlook'd, dark Mull! thy mighty
    Sound,
Where thwarting tides, with mingled
    roar,
Part thy swarth hills from Morven's
    shore.

VIII.

'Daughter,' she said, 'these seas
    behold,
Round twice a hundred islands roll'd,
From Hirt, that hears their northern
    roar,
To the green Ilay's fertile shore ;
Or mainland turn, where many a tower
Owns thy bold brother's feudal power,
Each on its own dark cape reclined,
And listening to its own wild wind,
From where Mingarry, sternly placed,
O'erawes the woodland and the waste,
To where Dunstaffnage hears the
    raging
Of Connal with his rocks engaging.
Think'st thou, amid this ample round,
A single brow but thine has frown'd,
To sadden this auspicious morn,
That bids the daughter of high Lorn

Impledge her spousal faith to wed
The heir of mighty Somerled !
Ronald, from many a hero sprung,
The fair, the valiant, and the young,
LORD OF THE ISLES, whose lofty name
A thousand bards have given to fame,
The mate of monarchs, and allied
On equal terms with England's pride.
From chieftain's tower to bondsman's
    cot,
Who hears the tale, and triumphs not?
The damsel dons her best attire,
The shepherd lights his beltane fire ;
Joy, joy! each warder's horn hath
    sung,
Joy, joy ! each matin bell hath rung ;
The holy priest says grateful mass,
Loud shouts each hardy galla-glass,
No mountain den holds outcast boor
Of heart so dull, of soul so poor,
But he hath flung his task aside,
And claim'd this morn for holy-tide ;
Yet, empress of this joyful day,
Edith is sad while all are gay.'

IX.

Proud Edith's soul came to her eye,
Resentment check'd the struggling
    sigh,
Her hurrying hand indignant dried
The burning tears of injured pride—
'Morag forbear ! or lend thy praise
To swell yon hireling harpers' lays ;
Make to yon maids thy boast of power,
That they may waste a wondering
    hour,
Telling of banners proudly borne,
Of pealing bell and bugle-horn,
Or, theme more dear, of robes of price,
Crownlets and gauds of rare device.
But thou, experienced as thou art,
Think'st thou with these to cheat the
    heart,
That, bound in strong affection's chain,
Looks for return and looks in vain ?
No ! sum thine Edith's wretched lot
In these brief words—He loves her not!

X.

'Debate it not; too long I strove
To call his cold observance love,
All blinded by the league that styled
Edith of Lorn—while yet a child
She tripp'd the heath by Morag's
    side—
The brave Lord Ronald's destined
    bride.
Ere yet I saw him, while afar
His broadsword blazed in Scotland's
    war,
Train'd to believe our fates the same,
My bosom throbb'd when Ronald's
    name
Came gracing Fame's heroic tale,
Like perfume on the summer gale.
What pilgrim sought our halls, nor
    told
Of Ronald's deeds in battle bold;
Who touch'd the harp to heroes' praise,
But his achievements swell'd the lays?
Even Morag—not a tale of fame
Was hers but closed with Ronald's
    name.
He came! and all that had been told
Of his high worth seem'd poor and
    cold,
Tame, lifeless, void of energy,
Unjust to Ronald and to me!

XI.

'Since then, what thought had Edith's
    heart
And gave not plighted love its part?
And what requital? cold delay,
Excuse that shunn'd the spousal day.
It dawns, and Ronald is not here!
Hunts he Bentalla's nimble deer,
Or loiters he in secret dell
To bid some lighter love farewell,
And swear, that though he may not
    scorn
A daughter of the House of Lorn,
Yet, when these formal rites are o'er,
Again they meet, to part no more?'

XII.

'Hush, daughter, hush! thy doubts
    remove,
More nobly think of Ronald's love.
Look, where beneath the castle grey
His fleet unmoor from Aros bay!
See'st not each galley's topmast bend,
As on the yards the sails ascend?
Hiding the dark-blue land, they rise
Like the white clouds on April skies;
The shouting vassals man the oars,
Behind them sink Mull's mountain
    shores,
Onward their merry course they keep
Through whistling breeze and foaming
    deep.
And mark the headmost, seaward cast,
Stoop to the freshening gale her mast,
As if she veil'd its banner'd pride
To greet afar her prince's bride!
Thy Ronald comes, and while in speed
His galley mates the flying steed,
He chides her sloth!' Fair Edith sigh'd,
Blush'd, sadly smiled, and thus replied:

XIII.

'Sweet thought, but vain! No, Morag!
    mark,
Type of his course, yon lonely bark,
That oft hath shifted helm and sail
To win its way against the gale.
Since peep of morn, my vacant eyes
Have view'd by fits the course she
    tries;
Now, though the darkening scud
    comes on,
And dawn's fair promises be gone,
And though the weary crew may see
Our sheltering haven on their lee,
Still closer to the rising wind
They strive her shivering sail to bind,
Still nearer to the shelves' dread verge
At every tack her course they urge,
As if they fear'd Artornish more
Than adverse winds and breakers
    roar.

XIV.

Sooth spoke the maid.   Amid the tide
The skiff she mark'd lay tossing sore,
And shifted oft her stooping side
In weary tack from shore to shore.
Yet on her destined course no more
She gain'd, of forward way,
Than what a minstrel may compare
To the poor meed which peasants
share,
Who toil the livelong day;
And such the risk her pilot braves,
That oft, before she wore,
Her boltsprit kiss'd the broken
waves,
Where in white foam the ocean raves
Upon the shelving shore.
Yet, to their destined purpose true,
Undaunted toil'd her hardy crew,
Nor look'd where shelter lay,
Nor for Artornish Castle drew,
Nor steer'd for Aros bay.

XV.

Thus while they strove with wind and
seas,
Borne onward by the willing breeze,
Lord Ronald's fleet swept by,
Streamer'd with siik, and trick'd with
gold,
Mann'd with the noble and the bold
Of Island chivalry.
Around their prows the ocean roars,
And chafes beneath their thousand
oars,
Yet bears them on their way:
So chafes the war-horse in his might,
That fieldward bears some valiant
knight,
Champs, till both bit and boss are white,
But, foaming, must obey.
On each gay deck they might behold
Lances of steel and crests of gold,
And hauberks with their burnish'd fold,
That shimmer'd fair and free;
And each proud galley, as she pass'd,
To the wild cadence of the blast
Gave wilder minstrelsy.

Full many a shrill triumphant note
Saline and Scallastle bade float
Their misty shores around;
And Morven's echoes answer'd well,
And Duart heard the distant swell
Come down the darksome Sound.

XVI.

So bore they on with mirth and pride,
And if that labouring bark hey spied,
'Twas with such idle eye
As nobles cast on lowly boor,
When, toiling in his task obscure,
They pass him careless by.
Let them sweep on with heedless eyes!
But, had they known what mighty
prize
In that frail vessel lay,
The famish'd wolf, that prowls the
wold,
Had scatheless pass'd the unguarded
fold,
Ere, drifting by these galleys bold,
Unchallenged were her way!
And thou, Lord Ronald, sweep thou on,
With mirth, and pride, and minstrel
tone!
But had'st thou known who sail'd so
nigh,
Far other glance were in thine eye!
Far other flush were on thy brow,
That, shaded by the bonnet, now
Assumes but ill the blithesome cheer
Of bridegroom when the bride is near!

XVII.

Yes, sweep they on!   We will not
leave,
For them that triumph, those who
grieve,
With that armada gay
Be laughter loud and jocund shout,
And bards to cheer the wassail rout,
With tale, romance, and lay;
And of wild mirth each clamorous art
Which, if it cannot cheer the heart,
May stupify and stun its smart,
For one loud busy day.

Yes, sweep they on!—But with that
    skiff
    Abides the minstrel tale,
Where there was dread of surge and
    cliff,
Labour that strain'd each sinew stiff,
    And one sad Maiden's wail.

XVIII.

All day with fruitless strife they toil'd,
With eve the ebbing currents boil'd
    More fierce from strait and lake ;
And midway through the channel met
Conflicting tides that foam and fret,
And high their mingled billows jet,
    As spears, that, in the battle set,
    Spring upward as they break.
Then, too, the lights of eve were past,
And louder sung the western blast
    On rocks of Inninmore ;
Rent was the sail, and strain'd the
    mast,
And many a leak was gaping fast,
And the pale steersman stood aghast,
    And gave the conflict o'er.

XIX.

'Twas then that One, whose lofty look
Nor labour dull'd nor terror shook,
    Thus to the Leader spoke :
'Brother, how hopest thou to abide
The fury of this wilder'd tide,
Or how avoid the rock's rude side,
    Until the day has broke ?
Didst thou not mark the vessel reel,
With quivering planks, and groaning
    keel,
    At the last billow's shock ?
Yet how of better counsel tell,
Though here thou see'st poor Isabel
    Half dead with want and fear ;
For look on sea, or look on land,
Or yon dark sky—on every hand
    Despair and death are near.
For her alone I grieve—on me
Danger sits light by land and sea,
    I follow where thou wilt ;

Either to bide the tempest's lour,
Or wend to yon unfriendly tower,
Or rush amid their naval power,
With war-cry wake their wassail-
    hour,
    And die with hand on hilt.'

XX.

That elder Leader's calm reply
    In steady voice was given,
'In man's most dark extremity
    Oft succour dawns from Heaven.
Edward, trim thou the shatter'd sail,
The helm be mine, and down the
    gale
    Let our free course be driven ;
So shall we 'scape the western bay,
The hostile fleet, the unequal fray,
So safely hold our vessel's way
    Beneath the Castle wall ;
For if a hope of safety rest,
'Tis on the sacred name of guest,
Who seeks for shelter, storm-dis-
    tress'd,
    Within a chieftain's hall.
If not—it best beseems our worth,
Our name, our right, our lofty birth,
    By noble hands to fall.'

XXI.

The helm, to his strong arm consign'd,
Gave the reef'd sail to meet the wind,
    And on her alter'd way,
Fierce bounding, forward sprung the
    ship,
Like greyhound starting from the slip
    To seize his flying prey.
Awaked before the rushing prow,
The mimic fires of ocean glow,
    Those lightnings of the wave :
Wild sparkles crest the broken tides,
And, flashing round, the vessel's sides
    With elvish lustre lave,
While, far behind, their livid light
To the dark billows of the night
    A gloomy splendour gave,

It seems as if old Ocean shakes
From his dark brow the lucid flakes
    In envious pageantry,
To match the meteor-light that streaks
    Grim Hecla's midnight sky.

XXII.

Nor lack'd they steadier light to keep
Their course upon the darken'd deep;
Artornish, on her frowning steep
    'Twixt cloud and ocean hung,
Glanced with a thousand lights of glee,
And landward far, and far to sea,
    Her festal radiance flung.
By that blithe beacon-light they steer'd,
    Whose lustre mingled well
With the pale beam that now appear'd,
As the cold moon her head uprear'd
    Above the eastern fell.

XXIII.

Thus guided, on their course they bore,
Until they near'd the mainland shore,
When frequent on the hollow blast
Wild shouts of merriment were cast,
And wind and wave and sea-birds'
    cry
With wassail sounds in concert vie,
Like funeral shrieks with revelry,
    Or like the battle-shout
By peasants heard from cliffs on high,
When Triumph, Rage, and Agony,
    Madden the fight and rout.
Now nearer yet, through mist and
    storm,
Dimly arose the Castle's form,
    And deepen'd shadow made,
Far lengthen'd on the main below,
Where, dancing in reflected glow,
    A hundred torches play'd,
Spangling the wave with lights as vain
As pleasures in this vale of pain,
    That dazzle as they fade.

XXIV.

Beneath the Castle's sheltering lee,
They staid their course in quiet sea.

Hewn in the rock, a passage there
Sought the dark fortress by a stair,
    So straight, so high, so steep,
With peasant's staff one valiant hand
Might well the dizzy pass have mann'd,
'Gainst hundreds arm'd with spear and
    brand,
    And plunged them in the deep.
His bugle then the helmsman wound;
Loud answer'd every echo round,
    From turret, rock, and bay;
The postern's hinges crash and groan,
And soon the Warder's cresset shone
On those rude steps of slippery stone,
    To light the upward way.
' Thrice welcome, holy Sire!' he said;
' Full long the spousal train have staid,
    And, vex'd at thy delay,
Fear'd lest, amidst these wildering
    seas,
The darksome night and freshening
    breeze
    Had driven thy bark astray.'

XXV.

' Warder,' the younger stranger said,
' Thine erring guess some mirth had
    made
In mirthful hour; but nights like these,
When the rough winds wake western
    seas,
Brook not of glee. We crave some aid
And needful shelter for this maid
    Until the break of day;
For, to ourselves, the deck's rude plank
Is easy as the mossy bank
    That 's breath'd upon by May.
And for our storm-toss'd skiff we
    seek
Short shelter in this leeward creek,
Prompt when the dawn the east shall
    streak
    Again to bear away.'
Answered the Warder,—' In what
    name
Assert ye hospitable claim?
    Whence come, or whither bound?

Hath Erin seen your parting sails?
Or come ye on Norweyan gales?
And seek ye England's fertile vales,
    Or Scotland's mountain ground?'

XXVI.

'Warriors—for other title none
For some brief space we list to own,
Bound by a vow—warriors are we;
In strife by land, and storm by sea,
    We have been known to fame;
And these brief words have import dear,
When sounded in a noble ear,
To harbour safe, and friendly cheer,
    That gives us rightful claim.
Grant us the trivial boon we seek,
And we in other realms will speak
    Fair of your courtesy;
Deny—and be your niggard Hold
Scorn'd by the noble and the bold,
Shunn'd by the pilgrim on the wold,
    And wanderer on the lea!'

XXVII.

'Bold stranger, no—'gainst claim like thine
No bolt revolves by hand of mine;
Though urged in tone that more express'd
A monarch than a suppliant guest.
Be what ye will, Artornish Hall
On this glad eve is free to all.
Though ye had drawn a hostile sword
'Gainst our ally, great England's Lord,
Or mail upon your shoulders borne
To battle with the Lord of Lorn,
Or, outlaw'd, dwelt by greenwood tree
With the fierce Knight of Ellerslie,
Or aided even the murderous strife
When Comyn fell beneath the knife
Of that fell homicide The Bruce,
This night had been a term of truce.
Ho, vassals! give these guests your care,
And show the narrow postern stair.'

XXVIII.

To land these two bold brethren leapt
(The weary crew their vessel kept)
And, lighted by the torches' flare,
That seaward flung their smoky glare,
The younger knight that maiden bare
    Half lifeless up the rock;
On his strong shoulder lean'd her head,
And down her long dark tresses shed,
As the wild vine in tendrils spread,
    Droops from the mountain oak.
Him follow'd close that elder Lord,
And in his hand a sheathed sword,
    Such as few arms could wield;
But when he boun'd him to such task,
Well could it cleave the strongest casque,
    And rend the surest shield.

XXIX.

The raised portcullis' arch they pass,
The wicket with its bars of brass,
    The entrance long and low,
Flank'd at each turn by loop-holes strait,
Where bowmen might in ambush wait
(If force or fraud should burst the gate)
    To gall an entering foe.
But every jealous post of ward
Was now defenceless and unbarr'd,
    And all the passage free
To one low-brow'd and vaulted room,
Where squire and yeoman, page and groom,
    Plied their loud revelry.

XXX.

And 'Rest ye here,' the Warder bade,
'Till to our Lord your suit is said.
And, comrades, gaze not on the maid,
And on these men who ask our aid,
    As if ye ne'er had seen
A damsel tired of midnight bark,
Or wanderers of a moulding stark,
    And bearing martial mien.'

But not for Eachin's reproof
Would page or vassal stand aloof,
　But crowded on to stare,
As men of courtesy untaught,
Till fiery Edward roughly caught
　From one, the foremost there,
His chequer'd plaid, and in its shroud,
To hide her from the vulgar crowd,
　Involved his sister fair.
His brother, as the clansman bent
His sullen brow in discontent,
　Made brief and stern excuse ;—
' Vassal, were thine the cloak of pall
That decks thy Lord in bridal hall,
　'Twere honour'd by her use.'

XXXI.

Proud was his tone, but calm ; his eye
Had that compelling dignity,
　His mien that bearing haught and
　　high,
　Which common spirits fear ;
Needed nor word nor signal more,
Nod, wink, and laughter, all were
　o'er ;
Upon each other back they bore,
　And gazed like startled deer.
But now appear'd the Seneschal,
Commission'd by his lord to call
The strangers to the Baron's hall,
　Where feasted fair and free
That Island Prince in nuptial tide,
With Edith there his lovely bride,
And her bold brother by her side,
And many a chief, the flower and
　　pride
　Of Western land and sea.

Here pause we, gentles, for a space ;
And, if our tale hath won your grace,
Grant us brief patience, and again
We will renew the minstrel strain.

—+—

Canto Second.

I.

FILL the bright goblet, spread the
　festive board !
Summon the gay, the noble, and the
　fair !
Through the loud hall in joyous
　concert pour'd
Let mirth and music sound the dirge
　of Care !
But ask thou not if Happiness be
　there,
If the loud laugh disguise convulsive
　throe,
Or if the brow the heart's true livery
　wear ;
Lift not the festal mask !—enough
　to know,
No scene of mortal life but teems
　with mortal woe.

II.

With beakers' clang, with harpers' lay,
With all that olden time deem'd gay,
The Island Chieftain feasted high ;
But there was in his troubled eye
A gloomy fire, and on his brow
Now sudden flush'd, and faded now,
Emotions such as draw their birth
From deeper source than festal mirth.
By fits he paused, and harper's strain
And jester's tale went round in vain,
Or fell but on his idle ear
Like distant sounds which dreamers
　hear.
Then would he rouse him, and employ
Each art to aid the clamorous joy,
　And call for pledge and lay,
And, for brief space, of all the crowd,
As he was loudest of the loud,
　Seem gayest of the gay.

III.

Yet nought amiss the bridal throng
Mark'd in brief mirth, or musing long;
The vacant brow, the unlistening ear,

They gave to thoughts of raptures near,
And his fierce starts of sudden glee
Seem'd bursts of bridegroom's ecstasy.
Nor thus alone misjudged the crowd,
Since lofty Lorn, suspicious, proud,
And jealous of his honour'd line,
And that keen knight, De Argentine,
(From England sent on errand high,
The western league more firm to tie,)
Both deem'd in Ronald's mood to find
A lover's transport-troubled mind.
But one sad heart, one tearful eye,
Pierced deeper through the mystery,
And watch'd, with agony and fear,
Her wayward bridegroom's varied cheer.

IV.

She watch'd, yet fear'd to meet his glance,
And he shunn'd hers; till when by chance
They met, the point of foeman's lance
Had given a milder pang!
Beneath the intolerable smart
He writhed, then sternly mann'd his heart
To play his hard but destined part,
And from the table sprang.
'Fill me the mighty cup!' he said,
'Erst own'd by royal Somerled;
Fill it, till on the studded brim
In burning gold the bubbles swim,
And every gem of varied shine
Glow doubly bright in rosy wine!
To you, brave lord, and brother mine
Of Lorn, this pledge I drink—
The union of Our House with thine,
By this fair bridal-link!'

V.

'Let it pass round!' quoth He of Lorn,
'And in good time; that winded horn
Must of the Abbot tell;
The laggard monk is come at last.'
Lord Ronald heard the bugle-blast,
And on the floor at random cast
The untasted goblet fell.
But when the Warder in his ear
Tells other news, his blither cheer
Returns like sun of May,
When through a thunder-cloud it beams!
Lord of two hundred isles, he seems
As glad of brief delay,
As some poor criminal might feel,
When, from the gibbet or the wheel,
Respited for a day.

VI.

'Brother of Lorn,' with hurried voice
He said, 'And you, fair lords, rejoice!
Here, to augment our glee,
Come wandering knights from travel far,
Well proved, they say, in strife of war,
And tempest on the sea.
Ho! give them at your board such place
As best their presences may grace,
And bid them welcome free!'
With solemn step, and silver wand,
The Seneschal the presence scann'd
Of these strange guests; and well he knew
How to assign their rank its due;
For though the costly furs
That erst had deck'd their caps were torn,
And their gay robes were overworn,
And soil'd their gilded spurs,
Yet such a high commanding grace
Was in their mien and in their face,
As suited best the princely dais,
And royal canopy;
And there he marshall'd them their place,
First of that company.

VII.

Then lords and ladies spake aside,
And angry looks the error chide,
That gave to guests unnamed, unknown,
A place so near their prince's throne;
But Owen Erraught said,

'For forty years a seneschal,
To marshal guests in bower and hall
   Has been my honour'd trade.
Worship and birth to me are known
By look, by bearing, and by tone,
Not by furr'd robe or broider'd zone;
   And 'gainst an oaken bough
I'll gage my silver wand of state,
That these three strangers oft have sate
   In higher place than now.'

VIII.

'I, too,' the aged Ferrand said,
'Am qualified by minstrel trade
   Of rank and place to tell;
Mark'd ye the younger stranger's eye,
My mates, how quick, how keen, how
   high,
   How fierce its flashes fell,
Glancing among the noble rout
As if to seek the noblest out,
Because the owner might not brook
On any save his peers to look?
   And yet it moves me more,
That steady, calm, majestic brow,
With which the elder chief even now
   Scann'd the gay presence o'er,
Like being of superior kind,
In whose high-toned impartial mind
Degrees of mortal rank and state
Seem objects of indifferent weight.
   The lady too—though closely tied
   The mantle veil both face and eye,
   Her motions' grace it could not hide,
   Nor could her form's fair sym-
     metry.'

IX.

Suspicious doubt and lordly scorn
Lour'd on the haughty front of Lorn.
From underneath his brows of pride,
The stranger guests he sternly eyed,
And whisper'd closely what the ear
Of Argentine alone might hear;
   Then question'd, high and brief,
If, in their voyage, aught they knew
Of the rebellious Scottish crew,
Who to Rath-Erin's shelter drew,
   With Carrick's outlaw'd Chief?

And if, their winter's exile o'er,
They harbour'd still by Ulster's shore,
Or launch'd their galleys on the main,
To vex their native land again?

X.

That younger stranger, fierce and
   high,
At once confronts the Chieftain's eye
   With look of equal scorn;
'Of rebels have we nought to show;
But if of Royal Bruce thou'dst know,
   I warn thee he has sworn,
Ere thrice three days shall come and
   go,
His banner Scottish winds shall blow,
Despite each mean or mighty foe,
   From England's every bill and bow,
   To Allaster of Lorn.'
Kindled the mountain Chieftain's ire,
But Ronald quench'd the rising fire;
'Brother, it better suits the time
To chase the night with Ferrand's
   rhyme,
Than wake, 'midst mirth and wine, the
   jars
That flow from these unhappy wars.'
'Content,' said Lorn; and spoke apart
With Ferrand, master of his art,
   Then whisper'd Argentine,
'The lay I named will carry smart
To these bold strangers' haughty heart,
   If right this guess of mine.'
He ceased, and it was silence all,
Until the minstrel waked the hall:

XI.

THE BROOCH OF LORN.

'Whence the brooch of burning gold,
That clasps the Chieftain's mantle-fold,
Wrought and chased with rare device,
Studded fair with gems of price,
On the varied tartans beaming,
As, through night's pale rainbow
   gleaming,
Fainter now, now seen afar,
Fitful shines the northern star!

Gem! ne'er wrought on Highland
 mountain,
Did the fairy of the fountain,
Or the mermaid of the wave,
Frame thee in some coral cave?
Did, in Iceland's darksome mine,
Dwarf's swart hands thy metal twine?
Or, mortal-moulded, comest thou here
From England's love, or France's fear?

XII.

'No!—thy splendours nothing tell
Foreign art or faëry spell.
Moulded thou for monarch's use,
By the overweening Bruce,
When the royal robe he tied
O'er a heart of wrath and pride;
Thence in triumph wert thou torn,
By the victor hand of Lorn!

When the gem was won and lost,
Widely was the war-cry toss'd!
Rung aloud Bendourish fell,
Answer'd Douchart's sounding dell,
Fled the deer from wild Teyndrum,
When the homicide, o'ercome,
Hardly 'scaped with scathe and scorn,
Left the pledge with conquering Lorn!

XIII.

'Vain was then the Douglas brand,
Vain the Campbell's vaunted hand,
Vain Kirkpatrick's bloody dirk,
Making sure of murder's work;
Barendown fled fast away,
Fled the fiery De la Haye,
When this brooch, triumphant borne,
Beam'd upon the breast of Lorn.

Farthest fled its former Lord,
Left his men to brand and cord,
Bloody brand of Highland steel,
English gibbet, axe, and wheel.
Let him fly from coast to coast,
Dogg'd by Comyn's vengeful ghost,
While his spoils, in triumph worn,
Long shall grace victorious Lorn!'

XIV.

As glares the tiger on his foes,
Hemm'd in by hunters, spears, and
 bows,
And, ere he bounds upon the ring,
Selects the object of his spring,—
Now on the bard, now on his Lord,
So Edward glared and grasp'd his
 sword;
But stern his brother spoke, 'Be still!
What! art thou yet so wild of will,
After high deeds and sufferings long,
To chafe thee for a menial's song?—
Well hast thou framed, Old Man, thy
 strains,
To praise the hand that pays thy pains;
Yet something might thy song have told
Of Lorn's three vassals, true and bold,
Who rent their Lord from Bruce's hold
As underneath his knee he lay,
And died to save him in the fray.
I've heard the Bruce's cloak and clasp
Was clench'd within their dying grasp,
What time a hundred foemen more
Rush'd in, and back the victor bore,
Long after Lorn had left the strife,
Full glad to 'scape with limb and life.
Enough of this; and, Minstrel, hold
As minstrel-hire this chain of gold,
For future lays a fair excuse
To speak more nobly of the Bruce.'

XV.

'Now, by Columba's shrine, I swear,
And every saint that's buried there,
'Tis he himself!' Lorn sternly cries,
'And for my kinsman's death he dies.'
As loudly Ronald calls, 'Forbear!
Not in my sight, while brand I wear,
O'ermatch'd by odds, shall warrior fall,
Or blood of stranger stain my hall!
This ancient fortress of my race
Shall be misfortune's resting-place,
Shelter and shield of the distress'd,
No slaughter-house for shipwreck'd
 guest.'

'Talk not to me,' fierce Lorn replied,
'Of odds or match! when Comyn died
Three daggers clash'd within his side!
Talk not to me of sheltering hall,
The Church of GOD saw Comyn fall!
On God's own altar stream'd his blood,
While o'er my prostrate kinsman
　　　stood
The ruthless murderer—e'en as now—
With armed hand and scornful brow!
Up, all who love me! blow on blow!
And lay the outlaw'd felons low!'

XVI.

Then upsprang many a mainland Lord,
Obedient to their Chieftain's word.
Barcaldine's arm is high in air,
And Kinloch-Alline's blade is bare,
Black Murthok's dirk has left its sheath,
And clench'd is Dermid's hand of death.
Their mutter'd threats of vengeance
　　　swell
Into a wild and warlike yell;
Onward they press with weapons high,
The affrighted females shriek and fly,
And, Scotland, then thy brightest ray
Had darken'd ere its noon of day,—
But every chief of birth and fame,
That from the Isles of Ocean came,
At Ronald's side that hour withstood
Fierce Lorn's relentless thirst for
　　　blood.

XVII.

Brave Torquil from Dunvegan high,
Lord of the misty hills of Skye,
Mac-Niel, wild Bara's ancient thane,
Duart, of bold Clan-Gillian's strain,
Fergus, of Canna's castled bay,
Mac-Duffith, Lord of Colonsay,
Soon as they saw the broadswords
　　　glance,
With ready weapons rose at once,
More prompt, that many an ancient
　　　feud,
Full oft suppress'd, full oft renew'd,
Glow'd 'twixt the chieftains of Argyle,
And many a lord of ocean's isle.

Wild was the scene—each sword was
　　　bare,
Back stream'd each chieftain's shaggy
　　　hair,
In gloomy opposition set,
Eyes, hands, and brandish'd weapons
　　　met;
Blue gleaming o'er the social board,
Flash'd to the torches many a sword;
And soon those bridal lights may shine
On purple blood for rosy wine.

XVIII.

While thus for blows and death pre-
　　　pared,
Each heart was up, each weapon
　　　bared,
Each foot advanced,—a surly pause
Still reverenced hospitable laws.
All menaced violence, but alike
Reluctant each the first to strike,
(For aye accursed in minstrel line
Is he who brawls 'mid song and
　　　wine,)
And, match'd in numbers and in might,
Doubtful and desperate seem'd the
　　　fight.
Thus threat and murmur died away,
Till on the crowded hall there lay
Such silence, as the deadly still
Ere bursts the thunder on the hill.
With blade advanced, each Chieftain
　　　bold
Show'd like the Sworder's form of old,
As wanting still the torch of life [1]
To wake the marble into strife.

XIX.

That awful pause the stranger maid,
And Edith, seized to pray for aid.
As to De Argentine she clung,
Away her veil the stranger flung,
And, lovely 'mid her wild despair,
Fast stream'd her eyes, wide flow'd
　　　her hair,
'O thou, of knighthood once the flower,
Sure refuge in distressful hour,

[1 Qu. touch of life?]

Thou, who in Judah well hast fought
For our dear faith, and oft hast sought
Renown in knightly exercise,
When this poor hand has dealt the
    prize,
Say, can thy soul of honour brook
On the unequal strife to look,
When, butcher'd thus in peaceful hall,
Those once thy friends, my brethren,
    fall!'
To Argentine she turn'd her word,
But her eye sought the Island Lord.
A flush like evening's setting flame
Glow'd on his cheek; his hardy frame,
As with a brief convulsion, shook:
With hurried voice and eager look,—
' Fear not,' he said, ' my Isabel !
What said I ?—Edith ! all is well ;
Nay, fear not ; I will well provide
The safety of my lovely bride—
My bride ?'—but there the accents
    clung
In tremor to his faltering tongue

XX.

Now rose De Argentine, to claim
The prisoners in his sovereign's name,
To England's crown, who, vassals
    sworn,
'Gainst their liege lord had weapon
    borne—
(Such speech, I ween, was but to hide
His care their safety to provide ;
For knight more true in thought and
    deed
Than Argentine ne'er spurr'd a
    steed)—
And Ronald, who his meaning guess'd,
Seem'd half to sanction the request.
This purpose fiery Torquil broke:
' Somewhat we 've heard of England's
    yoke,'
He said, ' and, in our islands, Fame
Hath whisper'd of a lawful claim,
That calls the Bruce fair Scotland's
    Lord,
Though dispossess'd by foreign sword.

This craves reflection—but though
    right
And just the charge of England's
    Knight,
Let England's crown her rebels seize
Where she has power ;—in towers
    like these,
'Midst Scottish Chieftains summon'd
    here
To bridal mirth and bridal cheer,
Be sure, with no consent of mine,
Shall either Lorn or Argentine
With chains or violence, in our sight,
Oppress a brave and banish'd Knight.'

XXI.

Then waked the wild debate again,
With brawling threat and clamour vain.
Vassals and menials, thronging in,
Lent their brute rage to swell the din ;
When, far and wide, a bugle-clang
From the dark ocean upward rang.
' The Abbot comes !' they cry at
    once,
' The holy man, whose favour'd
    glance
    Hath sainted visions known ;
Angels have met him on the way,
Beside the blessed martyrs' bay,
    And by Columba's stone.
His monks have heard their hymn-
    ings high
Sound from the summit of Dun-Y,
    To cheer his penance lone
When at each cross, on girth and wold,
(Their number thrice a hundred-fold,)
His prayer he made, his beads he told,
    With Aves many a one—
He comes our feuds to reconcile,
A sainted man from sainted isle ;
We will his holy doom abide,
The Abbot shall our strife decide.'

XXII.

Scarcely this fair accord was o'er,
When through the wide revolving door
    The black-stoled brethren wind ;

Twelve sandall'd monks, who relics
    bore,
With many a torch-bearer before,
    And many a cross behind.
Then sunk each fierce uplifted hand,
And dagger bright and flashing brand
    Dropp'd swiftly at the sight;
They vanish'd from the Churchman's
    eye,
As shooting stars, that glance and die,
    Dart from the vault of night.

XXIII.

The Abbot on the threshold stood,
And in his hand the holy rood;
Back on his shoulders flow'd his hood,
    The torch's glaring ray
Show'd, in its red and flashing light,
His wither'd cheek and amice white,
His blue eye glistening cold and
    bright,
    His tresses scant and grey.
'Fair Lords,' he said, 'Our Lady's
    love,
And peace be with you from above,
    And Benedicite!
—But what means this? no peace is
    here!—
Do dirks unsheathed suit bridal cheer?
    Or are these naked brands
A seemly show for Churchman's sight,
When he comes summon'd to unite
    Betrothed hearts and hands?'

XXIV.

Then, cloaking hate with fiery zeal,
Proud Lorn first answer'd the ap-
    peal;—
'Thou comest, O holy Man,
True sons of blessed church to greet,
But little deeming here to meet
    A wretch, beneath the ban
Of Pope and Church, for murder done
Even on the sacred altar-stone!—
Well mayst thou wonder we should
    know
Such miscreant here, nor lay him low,

Or dream of greeting, peace, or truce,
With excommunicated Bruce!
Yet well I grant, to end debate,
Thy sainted voice decide his fate.'

XXV.

Then Ronald pled the stranger's cause,
And knighthood's oath and honour's
    laws;
And Isabel, on bended knee,
Brought pray'rs and tears to back the
    plea:
And Edith lent her generous aid,
And wept, and Lorn for mercy pray'd.
'Hence,' he exclaim'd, 'degenerate
    maid!
Was't not enough to Ronald's bower
I brought thee, like a paramour,
Or bond-maid at her master's gate,
His careless cold approach to wait?
But the bold Lord of Cumberland,
The gallant Clifford, seeks thy hand;
His it shall be—Nay, no reply!
Hence! till those rebel eyes be dry.'
With grief the Abbot heard and saw,
Yet nought relax'd his brow of awe.

XXVI.

Then Argentine, in England's name,
So highly urged his sovereign's claim,
He waked a spark, that, long sup-
    press'd,
Had smoulder'd in Lord Ronald's
    breast;
And now, as from the flint the fire,
Flash'd forth at once his generous ire.
'Enough of noble blood,' he said,
'By English Edward had been shed,
Since matchless Wallace first had been
In mock'ry crown'd with wreaths of
    green,
And done to death by felon hand,
For guarding well his father's land.
Where's Nigel Bruce? and De la Haye,
And valiant Seton—where are they?
Where Somerville, the kind and free?
And Fraser, flower of chivalry?

Have they not been on gibbet bound,
Their quarters flung to hawk and
    hound,
And hold we here a cold debate,
To yield more victims to their fate?
What! can the English Leopard's
    mood
Never be gorged with northern blood?
Was not the life of Athole shed
To soothe the tyrant's sicken'd bed?
And must his word, till dying day,
Be nought but quarter, hang, and slay!
Thou frown'st, De Argentine; my
    gage
Is prompt to prove the strife I wage.'

XXVII.

'Nor deem,' said stout Dunvegan's
    knight,
'That thou shalt brave alone the fight!
By saints of isle and mainland both,
By Woden wild (my grandsire's
    oath),
Let Rome and England do their worst,
Howe'er attainted or accursed,
If Bruce shall e'er find friends again
Once more to brave a battle-plain,
If Douglas couch again his lance,
Or Randolph dare another chance,
Old Torquil will not be to lack
With twice a thousand at his back.
Nay, chafe not at my bearing bold,
Good Abbot! for thou know'st of old,
Torquil's rude thought and stubborn
    will
Smack of the wild Norwegian still;
Nor will I barter Freedom's cause
For England's wealth, or Rome's
    applause.'

XXVIII.

The Abbot seem'd with eye severe
The hardy Chieftain's speech to hear;
Then on King Robert turn'd the Monk,
But twice his courage came and sunk,
Confronted with the hero's look;
Twice fell his eye, his accents shook;

At length, resolved in tone and brow,
Sternly he question'd him—'And thou,
Unhappy! what hast thou to plead,
Why I denounce not on thy deed
That awful doom which canons tell
Shuts paradise, and opens hell;
Anathema of power so dread,
It blends the living with the dead,
Bids each good angel soar away,
And every ill one claim his prey;
Expels thee from the Church's care,
And deafens Heaven against thy
    prayer;
Arms every hand against thy life,
Bans all who aid thee in the strife,
Nay, each whose succour, cold and
    scant,
With meanest alms relieves thy want;
Haunts thee while living, and, when
    dead,
Dwells on thy yet devoted head,
Rends Honour's scutcheon from thy
    hearse,
Stills o'er thy bier the holy verse,
And spurns thy corpse from hallow'd
    ground,
Flung like vile carrion to the hound;
Such is the dire and desperate doom
For sacrilege, decreed by Rome;
And such the well-deservéd meed
Of thine unhallow'd, ruthless deed.'

XXIX.

'Abbot!' The Bruce replied, 'thy
    charge
It boots not to dispute at large.
This much, howe'er, I bid thee know,
No selfish vengeance dealt the blow,
For Comyn died his country's foe.
Nor blame I friends whose ill-timed
    speed
Fulfill'd my soon-repented deed,
Nor censure those from whose stern
    tongue
The dire anathema has rung.
I only blame mine own wild ire,
By Scotland's wrongs incensed to fire.

Heaven knows my purpose to atone,
Far as I may, the evil done,
And hears a penitent's appeal
From papal curse and prelate's zeal.
My first and dearest task achieved,
Fair Scotland from her thrall relieved,
Shall many a priest in cope and stole
Say requiem for Red Comyn's soul,
While I the blessed cross advance,
And expiate this unhappy chance
In Palestine, with sword and lance.
But, while content the Church should know
My conscience owns the debt I owe,
Unto De Argentine and Lorn
The name of traitor I return,
Bid them defiance stern and high,
And give them in their throats the lie!
These brief words spoke, I speak no more.
Do what thou wilt; my shrift is o'er.'

XXX.

Like man by prodigy amazed,
Upon the King the Abbot gazed;
Then o'er his pallid features glance
Convulsions of ecstatic trance.
His breathing came more thick and fast,
And from his pale blue eyes were cast
Strange rays of wild and wandering light;
Uprise his locks of silver white,
Flush'd is his brow, through every vein
In azure tide the currents strain,
And undistinguish'd accents broke
The awful silence ere he spoke.

XXXI.

'De Bruce! I rose with purpose dread
To speak my curse upon thy head,
And give thee as an outcast o'er
To him who burns to shed thy gore:
But, like the Midianite of old,
Who stood on Zophim, heaven-controll'd,

I feel within mine aged breast
A power that will not be repress'd.
It prompts my voice, it swells my veins,
It burns, it maddens, it constrains!—
De Bruce, thy sacrilegious blow
Hath at God's altar slain thy foe:
O'ermaster'd yet by high behest,
I bless thee, and thou shalt be bless'd!'
He spoke, and o'er the astonish'd throng
Was silence, awful, deep, and long.

XXXII.

Again that light has fired his eye,
Again his form swells bold and high,
The broken voice of age is gone,
'Tis vigorous manhood's lofty tone:—
' Thrice vanquish'd on the battle-plain,
Thy followers slaughter'd, fled, or ta'en,
A hunted wanderer on the wild,
On foreign shores a man exil'd,
Disown'd, deserted, and distress'd,
I bless thee, and thou shalt be bless'd!
Bless'd in the hall and in the field,
Under the mantle as the shield.
Avenger of thy country's shame,
Restorer of her injured fame,
Bless'd in thy sceptre and thy sword,
De Bruce, fair Scotland's rightful Lord,
Bless'd in thy deeds and in thy fame,
What lengthen'd honours wait thy name!
In distant ages, sire to son
Shall tell thy tale of freedom won,
And teach his infants, in the use
Of earliest speech, to falter Bruce.
Go, then, triumphant! sweep along
Thy course, the theme of many a song!
The Power, whose dictates swell my breast,
Hath bless'd thee, and thou shalt be bless'd!—
Enough—my short-lived strength decays,
And sinks the momentary blaze.

Heaven hath our destined purpose
　　broke,
Not here must nuptial vow be spoke;
Brethren, our errand here is o'er,
Our task discharged.　Unmoor, un-
　　moor!'
His priests received the exhausted
　　Monk,
As breathless in their arms he sunk.
Punctual his orders to obey,
The train refused all longer stay,
Embark'd, raised sail, and bore away.

—+—

Canto Third.

I.

HAST thou not mark'd, when o'er
　　thy startled head
Sudden and deep the thunder-peal
　　has roll'd,
How, when its echoes fell, a silence
　　dead
Sunk on the wood, the meadow,
　　and the wold?
The rye-grass shakes not on the
　　sod-built fold,
The rustling aspen's leaves are mute
　　and still,
The wall-flower waves not on the
　　ruin'd hold,
Till, murmuring distant first, then
　　near and shrill,
The savage whirlwind wakes, and
　　sweeps the groaning hill.

II.

Artornish! such a silence sunk
Upon thy halls, when that grey Monk
　　His prophet-speech had spoke;
And his obedient brethren's sail
Was stretch'd to meet the southern
　　gale
　　Before a whisper woke.

Then murmuring sounds of doubt and
　　fear,
Close pour'd in many an anxious ear,
　　The solemn stillness broke;
And still they gazed with eager guess,
Where, in an oriel's deep recess,
The Island Prince seem'd bent to press
What Lorn, by his impatient cheer,
And gesture fierce, scarce deign'd to
　　hear.

III.

Starting at length, with frowning look,
His hand he clench'd, his head he shook,
　　And sternly flung apart—
'And deem'st thou me so mean of mood,
As to forget the mortal feud,
And clasp the hand with blood imbrued
　　From my dear Kinsman's heart?
Is this thy rede?—a due return
For ancient league and friendship
　　sworn!
But well our mountain proverb shows
The faith of Islesmen ebbs and flows.
Be it even so; believe, ere long,
He that now bears shall wreak the
　　wrong.
Call Edith—call the Maid of Lorn!
My sister, slaves! For further scorn,
Be sure nor she nor I will stay.
Away, De Argentine, away!
We nor ally nor brother know,
In Bruce's friend, or England's foe.'

IV.

But who the Chieftain's rage can tell,
When, sought from lowest dungeon cell
To highest tower the castle round,
No Lady Edith was there found!
He shouted, 'Falsehood!—treachery[1]!
Revenge and blood! a lordly meed
To him that will avenge the deed!
A Baron's lands!'—His frantic mood
Was scarcely by the news withstood,
That Morag shared his sister's flight,
And that, in hurry of the night,
'Scaped noteless, and without remark,
Two strangers sought the Abbot's bark.

[1 Scott seems to have missed or dropt a line here.]

'Man every galley! fly—pursue!
The priest his treachery shall rue!
Ay, and the time shall quickly come
When we shall hear the thanks that
        Rome
Will pay his feigned prophecy!'
Such was fierce Lorn's indignant cry;
And Cormac Doil in haste obey'd,
Hoisted his sail, his anchor weigh'd
(For, glad of each pretext for spoil,
A pirate sworn was Cormac Doil).
But others, lingering, spoke apart,—
'The Maid has given her maiden heart
        To Ronald of the Isles,
And, fearful lest her brother's word
Bestow her on that English Lord,
She seeks Iona's piles,
And wisely deems it best to dwell
A votaress in the holy cell,
Until these feuds so fierce and fell
        The Abbot reconciles.'

v.

As impotent of ire, the hall
Echo'd to Lorn's impatient call,
'My horse, my mantle, and my train!
Let none who honours Lorn remain!'
Courteous, but stern, a bold request
To Bruce De Argentine express'd.
'Lord Earl,' he said, 'I cannot chuse
But yield such title to the Bruce,
Though name and earldom both are
        gone,
Since he braced rebel's armour on—
But, Earl or serf—rude phrase was
        thine
Of late, and launch'd at Argentine;
Such as compels me to demand
Redress of honour at thy hand.
We need not to each other tell
That both can wield their weapons well;
        Then do me but the soldier grace,
        This glove upon thy helm to place
            Where we may meet in fight;
        And I will say, as still I 've said,
        Though by ambition far misled,
            Thou art a noble knight.'

VI.

'And I,' the princely Bruce replied,
'Might term it stain on knighthood's
        pride
That the bright sword of Argentine
Should in a tyrant's quarrel shine;
        But, for your brave request,
Be sure the honour'd pledge you gave
In every battle-field shall wave
        Upon my helmet-crest;
Believe, that if my hasty tongue
Hath done thine honour causeless
        wrong,
        It shall be well redress'd.
Not dearer to my soul was glove,
Bestow'd in youth by lady's love,
        Than this which thou hast given!
Thus, then, my noble foe I greet;
Health and high fortune till we meet,
        And then—what pleases Heaven.'

VII.

Thus parted they; for now, with sound
Like waves roll'd back from rocky
        ground,
        The friends of Lorn retire;
Each mainland chieftain, with his train,
Draws to his mountain towers again,
Pondering how mortal schemes prove
        vain,
        And mortal hopes expire.
But through the castle double guard,
By Ronald's charge, kept wakeful
        ward,
Wicket and gate were trebly barr'd,
        By beam and bolt and chain;
Then of the guests, in courteous sort,
He pray'd excuse for mirth broke short,
And bade them in Artornish fort
        In confidence remain.
Now torch and menial tendance led
Chieftain and knight to bower and bed,
And beads were told, and Aves said,
        And soon they sunk away
Into such sleep, as wont to shed
Oblivion on the weary head,
        After a toilsome day.

VIII.

But soon uproused, the Monarch cried
To Edward slumbering by his side,
　'Awake. or sleep for aye !
Even now there jarr'd a secret door,
A taper-light gleams on the floor,
　Up, Edward, up, I say !
Some one glides in like midnight
　　ghost—
Nay, strike not ! 'tis our noble Host.'
Advancing then his taper's flame,
Ronald stept forth, and with him came
　Dunvegan's chief—each bent the
　　knee
　To Bruce in sign of fealty,
　　And proffer'd him his sword,
　And hail'd him, in a monarch's style,
　As king of mainland and of isle,
　　And Scotland's rightful lord.
'And O,' said Ronald, 'Own'd of
　　Heaven !
Say, is my erring youth forgiven,
By falsehood's arts from duty driven,
　Who rebel falchion drew,
Yet ever to thy deeds of fame,
Even while I strove against thy claim,
　Paid homage just and true ?'
'Alas ! dear youth, the unhappy time,'
Answer'd the Bruce, 'must bear the
　　crime,
　Since, guiltier far than you,
Even I'—he paused ; for Falkirk's woes
Upon his conscious soul arose.
The Chieftain to his breast he press'd,
And in a sigh conceal'd the rest.

IX.

They proffer'd aid, by arms and might,
To repossess him in his right ;
But well their counsels must be
　　weigh'd,
Ere banners raised and musters made,
For English hire and Lorn's intrigues
Bound many chiefs in southern leagues.
In answer, Bruce his purpose bold
To his new vassals frankly told.

'The winter worn in exile o'er,
I long'd for Carrick's kindred shore.
I thought upon my native Ayr,
And long'd to see the burly fare
That Clifford makes, whose lordly call
Now echoes through my father's hall.
But first my course to Arran led,
Where valiant Lennox gathers head,
And on the sea, by tempest toss'd,
Our barks dispersed, our purpose
　　cross'd,
Mine own, a hostile sail to shun,
Far from her destined course had run,
When that wise will, which masters
　　ours,
Compell'd us to your friendly towers.'

X.

Then Torquil spoke : 'The time craves
　　speed !
We must not linger in our deed,
But instant pray our Sovereign Liege,
To shun the perils of a siege.
The vengeful Lorn, with all his powers,
Lies but too near Artornish towers,
And England's light-arm'd vessels
　　ride,
Not distant far, the waves of Clyde,
Prompt at these tidings to unmoor,
And sweep each strait, and guard each
　　shore.
Then, till this fresh alarm pass by,
Secret and safe my Liege must lie
In the far bounds of friendly Skye,
Torquil thy pilot and thy guide.'
'Not so, brave Chieftain,' Ronald
　　cried ;
'Myself will on my Sovereign wait,
And raise in arms the men of Sleate,
Whilst thou, renown'd where chiefs
　　debate,
Shalt sway their souls by counsel
　　sage,
And awe them by thy locks of age.'
'And if my words in weight shall fail,
This ponderous sword shall turn the
　　scale.'

XI.

'The scheme,' said Bruce, 'contents
     me well;
Meantime, 'twere best that Isabel,
For safety, with my bark and crew,
Again to friendly Erin drew.
There Edward,too,shall with her wend,
In need to cheer her and defend,
And muster up each scatter'd friend.'
Here seem'd it as Lord Ronald's ear
Would other counsel gladlier hear;
But, all achieved as soon as plann'd,
Both barks, in secret arm'd and mann'd,
     From out the haven bore;
On different voyage forth they ply,
This for the coast of winged Skye [1],
     And that for Erin's shore.

XII.

With Bruce and Ronald bides the tale.
To favouring winds they gave the sail,
Till Mull's dark headlands scarce they
     knew,
And Ardnamurchan's hills were blue.
But then the squalls blew close and
     hard,
And, fain to strike the galley's yard,
     And take them to the oar,
With these rude seas, in weary plight,
They strove the livelong day and night,
Nor till the dawning had a sight
     Of Skye's romantic shore.
Where Coolin stoops him to the west,
They saw upon his shiver'd crest
     The sun's arising gleam;
But such the labour and delay,
Ere they were moor'd in Scavigh bay
(For calmer heaven compell'd to stay)
     He shot a western beam.
Then Ronald said, 'If true mine eye,
These are the savage wilds that lie
North of Strathnardill and Dunskye;
     No human foot comes here,
And, since these adverse breezes blow,
If my good Liege love hunter's bow,
What hinders that on land we go,
     And strike a mountain-deer?

---

[1] 'Insula alata.' George Buchanan.]

Allan, my page, shall with us wend;
A bow full deftly can he bend,
And, if we meet a herd, may send
     A shaft shall mend our cheer.'
Then each took bow and bolts in hand,
Their row-boat launch'd and leapt to
     land,
     And left their skiff and train,
Where a wild stream, with headlong
     shock,
Came brawling down its bed of rock,
     To mingle with the main.

XIII.

Awhile their route they silent made,
     As men who stalk for mountain-
     deer,
Till the good Bruce to Ronald said,
     'Saint Mary! what a scene is
     here!
I've traversed many a mountain-strand,
Abroad and in my native land,
And it has been my lot to tread
Where safety more than pleasure led;
Thus, many a waste I've wander'd o'er,
Clombe many a crag, cross'd many a
     moor,
     But, by my halidome,
A scene so rude, so wild as this,
Yet so sublime in barrenness,
Ne'er did my wandering footsteps press,
     Where'er I happ'd to roam.'

XIV.

No marvel thus the Monarch spake;
     For rarely human eye has known
A scene so stern as that dread lake,
     With its dark ledge of barren stone.
Seems that primeval earthquake's sway
Hath rent a strange and shatter'd way
     Through the rude bosom of the hill,
And that each naked precipice,
Sable ravine, and dark abyss,
     Tells of the outrage still.
The wildest glen, but this, can show
Some touch of Nature's genial glow;
On high Benmore green mosses grow,
And heath-bells bud in deep Glencroe,
     And copse on Cruchan-Ben;

But here,—above, around, below,
　On mountain or in glen,
Nor tree, nor shrub, nor plant, nor
　　flower,
Nor aught of vegetative power,
　The weary eye may ken.
For all is rocks at random thrown,
Black waves, bare crags, and banks of
　　stone,
　As if were here denied
The summer sun, the spring's sweet
　　dew,
That clothe with many a varied hue
　The bleakest mountain-side.

xv.

And wilder, forward as they wound,
Were the proud cliffs and lake profound.
Huge terraces of granite black
Afforded rude and cumber'd track;
　For from the mountain hoar,
Hurl'd headlong in some night of fear,
When yell'd the wolf and fled the deer,
　Loose crags had toppled o'er;
And some, chance-poised and balanced,
　　lay,
So that a stripling arm might sway
　A mass no host could raise,
In Nature's rage at random thrown,
Yet trembling like the Druid's stone
　On its precarious base.
The evening mists, with ceaseless
　　change,
Now clothed the mountains' lofty
　　range,
　Now left their foreheads bare,
And round the skirts their mantle furl'd,
Or on the sable waters curl'd,
Or on the eddying breezes whirl'd,
　Dispersed in middle air.
And oft, condensed, at once they lower,
When, brief and fierce, the mountain
　　shower
　Pours like a torrent down,
And when return the sun's glad beams,
Whiten'd with foam a thousand streams
　Leap from the mountain's crown.

xvi.

'This lake,' said Bruce, 'whose barriers
　　drear
Are precipices sharp and sheer,
Yielding no track for goat or deer,
　Save the black shelves we tread,
How term you its dark waves? and how
Yon northern mountain's pathless
　　brow,
　And yonder peak of dread,
That to the evening sun uplifts
The griesly gulfs and slaty rifts
　Which seam its shiver'd head?'
'Coriskin call the dark lake's name,
Coolin the ridge, as bards proclaim,
From old Cuchullin, chief of fame.
But bards, familiar in our isles
Rather with Nature's frowns than
　　smiles,
Full oft their careless humours please
By sportive names from scenes like
　　these.
I would old Torquil were to show
His maidens with their breasts of snow,
Or that my noble Liege were nigh
To hear his Nurse sing lullaby!
(The Maids—tall cliffs with breakers
　　white,
The Nurse—a torrent's roaring might,)
Or that your eye could see the mood
Of Corryvrekin's whirlpool rude,
When dons the Hag her whiten'd
　　hood!
'Tis thus our islesmen's fancy frames,
For scenes so stern, fantastic names.'

xvii.

Answer'd the Bruce, 'And musing mind
Might here a graver moral find.
These mighty cliffs, that heave on high
Their naked brows to middle sky,
Indifferent to the sun or snow,
Where nought can fade, and nought
　　can blow,
May they not mark a Monarch's fate,—
Raised high 'mid storms of strife and
　　state,

Beyond life's lowlier pleasures placed,
His soul a rock, his heart a waste?
O'er hope and love and fear aloft
High rears his crowned head—But
　　soft!
Look, underneath yon jutting crag
Are hunters and a slaughter'd stag.
Who may they be? But late you said
No steps these desert regions tread!'—

XVIII.

'So said I; and believed in sooth,'
Ronald replied, 'I spoke the truth.
Yet now I spy, by yonder stone,
Five men; they mark us, and come on;
And by their badge on bonnet borne,
I guess them of the land of Lorn,
Foes to my Liege.'　'So let it be;
I've faced worse odds than five to three;
But the poor page can little aid;
Then be our battle thus array'd
If our free passage they contest;
Cope thou with two, I'll match the rest.'
'Not so, my Liege, for, by my life,
This sword shall meet the treble strife;
My strength, my skill in arms, more
　　small,
And less the loss should Ronald fall.
But islesmen soon to soldiers grow,
Allan has sword as well as bow,
And were my Monarch's order given
Two shafts should make our number
　　even.'
'No! not to save my life!' he said;
'Enough of blood rests on my head
Too rashly spill'd—we soon shall
　　know
Whether they come as friend or foe.'

XIX.

Nigh came the strangers, and more
　　nigh;
Still less they pleased the Monarch's
　　eye.
Men were they all of evil mien,
Down-look'd. unwilling to be seen;
They moved with half-resolved pace,
And bent on earth each gloomy face.

The foremost two were fair array'd
With brogue and bonnet, trews and
　　plaid,
And bore the arms of mountaineers,
Daggers and broadswords, bows and
　　spears.
The three, that lagg'd small space
　　behind,
Seem'd serfs of more degraded kind;
Goat-skins or deer-hides o'er them
　　cast,
Made a rude fence against the blast;
Their arms and feet and heads were
　　bare,
Matted their beards, unshorn their
　　hair;
For arms, the caitiffs bore in hand
A club, an axe, a rusty brand.

XX.

Onward, still mute, they kept the track;
'Tell who ye be, or else stand back,'
Said Bruce; 'in deserts when they
　　meet
Men pass not as in peaceful street.'
Still, at his stern command, they stood,
And proffer'd greeting brief and rude,
But acted courtesy so ill
As seem'd of fear, and not of will.
'Wanderers we are, as you may be;
Men hither driven by wind and sea,
Who, if you list to taste our cheer,
Will share with you this fallow deer.
'If from the sea, where lies your bark?'
'Ten fathom deep in ocean dark!
Wreck'd yesternight: but we are men
Who little sense of peril ken.
The shades come down—the day is
　　shut—
Will you go with us to our hut?'—
'Our vessel waits us in the bay;
Thanks for your proffer—have good-
　　day.'
'Was that your galley, then, which
　　rode
Not far from shore when evening
　　glow'd?'

'It was.' 'Then spare your needless
    pain,
There will she now be sought in vain.
We saw her from the mountain head,
When, with St. George's blazon red,
A southern vessel bore in sight,
And yours raised sail, and took to flight.'

XXI.

'Now, by the rood, unwelcome news!'
Thus with Lord Ronald communed
    Bruce;
'Nor rests there light enough to show
If this their tale be true or no.
The men seem bred of churlish kind,
Yet mellow nuts have hardest rind;
We will go with them—food and fire
And sheltering roof our wants require.
Sure guard 'gainst treachery will we
    keep,
And watch by turns our comrades'
    sleep.—
Good fellows, thanks; your guests
    we'll be,
And well will pay the courtesy.
Come, lead us where your lodging
    lies,
— Nay, soft! we mix not companies.
Show us the path o'er crag and stone,
And we will follow you;—lead on.'

XXII.

They reach'd the dreary cabin, made
Of sails against a rock display'd,
    And there, on entering, found
A slender boy, whose form and mien
Ill suited with such savage scene,
In cap and cloak of velvet green,
    Low seated on the ground.
His garb was such as minstrels wear,
Dark was his hue, and dark his hair,
His youthful cheek was marr'd by
    care,
    His eyes in sorrow drown'd.
'Whence this poor boy?' As Ronald
    spoke,
The voice his trance of anguish broke:

As if awaked from ghastly dream,
He raised his head with start and
    scream,
    And wildly gazed around;
Then to the wall his face he turn'd,
And his dark neck with blushes burn'd.

XXIII.

'Whose is the boy?' again he said.
'By chance of war our captive made;
He may be yours, if you should hold
That music has more charms than gold;
For, though from earliest childhood
    mute,
The lad can deftly touch the lute,
    And on the rote and viol play,
    And well can drive the time away
      For those who love such glee;
    For me, the favouring breeze, when
      loud
    It pipes upon the galley's shroud,
      Makes blither melody.'
'Hath he, then, sense of spoken sound?'
    'Aye; so his mother bade us know,
A crone in our late shipwreck drown'd,
    And hence the silly stripling's woe.
More of the youth I cannot say,
Our captive but since yesterday;
When wind and weather wax'd so
    grim,
We little listed think of him.—
But why waste time in idle words?
Sit to your cheer—unbelt your swords.'
Sudden the captive turn'd his head,
And one quick glance to Ronald sped.
It was a keen and warning look,
And well the Chief the signal took.

XXIV.

'Kind host,' he said, 'our needs require
A separate board and separate fire;
For know, that on a pilgrimage
Wend I, my comrade and this page.
And, sworn to vigil and to fast
Long as this hallow'd task shall last,
We never doff the plaid or sword,
Or feast us at a stranger's board;

And never share one common sleep,
But one must still his vigil keep.
Thus, for our separate use, good friend,
We'll hold this hut's remoter end.'
'A churlish vow,' the eldest said,
'And hard, methinks, to be obey'd.
How say you, if, to wreak the scorn
That pays our kindness harsh return,
We should refuse to share our meal?'
'Then say we that our swords are steel,
And our vow binds us not to fast
Where gold or force may buy repast!'
Their host's dark brow grew keen and fell,
His teeth are clench'd, his features swell;
Yet sunk the felon's moody ire
Before Lord Ronald's glance of fire,
Nor could his craven courage brook
The Monarch's calm and dauntless look.
With laugh constrain'd,—'Let every man
Follow the fashion of his clan!
Each to his separate quarters keep,
And feed or fast, or wake or sleep.'

xxv.

Their fire at separate distance burns,
By turns they eat, keep guard by turns;
For evil seem'd that old man's eye,
Dark and designing, fierce yet shy.
Still he avoided forward look,
But slow and circumspectly took
A circling, never-ceasing glance,
By doubt and cunning mark'd at once,
Which shot a mischief-boding ray
From under eyebrows shagg'd and grey.
The younger, too, who seem'd his son,
Had that dark look the timid shun;
The half-clad serfs behind them sate,
And scowl'd a glare 'twixt fear and hate;

Till all, as darkness onward crept,
Couch'd down, and seem'd to sleep, or slept.
Nor he, that boy, whose powerless tongue
Must trust his eyes to wail his wrong,
A longer watch of sorrow made,
But stretch'd his limbs to slumber laid.

xxvi.

Not in his dangerous host confides
The King, but wary watch provides.
Ronald keeps ward till midnight past,
Then wakes the King, young Allan last;
Thus rank'd, to give the youthful page
The rest required by tender age.
What is Lord Ronald's wakeful thought,
To chase the languor toil had brought?
(For deem not that he deign'd to throw
Much care upon such coward foe.)
He thinks of lovely Isabel,
When at her foeman's feet she fell,
Nor less when, placed in princely selle,
She glanced on him with favouring eyes
At Woodstock when he won the prize.
Nor, fair in joy, in sorrow fair,
In pride of place as 'mid despair,
Must she alone engross his care.
His thoughts to his betrothed bride,
To Edith, turn—O how decide,
When here his love and heart are given,
And there his faith stands plight to Heaven!
No drowsy ward 'tis his to keep,
For seldom lovers long for sleep.
Till sung his midnight hymn the owl,
Answer'd the dog-fox with his howl,
Then waked the King—at his request
Lord Ronald stretch'd himself to rest.

xxvii.

What spell was good King Robert's, say,
To drive the weary night away?

His was the patriot's burning thought,
Of Freedom's battle bravely fought,
Of castles storm'd, of cities freed,
Of deep design and daring deed,
Of England's roses reft and torn,
And Scotland's cross in triumph worn,
Of rout and rally, war and truce,—
As heroes think, so thought the Bruce.
No marvel, 'mid such musings high,
Sleep shunn'd the Monarch's thought-
    ful eye.
Now over Coolin's eastern head
The greyish light begins to spread,
The otter to his cavern drew,
And clamour'd shrill the wakening
    mew;
Then watch'd the page—to needful rest
The King resign'd his anxious breast.

XXVIII.

To Allan's eyes was harder task,
The weary watch their safeties ask.
He trimm'd the fire, and gave to shine
With bickering light the splinter'd
    pine;
Then gazed awhile, where silent laid
Their hosts were shrouded by the plaid.
But little fear waked in his mind,
For he was bred of martial kind,
And, if to manhood he arrive,
May match the boldest knight alive.
Then thought he of his mother's tower,
His little sisters' greenwood bower,
How there the Easter-gambols pass,
And of Dan Joseph's lengthen'd mass.
But still before his weary eye
In rays prolong'd the blazes die—
Again he roused him—on the lake
Look'd forth, where now the twilight-
    flake
Of pale cold dawn began to wake.
On Coolin's cliffs the mist lay furl'd,
The morning breeze the lake had curl'd,
The short dark waves, heaved to the
    land,
With ceaseless plash kiss'd cliff or
    sand;—

It was a slumbrous sound – he turn'd
To tales at which his youth had burn'd,
Of pilgrim's path by demon cross'd,
Of sprightly elf or yelling ghost,
Of the wild witch's baneful cot,
And mermaid's alabaster grot,
Who bathes her limbs in sunless well,
Deep in Strathaird's enchanted cell.
Thither in fancy rapt he flies,
And on his sight the vaults arise;
That hut's dark walls he sees no more,
His foot is on the marble floor,
And o'er his head the dazzling spars
Gleam like a firmament of stars!
Hark! hears he not the sea-nymph
    speak
Her anger in that thrilling shriek!—
No! all too late, with Allan's dream
Mingled the captive's warning scream.
As from the ground he strives to start
A ruffian's dagger finds his heart!
Upward he casts his dizzy eyes, . . .
Murmurs his master's name, . . . and
    dies!

XXIX.

Not so awoke the King! his hand
Snatch'd from the flame a knotted
    brand,
The nearest weapon of his wrath;
With this he cross'd the murderer's
    path,
    And venged young Allan well!
The spatter'd brain and bubbling blood
Hiss'd on the half-extinguish'd wood,
    The miscreant gasp'd and fell!
Nor rose in peace the Island Lord;
One caitiff died upon his sword,
And one beneath his grasp lies prone,
In mortal grapple overthrown.
But while Lord Ronald's dagger drank
The life-blood from his panting flank,
The Father-ruffian of the band
Behind him rears a coward hand!
    O for a moment's aid,
Till Bruce, who deals no double blow,
Dash to the earth another foe,
    Above his comrade laid!

And it is gain'd—the captive sprung
On the raised arm, and closely clung,
    And, ere he shook him loose,
The master'd felon press'd the ground,
And gasp'd beneath a mortal wound,
      While o'er him stands the Bruce.

XXX.

' Miscreant! while lasts thy flitting
      spark,
Give me to know the purpose dark
That arm'd thy hand with murderous
      knife
Against offenceless stranger's life ?'
' No stranger thou!' with accent fell,
Murmur'd the wretch; ' I know thee
      well;
And know thee for the foeman sworn
Of my high chief, the mighty Lorn.'
' Speak yet again, and speak the truth
For thy soul's sake!—from whence
      this youth ?
His country, birth, and name declare,
And thus one evil deed repair.'
' Vex me no more! . . . my blood
      runs cold . . .
No more I know than I have told.
We found him in a bark we sought
With different purpose . . . and I
      thought ' . . .
Fate cut him short; in blood and broil,
As he had lived, died Cormac Doil.

XXXI.

Then resting on his bloody blade,
The valiant Bruce to Ronald said,
' Now shame upon us both! that boy
Lifts his mute face to heaven,
And clasps his hands, to testify
His gratitude to God on high
      For strange deliverance given.
His speechless gesture thanks hath
      paid
Which our free tongues have left
      unsaid !'
He raised the youth with kindly word,
But mark'd him shudder at the sword:

He cleansed it from its hue of death,
And plunged the weapon in its sheath.
' Alas, poor child! unfitting part
Fate doom'd, when with so soft a heart,
      And form so slight as thine,
She made thee first a pirate's slave,
Then, in his stead, a patron gave
      Of wayward lot like mine ;
A landless prince, whose wandering
      life
Is but one scene of blood and strife—
Yet scant of friends the Bruce shall be,
But he'll find resting-place for thee.
Come, noble Ronald! o'er the dead
Enough thy generous grief is paid,
And well has Allan's fate been wroke;
Come, wend we hence—the day has
      broke.
Seek we our bark ; I trust the tale
Was false, that she had hoisted sail.'

XXXII.

Yet, ere they left that charnel-cell,
The Island Lord bade sad farewell
To Allan :—' Who shall tell this tale,'
He said, ' in halls of Donagaile !
Oh, who his widow'd mother tell,
That, ere his bloom, her fairest fell!
Rest thee, poor youth! and trust my
      care
For mass and knell and funeral prayer;
While o'er those caitiffs, where they
      lie,
The wolf shall snarl, the raven cry !'
And now the eastern mountain's head
On the dark lake threw lustre red ;
Bright gleams of gold and purple streak
Ravine and precipice and peak—
(So earthly power at distance shows;
Reveals his splendour, hides his woes.)
O'er sheets of granite, dark and broad,
Rent and unequal, lay the road.
In sad discourse the warriors wind,
And the mute captive moves behind.

—◆—

Canto Fourth.

I.

STRANGER ! if e'er thine ardent step hath traced
The northern realms of ancient Caledon,
Where the proud Queen of Wilderness hath placed,
By lake and cataract, her lonely throne ;
Sublime but sad delight thy soul hath known,
Gazing on pathless glen and mountain high,
Listing where from the cliffs the torrents thrown
Mingle their echoes with the eagle's cry,
And with the sounding lake, and with the moaning sky.

Yes ! 'twas sublime, but sad. The loneliness
Loaded thy heart, the desert tired thine eye ;
And strange and awful fears began to press
Thy bosom with a stern solemnity.
Then hast thou wish'd some woodman's cottage nigh,
Something that show'd of life, though low and mean ;
Glad sight, its curling wreath of smoke to spy,
Glad sound, its cock's blithe carol would have been,
Or children whooping wild beneath the willows green.

Such are the scenes, where savage grandeur wakes
An awful thrill that softens into sighs ;
Such feelings rouse them by dim Rannoch's lakes,
In dark Glencoe such gloomy raptures rise :

Or farther, where, beneath the northern skies,
Chides wild Loch-Eribol his caverns hoar—
But, be the minstrel judge, they yield the prize
Of desert dignity to that dread shore
That sees grim Coolin rise, and hears Coriskin roar.

II.

Through such wild scenes the champion pass'd,
When bold halloo and bugle-blast
Upon the breeze came loud and fast.
'There,' said the Bruce, 'rung Edward's horn !
What can have caused such brief return ?
And see, brave Ronald,—see him dart
O er stock and stone like hunted hart,
Precipitate, as is the use,
In war or sport, of Edward Bruce.
—He marks us, and his eager cry
Will tell his news ere he be nigh.'

III.

Loud Edward shouts, ' What make ye here,
Warring upon the mountain-deer,
    When Scotland wants her King !
A bark from Lennox cross'd our track,
With her in speed I hurried back,
    These joyful news to bring—
The Stuart stirs in Teviotdale,
And Douglas wakes his native vale ;
Thy storm-toss'd fleet hath won its way
With little loss to Brodick-Bay,
And Lennox, with a gallant band,
Waits but thy coming and command
To waft them o'er to Carrick strand.
There are blithe news !—but mark the close !
Edward, the deadliest of our foes,
As with his host he northward pass'd,
Hath on the Borders breathed his last.'

P

IV.

Still stood the Bruce ; his steady cheek
Was little wont his joy to speak,
　　But then his colour rose :
' Now, Scotland ! shortly shalt thou see,
With God's high will, thy children free,
　　And vengeance on thy foes !
Yet to no sense of selfish wrongs,
Bear witness with me, Heaven, be longs
　　My joy o'er Edward's bier ;
I took my knighthood at his hand,
And lordship held of him, and land,
　　And well may vouch it here,
That, blot the story from his page,
Of Scotland ruin'd in his rage,
You read a monarch brave and sage,
　　And to his people dear.'—
' Let London's burghers mourn her Lord,
And Croydon monks his praise record,'
　　The eager Edward said ;
' Eternal as his own, my hate
Surmounts the bounds of mortal fate,
　　And dies not with the dead !
Such hate was his on Solway's strand,
When vengeance clench'd his palsied hand,
That pointed yet to Scotland's land
　　As his last accents pray'd
Disgrace and curse upon his heir,
If he one Scottish head should spare,
Till stretch'd upon the bloody lair
　　Each rebel corpse was laid !
Such hate was his, when his last breath
Renounced the peaceful house of death,
And bade his bones to Scotland's coast
Be borne by his remorseless host,
As if his dead and stony eye
Could still enjoy her misery !
Such hate was his—dark, deadly, long ;
Mine—as enduring, deep, and strong !'

V.

' Let women, Edward, war with words,
With curses monks, but men with swords :

Nor doubt of living foes, to sate
Deepest revenge and deadliest hate.
Now, to the sea ! behold the beach,
And see the galleys' pendants stretch
Their fluttering length down favouring gale !
Aboard, aboard ! and hoist the sail.
Hold we our way for Arran first,
Where meet in arms our friends dispersed ;
Lennox the loyal, De la Haye,
And Boyd the bold in battle-fray.
I long the hardy band to head,
And see once more my standard spread.
Does noble Ronald share our course,
Or stay to raise his island force ?'
' Come weal, come woe, by Bruce's side,'
Replied the Chief, ' will Ronald bide.
And since two galleys yonder ride,
Be mine, so please my liege, dismiss'd
To wake to arms the clans of Uist,
And all who hear the Minche's roar
On the Long Island's lonely shore.
The nearer Isles, with slight delay,
Ourselves may summon in our way ;
And soon on Arran's shore shall meet,
With Torquil's aid, a gallant fleet,
If aught avails their Chieftain's hest
Among the islesmen of the west.'

VI.

Thus was their venturous council said.
But, ere their sails the galleys spread,
Coriskin dark and Coolin high
Echoed the dirge's doleful cry.
Along that sable lake pass'd slow—
Fit scene for such a sight of woe—
The sorrowing islesmen, as they bore
The murder'd Allan to the shore.
At every pause, with dismal shout,
Their coronach of grief rung out,
And ever, when they moved again,
The pipes resumed their clamorous strain,
And, with the pibroch's shrilling wail,
Mourn'd the young heir of Donagaile.

Round and around, from cliff and cave,
His answer stern old Coolin gave,
Till high upon his misty side
Languish'd the mournful notes, and
    died.
For never sounds, by mortal made,
Attain'd his high and haggard head,
That echoes but the tempest's moan,
Or the deep thunder's rending groan.

VII.

Merrily, merrily bounds the bark,
    She bounds before the gale,
The mountain breeze from Ben-na-
    darch
    Is joyous in her sail!
With fluttering sound like laughter
    hoarse,
    The cords and canvas strain,
The waves, divided by her force,
In rippling eddies chased her course
    As if they laugh'd again.
Not down the breeze more blithely
    flew,
Skimming the wave, the light sea-mew,
    Than the gay galley bore
Her course upon that favouring wind,
And Coolin's crest has sunk behind,
    And Slapin's cavern'd shore.
'Twas then that warlike signals wake
Dunscaith's dark towers and Eisord's
    lake,
And soon, from Cavilgarrigh's head,
Thick wreaths of eddying smoke were
    spread;
A summons these of war and wrath
To the brave clans of Sleat and Strath,
    And, ready at the sight,
Each warrior to his weapons sprung,
And targe upon his shoulder flung,
    Impatient for the fight.
Mac-Kinnon's chief, in warfare grey,
Had charge to muster their array,
And guide their barks to Brodick-Bay.

VIII.

Signal of Ronald's high command,
A beacon gleam'd o'er sea and land,
From Canna's tower, that, steep and
    grey,
Like falcon-nest o'erhangs the bay.
Seek not the giddy crag to climb,
To view the turret scathed by time;
It is a task of doubt and fear
To aught but goat or mountain-deer
    But rest thee on the silver beach,
    And let the aged herdsman teach
        His tale of former day;
    His cur's wild clamour he shall
        chide,
    And for thy seat by ocean's side
        His varied plaid display;
    Then tell, how with their Chieftain
        came,
    In ancient times, a foreign dame
        To yonder turret grey.
Stern was her Lord's suspicious mind,
Who in so rude a jail confined
    So soft and fair a thrall!
And oft, when moon on ocean slept,
That lovely lady sate and wept
    Upon the castle-wall,
And turn'd her eye to southern climes,
And thought perchance of happier
    times,
And touch'd her lute by fits, and
    sung
Wild ditties in her native tongue.
And still, when on the cliff and bay
Placid and pale the moonbeams play,
    And every breeze is mute,
Upon the lone Hebridean's ear
Steals a strange pleasure mix'd with
    fear,
While from that cliff he seems to hear
    The murmur of a lute,
And sounds, as of a captive lone,
That mourns her woes in tongue
    unknown.
Strange is the tale—but all too long
Already hath it staid the song—
    Yet who may pass them by,
That crag and tower in ruins grey,
Nor to their hapless tenant pay
    The tribute of a sigh?

IX.

Merrily, merrily bounds the bark
  O'er the broad ocean driven,
Her path by Ronin's mountains dark
  The steersman's hand hath given.
And Ronin's mountains dark have
    sent
    Their hunters to the shore,
And each his ashen bow unbent,
    And gave his pastime o'er,
And at the Island Lord's command,
For hunting spear took warrior s brand.
On Scooreigg next a warning light
Summon'd her warriors to the fight ;
A numerous race, ere stern MacLeod
O'er their bleak shores in vengeance
    strode,
When all in vain the ocean-cave
Its refuge to his victims gave.
The Chief, relentless in his wrath,
With blazing heath blockades the path ;
In dense and stifling volumes roll'd,
The vapour fill'd the cavern'd hold !
The warrior-threat. the infant's plain,
The mother's screams, were heard in
    vain ;
The vengeful Chief maintains his fires,
Till in the vault a tribe expires !
The bones which strew that cavern's
    gloom
Too well attest their dismal doom.

X.

Merrily, merrily goes the bark
  On a breeze from the northward free,
So shoots through the morning sky
    the lark,
  Or the swan through the summer
    sea.
The shores of Mull on the eastward
    lay,
And Ulva dark and Colonsay,
And all the group of islets gay
  That guard famed Staffa round.
Then all unknown its columns rose,
Where dark and undisturb'd repose
  The cormorant had found,

And the shy seal had quiet home,
And welter'd in that wondrous dome,
Where, as to shame the temples deck'd
By skill of earthly architect,
Nature herself, it seem'd, would raise
A Minster to her Maker's praise !
Not for a meaner use ascend
Her columns, or her arches bend ;
Nor of a theme less solemn tells
That mighty surge that ebbs and
    swells,
And still, between each awful pause,
From the high vault an answer draws,
In varied tone prolong'd and high,
That mocks the organ's melody.
Nor doth its entrance front in vain
To old Iona's holy fane,
That Nature's voice might seem to say,
'. Well hast thou done, frail Child of
    clay !
Thy humble powers that stately shrine
Task'd high and hard—but witness
    mine !'

XI.

Merrily, merrily goes the bark,
  Before the gale she bounds ;
So darts the dolphin from the shark,
  Or the deer before the hounds.
They left Loch-Tua on their lee,
And they waken'd the men of the
    wild Tiree,
  And the Chief of the sandy Coll ;
They paused not at Columba's isle,
Though peal'd the bells from the holy
    pile
  With long and measured toll ;
No time for matin or for mass,
And the sounds of the holy summons
    pass
  Away in the billows' roll.
Lochbuie's fierce and warlike Lord
Their signal saw, and grasp'd his
    sword,
And verdant Ilay call'd her host,
And the clans of Jura's rugged coast
  Lord Ronald's call obey,

And Scarba's isle, whose tortured
      shore
Still rings to Corrievreken's roar,
      And lonely Colonsay;
—Scenes sung by him who sings no
      more!
His bright and brief career is o'er,
      And mute his tuneful strains;
Quench'd is his lamp of varied lore,
That loved the light of song to pour;
A distant and a deadly shore
      Has LEYDEN's cold remains!

XII.

Ever the breeze blows merrily,
But the galley ploughs no more the sea.
Lest, rounding wild Cantyre, they
      meet
The southern foeman's watchful fleet,
They held unwonted way;—
Up Tarbat's western lake they bore,
Then dragg'd their bark the isthmus
      o'er,
As far as Kilmaconnel's shore,
      Upon the eastern bay.
It was a wondrous sight to see
Topmast and pennon glitter free,
High raised above the greenwood tree,
As on dry land the galley moves,
By cliff and copse and alder groves.
Deep import from that selcouth sign
Did many a mountain Seer divine,
For ancient legends told the Gael
That when a royal bark should sail
      O'er Kilmaconnel moss,
Old Albyn should in fight prevail,
And every foe should faint and quail
      Before her silver Cross.

XIII.

Now launch'd once more, the inland sea
They furrow with fair augury,
      And steer for Arran's isle;
The sun, ere yet he sunk behind
Ben-Ghoil 'the Mountain of the Wind,'
Gave his grim peaks a greeting kind,
      And bade Loch Ranza smile.

Thither their destined course they
      drew;
It seem'd the isle her monarch knew,
So brilliant was the landward view,
      The ocean so serene;
Each puny wave in diamonds roll'd
O'er the calm deep, where hues of gold
      With azure strove and green.
The hill, the vale, the tree, the tower,
Glow'd with the tints of evening's
      hour,
      The beach was silver sheen,
The wind breathed soft as lover's sigh,
And, oft renew'd, seem'd oft to die,
      With breathless pause between.
O who, with speech of war and woes,
Would wish to break the soft repose
      Of such enchanting scene!

XIV.

Is it of war Lord Ronald speaks?
The blush that dyes his manly cheeks,
The timid look and downcast eye,
And faltering voice, the theme deny.
      And good King Robert's brow ex-
            press'd
      He ponder'd o'er some high request,
            As doubtful to approve;
      Yet in his eye and lip the while
      Dwelt the half-pitying glance and
            smile,
      Which manhood's graver mood be-
            guile
      When lovers talk of love.
Anxious his suit Lord Ronald pled;
'And for my bride betrothed,' he said,
'My Liege has heard the rumour spread,
Of Edith from Artornish fled.
Too hard her fate—I claim no right
To blame her for her hasty flight;
Be joy and happiness her lot!
But she hath fled the bridal-knot,
And Lorn recall'd his promised plight
In the assembled chieftains' sight.
      When, to fulfil our fathers' band,
      I proffer'd all I could, my hand,
      I was repulsed with scorn;

Mine honour I should ill assert,
And worse the feelings of my heart,
If I should play a suitor's part
Again, to pleasure Lorn.'

XV.

'Young Lord,' the Royal Bruce replied,
'That question must the Church decide;
Yet seems it hard, since rumours state
Edith takes Clifford for her mate,
The very tie which she hath broke,
To thee should still be binding yoke.
But, for my sister Isabel—
The mood of woman who can tell?
I guess the Champion of the Rock,
Victorious in the tourney shock,
That knight unknown, to whom the
    prize
She dealt,—had favour in her eyes;
But since our brother Nigel's fate,
Our ruin'd house and hapless state,
From worldly joy and hope estranged,
Much is the hapless mourner changed.
Perchance,' here smiled the noble King,
'This tale may other musings bring.
Soon shall we know: yon mountains
    hide
The little convent of Saint Bride;
There, sent by Edward, she must stay,
Till fate shall give more prosperous
    day;
And thither will I bear thy suit,
Nor will thine advocate be mute.'

XVI.

As thus they talk'd in earnest mood,
That speechless boy beside them stood.
He stoop'd his head against the mast,
And bitter sobs came thick and fast,
A grief that would not be repress'd,
But seem'd to burst his youthful breast.
His hands, against his forehead held,
As if by force his tears repell'd,
But through his fingers, long and slight,
Fast trill'd the drops of crystal bright.
Edward, who walk'd the deck apart,
First spied this conflict of the heart.

Thoughtless as brave, with bluntness
    kind
He sought to cheer the sorrower's
    mind;
By force the slender hand he drew
From those poor eyes that stream'd
    with dew.
As in his hold the stripling strove,
('Twas a rough grasp, though meant
    in love)
Away his tears the warrior swept,
And bade shame on him that he wept.
'I would to heaven thy helpless tongue
Could tell me who hath wrought thee
    wrong!
For, were he of our crew the best,
The insult went not unredress'd.
Come, cheer thee; thou art now of age
To be a warrior's gallant page;
Thou shalt be mine! a palfrey fair
O'er hill and holt my boy shall bear,
To hold my bow in hunting grove,
Or speed on errand to my love;
For well I wot thou wilt not tell
The temple where my wishes dwell.'

XVII.

Bruce interposed, 'Gay Edward, no,
This is no youth to hold thy bow,
To fill thy goblet, or to bear
Thy message light to lighter fair.
Thou art a patron all too wild
And thoughtless, for this orphan child.
See'st thou not how apart he steals,
Keeps lonely couch, and lonely meals?
Fitter by far in yon calm cell
To tend our sister Isabel,
With Father Augustin to share
The peaceful change of convent prayer,
Than wander wild adventures through
With such a reckless guide as you.'
'Thanks, brother!' Edward answer'd
    gay,
'For the high laud thy words convey!
But we may learn some future day
If thou or I can this poor boy
Protect the best, or best employ.

Meanwhile, our vessel nears the strand;
Launch we the boat, and seek the land.'

XVIII.

To land King Robert lightly sprung,
And thrice aloud his bugle rung
With note prolong'd and varied strain,
Till bold Ben-Ghoil replied again.
Good Douglas then, and De la Haye,
Had in a glen a hart at bay,
And Lennox cheer'd the laggard
    hounds,
When waked that horn the greenwood
    bounds.
'It is the foe!' cried Boyd, who came
In breathless haste with eye of flame,
' It is the foe! Each valiant lord
Fling by his bow, and grasp his sword!'
'Not so,' replied the good Lord James,
' That blast no English bugle claims.
Oft have I heard it fire the fight,
Cheer the pursuit, or stop the flight.
Dead were my heart, and deaf mine ear,
If Bruce should call, nor Douglas hear!
Each to Loch Ranza's margin spring;
That blast was winded by the King!'

XIX.

Fast to their mates the tidings spread,
And fast to shore the warriors sped.
Bursting from glen and greenwood tree,
High waked their loyal jubilee!
Around the royal Bruce they crowd,
And clasp'd his hands, and wept aloud.
Veterans of early fields were there,
Whose helmets press'd their hoary
    hair,
Whose swords and axes bore a stain
From life-blood of the red-hair'd Dane;
And boys, whose hands scarce brook'd
    to wield
The heavy sword or bossy shield.
Men too were there, that bore the scars
Impress'd in Albyn's woful wars,
At Falkirk's fierce and fatal fight,
Teyndrum's dread rout, and Methven's
    flight:

The might of Douglas there was seen,
There Lennox with his graceful mien;
Kirkpatrick, Closeburn's   dreaded
    Knight;
The Lindsay, fiery, fierce, and light;
The Heir of murder'd De la Haye,
And Boyd the grave, and Seton gay.
Around their King regain'd they
    press'd,
Wept, shouted, clasp'd him to their
    breast,
And young and old, and serf and lord,
And he who ne'er unsheathed a sword,
And he in many a peril tried,
Alike resolved the brunt to bide,
And live or die by Bruce's side!

XX.

Oh, War! thou hast thy fierce delight,
Thy gleams of joy, intensely bright!
Such gleams, as from thy polish'd shield
Fly dazzling o'er the battle-field!
Such transports wake, severe and high,
Amid the pealing conquest-cry;
Scarce less, when, after battle lost,
Muster the remnants of a host,
And as each comrade's name they tell,
Who in the well-fought conflict fell,
Knitting stern brow o'er flashing eye,
Vow to avenge them or to die!
Warriors!—and where are warriors
    found,
If not on martial Britain's ground?
And who, when waked with note of
    fire,
Love more than they the British
    lyre?—
Know ye not, hearts to honour dear!
That joy, deep-thrilling, stern, severe,
At which the heartstrings vibrate high,
And wake the fountains of the eye?
And blame ye, then, the Bruce, if trace
Of tear is on his manly face,
When, scanty relics of the train
That hail'd at Scone his early reign,
This patriot band around him hung,
And to his knees and bosom clung?

Blame ye the Bruce?—his brother
        blamed,
But shared   the   weakness, while
        ashamed :
With haughty laugh his head he turn'd,
And dash'd away the tear he scorn'd.

XXI.

'Tis morning, and the Convent bell
Long time had ceased its matin knell,
        Within thy walls, Saint Bride !
An aged Sister sought the cell
Assign'd to Lady Isabel,
        And hurriedly she cried,
'Haste, gentle Lady, haste ; there waits
A noble stranger at the gates ;
Saint Bride's poor vot'ress ne'er has
        seen
A Knight of such a princely mien ;
His errand, as he bade me tell,
Is with the Lady Isabel.'
The princess rose—for on her knee
Low bent she told her rosary—
' Let him by thee his purpose teach ;
I may not give a stranger speech.'
' Saint Bride forfend, thou royal Maid !'
The portress cross'd herself and said ;
' Not to be prioress might I
Debate his will, his suit deny.'
' Has earthly show, then, simple fool,
Power o'er a sister of thy rule,
And art thou, like the worldly train,
Subdued by splendours light and vain?'

XXII.

' No, Lady ! in old eyes like mine
Gauds have no glitter, gems no shine ;
Nor grace his rank attendants vain,
One youthful page is all his train.
It is the form, the eye, the word,
The bearing of that stranger Lord ;
His stature, manly, bold, and tall,
Built like a castle's battled wall,
Yet moulded in such just degrees,
His giant-strength seems lightsome
        ease.
Close as the tendrils of the vine
His locks upon his forehead twine,

Jet-black, save where some touch of
        grey
Has ta'en the youthful hue away ;
Weather and war their rougher trace
Have left on that majestic face.
But 'tis his dignity of eye !
There, if a suppliant, would I fly,
Secure, 'mid danger, wrongs, and grief,
Of sympathy, redress, relief—
That glance, if guilty, would I dread
More than the doom that spoke me
        dead !'
' Enough, enough,' the princess cried,
'' 'Tis Scotland's hope, her joy, her
        pride !
To meaner front was ne'er assign'd
Such mastery o'er the common mind—
Bestow'd thy high designs to aid,
How long, O Heaven ! how long
        delay'd !
Haste, Mona, haste, to introduce
My darling brother, royal Bruce !'

XXIII.

They met like friends who part in pain,
And meet in doubtful hope again.
But when subdued that fitful swell,
The Bruce survey'd the humble cell ;
' And this is thine, poor Isabel !—
That pallet-couch, and naked wall,
For room of state, and bed of pall ;
For costly robes and jewels rare,
A string of beads and zone of hair ;
And for the trumpet's sprightly call
To sport or banquet, grove or hall,
The bell's grim voice divides thy care,
'Twixt hours of penitence and prayer !
O ill for thee, my royal claim
From the First David's sainted name !
O woe for thee, that while he sought
His right, thy brother feebly fought !'

XXIV.

' Now lay these vain regrets aside,
And be the unshaken Bruce !' she cried.
' For more I glory to have shared
The woes thy venturous spirit dared,

When raising first thy valiant band
In rescue of thy native land,
Than had fair Fortune set me down
The partner of an empire's crown.
And grieve not that on Pleasure's
      stream
No more I drive in giddy dream,
For Heaven the erring pilot knew,
And from the gulf the vessel drew,
Tried me with judgments stern and
      great,
My house's ruin, thy defeat,
Poor Nigel's death, till, tamed, I own,
My hopes are fix'd on Heaven alone;
Nor e'er shall earthly prospects win
My heart to this vain world of sin.'

XXV.

' Nay, Isabel, for such stern choice,
First wilt thou wait thy brother's
      voice;
Then ponder if in convent scene
No softer thoughts might intervene—
Say they were of that unknown
      Knight,
Victor in Woodstock's tourney-fight—
Nay, if his name such blush you owe,
Victorious o'er a fairer foe !'
Truly his penetrating eye
Hath caught that blush's passing dye—
Like the last beam of evening thrown
On a white cloud—just seen and
      gone.
Soon with calm cheek and steady eye
The princess made composed reply :
' I guess my brother's meaning well;
For not so silent is the cell,
But we have heard the islesmen all
Arm in thy cause at Ronald's call,
And mine eye proves that Knight un-
      known
And the brave Island Lord are one.
Had then his suit been earlier made,
In his own name, with thee to aid,
(But that his plighted faith forbade)
I know not . . . But thy page so near?
This is no tale for menial's ear.'

XXVI.

Still stood that page, as far apart
   As the small cell would space afford;
With dizzy eye and bursting heart,
   He leant his weight on Bruce's
      sword,
The monarch's mantle too he bore,
And drew the fold his visage o'er.
'Fear not for him; in murderous strife,'
Said Bruce, 'his warning saved my
      life;
Full seldom parts he from my side,
And in his silence I confide,
Since he can tell no tale again.
He is a boy of gentle strain,
And I have purposed he shall dwell
In Augustin the chaplain's cell,
And wait on thee, my Isabel.
Mind not his tears; I've seen them flow,
As in the thaw dissolves the snow.
'Tis a kind youth, but fanciful,
Unfit against the tide to pull,
And those that with the Bruce would
      sail
Must learn to strive with stream and
      gale.
But forward, gentle Isabel—
My answer for Lord Ronald tell.'

XXVII.

' This answer be to Ronald given—
The heart he asks is fix'd on heaven.
My love was like a summer flower,
That wither'd in the wintry hour,
Born but of vanity and pride,
And with these sunny visions died.
If further press his suit, then say
He should his plighted troth obey,
Troth plighted both with ring and word,
And sworn on crucifix and sword.
Oh, shame thee, Robert ! I have seen
Thou hast a woman's guardian been !
Even in extremity's dread hour,
When press'd on thee the Southern
      power,
And safety, to all human sight,
Was only found in rapid flight,

Thou heard'st a wretched female plain
In agony of travail-pain,
And thou didst bid thy little band
Upon the instant turn and stand,
And dare the worst the foe might do,
Rather than, like a knight untrue,
Leave to pursuers merciless
A woman in her last distress.
And wilt thou now deny thine aid
To an oppress'd and injured maid,
Even plead for Ronald's perfidy,
And press his fickle faith on me ?—
So witness Heaven, as true I vow,
Had I those earthly feelings now,
Which could my former bosom move
Ere taught to set its hopes above,
I'd spurn each proffer he could bring,
Till at my feet he laid the ring,
The ring and spousal contract both,
And fair acquittal of his oath,
By her who brooks his perjured scorn,
The ill-requited Maid of Lorn !'

XXVIII.

With sudden impulse forward sprung
The page, and on her neck he hung;
Then, recollected instantly,
His head he stoop'd, and bent his knee,
Kiss'd twice the hand of Isabel,
Arose, and sudden left the cell.
The princess, loosen'd from his hold,
Blush'd angry at his bearing bold ;
   But good King Robert cried,
'Chafe not, by signs he speaks his mind,
He heard the plan my care design'd,
   Nor could his transports hide.
But, sister, now bethink thee well;
No easy choice the convent cell;
Trust, I shall play no tyrant part,
Either to force thy hand or heart,
Or suffer that Lord Ronald scorn,
Or wrong for thee, the Maid of Lorn.
But think,—not long the time has been
That thou wert wont to sigh unseen,
And wouldst the ditties best approve
That told some lay of hapless love.

Now are thy wishes in thy power,
And thou art bent on cloister bower !
O ! if our Edward knew the change,
How would his busy satire range,
With many a sarcasm varied still
On woman's wish, and woman's will!'

XXIX.

'Brother, I well believe,' she said,
'Even so would Edward's part be
   play'd.
Kindly in heart, in word severe,
A foe to thought, and grief, and fear,
He holds his humour uncontroll'd;
But thou art of another mould.
Say then to Ronald, as I say,
Unless before my feet he lay
The ring which bound the faith he
   swore,
By Edith freely yielded o'er,
He moves his suit to me no more.
Nor do I promise, even if now
He stood absolved of spousal vow,
That I would change my purpose
   made
To shelter me in holy shade.
Brother, for little space, farewell !
To other duties warns the bell.'

XXX.

'Lost to the world,' King Robert said,
When he had left the royal maid,
'Lost to the world by lot severe,
O what a gem lies buried here,
Nipp'd by misfortune's cruel frost,
The buds of fair affection lost !
But what have I with love to do ?
For sterner cares my lot pursue.
Pent in this isle we may not lie,
Nor would it long our wants supply.
Right opposite, the mainland towers
Of my own Turnberry court our
   powers ;
Might not my father's beadsman hoar,
Cuthbert, who dwells upon the shore,
Kindle a signal-flame, to show
The time propitious for the blow ?

It shall be so; some friend shall bear
Our mandate with despatch and care;
Edward shall find the messenger.
That fortress ours, the island fleet
May on the coast of Carrick meet.
O Scotland! shall it e'er be mine
To wreak thy wrongs in battle-line,
To raise my victor-head, and see
Thy hills, thy dales, thy people free?
That glance of bliss is all I crave,
Betwixt my labours and my grave!'
Then down the hill he slowly went,
Oft pausing on the steep descent,
And reach'd the spot where his bold train
Held rustic camp upon the plain.

—◆—

Canto Fifth.

I.

On fair Loch Ranza stream'd the early day;
Thin wreaths of cottage-smoke are upward curl'd
From the lone hamlet, which her inland bay
And circling mountains sever from the world.
And there the fisherman his sail unfurl'd,
The goat-herd drove his kids to steep Ben-Ghoil,
Before the hut the dame her spindle twirl'd,
Courting the sunbeam as she plied her toil,—
For, wake where'er he may, Man wakes to care and coil.

But other duties call'd each convent maid,
Roused by the summons of the moss-grown bell;
Sung were the matins, and the mass was said,
And every sister sought her separate cell,
Such was the rule, her rosary to tell.
And Isabel has knelt in lonely prayer;
The sunbeam, through the narrow lattice, fell
Upon the snowy neck and long dark hair,
As stoop'd her gentle head in meek devotion there.

II.

She raised her eyes, that duty done,
When glanced upon the pavement-stone,
Gemm'd and enchased, a golden ring,
Bound to a scroll with silken string,
With few brief words inscribed to tell,
'This for the Lady Isabel.'
Within, the writing farther bore,
''Twas with this ring his plight he swore,
With this his promise I restore;
To her who can the heart command
Well may I yield the plighted hand.
And O! for better fortune born,
Grudge not a passing sigh to mourn
Her who was Edith once of Lorn!'
One single flash of glad surprise
Just glanced from Isabel's dark eyes,
But vanish'd in the blush of shame,
That, as its penance, instant came.
'O thought unworthy of my race!
Selfish, ungenerous, mean, and base,
A moment's throb of joy to own,
That rose upon her hopes o'erthrown!
Thou pledge of vows too well believed,
Of man ingrate and maid deceived,
Think not thy lustre here shall gain
Another heart to hope in vain!
For thou shalt rest, thou tempting gaud,
Where worldly thoughts are over-awed,
And worldly splendours sink debased.'
Then by the cross the ring she placed.

III.

Next rose the thought,—its owner far,
How came it here through bolt and
     bar ?
But the dim lattice is ajar.
She looks abroad ; the morning dew
A light short step had brush'd anew,
     And there were footprints seen
On the carved buttress rising still,
Till on the mossy window-sill
     Their track effaced the green.
The ivy twigs were torn and fray'd,
As if some climber's steps to aid.
But who the hardy messenger,
Whose venturous path these signs
     infer ?
'Strange doubts are mine ! Mona,
     draw nigh ;
Nought 'scapes old Mona's curious
     eye—
What strangers, gentle mother, say,
Have sought these holy walls to-day?'
'None, Lady, none of note or name ;
Only your brother's foot-page came
At peep of dawn—I pray'd him pass
To chapel where they said the mass ;
But like an arrow he shot by,
And tears seem'd bursting from his eye.'

IV.

The truth at once on Isabel,
As darted by a sunbeam, fell.
''Tis Edith's self ! her speechless woe,
Her form, her looks, the secret show !
Instant, good Mona, to the bay,
And to my royal brother say,
I do conjure him seek my cell,
With that mute page he loves so well.'
'What ! know'st thou not his warlike
     host
At break of day has left our coast ?
My old eyes saw them from the tower.
At eve they couch'd in greenwood
     bower,
At dawn a bugle-signal, made
By their bold Lord, their ranks array'd ;

Up sprung the spears through bush
     and tree,
No time for benedicite !
Like deer that, rousing from their lair,
Just shake the dewdrops from their
     hair,
And toss their armed crests aloft,
Such matins theirs !' 'Good mother,
     soft—
Where does my brother bend his way?'
'As I have heard, for Brodick-Bay,
Across the isle ; of barks a score
Lie there, 'tis said, to waft them o'er,
On sudden news, to Carrick-shore.'
'If such their purpose, deep the need,'
Said anxious Isabel, 'of speed !
Call Father Augustine, good dame.'
The nun obey'd, the Father came.

V.

'Kind Father, hie without delay
Across the hills to Brodick-Bay.
This message to the Bruce be given ;
I pray him, by his hopes of Heaven,
That, till he speak with me, he stay !
Or, if his haste brook no delay,
That he deliver, on my suit,
Into thy charge that stripling mute.
Thus prays his sister Isabel,
For causes more than she may tell—
Away good father ! and take heed
That life and death are on thy speed.'
His cowl the good old priest did on,
Took his piked staff and sandall'd
     shoon,
And, like a palmer bent by eld,
O'er moss and moor his journey held.

VI.

Heavy and dull the foot of age,
And rugged was the pilgrimage ;
But none was there beside, whose care
Might such important message bear.
Through birchen copse he wander'd
     slow,
Stunted and sapless, thin and low ;
By many a mountain stream he pass'd,
From the tall cliffs in tumult cast,

Dashing to foam their waters dun,
And sparkling in the summer sun.
Round his grey head the wild curlew
In many a fearless circle flew.
O'er chasms he pass'd, where fractures wide
Crav'd wary eye and ample stride ;
He cross'd his brow beside the stone
Where Druids erst heard victims groan ;
And at the cairns upon the wild,
O'er many a heathen hero piled,
He breathed a timid prayer for those
Who died ere Shiloh's sun arose.
Beside Macfarlane's Cross he staid,
There told his hours within the shade,
And at the stream his thirst allay'd.
Thence onward journeying slowly still,
As evening closed he reach'd the hill,
Where, rising through the woodland green,
Old Brodick's gothic towers were seen:
From Hastings, late their English lord,
Douglas had won them by the sword.
The sun that sunk behind the isle
Now tinged them with a parting smile.

VII.

But though the beams of light decay,
'Twas bustle all in Brodick-Bay.
The Bruce's followers crowd the shore,
And boats and barges some unmoor,
Some raise the sail, some seize the oar ;
Their eyes oft turn'd where glimmer'd far
What might have seem'd an early star
On heaven's blue arch, save that its light
Was all too flickering, fierce, and bright.
Far distant in the south, the ray
Shone pale amid retiring day,
But as, on Carrick shore,
Dim seen in outline faintly blue,
The shades of evening closer drew,
It kindled more and more.

The monk's slow steps now press the sands,
And now amid a scene he stands
Full strange to churchman's eye;
Warriors, who, arming for the fight,
Rivet and clasp their harness light,
And twinkling spears, and axes bright,
And helmets flashing high.
Oft too, with unaccustom'd ears,
A language much unmeet he hears,
While, hastening all on board,
As stormy as the swelling surge
That mix'd its roar, the leaders urge
Their followers to the ocean verge,
With many a haughty word.

VIII.

Through that wild throng the Father pass'd
And reach'd the royal Bruce at last.
He leant against a stranded boat,
That the approaching tide must float,
And counted every rippling wave,
As higher yet her sides they lave,
And oft the distant fire he eyed,
And closer yet his hauberk tied,
And loosen'd in its sheath his brand.
Edward and Lennox were at hand,
Douglas and Ronald had the care
The soldiers to the barks to share.
The Monk approach'd and homage paid;
'And art thou come,' King Robert said,
'So far, to bless us ere we part?'
—'My Liege, and with a loyal heart!
But other charge I have to tell,'—
And spoke the hest of Isabel.
'Now, by Saint Giles,' the Monarch cried,
'This moves me much! this morning tide,
I sent the stripling to Saint Bride,
With my commandment there to bide.'
'Thither he came the portress show'd,
But there, my Liege, made brief abode.'

IX.

' 'Twas I,' said Edward, 'found employ
Of nobler import for the boy.

Deep pondering in my anxious mind,
A fitting messenger to find,
To bear thy written mandate o'er
To Cuthbert on the Carrick shore,
I chanced, at early dawn, to pass
The chapel gate to snatch a mass.
I found the stripling on a tomb
Low-seated, weeping for the doom
That gave his youth to convent gloom.
I told my purpose, and his eyes
Flash'd joyful at the glad surprise.
He bounded to the skiff, the sail
Was spread before a prosperous gale,
And well my charge he hath obey'd ;
For, see ! the ruddy signal made,
That Clifford, with his merry-men all,
Guards carelessly our father's hall.'

X.

' O wild of thought, and hard of heart !'
Answer'd the Monarch, ' on a part
Of such deep danger to employ
A mute, an orphan, and a boy !
Unfit for flight, unfit for strife,
Without a tongue to plead for life !
Now, were my right restored by
    Heaven,
Edward, my crown I would have
    given,
Ere, thrust on such adventure wild,
I perill'd thus the helpless child.'
Offended half, and half submiss,
' Brother and Liege, of blame like this,'
Edward replied, ' I little dream'd.
A stranger messenger, I deem'd,
Might safest seek the beadsman's cell,
Where all thy squires are known so
    well.
Noteless his presence, sharp his sense,
His imperfection his defence.
If seen, none can his errand guess ;
If ta'en, his words no tale express :
Methinks, too, yonder beacon's shine
Might expiate greater fault than mine.'
' Rash,' said King Robert, ' was the
    deed ;
But it is done. Embark with speed !

Good Father, say to Isabel
How this unhappy chance befell ;
If well we thrive on yonder shore,
Soon shall my care her page restore.
Our greeting to our sister bear,
And think of us in mass and prayer.'

XI.

' Ay !' said the Priest, ' while this
    poor hand
Can chalice raise or cross command,
While my old voice has accents' use,
Can Augustine forget the Bruce !'
Then to his side Lord Ronald press'd,
And whisper'd, ' Bear thou this
    request,
That, when by Bruce's side I fight
For Scotland's crown and freedom's
    right,
The princess grace her knight to bear
Some token of her favouring care ;
It shall be shown where England's best
May shrink to see it on my crest.
And for the boy—since weightier care
For royal Bruce the times prepare,
The helpless youth is Ronald's charge,
His couch my plaid, his fence my targe.'
He ceased ; for many an eager hand
Had urged the barges from the strand.
Their number was a score and ten,
They bore thrice threescore chosen
    men.
With such small force did Bruce at
    last
The die for death or empire cast !

XII.

Now on the darkening main afloat,
Ready and mann'd rocks every boat ;
Beneath their oars the ocean's might
Was dash'd to sparks of glimmering
    light.
Faint and more faint, as off they bore,
Their armour glanced against the
    shore,
And, mingled with the dashing tide,
Their murmuring voices distant died.

'God speed them!' said the Priest,
      as dark
On distant billows glides each bark;
'O Heaven! when swords for freedom
      shine,
And monarch's right, the cause is
      thine!
Edge doubly every patriot blow!
Beat down the banners of the foe!
And be it to the nations known
That Victory is from God alone!'
As up the hill his path he drew,
He turn'd his blessings to renew;
Oft turn'd, till on the darken'd coast
All traces of their course were lost;
Then slowly bent to Brodick tower,
To shelter for the evening hour.

XIII.

In night the fairy prospects sink,
Where Cumray's isles with verdant
      link
Close the fair entrance of the Clyde;
The woods of Bute, no more descried,
Are gone—and on the placid sea
The rowers ply their task with glee,
While hands that knightly lances bore
Impatient aid the labouring oar.
The half-faced moon shone dim and
      pale,
And glanced against the whiten'd sail;
But on that ruddy beacon-light
Each steersman kept the helm aright,
And oft, for such the King's command,
That all at once might reach the strand,
From boat to boat loud shout and hail
Warn'd them to crowd or slacken sail.
South and by west the armada bore,
And near at length the Carrick shore.
As less and less the distance grows,
High and more high the beacon rose;
The light, that seem'd a twinkling star,
Now blazed portentous, fierce, and far.
Dark-red the heaven above it glow'd,
Dark-red the sea beneath it flow'd,
Red rose the rocks on ocean's brim,
In blood-red light her islets swim;

Wild scream the dazzled sea-fowl gave,
Dropp'd from their crags on plashing
      wave;
The deer to distant covert drew,
The blackcock deem'd it day, and crew:
Like some tall castle given to flame,
O'er half the land the lustre came.
'Now, good my Liege, and brother
      sage,
What think ye of mine elfin page?'
'Row on!' the noble King replied,
'We'll learn the truth whate'er betide;
Yet sure the beadsman and the child
Could ne'er have waked that beacon
      wild.'

XIV.

With that the boats approach'd the
      land,
But Edward's grounded on the sand;
The eager Knight leap'd in the sea
Waist-deep, and first on shore was he,
Though every barge's hardy band
Contended which should gain the land,
When that strange light which, seen
      afar,
Seem'd steady as the polar star,
Now, like a prophet's fiery chair,
Seem'd travelling the realms of air.
Wide o'er the sky the splendour glows,
As that portentous meteor rose;
Helm, axe, and falchion glitter'd bright,
And in the red and dusky light
His comrade's face each warrior saw,
Nor marvell'd it was pale with awe.
Then high in air the beams were lost,
And darkness sunk upon the coast.
Ronald to Heaven a prayer address'd,
And Douglas cross'd his dauntless
      breast;
'Saint James protect us!' Lennox cried;
But reckless Edward spoke aside,
'Deem'st thou, Kirkpatrick, in that
      flame
Red Comyn's angry spirit came,
Or would thy dauntless heart endure
Once more to make assurance sure!'

'Hush!' said the Bruce, 'we soon
    shall know
If this be sorcerer's empty show,
Or stratagem of southern foe.
The moon shines out—upon the sand
Let every leader rank his band.'

XV.

Faintly the moon's pale beams supply
That ruddy light's unnatural dye;
The dubious cold reflection lay
On the wet sands and quiet bay.
Beneath the rocks King Robert drew
His scatter'd files to order due,
Till shield compact and serried spear
In the cool light shone blue and clear.
Then down a path that sought the tide,
That speechless page was seen to
    glide;
He knelt him lowly on the sand,
And gave a scroll to Robert's hand.
'A torch,' the Monarch cried, 'what,
    ho!
Now shall we Cuthbert's tidings know.'
But evil news the letters bare,—
The Clifford's force was strong and
    ware,
Augmented, too, that very morn,
By mountaineers who came with
    Lorn;
Long harrow'd by oppressor's hand,
Courage and faith had fled the land,
And over Carrick, dark and deep,
Had sunk dejection's iron sleep.
Cuthbert had seen that beacon-flame,
Unwitting from what source it came.
Doubtful of perilous event,
Edward's mute messenger he sent,
If Bruce deceived should venture o'er,
To warn him from the fatal shore.

XVI.

As round the torch the leaders crowd,
Bruce read these chilling news aloud.
'What council, nobles, have we
    now?
To ambush us in greenwood bough,
And take the chance which fate may
    send
To bring our enterprise to end?
Or shall we turn us to the main
As exiles, and embark again?'
Answer'd fierce Edward, 'Hap what
    may,
In Carrick Carrick's Lord must stay.
I would not minstrels told the tale
Wildfire or meteor made us quail.'
Answer'd the Douglas, 'If my Liege
May win yon walls by storm or siege,
Then were each brave and patriot heart
Kindled of new for loyal part.'
Answer'd Lord Ronald, 'Not for shame
Would I that aged Torquil came,
And found, for all our empty boast,
Without a blow we fled the coast.
I will not credit that this land,
So famed for warlike heart and hand,
The nurse of Wallace and of Bruce,
Will long with tyrants hold a truce.'
'Prove we our fate—the brunt we'll
    bide!'
So Boyd and Haye and Lennox cried:
So said, so vow'd, the leaders all;
So Bruce resolved: 'And in my hall
Since the bold Southern make their
    home,
The hour of payment soon shall come,
When with a rough and rugged host
Clifford may reckon to his cost.
Meantime, through well-known bosk
    and dell,
I'll lead where we may shelter well.'

XVII.

Now ask you whence that wondrous
    light,
Whose fairy glow beguiled their
    sight?
It ne'er was known—yet grey-hair'd
    eld
A superstitious credence held,
That never did a mortal hand
Wake its broad glare on Carrick
    strand;

Nay, and that on the self-same night
When Bruce cross'd o'er, still gleams
    the light.
Yearly it gleams o'er mount and moor,
And glittering wave and crimson'd
    shore—
But whether beam celestial, lent
By Heaven to aid the King's descent,
Or fire hell-kindled from beneath,
To lure him to defeat and death,
Or were it but some meteor strange,
Of such as oft through midnight range,
Startling the traveller late and lone,
I know not ; and it ne'er was known.

XVIII.

Now up the rocky pass they drew,
And Ronald, to his promise true,
Still made his arm the stripling's stay,
To aid him on the rugged way.
' Now cheer thee, simple Amadine !
Why throbs that silly heart of thine?'
That name the pirates to their slave
(In Gaelic 'tis the Changeling) gave;
' Dost thou not rest thee on my arm ?
Do not my plaid-folds hold thee
    warm ?
Hath not the wild bull's treble hide
This targe for thee and me supplied?
Is not Clan-Colla's sword of steel ?
And, trembler, canst thou terror feel ?
Cheer thee, and still that throbbing
    heart ;
From Ronald's guard thou shalt not
    part.'
O ! many a shaft, at random sent,
Finds mark the archer little meant !
And many a word, at random spoken,
May soothe or wound a heart that's
    broken !
Half sooth'd, half grieved, half
    terrified,
Close drew the page to Ronald's side ;
A wild delirious thrill of joy
Was in that hour of agony,
As up the steepy pass he strove,
Fear, toil, and sorrow lost in love !

XIX.

The barrier of that iron shore,
The rock's steep ledge, is now climb'd
    o'er ;
And from the castle's distant wall,
From tower to tower the warders
    call :
The sound swings over land and sea,
And marks a watchful enemy.
They gain'd the Chase, a wide domain
Left for the Castle's silvan reign.
Seek not the scene—the axe, the
    plough,
The boor's dull fence, have marr'd it
    now ;
But then, soft swept in velvet green
The plain with many a glade between,
Whose tangled alleys far invade
The depth of the brown forest shade.
Here the tall fern obscured the lawn,
Fair shelter for the sportive fawn ;
There, tufted close with copsewood
    green,
Was many a swelling hillock seen ;
And all around was verdure meet
For pressure of the fairies' feet.
The glossy holly loved the park,
The yew-tree lent its shadow dark,
And many an old oak, worn and bare,
With all its shiver'd boughs, was there.
Lovely between, the moonbeams fell
On lawn and hillock, glade and dell.
The gallant Monarch sigh'd to see
These glades so loved in childhood
    free,
Bethinking that, as outlaw now,
He ranged beneath the forest bough.

XX.

Fast o'er the moonlight Chase they
    sped.
Well knew the band that measured
    tread,
When, in retreat or in advance,
The serried warriors move at once ;
And evil were the luck, if dawn
Descried them on the open lawn.

Copses they traverse, brooks they
   cross,
Strain up the bank and o'er the moss.
From the exhausted page's brow
Cold drops of toil are streaming
   now ;
With effort faint and lengthen'd pause,
His weary step the stripling draws.
'Nay, droop not yet!' the warrior
   said;
'Come, let me give thee ease and aid!
Strong are mine arms, and little care
A weight so slight as thine to bear.
What ! wilt thou not?—capricious
   boy !
Then thine own limbs and strength
   employ.
Pass but this night, and pass thy care,
I 'll place thee with a lady fair,
Where thou shalt tune thy lute to tell
How Ronald loves fair Isabel !'
Worn out, dishearten'd, and dismay'd,
Here Amadine let go the plaid ;
His trembling limbs their aid refuse,
He sunk among the midnight dews !

XXI.

What may be done ?—the night is
   gone—
The Bruce's band moves swiftly on—
Eternal shame, if at the brunt
Lord Ronald grace not battle's front !
'See yonder oak, within whose trunk
Decay a darken'd cell hath sunk ;
Enter, and rest thee there a space,
Wrap in my plaid thy limbs, thy face,
I will not be, believe me, far ;
But must not quit the ranks of war.
Well will I mark the bosky bourne,
And soon, to guard thee hence, return.
Nay, weep not so, thou simple boy !
But sleep in peace, and wake in joy.'
In silvan lodging close bestow'd,
He placed the page, and onward strode
With strength put forth, o'er moss and
   brook,
And soon the marching band o'ertook.

XXII.

Thus strangely left, long sobb'd and
   wept
The page, till, wearied out, he slept.
A rough voice waked his dream—'Nay,
   here,
Here by this thicket, pass'd the deer—
Beneath that oak old Ryno staid—
What have we here?—a Scottish plaid,
And in its folds a stripling laid ?
Come forth ! thy name and business
   tell !
What, silent ? then I guess thee well,
The spy that sought old Cuthbert's cell,
Wafted from Arran yester morn—
Come, comrades, we will straight
   return.
Our Lord may choose the rack should
   teach
To this young lurcher use of speech.
Thy bow-string, till I bind him fast.'—
'Nay, but he weeps and stands aghast;
Unbound we 'll lead him, fear it not ;
'Tis a fair stripling, though a Scot.'
The hunters to the castle sped,
And there the hapless captive led.

XXIII.

Stout Clifford in the castle-court
Prepared him for the morning sport ;
And now with Lorn held deep dis-
   course,
Now gave command for hound and
   horse.
War-steeds and palfreys paw'd the
   ground,
And many a deer-dog howl'd around.
To Amadine, Lorn's well-known word
Replying to that Southern Lord,
Mix'd with this clanging din, might
   seem
The phantasm of a fever'd dream.
The tone upon his ringing ears
Came like the sounds which fancy
   hears,
When in rude waves or roaring winds
Some words of woe the muser finds,

Until more loudly and more near,
Their speech arrests the page's ear.

XXIV.

' And was she thus,' said Clifford, ' lost?
The priest should rue it to his cost!
What says the monk?' ' The holy Sire
Owns, that in masquer's quaint attire
She sought his skiff, disguised, un-
    known
To all except to him alone.
But, says the priest, a bark from Lorn
Laid them aboard that very morn,
And pirates seized her for their prey.
He proffer'd ransom-gold to pay,
And they agreed—but ere told o'er,
The winds blow loud, the billows roar;
They sever'd, and they met no more.
He deems—such tempest vex'd the
    coast—
Ship, crew, and fugitive, were lost.
So let it be, with the disgrace
And scandal of her lofty race!
Thrice better she had ne'er been born,
Than brought her infamy on Lorn!'

XXV.

Lord Clifford now the captive spied;—
' Whom, Herbert, hast thou there?'
    he cried.
' A spy we seized within the Chase,
A hollow oak his lurking place.'
' What tidings can the youth afford?'
' He plays the mute.' ' Then noose
    a cord—
Unless brave Lorn reverse the doom
For his plaid's sake.' ' Clan-Colla's
    loom,'
Said Lorn, whose careless glances trace
Rather the vesture than the face :
'Clan-Colla's dames such tartans twine;
Wearer nor plaid claims care of mine.
Give him, if my advice you crave,
His own scathed oak; and let him
    wave
In air, unless, by terror wrung,
A frank confession find his tongue.

Nor shall he die without his rite ;
Thou, Angus Roy, attend the sight,
And give Clan-Colla's dirge thy breath,
As they convey him to his death.'
' O brother! cruel to the last!'
Through the poor captive's bosom
    pass'd
The thought, but, to his purpose true,
He said not, though he sigh'd, ' Adieu!'

XXVI.

And will he keep his purpose still,
In sight of that last closing ill,
When one poor breath, one single
    word,
May freedom, safety, life, afford?
Can he resist the instinctive call,
For life that bids us barter all?—
Love, strong as death, his heart hath
    steel'd,
His nerves hath strung; he will not
    yield!
Since that poor breath, that little word,
May yield Lord Ronald to the sword.
Clan-Colla's dirge is pealing wide,
The griesly headsman 's by his side;
Along the greenwood Chase they bend,
And now their march has ghastly end!
That old and shatter'd oak beneath,
They destine for the place of death.
What thoughts are his, while all in vain
His eye for aid explores the plain ?
What thoughts, while, with a dizzy ear,
He hears the death-prayer mutter'd
    near ?
And must he die such death accurst,
Or will that bosom-secret burst ?
Cold on his brow breaks terror's dew,
His trembling lips are livid blue;
The agony of parting life
Has nought to match that moment's
    strife !

XXVII.

But other witnesses are nigh,
Who mock at fear, and death defy !
Soon as the dire lament was play'd,
It waked the lurking ambuscade.

The Island Lord look'd forth, and spied
The cause, and loud in fury cried,
'By Heaven, they lead the page to die,
And mock me in his agony!
They shall abye it!' On his arm
Bruce laid strong grasp, 'They shall
    not harm
A ringlet of the stripling's hair;
But, till I give the word, forbear.
Douglas, lead fifty of our force
Up yonder hollow water-course,
And couch thee midway on the wold,
Between the flyers and their hold:
A spear above the copse display'd,
Be signal of the ambush made.
Edward, with forty spearmen. straight
Through yonder copse approach the
    gate,
And, when thou hear'st the battle-din,
Rush forward, and the passage win,
Secure the drawbridge—storm the
    port,
And man and guard the castle-court.
The rest move slowly forth with me,
In shelter of the forest-tree,
Till Douglas at his post I see.'

XXVIII.

Like war-horse eager to rush on,
Compell'd to wait the signal blown,
Hid, and scarce hid, by greenwood
    bough,
Trembling with rage, stands Ronald
    now,
And in his grasp his sword gleams blue,
Soon to be dyed with deadlier hue.
Meanwhile the Bruce, with steady eye,
Sees the dark death-train moving by,
And, heedful, measures oft the space
The Douglas and his band must trace,
Ere they can reach their destined
    ground.
Now sinks the dirge's wailing sound,
Now cluster round the direful tree
That slow and solemn company,
While hymn mistuned and mutter'd
    prayer
The victim for his fate prepare.

What glances o'er the greenwood
    shade?
The spear that marks the ambuscade!
'Now, noble Chief! I leave thee loose;
Upon them, Ronald!' said the Bruce.

XXIX.

'The Bruce, the Bruce!' to well-
    known cry
His native rocks and woods reply.
'The Bruce, the Bruce!' in that dread
    word
The knell of hundred deaths was heard.
The astonish'd Southern gazed at first,
Where the wild tempest was to burst,
That waked in that presaging name.
Before, behind, around it came!
Half-arm'd, surprised, on every side
Hemm'd in, hew'd down, they bled
    and died.
Deep in the ring the Bruce engaged,
And fierce Clan-Colla's broadsword
    raged!
Full soon the few who fought were
    sped,
Nor better was their lot who fled,
And met, 'mid terror's wild career,
The Douglas's redoubted spear!
Two hundred yeomen on that morn
The castle left, and none return.

XXX.

Not on their flight press'd Ronald's
    brand,
A gentler duty claim'd his hand.
He raised the page, where on the plain
His fear had sunk him with the slain:
And twice, that morn, surprise well
    near
Betray'd the secret kept by fear;
Once, when, with life returning, came
To the boy's lip Lord Ronald's name,
And hardly recollection drown'd
The accents in a murmuring sound;
And once when scarce he could resist
The Chieftain's care to loose the vest,
Drawn tightly o'er his labouring
    breast.

But then the Bruce's bugle blew,
For martial work was yet to do.

XXXI.

A harder task fierce Edward waits.
Ere signal given, the castle gates
  His fury had assail'd ;
Such was his wonted reckless mood,
Yet desperate valour oft made good,
Even by its daring, venture rude,
  Where prudence might have fail'd.
Upon the bridge his strength he threw,
And struck the iron chain in two,
  By which its planks arose ;
The warder next his axe's edge
Struck down upon the threshold ledge,
'Twixt door and post a ghastly wedge !
  The gate they may not close.
Well fought the Southern in the fray,
Clifford and Lorn fought well that day,
But stubborn Edward forced his way
  Against a hundred foes.
Loud came the cry, ' The Bruce, the
    Bruce !'
No hope or in defence or truce,
  Fresh combatants pour in ;
Mad with success, and drunk with gore,
They drive the struggling foe before,
  And ward on ward they win.
Unsparing was the vengeful sword,
And limbs were lopp'd and life-
    blood pour'd,
The cry of death and conflict roar'd,
  And fearful was the din !
The startling horses plunged and flung,
Clamour'd the dogs till turrets rung,
  Nor sunk the fearful cry,
Till not a foeman was there found
Alive, save those who on the ground
  Groan'd in their agony !

XXXII.

The valiant Clifford is no more ;
On Ronald's broadsword stream'd
  his gore.
But better hap had he of Lorn,
Who, by the foemen backward borne,

Yet gain'd with slender train the port
Where lay his bark beneath the fort,
  And cut the cable loose.
Short were his shrift in that debate,
That hour of fury and of fate,
  If Lorn encounter'd Bruce !
Then long and loud the victor-shout
From turret and from tower rung out,
  The rugged vaults replied ;
And from the donjon tower on high,
The men of Carrick may descry
Saint Andrew's cross, in blazonry
  Of silver, waving wide !

XXXIII.

The Bruce hath won his father's hall !
' Welcome, brave friends and com-
    rades all,
  Welcome to mirth and joy !
The first, the last, is welcome here,
From lord and chieftain, prince and
    peer,
  To this poor speechless boy.
Great God ! once more my sire's abode
Is mine—behold the floor I trode
  In tottering infancy !
And there the vaulted arch, whose
    sound
Echoed my joyous shout and bound
In boyhood, and that rung around
  To youth's unthinking glee !
O first, to thee, all-gracious Heaven,
Then to my friends, my thanks be
    given !'
He paused a space, his brow he cross'd,
Then on the board his sword he toss'd,
Yet steaming hot ; with Southern gore
From hilt to point 'twas crimson'd o'er.

XXXIV.

' Bring here,' he said, 'the mazers four,
My noble fathers loved of yore.
Thrice let them circle round the board,
The pledge, fair Scotland's rights
    restored !
And he whose lip shall touch the wine,
Without a vow as true as mine,

To hold both lands and life at nought,
Until her freedom shall be bought,—
Be brand of a disloyal Scot,
And lasting infamy his lot!
Sit, gentle friends! our hour of glee
Is brief, we'll spend it joyously!
Blithest of all the sun's bright beams,
When betwixt storm and storm he
　　gleams.
Well is our country's work begun,
But more, far more, must yet be done.
Speed　messengers　the　country
　　through;
Arouse old friends, and gather new;
Warn Lanark's knights to gird their
　　mail,
Rouse the brave sons of Teviotdale,
Let Ettrick's archers sharp their darts,
The fairest forms, the truest hearts!
Call all, call all! from Reedswair-
　　Path,
To the wild confines of Cape-Wrath;
Wide let the news through Scotland
　　ring,
The Northern Eagle claps his wing!'

—◆◆—

Canto Sixth.

I.

O who, that shared them, ever
　　shall forget
The emotions of the spirit-rousing
　　time,
When breathless in the mart the
　　couriers met,
Early and late, at evening and at
　　prime;
When the loud cannon and the
　　merry chime
Hail'd news on news, as field on
　　field was won,
When Hope, long doubtful, soar'd
　　at length sublime,

And our glad eyes, awake as day
　　begun,
Watch'd Joy's broad banner rise, to
　　meet the rising sun!

O these were hours, when thrilling
　　joy repaid
A long, long course of darkness,
　　doubts, and fears!
The heart-sick faintness of the hope
　　delay'd,
The waste, the woe, the bloodshed,
　　and the tears
That track'd with terror twenty
　　rolling years,
All was forgot in that blithe jubilee!
Her downcast eye even pale Afflic-
　　tion rears,
To sigh a thankful prayer, amid
　　the glee,
That hail'd the Despot's fall, and
　　peace and liberty!

Such news o'er Scotland's hills
　　triumphant rode,
When 'gainst the invaders turn'd
　　the battle's scale,
When Bruce's banner had victorious
　　flow'd
O'er Loudoun's mountain, and in
　　Ury's vale;
When English blood oft deluged
　　Douglas-dale,
And fiery Edward routed stout St.
　　John,
When Randolph's war-cry swell'd
　　the southern gale,
And many a fortress, town, and
　　tower was won,
And Fame still sounded forth fresh
　　deeds of glory done.

II.

Blithe　tidings　flew　from　baron's
　　tower,
To peasant's cot, to forest-bower,

And waked the solitary cell
Where lone Saint Bride's recluses
    dwell.
Princess no more, fair Isabel,
    A vot'ress of the order now,
Say, did the rule that bid thee wear
Dim veil and woollen scapulaire,
And reft thy locks of dark-brown hair,
    That stern and rigid vow,
Did it condemn the transport high,
Which glisten'd in thy watery eye,
When minstrel or when palmer told
Each fresh exploit of Bruce the bold?—
And whose the lovely form that shares
Thy anxious hopes, thy fears, thy
    prayers ?
No sister she of convent shade;
So say these locks in lengthen'd braid,
So say the blushes and the sighs,
The tremors that unbidden rise,
When, mingled with the Bruce's fame,
The brave Lord Ronald's praises came.

III.

Believe, his father's castle won,
And his bold enterprise begun,
That Bruce's earliest cares restore
The speechless page to Arran's shore :
Nor think that long the quaint disguise
Conceal'd her from a sister's eyes ;
And sister-like in love they dwell
In that lone convent's silent cell.
There Bruce's slow assent allows
Fair Isabel the veil and vows ;
And there, her sex's dress regain'd,
The lovely Maid of Lorn remain'd,
Unnamed, unknown, while Scotland
    far
Resounded with the din of war ;
And many a month, and many a day,
In calm seclusion wore away.

IV.

These days, these months, to years
    had worn,
When tidings of high weight were
    borne
        To that lone island's shore ;

Of all the Scottish conquests made
By the First Edward's ruthless blade,
    His son retain'd no more,
Northward of Tweed, but Stirling's
    towers,
Beleaguer'd by King Robert's powers ;
    And they took term of truce,
If England's King should not relieve
The siege ere John the Baptist's eve,
    To yield them to the Bruce.
England was roused—on every side
Courier and post and herald hied,
    To summon prince and peer,
At Berwick-bounds to meet their Liege,
Prepared to raise fair Stirling's siege,
    With buckler, brand, and spear.
The term was nigh—they muster'd
    fast,
By beacon and by bugle-blast
    Forth marshall'd for the field ;
There rode each knight of noble name,
There England's hardy archers came,
The land they trode seem'd all on
    flame,
    With banner, blade, and shield !
And not famed England's powers alone,
Renown'd in arms, the summons own ;
    For Neustria's knights obey'd,
Gascogne hath lent her horsemen
    good,
And Cambria, but of late subdued,
Sent forth her mountain-multitude,
And Connoght pour'd from waste
    and wood
Her hundred tribes, whose sceptre
    rude
    Dark Eth O'Connor sway'd.

V.

Right to devoted Caledon
The storm of war rolls slowly on,
    With menace deep and dread ;
So the dark clouds, with gathering
    power,
Suspend awhile the threaten'd shower,
Till every peak and summit lower
    Round the pale pilgrim's head.

Not with such pilgrim's startled eye
King Robert mark'd the tempest nigh!
   Resolved the brunt to bide,
His royal summons warn'd the land,
That all who own'd their King's command
Should instant take the spear and brand,
   To combat at his side.
O who may tell the sons of fame,
That at King Robert's bidding came,
   To battle for the right!
From Cheviot to the shores of Ross,
From Solway-Sands to Marshal's-Moss,
   All boun'd them for the fight.
Such news the royal courier tells,
Who came to rouse dark Arran's dells;
But farther tidings must the ear
Of Isabel in secret hear.
These in her cloister walk, next morn,
Thus shared she with the Maid of Lorn:

VI.

'My Edith, can I tell how dear
Our intercourse of hearts sincere
   Hath been to Isabel?
Judge then the sorrow of my heart,
When I must say the words, We part!
   The cheerless convent-cell
Was not, sweet maiden, made for thee;
Go thou where thy vocation free
   On happier fortunes fell.
Nor, Edith, judge thyself betray'd
Though Robert knows that Lorn's high Maid
And his poor silent page were one.
Versed in the fickle heart of man,
Earnest and anxious hath he look'd
How Ronald's heart the message brook'd
That gave him, with her last farewell,
The charge of Sister Isabel,
To think upon thy better right,
And keep the faith his promise plight.

Forgive him for thy sister's sake,
At first if vain repinings wake—
   Long since that mood is gone:
Now dwells he on thy juster claims,
And oft his breach of faith he blames—
   Forgive him for thine own!'

VII.

'No! never to Lord Ronald's bower
Will I again as paramour'——
'Nay, hush thee, too impatient maid,
Until my final tale be said!
The good King Robert would engage
Edith once more his elfin page,
By her own heart, and her own eye,
Her lover's penitence to try—
Safe in his royal charge and free,
Should such thy final purpose be,
Again unknown to seek the cell,
And live and die with Isabel.'
Thus spoke the Maid: King Robert's eye
Might have some glance of policy:
Dunstaffnage had the monarch ta'en,
And Lorn had own'd King Robert's reign;
Her brother had to England fled,
And there in banishment was dead;
Ample, through exile, death, and flight,
O'er tower and land was Edith's right;
This ample right o'er tower and land
Were safe in Ronald's faithful hand.

VIII.

Embarrass'd eye and blushing cheek
Pleasure and shame, and fear bespeak!
Yet much the reasoning Edith made:
'Her sister's faith she must upbraid,
Who gave such secret, dark and dear,
In council to another's ear.
Why should she leave the peaceful cell?
How should she part with Isabel?
How wear that strange attire agen?
How risk herself 'midst martial men?
And how be guarded on the way?—
At least she might entreat delay.'

Kind Isabel, with secret smile,
Saw and forgave the maiden's wile,
Reluctant to be thought to move
At the first call of truant love.

IX.

Oh, blame her not! When zephyrs wake,
The aspen's trembling leaves must shake;
When beams the sun through April's shower,
It needs must bloom, the violet flower;
And Love, howe'er the maiden strive,
Must with reviving hope revive!
A thousand soft excuses came,
To plead his cause 'gainst virgin shame.
Pledged by their sires in earliest youth,
He had her plighted faith and truth—
Then, 'twas her Liege's strict command,
And she, beneath his royal hand,
A ward in person and in land :—
And, last, she was resolved to stay
Only brief space—one little day—
Close hidden in her safe disguise
From all, but most from Ronald's eyes—
But once to see him more!— nor blame
Her wish—to hear him name her name!
Then, to bear back to solitude
The thought he had his falsehood rued!
But Isabel, who long had seen
Her pallid cheek and pensive mien,
And well herself the cause might know,
Though innocent, of Edith's woe,
Joy'd, generous, that revolving time
Gave means to expiate the crime.
High glow'd her bosom as she said,
'Well shall her sufferings be repaid!'
Now came the parting hour—a band
From Arran's mountains left the land;
Their chief, Fitz-Louis, had the care
The speechless Amadine to bear
To Bruce, with honour, as behoved
To page the monarch dearly loved.

X.

The King had deem'd the maiden bright
Should reach him long before the fight,
But storms and fate her course delay:
It was on eve of battle-day,
When o'er the Gillie's-hill she rode.
The landscape like a furnace glow'd,
And far as e'er the eye was borne,
The lances waved like autumn-corn.
In battles four beneath their eye,
The forces of King Robert lie.
And one below the hill was laid,
Reserved for rescue and for aid;
And three, advanced, form'd vaward-line,
'Twixt Bannock's brook and Ninian's shrine.
Detach'd was each, yet each so nigh
As well might mutual aid supply.
Beyond, the Southern host appears,
A boundless wilderness of spears,
Whose verge or rear the anxious eye
Strove far, but strove in vain, to spy.
Thick flashing in the evening beam,
Glaives, lances, bills, and banners gleam;
And where the heaven join'd with the hill,
Was distant armour flashing still,
So wide, so far, the boundless host
Seem'd in the blue horizon lost.

XI.

Down from the hill the maiden pass'd,
At the wild show of war aghast;
And traversed first the rearward host,
Reserved for aid where needed most.
The men of Carrick and of Ayr,
Lennox and Lanark, too, were there,
And all the western land;
With these the valiant of the Isles
Beneath their chieftains rank'd their files,
In many a plaided band.
There, in the centre, proudly raised,
The Bruce's royal standard blazed,
And there Lord Ronald's banner bore
A galley driven by sail and oar.
A wild, yet pleasing contrast, made

Warriors in mail and plate array'd,
With the plumed bonnet and the plaid
   By these Hebrideans worn ;
But O ! unseen for three long years,
Dear was the garb of mountaineers
   To the fair Maid of Lorn !
For one she look'd—but he was far
Busied amid the ranks of war—
Yet with affection's troubled eye
She mark'd his banner boldly fly,
Gave on the countless foe a glance,
And thought on battle's desperate
   chance.

XII.

To centre of the vaward-line
Fitz-Louis guided Amadine.
Arm'd all on foot, that host appears
A serried mass of glimmering spears.
There stood the Marchers' warlike
   band,
The warriors there of Lodon's land ;
Ettrick and Liddell bent the yew,
A band of archers fierce, though few :
The men of Nith and Annan's vale,
And the bold spears of Teviotdale ;—
The dauntless Douglas these obey,
And the young Stuart's gentle sway.
North-eastward by Saint Ninian's
   shrine,
Beneath fierce Randolph's charge,
   combine
The warriors whom the hardy North
From Tay to Sutherland sent forth.
The rest of Scotland's war-array
With Edward Bruce to westward lay,
Where Bannock, with his broken bank
And deep ravine, protects their flank.
Behind them, screen'd by sheltering
   wood,
The gallant Keith, Lord Marshal, stood :
His men-at-arms bear mace and lance,
And plumes that wave, and helms
   that glance.
Thus fair divided by the King,
Centre, and right, and left-ward wing,
Composed his front ; nor distant far
Was strong reserve to aid the war.

And 'twas to front of this array,
Her guide and Edith made their way.

XIII.

Here must they pause ; for, in advance
As far as one might pitch a lance,
The Monarch rode along the van,
The foe's approaching force to scan,
His line to marshal and to range,
And ranks to square, and fronts to
   change.
Alone he rode—from head to heel
Sheathed in his ready arms of steel ;
Nor mounted yet on war-horse wight,
But, till more near the shock of fight,
Reining a palfrey low and light.
A diadem of gold was set
Above his bright steel basinet,
And clasp'd within its glittering twine
Was seen the glove of Argentine ;
Truncheon or leading staff he lacks,
Bearing, instead, a battle-axe.
He ranged his soldiers for the fight,
Accoutred thus, in open sight
Of either host. Three bowshots far,
Paused the deep front of England's
   war,
And rested on their arms awhile,
To close and rank their warlike file,
And hold high council, if that night
Should view the strife, or dawning light.

XIV.

O gay, yet fearful to behold,
Flashing with steel and rough with
   gold,
   And bristled o'er with bills and
     spears,
With plumes and pennons waving fair,
Was that bright battle-front ! for there
   Rode England's King and peers :
And who, that saw that monarch ride,
His kingdom battled by his side,
Could then his direful doom foretell !
Fair was his seat in knightly selle,
And in his sprightly eye was set
Some spark of the Plantagenet.

Though light and wandering was his
    glance,
It flash'd at sight of shield and lance.
'Know'st thou,' he said, 'De Argentine,
Yon knight who marshals thus their
    line?'
'The tokens on his helmet tell
The Bruce, my Liege: I know him
    well.'
'And shall the audacious traitor brave
The presence where our banners
    wave?'
'So please my Liege,' said Argentine,
'Were he but horsed on steed like mine,
To give him fair and knightly chance,
I would adventure forth my lance.'
'In battle-day,' the King replied,
'Nice tourney rules are set aside.
Still must the rebel dare our wrath?
Set on him, sweep him from our path!'
And, at King Edward's signal, soon
Dash'd from the ranks Sir Henry
    Boune.

XV.

Of Hereford's high blood he came,
A race renown'd for knightly fame.
He burn'd before his Monarch's eye
To do some deed of chivalry.
He spurr'd his steed, he couch'd his
    lance,
And darted on the Bruce at once.
As motionless as rocks, that bide
The wrath of the advancing tide,
The Bruce stood fast. Each breast
    beat high,
And dazzled was each gazing eye,
The heart had hardly time to think,
The eyelid scarce had time to wink,
While on the King, like flash of flame,
Spurr'd to full speed the war-horse
    came!
The partridge may the falcon mock
If that slight palfrey stand the shock;
But, swerving from the Knight's career,
Just as they met, Bruce shunn'd the
    spear.

Onward the baffled warrior bore
His course—but soon his course was
    o'er!
High in his stirrups stood the King,
And gave his battle-axe the swing.
Right on De Boune, the whiles he
    pass'd,
Fell that stern dint, the first, the last!
Such strength upon the blow was put,
The helmet crash'd like hazel-nut;
The axe-shaft, with its brazen clasp,
Was shiver'd to the gauntlet grasp.
Springs from the blow the startled
    horse,
Drops to the plain the lifeless corse;
First of that fatal field, how soon,
How sudden, fell the fierce De Boune!

XVI.

One pitying glance the Monarch sped
Where on the field his foe lay dead;
Then gently turn'd his palfrey's head,
And, pacing back his sober way,
Slowly he gain'd his own array.
There round their King the leaders
    crowd,
And blame his recklessness aloud,
That risk'd 'gainst each adventurous
    spear
A life so valued and so dear.
His broken weapon's shaft survey'd
The King, and careless answer made,
'My loss may pay my folly's tax;
I've broke my trusty battle-axe.'
'Twas then Fitz-Louis, bending low,
Did Isabel's commission show;
Edith, disguised at distance stands,
And hides her blushes with her hands.
The Monarch's brow has changed its
    hue,
Away the gory axe he threw,
While to the seeming page he drew,
    Clearing war's terrors from his
      eye.
Her hand with gentle ease he took,
With such a kind protecting look,
    As to a weak and timid boy

Might speak, that elder brother's care
And elder brother's love were there.

XVII.

'Fear not,' he said, 'young Amadine!'
Then whisper'd, 'Still that name be
    thine.
Fate plays her wonted fantasy,
Kind Amadine, with thee and me,
And sends thee here in doubtful hour.
But soon we are beyond her power;
For on this chosen battle-plain,
Victor or vanquish'd, I remain.
Do thou to yonder hill repair;
The followers of our host are there,
And all who may not weapons bear.
Fitz-Louis, have him in thy care.
Joyful we meet, if all go well;
If not, in Arran's holy cell
Thou must take part with Isabel;
For brave Lord Ronald, too, hath
    sworn
Not to regain the Maid of Lorn
(The bliss on earth he covets most),
Would he forsake his battle-post,
Or shun the fortune that may fall
To Bruce, to Scotland, and to all.
But, hark! some news these trumpets
    tell;
Forgive my haste—farewell! farewell!'
And in a lower voice he said,
'Be of good cheer; farewell, sweet
    maid!'

XVIII.

'What train of dust, with trumpet-
    sound
And glimmering spears, is wheeling
    round
Our leftward flank?' the Monarch
    cried
To Moray's Earl, who rode beside.
'Lo! round thy station pass the foes!
Randolph, thy wreath has lost a rose.'
The Earl his visor closed, and said,
'My wreath shall bloom, or life shall
    fade.

Follow my household!' And they go
Like lightning on the advancing foe.
'My Liege,' said noble Douglas then,
'Earl Randolph has but one to ten:
Let me go forth his band to aid!'
'Stir not. The error he hath made,
Let him amend it as he may;
I will not weaken mine array.'
Then loudly rose the conflict-cry,
And Douglas's brave heart swell'd
    high,—
'My Liege,' he said, 'with patient ear
I must not Moray's death-knell hear!'
'Then go—but speed thee back again.'
Forth sprung the Douglas with his
    train:
But, when they won a rising hill,
He bade his followers hold them still.
'See, see! the routed Southern fly!
The Earl hath won the victory.
Lo! where yon steeds run masterless,
His banner towers above the press.
Rein up; our presence would impair
The fame we come too late to share.'
Back to the host the Douglas rode,
And soon glad tidings are abroad,
That, Dayncourt by stout Randolph
    slain,
His followers fled with loosen'd rein.
That skirmish closed the busy day,
And couch'd in battle's prompt array,
Each army on their weapons lay.

XIX.

It was a night of lovely June,
High rode in cloudless blue the moon,
    Demayet smiled beneath her ray;
Old Stirling's towers arose in light,
And, twined in links of silver bright,
    Her winding river lay.
Ah, gentle planet! other sight
Shall greet thee next returning night.
Of broken arms and banners tore,
And marshes dark with human gore,
And piles of slaughter'd men and
    horse,
And Forth that floats the frequent
    corse,

And many a wounded wretch to plain
Beneath thy silver light in vain!
But now, from England's host, the cry
Thou hear'st of wassail revelry,
While from the Scottish legions pass
The murmur'd prayer, the early
 mass!
Here, numbers had presumption given;
There, bands o'ermatch'd sought aid
 from Heaven.

   xx.

On Gillie's-hill, whose height com-
 mands
The battle-field, fair Edith stands,
With serf and page unfit for war,
To eye the conflict from afar.
O! with what doubtful agony
She sees the dawning tint the sky!
Now on the Ochils gleams the sun,
And glistens now Demayet dun;
 Is it the lark that carols shrill,
 Is it the bittern's early hum?
No!—distant, but increasing still,
The trumpet's sound swells up the
 hill,
 With the deep murmur of the drum.
Responsive from the Scottish host,
Pipe-clang and bugle-sound were
 toss'd,
His breast and brow each soldier
 cross'd,
 And started from the ground;
Arm'd and array'd for instant fight,
Rose archer, spearman, squire, and
 knight,
And in the pomp of battle bright
 The dread battalia frown'd.

   xxi.

Now onward, and in open view,
The countless ranks of England drew,
Dark rolling like the ocean-tide
When the rough west hath chafed his
 pride,
And his deep roar sends challenge wide
 To all that bars his way!

In front the gallant archers trode,
The men-at-arms behind them rode,
And midmost of the phalanx broad
 The Monarch held his sway.
Beside him many a war-horse fumes,
Around him waves a sea of plumes,
Where many a knight in battle known,
And some who spurs had first braced
 on,
And deem'd that fight should see them
 won,
 King Edward's hests obey.
De Argentine attends his side,
With stout De Valence, Pembroke's
 pride,
Selected champions from the train
To wait upon his bridle-rein.
Upon the Scottish foe he gazed;
At once, before his sight amazed,
 Sunk banner, spear, and shield;
Each weapon point is downward sent,
Each warrior to the ground is bent.
'The rebels, Argentine, repent!
 For pardon they have kneel'd.'
'Ay! but they bend to other powers,
And other pardon sue than ours!
See where yon barefoot Abbot stands,
And blesses them with lifted hands!
Upon the spot where they have kneel'd
These men will die, or win the field.'
'Then prove we if they die or win!
Bid Gloster's Earl the fight begin.'

   xxii.

Earl Gilbert waved his truncheon high
 Just as the Northern ranks arose,
Signal for England's archery
 To halt and bend their bows.
Then stepp'd each yeoman forth a pace,
Glanced at the intervening space,
 And raised his left hand high;
To the right ear the cords they bring;
At once ten thousand bow-strings ring,
 Ten thousand arrows fly!
Nor paused on the devoted Scot
The ceaseless fury of their shot;
 As fiercely and as fast

Forth whistling came the grey-goose
    wing
As the wild hailstones pelt and ring
    Adown December's blast.
Nor mountain targe of tough bull-hide,
Nor lowland mail, that storm may bide;
Woe, woe to Scotland's banner'd pride
    If the fell shower may last!
Upon the right, behind the wood,
Each by his steed dismounted, stood
    The Scottish chivalry;
With foot in stirrup, hand on mane,
Fierce Edward Bruce can scarce
    restrain
His own keen heart, his eager train,
Until the archers gain'd the plain;
    Then 'Mount, ye gallants free!'
He cried; and, vaulting from the
    ground,
His saddle every horseman found.
On high their glittering crests they toss,
As springs the wild-fire from the moss;
The shield hangs down on every breast,
Each ready lance is in the rest,
    And loud shouts Edward Bruce,—
'Forth, Marshal! on the peasant foe!
We 'll tame the terrors of their bow,
    And cut the bow-string loose!'

        XXIII.

Then spurs were dash'd in chargers'
    flanks,
They rush'd among the archer ranks.
No spears were there the shock to let,
No stakes to turn the charge were set,
And how shall yeoman's armour slight
Stand the long lance and mace of might?
Or what may their short swords avail
'Gainst barbed horse and shirt of mail?
Amid their ranks the chargers sprung,
High o'er their heads the weapons
    swung,
And shriek and groan and vengeful
    shout
Give note of triumph and of rout!
Awhile, with stubborn hardihood,
Their English hearts the strife made
    good.

Borne down at length on every side,
Compell'd to flight, they scatter wide.
Let stags of Sherwood leap for glee,
And bound the deer of Dallom-Lee!
The broken bows of Bannock's shore
Shall in the greenwood ring no more!
Round Wakefield's merry May-pole
    now
The maids may twine the summer
    bough,
May northward look with longing
    glance
For those that wont to lead the dance,
For the blithe archers look in vain!
Broken, dispersed, in flight o'erta'en,
Pierc'd through, trode down, by
    thousands slain,
They cumber Bannock's bloody plain.

        XXIV.

The King with scorn beheld their flight.
'Are these,' he said, 'our yeomen
    wight?
Each braggart churl could boast before
Twelve Scottish lives his baldric bore!
Fitter to plunder chase or park
Than make a manly foe their mark.
Forward, each gentleman and knight!
Let gentle blood show generous might,
And chivalry redeem the fight!'
To rightward of the wild affray
The field show'd fair and level way;
    But, in mid-space, the Bruce's care
Had bored the ground with many a pit,
With turf and brushwood hidden yet,
    That form'd a ghastly snare.
Rushing, ten thousand horsemen came,
With spears in rest and hearts on flame,
    That panted for the shock!
With blazing crests and banners
    spread,
And trumpet-clang and clamour dread,
The wide plain thunder'd to their
    tread
    As far as Stirling rock.
Down! down! in headlong overthrow,
Horseman and horse, the foremost go,
    Wild floundering on the field!

The first are in destruction's gorge,
Their followers wildly o'er them urge;
　The knightly helm and shield,
The mail, the acton, and the spear,
Strong hand, high heart, are useless
　here!
Loud from the mass confused the cry
Of dying warriors swells on high,
And steeds that shriek in agony!
They came like mountain-torrent red
That thunders o'er its rocky bed;
They broke like that same torrent's
　wave
When swallow'd by a darksome cave.
Billows on billows burst and boil,
Maintaining still the stern turmoil,
And to their wild and tortured groan
Each adds new terrors of his own!

XXV.

Too strong in courage and in might
Was England yet, to yield the fight.
　Her noblest all are here;
Names that to fear were never known,
Bold Norfolk's Earl De Brotherton,
　And Oxford's famed De Vere.
There Gloster plied the bloody sword,
And Berkley, Grey, and Hereford;
　Bottetourt and Sanzavere,
Ross, Montague, and Mauley, came,
And Courtenay's pride, and Percy's
　fame—
Names known too well in Scotland's
　war
At Falkirk, Methven, and Dunbar,
Blazed broader yet in after years
At Cressy red and fell Poitiers.
Pembroke with these, and Argentine,
Brought up the rearward battle-line.
With caution o'er the ground they
　tread,
Slippery with blood and piled with
　dead,
Till hand to hand in battle set,
The bills with spears and axes met,
And, closing dark on every side,
Raged the full contest far and wide.

Then was the strength of Douglas tried,
Then proved was Randolph's generous
　pride,
And well did Stewart's actions grace
The sire of Scotland's royal race!
Firmly they kept their ground;
As firmly England onward press'd,
And down went many a noble crest,
And rent was many a valiant breast,
　And Slaughter revell'd round.

XXVI.

Unflinching foot 'gainst foot was set,
Unceasing blow by blow was met;
　The groans of those who fell
Were drown'd amid the shriller clang
That from the blades and harness rang,
　And in the battle-yell.
Yet fast they fell, unheard, forgot,
Both Southern fierce and hardy Scot;
And O! amid that waste of life,
What various motives fired the strife!
The aspiring Noble bled for fame,
The Patriot for his country's claim;
This Knight his youthful strength to
　prove,
And that to win his lady's love;
Some fought from ruffian thirst of blood,
From habit some, or hardihood.
But ruffian stern, and soldier good,
　The noble and the slave,
From various cause the same wild road,
On the same bloody morning, trode,
　To that dark inn, the grave!

XXVII.

The tug of strife to flag begins,
Though neither loses yet nor wins.
High rides the sun, thick rolls the dust,
And feebler speeds the blow and thrust.
Douglas leans on his war-sword now,
And Randolph wipes his bloody brow;
Nor less had toil'd each Southern
　knight,
From morn till mid-day in the fight.
Strong Egremont for air must gasp,
Beauchamp undoes his visor-clasp,

And Montague must quit his spear,
And sinks thy falchion, bold De Vere!
The blows of Berkley fall less fast,
And gallant Pembroke's bugle-blast
    Hath lost its lively tone;
Sinks, Argentine, thy battle-word,
And Percy's shout was fainter heard,
    'My merry-men, fight on!'

XXVIII.

Bruce, with the pilot's wary eye,
The slackening of the storm could spy.
    'One effort more, and Scotland's
      free!
    Lord of the Isles, my trust in thee
      Is firm as Ailsa Rock;
    Rush on with Highland sword and
      targe,
    I, with my Carrick spearmen
      charge:
    Now, forward to the shock!'
At once the spears were forward
    thrown,
Against the sun the broadswords shone;
The pibroch lent its maddening tone,
And loud King Robert's voice was
    known—
    'Carrick, press on! they fail, they fail!
    Press on, brave sons of Innisgail,
    The foe is fainting fast!
    Each strike for parent, child, and
      wife,
    For Scotland, liberty, and life,—
    The battle cannot last!'

XXIX.

The fresh and desperate onset bore
The foes three furlongs back and more,
Leaving their noblest in their gore.
    Alone, De Argentine
Yet bears on high his red-cross shield,
Gathers the relics of the field,
Renews the ranks where they have
    reel'd,
    And still makes good the line.
Brief strife, but fierce his efforts raise
A bright but momentary blaze.

Fair Edith heard the Southern shout,
Beheld them turning from the rout,
Heard the wild call their trumpets sent
In notes 'twixt triumph and lament.
That rallying force, combined anew,
Appear'd in her distracted view
To hem the Islesmen round;
    'O God! the combat they renew
      And is no rescue found!
And ye that look thus tamely on,
And see your native land o'erthrown,
O! are your hearts of flesh or stone?'

XXX.

The multitude that watch'd afar,
Rejected from the ranks of war,
Had not unmoved beheld the fight,
When strove the Bruce for Scotland's
    right;
Each heart had caught the patriot
    spark,
Old man and stripling, priest and clerk,
Bondsman and serf; even female hand
Stretch'd to the hatchet or the brand;
    But, when mute Amadine they
      heard
    Give to their zeal his signal-word,
      A frenzy fired the throng;
    'Portents and miracles impeach
    Our sloth—the dumb our duties
      teach—
    And he that gives the mute his
      speech
      Can bid the weak be strong.
To us, as to our lords, are given
A native earth, a promised heaven;
To us, as to our lords, belongs
The vengeance for our nation's wrongs;
The choice, 'twixt death or freedom,
    warms
Our breasts as theirs—To arms, to
    arms!'
To arms they flew,—axe, club, or
    spear, —
And mimic ensigns high they rear,
And, like a banner'd host afar,
Bear down on England's wearied war.

XXXI.

Already scatter'd o'er the plain,
Reproof, command, and counsel vain,
The rearward squadrons fled amain,
　　Or made but doubtful stay;
But when they mark'd the seeming
　　show
Of fresh and fierce and marshall'd foe,
　　The boldest broke array
O give their hapless prince his due!
In vain the royal Edward threw
　　His person 'mid the spears,
Cried 'Fight!' to terror and despair,
Menaced, and wept, and tore his hair,
　　And cursed their caitiff fears;
Till Pembroke turn'd his bridle rein,
And forced him from the fatal plain.
With them rode Argentine, until
They gain'd the summit of the hill,
　　But quitted there the train:
'In yonder field a gage I left,
I must not live of fame bereft;
　　I needs must turn again.
Speed hence, my Liege, for on your
　　trace
The fiery Douglas takes the chase,
　　I know his banner well.
God send my Sovereign joy and bliss
And many a happier field than this!
　　Once more, my Liege, farewell.'

XXXII.

Again he faced the battle-field,—
Wildly they fly, are slain, or yield.
'Now then,' he said, and couch'd his
　　spear,
'My course is run, the goal is near;
One effort more, one brave career,
　　Must close this race of mine.'
Then in his stirrups rising high,
He shouted loud his battle-cry,
　　'Saint James for Argentine!'
And, of the bold pursuers, four
The gallant knight from saddle bore;
But not unharm'd—a lance's point
Has found his breastplate's loosen'd
　　joint,
　　An axe has razed his crest;

Yet still on Colonsay's fierce lord,
Who press'd the chase with gory
　　sword,
　　He rode with spear in rest,
And through his bloody tartans bored,
　　And through his gallant breast.
Nail'd to the earth, the mountaineer
Yet writhed him up against the spear,
　　And swung his broadsword round!
—Stirrup, steel-boot, and cuish gave
　　way,
Beneath that blow's tremendous sway,
　　The blood gush'd from the wound;
And the grim Lord of Colonsay
　　Hath turn'd him on the ground,
And laugh'd in death-pang, that his
　　blade
The mortal thrust so well repaid.

XXXIII.

Now toil'd the Bruce, the battle done,
To use his conquest boldly won;
And gave command for horse and
　　spear
To press the Southern's scatter'd rear,
Nor let his broken force combine,
When the war-cry of Argentine
　　Fell faintly on his ear;
'Save, save his life,' he cried, 'O save
The kind, the noble, and the brave!'
The squadrons round free passage
　　gave,
　　The wounded knight drew near;
He raised his red-cross shield no more,
Helm, cuish, and breastplate stream'd
　　with gore;
Yet, as he saw the King advance,
He strove even then to couch his
　　lance—
　　The effort was in vain!
The spur-stroke fail'd to rouse the
　　horse;
Wounded and weary, in mid-course
　　He stumbled on the plain.
Then foremost was the generous Bruce
To raise his head, his helm to loose.
　　'Lord Earl, the day is thine!

Q

My Sovereign's charge, and adverse
    fate,
Have made our meeting all too late :
    Yet this may Argentine,
As boon from ancient comrade, crave—
A Christian's mass, a soldier's grave.'

XXXIV.

Bruce press'd his dying hand—its
    grasp
Kindly replied ; but, in his clasp,
    It stiffen'd and grew cold.
'And, O farewell !' the victor cried,
'Of chivalry the flower and pride,
    The arm in battle bold,
The courteous mien, the noble race,
The stainless faith, the manly face !
Bid Ninian's convent light their shrine
For late wake of De Argentine.
O'er better knight on death-bier laid,
Torch never gleam'd, nor mass was
    said !'

XXXV.

Nor for De Argentine alone
Through Ninian's church these torches
    shone,
And rose the death-prayer's awful
    tone.
That yellow lustre glimmer'd pale
On broken plate and bloodied mail,
Rent crest and shatter'd coronet,
Of Baron, Earl, and Banneret ;
And the best names that England
    knew
Claim'd in the death-prayer dismal due.
    Yet mourn not, Land of Fame !
Though ne'er the leopards on thy
    shield
Retreated from so sad a field,
    Since Norman William came.
Oft may thine annals justly boast
Of battles stern by Scotland lost ;
    Grudge not her victory,
When for her freeborn rights she
    strove ;
Rights dear to all who freedom love,
    To none so dear as thee !

XXXVI.

Turn we to Bruce, whose curious ear
Must from Fitz-Louis tidings hear ;
    With him, a hundred voices tell
    Of prodigy and miracle,
      ' For the mute page had spoke.'
'Page !' said Fitz-Louis, 'rather say
An angel sent from realms of day
    To burst the English yoke.
I saw his plume and bonnet drop,
When hurrying from the mountain top :
A lovely brow, dark locks that wave,
To his bright eyes new lustre gave,
A step as light upon the green
As if his pinions waved unseen !'
' Spoke he with none ?' ' With none—
    one word
Burst when he saw the Island Lord
Returning from the battle-field.'
' What answer made the Chief ?' ' He
    kneel'd,
Durst not look up, but mutter'd low,
Some mingled sounds that none might
    know,
And greeted him 'twixt joy and fear,
As being of superior sphere.'

XXXVII.

Even upon Bannock's bloody plain,
Heap'd then with thousands of the
    slain,
'Mid victor monarch's musings high,
Mirth laugh'd in good King Robert's
    eye.
' And bore he such angelic air,
Such noble front, such waving hair ?
Hath Ronald kneel'd to him ?' he said,
' Then must we call the church to aid ;
Our will be to the Abbot known,
Ere these strange news are wider
    blown ;
To Cambuskenneth straight ye pass,
And deck the church for solemn mass,
To pay for high deliverance given,
A nation's thanks to gracious Heaven.
Let him array, besides. such state,
As should on princes' nuptials wait ;

Ourself the cause, through fortune's
    spite,
That once broke short that spousal
    rite,
Ourself will grace, with early morn,
The bridal of the Maid of Lorn.'

    Go forth, my Song, upon thy
      venturous way;
    Go boldly forth; nor yet thy master
      blame,
    Who chose no patron for his
      humble lay,
    And graced thy numbers with no
      friendly name,
    Whose partial zeal might smooth
      thy path to fame.
    There was—and O! how many
      sorrows crowd
    Into these two brief words!—*there
      was* a claim

By generous friendship given—had
    fate allow'd,
It well had bid thee rank the proudest
    of the proud!

All angel now; yet little less than all,
    While still a pilgrim in our world
      below!
What 'vails it us that patience to
    recall,
Which hid its own to soothe all
    other woe;
What 'vails to tell, how Virtue's
    purest glow
Shone yet more lovely in a form so
    fair:
And, least of all, what 'vails the
    world should know
That one poor garland, twined to
    deck thy hair,
Is hung upon thy hearse, to droop
    and wither there!

END OF THE LORD OF THE ISLES.

Introduction and Notes to the Lord of the Isles.

INTRODUCTION TO THE EDITION OF 1833.

I COULD hardly have chosen a subject more popular in Scotland than anything connected with the Bruce's history, unless I had attempted that of Wallace. But I am decidedly of opinion that a popular, or what is called a *taking* title, though well qualified to ensure the publishers against loss, and clear their shelves of the original impression, is rather apt to be hazardous than otherwise to the reputation of the author. He who attempts a subject of distinguished popularity, has not the privilege of awakening the enthusiasm of his audience ; on the contrary, it is already awakened, and glows, it may be, more ardently than that of the author himself. In this case, the warmth of the author is inferior to that of the party whom he addresses, who has, therefore, little chance of being, in Bayes's phrase, 'elevated and surprised' by what he has thought of with more enthusiasm than the writer. The sense of this risk, joined to the consciousness of striving against wind and tide, made the task of composing the proposed poem somewhat heavy and hopeless ; but, like the prize-fighter in 'As You Like It,' I was to wrestle for my reputation, and not neglect any advantage. In a most agreeable pleasure-voyage, which I have tried to commemorate in the Introduction to the new edition of 'The Pirate,' I visited, in social and friendly company, the coasts and islands of Scotland, and made myself acquainted with the localities of which I meant to treat. But this voyage, which was in every other effect so delightful, was in its conclusion saddened by one of those instances of fate which so often mingle themselves with our pleasures. The accomplished and excellent person who had recommended to me the subject for 'The Lay of the Last Minstrel,' and to whom I proposed to inscribe what I already suspected might be the close of my poetical labours, was unexpectedly removed from the world, which she seemed only to have visited for purposes of kindness and benevolence. It is needless to say how the author's feelings, or the com-position of his trifling work, were affected by a circumstance which occasioned so many tears and so much sorrow. True it is, that 'The Lord of the Isles' was concluded, unwillingly and in haste, under the painful feeling of one who has a task which must be finished, rather than with the ardour of one who endeavours to perform that task well. Although the poem cannot be said to have made a favourable impression on the public, the sale of fifteen thousand copies enabled the author to retreat from the field with the honours of war.

In the meantime, what was necessarily to be considered as a failure was much reconciled to my feelings by the success attending my attempt in another species of composition. 'Waverley' had, under strict incognito, taken its flight from the press, just before I set out upon the voyage already mentioned ; it had now made its way to popularity, and the success of that work and the volumes which followed, was sufficient to have satisfied a greater appetite for applause than I have at any time possessed.

I may as well add in this place, that, being much urged by my intimate friend, now unhappily no more, William Erskine (a Scottish judge, by the title of Lord Kinedder), I agreed to write the little romantic tale called 'The Bridal of Triermain' ; but it was on the condition that he should make no serious effort to disown the composition, if report should lay it at his door. As he was more than suspected of a taste for poetry, and as I took care, in several places, to mix something which might resemble as far as was in my power) my friend's feeling and manner, the train easily caught, and two large editions were sold. A third being called for, Lord Kinedder became unwilling to aid any longer a deception which was going farther than he expected or desired, and the real author's name was given. Upon another occasion, I sent up another of these trifles, which, like schoolboys' kites, served to show how the wind of popular taste was setting. The manner was supposed to be that of a rude minstrel or scald, in opposition to 'The Bridal of Triermain,' which was designed to belong rather to the Italian school. This new fugitive piece was called 'Harold the Dauntless'; and I am still astonished at my having committed the gross error of selecting the very name which Lord Byron had made so famous. It encountered rather an odd fate. My ingenious friend, Mr. James Hogg, had published, about the same time, a work called 'The Poetic Mirror,' containing imitations of the principal living poets. There was in it a very good imitation of my own style, which bore such a resemblance to 'Harold the Dauntless,' that there was no discovering the original from the imitation; and I believe that many who took the trouble of thinking upon the subject, were rather of opinion that my ingenious friend was the true, and not the fictitious Simon Pure. Since this period, which was in the year 1817, the author has not been an intruder on the public by any poetical work of importance.

WALTER SCOTT.

ABBOTSFORD, *April* 1830.

NOTES.

NOTE I.

Thy rugged halls, Artornish! rung.
—P. 412.

THE ruins of the Castle of Artornish are situated upon a promontory, on the Morven, or mainland side of the Sound of Mull, a name given to the deep arm of the sea, which divides that island from the continent. The situation is wild and romantic in the highest degree, having on the one hand a high and precipitous chain of rocks overhanging the sea, and on the other the narrow entrance to the beautiful salt-water lake, called Loch Alline, which is in many places finely fringed with copsewood. The ruins of Artornish are not now very considerable, and consist chiefly of the remains of an old keep, or tower, with fragments of outward defences. But in former days it was a place of great consequence, being one of the principal strongholds which the Lords of the Isles, during the period of their stormy independence, possessed upon the mainland of Argyleshire. Here they assembled what popular tradition calls their parliaments, meaning, I suppose, their *cour plenière*, or assembly of feudal and patriarchal vassals and dependents. From this Castle of Artornish, upon the 19th day of October, 1461, John de Yle, designing himself Earl of Ross and Lord of the Isles, granted, in the style of an independent sovereign, a commission to his trusty and well-beloved cousins, Ronald of the Isles, and Duncan, Arch-Dean of the Isles, for empowering them to enter into a treaty with the most excellent Prince Edward, by the grace of God, King of France and England and Lord of Ireland. Edward IV, on his part, named Laurence, Bishop of Durham, the Earl of Worcester, the Prior of St. John's, Lord Wenlock, and Mr. Robert Stillington, keeper of the privy seal, his deputies and commissioners, to confer with those named by the Lord of the Isles. The conference terminated in a treaty, by which the Lord of the Isles agreed to become a vassal to the crown of England, and to assist Edward IV and James Earl of Douglas, then in banishment, in subduing the realm of Scotland.

The first article provides, that John de Isle, Earl of Ross, with his son Donald Balloch, and his grandson John de Isle, with all their subjects, men, people, and inhabitants, become vassals and liegemen to Edward IV of England, and assist him in his wars in Scotland or Ireland; and then follow the allowances to be made to the Lord of the Isles, in recompense of his military service, and the provisions for dividing such conquests as their united arms should make upon the mainland of Scotland among the confederates. These appear such curious illustrations of the period, that they are here subjoined :

'*Item*, The seid John Erle of Rosse shall, from the seid fest of Whittesontyde next comyng, yerely, duryng his lyf, have and take, for fees and wages in tyme of peas, of the seid most high and Christien prince c. marc sterlyng of Englysh money ; and in tyme of werre, as long as he shall entende with his myght and power in the said werres, in manner and fourme abovesaid, he shall have wages of cc. lb. sterlyng of English money ; and after the rate of the tyme that he shall be occupied in the seid werres.

'*Item*, The seid Donald shall, from the seid feste of Whittesontyde, have and take, during his lyf, yerly, in tyme of peas, for his fees and wages, xx l. sterlyng of Englysh money, and, when he shall be occupied and intend to the werre, with his myght and power, and in manner and fourme aboveseid, he shall have and take, for his wages yearly, xl l. sterlynge of Englysh money ; or for the rate of the tyme of werre——

'*Item*, The seid John, sonn and heire apparant of the said Donald, shall have and take, yerely, from the seid fest, for his fees and wages, in the tyme of peas, x l. sterlynge of Englysh money; and for tyme of werre, and his intendyng thereto, in manner and fourme aboveseid, he shall have, for his fees and wages, yearly xx l sterlynge of Englysh money; or after the rate of the tyme that he shall be occupied in the werre: And the seid John, th' Erle Donald and John, and eche of them, shall have good and sufficiaunt paiment of the seid fees and wages, as wel for tyme of peas as of werre, accordyng to thees articules and appoyntements. *Item*, It is appointed, according, concluded, and finally determined, that, if it so be that hereafter the said reaume of Scotlande, or the more part thereof, be conquered, subdued, and brought to the obeissance of the seid most high and Christien prince, and his heires, or successoures, of the seid Lionell, in fourme aboveseid descendyng, be the assistance, helpe, and aide of the said John Erle of Rosse, and Donald, and of James Erle of Douglas, then, the said fees and wages for the tyme of peas cessyng, the same erles and Donald shall have, by the graunte of the same most Christien prince, all the possessions of the said reaume beyonde Scottishe see, they to be departed equally betwix them: eche of them, his heires and successours, to holde his parte of the seid most Christien prince, his heires and successours, for evermore, in right of his coune of England, by homage and feaute to be done therefore.

'*Item*, If so be that, by th' aide and assistence of the seid James Erle of Douglas, the said reaume of Scotlande be conquered and subdued as above, then he shall have, enjoie, and inherite all his own possessions, landes, and inheritaunce, on this syde the Scottishe see; that is to saye, betwixt the seid Scottishe see and Englande, such he hath rejoiced and be possessed of before this; there to holde them of the said most high and Christien prince, his heires, and successours, as is abovesaid, for evermore, in right of the coroune of Englonde, as weel the said Erle of Douglas, as his heires and successours, by homage and feaute to be done therefore.'—RYMER'S *Fœdera Conventiones Literae et cujuscunque generis Acta Publica*, fol. vol. v. 1741.

Such was the treaty of Artornish; but it does not appear that the allies ever made any very active effort to realize their ambitious designs. It will serve to show both the power of these reguli, and their independence upon the crown of Scotland.

It is only farther necessary to say of the Castle of Artornish that it is almost opposite to the Bay of Aros, in the Island of the Mull, where there was another castle, occasional residence of the Lords of the Isles.

NOTE II.

Rude Heiskar's seal, through surges dark,
Will long pursue the minstrel's bark.
                        —P. 412.

The seal displays a taste for music, which could scarcely be expected from his habits and local predilections. They will long follow a boat in which any musical instrument is played, and even a tune simply whistled has attractions for them. The Dean of the Isles says of Heiskar, a small uninhabited rock, about twelve (Scottish) miles from the isle of Uist, that an infinite slaughter of seals takes place there.

NOTE III.

       —— *a turret's airy head,*
Slender and steep, and battled round,
O'erlook'd dark Mull! thy mighty
        Sound.—P. 414.

The Sound of Mull, which divides that island from the continent of Scotland, is one of the most striking scenes which the Hebrides afford to the traveller. Sailing from Oban to Aros, or Tobermory, through a narrow channel, yet deep enough to bear vessels of the largest burden, he has on his left the bold and mountainous shores of Mull; on the right those of that district of Argyleshire, called Morven, or Morvern, successively indented by deep salt-water lochs, running up many miles inland. To the south-eastward arise a prodigious range of mountains, among which Cruachan-Ben is pre-eminent; and to the north-east is the no less huge and picturesque range of the Ardnamurchan hills. Many ruinous castles, situated generally upon cliffs overhanging the ocean, add interest to the scene. Those of Donolly and Dunstaffnage are first passed, then that of Duart, formerly belonging to the chief of the warlike and powerful sept of Macleans, and the scene of Miss Baillie's beautiful tragedy, entitled 'The Family Legend.' Still passing on to the northward, Artornish and Aros become visible upon the opposite shores; and, lastly Mingarry, and other ruins of less distinguished note. In fine weather, a grander and more impressive scene, both from its natural beauties and associations with ancient history and tradition, can hardly be imagined. When the weather is rough, the passage is both difficult and dangerous, from the narrowness of the channel, and in part from the number of inland lakes, out of which sally forth a number of conflicting and thwarting tides, making the navigation perilous to open boats. The sudden flaws and gusts of wind which issue without a moment's warning from the mountain glens, are equally formidable. So that in unsettled weather, a stranger, if not much accustomed to the sea, may sometimes add to the other sublime sensations excited by the scene, that feeling of **dignity which arises from a sense of danger.**

NOTE IV.

——' these seas behold,
Round twice a hundred islands roll'd,
From Hirt, that hears their northern roar,
To the green Ilay's fertile shore.'— P. 414.

The number of the western isles of Scotland exceeds two hundred, of which St. Kilda is the most northerly, anciently called Hirth, or Hirt, probably from 'earth,' being in fact the whole globe to its inhabitants. Ilay, which now belongs almost entirely to Walter Campbell, Esq of Shawfield, is by far the most fertile of the Hebrides, and has been greatly improved under the spirited and sagacious management of the present proprietor. This was in ancient times the principal abode of the Lords of the Isles, being, if not the largest, the most important island of their archipelago. In Martin's time, some relics of their grandeur were yet extant. 'Loch-Finlagan, about three miles in circumference, affords salmon, trouts, and eels: this lake lies in the centre of the isle. The Isle Finlagan, from which this lake hath its name, is in it. It's famous for being once the court in which the great Mac-Donald, King of the Isles, had his residence; his houses, chapel, &c. are now ruinous. His guards de corps, called Luchttach, kept guard on the lake side nearest to the isle; the walls of their houses are still to be seen there. The high court of judicature, consisting of fourteen, sat always here; and there was an appeal to them from all the courts in the isles: the eleventh share of the sum in debate was due to the principal judge. There was a big stone of seven foot square, in which there was a deep impression made to receive the feet of Mac-Donald; for he was crowned King of the Isles standing in this stone, and swore that he would continue his vassals in the possession of their lands. and do exact justice to all his subjects: and then his father's sword was put into his hand. The Bishop of Argyle and seven priests anointed him king, in presence of all the heads of the tribes in the isles and continent, and were his vassals; at which time the orator rehearsed a catalogue of his ancestors,' &c.—MARTIN'S *Account of the Western Isles*, 8vo, London, 1716, pp. 240-1.

NOTE V.

——Mingarry, sternly placed,
O'erawes the woodland and the waste.
— P. 414.

The Castle of Mingarry is situated on the sea-coast of the district of Ardnamurchan. The ruins, which are tolerably entire, are surrounded by a very high wall, forming a kind of polygon, for the purpose of adapting itself to the projecting angles of a precipice overhanging the sea, on which the castle stands. It was anciently the residence of the Mac-Ians, a clan of Mac-Donalds, descended from Ian, or John, a grandson of Angus Og, Lord of the Isles. The last time that Mingarry was of military importance, occurs in the celebrated Leabhar dearg, or Red-book of Clanronald, a MS. renowned in the Ossianic controversy. Allaster Mac-Donald, commonly called Colquitto, who commanded the Irish auxiliaries sent over by the Earl of Antrim during the great civil war to the assistance of Montrose, began his enterprise in 1644 by taking the castles of Kinloch-Alline and Mingarry, the last of which made considerable resistance, as might, from the strength of the situation, be expected. In the meanwhile, Allaster Mac-Donald's ships, which had brought him over, were attacked in Loch Eisord, in Skye, by an armament sent round by the covenanting parliament, and his own vessel was taken. This circumstance is said chiefly to have induced him to continue in Scotland, where there seemed little prospect of raising an army in behalf of the King. He had no sooner moved eastward to join Montrose, a junction which he effected in the braes of Athole, than the Marquis of Argyle bes'eged the castle of Mingarry, but without success. Among other warriors and chiefs whom Argyle summoned to his camp to assist upon this occasion was John of Moidart, the Captain of Clanronald. Clanronald appeared; but, far from yielding effectual assistance to Argyle, he took the opportunity of being in arms to lay waste the district of Sunart, then belonging to the adherents of Argyle, and sent part of the spoil to relieve the Castle of Mingarry. Thus the castle was maintained until relieved by Allaster Mac-Donald (Colquitto), who had been detached for the purpose by Montrose. These particulars are hardly worth mentioning, were they not connected with the memorable successes of Montrose, related by an eyewitness, and hitherto unknown to Scottish historians.

NOTE VI.

The heir of mighty Somerled.— P. 414.

Somerled was thane of Argyle and Lord of the Isles, about the middle of the twelfth century. He seems to have exercised his authority in both capacities, independent of the crown of Scotland, against which he often stood in hostility. He made various incursions upon the western lowlands during the reign of Malcolm IV, and seems to have made peace with him upon the terms of an independent prince, about the year 1157. In 1164, he resumed the war against Malcolm, and invaded Scotland with a large, but probably a tumultuary army, collected in the isles, in the mainland of Argyleshire, and in the neighbouring provinces of Ireland. He was defeated and slain in an engagement with a very inferior force, near Renfrew. His son Gillicolane fell in the same battle. This mighty chieftain married a daughter of Olaus, King of Man. From him our genealogists deduce two dynasties, distinguished in the stormy history of the middle ages; the Lords of the Isles descended from his elder son Ronald,— and the Lords of Lorn, who took their surname of M'Dougal, as descended of his second son Dougal. That Somerled's territories upon the mainland, and upon the islands, should have been thus divided between his two sons, instead of passing to the elder exclusively, may illustrate the uncertainty of descent among the great Highland families, which we shall presently notice.

NOTE VII.

Lord of the Isles.—P. 414.

The representative of this independent principality, for such it seems to have been, though acknowledging occasionally the pre-eminence of the Scottish crown, was, at the period of the poem, Angus, called Angus Og; but the name has been, *euphoniae gratia*, exchanged for that of Ronald, which frequently occurs in the genealogy. Angus was a protector of Robert Bruce, whom he received in his Castle of Dunnaverty, during the time of his greatest distress. As I shall be equally liable to censure for attempting to decide a controversy which has long existed between three distinguished chieftains of this family, who have long disputed the representation of the Lord of the Isles, or for leaving a question of such importance altogether untouched, I choose, in the first place, to give such information as I have been able to derive from Highland genealogists, and which, for those who have patience to investigate such subjects, really contains some curious information concerning the history of the Isles. In the second place, I shall offer a few remarks upon the rules of succession at that period, without pretending to decide their bearing upon the question at issue, which must depend upon evidence which I have had no opportunity to examine.

'Angus Og,' says an ancient manuscript translated from the Gaelic, 'son of Angus Mor, son of Donald, son of Ronald, son of Somerled, high ch ef and superior Lord of Innisgall, (or the Isles of the Gael, the general name given to the Hebrides,) he married a daughter of Cunbui, namely, Cathan; she was mother to John, son of Angus, and with her came an unusual portion from Ireland, viz. twenty-four clans, of whom twenty-four families in Scotland are descended. Angus had another son, namely, young John Fraoch, whose descendants are called Clan-Ean of Glencoe, and the M'Donalds of Fraoch. This Angus Og died in Isla, where his body was interred. His son John succeeded to the inheritance of Innisgall. He had good descendants, namely, three sons procreate of Ann, daughter of Rodric, high chief of Lorn, and one daughter, Mary, married to John Maclean, Laird of Duart, and Lauchlan, his brother, Laird of Coll; she was interred in the church of the Black Nuns. The eldest sons of John were Ronald, Godfrey, and Angus. . . . He gave Ronald a great inheritance. These were the lands which he gave him, viz. from Kilcumin in Abertarf to the river Seil, and from thence to Beilli, north of Eig and Rum, and the two Uists, and from thence to the foot of the river Glaichan, and threescore long ships. John married afterwards Margaret Stewart, daughter to Robert Stewart, King of Scotland, called John Fernyear; she bore him three good sons, Donald of the Isles, the heir, John the Tainister (i. e. Thane), the second son, and Alexander Carrach. John had another son called Marcus, of whom the clan Macdonald of Cnoc, in Tirowen, are descended. This John lived long, and made donations to Icolumkill; he covered the chapel of Eorsay-Elan, the chapel of Finlagam, and the chapel of the Isle of Tsuibhne, and gave the proper furniture for the service of God, upholding the clergy and monks; he built or repaired the church of the Holy Cross immediately before his death. He died at his own castle of Arctorinish, many priests and monks took the sacrament at his funeral, and they embalmed the body of this dear man, and brought it to Icolumkill; the abbot, monks, and vicar, came as they ought to meet the King of Fiongal, and out of great respect to his memory mourned eight days and nights over it, and laid it in the same grave with his father, in the church of Oran, 1380.

'Ronald, son of John, was chief ruler of the Isles in his father's lifetime, and was old in the government at his father's death.

'He assembled the gentry of the Isles, brought the sceptre from Kildonan in Eig, and delivered it to his brother Donald, who was thereupon called M'Donald, and Donald Lord of the Isles, contrary to the opinion of the men of the Isles.

'Ronald, son of John, son of Angus Og, was a great supporter of the church and clergy; his descendants are called Clanronald. He gave the lands of Tiruma, in Uist, to the minister of it for ever, for the honour of God and Columkill; he was proprietor of all the lands of the north along the coast and the isles; he died in the year of Christ 1386, in his own mansion of Castle Tirim, leaving five children. Donald of the Isles, son of John, son of Angus Og, the brother of Ronald, took possession of Inisgall by the consent of his brother and the gentry thereof; they were all obedient to him: he married Mary Lesley, daughter to the Earl of Ross, and by her came the earldom of Ross to the M'Donalds. After his succession to that earldom, he was called M'Donald, Lord of the Isles and Earl of Ross. There are many things written of him in other places.

'He fought the battle of Garioch (i. e. Harlaw) against Duke Murdoch, the governor: the Earl of Mar commanded the army, in support of his claim to the earldom of Ross, which was ceded to him by King James the First, after his release from the King of England ; and Duke Murdoch, his two sons and retainers, were beheaded: he gave lands in Mull and Isla to the minister of Hi, and every privilege which the minister of Iona had formerly, besides vessels of gold and silver to Columkill for the monastery, and became himself one of the fraternity. He left issue, a lawful heir to Innisgall and Ross, namely, Alexander, the son of Donald: he died in Isla, and his body was interred in the south side of the temple of Oran. Alexander, called John of the Isles, son of Alexander of the Isles, son of Donald of the Isles. Angus, the third son of John, son of Angus Og, married the daughter of John, the son of Allan, which connexion caused some disagreement betwixt the two families about their marches and division of lands, the one party adhering to Angus, and the other to John : the differences increased so much that John obtained from Allan all the lands betwixt *Abhan Fahda* (i. e. the long river) and *old na sionnach* (i. e. the fox-burn brook) in the upper part of Cantyre. Allan went to the king to complain of his son-in-law ; in a short time thereafter, there happened to be a great meeting about this young Angus's lands to the north of Inverness, where he was murdered by his own harper Mac-Cairbre, by cutting his throat with a long knife. He [1] lived a year thereafter, and many of those concerned were delivered up to the king. Angus's wife was pregnant at the time of his murder, and she bore him a son who was named Donald, and called Donald Du. He was kept in confinement until he was thirty years of age, when he was released by the men of Glenco, by the strong hand. After this enlargement, he came to the Isles, and convened the gentry thereof. There happened great feuds betwixt these families while Donald Du was in confinement, insomuch that Mac-Cean of Ardnamurchan destroyed the greatest part of the posterity of John Mor of the Isles and Cantyre. For John Cathanach, son of John, son of Donald Balloch, son of John Mor, son of John, son of Angus Og (the chief of the descendants of John Mor), and John Mor, son of John Cathanach, and young John, son of John Cathanach, and young Donald Balloch, son of John Cathanach, were treacherously taken by Mac-Cean in the island of Finlagan, in Isla, and carried to Edinburgh, where he got them hanged at the Burrow-muir, and their bodies were buried in the Church of St. Anthony, called the New Church. There were none left alive at that time of the children of John Cathanach, except Alexander, the son of John Cathanach, and Agnes Flach, who concealed themselves in the glens of Ireland. Mac-Cean, hearing of their hiding-places, went to cut down the woods of these glens, in order to destroy Alexander, and extirpate the whole

race. At length Mac-Cean and Alexander met, were reconciled, and a marriage alliance took place ; Alexander married Mac-Cean's daughter, and she brought him good children. The Mac-Donalds of the north had also descendants ; for, after the death of John, Lord of the Isles, Earl of Ross, and the murder of Angus, Alexander, the son of Archibald, the son of Alexander of the Isles, took possession, and John was in possession of the earldom of Ross, and the north bordering country ; he married a daughter of the Earl of Moray, of whom some of the men of the north had descended. The Mac-Kenzies rose against Alexander, and fought the battle called *Blar na Paire*. Alexander had only a few of the men of Ross at the battle. He went after that battle to take possession of the Isles, and sailed in a ship to the south to see if he could find any of the posterity of John Mor alive, to rise along with him ; but Mac-Cean of Ardnamurchan watched him as he sailed past, followed him to Oransay and Colonsay, went to the house where he was, and he and Alexander, son of John Cathanach, murdered him there.

'A good while after these things fell out, Donald Galda, son of Alexander, son of Archibald, became major ; he, with the advice and direction of the Earl of Moray, came to the Isles, and Mac-Leod of the Lewis, and many of the gentry of the Isles, rose with him : they went by the promontory of Ardnamurchan, where they met Alexander, the son of John Cathanach, were reconciled to him, he joined his men with theirs against Mac-Cean of Ardnamurchan, came upon him at a place called the Silver Craig, where he and his three sons, and a great number of his people, were killed, and Donald Galda was immediately declared Mac-Donald : And, after the affair of Ardnamurchan, all the men of the Isles yielded to him, but he did not live above seven or eight weeks after it ; he died at Carnaborg, in Mull, without issue. He had three sisters, daughters of Alexander, son of Archibald, who were portioned in the north upon the continent, but the earldom of Ross was kept for them. Alexander, the son of Archibald, had a natural son, called John Cam, of whom is descended Achnacoichan, in Ramoeh, and Donald Gorm, son of Ronald, son of Alexander Duson, of John Cam. Donald Du, son of Angus, son of John of the Isles, son of Alexander of the Isles, son of Donald of the Isles, son of John of the Isles, son of Angus Og, namely, the true heir of the Isles and Ross, came after his release from captivity to the Isles, and convened the men thereof, and he and the Earl of Lennox agreed to raise a great army for the purpose of taking possession, and a ship came from England with a supply of money to carry on the war, which landed at Mull, and the money was given to Mac-Lean of Duart to be distributed among the commanders of the army, which they not receiving in proportion as it should have been distributed

---

[1] The murderer, I presume, not the man who was murdered.

among them, caused the army to disperse, which, when the Earl of Lennox heard, he disbanded his own men, and made it up with the king. Mac-Donald went to Ireland to raise men, but he died on his way to Dub in, at Drogheda, of a fever, without issue of either sons or daughters.'

In this history may be traced, though the Bard, or Seannachie, touches such a delicate discussion with a gentle hand, the point of difference between the three principal septs descended from the Lords of the Isles. The first question, and one of no easy solution, where so little evidence is produced, respects the nature of the connexion of John, called by the Archdean of the Isles 'the Good John of Ila,' and 'the last Lord of the Isles,' with Anne, daughter of Roderick Mac-Dougal, high-chief of Lorn. In the absence of positive evidence, presumptive must be resorted to, and I own it appears to render it in the highest degree improbable that this connexion was otherwise than legitimate. In the wars between David II and Edward Baliol, John of the Isles espoused the Baliol interest, to which he was probably determined by his alliance with Roderick of Lorn, who was, from every family predilection, friendly to Baliol and hostile to Bruce. It seems absurd to suppose, that between two chiefs of the same descent, and nearly equal power and rank, (though the Mac-Dougals had been much crushed by Robert Bruce,) such a connexion should have been that of concubinage; and it appears more likely that the tempting offer of an alliance with the Bruce family, when they had obtained the decided superiority in Scotland, induced 'the Good John of Ila ' to disinherit, to a certain extent, his eldest son Ronald, who came of a stock so unpopular as the Mc-Dougals, and to call to his succession his younger family, born of Margaret Stuart, daughter of Robert, afterwards King of Scotland. The setting aside of this elder branch of his family was most probably a condition of his new alliance, and his being received into favour with the dynasty he had always opposed. Nor were the laws of succession at this early period so clearly understood as to bar such transactions. The numerous and strange claims set up to the crown of Scotland, when vacant by the death of Alexander III, make it manifest how very little the indefeasible hereditary right of primogeniture was valued at that period. In fact, the title of the Bruces themselves to the crown, though justly the most popular, when assumed with the determination of asserting the independence of Scotland, was upon pure principle greatly inferior to that of Baliol. For Bruce, the competitor, claimed as son of Isabella, *second* daughter of David, Earl of Huntingdon; and John Baliol, as grandson of Margaret, the elder daughter of that same earl. So that the plea of Bruce was founded upon the very loose idea, that as the great-grandson of David I, King of Scotland, and the nearest

collateral relation of Alexander III, he was entitled to succeed in exclusion of the great-great-grandson of the same David, though by an elder daughter. This maxim savoured of the ancient practice of Scotland, which often called a brother to succeed to the crown as nearer in blood than a grandchild, or even a son of a deceased monarch. But, in truth, the maxims of inheritance in Scotland were sometimes departed from at periods when they were much more distinctly understood. Such a transposition took place in the family of Hamilton, in 1513, when the descendants of James, third Lord, by Lady Janet Home, were set aside, with an appanage of great value indeed, in order to call to the succession those which he had by a subsequent marriage with Janet Beatoun. In short, many other examples might be quoted to show that the question of legitimacy is not always determined by the fact of succession; and there seems reason to believe, that Ronald, descendant of 'John of Ila' by Anne of Lorn, was legitimate, and therefore Lord of the Isles *de jure*, though *de facto* his younger half-brother Donald, son of his father's second marriage with the Princess of Scotland, superseded him in his right, and apparently by his own consent. From this Donald so preferred is descended the family of Sleat, now Lords Mac-Donald. On the other hand, from Ronald, the excluded heir, upon whom a very large appanage was settled, descended the chiefs of Glengary and Clanronald, each of whom had large possessions and a numerous vassalage, and boasted a long descent of warlike ancestry. Their common ancestor Ronald was murdered by the Earl of Ross, at the Monastery of Elcho, A D 1346. I believe it has been subject of fierce dispute, whether Donald, who carried on the line of Glengary, or Allan of Moidart, the ancestor of the captains of Clanronald, was the eldest son of Ronald, the son of John of Isla. A humble Lowlander may be permitted to waive the discussion, since a Sennachie of no small note, who wrote in the sixteenth century, expresses himself upon this delicate topic in the following words :—

'I have now given you an account of everything you can expect of the descendants of the clan Colla, (i. e. the Mac-Donalds,) to the death of Donald Du at Drogheda, namely, the true line of those who possessed the Isles, Ross, and the mountainous countries of Scotland. It was Donald, the son of Angus, that was killed at Inverness (by his own harper Mac-i'Cairbre), son of John of the Isles, son of Alexander, son of Donald, son of John, son of Angus Og. And I know not which of his kindred or relations is the true heir, except these five sons of John, the son of Angus Og, whom I here set down for you, namely, Ronald and Godfrey, the two sons of the daughter of Mac-Donald of Lorn, and Donald and John Mor, and Alexander Carrach, the three sons of Margaret Stewart, daughter of Robert Stewart, King of Scotland.'—*Leabhar Dearg.*

Note VIII.

The House of Lorn.—P. 415.

The House of Lorn, as we observed in a former note, was, like the Lord of the Isles, descended from a son of Somerled, slain at Renfrew, in 1164. This son obtained the succession of his mainland territories, comprehending the greater part of the three districts of Lorn, in Argyleshire, and of course might rather be considered as petty princes than feudal barons. They assumed the patronymic appellation of Mac-Dougal, by which they are distinguished in the history of the middle ages. The Lord of Lorn who flourished during the wars of Bruce was Allaster (or Alexander) Mac-Dougal, called Allaster of Argyle. He had married the third daughter of John, called the Red Comyn[1], who was slain by Bruce in the Dominican Church at Dumfries, and hence he was a mortal enemy of that prince, and more than once reduced him to great straits during the early and distressed period of his reign, as we shall have repeated occasion to notice. Bruce, when he began to obtain an ascendency in Scotland, took the first opportunity in his power to requite these injuries. He marched into Argyleshire to lay waste the country. John of Lorn, son of the chieftain, was posted with his followers in the formidable pass between Dalmally and Bunawe. It is a narrow path along the verge of the huge and precipitous mountain, called Cruachan-Ben, and guarded on the other side by a precipice overhanging Loch Awe. The pass seems to the eye of a soldier as strong as it is wild and romantic to that of an ordinary traveller. But the skill of Bruce had anticipated this difficulty. While his main body, engaged in a skirmish with the men of Lorn, detained their attention to the front of their position, James of Douglas, with Sir Alexander Fraser, Sir William Wiseman, and Sir Andrew Grey, ascended the mountain with a select body of archery, and obtained possession of the heights which commanded the pass. A volley of arrows descending upon them directly warned the Argyleshire men of their perilous situation, and their resistance, which had hitherto been bold and manly, was changed into a precipitate flight. The deep and rapid river of Awe was then (we learn the fact from Barbour with some surprise) crossed by a bridge. This bridge the mountaineers attempted to demolish, but Bruce's followers were too close upon their rear; they were, therefore, without refuge and defence, and

were dispersed with great slaughter. John of Lorn, suspicious of the event, had early betaken himself to the galleys which he had upon the lake; but the feelings which Barbour assigns to him, while witnessing the rout and slaughter of his followers, exculpate him from the charge of cowardice.

> 'To Jhone off Lorne it suld displese
> I trow, quhen he his men mycht se,
> Owte off his schippis fra the se,
> Be slayne and chassyt in the hill,
> That he mycht set na help thar till.
> Bot it angrys als gretumly,
> To gud hartis that ar worthi,
> To se thar favis fulfill thair will
> As to thaim selff to thole the ill.'—B. VII. v. 394.

After this decisive engagement, Bruce laid waste Argyleshire, and besieged Dunstaffnage Castle, on the western shore of Lorn, compelled it to surrender, and placed in that principal stronghold of the Mac-Dougals a garrison and governor of his own. The elder Mac-Dougal, now wearied with the contest, submitted to the victor; but his son, 'rebellious,' says Barbour, 'as he wont to be,' fled to England by sea. When the wars between the Bruce and Baliol factions again broke out in the reign of David II, the Lords of Lorn were again found upon the losing side, owing to their hereditary enmity to the house of Bruce. Accordingly, upon the issue of that contest, they were deprived by David II and his successor of by far the greater part of their extensive territories, which were conferred upon Stewart, called the Knight of Lorn. The house of Mac-Dougal continued, however, to survive the loss of power, and affords a very rare, if not a unique, instance of a family of such unlimited power, and so distinguished during the middle ages, surviving the decay of their grandeur, and flourishing in a private station. The Castle of Dunolly, near Oban, with its dependencies, was the principal part of what remained to them, with their right of chieftainship over the families of their name and blood. These they continued to enjoy until the year 1715, when the representative incurred the penalty of forfeiture, for his accession to the insurrection of that period; thus losing the remains of his inheritance to replace upon the throne the descendants of those princes, whose accession his ancestors had opposed at the expense of their feudal grandeur. The estate was, however, restored about 1745, to the father of the present proprietor, whom family experience had taught the hazard of interfering with the established government, and who remained quiet upon that occasion. He therefore regained his property when many Highland chiefs lost theirs.

Nothing can be more wildly beautiful than the situation of Dunolly. The ruins are situated upon a bold and precipitous promontory, overhanging Loch Etive, and distant about a mile from the village and port of Oban. The principal part which remains is the donjon or keep; but fragments of other buildings, over-

---

[1] The aunt, according to Lord Hailes. But the genealogy is distinctly given by Wyntoun:—

> 'The thryd douchtyr of Red Cwmyn,
> Alysawndyr of Argayle syne
> Tuk, and weddyt til hys wyf,
> And on hyr he gat in-til hys lyfe
> Jhon of Lorne, the quhilk gat
> Ewyn of Lorne eftyr that.'

WYNTOUN'S *Chronicle*, Book VIII. Chap. vi. line 206.

grown with ivy, attest that it had been once a place of importance, as large apparently as Artornish or Dunstaffnage. These fragments enclose a courtyard, of which the keep probably formed one side ; the entrance being by a steep ascent from the neck of the isthmus, formerly cut across by a moat, and defended doubtless by outworks and a drawbridge. Beneath the castle stands the present mansion of the family, having on the one hand Loch Etive, with its islands and mountains, on the other two romantic eminences tufted with copsewood. There are other accompaniments suited to the scene ; in particular, a huge upright pillar, or detached fragment of that sort of rock called plum-pudding stone, upon the shore, about a quarter of a mile from the castle. It is called *Clach-na-cau*, or the Dog's Pillar, because Fingal is said to have used it as a stake to which he bound his celebrated dog Bran. Others say, that when the Lord of the Isles came upon a visit to the Lord of Lorn, the dogs brought for his sport were kept beside this pillar. Upon the whole, a more delightful and romantic spot can scarce be conceived ; and it receives a moral interest from the considerations attached to the residence of a family once powerful enough to confront and defeat Robert Bruce, and now sunk into the shade of private life. It is at present possessed by Patrick Mac-Dougal, Esq., the lineal and undisputed representative of the ancient Lords of Lorn. The heir of Dunolly fell lately in Spain, fighting under the Duke of Wellington,—a death well becoming his ancestry.

Note IX.

Awaked before the rushing prow,
The mimic fires of ocean glow,
Those lightnings of the wave.
—P. 417.

The phenomenon called by sailors Sea-fire, is one of the most beautiful and interesting which is witnessed in the Hebrides. At times the ocean appears entirely illuminated around the vessel, and a long train of lambent coruscations are perpetually bursting upon the sides of the vessel, or pursuing her wake through the darkness. These phosphoric appearances, concerning the origin of which naturalists are not agreed in opinion, seem to be called into action by the rapid motion of the ship through the water, and are probably owing to the water being saturated with fish-spawn, or other animal substances. They remind one strongly of the description of the sea-snakes in Mr. Coleridge's wild, but highly poetical ballad of 'The Ancient Mariner '—

'Beyond the shadow of the ship
I watch d the water-snakes,
They moved in tracks of shining white,
And when they rear'd, the elvish light
Fell off in hoary flakes.

Note X.

The dark fortress.—P. 418.

The fortress of a Hebridean chief was almost always on the sea-shore, for the facility of communication which the ocean afforded. Nothing can be more wild than the situations which they chose, and the devices by which the architects endeavoured to defend them. Narrow stairs and arched vaults were the usual mode of access ; and the drawbridge appears at Dunstaffnage, and elsewhere, to have fallen from the gate of the building to the top of such a staircase ; so that any one advancing with hostile purpose, found himself in a state of exposed and precarious elevation, with a gulf between him and the object of his attack.

These fortresses were guarded with equal care. The duty of the watch devolved chiefly upon an officer called the Cockman, who had the charge of challenging all who approached the castle. The very ancient family of Mac-Niel of Barra kept this attendant at their castle about a hundred years ago. Martin gives the following account of the difficulty which a tended his procuring entrance there:—
'The little island Kismul lies about a quarter of a mile from the south of this isle (Barra) ; it is the seat of Mackneil of Barra ; there is a stone wall round it two stories high, reaching the sea ; and within the wall there is an old tower and an hall, with other houses about it. There is a little magazine in the tower, to which no stranger has access. I saw the officer called the Cockman, and an old cock he is ; when I bid him ferry me over the water to the island, he told me that he was but an inferior officer, and his business being to attend in the tower ; but if (says he) the constable, who then stood on the wall, will give you access, I 'll ferry you over. I desired him to procure me the constable's permission, and I would reward him ; but having waited some hours for the constable's answer, and not receiving any, I was obliged to return without seeing this famous fort. Mackneil and his lady being absent, was the cause of this difficulty, and of my not seeing the place. I was told some weeks after, that the constable was very apprehensive of some design I might have in viewing the fort, and thereby to expose it to the conquest of a foreign power ; of which I supposed there was no great cause of fear.'

Note XI.

That keen knight, De Argentine.
—P. 421.

Sir Egidius, or Giles de Argentine, was one of the most accomplished knights of the period. He had served in the wars of Henry of Luxemburg with such high reputation, that he was, in popular estimation, the third worthy of the age. Those to whom fame assigned precedence over him were, Henry of Luxemburg himself, and Robert Bruce. Argentine had warred in Palestine, encountered thrice with the Saracens, and had slain two antagonists in each engagement :—an easy matter, he said, for one Christian knight to slay two Pagan dogs. His death corresponded with his high character. With Aymer de Valence, Earl of Pembroke, he was appointed to attend immediately upon the person of Edward II at Bannockburn. When the day was utterly lost they forced the king from the field. De Argentine saw the king safe from immediate danger, and then took his leave of him ; 'God be with you, sir,' he said, 'it is not my wont to fly.' So saying, he turned his horse, cried his war-cry, plunged into the midst of the combatants, and was slain. Baston, a rhyming monk who had been brought by Edward to celebrate his expected triumph, and who was compelled by the victors to compose a poem on his defeat, mentions with some feeling the death of Sir Giles de Argentine :

Nobilis Argenten, pugil inclyte, dulcis Egidi,
Vix scieram mentem cum te succumbere vidi.

'The first line mentions the three chief requisites of a true knight, noble birth, valour, and courteousness. Few Leonine couplets can be produced that have so much sentiment. I wish that I could have collected more ample memorials concerning a character altogether different from modern manners. Sir Giles d'Argentine was a hero of romance in real life.' So observes the excellent Lord Hailes.

NOTE XII.

'*Fill me the mighty cup !*' *he said,*
'*Erst own'd by royal Somerled.*'—P. 421.

A Hebridean drinking-cup, of the most ancient and curious workmanship, has been long preserved in the castle of Dunvegan, in Skye, the romantic seat of Mac-Leod of Mac-Leod, the chief of that ancient and powerful clan. The horn of Rorie More, preserved in the same family, and recorded by Dr. Johnson, is not to be compared with this piece of antiquity, which is one of the greatest curiosities in Scotland. The following is a pretty accurate description of its shape and dimensions, but cannot, I fear, be perfectly understood without a drawing.

This very curious piece of antiquity is nine inches and three-quarters in inside depth, and ten and a half in height on the outside, the extreme measure over the lips being four inches and a half. The cup is divided into two parts by a wrought ledge, beautifully ornamented, about three-fourths of an inch in breadth. Beneath this ledge the shape of the cup is rounded off, and terminates in a flat circle, like that of a tea-cup : four short feet support the whole. Above the projecting ledge the shape of the cup is nearly square, projecting outward at the brim. The cup is made of wood, (oak to all appearance,) but most curiously wrought and embossed with silver work, which projects from the vessel. There are a number of regular projecting sockets, which appear to have been set with stones ; two or three of them still hold pieces of coral, the rest are empty. At the four corners of the projecting ledge, or cornice, are four sockets, much larger, probably for pebbles or precious stones. The workmanship of the silver is extremely elegant, and appears to have been highly gilded. The ledge, brim, and legs of the cup are of silver. The family tradition bears that it was the property of Neil Ghlune-dhu, or Black-knee. But who this Neil was, no one pretends to say. Around the edge of the cup is a legend, perfectly legible, in the Saxon black-letter, which seems to run thus :

𝔘𝔣𝔬 : 𝔍𝔬𝔥𝔦𝔰 : 𝔐𝔦𝔠𝔥 : ‖ 𝔐𝔤𝔫 : 𝔓𝔫𝔠𝔦𝔭𝔦𝔰 : 𝔇𝔢 : ‖
𝔥𝔯 : 𝔐𝔞𝔫𝔞𝔢 : 𝔙𝔦𝔠𝔥 : ‖ 𝔏𝔦𝔞𝔥𝔦𝔞 : 𝔐𝔤𝔯𝔶𝔫𝔢𝔦𝔩 : ‖
𝔈𝔱 : 𝔖𝔭𝔞𝔱 : 𝔇𝔬 : 𝔍𝔥𝔲 : 𝔇𝔞 : ‖ 𝔆𝔩𝔢𝔞 : 𝔍𝔩𝔩𝔬𝔯𝔲 𝔒𝔭𝔞 : ‖
𝔣𝔢𝔠𝔦𝔱 : 𝔄𝔫𝔬 : 𝔇𝔦 : 𝔍𝔯 : 930 ‖ 𝔒𝔫𝔦𝔩𝔦 : 𝔒𝔦𝔪𝔦 :

The inscription may run thus at length : *Ufo Johannis Mich Magni Principis de Hr Manae Vich Liahia Magryneil et sperat Domino Ihesu dari clementiam illorum opera. Fecit Anno Domini 993 Onili Oimi.* Which may run in English : Ufo, the son of John, the son of Magnus, Prince of Man, the grandson of Liahia Macgryneil, trusts in the Lord Jesus that their works (i e. his own and those of his ancestors) will obtain mercy. Oneil Oimi made this in the year of God nine hundred and ninety-three.

But this version does not include the puzzling letters HR before the word Manae. Within the mouth of the cup the letters Jhs (Jesus) are repeated four times. From this and other circumstances it would seem to have been a chalice. This circumstance may perhaps account for the use of the two Arabic numerals 93. These figures were introduced by Pope Sylvester, A. D. 991, and might be used in a vessel formed for church service so early as 993. The workmanship of the whole cup is extremely elegant, and resembles, I am told, antiques of the same nature preserved in Ireland.

The cups thus elegantly formed, and highly valued, were by no means utensils of mere show. Martin gives the following account of the festivals of his time, and I have heard similar instances of brutality in the Lowlands at no very distant period.

'The manner of drinking used by the chief men of the Isles is called in their language Streah, i.e. a Round ; for the company sat in a circle, the cup-bearer fill'd the drink round to them, and all was drank out, whatever the liquor was, whether strong or weak ; they continued drinking sometimes twenty-four, sometimes forty-eight hours: It was reckoned a piece of manhood to drink until they became drunk, and there were two men with a barrow attending punctually on such occasions. They stood at the door until some became drunk, and they carry'd them upon the barrow to bed, and returned again to their post as long as any continued fresh, and so carried off the whole company, one by one, as they became drunk. Several of my acquaintance have been witnesses to this custom of drinking, but it is now abolished.'

This savage custom was not entirely done away within this last generation. I have heard of a gentleman who happened to be a water-drinker, and was permitted to abstain from the strong potations of the company. The bearers carried away one man after another, till no one was left but this Scottish Mirglip. They then came to do him the same good office, which, however, he declined as unnecessary, and proposed to walk to his bedroom. It was a permission he could not obtain. Never such a thing had happened, they said, in the castle ! that it was impossible but he must require their assistance, at any rate he must submit to receive it; and carried him off in the barrow accordingly. A classical penalty was sometimes imposed on those who balked the rules of good fellowship by evading their share of the banquet. The same author continues :—

'Among persons of distinction it was reckoned an affront put upon any company to broach a piece of wine, ale, or aquavitae, and not to see it all drank out at one meeting. If any man chance to go out from the company, though but for a few minutes, he is obliged, upon his return, and before he take his seat, to make an apology for his absence in rhyme; which if he cannot perform he is liable to such a share of the reckoning as the company thinks fit to impose : which custom obtains in many places still, and is called Bianchiz Bard, which, in their language, signifies the poet's congratulating the company.'

Few cups were better, at least more actively, employed in the rude hospitality of the period, than those of Dunvegan ; one of which we have just described. There is in the Leabhar Dearg, a song, intimating the overflowing gratitude of a bard of Clan-Ronald, after the exuberance of a Hebridean festival at the patriarchal fortress of Mac-Leod. The translation be'ng obviously very literal, has greatly flattened, as I am informed, the enthusiastic gratitude of the ancient bard; and it must be owned that the works of Homer or Virgil, to say nothing of Mac-Vuirich, might have suffered by their transfusion through such a medium. It is pretty plain, that when the tribute of poetical praise was bestowed, the horn of Rorie More had not been inactive.

Upon Sir Roderic Mor Macleod, by Niall Mor MacVuirich.

'The six nights I remained in the Dunvegan, it was not a show of hospitality I met with there, but a plentiful feast in thy fair hall among thy numerous host of heroes.

'The family placed all around under the protection of their great chief, raised by his prosperity and respect for his warlike feats, now enjoying the company of his friends at the feast,—Amidst the sound of harps, over-flowing cups, and happy youth unaccustomed to guile, or feud, partaking of the generous fare by a flaming fire.

'Mighty Chief, liberal to all in your princely mansion, filled with your numerous warlike host, whose generous wine would overcome the hardiest heroes, yet we continued to enjoy the feast, so happy our host, so generous our fare.'—*Translated by D. Mac-Intosh.*

It would be unpardonab'e in a modern bard, who has experienced the hospitality of Dunvegan Castle in the present day, to omit paying his own tribute of gratitude for a reception more elegant indeed, but not less kindly sincere, than Sir Roderick More himself could have afforded. But Johnson has already described a similar scene in the same ancient patriarchal residence of the Lords of Mac-Leod:—'Whatever is imaged in the wildest tales, if giants, dragons, and enchantment be excepted, would be felt by him, who, wandering in the mountains without a guide, or upon the sea without a pilot, should be carried, amidst his terror and uncertainty, to the hospitality and elegance of Raasay or Dunvegan.'

NOTE XIII.

*With solemn step, and silver wand,
The Seneschal the presence scann'd
Of these strange guests.—P. 421.*

The Sewer, to whom, rather than the Seneschal, the office of arranging the guests of an island chief appertained, was an officer of importance in the family of a Hebridean chief.—'Every family had commonly two stewards, which, in their language, were called Marischal Tach : the first of these served always at home, and was obliged to be versed in the pedigree of all the tribes in the isles, and in the highlands of Scotland; for it was his province to assign every man at table his seat according to his quality; and this was done without one word speaking, only by drawing a score with a white rod, which this Marischal had in his hand, before the person who was bid by him to sit down; and this was necessary to prevent disorder and contention; and though the Marischal might sometimes be mistaken, the master of the family incurred no censure by such an escape; but this custom has been laid aside

of late. They had also cup-bearers, who always filled and carried the cup round the company, and he himself always drank off the first draught. They had likewise purse-masters, who kept their money. Both these officers had an hereditary right to their office in writing, and each of them had a town and land for his service: some of those rights I have seen fair'y written on good parchment.'
—MARTIN'S *Western Isles.*

Note XIV.

*——the rebellious Scottish crew,
Who to Rath-Erin's shelter drew,
With Carrick's outlaw'd Chief?*—P. 422.

It must be remembered by all who have read the Scottish history, that after he had slain Comyn at Dumfries, and asserted his right to the Scottish crown, Robert Bruce was reduced to the greatest extremity by the English and their adherents. He was crowned at Scone by the general consent of the Scottish barons, but his authority endured but a short time. According to the phrase said to have been used by his wife, he was for that year 'a summer king, but not a winter one.' On the 29th March, 1306, he was crowned king at Scone. Upon the 19th June, in the same year, he was totally defeated at Methven, near Perth; and his most important adherents, with few exceptions, were either executed or compelled to embrace the English interest, for safety of their lives and fortunes. After this disaster, his life was that of an outlaw, rather than a candidate for monarchy. He separated himself from the females of his retinue, whom he sent for safety to the castle of Kildrummie, in Aberdeenshire, where they afterward became captives to England. From Aberdeenshire, Bruce retreated to the mountainous parts of Breadalbane, and approached the borders of Argyleshire. There, as mentioned in the Appendix, Note VIII, and more fully in Note XV, he was defeated by the Lord of Lorn, who had assumed arms against him in revenge of the death of his relative, John the Red Comyn. Escaped from this peril, Bruce, with his few attendants, subsisted by hunting and fishing, until the weather compelled them to seek better sustenance and shelter than the Highland mountains afforded. With great difficulty they crossed, from Rowardennan probably, to the western banks of Lochlomond, partly in a miserable boat, and partly by swimming. The valiant and loyal Earl of Lennox, to whose territories they had now found their way, welcomed them with tears, but was unable to assist them to make an effectual head. The Lord of the Isles, then in possession of great part of Cantyre, received the fugitive monarch and future restorer of his country's independence, in his castle of Dunnaverty, in that district. But treason, says Barbour, was so general,

that the King durst not abide there. Accordingly, with the remnant of his followers, Bruce embarked for Rath-Erin, or Rachrine, the Recina of Ptolemy, a small island, lying almost opposite to the shores of Ballycastle, on the coast of Ireland. The islanders at first fled from their new and armed guests, but upon some explanation submitted themselves to Bruce's sovereignty. He resided among them until the approach of spring 1307, when he again returned to Scotland, with the desperate resolution to reconquer his kingdom, or perish in the attempt. The progress of his success, from its commencement to its completion, forms the brightest period in Scottish history.

Note XV.

The Brooch of Lorn.—P. 422.

It has been generally mentioned in the preceding notes, that Robert Bruce, after his defeat at Methven, being hard pressed by the English, endeavoured, with the dispirited remnant of his followers, to escape from Breadalbane and the mountains of Perthshire into the Argyleshire Highlands. But he was encountered and repulsed, after a very severe engagement, by the Lord of Lorn. Bruce's personal strength and courage were never displayed to greater advantage than in this conflict. There is a tradition in the family of the Mac-Dougals of Lorn, that their chieftain engaged in personal battle with Bruce himself, while the latter was employed in protecting the retreat of his men; that Mac-Dougal was struck down by the king, whose strength of body was equal to his vigour of mind, and would have been slain on the spot, had not two of Lorn's vassals, a father and son, whom tradition terms Mac-Keoch, rescued him, by seizing the mantle of the monarch, and dragging him from above his adversary. Bruce rid himself of these foes by two blows of his redoubted battle-axe, but was so closely pressed by the other followers of Lorn, that he was forced to abandon the mantle, and brooch which fastened it, clasped in the dying grasp of the Mac-Keochs. A studded brooch, said to have been that which King Robert lost upon this occasion, was long preserved in the family of Mac-Dougal, and was lost in a fire which consumed their temporary residence.

The metrical history of Barbour throws an air of credibility upon the tradition, although it does not entirely coincide either in the names or number of the vassals by whom Bruce was assailed, and makes no mention of the personal danger of Lorn, or of the loss of Bruce's mantle. The last circumstance, indeed, might be warrantably omitted.

According to Barbour, the King, with his handful of followers, not amounting probably to three hundred men, encountered Lorn with about a thousand Argyleshire men, in Glen-

Douchart, at the head of Breadalbane, near Teyndrum. The place of action is still called Dalry, or the King's Field. The field of battle was unfavourable to Bruce's adherents, who were chiefly men-at-arms. Many of the horses were slain by the long pole-axes, of which the Argyleshire Scottish had learned the use from the Norwegians. At length Bruce commanded a retreat up a narrow and difficult pass, he himself bringing up the rear, and repeatedly turning and driving back the more venturous assailants. Lorn, observing the skill and valour used by his enemy in protecting the retreat of his followers, 'Methinks, Murthokson,' said he, addressing one of his followers, 'he resembles Gol Makmorn, protecting his followers from Fingal.' —'A most unworthy comparison,' observes the Archdeacon of Aberdeen, unsuspicious of the future fame of these names; 'he might with more propriety have compared the King to Sir Gaudefer de Layrs, protecting the foragers of Gadyrs against the attacks of Alexander.' Two brothers, the strongest among Lorn's followers, whose names Barbour calls Mackyn-Drosser, (interpreted Durward, or Porterson,) resolved to rid their chief of this formidable foe. A third person (perhaps the Mac-Keoch of the family tradition) associated himself with them for this purpose. They watched their opportunity until Bruce's party had entered a pass between a lake (Loch Dochart probably) and a precipice, where the King, who was the last of the party, had scarce room to manage his steed. Here his three foes sprung upon him at once. One seized his bridle, but received a wound which hewed off his arm; a second grasped Bruce by the stirrup and leg, and endeavoured to dismount him, but the King, putting spurs to his horse, threw him down, still holding by the stirrup. The third, taking advantage of an acclivity, sprung up behind him upon his horse. Bruce, however, whose personal strength is uniformly mentioned as exceeding that of most men, extricated himself from his grasp, threw him to the ground, and cleft his skull with his sword. By similar exertion he drew the stirrup from his grasp whom he had overthrown, and killed him also with his sword as he lay among the horse's feet. The story seems romantic, but this was the age of romantic exploit; and it must be remembered that Bruce was armed cap-a-pie, and the assailants were half-clad mountaineers. Barbour adds the following circumstance, highly characteristic of the sentiments of chivalry. Mac-Naughton, a Baron of Cowal, pointed out to the Lord of Lorn the deeds of valour which Bruce performed in this memorable retreat, with the highest expressions of admiration. 'It seems to give thee pleasure,' said Lorn, 'that be makes such havoc among our friends.' — 'Not so, by my faith,' replied Mac-Naughton; 'but be he friend or foe who achieves high deeds of chivalry, men should bear faithful witness to his valour; and never have I heard of one, who, by his knightly feats, has extricated himself from such dangers as have this day surrounded Bruce.'

NOTE XVI.

Wrought and chased with rare device,
Studded fair with gems of price.—P. 422.

Great art and expense was bestowed upon the *fibula*, or brooch, which secured the plaid, when the wearer was a person of importance. Martin mentions having seen a silver brooch of a hundred marks value. 'It was broad as any ordinary pewter plate, the whole curiously engraven with various animals, &c. There was a lesser buckle, which was wore in the middle of the larger, and above two ounces weight; it had in the centre a large piece of crystal, or some finer stone, and this was set all round with several finer stones of a lesser size.'—*Western Islands.* Pennant has given an engraving of such a brooch as Martin describes, and the workmanship of which is very elegant. It is said to have belonged to the family of Lochbuy.—See PENNANT'S *Tour,* vol. iii. p. 14.

NOTE XVII.

Vain was then the Douglas brand,
Vain the Campbell's vaunted hand.—P. 423.

The gallant Sir James, called the Good Lord Douglas, the most faithful and valiant of Bruce's adherents, was wounded at the battle of Dalry. Sir Nigel, or Neil Campbell, was also in that unfortunate skirmish. He married Marjorie, sister to Robert Bruce, and was among his most faithful followers. In a manuscript account of the house of Argyle, supplied, it would seem, as materials for Archbishop Spottiswoode's History of the Church of Scotland, I find the following passage concerning Sir Niel Campbell:— 'Moreover, when all the nobles in Scotland had left King Robert after his hard success, yet this noble knight was most faithful, and shrinked not, as it is to be seen in an indenture bearing these words:—*Memorandum quod cum ab incarnatione Domini* 1308 *conventum fuit et concordatum inter nobiles viros Dominum Alexandrum de Seatoun militem et Dominum Gilbertum de Haye militem et Dominum Nigellum Campbell militem apud monasterium de Cambuskenneth* 9° *Septembris qui tacta sancta eucharista, magnoque juramento facto, jurarunt se debere libertatem regni et Robertum nuper regem coronatum contra omnes mortales Francos Anglos Scotos defendere usque ad ultimum terminum vitae ipsorum.* Their sealles are appended to the indenture in greene wax, togithir with the seal of Gulfrid, Abbot of Cambuskenneth.'

Note XVIII.

When Comyn fell beneath the knife
Of that fell homicide The Bruce.—P. 419

Vain Kirkpatrick's bloody dirk,
Making sure of murder's work.—P. 423.

Every reader must recollect that the proximate cause of Bruce's asserting his right to the crown of Scotland, was the death of John, called the Red Comyn. The causes of this act of violence, equally extraordinary from the high rank both of the perpetrator and sufferer, and from the place where the slaughter was committed, are variously related by the Scottish and English historians, and cannot now be ascertained. The fact that they met at the high altar of the Minorites, or Greyfriars' Church in Dumfries, that their difference broke out into high and insulting language, and that Bruce drew his dagger and stabbed Comyn, is certain. Rushing to the door of the church, Bruce met two powerful barons, Kirkpatrick of Closeburn, and James de Lindsay, who eagerly asked him what tidings? 'Bad tidings,' answered Bruce; 'I doubt I have slain Comyn.'—'Doubtest thou?' said Kirkpatrick; 'I make sicker!' (i. e. sure.) With these words, he and Lindsay rushed into the church, and despatched the wounded Comyn. The Kirkpatricks of Closeburn assumed, in memory of this deed, a hand holding a dagger, with the memorable words, 'I make sicker.' Some doubt having been started by the late Lord Hailes as to the identity of the Kirkpatrick who completed this day's work with Sir Roger, then representative of the ancient family of Closeburn, my kind and ingenious friend, Mr. Charles Kirkpatricke Sharpe, has furnished me with the following memorandum, which appears to fix the deed with his ancestor:—

'The circumstances of the Regent Cummin's murder, from which the family of Kirkpatrick, in Nithsdale, is said to have derived its crest and motto, are well known to all conversant with Scottish history; but Lord Hailes has started a doubt as to the authenticity of this tradition, when recording the murder of Roger Kirkpatrick, in his own Castle of Caerlaverock, by Sir James Lindsay. "Fordun," says his Lordship, "remarks that Lindsay and Kirkpatrick were the heirs of the two men who accompanied Robert Brus at the fatal conference with Comyn. If Fordun was rightly informed as to this particular, an argument arises, in support of a notion which I have long entertained, that the person who struck his dagger in Comyn's heart, was *not* the representative of the honourable family of Kirkpatrick in Nithsdale. Roger de K. was made prisoner at the battle of Durham, in 1346. Roger de Kirkpatrick was alive on the 6th of August, 1357; for, on that day, Humphry, the son and heir of Roger de K., is proposed as one of the young gentlemen who were to be

hostages for David Bruce. Roger de K. Miles was present at the parliament held at Edinburgh, 25th September, 1357, and he is mentioned as alive 3rd October, 1357 (*Foedera*); it follows, of necessary consequence, that Roger de K., murdered in June 1357, must have been a different person."— *Annals of Scotland*, vol. ii. p. 242.

'To this it may be answered, that at the period of the regent's murder, there were only *two* families of the name of Kirkpatrick (nearly allied to each other) in existence— Stephen Kirkpatrick, styled in the Chartulary of Kelso (1278) *Dominus villae de Closeburn, Filius et haeres Domini A de de Kirkpatrick, Militis,* (whose father, Ivone de Kirkpatrick, witnesses a charter of Robert Brus, Lord of Annandale, before the year 1141.) had two sons, Sir Roger, who carried on the line of Closeburn, and Duncan, who married Isobel, daughter and heiress of Sir David Torthorwald of that Ilk; they had a charter of the lands of Torthorwald from King Robert Brus, dated 10th August, the year being omitted— Umphray, the son of Duncan and Isobel, got a charter of Torthorwald from the king, 16th July, 1322—his son, Roger of Torthorwald, got a charter from John the Grahame, son of Sir John Grahame of Moskessen, of an annual rent of 40 shillings, out of the lands of Overdryft, 1355—his son, William Kirkpatrick, grants a charter to John of Garroch, of the twa merk land of Glengip and Garvellgill, within the tenement of Wamphray, 22nd April, 1372. From this, it appears that the Torthorwald branch was not concerned in the affair of Comyn's murder, and the inflictions of Providence which ensued: Duncan Kirkpatrick, if we are to believe the Blind Minstrel, was the firm friend of Wallace, to whom he was related:—

"Ane Kyrk Patrick, that cruel was and keyne,
In Esdail wod that half yer he had beyne ;
With Ingliss men he couth nocht weyll accord,
Off Torthorowald he Barron was and Lord,
Off kyn he was, and Wallace modyr ner ;"—&c.

Bk. V. v. 920.

But this Baron seems to have had no share in the adventures of King Robert; the crest of his family, as it still remains on a carved stone built into a cottage wall, in the village of Torthorwald, bears some resemblance, says Grose, to a rose.

'Universal tradition, and all our later historians, have attributed the regent's deathblow to Sir Roger K. of Closeburn. The author of the MS. History of the Presbytery of Penpont, in the Advocates' Library, affirms, that the crest and motto were given by the King on that occasion; and proceeds to relate some circumstances respecting a grant to a cottager and his wife in the vicinity of Closeburn Castle, which are certainly authentic, and strongly vouch for the truth of the other report.—"The steep hill," (says he,) "called the Dune of Tynron, of a considerable height, upon the top of which there hath been some habitation or fort. There have been in ancient times, on all hands of it, very thick woods, and great about that place, which made it the more inaccessible, into which K. Ro. Bruce is said to have been conducted by Roger Kirkpatrick of Closeburn, after they had killed the Cumin at Dumfriess, which is nine miles from this place, whereabout it is probable that he did abide for some time thereafter; and it is reported, that during his abode there, he did often divert to a poor man's cottage, named Brownrig, situate in a small parcel of stoney ground, encompassed with thick woods, where he was content sometimes with such mean accommodation as the place could afford. The poor man's wife being advised to petition the King for somewhat, was so modest in her desires, that she sought no more but security for the croft in her husband's possession, and a liberty of pasturage for a very few cattle of different kinds on the hill, and the rest of the bounds. Of which priviledge that ancient family, by the injury of time, hath a long time been, and is, deprived: but the croft continues in the possession of the heirs and successours lineally descended of this Brownrig and his wife; so that this family, being more ancient than rich, doth yet continue in the name, and, as they say, retains the old charter."—*MS. History of the Presbytery of Penpont, in the Advocates' Library of Edinburgh.'*

NOTE XIX.

Barendown fled fast away,
Fled the fiery De la Haye.—P. 423.

These knights are enumerated by Barbour among the small number of Bruce's adherents, who remained in arms with him after the battle of Methven.

'With him was a bold baron,
Schyr William the Baroundoun,
.
Schyr Gilbert de la Haye alsua.'

There were more than one of the noble family of Hay engaged in Bruce's cause; but the principal was Gilbert de la Haye, Lord of Errol, a stanch adherent to King Robert's interest, and whom he rewarded by creating him hereditary Lord High Constable of Scotland, a title which he used 16th March, 1308, where, in a letter from the peers of Scotland to Philip the Fair of France, he is designed *Gilbertus de Hay Constabularius Scotiae.* He was slain at the battle of Halidoun-hill. Hugh de la Haye, his brother, was made prisoner at the battle of Methven.

NOTE XX.

Well hast thou framed, Old Man, thy
     strains,
To praise the hand that pays thy pains.
                              —P. 423.

The character of the Highland bards, however high in an earlier period of society, seems soon to have degenerated. The Irish affirm, that in their kindred tribes severe laws became necessary to restrain their avarice. In the Highlands they seem gradually to have sunk into contempt, as well as the orators, or men of speech, with whose office that of family poet was often united.—'The orators, in their language called Isdane, were in high esteem both in these islands and the continent; until within these forty years, they sat always among the nobles and chiefs of families in the streah, or circle. Their houses and little villages were sanctuaries, as well as churches, and they took place before doctors of physick. The orators, after the Druids were extinct, were brought in to preserve the genealogy of families, and to repeat the same at every succession of chiefs; and upon the occasion of marriages and births, they made epithalamiums and panegyricks, which the poet or bard pronounced. The orators, by the force of their eloquence, had a powerful ascendant over the greatest men in their time; for if any orator did but ask the habit, arms, horse, or any other thing belonging to the greatest man in these islands, it was readily granted them, sometimes out of respect, and sometimes for fear of being exclaimed against by a satyre, which, in those days, was reckoned a great dishonour. But these gentlemen becoming insolent, lost ever since both the profit and esteem which was formerly due to their character; for neither their panegyricks nor satyres are regarded to what they have been, and they are now allowed but a small salary. I must not omit to relate their way of study, which is very singular: They shut their doors and windows for a day's time, and lie on their backs, with a stone upon their belly, and plads about their heads, and their eyes being covered, they pump their brains for rhetorical encomium or panegyrick; and indeed they furnish such a style from this dark cell as is understood by very few; and if they purchase a couple of horses as the reward of their meditation, they think they have done a great matter. The poet, or bard, had a title to the bridegroom's upper garb, that is, the plad and bonnet; but now he is satisfied with what the bridegroom pleases to give him on such occasions.'— MARTIN'S *Western Isles.*

NOTE XXI.

Was't not enough to Ronald's bower
I brought thee, like a paramour.—P. 426.
It was anciently customary in the Highlands to bring the bride to the house of the

husband. Nay, in some cases the complaisance was stretched so far, that she remained there upon trial for a twelvemonth; and the bridegroom, even after this period of cohabitation, retained an option of refusing to fulfil his engagement. It is said that a desperate feud ensued between the clans of Mac-Donald of Sleate and Mac-Leod, owing to the former chief having availed himself of this license to send back to Dunvegan a sister, or daughter of the latter. Mac-Leod, resenting the indignity, observed, that since there was no wedding bonfire, there should be one to solemnize the divorce. Accordingly, he burned and laid waste the territories of Mac-Donald, who retaliated, and a deadly feud, with all its accompaniments, took place in form.

Note XXII.

*Since matchless Wallace first had been
In mock'ry crown'd with wreaths of green.*
— P. 426.

Stow gives the following curious account of the trial and execution of this celebrated patriot:—'William Wallace, who had oft-times set Scotland in great trouble, was taken and brought to London, with great numbers of men and women wondering upon him. He was lodged in the house of William Delect, a citizen of London, in Fenchurch-street. On the morrow, being the eve of St. Bartholomew, he was brought on horseback to Westminster. John Legrave and Geffrey, knights, the mayor, sheriffs, and aldermen of London, and many others, both on horseback and on foot, accompanying him; and in the great hall at Westminster, he being placed on the south bench, crowned with laurel, for that he had said in times past that he ought to bear a crown in that hall, as it was commonly reported; and being appeached for a traitor by Sir Peter Malorie, the king's justice, he answered, that he was never traitor to the King of England; but for other things whereof he was accused, he confessed them; and was after headed and quartered.'—Stow, *Chr.* p. 209. There is something singularly doubtful about the mode in which Wallace was taken. That he was betrayed to the English is indubitable; and popular fame charges Sir John Menteith with the indelible infamy. 'Accursed,' says Arnold Blair, 'be the day of nativity of John de Menteith, and may his name be struck out of the book of life.' But John de Menteith was all along a zealous favourer of the English interest, and was governor of Dumbarton Castle by commission from Edward the First; and therefore, as the accurate Lord Hailes has observed, could not be the friend and confidant of Wallace, as tradition states him to be. The truth seems to be, that Menteith, thoroughly engaged in the English interest, pursued Wallace closely, and made him prisoner through the treachery of an attendant, whom Peter Langtoft calls Jack Short.

' William Waleis is nomen that master was of theves,
Tiding to the king is comen that robbery mischeives,
Sir John of Menetest sued William so nigh,
He tok him when he ween'd least, on night, his
   leman him by,
That was through treason of *Jack Short* his man,
He was the encheson that Sir John so him ran,
Jack's brother had he s'ain, the Walleis that is said,
The more Jack was fain to do William that braid.'

From this it would appear that the infamy of seizing Wallace, must rest between a degenerate Scottish nobleman, the vassal of England, and a domestic, the obscure agent of his treachery; between Sir John Menteith, son of Walter, Earl of Menteith, and the traitor Jack Short.

Note XXIII.

*Where's Nigel Bruce? and De la Haye,
And valiant Seton—where are they?
Where Somerville, the kind and free?
And Fraser, flower of chivalry?*
— P. 426.

When these lines were written, the author was remote from the means of correcting his indistinct recollection concerning the individual fate of Bruce's followers, after the battle of Methven. Hugh de la Haye, and Thomas Somerville of Lintoun and Cowdaly, ancestor of Lord Somerville, were both made prisoners at that defeat, but neither was executed.

Sir Nigel Bruce was the younger brother of Robert, to whom he committed the charge of his wife and daughter, Marjorie, and the defence of his strong castle of Kildrummie, near the head of the Don, in Aberdeenshire. Kildrummie long resisted the arms of the Earls of Lancaster and Hereford, until the magazine was treacherously burnt. The garrison was then compelled to surrender at discretion, and Nigel Bruce, a youth remarkable for personal beauty, as well as for gallantry, fell into the hands of the unrelenting Edward. He was tried by a special commission at Berwick, was condemned, and executed.

Christopher Seatoun shared the same unfortunate fate. He also was distinguished by personal valour, and signalized himself in the fatal battle of Methven. Robert Bruce adventured his person in that battle like a knight of romance. He dismounted Aymer de Valence, Earl of Pembroke, but was in his turn dismounted by Sir Philip Mowbray. In this emergence Seatoun came to his aid, and remounted him. Langtoft mentions, that in this battle the Scottish wore white surplices, or shirts, over their armour, that those of rank might not be known. In this manner both Bruce and Seatoun escaped.

But the latter was afterwards betrayed to the English, through means, according to Barbour, of one MacNab, 'a disciple of Judas,' in whom the unfortunate knight reposed entire confidence. There was some peculiarity respecting his punishment; because, according to Matthew of Westminster, he was considered not as a Scottish subject, but an Englishman. He was therefore taken to Dumfries, where he was tried, condemned, and executed, for the murder of a soldier slain by him. His brother, John de Seton, had the same fate at Newcastle; both were considered as accomplices in the slaughter of Comyn, but in what manner they were particularly accessory to that deed does not appear.

The fate of Sir Simon Frazer, or Frizel, ancestor of the family of Lovat, is dwelt upon at great length, and with savage exultation, by the English historians. This knight, who was renowned for personal gallantry, and high deeds of chivalry, was also made prisoner, after a gallant defence, in the battle of Methven. Some stanzas of a ballad of the times, which, for the sake of rendering it intelligible, I have translated out of its rude orthography, give minute particulars of his fate. It was written immediately at the period, for it mentions the Earl of Athole as not yet in custody. It was first published by the indefatigable Mr. Ritson, but with so many contractions and peculiarities of character, as to render it illegible, excepting by antiquaries.

'This was before Saint Bartholomew's mass,
That Frizel was y-taken, were it more other less,
To Sir Thomas of Multon, gentil baron and free,
And to Sir Johan Jose be-take tho was he
            To hand
    He was y-fettered wele
    Both with iron and with steel
        To bringen of Scotland.

Soon thereafter the tiding to the king come,
He sent him to London, with mony armed groom,
He came in at Newgate, I tell you it on a-plight,
A garland of leaves on his head y-dight
            Of green,
    For he should be y-know,
    Both of high and of low,
        For traitour I ween.

Y-fettered were his legs under his horse's wombe,
Both with iron and with steel maucled were his hond,
A garland of pervynk [1] set upon his heved [2],
Much was the power that him was bereved,
            In land.
    So God me amend,
    Little he ween'd
        So to be brought in hand

This was upon our lady's even, forsooth I understand,
The justices sate for the knights of Scotland,
Sir Thomas of Multon, an kinde knyght and wise,
And Sir Ralph of Sandwich that mickle is told in price,
            And Sir Johan Abel,
    Moe I might tell by tale
    Both of great and of small
        Ye know sooth well.

[1] Periwinkle.   [2] Head.

Then said the justice, that gentil is and free,
Sir Simon Frizel the king's traiter hast thou be;
In water and in land that mony mighten see,
What sayst thou thereto, how will thou quite thee,
            Do say.
    So foul he him wist,
    Nede war on trust
        For to say nay.

With fetters and with gives [1] y-hot he was to-draw
From the Tower of London that many men might know,
In a kirtle of burel, a selcouth wise,
And a garland on his head of the new guise,
            Through Cheape
    Many men of England
    For to see Symond
        Thitherward can leap.

Though he cam to the gallows first he was on hung,
All quick beheaded that him thought long;
Then he was y-opened, his bowels y brend [2],
The heved to London-bridge was send
            To shende.
    So evermore mote I the,
    Some while weened he
        Thus little to stand

He rideth through the city, as I tell may,
With gamen and with solace that was their play,
To London-bridge he took the way,
Mony was the wives child that thereon lacketh a day [3],
            And said, alas!
    That he was y-born
    And so vilely forelorn,
        So fair man he was.

Now standeth the heved above the tu-brigge,
Fast by Wallace sooth for to segge;
After succour of Scotland long may he pry,
And after help of France what halt it to lie,
            I ween,
    Better him were in Scotland,
    With his axe in his hand,
        To play on the green,' &c.

The preceding stanzas contain probably as minute an account as can be found of the trial and execution of state criminals of the period. Superstition mingled its horrors with those of a ferocious state policy, as appears from the following singular narrative:—

'The Friday next, before the assumption of Our Lady, King Edward met Robert the Bruce at Saint Johnstoune, in Scotland, and with his company, of which company King Edward quelde seven thousand. When Robert the Bruce saw this mischief, and gan to flee, and hov'd in that place that men might not him find; but S. Simond Frisell pursued was so sore, so that he turned again and abode bataille, for he was a worthy knight and a bolde of bodye, and the Englishmen pursuede him sore on every side, and quelde the steed that Sir Simon Frisell rode upon, and then toke him and led him to the host. And S. Symond began for to flatter and speke fair, and saide, Lordys, I shall give you four thousand markes of silver, and myne horse and harness, and all my armoure and income. Tho' answered Thobaude of Pevenes, that was the kinges archer, Now, God me so

[1] Gyves.   [2] Burnt.   [3] Lamenteth.

helpe, it is for nought that thou speakest, for all the gold of England I would not let thee go without commandment of King Edward. And tho' he was led to the King, and the King would not see him, but commanded to lead him away to his doom in London, on Our Lady's even nativity. And he was hung and drawn, and his head smitten off, and hanged again with chains of iron upon the gallows, and his head was set at London-bridge upon a spear, and against Christmas the body was burnt, for encheson (*reason*) that the men that keeped the body saw many devils ramping with iron crooks, running upon the gallows, and horribly tormenting the body. And many that them saw, anon thereafter died for dread, or waxen mad, or sore sickness they had.'—*MS. Chronicle in the British Museum, quoted by Ritson.*

NOTE XXIV.

Was not the life of Athole shed
To soothe the tyrant's sicken'd bed?
—P. 427.

John de Strathbogie, Earl of Athole, had attempted to escape out of the kingdom, but a storm cast him upon the coast, when he was taken, sent to London, and executed, with circumstances of great barbarity, being first half strangled, then let down from the gallows while yet alive, barbarously dismembered, and his body burnt. It may surprise the reader to learn, that this was a *mitigated* punishment; for in respect that his mother was a grand-daughter of King John, by his natural son Richard, he was not drawn on a sledge to execution, 'that point was forgiven,' and he made the passage on horseback. Matthew of Westminster tells us that King Edward, then extremely ill, received great ease from the news that his relative was apprehended. '*Quo audito, Rex Angliae, etsi gravissimo morbo tunc langueret, levius tamen tulit dolorem.*' To this singular expression the text alludes.

NOTE XXV.

And must his word, till dying day,
Be nought but quarter, hang, and slay!
—P. 427.

This alludes to a passage in Barbour, singularly expressive of the vindictive spirit of Edward I. The prisoners taken at the castle of Kildrummie had surrendered upon condition that they should be at King Edward's disposal. 'But his will,' says Barbour, 'was always evil towards Scottishmen.' The news of the surrender of Kildrummie arrived when he was in his mortal sickness at Burgh-upon-Sands.

'And when he to the death was near,
The folk that at Kyldromy wer
Come with prisoners that they had tane,
And syne to the king are gane.
And for to comfort him they tauld
How they the castell to them yauld;
And how they till his will were brought,
To do off that whatever he thought;
And ask'd what men should off them do.
Then look'd he angryly them to,
He said, grinning, "HANGS AND DRAWS."
That was wonder of sic saws,
That he, that to the death was near,
Should answer upon sic maner,
Forouten moaning and mercy;
How might he trust on him to cry,
That sooth-fastly dooms all thing
To have mercy for his crying,
Off him that, throw his felony,
Into sic point had no mercy?'

There was much truth in the Leonine couplet, with which Matthew of Westminster concludes his encomium on the first Edward:—

'Scotos Edwardus, dum vixit, suppeditavit,
Tenuit, afflixit, depressit, dilaniavit.'

NOTE XXVI.

While I the blessed cross advance,
And expiate this unhappy chance
In Palestine, with sword and lance.
—P. 428.

Bruce uniformly professed, and probably felt, compunction for having violated the sanctuary of the church by the slaughter of Comyn; and finally, in his last hours, in testimony of his faith, penitence, and zeal, he requested James Lord Douglas to carry his heart to Jerusalem, to be there deposited in the Holy Sepulchre.

NOTE XXVII.

De Bruce! I rose with purpose dread
To speak my curse upon thy head.
—P. 428.

So soon as the notice of Comyn's slaughter reached Rome, Bruce and his adherents were excommunicated. It was published first by the Archbishop of York, and renewed at different times, particularly by Lambyrton, Bishop of St. Andrews, in 1308; but it does not appear to have answered the purpose which the English monarch expected. Indeed, for reasons which it may be difficult to trace, the thunders of Rome descended upon the Scottish mountains with less effect than in more fertile countries. Probably the comparative poverty of the benefices occasioned that fewer foreign clergy settled in Scotland; and the interest of the native churchmen were linked with that of their country. Many of the Scottish prelates, Lambyrton the primate particularly, declared for Bruce, while he was yet under the ban of the church, although he afterwards again changed sides.

NOTE XXVIII.

I feel within mine aged breast
A power that will not be repress'd.
　　　　　　—P. 428.

Bruce, like other heroes, observed omens, and one is recorded by tradition. After he had retreated to one of the miserable places of shelter, in which he could venture to take some repose after his disasters, he lay stretched upon a handful of straw, and abandoned himself to his melancholy meditations. He had now been defeated four times, and was upon the point of resolving to abandon all hopes of further opposition to his fate, and to go to the Holy Land. It chanced, his eye, while he was thus pondering, was attracted by the exertions of a spider, who, in order to fix his web, endeavoured to swing himself from one beam to another above his head. Involuntarily he became interested in the pertinacity with which the insect renewed his exertions, after failing six times; and it occurred to him that he would decide his own course according to the success or failure of the spider. At the seventh effort the insect gained his object; and Bruce, in like manner, persevered and carried his own. Hence it has been held unlucky or ungrateful, or both, in one of the name of Bruce to kill a spider.

The Archdeacon of Aberdeen, instead of the abbot of this tale, introduces an Irish Pythoness, who not only predicted his good fortune as he left the island of Rachrin, but sent her two sons along with him, to ensure her own family a share in it.

'Then in schort time men mycht thaim se
Schute all thair galayis to the se,
And ber to se baith ayr and ster.
And othyr thingis that mystir[1] wer.
And as the king apon the sand
Wes gangand wp and doun, bidand[2]
Till that his menye redy war,
His ost come rycht till him thar.
And quhen that scho him halyst had,
And priwé spek till him scho made;
And said, "Takis gud kep till my saw:
For or ye pass I sall yow schaw,
Off your forioun a gret party.
Bot our all speceally
A wyttring her I sall yow ma,
Quhat end that your purposs sall ta.
For in this land is nane trewly
Wate thingis to cum sa weill as I.
Ye pass now furth on your wiage,
To wenge the harme, and the owtrag,
That Ingliss men has to yow done;
Bot ye wat nocht quhatkyne forton
Ye mon drey in your werraying.
Bot wyt ye weill, with outyn lesing,
That fra ye now haiff takyn land,
Nane sa mychty, na sa strenth thi of hand,
Sall ger yow pass owt of your countré
Till all to yow abandownyt be.
With in schort tyme ye sall be king,
And haiff the land at your liking,
And ourcum your fayis all.
Bot fele anoyis thole ye sall,

---

[1] Needful.　　　[2] Biding, waiting.

Or that your purposs end haiff tane:
Bot ye sall thaim ourdryve ilkane.
And, that ye trow this sekerly,
My twa sonnys with yow sall I
Send to tak part of your trawaill;
For I wate weill thai sall nocht faill
To be rewardyt weill at rycht,
Quhen ye ar heyit to yowr mycht." '
　　　BARBOUR'S *Bruce*, Book III. v. 856.

NOTE XXIX.

A hunted wanderer on the wild,
On foreign shores a man exil'd.
　　　　　　—P. 428.

This is not metaphorical. The echoes of Scotland did actually

　　　　　　—'ring
With the bloodhounds that bayed for her fugitive
king.'

A very curious and romantic tale is told by Barbour upon this subject, which may be abridged as follows:—

When Bruce had again got footing in Scotland in the spring of 1307, he continued to be in a very weak and precarious condition, gaining, indeed, occasional advantages, but obliged to fly before his enemies whenever they assembled in force. Upon one occasion, while he was lying with a small party in the wilds of Cumnock, in Avrshire, Aymer de Valence, Earl of Pembroke, with his inveterate foe John of Lorn, came against him suddenly with eight hundred Highlanders, besides a large body of men-at-arms. They brought with them a slough-dog, or bloodhound, which, some say, had been once a favourite with the Bruce himself, and therefore was least likely to lose the trace.

Bruce, whose force was under four hundred men, continued to make head against the cavalry, till the men of Lorn had nearly cut off his retreat. Perceiving the danger of his situation, he acted as the celebrated and ill-requited Mina is said to have done in similar circumstances. He divided his force into three parts, appointed a place of rendezvous, and commanded them to retreat by different routes. But when John of Lorn arrived at the spot where they divided, he caused the hound to be put upon the trace, which immediately directed him to the pursuit of that party which Bruce headed. This, therefore, Lorn pursued with his whole force, paying no attention to the others. The king again subdivided his small body into three parts, and with the same result, for the pursuers attached themselves exclusively to that which he led in person. He then caused his followers to disperse, and retained only his foster-brother in his company. The slough-dog followed the trace, and, neglecting the others, attached himself and his attendants to the pursuit of the king. Lorn became convinced that his enemy was nearly in his power, and detached five of his most active attendants to follow him, and interrupt his flight. They did so with all the agility of mountaineers. 'What aid wilt thou make?' said Bruce to his single attendant, when he saw the five men gain ground on him. 'The best I can,' replied his foster-brother. 'Then,' said Bruce, 'here I make my stand.' The five pursuers came up fast. The king took three to himself, leaving the other two to his foster-brother. He slew the first whom he encountered him; but observing his foster-brother hard pressed, he sprung to his assistance, and despatched one of his assailants. Leaving him to deal with the survivor, he returned upon the other two, both of whom he slew before his foster-brother had despatched his single antagonist. When this hard encounter was over, with a courtesy, which in the whole work marks Bruce's character, he thanked his foster-brother for his aid. 'It likes you to say so,' answered his follower; 'but you yourself slew four of the five.'—'True,' said the king, 'but only because I had better opportunity than you. They were not apprehensive of me when they saw me encounter three, so I had a moment's time to spring to thy aid, and to return equally unexpectedly upon my own opponents.'

In the meanwhile Lorn's party approached rapidly, and the king and his foster-brother betook themselves to a neighbouring wood. Here they sat down, for Bruce was exhausted by fatigue, until the cry of the slough-hound came so near, that his foster-brother entreated Bruce to provide for his safety by retreating further. 'I have heard,' answered the king, 'that whosoever will wade a bow-shot length down a running stream, shall make the slough-hound lose scent.—Let us try the experiment, for were yon devilish hound silenced, I should care little for the rest.'

Lorn in the meanwhile advanced, and found the bodies of his slain vassals, over whom he made his moan, and threatened the most deadly vengeance. Then he followed the hound to the side of the brook, down which the king had waded a great way. Here the hound was at fault, and John of Lorn, after long attempting in vain to recover Bruce's trace, relinquished the pursuit.

'Others,' says Barbour, 'affirm, that upon this occasion the king's life was saved by an excellent archer who accompanied him, and who perceiving they would be finally taken by means of the bloodhound, hid himself in a thicket, and shot him with an arrow. In which way,' adds the metrical biographer, 'this escape happened I am uncertain, but at that brook the king escaped from his pursuers.'

' Quhen the chasseris relyit war,
And Jhon of Lorn had met thaim thar,
He tauld Schyr Aymer all the cass,
How that the king eschapyt wass;
And how that he his five men slew,
And syne to the wode him drew.
Quhen Schyr Aymer herd this, in hy
He sanyt him for the ferly :

And said ; " He is gretly to pryss ;
For I knaw nane that liffand is,
That at myscheyff gan help him swa.
I trow he suld be hard to sla,
And he war bodyn 1 ewynly."
On this wiss spak Schyr Aymery.'
BARBOUR'S *Bruce*, Book V. v. 391.

The English historians agree with Barbour as to the mode in which the English pursued Bruce and his followers, and the dexterity with which he evaded them. The following is the testimony of Harding, a great enemy to the Scottish nation :—

' The King Edward with hoost hym sought full sore,
But ay he fled into woodes and strayte forest,
And slewe his men at staytes and daungers thore,
And at marreys and mires was ay full prest
Englyshmen to kyll withoutyn any rest ;
In the mountaynes and cragges he slew ay where,
And in the nyght his foes he frayed full sere :

The King Edward with hornes and houndes him soght,
With menne on fote, through marris, mosse, and myre,
Through wodes also, and mountens (wher thei fought),
And euer the Kyng Edward hight men greate hyre,
Hym for to take and by myght conquere ;
But thei might hym not gette by force ne by train,
He satte by the fyre when thei went in the rain.'
HARDYNG'S *Chronicle*, pp. 303-4.

Peter Langtoft has also a passage concerning the extremities to which King Robert was reduced, which he entitles

De Roberto Brus et fuga circum circa fit.

' And wele I understode that the Kyng Robyn
Has drunken of that blode the drink of Dan Waryn.
Dan Waryn he les tounes that he held,
With wrong he mad a res, and misberyng of scheld,
Sithen into the forest he yede naked and wode,
Als a wild beast, ete of the gras that stode,
Thus of Dan Waryn in his boke men rede,
God gyf the King Robyn, that alle his kynde so spede,
Sir Robynet the Brus he durst noure abide,
That thei mad him restus, both in more and wodside,
To while he mad this train, and did umwhile outrage, &c.
PETER LANGTOFT'S *Chronicle*, vol. ii. 335.
8vo. London, 1810.

NOTE XXX.

For, glad of each pretext for spoil,
A pirate sworn was Cormac Doil.
—P. 430.

A sort of persons common in the isles, as may be easily believed, until the introduction of civil polity. Witness the Dean of the Isles' account of Ronay. 'At the north end of Raarsay, be half myle of sea frae it, layes ane ile callit Ronay, maire then a myle in lengthe, full of wood and heddir, with ane havein for heiland galeys in the middis of it, and the same havein is guid for fostering of

---

1 Matched.

theives, ruggairs, and reivairs, till a nail, upon the peilling and spulzeing of poor pepill. This ile perteins to M'Gillychallan of Raarsay by force, and to the bishope of the iles be heritage.'—SIR DONALD MUNRO'S *Description of the Western Islands of Scotland.* Edinburgh, 1805, p. 22.

NOTE XXXI.

'Alas! dear youth, the unhappy time,'
Answer'd the Bruce, 'must bear the crime,
Since, guiltier far than you,
Even I'—he paused; for Falkirk's woes
Upon his conscious soul arose.—P. 431.

I have followed the vulgar and inaccurate tradition, that Bruce fought against Wallace, and the array of Scotland, at the fatal battle of Falkirk. The story, which seems to have no better authority than that of Blind Harry, bears, that having made much slaughter during the engagement, he sat down to dine with the conquerors without washing the filthy witness from his hands.

'Fasting he was, and had been in great need,
Blooded were all his weapons and his weed;
Southeron lords scorn'd him in terms rude,
And said, Behold yon Scot eats his own blood.

Then rued he sore, for reason bad be known,
That blood and land alike should be his own;
With them he long was, ere he got away,
But contrair Scots he fought not from that day.'

The account given by most of our historians, of the conversation between Bruce and Wallace over the Carron river, is equally apocryphal. There is full evidence that Bruce was not at that time on the English side, nor present at the battle of Falkirk: nay, that he acted as a guardian of Scotland, along with John Comyn, in the name of Baliol, and in opposition to the English. He was the grandson of the competitor, with whom he has been sometimes confounded. Lord Hailes has well described, and in some degree apologized for, the earlier part of his life.—'His grandfather, the competitor, had patiently acquiesced in the award of Edward. His father, yielding to the times, had served under the English banners. But young Bruce had more ambition, and a more restless spirit. In his earlier years he acted upon no regular plan. By turns the partisan of Edward, and the vicegerent of Baliol, he seems to have forgotten or stifled his pretensions to the crown. But his character developed itself by degrees, and in maturer age became firm and consistent.'—*Annals of Scotland*, p. 290, quarto, London, 1776.

NOTE XXXII.

These are the savage wilds that lie
North of Strathnardill and Dunskye.
　　　　—P. 432.

The extraordinary piece of scenery which I have here attempted to describe is, I think,

unparalleled in any part of Scotland, at least in any which I have happened to visit. It lies just upon the frontier of the Laird of Mac-Leod's country, which is thereabouts divided from the estate of Mr. Maccallister of Strath-Aird, called Strathnardill by the Dean of the Isles. The following account of it is extracted from a journal kept during a tour through the Scottish islands:—

'The western coast of Sky is highly romantic, and at the same time displays a richness of vegetation in the lower grounds to which we have hitherto been strangers. We passed three salt-water lochs, or deep embayments, called Loch Bracadale, Loch Einort, and Loch ——, and about 11 o'clock opened Loch Slavig. We were now under the western termination of the high ridge of mountains called Cuillen, or Quillin, or Coolin, whose weather-beaten and serrated peaks we had admired at a distance from Dunvegan. They sunk here upon the sea, but with the same bold and peremptory aspect which their distant appearance indicated. They appeared to consist of precipitous sheets of naked rock, down which the torrents were leaping in a hundred lines of foam. The tops of the ridge, apparently inaccessible to human foot, were rent and split into the most tremendous pinnacles. Towards the base of these bare and precipitous crags the ground, enriched by the soil washed down from them, is comparatively verdant and productive. Where we passed within the small isle of Soa, we entered Loch Slavig, under the shoulder of one of these grisly mountains, and observed that the opposite side of the loch was of a milder character, the mountains being softened down into steep green declivities. From the bottom of the bay advanced a headland of high rocks, which divided its depth into two recesses, from each of which a brook issued. Here it had been intimated to us we would find some romantic scenery; but we were uncertain up which inlet we should proceed in search of it. We chose, against our better judgment, the southerly dip of the bay, where we saw a house which might afford us information. We found, upon inquiry, that there is a lake adjoining to each branch of the bay; and walked a couple of miles to see that near the farm-house, merely because the honest Highlander seemed jealous of the honour of his own loch, though we were speedily convinced it was not that which we were recommended to examine. It had no particular merit, excepting from its neighbourhood to a very high cliff, or precipitous mountain, otherwise the sheet of water had nothing differing from any ordinary low-country lake. We returned and re-embarked in our boat, for our guide shook his head at our proposal to climb over the peninsula, or rocky headland which divided the two lakes.

---

[1] This is the Poet's own journal.—LOCKHART.

In rowing round the headland, we were surprised at the infinite number of sea-fowl, then busy apparently with a shoal of fish.

'Arrived at the depth of the bay, we found that the discharge from this second lake forms a sort of waterfall, or rather a rapid stream, which rushes down to the sea with great fury and precipitation. Round this place were assembled hundreds of trouts and salmon, struggling to get up into the fresh water: with a net we might have had twenty salmon at a haul; and a sailor, with no better hook than a crooked pin, caught a dish of trouts during our absence. Advancing up this huddling and riotous brook, we found ourselves in a most extraordinary scene; we lost sight of the sea almost immediately after we had climbed over a low ridge of crags, and were surrounded by mountains of naked rock, of the boldest and most precipitous character. The ground on which we walked was the margin of a lake, which seemed to have sustained the constant ravage of torrents from these rude neighbours. The shores consisted of huge strata of naked granite, here and there intermixed with bogs, and heaps of gravel and sand piled in the empty water-courses. Vegetation there was little or none; and the mountains rose so perpendicularly from the water edge, that Borrowdale, or even Glencoe, is a jest to them. We proceeded a mile and a half up this deep, dark, and solitary lake, which was about two miles long, half a mile broad, and is, as we learned, of extreme depth. The murky vapours which enveloped the mountain ridges, obliged us by assuming a thousand varied shapes, changing their drapery into all sorts of forms, and sometimes clearing off all together. It is true, the mist made us pay the penalty by some heavy and downright showers, from the frequency of which a Highland boy, whom we brought from the farm, told us the lake was popularly called the Water-kettle. The proper name is Loch Corriskin, from the deep corrie, or hollow, in the mountains of Cuilin, which affords the basin for this wonderful sheet of water. It is as exquisite a savage scene as Loch Katrine is a scene of romantic beauty. After having penetrated so far as distinctly to observe the termination of the lake under an immense precipice, which rises abruptly from the water, we returned, and often stopped to admire the ravages which storms must have made in these recesses, where all human witnesses were driven to places of more shelter and security. Stones, or rather large masses and fragments of rocks of a composite kind, perfectly different from the strata of the lake, were scattered upon the bare rocky beach, in the strangest and most precarious situations, as if abandoned by the torrents which had borne them down from above. Some lay loose and tottering upon the ledges of the natural rock, with so little security, that the slightest push moved them, though their weight might exceed many tons. These detached rocks, or stones, were chiefly what is called plum-pudding stones. The bare rocks, which formed the shore of the lakes, were a species of granite. The opposite side of the lake seemed quite pathless and inaccessible, as a huge mountain, one of the detached ridges of the Cuilin hills, sinks in a profound and perpendicular precipice down to the water. On the left-hand side, which we traversed, rose a higher and equally inaccessible mountain, the top of which strongly resembled the shivered crater of an exhausted volcano. I never saw a spot in which there was less appearance of vegetation of any kind. The eye rested on nothing but barren and naked crags, and the rocks on which we walked by the side of the loch were as bare as the pavements of Cheapside. There are one or two small islets in the loch which seem to bear juniper, or some such low bushy shrub. Upon the whole, though I have seen many scenes of more extensive desolation, I never witnessed any in which it pressed more deeply upon the eye and the heart than at Loch Corriskin; at the same time that its grandeur elevated and redeemed it from the wild and dreary character of utter barrenness.'

Note XXXIII.

Men were they all of evil mien,
Down-look'd, unwilling to be seen.—P. 434.

The story of Bruce's meeting the banditti is copied, with such alterations as the fictitious narrative rendered necessary, from a striking incident in the monarch's history, told by Barbour, and which I shall give in the words of the hero's biographer. It is the sequel to the adventure of the bloodhound, narrated in Note XXIX. It will be remembered that the narrative broke off, leaving the Bruce escaped from his pursuers, but worn out with fatigue, and having no other attendant but his foster-brother.

'And the gude king held forth his way,
Betuix him and his man, quhill thai
Passyt owt throw the forest war ;
Syne in the more thai entryt thar.
It wes bathe hey, and lang, and breid ;
And or thai hailf it passyt had,
Thai saw on syd thre men cummand,
Lik to lycht men and wauerand.
Swerdis thai had, and axys als ;
And ane off thaim, apon his hals 1,
A mekill boundyn wethir bar.
Thai met the king, and hailst 2 him thar :
And the king thaim thar hailsing yauld 3 ;
And askyt thaim quethir thai wauld.
Thai said, Robert the Bruyss thai soucht
For mete with him giff that thai moucht,
Thar duelling with him wauld thai ma 4.
The king said, " Giff that ye will swa,
Haldys furth your way with me,
And I sall ger yow sone him se.

---

1 Neck, shoulders.   2 Hailed.
3 Yielded, returned.   4 Make.

Thai persawyt, be his speking,
That he wes the selwyn Robert king.
And chaungyt contenance and late [1];
And held nocht in the fyrst state.
For thai war fayis to the king;—
And thoucht to cum in to sculking,
And duell wth him, quhill that thai saw
Thar povnt, and bryng him than off daw.
Thai grantyt till his spek forthi [2].
Bot the king, that wes witty,
Persawyt weill, by thar hawing,
That thai luffyt him na thing :
And said, "Falowis, ye mon, all thre,
Forthir aqwent till that we be,
All be your selwyn furth ga ;
And, on the samyn wyss, we twa
Sall folow behind weill ner."
Quoth thai, "Schyr, it is na myster [3]
To trow in ws ony ill. —
"Nane do I, said he ; "bot I will,
That yhe ga fourth thus, quhill we
Better with othyr knawin be."—
"We grant, thai said, "sen ye will swa :"
And furth apon thair gate gan ga.
Thus yeid thai till the nycht wes ner,
And than the fornast cummyn wer
Til a waist housband houss : and thar
Thai slew the wethir that thai bar :
And slew fyr for to rost thar mete ;
And askyt the king giff he wald ete,
And rest him till the mete war dycht.
The king, that hungry was, Ik hycht,
Assentyt till thair spek in hy.
Bot he said, he wald anerry
At a fyr ; and that all thre
On na wyss with thaim till gyddre be.
In the end off the houss thai suld ma
Ane othyr fyr ; and thai did swa.
Thai drew thaim in the houss end,
And halff the wethir till him send.
And thai rostyt in hy thair mete ;
And fell rycht freschly for till ete.
For the king weill lang fastyt had ;
And had rycht mekill trawaill mad :
Tharfor he eyt full egrely.
And quhen he had etyn hastily,
He had to slep sa mekill will,
That he moucht set na let thar till.
For quhen the wanys [4] fillyt ar,
Men worthys [5] hewy euirmar ;
And to slepe drawys hewynes.
The king, that all fortrawaillyt [6] wes,
Saw that him worthyt slep nedwayis.
Till his fostyr-brodyr he sayis ;
"May I traist in the, me to waik,
Till Ik a little sleping tak?"—
"Ya, Schyr, he said, "till I may drey [7].'
The king then wynkyt a litill wey ;
And slepyt nocht full encrely ;
Bot gliffnyt wp oft sodanly.
For he had dreid off thai thre men,
That at the tothyr fyr war then.
That thai his fais war he wyst ;
Tharfor he slepyt as foule on twyst [8]
The king slepyt bot a litill than ;
Quhen sic slep fell on his man,
That he mycht nocht hald wp his ey,
Bot fell in slep, and rowtyt hey.
Now is the king in gret perile :
For slep he swa a litill quhile,
He sall be ded, for owtyn dreid.
For the thre tratours tuk gud heid,
That he on slep wes, and his man.
In full gret hy thai raiss wp than,
And drew the suerdis hastily ;
And went towart the king in hy,
Quhen that thai saw him sleip swa,
And slepand thoucht thei wald him sla.

The king wp blenkit hastily,
And saw his man slepand him by ;
And saw cummand the tothyr thre.
Deliuerly on fute gat he ;
And drew his suerd owt, and thaim mete.
And, as he yude, his fute he set
Apon his man, weill hewyly.
He waknyt, and raiss disily :
For the slep maistryt hym sway,
That or he gat wp, ane off thai,
That come for to sla the king,
Gaiff hym a strak in his rysing,
Swa that he mycht help him no mar.
The king sa straitly stad [1] wes thar,
That he wes neuir yeyt sa stad.
Ne war the arnyng [2] that he had,
He had been dede, for owtyn wer.
But nocht for thi [3] on sic maner
He helpyt him, in that bargayne [4],
That thai thre tratowris he has slan,
Throw Goddis grace, and his manheid.
His fostyr-brothyr thar was dede.
Then wes he wondre will of wayn [5],
Quhen he saw him left allane.
His fostyr-brodyr menyt he ;
And waryit [6] all the tothyr thre.
And syne hys way tuk him allane,
And rycht towart his tryst [7] is gane.'

The Bruce. Book V. v. 405.

NOTE XXXIV.

And mermaid's alabaster grot,
Who bathes her limbs in sunless well,
Deep in Strathaird's enchanted cell.

—P. 437.

Imagination can hardly conceive anything more beautiful than the extraordinary grotto discovered not many years since upon the estate of Alexander Mac-Allister, Esq., of Strathaird. It has since been much and deservedly ce'ebrated, and a full account of its beauties has been published by Dr. Mac-Leay of Oban. The general impression may perhaps be gathered from the following extract from a journal, which, written under the feelings of the moment, is likely to be more accurate than any attempt to recollect the impressions then received.—'The first entrance to this celebrated cave is rude and unpromising ; but the light of the torches, with which we were provided, was soon reflected from the roof, floor, and walls, which seem as if they were sheeted with marble, partly smooth, partly rough with frost-work and rustic ornaments, and partly seeming to be wrought into statuary. The floor forms a steep and difficult ascent, and might be fancifully compared to a sheet of water, which, while it rushed whitening and foaming down a declivity, had been suddenly arrested and consolidated by the spell of an enchanter. Upon attaining the summit of this ascent, the cave opens into a splendid gallery, adorned with the most dazzling crystallizations, and finally descends with rapidity to the brink of a pool, of the most

---

1 So dangerously situated
2 Had it not been for the armour he wore.
3 Nevertheless.   4 Fray, or dispute.
5 Much afflicted.   6 Cursed.
7 The place of rendezvous appointed for his soldiers.

---

1 Manner.   2 Therefore.   3 Need.   4 Veins.
5 Become.   6 Fatigued with travel.   7 Endure.
8 Bird on bough.

limpid water, about four or five yards broad. There opens beyond this pool a portal arch, formed by two columns of white spar, with beautiful chasing upon the sides, which promises a continuation of the cave. One of our sailors swam across, for there is no other mode of passing, and informed us (as indeed we partly saw by the light he carried) that the enchantment of Maccalister's cave terminates with this portal, a little beyond which there was only a rude cavern, speedily choked with stones and earth. But the pool, on the brink of which we stood, surrounded by the most fanciful mouldings, in a substance resembling white marble, and distinguished by the depth and purity of its waters, might have been the bathing grotto of a naiad. The groups of combined figures projecting, or embossed, by which the pool is surrounded, are exquisitely elegant and fanciful. A statuary might catch beautiful hints from the singular and romantic disposition of those stalactites. There is scarce a form, or group, on which active fancy may not trace figures or grotesque ornaments, which have been gradually moulded in this cavern by the dropping of the calcareous water hardening into petrifactions. Many of those fine groups have been injured by the senseless rage of appropriation of recent tourists; and the grotto has lost (I am informed), through the smoke of torches, something of that vivid silver tint which was originally one of its chief distinctions. But enough of beauty remains to compensate for all that may be lost.'—Mr. Mac-Allister of Strathaird has, with great propriety, built up the exterior entrance to this cave, in order that strangers may enter properly attended by a guide, to prevent any repetition of the wanton and selfish injury which this singular scene has already sustained.

Note XXXV.

Yet to no sense of selfish wrongs,
Bear witness with me, Heaven, belongs
My joy o'er Edward's bier.—P. 440.

The generosity which does justice to the character of an enemy, often marks Bruce's sentiments, as recorded by the faithful Barbour. He seldom mentions a fallen enemy without praising such good qualities as he might possess. I shall only take one instance. Shortly after Bruce landed in Carrick, in 1306, Sir Ingram Bell, the English governor of Ayr, engaged a wealthy yeoman, who had hitherto been a follower of Bruce, to undertake the task of assassinating him. The King learned this treachery, as he is said to have done other secrets of the enemy, by means of a female with whom he had an intrigue. Shortly after he was possessed of this information, Bruce, resorting to a small thicket at a distance from his men, with only

a single page to attend him, met the traitor, accompanied by two of his sons. They approached him with their wonted familiarity, but Bruce, taking his page's bow and arrow, commanded them to keep at a distance. As they still pressed forward with professions of zeal for his person and service, he, after a second warning, shot the father with the arrow; and being assaulted successively by the two sons, despatched first one, who was armed with an axe, then as the other charged him with a spear, avoided the thrust, struck the head from the spear, and cleft the skull of the assassin with a blow of his two-handed sword.

> ' He rushed down of blood all red,
> And when the king saw they were dead,
> All three lying, he wiped his brand.
> With that his boy came fast running,
> And said, " Our lord might lowyt[1] be
> That granted you might and poweste[2]
> To fell the felony and the pride,
> Of three in so little tide."
> The king said, " So our lord me see,
> They have been worthy men all three,
> Had they not been full of treason ;
> But that made their confusion."'
>
> 　　　BARBOUR'S *Bruce*, Bk. V. p. 152.

Note XXXVI.

Such hate was his on Solway's strand,
When vengeance clench'd his palsied hand,
That pointed yet to Scotland's land.—P. 440.

To establish his dominion in Scotland had been a favourite object of Edward's ambition, and nothing could exceed the pertinacity with which he pursued it, unless his inveterate resentment against the insurgents, who so frequently broke the English yoke when he deemed it most firmly riveted. After the battles of Falkirk and Methven, and the dreadful examples which he had made of Wallace and other champions of national independence, he probably concluded every chance of insurrection was completely annihilated. This was in 1306, when Bruce, as we have seen, was utterly expelled from Scotland: yet, in the conclusion of the same year, Bruce was again in arms and formidable; and in 1307, Edward, though exhausted by a long and wasting malady, put himself at the head of the army destined to destroy him utterly. This was, perhaps, partly in consequence of a vow which he had taken upon him, with all the pomp of chivalry, upon the day in which he dubbed his son a knight, for which see a subsequent note. But even his spirit of vengeance was unable to restore his exhausted strength. He reached Burgh-upon-Sands, a petty village of Cumberland, on the shores of the Solway Firth, and there, 6th July, 1307, expired in sight of the detested and devoted country of Scotland. His dying injunctions to his son required him to

---

　　1 Honoured.　　　　　　2 Power.

continue the Scottish war, and never to recall Gaveston. Edward II disobeyed both charges. Yet more to mark his animosity, the dying monarch ordered his bones to be carried with the invading army. Froissart, who probably had the authority of eye-witnesses, has given us the following account of this remarkable charge:—

'In the said forest, the old King Robert of Scotland dyd kepe hymselfe, whan King Edward the Fyrst conquered nygh all Scot-land; for he was so often chased, that none durst loge him in castell, nor fortresse, for feare of the said Kyng.

'And ever whan the King was returned into Ingland, than he would gather togerther agayn his people, and conquere townes, castells, and fortresses, iuste to Berwick, some by battle, and some by fair speech and love: and when the said King Edward heard thereof, than would he assemble his power, and wyn the realme of Scotland again; thus the chance went between these two foresaid Kings. It was shewed me, how that this King Robert wan and lost his realm v. times. So this continued till the said King Edward died at Berwick: and when he saw that he should die, he called before him his eldest son, who was King after him, and there, before all the barones, he caused him to swear, that as soon as he were dead, that he should take his body, and boyle it in a cauldron, till the flesh departed clean from the bones, and than to bury the flesh, and keep still the bones; and that as often as the Scotts should rebell against him, he should assemble the people against them, and carry with him the bones of his father; for he believed verily, that if they had his bones with them, that the Scotts should never attain any victory against them. The which thing was not accomplished, for when the King died his son carried him to London.'— BERNERS' FROISSART'S *Chronicle.* London, 1812, pp. 39-40.

Edward's commands were not obeyed, for he was interred in Westminster Abbey, with the appropriate inscription:—

'EDWARDUS PRIMUS SCOTORUM MALLEUS HIC EST. PACTUM SERVA.'

Yet some steps seem to have been taken towards rendering his body capable of occa-sional transportation, for it was exquisitely embalmed, as was ascertained when his tomb was opened some years ago. Edward II judged wisely in not carrying the dead body of his father into Scotland, since he would not obey his living counsels.

It ought to be observed, that though the order of the incidents is reversed in the poem, yet, in point of historical accuracy, Bruce had landed in Scotland, and obtained some successes of consequence, before the death of Edward I.

NOTE XXXVII.

——Canna's tower, that, steep and grey,
Like falcon-nest o'erhangs the bay.—P. 441.

The little island of Canna, or Cannay, adjoins to those of Rum and Muick, with which it forms one parish. In a pretty bay opening towards the east, there is a lofty and slender rock detached from the shore. Upon the summit are the ruins of a very small tower, scarcely accessible by a steep and precipitous path. Here, it is said, one of the kings, or Lords of the Isles, confined a beautiful lady, of whom he was jealous. The ruins are of course haunted by her restless spirit, and many romantic stories are told by the aged people of the island concerning her fate in life, and her appearances after death.

NOTE XXXVIII.

And Ronin's mountains dark have sent
Their hunters to the shore.—P. 442.

Ronin (popularly called Rum, a name which a poet may be pardoned for avoiding if possible) is a very rough and mountainous island, adjacent to those of Eigg and Cannay. There is almost no arable ground upon it, so that, except in the plenty of the deer, which of course are now nearly extirpated, it still deserves the description bestowed by the archdean of the Isles. 'Ronin, sixteen myle north-wast from the ile of Coll, lyes ane ile callit Ronin Ile, of sixteen myle long, and six in bredthe in the narrowest, ane forest of heigh mountains, and abundance of little deir in it, quhilk deir will never be slane dounewith, but the principal saittis man be in the height of the hill, because the deir will be callit upwart ay be the tainchell, or without tynchel they will pass upwart per-force. In this ile will be gotten about Britane als many wild nests upon the plane mure as men pleasis to gadder, and yet by resson the fowls hes few to start them except deir. This ile lyes from the west to the eist in lenth, and pertains to M'Kenabrey of Colla. Many solan geese are in this ile.'—MONRO'S *De-scription of the Western Isles*, p. 18.

NOTE XXXIX.

On Scooreigg next a warning light
Summon'd her warriors to the fight;
A numerous race, ere stern MacLeod
O'er their bleak shores in vengeance strode.
—P. 442.

These, and the following lines of the stanza, refer to a dreadful tale of feudal vengeance, of which unfortunately there are relics that still attest the truth. Scoor-Eigg is a high peak in the centre of the small Isle of Eigg, or Egg. It is well known to mineralogists, as affording many interesting specimens, and to others whom chance or curiosity may lead to the island, for the astonishing view of the mainland and neighbouring isles which it commands. I shall again avail myself of the journal I have quoted.

' 26th August, 1814.—At seven this morning we were in the Sound which divides the Isle of Rum from that of Eigg. The latter, although hilly and rocky, and traversed by a remarkably high and barren ridge, called Scoor-Rigg, has, in point of soil, a much more promising appearance. Southward of both lies the Isle of Muich, or Muck, a low and fertile island, and though the least, yet probably the most valuable of the three. We manned the boat, and rowed along the shore of Egg in quest of a cavern, which had been the memorable scene of a horrid feudal vengeance. We had rounded more than half the island, admiring the entrance of many a bold natural cave, which its rocks exhibited, without finding that which we sought, until we procured a guide. Nor, indeed, was it surprising that it should have escaped the search of strangers, as there are no outward indications more than might distinguish the entrance of a fox-earth. This noted cave has a very narrow opening, through which one can hardly creep on his knees and hands. It rises steep and lofty within, and runs into the bowels of the rock to the depth of 255 measured feet; the height at the entrance may be about three feet, but rises within to eighteen or twenty, and the breadth may vary in the same proportion. The rude and stony bottom of this cave is strewed with the bones of men, women, and children, the sad relics of the ancient inhabitants of the island, 200 in number, who were slain on the following occasion :—The Mac-Donalds of the Isle of Egg, a people dependent on Clan-Ranald, had done some injury to the Laird of Mac-Leod. The tradition of the isle says, that it was by a personal attack on the chieftain, in which his back was broken. But that of the other isles bears, more probably, that the injury was offered to two or three of the Mac-Leods, who, landing upon Eigg, and using some freedom with the young women, were seized by the islanders, bound hand and foot, and turned adrift in a boat, which the winds and waves safely conducted to Skye. To avenge the offence given, Mac-Leod sailed with such a body of men, as rendered resistance hopeless. The natives, fearing his vengeance, concealed themselves in this cavern, and, after a strict search, the Mac-Leods went on board their galleys, after doing what mischief they could, concluding the inhabitants had left the isle, and betaken themselves to the Long Island, or some of Clan-Ranald's other possessions. But next morning they espied from the vessels a man upon the island, and immediately landing again, they traced his retreat by the marks of his footsteps, a light snow being unhappily on the ground. Mac-Leod then surrounded the cavern, summoned

the subterranean garrison, and demanded that the individuals who had offended him should be delivered up to him. This was peremptorily refused. The chieftain then caused his people to divert the course of a rill of water, which, falling over the entrance of the cave, would have prevented his purposed vengeance. He then kindled at the entrance of the cavern a huge fire, composed of turf and fern, and maintained it with unrelenting assiduity, until all within were destroyed by suffocation. The date of this dreadful deed must have been recent, if one may judge from the fresh appearance of those relics. I brought off, in spite of the prejudice of our sailors, a skull from among the numerous specimens of mortality which the cavern afforded. Before re-embarking we visited another cave, opening to the sea, but of a character entirely different, being a large open vault, as high as that of a cathedral, and running back a great way into the rock at the same height. The height and width of the opening gives ample light to the whole. Here, after 1745, when the Catholic priests were scarcely tolerated, the priest of Eigg used to perform the Roman Catholic service, most of the islanders being of that persuasion. A huge ledge of rocks rising about half-way up one side of the cave, served for altar and pulpit ; and the appearance of a priest and Highland congregation in such an extraordinary place of worship, might have engaged the pencil of Salvator.'

NOTE XL.

——that wondrous dome,
Where, as to shame the temples deck'd
By skill of earthly architect,
Nature herself, it seem'd, would raise
A Minster to her Maker's praise!
—P. 442.

It would be unpardonable to detain the reader upon a wonder so often described, and yet so incapable of being understood by description. This palace of Neptune is even grander upon a second than the first view. The stupendous columns which form the sides of the cave, the depth and strength of the tide which rolls its deep and heavy swell up to the extremity of the vault—the variety of the tints formed by white, crimson, and yellow stalactites, or petrifactions, which occupy the vacancies between the base of the broken pillars which form the roof, and intersect them with a rich, curious, and variegated chasing, occupying each interstice—the corresponding variety below water, where the ocean rolls over a dark-red or violet-coloured rock, from which, as from a base, the basaltic columns arise—the tremendous noise of the swelling tide, mingling with the deep-toned echoes of the vault,—are circumstances elsewhere unparalleled.

Nothing can be more interesting than the varied appearance of the little archipelago of islets, of which Staffa is the most remarkable. This group, called in Gaelic Tresharnish, affords a thousand varied views to the voyager, as they appear in different positions with reference to his course. The variety of their shape contributes much to the beauty of these effects.

Note XLI.

Scenes sung by him who sings no more.
—P. 443.

The ballad, entitled 'Macphail of Colonsay, and the Mermaid of Corrievrekin,' [see Border Minstrelsy, vol. iv. p. 285,] was composed by John Leyden, from a tradition which he found while making a tour through the Hebrides about 1801, soon before his fatal departure for India, where, after having made farther progress in Oriental literature than any man of letters who had embraced those studies, he died a martyr to his zeal for knowledge, in the island of Java, immediately after the landing of our forces near Batavia, in August 1811.

Note XLII.

Up Tarbat's western lake they bore,
Then dragg'd their bark the isthmus o'er.
—P. 443.

The peninsula of Cantyre is joined to South Knapdale by a very narrow isthmus, formed by the western and eastern Loch of Tarbat. These two saltwater lakes, or bays, encroach so far upon the land, and the extremities come so near to each other, that there is not above a mile of land to divide them.

'It is not long,' says Pennant, 'since vessels of nine or ten tons were drawn by horses out of the west loch into that of the east, to avoid the dangers of the Mull of Cantyre, so dreaded and so little known was the navigation round that promontory. It is the opinion of many, that these little isthmuses, so frequently styled Tarbat in North Britain, took their name from the above circumstance; Tarruing, signifying to draw, and Bate, a boat. This too might be called, by way of pre-eminence, the Tarbat, from a very singular circumstance related by Torfœus. When Magnus, the barefooted king of Norway, obtained from Donald-bane of Scotland the cession of the Western Isles, or all those places that could be surrounded in a boat, he added to them the peninsula of Cantyre by this fraud: he placed himself in the stern of a boat, held the rudder, was drawn over this narrow track, and by this species of navigation wrested the country from his brother monarch.'—PENNANT'S *Scotland.* London, 1790, p. 190.

But that Bruce also made this passage, although at a period two or three years later than in the poem, appears from the evidence of Barbour, who mentions also the effect produced upon the minds of the Highlanders, from the prophecies current amongst them :—

' Bot to King Robert will we gang,
That we haff left wnspokyn of lang.
Quhen he had conwoyit to the se
His brodyr Eduuard, and his menye,
And othyr men off gret noblay.
To Tarbart thai held thair way,
In galayis ordanyt for thair far.
Bot thaim worthyt [1] draw thair schippis thar ;
And a myle wes betuix the seys ;
Bot that wes lompnyt [2] all with treis.
The King his schippis thar gert [3] draw,
And for the wynd couth [4] stoutly blaw
Apon thair bak, as thai wald ga,
He gert men rapys and mastis ta,
And set thaim in the schippis hey,
And sayllis to the toppis tey ;
And gert men gang thar by drawand.
The wynd thaim helpyt, that was blawand;
Swa that, in a litill space,
Thair flote all our drawin was.

And quhen thai, that in the Ilis war,
Hard tell how the gud King had thar
Gert hys schippis with saillis ga
Owt our betuix [the] Tarbart [is] twa,
Thai war abaysit [5] sa wrtely.
For thai wyst, throw auld prophecy,
That he suld ger [6] schippis sua
Betuix thai seis with saillis ga,
Suld wyne the Ilis sua till hand,
That nane with strenth suld him withstand.
Tharfor they come all to the King.
Wes nane withstud his bidding,
Owtakyn [7] Jhone of Lorne allayne.
Bot weill sone eftre wes he tayne ;
And present rycht to the King.
And thai that war of his leding,
That till the King had brokyn fay [8],
War all dede, and destroyit away.'
BARBOUR'S *Bruce.* Book X. v. 821.

Note XLIII.

The sun, ere yet he sunk behind
Ben-Ghoil, ' the Mountain of the Wind,'
Gave his grim peaks a greeting kind,
And bade Loch Ranza smile.—P. 443.

Loch Ranza is a beautiful bay, on the northern extremity of Arran, opening towards East Tarbat Loch. It is well described by Pennant :—' The approach was magnificent ; a fine bay in front, about a mile deep, having a ruined castle near the lower end, on a low far projecting neck of land, that forms another harbour, with a narrow passage ; but within has three fathom of water, even at the lowest ebb. Beyond is a little plain watered by a stream, and inhabited by the people of a small village. The whole is environed with a theatre of mountains ; and in the background the serrated crags of Grianan-Athol soar above.'—PENNANT'S *Tour to the Western Isles,* pp. 191-2. Ben-Ghaoil, ' the mountain of the winds,' is generally known by its English, and less poetical name, of Goatfield.

1 Were obliged to. 2 Laid with trees. 3 Caused.
4 Could. 5 Confounded. 6 Make.
7 Excepting. 8 Faith.

Note XLIV.

Each to Loch Ranza's margin spring;
That blast was winded by the King!
—P. 445.

The passage in Barbour, describing the landing of Bruce, and his being recognized by Douglas and those of his followers who had preceded him, by the sound of his horn, is in the original singularly simple and affecting.—The king arrived in Arran with thirty-three small row-boats. He interrogated a female if there had arrived any warlike men of late in that country. 'Surely, sir,' she replied, 'I can tell you of many who lately came hither, discomfited the English governor, and blockaded his castle of Brodick. They maintain themselves in a wood at no great distance.' The king, truly conceiving that this must be Douglas and his followers, who had lately set forth to try their fortune in Arran, desired the woman to conduct him to the wood. She obeyed.

> ' The king then blew his horn on high;
> And gert his men that were him by,
> Hold them still, and all privy;
> And syne again his horne blew he.
> James of Dowglas heard him blow,
> And at the last alone gan know,
> And said, " Soothly yon is the king;
> I know long whi.e since his blowing."
> The third time therewithall he blew,
> And then Sir Robert Boid it knew;
> And said, " Yon is the king, but dread,
> Go we forth till him, better speed."
> Then went they till the king in hye,
> And him inclined courteously.
> And blithly welcomed them the king,
> And was joyful of their meeting,
> And kissed them; and speared¹ syne
> How they had fared in hunting?
> And they him told all, but lesing²:
> Syne laud they God of their meeting.
> Syne with the king till his harbourye
> Went both joyfu' and jolly.'
>   BARBOUR'S *Bruce*, Book V. pp. 115-116.

Note XLV.

—— his brother blamed,
But shared the weakness, while ashamed;
With haughty laugh his head he turn'd,
And dash'd away the tear he scorn'd.
—P. 446.

The kind, and yet fiery character of Edward Bruce, is well painted by Barbour, in the account of his behaviour after the battle of Bannockburn. Sir Walter Ross, one of the very few Scottish nobles who fell in that battle, was so dearly beloved by Edward, that he wished the victory had been lost, so Ross had lived.

> ' Out-taken him, men has not seen
> Where he for any men made moaning.

And here the venerable Archdeacon intimates a piece of scandal. Sir Edward Bruce, it seems, loved Ross's sister, *par amours*, to the neglect of his own lady, sister to David de Strathbogie, Earl of Athole. This criminal passion had evil consequences; for, in resentment to the affront done to his sister, Athole attacked the guard which Bruce had left at Cambuskenneth, during the battle of Bannockburn, to protect his magazine of provisions, and slew Sir William Keith, the commander. For which treason he was forfeited.

In like manner, when in a sally from Carrickfergus, Neil Fleming, and the guards whom he commanded, had fallen, after the protracted resistance which saved the rest of Edward Bruce's army, he made such moan as surprised his followers:—

> ' Sic moan he made men had ferly¹,
> For he was not customably
> Wont for to moan men any thing,
> Nor would not hear men make moaning.

Such are the nice traits of character so often lost in general history.

Note XLVI.

Thou heard'st a wretched female plain
In agony of travail-pain,
And thou didst bid thy little band
Upon the instant turn and stand,
And dare the worst the foe might do,
Rather than, like a knight unitrue,
Leave to pursuers merciless
A woman in her last distress.—P. 448.

This incident, which illustrates so happily the chivalrous generosity of Bruce's character, is one of the many simple and natural traits recorded by Barbour. It occurred during the expedition which Bruce made to Ireland, to support the pretensions of his brother Edward to the throne of that kingdom. Bruce was about to retreat, and his host was arrayed for moving.

> ' The king has heard a woman cry,
> He asked what that was in hy².
> " It is the layndar³ sir." sai ane,
> " That her child-ill⁴ ri;ht now has ta'en,
> And must leave now behind us here.
> Therefore she makes an evil cheer⁵."
> The king said, " Certes⁶, it were pity
> That she in that point left should be,
> For certes I trow there is no man
> That he no will rue⁷ a woman than."
> His hosts all there arested he,
> And gert⁸ a tent soon stinted⁹ be,
> And gert her gang in hastily,
> And other women to be her by.
> While she was delivered he bade;
> And syne forth on his ways rade.
> And how she forth should carried be,
> Or he forth fure¹⁰, ordained he.
> This was a full great courtesy.
> That swilk a king and so mighty,
> Gert his men dwell on this manner,
> But for a poor lavender.'
>   BARBOUR'S *Bruce*, Book XVI. pp. 39-40.

¹ Wonder.	² Haste.	³ Laundress.
⁴ Child-bed.	⁵ Aspect.	⁶ Certainly. ⁷ Pity.
⁸ Caused.	⁹ Pitched.	¹⁰ Moved.

¹ Asked.   ² Without lying.

NOTE XLVII.

O'er chasms he pass'd, where fractures wide
Craved wary eye and ample stride.—P. 451.

The interior of the island of Arran abounds with beautiful Highland scenery. The hills, being very rocky and precipitous, afford some cataracts of great height, though of inconsiderable breadth. There is one pass over the river Machrai, renowned for the dilemma of a poor woman, who, being tempted by the narrowness of the ravine to step across, succeeded in making the first movement, but took fright when it became necessary to move the other foot, and remained in a posture equally ludicrous and dangerous, until some passenger assisted her to extricate herself. It is said she remained there some hours.

NOTE XLVIII.

He cross'd his brow beside the stone
Where Druids erst heard victims groan;
And at the cairns upon the wild,
O'er many a heathen hero piled.—P. 451.

The isle of Arran, like those of Man and Anglesea, abounds with many relics of heathen, and probably Druidical, superstition. There are high erect columns of unhewn stone, the most early of all monuments, the circles of rude stones, commonly entitled Druidical, and the cairns, or sepulchral piles, within which are usually found urns enclosing ashes. Much doubt necessarily rests upon the history of such monuments, nor is it possible to consider them as exclusively Celtic or Druidical. By much the finest circles of standing stones, excepting Stonehenge, are those of Stenhouse, at Stennis, in the island of Pomona, the principal isle of the Orcades. These, of course, are neither Celtic nor Druidical; and we are assured that many circles of the kind occur both in Sweden and Norway.

NOTE XLIX.

Old Brodick's gothic towers were seen:
From Hastings, late their English lord,
Douglas had won them by the sword.
—P. 451.

Brodick or Brathwick Castle, in the Isle of Arran, is an ancient fortress, near an open roadstead called Brodick-Bay, and not far distant from a tolerable harbour, closed in by the Island of Lamlash. This important place had been assailed a short time before Bruce's arrival in the island. James Lord Douglas, who accompanied Bruce to his retreat in Rachrine, seems, in the spring of 1306, to have tired of his abode there, and set out accordingly, in the phrase of the times, to see what adventure God would send him. Sir Robert Boyd accompanied him; and his

knowledge of the localities of Arran appears to have directed his course thither. They landed in the island privately, and appear to have laid an ambush for Sir John Hastings, the English governor of Brodwick, and surprised a considerable supply of arms and provisions, and nearly took the castle itself. Indeed, that they actually did so, has been generally averred by historians, although it does not appear from the narrative of Barbour. On the contrary, it would seem that they took shelter within a fortification of the ancient inhabitants, a rampart called *Tor an Schian.* When they were joined by Bruce, it seems probable that they had gained Brodick Castle. At least tradition says, that from the battlements of the tower he saw the supposed signal-fire on Turnberry-nook. The castle is now much modernized, but has a dignified appearance, being surrounded by flourishing plantations.

NOTE L.

Oft, too, with unaccustom'd ears,
A language much unmeet he hears.
—P. 451.

Barbour, with great simplicity, gives an anecdote, from which it would seem that the vice of profane swearing, afterwards too general among the Scottish nation, was, at this time, confined to military men. As Douglas, after Bruce's return to Scotland, was roving about the mountainous country of Tweeddale, near the water of Line, he chanced to hear some persons in a far n house say '*the devil.*' Concluding, from this hardy expression, that the house contained warlike guests, he immediately assailed it, and had the good fortune to make prisoners Thomas Randolph, afterwards the famous Earl of Murray, and Alexander Stuart, Lord Bonkle. Both were then in the English interest, and had come into that country with the purpose of driving out Douglas. They afterwards ranked among Bruce's most zealous adherents.

NOTE LI.

For, see! the ruddy signal made,
That Clifford, with his merry-men all,
Guards carelessly our father's hall.
—P. 452.

The remarkable circumstance by which Bruce was induced to enter Scotland, under the false idea that a signal-fire was lighted upon the shore near his maternal castle of Turnberry—the disappointment which he met with, and the train of success which arose out of that very disappointment, are too curious to be passed over unnoticed. The following is the narrative of Barbour. The introduction is a favourable specimen of his style, which seems to be in some degree the model for that of Gawain Douglas:—

'This wes in ver[1], quhen wynter tid,
With his blastis hidwyss to bid,
Was our drywyn : and byrdis smale,
As turturis and the nychtyngale,
Begouth[2] rycht sariely[3] to syng ;
And for to mak in thair singyng
Swete notis, and sownys ser[4],
And melodys plesand to her.
And the treis begouth to ma[5]
Burgeans[6], and brycht blomys alsua,
To wyn the helyng[7] off thair hewid,
That wykkyt wyntir had thaim rewid[8].
And all gressys beguth to spryng.
In to that tyme the nobill king,
With his flote, and a few menye[9],
Thre hundyr I trow thai mycht be
Is to the se, owte off Arane
A litill forouth[10], ewyn gane.

Thai rowit fast, with all thair mycht,
Till that apon thaim fell the nycht,
That woux myrk[11] apon gret maner,
Swa that thai wyst nocht quhar thai wer
For thai na nedill had, na stane ;
Bot rowyt alwayis in till ane,
Sterand all tyme apon the fyr,
That thai saw brynnand lycht and schyr[12]
It wes bot auentur[13] thaim led :
And thai in schort tyme sa thaim sped.
That at the fyr arywyt thai ;
And went to land bot mar delay.
And Cuthbert, that has sene the fyr,
Was full off angyr, and off ire :
For he durst nocht do it away ;
And wes alsua dowtand ay
That his lord suld pass to se.
Tharfor thair cummyn waytit he,
And met thaim at thair arywing.
He wes wele sone brocht to the King,
That speryt at him how he had done.
And he with sar hart tauld him sone,
How that he fand nane weill luffand ;
Bot all war fayis, that he fand :
And that the lord the Persy,
With ner thre hundre in cumpany,
Was in the castell thar besid,
Fulfillyt off dispyt and prid.
Bot ma than twa partis off his rowt
War herberyt in the toune without ;
"And dyspytyt yow mar, Schir King,
Than men may dispyt ony thing."
Than said the King, in full gret ire ;
"Tratour, quhy maid thow than the fyr ?"—
"A ! Schyr," said he, "sa God me se !
The fyr wes newyr maid for me.
Na, or the nycht, I wyst it nocht ;
Bot fra I wyst it, weill I thocht
That ye, and haly your menye,
In hy[14] suld put yow to the se.
For thi I cum to mete yow her,
To tell perellys that may aper."

The King wes off his spek angry,
And askyt his prywé men, in hy,
Quhat as thaim thoucht wes best to do,
Schyr Edward fryst answert thar to,
Hys brodyr that wes swa hardy,
And said : " I saw yow sekyrly
Thar sall na perell, that may be,
Dryve me eftsonys[15] to the se.
Myne auentur her tak will I,
Quhethir it be esfull or angry."—

"Brothyr," he said, "sen thou will sua,
It is gude that we saxyn ta
Dissese or ese, or payne or play,
Eftyr as God will ws purway[1].
And sen men sayis that the Persy
Myn heretage will occupy ;
And his menye sa ner ws lyis,
That ws dispytis mony wyss ;
Ga we and wenge[2] sum off the dispyte
And that may we haiff done alss tite[3].
For thai ly traistly[4], but dreding
Off ws, or off our her cummyng.
And thoucht we slepand slew thaim all,
Repruff tharof na man sall.
For werrayour na forss suld ma,
Quhethir he mycht ourcom his fa
Throw strenth or throw sutelté ;
Bot that gud faith ay haldyn be.' "

BARBOUR'S *Bruce*, Book IV. v. I.

NOTE LII.

*Now ask you whence that wondrous light,
Whose fairy glow beguiled their sight ?
It ne'er was known.*—P. 454.

The following are the words of an ingenious correspondent, to whom I am obliged for much information respecting Turnberry and its neighbourhood. ' The only tradition now remembered of the landing of Robert the Bruce in Carrick, relates to the fire seen by him from the Isle of Arran. It is still generally reported, and religiously believed by many, that this fire was really the work of supernatural power, unassisted by the hand of any mortal being ; and it is said that, for several centuries, the flame rose yearly on the same hour of the same night of the year, on which the king first saw it from the turrets of Brodick Castle ; and some go so far as to say, that if the exact time were known, it would be still seen. That this superstitious notion is very ancient, is evident from the place where the fire is said to have appeared, being called the Bogles' Brae, beyond the remembrance of man. In support of this curious belief, it is said that the practice of burning heath for the improvement of land was then unknown ; that a spunkie (Jack o'lanthorn) could not have been seen across the breadth of the Forth of Clyde, between Ayrshire and Arran ; and that the courier of Bruce was his kinsman, and never suspected of treachery.'—Letter from Mr. Joseph Train, of Newton Stuart, author of an ingenious Collection of Poems, illustrative of many ancient Traditions in Galloway and Ayrshire, Edinburgh, 1814. [Mr. Train made a journey into Ayrshire at Sir Walter Scott's request, on purpose to collect accurate information for the Notes to this poem ; and the reader will find more of the fruits of his labours in Note LIV. This is the same gentleman whose friendly assistance is so often acknowledged in the Notes and Introductions of the Waverley Novels.]

---

[1] Spring. [2] Began. [3] Loftily. [4] Several.
[5] Make. [6] Buds. [7] Covering.
[8] Bereaved. [9] Men. [10] Before. [11] Dark.
[12] Clear. [13] Adventure. [14] Haste. [15] Soon after.

[1] Prepare. [2] Avenge. [3] Quickly. [4] Confidently

R

NOTE LIII.

*They gain'd the Chase, a wide domain
Left for the Castle's silvan reign.*—P. 455.

The Castle of Turnberry, on the coast of Ayrshire, was the property of Robert Bruce, in right of his mother. Lord Hailes mentions the following remarkable circumstance concerning the mode in which he became proprietor of it:—'Martha, Countess of Carrick in her own right, the wife of Robert Bruce, Lord of Annandale, bare him a son, afterwards Robert I (11th July, 1274). The circumstances of her marriage were singular: happening to meet Robert Bruce in her domains, she became enamoured of him, and with some violence led him to her castle of Turnberry. A few days after she married him, without the knowledge of the relations of either party, and without the requisite consent of the king. The king instantly seized her castle and whole estates: She afterwards atoned by a fine for her feudal delinquency. Little did Alexander foresee that, from this union, the restorer of the Scottish monarchy was to arise.'—*Annals of Scotland*, vol. ii. p. 180. The same obliging correspondent, whom I have quoted in the preceding note, gives me the following account of the present state of the ruins of Turnberry:—'Turnberry Point is a rock projecting into the sea; the top of it is about eighteen feet above high-water mark. Upon this rock was built the castle. There is about twenty-five feet high of the wall next to the sea yet standing. Upon the land-side the wall is only about four feet high; the length has been sixty feet, and the breadth forty-five: it was surrounded by a ditch, but that is now nearly filled up. The top of the ruin, rising between forty and fifty feet above the water, has a majestic appearance from the sea. There is not much local tradition in the vicinity connected with Bruce or his history. In front, however, of the rock, upon which stands Culzean Castle, is the mouth of a romantic cavern, called the Cove of Colean, in which it is said Bruce and his followers concealed themselves immediately after landing, till they arranged matters for their farther enterprises. Burns mentions it in the poem of Hallowe'en. The only place to the south of Turnberry worth mentioning, with reference to Bruce's history, is the Weary Nuik, a little romantic green hill, where he and his party are said to have rested, after assaulting the castle.'

Around the Castle of Turnberry was a level plain of about two miles in extent, forming the castle park. There could be nothing, I am informed, more beautiful than the copsewood and verdure of this extensive meadow, before it was invaded by the ploughshare.

NOTE LIV.

The Bruce hath won his father's hall!
—P. 459.

I have followed the flattering and pleasing tradition, that the Bruce, after his descent upon the coast of Ayrshire, actually gained possession of his maternal castle. But the tradition is not accurate. The fact is, that he was only strong enough to alarm and drive in the outposts of the English garrison, then commanded, not by Clifford, as assumed in the text, but by Percy. Neither was Clifford slain upon this occasion, though he had several skirmishes with Bruce. He fell afterwards in the battle of Bannockburn. Bruce, after alarming the castle of Turnberry, and surprising some part of the garrison, who were quartered without the walls of the fortress, retreated into the mountainous part of Carrick, and there made himself so strong, that the English were obliged to evacuate Turnberry, and at length the Castle of Ayr. Many of his benefactions and royal gifts attest his attachment to the hereditary followers of his house, in this part of the country.

It is generally known that Bruce, in consequence of his distresses after the battle of Methven, was affected by a scorbutic disorder, which was then called a leprosy. It is said he experienced benefit from the use of a medicinal spring, about a mile north of the town of Ayr, called from that circumstance King's Ease[1]. The following is the tradition of the country, collected by Mr. Train:—'After Robert ascended the throne, he founded the priory of Dominican monks, every one of whom was under the obligation of putting up to Heaven a prayer once every week-day, and twice in holydays, for the recovery of the king; and, after his death, these masses were continued for the saving of his soul. The ruins of this old monastery are now nearly level with the ground. Robert likewise caused houses to be built round the well of King's Case, for eight lepers, and allowed eight bolls of oatmeal, and £28 Scotch money, per annum, to each person. These donations were laid upon the lands of Fullarton, and are now payable by the Duke of Portland. The farm of Shiels, in the neighbourhood of Ayr, has to give, if required, a certain quantity of straw to the lepers' beds, and so much to thatch their houses annually. Each leprous person had a drinking-horn provided him by the king, which continued to be hereditary in the house to which it was first granted. One of these identical horns, of very curious workmanship, was in the possession of the late Colonel Fullarton of that Ilk.'

My correspondent proceeds to mention some curious remnants of antiquity respecting

[1] Sir Walter Scott had misread Mr. Train's MS., which gave not *King's Ease*, but *King's Case*, i. e. *Casa Regis*, the name of the royal foundation described below. Mr. Train's kindness enabled Lockhart to make this correction.—1833.

this foundation. 'In compliment to Sir William Wallace, the great deliverer of his country, King Robert Bruce invested the descendants of that hero with the right of placing all the lepers upon the establishment of King's Case. This patronage continued in the family of Craigie, till it was sold along with the lands of the late Sir Thomas Wallace. The burgh of Ayr then purchased the right of applying the donations of King's Case to the support of the poor-house of Ayr. The lepers' charter-stone was a basaltic block, exactly the shape of a sheep's kidney, and weighing an Ayrshire boll of meal. The surface of this stone being as smooth as glass, there was not any other way of lifting it than by turning the hollow to the ground, there extending the arms along each side of the stone, and clasping the hands in the cavity. Young lads were always considered as deserving to be ranked among men, when they could lift the blue stone of King's Case. It always lay be ide the well, till a few years ago, when some English dragoons encamped at that place wantonly broke it, since which the fragments have been kept by the freemen of Prestwick in a place of security. There is one of these charter-stones at the village of Old Daily, in Carrick, which has become more celebrated by the following event, which happened only a few years ago:—The village of New Daily being now larger than the old place of the same name, the inhabitants insisted that the charter-stone should be removed from the old town to the new, but the people of Old Daily were unwilling to part with their ancient right. Demands and remonstrances were made on each side without effect, till at last man, woman, and child, of both villages, marched out and by one desperate engagement put an end to a war, the commencement of which no person then living remembered. Justice and victory, in this instance, being of the same party, the villagers of the old town of Daily now enjoy the pleasure of keeping the *blue-stane* unmolested. Ideal privileges are often attached to some of these stones. In Girvan, if a man can set his back against one of the above description, he is supposed not liable to be arrested for debt, nor can cattle, it is imagined, be poinded as long as they are fastened to the same stone. That stones were often used as symbols to denote the right of possessing land, before the use of written documents became general in Scotland is, I think, exceedingly probable. The charter-stone of Inverness is still kept with great care, set in a frame, and hooped with iron, at the market-place of that town. It is called by the inhabitants of that district Clack na Couddin. I think it is very likely that Carey has mentioned this stone in his poem of Craig Phaderick. This is only a conjecture, as I have never seen that work. While the famous marble chair was allowed to remain at Scoon, it was considered as the charter-stone of the kingdom of Scotland.'

NOTE LV.

'*Bring here,*' he said, '*the mazers four,*
My noble fathers loved of yore.'—P. 459.

These mazers were large drinking-cups, or goblets. Mention of them occurs in a curious inventory of the treasure and jewels of James III, which will be published, with other curious documents of antiquity, by my friend, Mr. Thomas Thomson, D. Register of Scotland, under the title of 'A Collection of Inventories, and other Records of the Royal Wardrobe, Jewel House,' &c. I copy the passage in which mention is made of the mazers, and also of a habiliment, called 'King Robert Bruce's serk,' i. e. *shirt*, meaning, perhaps, his shirt of mail; although no other arms are mentioned in the inventory. It might have been a relic of more sanctified description, a penance shirt perhaps.

Extract from '*Inventare of ane Parte of the Gold and Silver conyeit and unconyeit, Jowellis, and uther Stuff perteining to Umquhile oure Soverane Lords Fader, that he had in Depois the Tyme of his Deceis, and that come to the Handis of oure Soverane Lord that now is* M.CCCC. LXXXVIII.'

'Memorandum fundin in a bandit kist like a gardeviant [1], in the fyrst the grete chenye [2] of gold, contenand sevin score sex linkis.

Item, thre platis of silver.
Item, tuelf salfatis .
Item, fyftene discheis [4] ouregilt.
Item, a grete gilt plate.
Item, twa grete bassingis [5] ouregilt.
Item, FOUR MASARIS, CALLED KING ROBERT THE BROCIS, with a cover.
Item, a grete cok maid of silver.
Item, the hede of silver of ane of the coveris of masar.
Item, a fare dialle [6].
Item, twa kas.s of knyffis [7].
Item, a pare of auld kniffis.
Item, takin be the smyth that opinnit the lokkis, in gold fourty demyis.
Item, in Inglys grotis [8] . . . . xxiiii. li. and the said silver given again to the takaris of hym.
Item, ressavit in the clossat of Davidis tour, ane haly water-fat of silver, twa boxis, a cageat tume, a glas with rois-water, a dosoune of torchis, King ROBERT BRUCIS SERK.'

The real use of the antiquarian's studies is to bring the minute information which he collects to bear upon points of history. For example, in the inventory I have just quoted, there is given the contents of the *black kist*, or chest, belonging to James III, which was

---

[1] Gard-vin, or wine-cooler. [2] Chain.
[3] Salt-cellars, anciently the object of much curious workmanship.
[4] Dishes. [5] Basins. [6] Dial.
[7] Cases of knives. [8] English groats.

his strong box, and contained a quantity of treasure, in money and jewels, surpassing what might have been at the period expected of 'poor Scotland's gear.' This illustrates and authenticates a striking passage in the history of the house of Douglas, by Hume of Godscroft. The last Earl of Douglas (of the elder branch) had been reduced to monastic seclusion in the Abbey of Lindores, by James II. James III, in his distresses, would willingly have recalled him to public life, and made him his lieutenant. 'But he,' says Godscroft, 'laden with years and old age, and weary of troubles, refused, saying, Sir, you have keept mee, and your *black coffer* in Sterling, too long, neither of us can doe you any good: I, because my friends have forsaken me, and my followers and dependers are fallen from me, betaking themselves to other masters; and your black trunk is too farre from you, and your enemies are between you and it: or (as others say) because there was in it a sort of black coyne, that the king had caused to be coyned by the advice of his courtiers; which moneyes (saith he) sir, if you had put out at the first, the people would have taken it; and if you had employed mee in due time I might have done you service. But now there is none that will take notice of me, nor meddle with your money.'—HUME'S *History of the House of Douglas*, fol. Edin. 1644, p. 206.

NOTE LVI.

Arouse old friends, and gather new.
—P. 460.

As soon as it was known in Kyle, says ancient tradition, that Robert Bruce had landed in Carrick, with the intention of recovering the crown of Scotland, the Laird of Craigie, and forty-eight men in his immediate neighbourhood, declared in favour of their legitimate prince. Bruce granted them a tract of land, still retained by the freemen of Newton to this day. The original charter was lost when the pestilence was raging at Ayr; but it was renewed by one of the Jameses, and is dated at Faulkland. The freemen of Newton were formerly officers by rotation. The Provost of Ayr at one time was a freeman of Newton, and it happened to be his turn, while provost in Ayr, to be officer in Newton, both of which offices he discharged at the same time.

The forest of Selkirk, or Ettrick, at this period, occupied all the district which retains that denomination, and embraced the neighbouring dales of Tweeddale, and at least the Upper Ward of Clydesdale. All that tract was probably as waste as it is mountainous, and covered with the remains of the ancient Caledonian Forest, which is supposed to have stretched from Cheviot Hills as far as Hamilton, and to have comprehended even

a part of Ayrshire. At the fatal battle of Falkirk, Sir John Stewart of Bonkill, brother to the Steward of Scotland, commanded the archers of Selkirk Forest, who fell around the dead body of their leader. The English historians have commemorated the tall and stately persons, as well as the unswerving faith, of these foresters. Nor has their interesting fall escaped the notice of an elegant modern poetess, whose subject led her to treat of that calamitous engagement.

'The glance of the morn had sparkled bright
On their plumage green and their actons light;
The bugle was strung at each hunter's side,
As they had been bound to the chase to ride;
But the bugle is mute, and the shafts are spent,
The arm unnerved and the bow unbent.
And the tired forester is laid
Far, far from the clustering greenwood shade!
Sore have they toil'd—they are fallen asleep,
And their slumber is heavy, and dull, and deep!
When over their bones the grass shall wave,
When the wild winds over their tombs shall rave,
Memory shall lean on their graves, and tell
How Selkirk's hunters bold around old Stewart
fell!'

Wallace, or the Fight of Falkirk, by Miss HOLFORD. Lond. 4to, 1809, pp. 170-1.

NOTE LVII.

When Bruce's banner had victorious flow'd O'er Loudoun's mountain, and in Ury's vale.—P. 460.

The first important advantage gained by Bruce, after landing at Turnberry, was over Aymer de Valence, Earl of Pembroke, the same by whom he had been defeated near Methven. They met, as has been said, by appointment, at Loudonhill, in the west of Scotland. Pembroke sustained a defeat; and from that time Bruce was at the head of a considerable flying army. Yet he was subsequently obliged to retreat into Aberdeenshire, and was there assailed by Comyn, Earl of Buchan, desirous to avenge the death of his relative, the Red Comyn, and supported by a body of English troops under Philip de Moubray. Bruce was ill at the time of a scrofulous disorder, but took horse to meet his enemies, although obliged to be supported on either side. He was victorious, and it is said that the agitation of his spirits restored his health.

NOTE LVIII.

When English blood oft deluged Douglas-dale.—P. 460.

The 'good Lord James of Douglas,' during these commotions, often took from the English his own castle of Douglas, but being unable to garrison it, contented himself with destroying the fortifications, and retiring into the mountains. As a reward to his patriotism, it is said to have been prophesied, that how often soever Douglas Castle should be destroyed, it should always again arise more

magnificent from its ruins. Upon one of these occasions he used fearful cruelty, causing all the store of provisions, which the English had laid up in his castle, to be heaped together, bursting the wine and beer casks among the wheat and flour, slaughtering the cattle upon the same spot, and upon the top of the whole cutting the throats of the English prisoners. This pleasantry of the 'good Lord James' is commemorated under the name of the *Douglas's Larder*. A more pleasing tale of chivalry is recorded by Godscroft.—
'By this means, and such other exploits, he so affrighted the enemy, that it was counted a matter of great jeopardie to keep this castle, which began to be called the *adventurous* (or hazardous) *Castle of Douglas;* whereupon Sir John Walton being in suit of an English lady, she wrote to him, that when he had kept the adventurous Castle of Douglas seven years, then he might think himself worthy to be a suitor to her. Upon this occasion Walton took upon him the keeping of it, and succeeded to Thruswall, but he ran the same fortune with the rest that were before him. For Sir James, having first dressed an ambuscado near unto the place, he made fourteen of his men take so many sacks, and fill them with grass, as though it had been corn, which they carried in the way to Lanark, the chief market town in that county: so hoping to draw forth the captain by that bait, and either to take him or the castle, or both. Neither was this expectation frustrated, for the captain did bite, and came forth to have taken this victual (as he supposed). But ere he could reach these carriers, Sir James, with his company, had gotten between the castle and him; and these disguised carriers, seeing the captain following after them, did quickly cast off their sacks, mounted themselves on horseback, and met the captain with a sharp encounter, being so much the more amazed, as it was unlooked for: wherefore, when he saw these carriers metamorphosed into warriors, and ready to assault him, fearing that which was, that there was some train laid for them, he turned about to have retired to his castle, but there he also met with his enemies; between which two companies he and his whole followers were slain, so that none escaped: the captain afterwards being searched, they found (as it is reported) his mistress's letter about him.'—HUME's *History of the House of Douglas*, fol. pp. 29-30[1]

NOTE LIX.

And fiery Edward routed stout St. John.—P. 460.

'John de St. John, with 15,000 horsemen, had advanced to oppose the inroad of the Scots. By a forced march he endeavoured

[1] This is the foundation of the Author's last romance, *Castle Dangerous*.—LOCKHART.

to surprise them, but intelligence of his motions was timeously received. The courage of Edward Bruce, approaching to temerity, frequently enabled him to achieve what men of more judicious valour would never have attempted. He ordered the infantry, and the meaner sort of his army, to intrench themselves in strong narrow ground. He himself, with fifty horsemen well harnessed, issued forth under cover of a thick mist, surprised the English on their march, attacked and dispersed them.'—DALRYMPLE's *Annals of Scotland*. Edinburgh, quarto, 1779, p. 25.

NOTE LX.

When Randolph's war-cry swell'd the southern gale.—P. 460.

Thomas Randolph, Bruce's sister's son, a renowned Scottish chief, was in the early part of his life not more remarkable for consistency than Bruce himself. He espoused his uncle's party when Bruce first assumed the crown, and was made prisoner at the fatal battle of Methven, in which his relative's hopes appeared to be ruined. Randolph accordingly not only submitted to the English, but took an active part against Bruce; appeared in arms against him; and, in the skirmish where he was so closely pursued by the bloodhound, it is said his nephew took his standard with his own hand. But Randolph was afterwards made prisoner by Douglas in Tweeddale, and brought before King Robert. Some harsh language was exchanged between the uncle and nephew, and the latter was committed for a time to close custody. Afterwards, however, they were reconciled, and Randolph was created Earl of Moray about 1312. After this period he eminently distinguished himself, first by the surprise of Edinburgh Castle, and afterwards by many similar enterprises, conducted with equal courage and ability.

NOTE LXI.

—— Stirling's towers, Beleaguer'd by King Robert's powers; And they took term of truce.—P. 461.

When a long train of success, actively improved by Robert Bruce, had made him master of almost all Scotland, Stirling Castle continued to hold out. The care of the blockade was committed by the king to his brother Edward, who concluded a treaty with Sir Philip Mowbray, the governor, that he should surrender the fortress, if it were not succoured by the King of England before St. John the Baptist's day. The King severely blamed his brother for the impolicy of a treaty, which gave time to the King of England to advance to the relief of the castle with all his assembled forces, and obliged himself either to meet them in battle with an inferior force, or to retreat with dishonour. 'Let all England come,' answered the reckless Edward; 'we will fight them were they more.' The consequence was, of course, that each kingdom mustered its strength for the expected battle; and as the space agreed upon reached from Lent to Midsummer, full time was allowed for that purpose.

Note LXII.

*To summon prince and peer,
At Berwick-bounds to meet their Liege.*
—P. 461.

There is printed in Rymer's *Fœdera* the summons issued upon this occasion to the sheriff of York; and he mentions eighteen other persons to whom similar ordinances were issued. It seems to respect the infantry alone, for it is entitled, *De peditibus ad recussum Castri de Stryvelin a Scotis obsessi, properare faciendis.* This circumstance is also clear from the reasoning of the writ, which states: 'We have understood that our Scottish enemies and rebels are endeavouring to collect as strong a force as possible of infantry, in strong and marshy grounds, where the approach of cavalry would be difficult, between us and the castle of Stirling.'—It then sets forth Mowbray's agreement to surrender the castle, if not relieved before St. John the Baptist's day, and the king's determination, with divine grace, to raise the siege. 'Therefore,' the summons further bears, 'to remove our said enemies and rebels from such places as above mentioned, it is necessary for us to have a strong force of infantry fit for arms.' And accordingly the sheriff of York is commanded to equip and send forth a body of four thousand infantry, to be assembled at Werk, upon the tenth day of June first, under pain of the royal displeasure, &c.

Note LXIII.

*And Cambria, but of late subdued,
Sent forth her mountain-multitude.*
—P. 461.

Edward the First, with the usual policy of a conqueror, employed the Welsh, whom he had subdued, to assist him in his Scottish wars, for which their habits, as mountaineers, particularly fitted them. But this policy was not without its risks. Previous to the battle of Falkirk, the Welsh quarrelled with the English men-at-arms, and after bloodshed on both parts, separated themselves from his army, and the feud between them, at so dangerous and critical a juncture, was reconciled with difficulty. Edward II followed his father's example in this particular, and with no better success. They could not be brought to exert themselves in the cause of their conquerors. But they had an indifferent reward for their forbearance. Without arms, and clad only in scanty dresses of linen cloth, they appeared naked in the eyes even of the Scottish peasantry; and after the rout of Bannockburn, were massacred by them in great numbers, as they retired in confusion towards their own country. They were under command of Sir Maurice de Berkeley.

Note LXIV.

*And Connoght pour'd from waste and wood
Her hundred tribes, whose sceptre rude
Dark Eth O'Connor sway'd.*—P. 461.

There is in the *Fœdera* an invitation to Eth O'Connor, chief of the Irish of Connaught, setting forth that the king was about to move against his Scottish rebels, and therefore requesting the attendance of all the force he could muster, either commanded by himself in person, or by some nobleman of his race. These auxiliaries were to be commanded by Richard de Burgh, Earl of Ulster. Similar mandates were issued to the following Irish chiefs, whose names may astonish the unlearned, and amuse the antiquary.

'Eth O Donnuld, Duci Hibernicorum de Tyconil;
Demod O Kahan, Duci Hibernicorum de Fernetrew;
Doneval O Neel, Duci Hibernicorum de Tryowyn;
Neel Macbreen, Duci Hibernicorum de Kynallewan;
Eth. Offyn, Duci Hibernicorum de Turtery;
Admely Mac Anegus, Duci Hibernicorum de Onehagh;
Neel O Hanlan, Duci Hibernicorum de Erthere;
Bien Mac Mahun, Duci Hibernicorum de Uriel;
Lauercagh Mac Wyr, Duci Hibernicorum de Lougherin;
Gillys O Railly, Duci Hibernicorum de Bresfeny;
Geffrey O Fergy, Duci Hibernicorum de Montiragwil;
Felyn O Honughur, Duci Hibernicorum de Connach;
Donethuth O Bien, Duci Hibernicorum de Tothmund;
Dermod Mac Arthy, Duci Hibernicorum de Dessemound;
Denenol Carbragh;
Maur. Kenenagh Mac Murgh;
Murghugh O Bryn;
David O Tothvifl;
Dermod O Tonoghur, Doffaly;
Fyn O Dymsy;
Souethuth Mac Gillephatrick;
Lyssagh O Morth;
Gilbertus Ekelly, Duci Hibernicorum de Omany;
Mac Ethelau;
Omalan Helyn, Duci Hibernicorum Midie.'
RYMER'S *Fœdera*, vol. iii. pp. 476, 477.

NOTE LXV.

Their chief, Fitz-Louis.—P. 463.

Fitz-Louis, or Mac-Louis, otherwise called Fullarton, is a family of ancient descent in the Isle of Arran. They are said to be of French origin, as the name intimates. They attached themselves to Bruce upon his first landing; and Fergus Mac-Louis, or Fullarton, received from the grateful monarch a charter, dated 26th November, in the second year of his reign (1307), for the lands of Kilmichel, and others, which still remain in this very ancient and respectable family.

NOTE LXVI.

In battles four beneath their eye,
The forces of King Robert lie.—P. 463.

The arrangements adopted by King Robert for the decisive battle of Bannockburn are given very distinctly by Barbour, and form an edifying lesson to tacticians. Yet, till commented upon by Lord Hailes, this important passage of history has been generally and strangely misunderstood by historians. I will here endeavour to detail it fully.

Two days before the battle, Bruce selected the field of action, and took post there with his army, consisting of about 30,000 disciplined men, and about half the number of disorderly attendants upon the camp. The ground was called the New Park of Stirling; it was partly open, and partly broken by copses of wood and marshy ground. He divided his regular forces into four divisions. Three of these occupied a front line, separated from each other, yet sufficiently near for the purpose of communication. The fourth division formed a reserve. The line extended in a north-easterly direction from the brook of Bannock, which was so rugged and broken as to cover the right flank effectually, to the village of Saint Ninian's, probably in the line of the present road from Stirling to Kilsyth. Edward Bruce commanded the right wing, which was strengthened by a strong body of cavalry under Keith, the Mareschal of Scotland, to whom was committed the important charge of attacking the English archers; Douglas, and the young Steward of Scotland, led the central wing; and Thomas Randolph, Earl of Moray, the left wing. The King himself commanded the fourth division, which lay in reserve behind the others. The royal standard was pitched, according to tradition, in a stone, having a round hole for its reception, and thence called the Bore-stone. It is still shown on the top of a small eminence, called Brock's-brae, to the south-west of Saint Ninian's. His main body thus disposed, King Robert sent the followers of the camp, fifteen thousand and upwards in number, to the eminence in rear of his army, called from that circumstance the *Gillies'* (i.e. the servants') *Hill.*

The military advantages of this position were obvious. The Scottish left flank, protected by the brook of Bannock, could not be turned; or, if that attempt were made, a movement by the reserve might have covered it. Again, the English could not pass the Scottish army, and move towards Stirling, without exposing their flank to be attacked while in march.

If, on the other hand, the Scottish line had been drawn up east and west, and facing to the southward, as affirmed by Buchanan, and adopted by Mr. Nimmo, the author of the History of Stirlingshire, there appears nothing to have prevented the English approaching upon the carse, or level ground, from Falkirk, either from turning the Scottish left flank, or from passing their position, if they preferred it, without coming to an action, and moving on to the relief of Stirling. And the Gillies' Hill, if this less probable hypothesis be adopted, would be situated, not in the rear, as allowed by all the historians, but upon the left flank of Bruce's army. The only objection to the hypothesis above laid down, is, that the left flank of Bruce's army was thereby exposed to a sally from the garrison of Stirling. But, first, the garrison were bound to neutrality by terms of Mowbray's treaty; and Barbour even seems to censure, as a breach of faith, some secret assistance which they rendered their countrymen upon the eve of battle, in placing temporary bridges of doors and spars over the pools of water in the carse, to enable them to advance to the charge[1]. Secondly, had this not been the case, the strength of the garrison was probably not sufficient to excite apprehension. Thirdly, the adverse hypothesis leaves the rear of the Scottish army as much exposed to the Stirling garrison, as the left flank would be in the case supposed.

It only remains to notice the nature of the ground in front of Bruce's line of battle. Being part of a park, or chase, it was considerably interrupted with trees; and an extensive marsh, still visible, in some places rendered it inaccessible, and in all of difficult approach. More to the northward, where the natural impediments were fewer, Bruce fortified his position against cavalry, by digging a number of pits so close together, says Barbour, as to resemble the cells in a honeycomb. They were a foot in breadth, and between two and three feet deep, many rows of them being placed one behind the other. They were slightly covered with brushwood and green sods, so as not to be obvious to an impetuous enemy.

All the Scottish army were on foot, excepting a select body of cavalry stationed

---

[1] An assistance which (by the way) could not have been rendered, had not the English approached from the sou h-east; since, had their march been due north, the whole Scottish army must have been between them and the garrison.

with Edward Bruce on the right wing, under the immediate command of Sir Robert Keith, the Marshal of Scotland, who were destined for the important service of charging and dispersing the English archers.

Thus judiciously posted, in a situation fortified both by art and nature, Bruce awaited the attack of the English.

NOTE LXVII.

Beyond, the Southern host appears.
—P. 463.

Upon the 23rd June, 1314, the alarm reached the Scottish army of the approach of the enemy. Douglas and the Marshal were sent to reconnoitre with a body of cavalry:

'And soon the great host have they seen,
Where shields shining were so sheen,
And basinets burnished bright,
That gave against the sun great light.
They saw so fele 1 brawdyne 2 baners,
Standards and pennons and spears
And so fele knights upon steeds,
All flaming in their weeds,
And so fele bataills, and so broad,
And too so great room as they rode,
That the maist host, and the stoutest
Of Christendom, and the greatest,
Should be abaysit for to see
Their foes into such quantity.'

The Bruce, vol. ii. p. 111.

The two Scottish commanders were cautious in the account which they brought back to their camp. To the king in private they told the formidable state of the enemy; but in public reported that the English were indeed a numerous host, but ill commanded, and worse disciplined.

NOTE LXVIII.

With these the valiant of the Isles
Beneath their chieftains rank'd their files.
—P. 463.

The men of Argyle, the islanders, and the Highlanders in general, were ranked in the rear. They must have been numerous, for Bruce had reconciled himself with almost all their chieftains, excepting the obnoxious MacDougals of Lorn. The following deed, containing the submission of the potent Earl of Ross to the King, was never before published. It is dated in the third year of Robert's reign, that is, 1309.

'OBLIGACIO COMITIS ROSSENSIS PER HOMAGIUM FIDELITATEM ET SCRIPTUM.

'Universis christi fidelibus ad quorum noticiam presentes litere peruenerint Willielmus Comes de Ross salutem in domino sempiternam. Quia magnificus princeps Dominus

1 Many.   2 Displayed.

Robertus dei gracia Rex Scottorum Dominus meus ex innata sibi bonitate, inspirataque clemencia, et gracia speciali remisit michi pure rancorem animi sui, et relaxauit ac condonauit michi omnimodas transgressiones seu offensas contra ipsum et suos per me et meos vsque ad confeccionem literarum presencium perpetratas: Et terras meas et tenementa mea omnia graciose concessit. Et me nichilominus de terra de Dingwal et ferncroskry infra comitatum de Suthyrland de benigna liberalitate sua heriditarie infeodare curauit. Ego tantam principis beneuolenciam efficaciter attendens, et pro tot graciis michi factis, vicem sibi gratitudinis meis pro viribus de cetero digne . . . . vite cupiens exhibere, subicio et obligo me et heredes meos et homines meos vniuersos dicto Domino meo Regi per omnia . . . . erga suam regiam dignitatem, quod erimus de cetero fideles sibi et heredibus suis et fidele sibi seruicium auxilium et concilium . . . . contra omnes homines et feminas qui viuere poterint aut mori, et super h . . . Ego Willielmus pro me . . . . hominibus meis vniuersis dicto domino meo Regi . . . . manibus homagium sponte feci et super dei ewangelia sacramentum prestiti . . . . In quorum omnium testimonium sigillum meum, et sigilla Hugonis filii et heredis et Johannis filii mei vna cum sigillis venerabilium patrum Dominorum Dauid et Thome Moraviensis et Rossensis dei gracia episcoporum presentibus literis sunt appensa. Acta scripta et data apud Aldern in Morauia vltimo die mensis Octobris, Anno Regni dicti domini nostri Regis Roberti Tertio. Testibus venerabilibus patribus supradictis, Domino Bernardo Cancellario Regis, Dominis Willielmo de Haya, Johanne de Striuelyn, Willielmo Wysman, Johanne de Ffenton, Dauid de Berkeley, et Waltero de Berkeley militibus, magistro Waltero Heroc, Decano ecclesie Morauie, magistro Willielmo de Creswel eiusdem ecclesie precentore et multis aliis nobilibus clericis et laicis dictis die et loco congregatis.'

The copy of this curious document was supplied by my friend, Mr. Thomson, Deputy Register of Scotland, whose researches into our ancient records are daily throwing new and important light upon the history of the country.

NOTE LXIX.

The Monarch rode along the van.—P. 464.

The English vanguard, commanded by the Earls of Gloucester and Hereford, came in sight of the Scottish army upon the evening of the 23rd of June. Bruce was then riding upon a little palfrey, in front of his foremost line, putting his host in order. It was then that the personal encounter took place betwixt him and Sir Henry de Bohun, a gallant English knight, the issue of which had a great effect upon the spirits of both armies. It is thus recorded by Barbour :—

'And quhen Glosyster and Herfurd war
With thair bataill, approchand ner,
Befor thaim all thar come rydand,
With helm on heid, and sper in hand,
Schyr Henry the Boune, the worthi,
That wes a wycht knycht, and a hardy;
And to the Erle off Herfurd cusyne
Armyt in armys gud and fyne ;
Come on a sted, a bow schote ner,
Befor all othyr that thar wer :
And knew the King, for that he saw
Him swa ying his men on raw ;
And by the croune, that wes set
Alsua apon his bassynet.
And towart him he went in hy.
And [quhen] the King sua apertly
Saw him cum, forouth all his feris[1],
In hy[2] till him the hors he steris.
And quhen Schyr Henry saw the King
Cum on, for owtyn abaysing[3],
Till him he raid in full gret hy,
He thoucht that he suld weill lychtly
Wyn him, and haf him at his will,
Sen he him horsyt saw sa ill.
Sprent[4] thai samyn in till a ling[5].
Schyr Henry myssit the noble King,
And he, that in his sterapys stud,
With the ax that wes hard and gud,
With sa gret mayne[6] racht him a dynt,
That nothyr hat, na helm, mycht stynt,
The hewy[7] dusche[8] that he him gave,
That ner the heid till the harynys clave.
The hand ax schaft fruschit[9] in twa ;
And he doune to the erd gan ga
All flatlynys[10], for him faillyt mycht.'
This wes the fryst strak off the fycht.'

BARBOUR'S *Bruce*, Book VIII. v. 684.

The Scottish leaders remonstrated with the King upon his temerity. He only answered, 'I have broken my good battle-axe.'—The English vanguard retreated after witnessing this single combat. Probably their generals did not think it advisable to hazard an attack while its unfavourable issue remained upon their minds.

NOTE LXX.

'*What train of dust, with trumpet sound
And glimmering spears, is wheeling round
Our leftward flank ?*'—P. 466.

While the van of the English army advanced, a detached body attempted to relieve Stirling. Lord Hailes gives the following account of this manœuvre and the result, which is accompanied by circumstances highly characteristic of the chivalrous manners of the age, and displays that generosity which reconciles us even to their ferocity upon other occasions.

Bruce had enjoined Randolph, who commanded the left wing of his army, to be vigilant in preventing any advanced parties of the English from throwing succours into the castle of Stirling.

'Eight hundred horsemen, commanded by

Sir Robert Clifford, were detached from the English army ; they made a circuit by the low grounds to the east, and approached the castle. The King perceived their motions, and, coming up to Randolph, angrily exclaimed, "Thoughtless man! you have suffered the enemy to pass." Randolph hasted to repair his fault, or perish. As he advanced, the English cavalry wheeled to attack him. Randolph drew up his troops in a circular form, with their spears resting on the ground, and protended on every side. At the first onset, Sir William Daynecourt, an English commander of distinguished note, was slain. The enemy, far superior in numbers to Randolph, environed him, and pressed hard on his little band. Douglas saw his jeopardy, and requested the King's permission to go and succour him. "You shall not move from your ground," cried the King; "let Randolph extricate himself as he best may. I will not alter my order of battle, and lose the advantage of my position."—"In truth," replied Douglas, "I cannot stand by and see Randolph perish ; and, therefore, with your leave, I must aid him." The King unwillingly consented, and Douglas flew to the assistance of his friend. While approaching, he perceived that the English were falling into disorder, and that the perseverance of Randolph had prevailed over their impetuous courage. "Halt," cried Douglas, "those brave men have repulsed the enemy ; let us not diminish their glory by sharing it."'—DALRYMPLE'S *Annals of Scotland.* 4to, Edinburgh, 1779, pp. 44–45.

Two large stones erected at the north end of the village of Newhouse, about a quarter of a mile from the south part of Stirling, ascertain the place of this memorable skirmish. The circumstance tends, were confirmation necessary, to support the opinion of Lord Hailes, that the Scottish line had Stirling on its left flank. It will be remembered, that Randolph commanded infantry, Daynecourt cavalry. Supposing, therefore, according to the vulgar hypothesis, that the Scottish line was drawn up, facing to the south, in the line of the brook of Bannock, and consequently that Randolph was stationed with his left flank resting upon Milntown bog, it is morally impossible that his infantry, moving from that position, with whatever celerity, could cut off from Stirling a body of cavalry who had already passed St. Ninian's[1], or, in other words, were already between them and the town. Whereas, supposing Randolph's left to have approached St. Ninian's, the short movement to Newhouse could easily be executed, so as to intercept the English in the manner described.

---

1 Comrades.　2 Haste.　3 Without shrinking.
4 Spurred.　5 Line.　6 Strength, or force.
7 Heavy.　8 Clash.　9 Broke.　10 Flat.

1 Barbour says expressly, they avoided the New Park (where Bruce's army lay), and held 'well neath the Kirk,' which can only mean St. Ninian's.

Note LXXI.

Responsive from the Scottish host,
Pipe-clang and bugle-sound were toss'd.
                                    —P. 467.

There is an old tradition, that the well-known Scottish tune of 'Hey, tutti taitti,' was Bruce's march at the battle of Bannockburn. The late Mr. Ritson, no granter of propositions, doubts whether the Scots had any martial music, and quotes Froissart's account of each soldier in the host bearing a little horn, on which, at the onset, they would make such a horrible noise, as if all the devils of hell had been among them. He observes, that these horns are the only music mentioned by Barbour, and concludes, that it must remain a moot point whether Bruce's army were cheered by the sound even of a solitary bagpipe.—*Historical Essay prefixed to Ritson's Scottish Songs.*—It may be observed in passing, that the Scottish of this period certainly observed some musical cadence, even in winding their horns, since Bruce was at once recognized by his followers from his mode of blowing   See Note XLIV on Canto IV. But the tradition, true or false, has been the means of securing to Scotland one of the finest lyrics in the language, the celebrated war-song of Burns,—'Scots, wha hae wi' Wallace bled.'

Note LXXII.

Now onward, and in open view,
The countless ranks of England drew.
                                    —P. 467.

Upon the 24th of June, the English army advanced to the attack. The narrowness of the Scottish front, and the nature of the ground, did not permit them to have the full advantage of their numbers, nor is it very easy to find out what was their proposed order of battle. The vanguard, however, appeared a distinct body, consisting of archers and spearmen on foot, and commanded, as already said, by the Earls of Gloucester and Hereford. Barbour, in one place, mentions that they formed nine BATTLES or divisions; but from the following passage, it appears that there was no room or space for them to extend themselves, so that, except the vanguard, the whole army appeared to form one solid and compact body :—

> 'The English men, on either party,
> That as angels shone brightly,
> Were not array'd on such manner;
> For all their battles samyn[1] were
> In a schiltrum[2].   But whether it was

[1] Together.
[2] *Schiltrum.*—This word has been variously limited or extended in its signification. In general, it seems to imply a large body of men drawn up very closely together. But it has been limited to imply a round

Through the great straitness of the place
That they were in, to bide fighting;
Or that it was for abaysing[1];
I wete not.   But in a schiltrum
It seemed they were all and some;
Out ta'en the vaward anerly[2],
That right with a great company,
Be them selwyn, arrayed were.
Who had been by, might have seen there
That folk ourtake a mekill feild
On breadth, where many a shining shield,
And many a burnished bright armour,
And many a man of great valour,
Might in that great schiltrum be seen:
And many a bright banner and sheen.'
                    BARBOUR'S *Bruce*, vol. ii. p. 137.

Note LXXIII.

See where yon barefoot Abbot stands,
And blesses them with lifted hands!
                                    —P. 467.

'Maurice, abbot of Inchaffray, placing himself on an eminence, celebrated mass in sight of the Scottish army. He then passed along the front barefooted, and bearing a crucifix in his hands, and exhorting the Scots, in few and forcible words, to combat for their rights and their liberty. The Scots kneeled down. "They yield," cried Edward; "see, they implore mercy."—"They do," answered Ingelram de Umfraville, "but not ours. On that field they will be victorious, or die."—*Annals of Scotland*, vol. ii. p. 47.

Note LXXIV.

Forth, Marshal! on the peasant foe!
We'll tame the terrors of their bow,
And cut the bow-string loose!'—P. 468.

The English archers commenced the attack with their usual bravery and dexterity. But against a force, whose importance he had learned by fatal experience, Bruce was provided. A small but select body of cavalry were detached from the right, under command of Sir Robert Keith. They rounded, as I conceive, the marsh called Milntown bog, and, keeping the firm ground, charged the left flank and rear of the English archers. As the bowmen had no spears nor

or circular body of men so drawn up. I cannot understand it with this limitation in the present case. The schiltrum of the Scottish army at Falkirk was undoubtedly of a circular form, in order to resist the attacks of the English cavalry, on whatever quarter they might be charged. But it does not appear how, or why, the English, advancing to the attack at Bannockburn, should have arrayed themselves in a circular form. It seems more probable, that, by *schiltrum* in the present case, Barbour means to express an irregular mass into which the English army was compressed by the unwieldiness of its numbers, and the carelessness or ignorance of its leaders.
[1] Frightening.   [2] Alone.

long weapons fit to defend themselves against horse, they were instantly thrown into disorder, and spread through the who'e English army a confusion from which they never fairly recovered.

> 'The Inglis archeris schot sa fast,
> That mycht thair schot haff ony last,
> It had bene hard to Scottis men.
> Bot King Robert, that wele gan ken [1]
> That thair archeris war peralouss,
> And thair schot rycht hard and grewouss,
> Ordanyt, forouth [2] the assemblé,
> Hys marschell with a gret menye,
> Fyve hundre armyt in to stele,
> That on lycht horss war horsyt welle,
> For to pryk [3] amang the archeris ;
> And swa assaile thaim with thair speris,
> That thai na layser haiff to schute.
> This marschell that Ik of mute [4],
> That Schyr Robert of Keyth was cauld,
> As Ik befor her has yow tauld,
> Quhen he saw the bataillis sua
> Assembill, and to gidder ga,
> And saw the archeris schovt stoutly ;
> With all thaim off his cumpany,
> In hy apon thaim gan he rid ;
> And our tuk thaim at a sid [5] ;
> And ruschyt amang thaim sa rudly,
> Stekand thaim sa dispitously,
> And in sic fusoun [6] berand doun,
> And slayand thaim, for owtyn ransoun [7] ;
> That thai thaim scalyt [8] euirilkane [9].
> And fra that tyme furth thar wes nane
> That assemblyt schot to ma [10].
> Quhen Scottis archeris saw that thai sua
> War rebutyt [11], thai woux hardy,
> And with all thair mycht schot egrely
> Amang the horss men, that thar raid ;
> And woundis wid to thaim thai maid ;
> And slew of thaim a full gret dele.'
>
> BARBOUR'S *Bruce*, Book IX. v. 228.

Although the success of this manœuvre was evident, it is very remarkable that the Scottish generals do not appear to have profited by the lesson. Almost every subsequent battle which they lost against England, was decided by the archers, to whom the close and compact array of the Scottish phalanx afforded an exposed and unresisting mark. The bloody battle of Halidoun hill, fought scarce twenty years afterwards, was so completely gained by the archers, that the English are said to have lost only one knight, one esquire, and a few foot-soldiers. At the battle of Neville's Cross, in 1346, where David II was defeated and made prisoner, John de Graham, observing the loss which the Scots sustained from the English bowmen, offered to charge and disperse them, if a hundred men-at-arms were put under his command. ' *But*, to confess the truth,' says Fordun, ' he could not procure a single horseman for the service proposed.' Of such little use is experience in war, where its results are opposed by habit or prejudice.

[1] Know.   [2] Disjoined from the main body.
[3] Spur.   [4] That I speak of.   [5] Set upon their flank.
[6] Numbers.   [7] Ransom.   [8] Dispersed.
[9] Every one.   [10] Make.   [11] Driven back.

NOTE LXXV.

Each braggart churl could boast before
Twelve Scottish lives his baldric bore!
     — P. 468.

Roger Ascham quotes a similar Scottish proverb, ' whereby they give the whole praise of shooting honestly to Englishmen, saying thus, "that every English archer beareth under his girdle twenty-four Scottes." Indeed Toxophilus says before, and truly of the Scottish nation, "The Scottes surely be good men of warre in theyre owne feates as can be ; but as for shootinge, they can neither use it to any profite, nor yet challenge it for any praise." '—*Works of Ascham, edited by Bennet*, 4to, p. 110.

It is said, I trust incorrectly, by an ancient English historian, that the 'good Lord James of Douglas' dreaded the superiority of the English archers so much, that when he made any of them prisoner, he gave him the option of losing the forefinger of his right hand, or his right eye, either species of mutilation rendering him incapable to use the bow. I have mislaid the reference to this singular passage.

NOTE LXXVI.

Down! down! in headlong overthrow,
Horseman and horse, the foremost go.
     —P. 468.

It is generally alleged by historians, that the English men-at-arms fell into the hidden snare which Bruce had prepared for them. Barbour does not mention the circumstance. According to his account, Randolph, seeing the slaughter made by the cavalry on the right wing among the archers, advanced courageously against the main body of the English, and entered into close combat with them. Douglas and Stuart, who commanded the Scottish centre, led their division also to the charge, and the battle becoming general along the whole line, was obstinately maintained on both sides for a long space of time ; the Scottish archers doing great execution among the English men-at-arms, after the bowmen of England were dispersed.

NOTE LXXVII.

And steeds that shriek in agony.—P. 469.

I have been told that this line requires an explanatory note ; and, indeed, those who witness the silent patience with which horses submit to the most cruel usage, may be permitted to doubt, that, in moments of sudden and intolerable anguish, they utter a most melancholy cry. Lord Erskine, in a speech made in the House of Lords, upon a bill for enforcing humanity towards animals, noticed this remarkable fact, in language which I will not mutilate by attempting to repeat it. It was my fortune, upon one occasion, to hear a horse, in a moment of agony, utter a thrilling scream, which I still consider the most melancholy sound I ever heard.

NOTE LXXVIII.

*Lord of the Isles, my trust in thee
Is firm as Ailsa Rock;
Rush on with Highland sword and targe,
I, with my Carrick spearmen, charge.*
—P. 470.

When the engagement between the main bodies had lasted some time, Bruce made a decisive movement, by bringing up the Scottish reserve. It is traditionally said, that at this crisis, he addressed the Lord of the Isles in a phrase used as a motto by some of his descendants, 'My trust is constant in thee.' Barbour intimates, that the reserve 'assembled on one field,' that is, on the same line with the Scottish forces already engaged; which leads Lord Hailes to conjecture that the Scottish ranks must have been much thinned by slaughter, since, in that circumscribed ground, there was room for the reserve to fall into the line. But the advance of the Scottish cavalry must have contributed a good deal to form the vacancy occupied by the reserve.

NOTE LXXIX.

*To arms they flew,—axe, club, or spear,—
And mimic ensigns high they rear.*—P. 470.

The followers of the Scottish camp observed, from the Gillies' Hill in the rear, the impression produced upon the English army by the bringing up of the Scottish reserve, and, prompted by the enthusiasm of the moment, or the desire of plunder, assumed, in a tumultuary manner, such arms as they found nearest, fastened sheets to tent-poles and lances, and showed themselves like a new army advancing to battle.

'Yomen, and swanys [1], and pittaill [2],
That in the Park yemyt wictaill [3],
War left; quhen thai wyst but lesing [4],
That thair lordis, with fell fechtyng,
On thair fayis assemblyt wer;
Ane off thaim selwyn [5] that war thar
Capitane of thaim all thai maid.
And schetis, that war sumedele [6] brad,
Thai festnyt in steid off baneris,
Apon lang treys and speris:
And said that thai wald se the fycht;
And help thair lordis at thair mycht.
Quhen her till all assentyt wer,
In a rout assemblit er [7];
Fyftene thowsand thai war, or ma.
And than in gret hy gan thai ga,
With thair baneris, all in a rout,
As thai had men bene styth [8] and stout.

[1] Swains.   [2] Rabble.   [3] Kept the provisions.
[4] Lying.   [5] Selves.   [6] Somewhat.
[7] Are.   [8] Stiff.

Thai come, with all that assemblé,
Rycht quhill thai mycht the bataill se;
Than all at anys that gave a cry,
"Sla! sla! Apon thaim hastily!"
BARBOUR'S *Bruce,* Book IX. v. 410.

The unexpected apparition, of what seemed a new army, completed the confusion which already prevailed among the English, who fled in every direction, and were pursued with immense slaughter. The brook of Bannock, according to Barbour, was so choked with the bodies of men and horses, that it might have been passed dry-shod. The followers of the Scottish camp fell upon the disheartened fugitives, and added to the confusion and slaughter. Many were driven into the Forth, and perished there, which, by the way, could hardly have happened, had the armies been drawn up east and west; since, in that case, to get at the river, the English fugitives must have fled through the victorious army. About a short mile from the field of battle is a place called the Bloody Folds. Here the Earl of Gloucester is said to have made a stand, and died gallantly at the head of his own military tenants and vassals. He was much regretted by both sides; and it is said the Scottish would gladly have saved his life, but, neglecting to wear his surcoat with armorial bearings over his armour, he fell unknown, after his horse had been stabbed with spears.

Sir Marmaduke Twenge, an English knight, contrived to conceal himself during the fury of the pursuit, and when it was somewhat slackened, approached King Robert. 'Whose prisoner are you, Sir Marmaduke?' said Bruce, to whom he was personally known. 'Yours, sir,' answered the knight. 'I receive you,' answered the king, and, treating him with the utmost courtesy, loaded him with gifts, and dismissed him without ransom. The other prisoners were all well treated. There might be policy in this, as Bruce would naturally wish to acquire the good opinion of the English barons, who were at this time at great variance with their king. But it also well accords with his high chivalrous character.

NOTE LXXX.

O give their hapless prince his due!
—P. 471.

Edward II. according to the best authorities, showed, in the fatal field of Bannockburn, personal gallantry not unworthy of his great sire and greater son. He remained on the field till forced away by the Earl of Pembroke, when all was lost. He then rode to the Castle of Stirling, and demanded admittance; but the governor, remonstrating upon the imprudence of shutting himself up in that fortress, which must so soon surrender, he assembled around his person five hundred men-at-arms, and, avoiding the field of battle and the victorious army, fled towards Linlithgow, pursued by Douglas with about sixty horse. They were augmented by Sir Lawrence Abernethy with twenty more, whom Douglas met in the Torwood upon their way to join the English army, and whom he easily persuaded to desert the defeated monarch, and to assist in the pursuit. They hung upon Edward's flight as far as Dunbar, too few in number to assail him with effect, but enough to harass his retreat so constantly, that whoever fell an instant behind, was instantly slain or made prisoner. Edward's ignominious flight terminated at Dunbar, where the Earl of March, who still professed allegiance to him, 'received him full gently.' From thence, the monarch of so great an empire, and the late commander of so gallant and numerous an army, escaped to Bamborough in a fishing vessel.

Bruce, as will appear from the following document, lost no time in directing the thunders of Parliamentary censure against such part of his subjects as did not return to their natural allegiance after the battle of Bannockburn.

APUD MONASTERIUM DE CAMBUSKENNETH, VI DIE NOVEMBRIS, M,CCC,XIV.

Judicium Reditum apud Kambuskinet contra omnes illos qui tunc fuerunt contra fidem et pacem Domini Regis.

Anno gracie millesimo tricentisimo quarto decimo sexto die Novembris tenente parliamentum suum Excellentissimo principe Domino Roberto Dei gracia Rege Scottorum Illustri in monasterio de Cambuskyneth concordatum fuit finaliter Judicatum [ac super] hoc statutum de Concilio et Assensu Episcoporum et ceterorum Prelatorum Comitum Baronum et aliorum nobilium regni Scocie nec non et tocius communitatis regni predicti quod omnes qui contra fidem et pacem dicti domini regis in bello seu alibi mortui sunt [vel qui die] to die ad pacem ejus et fidem non venerant licet sepius vocati et legitime expectati fuissent de terris et tenementis et omni alio statu infra regnum Scocie perpetuo sint exheredati et habeantur de cetero tanquam inimici Regis et Regni ab omni vendicacione juris hereditarii vel juris alterius cujuscunque in posterum pro se et heredibus suis in perpetuum privati Ad perpetuam igitur rei memoriam et evidentem probacionem hujus Judicii et Statuti sigilla Episcoporum et aliorum Prelatorum nec non et comitum Baronum ac ceterorum nobilium dicti Regni presenti ordinacioni Judicio et statuto sunt appensa.

Sigillum Domini Regis
Sigillum Willelmi Episcopi Sancti Andree
Sigillum Roberti Episcopi Glascuensis
Sigillum Willelmi Episcopi Dunkeldensis
. . . Episcopi . . . . . .
. . . Episcopi . . . . . .
. . . Episcopi . . . . . .
Sigillum Alani Episcopi Sodorensis
Sigillum Johannis Episcopi Brechynensis
Sigillum Andree Episcopi Ergadiensis
Sigillum Frechardi Episcopi Cathanensis
Sigillum Abbatis de Scona
Sigillum Abbatis de Calco
Sigillum Abbatis de Abirbrothok
Sigillum Abbatis de Sancta Cruce
Sigillum Abbatis de Londoris
Sigillum Abbatis de Newbotill
Sigillum Abbatis de Cupro
Sigillum Abbatis de Paslet
Sigillum Abbatis de Dunfermelyn
Sigillum Abbatis de Lincluden
Sigillum Abbatis de Insula Missarum
Sigillum Abbatis de Sancto Columba
Sigillum Abbatis de Deer
Sigillum Abbatis de Dulce Corde
Sigillum Prioris de Coldinghame
Sigillum Prioris Sancte Andree
Sigillum Prioris de Pittinwem
Sigillum Prioris de Insula de Lochlevin
Sigillum Senescalli Scocie
Sigillum Willelmi Comitis de Ros
. . . .
. . . .
Sigillum Gilberti de la Haya Constabularii Scocie
Sigillum Roberti de Keth Mariscalli Scocie
Sigillum Hugonis de Ros
Sigillum Jacobi de Duglas
Sigillum Johannis de Sancto Claro
Sigillum Thome de Ros
Sigillum Alexandri de Settone
Sigillum Walteri Haliburtone
Sigillum Davidis de Balfour
Sigillum Duncani de Wallays
Sigillum Thome de Dischingtone
Sigillum Andree de Moravia
Sigillum Archibaldi de Betun
Sigillum Ranulphi de Lyill
Sigillum Malcomi de Balfour
Sigillum Normanni de Lesley
Sigillum Nigelli de Campo bello
Sigillum Morni de Musco Campo
. . . .
. . . .

NOTE LXXXI.

Nor for De Argentine alone,
Through Ninian's church these torches
shone,
And rose the death-prayer's awful tone.
—P. 472.

The remarkable circumstances attending the death of De Argentine have been already noticed (Note XI). Besides this renowned warrior, there fell many representatives of the noblest houses in England, which never sustained a more bloody and disastrous defeat. Barbour says that two hundred pairs of gilded spurs were taken from the field of battle; and that some were left the author can bear witness, who has in his possession a curious antique spur, dug up in the morass not long since.

> ' It wes forsuth a gret ferly,
> To se samyn [1] sa fele dede lie.
> Twa hundre payr of spuris reid [2],
> War tane of knichtis that war deid.'

I am now to take my leave of Barbour, not without a sincere wish that the public may encourage the undertaking of my friend Dr. Jamieson, who has issued proposals for publishing an accurate edition of his poem, and of Blind Harry's 'Wallace[3].' The only good edition of 'The Bruce' was published by Mr. Pinkerton, in 3 vols., in 1790; and, the learned editor having had no personal access to consult the manuscript, it is not without errors; and it has besides become scarce. Of 'Wallace' there is no tolerable edition; yet these two poems do no small honour to the early state of Scottish poetry, and 'The Bruce' is justly regarded as containing authentic historical facts.

The following list of the slain at Bannockburn, extracted from the continuator of Trivet's Annals, will show the extent of the national calamity.

LIST OF THE SLAIN.

Knights & Knights Bannerets.

Gilbert de Clare, Earl of Gloucester,
Robert de Clifford,
Payan Tybetot,
William Le Mareschal,
John Comyn,
William de Vescey,
John de Montfort,
Nicolas de Hasteleigh,
William Dayncourt,
Ægidius de Argenteyne,
Edmond Comyn,
John Lovel (the rich),
Edmund de Hastynge,
Milo de Stapleton,
Simon Ward,
Robert de Felton,
Michael Poyning,
Edmund Maulley.

Knights.

Henry de Boun,
Thomas de Ufford,
John de Elsingfelde,
John de Harcourt,
Walter de Hakelut,
Philip de Courtenay,
Hugo de Scales,
Radulph de Beauchamp,
John de Penbrigge,
With 33 others of the same rank, not named.

---

[1] Together.   [2] Red, or gilded.
[3] [The extracts from Barbour in this edition of Sir Walter Scott's poems have been uniformly corrected by the text of Dr. Jamieson's *Bruce*, published, along with Blind Harry's *Wallace*, Edin. 1820, 2 vols. 4to.—LOCKHART.]

PRISONERS.

Barons & Baronets.

Henry de Boun, Earl of Hereford,
Lord John Giffard,
William de Latimer,
Maurice de Berkeley,
Ingelram de Umfraville,
Marmaduke de Twenge,
John de Wyletone,
Robert de Maulee,
Henry Fitz-Hugh,
Thomas de Gray,
Walter de Beauchamp,
Richard de Charon,
John de Wevelmton,
Robert de Nevil,
John de Segrave,
Gilbert Peeche,
John de Clavering,
Antony de Lucy,
Radulph de Camys,
John de Evere,
Andrew de Abremhyn.

Knights.

Thomas de Berkeley,
The son of Roger Tyrrel,

Anselm de Mareschal,
Giles de Beauchamp,
John de Cyfrewast,
John Bluwet,
Roger Corbet,
Gilbert de Boun,
Bartholomew de Enefeld,
Thomas de Ferrers,
Radulph and Thomas Bottetort,
John and Nicholas de Kingstone (brothers),
William Lovel,
Henry de Wileton,
Baldwin de Frevill,
John de Clivedon [1],
Adomar la Zouche,
John de Merewode,
John Maufe [2],
Thomas and Odo Lele Ercedekene,
Robert Beaupel (the son),
John Mautravers, (the son),
William and William Giffard and 34 other knights, not named by the historian.

And in sum there were slain, along with the Earl of Gloucester, forty-two barons and bannerets. The number of earls barons, and bannerets made captive was twenty-two, and sixty-eight knights. Many clerks and e-quires were also there slain or taken. Roger de Northburge, keeper of the king's signet (*Custos Targiae Domini Regis*), was made prisoner with his two clerks, Roger de Wakenfelde and Thomas de Switon, upon which the king caused a seal to be made, and entitled it his *privy seal*, to distinguish the same from the signet so lost. The Earl of Hereford was exchanged against Bruce's queen, who had been detained in captivity ever since the year 1306. The *Targia*, or signet, was restored to England through the intercession of Ralph de Monthermer, ancestor of Lord Moira, who is said to have found favour in the eyes of the Scottish king.—*Continuation of* TRIVET'S *Annals, Hall's edit.* Oxford, 1712, vol. ii. p. 14.

Such were the immediate consequences of the field of Bannockburn. Its more remote effects, in completely establishing the national independence of Scotland, afford a boundless field for speculation.

---

[1] Supposed Clinton.   [2] Maule.

Harold the Dauntless.

INTRODUCTION.

THERE is a mood of mind we all have
    known
On drowsy eve, or dark and low'ring
    day,
When the tired spirits lose their
    sprightly tone,
And nought can chase the lingering
    hours away;
Dull on our soul falls Fancy's daz-
    zling ray,
And wisdom holds his steadier torch
    in vain,
Obscured the painting seems, mis-
    tuned the lay,
Nor dare we of our listless load
    complain,
For who for sympathy may seek that
    cannot tell of pain?

The jolly sportsman knows such
    drearihood
When bursts in deluge the autumnal
    rain,
Clouding that morn which threats
    the heath-cock's brood;
Of such, in summer's drought, the
    anglers plain,
Who hope the soft mild southern
    shower in vain;
But, more than all, the discontented
    fair,
Whom father stern and sterner aunt
    restrain
From county-ball, or race occurring
    rare,
While all her friends around their vest-
    ments gay prepare.

Ennui! or, as our mothers call'd
    thee, Spleen!
To thee we owe full many a rare
    device;
Thine is the sheaf of painted cards,
    I ween,
The rolling billiard-ball, the rattling
    dice,
The turning-lathe for framing gim-
    crack nice;
The amateur's blotch'd pallet thou
    mayst claim,
Retort, and air-pump threatening
    frogs and mice
(Murders disguised by philosophic
    name),
And much of trifling grave, and much
    of buxom game.

Then of the books, to catch thy
    drowsy glance
Compiled, what bard the catalogue
    may quote!
Plays, poems, novels, never read
    but once;—
But not of such the tale fair Edge-
    worth wrote,
That bears thy name, and is thine
    antidote;

And not of such the strain my
    Thomson sung,
Delicious dreams inspiring by his
    note,
What time to Indolence his harp he
    strung:
Oh! might my lay be rank'd that
    happier list among!

Each hath his refuge whom thy
    cares assail.
For me, I love my study-fire to trim
And con right vacantly some idle tale,
Displaying on the couch each list-
    less limb,
Till on the drowsy page the lights
    grow dim,
And doubtful slumber half supplies
    the theme,
While antique shapes of knight and
    giant grim,
Damsel and dwarf, in long pro-
    cession gleam,
And the romancer's tale becomes the
    reader's dream.

'Tis thus my malady I well may bear,
Albeit outstretch'd like Pope's own
    Paridel
Upon the rack of a too-easy chair,
And find, to cheat the time, a
    powerful spell
In old romaunts of errantry that tell,
Or later legends of the Fairy-folk,
Or Oriental tale of Afrite fell,
Of Genii, Talisman, and broad-
    wing'd Roc,
Though taste may blush and frown,
    and sober reason mock.

Oft at such season, too, will rhymes
    unsought
Arrange themselves in some ro-
    mantic lay;
The which, as things unfitting
    graver thought,
Are burnt or blotted on some wiser
    day

These few survive; and, proudly
    let me say,
Court not the critic's smile, nor
    dread his frown;
They well may serve to while an
    hour away,
Nor does the volume ask for more
    renown
Than Ennui's yawning smile what
    time she drops it down.

—◆—

Canto First.

I.

List to the valorous deeds that were
    done
By Harold the Dauntless, Count
    Witikind's son!

Count Witikind came of a regal strain,
And roved with his Norsemen the
    land and the main.
Woe to the realms which he coasted!
    for there
Was shedding of blood, and rending
    of hair,
Rape of maiden, and slaughter of priest,
Gathering of ravens and wolves to the
    feast:
When he hoisted his standard black,
Before him was battle, behind him
    wrack,
And he burn'd the churches, that
    heathen Dane,
To light his band to their barks again.

II.

On Erin's shores was his outrage
    known,
The winds of France had his banners
    blown;
Little was there to plunder, yet still
His pirates had foray'd on Scottish hill:

But upon merry England's coast
More frequent he sail'd, for he won
    the most.
So wide and so far his ravage they
    knew,
If a sail but gleam'd white 'gainst the
    welkin blue,
Trumpet and bugle to arms did call,
Burghers hasten'd to man the wall,
Peasants fled inland his fury to 'scape,
Beacons were lighted on headland
    and cape,
Bells were toll'd out, and aye as they
    rung,
Fearful and faintly the grey brothers
    sung,
'Bless us, Saint Mary from flood and
    from fire,
From famine and pest, and Count
    Witikind's ire!'

III.

He liked the wealth of fair England
    so well,
That he sought in her bosom as native
    to dwell.
He enter'd the Humber in fearful
    hour,
And disembark'd with his Danish
    power.
Three Earls came against him with
    all their train, —
Two hath he taken, and one hath he
    slain.
Count Witikind left the Humber's
    rich strand,
And he wasted and warr'd in North-
    umberland.
But the Saxon King was a sire in
    age,
Weak in battle, in council sage;
Peace of that heathen leader he sought,
Gifts he gave, and quiet he bought;
And the Count took upon him the
    peaceable style
Of a vassal and liegeman of Britain's
    broad isle.

IV.

Time will rust the sharpest sword,
Time will consume the strongest cord;
That which moulders hemp and steel
Mortal arm and nerve must feel.
Of the Danish band, whom Count
    Witikind led,
Many wax'd aged, and many were
    dead:
Himself found his armour full weighty
    to bear,
Wrinkled his brows grew, and hoary
    his hair;
He lean'd on a staff, when his step
    went abroad,
And patient his palfrey, when steed
    he bestrode.
As he grew feebler his wildness ceased,
He made himself peace with prelate
    and priest,—
Made his peace, and, stooping his head,
Patiently listed the counsel they said:
Saint Cuthbert's Bishop was holy
    and grave,
Wise and good was the counsel he
    gave.

V.

'Thou hast murder'd, robb'd, and
    spoil'd,
Time it is thy poor soul were assoil'd;
Priests didst thou slay, and churches
    burn,
Time it is now to repentance to turn;
Fiends hast thou worshipp'd, with
    fiendish rite,
Leave now the darkness, and wend
    into light:
O! while life and space are given,
Turn thee yet, and think of Heaven!'
That stern old heathen his head he
    raised,
And on the good prelate he stedfastly
    gazed;
'Give me broad lands on the Wear
    and the Tyne,
My faith I will leave, and I'll cleave
    unto thine.'

VI.

Broad lands he gave him on Tyne and
    Wear,
To be held of the Church by bridle
    and spear ;
Part of Monkwearmouth, of Tynedale
    part,
To better his will, and to soften his
    heart :
Count Witikind was a joyful man,
Less for the faith than the lands he
    wan.
The high church of Durham is dress'd
    for the day,
The clergy are rank'd in their solemn
    array :
There came the Count, in a bear-skin
    warm,
Leaning on Hilda his concubine's arm.
He kneel'd before Saint Cuthbert's
    shrine,
With patience unwonted at rites divine ;
He abjured the gods of heathen race,
And he bent his head at the font of
    grace.
But such was the grisly old proselyte's
    look,
That the priest who baptized him
    grew pale and shook ;
And the old monks mutter'd beneath
    their hood,
'Of a stem so stubborn can never
    spring good ! '

VII.

Up then arose that grim convertite,
Homeward he hied him when ended
    the rite ;
The Prelate in honour will with him
    ride,
And feast in his castle on Tyne's fair
    side.
Banners and banderols danced in the
    wind,
Monks rode before them, and spear-
    men behind ;

Onward they pass'd, till fairly did shine
Pennon and cross on the bosom of
    Tyne ;
And full in front did that fortress lower,
In darksome strength with its buttress
    and tower :
At the castle gate was young Harold
    there,
Count Witikind's only offspring and
    heir.

VIII.

Young Harold was fear'd for his
    hardihood,
His strength of frame, and his fury of
    mood.
Rude he was and wild to behold,
Wore neither collar nor bracelet of
    gold,
Cap of vair nor rich array,
Such as should grace that festal day :
His doublet of bull's hide was all
    unbraced,
Uncover'd his head, and his sandal
    unlaced :
His shaggy black locks on his brow
    hung low,
And his eyes glanced through them
    a swarthy glow ;
A Danish club in his hand he bore,
The spikes were clotted with recent
    gore ;
At his back a she-wolf, and her wolf-
    cubs twain,
In the dangerous chase that morning
    slain.
Rude was the greeting his father he
    made,
None to the Bishop, while thus he
    said :—

IX.

'What priest-led hypocrite art thou,
With thy humbled look and thy
    monkish brow,
Like a shaveling who studies to cheat
    his vow?

Canst thou be Witikind the Waster
   known,
Royal Eric's fearless son,
Haughty Gunhilda's haughtier lord,
Who won his bride by the axe and
   sword;
From the shrine of Saint Peter the
   chalice who tore,
And m lted to bracelets for Freya
   and Thor;
With one blow of his gauntlet who
   burst the skull,
Before Odin's stone, of the Mountain
   Bull?
Then ye worshipp'd with rites that to
   war-gods belong,
With the deed of the brave, and the
   blow of the strong;
And now, in thine age to dotage sunk,
Wilt thou patter thy crimes to a
   shaven monk,
Lay down thy mail-shirt for clothing
   of hair,
Fasting and scourge, like a slave, wilt
   thou bear?
Or, at best, be admitted in slothful
   bower
To batten with priest and with para-
   mour?
Oh! out upon thine endless shame!
Each Scald's high harp shall blast thy
   fame,
And thy son will refuse thee a father's
   name!'

X.

Ireful wax'd old Witikind's look,
His faltering voice with fury shook:
'Hear me, Harold of harden'd heart!
Stubborn and wilful ever thou wert.
Thine outrage insane I command thee
   to cease,
Fear my wrath and remain at peace.
Just is the debt of repentance I've paid,
Richly the Church has a recompense
   made,
And the truth of her doctrines I prove
   with my blade,

But reckoning to none of my actions
   I owe,
And least to my son such accounting
   will show.
Why speak I to thee of repentance or
   truth,
Who ne'er from thy childhood knew
   reason or ruth?
Hence! to the wolf and the bear in
   her den;
These are thy mates, and not rational
   men.'

XI.

Grimly smiled Harold, and coldly
   replied,
'We must honour our sires, if we fear
   when they chide.
For me, I am yet what thy lessons
   have made,
I was rock d in a buckler and fed
   from a blade;
An infant, was taught to clasp hands
   and to shout
From the roofs of the tower when the
   flame had broke out;
In the blood of slain foemen my
   finger to dip,
And tinge with its purple my cheek
   and my lip.
'Tis thou know'st not truth, that hast
   barter d in eld,
For a price, the brave faith that thine
   ancestors held.
When this wolf,'—and the carcass he
   flung on the plain,—
'Shall awake and give food to her
   nurslings again,
The face of his father will Harold
   review;
Till then, aged Heathen, young
   Christian, adieu!'

XII.

Priest, monk, and prelate, stood aghast,
As through the pageant the heathen
   pass'd.

A cross-bearer out of his saddle he
flung,
Laid his hand on the pommel, and
into it sprung.
Loud was the shriek, and deep the
groan,
When the holy sign on the earth was
thrown!
The fierce old Count unsheathed his
brand,
But the calmer Prelate stay'd his hand.
'Let him pass free! Heaven knows
its hour;
But he must own repentance's power,
Pray and weep, and penance bear,
Ere he hold land by the Tyne and
the Wear.'
Thus in scorn and in wrath from his
father is gone
Young Harold the Dauntless, Count
Witikind's son.

XIII.

High was the feasting in Witikind's
hall,
Revell'd priests, soldiers, and pagans,
and all;
And e'en the good Bishop was fain
to endure
The scandal, which time and instruction might cure:
It were dangerous, he deem'd, at the
first to restrain,
In his wine and his wassail, a half-
christen'd Dane.
The mead flow'd around, and the ale
was drain'd dry,
Wild was the laughter, the song, and
the cry;
With Kyrie Eleison, came clamor-
ously in
The war-songs of Danesmen, Norweyan, and Finn,
Till man after man the contention
gave o'er,
Outstretch'd on the rushes that strew'd
the hall floor;

And the tempest within, having ceased
its wild rout,
Gave place to the tempest that
thunder'd without.

XIV.

Apart from the wassail, in turret alone,
Lay flaxen-hair'd Gunnar, old Ermen-
garde's son;
In the train of Lord Harold that page
was the first,
For Harold in childhood had Ermen-
garde nursed;
And grieved was young Gunnar his
master should roam,
Unhoused and unfriended, an exile
from home.
He heard the deep thunder, the
plashing of rain,
He saw the red lightning through shot-
hole and pane;
'And oh!' said the Page, 'on the
shelterless wold
Lord Harold is wandering in dark-
ness and cold!
What though he was stubborn, and
wayward, and wild,
He endured me because I was Ermen-
garde's child,
And often from dawn till the set of
the sun,
In the chase, by his stirrup, unbidden
I run;
I would I were older, and knighthood
could bear,
I would soon quit the banks of the
Tyne and the Wear:
For my mother's command, with her
last parting breath,
Bade me follow her nursling in life
and to death.

XV.

'It pours and it thunders, it lightens
amain,
As if Lok, the Destroyer, had burst
from his chain!

Accursed by the Church, and expell'd
by his sire,
Nor Christian nor Dane give him
shelter or fire,
And this tempest what mortal may
houseless endure ?
Unaided, unmantled, he dies on the
moor !
Whate'er comes of Gunnar, he tarries
not here.'
He leapt from his couch and he grasp'd
to his spear ;
Sought the hall of the feast.   Undisturb'd by his tread,
The wassailers slept fast as the sleep
of the dead :
' Ungrateful and bestial ! ' his anger
broke forth,
' To forget 'mid your goblets the pride
of the North !
And you, ye cowl'd priests, who have
plenty in store,
Must give Gunnar for ransom a palfrey
and ore.'

XVI.

Then, heeding full little of ban or of
curse,
He has seized on the Prior of Jorvaux's
purse :
Saint Meneholt's Abbot next morning
has miss'd
His mantle, deep furr'd from the cape
to the wrist :
The Seneschal's keys from his belt he
has ta'en
(Well drench'd on that eve was old
Hildebrand's brain).
To the stable-yard he made his way,
And mounted the Bishop's palfrey
gay,
Castle and hamlet behind him has cast,
And right on his way to the moorland
has pass'd.
Sore snorted the palfrey, unused to
face
A weather so wild at so rash a pace ;

So long he snorted, so loud he neigh'd,
There answer'd a steed that was bound
beside,
And the red flash of lightning show'd
there where lay
His master, Lord Harold, outstretch'd
on the clay.

XVII.

Up he started, and thunder'd out,
' Stand ! '
And raised the club in his deadly
hand.
The flaxen-hair'd Gunnar his purpose
told,
Show'd the palfrey and proffer'd the
gold.
' Back, back, and home, thou simple
boy !
Thou canst not share my grief or joy :
Have I not mark'd thee wail and cry
When thou hast seen a sparrow die ?
And canst thou, as my follower should,
Wade ankle-deep through foeman's
blood,
Dare mortal and immortal foe,
The gods above, the fiends below,
And man on earth, more hateful still,
The very fountain-head of ill ?
Desperate of life, and careless of death,
Lover of bloodshed, and slaughter, and
scathe,
Such must thou be with me to roam,
And such thou canst not be ; back, and
home ! '

XVIII.

Young Gunnar shook like an aspen
bough
As he heard the harsh voice and beheld
the dark brow,
And half he repented his purpose and
vow.
But now to draw back were bootless
shame,
And he loved his master, so urged his
claim :

'Alas! if my arm and my courage be
    weak,
Bear with me a while for old Ermen-
    garde's sake;
Nor deem so lightly of Gunnar's faith
As to fear he would break it for peril
    of death.
Have I not risk'd it to fetch thee this
    gold,
This surcoat and mantle to fence thee
    from cold?
And, did I bear a baser mind,
What lot remains if I stay behind?
The priests' revenge, thy father's
    wrath,
A dungeon, and a shameful death.'

XIX.

With gentler look Lord Harold eyed
The Page, then turn'd his head aside;
And either a tear did his eyelash stain,
Or it caught a drop of the passing rain.
'Art thou an outcast, then?' quoth he;
'The meeter page to follow me.'
'Twere bootless to tell what climes
    they sought,
Ventures achieved, and battles fought;
How oft with few, how oft alone,
Fierce Harold's arm the field hath
    won.
Men swore his eye, that flash'd so red
When each other glance was quench'd
    with dread,
Bore oft a light of deadly flame,
That ne'er from mortal courage came.
Those limbs so strong, that mood so
    stern,
That loved the couch of heath and fern,
Afar from hamlet, tower, and town,
More than to rest on driven down;
That stubborn frame, that sullen mood,
Men deem'd must come of aught but
    good;
And they whisper'd, the great Master
    Fiend was at one
With Harold the Dauntless, Count
    Witikind's son.

XX.

Years after years had gone and fled,
The good old Prelate lies lapp'd in lead;
In the chapel still is shown
His sculptured form on a marble stone,
With staff and ring and scapulaire,
And folded hands in the act of
    prayer.
Saint Cuthbert's mitre is resting now
On the haughty Saxon, bold Aldingar's
    brow;
The power of his crozier he loved to
    extend
O'er whatever would break, or what-
    ever would bend;
And now hath he clothed him in cope
    and in pall,
And the Chapter of Durham has met
    at his call.
'And hear ye not, brethren,' the proud
    Bishop said,
'That our vassal, the Danish Count
    Witikind's dead?
All his gold and his goods hath he given
To holy Church for the love of Heaven,
And hath founded a chantry with
    stipend and dole,
That priests and that beadsmen may
    pray for his soul:
Harold his son is wandering abroad,
Dreaded by man and abhorr'd by God;
Meet it is not, that such should heir
The lands of the Church on the Tyne
    and the Wear,
And at her pleasure, her hallow'd hands
May now resume these wealthy lands.'

XXI.

Answer'd good Eustace, a canon old:
'Harold is tameless, and furious, and
    bold;
Ever renown blows a note of fame,
And a note of fear, when she sounds
    his name:
Much of bloodshed and much of scathe
Have been their lot who have waked
    his wrath.

Leave him these lands and lordships
 still,
Heaven in its hour may change his
 will;
But if reft of gold, and of living bare,
An evil counsellor is despair.'
More had he said, but the Prelate
 frown'd,
And murmur'd his brethren who sate
 around,
And with one consent have they given
 their doom,
That the Church should the lands of
 Saint Cuthbert resume.
So will'd the Prelate; and canon and
 dean
Gave to his judgment their loud amen.

—✦—

Canto Second.

I.

'TIS merry in greenwood—thus runs
 the old lay—
In the gladsome month of lively May,
When the wild birds' song on stem
 and spray
 Invites to forest bower;
Then rears the ash his airy crest,
Then shines the birch in silver vest,
And the beech in glistening leaves
 is drest,
And dark between shows the oak's
 proud breast,
 Like a chieftain's frowning tower;
Though a thousand branches join their
 screen,
Yet the broken sunbeams glance be-
 tween,
And tip the leaves with lighter green,
 With brighter tints the flower:
Dull is the heart that loves not then
The deep recess of the wildwood glen,
Where roe and red-deer find sheltering
 den,
 When the sun is in his power.

II.

Less merry, perchance, is the fading
 leaf
That follows so soon on the gather'd
 sheaf,
 When the greenwood loses the
 name;
Silent is then the forest bound,
Save the redbreast's note, and the
 rustling sound
Of frost-nipt leaves that are dropping
 round,
Or the deep-mouth'd cry of the distant
 hound
 That opens on his game:
Yet then, too, I love the forest wide,
Whether the sun in splendour ride,
And gild its many-colour'd side;
Or whether the soft and silvery haze,
In vapoury folds, o'er the landscape
 strays,
And half involves the woodland maze,
 Like an early widow's veil,
Where wimpling tissue from the gaze
The form half hides, and half betrays,
 Of beauty wan and pale.

III.

Fair Metelill was a woodland maid,
Her father a rover of greenwood shade,
 By forest statutes undismay'd,
 Who lived by bow and quiver;
Well known was Wulfstane's archery,
By merry Tyne both on moor and lea,
Through wooded Weardale's glens
 so free,
Well beside Stanhope's wildwood tree,
 And well on Ganlesse river.
Yet free though he trespass'd on wood-
 land game,
More known and more fear'd was the
 wizard fame
Of Jutta of Rookhope, the Outlaw's
 dame;
Fear'd when she frown'd was her eye
 of flame,
 More fear'd when in wrath she
 laugh'd;

For then, 'twas said, more fatal true
To its dread aim her spell-glance flew,
Than when from Wulfstane's bended
　　　yew
　　Sprung forth the grey-goose shaft.

IV.

Yet had this fierce and dreaded pair,
So Heaven decreed, a daughter fair ;
　　None brighter crown'd the bed,
In Britain's bounds, of peer or prince,
Nor hath, perchance, a lovelier since
　　In this fair isle been bred.
And nought of fraud, or ire, or ill,
Was known to gentle Metelill,
　　A simple maiden she ;
The spells in dimpled smile that lie,
And a downcast blush, and the darts
　　that fly
With the sidelong glance of a hazel
　　eye,
　　Were her arms and witchery.
So young, so simple was she yet,
She scarce could childhood's joys
　　forget,
And still she loved, in secret set
　　Beneath the greenwood tree,
To plait the rushy coronet,
And braid with flowers her locks of
　　jet,
　　As when in infancy ;
Yet could that heart, so simple, prove
The early dawn of stealing love :
　　Ah ! gentle maid, beware !
The power who, now so mild a guest,
Gives dangerous yet delicious zest
To the calm pleasures of thy breast,
Will soon, a tyrant o'er the rest,
　　Let none his empire share.

V.

One morn, in kirtle green array'd,
Deep in the wood the maiden stray'd,
　　And, where a fountain sprung,
She sate her down, unseen, to thread
The scarlet berry's mimic braid,
　　And while the beads she strung,

Like the blithe lark, whose carol gay
Gives a good-morrow to the day,
　　So lightsomely she sung :

VI.

SONG.

' Lord William was born in gilded
　　bower,
The heir of Wilton's lofty tower ;
Yet better loves Lord William now
To roam beneath wild Rookhope's
　　brow ;
And William has lived where ladies
　　fair
With gauds and jewels deck their
　　hair,
Yet better loves the dewdrops still
That pearl the locks of Metelill.

The pious Palmer loves, I wis,
Saint Cuthbert's hallow'd beads to
　　kiss ;
But I, though simple girl I be,
Might have such homage paid to me ;
For did Lord William see me suit
This necklace of the bramble's fruit,
He fain--but must not have his will--
Would kiss the beads of Metelill.

My nurse has told me many a tale,
How vows of love are weak and frail ;
My mother says that courtly youth
By rustic maid means seldom sooth.
What should they mean ? it cannot be
That such a warning's meant for me,
For nought, oh ! nought, of fraud or ill
Can William mean to Metelill !'

VII.

Sudden she stops, and starts to feel
A weighty hand, a glove of steel,
Upon her shrinking shoulders laid ;
Fearful she turn'd, and saw, dismay'd,
A Knight in plate and mail array'd,
His crest and bearing worn and
　　fray'd,
　　His surcoat soil'd and riven,

Form'd like that giant race of yore,
Whose long-continued crimes out-
    wore
      The sufferance of Heaven.
Stern accents made his pleasure known,
Though then he used his gentlest tone:
' Maiden,' he said, 'sing forth thy glee;
Start not, sing on, it pleases me.'

VIII.

Secured within his powerful hold,
To bend her knee, her hands to fold,
    Was all the maiden might;
And ' Oh! forgive,' she faintly said,
' The terrors of a simple maid,
    If thou art mortal wight!
But if—of such strange tales are told—
Unearthly warrior of the wold,
Thou comest to chide mine accents
    bold,
My mother, Jutta, knows the spell,
At noon and midnight pleasing well
    The disembodied ear;
Oh! let her powerful charms atone
For aught my rashness may have done,
    And cease thy grasp of fear.'
Then laugh'd the Knight; his
    laughter's sound
Half in the hollow helmet drown'd;
His barred visor then he raised,
And steady on the maiden gazed.
He smooth'd his brows, as best he
    might,
To the dread calm of autumn night,
    When sinks the tempest roar;
Yet still the cautious fishers eye
The clouds, and fear the gloomy sky,
    And haul their barks on shore.

IX.

' Damsel,' he said, ' be wise, and learn
Matters of weight and deep concern:
    From distant realms I come,
And, wanderer long, at length have
    plann'd
In this my native Northern land
    To seek myself a home.

Nor that alone; a mate I seek:
She must be gentle, soft, and meek;
    No lordly dame for me;
Myself am something rough of mood,
And feel the fire of royal blood,
And therefore do not hold it good
    To match in my degree.
Then, since coy maidens say my face
Is harsh, my form devoid of grace,
For a fair lineage to provide,
'Tis meet that my selected bride
    In lineaments be fair;
I love thine well; till now I ne'er
Look'd patient on a face of fear,
But now that tremulous sob and tear
    Become thy beauty rare.
One kiss—nay, damsel, coy it not!
And now go seek thy parents' cot,
And say, a bridegroom soon I come,
To woo my love and bear her home.'

X.

Home sprung the maid without a pause,
As leveret 'scaped from greyhound's
    jaws;
But still she lock'd, howe'er distress'd,
The secret in her boding breast;
Dreading her sire, who oft forbade
Her steps should stray to distant glade.
Night came: to her accustom'd nook
Her distaff aged Jutta took,
And by the lamp's imperfect glow
Rough Wulfstane trimm'd his shafts
    and bow.
Sudden and clamorous, from the
    ground
Upstarted slumbering brach and
    hound;
Loud knocking next the lodge alarms,
And Wulfstane snatches at his arms,
When open flew the yielding door,
And that grim Warrior press'd the
    floor.

XI.

'All peace be here! What! none
    replies?
Dismiss your fears and your surprise.

'Tis I; that Maid hath told my tale,—
Or, trembler, did thy courage fail?
It recks not; it is I demand
Fair Metelill in marriage band;
Harold the Dauntless I, whose name
Is brave men's boast and caitiff's
     shame.'
The parents sought each other's eyes,
With awe, resentment, and surprise:
Wulfstane, to quarrel prompt, began
The stranger's size and thewes to scan;
But as he scann'd, his courage sunk,
And from unequal strife he shrunk,
Then forth, to blight and blemish, flies
The harmful curse from Jutta's eyes;
Yet, fatal howsoe'er, the spell
On Harold innocently fell!
And disappointment and amaze
Were in the witch's wilder'd gaze.

XII.

But soon the wit of woman woke,
And to the Warrior mild she spoke:
'Her child was all too young.' 'A
     toy—
The refuge of a maiden coy.'
Again, 'A powerful baron's heir
Claims in her heart an interest fair.'
'A trifle—whisper in his ear,
That Harold is a suitor here!'
Baffled at length she sought delay:
'Would not the Knight till morning
     stay?
Late was the hour; he there might rest
Till morn, their lodge's honour'd
     guest.'
Such were her words; her craft might
     cast
Her honour'd guest should sleep his
     last:
'No, not to-night; but soon,' he
     swore,
'He would return, nor leave them
     more.'
The threshold then his huge stride
     crost,
And soon he was in darkness lost.

XIII.

Appall'd a while the parents stood,
Then changed their fear to angry mood,
And foremost fell their words of ill
On unresisting Metelill:
Was she not caution'd and forbid,
Forewarn'd, implored, accused, and
     chid,
And must she still to greenwood roam,
To marshal such misfortune home?
'Hence, minion! to thy chamber
     hence!
There prudence learn, and penitence.'
She went,—her lonely couch to steep
In tears which absent lovers weep;
Or, if she gain'd a troubled sleep,
Fierce Harold's suit was still the theme
And terror of her feverish dream.

XIV.

Scarce was she gone, her dame and
     sire
Upon each other bent their ire;
'A woodsman thou, and hast a spear,
And couldst thou such an insult bear?'
Sullen he said, 'A man contends
With men, a witch with sprites and
     fiends;
Not to mere mortal wight belong
Yon gloomy brow and frame so strong.
But thou—is this thy promise fair,
That your Lord William, wealthy
     heir
To Ulrick, Baron of Witton-le-Wear,
Should Metelill to altar bear?
Do all the spells thou boast'st as thine
Serve but to slay some peasant's kine,
His grain in autumn's storms to steep,
Or thorough fog and fen to sweep,
And hag-ride some poor rustic's sleep?
Is such mean mischief worth the
     fame
Of sorceress and witch's name?
Fame, which with all men's wish
     conspires,
With thy deserts and my desires,
To damn thy corpse to penal fires?

Out on thee, witch! aroint! aroint!
What now shall put thy schemes in
    joint?
What save this trusty arrow's point,
From the dark dingle when it flies,
And he who meets it gasps and dies.'

XV.

Stern she replied, 'I will not wage
War with thy folly or thy rage;
But ere the morrow's sun be low,
Wulfstane of Rookhope, thou shalt
    know
If I can venge me on a foe.
Believe the while, that whatsoe'er
I spoke, in ire, of bow and spear,
It is not Harold's destiny
The death of pilfer'd deer to die.
But he, and thou, and yon pale moon
(That shall be yet more pallid soon,
Before she sink behind the dell),
Thou, she, and Harold too, shall tell
What Jutta knows of charm or spell.'
Thus muttering, to the door she bent
Her wayward steps, and forth she
    went,
And left alone the moody sire
To cherish or to slake his ire.

XVI.

Far faster than belong'd to age
Has Jutta made her pilgrimage.
A priest has met her as she pass'd,
And cross'd himself and stood aghast:
She traced a hamlet; not a cur
His throat would ope, his foot would
    stir;
By crouch, by trembling and by groan,
They made her hated presence known!
But when she trode the sable fell,
Were wilder sounds her way to tell;
For far was heard the fox's yell,
The black-cock waked and faintly crew,
Scream'd o'er the moss the scared
    curlew;
Where o'er the cataract the oak
Lay slant, was heard the raven's croak;

The mountain-cat, which sought his
    prey,
Glared, scream'd, and started from
    her way.
Such music cheer'd her journey lone
To the deep dell and rocking stone:
There, with unhallow'd hymn of
    praise,
She call'd a God of heathen days:

XVII.

INVOCATION.

'From thy Pomeranian throne,
Hewn in rock of living stone,
Where, to thy godhead faithful yet,
Bend Esthonian, Finn, and Lett,
And their swords in vengeance whet,
That shall make thine altars wet,
Wet and red for ages more
With the Christians' hated gore,
Hear me! sovereign of the rock,
Hear me! mighty Zernebock!

Mightiest of the mighty known,
Here thy wonders have been shown;
Hundred tribes in various tongue
Oft have here thy praises sung;
Down that stone with Runic seam'd,
Hundred victims' blood hath stream'd!
Now one woman comes alone,
And but wets it with her own,
The last, the feeblest of thy flock;
Hear, and be present, Zernebock!

Hark! he comes! the night-blast cold
Wilder sweeps along the wold;
The cloudless moon grows dark and
    dim,
And bristling hair and quaking limb
Proclaim the Master Demon nigh,—
Those who view his form shall die!
Lo! I stoop and veil my head;
Thou who ridest the tempest dread,
Shaking hill and rending oak,
Spare me! spare me! Zernebock.

He comes not yet! Shall cold delay
The votaress at her need repay?

Thou—shall I call thee god or fiend?
Let others on thy mood attend
With prayer and ritual; Jutta's arms
Are necromantic words and charms;
Mine is the spell that, utter'd once,
Shall wake thy master from his trance,
Shake his red mansion-house of pain,
And burst his seven-times-twisted
    chain!
So! com'st thou ere the spell is
    spoke?
I own thy presence, Zernebock.'—

XVIII.

'Daughter of dust,' the deep voice
    said,
—Shook while it spoke the vale for
    dread,
Rock'd on the base that massive stone
The Evil Deity to own—
'Daughter of dust! not mine the
    power
Thou seek'st on Harold's fatal hour.
'Twixt heaven and hell there is a strife
Waged for his soul and for his life,
And fain would we the combat win,
And snatch him in his hour of sin.
There is a star now rising red,
That threats him with an influence
    dread:
Woman, thine arts of malice whet,
To use the space before it set.
Involve him with the Church in strife,
Push on adventurous chance his life;
Ourself will in the hour of need,
As best we may, thy counsels speed.'
So ceased the voice: for seven
    leagues round
Each hamlet started at the sound;
But slept again, as slowly died
Its thunders on the hill's brown side.

XIX.

'And is this all,' said Jutta stern,
'That thou canst teach and I can learn?
Hence! to the land of fog and waste,
There fittest is thine influence placed,

Thou powerless, sluggish Deity!
But ne'er shall Briton bend the knee
Again before so poor a god.'
She struck the altar with her rod;
Slight was the touch, as when at need
A damsel stirs her tardy steed;
But to the blow the stone gave place,
And, starting from its balanced base,
Roll'd thundering down the moon-
    light dell,—
Re-echo'd moorland, rock, and fell;
Into the moonlight tarn it dash'd,
Their shores the sounding surges
    lash'd,
    And there was ripple, rage, and
        foam;
But on that lake, so dark and lone,
Placid and pale the moonbeam shone
    As Jutta hied her home.

—◆—

Canto Third.

I.

GREY towers of Durham! there
    was once a time
I view'd your battlements with such
    vague hope
As brightens life in its first dawning
    prime;
Not that e'en then came within
    fancy's scope
A vision vain of mitre, throne, or
    cope;
Yet, gazing on the venerable hall,
Her flattering dreams would in
    perspective ope
Some reverend room, some pre-
    bendary's stall;
And thus Hope me deceived as she
    deceiveth all.

Well yet I love thy mix'd and
    massive piles,
Half church of God, half castle
    'gainst the Scot,

And long to roam these venerable aisles,
With records stored of deeds long since forgot;
There might I share my Surtees' happier lot,
Who leaves at will his patrimonial field
To ransack every crypt and hallow'd spot,
And from oblivion rend the spoils they yield,
Restoring priestly chant and clang of knightly shield.

Vain is the wish—since other cares demand
Each vacant hour, and in another clime;
But still that northern harp invites my hand,
Which tells the wonder of thine earlier time;
And fain its numbers would I now command
To paint the beauties of that dawning fair,
When Harold, gazing from its lofty stand
Upon the western heights of Beaurepaire,
Saw Saxon Eadmer's towers begirt by winding Wear.

II.

Fair on the half-seen streams the sunbeams danced,
Betraying it beneath the woodland bank,
And fair between the Gothic turrets glanced
Broad lights, and shadows fell on front and flank,
Where tower and buttress rose in martial rank,
And girdled in the massive donjon Keep,
And from their circuit peal'd o'er bush and bank
The matin bell with summons long and deep,
And echo answer'd still with long-resounding sweep.

III.

The morning mists rose from the ground,
Each merry bird awaken'd round,
As if in revelry;
Afar the bugles' clanging sound
Call'd to the chase the lagging hound;
The gale breathed soft and free,
And seem'd to linger on its way
To catch fresh odours from the spray,
And waved it in its wanton play
So light and gamesomely.
The scenes which morning beams reveal,
Its sounds to hear, its gales to feel
In all their fragrance round him steal,
It melted Harold's heart of steel,
And, hardly wotting why,
He doff'd his helmet's gloomy pride,
And hung it on a tree beside,
Laid mace and falchion by,
And on the greensward sate him down,
And from his dark habitual frown
Relax'd his rugged brow :—
Whoever hath the doubtful task
From that stern Dane a boon to ask,
Were wise to ask it now.

IV.

His place beside young Gunnar took,
And mark'd his master's softening look,
And in his eye's dark mirror spied
The gloom of stormy thoughts subside,
And cautious watch'd the fittest tide
To speak a warning word.
So when the torrent's billows shrink,
The timid pilgrim on the brink
Waits long to see them wave and sink,
Ere he dare brave the ford,

And often, after doubtful pause,
His step advances or withdraws :
Fearful to move the slumbering ire
Of his stern lord, thus stood the squire,
    Till Harold raised his eye,
That glanced as when athwart the
    shroud
Of the dispersing tempest-cloud
    The bursting sunbeams fly.

V.

' Arouse thee, son of Ermengarde,
Offspring of prophetess and bard !
Take harp, and greet this lovely prime
With some high strain of Runic rhyme,
Strong, deep, and powerful ! Peal
    it round
Like that loud bell's sonorous sound,
Yet wild by fits, as when the lay
Of bird and bugle hail the day.
Such was my grandsire Eric's sport
When dawn gleam'd on his martial
    court.
Heymar the Scald, with harp's high
    sound,
Summon'd the chiefs who slept around;
Couch'd on the spoils of wolf and
    bear,
They roused like lions from their
    lair,
Then rush'd in emulation forth
To enhance the glories of the North.
Proud Eric, mightiest of thy race,
Where is thy shadowy resting-place ?
In wild Valhalla hast thou quaff'd
From foeman's skull metheglin
    draught,
Or wanderest where thy cairn was
    piled
To frown o'er oceans wide and wild?
Or have the milder Christians given
Thy refuge in their peaceful heaven?
Where'er thou art, to thee are known
Our toils endured, our trophies won,
Our wars, our wanderings, and our
    woes.'
He ceased, and Gunnar's song arose:

VI.

SONG.

' Hawk and osprey scream'd for joy
O'er the beetling cliffs of Hoy,
Crimson foam the beach o'erspread,
The heath was dyed with darker red,
When o'er Eric, Inguar's son,
Dane and Northman piled the stone;
Singing wild the war-song stern,
" Rest thee, Dweller of the Cairn !"

Where eddying currents foam and boil
By Bersa's burgh and Græmsay's isle,
The seaman sees a martial form
Half-mingled with the mist and storm.
In anxious awe he bears away
To moor his bark in Stromna's bay,
And murmurs from the bounding stern,
" Rest thee, Dweller of the Cairn !"

What cares disturb the mighty dead ?
Each honour'd rite was duly paid ;
No daring hand thy helm unlaced,
Thy sword, thy shield, were near
    thee placed,
Thy flinty couch no tear profaned,
Without, with hostile blood was stain'd;
Within, 'twas lined with moss and fern;
Then rest thee, Dweller of the Cairn !—

He may not rest : from realms afar
Comes voice of battle and of war,
Of conquest wrought with bloody
    hand
On Carmel's cliffs and Jordan's strand,
When Odin's warlike son could daunt
The turban'd race of Termagaunt.'

VII.

' Peace,' said the Knight, ' the noble
    Scald
Our warlike fathers' deeds recall'd,
But never strove to soothe the son
With tales of what himself had done.
At Odin's board the bard sits high
Whose harp ne'er stoop'd to flattery:

But highest he whose daring lay
Hath dared unwelcome truths to say.'
With doubtful smile young Gunnar
    eyed
His master's looks, and nought re-
    plied ;
But well that smile his master led
To construe what he left unsaid.
' Is it to me, thou timid youth,
Thou fear'st to speak unwelcome
    truth ?
My soul no more thy censure grieves
Than frosts rob laurels of their leaves.
Say on ; and yet—beware the rude
And wild distemper of my blood ;
Loth were I that mine ire should
    wrong
The youth that bore my shield so long,
And who, in service constant still,
Though weak in frame, art strong in
    will.'
' Oh ! ' quoth the Page, ' even there
    depends
My counsel, there my warning tends ;
Oft seems as of my master's breast
Some demon were the sudden guest ;
Then at the first misconstrued word
His hand is on the mace and sword,
From her firm seat his wisdom driven,
His life to countless dangers given.
O ! would that Gunnar could suffice
To be the fiend's last sacrifice,
So that, when glutted with my gore,
He fled and tempted thee no more ! '

            VIII.

Then waved his hand, and shook his
    head
The impatient Dane, while thus he
    said :
' Profane not, youth—it is not thine
To judge the spirit of our line—
The bold Berserkar's rage divine,
Through whose inspiring, deeds are
    wrought
Past human strength and human
    thought.

When full upon his gloomy soul
The champion feels the influence roll,
He swims the lake, he leaps the wall,
Heeds not the depth, nor plumbs the
    fall,
Unshielded, mail-less, on he goes
Singly against a host of foes ;
Their spears he holds like wither'd
    reeds,
Their mail like maiden's silken weeds ;
One 'gainst a hundred will he strive,
Take countless wounds, and yet sur-
    vive.
Then rush the eagles to his cry
Of slaughter and of victory ;
And blood he quaffs like Odin's bowl,
Deep drinks his sword, deep drinks
    his soul ;
And all that meet him in his ire
He gives to ruin, rout. and fire ;
Then, like gorged lion, seeks some den,
And couches till he 's man agen.
Thou know'st the signs of look and limb,
When 'gins that rage to overbrim ;
Thou know'st when I am moved,
    and why ;
And when thou see'st me roll mine eye,
Set my teeth thus. and stamp my foot,
Regard thy safety and be mute ;
But else speak boldly out whate'er
Is fitting that a knight should hear.
I love thee, youth. Thy lay has power
Upon my dark and sullen hour ;—
So Christian monks are wont to say
Demons of old were charm'd away ;
Then fear not I will rashly deem
Ill of thy speech, whate'er the theme.'

            IX.

As down some strait in doubt and
    dread
The watchful pilot drops the lead,
And, cautious in the midst to steer,
The shoaling channel sounds with fear ;
So, lest on dangerous ground he
    swerved,
The Page his master's brow observed,

Pausing at intervals to fling
His hand o'er the melodious string,
And to his moody breast apply
The soothing charm of harmony,
While hinted half, and half exprest,
This warning song convey'd the rest:

SONG.

'Ill fares the bark with tackle riven,
And ill when on the breakers driven;
Ill when the storm-sprite shrieks in air,
And the scared mermaid tears her
     hair;
But worse when on her helm the hand
Of some false traitor holds command.

Ill fares the fainting Palmer, placed
'Mid Hebron's rocks or Rana's waste;
Ill when the scorching sun is high,
And the expected font is dry;
Worse when his guide o'er sand
     and heath,
The barbarous Copt, has plann'd his
     death.

Ill fares the Knight with buckler cleft,
And ill when of his helm bereft;
Ill when his steed to earth is flung,
Or from his grasp his falchion wrung;
But worse, if instant ruin token,
When he lists rede by woman spoken.'

X.

'How now, fond boy? Canst thou
     think ill,'
Said Harold, 'of fair Metelill?'
'She may be fair,' the Page replied,
     As through the strings he ranged,
'She may be fair; but yet,' he cried,
     And then the strain he changed,—

SONG.

'She may be fair,' he sang, 'but yet
     Far fairer have I seen
Than she, for all her locks of jet,
     And eyes so dark and sheen.

Were I a Danish knight in arms,
     As one day I may be,
My heart should own no foreign
     charms;
     A Danish maid for me!

I love my fathers' northern land,
     Where the dark pine-trees grow,
And the bold Baltic's echoing strand
     Looks o'er each grassy oe.
I love to mark the lingering sun,
     From Denmark loth to go,
And leaving on the billows bright,
To cheer the short-lived summer night,
     A path of ruddy glow.

But most the northern maid I love,
     With breast like Denmark's snow,
And form as fair as Denmark's pine,
Who loves with purple heath to twine
     Her locks of sunny glow;
And sweetly blends that shade of gold
     With the cheek's rosy hue,
And Faith might for her mirror hold
     That eye of matchless blue.

'Tis hers the manly sports to love
     That southern maidens fear,
To bend the bow by stream and grove,
     And lift the hunter's spear.
She can her chosen champion's flight
     With eye undazzled see,
Clasp him victorious from the strife,
Or on his corpse yield up her life;
     A Danish maid for me!'

XI.

Then smiled the Dane, 'Thou canst
     so well
The virtues of our maidens tell,
Half could I wish my choice had been
Blue eyes, and hair of golden sheen,
And lofty soul; yet what of ill
Hast thou to charge on Metelill?'
'Nothing on her,' young Gunnar said,
'But her base sire's ignoble trade.
Her mother, too—the general fame
Hath given to Jutta evil name,

And in her grey eye is a flame
Art cannot hide, nor fear can tame.
That sordid woodman's peasant cot
Twice have thine honour'd footsteps
    sought,
And twice return'd with such ill rede
As sent thee on some desperate deed.'

XII.

'Thou errest; Jutta wisely said,
He that comes suitor to a maid,
Ere link'd in marriage, should provide
Lands and a dwelling for his bride—
My father's, by the Tyne and Wear,
I have reclaim'd.' 'O, all too dear,
And all too dangerous the prize,
E'en were it won,' young Gunnar cries;
' And then this Jutta's fresh device,
That thou should'st seek, a heathen
    Dane,
From Durham's priests a boon to gain,
When thou hast left their vassals slain
In their own halls!' Flash'd Harold's
    eye,
Thunder'd his voice—' False Page,
    you lie !
The castle, hall and tower, is mine,
Built by old Witikind on Tyne.
The wild-cat will defend his den,
Fights for her nest the timid wren;
And think'st thou I'll forego my right
For dread of monk or monkish knight?
Up and away, that deepening bell
Doth of the Bishop's conclave tell.
Thither will I, in manner due,
As Jutta bade, my claim to sue ;
And, if to right me they are loth,
Then woe to church and chapter both!'

Now shift the scene, and let the
    curtain fall,
And our next entry be Saint Cuth-
    bert's hall.

—◆—

Canto Fourth.

I.

FULL many a bard hath sung the
    solemn gloom
Of the long Gothic aisle and stone-
    ribb'd roof,
O'er-canopying shrine, and gor-
    geous tomb,
Carved screen, and altar glimmering
    far aloof
And blending with the shade—a
    matchless proof
Of high devotion, which hath now
    wax'd cold ;
Yet legends say that Luxury's brute
    hoof
Intruded oft within such sacred fold,
Like step of Bel's false priest, track'd
    in his fane of old.

Well pleased am I, howe'er, that
    when the rout
Of our rude neighbours whilome
    deign'd to come,
Uncall'd, and eke unwelcome, to
    sweep out
And cleanse our chancel from the
    rags of Rome,
They spoke not on our ancient fane
    the doom
To which their bigot zeal gave o'er
    their own,
But spared the martyr'd saint and
    storied tomb,
Though papal miracles had graced
    the stone,
And though the aisles still loved the
    organ's swelling tone.

And deem not, though 'tis now my
    part to paint
A Prelate sway'd by love of power
    and gold,
That all who wore the mitre of our
    Saint
Like to ambitious Aldingar I hold;

S

Since both in modern times and
   days of old
It sate on those whose virtues might
   atone
Their predecessors' frailties trebly
   told:
Matthew and Morton we as such
   may own—
And such (if fame speak truth) the
   honour'd Barrington.

II.

But now to earlier and to ruder times,
As subject meet, I tune my rugged
   rhymes,
Telling how fairly the chapter was
   met,
And rood and books in seemly order
   set;
Huge brass-clasp'd volumes, which
   the hand
Of studious priest but rarely scann'd,
Now on fair carved desk display'd,
'Twas theirs the solemn scene to
   aid.
O'erhead with many a scutcheon
   graced,
And quaint devices interlaced,
A labyrinth of crossing rows,
The roof in lessening arches shows;
Beneath its shade, placed proud and
   high,
With footstool and with canopy,
Sate Aldingar,—and prelate ne'er
More haughty graced Saint Cuthbert's
   chair;
Canons and deacons were placed
   below,
In due degree and lengthen'd row.
Unmoved and silent each sat there,
Like image in his oaken chair;
Nor head, nor hand, nor foot they
   stirr'd,
Nor lock of hair, nor tress of beard;
And of their eyes severe alone
The twinkle show'd they were not
   stone.

III.

The Prelate was to speech address'd,
Each head sunk reverent on each
   breast;
But ere his voice was heard, without
Arose a wild tumultuous shout,
Offspring of wonder mix'd with fear,
Such as in crowded streets we hear
Hailing the flames, that, bursting
   out,
Attract yet scare the rabble rout.
Ere it had ceased, a giant hand
Shook oaken door and iron band,
Till oak and iron both gave way,
Clash'd the long bolts, the hinges
   bray,
And, ere upon angel or saint they can
   call,
Stands Harold the Dauntless in midst
   of the hall:

IV.

'Now save ye, my masters, both
   rocket and rood,
From Bishop with mitre to Deacon
   with hood!
For here stands Count Harold, old
   Witikind's son,
Come to sue for the lands which his
   ancestors won.'
The Prelate look'd round him with
   sore troubled eye,
Unwilling to grant, yet afraid to deny;
While each Canon and Deacon who
   heard the Dane speak,
To be safely at home would have
   fasted a week:
Then Aldingar roused him, and
   answer'd again,
'Thou suest for a boon which thou
   canst not obtain;
The Church hath no fiefs for an
   unchristen'd Dane.
Thy father was wise, and his treasure
   hath given,
That the priests of a chantry might
   hymn him to heaven;

And the fiefs which whilome he
　　possess'd as his due,
Have lapsed to the Church, and been
　　granted anew
To Anthony Conyers and Alberic
　　Vere,
For the service Saint Cuthbert's
　　bless'd banner to bear,
When the bands of the North come
　　to foray the Wear.
Then disturb not our conclave with
　　wrangling or blame,
But in peace and in patience pass
　　hence as ye came.'

V.

Loud laugh'd the stern Pagan—
　　'They're free from the care
Of fief and of service, both Conyers
　　and Vere;
Six feet of your chancel is all they
　　will need,
A buckler of stone and a corselet of
　　lead.
Ho, Gunnar!—the tokens!' and,
　　sever'd anew,
A head and a hand on the altar he
　　threw.
Then shudder'd with terror both
　　Canon and Monk,
They knew the glazed eye and the
　　countenance shrunk,
And of Anthony Conyers the half-
　　grizzled hair,
And the scar on the hand of Sir
　　Alberic Vere.
There was not a churchman or priest
　　that was there
But grew pale at the sight, and betook
　　him to prayer.

VI.

Count Harold laugh'd at their looks
　　of fear:
'Was this the hand should your
　　banner bear?

Was that the head should wear the
　　casque
In battle at the Church's task?
Was it to such you gave the place
Of Harold with the heavy mace?
Find me between the Wear and Tyne
A knight will wield this club of mine,—
Give him my fiefs, and I will say
There's wit beneath the cowl of grey.'
He raised it, rough with many a stain,
Caught from crush'd skull and
　　spouting brain;
He wheel'd it that it shrilly sung,
And the aisles echo'd as it swung,
Then dash'd it down with sheer
　　descent,
And split King Osric's monument.
'How like ye this music? How trow
　　ye the hand
That can wield such a mace may be
　　reft of its land?
No answer?—I spare ye a space to
　　agree,
And Saint Cuthbert inspire you,
　　a saint if he be.
Ten strides through your chancel, ten
　　strokes on your bell,
And again I am with you; grave
　　fathers, farewell.'

VII.

He turn'd from their presence, he
　　clash'd the oak door,
And the clang of his stride died away
　　on the floor;
And his head from his bosom the
　　Prelate uprears
With a ghost-seer's look when the
　　ghost disappears:
'Ye Priests of Saint Cuthbert, now
　　give me your rede,
For never of counsel had Bishop
　　more need!
Were the arch-fiend incarnate in
　　flesh and in bone,
The language, the look, and the
　　laugh were his own.

In the bounds of Saint Cuthbert there
   is not a knight
Dare confront in our quarrel yon
   goblin in fight ;
Then rede me aright to his claim to
   reply,
'Tis unlawful to grant, and 'tis death
   to deny.'

VIII.

On venison and malmsie that morning
   had fed
The Cellarer Vinsauf ; 'twas thus that
   he said :
' Delay till to-morrow the Chapter's
   reply :
Let the feast be spread fair, and the
   wine be pour'd high ;
If he 's mortal he drinks, if he drinks
   he is ours—
His bracelets of iron, his bed in our
   towers.'
This man had a laughing eye,
Trust not, friends, when such you spy;
A beaker's depth he well could drain,
Revel, sport, and jest amain ; .
The haunch of the deer and the grape's
   bright dye,
Never bard loved them better than I :
But sooner than Vinsauf fill'd me my
   wine,
Pass'd me his jest, and laugh'd at mine,
Though the buck were of Bearpark,
   of Bourdeaux the vine,
With the dullest hermit I'd rather dine
On an oaken cake and a draught of
   the Tyne.

IX.

Walwayn the leech spoke next : he
   knew
Each plant that loves the sun and dew,
But special those whose juice can gain
Dominion o'er the blood and brain ;
The peasant who saw him by pale
   moonbeam
Gathering such herbs by bank and
   stream,

Deem'd his thin form and soundless
   tread
Were those of wanderer from the dead.
' Vinsauf, thy wine,' he said, ' hath
   power,
Our gyves are heavy, strong our tower ;
Yet three drops from this flask of mine,
More strong than dungeons, gyves, or
   wine,
Shall give him prison under ground
More dark, more narrow, more
   profound.
Short rede, good rede, let Harold have,
A dog's death and a heathen's grave.'
I have lain on a sick man's bed,
Watching for hours for the leech's
   tread,
As if I deem'd that his presence alone
Were of power to bid my pain begone;
I have listed his words of comfort
   given,
As if to oracles from heaven ;
I have counted his steps from my
   chamber door,
And bless'd them when they were
   heard no more ;
But sooner than Walwayn my sick
   couch should nigh,
My choice were, by leech-craft un-
   aided, to die.

X.

' Such service done in fervent zeal
The Church may pardon and conceal,'
The doubtful Prelate said, ' but ne'er
The counsel ere the act should hear.
Anselm of Jarrow, advise us now,
The stamp of wisdom is on thy brow;
Thy days, thy nights, in cloister pent,
Are still to mystic learning lent ;
Anselm of Jarrow, in thee is my hope,
Thou well may'st give counsel to
   Prelate or Pope.'

XI.

Answer'd the Prior : ''Tis wisdom's use
Still to delay what we dare not refuse ;

Ere granting the boon he comes hither
    to ask,
Shape for the giant gigantic task ;
Let us see how a step so sounding
    can tread
In paths of darkness, danger, and dread ;
He may not, he will not, impugn our
    decree,
That calls but for proof of his chivalry ;
And were Guy to return, or Sir Bevis
    the Strong,
Our wilds have adventure might
    cumber them long ;
The Castle of Seven Shields '——
    ' Kind Anselm, no more !
The step of the Pagan approaches the
    door.'
The churchmen were hush'd. In his
    mantle of skin,
With his mace on his shoulder, Count
    Harold strode in ;
There was foam on his lips, there was
    fire in his eye,
For, chafed by attendance, his fury
    was nigh.
' Ho ! Bishop,' he said, ' dost thou
    grant me my claim ?
Or must I assert it by falchion and
    flame ? '

XII.

' On thy suit, gallant Harold,' the
    Bishop replied,
In accents which trembled, ' we may
    not decide,
Until proof of your strength and your
    valour we saw ;
'Tis not that we doubt them, but such
    is the law.'
' And would you, Sir Prelate, have
    Harold make sport
For the cowls and the shavelings that
    herd in thy court ?
Say what shall he do ? From the
    shrine shall he tear
The lead bier of thy patron, and heave
    it in air,

And through the long chancel make
    Cuthbert take wing,
With the speed of a bullet dismiss'd
    from the sling ? '
' Nay, spare such probation,' the
    Cellarer said,
' From the mouth of our minstrels thy
    task shall be read.
While the wine sparkles high in the
    goblet of gold,
And the revel is loudest, thy task shall
    be told ;
And thyself, gallant Harold, shall,
    hearing it, tell
That the Bishop, his cowls, and his
    shavelings, meant well.'

XIII.

Loud revell'd the guests, and the
    goblets loud rang,
But louder the minstrel, Hugh
    Meneville, sang ;
And Harold, the hurry and pride of
    whose soul,
E'en when verging to fury, own'd
    music's control,
Still bent on the harper his broad
    sable eye,
And often untasted the goblet pass'd
    by ;
Than wine, or than wassail, to him
    was more dear
The minstrel's high tale of enchant-
    ment to hear ;
And the Bishop that day might of
    Vinsauf complain
That his art had but wasted his wine-
    casks in vain.

XIV.

THE CASTLE OF THE SEVEN SHIELDS.

A BALLAD.

The Druid Urien had daughters seven,
Their skill could call the moon from
    heaven ;

So fair their forms and so high their
fame,
That seven proud kings for their
suitors came.

King Mador and Rhys came from
Powis and Wales,
Unshorn was their hair, and unpruned
were their nails ;
From Strath-Clwyde was Ewain, and
Ewain was lame,
And the red-bearded Donald from
Galloway came.

Lot, King of Lodon, was hunchback'd
from youth ;
Dunmail of Cumbria had never a tooth ;
But Adolf of Bambrough, Northumberland's heir,
Was gay and was gallant, was young
and was fair.

There was strife 'mongst the sisters,
for each one would have
For husband King Adolf, the gallant
and brave ;
And envy bred hate, and hate urged
them to blows,
When the firm earth was cleft, and
the Arch-fiend arose !

He swore to the maidens their wish
to fulfil ;
They swore to the foe they would
work by his will.
A spindle and distaff to each hath he
given,
' Now hearken my spell,' said the
Outcast of heaven.

' Ye shall ply these spindles at midnight hour,
And for every spindle shall rise a
tower,
Where the right shall be feeble, the
wrong shall have power,
And there shall ye dwell with your
paramour.'

Beneath the pale moonlight they sate
on the wold,
And the rhymes which they chanted
must never be told ;
And as the black wool from the distaff
they sped,
With blood from their bosom they
moisten'd the thread.

As light danced the spindles beneath
the cold gleam,
The castle arose like the birth of
a dream ;
The seven towers ascended like mist
from the ground,
Seven portals defend them, seven
ditches surround.

Within that dread castle seven
monarchs were wed,
But six of the seven ere the morning
lay dead ;
With their eyes all on fire, and their
daggers all red,
Seven damsels surround the Northumbrian's bed.

' Six kingly bridegrooms to death we
have done,
Six gallant kingdoms King Adolf hath
won,
Six lovely brides all his pleasure to do,
Or the bed of the seventh shall be
husbandless too.'

Well chanced it that Adolf the night
when he wed
Had confess'd and had sain'd him
ere boune to his bed ;
He sprung from the couch and his
broadsword he drew,
And there the seven daughters of
Urien he slew.

The gate of the castle he bolted and
seal'd,
And hung o'er each arch-stone a crown
and a shield ;

To the cells of Saint Dunstan then
    wended his way,
And died in his cloister an anchorite
    grey.

Seven monarchs' wealth in that castle
    lies stow'd,
The foul fiends brood o'er them like
    raven and toad ;
Whoever shall guesten these chambers
    within,
From curfew till matins, that treasure
    shall win.

But manhood grows faint as the
    world waxes old !
There lives not in Britain a champion
    so bold,
So dauntless of heart, and so prudent
    of brain,
As to dare the adventure that treasure
    to gain.

The waste ridge of Cheviot shall
    wave with the rye,
Before the rude Scots shall North-
    umberland fly,
And the flint clifts of Bambro' shall
    melt in the sun,
Before that adventure be perill'd and
    won.

xv.

'And is this my probation ?' wild
    Harold he said,
'Within a lone castle to press a lone
    bed ?
Good even, my Lord Bishop ; Saint
    Cuthbert to borrow,
The Castle of Seven Shields receives
    me to-morrow.'

—◆—

Canto Fifth.

I.

DENMARK'S sage courtier to her
    princely youth,
Granting his cloud an ouzel or
    a whale,
Spoke, though unwittingly, a partial
    truth ;
For Fantasy embroiders Nature's
    veil.
The tints of ruddy eve, or dawning
    pale,
Of the swart thunder-cloud, or
    silver haze,
Are but the ground-work of the
    rich detail
Which Fantasy with pencil wild
    portrays,
Blending what seems and is in the
    wrapt muser's gaze.

Nor are the stubborn forms of earth
    and stone
Less to the Sorceress's empire given ;
For not with unsubstantial hues
    alone,
Caught from the varying surge, or
    vacant heaven,
From bursting sunbeam, or from
    flashing levin,
She limns her pictures : on the
    earth, as air,
Arise her castles, and her car is
    driven ;
And never gazed the eye on scene
    so fair,
But of its boasted charms gave Fancy
    half the share.

II.

Up a wild pass went Harold, bent
    to prove,
Hugh Meneville, the adventure of
    thy lay ;

Gunnar pursued his steps in faith
    and love,
Ever companion of his master's
    way.
Midward their path, a rock of
    granite grey
From the adjoining cliff had made
    descent,
A barren mass, yet with her
    drooping spray
Had a young birch-tree crown'd its
    battlement,
Twisting her fibrous roots through
    cranny, flaw, and rent.

This rock and tree could Gunnar's
    thought engage
Till Fancy brought the tear-drop to
    his eye,
And at his master ask'd the timid
    Page,
'What is the emblem that a bard
    should spy
In that rude rock and its green
    canopy?'
And Harold said, 'Like to the
    helmet brave
Of warrior slain in fight it seems
    to lie,
And these same drooping boughs
    do o'er it wave
Not all unlike the plume his lady's
    favour gave.'

'Ah, no!' replied the Page; 'the
    ill-starr'd love
Of some poor maid is in the emblem
    shown,
Whose fates are with some hero's
    interwove,
And rooted on a heart to love
    unknown:
And as the gentle dews of heaven
    alone
Nourish those drooping boughs,
    and as the scathe

Of the red lightning rends both
    tree and stone,
So fares it with her unrequited faith;
Her sole relief is tears, her only
    refuge death.'

III.

'Thou art a fond fantastic boy,'
Harold replied, 'to females coy,
    Yet prating still of love;
Even so amid the clash of war
I know thou lovest to keep afar,
Though destined by thy evil star
    With one like me to rove,
Whose business and whose joys are
    found
Upon the bloody battle-ground.
Yet, foolish trembler as thou art,
Thou hast a nook of my rude heart,
And thou and I will never part;
Harold would wrap the world in flame
Ere injury on Gunnar came!'

IV.

The grateful Page made no reply,
But turn'd to Heaven his gentle eye,
And clasp'd his hands, as one who
    said,
'My toils, my wanderings are o'erpaid!'
Then in a gayer, lighter strain,
Compell'd himself to speech again;
    And, as they flow'd along,
His words took cadence soft and slow,
And liquid, like dissolving snow,
    They melted into song.

V.

'What though through fields of
    carnage wide
I may not follow Harold's stride,
Yet who with faithful Gunnar's pride
    Lord Harold's feats can see?
And dearer than the couch of pride,
He loves the bed of grey wolf's hide,
When slumbering by Lord Harold's
    side
    In forest, field, or lea.'

VI.

' Break off !' said Harold, in a tone
Where hurry and surprise were
        shown,
    With some slight touch of fear ;
' Break off, we are not here alone ;
A Palmer form comes slowly on !
By cowl, and staff, and mantle known,
        My monitor is near.
Now mark him, Gunnar, heedfully ;
He pauses by the blighted tree—
Dost see him, youth ? Thou could'st
        not see
When in the vale of Galilee
    I first beheld his form,
Nor when we met that other while
In Cephalonia's rocky isle
    Before the fearful storm ;
Dost see him now ? ' The Page,
        distraught
With terror, answer'd, ' I see nought,
    And there is nought to see,
Save that the oak's scathed boughs
        fling down
Upon the path a shadow brown,
That, like a pilgrim's dusky gown,
    Waves with the waving tree.'

VII.

Count Harold gazed upon the oak
As if his eyestrings would have broke,
    And then resolvedly said,
' Be what it will yon phantom grey,
Nor heaven, nor hell, shall ever say
That for their shadows from his
        way
    Count Harold turn'd dismay'd :
I'll speak him, though his accents fill
My heart with that unwonted thrill
    Which vulgar minds call fear.
I will subdue it !' Forth he strode,
    Paused where the blighted oak-tree
        show'd
Its sable shadow on the road,
And, folding on his bosom broad
    His arms, said, ' Speak, I hear.'

VIII.

The Deep Voice said, ' O wild of will,
Furious thy purpose to fulfil,
Heart-sear'd and unrepentant still,
How long, O Harold, shall thy tread
Disturb the slumbers of the dead ?
Each step in thy wild way thou
        makest
The ashes of the dead thou wakest ;
And shout in triumph o'er thy path
The fiends of bloodshed and of wrath.
In this thine hour, yet turn and hear !
For life is brief and judgment near.'

IX.

Then ceased The Voice.   The Dane
        replied
In tones where awe and inborn pride
For mastery strove : ' In vain ye chide
The wolf for ravaging the flock,
Or with its hardness taunt the rock ;
I am as they—my Danish strain
Sends streams of fire through every
        vein.
Amid thy realms of goule and ghost,
Say, is the fame of Eric lost,
Or Witikind's the Waster, known
Where fame or spoil was to be won ;
Whose galleys ne'er bore off a shore
    They left not black with flame ?
He was my sire, and, sprung of him,
That rover merciless and grim,
    Can I be soft and tame ?
Part hence, and with my crimes no
        more upbraid me,
I am that Waster's son, and am but
        what he made me.'

X.

The Phantom groan'd ; the mountain
        shook around,
The fawn and wild-doe started at the
        sound,
The gorse and fern did wildly round
        them wave,
As if some sudden storm the impulse
        gave.

'All thou hast said is truth; yet on
　　the head
Of that bad sire let not the charge be
　　laid,
That he, like thee, with unrelenting
　　pace,
From grave to cradle ran the evil race:
Relentless in his avarice and ire,
Churches and towns he gave to sword
　　and fire;
Shed blood like water, wasted every
　　land,
Like the destroying angel's burning
　　brand;
Fulfill'd whate'er of ill might be
　　invented,
Yes! all these things he did—he did,
　　but he repented!
Perchance it is part of his punishment
　　still,
That his offspring pursues his example
　　of ill.
But thou, when thy tempest of wrath
　　shall next shake thee,
Gird thy loins for resistance, my son,
　　and awake thee;
If thou yield'st to thy fury, how
　　tempted soever,
The gate of repentance shall ope for
　　thee never!'—

XI.

'He is gone,' said Lord Harold, and
　　gazed as he spoke;
'There is nought on the path but the
　　shade of the oak.
He is gone, whose strange presence
　　my feeling oppress'd,
Like the night-hag that sits on the
　　slumberer's breast.
My heart beats as thick as a fugitive's
　　tread,
And cold dews drop from my brow
　　and my head.
Ho! Gunnar, the flasket yon almoner
　　gave;
He said that three drops would recall
　　from the grave.

For the first time Count Harold owns
　　leech-craft has power,
Or, his courage to aid, lacks the juice
　　of a flower!'
The Page gave the flasket, which
　　Walwayn had fill'd
With the juice of wild roots that his
　　art had distill'd;
So baneful their influence on all that
　　had breath,
One drop had been frenzy, and two
　　had been death.
Harold took it, but drank not; for
　　jubilee shrill,
And music and clamour were heard
　　on the hill,
And down the steep pathway, o'er
　　stock and o'er stone,
The train of a bridal came blithe-
　　somely on;
There was song, there was pipe, there
　　was trimbrel, and still
The burden was 'Joy to the fair
　　Metelill!'

XII.

Harold might see from his high stance,
Himself unseen, that train advance
　　With mirth and melody;
On horse and foot a mingled throng,
Measuring their steps to bridal song
　　And bridal minstrelsy;
And ever when the blithesome rout
Lent to the song their choral shout,
Redoubling echoes roll'd about,
While echoing cave and cliff sent out
　　The answering symphony
Of all those mimic notes which dwell
In hollow rock and sounding dell.

XIII.

Joy shook his torch above the band,
By many a various passion fann'd;
As elemental sparks can feed
On essence pure and coarsest weed,
Gentle, or stormy, or refined,
Joy takes the colours of the mind.

Lightsome and pure, but unrepress'd,
He fired the bridegroom's gallant
　　breast ;
More feebly strove with maiden fear,
Yet still joy glimmer'd through the tear
On the bride's blushing cheek, that
　　shows
Like dewdrop on the budding rose ;
While Wulfstane's gloomy smile
　　declared
The glee that selfish avarice shared,
And pleased revenge and malice high
Joy's semblance took in Jutta's eye.
On dangerous adventure sped,
The witch deem'd Harold with the
　　dead,
For thus that morn her Demon said :
' If, ere the set of sun, be tied
The knot 'twixt bridegroom and his
　　bride,
The Dane shall have no power of ill
O'er William and o'er Metelill.'
And the pleased witch made answer,
　　' Then
Must Harold have pass'd from the
　　paths of men !
Evil repose may his spirit have ;
May hemlock and mandrake find root
　　in his grave ;
May his death-sleep be dogged by
　　dreams of dismay,
And his waking be worse at the
　　answering day ! '

XIV.

Such was their various mood of glee
Blent in one shout of ecstasy.
But still when Joy is brimming highest,
Of Sorrow and Misfortune nighest,
Of Terror with her ague cheek,
And lurking Danger, sages speak :
These haunt each path, but chief they lay
Their snares beside the primrose way.
Thus found that bridal band their path
Beset by Harold in his wrath.
Trembling beneath his maddening
　　mood,
High on a rock the giant stood ;

His shout was like the doom of death
Spoke o'er their heads that pass'd
　　beneath.
His destined victims might not spy
The reddening terrors of his eye,
The frown of rage that writhed his face,
The lip that foam'd like boar's in chase ;
But all could see—and, seeing, all
Bore back to shun the threaten'd fall—
The fragment which their giant foe
Rent from the cliff and heaved to throw.

XV.

Backward they bore : yet are there
　　two
　　　For battle who prepare ;
No pause of dread Lord William knew
Ere his good blade was bare ;
And Wulfstane bent his fatal yew,
But ere the silken cord he drew,
As hurl'd from Hecla's thunder, flew
　　　That ruin through the air !
Full on the outlaw's front it came,
And all that late had human name,
And human face, and human frame,
That lived, and moved, and had free
　　will
To choose the path of good or ill,
　　　Is to its reckoning gone ;
And nought of Wulfstane rests behind,
　　　Save that beneath that stone,
Half-buried in the dinted clay,
A red and shapeless mass there lay
　　　Of mingled flesh and bone !

XVI.

As from the bosom of the sky
　　　The eagle darts amain,
Three bounds from yonder summit high
　　　Placed Harold on the plain.
As the scared wild-fowl scream and fly,
　　　So fled the bridal train ;
As 'gainst the eagle's peerless might
The noble falcon dares the fight,
　　　But dares the fight in vain,
So fought the bridegroom ; from his
　　hand
The Dane's rude mace has struck his
　　brand,

Its glittering fragments strew the sand,
　　Its lord lies on the plain.
Now, Heaven! take noble William's
　　part,
And melt that yet unmelted heart,
Or, ere his bridal hour depart,
　　The hapless bridegroom 's slain !

XVII.

Count Harold's frenzied rage is high,
There is a death-fire in his eye,
Deep furrows on his brow are
　　trench'd,
His teeth are set, his hand is
　　clench'd,
The foam upon his lip is white,
His deadly arm is up to smite !
But, as the mace aloft he swung,
To stop the blow young Gunnar
　　sprung,
Around his master's knees he clung
　　And cried, ' In mercy spare !
O think upon the words of fear
Spoke by that visionary Seer ;
The crisis he foretold is here,
　　Grant mercy, or despair !'
This word suspended Harold's mood,
Yet still with arm upraised he stood,
And visage like the headsman's rude
　　That pauses for the sign.
' O mark thee with the blessed rood,'
The Page implored ; ' speak word of
　　good,
Resist the fiend, or be subdued !'
　　He sign'd the cross divine;
Instant his eye hath human light,
Less red, less keen, less fiercely bright;
His brow relax'd the obdurate frown,
The fatal mace sinks gently down,
　　He turns and strides away ;
Yet oft, like revellers who leave
Unfinish'd feast, looks back to grieve,
As if repenting the reprieve
　　He granted to his prey.
Yet still of forbearance one sign hath
　　he given,
And fierce Witikind's son made one
　　step towards heaven.

XVIII.

But though his dreaded footsteps part,
Death is behind and shakes his dart ;
Lord William on the plain is lying,
Beside him Metelill seems dying !
Bring odours, essences in haste—
And lo ! a flasket richly chased ;
But Jutta the elixir proves
Ere pouring it for those she loves ;
Then Walwayn's potion was not
　　wasted,
For when three drops the hag had
　　tasted,
　　So dismal was her yell,
Each bird of evil omen woke,
The raven gave his fatal croak,
And shriek'd the night-crow from the
　　oak,
The screech-owl from the thicket broke,
　　And flutter'd down the dell !
So fearful was the sound and stern,
The slumbers of the full-gorged erne
Were startled, and from furze and fern
　　Of forest and of fell,
The fox and famish'd wolf replied
(For wolves then prowl'd the Cheviot
　　side).
From mountain head to mountain head
The unhallow'd sounds around were
　　sped ;
But when their latest echo fled,
The sorceress on the ground lay dead.

XIX.

Such was the scene of blood and
　　woes
With which the bridal morn arose
　　Of William and of Metelill ;
But oft, when dawning 'gins to spread,
The summer morn peeps dim and red
　　Above the eastern hill,
Ere, bright and fair, upon his road
The King of Splendour walks abroad ;
So, when this cloud had pass'd away,
Bright was the noontide of their day,
And all serene its setting ray.

—✦—

Canto Sixth.

I.

WELL do I hope that this my minstrel tale
Will tempt no traveller from southern fields,
Whether in tilbury, barouche, or mail,
To view the Castle of these Seven Proud Shields.
Small confirmation its condition yields
To Meneville's high lay : no towers are seen
On the wild heath, but those that fancy builds,
And, save a fosse that tracks the moor with green,
Is nought remains to tell of what may there have been.

And yet grave authors, with the no small waste
Of their grave time, have dignified the spot
By theories, to prove the fortress placed
By Roman bands, to curb the invading Scot.
Hutchinson, Horsley, Camden, I might quote,
But rather choose the theory less civil
Of boors, who, origin of things forgot,
Refer still to the origin of evil,
And for their master-mason choose that master-fiend the Devil.

II.

Therefore, I say, it was on fiend-built towers
That stout Count Harold bent his wondering gaze,
When evening dew was on the heather flowers,
And the last sunbeams made the mountain blaze,
And tinged the battlements of other days
With the bright level light ere sinking down.
Illumined thus, the dauntless Dane surveys
The Seven Proud Shields that o'er the portal frown,
And on their blazons traced high marks of old renown.

A wolf North Wales had on his armour-coat,
And Rhys of Powis-land a couchant stag ;
Strath-Clwyd's strange emblem was a stranded boat,
Donald of Galloway's a trotting nag ;
A corn-sheaf gilt was fertile Lodon's brag ;
A dudgeon-dagger was by Dunmail worn ;
Northumbrian Adolf gave a sea-beat crag
Surmounted by a cross ; such signs were borne
Upon these antique shields, all wasted now and worn.

III.

These scann'd, Count Harold sought the castle-door
Whose ponderous bolts were rusted to decay ;
Yet till that hour adventurous knight forbore
The unobstructed passage to essay.
More strong than armed warders in array,
And obstacle more sure than bolt or bar,
Sate in the portal Terror and Dismay,
While Superstition, who forbade to war
With foes of other mould than mortal clay,
Cast spells across the gate, and barr'd the onward way.

Vain now those spells; for soon
  with heavy clank
The feebly-fasten'd gate was inward
  push'd,
And, as it oped, through that
  emblazon'd rank
Of antique shields, the wind of
  evening rush'd
With sound most like a groan, and
  then was hush'd.
Is none who on such spot such
  sounds could hear
But to his heart the blood had
  faster rush'd;
Yet to bold Harold's breast that
  throb was dear—
It spoke of danger nigh, but had no
  touch of fear.

IV.

Yet Harold and his Page no signs
  have traced
Within the castle, that of danger
  show'd;
For still the halls and courts were
  wild and waste,
As through their precincts the
  adventurers trode.
The seven huge towers rose stately,
  tall, and broad,
Each tower presenting to their
  scrutiny
A hall in which a king might make
  abode,
And fast beside, garnish'd both
  proud and high,
Was placed a bower for rest in which
  a king might lie.

As if a bridal there of late had
  been,
Deck'd stood the table in each
  gorgeous hall;
And yet it was two hundred years,
  I ween,
Since date of that unhallow'd festival.
Flagons, and ewers, and standing
  cups, were all

Of tarnish'd gold, or silver nothing
  clear,
With throne begilt, and canopy of
  pall,
And tapestry clothed the walls with
  fragments sear:
Frail as the spider's mesh did that
  rich woof appear.

V.

In every bower, as round a hearse,
  was hung
A dusky crimson curtain o'er the
  bed,
And on each couch in ghastly wise
  were flung
The wasted relics of a monarch
  dead;
Barbaric ornaments around were
  spread,
Vests twined with gold, and chains
  of precious stone,
And golden circlets, meet for
  monarch's head;
While grinn'd, as if in scorn amongst
  them thrown,
The wearer's fleshless skull, alike with
  dust bestrown.

For these were they who, drunken
  with delight,
On pleasure's opiate pillow laid
  their head,
For whom the bride's shy footstep,
  slow and light,
Was changed ere morning to the
  murderer's tread.
For human bliss and woe in the
  frail thread
Of human life are all so closely
  twined,
That till the shears of Fate the
  texture shred,
The close succession cannot be
  disjoin'd,
Nor dare we, from one hour, judge
  that which comes behind.

VI.

But where the work of vengeance
 had been done,
In that seventh chamber, was a
 sterner sight;
There of the witch-brides lay each
 skeleton,
Still in the posture as to death when
 dight.
For this lay prone, by one blow
 slain outright;
And that, as one who struggled
 long in dying;
One bony hand held knife, as if to
 smite;
One bent on fleshless knees, as
 mercy crying;
One lay across the door, as kill'd in
 act of flying.

The stern Dane smiled this charnel-
 house to see,
For his chafed thought return'd to
 Metelill;
And 'Well,' he said, 'hath woman's
 perfidy,
Empty as air, as water volatile,
Been here avenged. The origin of ill
Through woman rose, the Christian
 doctrine saith:
Nor deem I, Gunnar, that thy
 minstrel skill
Can show example where a woman's
 breath
Hath made a true-love vow, and,
 tempted, kept her faith.'

VII.

The minstrel-boy half smiled, half
 sigh'd,
And his half-filling eyes he dried,
And said, 'The theme I should but
 wrong,
Unless it were my dying song,
(Our Scalds have said, in dying hour
The Northern harp has treble power)
Else could I tell of woman's faith,
Defying danger, scorn, and death.

Firm was that faith, as diamond stone
Pure and unflaw'd, her love unknown,
And unrequited; firm and pure,
Her stainless faith could all endure;
From clime to clime, from place to place,
Through want, and danger, and
 disgrace,
A wanderer's wayward steps could
 trace.
All this she did, and guerdon none
Required, save that her burial-stone
Should make at length the secret
 known,
"Thus hath a faithful woman done."
Not in each breast such truth is laid,
But Eivir was a Danish maid.'

VIII.

'Thou art a wild enthusiast,' said
Count Harold, 'for thy Danish maid;
And yet, young Gunnar, I will own
Hers were a faith to rest upon.
But Eivir sleeps beneath her stone,
And all resembling her are gone.
What maid e'er show'd such constancy
In plighted faith, like thine to me?
But couch thee, boy; the darksome
 shade
Falls thickly round, nor be dismay'd
 Because the dead are by.
They were as we; our little day
O'erspent, and we shall be as they.
Yet near me, Gunnar, be thou laid,
Thy couch upon my mantle made,
That thou mayst think, should fear
 invade,
 Thy master slumbers nigh.'
Thus couch'd they in that dread abode,
Until the beams of dawning glow'd.

IX.

An alter'd man Lord Harold rose;
When he beheld that dawn unclose,
 There's trouble in his eyes,
And traces on his brow and cheek
Of mingled awe and wonder speak:
 'My page,' he said, 'arise;

Leave we this place, my page.' No
    more
He utter'd till the castle door
They cross'd, but there he paused and
    said,
'My wildness hath awaked the dead,
    Disturb'd the sacred tomb!
Methought this night I stood on high,
Where Hecla roars in middle sky,
And in her cavern'd gulfs could spy
    The central place of doom;
And there before my mortal eye
Souls of the dead came flitting by,
Whom fiends, with many a fiendish cry,
    Bore to that evil den!
My eyes grew dizzy, and my brain
Was wilder'd, as the elvish train,
With shriek and howl, dragg'd on
    amain
    Those who had late been men.

x.

'With haggard eyes and streaming
    hair,
Jutta the Sorceress was there,
And there pass'd Wulfstane, lately
    slain,
All crush'd and foul with bloody stain.
More had I seen, but that uprose
A whirlwind wild, and swept the
    snows;
And with such sound as when at need
A champion spurs his horse to speed,
Three armèd knights rush on, who lead
Caparison'd a sable steed.
Sable their harness, and there came
Through their closed visors sparks of
    flame.
The first proclaim'd, in sounds of fear,
"Harold the Dauntless, welcome here!"
The next cried, "Jubilee! we've won
Count Witikind the Waster's son!"
And the third rider sternly spoke,
"Mount, in the name of Zernebock!
From us, O Harold, were thy powers,
Thy strength, thy dauntlessness, are
    ours;

Nor think, a vassal thou of hell,
With hell can strive." The fiend
    spoke true!
My inmost soul the summons knew,
    As captives know the knell
That says the headsman's sword is bare,
And, with an accent of despair,
    Commands them quit their cell.
I felt resistance was in vain,
My foot had that fell stirrup ta'en,
My hand was on the fatal mane,
    When to my rescue sped
That Palmer's visionary form,
And, like the passing of a storm,
    The demons yell'd and fled!

xi.

'His sable cowl, flung back, reveal'd
The features it before conceal'd;
    And, Gunnar, I could find
In him whose counsels strove to stay
So oft my course on wilful way,
    My father Witikind!
Doom'd for his sins, and doom'd for
    mine,
A wanderer upon earth to pine
Until his son shall turn to grace,
And smooth for him a resting-place.
Gunnar, he must not haunt in vain
This world of wretchedness and pain:
I'll tame my wilful heart to live
In peace, to pity and forgive;
And thou, for so the Vision said,
Must in thy lord's repentance aid.
Thy mother was a prophetess,
He said, who by her skill could guess
How close the fatal textures join
Which knit thy thread of life with mine;
Then, dark, he hinted of disguise
She framed to cheat too curious eyes,
That not a moment might divide
Thy fated footsteps from my side.
Methought while thus my sire did
    teach,
I caught the meaning of his speech,
Yet seems its purport doubtful now.'
His hand then sought his thoughtful
    brow;

Then first he mark'd, that in the tower
His glove was left at waking hour.

XII.

Trembling at first, and deadly pale,
Had Gunnar heard the vision'd tale ;
But when he learn'd the dubious close,
He blush'd like any opening rose,
And, glad to hide his tell-tale cheek,
Hied back that glove of mail to seek ;
When soon a shriek of deadly dread
Summon'd his master to his aid.

XIII.

What sees Count Harold in that bower,
　So late his resting-place ?
The semblance of the Evil Power,
　Adored by all his race !
Odin in living form stood there,
His cloak the spoils of Polar bear ;
For plumy crest a meteor shed
Its gloomy radiance o'er his head,
Yet veil'd its haggard majesty
To the wild lightnings of his eye.
Such height was his, as when in stone
O'er Upsal's giant altar shown :
　So flow'd his hoary beard ;
Such was his lance of mountain-pine,
So did his sevenfold buckler shine ;
　But when his voice he rear'd,
Deep, without harshness, slow and
　strong,
The powerful accents roll'd along,
And, while he spoke, his hand was laid
On captive Gunnar's shrinking head.

XIV.

'Harold,' he said, 'what rage is thine,
To quit the worship of thy line,
　To leave thy Warrior-God ?
With me is glory or disgrace,
Mine is the onset and the chase,
Embattled hosts before my face
　Are wither'd by a nod.
Wilt thou then forfeit that high seat
Deserved by many a dauntless feat,
Among the heroes of thy line,
Eric and fiery Thorarine ?
Thou wilt not. Only I can give
The joys for which the valiant live,

Victory and vengeance ; only I
Can give the joys for which they die,
The immortal tilt, the banquet full,
The brimming draught from foeman's
　skull.
Mine art thou, witness this thy glove,
The faithful pledge of vassal's love.'

XV.

'Tempter,' said Harold, firm of heart,
'I charge thee, hence ! whate'er thou
　art,
I do defy thee, and resist
The kindling frenzy of my breast,
Waked by thy words ; and of my mail,
Nor glove, nor buckler, splent, nor nail,
Shall rest with thee—that youth
　release,
And God, or Demon, part in peace.'
'Eivir,' the Shape replied, 'is mine,
Mark'd in the birth hour with my sign.
Think'st thou that priest with drops
　of spray
Could wash that blood-red mark away ?
Or that a borrow'd sex and name
Can abrogate a Godhead's claim ?'
Thrill'd this strange speech through
　Harold's brain,
He clench'd his teeth in high disdain,
For not his new-born faith subdued
Some tokens of his ancient mood :
'Now, by the hope so lately given
Of better trust and purer heaven,
I will assail thee, fiend !' Then rose
His mace, and with a storm of blows
The mortal and the Demon close.

XVI.

Smoke roll'd above, fire flash'd around,
Darken'd the sky and shook the
　ground ;
　But not the artillery of hell,
The bickering lightning, nor the rock
Of turrets to the earthquake's shock,
　Could Harold's courage quell.
Sternly the Dane his purpose kept,
And blows on blows resistless heap'd,
　Till quail'd that Demon Form,

And—for his power to hurt or kill
Was bounded by a higher will—
    Evanish'd in the storm.
Nor paused the Champion of the North,
But raised, and bore his Eivir forth,
From that wild scene of fiendish strife,
To light, to liberty, and life!

XVII.

He placed her on a bank of moss,
    A silver runnel bubbled by,
And new-born thoughts his soul
    engross,
And tremors yet unknown across
    His stubborn sinews fly,
The while with timid hand the dew
Upon her brow and neck he threw,
And mark'd how life with rosy hue
On her pale cheek revived anew,
    And glimmer'd in her eye.
Inly he said, 'That silken tress
What blindness mine that could not
    guess!
Or how could page's rugged dress
That bosom's pride belie?
O, dull of heart, through wild and wave
In search of blood and death to rave,
    With such a partner nigh!'

XVIII.

Then in the mirror'd pool he peer'd,
Blamed his rough locks and shaggy
    beard,
The stains of recent conflict clear'd,
    And thus the Champion proved,
That he fears now who never fear'd,
    And loves who never loved.
And Eivir—life is on her cheek,
And yet she will not move or speak,
    Nor will her eyelid fully ope;
Perchance it loves, that half-shut eye,
Through its long fringe, reserved and
    shy,
Affection's opening dawn to spy;
And the deep blush, which bids its dye

O'er cheek, and brow, and bosom fly,
    Speaks shame-facedness and hope.

XIX.

But vainly seems the Dane to seek
For terms his new-born love to speak,
For words, save those of wrath and
    wrong,
Till now were strangers to his tongue;
So, when he raised the blushing maid,
In blunt and honest terms he said
('Twere well that maids, when lovers
    woo,
Heard none more soft, were all as true):
'Eivir! since thou for many a day
Hast follow'd Harold's wayward way,
It is but meet that in the line
Of after-life I follow thine.
To-morrow is Saint Cuthbert's tide,
And we will grace his altar's side,
A Christian knight and Christian bride;
And of Witikind's son shall the marvel
    be said,
That on the same morn he was
    christen'd and wed.

CONCLUSION.

And now, Ennui, what ails thee,
    weary maid?
And why these listless looks of
    yawning sorrow?
No need to turn the page, as if
    'twere lead,
Or fling aside the volume till to-
    morrow.
Be cheer'd; 'tis ended—and I will
    not borrow,
To try thy patience more, one
    anecdote
From Bartholine, or Perinskiold,
    or Snorro.
Then pardon thou thy minstrel, who
    hath wrote
A Tale six cantos long, yet scorn'd
    to add a note.

END OF HAROLD THE DAUNTLESS.

The Bridal of Triermain.

INTRODUCTION.

I.

Come, Lucy! while 'tis morning hour
The woodland brook we needs must
pass;
So, ere the sun assume his power,
We shelter in our poplar bower,
Where dew lies long upon the flower,
Though vanish'd from the velvet
grass.
Curbing the stream, this stony ridge
May serve us for a silvan bridge;
For here, compell'd to disunite,
Round petty isles the runnels
glide,
And chafing off their puny spite,
The shallow murmurers waste their
might,
Yielding to footstep free and light
A dry-shod pass from side to side.

II.

Nay, why this hesitating pause?
And, Lucy, as thy step withdraws,
Why sidelong eye the streamlet's brim?
Titania's foot without a slip,
Like thine, though timid, light, and
slim,
From stone to stone might safely trip,
Nor risk the glow-worm clasp to dip
That binds her slipper's silken rim.
Or trust thy lover's strength: nor fear
That this same stalwart arm of mine,

Which could yon oak's prone trunk
uprear,
Shall shrink beneath the burden dear
Of form so slender, light, and fine;
So! now, the danger dared at last,
Look back, and smile at perils past!

III.

And now we reach the favourite glade,
Paled in by copsewood, cliff, and
stone,
Where never harsher sounds invade,
To break affection's whispering tone,
Than the deep breeze that waves the
shade,
Than the small brooklet's feeble
moan.
Come! rest thee on thy wonted seat;
Moss'd is the stone, the turf is green,
A place where lovers best may meet
Who would not that their love be
seen.
The boughs, that dim the summer sky,
Shall hide us from each lurking spy,
That fain would spread the invidious
tale,
How Lucy of the lofty eye,
Noble in birth, in fortunes high,
She for whom lords and barons sigh,
Meets her poor Arthur in the dale.

IV.

How deep that blush!—how deep
that sigh!
And why does Lucy shun mine eye?

Is it because that crimson draws
Its colour from some secret cause,
Some hidden movement of the breast
She would not that her Arthur guess'd?
O! quicker far is lovers' ken
Than the dull glance of common men,
And, by strange sympathy, can spell
The thoughts the loved one will not
tell!
And mine, in Lucy's blush, saw met
The hues of pleasure and regret;
  Pride mingled in the sigh her voice,
    And shared with Love the crimson
    glow;
  Well pleased that thou art Arthur's
    choice,
    Yet shamed thine own is placed
    so low:
  Thou turn'st thy self-confessing
    cheek,
    As if to meet the breeze's cooling;
  Then, Lucy, hear thy tutor speak,
    For Love, too, has his hours of
    schooling.

v.

Too oft my anxious eye has spied
That secret grief thou fain wouldst
  hide,
The passing pang of humbled pride;
  Too oft, when through the splendid
    hall,
  The load-star of each heart and eye,
My fair one leads the glittering ball,
Will her stol'n glance on Arthur fall,
  With such a blush and such a sigh!
Thou wouldst not yield, for wealth
  or rank,
  The heart thy worth and beauty
    won,
Nor leave me on this mossy bank,
  To meet a rival on a throne:
Why, then, should vain repinings
  rise,
That to thy lover fate denies
A nobler name, a wide domain,
A Baron's birth, a menial train,

Since Heaven assign'd him, for his
  part,
A lyre, a falchion, and a heart?

VI.

My sword—its master must be dumb;
  But, when a soldier names my
    name,
Approach, my Lucy! fearless come,
  Nor dread to hear of Arthur's
    shame.
My heart! 'mid all yon courtly crew,
  Of lordly rank and lofty line,
Is there to love and honour true,
  That boasts a pulse so warm as
    mine?
They praised thy diamonds' lustre
  rare—
  Match'd with thine eyes, I thought
    it faded;
They praised the pearls that bound
  thy hair—
  I only saw the locks they braided;
They talk'd of wealthy dower and land,
  And titles of high birth the token—
I thought of Lucy's heart and hand,
  Nor knew the sense of what was
    spoken.
And yet, if rank'd in Fortune's roll,
  I might have learn'd their choice
    unwise,
Who rate the dower above the soul,
  And Lucy's diamonds o'er her eyes.

VII.

My lyre—it is an idle toy,
  That borrows accents not its own,
Like warbler of Colombian sky,
  That sings but in a mimic tone.
Ne'er did it sound o'er sainted well,
Nor boasts it aught of Border spell;
Its strings no feudal slogan pour,
Its heroes draw no broad claymore;
No shouting clans applauses raise,
Because it sung their father's praise;
On Scottish moor, or English down,
It ne'er was graced with fair renown;

Nor won—best meed to minstrel true—
One favouring smile from fair Buc-
CLEUCH!
By one poor streamlet sounds its tone,
And heard by one dear maid alone.

VIII.

But, if thou bid'st, these tones shall tell
Of errant knight, and damozelle;
Of the dread knot a Wizard tied,
In punishment of maiden's pride,
In notes of marvel and of fear,
That best may charm romantic ear.
For Lucy loves (like COLLINS, ill-
starred name,
Whose lay's requital was that tardy
fame,
Who bound no laurel round his living
head,
Should hang it o'er his monument when
dead)
For Lucy loves to tread enchanted
strand,
And thread, like him, the maze of fairy
land;
Of golden battlements to view the
gleam,
And slumber soft by some Elysian
stream;
Such lays she loves; and, such my
Lucy's choice,
What other song can claim her Poet's
voice?

Canto First.

I.

WHERE is the maiden of mortal strain
That may match with the Baron of
Triermain?
She must be lovely, and constant, and
kind,
Holy and pure, and humble of mind,
Blithe of cheer, and gentle of mood,
Courteous. and generous, and noble
of blood;

Lovely as the sun's first ray
When it breaks the clouds of an April
day;
Constant and true as the widow'd dove,
Kind as a minstrel that sings of love;
Pure as the fountain in rocky cave,
Where never sunbeam kiss'd the wave;
Humble as maiden that loves in vain,
Holy as hermit's vesper strain;
Gentle as breeze that but whispers and
dies,
Yet blithe as the light leaves that
dance in its sighs;
Courteous as monarch the morn he is
crown'd,
Generous as spring-dews that bless
the glad ground;
Noble her blood as the currents that met
In the veins of the noblest Plantagenet:
Such must her form be, her mood,
and her strain,
That shall match with Sir Roland of
Triermain.

II.

Sir Roland de Vaux he hath laid him
to sleep,
His blood it was fever'd, his breathing
was deep.
He had been pricking against the Scot,
The foray was long, and the skirmish
hot;
His dinted helm and his buckler's plight
Bore token of a stubborn fight.
All in the castle must hold them still,
Harpers must lull him to his rest
With the slow soft tunes he loves the
best,
Till sleep sink down upon his breast
Like the dew on a summer hill.

III.

It was the dawn of an autumn day;
The sun was struggling with frost-fog
grey,
That like a silvery crape was spread
Round Skiddaw's dim and distant
head,

And faintly gleam'd each painted pane
Of the lordly halls of Triermain,
    When that Baron bold awoke.
Starting he woke, and loudly did call,
Rousing his menials in bower and hall,
    While hastily he spoke.

IV.

'Hearken, my minstrels! which of ye all
Touch'd his harp with that dying fall,
    So sweet, so soft, so faint,
It seem'd an angel's whisper'd call
    To an expiring saint?
And hearken, my merry-men! what
      time or where
Did she pass, that maid with her
      heavenly brow,
With her look so sweet and her eyes
      so fair,
And her graceful step and her angel air,
And the eagle plume in her dark-brown
      hair,
    That pass'd from my bower e'en
      now?'

V.

Answer'd him Richard de Bretville—
    he
Was chief of the Baron's minstrelsy:
'Silent, noble chieftain, we
    Have sat since midnight close,
When such lulling sounds as the
      brooklet sings
Murmur'd from our melting strings,
    And hush'd you to repose.
    Had a harp-note sounded here
It had caught my watchful ear,
Although it fell as faint and shy
As bashful maiden's half-form'd sigh,
    When she thinks her lover near.'
Answer'd Philip of Fasthwaite tall—
He kept guard in the outer hall:
'Since at eve our watch took post,
Not a foot has thy portal cross'd;
    Else had I heard the steps, though low
And light they fell, as when earth
      receives,
In morn of frost, the wither'd leaves
    That drop when no winds blow.'

VI.

'Then come thou hither, Henry, my
      page,
Whom I saved from the sack of
      Hermitage,
When that dark castle, tower, and spire,
Rose to the skies a pile of fire,
    And redden'd all the Nine-stane Hill,
And the shrieks of death, that wildly
      broke
Through devouring flame and smoth-
      ering smoke,
    Made the warrior's heart-blood chill.
The trustiest thou of all my train,
My fleetest courser thou must rein,
      And ride to Lyulph's tower,
And from the Baron of Triermain
      Greet well that sage of power.
He is sprung from Druid sires,
And British bards that tuned their lyres
To Arthur's and Pendragon's praise,
And his who sleeps at Dunmailraise.
Gifted like his gifted race,
He the characters can trace,
Graven deep in elder time
Upon Helvellyn's cliffs sublime;
Sign and sigil well doth he know,
And can bode of weal and woe,
Of kingdoms' fall, and fate of wars,
From mystic dreams and course of stars.
He shall tell if middle earth
To that enchanting shape gave birth,
Or if 'twas but an airy thing,
Such as fantastic slumbers bring,
Fram'd from the rainbow's varying
      dyes
Or fading tints of western skies.
For, by the Blessed Rood I swear,
If that fair form breathe vital air,
No other maiden by my side
Shall ever rest De Vaux's bride!'

VII.

The faithful Page he mounts his steed,
And soon he cross'd green Irthing's
      mead,
Dash'd o'er Kirkoswald's verdant plain,
And Eden barr'd his course in vain.

He pass'd red Penrith's Table Round,
For feats of chivalry renown'd,
Left Mayburgh's mound and stones of
    power,
By Druids raised in magic hour,
And traced the Eamont's winding way,
Till Ulfo's lake beneath him lay.

VIII.

Onward he rode, the pathway still
Winding betwixt the lake and hill;
Till, on the fragment of a rock,
Struck from its base by lightning
    shock,
He saw the hoary Sage:
The silver moss and lichen twined,
With fern and deer-hair check'd and
    lined,
    A cushion fit for age;
And o'er him shook the aspen-tree,
A restless, rustling canopy.
Then sprung young Henry from his
    selle,
    And greeted Lyulph grave;
And then his master's tale did tell,
And then for counsel crave.
The Man of Years mused long and deep,
Of time's lost treasures taking keep,
And then, as rousing from a sleep,
    His solemn answer gave.

IX.

'That maid is born of middle earth,
    And may of man be won,
Though there have glided since her
    birth
    Five hundred years and one.
But where's the knight in all the north
That dare the adventure follow forth,
So perilous to knightly worth,
    In the valley of Saint John?
Listen, youth, to what I tell,
And bind it on thy memory well;
Nor muse that I commence the rhyme
Far distant 'mid the wrecks of time.
The mystic tale, by bard and sage,
Is handed down from Merlin's age.

X.

LYULPH'S TALE.

'King Arthur has ridden from merry
    Carlisle
    When Pentecost was o'er:
He journey'd like errant-knight the
    while,
And sweetly the summer sun did smile
    On mountain, moss, and moor.
Above his solitary track
Rose Glaramara's ridgy back,
Amid whose yawning gulfs the sun
Cast umber'd radiance red and dun,
Though never sunbeam could discern
The surface of that sable tarn,
In whose black mirror you may spy
The stars, while noontide lights the sky.
The gallant King he skirted still
The margin of that mighty hill;
Rock upon rocks incumbent hung,
And torrents, down the gullies flung,
Join'd the rude river that brawl'd on,
Recoiling now from crag and stone,
Now diving deep from human ken,
And raving down its darksome glen,
The Monarch judged this desert wild,
With such romantic ruin piled,
Was theatre by Nature's hand
For feat of high achievement plann'd.

XI.

'O rather he chose, that Monarch bold,
    On vent'rous quest to ride,
In plate and mail, by wood and wold,
Than, with ermine trapp'd and cloth
    of gold,
    In princely bower to bide:
The bursting crash of a foeman's spear
    As it shiver'd against his mail,
Was merrier music to his ear
    Than courtier's whisper'd tale:
And the clash of Caliburn more dear,
    When on the hostile casque it rung,
      Than all the lays
      To their monarch's praise
That the harpers of Reged sung.

He loved better to rest by wood or
    river,
Than in bower of his bride, Dame
    Guenever,
For he left that lady, so lovely of cheer,
To follow adventures of danger and
    fear ;
And the frank-hearted Monarch full
    little did wot
That she smiled, in his absence, on
    brave Lancelot.

XII.

' He rode, till over down and dell
The shade more broad and deeper fell;
And though around the mountain's
    head
Flow'd streams of purple, and gold,
    and red,
Dark at the base, unblest by beam
Frown'd the black rocks, and roar'd
    the stream.
With toil the King his way pursued
By lonely Threlkeld's waste and wood,
Till on his course obliquely shone
The narrow valley of SAINT JOHN,
Down sloping to the western sky,
Where lingering sunbeams love to lie.
Right glad to feel those beams again,
The King drew up his charger's rein;
With gauntlet raised he screen'd his
    sight,
As dazzled with the level light,
And, from beneath his glove of mail,
Scann'd at his ease the lovely vale,
While 'gainst the sun his armour bright
Gleam'd ruddy like the beacon's light.

XIII.

' Paled in by many a lofty hill,
The narrow dale lay smooth and still,
And, down its verdant bosom led,
A winding brooklet found its bed.
But, midmost of the vale, a mound
Arose with airy turrets crown'd,
Buttress, and rampire's circling bound,
    And mighty keep and tower;

Seem'd some primeval giant's hand
The castle's massive walls had plann'd,
A ponderous bulwark to withstand
    Ambitious Nimrod's power.
Above the moated entrance slung,
The balanced drawbridge trembling
    hung,
    As jealous of a foe ;
Wicket of oak, as iron hard,
With iron studded, clench'd, and barr'd,
And prong'd portcullis, join'd to guard
    The gloomy pass below.
But the grey walls no banners crown'd,
Upon the watch-tower's airy round
No warder stood his horn to sound,
No guard beside the bridge was found,
And, where the Gothic gateway
    frown'd,
    Glanced neither bill nor bow.

XIV.

' Beneath the castle's gloomy pride
In ample round did Arthur ride
Three times ; nor living thing he spied,
    Nor heard a living sound,
Save that, awakening from her dream,
The owlet now began to scream,
In concert with the rushing stream,
    That wash'd the battled mound.
He lighted from his goodly steed,
And he left him to graze on bank and
    mead ;
And slowly he climb'd the narrow way
That reach'd the entrance grim and grey,
And he stood the outward arch below,
And his bugle-horn prepared to blow,
    In summons blithe and bold,
Deeming to rouse from iron sleep
The guardian of this dismal Keep,
    Which well he guess'd the hold
Of wizard stern, or goblin grim,
Or pagan of gigantic limb,
    The tyrant of the wold.

XV.

' The ivory bugle's golden tip
Twice touch'd the Monarch's manly lip,
    And twice his hand withdrew.

Think not but Arthur's heart was
    good!
His shield was cross'd by the blessed
    rood,
Had a pagan host before him stood
    He had charged them through
      and through;
Yet the silence of that ancient place
Sunk on his heart, and he paused a
    space
    Ere yet his horn he blew.
But, instant as its 'larum rung,
The castle gate was open flung,
Portcullis rose with crashing groan
Full harshly up its groove of stone;
The balance-beams obey'd the blast,
And down the trembling drawbridge
    cast;
The vaulted arch before him lay,
With nought to bar the gloomy way,
And onward Arthur paced, with hand
On Caliburn's resistless brand.

XVI.

'An hundred torches, flashing bright,
Dispell'd at once the gloomy night
    That lour'd along the walls,
And show'd the King's astonish'd
    sight
    The inmates of the halls.
Nor wizard stern, nor goblin grim,
Nor giant huge of form and limb,
    Nor heathen knight, was there;
But the cressets, which odours flung
    aloft,
Show'd by their yellow light and soft,
    A band of damsels fair.
Onward they came, like summer wave
    That dances to the shore;
An hundred voices welcome gave,
    And welcome o'er and o'er!
An hundred lovely hands assail
The bucklers of the Monarch's mail,
And busy labour'd to unhasp
Rivet of steel and iron clasp.
One wrapp'd him in a mantle fair,
And one flung odours on his hair;

His short curl'd ringlets one smooth'd
    down,
One wreath'd them with a myrtle
    crown.
A bride upon her wedding-day
Was tended ne'er by troop so gay.

XVII.

'Loud laugh'd they all,—the King, in
    vain,
With questions task'd the giddy train;
Let him entreat, or crave, or call,
'Twas one reply—loud laugh'd they all.
Then o'er him mimic chains they fling,
Framed of the fairest flowers of spring.
While some their gentle force unite
Onward to drag the wondering knight;
Some, bolder urge his pace with blows,
Dealt with the lily or the rose.
Behind him were in triumph borne
The warlike arms he late had worn.
Four of the train combined to rear
The terrors of Tintadgel's spear;
Two, laughing at their lack of strength,
Dragg'd Caliburn in cumbrous length;
One, while she aped a martial stride,
Placed on her brows the helmit's pride;
Then scream'd, 'twixt laughter and
    surprise,
To feel its depth o'erwhelm her eyes.
With revel-shout, and triumph-song,
Thus gaily march'd the giddy throng.

XVIII.

'Through many a gallery and hall
They led, I ween, their royal thrall;
At length, beneath a fair arcade
Their march and song at once they
    staid.
The eldest maiden of the band
    (The lovely maid was scarce
      eighteen)
Raised, with imposing air, her hand,
And reverent silence did command,
    On entrance of their Queen,
And they were mute.— But as a glance
They steal on Arthur's countenance
    Bewilder'd with surprise,

Their smother'd mirth again 'gan speak,
In archly dimpled chin and cheek,
  And laughter-lighted eyes.

XIX.

' The attributes of those high days
Now only live in minstrel lays ;
For Nature, now exhausted, still
Was then profuse of good and ill.
Strength was gigantic, valour high,
And wisdom soar'd beyond the sky,
And beauty had such matchless beam
As lights not now a lover's dream.
Yet e'en in that romantic age,
    Ne'er were such charms by mortal
        seen,
As Arthur's dazzled eyes engage,
When forth on that enchanted stage,
With glittering train of maid and page,
    Advanced the castle's Queen !
While up the hall she slowly pass'd
Her dark eye on the King she cast,
    That flash'd expression strong ;
The longer dwelt that lingering look,
Her cheek the livelier colour took,
And scarce the shame-faced King
        could brook
    The gaze that lasted long.
A sage, who had that look espied,
Where kindling passion strove with
        pride,
    Had whisper'd, "Prince, beware!
From the chafed tiger rend the prey,
Rush on the lion when at bay,
Bar the fell dragon's blighted way,
    But shun that lovely snare !"

XX.

' At once, that inward strife suppress'd,
The dame approach'd her warlike
        guest,
With greeting in that fair degree,
Where female pride and courtesy
Are blended with such passing art
As awes at once and charms the heart.
A courtly welcome first she gave,
Then of his goodness 'gan to crave
    Construction fair and true

Of her light maidens' idle mirth,
Who drew from lonely glens their
        birth,
Nor knew to pay to stranger worth
    And dignity their due ;
And then she pray'd that he would rest
That night her castle's honour'd guest.
The Monarch meetly thanks express'd;
The banquet rose at her behest ;
With lay and tale, and laugh and jest,
    Apace the evening flew.

XXI.

' The Lady sate the Monarch by,
Now in her turn abash'd and shy,
And with indifference seem'd to hear
The toys he whisper'd in her ear.
Her bearing modest was and fair,
Yet shadows of constraint were there,
That show'd an over-cautious care
    Some inward thought to hide;
Oft did she pause in full reply,
And oft cast down her large dark eye,
Oft check'd the soft voluptuous sigh
    That heav'd her bosom's pride.
Slight symptoms these, but shepherds
        know
How hot the mid-day sun shall glow
    From the mist of morning sky;
And so the wily Monarch guess'd
That this assumed restraint express'd
More ardent passions in the breast
    Than ventured to the eye.
Closer he press'd, while beakers rang,
While maidens laugh'd and minstrels
        sang,
    Still closer to her ear—
But why pursue the common tale ?
Or wherefore show how knights
        prevail
    When ladies dare to hear ?
Or wherefore trace, from what slight
        cause
Its source one tyrant passion draws,
    Till, mastering all within,
Where lives the man that has not tried
How mirth can into folly glide,
    And folly into sin ?'

Canto Second.

I.

LYULPH'S TALE, CONTINUED.

ANOTHER day, another day,
And yet another, glides away !
The Saxon stern, the pagan Dane,
Maraud on Britain's shores again.
Arthur, of Christendom the flower,
Lies loitering in a lady's bower ;
The horn, that foemen wont to fear,
Sounds but to wake the Cumbrian deer,
And Caliburn, the British pride,
Hangs useless by a lover's side.

II.

' Another day, another day,
And yet another, glides away !
Heroic plans in pleasure drown'd,
He thinks not of the Table Round ;
In lawless love dissolved his life,
He thinks not of his beauteous wife :
Better he loves to snatch a flower
From bosom of his paramour,
Than from a Saxon knight to wrest
The honours of his heathen crest !
Better to wreathe, 'mid tresses brown,
The heron's plume her hawk struck
down,
Than o'er the altar give to flow
The banners of a Paynim foe.
Thus, week by week, and day by day,
His life inglorious glides away :
But she, that soothes his dream, with
fear
Beholds his hour of waking near !

III.

' Much force have mortal charms to stay
Our peace in Virtue's toilsome way ;
But Guendolen's might far outshine
Each maid of merely mortal line.
Her mother was of human birth,
Her sire a Genie of the earth,
In days of old deem'd to preside
O'er lovers' wiles and beauty's pride,
By youths and virgins worshipp'd
long
With festive dance and choral song,
Till, when the cross to Britain came,
On heathen altars died the flame.
Now, deep in Wastdale solitude,
The downfall of his rights he rued,
And, born of his resentment heir,
He train'd to guile that lady fair,
To sink in slothful sin and shame
The champions of the Christian name.
Well skill'd to keep vain thoughts alive,
And all to promise, nought to give ;
The timid youth had hope in store,
The bold and pressing gain'd no more.
As wilder'd children leave their home
After the rainbow's arch to roam,
Her lovers barter'd fair esteem,
Faith, fame, and honour, for a dream.

IV.

' Her sire's soft arts the soul to tame
She practised thus, till Arthur came ;
Then frail humanity had part,
And all the mother claim'd her heart.
Forgot each rule her father gave,
Sunk from a princess to a slave,
Too late must Guendolen deplore ;
He, that has all, can hope no more !
Now must she see her lover strain,
At every turn, her feeble chain ;
Watch, to new-bind each knot, and
shrink
To view each fast-decaying link.
Art she invokes to Nature's aid,
Her vest to zone, her locks to braid ;
Each varied pleasure heard her call,
The feast, the tourney, and the ball :
Her storied lore she next applies,
Taxing her mind to aid her eyes ;
Now more than mortal wise, and then
In female softness sunk again ;
Now, raptured, with each wish com-
plying,
With feign'd reluctance now denying :
Each charm she varied, to retain
A varying heart, and all in vain !

v.

'Thus in the garden's narrow bound,
Flank'd by some castle's Gothic round,
Fain would the artist's skill provide
The limits of his realms to hide.
The walks in labyrinths he twines,
Shade after shade with skill combines,
With many a varied flowery knot,
And copse, and arbour, decks the spot,
Tempting the hasty foot to stay,
And linger on the lovely way;
Vain art! vain hope! 'tis fruitless all!
At length we reach the bounding wall,
And, sick of flower and trim-dress'd
    tree,
Long for rough glades and forest free.

vi.

'Three summer months had scantly
    flown
When Arthur, in embarrass'd tone,
Spoke of his liegemen and his throne;
Said, all too long had been his stay,
And duties, which a monarch sway,
Duties, unknown to humbler men,
Must tear her knight from Guendolen.
She listen'd silently the while,
Her mood express'd in bitter smile;
Beneath her eye must Arthur quail,
And oft resume the unfinish'd tale,
Confessing, by his downcast eye,
The wrong he sought to justify.
He ceased. A moment mute she gazed,
And then her looks to heaven she rais'd;
One palm her temples veiled, to hide
The tear that sprung in spite of pride;
The other for an instant press'd
The foldings of her silken vest!

vii.

'At her reproachful sign and look,
The hint the Monarch's conscience
    took.
Eager he spoke—" No, lady, no!
Deem not of British Arthur so,
Nor think he can deserter prove
To the dear pledge of mutual love.

I swear by sceptre and by sword,
As belted knight and Britain's lord,
That if a boy shall claim my care,
That boy is born a kingdom's heir;
But if a maiden Fate allows,
To choose that maid a fitting spouse,
A summer-day in lists shall strive
My knights, the bravest knights alive,
And he, the best and bravest tried,
Shall Arthur's daughter claim for bride."
He spoke, with voice resolved and
    high;
The lady deign'd him not reply.

viii.

' At dawn of morn, ere on the brake
His matins did a warbler make,
Or stirr'd his wing to brush away
A single dewdrop from the spray,
Ere yet a sunbeam, through the mist,
The castle-battlements had kiss'd,
The gates revolve the drawbridge falls,
And Arthur sallies from the walls.
Doff'd his soft garb of Persia's loom,
And steel from spur to helmet-plume,
His Lybian steed full proudly trode,
And joyful neigh'd beneath his load.
The Monarch gave a passing sigh
To penitence and pleasures by,
When, lo! to his astonish'd ken
Appear'd the form of Guendolen.

ix.

' Beyond the outmost wall she stood,
Attired like huntress of the wood :
Sandall'd her feet, her ankles bare,
And eagle-plumage deck'd her hair;
Firm was her look. her bearing bold,
And in her hand a cup of gold.
"Thou goest !" she said, "and ne'er
    again
Must we two meet, in joy or pain.
Full fain would I this hour delay,
Though weak the wish —yet, wilt thou
    stay ?
No! thou look'st forward. Still, attend!
Part we like lover and like friend."

She raised the cup—" Not this the juice
The sluggish vines of earth produce ;
Pledge we, at parting, in the draught
Which Genii love !" She said, and
    quaff'd ;
And strange unwonted lustres fly
From her flush'd cheek and sparkling
    eye.

x.

' The courteous Monarch bent him low,
And, stooping down from saddlebow,
Lifted the cup, in act to drink.
A drop escaped the goblet's brink—
Intense as liquid fire from hell,
Upon the charger's neck it fell.
Screaming with agony and fright,
He bolted twenty feet upright !
The peasant still can show the dint
Where his hoofs lighted on the flint.
From Arthur's hand the goblet flew,
Scattering a shower of fiery dew,
That burn'd and blighted where it fell !
The frantic steed rush'd up the dell,
As whistles from the bow the reed ;
Nor bit nor rein could check his speed
    Until he gain'd the hill ;
Then breath and sinew fail'd apace,
And, reeling from the desperate race,
    He stood, exhausted, still.
The Monarch, breathless and amazed,
Back on the fatal castle gazed :
Nor tower nor donjon could he spy,
Darkening against the morning sky ;
But, on the spot where once they
    frown'd,
The lonely streamlet brawl'd around
A tufted knoll, where dimly shone
Fragments of rock and rifted stone.
Musing on this strange hap the while,
The King wends back to fair Carlisle ;
And cares, that cumber royal sway,
Wore memory of the past away.

xi.

'Full fifteen years and more were sped,
Each brought new wreaths to Arthur's
    head.

Twelve bloody fields, with glory fought,
The Saxons to subjection brought :
Rython, the mighty giant, slain
By his good brand, relieved Bretagne:
The Pictish Gillamore in fight,
And Roman Lucius, own'd his might ;
And wide were through the world
    renown'd
The glories of his Table Round.
Each knight who sought adventurous
    fame,
To the bold court of Britain came,
And all who suffer'd causeless wrong,
From tyrant proud, or faitour strong,
Sought Arthur's presence, to complain,
Nor there for aid implored in vain.

xii.

' For this the King, with pomp and
    pride,
Held solemn court at Whitsuntide,
    And summon'd Prince and Peer,
All who owed homage for their land,
Or who craved knighthood from his
    hand,
Or who had succour to demand,
    To come from far and near.
At such high tide were glee and game
Mingled with feats of martial fame,
For many a stranger champion came
    In lists to break a spear ;
And not a knight of Arthur's host,
Save that he trode some foreign coast,
But at this feast of Pentecost
    Before him must appear.
Ah, Minstrels ! when the Table Round
Arose, with all its warriors crown'd,
There was a theme for bards to sound
    In triumph to their string !
Five hundred years are past and gone,
But Time shall draw his dying groan
Ere he behold the British throne
    Begirt with such a ring !

xiii.

' The heralds named the appointed spot,
As Caerleon or Camelot,
    Or Carlisle fair and free.

At Penrith, now, the feast was set,
And in fair Eamont's vale were met
 The flower of Chivalry.
There Galaad sate with manly grace,
Yet maiden meekness in his face ;
There Morolt of the iron mace,
 And love-lorn Tristrem there :
And Dinadam with lively glance,
And Lanval with the fairy lance,
And Mordred with his look askance,
 Brunor and Bevidere.
Why should I tell of numbers more ?
Sir Cay, Sir Banier, and Sir Bore,
 Sir Carodac the keen,
The gentle Gawain's courteous lore,
Hector de Mares and Pellinore,
And Lancelot, that evermore
 Look'd stol'n-wise on the Queen.

XIV.

'When wine and mirth did most abound,
And harpers play'd their blithest round,
A shrilly trumpet shook the ground,
 And marshals cleared the ring ;
A maiden, on a palfrey white,
Heading a band of damsels bright,
Paced through the circle, to alight
 And kneel before the King.
Arthur, with strong emotion, saw
Her graceful boldness check'd by
 awe,
Her dress, like huntress of the wold,
Her bow and baldric trapp'd with
 gold,
Her sandall'd feet, her ankles bare,
And the eagle-plume that deck'd her
 hair.
Graceful her veil she backward flung ;
The King, as from his seat he sprung,
 Almost cried, " Guendolen ! "
But 'twas a face more frank and wild,
Betwixt the woman and the child,
Where less of magic beauty smiled
 Than of the race of men ;
And in the forehead's haughty grace
The lines of Britain's royal race,
 Pendragon's, you might ken.

XV.

' Faltering, yet gracefully, she said—
" Great Prince ! behold an orphan
 maid,
In her departed mother's name,
A father's vow'd protection claim !
The vow was sworn in desert lone,
In the deep valley of Saint John."
At once the King the suppliant raised,
And kiss'd her brow, her beauty
 praised ;
His vow, he said, should well be kept,
Ere in the sea the sun was dipp'd ;
Then, conscious, glanced upon his
 queen ;
But she, unruffled at the scene
Of human frailty, construed mild,
Look'd upon Lancelot, and smiled.

XVI.

'"Up ! up ! each knight of gallant crest,
 Take buckler, spear, and brand !
He that to-day shall bear him best
 Shall win my Gyneth's hand.
And Arthur's daughter, when a bride,
 Shall bring a noble dower ;
Both fair Strath-Clyde and Reged
 wide,
 And Carlisle town and tower."
Then might you hear each valiant
 knight
To page and squire that cried,
" Bring my armour bright, and my
 courser wight !
'Tis not each day that a warrior's might
 May win a royal bride."
Then cloaks and caps of maintenance
 In haste aside they fling ;
The helmets glance, and gleams the
 lance,
And the steel-weaved hauberks ring.
Small care had they of their peaceful
 array,—
 They might gather it that wolde ;
For brake and bramble glitter'd gay
 With pearls and cloth of gold.

XVII.

'Within trumpet sound of the Table
Round
Were fifty champions free,
And they all arise to fight that prize,
They all arise but three.
Nor love's fond troth, nor wedlock's
oath,
One gallant could withhold,
For priests will allow of a broken vow
For penance or for gold.
But sigh and glance from ladies bright
Among the troop were thrown,
To plead their right, and true-love
plight,
And 'plain of honour flown.
The knights they busied them so fast,
With buckling spur and belt,
That sigh and look, by ladies cast,
Were neither seen nor felt.
From pleading, or upbraiding glance,
Each gallant turns aside,
And only thought, "If speeds my lance,
A queen becomes my bride!
She has fair Strath-Clyde, and Reged
wide,
And Carlisle tower and town ;
She is the loveliest maid, beside,
That ever heir'd a crown."
So in haste their coursers they bestride,
And strike their visors down.

XVIII.

'The champions, arm'd in martial sort,
Have throng'd into the list,
And but three knights of Arthur's court
Are from the tourney miss'd.
And still these lovers' fame survives
For faith so constant shown,—
There were two who loved their
neighbours' wives,
And one who loved his own.
The first was Lancelot de Lac,
The second Tristrem bold,
The third was valiant Carodac,
Who won the cup of gold,

What time, of all King Arthur's crew
(Thereof came jeer and laugh)
He, as the mate of lady true,
Alone the cup could quaff.
Though envy's tongue would fain
surmise
That, but for very shame,
Sir Carodac, to fight that prize,
Had given both cup and dame ;
Yet, since but one of that fair court
Was true to wedlock's shrine,
Brand him who will with base report,
He shall be free from mine.

XIX.

' Now caracoled the steeds in air,
Now plumes and pennons wanton'd
fair,
As all around the lists so wide
In panoply the champions ride.
King Arthur saw, with startled eye,
The flower of chivalry march by,
The bulwark of the Christian creed,
The kingdom's shield in hour of need.
Too late he thought him of the woe
Might from their civil conflict flow ;
For well he knew they would not part
Till cold was many a gallant heart.
His hasty vow he 'gan to rue,
And Gyneth then apart he drew ;
To her his leading-staff resign'd,
But added caution grave and kind.

XX.

' " Thou see'st, my child, as promise-
bound,
I bid the trump for tourney sound.
Take thou my warder, as the queen
And umpire of the martial scene ;
But mark thou this : as Beauty bright
Is polar star to valiant knight,
As at her word his sword he draws,
His fairest guerdon her applause,
So gentle maid should never ask
Of knighthood vain and dangerous
task ;
And Beauty's eyes should ever be
Like the twin stars that soothe the sea,

And Beauty's breath shall whisper
    peace,
And bid the storm of battle cease.
I tell thee this, lest all too far
These knights urge tourney into war.
Blithe at the trumpet let them go,
And fairly counter blow for blow:
No striplings these, who succour need
For a razed helm or falling steed.
But, Gyneth, when the strife grows
    warm,
And threatens death or deadly harm,
Thy sire entreats thy king commands,
Thou drop the warder from thy hands.
Trust thou thy father with thy fate,
Doubt not he choose thee fitting mate;
Nor be it said, through Gyneth's pride
A rose of Arthur's chaplet died."

XXI.

'A proud and discontented glow
O'ershadow'd Gyneth's brow of snow;
    She put the warder by:
" Reserve thy boon, my liege," she
    said,
"Thus chaffer'd down and limited,
Debased and narrow'd, for a maid
    Of less degree than I.
No petty chief, but holds his heir
At a more honour'd price and rare
    Than Britain's King holds me !
Although the sun-burn'd maid, for
    dower,
Has but her father's rugged tower,
    His barren hill and lee.
King Arthur swore, *By crown and*
    sword,
As belted knight and Britain's lord,
That a whole summer's day should
    strive
His knights, the bravest knights alive !
Recall thine oath ! and to her glen
Poor Gyneth can return agen;
Not on thy daughter will the stain,
That soils thy sword and crown,
    remain.
But think not she will e'er be bride
Save to the bravest, proved and tried;

Pendragon's daughter will not fear
For clashing sword or splinter'd spear,
    Nor shrink though blood should
      flow;
And all too well sad Guendolen
Hath taught the faithlessness of men,
That child of hers should pity, when
    Their meed they undergo."

XXII.

'He frown'd and sigh'd, the Monarch
    bold :
"I give what I may not withhold;
For not for danger. dread, or death,
Must British Arthur break his faith.
Too late I mark thy mother's art
Hath taught thee this relentless part
I blame her not, for she had wrong,
But not to these my faults belong.
Use, then, the warder as thou wilt;
But trust me, that, if life be spilt,
In Arthur's love, in Arthur's grace,
Gyneth shall lose a daughter's place."
With that he turn'd his head aside,
Nor brook'd to gaze upon her pride,
As, with the truncheon raised, she sate
The arbitress of mortal fate;
Nor brook'd to mark, in ranks disposed,
How the bold champions stood
    opposed,
For shrill the trumpet-flourish fell
Upon his ear like passing bell !
Then first from sight of martial fray
Did Britain's hero turn away.

XXIII.

'But Gyneth heard the clangour high
As hears the hawk the partridge cry.
Oh, blame her not; the blood was hers
That at the trumpet's summons stirs !
And e'en the gentlest female eye
Might the brave strife of chivalry
    Awhile untroubled view;
So well accomplish'd was each knight,
To strike and to defend in fight,
Their meeting was a goodly sight,
    While plate and mail held true.

The lists with painted plumes were
    strown,
Upon the wind at random thrown,
But helm and breastplate bloodless
    shone,
It seem'd their feather'd crests alone
    Should this encounter rue.
And ever, as the combat grows,
The trumpet's cheery voice arose,
Like lark's shrill song the flourish flows,
Heard while the gale of April blows
    The merry greenwood through.

XXIV.

' But soon to earnest grew their game,
The spears drew blood, the swords
    struck flame,
And, horse and man, to ground there
    came
    Knights, who shall rise no more !
Gone was the pride the war that graced,
Gay shields were cleft, and crests
    defaced,
And steel coats riven, and helms
    unbraced,
    And penrons stream'd with gore.
Gone, too, were fence and fair array,
And desperate strength made deadly
    way
At random through the bloody fray,
And blows were dealt with headlong
    sway,
    Unheeding where they fell ;
And now the trumpet's clamours seem
Like the shrill sea-bird's wailing
    scream,
Heard o'er the whirlpool's gulfing
    stream,
    The sinking seaman's knell !

XXV.

' Seem'd in this dismal hour, that Fate
Would Camlan's ruin antedate,
    And spare dark Mordred's crime ;
Already gasping on the ground
Lie twenty of the Table Round,
    Of chivalry the prime.

Arthur, in anguish, tore away
From head and beard his tresses grey,
And she, proud Gyneth, felt dismay,
    And quaked with ruth and fear ;
But still she deem'd her mother's shade
Hung o'er the tumult, and forbade
The sign that had the slaughter staid,
    And chid the rising tear.
Then Brunor, Taulas, Mador, fell,
Helias the White, and Lionel,
    And many a champion more ;
Rochemont and Dinadam are down,
And Ferrand of the Forest Brown
    Lies gasping in his gore.
Vanoc, by mighty Morolt press'd
Even to the confines of the list,
Young Vanoc of the beardless face
(Fame spoke the youth of Merlin's
    race)
O'erpower'd at Gyneth's footstool bled,
His heart's-blood dyed her sandals red.
But then the sky was overcast,
Then howl'd at once a whirlwind's
    blast,
    And, rent by sudden throes,
Yawn'd in mid lists the quaking earth,
And from the gulf, tremendous birth !
    The form of Merlin rose.

XXVI.

' Sternly the Wizard Prophet eyed
The dreary lists with slaughter dyed,
    And sternly raised his hand :
"Madmen," he said, "your strife
    forbear ;
And thou, fair cause of mischief, hear
    The doom thy fates demand !
Long shall close in stony sleep
Eyes for ruth that would not weep ;
Iron lethargy shall seal
Heart that pity scorn'd to feel.
Yet, because thy mother's art
Warp'd thine unsuspicious heart,
And for love of Arthur's race,
Punishment is blent with grace,
Thou shalt bear thy penance lone
In the Valley of Saint John,

T

And this weird[1] shall overtake thee ;
Sleep, until a knight shall wake thee,
For feats of arms as far renown'd
As warrior of the Table Round.
Long endurance of thy slumber
Well may teach the world to number
All their woes from Gyneth's pride,
When the Red Cross champions
   died."

XXVII.

'As Merlin speaks, on Gyneth's eye
Slumber's load begins to lie ;
Fear and anger vainly strive
Still to keep its light alive.
Twice, with effort and with pause,
O'er her brow her hand she draws ;
Twice her strength in vain she tries,
From the fatal chair to rise ;
Merlin's magic doom is spoken,
Vanoc's death must now be wroken.
Slow the dark-fringed eyelids fall,
Curtaining each azure ball,
Slowly as on summer eves
Violets fold their dusky leaves.
The weighty baton of command
Now bears down her sinking hand,
On her shoulder droops her head ;
Net of pearl and golden thread,
Bursting, gave her locks to flow
O'er her arm and breast of snow.
And so lovely seem'd she there,
Spell-bound in her ivory chair,
That her angry sire, repenting,
Craved stern Merlin for relenting,
And the champions, for her sake,
Would again the contest wake ;
Till, in necromantic night,
Gyneth vanish'd from their sight.

XXVIII.

'Still she bears her weird alone,
In the Valley of Saint John ;
And her semblance oft will seem,
Mingling in a champion's dream,

[1] Doom.

Of her weary lot to 'plain,
A..d crave his aid to burst her chain.
While her wondrous tale was new,
Warriors to her rescue drew,
East and west, and south and north,
From the Liffy, Thames, and Forth.
Most have sought in vain the glen,
Tower nor castle could they ken ;
Not at every time or tide,
Nor by every eye, descried.
Fast and vigil must be borne,
Many a night in watching worn,
Ere an eye of mortal powers
Can discern those magic towers.
Of the persevering few,
Some from hopeless task withdrew,
When they read the dismal threat
Graved upon the gloomy gate.
Few have braved the yawning door,
And those few return'd no more.
In the lapse of time forgot,
Wellnigh lost is Gyneth's lot ;
Sound her sleep as in the tomb,
Till waken'd by the trump of doom.'

END OF LYULPH'S TALE.

I.

HERE pause my tale ! for all too soon,
My Lucy, comes the hour of noon.
Already from thy lofty dome
Its courtly inmates 'gin to roam,
And each, to kill the goodly day
That God has granted them, his way
   Of lazy sauntering has sought ;
      Lordlings and witlings not a few,
   Incapable of doing aught,
      Yet ill at ease with nought to do.
Here is no longer place for me ;
For, Lucy, thou wouldst blush to see
   Some phantom, fashionably thin,
   With limb of lath and kerchief'd chin,
   And lounging gape, or sneering grin,
Steal sudden on our privacy.
And how should I, so humbly born,
Endure the graceful spectre's scorn!

Faith! ill, I fear, while conjuring wand
Of English oak is hard at hand.

II.

Or grant the hour be all too soon
For Hessian boot and pantaloon,
And grant the lounger seldom strays
Beyond the smooth and gravell'd maze,
Laud we the gods, that Fashion's train
Holds hearts of more adventurous
        strain.
Artists are hers, who scorn to trace
Their rules from Nature's boundless
        grace,
But their right paramount assert
To limit her by pedant art,
Damning whate'er of vast and fair
Exceeds a canvas three feet square.
This thicket, for their *gumption* fit,
May furnish such a happy *bit*.
Bards, too, are hers, wont to recite
Their own sweet lays by waxen light,
Half in the salver's tingle drown'd,
While the *chasse-café* glides around;
And such may hither secret stray,
To labour an extempore:
Or sportsman, with his boisterous
        hollo,
May here his wiser spaniel follow;
Or stage-struck Juliet may presume
To choose this bower for tiring-room;
And we alike must shun regard,
From painter, player, sportsman, bard.
Insects that skim in Fashion's sky,
Wasp, blue-bottle, or butterfly,
Lucy, have all alarms for us,
For all can hum and all can buzz.

III.

But oh, my Lucy, say how long
We still must dread this trifling throng,
And stoop to hide, with coward art,
The genuine feelings of the heart!
No parents thine whose just command
Should rule their child's obedient
        hand;
Thy guardians, with contending voice
Press each his individual choice.

And which is Lucy's? Can it be
That puny fop, trimm'd cap-a-pie,
Who loves in the saloon to show
The arms that never knew a foe;
Whose sabre trails along the ground,
Whose legs in shapeless boots are
        drown'd;
A new Achilles, sure! the steel
Fled from his breast to fence his heel;
One, for the simple manly grace
That wont to deck our martial race,
    Who comes in foreign trashery
        Of tinkling chain and spur,
    A walking haberdashery,
        Of feathers, lace, and fur:
In Rowley's antiquated phrase,
Horse-milliner of modern days?

IV.

    Or is it he, the wordy youth,
        So early train'd for statesman's
            part,
    Who talks of honour, faith, and
            truth,
        As themes that he has got by
            heart;
Whose ethics Chesterfield can teach,
Whose logic is from Single-speech;
Who scorns the meanest thought to
        vent,
Save in the phrase of Parliament;
Who, in a tale of cat and mouse,
Calls 'order,' and 'divides the house,'
Who 'craves permission to reply,'
Whose 'noble friend is in his eye;'
Whose loving tender some have
        reckon'd
A motion, you should gladly second?

V.

What! neither? Can there be a third,
To such resistless swains preferr'd?
O why, my Lucy, turn aside,
With that quick glance of injured
        pride?
Forgive me, love, I cannot bear
That alter'd and resentful air.

Were all the wealth of Russell mine,
And all the rank of Howard's line,
All would I give for leave to dry
That dewdrop trembling in thine eye.
Think not I fear such fops can wile
From Lucy more than careless smile;
But yet if wealth and high degree
Give gilded counters currency,
Must I not fear, when rank and birth
Stamp the pure ore of genuine worth?
Nobles there are, whose martial fires
Rival the fame that raised their sires,
And patriots, skill'd through storms
    of fate
To guide and guard the reeling state.
Such, such there are: if such should
    come,
Arthur must tremble and be dumb,
Self-exiled seek some distant shore,
And mourn till life and grief are o'er.

VI.

What sight, what signal of alarm,
That Lucy clings to Arthur's arm?
Or is it, that the rugged way
Makes Beauty lean on lover's stay?
Oh, no! for on the vale and brake
Nor sight nor sounds of danger wake,
And this trim sward of velvet green
Were carpet for the Fairy Queen.
That pressure slight was but to tell
That Lucy loves her Arthur well,
And fain would banish from his mind
Suspicious fear and doubt unkind.

VII.

But wouldst thou bid the demons fly
Like mist before the dawning sky,
There is but one resistless spell—
Say, wilt thou guess, or must I tell?
'Twere hard to name, in minstrel
    phrase,
A landaulet and four blood-bays,
But bards agree this wizard band
Can but be bound in Northern land.
'Tis there—nay, draw not back thy
    hand!

'Tis there this slender finger round
Must golden amulet be bound,
Which, bless'd with many a holy
    prayer,
Can change to rapture lovers' care,
And doubt and jealousy shall die,
And fears give place to ecstasy.

VIII.

Now, trust me, Lucy, all too long
Has been thy lover's tale and song.
O, why so silent, love, I pray?
Have I not spoke the livelong day?
And will not Lucy deign to say
    One word her friend to bless.
I ask but one, a simple sound,
Within three little letters bound,
    O, let the word be *Yes!*

—◆—

INTRODUCTION TO CANTO
THIRD.

I.

Long loved, long woo'd, and lately won,
My life's best hope, and now mine own!
Doth not this rude and Alpine glen
Recall our favourite haunts agen?
A wild resemblance we can trace,
Though reft of every softer grace,
As the rough warrior's brow may bear
A likeness to a sister fair.
Full well advised our Highland host,
That this wild pass on foot be cross'd,
While round Ben-Cruach's mighty
    base
Wheel the slow steeds and lingering
    chaise.
The keen old carle, with Scottish pride,
He praised his glen and mountains
    wide;
An eye he bears for Nature's face,
Ay, and for woman's lovely grace,
Even in such mean degree we find
The subtle Scot's observing mind;

For, nor the chariot nor the train
Could gape of vulgar wonder gain,
But when old Allan would expound
Of Beal-na-paish [1] the Celtic sound,
His bonnet doff'd, and bow, applied
His legend to my bonny bride;
While Lucy blush'd beneath his eye,
Courteous and cautious, shrewd and
    sly.

        II.

Enough of him. Now, ere we lose,
Plunged in the vale, the distant views,
Turn thee, my love! look back once
    more
To the blue lake's retiring shore.
On its smooth breast the shadows
    seem
Like objects in a morning dream,
What time the slumberer is aware
He sleeps, and all the vision's air:
Even so, on yonder liquid lawn,
In hues of bright reflection drawn,
Distinct the shaggy mountains lie,
Distinct the rocks, distinct the sky:
The summer-clouds so plain we note
That we might count each dappled
    spot:
We gaze and we admire, yet know
The scene is all delusive show.
Such dreams of bliss would Arthur
    draw
When first his Lucy's form he saw;
Yet sigh'd and sicken'd as he drew,
Despairing they could e'er prove true!

        III.

But, Lucy, turn thee now, to view
    Up the fair glen, our destined way:
The fairy path that we pursue,
Distinguish'd but by greener hue,
    Winds round the purple brae,
While Alpine flowers of varied dye
For carpet serve, or tapestry.
See how the little runnels leap,
In threads of silver, down the steep,
    To swell the brooklet's moan!

---

[1] Beal-na-paish, the Vale of the Bridal.

Seems that the Highland Naiad
    grieves,
Fantastic while her crown she weaves,
Of rowan, birch, and alder leaves,
    So lovely, and so lone.
There's no illusion there; these
    flowers,
That wailing brook, these lovely
    bowers,
    Are, Lucy, all our own;
And since thine Arthur call'd thee wife,
Such seems the prospect of his life,
A lovely path, on-winding still,
By gurgling brook and sloping hill.
'Tis true, that mortals cannot tell
What waits them in the distant dell;
But be it hap, or be it harm,
We tread the pathway arm in arm.

        IV.

And now, my Lucy, wot'st thou why
I could thy bidding twice deny,
When twice you pray'd I would again
Resume the legendary strain
Of the bold Knight of Triermain?
At length yon peevish vow you swore,
That you would sue to me no more,
Until the minstrel fit drew near,
And made me prize a listening ear.
But, loveliest, when thou first didst
    pray
Continuance of the knightly lay,
Was it not on the happy day
    That made thy hand mine own?
When, dizzied with mine ecstasy,
Nought past, or present, or to be,
Could I or think on, hear, or see,
    Save, Lucy, thee alone!
A giddy draught my rapture was,
As ever chemist's magic gas.

        V.

Again the summons I denied
In yon fair capital of Clyde:
My Harp—or let me rather choose
The good old classic form—my Muse,
(For Harp's an over-scutchèd phrase,
Worn out by bards of modern days)

My Muse, then—seldom will she wake,
Save by dim wood and silent lake ;
She is the wild and rustic Maid,
Whose foot unsandall'd loves to tread
Where the soft greensward is inlaid
    With varied moss and thyme ;
And, lest the simple lily-braid
That coronets her temples fade,
She hides her still in greenwood shade
    To meditate her rhyme.

VI.

And now she comes. The murmur dear
Of the wild brook hath caught her ear,
   The glade hath won her eye ;
She longs to join with each blithe rill
That dances down the Highland hill
   Her blither melody.
And now, my Lucy's way to cheer,
She bids Ben-Cruach's echoes hear
How closed the tale my love whilere
   Loved for its chivalry.
List how she tells, in notes of flame,
'Childe Roland to the dark tower
   came !'

Canto Third.

I.

BEWCASTLE now must keep the Hold,
   Speir-Adam's steeds must bide in
    stall,
Of Hartley-burn the bowmen bold
   Must only shoot from battled wall ;
And Liddesdale may buckle spur,
   And Teviot now may belt the brand,
Taras and Ewes keep nightly stir,
   And Eskdale foray Cumberland.
Of wasted fields and plunder'd flocks
   The Borderers bootless may com-
    plain ;
They lack the sword of brave de Vaux,
   There comes no aid from Triermain.

That lord, on high adventure bound,
   Hath wander'd forth alone,
And day and night keeps watchful
    round
   In the valley of Saint John.

II.

When first began his vigil bold,
The moon twelve summer nights was
    old,
   And shone both fair and full ;
High in the vault of cloudless blue,
O'er streamlet, dale, and rock, she
    threw
   Her light composed and cool.
Stretch'd on the brown hill's heathy
    breast,
   Sir Roland eyed the vale ;
Chief where, distinguish'd from the
    rest,
Those clustering rocks uprear'd their
    crest,
The dwelling of the fair distress'd,
   As told grey Lyulph's tale.
Thus as he lay, the lamp of night
Was quivering on his armour bright,
   In beams that rose and fell,
And danced upon his buckler's boss,
That lay beside him on the moss,
   As on a crystal well.

III.

Ever he watch'd, and oft he deem'd,
While on the mound the moonlight
    stream'd,
   It alter'd to his eyes ;
Fain would he hope the rocks 'gan
    change
To buttress'd walls their shapeless
    range,
Fain think, by transmutation strange,
   He saw grey turrets rise.
But scarce his heart with hope throbb'd
    high,
Before the wild illusions fly
   Which fancy had conceived,
Abetted by an anxious eye
   That long'd to be deceived.

It was a fond deception all,
Such as, in solitary hall,
　　Beguiles the musing eye,
When, gazing on the sinking fire,
Bulwark, and battlement, and spire,
　　In the red gulf we spy.
For, seen by moon of middle night,
Or by the blaze of noontide bright,
Or by the dawn of morning light,
　　Or evening's western flame,
In every tide, at every hour,
In mist, in sunshine, and in shower,
　　The rocks remain'd the same.

IV.

Oft has he traced the charmed mound,
Oft climb'd its crest, or paced it round,
　　Yet nothing might explore,
Save that the crags so rudely piled,
At distance seen, resemblance wild
　　To a rough fortress bore.
Yet still his watch the warrior keeps,
Feeds hard and spare, and seldom
　　　sleeps,
　　And drinks but of the well:
Ever by day he walks the hill,
And when the evening gale is chill,
　　He seeks a rocky cell,
Like hermit poor to bid his bead,
And tell his Ave and his Creed,
Invoking every saint at need,
　　For aid to burst his spell.

V.

And now the moon her orb has hid,
And dwindled to a silver thread,
　　Dim seen in middle heaven,
While o'er its curve careering fast,
Before the fury of the blast
　　The midnight clouds are driven.
The brooklet raved, for on the hills
The upland showers had swoln the
　　　rills,
　　And down the torrents came;
Mutter'd the distant thunder dread,
And frequent o'er the vale was spread
　　A sheet of lightning flame.

De Vaux, within his mountain cave,
(No human step the storm durst brave)
To moody meditation gave
　　Each faculty of soul,
Till, lull'd by distant torrent sound,
And the sad winds that whistled round,
Upon his thoughts, in musing drown'd,
　　A broken slumber stole.

VI.

'Twas then was heard a heavy sound
　　(Sound strange and fearful there to
　　　hear,
'Mongst desert hills, where, leagues
　　　around,
　　Dwelt but the gorcock and the
　　　deer):
As, starting from his couch of fern,
Again he heard, in clangor stern,
　　That deep and solemn swell,—
Twelve times, in measured tone, it
　　　spoke,
Like some proud minster's pealing
　　　clock,
　　Or city's larum-bell,—
What thought was Roland's first when
　　　fell,
In that deep wilderness, the knell
　　Upon his startled ear?
To slander warrior were I loth,
Yet must I hold my minstrel troth,—
　　It was a thought of fear.

VII.

But lively was the mingled thrill
That chased that momentary chill,
　　For Love's keen wish was there,
And eager Hope, and Valour high,
And the proud glow of Chivalry,
　　That burn'd to do and dare.
Forth from the cave the warrior rush'd,
Long ere the mountain-voice was
　　　hush'd,
　　That answer'd to the knell;
For long and far the unwonted sound,
Eddying in echoes round and round,
　　Was toss'd from fell to fell;

And Glaramara answer flung,
And Grisdale-pike responsive rung,
And Legbert heights their echoes swung
    As far as Derwent's dell.

VIII.

Forth upon trackless darkness gazed
The Knight, bedeafen'd and amazed,
    Till all was hush'd and still,
Save the swoln torrent's sullen roar,
And the night-blast that wildly bore
    Its course along the hill.
Then on the northern sky there came
A light, as of reflected flame,
    And over Legbert-head,
As if by magic art controll'd,
A mighty meteor slowly roll'd
    Its orb of fiery red ;
Thou wouldst have thought some demon dire
Came, mounted on that car of fire,
    To do his errand dread.
Far on the sloping valley's course,
On thicket, rock, and torrent hoarse,
Shingle and Scrae, and Fell and Force,
    A dusky light arose :
Display'd, yet alter'd was the scene ;
Dark rock, and brook of silver sheen,
Even the gay thicket's summer green,
    In bloody tincture glows.

IX.

De Vaux had mark'd the sunbeams set,
    At eve, upon the coronet
        Of that enchanted mound,
And seen but crags at random flung,
That, o'er the brawling torrent hung,
    In desolation frown'd.
What sees he by that meteor's lour ?
A banner'd Castle, keep, and tower,
    Return the lurid gleam,
With battled walls and buttress fast,
And barbican and ballium vast,
And airy flanking towers, that cast
    Their shadows on the stream.

'Tis no deceit ! distinctly clear
Crenell and parapet appear,
While o'er the pile that meteor drear
    Makes momentary pause ;
Then forth its solemn path it drew,
And fainter yet and fainter grew
Those gloomy towers upon the view,
    As its wild light withdraws.

X.

Forth from the cave did Roland rush,
O'er crag and stream, through brier and bush ;
    Yet far he had not sped
Ere sunk was that portentous light
Behind the hills, and utter night
    Was on the valley spread.
He paused perforce, and blew his horn,
And on the mountain-echoes borne
    Was heard an answering sound,
A wild and lonely trumpet-note ;
In middle air it seem'd to float
    High o'er the battled mound ;
And sounds were heard, as when a guard
Of some proud castle, holding ward,
    Pace forth their nightly round.
The valiant Knight of Triermain
Rung forth his challenge-blast again,
    But answer came there none ;
And 'mid the mingled wind and rain,
Darkling he sought the vale in vain,
    Until the dawning shone ;
And when it dawn'd, that wondrous sight,
Distinctly seen by meteor light—
    It all had pass'd away ;
And that enchanted mount once more
A pile of granite fragments bore,
    As at the close of day.

XI.

Steel'd for the deed, De Vaux's heart
Scorn'd from his vent'rous quest to part,
    He walks the vale once more ;
But only sees, by night or day,
That shatter'd pile of rocks so grey,
    Hears but the torrent's roar.

Till when, through hills of azure borne,
The moon renew'd her silver horn,
Just at the time her waning ray
Had faded in the dawning day,
    A summer mist arose;
Adown the vale the vapours float,
And cloudy undulations moat
That tufted mound of mystic note,
    As round its base they close.
And higher now the fleecy tide
Ascends its stern and shaggy side,
Until the airy billows hide
    The rock's majestic isle;
It seem'd a veil of filmy lawn,
By some fantastic fairy drawn
    Around enchanted pile.

XII.

The breeze came softly down the brook,
    And, sighing as it blew,
The veil of silver mist it shook,
And to De Vaux's eager look
    Renew'd that wondrous view.
For, though the loitering vapour braved
The gentle breeze, yet oft it waved
    Its mantle's dewy fold;
And still, when shook that filmy screen,
Were towers and bastions dimly seen,
And Gothic battlements between
    Their gloomy length unroll'd.
Speed, speed, De Vaux, ere on thine eye
Once more the fleeting vision die!
    The gallant knight 'gan speed
As prompt and light as, when the hound
Is opening, and the horn is wound,
    Careers the hunter's steed.
Down the steep dell his course amain
    Hath rivall'd archer's shaft;
But ere the mound he could attain,
The rocks their shapeless form regain,
And, mocking loud his labour vain,
    The mountain spirits laugh'd.
Far up the echoing dell was borne
Their wild unearthly shout of scorn.

XIII.

Wroth wax'd the Warrior: 'Am I then
Fool'd by the enemies of men,
Like a poor hind, whose homeward way
Is haunted by malicious fay?
Is Triermain become your taunt,
De Vaux your scorn? False fiends, avaunt!'
A weighty curtal-axe he bare;
The baleful blade so bright and square,
And the tough shaft of heben wood,
Were oft in Scottish gore imbrued.
Backward his stately form he drew,
And at the rocks the weapon threw,
Just where one crag's projected crest
Hung proudly balanced o'er the rest.
Hurl'd with main force, the weapon's shock
Rent a huge fragment of the rock.
If by mere strength, 'twere hard to tell,
Or if the blow dissolved some spell,
But down the headlong ruin came,
With cloud of dust and flash of flame.
Down bank, o'er bush, its course was borne,
Crush'd lay the copse, the earth was torn,
Till staid at length, the ruin dread
Cumber'd the torrent's rocky bed,
And bade the waters' high swoln tide
Seek other passage for its pride.

XIV.

When ceased that thunder, Triermain
Survey'd the mound's rude front again;
And, lo! the ruin had laid bare,
Hewn in the stone. a winding stair,
Whose moss'd and fractured steps might lend
The means the summit to ascend;
And by whose aid the brave De Vaux
Began to scale these magic rocks,
    And soon a platform won,

Where, the wild witchery to close,
Within three lances' length arose
    The Castle of Saint John!
No misty phantom of the air,
No meteor-blazon'd show was there;
In morning splendour, full and fair,
    The massive fortress shone.

xv.

Embattled high and proudly tower'd,
Shaded by pond'rous flankers, lower'd
    The portal's gloomy way.
Though for six hundred years and
    more
Its strength had brook'd the tempest's
    roar,
The scutcheon'd emblems which it
    bore
    Had suffer'd no decay:
But from the eastern battlement
A turret had made sheer descent,
And, down in recent ruin rent,
    In the mid-torrent lay.
Else, o'er the Castle's brow sublime,
Insults of violence or of time
    Unfelt had pass'd away.
In shapeless characters of yore,
The gate this stern inscription bore:—

xvi.

'Patience waits the destined day,
Strength can clear the cumber'd way.
Warrior, who hast waited long,
Firm of soul, of sinew strong,
It is given to thee to gaze
On the pile of ancient days.
Never mortal builder's hand
This enduring fabric plann'd;
Sign and sigil, word of power,
From the earth raised keep and tower.
View it o'er, and pace it round,
Rampart, turret, battled mound.
Dare no more! To cross the gate
Were to tamper with thy fate;
Strength and fortitude were vain,
View it o'er—and turn again.'

xvii.

'That would I,' said the Warrior bold,
'If that my frame were bent and old,
And my thin blood dropp'd slow and
    cold
    As icicle in thaw;
But while my heart can feel it dance,
Blithe as the sparkling wine of France,
And this good arm wields sword or
    lance,
    I mock these words of awe!'
He said; the wicket felt the sway
Of his strong hand, and straight gave
    way,
And, with rude crash and jarring bray,
    The rusty bolts withdraw;
But o'er the threshold as he strode,
And forward took the vaulted road,
An unseen arm, with force amain,
The ponderous gate flung close again,
    And rusted bolt and bar
Spontaneous took their place once
    more,
While the deep arch with sullen roar
    Return'd their surly jar.
'Now closed is the gin and the prey
    within
    By the Rood of Lanercost!
But he that would win the war-wolf's
    skin
    May rue him of his boast.'
Thus muttering, on the Warrior went,
By dubious light down steep descent.

xviii.

Unbarr'd, unlock'd, unwatch'd, a port
Led to the Castle's outer court:
There the main fortress, broad and tall,
Spread its long range of bower and hall,
    And towers of varied size,
Wrought with each ornament extreme
That Gothic art, in wildest dream
    Of fancy, could devise;
But full between the Warrior's way
And the main portal arch, there lay
    An inner moat;
    Nor bridge nor boat

Affords De Vaux the means to cross
The clear, profound, and silent fosse.
His arms aside in haste he flings,
Cuirass of steel and hauberk rings,
And down falls helm, and down the
　　shield,
Rough with the dints of many a field.
Fair was his manly form, and fair
His keen dark eye, and close curl'd
　　hair,
When, all unarm'd, save that the brand
Of well-proved metal graced his hand,
With nought to fence his dauntless
　　breast
But the close gipon's under-vest,
Whose sullied buff the sable stains
Of hauberk and of mail retains,
Roland De Vaux upon the brim
Of the broad moat stood prompt to
　　swim.

XIX.

Accoutred thus he dared the tide,
And soon he reach'd the farther side,
　　And enter'd soon the hold,
And paced a hall, whose walls so wide
Were blazon'd all with feats of pride,
　　By warriors done of old.
In middle lists they counter'd here,
　　While trumpets seem'd to blow;
And there, in den or desert drear,
　　They quell'd gigantic foe,
Braved the fierce griffon in his ire,
Or faced the dragon's breath of fire.
Strange in their arms, and strange in
　　face,
Heroes they seem'd of ancient race,
Whose deeds of arms, and race, and
　　name,
Forgotten long by later fame,
　　Were here depicted, to appal
Those of an age degenerate,
Whose bold intrusion braved their fate
　　In this enchanted hall.
For some short space the venturous
　　knight
With these high marvels fed his sight,

Then sought the chamber's upper end,
Where three broad easy steps ascend
　　To an arch'd portal door,
In whose broad folding leaves of state
Was framed a wicket window-grate,
　　And, ere he ventured more,
The gallant Knight took earnest view
The grated wicket-window through.

XX.

Oh, for his arms! Of martial weed
Had never mortal Knight such need!
He spied a stately gallery; all
Of snow-white marble was the wall,
　　The vaulting, and the floor;
And, contrast strange! on either hand
There stood array'd in sable band
　　Four maids whom Afric bore;
And each a Lybian tiger led,
Held by as bright and frail a thread
　　As Lucy's golden hair,—
For the leash that bound these mon-
　　sters dread
　　Was but of gossamèr.
Each maiden's short barbaric vest
Left all unclosed the knee and breast,
　　And limbs of shapely jet;
White was their vest and turban's fold,
On arms and ankles rings of gold
　　In savage pomp were set;
A quiver on their shoulders lay,
And in their hand an assagay.
Such and so silent stood they there,
　　That Roland wellnigh hoped
He saw a band of statues rare,
Station'd the gazer's soul to scare;
　　But when the wicket oped,
Each grisly beast 'gan upward draw,
Roll'd his grim eye, and spread his
　　claw,
Scented the air, and licked his jaw;
While these weird maids, in Moorish
　　tongue,
A wild and dismal warning sung.

XXI.

'Rash adventurer, bear thee back!
　　Dread the spell of Dahomay!

Fear the race of Zaharak,
  Daughters of the burning day!

'When the whirlwind's gusts are
    wheeling,
  Ours it is the dance to braid;
Zarah's sands in pillars reeling
  Join the measure that we tread,
When the moon has donn'd her cloak,
  And the stars are red to see,
Shrill when pipes the sad siroc,
  Music meet for such as we.

'Where the shatter'd columns lie,
  Showing Carthage once had been,
If the wandering Santon's eye
  Our mysterious rites hath seen,—
Oft he cons the prayer of death,
  To the nations preaches doom,
"Azrael's brand hath left the sheath!
  Moslems, think upon the tomb!"

'Ours the scorpion, ours the snake,
  Ours the hydra of the fen,
Ours the tiger of the brake,
  All that plague the sons of men.
Ours the tempest's midnight wrack,
  Pestilence that wastes by day:
Dread the race of Zaharak!
  Fear the spell of Dahomay!'

XXII.

Uncouth and strange the accents shrill
  Rung those vaulted roofs among,
Long it was ere, faint and still,
  Died the far-resounding song.
While yet the distant echoes roll,
The Warrior communed with his soul:
  'When first I took this venturous
      quest,
    I swore upon the rood,
  Neither to stop, nor turn, nor rest,
    For evil or for good.
My forward path too well I ween,
Lies yonder fearful ranks between!
For man unarm'd, 'tis bootless hope
With tigers and with fiends to cope;
Yet, if I turn, what waits me there,
Save famine dire and fell despair?

Other conclusion let me try,
Since, choose howe'er I list, I die.
Forward, lies faith and knightly fame;
Behind, are perjury and shame.'
In life or death I hold my word!'
With that he drew his trusty sword,
Caught down a banner from the wall,
And enter'd thus the fearful hall.

XXIII.

On high each wayward maiden threw
  Her swarthy arm, with wild halloo—
On either side a tiger sprung:
Against the leftward foe he flung
The ready banner, to engage
With tangling folds the brutal rage;
The right-hand monster in mid air
He struck so fiercely and so fair,
Through gullet and through spinal
      bone,
The trenchant blade had sheerly gone.
His grisly brethren ramp'd and yell'd,
But the slight leash their rage withheld,
Whilst, 'twixt their ranks, the danger-
      ous road
Firmly, though swift, the champion
      strode.
Safe to the gallery's bound he drew,
Safe pass'd an open portal through;
And when against pursuit he flung
The gate, judge if the echoes rung!
Onward his daring course he bore,
While, mix'd with dying growl and
      roar,
Wild jubilee and loud hurra
Pursued him on his venturous way.

XXIV.

'Hurra, hurra! our watch is done!
We hail once more the tropic sun.
Pallid beams of northern day,
Farewell, farewell! Hurra, hurra!

'Five hundred years o'er this cold
      glen
Hath the pale sun come round agen;
Foot of man, till now, hath ne'er
Dared to cross the Hall of Fear.

'Warrior! thou, whose dauntless
    heart
Gives us from our ward to part,
Be as strong in future trial,
Where resistance is denial.

' Now for Afric's glowing sky,
Zwenga wide and Atlas high,
Zaharak and Dahomay!
Mount the winds! Hurra, hurra!'

XXV.

The wizard song at distance died,
  As if in ether borne astray,
While through waste halls and
    chambers wide
The knight pursued his steady way,
Till to a lofty dome he came,
That flash'd, with such a brilliant flame,
As if the wealth of all the world
Were there in rich confusion hurl'd.
For here the gold, in sandy heaps,
With duller earth, incorporate, sleeps ;
Was there in ingots piled ; and there
Coin'd badge of empery it bare ;
Yonder, huge bars of silver lay,
Dimm'd by the diamond's neighbouring
    ray,
Like the pale moon in morning day ;
And in the midst four maidens stand,
The daughters of some distant land.
Their hue was of the dark-red dye,
That fringes oft a thunder sky ;
Their hands palmetto baskets bare,
And cotton fillets bound their hair ;
Slim was their form, their mien was shy,
To earth they bent the humbled eye,
Folded their arms, and suppliant
    kneel'd,
And thus their proffer'd gifts reveal'd.

XXVI.

CHORUS.

'See the treasures Merlin piled,
Portion meet for Arthur's child.
Bathe in wealth's unbounded stream,
Wealth that avarice ne'er could
    dream !'

FIRST MAIDEN.

' See these clots of virgin gold !
Sever'd from the sparry mould,
Nature's mystic alchemy
In the mine thus bade them lie ;
And their orient smile can win
Kings to stoop, and saints to sin.'

SECOND MAIDEN.

' See these pearls, that long have slept ;
These were tears by Naiads wept
For the loss of Marinel.
Tritons in the silver shell
Treasured them, till hard and white
As the teeth of Amphitrite.'

THIRD MAIDEN.

' Does a livelier hue delight ?
Here are rubies blazing bright,
Here the emerald's fairy green,
And the topaz glows between ;
Here their varied hues unite,
In the changeful chrysolite.'

FOURTH MAIDEN.

' Leave these gems of poorer shine,
Leave them all, and look on mine !
While their glories I expand,
Shade thine eyebrows with thy hand.
Mid-day sun and diamond's blaze
Blind the rash beholder's gaze.'

CHORUS.

' Warrior, seize the splendid store ;
Would 'twere all our mountains bore !
We should ne'er in future story
Read, Peru, thy perish'd glory !'

XXVII.

Calmly and unconcern'd, the knight
Waved aside the treasures bright :—
' Gentle maidens, rise, I pray !
Bar not thus my destined way.
Let these boasted brilliant toys
Braid the hair of girls and boys !
Bid your streams of gold expand
O'er proud London's thirsty land.

De Vaux of wealth saw never need,
Save to purvey him arms and steed,
And all the ore he deign'd to hoard
Inlays his helm, and hilts his sword.'
Thus gently parting from their hold,
He left, unmoved, the dome of gold.

XXVIII.

And now the morning sun was high,
De Vaux was weary, faint, and dry;
When, lo! a plashing sound he hears,
A gladsome signal that he nears
    Some frolic water-run;
And soon he reach'd a court-yard
    square,
Where, dancing in the sultry air,
Toss'd high aloft, a fountain fair
    Was sparkling in the sun.
On right and left, a fair arcade,
In long perspective view display'd
Alleys and bowers, for sun or shade :
    But, full in front, a door,
Low-brow'd and dark, seem'd as it led
To the lone dwelling of the dead,
    Whose memory was no more.

XXIX.

Here stopp'd De Vaux an instant's
    space,
To bathe his parched lips and face,
    And mark'd with well-pleased eye,
Refracted on the fountain stream,
In rainbow hues the dazzling beam
    Of that gay summer sky.
His senses felt a mild control,
Like that which lulls the weary soul,
    From contemplation high
Relaxing, when the ear receives
The music that the greenwood leaves
    Make to the breezes' sigh.

XXX.

And oft in such a dreamy mood,
    The half-shut eye can frame
Fair apparitions in the wood
As if the nymphs of field and flood
    In gay procession came.

Are these of such fantastic mould,
    Seen distant down the fair arcade,
These maids enlink'd in sister-fold,
    Who, late at bashful distance staid,
    Now tripping from the greenwood
      shade,
Nearer the musing champion draw,
And, in a pause of seeming awe,
    Again stand doubtful now ?
Ah, that sly pause of witching powers
That seems to say, ' To please be ours,
    Be yours to tell us how.'
Their hue was of the golden glow
That suns of Candahar bestow,
O'er which in slight suffusion flows
A frequent tinge of paly rose ;
Their limbs were fashion'd fair and free,
In nature's justest symmetry;
And, wreathed with flowers, with
    odours graced,
Their raven ringlets reach'd the waist :
In eastern pomp, its gilding pale
The hennah lent each shapely nail,
And the dark sumah gave the eye
More liquid and more lustrous dye.
The spotless veil of misty lawn,
In studied disarrangement, drawn
    The form and bosom o'er,
To win the eye, or tempt the touch,
For modesty show'd all too much—
    Too much, yet promised more.

XXXI.

' Gentle knight, a while delay,'
Thus they sung, ' thy toilsome way,
While we pay the duty due
To our Master and to you.
Over avarice, over fear,
Love triumphant led thee here ;
Warrior, list to us, for we
Are slaves to love, are friends to thee.
Though no treasured gems have we,
To proffer on the bended knee,
Though we boast nor arm nor heart,
For the assagay or dart,
Swains allow each simple girl
Ruby lip and teeth of pearl;

Or, if dangers more you prize,
Flatterers find them in our eyes.

' Stay, then, gentle warrior, stay,
Rest till evening steal on day;
Stay, O, stay! in yonder bowers
We will braid thy locks with flowers,
Spread the feast and fill the wine,
Charm thy ear with sounds divine,
Weave our dances till delight
Yield to languor, day to night.
Then shall she you most approve,
Sing the lays that best you love,
Soft thy mossy couch shall spread,
Watch thy pillow, prop thy head,
Till the weary night be o'er;
Gentle warrior, wouldst thou more?
Wouldst thou more, fair warrior? she
Is slave to love and slave to thee.'

XXXII.

O do not hold it for a crime
In the bold hero of my rhyme,
    For Stoic look,
    And meet rebuke,
He lack'd the heart or time;
As round the band of sirens trip,
He kiss'd one damsel's laughing lip,
And press'd another's proffer'd hand.
Spoke to them all in accents bland,
But broke their magic circle through;
' Kind maids,' he said, ' adieu, adieu!
My fate, my fortune, forward lies.'
He said, and vanish'd from their eyes;
But, as he dared that darksome way,
Still heard behind their lovely lay:
' Fair Flower of Courtesy, depart!
Go, where the feelings of the heart
With the warm pulse in concord
    move;
Go, where virtue sanctions love!'

XXXIII.

Downward De Vaux through dark-
    some ways
    And ruin'd vaults has gone,
Till issue from their wilder'd maze,
    Or safe retreat, seem'd none;

And e'en the dismal path he strays
    Grew worse as he went on.
For cheerful sun, for living air,
Foul vapours rise and mine-fires glare,
Whose fearful light the dangers show'd
That dogg'd him on that dreadful road.
Deep pits, and lakes of waters dun,
They show d, but show'd not how to
    shun.
These scenes of desolate despair,
These smothering clouds of poison'd
    air,
How gladly had De Vaux exchanged,
Though 'twere to face yon tigers
    ranged!
Nay, soothful bards have said
So perilous his state seem'd now,
He wish'd him under arbour bough
    With Asia's willing maid.
When, joyful sound! at distance near
A trumpet flourish'd loud and clear,
And as it ceased, a lofty lay
Seem'd thus to chide his lagging way.

XXXIV.

' Son of Honour, theme of story,
Think on the reward before ye!
Danger, darkness, toil despise;
'Tis ambition bids thee rise.

' He that would her heights ascend,
Many a weary step must wend;
Hand and foot and knee he tries;
Thus ambition's minions rise.

'Lag not now, though rough the way,
Fortune's mood brooks no delay;
Grasp the boon that's spread before
    ye,
Monarch's power, and conqueror's
    glory!'

It ceased. Advancing on the sound,
A steep ascent the wanderer found,
    And then a turret stair:
Nor climb'd he far its steepy round
    Till fresher blew the air,

And next a welcome glimpse was given,
That cheer'd him with the light of
       heaven.
At length his toil had won
A lofty hall with trophies dress'd,
Where, as to greet imperial guest,
Four maidens stood, whose crimson
       vest
     Was bound with golden zone.

XXXV.

Of Europe seem'd the damsels all;
The first a nymph of lively Gaul,
Whose easy step and laughing eye
    Her borrow'd air of awe belie;
    The next a maid of Spain,
Dark-eyed, dark-hair'd, sedate, yet
       bold;
White ivory skin and tress of gold,
Her shy and bashful comrade told
     For daughter of Almaine.
These maidens bore a royal robe,
With crown, with sceptre, and with
       globe,
     Emblems of empery;
The fourth a space behind them stood,
And leant upon a harp, in mood
     Of minstrel ecstasy.
Of merry England she, in dress
Like ancient British Druidess.
Her hair an azure fillet bound,
Her graceful vesture swept the ground,
     And, in her hand display'd,
A crown did that fourth maiden hold,
But unadorn'd with gems and gold,
     Of glossy laurel made.

XXXVI.

At once to brave De Vaux knelt down
    These foremost maidens three,
And proffer'd sceptre, robe, and crown,
    Liegedom and seignorie,
O'er many a region wide and fair,
Destined, they said, for Arthur's heir;
    But homage would he none:
'Rather,' he said, ' De Vaux would ride,
A warden of the Border-side,

In plate and mail, than, robed in pride,
    A monarch's empire own;
Rather, far rather, would he be
A free-born knight of England free,
    Than sit on despot's throne.'
So pass'd he on, when that fourth maid,
    As starting from a trance,
Upon the harp her finger laid;
Her magic touch the chords obey'd,
    Their soul awaked at once!

SONG OF THE FOURTH MAIDEN.

' Quake to your foundations deep,
Stately towers, and banner'd keep,
Bid your vaulted echoes moan,
As the dreaded step they own.

' Fiends, that wait on Merlin's spell,
Hear the foot-fall! mark it well!
Spread your dusky wings abroad,
Boune ye for your homeward road!

' It is his, the first who e'er
Dared the dismal Hall of Fear;
His, who hath the snares defied
Spread by pleasure, wealth, and pride.

'Quake to your foundations deep,
Bastion huge, and turret steep!
Tremble, keep! and totter, tower!
This is Gyneth's waking hour.'

XXXVII.

Thus while she sung, the venturous
       knight
Has reach'd a bower, where milder
       light
    Through crimson curtains fell;
Such soften'd shade the hill receives,
Her purple veil when twilight leaves
    Upon its western swell.
That bower, the gazer to bewitch,
Hath wondrous store of rare and rich
    As e'er was seen with eye;
For there by magic skill, I wis,
Form of each thing that living is
    Was limn'd in proper dye.

All seem'd to sleep—the timid hare
On form, the stag upon his lair,
The eagle in her eyrie fair
    Between the earth and sky.
But what of pictured rich and rare
Could win De Vaux's eye-glance,
    where,
Deep slumbering in the fatal chair,
    He saw King Arthur's child!
Doubt, and anger, and dismay,
From her brow had pass'd away,
Forgot was that fell tourney-day,
    For, as she slept, she smiled:
It seem'd, that the repentant Seer
Her sleep of many a hundred year
    With gentle dreams beguiled

XXXVIII.

That form of maiden loveliness,
    'Twixt childhood and 'twixt youth,
That ivory chair, that silvan dress,
The arms and ankles bare, express
    Of Lyulph's tale the truth.
Still upon her garment's hem
Vanoc's blood made purple gem,
And the warder of command
Cumber'd still her sleeping hand;
Still her dark locks dishevell'd flow
From net of pearl o'er breast of snow;
And so fair the slumberer seems,
That De Vaux impeach'd his dreams,
Vapid all and void of might,
Hiding half her charms from sight.
Motionless a while he stands,
Folds his arms and clasps his hands,
Trembling in his fitful joy,
Doubtful how he should destroy
    Long-enduring spell;
Doubtful, too, when slowly rise
Dark-fringed lids of Gyneth's eyes,
    What these eyes shall tell.
'Saint George! Saint Mary! can it be,
That they will kindly look on me!'

XXXIX.

Gently, lo! the warrior kneels,
Soft that lovely hand he steals.

Soft to kiss, and soft to clasp—
But the warder leaves his grasp;
    Lightning flashes, rolls the
        thunder!
Gyneth startles from her sleep,
Totters tower, and trembles keep,
    Burst the castle-walls asunder!
Fierce and frequent were the shocks,—
    Melt the magic halls away;
But beneath their mystic rocks,
In the arms of bold De Vaux,
    Safe the princess lay;
Safe and free from magic power,
Blushing like the rose's flower
    Opening to the day;
And round the champion's brows were
    bound
The crown that Druidess had wound,
    Of the green laurel-bay.
And this was what remain'd of all
The wealth of each enchanted hall,
    The garland and the dame:
But where should warrior seek the
    meed,
Due to high worth for daring deed,
    Except from love and fame!

CONCLUSION.

I.

My Lucy, when the maid is won,
The minstrel's task, thou know'st, is
    done;
    And to require of bard
That to his dregs the tale should run,
    Were ordinance too hard.
Our lovers, briefly be it said,
Wedded as lovers wont to wed,
    When tale or play is o'er;
Lived long and blest, loved fond and
    true,
    And saw a numerous race renew
The honours that they bore.
Know, too, that when a pilgrim strays,
In morning mist or evening maze,
    Along the mountain lone,

That fairy fortress often mocks
His gaze upon the castled rocks
    Of the Valley of Saint John ;
But never man since brave De Vaux
    The charmed portal won.
'Tis now a vain illusive show,
That melts whene'er the sunbeams glow
    Or the fresh breeze hath blown.

II.

But see, my love, where far below
Our lingering wheels are moving slow,
    The whiles, up-gazing still,
Our menials eye our steepy way,
Marvelling, perchance, what whim can
    stay
Our steps, when eve is sinking grey,
    On this gigantic hill.
So think the vulgar : Life and time
Ring all their joys in one dull chime
    Of luxury and ease ;

And, O ! beside these simple knaves,
How many better born are slaves
    To such coarse joys as these !
Dead to the nobler sense that glows
When nature's grander scenes unclose !
But, Lucy, we will love them yet,
The mountain's misty coronet,
    The greenwood, and the wold ;
And love the more that of their maze
Adventure high of other days
    By ancient bards is told,
Bringing, perchance, like my poor
    tale,
Some moral truth in fiction's veil :
Nor love them less, that o'er the hill
The evening breeze, as now, comes
    chill ;—
    My love shall wrap her warm,
And, fearless of the slippery way,
While safe she trips the heathy brae,
    Shall hang on Arthur's arm.

END OF THE BRIDAL OF TRIERMAIN.

Introduction and Notes to The Bridal of Triermain.

INTRODUCTION TO THE FIRST EDITION.[1]

In the *Edinburgh Annual Register* for the year 1809, Three Fragments were inserted, written in imitation of Living Poets. It must have been apparent that, by these prolusions, nothing burlesque, or disrespectful to the authors, was intended, but that they were offered to the public as serious, though certainly very imperfect, imitations of that style of composition, by which each of the writers is supposed to be distinguished. As these exercises attracted a greater degree of attention than the author anticipated, he has been induced to complete one of them, and present it as a separate publication[2].

It is not in this place that an examination of the works of the master whom he has here adopted as his model, can, with propriety, be introduced; since his general acquiescence in the favourable suffrage of the public must necessarily be inferred from the attempt he has now made. He is induced, by the nature of his subject, to offer a few remarks on what has been called Romantic Poetry;—the popularity of which has been revived in the present day, under the auspices, and by the unparalleled success, of one individual.

The original purpose of poetry is either religious or historical, or, as must frequently happen, a mixture of both. To modern readers, the poems of Homer have many of the features of pure romance; but in the estimation of his contemporaries, they probably derived their chief value from their supposed historical authenticity. The same may be generally said of the poetry of all early ages. The marvels and miracles which the poet blends with his song, do not exceed in number or extravagance the figments of the historians of the same period of society; and, indeed, the difference betwixt poetry and prose, as the vehicles of historical truth, is always of late introduction. Poets, under various denominations of Bards, Scalds, Chroniclers, and so forth, are the first historians of all nations. Their intention is to relate the events they have witnessed, or the traditions that have reached them; and they clothe the relation in rhyme, merely as the means of rendering it more solemn in the narrative or more easily committed to memory. But as the poetical historian improves in the art of conveying information, the authenticity of his narrative unavoidably declines. He is tempted to dilate and dwell upon the events that are interesting to his imagination, and, conscious how indifferent his audience is to the naked truth of his poem, his history gradually becomes a romance.

It is in this situation that those epics are found, which have been generally regarded as the standards of poetry; and it has happened somewhat strangely, that the moderns have pointed out as the characteristics and peculiar excellencies of narrative poetry the very circumstances which the authors themselves adopted, only because their art involved the duties of the historian as well as the poet. It cannot be believed, for example, that Homer selected the siege of Troy as the most appropriate subject for poetry; his purpose was to write the early history of his country; the event he has chosen, though not very fruitful in varied incident, nor perfectly well adapted for poetry, was nevertheless combined with traditionary and genealogical

---

[1] Published in March 1813.

[2] Being much urged by my intimate friend, now unhappily no more, William Erskine, I agreed to write the little romantic tale called 'The Bridal of Triermain'; but it was on the condition that he should make no serious effort to disown the composition, if report should lay it at his door. As he was more than suspected of a taste for poetry, and as I took care, in several places, to mix something which might resemble (as far as was in my power) my friend's feeling and manner, the train easily caught; and two large editions were sold. A third being called for, Lord Kinedder became unwilling to aid any longer a deception which was going farther than he expected or desired, and the real author's name was given.

anecdotes extremely interesting to those who were to listen to him ; and this he has adorned by the exertions of a genius, which, if it has been equalled, has certainly been never surpassed. It was not till comparatively a late period that the general accuracy of his narrative, or his purpose in composing it was brought into question. Δοκεῖ πρῶτος [ὁ Ἀναξαγόρας] (καθά φησι Φαβωρῖνος ἐν παντοδαπῇ Ἱστορίᾳ) τὴν Ὁμήρου ποίησιν ἀπο- φήνασθαι εἶναι περὶ ἀρετῆς καὶ δικαιοσύνης[1]. But whatever theories might be framed by speculative men, his work was of an historical, not of an allegorical nature. Ἐναντίλλετο μετὰ τοῦ Μέντεω καὶ ὅπου ἑκάστοτε ἀφίκοιτο, πάντα τὰ ἐπιχώρια διερωτᾶτο, καὶ ἱστορέων ἐπυνθάνετο· εἰκὸς δέ μιν ἦν καὶ μνημοσύνη πάν- των γράφεσθαι[2]. Instead of recommending the choice of a subject similar to that of Homer, it was to be expected that critics should have exhorted the poets of these latter days to adopt or invent a narrative in itself more susceptible of poetical ornament, and to avail themselves of that advantage in order to compensate, in some degree, the inferiority of genius. The contrary course has been inculcated by almost all the writers upon the *Epopoeia;* with what success, the fate of Homer's numerous imitators may best show. The *ultimum supplicium* of criticism was inflicted on the author if he did not choose a subject which at once deprived him of all claim to originality, and placed him, if not in actual contest, at least in fatal comparison, with those giants in the land whom it was most his interest to avoid. The celebrated receipt for writing an epic poem, which appeared in *The Guardian,* was the first instance in which common sense was applied to this department of poetry ; and, indeed, if the question be considered on its own merits, we must be satisfied that narrative poetry, if strictly confined to the great occur- rences of history, would be deprived of the individual interest which it is so well calculated to excite.

Modern poets may therefore be pardoned in seeking simpler subjects of verse, more interesting in proportion to their simplicity. Two or three figures, well grouped, suit the artist better than a crowd, for whatever purpose assembled. For the same reason, a scene immediately presented to the imagina- tion, and directly brought home to the feel- ings, though involving the fate of but one or two persons, is more favourable for poetry than the political struggles and convulsions which influence the fate of kingdoms. The former are within the reach and compre- hension of all, and, if depicted with vigour, seldom fail to fix attention : the other, if more sublime, are more vague and distant,

less capable of being distinctly understood, and infinitely less capable of exciting those sentiments which it is the very purpose of poetry to inspire. To generalize is always to destroy effect. We would, for example, be more interested in the fate of an individual soldier in combat, than in the grand event of a general action ; with the happiness of two lovers raised from misery and anxiety to peace and union, than with the successful exertions of a whole nation. From what causes this may originate, is a separate and obviously an immaterial consideration. Be- fore ascribing this peculiarity to causes decidedly and odiously selfish, it is proper to recollect, that while men see only a limited space, and while their affections and conduct are regulated, not by aspiring to an universal good, but by exerting their power of making themselves and others happy within the limited scale allotted to each individual, so long will individual history and individual virtue be the readier and more accessible road to general interest and attention ; and, perhaps, we may add, that it is the more useful, as well as the more accessible, inasmuch as it affords an example capable of being easily imitated.

According to the author's idea of Romantic Poetry as distinguished from Epic, the former comprehends a fictitious narrative, framed and combined at the pleasure of the writer ; beginning and ending as he may judge best: which neither exacts nor refuses the use of supernatural machinery ; which is free from the technical rules of the *Epée* ; and is subject only to those which good sense, good taste, and good morals, apply to every species of poetry without exception. The date may be in a remote age, or in the present ; the story may detail the adventures of a prince or of a peasant. In a word, the author is absolute master of his country and its inhabitants, and everything is permitted to him, excepting to be heavy or prosaic, for which, free and unembarrassed as he is, he has no manner of apology. Those, it is probable, will be found the peculiarities of this species of com- position ; and before joining the outcry against the vitiated taste that fosters and encourages it, the justice and grounds of it ought to be made perfectly apparent. If the want of sieges, and battles, and great military evo- lutions, in our poetry, is complained of, let us reflect, that the campaigns and heroes of our days are perpetuated in a record that neither requires nor admits of the aid of fiction ; and if the complaint refers to the inferiority of our bards, let us pay a just tribute to their modesty, limiting them, as it does, to subjects which, however indifferently treated, have still the interest and charm of novelty, and which thus prevents them from adding insipidity to their other more insuperable defects.

---

1 Diogenes Laertius, lib. ii. Anaxag. Segm. II.
2 Homeri Vita, in Herod. Henr. Steph. 1570, p. 356.

NOTES.

Note I.

Like Collins, thread the maze of fairy land.
—P. 555.

COLLINS, according to Johnson, 'by indulging some peculiar habits of thought, was eminently delighted with those flights of imagination which pass the bounds of nature, and to which the mind is reconciled only by a passive acquiescence in popular traditions. He loved fairies, genii, giants, and monsters; he delighted to rove through the meanders of enchantment, to gaze on the magnificence of golden palaces, to repose by the waterfalls of Elysian gardens.'

Note II.

The Baron of Triermain.—P. 555.

Triermain was a fief of the Barony of Gilsland, in Cumberland; it was possessed by a Saxon family at the time of the Conquest, but, 'after the death of Gilmore, Lord of Tryermaine and Torcrossock, Hubert Vaux gave Tryermaine and Torcrossock to his second son, Ranulph Vaux; which Ranulph afterwards became heir to his elder brother Robert, the founder of Lanercost, who died without issue. Ranulph, being Lord of all Gilsland, gave Gilmore's lands to his younger son, named Roland, and let the Barony descend to his eldest son Robert, son of Ranulph. Roland had issue Alexander, and he Ranulph, after whom succeeded Robert, and they were named Rolands successively, that were lords thereof, until the reign of Edward the Fourth. That house gave for arms, Vert, a bend dexter, chequy, or and gules.'—BURN's *Antiquities of Westmoreland and Cumberland*, vol. ii. p. 482.

This branch of Vaux, with its collateral alliances, is now represented by the family of Braddyl of Conished Priory, in the county palatine of Lancaster; for it appears that about the time above mentioned, the house of Triermain was united to its kindred family Vaux of Caterlen, and, by marriage with the heiress of Delamore and Leybourne, became the representative of those ancient and noble families. The male line failing in John de Vaux, about the year 1665, his daughter and heiress, Mabel, married Christopher Richmond, Esq., of Highhead Castle, in the county of Cumberland, descended from an ancient family of that name, Lords of Corby Castle, in the same county, soon after the Conquest, and which they alienated about the 15th of Edward the Second, to Andrea de Harcla, Earl of Carlisle. Of this family was Sir Thomas de Raigemont (miles auratus), in the reign of King Edward the First, who appears to have greatly distinguished himself at the siege of Kaerlaveroc, with William, Baron of Leybourne. In an ancient heraldic poem, now extant, and preserved in the British Museum, describing that siege, his arms are stated to be, Or, 2 Bars Gemelles Gules, and a Chief Or, the same borne by his descendants at the present day. The Richmonds removed to their Castle of Highhead in the reign of Henry the Eighth, when the then representative of the family married Margaret, daughter of Sir Hugh Lowther, by the Lady Dorothy de Clifford, only child by a second marriage of Henry Lord Clifford, great grandson of John Lord Clifford, by Elizabeth Percy, daughter of Henry (surnamed Hotspur) by Elizabeth Mortimer, which said Elizabeth was daughter of Edward Mortimer, third Earl of Marche, by Philippa, sole daughter and heiress of Lionel, Duke of Clarence.

The third in descent from the above-mentioned John Richmond, became the representative of the families of Vaux, of Triermain, Caterlen, and Torcrossock, by his marriage with Mabel de Vaux, the heiress of them. His grandson, Henry Richmond, died without issue, leaving five sisters co-heiresses, four of whom married; but Margaret, who married William Gale, Esq., of Whitehaven, was the only one who had male issue surviving. She had a son, and a daughter married to Henry Curwen of Workington, Esq., who represented the county of Cumberland for many years in Parliament, and by her had a daughter, married to John Christian, Esq (now Curwen). John, son and heir of William Gale, married Saran, daughter and heiress of Christopher Wilson of Bardsea Hall, in the county of Lancaster, by Thomas Braddyl, aunt and co-heiress of Thomas Braddyl, Esq., of Braddyl, and Conishead Priory, in the same county, and had issue four sons and two daughters. 1st, William Wilson, died an infant; 2nd, Wilson, who upon the death of his cousin, Thomas Braddyl, without issue, succeeded to his estates, and took the name of Braddyl, in pursuance of his will, by the King's sign-manual; 3rd, William, died young; and, 4th, Henry Richmond, a lieutenant-general of the army, married Sarah, daughter of the Rev. R. Baldwin; Margaret married Richard Greaves Townley, Esq. of Fulbourne, in the county of Cambridge, and of Bellfield, in the county of Lancaster; Sarah married to George Bigland of Bigland Hall, in the same county. Wilson Braddyl, eldest son of John Gale, and grandson of Margaret Richmond, married Jane, daughter and heiress of Matthias Gale, Esq., of Catgill Hall, in the county of Cumberland, by Jane, daughter and heiress of the Rev. S. Bennet, D.D.; and, as the eldest surviving male branch of the families above-mentioned, he quarters, in addition to his own, their paternal coats in the following order, as appears by the records in the College of Arms. 1st, Argent, a fess azure, between 3 saltiers of the same, charged with an anchor between 2 lions' heads erased, or,—Gale. 2nd, Or, 2 bars gemelles gules, and a chief or,—Richmond. 3rd, Or, a fess chequey, or and gules between 9 gerbes gules,—Vaux of Caterlen. 4th, Gules, a fess chequey, or and gules between 9 gerbes or,—Vaux of Torcrossock. 5th, Argent, (not vert, as stated by Burn,) a bend chequey, or and gules, for Vaux of Triermain. 6th, Gules, a cross patonce, or, Delamore. 7th, Gules, 6 lions rampant argent, 3, 2, and 1,—Leybourne.—This more detailed genealogy of the family of Triermain was obligingly sent to the author by Major Braddyll of Conishead Priory.

_____

Note III.

He pass'd Red Penrith's Table Round.
—P. 557.

A circular intrenchment, about half a mile from Penrith, is thus popularly termed. The circle within the ditch is about one hundred and sixty paces in circumference, with openings, or approaches, directly opposite to each other. As the ditch is on the inner side, it could not be intended for the purpose of defence, and it has reasonably been conjectured that the enclosure was designed for the solemn exercise of feats of chivalry, and the embankment around for the convenience of the spectators.

_____

Note IV.

Mayburgh's mound.—P. 557.

Higher up the river Eamont than Arthur's Round Table, is a prodigious enclosure of great antiquity, formed by a collection of stones upon the top of a gently sloping hill, called Mayburgh. In the plain which it encloses there stands erect an unhewn stone of twelve feet in height. Two similar masses are said to have been destroyed during the memory of man. The whole appears to be a monument of Druidical times.

_____

Note V.

The Monarch, breathless and amazed,
Back on the fatal castle gazed:
Nor tower nor donjon could he spy,
Darkening against the morning sky.
—P. 563.

—'We now gained a view of the Vale of St. John's, a very narrow dell, hemmed in by mountains, through which a small brook makes many meanderings, washing little enclosures of grass-ground, which stretch up

the rising of the hills. In the widest part of the dale you are struck with the appearance of an ancient ruined castle, which seems to stand upon the summit of a little mount, the mountains around forming an amphitheatre. This massive bulwark shows a front of various towers, and makes an awful, rude, and Gothic appearance, with its lofty turrets and ragged battlements; we traced the galleries, the bending arches, the buttresses. The greatest antiquity stands characterized in its architecture; the inhabitants near it assert it is an antediluvian structure.

'The traveller's curiosity is roused, and he prepares to make a nearer approach, when that curiosity is put upon the rack, by his being assured, that, if he advances, certain genii who govern the place, by virtue of their supernatural art and necromancy, will strip it of all its beauties, and by enchantment, transform the magic walls. The vale seems adapted for the habitation of such beings; its gloomy recesses and retirements look like haunts of evil spirits. There was no delusion in the report; we were soon convinced of its truth; for this piece of antiquity, so venerable and noble in its aspect, as we drew near, changed its figure, and proved no other than a shaken massive pile of rocks, which stand in the midst of this little vale, disunited from the adjoining mountains, and have so much the real form and resemblance of a castle, that they bear the name of the Castle Rocks of St. John.'—HUTCHINSON'S *Excursion to the Lakes*, p. 121.

_____

Note VI.

The flower of Chivalry.
There Galaad sate with manly grace,
Yet maiden meekness in his face;
There Morolt of the iron mace,
And love-lorn Tristrem there.
—P. 564.

The characters named in the stanza are all of them more or less distinguished in the romances which treat of King Arthur and his Round Table, and their names are strung together according to the established custom of minstrels upon such occasions; for example, in the ballad of the Marriage of Sir Gawaine—

'Sir Lancelot, Sir Stephen bolde,
   They rode with them that daye,
And, foremost of the companye,
   There rode the stewarde Kaye.

'Soe did Sir Banier, and Sir Bore,
   And eke Sir Garratte keen,
Sir Tristrem too, that gentle knight,
   To the forest fresh and greene.'

Note VII.

Lancelot, that ever more
Look'd stolen-wise on the Queen.—P. 564.

Upon this delicate subject hear Richard Robinson, citizen of London, in his Assertion of King Arthur:—'But as it is a thing sufficiently apparent that she (Guenever, wife of King Arthur) was beautiful, so it is a thing doubted whether she was chaste, yea or no. Truly, so far as I can with honestie, I would spare the impayred honour and fame of noble women. But yet the truth of the historie pluckes me by the eare, and willeth not onely, but commandeth me to declare what the ancients have deemed of her. To wrestle or contend with so great authoritie were indeede unto mei a controversie, and that greate.'—*Assertion of King Arthure. Imprinted by John Wolfe, London*, 1582.

NOTE VIII.

There were two who loved their neighbours'
    wives,
And one who loved his own.—P. 565.

'In our forefathers' tyme, when Papistrie, as a standyng poole, covered and overflowed all England, fewe books were read in our tongue, savying certaine bookes of chevalrie, as they said, for pastime and pleasure; which, as some say, were made in the monasteries, by idle monks or wanton chanons. As one, for example, *La Morte d'Arthure*; the whole pleasure of which book standeth in two speciall poynts, in open manslaughter and bold bawdrye; in which booke they be counted the noblest knightes that do kill most men without any quarrell, and commit fowlest adoulteries by sutlest shiftes; as Sir Launcelot, with the wife of King Arthur, his master; Sir Tristram, with the wife of King Marke, his uncle; Sir Lamerocke, with the wife of King Lote, that was his own aunt. This is good stuffe for wise men to laugh at; or honest men to take pleasure at; yet I know when God's Bible was banished the Court, and La Morte d'Arthure received into the Prince's chamber.' — ASCHAM'S *Schoolmaster.*

The Vision of Don Roderick.

—✦—

TO

JOHN WHITMORE, Esq.,

AND TO

THE COMMITTEE OF SUBSCRIBERS FOR RELIEF OF THE PORTUGUESE SUFFERERS,
IN WHICH HE PRESIDES,

THIS POEM,

(THE VISION OF DON RODERICK,)

COMPOSED FOR THE BENEFIT OF THE FUND UNDER THEIR MANAGEMENT,
IS RESPECTFULLY INSCRIBED

BY

WALTER SCOTT.

I.

I.

Lives there a strain, whose sounds
    of mounting fire
  May rise distinguish'd o'er the
    din of war;
Or died it with yon master of the lyre,
  Who sung beleaguer'd Ilion's evil
    star?
Such, Wellington, might reach thee
    from afar,
  Wafting its descant wide o'er
    ocean's range;
Nor shouts, nor clashing arms, its
    mood could mar,
  All as it swell'd 'twixt each loud
    trumpet-change,
That clangs to Britain victory, to
    Portugal revenge!

II.

Yes, such a strain, with all o'er-
    pouring measure,
  Might melodize with each tumul-
    tuous sound,
Each voice of fear or triumph, woe
    or pleasure,
  That rings Mondego's ravaged
    shores around;
The thundering cry of hosts with
    conquest crown'd,
  The female shriek, the ruin'd
    peasant's moan,
The shout of captives from their
    chains unbound,
  The foil'd oppressor's deep and
    sullen groan,
A nation's choral hymn for tyranny
    o'erthrown.

III.

But we, weak minstrels of a laggard
    day,
  Skill'd but to imitate an elder page,
Timid and raptureless, can we repay
  The debt thou claim'st in this
    exhausted age?
Thou giv'st our lyres a theme that
    might engage
  Those that could send thy name
    o'er sea and land,
While sea and land shall last; for
    Homer's rage
  A theme; a theme for Milton's
    mighty hand!
How much unmeet for us, a faint
    degenerate band.

IV.

Ye mountains stern, within whose
    rugged breast
  The friends of Scottish freedom
    found repose;
Ye torrents, whose hoarse sounds
    have soothed their rest,
  Returning from the field of
    vanquish'd foes;
Say, have ye lost each wild
    majestic close,
  That erst the choir of Bards or
    Druids flung;
What time their hymn of victory
    arose,
  And Cattraeth's glens with voice
    of triumph rung,
And mystic Merlin harp'd, and grey-
    hair'd Llywarch sung!

V.

Oh, if your wilds such minstrelsy
    retain,
  As sure your changeful gales
    seem oft to say,
When sweeping wild and sinking
    soft again,
  Like trumpet-jubilee, or harp's
    wild sway;

If ye can echo such triumphant lay,
  Then lend the note to him has
    loved you long;
Who pious gather'd each tradition
    grey,
  That floats your solitary wastes
    along,
And with affection vain gave them
    new voice in song.

VI.

For not till now, how oft soe'er
    the task
  Of truant verse hath lighten'd
    graver care,
From muse or sylvan was he wont
    to ask,
  In phrase poetic, inspiration fair;
Careless he gave his numbers to
    the air;
  They came unsought for if ap-
    plauses came;
Nor for himself prefers he now the
    prayer:
  Let but his verse befit a hero's
    fame,
Immortal be the verse—forgot the
    poet's name!

VII.

Hark, from yon misty cairn their
    answer tost:
  'Minstrel, the fame of whose
    romantic lyre,
Capricious-swelling now, may soon
    be lost,
  Like the light flickering of a
    cottage fire;
If to such task presumptuous thou
    aspire,
  Seek not from us the meed to
    warrior due:
Age after age has gather'd son to sire,
  Since our grey cliffs the din of
    conflict knew,
Or, pealing through our vales, vic-
    torious bugles blew

VIII.

'Decay'd our old traditionary lore,
 Save where the lingering fays
 renew their ring,
By milk-maid seen beneath the
 hawthorn hoar,
 Or round the marge of Minch-
 more's haunted spring;
Save where their legends grey-
 hair'd shepherds sing,
 That now scarce win a listening
 ear but thine,
Of feuds obscure, and Border
 ravaging,
 And rugged deeds recount in
 rugged line,
Of moonlight foray made on Teviot.
 Tweed, or Tyne.

IX.

'No; search romantic lands, where
 the near Sun
 Gives with unstinted boon ethereal flame,
Where the rude villager, his labour
 done,
 In verse spontaneous chants
 some favour'd name,
Whether Olalia's charms his tribute
 claim,
 Her eye of diamond, and her
 locks of jet;
Or whether, kindling at the deeds
 of Græme,
 He sing, to wild Morisco measure
 set,
Old Albin's red claymore, green Erin's
 bayonet!

X.

'Explore those regions, where the
 flinty crest
 Of wild Nevada ever gleams
 with snows,
Where in the proud Alhambra's
 ruin'd breast
 Barbaric monuments of pomp
 repose;

Or where the banners of more
 ruthless foes
 Than the fierce Moor float o'er
 Toledo's fane,
From whose tall towers even now
 the patriot throws
 An anxious glance, to spy upon
 the plain
The blended ranks of England, Por-
 tugal, and Spain.

XI.

'There, of Numantian fire a swarthy
 spark
 Still lightens in the sun-burnt
 native's eye;
The stately port, slow step, and
 visage dark,
 Still mark enduring pride and
 constancy.
And, if the glow of feudal chivalry
 Beam not, as once, thy nobles'
 dearest pride,
Iberia! oft thy crestless peasantry
 Have seen the plumed Hidalgo
 quit their side,
Have seen, yet dauntless stood—
 'gainst fortune fought and died.

XII.

'And cherish'd still by that un-
 changing race,
 Are themes for minstrelsy more
 high than thine;
Of strange tradition many a mystic
 trace,
 Legend and vision, prophecy and
 sign;
Where wonders wild of Arabesque
 combine
 With Gothic imagery of darker
 shade,
Forming a model meet for minstrel
 line.
 Go, seek such theme!' The
 Mountain Spirit said:
With filial awe I heard; I heard,
 and I obey'd.

II.

I.

REARING their crests amid the
  cloudless skies,
　And darkly clustering in the pale
　　moonlight,
Toledo's holy towers and spires
  arise,
　As from a trembling lake of silver
　　white.
Their mingled shadows intercept
  the sight
　Of the broad burial-ground out-
　　stretch'd below,
And nought disturbs the silence
  of the night;
　All sleeps in sullen shade, or
　　silver glow,
All save the heavy swell of Teio's
  ceaseless flow.

II.

All save the rushing swell of Teio's
  tide,
　Or, distant heard, a courser's
　　neigh or tramp;
Their changing rounds as watchful
  horsemen ride,
　To guard the limits of King
　　Roderick's camp.
For, through the river's night-fog
  rolling damp,
　Was many a proud pavilion
　　dimly seen,
Which glimmer'd back, against the
  moon's fair lamp,
　Tissues of silk and silver twisted
　　sheen,
And standards proudly pitch'd, and
  warders arm'd between.

III.

But of their monarch's person
  keeping ward,
　Since last the deep-mouth'd bell
　　of vespers toll'd,
The chosen soldiers of the royal
  guard

The post beneath the proud
  cathedral hold:
A band unlike their Gothic sires of
  old,
　Who, for the cap of steel and
　　iron mace,
Bear slender darts, and casques
  bedeckt with gold,
　While silver-studded belts their
　　shoulders grace,
Where ivory quivers ring in the
  broad falchion's place.

IV.

In the light language of an idle court,
　They murmur'd at their master's
　　long delay,
And held his lengthen'd orisons in
  sport:
　'What! will Don Roderick here
　　till morning stay,
To wear in shrift and prayer the
  night away?
　And are his hours in such dull
　　penance past,
For fair Florinda's plunder'd charms
  to pay?'
　Then to the east their weary
　　eyes they cast,
And wish'd the lingering dawn would
  glimmer forth at last.

V.

But, far within, Toledo's prelate lent
　An ear of fearful wonder to the
　　King;
The silver lamp a fitful lustre sent.
　So long that sad confession
　　witnessing:
For Roderick told of many a hidden
  thing,
　Such as are lothly utter'd to the air,
When fear, remorse, and shame
  the bosom wring,
　And guilt his secret burden
　　cannot bear,
And conscience seeks in speech a
  respite from despair.

VI.

Full on the prelate's face and silver
  hair
  The stream of failing light was
  feebly roll'd :
But Roderick's visage, though his
  head was bare,
  Was shadow'd by his hand and
  mantle's fold.
While of his hidden soul the sins
  he told,
  Proud Alaric's descendant could
  not brook,
That mortal man his bearing should
  behold,
  Or boast that he had seen, when
  conscience shook,
Fear tame a monarch's brow, remorse
  a warrior's look.

VII.

The old man's faded cheek wax'd
  yet more pale
  As many a secret sad the king
  bewray'd,
As sign and glance eked out the
  unfinish'd tale,
  When in the midst his faltering
  whisper staid.
'Thus royal Witiza was slain,' he
  said ;
  'Yet, holy father, deem not it
  was I.'
Thus still ambition strives her
  crimes to shade.
  'Oh! rather deem 'twas stern
  necessity ;
Self-preservation bade, and I must
  kill or die.

VIII.

'And if Florinda's shrieks alarm'd
  the air,
  If she invoked her absent sire in
  vain,
And on her knees implored that
  I would spare,
  Yet, reverend priest, thy sentence
  rash refrain.

All is not as it seems ; the female train
  Know by their bearing to disguise
  their mood :'
But conscience here, as if in high
  disdain,
  Sent to the monarch's cheek the
  burning blood ;
He stay'd his speech abrupt, and up
  the prelate stood.

IX.

'O harden'd offspring of an iron race!
  What of thy crimes, Don
  Roderick, shall I say ?
What alms, or prayers, or penance,
  can efface
  Murder's dark spot, wash treason's
  stain away !
For the foul ravisher how shall I pray,
  Who, scarce repentant, makes his
  crime his boast ?
How hope Almighty vengeance
  shall delay,
  Unless in mercy to yon Christian
  host,
He spare the shepherd, lest the
  guiltless sheep be lost.'

X.

Then kindled the dark tyrant in
  his mood,
  And to his brow return'd its
  dauntless gloom ;
'And welcome then,' he cried, ' be
  blood for blood,
  For treason treachery, for dishonour doom !
Yet will I know whence come they,
  or by whom.
  Show, for thou canst ; give forth
  the fated key,
And guide me, priest, to that
  mysterious room,
  Where, if aught true in old
  tradition be,
His nation's future fates a Spanish
  king shall see.'

XI.

'Ill-fated prince! recall the desperate
    word,
    Or pause ere yet the omen thou
      obey!
Bethink, yon spell-bound portal
    would afford
    Never to former monarch
      entrance-way;
Nor shall it ever ope, old records say,
    Save to a king, the last of all his
      line,
What time his empire totters to
    decay,
    And treason digs, beneath, her
      fatal mine,
And, high above, impends avenging
    wrath divine.'

XII.

'Prelate! a monarch's fate brooks
    no delay;
    Lead on!' The ponderous key
      the old man took,
And held the winking lamp, and led
    the way,
    By winding stair, dark aisle, and
      secret nook,
Then on an ancient gateway bent
    his look:
    And, as the key the desperate
      king essay'd,
Low mutter'd thunders the
    cathedral shook,
    And twice he stopp'd, and twice
      new effort made,
Till the huge bolts roll'd back, and the
    loud hinges bray'd.

XIII.

Long, large, and lofty, was that
    vaulted hall;
    Roof, walls, and floor, were all of
      marble stone,
Of polish'd marble, black as funeral
    pall,
    Carved o'er with signs and char-
      acters unknown.
A paly light as of the dawning shone
Through the sad bounds, but whence
    they could not spy;
    For window to the upper air was
      none;
Yet by that light Don Roderick
    could descry
Wonders that ne'er till then were seen
    by mortal eye.

XIV.

Grim sentinels, against the upper
    wall,
    Of molten bronze, two statues held
      their place;
Massive their naked limbs, their
    stature tall,
    Their frowning foreheads golden
      circles grace.
Moulded they seem'd for kings of
    giant race,
    That lived and sinn'd before the
      avenging flood;
This grasp'd a scythe, that rested
    on a mace;
    This spread his wings for flight,
      that pondering stood;
Each stubborn seem'd and stern,
    immutable of mood.

XV.

Fix'd was the right-hand giant's
    brazen look
    Upon his brother's glass of shifting
      sand,
As if its ebb he measured by a book,
    Whose iron volume loaded his
      huge hand;
In which was wrote of many a fallen
    land,
    Of empires lost, and kings to exile
      driven:
And o'er that pair their names in
    scroll expand—
    'Lo, Destiny and Time! to whom
      by Heaven
The guidance of the earth is for a
    season given.'

XVI.

Even while they read, the sand-glass
　　wastes away;
　And, as the last and lagging grains
　　did creep,
That right-hand giant 'gan his club
　　upsway,
　As one that startles from a heavy
　　sleep.
Full on the upper wall the mace's
　　sweep
　At once descended with the force
　　of thunder,
And hurtling down at once, in
　　crumbled heap,
　The marble boundary was rent
　　asunder,
And gave to Roderick's view new
　　sights of fear and wonder.

XVII.

For they might spy, beyond that
　　mighty breach,
　Realms as of Spain in vision'd
　　prospect laid,
Castles and towers, in due propor-
　　tion each,
　As by some skilful artist's hand
　　portray'd:
Here, crossed by many a wild
　　Sierra's shade,
　And boundless plains that tire the
　　traveller's eye;
There, rich with vineyard and with
　　olive glade,
　Or deep-embrown'd by forests
　　huge and high,
Or wash'd by mighty streams, that
　　slowly murmur'd by.

XVIII.

And here, as erst upon the antique
　　stage,
　Pass'd forth the band of masquers
　　trimly led,
In various forms, and various
　　equipage,
　While fitting strains the hearer's
　　fancy fed;

So, to sad Roderick's eye in order
　　spread,
　Successive pageants fill'd that
　　mystic scene,
Showing the fate of battles ere they
　　bled,
　And issue of events that had not
　　been;
And, ever and anon, strange sounds
　　were heard between.

XIX.

First shrill'd an unrepeated female
　　shriek!
　It seemed as if Don Roderick knew
　　the call.
For the bold blood was blanching
　　in his cheek.
　Then answer'd kettle-drum and
　　atabal,
Gong-peal and cymbal-clank the ear
　　appal,
　The Tecbir war-cry, and the
　　Lelie's yell,
Ring wildly dissonant along the hall.
　Needs not to Roderick their dread
　　import tell;
'The Moor!' he cried, 'the Moor!—
　　ring out the tocsin bell!

XX.

'They come, they come, I see the
　　groaning lands
　White with the turbans of each
　　Arab horde;
Swart Zaarah joins her misbelieving
　　bands,
　Alla and Mahomet their battle-
　　word,
The choice they yield, the Koran
　　or the Sword;
　See how the Christians rush to
　　arms amain!
In yonder shout the voice of conflict
　　roar'd,
　The shadowy hosts are closing
　　on the plain—
Now, God and Saint Iago strike, for
　　the good cause of Spain!

XXI.

'By Heaven, the Moors prevail!
　the Christians yield!
　Their coward leader gives for
　　flight the sign!
The sceptred craven mounts to quit
　　the field—
　Is not yon steed Orelio? Yes, 'tis
　　mine!
But never was she turn'd from battle-
　　line:
　Lo! where the recreant spurs o'er
　　stock and stone!
Curses pursue the slave, and wrath
　　divine!
　Rivers ingulph him!' 'Hush,' in
　　shuddering tone,
The Prelate said; 'rash Prince, yon
　vision'd form's thine own.'

XXII.

Just then, a torrent cross'd the flier's
　　course;
　The dangerous ford the kingly
　　Likeness tried;
But the deep eddies whelm'd both
　　man and horse,
　Swept like benighted peasant
　　down the tide;
And the proud Moslemah spread far
　　and wide,
　As numerous as their native locust
　　band;
Berber and Ismael's sons the spoils
　　divide,
　With naked scimitars mete out
　　the land,
And for the bondsmen base the free-
　born natives brand.

XXIII.

Then rose the grated Harem, to
　　enclose
　The loveliest maidens of the
　　Christian line;
Then, menials, to their misbelieving
　foes,

Castile's young nobles held for-
　　bidden wine;
Then, too, the holy cross, salvation's
　　sign,
　By impious hands was from the
　　altar thrown,
And the deep aisles of the polluted
　　shrine
　Echo'd, for holy hymn and organ-
　　tone,
The Santon's frantic dance, the Fakir's
　gibbering moan.

XXIV.

How fares Don Roderick? E'en as
　　one who spies
　Flames dart their glare o'er mid-
　　night's sable woof,
And hears around his children's
　　piercing cries,
　And sees the pale assistants stand
　　aloof;
While cruel conscience brings him
　　bitter proof,
　His folly or his crime have caused
　　his grief;
And while above him nods the
　　crumbling roof,
　He curses earth and Heaven,
　　himself in chief—
Desperate of earthly aid, despairing
　Heaven's relief!

XXV.

That scythe-arm'd giant turn'd his
　　fatal glass
　And twilight on the landscape
　　closed her wings;
Far to Asturian hills the war-sounds
　　pass,
　And in their stead rebeck or
　　timbrel rings;
And to the sound the bell-deck'd
　　dancer springs,
　Bazaars resound as when their
　　marts are met,

In tourney light the Moor his jerrid
    flings,
    And on the land as evening
        seem'd to set,
The Imaum's chant was heard from
    mosque or minaret.

XXVI.

So pass'd that pageant. Ere another
    came,
    The visionary scene was wrapp'd
        in smoke,
Whose sulph'rous wreaths were
    cross'd by sheets of flame;
    With every flash a bolt explosive
        broke,
Till Roderick deem'd the fiends
    had burst their yoke,
    And waved 'gainst heaven the
        infernal gonfalone!
For War a new and dreadful lan-
    guage spoke,
    Never by ancient warrior heard
        or known;
Lightning and smoke her breath, and
    thunder was her tone.

XXVII.

From the dim landscape roll the
    clouds away—
    The Christians have regain'd
        their heritage;
Before the Cross has waned the
    Crescent's ray
    And many a monastery decks the
        stage,
And lofty church, and low-brow'd
    hermitage.
    The land obeys a hermit and a
        knight,—
The genii those of Spain for many
    an age;
    This clad in sackcloth, that in
        armour bright,
And that was Valour named, this
    Bigotry was hight.

XXVIII.

Valour was harness'd like a chief
    of old,
    Arm'd at all points, and prompt
        for knightly gest;
His sword was temper'd in the
    Ebro cold,
    Morena's eagle plume adorn'd
        his crest,
The spoils of Afric's lion bound his
    breast.
    Fierce he stepp'd forward and
        flung down his gage;
As if of mortal kind to brave the best.
    Him follow'd his companion, dark
        and sage,
As he, my master, sung the dangerous
    Archimage.

XXIX.

Haughty of heart and brow the
    warrior came,
    In look and language proud as
        proud might be,
Vaunting his lordship, lineage,
    fights, and fame:
    Yet was that barefoot monk more
        proud than he:
And as the ivy climbs the tallest tree,
    So round the loftiest soul his toils
        he wound,
And with his spells subdued the
    fierce and free,
    Till ermined age, and youth in
        arms renown'd,
Honouring his scourge and hair-cloth,
    meekly kiss'd the ground.

XXX.

And thus it chanced that Valour
    peerless knight,
    Who ne'er to king or kaiser
        veil'd his crest,
Victorious still in bull-feast or in
    fight,
    Since first his limbs with mail he
        did invest,

Stoop'd ever to that anchoret's
   behest;
   Nor reason'd of the right, nor of
     the wrong,
But at his bidding laid the lance
   in rest,
   And wrought fell deeds the
     troubled world along,
For he was fierce as brave, and piti-
   less as strong.

XXXI.

Oft his proud galleys sought some
   new-found world,
   That latest sees the sun, or first
     the morn;
Still at that Wizard's feet their
   spoils he hurl'd—
   Ingots of ore from rich Potosi
     borne,
Crowns by Caciques, aigrettes by
   Omrahs worn,
   Wrought of rare gems, but broken,
     rent, and foul;
Idols of gold from heathen temples
   torn,
   Bedabbled all with blood. With
     grisly scowl
The hermit mark'd the stains, and
   smiled beneath his cowl.

XXXII.

Then did he bless the offering, and
   bade make
   Tribute to Heaven of gratitude
     and praise;
And at his word the choral hymns
   awake,
   And many a hand the silver
     censer sways;
But, with the incense-breath these
   censers raise,
   Mix steams from corpses smoul-
     dering in the fire;
The groans of prison'd victims mar
   the lays,

And shrieks of agony confound
     the quire;
While, 'mid the mingled sounds, the
   darken'd scenes expire.

XXXIII.

Preluding light, were strains of
   music heard,
   As once again revolved that
     measured sand;
Such sounds as when, for sylvan
   dance prepared,
   Gay Xeres summons forth her
     vintage band;
When for the light bolero ready
   stand
   The mozo blithe, with gay mu-
     chacha met,
He conscious of his broider'd cap
   and band,
   She of her netted locks and light
     corsette,
Each tiptoe perch'd to spring, and
   shake the castanet.

XXXIV.

And well such strains the opening
   scene became;
   For Valour had relax'd his ardent
     look,
And at a lady's feet, like lion tame,
   Lay stretch'd, full loth the weight
     of arms to brook;
And soften'd Bigotry, upon his book,
   Patter'd a task of little good or ill:
But the blithe peasant plied his
   pruning-hook,
   Whistled the muleteer o'er vale
     and hill,
And rung from village-green the
   merry seguidille.

XXXV.

Grey royalty, grown impotent of toil,
   Let the grave sceptre slip his
     lazy hold;

And, careless, saw his rule become
the spoil
   Of a loose female and her minion
bold.
But peace was on the cottage and
the fold,
   From court intrigue, from bickering faction far;
Beneath the chestnut-tree love's
tale was told,
   And to the tinkling of the light
guitar,
Sweet stoop'd the western sun, sweet
rose the evening star.

XXXVI.

As that sea-cloud, in size like
human hand,
   When first from Carmel by the
Tishbite seen,
Came slowly overshadowing Israel's
land,
   A while, perchance, bedeck'd
with colours sheen,
While yet the sunbeams on its
skirts had been,
   Limning with purple and with
gold its shroud,
Till darker folds obscured the blue
serene,
   And blotted heaven with one
broad sable cloud,
Then sheeted rain burst down, and
whirlwinds howl'd aloud:

XXXVII.

Even so, upon that peaceful scene
was pour'd,
   Like gathering clouds, full many
a foreign band,
And he, their leader, wore in sheath
his sword,
   And offer'd peaceful front and
open hand,
Veiling the perjured treachery he
plann'd

By friendship's zeal and honour's
specious guise,
Until he won the passes of the land;
   Then burst were honour's oath,
and friendship's ties!
He clutch'd his vulture-grasp, and
call'd fair Spain his prize.

XXXVIII.

An iron crown his anxious forehead
bore;
   And well such diadem his heart
became.
Who ne'er his purpose for remorse
gave o'er,
   Or check'd his course for piety
or shame;
Who, train'd a soldier, deem'd a
soldier's fame
   Might flourish in the wreath of
battles won,
Though neither truth nor honour
deck'd his name;
   Who, placed by fortune on a
monarch's throne,
Reck'd not of monarch's faith, or
mercy's kingly tone.

XXXIX.

From a rude isle his ruder lineage
came,
   The spark that, from a suburb-
hovel's hearth
Ascending, wraps some capital in
flame,
   Hath not a meaner or more sordid
birth.
And for the soul that bade him waste
the earth,
   The sable land-flood from some
swamp obscure,
That poisons the glad husband-field
with dearth,
   And by destruction bids its fame
endure,
Hath not a source more sullen, stagnant, and impure.

XL.

Before that leader strode a shadowy
form ;
  Her limbs like mist, her torch like
    meteor show'd,
With which she beckon'd him
    through fight and storm,
  And all he crush'd that cross'd his
    desperate road,
Nor thought, nor fear'd, nor look'd
    on what he trode.
  Realms could not glut his pride,
    blood could not slake,
So oft as e'er she shook her torch
    abroad—
  It was Ambition bade her terrors
    wake,
Nor deign'd she, as of yore, a milder
    form to take.

XLI.

No longer now she spurn'd at mean
    revenge,
  Or staid her hand for conquer'd
    foeman's moan ;
As when, the fates of aged Rome to
    change,
  By Cæsar's side she cross'd the
    Rubicon.
Nor joy'd she to bestow the spoils
    she won,
  As when the banded powers of
    Greece were task'd
To war beneath the youth of Mace-
    don :
  No seemly veil her modern minion
    ask'd,
He saw her hideous face, and loved
    the fiend unmask'd.

XLII.

That prelate mark'd his march : On
    banners, blazed
  With battles won in many a distant
    land,
On eagle-standards and on arms he
    gazed ;

'And hopest thou then,' he said,
  'thy power shall stand?
Oh, thou hast builded on the shifting
    sand,
  And thou hast temper'd it with
    slaughter's flood ;
And know, fell scourge in the
    Almighty's hand,
  Gore-moisten'd trees shall perish
    in the bud,
And by a bloody death shall die the
    man of blood !'

XLIII.

The ruthless leader beckon'd from
    his train
  A wan fraternal shade, and bade
    him kneel,
And paled his temples with the
    crown of Spain,
  While trumpets rang, and heralds
    cried, ' Castile !'
Not that he loved him ; no ! in no
    man's weal,
  Scarce in his own, e'er joy'd that
    sullen heart ;
Yet round that throne he bade his
    warriors wheel
  That the poor puppet might per-
    form his part,
And be a sceptred slave, at his stern
    beck to start.

XLIV.

But on the natives of that land mis-
    used,
  Not long the silence of amazement
    hung,
Nor brook'd they long their friendly
    faith abused ;
  For, with a common shriek, the
    general tongue
Exclaim'd, ' To arms !' and fast to
    arms they sprung.
  And Valour woke, that genius of
    the land !
Pleasure, and ease, and sloth, aside
    he flung,

As burst th' awakening Nazarite
his band,
When 'gainst his treacherous foes he
clench'd his dreadful hand.

XLV.

That mimic monarch now cast
anxious eye
Upon the Satraps that begirt him
round,
Now doff'd his royal robe in act to fly,
And from his brow the diadem
unbound.
So oft, so near, the patriot bugle
wound,
From Tarik's walls to Bilboa's
mountains blown,
These martial satellites hard labour
found,
To guard a while his substituted
throne,
Light recking of his cause, but battling
for their own.

XLVI.

From Alpuhara's peak that bugle
rung,
And it was echo'd from Corunna's
wall;
Stately Seville responsive war-shot
flung,
Grenada caught it in her Moorish
hall;
Galicia bade her children fight or fall,
Wild Biscay shook his mountain-
coronet,
Valencia roused her at the battle-call,
And, foremost still where Valour's
sons are met,
First started to his gun each fiery
Miquelet.

XLVII.

But unappall'd and burning for the
fight,
The invaders march, of victory
secure;

Skilful their force to sever or unite,
And train'd alike to vanquish or
endure.
Nor skilful less, cheap conquest to
ensure,
Discord to breathe, and jealousy
to sow,
To quell by boasting, and by bribes
to lure;
While nought against them bring
the unpractised foe,
Save hearts for Freedom's cause, and
hands for Freedom's blow.

XLVIII.

Proudly they march; but, O! they
march not forth
By one hot field to crown a brief
campaign,
As when their eagles, sweeping
through the north,
Destroy'd at every stoop an
ancient reign!
Far other fate had Heaven decreed
for Spain;
In vain the steel, in vain the torch
was plied,
New patriot armies started from the
slain,
High blazed the war, and long,
and far, and wide,
And oft the God of battles blest the
righteous side.

XLIX.

Nor unatoned, where freedom's foes
prevail,
Remain'd their savage waste.
With blade and brand,
By day the invaders ravaged hill
and dale,
But, with the darkness, the
guerilla band
Came like night's tempest, and
avenged the land,
And claim'd for blood the re-
tribution due,

Probed the hard heart, and lopp'd
the murd'rous hand;
And dawn, when o'er the scene
her beams she threw,
Midst ruins they had made, the spoilers'
corpses knew.

L.

What minstrel verse may sing, or
tongue may tell,
Amid the vision'd strife from sea to
sea,
How oft the patriot banners rose or
fell,
Still honour'd in defeat as victory!
For that sad pageant of events
to be,
Show'd every form of fight by
field and flood;
Slaughter and ruin, shouting forth
their glee,
Beheld, while riding on the
tempest scud,
The waters choked with slain, the earth
bedrench'd with blood!

LI.

Then Zaragoza—blighted be the
tongue
That names thy name without the
honour due;
For never hath the harp of minstrel
rung
Of faith so felly proved, so firmly
true!
Mine, sap, and bomb, thy shatter'd
ruins knew,
Each art of war's extremity had
room,
Twice from thy half-sack'd streets
the foe withdrew,
And when at length stern fate
decreed thy doom,
They won not Zaragoza, but her
children's bloody tomb.

LII.

Yet raise thy head, sad city! though
in chains,
Enthrall'd thou canst not be!
Arise, and claim
Reverence from every heart where
freedom reigns,
For what thou worshippest! Thy
sainted dame,
She of the Column, honour'd be her
name,
By all, whate'er their creed, who
honour love!
And, like the sacred relics of the flame
That gave some martyr to the
bless'd above,
To every loyal heart may thy sad
embers prove!

LIII.

Nor thine alone such wreck. Gerona
fair!
Faithful to death thy heroes shall
be sung,
Manning the towers while o'er their
heads the air
Swart as the smoke from raging
furnace hung;
Now thicker dark'ning where the
mine was sprung,
Now briefly lighten'd by the
cannon's flare,
Now arch'd with fire-sparks as the
bomb was flung,
And redd'ning now with conflagration's glare,
While by the fatal light the foes for
storm prepare.

LIV.

While all around was danger, strife,
and fear,
While the earth shook, and dark-
en'd was the sky,
And wide destruction stunn'd the
listening ear,

Appall'd the heart, and stupified
the eye,
Afar was heard that thrice-repeated
cry,
  In which old Albion's heart and
  tongue unite,
Whene'er her soul is up, and pulse
beats high,
  Whether it hail the wine cup or
  the fight,
And bid each arm be strong, or bid
each heart be light.

LV.

Don Roderick turn'd him as the shout
grew loud :
  A varied scene the changeful
  vision show'd,
For, where the ocean mingled with
the cloud,
  A gallant navy stemm'd the
  billows broad.
From mast and stern Saint George's
symbol flow'd,
  Blent with the silver cross to
  Scotland dear ;
Mottling the sea their landward
barges row'd ;
  And flash'd the sun on bayonet,
  brand, and spear,
And the wild beach return'd the sea-
man's jovial cheer.

LVI.

It was a dread yet spirit-stirring
sight !
  The billows foam'd beneath a
  thousand oars ;
Fast as they land the red-cross
ranks unite,
  Legions on legions bright'ning all
  the shores.
Then banners rise, and cannon signal roars,
  Then peals the warlike thunder
  of the drum,

Thrills the loud fife, the trumpet-
flourish pours,
  And patriot hopes awake, and
  doubts are dumb,
For, bold in freedom's cause, the bands
of ocean come !

LVII.

A various host they came, whose
ranks display
  Each mode in which the warrior
  meets the fight,
The deep battalion locks its firm
array,
  And meditates his aim the marksman light ;
Far glance the light of sabres flashing bright,
  Where mounted squadrons shake
  the echoing mead ;
Lacks not artillery breathing flame
and night,
  Nor the fleet ordnance whirl'd by
  rapid steed,
That rivals lightning's flash in ruin and
in speed.

LVIII.

A various host — from kindred
realms they came,
  Brethren in arms, but rivals in
  renown ;
For yon fair bands shall merry England claim,
  And with their deeds of valour
  deck her crown.
Hers their bold port, and hers their
martial frown,
  And hers their scorn of death in
  freedom's cause,
Their eyes of azure, and their locks
of brown,
  And the blunt speech that bursts
  without a pause,
And freeborn thoughts, which league
the soldier with the laws.

LIX.

And O! loved warriors of the Min-
strel's land!
 Yonder your bonnets nod, your
  tartans wave!
The rugged form may mark the
mountain band,
 And harsher features, and a mien
  more grave;
But ne'er in battle-field throbb'd
heart so brave,
 As that which beats beneath the
  Scottish plaid;
And when the pibroch bids the
battle rave,
 And level for the charge your
  arms are laid,
Where lives the desperate foe that for
such onset staid?

LX.

Hark! from yon stately ranks what
laughter rings
 Mingling wild mirth with war's
  stern minstrelsy,
His jest while each blithe comrade
round him flings,
 And moves to death with military
  glee:
Boast, Erin, boast them! tameless,
frank, and free,
 In kindness warm, and fierce in
  danger known,
Rough nature's children, humorous
as she:
 And He, yon Chieftain—strike the
  proudest tone
Of thy bold harp, green Isle! the Hero
is thine own.

LXI.

Now on the scene Vimeira should be
shown,
 On Talavera's fight should Roderick gaze,
And hear Corunna wail her battle
won,
 And see Busaco's crest with lightning blaze:

But shall fond fable mix with heroes'
praise?
 Hath fiction's stage for truth's
  long triumphs room?
And dare her wild-flowers mingle
with the bays,
 That claim a long eternity to bloom
Around the warrior's crest, and o'er
the warrior's tomb!

LXII.

Or may I give adventurous fancy
scope,
 And stretch a bold hand to the
  awful veil
That hides futurity from anxious
hope,
 Bidding beyond it scenes of glory
  hail,
And painting Europe rousing at
the tale
 Of Spain's invaders from her
  confines hurl'd,
While kindling nations buckle on
their mail,
 And Fame, with clarion-blast and
  wings unfurl'd,
To freedom and revenge awakes an
injured world?

LXIII.

O vain, though anxious, is the
glance I cast,
 Since fate has mark'd futurity
  her own:
Yet fate resigns to worth the
glorious past,
 The deeds recorded, and the
  laurels won.
Then, though the vault of destiny
be gone,
 King, prelate, all the phantasms
  of my brain,
Melted away like mist-wreaths in
the sun,
 Yet grant for faith, for valour,
  and for Spain,
One note of pride and fire, a patriot's
parting strain!

III.

I.

'Who shall command Estrella's
        mountain-tide
    Back to the source, when tempest-
        chafed, to hie?
Who, when Gascogne's vex'd gulf
        is raging wide,
    Shall hush it as a nurse her
        infant's cry?
His magic power let such vain
        boaster try,
    And when the torrent shall his
        voice obey,
    And Biscay's whirlwinds list his
        lullaby,
    Let him stand forth and bar mine
        eagles' way,
And they shall heed his voice, and at
        his bidding stay.

II.

'Else ne'er to stoop, till high on
        Lisbon's towers
    They close their wings, the
        symbol of our yoke,
And their own sea hath whelm'd
        yon red-cross powers!'
    Thus, on the summit of Alverca's
        rock,
    To marshal, duke, and peer, Gaul's
        leader spoke.
    While downward on the land
        his legions press,
Before them it was rich with vine
        and flock,
    And smiled like Eden in her
        summer dress;
Behind their wasteful march, a
        reeking wilderness.

III.

And shall the boastful chief main-
        tain his word,
    Though Heaven hath heard the
        wailings of the land,
Though Lusitania whet her venge-
        ful sword,
    Though Britons arm, and Wel-
        lington command!
No! grim Busaco's iron ridge shall
        stand
    An adamantine barrier to his force;
    And from its base shall wheel his
        shatter'd band,
    As from the unshaken rock the
        torrent hoarse
Bears off its broken waves, and seeks
        a devious course.

IV.

Yet not because Alcoba's mountain-
        hawk
    Hath on his best and bravest
        made her food,
In numbers confident, yon chief
        shall baulk
    His lord's imperial thirst for spoil
        and blood:
For full in view the promised
        conquest stood,
    And Lisbon's matrons from their
        walls, might sum
The myriads that had half the world
        subdued,
    And hear the distant thunders of
        the drum,
That bids the bands of France to storm
        and havoc come.

V.

Four moons have heard these
        thunders idly roll'd,
    Have seen these wistful myriads
        eye their prey,
As famish'd wolves survey a guarded
        fold—
    But in the middle path a Lion lay!
At length they move—but not to
        battle-fray,
    Nor blaze yon fires where meets
        the manly fight;
Beacons of infamy, they light the
        way

Where cowardice and cruelty
unite
To damn with double shame their
ignominious flight !

VI.

O triumph for the fiends of lust and
wrath !
Ne'er to be told, yet ne'er to be
forgot,
What wanton horrors mark'd their
wreckful path !
The peasant butcher'd in his
ruin'd cot,
The hoary priest even at the altar
shot,
Childhood and age given o'er to
sword and flame,
Woman to infamy;—no crime forgot,
By which inventive demons might
proclaim
Immortal hate to man, and scorn
of God's great name !

VII.

The rudest sentinel, in Britain born,
With horror paused to view the
havoc done,
Gave his poor crust to feed some
wretch forlorn,
Wiped his stern eye, then fiercer
grasp'd his gun.
Nor with less zeal shall Britain's
peaceful son
Exult the debt of sympathy to pay ;
Riches nor poverty the tax shall
shun,
Nor prince nor peer, the wealthy
nor the gay,
Nor the poor peasant's mite, nor
bard's more worthless lay.

VIII.

But thou—unfoughten wilt thou
yield to fate,
Minion of fortune, now miscall'd
in vain !
Can vantage-ground no confidence
create,
Marcella's pass, nor Guarda's
mountain-chain ?
Vainglorious fugitive ! yet turn
again !
Behold, where, named by some
prophetic seer,
Flows Honour's Fountain [1], as foredoom'd the stain
From thy dishonour'd name and
arms to clear—
Fallen child of fortune, turn, redeem
her favour here !

IX.

Yet, ere thou turn'st, collect each
distant aid ;
Those chief that never heard
the lion roar !
Within whose souls lives not a
trace portray'd,
Of Talavera, or Mondego's shore !
Marshal each band thou hast, and
summon more ;
Of war's fell stratagems exhaust
the whole ;
Rank upon rank, squadron on
squadron pour,
Legion on legion on thy foeman
roll,
And weary out his arm ; thou canst
not quell his soul.

X.

O vainly gleams with steel Agueda's
shore,
Vainly thy squadrons hide As-
suava's plain,
And front the flying thunders as
they roar,
With frantic charge and tenfold
odds, in vain !
And what avails thee that, for
Cameron slain,
Wild from his plaided ranks the
yell was given ?

---

[1] *Sc.* Fuentes d'Honoro.

Vengeance and grief gave mountain-
 rage the rein,
 And, at the bloody spear-point
 headlong driven,
Thy despot's giant guards fled like
 the rack of heaven.

XI.

Go, baffled boaster, teach thy
 haughty mood
 To plead at thine imperious
 master's throne;
Say, thou hast left his legions in
 their blood,
 Deceived his hopes, and frustrated
 thine own;
Say, that thine utmost skill and
 valour shown,
 By British skill and valour were
 outvied;
Last say, thy conqueror was Wellington!
 And if he chafe, be his own
 fortune tried—
God and our cause to friend, the
 venture we'll abide.

XII.

But you, ye heroes of that well-
 fought day,
 How shall a bard, unknowing
 and unknown,
His meed to each victorious leader
 pay,
 Or bind on every brow the laurels
 won?
Yet fain my harp would wake its
 boldest tone,
 O'er the wide sea to hail Cadogan
 brave;
And he, perchance, the minstrel-
 note might own,
 Mindful of meeting brief that
 fortune gave
'Mid yon far western isles that hear
 the Atlantic rave.

XIII.

Yes! hard the task, when Britons
 wield the sword,
 To give each chief and every field
 its fame:
Hark! Albuera thunders Beresford,
 And red Barosa shouts for daunt-
 less Græme!
O for a verse of tumult and of flame,
 Bold as the bursting of their
 cannon sound,
To bid the world re-echo to their
 fame!
For never upon gory battle-ground
With conquest's well bought wreath
 were braver victors crown'd!

XIV.

O who shall grudge him Albuera's
 bays,
 Who brought a race regenerate
 to the field,
Roused them to emulate their
 fathers' praise,
 Temper'd their headlong rage,
 their courage steel'd,
And raised fair Lusitania's fallen
 shield,
 And gave new edge to Lusitania's
 sword,
And taught her sons forgotten arms
 to wield!
 Shiver'd my harp, and burst its
 every chord,
If it forget thy worth, victorious
 Beresford!

XV.

Not on that bloody field of battle
 won,
 Though Gaul's proud legions
 roll'd like mist away,
Was half his self-devoted valour
 shown;
 He gaged but life on that illustrious day;

But when he toil'd those squadrons
  to array,
  Who fought like Britons in the
    bloody game,
Sharper than Polish pike or assagay,
  He braved the shafts of censure
    and of shame,
And, dearer far than life, he pledged
    a soldier's fame.

xvi.

Nor be his praise o'erpast who
  strove to hide
  Beneath the warrior's vest affec-
    tion's wound,
Whose wish Heaven for his country's
  weal denied ;
  Danger and fate he sought, but
    glory found.
From clime to clime, where'er war's
  trumpets sound,
  The wanderer went ; yet, Cale-
    donia, still
Thine was his thought in march and
  tented ground ;
  He dream'd 'mid Alpine cliffs of
    Athole's hill,
And heard in Ebro's roar his Lyn-
  doch's lovely rill.

xvii.

O hero of a race renown'd of old,
  Whose war-cry oft has waked
    the battle-swell,

Since first distinguish'd in the onset
    bold,
  Wild sounding when the Roman
    rampart fell !
By Wallace' side it rung the
    Southron's knell,
  Alderne, Kilsythe, and Tibber,
    own'd its fame,
Tummell's rude pass can of its
    terrors tell,
  But ne'er from prouder field arose
    the name,
Than when wild Ronda learn'd the
  conquering shout of Græme !

xviii.

But all too long, through seas un-
    known and dark,
  (With Spenser's parable I close
    my tale)
By shoal and rock hath steer'd my
    venturous bark,
  And landward now I drive before
    the gale.
And now the blue and distant shore
    I hail,
  And nearer now I see the port
    expand,
And now I gladly furl my weary sail,
  And as the prow light touches
    on the strand,
I strike my red-cross flag and bind
  my skiff to land.

END OF THE VISION OF DON RODERICK

Notes to the Vision of Don Roderick.

——◆◆——

Quid dignum memorare tuis, Hispania, terris,
Vox humana valet!—CLAUDIAN.

——◆◆——

THE poem is founded upon a Spanish tradition particularly detailed in the following Notes, but bearing in general that Don Roderick, the last Gothic King of Spain, when the Invasion of the Moors was impending, had the temerity to descend into an ancient vault near Toledo, the opening of which had been denounced as fatal to the Spanish Monarchy. The legend adds that his rash curiosity was mortified by an emblematical representation of those Saracens who, in the year, 714, defeated him in battle, and reduced Spain under their dominion. I have presumed to prolong the vision of the revolutions of Spain down to the present eventful crisis of the Peninsula; and to divide it, by a supposed change of scene, into three periods. The first of these represents the Invasion of the Moors, the defeat and death of Roderick, and closes with the peaceful occupation of the country by the victors. The second period embraces the state of the Peninsula, when the conquests of the Spaniards and Portuguese in the East and West Indies had raised to the highest pitch the renown of their arms,—sullied, however, by superstition and cruelty. An allusion to the inhumanities of the Inquisition terminates this picture. The last part of the poem opens with the state of Spain previous to the unparalleled treachery of Bonaparte; gives a sketch of the usurpation attempted upon that unsuspicious and friendly kingdom, and terminates with the arrival of the British succours. It may be farther proper to mention that the object of the poem is less to commemorate or detail particular incidents than to exhibit a general and impressive picture of the several periods brought upon the stage.

I am too sensible of the respect due to the public, especially by one who has already experienced more than ordinary indulgence, to offer any apology for the inferiority of the poetry to the subject it is chiefly designed to commemorate. Yet I think it proper to mention that while I was hastily executing a work, written for a temporary purpose, and on passing events, the task was most cruelly interrupted by the successive deaths of Lord President Blair, and Lord Viscount Melville. In those distinguished characters I had not only to regret persons whose lives were most important to Scotland, but also whose notice and patronage honoured my entrance upon active life; and, I may add with melancholy pride, who permitted my more advanced age to claim no common share in their friendship. Under such interruptions the preceding verses, which my best and happiest efforts must have left far unworthy of their theme, have, I am myself sensible, an appearance of negligence and incoherence which in other circumstances I might have been able to remove.

EDINBURGH, *June* 24, 1811.

NOTES.

NOTE I.

*And Cattraeth's glens with voice of
    triumph rung,
And mystic Merlin harp'd, and grey-hair'd
    Llywarch sung!*—P. 591.

THIS locality may startle those readers who do not recollect that much of the ancient poetry preserved in Wales refers less to the history of the Principality to which that name is now limited, than to events which happened in the north-west of England, and south-west of Scotland, where the Britons for a long time made a stand against the Saxons. The battle of Cattraeth, lamented by the celebrated Aneurin, is supposed, by the learned Dr. Leyden, to have been fought on the skirts of Ettrick Forest. It is known to the English reader by the paraphrase of Gray, beginning,

'Had I but the torrent's might,
With headlong rage and wild affright,' &c.

But it is not so generally known that the champions, mourned in this beautiful dirge, were the British inhabitants of Edinburgh, who were cut off by the Saxons of Deiria, or Northumberland, about the latter part of the sixth century.—TURNER'S *History of the Anglo-Saxons*, edition 1799, vol. i. p. 222. Llywarch, the celebrated bard and monarch, was Prince of Argood, in Cumberland; and his youthful exploits were performed upon the Border, although in his age he was driven into Powys by the successes of the Anglo-Saxons. As for Merlin Wyllt, or the Savage, his name of Caledonia, and his retreat into the Caledonian wood, appropriate him to Scotland. Fordun dedicates the thirty-first chapter of the third book of his Scoto-Chronicon, to a narration of the death of this celebrated bard and prophet near Drumelzier, a village upon Tweed, which is supposed to have derived its name (*quasi Tumulus Merlini*) from the event. The particular spot in which he is buried is still shown, and appears, from the following quotation, to have partaken of his prophetic qualities :—
'There is one thing remarkable here, which is, that the burn called Pausayl runs by the east side of this churchyard into the Tweed; at the side of which burn, a little below the churchyard, the famous prophet Merlin is said to be buried. The particular place of his grave, at the root of a thorn tree, was shown me, many years ago, by the old and reverend minister of the place, Mr. Richard Brown; and here was the old prophecy fulfilled, delivered in Scots rhyme, to this purpose :—

"When Tweed and Pausayl meet at Merlin's grave,
Scotland and England shall one Monarch have."

'For, the same day that our King James the Sixth was crowned King of England, the river Tweed, by an extraordinary flood, so far overflowed its banks, that it met and joined with the Pausayl at the said grave,' which was never before observed to fall out.' —PENNYCUICK'S *Description of Tweeddale.* Edin. 1715, iv. p. 26.

NOTE II.

——*Minchmore's haunted spring.*—P. 592.

A belief in the existence and nocturnal revels of the fairies still lingers among the vulgar in Selkirkshire. A copious fountain upon the ridge of Minchmore, called the Cheesewell, is supposed to be sacred to these fanciful spirits, and it was customary to propitiate them by throwing in something upon passing it. A pin was the usual oblation; and the ceremony is still sometimes practised, though rather in jest than earnest.

NOTE III.

——*the rude villager, his labour done,
In verse spontaneous chants some favour'd name.*—P. 592.

The flexibility of the Italian and Spanish languages, and perhaps the liveliness of their genius, renders these countries distinguished for the talent of improvisation, which is found even among the lowest of the people. It is mentioned by Baretti and other travellers.

NOTE IV.

——*Kindling at the deeds of Græme.* —P. 592.

Over a name sacred for ages to heroic verse, a poet may be allowed to exercise some power. I have used the freedom, here and elsewhere, to alter the orthography of the name of my gallant countryman, in order to apprize the Southern reader of its legitimate sound ;—Grahame being, on the other side of the Tweed, usually pronounced as a dissyllable.

NOTE V.

*What! will Don Roderick here till
morning stay,
To wear in shrift and prayer the night
away?
And are his hours in such dull penance
past,
For fair Florinda's plunder'd charms to
pay?*—P. 593.

Almost all the Spanish historians, as well as the voice of tradition, ascribe the invasion of the Moors to the forcible violation committed by Roderick upon Florinda, called by the Moors, Caba or Cava. She was the daughter of Count Julian, one of the Gothic monarch's principal lieutenants, who, when the crime was perpetrated, was engaged in the defence of Ceuta against the Moors. In his indignation at the ingratitude of his sovereign, and the dishonour of his daughter, Count Julian forgot the duties of a Christian and a patriot, and, forming an alliance with Musa, then the Caliph's lieutenant in Africa, he countenanced the invasion of Spain by a body of Saracens and Africans, commanded by the celebrated Tarik ; the issue of which was the defeat and death of Roderick, and the occupation of almost the whole peninsula by the Moors. Voltaire, in his General History, expresses his doubts of this popular story, and Gibbon gives him some countenance; but the universal tradition is quite sufficient for the purposes of poetry. The Spaniards, in detestation of Florinda's memory, are said, by Cervantes, never to bestow that name upon any human female, reserving it for their dogs. Nor is the tradition less inveterate among the Moors, since the same author mentions a promontory on the coast of Barbary, called 'The Cape of the Caba Rumia, which, in our tongue, is the Cape of the Wicked Christian Woman; and it is a tradition among the Moors, that Caba, the daughter of Count Julian, who was the cause of the loss of Spain, lies buried there, and they think it ominous to be forced into that bay; for they never go in otherwise than by necessity.'

NOTE VI.

And guide me, priest, to that mysterious room,
Where, if aught true in old tradition be,
His nation's future fates a Spanish king
shall see.—P. 594.

The transition of an incident from history to tradition, and from tradition to fable and romance, becoming more marvellous at each step from its original simplicity, is not ill exemplified in the account of the 'Fated Chamber' of Don Roderick, as given by his namesake, the historian of Toledo, contrasted with subsequent and more romantic accounts of the same subterranean discovery. I give the Archbishop of Toledo's tale in the words of Nonius, who seems to intimate (though very modestly), that the *fatale palatium* of which so much had been said, was only the ruins of a Roman amphitheatre.

'Extra muros, septentrionem versus, vestigia magni olim theatri sparsa visuntur. Auctor est Rodericus, Toletanus Archiepiscopus ante Arabum in Hispanias irruptionem, hic *fatale palatium* fuisse; quod invicti vectes aeterna ferri robora claudebant, ne reseratum Hispaniae excidium adferret; quod in fatis non vulgus solum, sed et prudentissimi quique credebant. Sed Roderici ultimi Gothorum Regis animum infelix curiositas subiit, sciendi quid sub tot vetitis claustris observaretur; ingentes ibi superiorum regum opes et arcanos thesauros servari ratus. Seras et pessulos perfringi curat, invitis omnibus; nihil praeter arculam repertum, et in ea linteum, quo explicato novae et insolentes hominum facies habitusque apparuere, cum inscriptione Latina, *Hispaniae excidium ab illa gente imminere;* Vultus habitusque Maurorum erant. Quamobrem ex Africa tantam cladem instare regi caeterisque persuasum; nec falso ut Hispaniae annales etiamnum queruntur.'—*Hispania Ludovic. Nonij,* cap. lix.

But, about the term of the expulsion of the Moors from Grenada, we find, in the *Historia Verdadeyra del Rey Don Rodrigo,* a (pretended) translation from the Arabic of the sage Alcayde Abulcacim Tarif Abentarique, a legend which puts to shame the modesty of the historian Roderick, with his chest and prophetic picture. The custom of ascribing a pretended Moorish original to these legendary histories, is ridiculed by Cervantes, who affects to translate the History of the Knight of the Woful Figure, from the Arabic of the sage Cid Hamet Benengeli. As I have been indebted to the *Historia Verdadeyra* for some of the imagery employed in the text, the following literal translation from the work itself may gratify the inquisitive reader :—

'One mile on the east side of the city of Toledo, among some rocks, was situated an ancient tower, of a magnificent structure, though much dilapidated by time, which consumes all : four estadoes (i. e. four times a man's height) below it, there was a cave with a very narrow entrance, and a gate cut out of the solid rock, lined with a strong covering of iron, and fastened with many locks; above the gate some Greek letters are engraved, which, although abbreviated, and of doubtful meaning, were thus interpreted, according to the exposition of learned men :—"The King who opens this cave, and can discover the wonders, will discover both good and evil things." Many Kings desired to know the mystery of this tower, and sought to find out the manner with much care; but when they opened the gate, such a tremendous noise arose in the cave, that it appeared as if the earth was bursting; many of those present sickened with fear, and others lost their lives. In order to prevent such great perils (as they supposed a dangerous enchantment was contained within), they secured the gate with new locks, concluding that, though a King was destined to open it, the fated time was not yet arrived. At last King Don Rodrigo, led on by his evil fortune and unlucky destiny, opened the tower; and some bold attendants, whom he had brought with him, entered, although agitated with fear. Having proceeded a good way, they fled back to the entrance, terrified with a frightful vision which they had beheld. The King was greatly moved, and ordered many torches, so contrived that the tempest in the cave could not extinguish them, to be lighted. Then the King entered, not without fear, before all the others. They discovered, by degrees, a splendid hall, apparently built in a very sumptuous manner; in the middle stood a Bronze Statue of very ferocious appearance, which held a battle-axe in its hands. With this he struck the floor violently, giving it such heavy blows, that the noise in the cave was occasioned by the motion of the air. The King, greatly affrighted and astonished, began to conjure this terrible vision, promising that he would return without doing any injury in the cave, after he had obtained a sight of what was contained in it. The statue ceased to strike the floor, and the King, with his followers, somewhat assured, and recovering their courage, proceeded into the hall; and on the left of the statue they found this inscription on the wall, "Unfortunate King, thou hast entered here in evil hour." On the right side of the wall these words were inscribed, "By strange nations thou shalt be dispossessed, and thy subjects foully degraded." On the shoulders of the statue other words were written, which said, "I call upon the Arabs." And upon his breast was written, "I do my office" At the entrance of the hall there was placed a round bowl, from which a great noise, like the fall of waters, proceeded. They found no other thing in the hall: and when the King, sorrowful and greatly affected, had scarcely turned about to leave the cavern, the statue again commenced its accustomed blows upon the floor. After they had mutually promised to conceal what they had seen, they again closed the tower, and blocked up the gate of the cavern with earth, that no memory might remain in the world of such a portentous and evil-boding prodigy. The ensuing midnight they heard great cries and clamour from the cave, resounding like the noise of battle, and the ground shaking with a tremendous roar; the whole edifice of the old tower fell to the ground, by which they were greatly affrighted, the vision which they had beheld appearing to them as a dream.

'The King having left the tower, ordered wise men to explain what the inscriptions signified; and having consulted upon and studied their meaning, they declared that the statue of bronze, with the motion which it made with its battle-axe, signified Time; and that its office, alluded to in the inscription on its breast, was, that he never rests a single moment. The words on the shoulders, "I call upon the Arabs," they expounded, that, in time, Spain would be conquered by the Arabs. The words upon the left wall signified the destruction of King Rodrigo; those on the right, the dreadful calamities which were to fall upon the Spaniards and Goths, and that the unfortunate King would be dispossessed of all his states. Finally, the letters on the portal indicated, that good would betide to the conquerors, and evil to the conquered, of which experience proved the truth.'—*Historia Verdadeyra del Rey Don Rodrigo.* Quinta impression. Madrid, 1654, iv. p. 23.

NOTE VII.

The Tecbir war-cry, and the Lelie's yell.
—P. 596.

The Tecbir (derived from the words *Alla acbar*, God is most mighty) was the original war-cry of the Saracens. It is celebrated by Hughes in the Siege of Damascus:—

'We heard the Tecbir; so these Arabs call
   Their shout of onset, when, with loud appeal,
   They challenge Heaven, as if demanding conquest.

The *Lelie*, well known to the Christians during the crusades, is the shout of *Alla illa Alla*, the Mahomedan confession of faith. It is twice used in poetry by my friend Mr. W. Stewart Rose, in the romance of Partenopex, and in the Crusade of St. Lewis.

NOTE VIII.

By Heaven, the Moors prevail! the Christians yield!
   Their coward leader gives for flight the sign!
The sceptred craven mounts to quit the field—
   Is not yon steed Orelio?—Yes, 'tis mine!
   —P. 597.

Count Julian, the father of the injured Florinda, with the connivance and assistance of Oppas, Archbishop of Toledo, invited, in 713, the Saracens into Spain. A considerable army arrived under the command of Tarif, or Tarif, who bequeathed the well-known name of Gibraltar (*Gibel al Tarik*, or the mountain of Tarik) to the place of his landing. He was joined by Count Julian, ravaged Andalusia, and took Seville. In 714 they returned with a still greater force, and Roderick marched into Andalusia at the head of a great army, to give them battle. The field was chosen near Xeres, and Mariana gives the following account of the action:—

'Both armies being drawn up, the King, according to the custom of the Gothic kings when they went to battle, appeared in an ivory chariot, clothed in cloth of gold, encouraging his men; Tarif, on the other side, did the same. The armies, thus prepared, waited only for the signal to fall on; the Goths gave the charge, their drums and trumpets sounding, and the Moors received it with the noise of kettle-drums. Such were the shouts and cries on both sides, that the mountains and valleys seemed to meet. First, they began with slings, darts, javelins, and lances, then came to the swords; a long time the battle was dubious; but the Moors seemed to have the worst, till D. Oppas, the archbishop, having to that time concealed his treachery, in the heat of the fight, with a great body of his followers went over to the infidels. He joined Count Julian, with whom was a great number of Goths, and both together fell upon the flank of our army. Our men, terrified with that unparalleled treachery, and tired with fighting, could no longer sustain that charge, but were easily put to flight. The King performed the part not only of a wise general, but of a resolute soldier, relieving the weakest, bringing on fresh men in place of those that were tired, and stopping those that turned their backs. At length, seeing no hopes left, he alighted out of his chariot for fear of being taken, and mounting on a horse called Orelia, he withdrew out of the battle. The Goths, who still stood, missing him, were most part put to the sword, the rest betook themselves to flight. The camp was immediately entered, and the baggage taken. What number was killed was not known : I suppose they were so many it was hard to count them ; for this single battle robbed Spain of all its glory, and in it perished the renowned name of the Goths. The King's horse, upper garment, and buskins, covered with pearls and precious stones, were found on the bank of the river Guadelite, and there being no news of him afterwards, it was supposed he was drowned passing the river.'—MARIANA's *History of Spain*, book vi. chap. 9.

Orelia, the courser of Don Roderick, mentioned in the text, and in the above quotation, was celebrated for her speed and form. She is mentioned repeatedly in Spanish romance, and also by Cervantes.

NOTE IX.

When for the light bolero ready stand,
The mozo blithe, with gay muchacha met.
—P. 599.

The bolero is a very light and active dance, much practised by the Spaniards, in which castanets are always used. *Mozo* and *muchacha* are equivalent to our phrase of lad and lass.

NOTE X.

While trumpets rang, and heralds cried
'*Castile!*'—P. 601.

The heralds, at the coronation of a Spanish monarch, proclaim his name three times, and repeat three times the word *Castilla, Castilla, Castilla*; which, with all other ceremonies, was carefully copied in the mock inauguration of Joseph Bonaparte.

NOTE XI.

High blazed the war, and long, and far,
and wide.—P. 602.

Those who were disposed to believe that mere virtue and energy are able of themselves to work forth the salvation of an oppressed people, surprised in a moment of confidence, deprived of their officers, armies, and for-tresses, who had every means of resistance to seek in the very moment when they were to be made use of, and whom the numerous treasons among the higher orders deprived of confidence in their natural leaders,—those who entertained this enthusiastic but delusive opinion may be pardoned for expressing their disappointment at the protracted warfare in the Peninsula. There are, however, another class of persons, who, having themselves the highest dread or veneration, or something allied to both, for the power of the modern Attila, will nevertheless give the heroical Spaniards little or no credit for the long, stubborn, and unsubdued resistance of three years to a power before whom their former well-prepared, well-armed, and numerous adversaries fell in the course of as many months. While these gentlemen plead for deference to Bonaparte, and crave

'Respect for his great place, and bid the devil
Be duly honour'd for his burning throne,'

it may not be altogether unreasonable to claim some modification of censure upon those who have been long and to a great extent successfully resisting this great enemy of mankind. That the energy of Spain has not uniformly been directed by conduct equal to its vigour, has been too obvious; that her armies, under their complicated disadvantages, have shared the fate of such as were defeated after taking the field with every possible advantage of arms and discipline, is surely not to be wondered at. But that a nation, under the circumstances of repeated discomfiture, internal treason, and the mismanagement incident to a temporary and hastily adopted government, should have wasted, by its stubborn, uniform, and prolonged resistance, myriads after myriads of those soldiers who had overrun the world —that some of its provinces should, like Galicia, after being abandoned by their allies, and overrun by their enemies, have recovered their freedom by their own unas-sisted exertions ; that others, like Catalonia, undismayed by the treason which betrayed some fortresses, and the force which subdued others, should not only have continued their resistance, but have attained over their victorious enemy a superiority, which is even now enabling them to besiege and retake the places of strength which had been wrested from them, is a tale hitherto untold in the revolutionary war. To say that such a people cannot be subdued, would be presumption similar to that of those who protested that Spain could not defend herself for a year, or Portugal for a month; but that a resistance which has been continued for so long a space, when the usurper, except during the short-lived Austrian campaign, had no other enemies on the continent, should be now less successful, when repeated defeats have broken the reputation of the French armies, and when they are likely (it would seem almost in desperation) to seek occupation elsewhere, is a prophecy as improbable as ungracious. And while we are in the humour of severely censuring our allies, gallant and devoted as they have shown themselves in the cause of national liberty, because they may not instantly adopt those measures which we in our wisdom may deem essential to success, it might be well if we endeavoured first to resolve the previous questions,—First, Whether we do not at this moment know much less of the Spanish armies than those of Portugal, which were so promptly condemned as totally inadequate to assist in the preservation of their country? Second, Whether, independently of any right we have to offer more than advice and assistance to our independent allies, we can expect that they should renounce entirely the national pride, which is inseparable from patriotism, and at once condescend not only to be saved by our assistance, but to be saved in our own way? Third, Whether, if it be an object (as undoubtedly it is a main one) that the Spanish troops should be trained under British discipline, to the flexibility of movement, and power of rapid concert and combination, which is essential to modern war—such a consummation is likely to be produced by abusing them in newspapers and periodical publications? Lastly, since the undoubted authority of British officers makes us now acquainted with part of the horrors that attend invasion, and which the providence of God, the valour of our navy, and perhaps the very efforts of these Spaniards, have hitherto diverted from us, it may be modestly questioned whether we ought to be too forward to estimate and condemn the feeling of temporary stupefaction which they create; lest, in so doing, we should resemble the worthy clergyman who, while he had himself never snuffed a candle with his fingers, was disposed severely to criticise the conduct of a martyr, who winced a little among his flames.

Note XII.

They won not Zaragoza, but her children's bloody tomb.—P. 603.

The interesting account of Mr. Vaughan has made most readers acquainted with the first siege of Zaragoza[1]. The last and fatal siege of that gallant and devoted city is detailed with great eloquence and precision in the 'Edinburgh Annual Register' for 1809,—a work in which the affairs of Spain have been treated of with attention corresponding to their deep interest, and to the peculiar sources of information open to the historian. The following are a few brief extracts from this splendid historical narrative:—

'A breach was soon made in the mud walls, and then, as in the former siege, the war was carried on in the streets and houses; but the French had been taught by experience, that in this species of warfare the Zaragozans derived a superiority from the feeling and principle which inspired them, and the cause for which they fought. The only means of conquering Zaragoza was to destroy it house

[1] See Narrative of the Siege of Zaragoza, by Richard Charles Vaughan, Esq., 1809.

by house, and street by street; and upon this system of destruction they proceeded. Three companies of miners, and eight companies of sappers, carried on this subterraneous war; the Spaniards, it is said, attempted to oppose them by countermines; these were operations to which they were wholly unused, and, according to the French statement, their miners were every day discovered and suffocated. Meantime, the bombardment was incessantly kept up. "Within the last forty-eight hours," said Palafox in a letter to his friend General Doyle, "6000 shells have been thrown in. Two-thirds of the town are in ruins, but we shall perish under the ruins of the remaining third rather than surrender. In the course of the siege, above 17,000 bombs were thrown at the town; the stock of powder with which Zaragoza had been stored was exhausted; they had none at last but what they manufactured day by day; and no other cannon-balls than those which were shot into the town, and which they collected and fired back upon the enemy.'

In the midst of these horrors and privations, the pestilence broke out in Zaragoza. To various causes, enumerated by the annalist, he adds, 'scantiness of food, crowded quarters, unusual exertion of body, anxiety of mind, and the impossibility of recruiting their exhausted strength by needful rest, in a city which was almost incessantly bombarded, and where every hour their sleep was broken by the tremendous explosion of mines. There was now no respite, either by day or night, for this devoted city; even the natural order of light and darkness was destroyed in Zaragoza; by day it was involved in a red sulphureous atmosphere of smoke, which hid the face of heaven; by night, the fire of cannons and mortars, and the flames of burning houses, kept it in a state of terrific illumination.

'When once the pestilence had begun, it was impossible to check its progress, or confine it to one quarter of the city. Hospitals were immediately established,—there were above thirty of them; as soon as one was destroyed by the bombardment, the patients were removed to another, and thus the infection was carried to every part of Zaragoza. Famine aggravated the evil; the city had probably not been sufficiently provided at the commencement of the siege, and of the provisions which it contained, much was destroyed in the daily ruin which the mines and bombs effected. Had the Zaragozans and their garrison proceeded according to military rules, they would have surrendered before the end of January; their batteries had then been demolished, there were open breaches in many parts of their weak walls, and the enemy were already within the city. On the 30th, above sixty houses were blown up, and the French obtained possession of the monasteries of the Augustines and Las Monicas, which adjoined each other, two of the last defensible places left. The enemy forced their way into the church; every column, every chapel, every altar, became a point of defence, which was repeatedly attacked, taken, and retaken; the pavement was covered with blood, the aisles and body of the church strewed with the dead, who were trampled under foot by the combatants. In the midst of this conflict, the roof, shattered by repeated bombs, fell in; the few who were not crushed, after a short pause, which this tremendous shock, and their own unexpected escape, occasioned, renewed the fight with rekindled fury: fresh parties of the enemy poured in; monks, and citizens, and soldiers, came to the defence, and the contest was continued upon the ruins, and the bodies of the dead and the dying.'

Yet, seventeen days after sustaining these extremities, did the heroic inhabitants of Zaragoza continue their defence; nor did they then surrender until their despair had extracted from the French generals a capitulation, more honourable than has been granted to fortresses of the first order.

Who shall venture to refuse the Zaragozans the eulogium conferred upon them by the eloquence of Wordsworth!—' Most gloriously have the citizens of Zaragoza proved that the true army of Spain, in a contest of this nature, is the whole people. The same city has also exemplified a melancholy, yea, a dismal truth,—yet consolatory and full of joy,—that when a people are called suddenly to fight for their liberty, and are sorely pressed upon, their best field of battle is the floors upon which their children have played; the chambers where the family of each man has slept (his own or his neighbours); upon or under the roofs by which they have been sheltered; in the gardens of their recreation; in the street, or in the market-place; before the altars of their temples, and among their congregated dwellings, blazing or uprooted. 'The government of Spain must never forget Zaragoza for a moment. Nothing is wanting to produce the same effects everywhere but a leading mind, such as that city was blessed with. In the latter contest this has been proved; for Zaragoza contained, at that time, bodies of men from almost all parts of Spain. The narrative of those two sieges should be the manual of every Spaniard. He may add to it the ancient stories of Numantia and Saguntum; let him sleep upon the book as a pillow, and, if he be a devout adherent to the religion of his country, let him wear it in his bosom for his crucifix to rest upon.'—WORDSWORTH *on the Convention of Cintra.*

NOTE XIII.

——the vault of destiny.—P. 605.

Before finally dismissing the enchanted cavern of Don Roderick, it may be noticed that the legend occurs in one of Calderon's plays, entitled, *La Virgin del Sagrario.* The scene opens with the noise of the chase, and Recisundo, a predecessor of Roderick upon the Gothic throne, enters pursuing a stag. The animal assumes the form of a man, and defies the king to enter the cave, which forms the bottom of the scene, and engage with him in single combat. The king accepts the challenge, and they engage accordingly, but without advantage on either side, which induces the Genie to inform Recisundo, that he is not the monarch for whom the adventure of the enchanted cavern is reserved, and he proceeds to predict the downfall of the Gothic monarchy, and of the Christian religion, which shall attend the discovery of its mysteries. Recisundo, appalled by these prophecies, orders the cavern to be secured by a gate and bolts of iron. In the second part of the same play, we are informed that Don Roderick had removed the barrier, and transgressed the prohibition of his ancestor, and had been apprized by the prodigies which he discovered of the approaching ruin of his kingdom.

NOTE XIV.

While downward on the land his legions press,
Before them it was rich with vine and flock,
And smiled like Eden in her summer dress;
Behind their wasteful march, a reeking wilderness.— P. 606.

I have ventured to apply to the movements of the French army that sublime passage in the prophecies of Joel, which seems applicable to them in more respects than that I have adopted in the text. One would think their ravages, their military appointments, the terror which they spread among invaded nations, their military discipline, their arts of political intrigue and deceit, were distinctly pointed out in the following verses of Scripture:—

' 2. A day of darkness and of gloominesse, a day of clouds and of thick darknesse, as the morning spread upon the mountains: a great people and a strong, there hath not been ever the like, neither shall be any more after it, even to the yeares of many generations. 3. A fire devoureth before them, and behind them a flame burneth: the land is as the garden of Eden before them, and behinde them a desolate wildernesse, yea, and nothing shall escape them. 4. The appearance of them is as the appearance of horses and as horsemen, so shall they runne. 5. Like the noise of chariots on the tops of mountains, shall they leap, like the noise of a flame of fire that devoureth the stubble, as a strong people set in battel array. 6. Before their face shall the people be much pained; all faces shall gather blacknesse. 7. They shall run like mighty men, they shall climb the wall like men of warre, and they shall march every one in his wayes, and they shall not break their ranks. 8. Neither shall one thrust another, they shall walk every one in his path: and when they fall upon the sword, they shall not be wounded. 9. They shall run to and fro in the citie; they shall run upon the wall, they shall climbe up upon the houses: they shall enter in at the windows like a thief. 10. The earth shall quake before them, the heavens shall tremble, the sunne and the moon shall be dark, and the starres shall withdraw their shining.'

In verse 20th also, which announces the retreat of the northern army, described in such dreadful colours, into a 'land barren and desolate,' and the dishonour with which God afflicted them for having 'magnified themselves to do great things,' there are particulars not inapplicable to the retreat of Massena;—Divine Providence having, in all ages, attached disgrace as the natural punishment of cruelty and presumption.

Note XV.

The rudest sentinel, in Britain born,
  With horror paused to view the havoc done,
Gave his poor crust to feed some wretch for-
  lorn.—P. 607.

Even the unexampled gallantry of the British army in the campaign of 1810-11, although they never fought but to conquer, will do them less honour in history than their humanity, attentive to soften to the utmost of their power the horrors which war, in its mildest aspect, must always inflict upon the defenceless inhabitants of the country in which it is waged, and which, on this occasion, were tenfold augmented by the barbarous cruelties of the French. Soup kitchens were established by subscription among the officers, wherever the troops were quartered for any length of time. The commissaries contributed the heads, feet, &c. of the cattle slaughtered for the soldiery: rice, vegetables, and bread, where it could be had, were purchased by the officers. Fifty or sixty starving peasants were daily fed at one of these regimental establishments, and carried home the relics to their famished households. The emaciated wretches, who could not crawl from weakness, were speedily employed in pruning their vines. While pursuing Massena, the soldiers evinced the same spirit of humanity, and in many instances, when reduced themselves to short allowance, from having out-marched their supplies, they shared their pittance with the starving inhabitants, who had ventured back to view the ruins of their habitations, burnt by the retreating enemy, and to bury the bodies of their relations whom they had butchered. Is it possible to know such facts without feeling a sort of confidence, that those who so well deserve victory are most likely to attain it? —It is not the least of Lord Wellington's military merits, that the slightest disposition towards marauding meets immediate punishment. Independently of all moral obligation, the army which is most orderly in a friendly country, has always proved most formidable to an armed enemy.

Note XVI.

Vainglorious fugitive!—P. 607.

The French conducted this memorable retreat with much of the *fanfarronade* proper to their country, by which they attempt to impose upon others, and perhaps on themselves, a belief that they are triumphing in the very moment of their discomfiture. On the 30th March, 1811, their rear-guard was overtaken near Pega by the British cavalry. Being well posted, and conceiving themselves safe from infantry (who were indeed many miles in the rear), and from artillery, they indulged themselves in parading their bands of music, and actually performed 'God save the King.' Their minstrelsy was, however, deranged by the undesired accompaniment of the British horse-artillery, on whose part in the concert they had not calculated. The surprise was sudden, and the rout complete; for the artillery and cavalry did execution upon them for about four miles, pursuing at the gallop as often as they got beyond the range of the guns.

Note XVII.

Vainly thy squadrons hide Assuava's
  plain,
And front the flying thunders as they roar,
  With frantic charge and tenfold odds, in
  vain!—P. 607.

In the severe action of Fuentes d' Honoro, upon May 5, 1811, the grand mass of the French cavalry attacked the right of the British position, covered by two guns of the horse-artillery, and two squadrons of cavalry. After suffering considerably from the fire of the guns, which annoyed them in every attempt at formation, the enemy turned their wrath entirely towards them, distributed brandy among their troopers, and advanced to carry the field-pieces with the desperation of drunken fury. They were in nowise checked by the heavy loss which they sustained in this daring attempt, but closed, and fairly mingled with the British cavalry, to whom they bore the proportion of ten to one. Captain Ramsay (let me be permitted to name a gallant countryman), who commanded the two guns, dismissed them at the gallop, and putting himself at the head of the mounted artillerymen, ordered them to fall upon the French, sabre in hand. This very unexpected conversion of artillerymen into dragoons, contributed greatly to the defeat of the enemy already disconcerted by the reception they had met from the two British squadrons; and the appearance of some small reinforcements, notwithstanding the immense disproportion of force, put them to absolute rout. A colonel or major of their cavalry, and many prisoners (almost all intoxicated), remained in our possession. Those who consider for a moment the difference of the services, and how much an artilleryman is necessarily and naturally led to identify his own safety and utility with abiding by the tremendous implement of war, to the exercise of which he is chiefly, if not exclusively, trained, will know how to estimate the presence of mind which commanded so bold a manœuvre, and the steadiness and confidence with which it was executed.

Note XVIII.

And what avails thee that, for Cameron slain,
Wild from his plaided ranks the yell was given?—P. 607.

The gallant Colonel Cameron was wounded mortally during the desperate contest in the streets of the village called Fuentes d'Honoro. He fell at the head of his native Highlanders, the 71st and 79th, who raised a dreadful shriek of grief and rage. They charged, with irresistible fury, the finest body of French grenadiers ever seen, being a part of Bonaparte's selected guard. The officer who led the French, a man remarkable for stature and symmetry, was killed on the spot. The Frenchman who stepped out of his rank to take aim at Colonel Cameron was also bayoneted, pierced with a thousand wounds, and almost torn to pieces by the furious Highlanders, who, under the command of Colonel Cadogan, bore the enemy out of the contested ground at the point of the bayonet. Massena pays my countrymen a singular compliment in his account of the attack and defence of this village, in which he says the British lost many officers, *and Scotch.*

Note XIX.

O who shall grudge him Albuera's bays,
Who brought a race regenerate to the field,
Roused them to emulate their fathers' praise,
Temper'd their headlong rage, their courage steel'd,
And raised fair Lusitania's fallen shield.
—P. 608.

Nothing during the war of Portugal seems, to a distinct observer, more deserving of praise, than the self-devotion of Field-Marshal Beresford, who was contented to undertake all the hazard of obloquy which might have been founded upon any miscarriage in the highly important experiment of training the Portuguese troops to an improved state of discipline. In exposing his military reputation to the censure of imprudence from the most moderate, and all manner of unutterable calumnies from the ignorant and malignant, he placed at stake the dearest pledge which a military man had to offer, and nothing but the deepest conviction of the high and essential importance attached to success can be supposed an adequate motive. How great the chance of miscarriage was supposed, may be estimated from the general opinion of officers of unquestioned talents and experience, possessed of every opportunity of information; how completely the experiment has succeeded, and how much the spirit and patriotism of our ancient allies had been underrated, is evident, not only from those victories in which they have borne a distinguished share, but from the liberal and highly honourable manner in which these opinions have been retracted. The success of this plan, with all its important consequences, we owe to the indefatigable exertions of Field-Marshal Beresford.

Note XX.

——a race renown'd of old,
Whose war-cry oft has waked the battle-swell.

· · · · · · · · · · · ·
——the conquering shout of Græme.
—P. 609.

This stanza alludes to the various achievements of the warlike family of Græme, or Grahame. They are said, by tradition, to have descended from the Scottish chief, under whose command his countrymen stormed the wall built by the Emperor Severus between the Firths of Forth and Clyde, the fragments of which are still popularly called Græme's Dyke. Sir John the Græme, 'the hardy, wight, and wise,' is well known as the friend of Sir William Wallace. Alderne, Kilsythe, and Tibbermuir, were scenes of the victories of the heroic Marquis of Montrose. The pass of Killiecrankie is famous for the action between King William's forces and the Highlanders in 1689,

'Where glad Dundee in faint huzzas expired.'

It is seldom that one line can number so many heroes, and yet more rare when it can appeal to the glory of a living descendant in support of its ancient renown.
The allusions to the private history and character of General Grahame may be illustrated by referring to the eloquent and affecting speech of Mr. Sheridan, upon the vote of thanks to the Victor of Barosa.

The Field of Waterloo:

A POEM.

'Though Valois braved young Edward's gentle hand,
And Albert rush'd on Henry's way-worn band,
With Europe's chosen sons, in arms renown'd,
Yet not on Vere's bold archers long they look'd,
Nor Audley's squires nor Mowbray's yeomen brook'd,—
They saw their standard fall, and left their monarch bound.'

AKENSIDE.

TO

HER GRACE

THE DUCHESS OF WELLINGTON,

PRINCESS OF WATERLOO,

THE FOLLOWING VERSES

ARE MOST RESPECTFULLY INSCRIBED

BY

THE AUTHOR.

It may be some apology for the imperfections of this poem, that it was composed hastily, and during a short tour upon the Continent, when the Author's labours were liable to frequent interruption; but its best apology is, that it was written for the purpose of assisting the Waterloo Subscription.

ABBOTSFORD, 1815.

I.

FAIR Brussels, thou art far behind,
Though, lingering on the morning
    wind,
  We yet may hear the hour
Peal'd over orchard and canal,
With voice prolong'd and measured
    fall,
    From proud Saint Michael's
    tower;

Thy wood, dark Soignies, holds us
    now,
Where the tall beeches' glossy bough
    For many a league around,
With birch and darksome oak between,
Spreads deep and far a pathless screen
    Of tangled forest ground.
Stems planted close by stems defy
The adventurous foot—the curious eye
    For access seeks in vain;

And the brown tapestry of leaves,
Strew'd on the blighted ground,
    receives
Nor sun, nor air, nor rain.
No opening glade dawns on our way,
No streamlet, glancing to the ray,
    Our woodland path has cross'd ;
And the straight causeway which we
    tread
Prolongs a line of dull arcade,
Unvarying through the unvaried shade
    Until in distance lost.

II.

A brighter, livelier scene succeeds ;
In groups the scattering wood recedes,
Hedge-rows, and huts, and sunny
    meads,
    And corn-fields glance between ;
The peasant, at his labour blithe,
Plies the hook'd staff and shorten'd
    scythe :
    But when these ears were green,
Placed close within destruction's
    scope,
Full little was that rustic's hope
    Their ripening to have seen !
And, lo, a hamlet and its fane—
Let not the gazer with disdain
    Their architecture view ;
For yonder rude ungraceful shrine
And disproportion'd spire are thine,
    Immortal WATERLOO !

III.

Fear not the heat, though full and
    high
The sun has scorch'd the autumn sky,
And scarce a forest straggler now
To shade us spreads a greenwood
    bough ;
These fields have seen a hotter day
Than e'er was fired by sunny ray.
Yet one mile on—yon shatter'd hedge
Crests the soft hill whose long smooth
    ridge
    Looks on the field below,

And sinks so gently on the dale,
That not the folds of Beauty's veil
    In easier curves can flow.
Brief space from thence the ground
    again,
Ascending slowly from the plain,
    Forms an opposing screen,
Which with its crest of upland ground
Shuts the horizon all around.
    The soften'd vale between
Slopes smooth and fair for courser's
    tread ;—
Not the most timid maid need dread
To give her snow-white palfrey head
    On that wide stubble-ground ;
Nor wood, nor tree, nor bush is there,
Her course to intercept or scare,
    Nor fosse nor fence is found,
Save where, from out her shatter'd
    bowers,
Rise Hougomont's dismantled towers.

IV.

Now, see'st thou aught in this lone
    scene
Can tell of that which late hath been ?—
    A stranger might reply,
' The bare extent of stubble-plain
Seems lately lighten'd of its grain ;
And yonder sable tracks remain
Marks of the peasant's ponderous wain,
    When harvest-home was nigh.
On these broad spots of trampled
    ground,
Perchance the rustics danced such
    round
    As Teniers loved to draw ;
And where the earth seems scorch'd
    by flame,
To dress the homely feast they came,
And toil'd the kerchief'd village dame
    Around her fire of straw.'

V.

So deem'st thou ; so each mortal deems,
Of that which is from that which seems :
    But other harvest here,

Than that which peasant's scythe
demands,
Was gather'd in by sterner hands,
  With bayonet, blade, and spear.
No vulgar crop was theirs to reap,
No stinted harvest thin and cheap!
Heroes before each fatal sweep
  Fell thick as ripen'd grain;
And ere the darkening of the day,
Piled high as autumn shocks, there lay
The ghastly harvest of the fray,
  The corpses of the slain.

VI.

Ay, look again: that line, so black
And trampled, marks the bivouac;
Yon deep-graved ruts the artillery's
track,
  So often lost and won;
And close beside, the harden'd mud
Still shows where, fetlock-deep in
blood,
The fierce dragoon through battle's
flood
  Dash'd the hot war-horse on.
These spots of excavation tell
The ravage of the bursting shell;
And feel'st thou not the tainted steam,
That reeks against the sultry beam,
  From yonder trenched mound?
The pestilential fumes declare
That Carnage has replenish'd there
  Her garner-house profound.

VII.

Far other harvest-home and feast,
Than claims the boor from scythe
released,
  On these scorch'd fields were
known!
Death hover'd o'er the maddening rout,
And, in the thrilling battle-shout,
Sent for the bloody banquet out
  A summons of his own.
Through rolling smoke the Demon's
eye
Could well each destined guest espy,
Well could his ear in ecstasy
  Distinguish every tone

That fill'd the chorus of the fray—
From cannon-roar and trumpet-bray,
From charging squadrons' wild hurra,
From the wild clang that mark'd their
  way—
  Down to the dying groan
And the last sob of life's decay
  When breath was all but flown.

VIII.

Feast on, stern foe of mortal life,
Feast on! but think not that a strife,
With such promiscuous carnage rife,
  Protracted space may last;
The deadly tug of war at length
Must limits find in human strength,
  And cease when these are past.
Vain hope! that morn's o'erclouded
  sun
Heard the wild shout of fight begun
  Ere he attain'd his height,
And through the war-smoke, volumed
  high,
Still peals that unremitted cry,
  Though now he stoops to night.
For ten long hours of doubt and dread,
Fresh succours from the extended head
Of either hill the contest fed;
  Still down the slope they drew,
The charge of columns paused not,
Nor ceased the storm of shell and shot;
  For all that war could do
Of skill and force was proved that day,
And turn'd not yet the doubtful fray
  On bloody Waterloo.

IX.

Pale Brussels! then what thoughts
  were thine,
When ceaseless from the distant line
  Continued thunders came!
Each burgher held his breath to hear
These forerunners of havoc near,
  Of rapine and of flame.
What ghastly sights were thine to
  meet,
When rolling through thy stately
  street,

The wounded show'd their mangled
    plight
In token of the unfinish'd fight,
And from each anguish-laden wain
The blood-drops laid thy dust like rain !
How often in the distant drum
Heard'st thou the fell Invader come,
While Ruin, shouting to his band,
Shook high her torch and gory
    brand !—
Cheer thee, fair City ! From yon stand,
Impatient, still his outstretch'd hand
    Points to his prey in vain,
While maddening in his eager mood,
And all unwont to be withstood,
    He fires the fight again.

x.

' On ! on !' was still his stern exclaim ;
' Confront the battery's jaws of flame !
    Rush on the levell'd gun !
My steel-clad cuirassiers, advance !
Each Hulan forward with his lance !
My Guard, my Chosen, charge for
    France,
    France and Napoleon !'
Loud answer'd their acclaiming shout,
Greeting the mandate which sent out
Their bravest and their best to dare
The fate their leader shunn'd to share.
But HE, his country's sword and shield,
Still in the battle-front reveal'd
Where danger fiercest swept the field,
    Came like a beam of light ;
In action prompt, in sentence brief,
' Soldiers, stand firm,' exclaim'd the
    Chief,
    ' England shall tell the fight !'

xi.

On came the whirlwind, like the last
But fiercest sweep of tempest-blast—
On came the whirlwind ! steel-gleams
    broke
Like lightning through the rolling
    smoke ;
    The war was waked anew ;

Three hundred cannon-mouths roar'd
    loud,
And from their throats, with flash and
    cloud,
    Their showers of iron threw.
Beneath their fire, in full career,
Rush'd on the ponderous cuirassier,
The lancer couch'd his ruthless spear,
And hurrying as to havoc near,
    The cohorts' eagles flew.
In one dark torrent, broad and strong,
The advancing onset roll'd along,
Forth harbinger'd by fierce acclaim,
That, from the shroud of smoke and
    flame,
Peal'd wildly the imperial name.

xii.

But on the British heart were lost
The terrors of the charging host ;
For not an eye the storm that view'd
Changed its proud glance of fortitude,
Nor was one forward footstep staid,
As dropp'd the dying and the dead.
Fast as their ranks the thunders tear,
Fast they renew'd each serried square,
And on the wounded and the slain
Closed their diminish'd files again,
Till from their line, scarce spears'
    lengths three,
Emerging from the smoke they see
Helmet, and plume, and panoply ;
    Then waked their fire at once !
Each musketeer's revolving knell
As fast, as regularly fell,
As when they practise to display
Their discipline on festal day ;
    Then down went helm and lance !
Down were the eagle banners sent,
Down reeling steeds and riders went,
Corslets were pierced, and pennons
    rent,
    And, to augment the fray,
Wheel'd full against their staggering
    flanks,
The English horsemen's foaming ranks
    Forced their resistless way.

Then to the musket-knell succeeds
The clash of swords, the neigh of steeds;
As plies the smith his clanging trade,
Against the cuirass rang the blade;
And while amid their close array
The well-served cannon rent their
    way,
And while amid their scatter'd band
Raged the fierce rider's bloody brand,
Recoil'd in common rout and fear
Lancer and guard and cuirassier,
Horsemen and foot, a mingled host,
Their leaders fall'n, their standards lost.

XIII.

Then, WELLINGTON, thy piercing eye
This crisis caught of destiny;
    The British host had stood
That morn 'gainst charge of sword
    and lance
As their own ocean-rocks hold stance,
But when thy voice had said, 'Ad-
    vance!'
    They were their ocean's flood.
O thou, whose inauspicious aim
Hath wrought thy host this hour of
    shame,
Think'st thou thy broken bands will
    bide
The terrors of yon rushing tide?
Or will thy Chosen brook to feel
The British shock of levell'd steel,
    Or dost thou turn thine eye
Where coming squadrons gleam afar,
And fresher thunders wake the war,
    And other standards fly?
Think not that in yon columns, file
Thy conquering troops from Distant
    Dyle—
    Is Blucher yet unknown?
Or dwells not in thy memory still,
(Heard frequent in thine hour of ill)
What notes of hate and vengeance
    thrill
    In Prussia's trumpet tone?
What yet remains? shall it be thine
To head the relics of thy line

    In one dread effort more?
The Roman lore thy leisure loved,
And thou canst tell what fortune proved
    That Chieftain, who, of yore,
Ambition's dizzy paths essay'd,
And with the gladiators' aid
    For empire enterprised:
He stood the cast his rashness play'd,
Left not the victims he had made,
Dug his red grave with his own blade
And on the field he lost was laid,
    Abhorr'd—but not despised.

XIV.

But if revolves thy fainter thought
On safety, howsoever bought,
Then turn thy fearful rein and ride,
Though twice ten thousand men have
    died
    On this eventful day,
To gild the military fame
Which thou, for life, in traffic tame
    Wilt barter thus away.
Shall future ages tell this tale
Of inconsistence faint and frail?
And art thou he of Lodi's bridge,
Marengo's field, and Wagram's ridge!
    Or is thy soul like mountain-tide,
That, swell'd by winter storm and
    shower,
Rolls down in turbulence of power,
    A torrent fierce and wide;
Reft of these aids, a rill obscure,
Shrinking unnoticed, mean and poor,
    Whose channel shows display'd
The wrecks of its impetuous course,
But not one symptom of the force
    By which these wrecks were
    made!

XV.

Spur on thy way! since now thine ear
Has brook'd thy veterans' wish to hear,
    Who, as thy flight they eyed,
Exclaim'd, while tears of anguish came,
Wrung forth by pride, and rage, and
    shame,
    'O that he had but died!'

But yet, to sum this hour of ill,
Look, ere thou leavest the fatal hill,
 Back on yon broken ranks
Upon whose wild confusion gleams
The moon, as on the troubled streams
 When rivers break their banks,
And, to the ruin'd peasant's eye,
Objects half seen roll swiftly by,
 Down the dread current hurl'd :
So mingle banner, wain, and gun,
Where the tumultuous flight rolls on
Of warriors, who, when morn begun,
 Defied a banded world.

XVI.

List ! frequent to the hurrying rout
The stern pursuers' vengeful shout
Tells that upon their broken rear
Rages the Prussian's bloody spear.
 So fell a shriek was none,
When Beresina's icy flood
Redden'd and thaw'd with flame and
 blood,
And, pressing on thy desperate way,
Raised oft and long their wild hurra,
 The children of the Don.
Thine ear no yell of horror cleft
So ominous, when, all bereft
Of aid, the valiant Polack left—
Ay, left by thee—found soldier's grave
In Leipsic's corpse-encumber'd wave.
Fate, in those various perils past,
Reserved thee still some future cast ;
On the dread die thou now hast
 thrown,
Hangs not a single field alone,
Nor one campaign ; thy martial fame,
Thy empire, dynasty, and name,
 Have felt the final stroke ;
And now, o'er thy devoted head
The last stern vial's wrath is shed,
 The last dread seal is broke.

XVII.

Since live thou wilt, refuse not now
Before these demagogues to bow,

Late objects of thy scorn and hate,
Who shall thy once imperial fate
Make wordy theme of vain debate
Or shall we say thou stoop'st less low
In seeking refuge from the foe
Against whose heart, in prosperous life,
Thine hand hath ever held the knife ?
 Such homage hath been paid
By Roman and by Grecian voice,
And there were honour in the choice,
 If it were freely made.
Then safely come : in one so low,
So lost, we cannot own a foe ;
Though dear experience bid us end
In thee we ne'er can hail a friend.
Come, howsoe'er : but do not hide
Close in thy heart that germ of pride,
Erewhile, by gifted bard espied,
 That ' yet imperial hope ' ;
Think not that for a fresh rebound,
To raise ambition from the ground,
 We yield thee means or scope.
In safety come : but ne'er again
Hold type of independent reign ;
 No islet calls thee lord,
We leave thee no confederate band,
No symbol of thy lost command,
To be a dagger in the hand
 From which we wrench'd the
 sword.

XVIII.

Yet even in yon sequester'd spot
May worthier conquest be thy lot
 Than yet thy life has known ;
Conquest, unbought by blood or harm,
That needs nor foreign aid nor arm,
 A triumph all thine own.
Such waits thee when thou shalt
 control
Those passions wild, that stubborn
 soul,
 That marr'd thy prosperous scene :
Hear this from no unmoved heart,
Which sighs, comparing what thou art
 With what thou might'st have
 been !

XIX.

Thou, too, whose deeds of fame renew'd
Bankrupt a nation's gratitude,
To thine own noble heart must owe
More than the meed she can bestow.
For not a people's just acclaim,
Not the full hail of Europe's fame,
Thy Prince's smiles, thy State's decree,
The ducal rank, the garter'd knee,—
Not these such pure delight afford
As that, when hanging up thy sword,
Well may'st thou think, ' This honest steel
Was ever drawn for public weal ;
And, such was rightful Heaven's decree,
Ne'er sheathed unless with victory ! '

XX.

Look forth once more with soften'd heart,
Ere from the field of fame we part ;
Triumph and sorrow border near,
And joy oft melts into a tear.
Alas ! what links of love that morn
Has war's rude hand asunder torn !
For ne'er was field so sternly fought,
And ne'er was conquest dearer bought.
Here piled in common slaughter sleep
Those whom affection long shall weep :
Here rests the sire, that ne'er shall strain
His orphans to his heart again ;
The son, whom on his native shore
The parent's voice shall bless no more ;
The bridegroom, who has hardly press'd
His blushing consort to his breast ;
The husband, whom through many a year
Long love and mutual faith endear.
Thou canst not name one tender tie,
But here dissolved its relics lie !
O ! when thou see'st some mourner's veil
Shroud her thin form and visage pale ;

Or mark'st the matron's bursting tears
Stream when the stricken drum she hears ;
Or see'st how manlier grief, suppress'd,
Is labouring in a father's breast,—
With no enquiry vain pursue
The cause, but think on Waterloo !

XXI.

Period of honour as of woes,
What bright careers 'twas thine to close !
Mark'd on thy roll of blood what names
To Briton's memory, and to Fame's,
Laid there their last immortal claims !
Thou saw'st in seas of gore expire
Redoubted Picton's soul of fire,
Saw'st in the mingled carnage lie
All that of Ponsonby could die,
De Lancey change Love's bridal-wreath
For laurels from the hand of Death,
Saw'st gallant Miller's failing eye
Still bent where Albion's banners fly,
And Cameron in the shock of steel
Die like the offspring of Lochiel ;
And generous Gordon 'mid the strife
Fall while he watch'd his leader's life.
Ah ! though her guardian angel's shield
Fenced Britain's hero through the field,
Fate not the less her power made known,
Through his friends' hearts to pierce his own !

XXII.

Forgive, brave Dead, the imperfect lay !
Who may your names, your numbers, say ?
What high-strung harp, what lofty line,
To each the dear-earn'd praise assign,
From high-born chiefs of martial fame
To the poor soldier's lowlier name ?
Lightly ye rose that dawning day,
From your cold couch of swamp and clay,
To fill, before the sun was low,
The bed that morning cannot know.

Oft may the tear the green sod steep,
And sacred be the heroes' sleep,
    Till time shall cease to run ;
And ne'er beside their noble grave,
May Briton pass and fail to crave
A blessing on the fallen brave
    Who fought with Wellington !

XXIII.

Farewell, sad Field ! whose blighted face
Wears desolation's withering trace ;
Long shall my memory retain
Thy shatter'd huts and trampled grain,
With every mark of martial wrong,
That scathe thy towers, fair Hougomont !
Yet though thy garden's green arcade
The marksman's fatal post was made,
Though on thy shatter'd beeches fell
The blended rage of shot and shell,
Though from thy blacken'd portals torn,
Their fall thy blighted fruit-trees mourn,
Has not such havoc brought a name
Immortal in the rolls of fame ?
Yes, Agincourt may be forgot,
And Cressy be an unknown spot,
    And Blenheim's name be new ;
But still in story and in song,
For many an age remember'd long,
Shall live the towers of Hougomont,
    And field of Waterloo.

———

STERN tide of human Time ! that know'st not rest,
But, sweeping from the cradle to the tomb,
Bear'st ever downward on thy dusky breast
Successive generations to their doom;
While thy capacious stream has equal room

For the gay bark where pleasure's streamers sport,
And for the prison-ship of guilt and gloom,
The fisher-skiff, and barge that bears a court,
Still wafting onward all to one dark silent port ;—

Stern tide of Time ! through what mysterious change
Of hope and fear have our frail barks been driven !
For ne'er before, vicissitude so strange
Was to one race of Adam's offspring given.
And sure such varied change of sea and heaven
Such unexpected bursts of joy and woe,
Such fearful strife as that where we have striven,
Succeeding ages ne'er again shall know,
Until the awful term when thou shalt cease to flow !

Well hast thou stood, my Country! the brave fight
Hast well maintain'd through good report and ill ;
In thy just cause and in thy native might,
And in Heaven's grace and justice constant still ;
Whether the banded prowess, strength, and skill
Of half the world against thee stood array'd,
Or when, with better views and freer will,
Beside thee Europe's noblest drew the blade,
Each emulous in arms the Ocean Queen to aid.

Well art thou now repaid; though slowly rose
And struggled long with mists thy blaze of fame,
While like the dawn that in the orient glows
On the broad wave its earlier lustre came ;
Then eastern Egypt saw the growing flame,
And Maida's myrtles gleam'd beneath its ray,
Where first the soldier, stung with generous shame,
Rivall'd the heroes of the wat'ry way,
And wash'd in foemen's gore unjust reproach away.

Now, Island Empress, wave thy crest on high,
And bid the banner of thy patron flow,
Gallant Saint George, the flower of Chivalry,
For thou hast faced, like him, a dragon foe,
And rescued innocence from over-throw,
And trampled down, like him, tyrannic might,
And to the gazing world mayst proudly show
The chosen emblem of thy sainted Knight,
Who quell'd devouring pride, and vindicated right.

Yet 'mid the confidence of just renown,
Renown dear-bought, but dearest thus acquired,
Write, Britain, write the moral lesson down :
'Tis not alone the heart with valour fired,
The discipline so dreaded and admired,
In many a field of bloody conquest known ;
Such may by fame be lured, by gold be hired ;
'Tis constancy in the good cause alone,
Best justifies the meed thy valiant sons have won.

END OF THE FIELD OF WATERLOO.

Notes to the Field of Waterloo.

NOTE I.

The peasant, at his labour blithe,
Flies the hook'd staff and shorten'd scythe.
—P. 620.

THE reaper in Flanders carries in his left hand a stick with an iron hook, with which he collects as much grain as he can cut at one sweep with a short scythe, which he holds in his right hand. They carry on this double process with great spirit and dexterity.

NOTE II.

Pale Brussels! then what thoughts were thine.—P. 621.

It was affirmed by the prisoners of war, that Bonaparte had promised his army, in case of victory, twenty-four hours' plunder of the city of Brussels.

NOTE III.

' On! On!' was still his stern exclaim.
—P. 622.

The characteristic obstinacy of Napoleon was never more fully displayed than in what we may be permitted to hope will prove the last of his fields. He would listen to no advice, and allow of no obstacles. An eye-witness has given the following account of his demeanour towards the end of the action :—

' It was near seven o'clock; Bonaparte, who till then had remained upon the ridge of the hill whence he could best behold what passed, contemplated with a stern countenance the scene of this horrible slaughter. The more that obstacles seemed to multiply, the more his obstinacy seemed to increase. He became indignant at these unforeseen difficulties; and, far from fearing to push to extremities an army whose confidence in him was boundless, he ceased not to pour down fresh troops, and to give orders to march forward—to charge with the bayonet—to carry by storm. He was repeatedly informed, from different points, that the day went against him, and that the

troops seemed to be disordered; to which he only replied,—"*En-avant! En-avant!*" '

'One general sent to inform the Emperor that he was in a position which he could not maintain, because it was commanded by a battery, and requested to know, at the same time, in what way he should protect his division from the murderous fire of the English artillery. "Let him storm the battery," replied Bonaparte, and turned his back on the aide-de-camp who brought the message.' — *Relation de la Bataille de Mont-St. Jean. Par un Témoin Oculaire.* Paris. 1815, 8vo, p. 51.

NOTE IV.

The fate their leader shunn'd to share.
—P. 622.

It has been reported that Bonaparte charged at the head of his guards, at the last period of this dreadful conflict. This, however, is not accurate. He came down indeed to a hollow part of the high road, leading to Charleroi, within less than a quarter of a mile of the farm of La Haye Sainte, one of the points most fiercely disputed. Here he harangued the guards, and informed them that his preceding operations had destroyed the British infantry and cavalry, and that they had only to support the fire of the artillery, which they were to attack with the bayonet. This exhortation was received with shouts of *Vive l'Empereur*, which were heard over all our line, and led to an idea that Napoleon was charging in person. But the guards were led on by Ney; nor did Bonaparte approach nearer the scene of action than the spot already mentioned, which the rising banks on each side rendered secure from all such balls as did not come in a straight line. He witnessed the earlier part of the battle from places yet more remote, particularly from an observatory which had been placed there by the King of the Netherlands, some weeks before, for the purpose of surveying the country. It is not meant to infer from these particulars that Napoleon showed, on that memorable occasion, the least deficiency in personal courage; on the contrary, he evinced the greatest composure and presence of mind during the whole action. But it is no less true that report has erred in ascribing to him any desperate efforts of valour for recovery of the battle; and it is remarkable that during the whole carnage, none of his suite were either killed or wounded, whereas scarcely one of the Duke of Wellington's personal attendants escaped unhurt.

NOTE V.

England shall tell the fight!—P. 622.

In riding up to a regiment which was hard pressed, the Duke called to the men, 'Soldiers, we must never be beat,—what will they say in England?' It is needless to say how this appeal was answered.

NOTE VI.

As plies the smith his clanging trade.
—P. 623.

A private soldier of the 95th regiment compared the sound which took place immediately upon the British cavalry mingling with those of the enemy, to '*a thousand tinkers at work mending pots and kettles*.'

NOTE VII.

The British shock of levell'd steel.—P. 623.

No persuasion or authority could prevail upon the French troops to stand the shock of the bayonet. The Imperial Guards, in particular, hardly stood till the British were within thirty yards of them, although the French author, already quoted, has put into their mouths the magnanimous sentiment, 'The Guards never yield—they die.' The same author has covered the plateau, or eminence, of St. Jean, which formed the British position, with redoubts and retrenchments which never had an existence. As the narrative, which is in many respects curious, was written by an eye-witness, he was probably deceived by the appearance of a road and ditch which run along part of the hill. It may be also mentioned, in criticising this work, that the writer mentions the Château of Hougomont to have been carried by the French, although it was resolutely and successfully defended during the whole action. The enemy, indeed, possessed themselves of the wood by which it is surrounded, and at length set fire to the house itself; but the British (a detachment of the Guards, under the command of Colonel Macdonnell, and afterwards of Colonel Home) made good the garden, and thus preserved, by their desperate resistance, the post which covered the return of the Duke of Wellington's right flank.

Ballads

TRANSLATED OR IMITATED

From the German.

—◆—

WILLIAM AND HELEN.

FROM heavy dreams fair Helen rose,
   And eyed the dawning red:
'Alas, my love, thou tarriest long!
   O art thou false or dead?'

With gallant Fred'rick's princely
     power
   He sought the bold Crusade;
But not a word from Judah's wars
   Told Helen how he sped.

With Paynim and with Saracen
   At length a truce was made,
And every knight return'd to dry
   The tears his love had shed.

Our gallant host was homeward bound
   With many a song of joy;
Green waved the laurel in each plume,
   The badge of victory.

And old and young, and sire and son,
   To meet them crowd the way,
With shouts, and mirth, and melody,
   The debt of love to pay.

Full many a maid her true-love met,
   And sobb'd in his embrace,
And flutt'ring joy in tears and smiles
   Array'd full many a face.

Nor joy nor smile for Helen sad;
   She sought the host in vain;
For none could tell her William's
     fate,
   If faithless, or if slain.

The martial band is past and gone;
   She rends her raven hair,
And in distraction's bitter mood
   She weeps with wild despair.

'O rise, my child,' her mother said,
   'Nor sorrow thus in vain;
A perjured lover's fleeting heart
   No tears recall again.'

'O mother, what is gone, is gone,
   What's lost for ever lorn:
Death, death alone can comfort me;
   O had I ne'er been born!

'O break, my heart—O break at once!
   Drink my life-blood, Despair!
No joy remains on earth for me,
   For me in heaven no share.'

'O enter not in judgment, Lord!'
   The pious mother prays;
'Impute not guilt to thy frail child!
   She knows not what she says.

'O say thy pater noster, child!
  O turn to God and grace!
His will, that turn'd thy bliss to bale,
  Can change thy bale to bliss.'

'O mother, mother, what is bliss?
  O mother, what is bale?
My William's love was heaven on earth,
  Without it earth is hell.

'Why should I pray to ruthless
    Heaven,
  Since my loved William's slain?
I only pray'd for William's sake,
  And all my prayers were vain.'

'O take the sacrament, my child,
  And check these tears that flow;
By resignation's humble prayer,
  O hallow'd be thy woe!'

'No sacrament can quench this fire,
  Or slake this scorching pain;
No sacrament can bid the dead
  Arise and live again.

'O break, my heart—O break at once!
  Be thou my god, Despair!
Heaven's heaviest blow has fallen on
    me,
  And vain each fruitless prayer.'

'O enter not in judgment, Lord,
  With thy frail child of clay!
She knows not what her tongue has
    spoke;
  Impute it not, I pray!

'Forbear, my child, this desperate woe,
  And turn to God and grace;
Well can devotion's heavenly glow
  Convert thy bale to bliss.'

'O mother, mother, what is bliss?
  O mother, what is bale?
Without my William what were
    heaven,
  Or with him what were hell?'

Wild she arraigns the eternal doom,
  Upbraids each sacred power,
Till, spent, she sought her silent room,
  All in the lonely tower.

She beat her breast, she wrung her
    hands,
  Till sun and day were o'er,
And through the glimmering lattice
    shone
  The twinkling of the star.

Then, crash! the heavy drawbridge fell
  That o'er the moat was hung;
And, clatter! clatter! on its boards
  The hoof of courser rung.

The clank of echoing steel was heard
  As off the rider bounded;
And slowly on the winding stair
  A heavy footstep sounded.

And hark! and hark! a knock—tap!
    tap!
  A rustling stifled noise;
Door-latch and tinkling staples ring;
  At length a whispering voice:

'Awake, awake, arise, my love!
  How, Helen, dost thou fare?
Wak'st thou, or sleep'st? laugh'st
    thou, or weep'st?
  Hast thought on me, my fair?'

'My love! my love!—so late by night!
  I waked, I wept for thee:
Much have I borne since dawn of morn;
  Where, William, couldst thou be?'

'We saddle late—from Hungary
  I rode since darkness fell;
And to its bourne we both return
  Before the matin-bell.'

'O rest this night within my arms,
  And warm thee in their fold!
Chill howls through hawthorn bush
    the wind:
  My love is deadly cold.'

x

'Let the wind howl through hawthorn
　　bush !
　This night we must away ;
The steed is wight, the spur is bright ;
　I cannot stay till day.

'Busk, busk, and boune ! thou mount'st
　　behind
　Upon my black barb steed :
O'er stock and stile, a hundred miles,
　We haste to bridal bed.'

'To-night—to-night a hundred miles ?
　O dearest William, stay !
The bell strikes twelve—dark, dismal
　　hour !
　O wait, my love, till day !'

'Look here, look here—the moon
　　shines clear—
　Full fast I ween we ride ;
Mount and away ! for ere the day
　We reach our bridal bed.

'The black barb snorts, the bridle rings ;
　Haste, busk, and boune, and seat
　　thee !
The feast is made, the chamber spread,
　The bridal guests await thee.'

Strong love prevail'd.　She busks, she
　　bounes,
　She mounts the barb behind,
And round her darling William's waist
　Her lily arms she twined.

And, hurry ! hurry ! off they rode,
　As fast as fast might be ;
Spurn'd from the courser's thundering
　　heels
　The flashing pebbles flee.

And on the right, and on the left,
　Ere they could snatch a view,
Fast, fast each mountain, mead, and
　　plain,
　And cot, and castle flew.

'Sit fast—dost fear ? The moon shines
　　clear ;
　Fleet goes my barb—keep hold !
Fear'st thou ?' 'O no !' she faintly said ;
　'But why so stern and cold ?

'What yonder rings ? what yonder
　　sings ?
　Why shrieks the owlet grey ?'
''Tis death-bells' clang, 'tis funeral
　　song,
　The body to the clay.

'With song and clang, at morrow's
　　dawn,
　Ye may inter the dead :
To-night I ride, with my young bride,
　To deck our bridal bed.

'Come with thy choir, thou coffin'd
　　guest,
　To swell our nuptial song !
Come, priest, to bless our marriage
　　feast !
　Come all, come all along !'

Ceased clang and song ; down sunk
　　the bier ;
　The shrouded corpse arose :
And, hurry ! hurry ! all the train
　The thundering steed pursues.

And, forward ! forward ! on they go ;
　High snorts the straining steed ;
Thick pants the rider's labouring
　　breath,
　As headlong on they speed.

'O William, why this savage haste ?
　And where thy bridal bed ?'
''Tis distant far, low, damp, and chill,
　And narrow, trustless maid.'

'No room for me ?' 'Enough for both ;
　Speed, speed, my barb, thy course !'
O'er thundering bridge, through boil-
　　ing surge
　He drove the furious horse.

Tramp! tramp! along the land they
    rode,
Splash! splash! along the sea;
The scourge is wight, the spur is
    bright,
    The flashing pebbles flee.

Fled past on right and left how fast
    Each forest, grove, and bower!
On right and left fled past how fast
    Each city, town, and tower!

'Dost fear? dost fear? The moon
    shines clear,
    Dost fear to ride with me?
Hurrah! hurrah! the dead can ride!'
    'O William, let them be!

'See there, see there! What yonder
    swings,
    And creaks 'mid whistling rain?'
'Gibbet and steel, th' accursed wheel;
    A murderer in his chain.

'Hollo! thou felon, follow here:
    To bridal bed we ride;
And thou shalt prance a fetter dance
    Before me and my bride.'

And, hurry! hurry! clash! clash!
    clash!
    The wasted form descends;
And fleet as wind through hazel bush
    The wild career attends.

Tramp! tramp! along the land they
    rode,
Splash! splash! along the sea;
The scourge is red, the spur drops
    blood,
    The flashing pebbles flee.

How fled what moonshine faintly
    show'd!
How fled what darkness hid!
How fled the earth beneath their feet,
    The heaven above their head!

'Dost fear? dost fear? The moon
    shines clear,
    And well the dead can ride;
Does faithful Helen fear for them?'
    'O leave in peace the dead!'

'Barb! barb! methinks I hear the cock;
    The sand will soon be run:
Barb! barb! I smell the morning air;
    The race is wellnigh done.'

Tramp! tramp! along the land they
    rode,
Splash! splash! along the sea;
The scourge is red, the spur drops
    blood,
    The flashing pebbles flee.

'Hurrah! hurrah! well ride the dead;
    The bride, the bride is come;
And soon we reach the bridal bed,
    For, Helen, here's my home.'

Reluctant on its rusty hinge
    Revolved an iron door,
And by the pale moon's setting beam
    Were seen a church and tower.

With many a shriek and cry, whiz
    round
    The birds of midnight, scared;
And rustling like autumnal leaves
    Unhallow'd ghosts were heard.

O'er many a tomb and tombstone pale
    He spurr'd the fiery horse,
Till sudden at an open grave
    He check'd the wondrous course.

The falling gauntlet quits the rein,
    Down drops the casque of steel,
The cuirass leaves his shrinking side,
    The spur his gory heel.

The eyes desert the naked skull,
    The mould'ring flesh the bone,
Till Helen's lily arms entwine
    A ghastly skeleton.

The furious barb snorts fire and foam,
   And, with a fearful bound,
Dissolves at once in empty air,
   And leaves her on the ground.

Half seen by fits, by fits half heard,
   Pale spectres flit along,
Wheel round the maid in dismal dance,
   And howl the funeral song;

'E'en when the heart's with anguish
   cleft,
   Revere the doom of Heaven!
Her soul is from her body reft:
   Her spirit be forgiven!'

—•◦•—

THE WILD HUNTSMAN.

THE Wildgrave winds his bugle-horn,
   To horse, to horse! halloo, halloo!
His fiery courser snuffs the morn,
   And thronging serfs their lord
   pursue.

The eager pack, from couples freed,
   Dash through the bush, the brier,
   the brake;
While, answering hound, and horn,
   and steed,
   The mountain echoes startling wake.

The beams of God's own hallow'd day
   Had painted yonder spire with gold,
And, calling sinful man to pray,
   Loud, long, and deep the bell had
   toll'd.

But still the Wildgrave onward rides;
   Halloo, halloo! and, hark again!
When, spurring from opposing sides,
   Two Stranger Horsemen join the
   train.

Who was each Stranger, left and right,
   Well may I guess, but dare not tell;
The right-hand steed was silver white,
   The left, the swarthy hue of hell.

The right-hand Horseman, young and
   fair,
   His smile was like the morn of May;
The left, from eye of tawny glare,
   Shot midnight lightning's lurid ray.

He waved his huntsman's cap on high,
   Cried, 'Welcome, welcome, noble
   lord!
What sport can earth, or sea, or sky,
   To match the princely chase, afford?'

'Cease thy loud bugle's clanging knell,'
   Cried the fair youth, with silver
   voice;
'And for devotion's choral swell,
   Exchange the rude unhallow'd noise.

'To-day, the ill-omen'd chase forbear,
   Yon bell yet summons to the fane;
To-day the Warning Spirit hear,
   To-morrow thou mayst mourn in
   vain.'

'Away, and sweep the glades along!'
   The Sable Hunter hoarse replies;
'To muttering monks leave matin-song,
   And bells, and books, and mysteries.'

The Wildgrave spurr'd his ardent
   steed,
   And, launching forward with a
   bound,
'Who, for thy drowsy priestlike rede,
   Would leave the jovial horn and
   hound?

'Hence, if our manly sport offend!
   With pious fools go chant and pray:
Well hast thou spoke, my dark-brow'd
   friend:
   Halloo, halloo! and hark away!'

The Wildgrave spurr'd his courser
   light,
   O'er moss and moor, o'er holt and
   hill;
And on the left and on the right,
   Each Stranger Horseman follow'd
   still.

Up springs, from yonder tangled thorn,
　A stag more white than mountain
　　snow;
And louder rung the Wildgrave's horn,
　'Hark forward, forward! holla, ho!'

A heedless wretch has cross'd the way;
　He gasps the thundering hoofs
　　below;—
But, live who can, or die who may,
　Still, 'forward, forward!' on they go.

See, where yon simple fences meet,
　A field with Autumn's blessings
　　crown'd:
See, prostrate at the Wildgrave's feet,
　A husbandman with toil embrown'd:

' O mercy, mercy, noble lord!
　Spare the poor's pittance,' was his
　　cry,
' Earn'd by the sweat these brows have
　　pour'd,
　In scorching hour of fierce July.'

Earnest the right-hand Stranger
　　pleads,
　The left still cheering to the prey;
The impetuous Earl no warning heeds,
　But furious holds the onward way.

' Away, thou hound! so basely born,
　Or dread the scourge's echoing
　　blow!'
Then loudly rung his bugle-horn,
　' Hark forward, forward! holla, ho!'

So said, so done: A single bound
　Clears the poor labourer's humble
　　pale:
Wild follows man, and horse, and
　　hound,
　Like dark December's stormy gale.

And man and horse, and hound and
　　horn,
　Destructive sweep the field along;
While, joying o'er the wasted corn,
　Fell Famine marks the maddening
　　throng.

Again uproused, the timorous prey
　Scours moss and moor, and holt
　　and hill;
Hard run, he feels his strength decay,
　And trusts for life his simple skill.

Too dangerous solitude appear'd;
　He seeks the shelter of the crowd;
Amid the flock's domestic herd
　His harmless head he hopes to
　　shroud.

O'er moss and moor, and holt and hill,
　His track the steady blood-hounds
　　trace;
O'er moss and moor, unwearied still,
　The furious Earl pursues the chase.

Full lowly did the herdsman fall;
　' O spare, thou noble Baron, spare
These herds, a widow's little all;
　These flocks, an orphan's fleecy
　　care!'

Earnest the right-hand Stranger
　　pleads,
　The left still cheering to the prey;
The Earl nor prayer nor pity heeds,
　But furious keeps the onward way.

' Unmanner'd dog! To stop my sport
　Vain were thy cant and beggar
　　whine,
Though human spirits, of thy sort,
　Were tenants of these carrion kine!'

Again he winds his bugle-horn,
　' Hark forward, forward! holla, ho!'
And through the herd, in ruthless scorn,
　He cheers his furious hounds to go.

In heaps the throttled victims fall;
　Down sinks their mangled herdsman
　　near;
The murderous cries the stag appal,
　Again he starts, new-nerved by
　　fear.

With blood besmear'd, and white with
    foam,
  While big the tears of anguish pour,
He seeks, amid the forest's gloom,
  The humble hermit's hallow'd bower.

But man and horse, and horn and
    hound,
  Fast rattling on his traces go;
The sacred chapel rung around
  With, ' Hark away! and, holla, ho!'

All mild, amid the rout profane,
  The holy hermit pour'd his prayer;
' Forbear with blood God's house to
    stain;
  Revere his altar, and forbear!

' The meanest brute has rights to plead,
  Which, wrong'd by cruelty, or pride,
Draw vengeance on the ruthless head:
  Be warn'd at length, and turn aside.'

Still the Fair Horseman anxious pleads;
  The Black, wild whooping, points
    the prey:
Alas! the Earl no warning heeds,
  But frantic keeps the forward way.

' Holy or not, or right or wrong,
  Thy altar, and its rites, I spurn;
Not sainted martyrs' sacred song,
  Not God himself, shall make me
    turn!'

He spurs his horse, he winds his horn,
  ' Hark forward, forward! holla, ho!'
But off, on whirlwind's pinions borne,
  The stag, the hut, the hermit, go.

And horse and man, and horn and
    hound,
  And clamour of the chase, was gone;
For hoofs, and howls, and bugle-sound,
  A deadly silence reign'd alone.

Wild gazed the affrighted Earl around;
  He strove in vain to wake his horn,
In vain to call: for not a sound
  Could from his anxious lips be borne.

He listens for his trusty hounds;
  No distant baying reach'd his ears:
His courser, rooted to the ground,
  The quickening spur unmindful
    bears.

Still dark and darker frown the shades,
  Dark as the darkness of the grave;
And not a sound the still invades,
  Save what a distant torrent gave.

High o'er the sinner's humbled head
  At length the solemn silence broke;
And, from a cloud of swarthy red,
  The awful voice of thunder spoke.

' Oppressor of creation fair!
  Apostate Spirits' harden'd tool!
Scorner of God! Scourge of the poor!
  The measure of thy cup is full.

' Be chased for ever through the wood;
  For ever roam the affrighted wild;
And let thy fate instruct the proud,
  God's meanest creature is his child.'

'Twas hush'd: One flash, of sombre
    glare,
  With yellow tinged the forests
    brown;
Uprose the Wildgrave's bristling hair,
  And horror chill'd each nerve and
    bone.

Cold pour'd the sweat in freezing rill;
  A rising wind began to sing;
And louder, louder, louder still,
  Brought storm and tempest on its
    wing.

Earth heard the call; her entrails rend;
  From yawning rifts, with many
    a yell,
Mix'd with sulphureous flames, ascend
  The misbegotten dogs of hell.

What ghastly Huntsman next arose,
  Well may I guess, but dare not tell;
His eye like midnight lightning glows,
  His steed the swarthy hue of hell.

The Wildgrave flies o'er bush and
　　thorn,
　With many a shriek of helpless
　　woe ;
Behind him hound, and horse, and
　　horn,
　And 'Hark away!' and 'Holla, ho!'

With wild despair's reverted eye,
　Close, close behind, he marks the
　　throng.
With bloody fangs and eager cry ;
　In frantic fear he scours along.

Still, still shall last the dreadful chase,
　Till time itself shall have an end;
By day, they scour earth's cavern'd
　　space,
　At midnight's witching hour, ascend.

This is the horn, and hound, and horse,
　That oft the lated peasant hears ;
Appall'd, he signs the frequent cross,
　When the wild din invades his ears.

The wakeful priest oft drops a tear
　For human pride, for human woe,
When, at his midnight mass, he hears
　The infernal cry of 'Holla, ho !'

—◆—

THE FIRE-KING.

'The blessing of the evil genii, which are
curses, were upon him.'—*Eastern Tale.*

BOLD knights and fair dames, to my
　　harp give an ear,
Of love, and of war, and of wonder
　　to hear ;
And you haply may sigh, in the midst
　　of your glee,
At the tale of Count Albert, and fair
　　Rosalie.

O see you that castle, so strong and
　　so high ?
And see you that lady, the tear in
　　her eye ?
And see you that palmer, from
　　Palestine's land,
The shell on his hat, and the staff
　　in his hand ?

'Now palmer, grey palmer, O tell
　　unto me,
What news bring you home from the
　　Holy Countrie ?
And how goes the warfare by Galilee's
　　strand ?
And how fare our nobles, the flower
　　of the land ?'

'O well goes the warfare by Galilee's
　　wave,
For Gilead, and Nablous, and Ramah
　　we have ;
And well fare our nobles by Mount
　　Lebanon,
For the Heathen have lost, and the
　　Christians have won.'

A fair chain of gold 'mid her ringlets
　　there hung ;
O'er the palmer's grey locks the fair
　　chain has she flung :
'O palmer, grey palmer, this chain
　　be thy fee,
For the news thou hast brought from
　　the Holy Countrie.

'And, palmer, good palmer, by Gali-
　　lee's wave,
O saw ye Count Albert, the gentle
　　and brave ?
When the Crescent went back, and
　　the Red-cross rush'd on,
O saw ye him foremost on Mount
　　Lebanon ?'

'O lady, fair lady, the tree green it
　　grows ;
O lady, fair lady, the stream pure it
　　flows ;

Your castle stands strong, and your
   hopes soar on high;
But, lady, fair lady, all blossoms to die.

'The green boughs they wither, the
   thunderbolt falls,
It leaves of your castle but levin-
   scorch'd walls;
The pure stream runs muddy; the
   gay hope is gone;
Count Albert is prisoner on Mount
   Lebanon.'

O she's ta'en a horse, should be fleet
   at her speed;
And she's ta'en a sword, should be
   sharp at her need;
And she has ta'en shipping for
   Palestine's land,
To ransom Count Albert from
   Soldanrie's hand.

Small thought had Count Albert on
   fair Rosalie,
Small thought on his faith, or his
   knighthood, had he:
A heathenish damsel his light heart
   had won,
The Soldan's fair daughter of Mount
   Lebanon.

'O Christian, brave Christian, my
   love wouldst thou be,
Three things must thou do ere I
   hearken to thee:
Our laws and our worship on thee
   shalt thou take;
And this thou shalt first do for
   Zulema's sake.

'And, next, in the cavern, where
   burns evermore
The mystical flame which the Curd-
   mans adore,
Alone, and in silence, three nights
   shalt thou wake;
And this thou shalt next do for
   Zulema's sake.

'And, last, thou shalt aid us with
   counsel and hand,
To drive the Frank robber from
   Palestine's land;
For my lord and my love then Count
   Albert I'll take,
When all this is accomplish'd for
   Zulema's sake.'

He has thrown by his helmet, and
   cross-handled sword,
Renouncing his knighthood, denying
   his Lord;
He has ta'en the green caftan, and
   turban put on,
For the love of the maiden of fair
   Lebanon.

And in the dread cavern, deep deep
   under ground,
Which fifty steel gates and steel
   portals surround,
He has watch'd until daybreak, but
   sight saw he none,
Save the flame burning bright on its
   altar of stone.

Amazed was the Princess, the Soldan
   amazed,
Sore murmur'd the priests as on
   Albert they gazed;
They search'd all his garments, and,
   under his weeds,
They found, and took from him, his
   rosary beads.

Again in the cavern, deep deep under
   ground,
He watch'd the lone night, while the
   winds whistled round;
Far off was their murmur, it came not
   more nigh,
The flame burn'd unmoved, and nought
   else did he spy.

Loud murmur'd the priests, and
   amazed was the King,
While many dark spells of their
   witchcraft they sing;

They search'd Albert's body, and, lo! on his breast
Was the sign of the Cross, by his father impress'd.

The priests they erase it with care and with pain,
And the recreant return'd to the cavern again;
But, as he descended, a whisper there fell:
It was his good angel, who bade him farewell!

High bristled his hair, his heart flutter'd and beat,
And he turn'd him five steps, half resolved to retreat;
But his heart it was harden'd, his purpose was gone,
When he thought of the Maiden of fair Lebanon.

Scarce pass'd he the archway, the threshold scarce trode,
When the winds from the four points of heaven were abroad,
They made each steel portal to rattle and ring,
And, borne on the blast, came the dread Fire-King.

Full sore rock'd the cavern whene'er he drew nigh,
The fire on the altar blazed bickering and high;
In volcanic explosions the mountains proclaim
The dreadful approach of the Monarch of Flame.

Unmeasured in height, undistinguish'd in form,
His breath it was lightning, his voice it was storm;
I ween the stout heart of Count Albert was tame,
When he saw in his terrors the Monarch of Flame.

In his hand a broad falchion blue-glimmer'd through smoke,
And Mount Lebanon shook as the monarch he spoke:
'With this brand shalt thou conquer, thus long, and no more,
Till thou bend to the Cross, and the Virgin adore.'

The cloud-shrouded Arm gives the weapon; and see!
The recreant receives the charm'd gift on his knee:
The thunders growl distant, and faint gleam the fires,
As, borne on the whirlwind, the phantom retires.

Count Albert has arm'd him the Paynim among,
Though his heart it was false, yet his arm it was strong;
And the Red-cross wax'd faint, and the Crescent came on,
From the day he commanded on Mount Lebanon.

From Lebanon's forests to Galilee's wave,
The sands of Samaar drank the blood of the brave;
Till the Knights of the Temple, and Knights of Saint John,
With Salem's King Baldwin, against him came on.

The war-cymbals clatter'd, the trumpets replied,
The lances were couch'd, and they closed on each side;
And horsemen and horses Count Albert o'erthrew,
Till he pierced the thick tumult King Baldwin unto.

Against the charm'd blade which Count Albert did wield,
The fence had been vain of the King's Red-cross shield;

But a Page thrust him forward the
    monarch before,
And cleft the proud turban the rene-
    gade wore.

So fell was the dint, that Count
    Albert stoop'd low
Before the cross'd shield, to his steel
    saddlebow;
And scarce had he bent to the Red-
    cross his head,
'*Bonne Grace, Notre Dame!*' he un-
    wittingly said.

Sore sigh'd the charm'd sword, for its
    virtue was o'er,
It sprung from his grasp, and was
    never seen more;
But true men have said, that the
    lightning's red wing
Did waft back the brand to the dread
    Fire-King.

He clench'd his set teeth, and his
    gauntleted hand;
He stretch'd, with one buffet, that
    Page on the strand.
As back from the stripling the broken
    casque roll'd,
You might see the blue eyes, and the
    ringlets of gold.

Short time had Count Albert in horror
    to stare
On those death-swimming eyeballs,
    that blood-clotted hair;
For down came the Templars, like
    Cedron in flood,
And dyed their long lances in Saracen
    blood.

The Saracens, Curdmans, and Ish-
    maelites yield
To the scallop, the saltier, and
    crossleted shield;
And the eagles were gorged with the
    infidel dead,
From Bethsaida's fountains to Naph-
    thali's head.

The battle is over on Bethsaida's plain.
Oh, who is yon Paynim lies stretch'd
    'mid the slain?
And who is yon Page lying cold at
    his knee?
Oh, who but Count Albert and fair
    Rosalie!

The Lady was buried in Salem's
    bless'd bound,
The Count he was left to the vulture
    and hound:
Her soul to high mercy Our Lady
    did bring;
His went on the blast to the dread
    Fire-King.

Yet many a minstrel, in harping, can
    tell,
How the Red-cross it conquer'd, the
    Crescent it fell:
And lords and gay ladies have sigh'd,
    'mid their glee,
At the tale of Count Albert and fair
    Rosalie.

—++—

FREDERICK AND ALICE.

FREDERICK leaves the land of France,
    Homeward hastes his steps to
    measure,
Careless casts the parting glance
    On the scene of former pleasure.

Joying in his prancing steed,
    Keen to prove his untried blade,
Hope's gay dreams the soldier lead
    Over mountain, moor, and glade.

Helpless, ruin'd, left forlorn,
    Lovely Alice wept alone;
Mourn'd o'er love's fond contract torn,
    Hope, and peace, and honour flown.

Mark her breast's convulsive throbs !
  See, the tear of anguish flows !
Mingling soon with bursting sobs,
  Loud the laugh of frenzy rose.

Wild she cursed, and wild she pray'd ;
  Seven long days and nights are o'er ;
Death in pity brought his aid,
  As the village bell struck four.

Far from her, and far from France,
  Faithless Frederick onward rides ;
Marking, blithe, the morning's glance
  Mantling o'er the mountain's sides.

Heard ye not the boding sound,
  As the tongue of yonder tower,
Slowly, to the hills around,
  Told the fourth, the fated hour ?

Starts the steed, and snuffs the air,
  Yet no cause of dread appears ;
Bristles high the rider's hair,
    Struck with strange mysterious
      fears.

Desperate, as his terrors rise,
  In the steed the spur he hides ;
From himself in vain he flies ;
  Anxious, restless, on he rides.

Seven long days, and seven long nights,
  Wild he wander'd, woe the while !
Ceaseless care and causeless fright
  Urge his footsteps many a mile.

Dark the seventh sad night descends :
  Rivers swell, and rain-streams pour ;
While the deafening thunder lends
  All the terrors of its roar.

Weary, wet, and spent with toil,
  Where his head shall Frederick hide ?
Where, but in yon ruin'd aisle,
  By the lightning's flash descried.

To the portal, dank and low,
  Fast his steed the wanderer bound ;
Down a ruin'd staircase slow,
  Next his darkling way he wound.

Long drear vaults before him lie !
  Glimmering lights are seen to glide !
'Blessed Mary, hear my cry !
  Deign a sinner's steps to guide !'

Often lost their quivering beam,
  Still the lights move slow before,
Till they rest their ghastly gleam
  Right against an iron door.

Thundering voices from within,
  Mix'd with peals of laughter, rose ;
As they fell, a solemn strain
  Lent its wild and wondrous close !

Midst the din, he seem'd to hear
  Voice of friends, by death removed:
Well he knew that solemn air,—
  'Twas the lay that Alice loved.

Hark ! for now a solemn knell
  Four times on the still night broke
Four times, at its deaden'd swell,
  Echoes from the ruins spoke.

As the lengthen'd clangours die,
  Slowly opes the iron door !
Straight a banquet met his eye,
  But a funeral's form it wore !

Coffins for the seats extend ;
  All with black the board was spread ;
Girt by parent, brother, friend,
  Long since number'd with the dead.

Alice, in her grave-clothes bound,
  Ghastly smiling, points a seat ;
All arose, with thundering sound ;
  All the expected stranger greet.

High their meagre arms they wave,
  Wild their notes of welcome swell ;
'Welcome, traitor, to the grave !
  Perjured, bid the light farewell !'

—++—

THE BATTLE OF SEMPACH.

'Twas when among our linden-trees
 The bees had housed in swarms
(And grey-hair'd peasants say that
  these
 Betoken foreign arms);

Then look'd we down to Willisow,—
 The land was all in flame;
We knew the Archduke Leopold
 With all his army came.

The Austrian nobles made their vow,
 So hot their heart and bold,
' On Switzer carles we'll trample now,
 And slay both young and old.'

With clarion loud, and banner proud,
 From Zurich on the lake,
In martial pomp and fair array,
 Their onward march they make.

' Now list, ye lowland nobles all :
 Ye seek the mountain strand,
Nor wot ye what shall be your lot
 In such a dangerous land.

' I rede ye, shrive ye of your sins,
 Before ye farther go ;
A skirmish in Helvetian hills
 May send your souls to woe.'

'But where now shall we find a priest
 Our shrift that he may hear ?'
' The Switzer priest [1] has ta'en the field,
 He deals a penance drear.

' Right heavily upon your head
 He 'll lay his hand of steel ;
And with his trusty partisan
 Your absolution deal.'

'Twas on a Monday morning then,
 The corn was steep'd in dew,
And merry maids had sickles ta'en,
 When the host to Sempach drew.

The stalwart men of fair Lucerne
 Together have they join'd ;
The pith and core of manhood stern,
 Was none cast looks behind.

It was the Lord of Hare-castle,
 And to the Duke he said,
' Yon little band of brethren true
 Will meet us undismay'd.'

' O Hare-castle [2], thou heart of hare !'
 Fierce Oxenstern replied.
'Shalt see then how the game will fare,'
 The taunted knight replied.

There was lacing then of helmets bright,
 And closing ranks amain ;
The peaks they hew'd from their boot-
  points
 Might wellnigh load a wain [3].

And thus they to each other said.
 ' Yon handful down to hew
Will be no boastful tale to tell,
 The peasants are so few.'

The gallant Swiss Confederates there
 They pray'd to God aloud,
And he display'd his rainbow fair
 Against a swarthy cloud.

Then heart and pulse throbb'd more
  and more
 With courage firm and high,
And down the good Confederates bore
 On the Austrian chivalry.

The Austrian Lion [4] 'gan to growl,
 And toss his mane and tail ;
And ball, and shaft, and crossbow bolt,
 Went whistling forth like hail.

---

[1] All the Swiss clergy who were able to bear arms fought in this patriotic war.

[2] In the original, *Haasenstein*, or *Hare-stone*.

[3] This seems to allude to the preposterous fashion, during the middle ages, of wearing boots with the points or peaks turned upwards, and so long, that in some cases they were fastened to the knees of the wearer with small chains. When they alighted to fight upon foot, it would seem that the Austrian gentlemen found it necessary to cut off these peaks, that they might move with the necessary activity.

[4] A pun on the Archduke's name, LEOPOLD.

Lance, pike, and halbert mingled there,
  The game was nothing sweet;
The boughs of many a stately tree
  Lay shiver'd at their feet.

The Austrian men-at-arms stood fast,
  So close their spears they laid;
It chafed the gallant Winkelried,
  Who to his comrades said:

'I have a virtuous wife at home,
  A wife and infant son;
I leave them to my country's care,—
  This field shall soon be won.

'These nobles lay their spears right thick,
  And keep full firm array,
Yet shall my charge their order break,
  And make my brethren way.'

He rush'd against the Austrian band
  In desperate career,
And with his body, breast, and hand,
  Bore down each hostile spear.

Four lances splinter'd on his crest,
  Six shiver'd in his side;
Still on the serried files he press'd,
  He broke their ranks, and died.

This patriot's self-devoted deed
  First tamed the Lion's mood,
And the four forest cantons freed
  From thraldom by his blood.

Right where his charge had made a lane,
  His valiant comrades burst,
With sword, and axe, and partisan,
  And hack, and stab, and thrust.

The daunted Lion 'gan to whine,
  And granted ground amain,
The Mountain Bull [1] he bent his brows,
  And gored his sides again.

---

[1] A pun on the URUS, or wild bull, which gives name to the Canton of Uri.

Then lost was banner, spear, and shield
  At Sempach in the flight,
The cloister vaults at Konig's-field
  Hold many an Austrian knight.

It was the Archduke Leopold,
  So lordly would he ride,
But he came against the Switzer churls,
  And they slew him in his pride.

The heifer said unto the bull,
  'And shall I not complain?
There came a foreign nobleman
  To milk me on the plain.

'One thrust of thine outrageous horn
  Has gall'd the knight so sore,
That to the churchyard he is borne
  To range our glens no more.'

An Austrian noble left the stour,
  And fast the flight 'gan take;
And he arrived in luckless hour
  At Sempach on the lake.

He and his squire a fisher call'd
  (His name was Hans Von Rot)—
'For love, or meed, or charity,
  Receive us in thy boat!'

Their anxious call the fisher heard,
  And, glad the meed to win,
His shallop to the shore he steer'd,
  And took the flyers in.

And while against the tide and wind
  Hans stoutly row'd his way,
The noble to his follower sign'd
  He should the boatman slay.

The fisher's back was to them turn'd,
  The squire his dagger drew,
Hans saw his shadow in the lake,
  The boat he overthrew.

He 'whelm'd the boat, and as they strove,
  He stunn'd them with his oar;
'Now, drink ye deep, my gentle sirs,
  You 'll ne'er stab boatman more.

'Two gilded fishes in the lake
  This morning have I caught,
Their silver scales may much avail,
  Their carrion flesh is naught.'

It was a messenger of woe
  Has sought the Austrian land:
'Ah! gracious lady, evil news!
  My lord lies on the strand.

'At Sempach, on the battle-field,
  His bloody corpse lies there.'
'Ah, gracious God!' the lady cried,
  'What tidings of despair!'

Now would you know the minstrel
    wight
Who sings of strife so stern,
Albert the Souter is he hight,
  A burgher of Lucerne.

A merry man was he, I wot,
  The night he made the lay,
Returning from the bloody spot
  Where God had judged the day.

—◆◆—

THE NOBLE MORINGER.

O will you hear a knightly tale of
  old Bohemian day?
It was the noble Moringer in wedlock
  bed he lay;
He halsed and kiss'd his dearest
  dame, that was as sweet as May,
And said, 'Now, lady of my heart,
  attend the words I say.

''Tis I have vow'd a pilgrimage unto
  a distant shrine,
And I must seek Saint Thomas-land,
  and leave the land that's mine;
Here shalt thou dwell the while in state,
  so thou wilt pledge thy fay,
That thou for my return wilt wait
  seven twelvemonths and a day.'

Then out and spoke that Lady bright,
  sore troubled in her cheer,
'Now tell me true, thou noble knight,
  what order takest thou here?
And who shall lead thy vassal band,
  and hold thy lordly sway,
And be thy lady's guardian true when
  thou art far away?'

Out spoke the noble Moringer, 'Of
  that have thou no care,
There's many a valiant gentleman of
  me holds living fair;
The trustiest shall rule my land, my
  vassals and my state,
And be a guardian tried and true
  to thee, my lovely mate.

'As Christian man, I needs must keep
  the vow which I have plight;
When I am far in foreign land,
  remember thy true knight;
And cease, my dearest dame, to grieve,
  for vain were sorrow now,
But grant thy Moringer his leave,
  since God hath heard his vow.'

It was the noble Moringer from bed
  he made him boune,
And met him there his Chamberlain,
  with ewer and with gown:
He flung the mantle on his back,
  'twas furr'd with miniver,
He dipp'd his hand in water cold,
  and bathed his forehead fair.

'Now hear,' he said, 'Sir Chamberlain,
  true vassal art thou mine,
And such the trust that I repose in
  that proved worth of thine,
For seven years shalt thou rule my
  towers, and lead my vassal train,
And pledge thee for my Lady's faith
  till I return again.'

The Chamberlain was blunt and true,
  and sturdily said he,
'Abide, my lord, and rule your own,
  and take this rede from me;

That woman's faith 's a brittle trust—
    seven twelvemonths didst thou
    say?
I 'll pledge me for no lady's truth be-
    yond the seventh fair day.'

The noble Baron turn'd him round,
    his heart was full of care,
His gallant Esquire stood him nigh,
    he was Marstetten's heir,
To whom he spoke right anxiously,
    ' Thou trusty squire to me,
Wilt thou receive this weighty trust
    when I am o'er the sea?

' To watch and ward my castle strong,
    and to protect my land,
And to the hunting or the host to
    lead my vassal band;
And pledge thee for my Lady's faith
    till seven long years are gone,
And guard her as Our Lady dear
    was guarded by Saint John?'

Marstetten's heir was kind and true,
    but fiery, hot, and young,
And readily he answer made with too
    presumptuous tongue:
' My noble lord, cast care away, and
    on your journey wend,
And trust this charge to me until
    your pilgrimage have end.

' Rely upon my plighted faith, which
    shall be truly tried,
To guard your lands, and ward your
    towers, and with your vassals
    ride;
And for your lovely Lady's faith, so
    virtuous and so dear,
I 'll gage my head it knows no change,
    be absent thirty year.'

The noble Moringer took cheer when
    thus he heard him speak,
And doubt forsook his troubled brow,
    and sorrow left his cheek;

A long adieu he bids to all, hoists
    topsails, and away,
And wanders in Saint Thomas-land
    seven twelvemonths and a day.

It was the noble Moringer within an
    orchard slept,
When on the Baron's slumbering
    sense a boding vision crept;
And whisper'd in his ear a voice, ''Tis
    time, Sir Knight, to wake,
Thy Lady and thy heritage another
    master take.

' Thy tower another banner knows,
    thy steeds another rein,
And stoop them to another's will thy
    gallant vassal train;
And she, the Lady of thy love, so
    faithful once and fair,
This night within thy fathers' hall
    she weds Marstetten's heir.'

It is the noble Moringer starts up
    and tears his beard,
' Oh would that I had ne'er been born!
    what tidings have I heard!
To lose my lordship and my lands
    the less would be my care,
But, God! that e'er a squire untrue
    should wed my Lady fair.

' O good Saint Thomas, hear,' he pray'd,
    ' my patron Saint art thou,
A traitor robs me of my land even
    while I pay my vow!
My wife he brings to infamy that was
    so pure of name,
And I am far in foreign land, and must
    endure the shame.'

It was the good Saint Thomas, then,
    who heard his pilgrim's prayer,
And sent a sleep so deep and dead
    that it o'erpower'd his care;
He waked in fair Bohemian land
    outstretch'd beside a rill,
High on the right a castle stood, low
    on the left a mill.

The Moringer he started up as one from
    spell unbound,
And dizzy with surprise and joy gazed
    wildly all around ;
'I know my fathers' ancient towers,
    the mill, the stream I know,
Now blessed be my patron Saint who
    cheer'd his pilgrim's woe !'

He leant upon his pilgrim staff, and
    to the mill he drew,
So alter'd was his goodly form that
    none their master knew ;
The Baron to the miller said, 'Good
    friend, for charity,
Tell a poor palmer in your land what
    tidings may there be ?'

The miller answered him again, 'He
    knew of little news,
Save that the Lady of the land did
    a new bridegroom choose ;
Her husband died in distant land,
    such is the constant word ;
His death sits heavy on our souls,
    he was a worthy Lord.

'Of him I held the little mill which
    wins me living free ;
God rest the Baron in his grave, he
    still was kind to me !
And when Saint Martin's tide comes
    round, and millers take their toll,
The priest that prays for Moringer
    shall have both cope and stole.'

It was the noble Moringer to climb
    the hill began,
And stood before the bolted gate
    a woe and weary man ;
'Now help me, every saint in heaven
    that can compassion take,
To gain the entrance of my hall this
    woful match to break.'

His very knock it sounded sad, his
    call was sad and slow,
For heart and head, and voice and
    hand, were heavy all with woe ;

And to the warder thus he spoke :
    'Friend, to thy Lady say,
A pilgrim from Saint Thomas-land
    craves harbour for a day.

'I've wander'd many a weary step,
    my strength is wellnigh done,
And if she turn me from her gate
    I'll see no morrow's sun ;
I pray, for sweet Saint Thomas' sake,
    a pilgrim's bed and dole,
And for the sake of Moringer's, her
    once-loved husband's soul.'

It was the stalwart warder then he
    came his dame before,
'A pilgrim, worn and travel-toil'd,
    stands at the castle-door ;
And prays, for sweet Saint Thomas'
    sake, for harbour and for dole,
And for the sake of Moringer, thy
    noble husband's soul.'

The Lady's gentle heart was moved ;
    'Do up the gate,' she said,
'And bid the wanderer welcome be
    to banquet and to bed ;
And since he names my husband's
    name, so that he lists to stay,
These towers shall be his harbourage
    a twelvemonth and a day.'

It was the stalwart warder then un-
    did the portal broad ;
It was the noble Moringer that o'er
    the threshold strode ;
'And have thou thanks, kind heaven,'
    he said, 'though from a man
    of sin,
That the true lord stands here once
    more his castle-gate within.'

Then up the halls paced Moringer, his
    step was sad and slow ;
It sat full heavy on his heart, none
    seem'd their Lord to know ;
He sat him on a lowly bench, oppress'd
    with woe and wrong,
Short space he sat, but ne'er to him
    seem'd little space so long.

Now spent was day, and feasting o'er,
    and come was evening hour,
The time was nigh when new-made
    brides retire to nuptial bower;
'Our castle's wont,' a bridesman said,
    'hath been both firm and long,
No guest to harbour in our halls till he
    shall chant a song.'

Then spoke the youthful bridegroom
    there as he sat by the bride,
'My merry minstrel folk,' quoth he,
    'lay shalm and harp aside;
Our pilgrim guest must sing a lay, the
    castle's rule to hold,
And well his guerdon will I pay with
    garment and with gold.'

'Chill flows the lay of frozen age,'
    'twas thus the pilgrim sung;
'Nor golden meed nor garment gay
    unlocks his heavy tongue;
Once did I sit, thou bridegroom gay, at
    board as rich as thine,
And by my side as fair a bride with
    all her charms was mine.

'But time traced furrows on my face,
    and I grew silver-hair'd,
For locks of brown, and cheeks of youth,
    she left this brow and beard;
Once rich, but now a palmer poor,
    I tread life's latest stage,
And mingle with your bridal mirth
    the lay of frozen age.'

It was the noble Lady there this woful
    lay that hears,
And for the aged pilgrim's grief her
    eye was dimm'd with tears;
She bade her gallant cupbearer a golden
    beaker take,
And bear it to the palmer poor to
    quaff it for her sake.

It was the noble Moringer that dropp'd
    amid the wine
A bridal ring of burning gold so costly
    and so fine:

Now listen, gentles, to my song, it
    tells you but the sooth,
'Twas with that very ring of gold he
    pledged his bridal truth.

Then to the cupbearer he said, 'Do me
    one kindly deed,
And should my better days return,
    full rich shall be thy meed;
Bear back the golden cup again to
    yonder bride so gay,
And crave her of her courtesy to
    pledge the palmer grey.'

The cupbearer was courtly bred, nor
    was the boon denied,
The golden cup he took again, and
    bore it to the bride;
'Lady,' he said, 'your reverend guest
    sends this, and bids me pray,
That, in thy noble courtesy, thou
    pledge the palmer grey.'

The ring hath caught the Lady's eye,
    she views it close and near,
Then might you hear her shriek aloud,
    'The Moringer is here!'
Then might you see her start from
    seat, while tears in torrents fell,
But whether 'twas for joy or woe, the
    ladies best can tell.

But loud she utter'd thanks to Heaven,
    and every saintly power,
That had return'd the Moringer before
    the midnight hour;
And loud she utter'd vow on vow, that
    never was there bride
That had like her preserved her troth,
    or been so sorely tried.

'Yes, here I claim the praise,' she said,
    'to constant matrons due,
Who keep the troth that they have
    plight, so stedfastly and true;

For count the term howe'er you will,
   so that you count aright,
Seven twelvemonths and a day are out
   when bells toll twelve to-night.'

It was Marstetten then rose up, his
   falchion there he drew,
He kneel d before the Moringer, and
   down his weapon threw;
'My oath and knightly faith are broke,'
   these were the words he said,
'Then take, my liege, thy vassal's sword,
   and take thy vassal's head.'

The noble Moringer he smiled, and
   then aloud did say,
' He gathers wisdom that hath roam'd
   seven twelvemonths and a day;
My daughter now hath fifteen years,
   fame speaks her sweet and fair,
I give her for the bride you lose, and
   name her for my heir.

'The young bridegroom hath youthful
   bride, the old bridegroom the old,
Whose faith was kept till term and tide
   so punctually were told;
But blessings on the warder kind that
   oped my castle-gate,
For had I come at morrow tide, I came
   a day too late.'

—◆—

THE ERL-KING.

FROM THE GERMAN OF GOETHE.

O, who rides by night thro' the woodland so wild ?
It is the fond father embracing his
   child;
And close the boy nestles within his
   loved arm,
To hold himself fast, and to keep
   himself warm.

' O father, see yonder ! see yonder !'
   he says;
' My boy, upon what dost thou fearfully gaze ?'
' O, 'tis the Erl-King with his crown
   and his shroud.'
' No, my son, it is but a dark wreath
   of the cloud.'

(*The Erl-King speaks.*)

' O come and go with me, thou loveliest
   child ;
By many a gay sport shall thy time be
   beguiled ;
My mother keeps for thee full many
   a fair toy,
And many a fine flower shall she pluck
   for my boy.'

' O father, my father, and did you
   not hear
The Erl-King whisper so low in my
   ear ?'
' Be still, my heart's darling—my child,
   be at ease ;
It was but the wild blast as it sung
   thro' the trees.'

Erl-King.

' O wilt thou go with me, thou loveliest
   boy ?
My daughter shall tend thee with care
   and with joy ;
She shall bear thee so lightly thro'
   wet and thro' wild,
And press thee, and kiss thee, and
   sing to my child.'

' O father, my father, and saw you not
   plain
The Erl-King's pale daughter glide
   past thro' the rain ?'
' O yes, my loved treasure, I knew it
   full soon ;
It was the grey willow that danced to
   the moon.'

Erl-King.

'O come and go with me, no longer
    delay,
Or else, silly child, I will drag thee
    away.'
'O father! O father! now, now, keep
    your hold,
The Erl-King has seized me—his grasp
    is so cold!'

Sore trembled the father; he spurr'd
    thro' the wild,
Clasping close to his bosom his shud-
    dering child;
He reaches his dwelling in doubt and
    in dread,
But, clasp'd to his bosom, the infant
    was dead.

END OF BALLADS FROM THE GERMAN.

𝔑otes to 𝔅allads from t𝔥e 𝔊erman.

— ✦ —

INTRODUCTORY NOTE.

In early youth I had been an eager student of Ballad Poetry, and the tree is still in my recollection beneath which I lay and first entered upon the enchanting perusal of Percy's 'Reliques of Ancient Poetry,' although it has long perished in the general blight which affected the whole race of Oriental platanus to which it belonged. The taste of another person had strongly encouraged my own researches into this species of legendary lore. But I had never dreamed of an attempt to imitate what gave me so much pleasure.

I had, indeed, tried the metrical translations which were occasionally recommended to us at the High School. I got credit for attempting to do what was enjoined, but very little for the mode in which the task was performed, and I used to feel not a little mortified when my versions were placed in contrast with others of admitted merit. At one period of my schoolboy days I was so far left to my own desires as to become guilty of Verses on a Thunderstorm, which were much approved of, until a malevolent critic sprung up, in the shape of an apothecary's blue-buskined wife, who affirmed that my most sweet poetry was stolen from an old magazine. I never forgave the imputation, and even now I acknowledge some resentment against the poor woman's memory. She indeed accused me unjustly, when she said I had stolen my brooms ready made ; but as I had, like most premature poets, copied all the words and ideas of which my verses consisted, she was so far right. I made one or two faint attempts at verse, after I had undergone this sort of daw-plucking at the hands of the apothecary's wife ; but some friend or other always advised me to put my verses in the fire, and, like Dorax in the play, I submitted, though 'with a swelling heart.' In short, excepting the usual tribute to a mistress's eyebrow, which is the language of passion rather than poetry, I had not for ten years indulged the wish to couple so much as *love* and *dove*, when, finding Lewis in possession of so much

reputation, and conceiving that, if I fell behind him in poetical powers, I considerably exceeded him in general information, I suddenly took it into my head to attempt the style of poetry by which he had raised himself to fame.

This idea was hurried into execution, in consequence of a temptation which others, as well as the author, found it difficult to resist. The celebrated ballad of 'Lenoré,' by Bürger, was about this time introduced into England ; and it is remarkable, that, written as far back as 1775, it was upwards of twenty years before it was known in Britain, though calculated to make so strong an impression. The wild character of the tale was such as struck the imagination of all who read it, although the idea of the lady's ride behind the spectre horseman had been long before hit upon by an English ballad-maker. But this pretended English original, if in reality it be such, is so dull, flat, and prosaic, as to leave the distinguished German author all that is valuable in his story, by clothing it with a fanciful wildness of expression, which serves to set forth the marvellous tale in its native terror. The ballad of 'Lenoré' accordingly possessed general attractions for such of the English as understood the language in which it is written ; and, as if there had been a charm in the ballad, no one seemed to cast his eyes upon it without a desire to make it known by translation to his own countrymen, and six or seven versions were accordingly presented to the public. Although the present author was one of those who intruded his translation on the world at this time, he may fairly exculpate himself from the rashness of entering the lists against so many rivals. The circumstances which threw him into this competition were quite accidental, and of a nature tending to show how much the destiny of human life depends upon unimportant occurrences, to which little consequence is attached at the moment.

About the summer of 1793 or 1794, the celebrated Miss Laetitia Aikin, better known as Mrs. Barbauld, paid a visit to Edinburgh, and was received by such literary society as the place then boasted, with the hospitality to which her talents and her worth entitled her. Among others, she was kindly welcomed by the late excellent and admired Professor Dugald Stewart, his lady, and family. It was in their evening society that Miss Aikin drew from her pocket-book a version of 'Lenoré,' executed by William Taylor, Esq., of Norwich, with as much freedom as was consistent with great spirit and scrupulous fidelity. She read this composition to the company, who were electrified by the tale. It was the more successful, that Mr. Taylor had boldly copied the imitative harmony of the German, and described the spectral journey in language resembling that of the original. Bürger had thus painted the ghostly career:

'Und hurre, hurre, hop, hop, hop,
Ging's fort in sausendem Galopp,
Dass Ross und Reiter schnoben,
Und Kies und Funken stoben.'

The words were rendered by the kindred sounds in English:

'Tramp, tramp, across the land they speede,
Splash, splash, across the sea;
Hurrah, the dead can ride apace!
Dost fear to ride with me?'

When Miss Aikin had finished her recitation, she replaced in her pocket-book the paper from which she had read it, and enjoyed the satisfaction of having made a strong impression on the hearers, whose bosoms thrilled yet the deeper, as the ballad was not to be more closely introduced to them.

The author was not present upon this occasion, although he had then the distinguished advantage of being a familiar friend and frequent visitor of Professor Stewart and his family. But he was absent from town while Miss Aikin was in Edinburgh, and it was not until his return that he found all his friends in rapture with the intelligence and good sense of their visitor, but in particular with the wonderful translation from the German, by means of which she had delighted and astonished them. The enthusiastic description given of Bürger's ballad, and the broken account of the story, of which only two lines were recollected, inspired the author, who had some acquaintance, as has been said, with the German language, and a strong taste for popular poetry, with a desire to see the original. This was not a wish easily gratified; German works were at that time seldom found in London for sale—in Edinburgh never. A lady of noble German descent,[1] whose friendship I have enjoyed for many years, found means, however, to procure me a copy of Bürger's works from Hamburgh.

[1] Born Countess Harriet Bruhl of Martinskirchen, and married to Hugh Scott, Esq., of Harden, afterwards Lord Polwarth, the author's relative, and much-valued friend almost from infancy.

The perusal of the original rather exceeded than disappointed the expectations which the report of Mr. Stewart's family had induced me to form. At length, when the book had been a few hours in my possession, I found myself giving an animated account of the poem to a friend, and rashly added a promise to furnish a copy in English ballad verse.

I well recollect that I began my task after supper, and finished it about daybreak the next morning, by which time the ideas which the task had a tendency to summon up were rather of an uncomfortable character. As my object was much more to make a good translation of the poem for those whom I wished to please, than to acquire any poetical fame for myself, I retained in my translation the two lines which Mr. Taylor had rendered with equal boldness and felicity.

My attempt succeeded far beyond my expectations; and it may readily be believed that I was induced to persevere in a pursuit which gratified my own vanity, while it seemed to amuse others. I accomplished a translation of 'Der Wilde Jäger'—a romantic ballad founded on a superstition universally current in Germany, and known also in Scotland and France. In this I took rather more license than in versifying 'Lenoré'; and I balladized one or two other poems of Bürger with more or less success. In the course of a few weeks, my own vanity, and the favourable opinion of friends, interested by the temporary revival of a species of poetry containing a germ of popularity of which perhaps they were not themselves aware, urged me to the decisive step of sending a selection, at least, of my translations to the press, to save the numerous applications which were made for copies. When was there an author deaf to such a recommendation? In 1796, the present author was prevailed on, 'by request of friends,' to indulge his own vanity by publishing the translation of 'Lenoré,' with that of 'The Wild Huntsman,' in a thin quarto.

The fate of this, my first publication, was by no means flattering. I distributed so many copies among my friends as, according to the booksellers, materially to interfere with the sale; and the number of translations which appeared in England about the same time, including that of Mr. Taylor, to which I had been so much indebted, and which was published in 'The Monthly Magazine,' were sufficient to exclude a provincial writer from competition. However different my success might have been, had I been fortunate enough to have led the way in the general scramble for precedence, my efforts sunk unnoticed when launched at the same time with those of Mr. Taylor (upon whose property I had committed the kind of piracy already noticed, and who generously forgave me the invasion of his rights); of my ingenious and amiable friend of many years,

William Robert Spencer; of Mr. Pye, the laureate of the day, and many others besides. In a word, my adventure, where so many pushed off to sea, proved a dead loss, and a great part of the edition was condemned to the service of the trunk-maker. Nay, so complete was the failure of the unfortunate ballads, that the very existence of them was soon forgotten; and, in a newspaper, in which I very lately read, to my no small horror, a most appalling list of my own various publications, I saw this, my first offence, had escaped the industrious collector, for whose indefatigable research I may in gratitude wish a better object.

The failure of my first publication did not operate, in any unpleasant degree, either on my feelings or spirits. I was coldly received by strangers, but my reputation began rather to increase among my own friends, and, on the whole, I was more bent to show the world that it had neglected something worth notice, than to be affronted by its indifference. Or rather, to speak candidly, I found pleasure in the literary labour in which I had, almost by accident, become engaged, and laboured, less in the hope of pleasing others, though certainly without despair of doing so, than in the pursuit of a new and agreeable amusement to myself. I pursued the German language keenly, and, though far from being a correct scholar, became a bold and daring reader, nay, even translator, of various dramatic pieces from that tongue.

The want of books at that time (about 1796) was a great interruption to the rapidity of my movements; for the young do not know, and perhaps my own contemporaries may have forgotten, the difficulty with which publications were then procured from the continent. The worthy and excellent friend, of whom I gave a sketch many years afterwards in the person of Jonathan Oldbuck, procured me Adelung's Dictionary, through the mediation of Father Pepper, a monk of the Scotch College of Ratisbon. Other wants of the same nature were supplied by Mrs. Scott of Harden, whose kindness in a similar instance I have had already occasion to acknowledge. Through this lady's connections on the continent, I obtained copies of Bürger, Schiller, Goethe, and other standard German works; and though the obligation be of a distant date, it still remains impressed on my memory, after a life spent in a constant interchange of friendship and kindness with that family which is, according to Scottish ideas, the head of my house.

Being thus furnished with the necessary originals, I began to translate on all sides, certainly without anything like an accurate knowledge of the language; and, although the dramas of Goethe, Schiller, and others, powerfully attracted one whose early attention to the German had been arrested by Mackenzie's Dissertation, and the play of 'The Robbers,' yet the ballad poetry, in which I had made a bold essay, was still my favourite. I was yet more delighted on finding that the old English, and especially the Scottish language, were so nearly similar to the German, not in sound merely, but in the turn of phrase, that they were capable of being rendered line for line, with very little variation.

NOTES.

WILLIAM AND HELEN.

(IMITATED FROM THE 'LENORÉ' OF BÜRGER.)

P. 630.

The author had resolved to omit this version of a well-known Poem, in any collection which he might make of his poetical trifles. But the publishers having pleaded for its admission, the author has consented, though not unaware of the disadvantage at which this youthful essay (for it was written in 1795) must appear with those which have been executed by much more able hands, in particular that of Mr. Taylor of Norwich, and that of Mr. Spencer.

The translation of this ballad was written long before the author saw any other, and originated in the following circumstances :—

A lady of high rank in the literary world read this romantic tale, as translated by Mr. Taylor, in the house of the celebrated Professor Dugald Stewart, of Edinburgh. The author was not present, nor indeed in Edinburgh at the time; but a gentleman who had the pleasure of hearing the ballad, afterwards told him the story, and repeated the remarkable chorus—

> 'Tramp, tramp, across the land they speede,
> Splash, splash, across the sea;
> Hurrah, the dead can ride apace!
> Dost fear to ride with me?'

In attempting a translation, then intended only to circulate among friends, the present author did not hesitate to make use of this impressive stanza; for which freedom he has since obtained the forgiveness of the ingenious gentleman to whom it properly belongs.

Ballads from the German. 653

THE WILD HUNTSMAN.

P. 634.

This is a translation, or rather an imitation, of the *Wilde Jäger* of the German poet Bürger. The tradition upon which it is founded bears, that formerly a Waldgrave, or keeper of a royal forest, named Faulkenburg, was so much addicted to the pleasures of the chase, and otherwise so extremely profligate and cruel, that he not only followed this unhallowed amusement on the Sabbath, and other days consecrated to religious duty, but accompanied it with the most unheard-of oppression upon the poor peasants, who were under his vassalage. When this second Nimrod died, the people adopted a superstition, founded probably on the many various uncouth sounds heard in the depth of a German forest, during the silence of the night. They conceived they still heard the cry of the Waldgrave's hounds; and the well-known cheer of the deceased hunter, the sounds of his horses' feet, and the rustling of the branches before the game, the pack, and the sportsmen, are also distinctly discriminated; but the phantoms are rarely, if ever, visible. Once, as a benighted *Chasseur* heard this infernal chase pass by him, at the sound of the halloo, with which the Spectre Huntsman cheered his hounds, he could not refrain from crying, *'Gluck zu Falkenburgh!'* [Good sport to ye, Falkenburgh!] 'Dost thou wish me good sport?' answered a hoarse voice; 'thou shalt share the game;' and there was thrown at him what seemed to be a huge piece of foul carrion. The daring *Chasseur* lost two of his best horses soon after, and never perfectly recovered the personal effects of this ghostly greeting. This tale, though told with some variations, is universally believed all over Germany.

The French had a similar tradition concerning an aërial hunter, who infested the forest of Fountainbleau. He was sometimes visible; when he appeared as a huntsman, surrounded with dogs, a tall grisly figure. Some account of him may be found in 'Sully's Memoirs,' who says he was called *Le Grand Veneur.* At one time he chose to hunt so near the palace that the attendants, and, if I mistake not, Sully himself, came out into the court, supposing it was the sound of the king returning from the chase. This phantom is elsewhere called Saint Hubert.

The superstition seems to have been very general, as appears from the following fine poetical description of this phantom chase, as it was heard in the wilds of Ross shire.

'Ere since of old, the haughty thanes of Ross,—
So to the simple swain tradition tells,—
Were wont with clans, and ready vassals throng'd,
To wake the bounding stag, or guilty wolf,
There oft is heard, at midnight, or at noon,
Beginning faint, but rising still more loud,

And nearer, voice of hunters, and of hounds,
And horns, hoarse winded, blowing far and keen :—
Forthwith the hubbub multiplies; the gale
Labours with wilder shrieks, and rifer din
Of hot pursuit; the broken cry of deer
Mangled by throttling dogs; the shouts of men,
And hoofs, thick beating on the hollow hill.
Sudden the grazing heifer in the vale
Starts at the noise, and both the herdsman's ears
Tingle with inward dread. Aghast, he eyes
The mountain's height, and all the ridges round,
Yet not one trace of living wight discerns,
Nor knows, o'erawed, and trembling as he stands,
To what, or whom, he owes his idle fear,
To ghost, to witch, to fairy, or to fiend;
But wonders, and no end of wondering finds.
Albania—reprinted in *Scottish Descriptive Poems*, pp. 167, 168.

A posthumous miracle of Father Lesley, a Scottish capuchin, related to his being buried on a hill haunted by these unearthly cries of hounds and huntsmen. After his sainted relics had been deposited there, the noise was never heard more. The reader will find this, and other miracles, recorded in the life of Father Bonaventura, which is written in the choicest Italian.

THE FIRE-KING.

P. 637.

This ballad was written at the request of Mr. Lewis, to be inserted in his 'Tales of Wonder.' It is the third in a series of four ballads, on the subject of Elementary Spirits. The story is, however, partly historical; for it is recorded that, during the struggles of the Latin kingdom of Jerusalem, a Knight-Templar, called Saint-Alban, deserted to the Saracens, and defeated the Christians in many combats, till he was finally routed and slain, in a conflict with King Baldwin, under the walls of Jerusalem.

FREDERICK AND ALICE.

P. 640.

This tale is imitated, rather than translated, from a fragment introduced in Goethe's 'Claudina von Villa Bella,' where it is sung by a member of a gang of banditti, to engage the attention of the family, while his companions break into the castle. It owes any little merit it may possess to my friend Mr. Lewis, to whom it was sent in an extremely rude state; and who, after some material improvements, published it in his 'Tales of Wonder.'

THE BATTLE OF SEMPACH.

P. 642.

These verses are a literal translation of an ancient Swiss ballad upon the battle of Sempach, fought July 9, 1386, being the victory by which the Swiss cantons established their independence; the author, Albert Tchudi, denominated the Souter, from his profession of a shoemaker. He was a citizen of Lucerne, esteemed highly among his countrymen, both for his powers as a *Meister-Singer*, or minstrel, and his courage as a soldier; so that he might share the praise conferred by Collins on Aeschylus, that—

> 'Not alone he nursed the poet's flame,
> But reach'd from Virtue's hand the patriot steel.'

The circumstance of their being written by a poet returning from the well-fought field he describes, and in which his country's fortune was secured, may confer on Tchudi's verses an interest which they are not entitled to claim from their poetical merit. But ballad poetry, the more literally it is translated, the more it loses its simplicity, without acquiring either grace or strength; and, therefore, some of the faults of the verses must be imputed to the translator's feeling it a duty to keep as closely as possible to his original. The various puns, rude attempts at pleasantry, and disproportioned episodes, must be set down to Tchudi's account, or to the taste of his age.

The military antiquary will derive some amusement from the minute particulars which the martial poet has recorded. The mode in which the Austrian men-at-arms received the charge of the Swiss was by forming a phalanx, which they defended with their long lances. The gallant Winkelried, who sacrificed his own life by rushing among the spears, clasping in his arms as many as he could grasp, and thus opening a gap in those iron battalions, is celebrated in Swiss history. When fairly mingled together, the unwieldy length of their weapons, and cumbrous weight of their defensive armour, rendered the Austrian men-at-arms a very unequal match for the light-armed mountaineers. The victories obtained by the Swiss over the German chivalry, hitherto deemed as formidable on foot as on horseback, led to important changes in the art of war. The poet describes the Austrian knights and squires as cutting the peaks from their boots ere they could act upon foot, in allusion to an inconvenient piece of foppery, often mentioned in the middle ages. Leopold III, Archduke of Austria, called 'The handsome man-at-arms,' was slain in the battle of Sempach, with the flower of his chivalry.

THE NOBLE MORINGER.

P. 644.

The original of these verses occurs in a collection of German popular songs, entitled 'Sammlung Deutschen Volkslieder,' Berlin, 1807, published by Messrs. Busching and Von der Hagen, both, and more especially the last, distinguished for their acquaintance with the ancient popular poetry and legendary history of Germany.

In the German editor's notice of the ballad, it is stated to have been extracted from a manuscript Chronicle of Nicolaus Thomann, chaplain to Saint Leonard in Weisenhorn, which bears the date 1533; and the song is stated by the author to have been generally sung in the neighbourhood at that early period. Thomann, as quoted by the German editor, seems faithfully to have believed the event he narrates. He quotes tombstones and obituaries to prove the existence of the personages of the ballad, and discovers that there actually died, on the 11th of May, 1349, a Lady Von Neuffen, Countess of Marstetten, who was, by birth, of the house of Moringer. This lady he supposes to have been Moringer's daughter, mentioned in the ballad. He quotes the same authority for the death of Berckhold Von Neuffen in the same year. The editors, on the whole, seem to embrace the opinion of Professor Smith of Ulm, who, from the language of the ballad, ascribes its date to the 15th century.

The legend itself turns on an incident not peculiar to Germany, and which, perhaps, was not unlikely to happen in more instances than one, when crusaders abode long in the Holy Land, and their disconsolate dames received no tidings of their fate. A story, very similar in circumstances, but without the miraculous machinery of Saint Thomas, is told of one of the ancient Lords of Haighhall in Lancashire, the patrimonial inheritance of the late Countess of Balcarras; and the particulars are represented on stained glass upon a window in that ancient manorhouse.

THE ERL-KING.

P. 648.

The Erl-King is a goblin that haunts the Black Forest in Thuringia. To be read by a candle particularly long in the snuff.

Imitations of the Ancient Ballad.

(CONTRIBUTED TO 'THE MINSTRELSY OF THE SCOTTISH BORDER.')

—◆◆—

THOMAS THE RHYMER.

PART I. (ANCIENT.)

TRUE THOMAS lay on Huntlie bank;
    A ferlie he spied wi' his ee;
And there he saw a ladye bright
    Come riding down by the Eildon-
        tree.

Her shirt was o' the grass-green silk,
    Her mantle o' the velvet fyne;
At ilka tett of her horse's mane,
    Hung fifty siller bells and nine.

True Thomas he pull'd aff his cap,
    And louted low down to his knee,
'All hail, thou mighty Queen of
       Heaven!
    For thy peer on earth I never did see.'

'O no, O no, Thomas,' she said,
    'That name does not belang to me;
I am but the Queen of fair Elfland,
    That am hither come to visit thee.

'Harp and carp, Thomas,' she said,
    'Harp and carp along wi' me;
And if ye dare to kiss my lips,
    Sure of your bodie I will be.'

'Betide me weal, betide me woe,
    That weird shall never daunton me;'
Syne he has kiss'd her rosy lips
    All underneath the Eildon-tree.

'Now ye maun go wi' me,' she said,
    'True Thomas, ye maun go wi' me;
And ye maun serve me seven years,
    Thro' weal or woe as may chance
       to be.'

She mounted on her milk-white steed·
    She's ta'en true Thomas up behind:
And aye, whene'er her bridle rung,
    The steed flew swifter than the wind.

O they rade on, and farther on;
    The steed gaed swifter than the wind;
Until they reach'd a desert wide,
    And living land was left behind.

'Light down, light down now, true
       Thomas,
    And lean your head upon my knee;
Abide and rest a little space,
    And I will show you ferlies three.

'O see ye not yon narrow road,
    So thick beset with thorns and briers?
That is the path of righteousness,
    Though after it but few inquires.

'And see ye not that braid braid road,
 That lies across that lily leven?
That is the path of wickedness,
 Though some call it the road to
  heaven.

'And see ye not that bonny road,
 That winds about the fernie brae?
That is the road to fair Elfland,
 Where thou and I this night maun
  gae.

'But, Thomas, ye maun hold your
  tongue,
 Whatever ye may hear or see;
For, if ye speak word in Elfyn land,
 Ye'll ne'er get back to your ain
  countrie.'

O they rade on, and farther on,
 And they waded through rivers
  aboon the knee,
And they saw neither sun nor moon,
 But they heard the roaring of the sea.

It was mirk mirk night, and there was
  nae stern light,
 And they waded through red blude
  to the knee;
For a' the blude that's shed on earth
 Rins through the springs o' that
  countrie.

Syne they came on to a garden green,
 And she pu'd an apple frae a tree—
'Take this for thy wages, true Thomas;
 It will give thee the tongue that
  can never lie.'

'My tongue is mine ain,' true Thomas
  said;
 'A gudely gift ye wad gie to me!
I neither dought to buy nor sell,
 At fair or tryst where I may be.

'I dought neither speak to prince or
  peer,
 Nor ask of grace from fair ladye.'
'Now hold thy peace!' the lady said,
 'For as I say, so must it be.'

He has gotten a coat of the even cloth,
 And a pair of shoes of velvet green;
And till seven years were gane and past
 True Thomas on earth was never
  seen.

Part II. (Modernized from the Prophecies.)

When seven years were come and gane,
 The sun blink'd fair on pool and
  stream;
And Thomas lay on Huntlie bank,
 Like one awaken'd from a dream.

He heard the trampling of a steed,
 He saw the flash of armour flee,
And he beheld a gallant knight
 Come riding down by the Eildon-
  tree.

He was a stalwart knight, and strong;
 Of giant make he 'pear'd to be:
He stirr'd his horse, as he were wode,
 Wi' gilded spurs, of faushion free.

Says 'Well met, well met, true
  Thomas!
 Some uncouth ferlies show to me.'
Says 'Christ thee save, Corspatrick
  brave!
 Thrice welcome, good Dunbar, to me!

'Light down, light down, Corspatrick
  brave!
 And I will show thee curses three,
Shall gar fair Scotland greet and grane,
 And change the green to the black
  livery.

'A storm shall roar this very hour,
 From Ross's hills to Solway sea.'
'Ye lied, ye lied, ye warlock hoar!
 For the sun shines sweet on fauld
  and lee.'

He put his hand on the Earlie's head;
  He show'd him a rock beside the sea,
Where a king lay stiff beneath his
    steed,
  And steel-dight nobles wiped their
    ee.

'The neist curse lights on Branxton
    hills:
  By Flodden's high and heathery side,
Shall wave a banner red as blude,
  And chieftains throng wi' meikle
    pride.

'A Scottish King shall come full keen,
  The ruddy lion beareth he;
A feather'd arrow sharp, I ween,
  Shall make him wink and warre to
    see.

'When he is bloody, and all to-bledde,
  Thus to his men he still shall say—
" For God's sake, turn ye back again,
  And give yon southern folk a fray!
Why should I lose? the right is mine!
  My doom is not to die this day."

' Yet turn ye to the eastern hand,
  And woe and wonder ye sall see;
How forty thousand spearmen stand,
  Where yon rank river meets the sea.

' There shall the lion lose the gylte,
  And the libbards bear it clean away;
At Pinkyn Cleuch there shall be spilt
  Much gentil bluid that day.'

' Enough, enough, of curse and ban;
  Some blessings show thou now to me,
Or, by the faith o' my bodie,' Cors-
    patrick said,
  ' Ye shall rue the day ye e'er saw me!'

'The first of blessings I shall thee show,
  Is by a burn [1] that 's call'd of bread;
Where Saxon men shall tine the bow,
  And find their arrows lack the head.

Bannock-burn.

' Beside that brigg, out-ower that burn,
  Where the water bickereth bright
    and sheen,
Shall many a fallen courser spurn,
  And knights shall die in battle keen.

' Beside a headless cross of stone,
  The libbards there shall lose the gree:
The raven shall come, the erne shall go,
  And drink the Saxon bluid sae free.
The cross of stone they shall not know,
  So thick the corses there shall be.'

' But tell me now,' said brave Dunbar,
  ' True Thomas, tell now unto me,
What man shall rule the isle Britain,
  Even from the north to the southern
    sea?'

' A French Queen shall bear the son,
  Shall rule all Britain to the sea;
He of the Bruce's blood shall come,
  As near as in the ninth degree.

' The waters worship shall his race;
  Likewise the waves of the farthest
    sea;
For they shall ride over ocean wide,
  With hempen bridles, and horse of
    tree.'

PART III. (MODERN.)

WHEN seven years more were come
    and gone,
  Was war through Scotland spread,
And Ruberslaw show'd high Dunyon
  His beacon blazing red.

Then all by bonny Coldingknow,
  Pitch'd pallions took their room,
And crested helms, and spears a-rowe,
  Glanced gaily through the broom.

The Leader, rolling to the Tweed,
  Resounds the ensenzie;
They roused the deer from Cadden-
    head,
  To distant Torwoodlee.

The feast was spread in Ercildoune,
　In Learmont's high and ancient hall:
And there were knights of great re-
　nown,
　And ladies laced in pall.

Nor lacked they, while they sat at dine,
　The music nor the tale,
Nor goblets of the blood-red wine,
　Nor mantling quaighs of ale.

True Thomas rose with harp in hand.
　When as the feast was done:
(In minstrel strife in Fairy Land
　The elfin harp he won.)

Hush'd were the throng, both limb
　and tongue,
And harpers for envy pale;
And armed lords lean'd on their swords,
　And hearken'd to the tale.

In numbers high, the witching tale
　The prophet pour'd along;
No after bard might e'er avail
　Those numbers to prolong.

Yet fragments of the lofty strain
　Float down the tide of years,
As, buoyant on the stormy main,
　A parted wreck appears.

He sung King Arthur's Table Round:
　The Warrior of the Lake;
How courteous Gawaine met the
　wound,
　And bled for ladies' sake.

But chief, in gentle Tristrem's praise,
　The notes melodious swell;
Was none excell'd in Arthur's days,
　The knight of Lionelle.

For Marke, his cowardly uncle's right,
　A venom'd wound he bore;
When fierce Morholde he slew in fight
　Upon the Irish shore.

No art the poison might withstand;
　No medicine could be found,
Till lovely Isolde's lily hand
　Had probed the rankling wound.

With gentle hand and soothing tongue
　She bore the leech's part;
And, while she o'er his sick-bed hung,
　He paid her with his heart.

O fatal was the gift, I ween!
　For, doom'd in evil tide,
The maid must be rude Cornwall's
　queen,
　His cowardly uncle's bride.

Their loves, their woes, the gifted bard
　In fairy tissue wove;
Where lords and knights and ladies
　bright
　In gay confusion strove.

The Garde Joyeuse amid the tale
　High rear'd its glittering head;
And Avalon's enchanted vale
　In all its wonders spread.

Brangwain was there, and Segramore,
　And fiend-born Merlin's gramarye;
Of that famed wizard's mighty lore,
　O who could sing but he?

Through many a maze the winning song
　In changeful passion led,
Till bent at length the listening throng
　O'er Tristrem's dying bed.

His ancient wounds their scars expand,
　With agony his heart is wrung:
O where is Isolde's lilye hand,
　And where her soothing tongue?

She comes! she comes! like flash of
　flame
　Can lovers' footsteps fly:
She comes! she comes! She only came
　To see her Tristrem die.

She saw him die; her latest sigh
　Join'd in a kiss his parting breath;
The gentlest pair that Britain bare
　United are in death.

There paused the harp: its lingering
　　sound
　Died slowly on the ear;
The silent guests still bent around,
　For still they seem'd to hear.

Then woe broke forth in murmurs
　　weak:
　Nor ladies heaved alone the sigh;
But, half ashamed, the rugged cheek
　Did many a gauntlet dry.

On Leader's stream and Learmont's
　　tower
　The mists of evening close;
In camp, in castle, or in bower
　Each warrior sought repose.

Lord Douglas in his lofty tent
　Dream'd o'er the woeful tale;
When footsteps light across the bent
　The warrior's ears assail.

He starts, he wakes: 'What, Richard,
　　ho!
　Arise, my page, arise!
What venturous wight at dead of night
　Dare step where Douglas lies?'

Then forth they rush'd: by Leader's
　　tide,
　A selcouth sight they see—
A hart and hind pace side by side,
　As white as snow on Fairnalie.

Beneath the moon with gesture proud
　They stately move and slow;
Nor scare they at the gathering crowd,
　Who marvel as they go.

To Learmont's tower a message sped,
　As fast as page might run;
And Thomas started from his bed,
　And soon his clothes did on.

First he woxe pale, and then woxe red!
　Never a word he spake but three;—
'My sand is run; my thread is spun;
　This sign regardeth me.'

The elfin harp his neck around,
　In minstrel guise, he hung;
And on the wind in doleful sound
　Its dying accents rung.

Then forth he went; yet turn'd him oft
　To view his ancient hall:
On the grey tower in lustre soft
　The autumn moonbeams fall;

And Leader's waves like silver sheen
　Danced shimmering in the ray;
In deepening mass, at distance seen,
　Broad Soltra's mountains lay.

'Farewell, my fathers' ancient tower!
　A long farewell,' said he:
'The scene of pleasure, pomp, or power
　Thou never more shalt be.

'To Learmont's name no foot of earth
　Shall here again belong,
And on thy hospitable hearth
　The hare shall leave her young.

'Adieu! adieu!' again he cried,
　All as he turn'd him roun'—
'Farewell to Leader's silver tide!
　Farewell to Ercildoune!'

The hart and hind approach'd the place,
　As lingering yet he stood;
And there, before Lord Douglas' face,
　With them he cross'd the flood.

Lord Douglas leap'd on his berry-
　　brown steed,
　And spurr'd him the Leader o'er;
But, though he rode with lightning
　　speed,
　He never saw them more.

Some said to hill, and some to glen,
　Their wondrous course had been;
But ne'er in haunts of living men
　Again was Thomas seen.

GLENFINLAS;

OR,

LORD RONALD'S CORONACH.

'For them the viewless forms of air obey,
  Their bidding heed, and at their beck repair;
They know what spirit brews the stormful day,
And heartless oft, like moody madness stare,
To see the phantom-train their secret work prepare.'

COLLINS.

O HONE a rie'! O hone a rie'!
  The pride of Albin's line is o'er,
And fall'n Glenartney's stateliest tree;
  We ne'er shall see Lord Ronald
      more!

O, sprung from great Macgillianore,
  The chief that never fear'd a foe,
How matchless was thy broad clay-
      more,
  How deadly thine unerring bow!

Well can the Saxon widows tell,
  How on the Teith's resounding shore
The boldest Lowland warriors fell,
  As down from Lenny's pass you bore.

But o'er his hills, in festal day,
  How blazed Lord Ronald's beltane-
      tree,
While youths and maids the light
      strathspey
  So nimbly danced with Highland
      glee!

Cheer'd by the strength of Ronald's
      shell,
  E'en age forgot his tresses hoar;
But now the loud lament we swell,
  O ne'er to see Lord Ronald more!

From distant isles a chieftain came,
  The joys of Ronald's halls to find,
And chase with him the dark-brown
      game,
  That bounds o'er Albin's hills of
      wind.

'Twas Moy; whom in Columba's isle
  The seer's prophetic spirit found,
As, with a minstrel's fire the while,
  He waked his harp's harmonious
      sound.

Full many a spell to him was known,
  Which wandering spirits shrink to
      hear;
And many a lay of potent tone,
  Was never meant for mortal ear.

For there, 'tis said, in mystic mood,
  High converse with the dead they
      hold,
And oft espy the fated shroud,
  That shall the future corpse enfold.

O so it fell, that on a day,
  To rouse the red deer from their den,
The Chiefs have ta'en their distant way,
  And scour'd the deep Glenfinlas glen.

No vassals wait their sports to aid,
  To watch their safety, deck their
      board;
Their simple dress the Highland plaid,
  Their trusty guard the Highland
      sword.

Three summer days, through brake
      and dell,
  Their whistling shafts successful
      flew;
And still, when dewy evening fell,
  The quarry to their hut they drew.

In grey Glenfinlas' deepest nook
  The solitary cabin stood,
Fast by Moneira's sullen brook,
  Which murmurs through that lonely
      wood.

Soft fell the night, the sky was calm,
  When three successive days had
      flown;
And summer mist in dewy balm
  Steep'd heathy bank and mossy
      stone.

The moon, half-hid in silvery flakes,
　　Afar her dubious radiance shed,
Quivering on Katrine's distant lakes.
　　And resting on Benledi's head.

Now in their hut, in social guise,
　　Their silvan fare the Chiefs enjoy ;
And pleasure laughs in Ronald's eyes,
　　As many a pledge he quaffs to Moy.

'What lack we here to crown our bliss,
　　While thus the pulse of joy beats
　　　high ?
What, but fair woman's yielding kiss,
　　Her panting breath and melting eye ?

'To chase the deer of yonder shades,
　　This morning left their father's pile
The fairest of our mountain maids,
　　The daughters of the proud Glengyle.

'Long have I sought sweet Mary's heart,
　　And dropp'd the tear, and heaved
　　　the sigh :
But vain the lover's wily art,
　　Beneath a sister's watchful eye.

' But thou mayst teach that guardian
　　　fair,
　　While far with Mary I have flown,
Of other hearts to cease her care,
　　And find it hard to guard her own.

'Touch but thy harp—thou soon shalt
　　　see
　　The lovely Flora of Glengyle,
Unmindful of her charge and me,
　　Hang on thy notes 'twixt tear and
　　　smile.

' Or, if she choose a melting tale,
　　All underneath the greenwood
　　　bough,
Will good Saint Oran's rule prevail,
　　Stern huntsman of the rigid brow ? '

'Since Enrick's fight, since Morna's
　　　death,
　　No more on me shall rapture rise,
Responsive to the panting breath,
　　Or yielding kiss, or melting eyes.

' E'en then, when o'er the heath of woe,
　　Where sunk my hopes of love and
　　　fame,
I bade my harp's wild wailings flow,
　　On me the Seer's sad spirit came.

' The last dread curse of angry heaven,
　　With ghastly sights and sounds of
　　　woe,
To dash each glimpse of joy, was given ;
　　The gift—the future ill to know.

' The bark thou saw'st yon summer morn
　　So gaily part from Oban's bay,
My eye beheld her dash'd and torn,
　　Far on the rocky Colonsay.

' Thy Fergus too, thy sister's son,—
　　Thou saw'st with pride the gallant's
　　　power,
As marching 'gainst the Lord of Downe
　　He left the skirts of huge Benmore.

' Thou only saw'st their tartans wave,
　　As down Benvoirlich's side they
　　　wound,
Heard'st but the pibroch answering
　　　brave
　　To many a target clanking round.

'I heard the groans, I mark'd the tears,
　　I saw the wound his bosom bore,
When on the serried Saxon spears
　　He pour'd his clan's resistless roar.

' And thou who bidst me think of bliss,
　　And bidst my heart awake to glee,
And court like thee the wanton kiss—
　　That heart, O Ronald, bleeds for thee !

' I see the death-damps chill thy brow ;
　　I hear thy Warning Spirit cry ;
The corpse-lights dance ! they're gone !
　　　and now—
　　No more is given to gifted eye ! '

' Alone enjoy thy dreary dreams,
　　Sad prophet of the evil hour !
Say, should we scorn joy's transient
　　　beams,
　　Because to-morrow's storm may lour?

'Or false or sooth thy words of woe,
  Clangillian's Chieftain ne'er shall
    fear;
His blood shall bound at rapture's glow,
  Though doom'd to stain the Saxon
    spear.

'E'en now, to meet me in yon dell,
  My Mary's buskins brush the dew.'
He spoke, nor bade the Chief farewell,
  But called his dogs, and gay with-
    drew.

Within an hour return'd each hound;
  In rush'd the rousers of the deer;
They howl'd in melancholy sound,
  Then closely couch'd beside the
    Seer.

No Ronald yet—though midnight
    came,
  And sad were Moy's prophetic
    dreams,
As, bending o'er the dying flame,
  He fed the watch-fire's quivering
    gleams.

Sudden the hounds erect their ears,
  And sudden cease their moaning
    howl;
Close press'd to Moy, they mark their
    fears
  By shivering limbs and stifled growl.

Untouch'd, the harp began to ring,
  As softly, slowly, oped the door;
And shook responsive every string,
  As, light, a footstep press'd the floor.

And by the watch-fire's glimmering
    light,
  Close by the minstrel's side was seen
An huntress maid in beauty bright,
  All dropping wet her robes of green.

All dropping wet her garments seem;
  Chill'd was her cheek, her bosom bare,
As, bending o'er the dying gleam,
  She wrung the moisture from her
    hair.

With maiden blush, she softly said,
  'O gentle huntsman, hast thou seen,
In deep Glenfinlas' moonlight glade,
  A lovely maid in vest of green:

'With her a Chief in Highland pride;
  His shoulders bear the hunter's bow,
The mountain dirk adorns his side,
  Far on the wind his tartans flow?'

'And who art thou? and who are they?'
  All ghastly gazing, Moy replied:
'And why, beneath the moon's pale ray,
  Dare ye thus roam Glenfinlas' side?'

'Where wild Loch Katrine pours her
    tide,
  Blue, dark, and deep, round many
    an isle,
Our father's towers o'erhang her side,
  The castle of the bold Glengyle.

'To chase the dun Glenfinlas deer
  Our woodland course this morn we
    bore,
And haply met, while wandering here,
  The son of great Macgillianore.

'O aid me, then, to seek the pair,
  Whom, loitering in the woods, I
    lost;
Alone, I dare not venture there,
  Where walks, they say, the shrieking
    ghost.'

'Yes, many a shrieking ghost walks
    there;
  Then, first, my own sad vow to keep,
Here will I pour my midnight prayer,
  Which still must rise when mortals
    sleep.'

'O first, for pity's gentle sake,
  Guide a lone wanderer on her way!
For I must cross the haunted brake,
  And reach my father's towers ere
    day.'

'First, three times tell each Ave-bead,
  And thrice a Pater-noster say,
Then kiss with me the holy rede;
  So shall we safely wend our way.'

'O shame to knighthood, strange and
    foul!
Go, doff the bonnet from thy brow,
And shroud thee in the monkish cowl,
  Which best befits thy sullen vow.

'Not so, by high Dunlathmon's fire,
  Thy heart was froze to love and joy,
When gaily rung thy raptured lyre
  To wanton Morna's melting eye.'

Wild stared the minstrel's eyes of
    flame,
  And high his sable locks arose,
And quick his colour went and came,
  As fear and rage alternate rose.

'And thou! when by the blazing oak
I lay, to her and love resign'd,
Say, rode ye on the eddying smoke,
  Or sail'd ye on the midnight wind?

'Not thine a race of mortal blood,
  Nor old Glengyle's pretended line;
Thy dame, the Lady of the Flood—
  Thy sire, the Monarch of the Mine.'

He mutter'd thrice Saint Oran's rhyme,
  And thrice Saint Fillan's powerful
    prayer;
Then turn'd him to the eastern clime,
  And sternly shook his coal-black hair.

And, bending o'er his harp, he flung
  His wildest witch-notes on the wind;
And loud and high and strange they
    rung,
  As many a magic change they find.

Tall wax'd the Spirit's altering form,
  Till to the roof her stature grew;
Then, mingling with the rising storm,
  With one wild yell away she flew.

Rain beats, hail rattles, whirlwinds
    tear:
  The slender hut in fragments flew;
But not a lock of Moy's loose hair
  Was waved by wind, or wet by dew.

Wild mingling with the howling gale,
  Loud bursts of ghastly laughter rise;
High o'er the minstrel's head they sail,
  And die amid the northern skies.

The voice of thunder shook the wood,
  As ceased the more than mortal yell;
And, spattering foul, a shower of blood
  Upon the hissing firebrands fell.

Next dropp'd from high a mangled arm;
  The fingers strain'd an half-drawn
    blade:
And last, the life-blood streaming warm,
  Torn from the trunk, a gasping head.

Oft o'er that head, in battling field,
  Stream'd the proud crest of high
    Benmore;
That arm the broad claymore could
    wield,
  Which dyed the Teith with Saxon
    gore.

Woe to Moneira's sullen rills!
  Woe to Glenfinlas dreary glen!
There never son of Albin's hills
  Shall draw the hunter's shaft agen!

E'en the tired pilgrim's burning feet
  At noon shall shun that sheltering
    den,
Lest, journeying in their rage, he meet
  The wayward Ladies of the Glen.

And we—behind the Chieftain's shield
  No more shall we in safety dwell;
None leads the people to the field—
  And we the loud lament must swell.

O hone a rie'! O hone a rie'!
  The pride of Albin's line is o'er!
And fall'n Glenartney's stateliest tree;
  We ne'er shall see Lord Ronald
    more!

Y

THE EVE OF SAINT JOHN.

THE Baron of Smaylho'me rose with day,
  He spurr'd his courser on,
Without stop or stay, down the rocky way,
  That leads to Brotherstone.

He went not with the bold Buccleuch,
  His banner broad to rear ;
He went not 'gainst the English yew
  To lift the Scottish spear.

Yet his plate-jack was braced, and his helmet was laced,
  And his vaunt-brace of proof he wore ;
At his saddle-gerthe was a good steel sperthe,
  Full ten pound weight and more.

The Baron return'd in three days' space,
  And his looks were sad and sour ;
And weary was his courser's pace,
  As he reach'd his rocky tower.

He came not from where Ancram Moor
  Ran red with English blood ;
Where the Douglas true and the bold Buccleuch
  'Gainst keen Lord Evers stood.

Yet was his helmet hack'd and hew'd,
  His acton pierced and tore,
His axe and his dagger with blood imbrued,—
  But it was not English gore.

He lighted at the Chapellage,
  He held him close and still ;
And he whistled thrice for his little foot-page,
  His name was English Will.

' Come thou hither, my little foot-page,
  Come hither to my knee ;
Though thou art young, and tender of age,
  I think thou art true to me.

' Come, tell me all that thou hast seen,
  And look thou tell me true !
Since I from Smaylho'me tower have been,
  What did thy lady do ?'

' My lady each night sought the lonely light
  That burns on the wild Watchfold ;
For, from height to height, the beacons bright
  Of the English foemen told.

' The bittern clamour'd from the moss,
  The wind blew loud and shrill ;
Yet the craggy pathway she did cross
  To the eiry Beacon Hill.

' I watch'd her steps, and silent came
  Where she sat her on a stone ;
No watchman stood by the dreary flame,
  It burnèd all alone.

' The second night I kept her in sight
  Till to the fire she came,
And, by Mary's might ! an armed Knight
  Stood by the lonely flame.

' And many a word that warlike lord
  Did speak to my lady there ;
But the rain fell fast, and loud blew the blast,
  And I heard not what they were.

' The third night there the sky was fair,
  And the mountain-blast was still,
As again I watch'd the secret pair
  On the lonesome Beacon Hill.

' And I heard her name the midnight hour,
  And name this holy eve,
And say "Come this night to thy lady's bower ;
  Ask no bold Baron's leave.

'"He lifts his spear with the bold Buccleuch ;
  His lady is all alone ;
The door she'll undo to her knight so true
  On the eve of good Saint John."

'"I cannot come, I must not come,
  I dare not come to thee ;
On the eve of Saint John I must wander alone,
  In thy bower I may not be."

'"Now out on thee, fainthearted knight !
  Thou shouldst not say me nay ;
For the eve is sweet, and when lovers meet
  Is worth the whole summer's day.

'"And I'll chain the blood-hound, and the warder shall not sound,
And rushes shall be strew'd on the stair ;
So, by the black rood-stone, and by holy Saint John,
  I conjure thee, my love, to be there !"

'"Though the blood-hound be mute, and the rush beneath my foot,
And the warder his bugle should not blow,
Yet there sleepeth a priest in the chamber to the east,
  And my footstep he would know.

'"O fear not the priest, who sleepeth to the east,
  For to Dryburgh the way he has ta'en ;
And there to say mass, till three days do pass,
  For the soul of a knight that is slayne."

'He turn'd him around, and grimly he frown'd,
  Then he laugh'd right scornfully—
"He who says the mass-rite for the soul of that knight
  May as well say mass for me.

'"At the lone midnight hour, when bad spirits have power,
  In thy chamber will I be."
With that he was gone, and my lady left alone,
  And no more did I see.'

Then changed, I trow, was that bold Baron's brow,
  From the dark to the blood-red high—
'Now tell me the mien of the knight thou hast seen,
  For, by Mary, he shall die ! '

'His arms shone full bright in the beacon's red light ;
  His plume it was scarlet and blue ;
On his shield was a hound in a silver leash bound,
  And his crest was a branch of the yew.'

'Thou liest, thou liest, thou little foot-page,
  Loud dost thou lie to me !
For that knight is cold, and low laid in the mould,
  All under the Eildon-tree.'

'Yet hear but my word, my noble lord !
  For I heard her name his name ;
And that lady bright, she called the knight
  Sir Richard of Coldinghame.'

The bold Baron's brow then changed, I trow,
  From high blood-red to pale—
'The grave is deep and dark, and the corpse is stiff and stark,
  So I may not trust thy tale.

'Where fair Tweed flows round holy Melrose,
  And Eildon slopes to the plain,
Full three nights ago, by some secret foe,
  That gay gallant was slain.

'The varying light deceived thy sight,
    And the wild winds drown'd the
        name;
For the Dryburgh bells ring and the
        white monks do sing
    For Sir Richard of Coldinghame !'

He pass'd the court-gate, and he oped
        the tower-grate,
    And he mounted the narrow stair
To the bartizan-seat, where, with
        maids that on her wait
    He found his lady fair.

That lady sat in mournful mood,
    Look'd over hill and vale,
Over Tweed's fair flood and Mertoun's
        wood
    And all down Teviotdale.

'Now hail, now hail, thou lady bright !'
'Now hail, thou Baron true !
What news, what news from Ancram
        fight?
    What news from the bold Buc-
        cleuch?'

'The Ancram Moor is red with gore,
    For many a southron fell;
And Buccleuch has charged us ever-
        more
    To watch our beacons well.'

The lady blush'd red, but nothing she
        said;
    Nor added the Baron a word .
Then she stepp'd down the stair to
        her chamber fair,
    And so did her moody lord.

In sleep the lady mourn'd, and the
        Baron toss'd and turn'd,
    And oft to himself he said,
'The worms around him creep, and
        his bloody grave is deep—
    It cannot give up the dead !'

It was near the ringing of matin-bell,
    The night was wellnigh done,
When a heavy sleep on that Baron fell,
    On the eve of good Saint John.

The lady look'd through the chamber
        fair,
    By the light of a dying flame;
And she was aware of a knight stood
        there—
    Sir Richard of Coldinghame !

'Alas! away, away !' she cried,
    'For the holy Virgin's sake !'
'Lady, I know who sleeps by thy side ;
    But, lady, he will not awake.

'By Eildon-tree, for long nights three,
    In bloody grave have I lain ;
The mass and the death-prayer are
        said for me,
    But, lady, they are said in vain.

'By the Baron's brand, near Tweed's
        fair strand,
    Most foully slain I fell;
And my restless sprite on the beacon's
        height
    For a space is doom'd to dwell.

'At our trysting-place, for a certain
        space,
    I must wander to and fro ;
But I had not had power to come to
        thy bower
    Had'st thou not conjured me so.'

Love master'd fear; her brow she
        cross'd—
    'How, Richard, hast thou sped ?
And art thou saved, or art thou lost?'
    The vision shook his head !

'Who spilleth life shall forfeit life;
    So bid thy lord believe :
That lawless love is guilt above,
    This awful sign receive.'

He laid his left palm on an oaken beam,
  His right upon her hand—
The lady shrunk, and fainting sunk,
  For it scorch'd like a fiery brand.

The sable score of fingers four
  Remains on that board impress'd;
And for evermore that lady wore
  A covering on her wrist.

There is a nun in Dryburgh bower,
  Ne'er looks upon the sun;
There is a monk in Melrose tower,
  He speaketh word to none;

That nun who ne'er beholds the day,
  That monk who speaks to none—
That nun was Smaylho'me's Lady gay,
  That monk the bold Baron.

—◦—

CADYOW CASTLE.

ADDRESSED TO

THE RIGHT HONOURABLE

LADY ANNE HAMILTON.

WHEN princely Hamilton's abode
  Ennobled Cadyow's Gothic towers,
The song went round, the goblet flow'd,
  And revel sped the laughing hours.

Then, thrilling to the harp's gay sound,
  So sweetly rung each vaulted wall,
And echoed light the dancer's bound,
  As mirth and music cheer'd the hall.

But Cadyow's towers, in ruins laid,
  And vaults, by ivy mantled o'er,
Thrill to the music of the shade,
  Or echo Evan's hoarser roar.

Yet still of Cadyow's faded fame
  You bid me tell a minstrel tale,
And tune my harp of Border frame
  On the wild banks of Evandale.

For thou, from scenes of courtly pride,
  From pleasure's lighter scenes,
    canst turn,
To draw oblivion's pall aside,
  And mark the long-forgotten urn.

Then, noble maid! at thy command,
  Again the crumbled halls shall rise;
Lo! as on Evan's banks we stand,
  The past returns—the present flies.

Where with the rock's wood cover'd
    side
  Were blended late the ruins green,
Rise turrets in fantastic pride,
  And feudal banners flaunt between.

Where the rude torrent's brawling
    course
  Was shagg'd with thorn and tang-
    ling sloe,
The ashler buttress braves its force,
  And ramparts frown in 'battled row.

'Tis night: the shade of keep and spire
  Obscurely dance on Evan's stream;
And on the wave the warder's fire
  Is chequering the moonlight beam.

Fades slow their light—the east is grey;
  The weary warder leaves his tower;
Steeds snort, uncoupled stag-hounds
    bay,
  And merry hunters quit the bower.

The drawbridge falls—they hurry
    out—
  Clatters each plank and swinging
    chain,
As, dashing o'er, the jovial rout
  Urge the shy steed, and slack the
    rein.

First of his troop the Chief[1] rode on;
  His shouting merry-men throng
    behind;
The steed of princely Hamilton
  Was fleeter than the mountain wind.

---

1 The head of the family of Hamilton, at this period,
was James, Earl of Arran, Duke of Chatelherault in
France, and first peer of the Scottish realm. In 1569
he was appointed by Queen Mary her lieutenant-
general in Scotland.

From the thick copse the roebucks
    bound,
  The startled red-deer scuds the
    plain,
For the hoarse bugle's warrior-sound
  Has roused their mountain haunts
    again.

Through the huge oaks of Evandale,
  Whose limbs a thousand years have
    worn,
What sullen roar comes down the
    gale
  And drowns the hunter's pealing
    horn?

Mightiest of all the beasts of chase
  That roam in woody Caledon,
Crashing the forest in his race,
  The Mountain Bull comes thunder-
    ing on.

Fierce on the hunter's quiver'd band
  He rolls his eyes of swarthy glow,
Spurns with black hoof and horn the
    sand,
  And tosses high his mane of snow.

Aim'd well the Chieftain's lance has
    flown—
  Struggling in blood the savage lies;
His roar is sunk in hollow groan—
  Sound, merry huntsmen! sound
    the pryse.

'Tis noon: against the knotted oak
  The hunters rest the idle spear;
Curls through the trees the slender
    smoke,
  Where yeomen dight the woodland
    cheer.

Proudly the Chieftain mark'd his clan,
  On greenwood lap all careless
    thrown,
Yet miss'd his eye the boldest man
  That bore the name of Hamilton.

'Why fills not Bothwellhaugh his
    place,
  Still wont our weal and woe to share?
Why comes he not our sport to grace?
  Why shares he not our hunter's
    fare?'

Stern Claud replied with darkening
    face
  (Grey Paisley's haughty lord was he)
'At merry feast or buxom chase
  No more the warrior wilt thou see.

'Few suns have set since Woodhouse-
    lee
  Saw Bothwellhaugh's bright goblets
    foam,
When to his hearths in social glee
  The war-worn soldier turn'd him
    home.

'There, wan from her maternal throes,
  His Margaret, beautiful and mild,
Sate in her bower, a pallid rose,
  And peaceful nursed her new-born
    child.

'O change accursed! past are those
    days;
  False Murray's ruthless spoilers
    came,
And, for the hearth's domestic blaze,
  Ascends destruction's volumed
    flame.

'What sheeted phantom wanders wild,
  Where mountain Eske through
    woodland flows,
Her arms enfold a shadowy child—
  Oh! is it she, the pallid rose?

'The wilder'd traveller sees her glide,
  And hears her feeble voice with awe;
"Revenge," she cries, "on Murray's
    pride!
  And woe for injured Bothwell-
    haugh!"'

He ceased; and cries of rage and grief
  Burst mingling from the kindred
    band,
And half arose the kindling Chief,
  And half unsheathed his Arran brand.

But who, o'er bush, o'er stream and
    rock,
  Rides headlong, with resistless
    speed,
Whose bloody poniard's frantic stroke
  Drives to the leap his jaded steed,

Whose cheek is pale, whose eyeballs
    glare,
  As one some vision'd sight that saw,
Whose hands are bloody, loose his
    hair?—
  'Tis he! 'tis he! 'tis Bothwellhaugh.

From gory selle, and reeling steed,
  Sprung the fierce horseman with a
    bound,
And, reeking from the recent deed,
  He dash'd his carbine on the ground.

Sternly he spoke: ''Tis sweet to hear
  In good greenwood the bugle blown,
But sweeter to Revenge's ear,
  To drink a tyrant's dying groan.

'Your slaughter'd quarry proudly
    trode,
  At dawning morn, o'er dale and
    down,
But prouder base-born Murray rode
  Through old Linlithgow's crowded
    town.

'From the wild Border's humbled side,
  In haughty triumph marchèd he,
While Knox relax'd his bigot pride
  And smiled the traitorous pomp to
    see.

'But can stern Power, with all his
    vaunt,
  Or Pomp, with all her courtly glare,
The settled heart of Vengeance daunt,
  Or change the purpose of Despair?

'With hackbut bent, my secret stand,
  Dark as the purposed deed, I chose,
And mark'd where, mingling in his
    band,
  Troop'd Scottish pikes and English
    bows.

'Dark Morton, girt with many a spear,
  Murder's foul minion, led the van;
And clash'd their broadswords in the
    rear
  The wild Macfarlanes' plaided clan.

'Glencairn and stout Parkhead were
    nigh,
  Obsequious at their Regent's rein,
And haggard Lindesay's iron eye,
  That saw fair Mary weep in vain.

''Mid pennon'd spears, a steely grove,
  Proud Murray's plumage floated
    high;
Scarce could his trampling charger
    move,
  So close the minions crowded nigh.

'From the raised vizor's shade, his eye
  Dark-rolling glanced the ranks along,
And his steel truncheon, waved on
    high,
  Seem'd marshalling the iron throng.

'But yet his sadden'd brow confess'd
  A passing shade of doubt and awe;
Some fiend was whispering in his
    breast;
  "Beware of injured Bothwell-
    haugh!"

'—The death-shot parts! the charger
    springs,
  Wild rises tumult's startling roar,
And Murray's plumy helmet rings—
  Rings on the ground, to rise no more.

'What joy the raptured youth can feel
  To hear her love the loved one tell!
Or he who broaches on his steel
  The wolf by whom his infant fell!

'But dearer to my injured eye
  To see in dust proud Murray roll;
And mine was ten times trebled joy,
  To hear him groan his felon soul.

' My Margaret's spectre glided near,
  With pride her bleeding victim saw,
And shriek'd in his death-deafen'd ear
" Remember injured Bothwellhaugh!"

' Then speed thee, noble Chatlerault,
  Spread to the wind thy banner'd
    tree!
Each warrior bend his Clydesdale
    bow! —
  "Murray is fall'n, and Scotland
    free!"'

Vaults every warrior to his steed;
  Loud bugles join their wild acclaim:
' Murray is fall'n, and Scotland freed!
  Couch, Arran! couch thy spear of
    flame!'

But, see! the minstrel vision fails—
  The glimmering spears are seen no
    more;
The shouts of war die on the gales,
  Or sink in Evan's lonely roar.

For the loud bugle, pealing high,
  The blackbird whistles down the
    vale,
And sunk in ivied ruins lie
  The banner'd towers of Evandale.

For Chiefs, intent on bloody deed,
  And Vengeance shouting o'er the
    slain,
Lo! high-born Beauty rules the steed,
  Or graceful guides the silken rein.

And long may Peace and Pleasure own
  The maids who list the minstrel's
    tale;
Nor e'er a ruder guest be known
  On the fair banks of Evandale!

THE GRAY BROTHER.

THE Pope he was saying the high,
    high mass,
  All on Saint Peter's day,
With the power to him given, by the
    saints in heaven,
  To wash men's sins away.

The Pope he was saying the blessed
    mass,
  And the people kneel'd around,
And from each man's soul his sins did
    pass,
  As he kiss'd the holy ground.

And all, among the crowded throng,
  Was still, both limb and tongue,
While, through vaulted roof and aisles
    aloof,
  The holy accents rung.

At the holiest word he quiver'd for fear,
  And falter'd in the sound,
And, when he would the chalice rear,
  He dropp'd it to the ground.

' The breath of one of evil deed
  Pollutes our sacred day;
He has no portion in our creed,
  No part in what I say.

' A being, whom no blessed word
  To ghostly peace can bring;
A wretch, at whose approach abhorr'd,
  Recoils each holy thing.

' Up, up, unhappy! haste, arise!
  My adjuration fear!
I charge thee not to stop my voice,
  Nor longer tarry here!'

Amid them all a pilgrim kneel'd,
  In gown of sackcloth grey;
Far journeying from his native field,
  He first saw Rome that day.

For forty days and nights so drear,
  I ween he had not spoke,
And, save with bread and water clear,
  His fast he ne'er had broke.

Amid the penitential flock,
  Seem'd none more bent to pray;
But, when the Holy Father spoke,
  He rose and went his way.

Again unto his native land
  His weary course he drew,
To Lothian's fair and fertile strand,
  And Pentland's mountains blue.

His unblest feet his native seat,
  'Mid Eske's fair woods, regain;
Thro' woods more fair no stream more sweet
  Rolls to the eastern main.

And lords to meet the pilgrim came,
  And vassals bent the knee;
For all 'mid Scotland's chiefs of fame,
  Was none more famed than he.

And boldly for his country still
  In battle he had stood,
Ay, even when on the banks of Till
  Her noblest pour'd their blood.

Sweet are the paths, O passing sweet,
  By Eske's fair streams that run,
O'er airy steep, through copsewood deep,
  Impervious to the sun;

There the rapt poet's step may rove
  And yield the muse the day,
There Beauty led by timid Love
  May shun the tell-tale ray,—

From that fair dome where suit is paid
  By blast of bugle free,
To Auchendinny's hazel glade
  And haunted Woodhouselee.

Who knows not Melville's beechy grove,
  And Roslin's rocky glen,
Dalkeith which all the virtues love,
  And classic Hawthornden?

Yet never a path, from day to day,
  The pilgrim's footsteps range,
Save by the solitary way
  To Burndale's ruin'd grange.

A woful place was that, I ween,
  As sorrow could desire;
For nodding to the fall was each crumbling wall,
  And the roof was scathed with fire.

It fell upon a summer's eve,
  While, on Carnethy's head,
The last faint gleams of the sun's low beams
  Had streak'd the grey with red;

And the convent bell did vespers tell
  Newbattle's oaks among,
And mingled with the solemn knell
  Our Ladye's evening song:

The heavy knell, the choir's faint swell,
  Came slowly down the wind,
And on the pilgrim's ear they fell,
  As his wonted path he did find.

Deep sunk in thought, I ween, he was,
  Nor ever raised his eye,
Until he came to that dreary place,
  Which did all in ruins lie.

He gazed on the walls so scathed with fire,
  With many a bitter groan—
And there was aware of a Gray Friar,
  Resting him on a stone.

'Now, Christ thee save!' said the Gray Brother;
  'Some pilgrim thou seemest to be.'
But in sore amaze did Lord Albert gaze,
  Nor answer again made he.

'O come ye from east, or come ye
 from west,
 Or bring reliques from over the sea?
Or come ye from the shrine of
 Saint James the divine,
 Or Saint John of Beverley?'

'I come not from the shrine of
 Saint James the divine,
 Nor bring reliques from over the sea;
I bring but a curse from our father,
 the Pope,
 Which for ever will cling to me.'

'Now, woful pilgrim, say not so!
 But kneel thee down to me,
And shrive thee so clean of thy deadly
 sin,
 That absolvèd thou mayst be.'

'And who art thou, thou Gray Brother,
 That I should shrive to thee,
When He, to whom are given the keys
 of earth and heaven,
 Has no power to pardon me?'

'O I am sent from a distant clime,
 Five thousand miles away,
And all to absolve a foul foul crime,
 Done *here* ' twixt night and day.'

The pilgrim kneel'd him on the sand,
 And thus began his saye—
When on his neck an ice-cold hand
 Did that Gray Brother laye—

.   .   .   .   .   .

END OF IMITATIONS OF THE ANCIENT BALLAD.

Notes to Imitations of the Ancient Ballad.

◆◆

THOMAS THE RHYMER.

INTRODUCTORY NOTE.

PART I.—ANCIENT.

FEW personages are so renowned in tradition as Thomas of Ercildoune, known by the appellation of *The Rhymer*. Uniting, or supposed to unite, in his person, the powers of poetical composition, and of vaticination, his memory, even after the lapse of five hundred years, is regarded with veneration by his countrymen. To give anything like a certain history of this remarkable man would be indeed difficult; but the curious may derive some satisfaction from the particulars here brought together.

It is agreed on all hands that the residence, and probably the birthplace, of this ancient bard, was Ercildoune, a village situated upon the Leader, two miles above its junction with the Tweed. The ruins of an ancient tower are still pointed out as the Rhymer's castle. The uniform tradition bears, that his sirname was Lermont, or Learmont; and that the appellation of *The Rhymer* was conferred on him in consequence of his poetical compositions. There remains, nevertheless, some doubt upon the subject. In a charter, which is subjoined at length [1], the son of our poet designed himself 'Thomas of Ercildoun, son and heir of Thomas Rymour of Ercildoun,' which seems to imply that the father did not bear the hereditary name of Learmont; or, at least, was better known and distinguished by the epithet which he had acquired by his personal accomplishments. I must, however, remark that, down to a very late period, the practice of distinguishing the parties, even in formal writings, by the epithets which had been bestowed on them from personal circumstances, instead of the proper sirnames of their families, was common, and indeed necessary, among the Border clans. So early

as the end of the thirteenth century, when sirnames were hardly introduced in Scotland, this custom must have been universal. There is, therefore, nothing inconsistent in supposing our poet's name to have been actually Learmont, although, in this charter, he is distinguished by the popular appellation of *The Rhymer*.

We are better able to ascertain the period at which Thomas of Ercildoune lived, being the latter end of the thirteenth century. I am inclined to place his death a little farther back than Mr. Pinkerton, who supposes that he was alive in 1300 (*List of Scottish Poets*), which is hardly, I think, consistent with the charter already quoted, by which his son, in 1299, for himself and his heirs, conveys to the convent of the Trinity of Soltra, the tenement which he possessed by inheritance (*hereditarie*) in Ercildoune, with all claim which he or his predecessors could pretend thereto. From this we may infer that the Rhymer was now dead, since we find the son disposing of the family property. Still, however, the argument of the learned historian will remain unimpeached as to the time of the poet's birth. For if, as we learn from Barbour, his prophecies were held in reputation as early as 1306, when Bruce slew the Red Cummin, the sanctity, and (let me add to Mr. Pinkerton's words) the uncertainty of antiquity, must have already involved his character and writings. In a charter of Peter de Haga de Bemersyde, which unfortunately wants a date, the Rhymer, a near neighbour, and, if we may trust tradition, a friend of the family, appears as a witness.—*Chartulary of Melrose.*

It cannot be doubted that Thomas of Ercildoune was a remarkable and important person in his own time, since, very shortly after his death, we find him celebrated as a prophet and as a poet. Whether he himself made any pretensions to the first of these characters, or whether it was gratuitously conferred upon him by the credulity of pos-

---

[1] Note I, p. 680.

terity, it seems difficult to decide. If we may believe Mackenzie, Learmont only versified the prophecies delivered by Eliza, an inspired nun of a convent at Haddington. But of this there seems not to be the most distant proof. On the contrary, all ancient authors, who quote the Rhymer's prophecies, uniformly suppose them to have been emitted by himself. Thus, in Winton's *Chronicle*—

> ' Of this fycht quilum spak Thomas
> Of Ersyldoune, that sayd in derne,
> There suld meit stalwartly, starke and sterne.
> He sayd it in his prophecy ;
> But how he wist it was *ferly*.'
> Book VIII, chap. 32.

There could have been no *ferly* (marvel), in Winton's eyes at least, how Thomas came by his knowledge of future events, had he ever heard of the inspired nun of Haddington, which, it cannot be doubted, would have been a solution of the mystery much to the taste of the Prior of Lochleven.

Whatever doubts, however, the learned might have as to the source of the Rhymer's prophetic skill, the vulgar had no hesitation to ascribe the whole to the intercourse between the bard and the Queen of Faëry. The popular tale bears that Thomas was carried off, at an early age, to the Fairy Land, where he acquired all the knowledge which made him afterwards so famous. After seven years' residence, he was permitted to return to the earth, to enlighten and astonish his countrymen by his prophetic powers ; still, however, remaining bound to return to his royal mistress, when she should intimate her pleasure. Accordingly, while Thomas was making merry with his friends in the Tower of Ercildoune, a person came running in, and told, with marks of fear and astonishment, that a hart and hind had left the neighbouring forest, and were, composedly and slowly, parading the street of the village. The prophet instantly arose, left his habitation, and followed the wonderful animals to the forest, whence he was never seen to return. According to the popular belief, he still 'drees his weird' in Fairy Land, and is one day expected to revisit earth. In the meanwhile, his memory is held in the most profound respect. The Eildon-tree, from beneath the shade of which he delivered his prophecies, now no longer exists ; but the spot is marked by a large stone, called Eildon-tree Stone. A neighbouring rivulet takes the name of the Bogle Burn (Goblin Brook) from the Rhymer's supernatural visitants. The veneration paid to his dwelling-place even attached itself in some degree to a person, who within the memory of man, chose to set up his residence in the ruins of Learmont's tower. The name of this man was Murray, a kind of herbalist ; who, by dint of some knowledge in simples, the possession of a musical clock, an electrical machine, and a stuffed alligator, added to a supposed communication with Thomas the Rhymer, lived for many years in very good credit as a wizard.

It seemed to the Editor unpardonable to dismiss a person so important in Border tradition as the Rhymer, without some farther notice than a simple commentary upon the ancient ballad. It is given from a copy, obtained from a lady residing not far from Ercildoune, corrected and enlarged by one in Mrs. Brown's MSS. The former copy, however, as might be expected, is far more minute as to local description. To this old tale the Editor has ventured to add a Second Part, consisting of a kind of cento, from the printed prophecies vulgarly ascribed to the Rhymer ; and a Third Part, entirely modern, founded upon the tradition of his having returned with the hart and hind to the Land of Faëry. To make his peace with the more severe antiquaries, the Editor has furnished the Second Part with some remarks on Learmont's prophecies.

Part II.—Adapted.

The prophecies ascribed to Thomas of Ercildoune have been the principal means of securing to him remembrance 'amongst the sons of his people.' The author of *Sir Tristrem* would long ago have joined, in the vale of oblivion, 'Clerk of Tranent, who wrote the adventures of *Schir Gawain*,' if, by good hap, the same current of ideas respecting antiquity, which causes Virgil to be regarded as a mag'cian by the Lazaroni of Naples, had not exalted the bard of Ercildoune to the prophetic character. Perhaps, indeed, he himself affected it during his life. We know at least, for certain, that a belief in his supernatural knowledge was current soon after his death. His prophecies are alluded to by Barbour by Winton, and by Henry the Minstrel, or *Blind Harry*, as he is usually termed. None of these authors, however, give the words of any of the Rhymer's vaticinations, but merely narrate, historically, his having predicted the events of which they speak. The earliest of the prophecies ascribed to him, which is now extant, is quoted by Mr. Pinkerton from a MS. It is supposed to be a response from Thomas of Ercildoune to a question from the heroic Countess of March, renowned for the defence of the castle of Dunbar against the English, and termed, in the familiar dialect of her time, *Black Agnes* of Dunbar. This prophecy is remarkable, in so far as it bears very little resemblance to any verses published in the printed copy of the Rhymer's supposed prophecies. The verses are as follows :—

> ' *La Countesse de Donbar demande a Thomas de*
> *Essedoune quae t la guerre d'Escoce prendreit*
> *fyn. E yl i'a repoundy et dyt.*
>
> When man is mad a kyng of a capped man ;
> When man is levere other mones thyng than his owen
> When londe thouys forest, ant forest is felde ;
> When hares kendles o' the her'stane ;
> When Wyt and Wille werres togedere

When mon makes stables of kyrkes, and steles castels
    with stye;
When Rokesboroughe nys no burgh ant market is at
    Forwyleye;
When Bambourne is donged with dede men;
When men ledes men in ropes to buyen and to sellen;
When a quarter of whaty whete is chaunged for a colt
    of ten markes;
When prude (pride) prikes and pees is leyd in prisoun;
When a Scot ne me hym hude ase hare in forme that
    the English ne shall hym fynde;
When rycht ant wronge astente the togedere;
When laddes weddeth lovedies;
When Scottes flen so faste, that, for faute of shep, hy
    drowneth hemselve;
When shal this be?
Nouther in thine tyme ne in mine;
Ah comen ant gone
Withinne twenty winter ant one.'

    PINKERTON'S *Poems, from* MAITLAND'S *MSS.*
      quoting from Harl. Lib. 2253, f. 127.

As I have never seen the MS. from which
Mr. Pinkerton makes this extract, and as the
date of it is fixed by him (certainly one of the
most able antiquaries of our age) to the
reign of Edward I or II, it is with great
diffidence that I hazard a contrary opinion.
There can, however, I believe, be little doubt
that these prophetic verses are a forgery, and
not the production of our Thomas the Rhymer.
But I am inclined to believe them of a later
date than the reign of Edward I or II.
The gallant defence of the castle of Dunbar,
by Black Agnes, took place in the year 1337.
The Rhymer died previous to the year 1299
(see the charter, by his son, Note I, p. 680).
It seems, therefore, very improbable, that
the Countess of Dunbar could ever have
an opportunity of consulting Thomas the
Rhymer, since that would infer that she was
married, or at least engaged in state matters,
previous to 1299; whereas she is described as
a young, or a middle-aged woman, at the
period of her being besieged in the fortress,
which she so well defended. If the editor
might indulge a conjecture, he would suppose
that the prophecy was contrived for the
encouragement of the English invaders during
the Scottish wars; and that the names of the
Countess of Dunbar, and of Thomas of Ercildoune, were used for the greater credit of the
forgery. According to this hypothesis, it
seems likely to have been composed after the
siege of Dunbar, which had made the name
of the Countess well known, and consequently
in the reign of Edward III. The whole tendency of the prophecy is to aver that there
shall be no end of the Scottish war (concerning
which the question was proposed) till a final
conquest of the country by England, attended
by all the usual severities of war. 'When the
cultivated country shall become forest,' says
the prophecy;—'when the wild animals shall
inhabit the abode of men;—when Scots shall
not be able to escape the English, should
they crouch as hares in their form'—all these
denunciations seem to refer to the time of
Edward III, upon whose victories the prediction was probably founded. The mention of
the exchange betwixt a colt worth ten marks,

and a quarter of 'whaty [indifferent] wheat,'
seems to allude to the dreadful famine, about
the year 1388. The independence of Scotland
was, however, as impregnable to the mines of
superstition, as to the steel of our more powerful and more wealthy neighbours. The war
of Scotland is, thank God, at an end; but it
is ended without her people having either
crouched like hares in their form, or being
drowned in their flight, 'for faute of ships,'—
thank God for that too.—The prophecy
quoted in the preceding page is probably of
the same date, and intended for the same
purpose.
A minute search of the records of the time
would, probably, throw additional light upon
the allusions contained in these ancient
legends. Among various rhymes of prophetic
import, which are at this day current amongst
the people of Teviotdale, is one, supposed to
be pronounced by Thomas the Rhymer,
presaging the destruction of his habitation
and family:—

' The hare sall kittle [litter] on my hearth stane,
  And there will never be a Laird Learmont again.'

The first of these lines is obviously borrowed
from that in the MS. of the Harl. Library—
'When hares kendles o' the her'stane '—an
emphatic image of desolation. It is also
inaccurately quoted in the prophecy of Waldhave, published by Andro Hart, 1613:—

' This is a true talking that Thomas tells,
  The hare shall hirple on the hard [hearth] stane.'

Spottiswoode, an honest, but credulous
historian, seems to have been a firm believer
in the authenticity of the prophetic wares
vended in the name of Thomas of Ercildoune.
'The prophecies, yet extant in Scottish rhymes,
whereupon he was commonly called *Thomas
the Rhymer*, may justly be admired; having
foretold, so many ages before the union of
England and Scotland in the ninth degree of
the Bruce's blood, with the succession of
Bruce himself to the crown, being yet a child,
and other divers particulars, which the event
hath ratified and made good. Boethius, in his
story, relateth his prediction of King Alexander's death, and that he did foretel the same to
the Earl of March, the day before it fell out;
saying, "That before the next day at noon,
such a tempest should blow, as Scotland had
not felt for many years before." The next
morning, the day being clear, and no change
appearing in the air, the nobleman did
challenge Thomas of his saying, calling him
an impostor. He replied, that noon was not
yet passed. About which time a post came
to advertise the earl of the king his sudden
death. "Then," said Thomas, "this is the
tempest I foretold; and so it shall prove to
Scotland." Whence, or how, he had this knowledge, can hardly be affirmed; but sure it is,
that he did divine and answer truly of many
things to come.'—SPOTTISWOODE, p. 47.
Besides that notable voucher, Master Hector

Boece, the good archbishop might, had he been so minded, have referred to Fordun for the prophecy of King Alexander's death. That historian calls our bard '*ruralis ille vates.*'—FORDUN, lib. x, cap. 40.

What Spottiswoode calls 'the prophecies extant in Scottish rhyme,' are the metrical productions ascribed to the seer of Ercildoune, which, with many other compositions of the same nature, bearing the names of Bede, Merlin, Gildas, and other approved sooth-sayers, are contained in one small volume, published by Andro Hart, at Edinburgh, 1615. Nisbet the herald (who claims the prophet of Ercildoune as a brother-professor of his art, founding upon the various allegorical and emblematical allusions to heraldry) intimates the existence of some earlier copy of his pro-phecies than that of Andro Hart, which, how-ever, he does not pretend to have seen[1]. The late excellent Lord Hailes made these compo-sitions the subject of a dissertation, published in his *Remarks on the History of Scotland.* His attention is chiefly directed to the cele-brated prophecy of our bard, mentioned by Bishop Spottiswoode, bearing that the crowns of England and Scotland should be united in the person of a King, son of a French Queen, and related to the Bruce in the ninth degree. Lord Hailes plainly proves that this prophecy is perverted from its original purpose in order to apply it to the succession of James VI. The groundwork of the forgery is to be found in the prophecies of Berlington, con-tained in the same collection, and runs thus:—

'Of Bruce's left side shall spring out a leafe,
As neere as the ninth degree;
And shall be fleemed of faire Scotland,
In France farre beyond the sea.
And then shall come again ryding,
With eyes that many men may see.
At Aberladie he shall light,
With hempen helteres and horse of tre.

. . . .

However it happen for to fall,
The lyon shall be lord of all;
The French Quen shall bearre the sonne,
Shall rule all Britainne to the sea;
Ane from the Bruce's blood shal come also,
As neer as the ninth degree.

. . . .

Yet shal there come a keene knight over the salt sea,
A keene man of courage and bold man of armes;
A duke's son dowbled [i. e. dubbed], a born man in France,
That shall our mirths augment, and mend all our harmes;
After the date of our Lord 1513, and thrice three thereafter;
Which shall brooke all the broad isle to himself,
Between thirteen and thrice three the threip shall be ended,
The Saxons shall never recover after.'

There cannot be any doubt that this pro-phecy was intended to excite the confidence of the Scottish nation in the Duke of Albany, regent of Scotland, who arrived from France

[1] See Note III, p. 682.

in 1515, two years after the death of James IV in the fatal field of Flodden. The Regent was descended of Bruce by the left, i.e. by the female side, within the ninth degree. His mother was daughter of the Earl of Boulogne, his father banished from his country—'fleemit of fair Scotland.' His arrival must necessarily be by sea, and his landing was expected at Aberlady, in the Frith of Forth. He was a duke's son, dubbed knight; and nine years, from 1513, are allowed him by the pretended prophet for the accomplishment of the salva-tion of his country, and the exaltation of Scotland over her sister and rival. All this was a pious fraud, to excite the confidence and spirit of the country.

The prophecy, put in the name of our Thomas the Rhymer, as it stands in Hart's book, refers to a later period. The narrator meets the Rhymer *upon a land beside a lee,* who shows him many emblematical visions, described in no mean strain of poetry. They chiefly relate to the fields of Flodden and Pinkie, to the national distress which followed these defeats, and to future halcyon days, which are promised to Scotland. One quota-tion or two will be sufficient to establish this fully:—

'Our Scottish King sal come ful keene,
The red lyon beareth he;
A feddered arrow sharp, I ween,
Shall make him winke and warre to see.
Out of the field he shall be led,
When he is bludie and woe for blood;
Yet to his men shall he say,
"For God's love turn you againe,
And give yon sutherne folk a frey!
Why should I lose, the right is mine?
My date is not to die this day."'

Who can doubt, for a moment, that this refers to the battle of Flodden, and to the popular reports concerning the doubtful fate of James IV? Allusion is immediately after-wards made to the death of George Douglas, heir-apparent of Angus, who fought and fell with his sovereign:—

'The sternes three that day shall die,
That bears the harte in silver sheen.'

The well-known arms of the Douglas family are the heart and three stars. In another place, the battle of Pinkie is expressly men-tioned by name:—

'At Pinken Cluch there shall be spilt
Much gentle blood that day;
There shall the bear lose the guilt,
And the eagill bear it away.'

To the end of all this allegorical and mysti-cal rhapsody, is interpolated, in the later edition by Andro Hart, a new edition of Ber-lington's verses, before quoted, altered and manufactured, so as to bear reference to the accession of James VI, which had just then taken place. The insertion is made with a peculiar degree of awkwardness, betwixt a question, put by the narrator, concerning the name and abode of the person who showed him these strange matters, and the answer of the prophet to that question :—

> 'Then to the Beirne could I say,
> Where dwells thou, or in what countrie?
> [Or who shall rule the isle of Britane,
> From the north to the south sey?
> A French queene shall bear the sonne,
> Shall rule all Britaine to the sea ;
> Which of the Bruce's blood shall come,
> As neere as the nint degree :
> I frained fast what was his name,
> Where that he came, from what country.]
> In Erslingtoun I dwell at hame,
> Thomas Rymour men cals me.'

There is surely no one who will not conclude, with Lord Hailes, that the eight lines enclosed in brackets are a clumsy interpolation, borrowed from Berlington, with such alterations as might render the supposed prophecy applicable to the union of the crowns.

While we are on this subject, it may be proper briefly to notice the scope of some of the other predictions, in Hart's Collection. As the prophecy of Berlington was intended to raise the spirits of the nation during the regency of Albany, so those of Sybilla and Eltraine refer to that of the Earl of Arran, afterwards Duke of Chatelherault, during the minority of Mary, a period of similar calamity. This is obvious from the following verses :—

> 'Take a thousand in calculation,
> And the longest of the lyon,
> Four crescents under one crowne,
> With Saint Andrew's croce thrise,
> Then threescore and thrise three :
> Take tent to Merling truely,
> Then shall the wars ended be,
> And never again rise.
> In that yere there shall a king,
> A duke, and no crown'd king :
> Becaus the prince shall be yong,
> And tender of yeares.'

The date, above hinted at, seems to be 1549, when the Scottish Regent, by means of some succours derived from France, was endeavouring to repair the consequences of the fatal battle of Pinkie. Allusion is made to the supply given to the ' Moldwarte [England] by the fained hart' (the Earl of Angus). The Regent is described by his bearing the antelope ; large supplies are promised from France, and complete conquest predicted to Scotland and her allies. Thus was the same hackneyed stratagem repeated, whenever the interest of the rulers appeared to stand in need of it. The Regent was not, indeed, till after this period, created Duke of Chatelherault ; but that honour was the object of his hopes and expectations.

The name of our renowned soothsayer is liberally used as an authority throughout all the prophecies published by Andro Hart. Besides those expressly put in his name, Gildas, another assumed personage, is supposed to derive his knowledge from him ; for he concludes thus :—

> 'True Thomas me told in a troublesome time,
> In a harvest morn at Eldoun hills.'
> *The Prophecy of Gildas.*

In the prophecy of Berlington, already quoted, we are told,

> 'Marvellous Merlin, that many men of tells,
> And Thomas's sayings comes all at once.'

While I am upon the subject of these prophecies, may I be permitted to call the attention of antiquaries to Merdwynn Wyllt, or *Merlin the Wild*, in whose name, and by no means in that of Ambrose Merlin, the friend of Arthur, the Scottish prophecies are issued ? That this personage resided at Drummelziar, and roamed, like a second Nebuchadnezzar, the woods of Tweeddale, in remorse for the death of his nephew, we learn from Fordun. In the *Scotichronicon*, lib. iii, cap. 31, is an account of an interview betwixt St. Kentigern and Merlin, then in this distracted and miserable state. He is said to have been called *Lailoken*, from his mode of life. On being commanded by the saint to give an account of himself, he says that the penance which he performs was imposed on him by a voice from heaven, during a bloody contest betwixt Lidel and Carwanolow, of which battle he had been the cause. According to his own prediction, he perished at once by wood, earth, and water ; for, being pursued with stones by the rustics, he fell from a rock into the river Tweed, and was transfixed by a sharp stake, fixed there for the purpose of extending a fishing-net :—

> 'Sude perfossus, lapide percussus, et unda,
> Haec tria Merlinum fertur inire necem.
> Sicque ruit, mersusque fuit lignoque prehensus,
> Et fecit vatem per terna pericula verum.'

But, in a metrical history of Merlin of Caledonia, compiled by Geoffrey of Monmouth from the traditions of the Welsh bards, this mode of death is attributed to a page, whom Merlin's sister, desirous to convict the prophet of falsehood, because he had betrayed her intrigues, introduced to him, under three various disguises, inquiring each time in what manner the person should die. To the first demand Merlin answered, the party should perish by a fall from a rock ; to the second, that he should die by a tree ; and to the third, that he should be drowned. The youth perished, while hunting, in the mode imputed by Fordun to Merlin himself.

Fordun, contrary to the French authorities, confounds this person with the Merlin of Arthur ; but concludes by informing us, that many believed him to be a different person. The grave of Merlin is pointed out at Drummelziar, in Tweeddale, beneath an aged thorn-tree. On the east side of the churchyard the brook, called Pausayl, falls into the Tweed ; and the following prophecy is said to have been current concerning their union :—

> 'When Tweed and Pausayl join at Merlin's grave,
> Scotland and England shall one monarch have.'

On the day of the coronation of James VI, the Tweed accordingly overflowed, and joined the Pausayl at the prophet's grave.—PENNYCUICK'S *History of Tweeddale*, p. 26.

These circumstances would seem to infer a communication betwixt the south-west of Scotland and Wales, of a nature peculiarly intimate; for I presume that Merlin would retain sense enough to choose for the scene of his wanderings a country having a language and manners similar to his own.

Be this as it may, the memory of Merlin Sylvester, or the Wild, was fresh among the Scots during the reign of James V. Waldhave[1], under whose name a set of prophecies was published, describes himself as lying upon Lomond Law; he hears a voice, which bids him stand to his defence; he looks around, and beholds a flock of hares and foxes[2] pursued over the mountain by a savage figure, to whom he can hardly give the name of man. At the sight of Waldhave, the apparition leaves the objects of his pursuit, and assaults him with a club. Waldhave defends himself with his sword, throws the savage to the earth, and refuses to let him arise till he swear, by the law and lead he lives upon, 'to do him no harm.' This done, he permits him to arise, and marvels at his strange appearance:—

> 'He was formed like a freike [man] all his four quarters;
> And then his chin and his face haired so thick,
> With haire growing so grime, fearful to see.'

He answers briefly to Waldhave's inquiry concerning his name and nature, that he 'drees his weird,' i.e. does penance in that wood; and, having hinted that questions as to his own state are offensive, he pours forth an obscure rhapsody concerning futurity, and concludes:—

> 'Go musing upon Merlin if thou wilt:
> For I mean no more, man, at this time.'

This is exactly similar to the meeting betwixt Merlin and Kentigern in Fordun. These prophecies of Merlin seem to have been in request in the minority of James V; for among the amusements with which Sir David Lindsay diverted that prince during his infancy, are,

> 'The prophecies of Rymer, Bede, and Merlin.
> SIR DAVID LINDSAY'S *Epistle to the King*.

And we find, in Waldhave, at least one allusion to the very ancient prophecy, addressed to the Countess of Dunbar:—

> 'This is a true token that Thomas of tells,
> When a ladde with a ladye shall go over the fields.'

The original stands thus:—

> 'When laddes weddeth lovedies.'

Another prophecy of Merlin seems to have been current about the time of the Regent Morton's execution. When that nobleman

was committed to the charge of his accuser, Captain James Stewart, newly created Earl of Arran, to be conducted to his trial at Edinburgh, Spottiswoode says that he asked, '"Who was Earl of Arran?" and being answered that Captain James was the man, after a short pause, he said, "And is it so? I know then what I may look for?" meaning, as was thought, that the old prophecy of the "Falling of the heart by the mouth of Arran" should then be fulfilled. Whether this was his mind or not, it is not known; but some spared not, at the time when the Hamiltons were banished, in which business he was held too earnest, to say, that he stood in fear of that prediction, and went that course only to disappoint it. But if so it was, he did find himself now deluded; for he fell by the mouth of another Arran than he imagined.'— SPOTTISWOODE, p. 313. The fatal words alluded to seem to be these in the prophecy of Merlin:—

> 'In the mouthe of Arrane a selclouth shall fall,
> Two bloodie hearts shall be taken with a false traine,
> And derfly dung down without any dome.'

To return from these desultory remarks, into which I have been led by the celebrated name of Merlin, the style of all these prophecies, published by Hart, is very much the same. The measure is alliterative, and somewhat similar to that of *Pierce Plowman's Visions*; a circumstance which might entitle us to ascribe to some of them an earlier date than the reign of James V, did we not know that *Sir Galloran of Galloway* and *Gawaine and Gologras*, two romances rendered almost unintelligible by the extremity of affected alliteration, are perhaps not prior to that period. Indeed, although we may allow that, during much earlier times, prophecies, under the names of those celebrated soothsayers, have been current in Scotland, yet those published by Hart have obviously been so often vamped and re-vamped, to serve the political purposes of different periods, that it may be shrewdly suspected, that, as in the case of Sir John Cutler's transmigrated stockings, very little of the original materials now remains. I cannot refrain from indulging my readers with the publisher's title to the last prophecy, as it contains certain curious information concerning the Queen of Sheba, who is identified with the Cumaean Sibyl: 'Here followeth a prophecie, pronounced by a noble queene and matron, called Sybilla, Regina Austri, that came to Solomon. Through the which she compiled four bookes, at the instance of the said King Sol, and others divers: and the fourth book was directed to a noble king, called Baldwine, King of the broad isle of Britain; in the which she maketh mention of two noble princes and emperours, the which is called Leones. How these two shall subdue and overcome all earthlie princes to their diademe and crowne, and also be glorified and crowned in the heaven among saints. The

---

[1] I do not know whether the person here meant be Waldhave, an abbot of Melrose, who died in the odour of sanctity about 1160.
[2] See Note IV, p. 682.

first of these two is Constantinus Magnus; that was Leprosus, the son of Saint Helena, that found the croce. The second is the sixt king of the name of Steward of Scotland, the which is our most noble king.' With such editors and commentators, what wonder that the text became unintelligible, even beyond the usual oracular obscurity of prediction?

If there still remain, therefore, among these predictions, any verses having a claim to real antiquity, it seems now impossible to discover them from those which are comparatively modern. Nevertheless, as there are to be found, in these compositions, some uncommonly wild and masculine expressions, the Editor has been induced to throw a few passages together, into the sort of ballad to which this disquisition is prefixed. It would, indeed, have been no difficult matter for him, by a judicious selection, to have excited, in favour of Thomas of Ercildoune, a share of the admiration bestowed by sundry wise persons upon Mass Robert Fleming. For example :—

'But then the lilye shal be loused when they least think;
Then clear king's blood shal quake for fear of death;
For churls shal chop off heads of their chief beirns,
And carfe of the crowns that Christ hath appointed.

. . . .

Thereafter, on every side, sorrow shal arise ;
The barges of clear barons down shal be sunken,
Seculars shall sit in spiritual seats,
Occupying offices anointed as they were.'

Taking the lily for the emblem of France, can there be a more plain prophecy of the murder of her monarch, the destruction of her nobility, and the desolation of her hierarchy?

But, without looking farther into the signs of the times, the Editor, though the least of all the prophets, cannot help thinking that every true Briton will approve of his application of the last prophecy quoted in the ballad.

Hart's collection of prophecies was frequently reprinted during the last century, probably to favour the pretensions of the unfortunate family of Stuart. For the prophetic renown of Gildas and Bede, see Fordun, lib. iii.

Before leaving the subject of Thomas's predictions, it may be noticed that sundry rhymes, passing for his prophetic effusions, are still current among the vulgar. Thus, he is said to have prophesied of the very ancient family of Haig of Bemerside,

'Betide, betide, whate'er betide,
Haig shall be Haig of Bemerside.'

The grandfather of the present proprietor of Bemerside had twelve daughters, before his lady brought him a male heir. The common people trembled for the credit of their favourite soothsayer. The late Mr. Haig was at length born, and their belief in the prophecy confirmed beyond a shadow of doubt.

Another memorable prophecy bore, that the Old Kirk at Kelso, constructed out of the ruins of the Abbey, should ' fall when at the fullest.' At a very crowded sermon, about thirty years ago, a piece of lime fell from the roof of the church. The alarm for the fulfilment of the words of the seer became universal ; and happy were they who were nearest the door of the predestined edifice. The church was in consequence deserted, and has never since had an opportunity of tumbling upon a full congregation. I hope, for the sake of a beautiful specimen of Saxo-Gothic architecture, that the accomplishment of this prophecy is far distant.

Another prediction, ascribed to the Rhymer, seems to have been founded on that sort of insight into futurity, possessed by most men of a sound and combining judgment. It runs thus :—

'At Eldon Tree if you shall be,
A brigg ower Tweed you there may see.

The spot in question commands an extensive prospect of the course of the river ; and it was easy to foresee that when the country should become in the least degree improved, a bridge would be somewhere thrown over the stream. In fact, you now see no less than three bridges from that elevated situation.

Corspatrick (Comes Patrick), Earl of March, but more commonly taking his title from his castle of Dunbar, acted a noted part during the wars of Edward I in Scotland. As Thomas of Ercildoune is said to have delivered to him his famous prophecy of King Alexander's death, the Editor has chosen to introduce him into the ballad. All the prophetic verses are selected from Hart's publication.

Part III.—Modern.

Thomas the Rhymer was renowned among his contemporaries as the author of the celebrated romance of *Sir Tristrem.* Of this once-admired poem only one copy is now known to exist, which is in the Advocates' Library. The Editor, in 1804, published a small edition of this curious work ; which, if it does not revive the reputation of the bard of Ercildoune, is at least the earliest specimen of Scottish poetry hitherto published. Some account of this romance has already been given to the world in Mr. Ellis's *Specimens of Ancient Poetry,* vol. i. p. 165, iii. p. 410 ; a work to which our predecessors and our posterity are alike obliged ; the former, for the preservation of the best-selected examples of their poetical taste ; and the latter for a history of the English language, which will only cease to be interesting with the existence of our mother-tongue, and all that genius and learning have recorded in it.

It is sufficient here to mention, that so great was the reputation of the romance of *Sir Tristrem*, that few were thought capable of reciting it after the manner of the author—a circumstance alluded to by Robert de Brunne, the annalist :—

> 'I see in song, in sedgeyng tale,
> Of Erceldoun, and of Kendale,
> Now thame says as they thame wroght,
> And in thare saying it semes nocht.
> That thou may here in Sir Tristrem,
> Over gestes it has the steme,
> Over all that is or was ;
> If men it said as made Thomas,' &c.

It appears, from a very curious MS. of the thirteenth century, *penes* Mr. Douce of London, containing a French metrical romance of *Sir Tristrem*, that the work of our Thomas the Rhymer was known, and referred to, by the minstrels of Normandy and Bretagne. Having arrived at a part of the romance where reciters were wont to differ in the mode of telling the story, the French bard expressly cites the authority of the poet of Erceldoune :—

> 'Plusurs de nos granter ne volent,
> Co que del naim dire se solent,
> Ki femme Kaherdin dut aimer,
> Li naim redut Tristram narrer,
> E entusché par grant engin,
> Quant il afole Kaherdin ;
> Pur cest plai e pur cest mal,
> Enveiad Tristram Guvernal.
> En Engleterre pur Ysolt :
> THOMAS ico granter ne volt,
> Et si volt par raisun mostrer,
> Qu' ico ne put pas esteer,' &c.

The tale of *Sir Tristrem*, as narrated in the Edinburgh MS., is totally different from the voluminous romance in prose, originally compiled on the same subject by Rusticien de Puise, and analyzed by M. de Tressan ; but agrees in every essential particular with the metrical performance just quoted, which is a work of much higher antiquity.

<hr>

NOTES.

Note I.—P. 673.

From the Chartulary of the Trinity House of Soltra. Advocates' Library, W. 4. 14.

ERSYLTON.

Omnibus has literas visuris vel audituris Thomas de Ercildoun filius et heres Thomae Rymour de Ercildoun salutem in Domino. Noveritis me per fustem et baculum in pleno judicio resignasse ac per presentes quietem clamasse pro me et heredibus meis Magistro domus Sanctae Trinitatis de Soltre et fratribus ejusdem domus totam terram meam cum omnibus pertinentibus suis quam in tenemento de Ercildoun hereditarie tenui renunciando de toto pro me et heredibus meis omni jure et clameo quae ego seu antecessores mei in eadem terra alioque tempore de perpetuo habuimus sive de futuro habere possumus. In cujus rei testimonio presentibus his sigillum meum apposui data apud Ercildoun die Martis proximo post festum Sanctorum Apostolorum Symonis et Jude Anno Domini Millesimo cc. Nonagesimo Nono.

<hr>

Note II.

Thomas the Rhymer, Part I.—P. 655.

The reader is here presented, from an old, and unfortunately an imperfect MS., with the undoubted original of Thomas the Rhymer's intrigue with the Queen of Faëry. It will afford great amusement to those who would study the nature of traditional poetry, and the changes effected by oral tradition, to compare this ancient romance with the ballad of the text. The same incidents are narrated, even the expression is often the same ; yet the poems are as different in appearance as if the older tale had been regularly and systematically modernised by a poet of the present day.

Incipit Prophesia Thomae de Erseldoun.

> 'In a lande as I was lent,
> In the gryking of the day,
> Ay alone as I went,
> In Huntle bankys me for to play ;
> I saw the throstyl, and the jay,
> Ye mawes movyde of her song,
> Ye wodwale sange notes gay,
> That al the wod about range.
> In that longyng as I lay,
> Undir nethe a dern tre,
> I was war of a lady gay,
> Come rydyng ouyr a fair le :
> Zogh I suld sitt to domysday,
> With my tong to wrabbe and wry,
> Certenly all hyr aray,
> It beth neuyer discryuyd for me.
> Hyr palfra was dappyll gray,
> Sycke on say neuer none ;
> As the son in somers day,
> All abowte that lady schone.
> Hyr sadel was of a rewel bone,
> A semly syght it was to se,
> Bryht with mony a precyous stone,
> And compasyd all with crapste ;
> Stones of oryens, gret plente.
> Her hair about her hede it hang,
> She rode ouer the farnyle,
> A while she blew, a while she sang,
> Her girths of nobil silke they were,
> Her boculs were of beryl stone,
> Sadyll and brydil war . . . ;
> With sylk and sendel about bedone,
> Hyr patyrel was of a pall fyne,
> And hyr croper of the arase,
> Her brydil was of gold fine,
> On euery syde forsothe hang bells thre,
> Her brydil reynes . . . .
> A semly syzt . . . .
> Crop and patyrel. . . .
> In every joynt. . . .
> She led thre grew houndes in a leash,
> And ratches cowpled by her ran ;
> She bar an horn about her halse,
> And undir her gyrdil mene flene.

Thomas lay and sa . . . .
In the bankes of . . . . .
He sayd Yonder is Mary of Might,
That bar the child that died for me,
Certes bot I may speke with that lady bright,
Myd my hert wil breke in three;
I schal me hye with all my might,
Hyr to mete at Eldyn Tre.
Thomas rathly up her rase,
And ran ouer mountayn hye,
If it he sothe the story says,
He met her euyn at Eldyn Tre.
Thomas knelyd down on his kne
Undir nethe the grenewood spray,
And sayd, Lovely lady, thou rue on me,
Queen of Heaven as you may well be.
But I am a lady of another countrie,
If I be pareld most of prise,
I ride after the wild fee,
My ratches rinnen at my devys.
If thou be pareld most of prise,
And rides a lady in strang foly,
Lovely lady, as thou art wise,
Giue you me leue to lige ye by.
Do way, Thomas, that were foly,
I pray ye, Thomas, late me be,
That sin will fordo all my bewtie.
Lovely ladye. rewe on me,
And euer more I shall with ye dwell,
Here my trowth I plyght to thee,
Where you believes in heuin or hell.
Thomas, and you myght lyge me by,
Undir nethe this grene wood spray,
Thou would tell full hastely,
That thou had layn by a lady gay.
Lady, mote I lyge by the,
Undir nethe the grene wode tre,
For all the gold in chrystenty,
Suld you neuer be wryede for me.
Man on molde you will me marre,
And yet bot you may haf your will,
Trow you well, Thomas, you cheuyst ye warre;
For all my bewtie wilt you spill.
Down lyghtyd that lady bryȝt,
Undir nethe the grene wode spray,
And as ye story sayth full ryȝt,
Seuyn tymes by her he lay.
She sayd, Man, you lyst thi play,
What berde in bouyr may dele with thee,
That maries me all this long day ;
I pray ye, Thomas, let me be.
Thomas stode up in the stede,
And behelde the lady gay,
Her heyre hang down about hyr hede,
The tane was blak, the other gray,
Her eyn semyt onte before was gray,
Her gay clethyng was all away,
That he before had sene in that stede ;
Hyr body as blow as ony bede.
Thomas sighede, and sayd, Allas,
Me thynke this a dullfull syght,
That thou art fadyd in the face,
Before you shone as son so bryȝt.
Tak thy leue, Thomas, at son and mone,
At gresse, and at euery tre,
This twelmonth sall you with me gone,
Medyl erth you sall not se.
Alas, he seyd, ful wo is me,
I trow my dedes will werke me care,
Jesu, my sole tak to ye,
Whedir so euyr my body sal fare.
She rode furth with all her myȝt,
Undir nethe the derne lee,
It was as derke down at midniȝt,
And euyr in water unto the kne ;
Through the space of days thre,
He herde but swowyng of a flode
Thomas sayd, Ful wo is me,
Now I spyll for fawte of fode ;
To a garden lede him tyte,
There was fruyte in grete plente,
Peyres and appless ther were rype,
The date and the damese,

The figge and als fylbert tre ;
The nyghtyngale breuyng in her neste,
The papigaye about gan fle,
The turostylcock sang wald hafe no rest.
He pressed to pulle fruyt wi.h his hand,
As man for faute that was faynt ;
She seyd, Thomas, let al stand,
Or els the deuyl wil the ataynt.
Sche seyd, Thomas. I the hyȝt,
To lay th ihede upon my kne,
And thou shalt see fayrer syȝt,
Than euyr sawe man in their kintre.
Sees thou, Thomas, yon fayr way,
That lyggs ouyr yone fayr playn?
Yonder is the way to heuyn for ay,
Whan synful sawies haf derayed their payne.
Sees thou, Thomas, yon secund way,
That lygges lawe undir the ryse?
Streight is the way, sothly to say,
To the joyes of paradyce.
Sees thou, Thomas, yon thyrd way,
That lygges ouyr yone how ?
Wide is the way, sothly to say,
To the brynyng fyres of helle.
Sees thou, Thomas, yone fayr castell,
That standes ouyr yone fair hill ?
Of town and tower it beereth the belle,
In middell erth is none like theretill.
Whan thou comyst in yone castell gaye,
I pray thee curteis man to be ;
What so any man to you say,
Loke thu answer none but me.
My lord is servyd at yche messe,
With xxx kniȝtes feir and fre ;
I shall say syttyng on the dese,
I toke thy speche beyonde the le.
Thomas stode as still as stone,
And behelde that ladye gaye;
Than was sche fayr, and ryche anone,
And also ryal on hir palfreye.
The grewhoundes had fylde thaim on the dere,
The raches coupled, by my fay,
She blewe her horne Thomas to chere,
To the castell she went her way.
The ladye into the hall went,
Thomas folowyd at her hand ;
Thar kept her mony a lady gent,
With curtasy and lawe.
Harp and fedyl both he fande,
The getern and the sawtry,
Lut and rybid ther gon gan,
Thair was al maner of mynstralsy,
The most fertly that Thomas thoȝt,
When he com emyddes the flore,
Fourty hertes to quarry were broght,
That had been befor both long and store.
Lymors lay lappyng blode,
And kokes standyng with dressyng knyfe.
And dressyd dere as thai wer wode,
And rewell was thair wonder.
Knyghtes dansyd by two and thre,
All that leue long day.
Ladyes that were gret of gre,
Sat and sang of rych aray.
Thomas sawe much more in that place,
Than I can descryve,
Til on a day, alas, alas,
My lovelye ladye sayd to me,
Busk ye, Thomas, you must agayn,
Here you may no longer be :
Hy then ȝerne that you were at hame,
I sal ye bryng to Eldyn Tre.
Thomas answerd with heuy cher,
And said, Lowely ladye, lat ma be,
For I say ye certenly here
Haf I be bot the space of dayes three.
Sothly, Thomas, as I telle ye,
You hath ben here thre yeres,
And here you may no longer be ;
And I sal telle ye a skele,
To-morrowe of helle ye foule comen
Amang our folke shall chuse his fee ;
For you art a larg man and an hende,

> Trowe you wele he will chuse thee.
> Fore all the golde that may be,
> Fro hens unto the worldes ende,
> Sall you not be betrayed by me,
> And thairfor sall you hens wende.
> She bro_ght hym euyn to Eldyn Tre,
> Undir nethe the grene wode spray,
> In Huntle bankes was fayr to be,
> Ther breddes syng both ny_t and day.
> Ferre ouyr yon montayns gray,
> Ther hathe my facon ;
> Fare wele, Thomas, I wende my way.'

The Elfin Queen, after restoring Thomas to earth, pours forth a string of prophecies, in which we distinguish references to the events and personages of the Scottish wars of Edward III. The battles of Dupplin and Halidon are mentioned, and also Black Agnes, Countess of Dunbar. There is a copy of this poem in the Museum of the Cathedral of Lincoln, another in the collection in Peterborough, but unfortunately they are all in an imperfect state. Mr. Jamieson, in his curious Collection of Scottish Ballads and Songs, has an entire copy of this ancient poem, with all the collations. The *lacunae* of the former editions have been supplied from his copy.

***

Note III.

ALLUSIONS TO HERALDRY.—P. 676.

'The muscle is a square figure like a lozenge, but it is always voided of the field. They are carried as principal figures by the name of Learmont. Learmont of Earlstoun, in the Merss, carried or on a bend azure three muscles ; of which family was Sir Thomas Learmont, who is well known by the name of Thomas the Rhymer, because he wrote his prophecies in rhime. This prophetick herauld lived in the days of King Alexander the Third, and prophesied of his death, and of many other remarkable occurrences ; particularly of the union of Scotland with England, which was not accomplished until the reign of James the Sixth, some hundred years after it was foretold by this gentleman, whose prophecies are much esteemed by many of the vulgar even at this day. I was promised by a friend a sight of his prophecies, of which there is everywhere to be had an epitome, which, I suppose, is erroneous, and differs in many things from the original, it having been oft reprinted by some unskilful persons. Thus many things are amissing in the small book which are to be met with in the original, particularly these two lines concerning his neighbour, Bemerside :—

> " Tyde what may betide,
> Haig shall be laird of Bemerside."

And indeed his prophecies concerning that ancient family have hitherto been true ; for, since that time to this day, the Haigs have been lairds of that place. They carrie, Azure a saltier cantoned with two stars in chief and in base argent, as many crescents in the flanques or ; and for crest a rock proper, with this motto, taken from the above-written rhyme—"Tide what may."'—NISBET *On Marks of Cadency*, p. 158.—He adds, 'that Thomas' meaning may be understood by heraulds when he speaks of kingdoms whose insignia seldom vary, but that individual families cannot be discovered, either because they have altered their bearings, or because they are pointed out by their crests and exterior ornaments, which are changed at the pleasure of the bearer.' Mr. Nisbet, however, comforts himself for this obscurity by reflecting that ' we may certainly conclude, from his writings, that herauldry was in good esteem in his days, and well known to the vulgar.'—*Ibid.* p. 160.—It may be added, that the publication of predictions, either printed or hieroglyphical, in which noble families were pointed out by their armorial bearings, was, in the time of Queen Elizabeth, extremely common ; and the influence of such predictions on the minds of the common people was so great as to occasion a prohibition, by statute, of prophecy by reference to heraldic emblems. Lord Henry Howard also (afterwards Earl of Northampton) directs against this practice much of the reasoning in his learned treatise, entitled, ' A Defensation against the Poyson of pretended Prophecies.'

***

Note IV.—P. 678.

The strange occupation in which Waldhave beholds Merlin engaged, derives some illustration from a curious passage in Geoffrey of Monmouth's life of Merlin, above quoted. The poem, after narrating that the prophet had fled to the forest in a state of distraction, proceeds to mention that, looking upon the stars one clear evening, he discerned from his astrological knowledge, that his w.fe, Guendolen, had resolved, upon the next morning, to take another husband. As he had presaged to her that this would happen, and had promised her a nuptial gift (cautioning her, however, to keep the bridegroom out of his sight), he now resolved to make good his word. Accordingly, he collected all the stags and lesser game in his neighbourhood ; and, having seated himself upon a buck, drove the herd before him to the capital of Cumberland, where Guendolen resided. But her lover's curiosity leading him to inspect too nearly this extraordinary cavalcade, Merlin's rage was awakened, and he slew him with the strike of an antler of the stag. The original runs thus :—

' Dixerat : et silvas et saltus circuit omnes,
Cervorumque greges agmen collegit in unum,
Et damas, capreasque simul ; cervoque reseuit
Et, veniente die, compellens agmina prae se,
Festinans vadit quo nubit Guendolaena,
Postquam venit eo, pacienter ipse coegit
Cervos ante fores proclamans. " Guendolaena,
Guendolaena, veni, te talia munera spectant."
Ocius ergo venit subridens Guendolaena,
Gestarique virum cervo miratur, et illum
Sic parere viro, tantum quoque posse ferarum
Uniri numerum quas prae se solus agebat,
Sicut pastor oves, quas ducere suevit ad herbas.
Stabat ab excelsa sponsus spectando fenestra,
In solio mirans equitem, risumque movebat.
Ast ubi vidit eum vates, animoque quis esset
Calluit, extemplo divulsit cornua cervo

Quo gestabatur, vibrataque jecit in illum,
Et caput illius penitus contrivit, eumque
Reddidit exanimem, vitamque fugavit in auras ;
Ocius inde suum, talorum verbere, cervum
Diffugiens egit, silvasque redire paravit.'

For a perusal of this curious poem, accurately copied from a MS. in the Cotton Librar , nearly coeval with the author, I was indebted to my learned friend, the late Mr. Ritson. There is an excellent paraphrase of it in the curious and entertaining *Specimens of Early English Romances*, published by Mr. Ellis.

GLENFINLAS ; OR, LORD RONALD'S CORONACH [1].

INTRODUCTORY NOTE.

THE simple tradition upon which this ballad is founded runs thus : While two Highland hunters were passing the night in a solitary *bothy* (a hut built for the purpose of hunting) and making merry over their venison and whisky, one of them expressed a wish that they had pretty lasses to complete their party. The words were scarcely uttered, when two beautiful young women, habited in green, entered the hut, dancing and singing. One of the hunters was seduced by the siren who attached herself particularly to him, to leave the hut : the other remained, and, suspicious of the fair seducers, continued to play upon a trump, or Jew's harp, some strain, consecrated to the Virgin Mary. Day at length came, and the temptress vanished. Searching in the forest, he found the bones of his unfortunate friend, who had been torn to pieces and devoured by the fiend into whose toils he had fallen. The place was from thence called the Glen of the Green Women.

Glenfinlas is a tract of forest-ground, lying in the Highlands of Perthshire, not far from Callender in Menteith. It was formerly a royal forest, and now belongs to the Earl of Moray. This country, as well as the adjacent district of Balquidder, was, in times of yore, chiefly inhabited by the Macgregors. To the west of the Forest of Glenfinlas lies Loch Katrine, and its romantic avenue, called the Troshachs. Benledi, Benmore, and Benvoirlich, are mountains in the same district, and at no great distance from Glenfinlas. The river Teith passes Callender and

the Castle of Doune, and joins the Forth near Stirling. The Pass of Lenny is immediately above Callender, and is the principal access to the Highlands from that town. Glenartney is a forest, near Benvoirlich. The whole forms a sublime tract of Alpine scenery.

This ballad first appeared in the *Tales of Wonder*. The ballad called 'Glenfinlas' was, I think, the first original poem which I ventured to compose. As it is supposed to be a translation from the Gaelic, I considered myself as liberated from imitating the antiquated language and rude rhythm of the Minstrel ballad. A versification of an Ossianic fragment came nearer to the idea I had formed of my task ; for although controversy may have arisen concerning the authenticity of these poems, yet I never heard it disputed, by those whom an accurate knowledge of the Gaelic rendered competent judges, that in their spirit and diction they nearly resemble fragments of poetry extant in that language, to the genuine antiquity of which no doubt can attach. Indeed, the celebrated dispute on that subject is something like the more bloody, though scarce fiercer controversy, about the Popish Plot in Charles the Second's time, concerning which Dryden has said—

' Succeeding times will equal folly call,
Believing nothing, or believing all.'

The Celtic people of Erin and Albyn had, in short, a style of poetry properly called national, though MacPherson was rather an excellent poet than a faithful editor and translator. This style and fashion of poetry, existing in a different language, was supposed to give the original of ' Glenfinlas,' and the author was to pass for one who had used his best command of English to do the Gaelic model justice. In one point, the inci-

---

[1] *Coronach* is the lamentation for a deceased warrior, sung by the aged of the clan.

dents of the poem were irreconcilable with the costume of the times in which they were laid. The ancient Highland chieftains, when they had a mind to 'hunt the dun deer down,' did not retreat into solitary bothies, or trust the success of the chase to their own unassisted exertions, without a single gillie to help them; they assembled their clan, and all partook of the sport, forming a ring, or enclosure, called the Tinchell, and driving the prey towards the most distinguished persons of the hunt. This course would not have suited me, so Ronald and Moy were cooped up in their solitary wigwam, like two moor-fowl-shooters of the present day.

After 'Glenfinlas,' I undertook another ballad, called 'The Eve of St. John.' The incidents are mostly entirely imaginary, but the scene was that of my early childhood. Some idle persons had of late years, during the proprietor's absence, torn the iron-grated door of Smailholm Tower from its hinges, and thrown it down the rock. I was an earnest suitor to my friend and kinsman, Mr. Scott of Harden, already mentioned, that the dilapidation might be put a stop to, and the mischief repaired. This was readily promised, on condition that I should make a ballad, of which the scene should lie at Smai.holm Tower, and among the crags where it is situated. The ballad was approved of, as well as its companion 'Glenfinlas'; and I remember that they procured me many marks of attention and kindness from Duke John of Roxburghe, who gave me the unlimited use of that celebrated collection of volumes from which the Roxburghe Club derives its name.

Thus I was set up for a poet, like a pedlar who has got two ballads to begin the world upon, and I hastened to make the round of all my acquaintances, showing my precious wares, and requesting criticism—a boon which no author asks in vain. For it may be observed, that, in the fine arts, those who are in no respect able to produce any specimens themselves, hold themselves not the less entitled to decide upon the works of others; and, no doubt, with justice to a certain degree; for the merits of composition produced for the express purpose of pleasing the world at large, can only be judged of by the opinion of individuals, and perhaps, as in the case of Molière's old woman, the less sophisticated the person consulted so much the better. But I was ignorant, at the time I speak of, that though the applause of the many may justly appreciate the general merits of a piece, it is not so safe to submit such a performance to the more minute criticism of the same individuals, when each in turn, having seated himself in the censor's chair, has placed his mind in a critical attitude, and delivers his opinion sententiously and *ex cathedrâ*. General applause was in almost every case freely tendered, but the abatements in the way of proposed alterations and cor-

rections were cruelly puzzling. It was in vain the young author, listening with becoming modesty and with a natural wish to please, cut and carved, tinkered and coopered, upon his unfortunate ballads, or trust that he placed, displaced, replaced, and misplaced; every one of his advisers was displeased with the concessions made to his co-assessors, and the author was blamed by some one, in almost every case, for having made two holes in attempting to patch up one.

At last, after thinking seriously on the subject, I wrote out a fair copy (of 'Glenfinlas,' I think), and marked all the various corrections which had been proposed. On the whole, I found that I had been required to alter every verse, almost every line, and the only stanzas of the whole ballad which escaped criticism were two which could neither be termed good nor bad, speaking of them as poetry, but were of a mere commonplace character, absolutely necessary for conducting the business of the tale. This unexpected result, after about a fortnight's anxiety, led me to adopt a rule from which I have seldom departed during more than thirty years of literary life. When a friend, whose judgment I respect, has decided, and upon good advisement told me, that a manuscript was worth nothing, or at least possessed no redeeming qualities sufficient to atone for its defects, I have generally cast it aside; but I am little in the custom of paying attention to minute criticisms, or of offering such to any friend who may do me the honour to consult me. I am convinced that, in general, in removing even errors of a trivial or venial kind, the character of originality is lost, which, upon the whole, may be that which is most valuable in the production.

About the time that I shook hands with criticism, and reduced my ballads back to the original form, stripping them without remorse of those 'lendings' which I had adopted at the suggestion of others, an opportunity unexpectedly offered of introducing to the world what had hitherto been confined to a circle of friends. Lewis had announced a collection, first intended to bear the title of *Tales of Terror*, and afterwards published under that of *Tales of Wonder*. As this was to be a collection of tales turning on the preternatural, there were risks in the plan of which the ingenious editor was not aware. The supernatural, though appealing to certain powerful emotions very widely and deeply sown amongst the human race, is, nevertheless, a spring which is peculiarly apt to lose its elasticity by being too much pressed on, and a collection of ghost stories is not more likely to be terrible, than a collection of jests to be merry or entertaining. But although the very title of the proposed work carried in it an obstruction to its effect, this was far from being suspected at the time, for the popularity of the editor, and of his compositions, seemed a warrant for his success. The distinguished favour with which the 'Castle Spectre' was received upon the stage, seemed an additional pledge for the safety of his new attempt. I readily agreed to contribute the ballads of 'Glenfinlas' and of 'The Eve of Saint John,' with one or two others of less merit; and my friend Dr. Leyden became also a contributor. Mr. Southey, a tower of strength, added 'The Old Woman of Berkeley,' 'Lord William,' and several other interesting ballads of the same class, to the proposed collection.

In the meantime, my friend Lewis found it no easy matter to discipline his northern recruits. He was a martinet, if I may so term him, in the accuracy of rhymes and of numbers; I may add, he had a right to be so, for few persons have exhibited more mastery of rhyme, or greater command over the melody of verse. He was, therefore, rigid in exacting similar accuracy from others, and as I was quite unaccustomed to the mechanical part of poetry, and used rhymes which were merely permissible, as readily as those which were legitimate, contests often arose amongst us, which were exasperated by the pertinacity of my Mentor, who, as all who knew him can testify, was no granter of propositions. The lectures which I underwent from my friend Lewis did not at the time produce any effect on my inflexibility, though I did not forget them at a future period.

The proposed publication of the *Tales of Wonder* was, from one reason or another, postponed till the year 1801, a circumstance by which, of itself, the success of the work was considerably impeded; for protracted expectation always leads to disappointment. But besides, there were circumstances of various kinds which contributed to its depreciation, some of which were imputable to the editor, or author, and some to the bookseller.

The former remained insensible of the passion for ballads and ballad-mongers having been for some time on the wane, and that with such alteration in the public taste, the chance of success in that line was diminished. What had been at first received as simple and natural, was now sneered at as puerile and extravagant. Another objection was, that my friend Lewis had a high but mistaken opinion of his own powers of humour. The truth was, that though he could throw some gaiety into his lighter pieces, after the manner of the French writers, his attempts at what is called pleasantry in English wholly wanted the quality of humour, and were generally failures. But this he would not allow; and the *Tales of Wonder* were filled, in a sense, with attempts at comedy, which might be generally accounted abortive.

Another objection, which might have been more easily foreseen, subjected the editor to a charge of which Mat Lewis was entirely incapable—that of collusion with his publisher in an undue attack on the pockets of the public. The *Tales of Wonder* formed a work in royal octavo, and were, by large printing, *driven out*, as it is technically termed, to two volumes, which were sold at a high price. Purchasers murmured at finding that this size had been attained by the insertion of some of the best-known pieces of the English language, such as Dryden's 'Theodore and Honoria,' Parnell's 'Hermit,' Lisle's 'Porsenna, King of Russia,' and many other popular poems of old date, and generally known, which ought not in conscience to have made part of a set of tales, 'written and collected' by a modern author. His bookseller was also accused in the public prints, whether truly or not I am uncertain, of having attempted to secure to himself the entire profits of the large sale which he expected, by refusing to his brethren the allowances usually, if not in all cases, made to the retail trade.

Lewis, one of the most liberal as well as benevolent of mankind, had not the least participation in these proceedings of his bibliopolist; but his work sunk under the obloquy which was heaped on it by the offended parties. The book was termed 'Tales of Plunder,' was censured by reviewers, and attacked in newspapers and magazines. A very clever parody was made on the style and the person of the author, and the world laughed as willingly as if it had never applauded.

Thus, owing to the failure of the vehicle I had chosen, my efforts to present myself before the public as an original writer proved as vain as those by which I had previously endeavoured to distinguish myself as a translator. Like Lord Home, however, at the battle of Flodden, I did so far well, that I was able to stand and save myself; and amidst the general depreciation of the *Tales of Wonder*, my small share of the obnoxious publication was dismissed without much censure, and in some cases obtained praise from the critics.

The consequence of my escape made me naturally more daring, and I attempted, in my own name, a collection of ballads of various kinds, both ancient and modern, to be connected by the common tie of relation to the Border districts in which I had gathered the materials. The original preface explains my purpose, and the assistance of various kinds which I met with. The edition was curious, as being the first work printed by my friend and schoolfellow, Mr. James Ballantyne, who, at that period, was editor of a provincial newspaper, called *The Kelso Mail*. When the book came out, in 1802, the imprint, Kelso, was read with wonder by amateurs of typography, who had never heard of such a place, and were astonished at the example of handsome printing which so obscure a town produced.

As for the editorial part of the task, my attempt to imitate the plan and style of Bishop Percy, observing only more strict fidelity concerning my originals, was favourably received by the public, and there was a demand within a short space for a second edition, to which I proposed to add a third volume. Messrs. Cadell and Davies, the first publishers of the work, declined the publication of this second edition, which was undertaken, at a very liberal price, by the well-known firm of Messrs. Longman and Rees of Paternoster Row. My progress in the literary career, in which I might now be considered as seriously engaged, the reader will find briefly traced in the Introduction to 'The Lay of the Last Minstrel.'

In the meantime, the Editor has accomplished his proposed task of acquainting the reader with some particulars respecting the modern imitations of the Ancient Ballad, and the circumstances which gradually, and almost insensibly, engaged himself in that species of literary employment.

WALTER SCOTT.

ABBOTSFORD, *April*, 1830.

NOTES.

NOTE I.

How blazed Lord Ronald's beltane-tree.
—P. 660.

The fires lighted by the Highlanders, on the first of May, in compliance with a custom derived from the Pagan times, are termed *The Beltane-tree.* It is a festival celebrated with various superstitious rites, both in the north of Scotland and in Wales.

NOTE II.

The seer's prophetic spirit found.—P. 660.

I can only describe the second sight by adopting Dr. Johnson's definition, who calls it 'An impression, either by the mind upon the eye, or by the eye upon the mind, by which things distant and future are perceived and seen as if they were present.' To which I would only add, that the spectral appearances, thus presented, usually presage misfortune; that the faculty is painful to those who suppose they possess it; and that they usually acquire it while themselves under the pressure of melancholy.

NOTE III.

Will good St. Oran's rule prevail.—P. 661.

St. Oran was a friend and follower of St. Columba, and was buried at Icolmkill. His pretensions to be a saint were rather dubious. According to the legend, he consented to be buried alive, in order to propitiate certain demons of the soil, who obstructed the attempts of Columba to build a chapel. Columba caused the body of his friend to be dug up, after three days had elapsed; when Oran, to the horror and scandal of the assistants, declared that there was neither a God, a judgment, nor a future state! He had no time to make further discoveries, for Columba caused the earth once more to be shovelled over him with the utmost despatch. The chapel, however, and the cemetery, was called *Relig Ouran*; and, in memory of his rigid celibacy, no female was permitted to pay her devotions, or be buried in that place. This is the rule alluded to in the poem.

NOTE IV.

And thrice St. Fillan's powerful prayer.
—P. 663.

St. Fillan has given his name to many chapels, holy fountains, &c., in Scotland. He was, according to Camerarius, an Abbot of Pittenweem, in Fife; from which situation he retired, and died a hermit in the wilds of Glenurchy, A.D. 649. While engaged in transcribing the Scriptures, his left hand was observed to send forth such a splendour, as to afford light to that with which he wrote; a miracle which saved many candles to the convent, as St. Fillan used to spend whole nights in that exercise. The 9th of January was dedicated to this saint, who gave his name to Kilfillan, in Renfrew, and St. Phillans, or Forgend, in Fife. Lesley, lib. 7, tells us, that Robert the Bruce was possessed of Fillan's miraculous and luminous arm, which he enclosed in a silver shrine, and had it carried at the head of his army. Previous to the battle of Bannockburn, the king's chaplain, a man of little faith, abstracted the relic, and deposited it in a place of security, lest it should fall into the hands of the English. But, lo! while Robert was addressing his prayers to the empty casket, it was observed to open and shut suddenly; and, on inspection, the saint was found to have himself deposited his arm in the shrine as an assurance of victory. Such is the tale of Lesley. But though Bruce little needed that the arm of St. Fillan should assist his own, he dedicated to him, in gratitude, a priory at Killin, upon Loch Tay.

In the *Scots Magazine* for July, 1802, there is a copy of a very curious crown grant, dated July 11. 1487, by which James III confirms, to Malice Doire, an inhabitant of Strathfillan, in Perthshire, the peaceable exercise and enjoyment of a relic of St. Fillan, being apparently the head of a pastoral staff called the Quegrich, which he and his predecessors are said to have possessed since the days of Robert Bruce. As the Quegrich was used to cure diseases, this document is prob-

ably the most ancient patent ever granted for a quack medicine. The ingenious correspondent, by whom it is furnished, farther observes, that additional particulars concerning St. Fillan are to be found in BELLENDEN'S *Boece*, Book 4, folio ccxiii, and PENNANT'S *Tour in Scotland*, 1772, pp. 11, 15.

THE EVE OF SAINT JOHN.

SMAYLHO'ME, or Smallholm Tower, the scene of 'The Eve of Saint John,' is situated on the northern boundary of Roxburghshire, among a cluster of wild rocks, called Sandiknow-Crags, the property of Hugh Scott, Esq. of Harden (afterwards Lord Polwarth). The tower is a high square building, surrounded by an outer wall, now ruinous. The circuit of the outer court, being defended on three sides, by a precipice and morass, is accessible only from the west, by a steep and rocky path. The apartments, as is usual in a Border keep, or fortress, are placed one above another, and communicate by a narrow stair; on the roof are two bartizans, or platforms, for defence or pleasure. The inner door of the tower is wood, the outer an iron gate; the distance between them being nine feet, the thickness, namely, of the wall. From the elevated situation of Smaylholme Tower, it is seen many miles in every direction. Among the crags by which it is surrounded, one, more eminent, is called the *Watchfold*, and is said to have been the station of a beacon in the times of war with England. Without the tower-court is a ruined chapel. Brotherstone is a heath in the neighbourhood of Smaylho'me Tower.

This ballad was first printed in Mr. Lewis's *Tales of Wonder*. It is here published, with some additional illustrations, particularly an account of the battle of Ancram Moor; which seemed proper in a work upon Border antiquities. The catastrophe of the tale is founded upon a well-known Irish tradition. This ancient fortress and its vicinity formed the scene of the Editor's infancy, and seemed to claim from him this attempt to celebrate them in a Border tale.

NOTE I.

BATTLE OF ANCRAM MOOR.—P. 664.

Lord Evers and Sir Brian Latoun, during the year 1544, committed the most dreadful ravages upon the Scottish frontiers, compelling most of the inhabitants, and especially

the men of Liddesdale, to take assurance under the King of England. Upon the 17th November, in that year, the sum total of their depredations stood thus, in the bloody ledger of Lord Evers:—

Towns, towers, barnekynes, paryshe churches, bastill houses, burned and destroyed	192
Scots slain	403
Prisoners taken	816
Nolt (cattle)	10,386
Shepe	12,492
Nags and geldings	1296
Gayt	200
Bolls of corn	850

Insight gear, &c. (furniture) an incalculable quantity.

MURDIN'S *State Papers*, vol. i. p. 51.

For these services Sir Ralph Evers was made a Lord of Parliament. See a strain of exulting congratulation upon his promotion poured forth by some contemporary minstrel, in vol. i. p. 417 of *The Border Minstrelsy*.

The King of England had promised to these two barons a feudal grant of the country, which they had thus reduced to a desert; upon hearing which, Archibald Douglas, the seventh Earl of Angus, is said to have sworn to write the deed of investiture upon their skins, with sharp pens and bloody ink, in resentment for their having defaced the tombs of his ancestors at Melrose.—GODSCROFT. In 1545, Lord Evers and Latoun again entered Scotland, with an army consisting of 3000 mercenaries, 1500 English Borderers, and 700 assured Scottish men, chiefly Armstrongs, Turnbulls, and other broken clans. In this second incursion, the English generals even exceeded their former cruelty. Evers burned the tower of Broomhouse, with its lady (a noble and aged woman, says Lesley) and her whole family. The English penetrated as far as Melrose, which they had destroyed last year, and which they now again pillaged. As they returned towards Jedburgh, they were followed by Angus at the head of 1000 horse, who was shortly after joined by the famous

Norman Lesley, with a body of Fife-men. The English, being probably unwilling to cross the Teviot while the Scots hung upon their rear, halted upon Ancram Moor, above the village of that name; and the Scottish general was deliberating whether to advance or retire, when Sir Walter Scott, of Buccleuch, came up at full speed with a small but chosen body of his retainers, the rest of whom were near at hand. By the advice of this experienced warrior (to whose conduct Pitscottie and Buchanan ascribe the success of the engagement), Angus withdrew from the height which he occupied, and drew up his forces behind it, upon a piece of low flat ground, called Panier-heugh, or Paniel-heugh. The spare horses being sent to an eminence in their rear, appeared to the English to be the main body of the Scots in the act of flight. Under this persuasion, Evers and Latoun hurried precipitately forward, and having ascended the hill, which their foes had abandoned, were no less dismayed than astonished to find the phalanx of Scottish spearmen drawn up, in firm array upon the flat ground below. The Scots in their turn became the assailants. A heron, roused from the marshes by the tumult, soared away betwixt the encountering armies. 'O!' exclaimed Angus, 'that I had here my white goss-hawk, that we might all yoke at once!'—GODSCROFT. The English, breathless and fatigued, having the setting sun and wind full in their faces, were unable to withstand the resolute and desperate charge of the Scottish lances. No sooner had they begun to waver, than their own allies, the assured Borderers, who had been waiting the event, threw aside their red crosses, and, joining their countrymen, made a most merciless slaughter among the English fugitives, the pursuers calling upon each other to 'Remember Broomhouse!'—LESLEY, p. 478.

In the battle fell Lord Evers and his son, together with Sir Brian Latoun, and 800 Englishmen, many of whom were persons of rank. A thousand prisoners were taken. Among these was a patriotic alderman of London, Read by name, who, having contumaciously refused to pay his portion of a benevolence demanded from the city by Henry VIII, was sent by royal authority to serve against the Scots. These, at settling his ransom, he found still more exorbitant in their exactions than the monarch.—REDPATH'S *Border History*, p. 563.

Evers was much regretted by King Henry, who swore to avenge his death upon Angus, against whom he conceived himself to have particular grounds of resentment, on account of favours received by the earl at his hands. The answer of Angus was worthy of a Douglas: 'Is our brother-in-law offended,' said he, 'that I, as a good Scotsman, have avenged my ravaged country, and the defaced tombs of my ancestors, upon Ralph Evers?

They were better men than he, and I was bound to do no less—and will he take my life for that? Little knows King Henry the skirts of Kirnetable: I can keep myself there against all his English host.'—GODSCROFT.

Such was the noted battle of Ancram Moor. The spot on which it was fought is called Lilyard's Edge, from an Amazonian Scottish woman of that name, who is reported, by tradition, to have distinguished herself in the same manner as Squire Witherington. The old people point out her monument, now broken and defaced. The inscription is said to have been legible within this century, and to have run thus:

'Fair maiden Lylliard lies under this stane,
  Little was her stature, but great was her fame;
Upon the English louns she laid mony thumps,
And, when her legs were cutted off, she fought upon
  her stumps.'

Vide *Account of the Parish of Melrose*.

It appears, from a passage in Stowe, that an ancestor of Lord Evers held also a grant of Scottish lands from an English monarch. 'I have seen,' says the historian, 'under the broad-seale of the said King Edward I, a manor, called Ketnes, in the county of Forfare, in Scotland, and neere the furthest part of the same nation northward, given to John Ure and his heires, ancestor to the Lord Ure, that now is, for his service done in these partes, with market, &c. dated at Lanercost, the 20th day of October, anno regis, 34.'—STOWE'S *Annals*, p. 210. This grant, like that of Henry, must have been dangerous to the receiver.

NOTE II.

That nun who ne'er beholds the day.—P. 667.

The circumstance of the nun, 'who never saw the day,' is not entirely imaginary. About fifty years ago an unfortunate female wanderer took up her residence in a dark vault, among the ruins of Dryburgh Abbey, which, during the day, she never quitted. When night fell, she issued from this miserable habitation, and went to the house of Mr. Haliburton of Newmains, the Editor's great-grandfather, or to that of Mr. Erskine of Sheilfield, two gentlemen of the neighbourhood. From their charity, she obtained such necessaries as she could be prevailed upon to accept. At twelve, each night, she lighted her candle, and returned to her vault, assuring her friendly neighbours, that, during her absence, her habitation was arranged by a spirit, to whom she gave the uncouth name of *Fatlips*; describing him as a little man, wearing heavy iron shoes, with which he trampled the clay floor of the vault, to dispel the damps. This circumstance caused her to be regarded, by the well-informed, with compassion, as deranged in her understanding;

and by the vulgar, with some degree of terror. The cause of her adopting this extraordinary mode of life she would never explain. It was, however, believed to have been occasioned by a vow, that during the absence of a man to whom she was attached, she would never look upon the sun. Her lover never returned. He fell during the civil war of 1745-6, and she never more would behold the light of day.

The vault, or rather dungeon, in which this unfortunate woman lived and died, passes still by the name of the supernatural being, with which its gloom was tenanted by her disturbed imagination, and few of the neighbouring peasants dare enter it by night.—1803.

CADYOW CASTLE.

THE ruins of Cadyow, or Cadzow Castle, the ancient baronial residence of the family of Hamilton, are situated upon the precipitous banks of the river Evan, about two miles above its junction with the Clyde. It was dismantled, in the conclusion of the Civil Wars, during the reign of the unfortunate Mary, to whose cause the house of Hamilton devoted themselves with a generous zeal, which occasioned their temporary obscurity, and, very nearly, their total ruin. The situation of the ruins, embosomed in wood, darkened by ivy and creeping shrubs, and overhanging the brawling torrent, is romantic in the highest degree. In the immediate vicinity of Cadyow is a grove of immense oaks, the remains of the Caledonian Forest, which anciently extended through the south of Scotland, from the eastern to the Atlantic Ocean. Some of these trees measure twenty-five feet, and upwards, in circumference ; and the state of decay in which they now appear shows that they have witnessed the rites of the Druids. The whole scenery is included in the magnificent and extensive park of the Duke of Hamilton. There was long preserved in this forest the breed of the Scottish wild cattle, until their ferocity occasioned their being extirpated, about forty years ago[1]. Their appearance was beautiful, being milk-white, with black muzzles, horns, and hoofs. The bulls are described by ancient authors as having white manes ; but those of latter days had lost that peculiarity, perhaps by intermixture with the tame breed.

In detailing the death of the Regent Murray, which is made the subject of the ballad, it would be injustice to my reader to use other words than those of Dr. Robertson, whose account of that memorable event forms a beautiful piece of historical painting.

'Hamilton of Bothwellhaugh was the person who committed this barbarous action. He had been condemned to death soon after the battle of Langside, as we have already related, and owed his life to the Regent's clemency. But part of his estate had been bestowed upon one of the Regent's favourites, who seized his house, and turned out his wife, naked, in a cold night, into the open fields, where, before next morning, she became furiously mad. This injury made a deeper impression on him than the benefit he had received, and from that moment he vowed to be revenged of the Regent. Party rage strengthened and inflamed his private resentment. His kinsmen, the Hamiltons, applauded the enterprise. The maxims of that age justified the most desperate course he could take to obtain vengeance. He followed the Regent for some time, and watched for an opportunity to strike the blow. He resolved at last to wait till his enemy should arrive at Linlithgow, through which he was to pass in his way from Stirling to Edinburgh. He took his stand in a wooden gallery, which had a window towards the street ; spread a feather-bed on the floor to hinder the noise of his feet from being heard ; hung up a black cloth behind him, that his shadow might not be observed from without ; and, after all this preparation, calmly expected the Regent's approach, who had lodged, during the night, in a house not far distant. Some indistinct information of the danger which threatened him had been conveyed to the Regent, and he paid so much regard to it, that he resolved to return by the same gate through which he had entered, and to fetch a compass round the town. But, as the crowd about the gate was great, and he himself unacquainted with fear, he proceeded directly along the street ; and the throng of people obliging him to move very slowly, gave the assassin time to take so true an aim, that he shot him, with a single bullet, through the lower part of his belly, and killed the horse of a gentleman who rode on his other side. His followers instantly endeavoured to break into the house whence the blow had come ; but they found the door strongly barricaded, and, before it could be forced open, Hamilton had mounted a fleet horse, which stood ready

---

[1] Counting from the appearance of *The Border Minstrelsy,* 1802-3, Lockhart points out that so late as *circ.* 1830 a herd of those cattle still remained in Cadzow Forest.

for him at a back passage, and was got far beyond their reach. The Regent died the same night of his wound.'—*History of Scotland*, Book v.

Bothwellhaugh rode straight to Hamilton, where he was received in triumph; for the ashes of the houses in Clydesdale, which had been burned by Murray's army, were yet smoking; and party prejudice, the habits of the age, and the enormity of the provocation, seemed to his kinsmen to justify the deed. After a short abode at Hamilton, this fierce and determined man left Scotland, and served in France, under the patronage of the family of Guise, to whom he was doubtless recommended by having avenged the cause of their niece, Queen Mary, upon her ungrateful brother. De Thou has recorded, that an attempt was made to engage him to assassinate Gaspar de Coligni, the famous Admiral of France, and the buckler of the Huguenot cause. But the character of Bothwellhaugh was mistaken. He was no mercenary trader in blood, and rejected the offer with contempt and indignation. He had no authority, he said, from Scotland to commit murders in France; he had avenged his own just quarrel, but he would neither, for price nor prayer, avenge that of another man.—*Thuanus*, cap. 46.

The Regent's death happened January 23, 1569. It is applauded or stigmatized, by contemporary historians, according to their religious or party prejudices. The triumph of Blackwood is unbounded. He not only extols the pious feat of Bothwellhaugh, 'who,' he observes, 'satisfied, with a single ounce of lead, him whose sacrilegious avarice had stripped the metropolitan church of St. Andrews of its covering'; but he ascribes it to immediate divine inspiration, and the escape of Hamilton to little less than the miraculous interference of the Deity.— JEBB, vol. ii. p. 263. With equal injustice, it was, by others, made the ground of a general national reflection; for, when Mather urged Berney to assassinate Burleigh, and quoted the examples of Poltrot and Bothwellhaugh, the other conspirator answered, 'that neyther Poltrot nor Hambleton did attempt their enterpryse, without some reason or consideration to lead them to it; as the one, by hyre, and promise of preferment or rewarde; the other, upon desperate mind of revenge, for a lyttle wrong done unto him, as the report goethe, according to the vyle trayterous dysposysyon of the hoole natyon of the Scottes.'—MURDIN'S *State Papers*, vol. i. p. 197.

NOTE I.

Sound the pryse!—P. 668.

Pryse—The note blown at the death of the game. 'In Caledonia olim frequens erat sylvestris quidam bos, nunc vero rarior, qui, colore candidissimo, jubam densam et de-

missam instar leonis gestat, truculentus ac ferus ab humano genere abhorrens, ut quaecunque homines vel manibus contrectarint, vel halitu perflaverint, ab iis multos post dies omnino abstinuerunt. Ad hoc tanta audacia huic bovi indita erat, ut non solum irritatus equites furenter prosterneret, sed ne tantillum lacessitus omnes promiscue homines cornibus ac ungulis peterit; ac canum, qui apud nos ferocissimi sunt, impetus plane contemneret. Ejus carnes cartilaginosae, sed saporis suavissimi. Erat olim per illam vastissimam Caledoniae sylvam frequens, sed humana ingluvie jam assumptus tribus tantum locis est reliquus, Strivilingii, Cumbernaldiae, et Kincarniae.'—LESLAEUS, *Scotiae Descriptio*, p. 13.—[See a note on *Castle Dangerous*, Waverley Novels.]

NOTE II.

Stern Claud replied.—P. 668.

Lord Claud Hamilton, second son of the Duke of Chatelherault, and commendator of the Abbey of Paisley, acted a distinguished part during the troubles of Queen Mary's reign, and remained unalterably attached to the cause of that unfortunate princess. He led the van of her army at the fatal battle of Langside, and was one of the commanders at the Raid of Stirling, which had so nearly given complete success to the Queen's faction. He was ancestor of the present [1803] Marquis of Abercorn.

NOTE III.

Woodhouselee.—P. 668.

This barony, stretching along the banks of the Esk, near Auchendinny, belonged to Bothwellhaugh, in right of his wife. The ruins of the mansion, from whence she was expelled in the brutal manner which occasioned her death, are still to be seen in a hollow glen beside the river. Popular report tenants them with the restless ghost of the Lady Bothwellhaugh; whom, however, it confounds with Lady Anne Bothwell, whose *Lament* is so popular. This spectre is so tenacious of her rights, that, a part of the stones of the ancient edifice having been employed in building or repairing the present Woodhouselee, she has deemed it a part of her privilege to haunt that house also; and, even of very late years, has excited considerable disturbance and terror among the domestics. This is a more remarkable vindication of the *rights of ghosts*, as the present Woodhouselee, which gives his title to the Honourable Alexander Fraser Tytler, a senator of the College of Justice, is situated on the slope of the Pentland hills, distant at least four miles from her proper abode. She always appears in white, and with her child in her arms.

Note IV.

Drives to the leap his jaded steed.—P. 669.

Birrel informs us, that Bothwellhaugh, being closely pursued, 'after that spur and wand had failed him, he drew forth his dagger, and strocke his horse behind, whilk caused the horse to leap a very brode stanke [i.e. ditch], by whilk means he escapit, and gat away from all the rest of the horses.'—BIRREL's *Diary*, p. 18.

Note V.

From the wild Border's humbled side.
—P. 669.

Murray's death took place shortly after an expedition to the Borders; which is thus commemorated by the author of his Elegy :—

'So having stablischt all thing in this sort,
To Liddisdaill agane he did resort,
Throw Ewisdail, Eskdail, and all the daills rode he,
And also lay three nights in Cannabie,
Whair na prince lay thir hundred yeiris before.
Nae thief durst stir, they did him feir sa sair ;
And. that thay suld na mair thair thift allege,
Threescore and twelf he brocht of thame in pledge,
Syne wardit thame, whilk maid the rest keep ordour :
Than mycht the rasch-bus keep ky on the Border.'
Scottish Poems, 16th century, p. 232.

Note VI.

With hackbut bent.—P. 669.

Hackbut bent—Gun cock'd. The carbine, with which the Regent was shot, is preserved at Hamilton Palace. It is a brass piece, of a middling length, very small in the bore, and, what is rather extraordinary, appears to have been rifled or indented in the barrel. It had a matchlock, for which a modern firelock has been injudiciously substituted.

Note VII.

The wild Macfarlanes' plaided clan.
—P. 669.

This clan of Lennox Highlanders were attached to the Regent Murray. Hollinshed, speaking of the bataile of Langside, says, 'In this bataile the vallancie of an Heiland gentleman, named Macfarlane, stood the Regent's part in great steede ; for, in the hottest brunte of the fighte, he came up with two hundred of his friendes and countrymen, and so manfully gave in upon the flankes of the Queen's people, that he was a great cause of the disordering of them. This Macfarlane had been lately before, as I have

heard, condemned to die, for some outrage by him committed, and obtayning pardon through suyte of the Countess of Murray, he recompensed that clemencie by this piece of service now at this batayle.' Calderwood's account is less favourable to the Macfarlanes. He states that 'Macfarlane, with his Highlandmen, fled from the wing where they were set. The Lord Lindsay, who stood nearest to them in the Regent's battle, said, 'Let them go! I shall fill their place better :' and so, stepping forward, with a company of fresh men, charged the enemy, whose spears were now spent, with long weapons, so that they were driven back by force, being before almost overthrown by the avaunt-guard and harquebusiers, and so were turned to flight.' —CALDERWOOD's *MS. apud* KEITH, p. 480. Melville mentions the flight of the vanguard, but states it to have been commanded by Morton, and composed chiefly of commoners of the barony of Renfrew.

Note VIII.

Glencairn and stout Parkhead were nigh.
—P. 669.

The Earl of Glencairn was a steady adherent of the Regent. George Douglas of Parkhead was a natural brother of the Earl of Morton, whose horse was killed by the same ball by which Murray fell.

Note IX.

*——haggard Lindesay's iron eye,
That saw fair Mary weep in vain.*—P. 669.

Lord Lindsay, of the Byres, was the most ferocious and brutal of the Regent's faction, and, as such, was employed to extort Mary's signature to the deed of resignation presented to her in Lochleven Castle. He discharged his commission with the most savage rigour ; and it is even said, that when the weeping captive, in the act of signing, averted her eyes from the fatal deed, he pinched her arm with the grasp of his iron glove.

Note X.

So close the minions crowded nigh.—P. 669.

Not only had the Regent notice of the intended attempt upon his life, but even of the very house from which it was threatened. With that infatuation at which men wonder, aiter such events have happened, he deemed it would be a sufficient precaution to ride briskly past the dangerous spot. But even this was prevented by the crowd : so that Bothwellhaugh had time to take a deliberate aim.—SPOTTISWOODE, p. 233. BUCHANAN.

THE GRAY BROTHER.

THE imperfect state of this ballad, which was written several years ago, is not a circumstance affected for the purpose of giving it that peculiar interest which is often found to arise from ungratified curiosity. On the contrary, it was the Editor's intention to have completed the tale, if he had found himself able to succeed to his own satisfaction. Yielding to the opinion of persons, whose judgment, if not biassed by the partiality of friendship, is entitled to deference, he has preferred inserting these verses as a fragment, to his intention of entirely suppressing them.

The tradition, upon which the tale is founded, regards a house upon the barony of Gilmerton, near Lasswade, in Mid-Lothian. This building, now called Gilmerton Grange, was originally named Burndale, from the following tragic adventure. The barony of Gilmerton belonged, of yore, to a gentleman named Heron, who had one beautiful daughter. This young lady was seduced by the Abbot of Newbattle, a richly endowed abbey, upon the banks of the South Esk, now a seat of the Marquis of Lothian. Heron came to the knowledge of this circumstance, and learned also, that the lovers carried on their guilty intercourse by the connivance of the lady's nurse, who lived at this house of Gilmerton Grange, or Burndale. He formed a resolution of bloody vengeance, undeterred by the supposed sanctity of the clerical character, or by the stronger claims of natural affection. Choosing, therefore, a dark and windy night, when the objects of his vengeance were engaged in a stolen interview, he set fire to a stack of dried thorns, and other combustibles, which he had caused to be piled against the house, and reduced to a pile of glowing ashes the dwelling, with all its inmates[1].

The scene with which the ballad opens was suggested by the following curious passage, extracted from the Life of Alexander Peden, one of the wandering and persecuted teachers of the sect of Cameronians, during the reign of Charles II and his successor, James. This person was supposed by his followers, and, perhaps, really believed himself, to be possessed of supernatural gifts; for the wild scenes which they frequented, and the constant dangers which were incurred through their proscription, deepened upon their minds the gloom of superstition, so general in that age.

'About the same time he [Peden] came to

Andrew Normand's house, in the parish of Alloway, in the shire of Ayr, being to preach at night in his barn. After he came in, he halted a little, leaning upon a chair-back, with his face covered; when he lifted up his head, he said, "They are in this house that I have not one word of salvation unto"; he halted a little again, saying, "This is strange, that the devil will not go out, that we may begin our work!" Then there was a woman went out, ill-looked upon almost all her life, and to her dying hour, for a witch, with many presumptions of the same. It escaped me, in the former passages, what John Muirhead (whom I have often mentioned) told me, that when he came from Ireland to Galloway, he was at family-worship, and giving some notes upon the Scripture read, when a very ill-looking man came, and sat down within the door, at the back of the *hallan* [partition of the cottage]: immediately he halted and said, "There is some unhappy body just now come into this house. I charge him to go out, and not stop my mouth!" This person went out, and he *insisted* [went on], yet he saw him neither come in nor go out.'—*The Life and Prophecies of Mr. Alexander Peden, late Minister of the Gospel at New Glenluce, in Galloway,* part ii. § 26.

A friendly correspondent remarks, 'that the incapacity of proceeding in the performance of a religious duty, when a contaminated person is present, is of much higher antiquity than the era of the Reverend Mr. Alexander Peden.'—Vide *Hygini Fabulas,* cap. 26. 'Medea Corintho exul, Athenas, ad Aegeum Pandionis filium devenit in hospitium, eique nupsit... Postea sacerdos Dianae Medeam exagitare coepit, regique negabat sacra caste facere posse, eo quod in ea civitate esset mulier venefica et scelerata; tunc exulatur.'

NOTE I.

From that fair dome where suit is paid By blast of bugle free.—P. 671.

The barony of Pennycuik, the property of Sir George Clerk, Bart., is held by a singular tenure; the proprietor being bound to sit upon a large rocky fragment called the Buckstane, and wind three blasts of a horn, when the King shall come to hunt on the Borough Muir, near Edinburgh. Hence the family have adopted as their crest a demi-forester proper, winding a horn, with the motto, *Free for a Blast.* The beautiful mansion-house of Pennycuik is much admired, both on account of the architecture and surrounding scenery.

---

[1] This tradition was communicated to me by John Clerk, Esq. of Eldin, author of an *Essay upon Naval Tactics.*

NOTE II.

Auchendinny's hazel glade.—P. 671.

Auchendinny, situated upon the Eske, below Pennycuik, the present residence of the ingenious H. Mackenzie, Esq., author of the *Man of Feeling*, &c.—Edition 1803.

NOTE III.

Haunted Woodhouselee.—P. 671.

For the traditions connected with this ruinous mansion, see Ballad of 'Cadyow Castle,' Note III, p. 690.

NOTE IV.

Melville's beechy grove.—P. 671.

Melville Castle, the seat of the Right Honourable Lord Melville, to whom it gives the title of Viscount, is delightfully situated upon the Eske, near Lasswade.

NOTE V.

Roslin's rocky glen.—P. 671.

The ruins of Roslin Castle, the baronial residence of the ancient family of St. Clair. The Gothic chapel, which is still in beautiful preservation, with the romantic and woody dell in which they are situated, belong to the Right Honourable the Earl of Rosslyn, the representative of the former Lords of Roslin.

NOTE VI.

Dalkeith.—P. 671.

The village and castle of Dalkeith belonged of old to the famous Earl of Morton, but is now the residence of the noble family of Buccleuch. The park extends along the Eske, which is there joined by its sister stream of the same name.

NOTE VII.

Classic Hawthornden.—P. 671.

Hawthornden, the residence of the poet Drummond. A house of more modern date is enclosed, as it were, by the ruins of the ancient castle, and overhangs a tremendous precipice upon the banks of the Eske, perforated by winding caves, which in former times were a refuge to the oppressed patriots of Scotland. Here Drummond received Ben Jonson, who journeyed from London on foot in order to visit him. The beauty of this striking scene has been much injured of late years by the indiscriminate use of the axe. The traveller now looks in vain for the leafy bower,

'Where Jonson sat in Drummond's social shade.

Upon the whole, tracing the Eske from its source till it joins the sea at Musselburgh, no stream in Scotland can boast such a varied succession of the most interesting objects, as well as of the most romantic and beautiful scenery. 1803. . .—The beautiful scenery of Hawthornden has, since the above note was written, recovered all its proper ornament of wood. 1831.

Miscellaneous Poems.

ARRANGED IN CHRONOLOGICAL ORDER.)

—◆—

HIS FIRST LINES.

(1782.)

(*Preserved by his Mother.*)

In awful ruins Ætna thunders nigh,
And sends in pitchy whirlwinds to
　the sky
Black clouds of smoke, which, still as
　they aspire,
From their dark sides there bursts
　the glowing fire;
At other times huge balls of fire are
　toss'd
That lick the stars, and in the smoke
　are lost:
Sometimes the mount, with vast con-
　vulsions torn,
Emits huge rocks, which instantly
　are borne
With loud explosions to the starry
　skies,
The stones made liquid as the huge
　mass flies,
Then back again with greater weight
　recoils,
While Ætna thundering from the
　bottom boils.

ON A THUNDERSTORM.

(1783.)

(*Preserved by his Schoolmaster.*)

Loud o'er my head though awful
　thunders roll,
And vivid lightnings flash from pole
　to pole,
Yet 'tis thy voice, my God, that bids
　them fly,
Thy arm directs those lightnings
　through the sky.
Then let the good thy mighty name
　revere,
And harden'd sinners thy just venge-
　ance fear.

—◆—

ON THE SETTING SUN.

(1783.)

(*Preserved by his Schoolmaster.*)

Those evening clouds, that setting ray,
And beauteous tints, serve to display
　Their great Creator's praise;
Then let the short-lived thing call'd
　man,
Whose life's comprised within a span,
　To him his homage raise.

We often praise the evening clouds,
  And tints so gay and bold,
But seldom think upon our God,
  Who tinged these clouds with gold!

—++—

THE VIOLET.

(1797.)

THE violet in her greenwood bower,
  Where birchen boughs with hazels
    mingle,
May boast itself the fairest flower
  In glen, or copse, or forest dingle.

Though fair her gems of azure hue,
  Beneath the dewdrop's weight re-
    clining;
I've seen an eye of lovelier blue,
  More sweet through wat'ry lustre
    shining.

The summer sun that dew shall dry,
  Ere yet the day be past its morrow;
Nor longer in my false love's eye
  Remain'd the tear of parting sorrow.

—++—

TO A LADY

WITH FLOWERS FROM THE ROMAN
WALL.

(1797.)

TAKE these flowers which, purple
    waving,
  On the ruin'd rampart grew,
Where, the sons of freedom braving,
  Rome's imperial standards flew.

Warriors from the breach of danger
  Pluck no longer laurels there;
They but yield the passing stranger
  Wild-flower wreaths for Beauty's
    hair.

BOTHWELL'S SISTERS THREE.

A FRAGMENT.

(1799.)

WHEN fruitful Clydesdale's apple-
    bowers
  Are mellowing in the noon,
When sighs round Pembroke's ruin'd
    towers
  The sultry breath of June,

When Clyde, despite his sheltering
    wood,
  Must leave his channel dry,
And vainly o'er the limpid flood
  The angler guides his fly,—

If chance by Bothwell's lovely braes
  A wanderer thou hast been,
Or hid thee from the summer's blaze
  In Blantyre's bowers of green,

Full where the copsewood opens wild
  Thy pilgrim step hath staid,
Where Bothwell's towers, in ruin piled
  O'erlook the verdant glade,

And many a tale of love and fear
  Hath mingled with the scene—
Of Bothwell's banks that bloom'd so
    dear,
  And Bothwell's bonny Jean—

O, if with rugged minstrel lays
  Unsated be thy ear,
And thou of deeds of other days
  Another tale wilt hear,—

Then all beneath the spreading beech,
  Flung careless on the lea,
The Gothic muse the tale shall teach
  Of Bothwell's sisters three.

Wight Wallace stood on Deckmont
    head,
  He blew his bugle round,
Till the wild bull in Cadyow wood
  Has started at the sound.

Z

Saint George's cross, o'er Bothwell
     hung,
     Was waving far and wide,
And from the lofty turret flung
     Its crimson blaze on Clyde;

And rising at the bugle blast
     That marked the Scottish foe,
Old England's yeomen muster'd fast,
     And bent the Norman bow.

Tall in the midst Sir Aylmer rose,
     Proud Pembroke's Earl was he—
While ——   .   .   .   .

—*—

THE COVENANTER'S FATE.

(1799.)

.   .   .   .   .

And ne'er but once, my son, he says,
     Was yon sad cavern trod,—
In persecution's iron days,
     When the land was left by God.

From Bewlie bog, with slaughter red,
     A wanderer hither drew,
And oft he stopt and turn'd his head,
     As by fits the night wind blew;

For trampling round by Cheviot edge
     Were heard the troopers keen,
And frequent from the Whitelaw ridge
     The death-shot flash'd between.

The moonbeams through the misty
     shower
     On yon dark cavern fell;
Through the cloudy night the snow
     gleam'd white,
     Which sunbeam ne'er could quell.

'Yon cavern dark is rough and rude,
     And cold its jaws of snow;
But more rough and rude are the
     men of blood,
     That hunt my life below!

'Yon spell-bound den, as the aged tell,
     Was hewn by demon's hands;
But I had lourd melle with the fiends
     of hell
Than with Clavers and his band.'

He heard the deep-mouth'd blood-
     hound bark,
     He heard the horses neigh,
He plunged him in the cavern dark,
     And downward sped his way.

Now faintly down the winding path
     Came the cry of the faulting hound,
And the mutter'd oath of baulked
     wrath
     Was lost in hollow sound.

He threw him on the flinted floor,
     And held his breath for fear;
He rose and bitter cursed his foes,
     As the sounds died on his ear:

'O bare thine arm, thou battling Lord,
     For Scotland's wandering band;
Dash from the oppressor's grasp the
     sword,
     And sweep him from the land!

'Forget not thou thy people's groans
     From dark Dunnotter's tower,
Mix'd with the seafowl's shrilly moans,
     And ocean's bursting roar!

'O, in fell Clavers' hour of pride,
     Even in his mightiest day,
As bold ne strides through conquest's
     tide,
     O stretch him on the clay!

'His widow and his little ones,
     O from their tower of trust
Remove its strong foundation stones,
     And crush them in the dust!'

'Sweet prayers to me!' a voice replied;
     'Thrice welcome, guest of mine!'
And glimmering on the cavern side
     A light was seen to shine.

An aged man, in amice brown,
 Stood by the wanderer's side ;
By powerful charm, a dead man's arm
 The torch's light supplied.

From each stiff finger, stretch'd
 upright,
 Arose a ghastly flame,
That waved not in the blast of night
 Which through the cavern came.

O, deadly blue was that taper's hue,
 That flamed the cavern o'er,
But more deadly blue was the ghastly
 hue
 Of his eyes who the taper bore.

He laid on his head a hand like lead,
 As heavy, pale, and cold—
'Vengeance be thine, thou guest of
 mine,
 If thy heart be firm and bold.

'But if faint thy heart, and caitiff fear
 Thy recreant sinews know,
The mountain erne thy heart shall tear,
 Thy nerves the hooded crow.'

The wanderer raised him undismay'd :
 'My soul, by dangers steel'd,
Is stubborn as my border blade,
 Which never knew to yield.

'And if thy power can speed the hour
 Of vengeance on my foes,
Theirs be the fate from bridge and gate
 To feed the hooded crows.'

The Brownie look'd him in the face,
 And his colour fled with speed—
'I fear me,' quoth he, 'uneath it will be
 To match thy word with deed.

'In ancient days when English bands
 Sore ravaged Scotland fair,
The sword and shield of Scottish land
 Was valiant Halbert Kerr.

'A warlock loved the warrior well,
 Sir Michael Scott by name,
And he sought for his sake a spell to
 make,
 Should the Southern foemen tame.

'"Look thou," he said, "from Cess-
 ford head,
 As the July sun sinks low,
And when glimmering white on
 Cheviot's height
Thou shalt spy a wreath of snow,
The spell is complete which shall
 bring to thy feet
 The haughty Saxon foe."

'For many a year wrought the wizard
 here,
 In Cheviot's bosom low,
Till the spell was complete, and in
 July's heat
Appear'd December's snow ;
But Cessford's Halbert never came
 The wondrous cause to know.

'For years before in Bowden aisle
 The warrior's bones had lain ;
And after short while, by female guile,
 Sir Michael Scott was slain.

'But me and my brethren in this cell
 His mighty charms retain ;
And he that can quell the powerful
 spell
 Shall o'er broad Scotland reign.'

He led him through an iron door
 And up a winding stair,
And in wild amaze did the wanderer
 gaze
 On the sight which open'd there.

Through the gloomy night flash'd
 ruddy light,—
 A thousand torches glow ;
The cave rose high, like the vaulted sky,
 O'er stalls in double row.

In every stall of that endless hall
  Stood a steed in barbing bright;
At the foot of each steed, all arm'd
    save the head,
  Lay stretch'd a stalwart knight.

In each mail'd hand was a naked brand;
  As they lay on the black bull's hide,
Each visage stern did upwards turn,
  With eyeballs fix'd and wide.

A launcegay strong, full twelve ells
    long,
  By every warrior hung;
At each pommel there, for battle yare,
  A Jedwood axe was slung.

The casque hung near each cavalier;
  The plumes waved mournfully
At every tread which the wanderer
    made
  Through the hall of gramarye.

The ruddy beam of the torches' gleam
  That glared the warriors on,
Reflected light from armour bright,
  In noontide splendour shone.

And onward seen in lustre sheen,
  Still lengthening on the sight,
Through the boundless hall stood
    steeds in stall,
  And by each lay a sable knight.

Still as the dead lay each horseman
    dread,
  And moved nor limb nor tongue;
Each steed stood stiff as an earthfast
    cliff,
  Nor hoof nor bridle rung.

No sounds through all the spacious hall
  The deadly still divide,
Save where echoes aloof from the
    vaulted roof
  To the wanderer's step replied.

At length before his wondering eyes,
  On an iron column borne,
Of antique shape, and giant size,
  Appear'd a sword and horn.

'Now choose thee here,' quoth his
    leader,
  'Thy venturous fortune try;
Thy woe and weal, thy boot and bale,
  In yon brand and bugle lie.'

To the fatal brand he mounted his hand,
  But his soul did quiver and quail;
The life-blood did start to his shudder-
    ing heart,
  And left him wan and pale.

The brand he forsook, and the horn
    he took
  To 'say a gentle sound;
But so wild a blast from the bugle brast,
  That the Cheviot rock'd around.

From Forth to Tees, from seas to seas,
  The awful bugle rung;
On Carlisle wall, and Berwick withal,
  To arms the warders sprung.

With clank and clang the cavern rang,
  The steeds did stamp and neigh;
And loud was the yell as each warrior
    fell
  Sterte up with hoop and cry.

'Woe, woe,' they cried, 'thou caitiff
    coward,
  'That ever thou wert born!
Why drew ye not the knightly sword
  Before ye blew the horn?'

The morning on the mountain shone,
  And on the bloody ground,
Hurl'd from the cave with shiver'd
    bone,
  The mangled wretch was found.

And still beneath the cavern dread,
  Among the glidders grey,
A shapeless stone with lichens spread
  Marks where the wanderer lay.

AT FLODDEN.

A FRAGMENT.

(1799.)

Go sit old Cheviot's crest below,
And pensive mark the lingering snow
In all his scaurs abide,
And slow dissolving from the hill
In many a sightless, soundless rill,
  Feed sparkling Bowmont's tide.

Fair shines the stream by bank and lea,
As wimpling to the eastern sea
  She seeks Till's sullen bed,
Indenting deep the fatal plain,
Where Scotland's noblest, brave in
  vain,
  Around their monarch bled.

And westward hills on hills you see,
Even as old Ocean's mightiest sea
  Heaves high her waves of foam,
Dark and snow-ridged from Cutsfeld's
  wold
To the proud foot of Cheviot roll'd,
  Earth's mountain billows come.

.   .   .   .   .

—+—

A SONG OF VICTORY.

(1800.)

(*From ' The House of Aspen.'*)

Joy to the victors! the sons of old
  Aspen!
  Joy to the race of the battle and
  scar!
Glory's proud garland triumphantly
  grasping;
  Generous in peace, and victorious
  in war.

Honour acquiring,
  Valour inspiring,
Bursting, resistless, through foemen
  they go:
  War-axes wielding,
  Broken ranks yielding,
Till from the battle proud Roderic
  retiring,
Yields in wild rout the fair palm to his
  foe.

Joy to each warrior, true follower of
  Aspen!
  Joy to the heroes that gain'd the
  bold day!
Health to our wounded, in agony
  gasping;
  Peace to our brethren that fell in
  the fray!
  Boldly this morning,
  Roderic's power scorning,
Well for their chieftain their blades
  did they wield:
  Joy blest them dying,
  As Maltingen flying,
Low laid his banners, our conquest
  adorning,
Their death-clouded eyeballs descried
  on the field!

Now to our home, the proud mansion
  of Aspen,
  Bend we, gay victors, triumphant
  away;
There each fond damsel, her gallant
  youth clasping,
  Shall wipe from his forehead the
  stains of the fray.
  Listening the prancing
  Of horses advancing;
E'en now ot the turrets our maidens
  appear.
  Love our hearts warming,
  Songs the night charming,
Round goes the grape in the goblet
  gay dancing;
Love, wine, and song, our blithe
  evening shall cheer!

RHEIN-WEIN LIED.

(1800.)

(From 'The House of Aspen.')

WHAT makes the troopers' frozen
    courage muster?
    The grapes of juice divine.
Upon the Rhine, upon the Rhine they
    cluster:
    Oh, blessed be the Rhine!

Let fringe and furs, and many a rabbit-
    skin, sirs,
    Bedeck your Saracen;
He 'll freeze without what warms our
    hearts within, sirs,
    When the night-frost crusts the fen.

But on the Rhine, but on the Rhine
    they cluster,
    The grapes of juice divine,
That make our troopers' frozen courage
    muster:
    Oh, blessed be the Rhine!

—◆—

THE REIVER'S WEDDING.

(1802.)

O WILL ye hear a mirthful bourd?
    Or will ye hear of courtesie?
Or will ye hear how a gallant lord
    Was wedded to a gay ladye?

'Ca' out the kye,' quo' the village herd,
    As he stood on the knowe,
'Ca' this ane's nine and that ane's ten,
    And bauld Lord William's cow.'

'Ah! by my sooth,' quoth William
    then,
    'And stands it that way now,
When knave and churl have nine an
    ten,
    That the Lord has but his cow?

'I swear by the light of the Michael-
    mas moon,
    And the might of Mary high,
And by the edge of my braidsword
    brown,
    They shall soon say Harden's kye.'

He took a bugle frae his side,
    With names carved o'er and o'er;
Full many a chief of meikle pride
    That Border bugle bore,—

He blew a note baith sharp and hie,
    Till rock and water rang around—
Three score of moss-troopers and three
    Have mounted at that bugle sound.

The Michaelmas moon had enter'd
    then,
    And ere she wan the full,
Ye might see by her light in Harden
    glen
    A bow o' kye and a bassen'd bull.

And loud and loud in Harden tower
    The quaigh gaed round wi' meikle
    glee;
For the English beef was brought in
    bower
    And the English ale flow'd merrilie.

And mony a guest from Teviotside
    And Yarrow's Braes was there;
Was never a lord in Scotland wide
    That made more dainty fare.

They ate, they laugh'd, they sang and
    quaff'd,
    Till nought on board was seen,
When knight and squire were boune
    to dine,
    But a spur of silver sheen.

Lord William has ta'en his berry
    brown steed,
    A sore shent man was he;
'Wait ye, my guests, a little speed;
    Weel feasted ye shall be.'

He rode him down by Falsehope burn,
  His cousin dear to see,
With him to take a riding turn—
  Wat-draw-the-sword was he.

And when he came to Falsehope glen,
  Beneath the trysting-tree,
On the smooth green was carved plain,
  'To Lochwood bound are we.'

'O if they be gane to dark Lochwood
  To drive the Warden's gear,
Betwixt our names, I ween, there's
    feud;
  I'll go and have my share:

'For little reck I for Johnstone's feud,
  The Warden though he be.'
So Lord William is away to dark
    Lochwood,
  With riders barely three.

The Warden's daughters in Lochwood
    sate,
  Were all both fair and gay,
All save the Lady Margaret,
  And she was wan and wae.

The sister, Jean, had a full fair skin,
  And Grace was bauld and braw;
But the leal-fast heart her breast within
  It weel was worth them a'.

Her father's pranked her sisters twa
  With meikle joy and pride;
But Margaret maun seek Dundrennan's
    wa'—
  She ne'er can be a bride.

On spear and casque by gallants gent
  Her sisters' scarfs were borne,
But never at tilt or tournament
  Were Margaret's colours worn.

Her sisters rode to Thirlstane bower,
  But she was left at hame
To wander round the gloomy tower,
  And sigh young Harden's name.

'Of all the knights, the knight most
    fair,
  From Yarrow to the Tyne,'
Soft sigh'd the maid, 'is Harden's heir,
  But ne'er can he be mine;

'Of all the maids, the foulest maid,
  From Teviot to the Dee,
Ah!' sighing sad, that lady said,
  'Can ne'er young Harden's be.'

She looked up the briery glen,
  And up the mossy brae,
And she saw a score of her father's men
  Yclad in the Johnstone grey.

O fast and fast they downwards sped
  The moss and briers among,
And in the midst the troopers led
  A shackled knight along.

. . . . . .

—◆◆—

WAR-SONG OF THE ROYAL EDINBURGH LIGHT DRAGOONS.

(1802.)

To horse! to horse! the standard flies,
  The bugles sound the call;
The Gallic navy stems the seas,
The voice of battle's on the breeze,
  Arouse ye, one and all!

From high Dunedin's towers we come,
  A band of brothers true;
Our casques the leopard's spoils sur-
    round,
With Scotland's hardy thistle crown'd;
  We boast the red and blue[1].

Though tamely crouch to Gallia's frown
  Dull Holland's tardy train;
Their ravish'd toys though Romans
    mourn;
Though gallant Switzers vainly spurn,
  And, foaming, gnaw the chain;

---

[1] The royal colours.

Oh! had they mark'd the avenging call [1]
Their brethren's murder gave,
Disunion ne'er their ranks had mown,
Nor patriot valour, desperate grown,
Sought freedom in the grave!

Shall we, too, bend the stubborn head.
In Freedom's temple born,
Dress our pale cheek in timid smile,
To hail a master in our isle,
Or brook a victor's scorn?

No! though destruction o'er the land
Come pouring as a flood,
The sun, that sees our falling day,
Shall mark our sabres' deadly sway,
And set that night in blood.

For gold let Gallia's legions fight,
Or plunder's bloody gain;
Unbribed, unbought, our swords we draw,
To guard our king, to fence our law,
Nor shall their edge be vain.

If ever breath of British gale
Shall fan the tri-color,
Or footstep of invader rude,
With rapine foul, and red with blood,
Pollute our happy shore,—

Then farewell home! and farewell friends!
Adieu each tender tie!
Resolved, we mingle in the tide,
Where charging squadrons furious ride,
To conquer or to die.

1 The allusion is to the massacre of the Swiss Guards, on the fatal 10th August, 1792. It is painful, but not useless, to remark, that the passive temper with which the Swiss regarded the death of their bravest country-men, mercilessly slaughtered in discharge of their duty, encouraged and authorized the progressive injustice, by which the Alps, once the seat of the most virtuous and free people upon the Continent, have, at length, been converted into the citadel of a foreign and military despot. A state degraded is half enslaved. [1812.]

To horse! to horse! the sabres gleam;
High sounds our bugle-call;
Combined by honour's sacred tie,
Our word is *Laws and Liberty!*
March forward, one and all!

—◦◦—

THE BARD'S INCANTATION.

(Written under threat of an invasion in the Autumn of 1804.)

THE forest of Glenmore is drear,
It is all of black pine and the dark oak-tree;
And the midnight wind to the moun-tain deer
Is whistling the forest lullaby:
The moon looks through the drifting storm,
But the troubled lake reflects not her form,
For the waves roll whitening to the land,
And dash against the shelvy strand.

There is a voice among the trees,
That mingles with the groaning oak—
That mingles with the stormy breeze,
And the lake-waves dashing against the rock;
There is a voice within the wood,
The voice of the bard in fitful mood;
His song was louder than the blast,
As the bard of Glenmore through the forest past.

'Wake ye from your sleep of death,
Minstrels and bards of other days!
For the midnight wind is on the heath,
And the midnight meteors dimly blaze:

The Spectre with his Bloody Hand
Is wandering through the wild woodland;
The owl and the raven are mute for
dread,
And the time is meet to awake the
dead!

'Souls of the mighty, wake and say,
    To what high strain your harps
        were strung,
When Lochlin plow'd her billowy way,
    And on your shores her Norsemen
        flung?
Her Norsemen train'd to spoil and
    blood,
Skill'd to prepare the Raven's food,
All, by your harpings, doom'd to die
On bloody Largs and Loncarty.

'Mute are ye all? No murmurs strange
    Upon the midnight breeze sail by;
Nor through the pines, with whistling
        change
    Mimic the harp's wild harmony!
Mute are ye now? Ye ne'er were mute,
When Murder with his bloody foot,
And Rapine with his iron hand,
Were hovering near yon mountain
    strand.

'O yet awake the strain to tell,
    By every deed in song enroll'd,
By every chief who fought or fell,
    For Albion's weal in battle bold:
From Coilgach[1], first who roll'd his car
Through the deep ranks of Roman war,
To him, of veteran memory dear.
Who victor died on Aboukir.

'By all their swords, by all their scars,
    By all their names, a mighty spell!
By all their wounds, by all their wars,
    Arise, the mighty strain to tell!
For fiercer than fierce Hengist's strain,
More impious than the heathen Dane,
More grasping than all-grasping Rome,
Gaul's ravening legions hither come!'

---

[1] The Galgacus of Tacitus.

The wind is hush'd, and still the lake—
    Strange murmurs fill my tinkling
        ears,
Bristles my hair, my sinews quake,
    At the dread voice of other years:
'When targets clash'd, and bugles
        rung,
And blades round warriors heads
        were flung,
The foremost of the band were we,
And hymn'd the joys of Liberty!'

—•+•—

HELLVELLYN.

(1805.)

I CLIMB'D the dark brow of the mighty
        Hellvellyn,
    Lakes and mountains beneath me
        gleam'd misty and wide;
All was still, save by fits, when the
        eagle was yelling,
    And starting around me the echoes
        replied.
On the right, Striden-edge round the
        Red-tarn was bending,
And Catchedicam its left verge was
        defending,
One huge nameless rock in the front
        was ascending,
    When I mark'd the sad spot where
        the wanderer had died.

Dark green was that spot 'mid the
        brown mountain-heather,
    Where the Pilgrim of Nature lay
        stretch'd in decay,
Like the corpse of an outcast abandon'd
        to weather,
    Till the mountain winds wasted
        the tenantless clay.
Nor yet quite deserted, though lonely
        extended,
For, faithful in death, his mute
        favourite attended,

The much-loved remains of her master
    defended,
    And chased the hill-fox and the
        raven away.

How long didst thou think that his
    silence was slumber?
    When the wind waved his garment,
        how oft didst thou start?
How many long days and long weeks
    didst thou number,
    Ere he faded before thee, the friend
        of thy heart?
And, oh, was it meet, that—no re-
    quiem read o'er him—
No mother to weep, and no friend
    to deplore him,
And thou, little guardian, alone
    stretch'd before him—
    Unhonour'd the Pilgrim from life
        should depart?

When a Prince to the fate of the
    Peasant has yielded,
    The tapestry waves dark round the
        dim-lighted hall;
With scutcheons of silver the coffin
    is shielded,
    And pages stand mute by the cano-
        pied pall:
Through the courts, at deep midnight,
    the torches are gleaming;
In the proudly-arch'd chapel the
    banners are beaming,
Far adown the long aisle sacred music
    is streaming,
    Lamenting a Chief of the people
        should fall.

But meeter for thee, gentle lover of
    nature,
    To lay down thy head like the meek
        mountain lamb,
When, wilder'd, he drops from some
    cliff huge in stature,
    And draws his last sob by the side
        of his dam.

And more stately thy couch by this
    desert lake lying,
Thy obsequies sung by the grey plover
    flying,
With one faithful friend but to witness
    thy dying,
    In the arms of Hellvellyn and
    Catchedicam.

THE DYING BARD.

(1806.)

DINAS EMLINN, lament; for the
    moment is nigh,
When mute in the woodlands thine
    echoes shall die:
No more by sweet Teivi Cadwallon
    shall rave,
And mix his wild notes with the wild
    dashing wave.

In spring and in autumn thy glories
    of shade
Unhonour'd shall flourish, unhonour'd
    shall fade;
For soon shall be lifeless the eye and
    the tongue,
That view'd them with rapture, with
    rapture that sung.

Thy sons, Dinas Emlinn, may march
    in their pride,
And chase the proud Saxon from
    Prestatyn's side;
But where is the harp shall give life
    to their name?
And where is the bard shall give
    heroes their fame?

And oh, Dinas Emlinn! thy daughters
    so fair,
Who heave the white bosom, and
    wave the dark hair;
What tuneful enthusiast shall worship
    their eye,
When half of their charms with Cad-
    wallon shall die?

Then adieu, silver Teivi! I quit thy
      loved scene,
To join the dim choir of the bards who
      have been ;
With Lewarch, and Meilor, and Merlin
      the Old,
And sage Taliessin, high harping to
      hold.

And adieu, Dinas Emlinn! still green
      be thy shades,
Unconquer'd thy warriors, and match-
      less thy maids!
And thou, whose faint warblings my
      weakness can tell,
Farewell, my loved Harp! my last
      treasure, farewell!

—◆—

THE NORMAN HORSE-SHOE.

(1806.)

RED glows the forge in Striguil's
      bounds,
And hammers din, and anvil sounds,
And armourers, with iron toil,
Barb many a steed for battle's broil.
Foul fall the hand which bends the
      steel
Around the courser's thundering heel,
That e'er shall dint a sable wound
On fair Glamorgan's velvet ground ?

From Chepstow's towers, ere dawn
      of morn,
Was heard afar the bugle-horn ;
And forth, in banded pomp and pride,
Stout Clare and fiery Neville ride.
They swore their banners broad
      should gleam,
In crimson light, on Rymny's stream ;
They vow'd Caerphili's sod should
      feel
The Norman charger's spurning heel.

And sooth they swore : the sun arose,
And Rymny's wave with crimson
      glows ;
For Clare's red banner, floating wide,
Roll'd down the stream to Severn's tide!
And sooth they vow'd : the trampled
      green
Show'd where hot Neville's charge
      had been :
In every sable hoof-tramp stood
A Norman horseman's curdling blood!

Old Chepstow's brides may curse the
      toil
That arm'd stout Clare for Cambrian
      broil ;
Their orphans long the art may rue,
For Neville's war-horse forged the
      shoe.
No more the stamp of armed steed
Shall dint Glamorgan's velvet mead ;
Nor trace be there, in early spring,
Save of the Fairies' emerald ring.

—◆—

THE MAID OF TORO.

(1806.)

(*An earlier version, of date 1800,
appears in 'The House of Aspen.'*)

O, LOW shone the sun on the fair
      lake of Toro,
      And weak were the whispers that
            waved the dark wood,
All as a fair maiden, bewilder'd in
      sorrow,
      Sorely sigh'd to the breezes, and
            wept to the flood.
' O saints! from the mansions of bliss
      lowly bending ;
      Sweet Virgin! who hearest the
            suppliant's cry,
Now grant my petition, in anguish
      ascending,
      My Henry restore, or let Eleanor
            die!'

All distant and faint were the sounds
of the battle,
  With the breezes they rise, with
the breezes they fail,
Till the shout, and the groan, and
the conflict's dread rattle,
  And the chase's wild clamour, came
loading the gale.
Breathless she gazed on the woodlands
so dreary;
  Slowly approaching a warrior was
seen;
Life's ebbing tide mark'd his footsteps
so weary,
  Cleft was his helmet, and woe was
his mien.

'O save thee, fair maid, for our armies
are flying!
  O save thee, fair maid, for thy
guardian is low!
Deadly cold on yon heath thy brave
Henry is lying,
  And fast through the woodland
approaches the foe.'
Scarce could he falter the tidings of
sorrow,
  And scarce could she hear them,
benumb'd with despair;
And when the sun sank on the sweet
lake of Toro,
  For ever he set to the brave and
the fair.

—◦—

THE PALMER.
(1806.)

' O OPEN the door, some pity to show,
  Keen blows the northern wind!
The glen is white with the drifted snow,
  And the path is hard to find.

' No outlaw seeks your castle gate,
  From chasing the King's deer,
Though even an outlaw's wretched
state
  Might claim compassion here.

' A weary Palmer, worn and weak,
  I wander for my sin;
O open, for Our Lady's sake!
  A pilgrim's blessing win!

' I 'll give you pardons from the Pope,
  And reliques from o'er the sea;
Or if for these you will not ope,
  Yet open for charity.

' The hare is crouching in her form,
  The hart beside the hind;
An aged man, amid the storm,
  No shelter can I find.

' You hear the Ettrick's sullen roar,
  Dark, deep, and strong is he,
And I must ford the Ettrick o'er,
  Unless you pity me.

' The iron gate is bolted hard,
  At which I knock in vain;
The owner's heart is closer barr'd,
  Who hears me thus complain.

' Farewell, farewell! and Mary grant,
  When old and frail you be,
You never may the shelter want
  That 's now denied to me.'

The Ranger on his couch lay warm,
  And heard him plead in vain;
But oft amid December's storm
  He 'll hear that voice again:

For lo, when through the vapours dank
  Morn shone on Ettrick fair,
A corpse amid the a'ders rank,
  The Palmer welter'd there.

—◦—

THE MAID OF NEIDPATH.
(1806.)

O LOVERS' eyes are sharp to see,
  And lovers' ears in hearing;
And love, in life's extremity,
  Can lend an hour of cheering.

Disease had been in Mary's bower,
And slow decay from mourning,
Though now she sits on Neidpath's
tower,
To watch her love's returning.

All sunk and dim her eyes so bright,
Her form decay'd by pining,
Till through her wasted hand, at night,
You saw the taper shining;
By fits, a sultry hectic hue
Across her cheek was flying;
By fits, so ashy pale she grew,
Her maidens thought her dying.

Yet keenest powers to see and hear
Seem'd in her frame residing;
Before the watch-dog prick'd his ear
She heard her lover's riding;
Ere scarce a distant form was ken'd,
She knew, and waved to greet him;
And o'er the battlement did bend,
As on the wing to meet him.

He came—he pass'd—an heedless
gaze,
As o'er some stranger glancing;
Her welcome, spoke in faltering phrase,
Lost in his courser's prancing.
The castle arch, whose hollow tone
Returns each whisper spoken,
Could scarcely catch the feeble moan
Which told her heart was broken.

—◆—

WANDERING WILLIE.

(1806.)

ALL joy was bereft me the day that
you left me,
And climb'd the tall vessel to sail
yon wide sea;
O weary betide it! I wander'd beside it,
And bann'd it for parting my Willie
and me.

Far o'er the wave hast thou follow'd
thy fortune,
Oft fought the squadrons of France
and of Spain,
Ae kiss of welcome's worth twenty
at parting,
Now I hae gotten my Willie again.

When the sky it was mirk, and the
winds they were wailing,
I sat on the beach wi' the tear in
my ee,
And thought o' the bark where my
Willie was sailing,
And wish'd that the tempest could
a' blaw on me.

Now that thy gallant ship rides at her
mooring,
Now that my wanderer's in safety
at hame,
Music to me were the wildest winds'
roaring,
That e'er o'er Inch-Keith drove the
dark ocean faem.

When the lights they did blaze, and
the guns they did rattle,
And blithe was each heart for the
great victory,
In secret I wept for the dangers of
battle,
And thy glory itself was scarce
comfort to me.

But now shalt thou tell, while I
eagerly listen,
Of each bold adventure, and every
brave scar;
And trust me, I'll smile, though my
een they may glisten;
For sweet after danger's the tale
of the war.

And oh, how we doubt when there's
distance 'tween lovers,
When there's naething to speak to
the heart thro' the ee;

How often the kindest and warmest
prove rovers,
And the love of the faithfullest ebbs
like the sea.

Till, at times—could I help it ? I pined
and I ponder'd,
If love could change notes like the
bird on the tree;
Now I 'll ne'er ask if thine eyes may
hae wander'd,
Enough, thy leal heart has been
constant to me.

Welcome, from sweeping o'er sea
and through channel,
Hardships and danger despising for
fame,
Furnishing story for glory's bright
annal,
Welcome, my wanderer, to Jeanie
and hame !

Enough, now thy story in annals of
glory
Has humbled the pride of France,
Holland, and Spain ;
No more shalt thou grieve me, no
more shalt thou leave me,
I never will part with my Willie again.

——◆——

HEALTH TO LORD MELVILLE.

(1806.)

SINCE here we are set in array round
the table,
Five hundred good fellows well met
in a hall,
Come listen, brave boys, and I 'll sing
as I 'm able
How innocence triumph'd and pride
got a fall.
But push round the claret—
Come, stewards, don't spare it—
With rapture you'll drink to the toast
that I give ;
Here, boys,
Off with it merrily—
Melville for ever, and long may he live!

What were the Whigs doing, when
boldly pursuing,
Pitt banish'd Rebellion, gave
Treason a string ?
Why, they swore on their honour,
for Arthur O'Connor,
And fought hard for Despard
against country and king.
Well, then, we knew boys,
Pitt and Melville were true boys,
And the tempest was raised by the
friends of Reform.
Ah, woe !
Weep to his memory ;
Low lies the pilot that weather'd the
storm !

And pray, don't you mind when the
Blues first were raising,
And we scarcely could think the
house safe o'er our heads ?
When villains and coxcombs, French
politics praising,
Drove peace from our tables and
sleep from our beds ?
Our hearts they grew bolder
When, musket on shoulder,
Stepp'd forth our old Statesmen
example to give.
Come, boys, never fear,
Drink the Blue grenadier—
Here 's to old Harry, and long may he
live !

They would turn us adrift; though
rely, sir, upon it—
Our own faithful chronicles warrant
us that
The free mountaineer and his bonny
blue bonnet
Have oft gone as far as the regular's
hat.
We laugh at their taunting,
For all we are wanting
Is licence our life for our country to give.
Off with it merrily,
Horse, foot, and artillery,
Each loyal Volunteer, long may he live !

'Tis not us alone, boys—the Army
    and Navy
  Have each got a slap 'mid their
    politic pranks ;
Cornwallis cashier'd, that watch'd
    winters to save ye,
  And the Cape call'd a bauble,
    unworthy of thanks.
    But vain is their taunt,
    No soldier shall want
The thanks that his country to valour
    can give :
    Come, boys,
    Drink it off merrily,—
Sir David and Popham, and long may
    they live !

And then our revenue—Lord knows
    how they view'd it,
  While each petty statesman talk'd
    lofty and big;
But the beer-tax was weak, as if
    Whitbread had brew'd it,
  And the pig-iron duty a shame to
    a pig.
    In vain is their vaunting,
    Too surely there's wanting
What judgment, experience, and
    steadiness give :
    Come, boys,
    Drink about merrily,—
Health to sage Melville, and long may
    he live !

Our King, too—our Princess—I dare
    not say more, sir,—
  May Providence watch them with
    mercy and might !
While there's one Scottish hand that
    can wag a claymore, sir,
  They shall ne'er want a friend to
    stand up for their right.
    Be damn'd he that dare not,—
    For my part, I'll spare not
To beauty afflicted a tribute to
    give :

Fill it up steadily,
    Drink it off readily,—
Here's to the Princess, and long may
    she live !

And since we must not set Auld
    Reekie in glory,
  And make her brown visage as
    light as her heart;
Till each man illumine his own upper
    story,
  Nor law-book nor lawyer shall force
    us to part.
    In Grenville and Spencer,
    And some few good men, sir,
High talents we honour, slight dif-
    ference forgive;
    But the Brewer we'll hoax,
    Tallyho to the Fox,
And drink Melville for ever, as long
    as we live !

—◆◆—

HUNTING SONG.

(1808.)

(*This song appears in the Appendix to
the General Preface of Waverley,* 1814.)

WAKEN, lords and ladies gay,
On the mountain dawns the day,
All the jolly chase is here,
With hawk, and horse, and hunting-
    spear !
Hounds are in their couples yelling,
Hawks are whistling, horns are
    knelling,
Merrily, merrily, mingle they,
'Waken, lords and ladies gay.'

Waken, lords and ladies gay,
The mist has left the mountain grey,
Springlets in the dawn are steaming,
Diamonds on the brake are gleaming :

And foresters have busy been,
To track the buck in thicket green;
Now we come to chant our lay,
'Waken, lords and ladies gay.'

Waken, lords and ladies gay,
To the greenwood haste away;
We can show you where he lies,
Fleet of foot, and tall of size;
We can show the marks he made,
When 'gainst the oak his antlers fray'd;
You shall see him brought to bay,
'Waken, lords and ladies gay.'

Louder, louder chant the lay,
Waken, lords and ladies gay!
Tell them youth, and mirth, and glee,
Run a course as well as we;
Time, stern huntsman! who can baulk,
Stanch as hound, and fleet as hawk:
Think of this, and rise with day,
Gentle lords and ladies gay.

—◦—

THE RESOLVE.

(1808.)

(In imitation of an Old English Poem.)

My wayward fate I needs must 'plain,
Though bootless be the theme;
I loved, and was beloved again,
Yet all was but a dream:
For, as her love was quickly got,
So it was quickly gone;
No more I'll bask in flame so hot,
But coldly dwell alone.

Not maid more bright than maid was e'er
My fancy shall beguile,
By flattering word, or feigned tear,
By gesture, look, or smile:
No more I'll call the shaft fair shot,
Till it has fairly flown,
Nor scorch me at a flame so hot;
I'll rather freeze alone.

Each ambush'd Cupid I'll defy,
In cheek, or chin, or brow,
And deem the glance of woman's eye
As weak as woman's vow:
I'll lightly hold the lady's heart,
That is but lightly won;
I'll steel my breast to beauty's art,
And learn to live alone.

The flaunting torch soon blazes out,
The diamond's ray abides;
The flame its glory hurls about,
The gem its lustre hides;
Such gem I fondly deem'd was mine,
And glow'd a diamond stone,
But, since each eye may see it shine,
I'll darkling dwell alone.

No waking dream shall tinge my thought
With dyes so bright and vain,
No silken net, so slightly wrought,
Shall tangle me again:
No more I'll pay so dear for wit,
I'll live upon mine own,
Nor shall wild passion trouble it,
I'll rather dwell alone.

And thus I'll hush my heart to rest—
'Thy loving labour's lost;
Thou shalt no more be wildly blest,
To be so strangely crost;
The widow'd turtles mateless die,
The phœnix is but one;
They seek no loves, no more will I—
I'll rather dwell alone.'

—◦—

EPITAPH

*For a monument in Lichfield Cathedral,
at the burial-place of the family of
Miss Seward.*

(1808.)

Amid these aisles, where once his precepts show'd
The Heavenward pathway which in life he trod,

This simple tablet marks a Father's
    bier,
And those he loved in life, in death
    are near ;
For him, for them, a Daughter bade
    it rise,
Memorial of domestic charities.
Still wouldst thou know why o'er the
    marble spread,
In female grace the willow droops
    her head ;
Why on her branches, silent and
    unstrung,
The minstrel harp is emblematic hung ;
What poet's voice is smother'd here
    in dust
Till waked to join the chorus of the
    just,—
Lo ! one brief line an answer sad
    supplies,
Honour'd, beloved, and mourn'd, here
    Seward lies ;
Her worth, her warmth of heart, let
    friendship say,—
Go seek her genius in her living lay.

—◦—

PROLOGUE

*To Miss Baillie's Play of ' The Family
Legend.'*

(1809.)

'Tis sweet to hear expiring Summer's
    sigh,
Through forests tinged with russet,
    wail and die ;
'Tis sweet and sad the latest notes to
    hear
Of distant music, dying on the ear ;
But far more sadly sweet, on foreign
    strand,
We list the legends of our native land,
Link'd as they come with every
    tender tie,
Memorials dear of youth and infancy.

Chief, thy wild tales, romantic
    Caledon,
Wake keen remembrance in each
    hardy son.
Whether on India's burning coasts
    he toil,
Or till Acadia's winter-fetter'd soil,
He hears with throbbing heart and
    moisten'd eyes,
And, as he hears, what dear illusions
    rise !
It opens on his soul his native
    dell,
The woods wild waving, and the
    water's swell ;
Tradition's theme, the tower that
    threats the plain,
The mossy cairn that hides the hero
    slain ;
The cot, beneath whose simple porch
    were told,
By grey-hair'd patriarch, the tales of
    old,
The infant group, that hush'd their
    sports the while,
And the dear maid who listen'd with
    a smile.
The wanderer, while the vision warms
    his brain,
Is denizen of Scotland once again.

Are such keen feelings to the crowd
    confined,
And sleep they in the poet's gifted
    mind ?
Oh no ! For she, within whose
    mighty page
Each tyrant Passion shows his woe
    and rage,
Has felt the wizard influence they
    inspire,
And to your own traditions tuned
    her lyre.
Yourselves shall judge : whoe'er has
    raised the sail
By Mull's dark coast, has heard this
    evening's tale.

The plaided boatman, resting on his oar,
Points to the fatal rock amid the roar
Of whitening waves, and tells whate'er to-night
Our humble stage shall offer to your sight;
Proudly preferr'd that first our efforts give
Scenes glowing from her pen to breathe and live;
More proudly yet, should Caledon approve
The filial token of a Daughter's love.

—◆—

THE POACHER.

(1809.)

(In imitation of Crabbe.)

WELCOME, grave stranger, to our green retreats,
Where health with exercise and freedom meets!
Thrice welcome, Sage, whose philosophic plan
By nature's limits metes the rights of man;
Generous as he, who now for freedom bawls,
Now gives full value for true Indian shawls:
O'er court, o'er customhouse, his shoe who flings,
Now bilks excisemen, and now bullies kings.
Like his, I ween, thy comprehensive mind
Holds laws as mouse-traps baited for mankind:
Thine eye, applausive, each sly vermin sees,
That baulks the snare, **yet** battens on the cheese;

Thine ear has heard, with scorn instead of awe,
Our buckskinn'd justices expound the law,
Wire-draw the acts that fix for wires the pain,
And for the netted partridge noose the swain;
And thy vindictive arm would fain have broke
The last light fetter of the feudal yoke,
To give the denizens of wood and wild,
Nature's free race, to each her free-born child.
Hence hast thou mark'd, with grief, fair London's race,
Mock'd with the boon of one poor Easter chase,
And long'd to send them forth as free as when
Pour'd o'er Chantilly the Parisian train,
When musket, pistol, blunderbuss, combined,
And scarce the field-pieces were left behind!
A squadron's charge each leveret's heart dismay'd,
On every covey fired a bold brigade;
La Douce Humanité approved the sport,
For great the alarm indeed, yet small the hurt;
Shouts patriotic solemnized the day,
And Seine re-echo'd *Vive la Liberté!*
But mad *Citoyen*, meek *Monsieur* again,
With some few added links resumes his chain.
Then, since such scenes to France no more are known,
Come, view with me a hero of thine own!
One, whose free actions vindicate the cause
Of silvan liberty o'er feudal laws.

Seek we yon glades, where the
proud oak o'ertops
Wide-waving seas of birch and hazel
copse,
Leaving between deserted isles of land,
Where stunted heath is patch'd with
ruddy sand ;
And lonely on the waste the yew is
seen,
Or straggling hollies spread a brighter
green.
Here, little worn, and winding dark
and steep,
Our scarce mark'd path descends yon
dingle deep :
Follow—but heedful, cautious of a trip ;
In earthly mire philosophy may slip.
Step slow and wary o'er that swampy
stream,
Till, guided by the charcoal's smother-
ing steam,
We reach the frail yet barricaded door
Of hovel form'd for poorest of the
poor ;
No hearth the fire, no vent the smoke
receives,
The walls are wattles, and the cover-
ing leaves ;
For, if such hut, our forest statutes say,
Rise in the progress of one night and
day,
(Though placed where still the Con-
queror's hests o'erawe,
And his son's stirrup shines the badge
of law,)
The builder claims the unenviable boon,
To tenant dwelling, framed as slight
and soon
As wigwam wild, that shrouds the
native frore
On the bleak coast of frost-barr'd
Labrador.

Approach, and through the un-
latticed window peep—
Nay, shrink not back, the inmate is
asleep ;

Sunk 'mid yon sordid blankets, till
the sun
Stoop to the west, the plunderer's
toils are done.
Loaded and primed, and prompt for
desperate hand,
Rifle and fowling-piece beside him
stand ;
While round the hut are in disorder laid
The tools and booty of his lawless trade;
For force or fraud, resistance or escape,
The crow, the saw, the bludgeon, and
the crape.
His pilfer'd powder in yon nook he
hoards,
And the filch'd lead the church's roof
affords
(Hence shall the rector's congregation
fret,
That while his sermon's dry his walls
are wet).
The fish-spear barb'd, the sweeping
net are there,
Doe-hides, and pheasant plumes, and
skins of hare,
Cordage for toils, and wiring for the
snare.
Barter'd for game from chase or
warren won,
Yon cask holds moonlight, run when
moon was none ;
And late-snatch'd spoils lie stow'd in
hutch apart,
To wait the associate higgler's evening
cart.

Look on his pallet foul, and mark
his rest :
What scenes perturb'd are acting in
his breast !
His sable brow is wet and wrung
with pain,
And his dilated nostril toils in vain ;
For short and scant the breath each
effort draws,
And 'twixt each effort Nature claims
a pause.

Beyond the loose and sable neckcloth
   stretch'd,
His sinewy throat seems by convulsion twitch'd,
While the tongue falters, as to utterance loth,
Sounds of dire import—watchword,
   threat, and oath.
Though, stupified by toil, and drugg'd
   with gin,
The body sleep, the restless guest
   within
Now plies on wood and wold his
   lawless trade,
Now in the fangs of justice wakes
   dismay'd.

'Was that wild start of terror and
   despair,
Those bursting eyeballs, and that
   wilder'd air,
Signs of compunction for a murder'd
   hare?
Do the locks bristle and the eyebrows
   arch
For grouse or partridge massacred in
   March?'

No, scoffer, no! Attend, and mark
   with awe,
There is no wicket in the gate of law!
He that would e'er so lightly set ajar
That awful portal, must undo each bar:
Tempting occasion, habit, passion,
   pride,
Will join to storm the breach, and
   force the barrier wide.

That ruffian, whom true men avoid
   and dread,
Whom bruisers, poachers, smugglers,
   call Black Ned,
Was Edward Mansell once,—the light-
   est heart
That ever play'd on holiday his part!
The leader he in every Christmas game,
The harvest-feast grew blither when
   he came,

And liveliest on the chords the bow
   did glance
When Edward named the tune and
   led the dance.
Kind was his heart, his passions quick
   and strong,
Hearty his laugh, and jovial was his
   song;
And if he loved a gun, his father swore,
''Twas but a trick of youth would
   soon be o'er,
Himself had done the same some
   thirty years before.'

But he whose humours spurn law's
   awful yoke
Must herd with those by whom law's
   bonds are broke:
The common dread of justice soon allies
The clown, who robs the warren. or
   excise,
With sterner felons train'd to act
   more dread,
Even with the wretch by whom his
   fellow bled.
Then, as in plagues the foul conta-
   gions pass,
Leavening and festering the corrupted
   mass,
Guilt leagues with guilt, while mutual
   motives draw,
Their hope impunity, their fear the law;
Their foes, their friends, their rendez-
   vous the same,
Till the revenue baulk'd, or pilfer'd
   game,
Flesh the young culprit, and example
   leads
To darker villany, and direr deeds.

Wild howl'd the wind the forest
   glades along,
And oft the owl renew'd her dismal
   song;
Around the spot where erst he felt
   the wound,
Red William's spectre walk'd his
   midnight round.

When o'er the swamp he cast his
    blighting look,
From the green marshes of the stag-
    nant brook
The bittern's sullen shout the sedges
    shook!
The waning moon, with storm-pre-
    saging gleam,
Now gave and now withheld her
    doubtful beam;
The old Oak stoop'd his arms, then
    flung them high,
Bellowing and groaning to the troubled
    sky;
'Twas then, that, couch'd amid the
    brushwood sere,
In Malwood-walk young Mansell
    watch'd the deer:
The fattest buck received his deadly
    shot,
The watchful keeper heard, and sought
    the spot.
Stout were their hearts, and stubborn
    was their strife;
O'erpower'd at length, the Outlaw
    drew his knife.
Next morn a corpse was found upon
    the fell—
The rest his waking agony may tell!

—◆◆—

OH SAY NOT, MY LOVE.

(1810?)

(*In imitation of Moore.*)

Oh say not, my love, with that
    mortified air,
  That your spring-time of pleasure
    is flown,
Nor bid me to maids that are younger
    repair
  For those raptures that still are
    thine own.

Though April his temples may wreathe
    with the vine,
  Its tendrils in infancy curl'd,
'Tis the ardour of August matures us
    the wine,
  Whose lifeblood enlivens the world.

Though thy form, that was fashion'd
    as light as a fay's,
  Has assumed a proportion more
    round,
And thy glance, that was bright as
    a falcon's at gaze,
  Looks soberly now on the ground;

Enough, after absence to meet me
    again,
  Thy steps still with ecstasy move;
Enough, that those dear sober glances
    retain
  For me the kind language of love.

—◆◆—

THE BOLD DRAGOON.

(1812.)

'Twas a Maréchal of France, and he
    fain would honour gain,
And he long'd to take a passing glance
    at Portugal from Spain;
  With his flying guns, this gallant
    gay,
  And boasted corps d'armée—
O he fear'd not our dragoons, with
    their long swords, boldly riding,
Whack, fal de ral, &c.

To Campo Mayor come, he had quietly
    sat down,
Just a fricassee to pick, while his
    soldiers sack'd the town,
  When, 'twas peste! morbleu!
    mon General,
  Hear the English bugle-call!
And behold the light dragoons, with
    their long swords, boldly riding,
Whack, fal de ral, &c.

Right about went horse and foot,
    artillery and all,
And, as the devil leaves a house, they
    tumbled through the wall ;
    They took no time to seek the door,
    But, best foot set before—
O they ran from our dragoons, with
    their long swords, boldly riding,
    Whack, fal de ral, &c.

Those valiant men of France they had
    scarcely fled a mile,
When on their flank there sous'd at
    once the British rank and file ;
For Long, De Grey, and Otway,
    then
    Ne'er minded one to ten,
But came on like light dragoons, with
    their long swords, boldly riding,
    Whack, fal de ral, &c.

Three hundred British lads they made
    three thousand reel,
Their hearts were made of English oak,
    their swords of Sheffield steel,
    Their horses were in Yorkshire
    bred,
    And Beresford them led ;
So huzza for brave dragoons, with
    their long swords, boldly riding,
    Whack, fal de ral, &c.

Then here's a health to Wellington, to
    Beresford, to Long,
And a single word of Bonaparte before
    I close my song :
    The eagles that to fight he brings
    Should serve his men with wings,
When they meet the bold dragoons,
    with their long swords, boldly
    riding,
    Whack, fal de ral, &c.

—◆◆—

ON THE MASSACRE OF GLENCOE.

(*Pub.* 1814.)

'O TELL me, Harper, wherefore flow
Thy wayward notes of wail and woe,
Far down the desert of Glencoe,
    Where none may list their melody?
Say, harp'st thou to the mists that
    fly,
Or to the dun-deer glancing by,
Or to the eagle, that from high
    Screams chorus to thy min-
    strelsy ?'—

'No, not to these, for they have rest,—
The mist-wreath has the mountain-
    crest,
The stag his lair, the erne her nest,
    Abode of lone security.
But those for whom I pour the lay,
Not wild-wood deep, nor mountain
    grey,
Not this deep dell, that shrouds from
    day,
    Could screen from treach'rous
    cruelty.

'Their flag was furl'd, and mute their
    drum,
The very household dogs were dumb,
Unwont to bay at guests that come
    In guise of hospitality.
His blithest notes the piper plied,
Her gayest snood the maiden tied,
The dame her distaff flung aside,
    To tend her kindly housewifery.

'The hand that mingled in the meal
At midnight drew the felon steel,
And gave the host's kind breast to feel
    Meed for his hospitality !
The friendly hearth which warm'd
    that hand,
At midnight arm'd it with the brand,
That bade destruction's flames expand
    Their red and fearful blazonry.

'Then woman's shriek was heard in vain,
Nor infancy's unpitied plain,
More than the warrior's groan, could gain
 Respite from ruthless butchery!
The winter wind that whistled shrill,
The snows that night that cloked the hill,
Though wild and pitiless, had still
 Far more than Southern clemency.

'Long have my harp's best notes been gone,
Few are its strings, and faint their tone,
They can but sound in desert lone
 Their grey-hair'd master's misery.
Were each grey hair a minstrel string
Each chord should imprecations fling,
Till startled Scotland loud should ring,
 “Revenge for blood and treachery!”'

—✦—

FOR A' THAT AN' A' THAT.

(1814.)

(*A New Song to an Old Tune.*)

THOUGH right be aft put down by strength,
 As mony a day we saw that,
The true and leilfu' cause at length
 Shall bear the grie for a' that.
For a' that an' a' that,
 Guns, guillotines, and a' that,
The fleur-de-lis, that lost her right,
 Is queen again for a' that!

We'll twine her in a friendly knot
 With England's rose, and a' that;
The shamrock shall not be forgot,
 For Wellington made braw that.
The thistle, though her leaf be rude,
 Yet faith we'll no misca' that,
She shelter'd in her solitude
 The fleur-de-lis, for a' that.

The Austrian vine, the Prussian pine
 (For Blucher's sake, hurra that),
The Spanish olive, too, shall join,
 And bloom in peace for a' that.
Stout Russia's hemp, so surely twined,
 Around our wreath we'll draw that,
And he that would the cord unbind
 Shall have it for his gra-vat!

Or, if to choke sae puir a sot,
 Your pity scorn to thraw that,
The devil's elbow be his lot
 Where he may sit and claw that.
In spite of slight, in spite of might,
 In spite of brags, an' a' that,
The lads that battled for the right
 Have won the day, an' a' that!

There's ae bit spot I had forgot,
 America they ca' that!
A coward plot her rats had got
 Their father's flag to gnaw that:
Now see it fly top-gallant high,
 Atlantic winds shall blaw that,
And Yankee loon, beware your croun,
 There's kames in hand to claw that!

For on the land, or on the sea,
 Where'er the breezes blaw that,
The British flag shall bear the grie,
 And win the day for a' that!

—✦—

SONG

FOR THE ANNIVERSARY MEETING OF
THE PITT CLUB OF SCOTLAND.

(1814.)

O, DREAD was the time, and more dreadful the omen,
 When the brave on Marengo lay slaughter'd in vain,
And beholding broad Europe bow'd down by her foemen,
 Pitt closed in his anguish the map of her reign!

Not the fate of broad Europe could
    bend his brave spirit
  To take for his country the safety of
    shame;
O, then in her triumph remember his
    merit,
  And hallow the goblet that flows to
    his name.

Round the husbandman's head, while
    he traces the furrow,
  The mists of the winter may mingle
    with rain,
He may plough it with labour, and
    sow it in sorrow,
  And sigh while he fears he has
    sow'd it in vain;
He may die ere his children shall reap
    in their gladness,
  But the blithe harvest-home shall
    remember his claim;
And their jubilee-shout shall be soften'd
    with sadness,
  While they hallow the goblet that
    flows to his name.

Though anxious and timeless his life
    was expended,
  In toils for our country preserved
    by his care,
Though he died ere one ray o'er the
    nations ascended,
  To light the long darkness of doubt
    and despair;
The storms he endured in our Britain's
    December,
  The perils his wisdom foresaw and
    o'ercame,
In her glory's rich harvest shall
    Britain remember,
  And hallow the goblet that flows to
    his name.

Nor forget His grey head, who, all
    dark in affliction,
  Is deaf to the tale of our victories
    won,

And to sounds the most dear to
    paternal affection,
  The shout of his people applauding
    his Son;
By his firmness unmoved in success
    and disaster,
  By his long reign of virtue, remember
    his claim!
With our tribute to Pitt join the praise
    of his Master,
  Though a tear stain the goblet that
    flows to his name.

Yet again fill the wine-cup, and
    change the sad measure,
  The rites of our grief and our
    gratitude paid,
To our Prince, to our Heroes, devote
    the bright treasure,
  The wisdom that plann'd, and the
    zeal that obey'd.
Fill Wellington's cup till it beam like
    his glory,
  Forget not our own brave Dalhousie
    and Græme;
A thousand years hence hearts shall
    bound at their story,
  And hallow the goblet that flows
    to their fame.

—♦—

PHAROS' LOQUITUR.

(1814.)

FAR in the bosom of the deep,
O'er these wild shelves my watch
    I keep;
A ruddy gem of changeful light,
Bound on the dusky brow of night,
The seaman bids my lustre hail,
And scorns to strike his timorous sail.

—♦—

ADDRESS

TO RANALD MACDONALD OF STAFFA.

(1814.)

STAFFA, sprung from high Macdonald,
Worthy branch of old Clan-Ranald,
Staffa, king of all kind fellows,
Well befall thy hills and valleys,
Lakes and inlets, deeps and shallows,
Cliffs of darkness, caves of wonder,
Echoing the Atlantic thunder;
Mountains which the grey mist covers,
Where the Chieftain spirit hovers,
Pausing while his pinions quiver,
Stretch'd to quit our land for ever!
Each kind influence reign above thee!
Warmer heart, 'twixt this and Jaffa
Beats not, than in heart of Staffa!

—◆◆—

EPISTLE

TO HIS GRACE THE DUKE OF
BUCCLEUCH.

Lighthouse Yacht in the Sound of Lerwick,
August 8, 1814.

HEALTH to the chieftain from his
    clansman true!
From her true minstrel, health to fair
    Buccleuch!
Health from the isles, where dewy
    Morning weaves
Her chaplet with the tints that Twi-
    light leaves;
Where late the sun scarce vanish'd
    from the sight,
And his bright pathway graced the
    short-lived night,
Though darker now as autumn's shades
    extend,
The north winds whistle and the mists
    ascend!

Health from the land where eddying
    whirlwinds toss
The storm-rock'd *cradle* of the Cape
    of Noss;
On outstretch'd cords the giddy engine
    slides,
His own strong arm the bold adven-
    turer guides,
And he that lists such desperate feat
    to try,
May, like the sea-mew, skim 'twixt
    surf and sky,
And feel the mid-air gales around him
    blow,
And see the billows rage five hundred
    feet below.

Here, by each stormy peak and
    desert shore,
The hardy islesman tugs the daring
    oar,
Practised alike his venturous course
    to keep
Through the white breakers or the
    pathless deep,
By ceaseless peril and by toil to
    gain
A wretched pittance from the niggard
    main.
And when the worn-out drudge old
    ocean leaves
What comfort greets him, and what
    hut receives?
Lady! the worst your presence ere
    has cheer'd
(When want and sorrow fled as you
    appear'd)
Were to a Zetlander as the high dome
Of proud Drumlanrig to my humble
    home.
Here rise no groves, and here no
    gardens blow,
Here even the hardy heath scarce
    dares to grow;
But rocks on rocks, in mist and storm
    array'd,
Stretch far to sea their giant colonnade,

With many a cavern seam'd, the
 dreary haunt
Of the dun seal and swarthy cormorant.
Wild round their rifted brows, with
 frequent cry
As of lament, the gulls and gannets
 fly,
And from their sable base, with sullen
 sound,
In sheets of whitening foam the waves
 rebound.

Yet even these coasts a touch of
 envy gain
From those whose land has known
 oppression's chain;
For here the industrious Dutchman
 comes once more
To moor his fishing craft by Bressay's
 shore;
Greets every former mate and brother
 tar,
Marvels how Lerwick 'scaped the rage
 of war,
Tells many a tale of Gallic outrage
 done,
And ends by blessing God and Wellington.
Here too the Greenland tar, a fiercer
 guest,
Claims a brief hour of riot, not of
 rest;
Proves each wild frolic that in wine
 has birth,
And wakes the land with brawls and
 boisterous mirth.
A sadder sight on yon poor vessel's
 prow—
The captive Norseman sits in silent
 woe,
And eyes the flags of Britain as they
 flow.
Hard fate of war, which bade her terrors sway
His destined course, and seize so mean
 a prey;

A bark with planks so warp'd and
 seams so riven,
She scarce might face the gentlest airs
 of heaven:
Pensive he sits, and questions oft if
 none
Can list his speech, and understand
 his moan;
In vain: no Islesman now can use the
 tongue
Of the bold Norse, from whom their
 lineage sprung.
Not thus of old the Norsemen hither
 came,
Won by the love of danger or of fame;
On every stormbeat cape a shapeless
 tower
Tells of their wars, their conquests,
 and their power;
For ne'er for Grecia's vales, nor Latian
 land,
Was fiercer strife than for this barren
 strand;
A race severe—the isle and ocean lords
Loved for its own delight the strife of
 swords;
With scornful laugh the mortal pang
 defied,
And blest their gods that they in battle
 died.

Such were the sires of Zetland's
 simple race,
And still the eye may faint resemblance
 trace
In the blue eye, tall form, proportion
 fair,
The limbs athletic, and the long light
 hair
(Such was the mien, as Scald and Min-
 strel sings,
Of fair-hair'd Harold, first of Norway's
 Kings);
But, their high deeds to scale these
 crags confined,
Their only warfare is with waves and
 wind.

Why should I talk of Mousa's castled
    coast?
Why of the horrors of the Sumburgh
    Rost?
May not these bald disjointed lines
    suffice,
Penn'd while my comrades whirl the
    rattling dice—
While down the cabin skylight lessen-
    ing shine
The rays, and eve is chased with mirth
    and wine?
Imagined, while down Mousa's desert
    bay
Our well-trimm'd vessel urged her
    nimble way,
While to the freshening breeze she
    lean'd her side,
And bade her bowsprit kiss the foamy
    tide?

Such are the lays that Zetland Isles
    supply;
Drench'd with the drizzly spray and
    dropping sky,
Weary and wet, a sea-sick minstrel I.

                W. Scott.

———

P. S.
       Kirkwall, Orkney, August 13, 1814.

In respect that your Grace has com-
    mission'd a Kraken,
You will please be inform'd that they
    seldom are taken;
It is January two years, the Zetland
    folks say,
Since they saw the last Kraken in
    Scalloway bay;
He lay in the offing a fortnight or
    more,
But the devil a Zetlander put from the
    shore,

Though bold in the seas of the North
    to assail
The morse and the sea-horse, the
    grampus and whale.
If your grace thinks I'm writing the
    thing that is not,
You may ask at a namesake of ours,
    Mr. Scott
(He's not from our clan, though his
    merits deserve it,
But springs, I'm informed, from the
    Scotts of Scotstarvet`;
He question'd the folks who beheld it
    with eyes,
But they differ'd confoundedly as to
    its size.
For instance, the modest and diffident
    swore
That it seem'd like the keel of a ship,
    and no more;
Those of eyesight more clear, or of
    fancy more high,
Said it rose like an island 'twixt ocean
    and sky;
But all of the hulk had a steady opinion
That 'twas sure a *live* subject of Nep-
    tune's dominion.
And I think, my Lord Duke, your
    Grace hardly would wish,
To cumber your house, such a kettle
    of fish.
Had your order related to nightcaps
    or hose,
Or mittens of worsted, there's plenty
    of those.
Or would you be pleased but to fancy
    a whale?
And direct me to send it—by sea or
    by mail!
The season, I'm told, is nigh over, but
    still
I could get you one fit for the lake at
    Bowhill.
Indeed, as to whales, there's no need
    to be thrifty,
Since one day last fortnight two
    hundred and fifty,

Pursued by seven Orkneymen's boats
and no more,
Betwixt Truffness and Luffness were
drawn on the shore!
You'll ask if I saw this same won-
derful sight;
I own that I did not, but easily might—
For this mighty shoal of leviathans
lay
On our lee-beam a mile, in the loop
of the bay,
And the islesmen of Sanda were all
at the spoil,
And *flinching* (so term it) the blubber
to boil;
(Ye spirits of lavender, drown the
reflection
That awakes at the thoughts of this
odorous dissection).
To see this huge marvel full fain would
we go,
But Wilson, the wind, and the current,
said no.
We have now got to Kirkwall, and
needs I must stare
When I think that in verse I have
once call'd it *fair*;
'Tis a base little borough, both dirty
and mean.
There is nothing to hear, and there's
nought to be seen,
Save a church, where, of old times, a
prelate harangued,
And a palace that's built by an earl
that was hang'd.
But, farewell to Kirkwall—aboard we
are going,
The anchor's a-peak, and the breezes
are blowing;
Our commodore calls all his band to
their places,
And 'tis time to release you—good
night to your Graces!

—◆◆—

THE A. OF WA . . . . . .

(*Author of Waverley.*)

No, John, I will not own the book—
I won't, you Piccaroon.
When next I try Saint Grubby's brook,
'The A of Wa—' shall bait the hook—
And flat-fish bite as soon
As if before them they had got
The worn-out wriggler

WALTER SCOTT.

—◆◆—

FAREWELL TO MACKENZIE,

HIGH CHIEF OF KINTAIL.

(1815.)

(*From the Gaelic.*)

'FAREWELL to Mackenneth, great Earl
of the North,
The Lord of Lochcarron, Glenshiel,
and Seaforth;
To the Chieftain this morning his
course who began,
Launching forth on the billows his
bark like a swan.
For a far foreign land he has hoisted
his sail,
Farewell to Mackenzie, High Chief
of Kintail!

O swift be the galley, and hardy her
crew,
May her captain be skilful, her mari-
ners true,
In danger undaunted, unwearied by
toil,
Though the whirlwind should rise,
and the ocean should boil:
On the brave vessel's gunnel I drank
his bonail[1],
And farewell to Mackenzie, High
Chief of Kintail!

---

[1] *Bon-allez.*

Awake in thy chamber, thou sweet
    southland gale !
Like the sighs of his people, breathe
    soft on his sail ;
Be prolong'd as regret, that his vassals
    must know,
Be fair as their faith, and sincere as
    their woe :
Be so soft, and so fair, and so faithful,
    sweet gale,
Wafting onward Mackenzie, High
    Chief of Kintail !

Be his pilot experienced, and trusty,
    and wise,
To measure the seas and to study
    the skies :
May he hoist all his canvas from
    streamer to deck,
But O ! crowd it higher when wafting
    him back—
Till the cliffs of Skooroora, and Conan's
    glad vale,
Shall welcome Mackenzie, High Chief
    of Kintail ! '

———

So sung the old Bard, in the grief
    of his heart,
When he saw his loved Lord from
    his people depart.
Now mute on thy mountains, O Albyn,
    are heard
Nor the voice of the song, nor the
    harp of the bard ;
Or its strings are but waked by the
    stern winter gale,
As they mourn for Mackenzie, last Chief
    of Kintail.

From the far Southland Border a
    Minstrel came forth,
And he waited the hour that some
    Bard of the north
His hand on the harp of the ancient
    should cast,
And bid its wild numbers mix high
    with the blast ;

But no bard was there left in the land
    of the Gael
To lament for Mackenzie, last Chief
    of Kintail.

And shalt thou then sleep, did the
    Minstrel exclaim,
Like the son of the lowly, unnoticed
    by fame ?
No, son of Fitzgerald ! in accents of
    woe
The song thou hast loved o'er thy
    coffin shall flow,
And teach thy wild mountains to join
    in the wail
That laments for Mackenzie, last Chief
    of Kintail.

In vain, the bright course of thy
    talents to wrong,
Fate deaden'd thine ear and imprison'd
    thy tongue ;
For brighter o'er all her obstructions
    arose
The glow of the genius they could
    not oppose ;
And who in the land of the Saxon or
    Gael
Might match with Mackenzie, High
    Chief of Kintail ?

Thy sons rose around thee in light
    and in love,
All a father could hope, all a friend
    could approve ;
What 'vails it the tale of thy sorrows
    to tell,—
In the spring-time of youth and of
    promise they fell !
Of the line of Fitzgerald remains
    not a male
To bear the proud name of the Chief
    of Kintail.

And thou, gentle Dame, who must
    bear, to thy grief,
For thy clan and thy country the
    cares of a Chief,

Whom brief rolling moons in six
    changes have left,
Of thy husband, and father, and
    brethren bereft,
To thine ear of affection, how sad
    is the hail,
That salutes thee the Heir of the
    line of Kintail!

—◆—

WAR-SONG OF LACHLAN,

HIGH CHIEF OF MACLEAN.

(1815.)

(From the Gaelic.)

A WEARY month has wander'd o'er
Since last we parted on the shore;
Heaven! that I saw thee, love, once
    more,
    Safe on that shore again!
'Twas valiant Lachlan gave the word—
Lachlan, of many a galley lord:
He call'd his kindred bands on board,
    And launch'd them on the main.

Clan-Gillian is to ocean gone—
Clan-Gillian, fierce in foray known;
Rejoicing in the glory won
    In many a bloody broil:
For wide is heard the thundering fray,
The rout, the ruin, the dismay,
When from the twilight glens away
    Clan-Gillian drives the spoil.

Woe to the hills that shall rebound
Our banner'd bagpipes' maddening
    sound;
Clan-Gillian's onset echoing round
    Shall shake their inmost cell.
Woe to the bark whose crew shall gaze
Where Lachlan's silken streamer plays!
The fools might face the lightning's
    blaze
    As wisely and as well!

—◆—

SAINT CLOUD.

(Paris, September 5, 1815.)

SOFT spread the southern summer night
    Her veil of darksome blue;
Ten thousand stars combined to light
    The terrace of Saint Cloud.

The evening breezes gently sigh'd,
    Like breath of lover true,
Bewailing the deserted pride
    And wreck of sweet Saint Cloud.

The drum's deep roll was heard afar,
    The bugle wildly blew
Good-night to Hulan and Hussar,
    That garrison Saint Cloud.

The startled Naiads from the shade
    With broken urns withdrew,
And silenced was that proud cascade,
    The glory of Saint Cloud.

We sate upon its steps of stone,
    Nor could its silence rue,
When waked, to music of our own,
    The echoes of Saint Cloud.

Slow Seine might hear each lovely note
    Fall light as summer dew,
While through the moonless air they
    float,
    Prolong'd from fair Saint Cloud.

And sure a melody more sweet
    His waters never knew,
Though music's self was wont to meet
    With Princes at Saint Cloud.

Nor then, with more delighted ear,
    The circle round her drew,
Than ours, when gather'd round to hear
    Our songstress at Saint Cloud.

Few happy hours poor mortals pass,—
    Then give those hours their due,
And rank among the foremost class
    Our evenings at Saint Cloud.

THE DANCE OF DEATH.

(1815.)

NIGHT and morning were at meeting
  Over Waterloo ;
Cocks had sung their earliest greeting ;
  Faint and low they crew,
For no paly beam yet shone
On the heights of Mount Saint John ;
Tempest-clouds prolong'd the sway
Of timeless darkness over day ;
Whirlwind, thunder-clap, and shower,
Mark'd it a predestined hour.
Broad and frequent through the night
Flash'd the sheets of levin-light ;
Muskets, glancing lightnings back,
Show'd the dreary bivouac
  Where the soldier lay,
Chill and stiff, and drench'd with
  rain,
Wishing dawn of morn again,
  Though death should come with day.

'Tis at such a tide and hour,
Wizard, witch, and fiend have power,
And ghastly forms through mist and
  shower
  Gleam on the gifted ken ;
And then the affrighted prophet's ear
Drinks whispers strange of fate and
  fear,
Presaging death and ruin near
  Among the sons of men ;—
Apart from Albyn's war-array,
'Twas then grey Allan sleepless lay ;
Grey Allan, who, for many a day,
  Had follow'd stout and stern,
Where, through battle's rout and reel,
Storm of shot and hedge of steel,
Led the grandson of Lochiel,
  Valiant Fassiefern.
Through steel and shot he leads no
  more,
Low laid 'mid friends' and foemen's
  gore—

But long his native lake's wild shore,
And Sunart rough, and high Ard-
    gower,
  And Morven long shall tell,
And proud Bennevis hear with awe,
How, upon bloody Quatre-Bras,
Brave Cameron heard the wild hurra
  Of conquest as he fell.

Lone on the outskirts of the host
The weary sentinel held post,
And heard, through darkness far aloof,
The frequent clang of courser's hoof,
Where held the cloak'd patrol their
    course,
And spurr'd 'gainst storm the swerv-
    ing horse.
But there are sounds in Allan's ear
Patrol nor sentinel may hear,
And sights before his eye aghast
Invisible to them have pass'd,
  When down the destined plain,
'Twixt Britain and the bands of France,
Wild as marsh-borne meteor's glance,
Strange phantoms wheel'd a revel
    dance,
  And doom'd the future slain.
Such forms were seen, such sounds
    were heard,
When Scotland's James his march
    prepared
For Flodden's fatal plain ;
Such, when he drew his ruthless sword,
As Choosers of the Slain, adored
  The yet unchristen'd Dane.
An indistinct and phantom band,
They wheel'd their ring-dance hand
    in hand,
  With gestures wild and dread :
The Seer, who watch'd them ride
    the storm,
Saw through their faint and shadowy
    form
  The lightning's flash more red ;
And still their ghastly roundelay
Was of the coming battle-fray,
  And of the destined dead :

SONG.

'Wheel the wild dance
While lightnings glance,
    And thunders rattle loud,
And call the brave
To bloody grave,
    To sleep without a shroud.

' Our airy feet,
So light and fleet,
    They do not bend the rye
That sinks its head when whirlwinds
        rave,
And swells again in eddying wave
    As each wild gust blows by ;
But still the corn,
At dawn of morn,
    Our fatal steps that bore,
At eve lies waste
A trampled paste
    Of blackening mud and gore.

'Wheel the wild dance
While lightnings glance,
    And thunders rattle loud,
And call the brave
To bloody grave,
    To sleep without a shroud.

'Wheel the wild dance !
Brave sons of France,
    For you our ring makes room ;
Make space full wide
For martial pride,
    For banner, spear, and plume.
Approach, draw near,
Proud cuirassier !
    Room for the men of steel !
Through crest and plate
The broadsword's weight
    Both head and heart shall feel.

'Wheel the wild dance
While lightnings glance,
    And thunders rattle loud,
And call the brave
To bloody grave,
    To sleep without a shroud.

' Sons of the spear !
You feel us near
    In many a ghastly dream ;
With fancy's eye
Our forms you spy,
    And hear our fatal scream.
With clearer sight
Ere falls the night,
    Just when to weal or woe
Your disembodied souls take flight
On trembling wing—each startled
        sprite
    Our choir of death shall know.

'Wheel the wild dance
While lightnings glance,
    And thunders rattle loud,
And call the brave
To bloody grave,
    To sleep without a shroud.

'Burst, ye clouds, in tempest showers,
Redder rain shall soon be ours !
    See ! the east grows wan—
Yield we place to sterner game,
Ere deadlier bolts and direr flame
Shall the welkin's thunders shame :
Elemental rage is tame
    To the wrath of man.'

At morn, grey Allan's mates with
        awe
Heard of the vision'd sights he saw,
    The legend heard him say ;
But the Seer's gifted eye was dim,
Deafen'd his ear, and stark his limb,
    Ere closed that bloody day
He sleeps far from his Highland
        heath,—
But often of the Dance of Death
    His comrades tell the tale,
On picquet-post, when ebbs the night,
And waning watch-fires glow less
        bright,
    And dawn is glimmering pale.

ROMANCE OF DUNOIS.

(1815.)

(*From the French of Hortense Beau-harnois, Ex-Queen of Holland.*)

IT was Dunois, the young and brave,
　　was bound for Palestine,
But first he made his orisons before
　　Saint Mary's shrine :
'And grant, immortal Queen of
　　Heaven,' was still the soldier's
　　prayer,
'That I may prove the bravest knight,
　　and love the fairest fair.'

His oath of honour on the shrine he
　　graved it with his sword,
And follow'd to the Holy Land the
　　banner of his Lord ;
Where, faithful to his noble vow, his
　　war-cry fill'd the air,
'Be honour'd aye the bravest knight,
　　beloved the fairest fair.'

They owed the conquest to his arm, and
　　then his Liege-Lord said,
'The heart that has for honour beat
　　by bliss must be repaid.
My daughter Isabel and thou shall be
　　a wedded pair,
For thou art bravest of the brave, she
　　fairest of the fair.'

And then they bound the holy knot
　　before Saint Mary's shrine,
That makes a paradise on earth, if
　　hearts and hands combine ;
And every lord and lady bright, that
　　were in chapel there,
Cried, 'Honour'd be the bravest knight,
　　beloved the fairest fair !'

—✦—

THE TROUBADOUR.

(1815.)

(*From the French of Hortense Beau-harnois.*)

GLOWING with love, on fire for fame,
　　A Troubadour that hated sorrow,
Beneath his Lady's window came,
　　And thus he sung his last good-
　　　morrow :
'My arm it is my country's right,
　　My heart is in my true-love's bower ;
Gaily for love and fame to fight
　　Befits the gallant Troubadour.'

And while he march'd with helm on
　　head
　　And harp in hand, the descant rung,
As, faithful to his favourite maid,
　　The minstrel-burden still he sung :
'My arm it is my country's right,
　　My heart is in my lady's bower ;
Resolved for love and fame to fight,
　　I come, a gallant Troubadour.'

Even when the battle-roar was deep,
　　With dauntless heart he hew'd his
　　　way,
'Mid splintering lance and falchion-
　　sweep,
　　And still was heard his warrior-lay :
'My life it is my country's right,
　　My heart is in my lady's bower ;
For love to die, for fame to fight,
　　Becomes the valiant Troubadour.'

Alas ! upon the bloody field
　　He fell beneath the foeman's glaive,
But still reclining on his shield,
　　Expiring sung the exulting stave :
'My life it is my country's right,
　　My heart is in my lady's bower ;
For love and fame to fall in fight
　　Becomes the valiant Troubadour.'

—✦—

2 A

FROM THE FRENCH.

(1815.)

It chanced that Cupid on a season,
　By Fancy urged, resolved to wed,
But could not settle whether Reason
　Or Folly should partake his bed.

What does he then?—Upon my life,
　'Twas bad example for a deity—
He takes me Reason for a wife,
　And Folly for his hours of gaiety.

Though thus he dealt in petty treason,
　He loved them both in equal mea-
　　sure;
Fidelity was born of Reason,
　And Folly brought to bed of Pleasure.

———

LINES

ON THE LIFTING OF THE BANNER OF THE HOUSE OF BUCCLEUCH, AT A GREAT FOOTBALL MATCH ON CARTERHAUGH.

(1815.)

From the brown crest of Newark its
　　summons extending,
　Our signal is waving in smoke and
　　in flame;
And each forester blithe, from his
　　mountain descending,
　Bounds light o'er the heather to
　　join in the game.

CHORUS.

Then up with the Banner, let forest
　　winds fan her,
　She has blazed over Ettrick eight
　　ages and more;
In sport we'll attend her, in battle
　　defend her,
　With heart and with hand, like our
　　fathers before.

When the Southern invader spread
　　waste and disorder,
　At the glance of her crescents he
　　paused and withdrew,
For around them were marshall'd the
　　pride of the Border,
　The Flowers of the Forest, the
　　Bands of Buccleuch.
　　Then up with the Banner, &c.

A Stripling's weak hand to our revel
　　has borne her,
　No mail-glove has grasp'd her, no
　　spearmen surround;
But ere a bold foeman should scathe
　　or should scorn her,
　A thousand true hearts would be
　　cold on the ground.
　　Then up with the Banner, &c.

We forget each contention of civil
　　dissension,
　And hail, like our brethren, Home,
　　Douglas, and Car:
And Elliot and Pringle in pastime
　　shall mingle,
　As welcome in peace as their fathers
　　in war.
　　Then up with the Banner, &c.

Then strip, lads, and to it, though
　　sharp be the weather,
　And if, by mischance, you should
　　happen to fall,
There are worse things in life than
　　a tumble on heather,
　And life is itself but a game at football.
　　Then up with the Banner, &c.

And when it is over, we'll drink a
　　blithe measure
　To each Laird and each Lady that
　　witness'd our fun,
And to every blithe heart that took
　　part in our pleasure,
　To the lads that have lost and the
　　lads that have won.
　　Then up with the Banner, &c.

May the Forest still flourish, both
Borough and Landward,
From the hall of the Peer to the
Herd's ingle-nook;
And huzza! my brave hearts, for
Buccleuch and his standard,
For the King and the Country, the
Clan and the Duke!

Then up with the Banner, let forest
winds fan her,
She has blazed over Ettrick eight
ages and more;
In sport we'll attend her, in battle
defend her,
With heart and with hand, like our
fathers before.

—◆—

LULLABY OF AN INFANT CHIEF.

(1815.)

O HUSH thee, my babie, thy sire was
a knight,
Thy mother a lady, both lovely and
bright;
The woods and the glens, from the
towers which we see,
They all are belonging, dear babie, to
thee.
    O ho ro, i ri ri, cadul gu lo,
    O ho ro, i ri ri, &c

O fear not the bugle, though loudly
it blows,
It calls but the warders that guard thy
repose;
Their bows would be bended, their
blades would be red,
Ere the step of a foeman drew near
to thy bed.
    O ho ro, i ri ri, &c.

O hush thee, my babie, the time soon
will come
When thy sleep shall be broken by
trumpet and drum;
Then hush thee, my darling, take rest
while you may,
For strife comes with manhood, and
waking with day.
    O ho ro, i ri ri, &c.

—◆—

THE RETURN TO ULSTER.

(1816.)

ONCE again,—but how changed since
my wand'rings began—
I have heard the deep voice of the
Lagan and Bann,
And the pines of Clanbrassil resound
to the roar
That wearies the echoes of fair Tulla-
more.
Alas! my poor bosom, and why
shouldst thou burn?
With the scenes of my youth can
its raptures return?
Can I live the dear life of delusion again,
That flow'd when these echoes first
mix'd with my strain?

It was then that around me, though
poor and unknown,
High spells of mysterious enchantment
were thrown;
The streams were of silver, of diamond
the dew,
The land was an Eden, for fancy was
new.
I had heard of our bards, and my soul
was on fire
At the rush of their verse, and the
sweep of their lyre:
To me 'twas not legend, nor tale to the
ear,
But a vision of noontide, distinguish'd
and clear.

Ultonia's old heroes awoke at the call,
And renew'd the wild pomp of the
    chase and the hall;
And the standard of Fion flash'd fierce
    from on high,
Like a burst of the sun when the
    tempest is nigh.
It seem'd that the harp of green Erin
    once more
Could renew all the glories she
    boasted of yore.
Yet why at remembrance, fond heart,
    shouldst thou burn?
They were days of delusion, and
    cannot return.

But was she, too, a phantom, the Maid
    who stood by,
And listed my lay, while she turn'd
    from mine eye?
Was she, too, a vision, just glancing to
    view,
Then dispersed in the sunbeam, or
    melted to dew?
Oh! would it had been so,—oh!
    would that her eye
Had been but a star-glance that
    shot through the sky,
And her voice, that was moulded to
    melody's thrill,
Had been but a zephyr, that sigh'd
    and was still!

Oh! would it had been so,—not then
    this poor heart
Had learn'd the sad lesson, to love
    and to part;
To bear, unassisted, its burthen of care,
While I toil'd for the wealth I had no
    one to share.
Not then had I said, when life's
    summer was done,
And the hours of her autumn were
    fast speeding on,
'Take the fame and the riches ye
    brought in your train,
And restore me the dream of my
    spring-tide again.'

JOCK OF HAZELDEAN.

(1816.)

'Why weep ye by the tide, ladie?
    Why weep ye by the tide?
I'll wed ye to my youngest son,
    And ye sall be his bride:
And ye sall be his bride, ladie,
    Sae comely to be seen'—
But aye she loot the tears down fa'
    For Jock of Hazeldean.[1]

'Now let this wilfu' grief be done,
    And dry that cheek so pale;
Young Frank is chief of Errington,
    And lord of Langley-dale;
His step is first in peaceful ha',
    His sword in battle keen'—
But aye she loot the tears down fa'
    For Jock of Hazeldean.

'A chain of gold ye sall not lack,
    Nor braid to bind your hair;
Nor mettled hound, nor managed
    hawk,
    Nor palfrey fresh and fair;
And you, the foremost o' them a',
    Shall ride our forest queen'—
But aye she loot the tears down fa'
    For Jock of Hazeldean.

The kirk was deck'd at morning-tide,
    The tapers glimmer'd fair;
The priest and bridegroom wait the
    bride,
    And dame and knight are there.
They sought her baith by bower and
    ha';
    The ladie was not seen!
She's o'er the Border, and awa'
    Wi' Jock of Hazeldean.

---

1 The first stanza is ancient.

PIBROCH OF DONUIL DHU.

(1816.)

PIBROCH of Donuil Dhu,
 Pibroch of Donuil,
Wake thy wild voice anew,
 Summon Clan-Conuil.
Come away, come away,
 Hark to the summons!
Come in your war array,
 Gentles and commons.

Come from deep glen, and
 From mountain so rocky,
The war-pipe and pennon
 Are at Inverlochy.
Come every hill-plaid, and
 True heart that wears one,
Come every steel blade, and
 Strong hand that bears one.

Leave untended the herd,
 The flock without shelter;
Leave the corpse uninterr'd,
 The bride at the altar;
Leave the deer, leave the steer,
 Leave nets and barges:
Come with your fighting gear,
 Broadswords and targes.

Come as the winds come, when
 Forests are rended,
Come as the waves come, when
 Navies are stranded:
Faster come, faster come,
 Faster and faster,
Chief, vassal, page and groom,
 Tenant and master.

Fast they come, fast they come;
 See how they gather!
Wide waves the eagle plume,
 Blended with heather.
Cast your plaids, draw your blades,
 Forward, each man, set!
Pibroch of Donuil Dhu,
 Knell for the onset!

NORA'S VOW.

(1816.)

(*From the Gaelic.*)

HEAR what Highland Nora said,—
'The Earlie's son I will not wed,
Should all the race of nature die,
And none be left but he and I.
For all the gold, for all the gear,
And all the lands both far and near
That ever valour lost or won,
I would not wed the Earlie's son.'

'A maiden's vows,' old Callum spoke,
'Are lightly made and lightly broke;
The heather on the mountain's height
Begins to bloom in purple light;
The frost-wind soon shall sweep away
That lustre deep from glen and brae;
Yet Nora, ere its bloom be gone,
May blithely wed the Earlie's son.'

'The swan,' she said, 'the lake's clear
  breast
May barter for the eagle's nest;
The Awe's fierce stream may back-
  ward turn,
Ben-Cruaichan fall, and crush Kil-
  churn;
Our kilted clans, when blood is high,
Before their foes may turn and fly;
But I, were all these marvels done,
Would never wed the Earlie's son.'

Still in the water-lily's shade
Her wonted nest the wild-swan made;
Ben-Cruaichan stands as fast as ever,
Still downward foams the Awe's fierce
  river;
To shun the clash of foeman's steel
No Highland brogue has turn'd the
  heel;
But Nora's heart is lost and won,
—She's wedded to the Earlie's son!

MACGREGOR'S GATHERING.

(1816.)

THE moon's on the lake, and the mist's
  on the brae,
And the Clan has a name that is
  nameless by day ;
    Then gather, gather, gather,
      Grigalach !
    Gather, gather, gather, &c.

Our signal for fight, that from monarchs
  we drew,
Must be heard but by night in our
  vengeful haloo !
    Then haloo, Grigalach ! haloo,
      Grigalach !
    Haloo, haloo, haloo, Grigalach, &c.

Glen Orchy's proud mountains, Coal-
  chuirn and her towers,
Glenstrae and Glenlyon no longer
  are ours ;
    We're landless, landless, landless,
      Grigalach !
    Landless, landless, landless, &c.

But doom'd and devoted by vassal and
  lord,
MacGregor has still both his heart and
  his sword !
    Then courage, courage, courage,
      Grigalach !
    Courage, courage, courage, &c.

If they rob us of name, and pursue us
  with beagles,
Give their roofs to the flame, and their
  flesh to the eagles !
    Then vengeance, vengeance,
      vengeance, Grigalach !
    Vengeance, vengeance, ven-
      geance, &c.

While there's leaves in the forest, and
  foam on the river,
MacGregor, despite them, shall flourish for ever !

Come then, Grigalach, come then,
  Grigalach,
Come then, come then, come
  then, &c.

Through the depths of Loch Katrine
  the steed shall career,
O'er the peak of Ben-Lomond the
  galley shall steer,
And the rocks of Craig-Royston like
  icicles melt,
Ere our wrongs be forgot, or our
  vengeance unfelt !
    Then gather, gather, gather,
      Grigalach !
    Gather, gather, gather, &c.

———◆◆———

VERSES

ON THE OCCASION OF A BANQUET GIVEN
BY THE CITY OF EDINBURGH TO THE
GRAND-DUKE NICHOLAS OF RUSSIA
AND HIS SUITE, DEC. 19, 1816.)

GOD protect brave Alexander,
Heaven defend the noble Czar,
Mighty Russia's high Commander,
First in Europe's banded war ;
For the realms he did deliver
From the tyrant overthrown,
Thou, of every good the Giver,
Grant him long to bless his own !
Bless him, 'mid his land's disaster,
For her rights who battled brave ;
Of the land of foemen master,
Bless him who their wrongs forgave.

O'er his just resentment victor,
Victor over Europe's foes,
Late and long supreme director,
Grant in peace his reign may close.
Hail ! then, hail ! illustrious stranger ;
Welcome to our mountain strand ;
Mutual interests, hopes, and danger,
Link us with **thy** native land.

Freemen's force, or false beguiling,
Shall that union ne'er divide,
Hand in hand while peace is smiling,
And in battle side by side.

—◆◆—

THE SEARCH AFTER HAPPINESS;

OR THE QUEST OF SULTAUN SOLIMAUN.

(1817.)

(In imitation of Byron.)

I.

OH for a glance of that gay Muse's
eye
That lighten'd on Bandello's laugh-
ing tale,
And twinkled with a lustre shrewd
and sly
When Giam Battista[1] bade her vision
hail!—
Yet fear not, ladies, the *naïve* detail
Given by the natives of that land
canorous;
Italian license loves to leap the pale,
We Britons have the fear of shame
before us,
And, if not wise in mirth, at least must
be decorous.

II.

In the far eastern clime, no great
while since,
Lived Sultaun Solimaun, a mighty
prince,
Whose eyes, as oft as they perform'd
their round,
Beheld all others fix'd upon the ground;
Whose ears received the same unvaried
phrase,
'Sultaun! thy vassal hears, and he
obeys!'
All have their tastes—this may the
fancy strike
Of such grave folks as pomp and
grandeur like;

---

[1] The hint of this tale is taken from *La Camiscia Magica*, a novel of Giam Battista Casti.

For me, I love the honest heart and
warm
Of Monarch who can amble round his
farm,
Or, when the toil of state no more
annoys,
In chimney corner seek domestic
joys.
I love a prince will bid the bottle pass,
Exchanging with his subjects glance
and glass;
In fitting time, can, gayest of the gay,
Keep up the jest, and mingle in the
lay.
Such Monarchs best our free-born
humours suit,
But Despots must be stately, stern,
and mute.

III.

This Solimaun, Serendib had in sway—
And where's Serendib? may some
critic say.
Good lack, mine honest friend, consult
the chart,
Scare not my Pegasus before I start!
If Rennell has it not, you'll find, may-
hap,
The isle laid down in Captain Sind-
bad's map,
Famed mariner! whose merciless nar-
rations
Drove every friend and kinsman out
of patience,
Till, fain to find a guest who thought
them shorter,
He deign'd to tell them over to a
porter:
The last edition see, by Long. and Co.,
Rees, Hurst, and Orme, our fathers
in the Row.

IV.

Serendib found, deem not my tale
a fiction—
This Sultaun, whether lacking contradiction—

(A sort of stimulant which hath its uses,
To raise the spirits and reform the
    juices,—
Sovereign specific for all sorts of cures
In my wife's practice, and perhaps in
    yours,)
The Sultaun lacking this same whole-
    some bitter,
Or cordial smooth for prince's palate
    fitter—
Or if some Mollah had hag-rid his
    dreams
With Degial, Ginnistan, and such wild
    themes
Belonging to the Mollah's subtle craft,
I wot not—but the Sultaun never
    laugh'd,
Scarce ate or drank, and took a
    melancholy
That scorn'd all remedy—profane or
    holy;
In his long list of melancholies, mad,
Or mazed, or dumb, hath Burton none
    so bad [1].

v.

Physicians soon arrived, sage, ware,
    and tried,
    As e'er scrawl'd jargon in a darken'd
        room;
With heedful glance the Sultaun's
    tongue they eyed,
Peep'd in his bath, and God knows
    where beside,
    And then in solemn accent spoke
        their doom,
'His majesty is very far from well.'
Then each to work with his specific
    fell:
The Hakim Ibrahim *instanter* brought
His unguent Mahazzim al Zerdukkaut,
While Roompot, a practitioner more
    wily,
Relied on his Munaskif al fillfily [2].

---

[1] See Burton's 'Anatomy of Melancholy.'
[2] For these hard words see D'Herbelot, or the
learned editor of the 'Recipes of Avicenna.'

More and yet more in deep array
    appear,
And some the front assail, and some
    the rear;
Their remedies to reinforce and vary
Came surgeon eke, and eke apothecary;
Till the tired Monarch, though of
    words grown chary,
Yet dropt, to recompense their fruit-
    less labour,
Some hint about a bowstring or a sabre.
There lack'd, I promise you, no longer
    speeches
To rid the palace of those learned
    leeches.

VI.

Then was the council call'd: by their
    advice
(They deem'd the matter ticklish all,
    and nice,
    And sought to shift it off from their
        own shoulders)
Tartars and couriers in all speed were
    sent
To call a sort of Eastern Parliament
    Of feudatory chieftains and free-
        holders:
Such have the Persians at this very
    day,
My gallant Malcolm calls them *cou-
    roultai* [3];
I'm not prepared to show in this slight
    song
That to Serendib the same forms
    belong,—
E'en let the learn'd go search, and tell
    me if I'm wrong.

VII.

The Omrahs [4], each with hand on
    scymitar,
Gave, like Sempronius, still their voice
    for war—

---

[3] See Sir John Malcolm's admirable History of
Persia.
[4] Nobility.

'The sabre of the Sultaun in its sheath
Too long has slept, nor own'd the
    work of death;
Let the Tambourgi bid his signal rattle,
Bang the loud gong, and raise the
    shout of battle!
This dreary cloud that dims our sover-
    eign's day
Shall from his kindled bosom flit away,
When the bold Lootie wheels his
    courser round,
And the arm'd elephant shall shake
    the ground.
Each noble pants to own the glorious
    summons;
And for the charges—lo! your faith-
    ful Commons!'
The Riots who attended in their places
    (Serendib language calls a farmer
    Riot)
Look'd ruefully in one another's faces,
    From this oration auguring much
    disquiet,
Double assessment, forage, and free
    quarters;
And, fearing these as Chinamen the
    Tartars,
Or as the whisker'd vermin fear the
    mousers,
Each fumbled in the pocket of his
    trousers.

VIII.

And next came forth the reverend
    Convocation,
    Bald heads, white beards, and many
    a turban green,
Imaum and Mollah there of every
    station,
    Santon, Fakir, and Calendar were
    seen.
Their votes were various: some ad-
    vised a Mosque
    With fitting revenues should be
    erected,
With seemly gardens and with gay
    Kiosque,
    To recreate a band of priests selected;

Others opined that through the realms
    a dole
    Be made to holy men, whose prayers
    might profit
The Sultaun's weal in body and in
    soul.
    But their long-headed chief, the
    Sheik Ul-Sofit,
More closely touch'd the point:—'Thy
    studious mood,'
Quoth he, 'O Prince! hath thicken'd
    all thy blood,
And dull'd thy brain with labour
    beyond measure;
Wherefore relax a space and take thy
    pleasure,
And toy with beauty, or tell o'er thy
    treasure;
From all the cares of state, my Liege,
    enlarge thee,
And leave the burden to thy faithful
    clergy.'

IX.

These counsels sage availèd not a
    whit,
    And so the patient (as is not un-
    common
Where grave physicians lose their
    time and wit)
    Resolved to take advice of an old
    woman;
His mother she, a dame who once
    was beauteous,
And still was called so by each subject
    duteous.
Now, whether Fatima was witch in
    earnest,
    Or only made believe, I cannot
    say;
But she profess'd to cure disease the
    sternest
    By dint of magic amulet or lay;
And, when all other skill in vain was
    shown,
She deem'd it fitting time to use her
    own.

X.

'*Sympathia magica* hath wonders done'
(Thus did old Fatima bespeak her son),
' It works upon the fibres and the pores,
And thus, insensibly, our health restores,
And it must help us here. Thou must endure
The ill, my son, or travel for the cure.
Search land and sea, and get, where'er you can,
The inmost vesture of a happy man,—
I mean his *shirt*, my son ; which, taken warm
And fresh from off his back, shall chase your harm,
Bid every current of your veins rejoice,
And your dull heart leap light as shepherd-boy's.'
Such was the counsel from his mother came ;—
I know not if she had some under-game,
As Doctors have, who bid their patients roam
And live abroad, when sure to die at home ;
Or if she thought, that, somehow or another,
Queen-Regent sounded better than Queen-Mother ;
But, says the Chronicle (who will, go look it),
That such was her advice. The Sultaun took it.

XI.

All are on board—the Sultaun and his train,
In gilded galley prompt to plough the main.
   The old Rais [1] was the first who questioned, 'Whither?'
They paused : ' Arabia,' thought the pensive Prince,

---

[1] Master of the vessel.

' Was call'd The Happy many ages since—
   For Mokha, Rais.' And they came safely thither.
But not in Araby, with all her balm,
Not where Judea weeps beneath her palm,
Not in rich Egypt, not in Nubian waste,
Could there the step of happiness be traced.
One Copt alone profess'd to have seen her smile,
When Bruce his goblet fill'd at infant Nile :
She bless'd the dauntless traveller as he quaff'd,
But vanish'd from him with the ended draught.

XII.

' Enough of turbans,' said the weary King,
' These dolimans of ours are not the thing ;
Try we the Giaours, these men of coat and cap, I
Incline to think some of them must be happy ;
At least, they have as fair a cause as any can,
They drink good wine and keep no Ramazan.
Then northward, ho !' The vessel cuts the sea,
And fair Italia lies upon her lee.
But fair Italia, she who once unfurl'd
Her eagle banners o'er a conquer'd world,
Long from her throne of domination tumbled,
Lay, by her quondam vassals, sorely humbled ;
The Pope himself look'd pensive, pale, and lean,
And was not half the man he once had been.

'While these the priest and those the noble fleeces,
Our poor old boot [1],' they said, 'is torn to pieces.
Its tops [2] the vengeful claws of Austria feel,
And the Great Devil is rending toe and heel [3].
If happiness you seek, to tell you truly,
We think she dwells with one Giovanni Bulli ;
A tramontane, a heretic,—the buck,
Poffaredio ! still has all the luck ;
By land or ocean never strikes his flag—
And then—a perfect walking money-bag.'
Off set our Prince to seek John Bull's abode,
But first took France—it lay upon the road.

XIII.

Monsieur Baboon, after much late commotion,
Was agitated like a settling ocean,
Quite out of sorts, and could not tell what ail'd him,
Only the glory of his house had fail'd him ;
Besides, some tumours on his noddle biding,
Gave indication of a recent hiding [4].
Our Prince, though Sultauns of such things are heedless,
Thought it a thing indelicate and needless
  To ask, if at that moment he was happy.
And Monsieur, seeing that he was *comme il faut,*

---

[1] The well-known resemblance of Italy in the map.
[2] Florence, Venice, &c.
[3] The Calabrias, infested by bands of assassins. One of the leaders was called Fra Diavolo, i. e. Brother Devil.
[4] Or drubbing ; so called in the Slang Dictionary.

A loud voice mustered up, for ' *Vive le Roi !* '
Then whisper'd, ' 'Ave you any news of Nappy ?'
The Sultaun answer'd him with a cross question,—
  ' Pray, can you tell me aught of one John Bull,
That dwells somewhere beyond your herring-pool ?'
The query seem'd of difficult digestion,
The party shrugg'd, and grinn'd, and took his snuff,
And found his whole good-breeding scarce enough.

XIV.

Twitching his visage into as many puckers
As damsels wont to put into their tuckers
(Ere liberal Fashion damn'd both lace and lawn,
And bade the veil of modesty be drawn),
Replied the Frenchman, after a brief pause,
' Jean Bool !—I vas not know him— Yes, I vas—
I vas remember dat, von year or two,
I saw him at von place call'd Vaterloo—
Ma foi ! il s'est tres joliment battu,
Dat is for Englishman,—m'entendez-vous ?
But den he had wit him one damn son-gun,
Rogue I no like—dey call him Vellington.'
Monsieur's politeness could not hide his fret,
So Solimaun took leave, and cross'd the strait.

XV.

John Bull was in his very worst of moods,
Raving of sterile farms and unsold goods ;

His sugar-loaves and bales about he
    threw,
And on his counter beat the devil's
    tattoo.
His wars were ended, and the victory
    won,
But then, 'twas reckoning-day with
    honest John;
And authors vouch, 'twas still this
    Worthy's way,
'Never to grumble till he came to
    pay;
And then he always thinks, his tem-
    per's such,
The work too little, and the pay too
    much[1].'
    Yet, grumbler as he is, so kind and
      hearty,
That when his mortal foe was on the
    floor,
And past the power to harm his quiet
    more,
    Poor John had wellnigh wept for
      Bonaparte!
Such was the wight whom Solimaun
    salaam'd,—
'And who are you,' John answer'd,
    'and be d—d?'

XVI.

'A stranger, come to see the happiest
    man—
So, signior, all avouch—in Fran-
    gistan[2].'
'Happy? my tenants breaking on my
    hand;
Unstock'd my pastures, and untill'd
    my land;
Sugar and rum a drug, and mice and
    moths
The sole consumers of my good broad-
    cloths—
Happy?—Why, cursed war and
    racking tax
Have left us scarcely raiment to our
    backs.'

---

[1] See 'The True Born Englishman,' by Daniel De
Foe.   [2] Europe.

'In that case, signior, I may take my
    leave;
I came to ask a favour—but I grieve'—
'Favour?' said John, and eyed the
    Sultaun hard,
'It's my belief you come to break the
    yard!—
But, stay, you look like some poor
    foreign sinner,—
Take that to buy yourself a shirt and
    dinner.'
With that he chuck'd a guinea at
    his head;
But, with due dignity, the Sultaun said,
'Permit me, sir, your bounty to decline;
A *shirt* indeed I seek, but none of thine.
Signior, I kiss your hands, so fare
    you well.'
'Kiss and be d—d,' quoth John, 'and
    go to hell!'

XVII.

Next door to John there dwelt his
    sister Peg,
Once a wild lass as ever shook a leg
When the blithe bagpipe blew—but,
    soberer now,
She *doucely* span her flax and milk'd
    her cow.
And whereas erst she was a needy
    slattern,
Nor now of wealth or cleanliness a
    pattern,
Yet once a month her house was
    partly swept,
And once a week a plenteous board
    she kept.
And whereas, eke, the vixen used her
    claws
    And teeth, of yore, on slender
      provocation,
She now was grown amenable to laws,
    A quiet soul as any in the nation;
The sole remembrance of her warlike
    joys
Was in old songs she sang to please
    her boys

John Bull, whom, in their years of
early strife,
She wont to lead a cat-and-doggish
life,
Now found the woman, as he said,
a neighbour,
Who look'd to the main chance,
declined no labour,
Loved a long grace, and spoke a
northern jargon,
And was d——d close in making of a
bargain.

XVIII.

The Sultaun enter'd, and he made his
leg,
And with decorum curtsey'd sister Peg
(She loved a book, and knew a thing
or two,
And guess'd at once with whom she
had to do).
She bade him 'Sit into the fire,' and
took
Her dram, her cake, her kebbuck from
the nook;
Ask'd him 'about the news from
Eastern parts;
And of her absent bairns, puir
Highland hearts!
If peace brought down the price of
tea and pepper,
And if the *nitmugs* were grown *ony*
cheaper;—
Were there nae *speerings* of our
Mungo Park—
Ye'll be the gentleman that wants
the sark?
If ye wad buy a web o' auld wife's
spinnin',
I'll warrant ye it's a weel-wearing
linen!'

XIX.

Then up got Peg, and round the
house 'gan scuttle
In search of goods her customer
to nail,

Until the Sultaun strain'd his princely
throttle,
And hollo'd, 'Ma'am, that is not
what I ail.
Pray, are you happy, ma'am, in this
snug glen?'
'Happy?' said Peg; 'what for d'ye
want to ken?
Besides, just think upon this bygane
year,
Grain wadna pay the yoking of the
pleugh.'
'What say you to the present?'
'Meal's sae dear,
To mak' their *brose* my bairns have
scarce aneugh.'
'The devil take the shirt,' said
Solimaun,
'I think my quest will end as it
began.
Farewell, ma'am; nay, no ceremony,
I beg.'
'Ye'll no be for the linen then?' said
Peg.

XX.

Now for the land of verdant Erin
The Sultaun's royal bark is steering,
The Emerald Isle, where honest
Paddy dwells,
The cousin of John Bull, as story tells.
For a long space had John, with
words of thunder,
Hard looks, and harder knocks, kept
Paddy under,
Till the poor lad, like boy that's flogg'd
unduly,
Had gotten somewhat restive and
unruly.
Hard was his lot and lodging, you'll
allow,
A wigwam that would hardly serve
a sow;
His landlord, and of middle-men two
brace,
Had screw'd his rent up to the
starving-place;

His garment was a top-coat, and an
    old one,
His meal was a potato, and a cold
    one ;
But still for fun or frolic, and all that,
In the round world was not the
    match of Pat.

XXI.

The Sultaun saw him on a holiday,
Which is with Paddy still a jolly day ;
When mass is ended, and his load of
    sins
Confess'd, and Mother Church hath
    from her binns
Dealt forth a bonus of imputed merit,
Then is Pat's time for fancy, whim,
    and spirit !
To jest, to sing, to caper fair and free,
And dance as light as leaf upon the
    tree.
'By Mahomet,' said Sultaun Soli-
    maun,
' That ragged fellow is our very man !
Rush in and seize him—do not do
    him hurt,
But, will he nill he, let me have
    his *shirt*.'—

XXII.

Shilala their plan was wellnigh after
    baulking
(Much less provocation will set it
    a-walking),
But the odds that foil'd Hercules
    foil'd Paddy Whack ;
They seized, and they floor'd, and
    they stripp'd him—Alack !
Up-bubboo ! Paddy had not a shirt
    to his back !
And the King, disappointed, with
    sorrow and shame,
Went back to Serendib as sad as he
    came.

—+—

MR. KEMBLE'S FAREWELL ADDRESS

ON TAKING LEAVE OF THE EDINBURGH
STAGE.

(1817.)

As the worn war-horse, at the
    trumpet's sound,
Erects his mane, and neighs, and paws
    the ground—
Disdains the ease his generous lord
    assigns,
And longs to rush on the embattled
    lines,
So I, your plaudits ringing on mine ear,
Can scarce sustain to think our parting
    near ;
To think my scenic hour for ever past,
And that these valued plaudits are
    my last.
Why should we part, while still some
    powers remain,
That in your service strive not yet
    in vain ?
Cannot high zeal the strength of
    youth supply,
And sense of duty fire the fading eye ;
And all the wrongs of age remain
    subdued
Beneath the burning glow of gratitude ?
Ah, no ! the taper, wearing to its close,
Oft for a space in fitful lustre glows
But all too soon the transient gleam is
    past,
It cannot be renew'd, and will not last ;
Even duty, zeal, and gratitude, can
    wage
But short-lived conflict with the frosts
    of age.
Yes ! It were poor, remembering what
    I was,
To live a pensioner on your applause,
To drain the dregs of your endurance
    dry,
And take, as alms, the praise I once
    could buy ;

Till every sneering youth around
 inquires,
'Is this the man who once could
 please our sires?'
And scorn assumes compassion's
 doubtful mien
To warn me off from the encumber'd
 scene.
This must not be;—and higher duties
 crave
Some space between the theatre and
 the grave,
That, like the Roman in the Capitol,
I may adjust my mantle ere I fall:
My life's brief act in public service
 flown,
The last, the closing scene, must be
 my own.

 Here, then, adieu! while yet some
  well-graced parts
May fix an ancient favourite in your
 hearts,
Not quite to be forgotten, even when
You look on better actors, younger
 men:
And if your bosoms own this kindly
 debt
Of old remembrance, how shall mine
 forget—
O, how forget!—how oft I hither came
In anxious hope, how oft return'd
 with fame!
How oft around your circle this weak
 hand
Has waved immortal Shakespeare's
 magic wand
Till the full burst of inspiration came,
And I have felt, and you have fann'd
 the flame!
By mem'ry treasured, while her reign
 endures,
Those hours must live—and all their
 charms are yours.

 O favour'd Land! renown'd for
  arts and arms,
For manly talent and for female charms,

Could this full bosom prompt the
 sinking line,
What fervent benedictions now were
 thine!
But my last part is play'd, my knell is
 rung,
When e'en your praise falls faltering
 from my tongue;
And all that you can hear, or I can
 tell,
Is—Friends and Patrons, hail, and
 FARE YOU WELL.

—◦◦—

LINES

WRITTEN FOR MISS SMITH.

(1817.)

When the lone pilgrim views afar
The shrine that is his guiding star,
With awe his footsteps print the road
Which the loved saint of yore has trod.
As near he draws, and yet more near,
His dim eye sparkles with a tear;
The Gothic fane's unwonted show,
The choral hymn, the tapers' glow,
Oppress his soul; while they delight
And chasten rapture with affright.
No longer dare he think his toil
Can merit aught his patron's smile;
Too light appears the distant way,
The chilly eve, the sultry day—
All these endured no favour claim,
But murmuring forth the sainted name,
He lays his little offering down,
And only deprecates a frown.

 We too, who ply the Thespian art,
Oft feel such bodings of the heart,
And, when our utmost powers are
 strain'd,
Dare hardly hope your favour gain'd.
She, who from sister climes has sought
The ancient land where Wallace
 fought—

Land long renown'd for arms and arts,
And conquering eyes and dauntless
  hearts—
She, as the flutterings *here* avow,
Feels all the pilgrim's terrors *now*;
Yet sure on Caledonian plain
The stranger never sued in vain.
'Tis yours the hospitable task
To give the applause she dare not ask;
And they who bid the pilgrim speed,
The pilgrim's blessing be their meed.

THE DREARY CHANGE.

(1817.)

THE sun upon the Weirdlaw Hill,
  In Ettrick's vale, is sinking sweet;
The westland wind is hush and still,
  The lake lies sleeping at my feet.
Yet not the landscape to mine eye
  Bears those bright hues that once
    it bore;
Though evening, with her richest dye,
  Flames o'er the hills of Ettrick's
    shore.

With listless look along the plain,
  I see Tweed's silver current glide,
And coldly mark the holy fane
  Of Melrose rise in ruin'd pride.
The quiet lake, the balmy air,
  The hill, the stream, the tower,
    the tree,—
Are they still such as once they were?
Or is the dreary change in me?

Alas, the warp'd and broken board,
  How can it bear the painter's dye!
The harp of strain'd and tuneless chord,
  How to the minstrel's skill reply!
To aching eyes each landscape lowers,
  To feverish pulse each gale blows
    chill;
And Araby's or Eden's bowers
  Were barren as this moorland hill.

MARCH OF THE MONKS OF BANGOR.

(1817.)

WHEN the heathen trumpet's clang
Round beleaguer'd Chester rang,
Veilèd nun and friar grey
March'd from Bangor's fair Abbaye;
High their holy anthem sounds,
Cestria's vale the hymn rebounds,
Floating down the silvan Dee,
            O miserere, Domine!

On the long procession goes,
Glory round their crosses glows,
And the Virgin-mother mild
In their peaceful banner smiled;
Who could think such saintly band
Doom'd to feel unhallow'd hand?
Such was the Divine decree,
            O miserere, Domine!

Bands that masses only sung,
Hands that censers only swung,
Met the northern bow and bill,
Heard the war-cry wild and shrill:
Woe to Brockmael's feeble hand,
Woe to Olfrid's bloody brand,
Woe to Saxon cruelty,
            O miserere, Domine!

Weltering amid warriors slain,
Spurn'd by steeds with bloody mane,
Slaughter'd down by heathen blade,
Bangor's peaceful monks are laid:
Word of parting rest unspoke,
Mass unsung, and bread unbroke;
For their souls for charity,
            Sing, *miserere, Domine!*

Bangor! o'er the murder wail!
Long thy ruins told the tale,
Shatter'd towers and broken arch
Long recall'd the woful march:
On thy shrine no tapers burn,
Never shall thy priests return;
The pilgrim sighs and sings for thee,
            O miserere, Domine!

EPISTLE

TO HIS GRACE THE DUKE OF BUCCLEUCH,

AT DRUMLANRIG CASTLE.

Sanquhar, 2 o'clock, July 30, 1817.

FROM Ross, where the clouds on
  Benlomond are sleeping—
From Greenock, where Clyde to the
  Ocean is sweeping—
From Largs, where the Scots gave
  the Northmen a drilling—
From Ardrossan, whose harbour cost
  many a shilling—
From Old Cumnock, where beds are
  as hard as a plank, sir—
From a chop and green pease, and
  a chicken in Sanquhar,
This eve, please the Fates, at Drum-
  lanrig we anchor.

WALTER SCOTT.

—◆—

EPILOGUE TO 'THE APPEAL.'

(*Spoken by Mrs. Henry Siddons,
Feb.* 16, 1818.)

A CAT of yore (or else old Æsop
  lied)
Was changed into a fair and blooming
  bride,
But spied a mouse upon her marriage-
  day,
Forgot her spouse, and seized upon
  her prey ;
Even thus my bridegroom lawyer, as
  you saw,
Threw off poor me, and pounced upon
  papa.
His neck from Hymen's mystic knot
  made loose,
He twisted round my sire's the literal
  noose.

Such are the fruits of our dramatic
  labour
Since the New Jail became our next-
  door neighbour.

Yes, times *are* changed ; for, in
  your fathers' age,
The lawyers were the patrons of the
  stage ;
However high advanced by future fate,
There stands the bench [*points to the
  Pit*] that first received their
  weight.
The future legal sage, 'twas ours to
  see,
Doom though unwigg'd, and plead
  without a fee.

But now, astounding each poor
  mimic elf,
Instead of lawyers comes the law
  herself ;
Tremendous neighbour, on our right
  she dwells,
Builds high her towers and excavates
  her cells ;
While on the left she agitates the
  town,
With the tempestuous question, Up
  or down ?
'Twixt Scylla and Charybdis thus
  stand we,
Law's final end, and law's uncertainty.
But, soft ! who lives at Rome the Pope
  must flatter,
And jails and lawsuits are no jesting
  matter.
Then—just farewell ! We wait with
  serious awe
Till your applause or censure gives
  the law.
Trusting our humble efforts may
  assure ye,
We hold you Court and Counsel,
  Judge and Jury.

—◆—

MACKRIMMON'S LAMENT.

(1818.)

MACLEOD's wizard flag from the grey
    castle sallies,
The rowers are seated, unmoor'd are
    the galleys ;
Gleam war-axe and broadsword, clang
    target and quiver,
As Mackrimmon sings, 'Farewell to
    Dunvegan for ever !
Farewell to each cliff, on which
    breakers are foaming ;
Farewell, each dark glen, in which
    red-deer are roaming ;
Farewell, lonely Skye, to lake, moun-
    tain, and river ;
Macleod may return, but Mackrimmon
    shall never !

' Farewell the bright clouds that on
    Quillan are sleeping ;
Farewell the bright eyes in the Dun
    that are weeping ;
To each minstrel delusion, farewell
    and for ever !
Mackrimmon departs, to return to
    you never !
The Banshee's wild voice sings the
    death-dirge before me,
The pall of the dead for a mantle
    hangs o'er me ;
But my heart shall not flag, and my
    nerves shall not shiver,
Though devoted I go—to return again
    never !

'Too oft shall the notes of Mack-
    rimmon's bewailing
Be heard when the Gael on their
    exile are sailing ;
Dear land ! to the shores, whence
    unwilling we sever,
Return—return—return shall we
    never !

Cha till, cha till, cha till sin tuille!
Cha till, cha till, cha till sin tuille,
Cha till, cha till, cha till sin tuille,
Gea thillis Macleod, cha till Mack-
    rimmon !'

DONALD CAIRD'S COME AGAIN.

(1818.)

CHORUS.

DONALD CAIRD's come again !
Donald Caird's come again !
Tell the news in brugh and glen,
Donald Caird's come again !

Donald Caird can lilt and sing,
Blithely dance the Hieland fling,
Drink till the gudeman be blind,
Fleech till the gudewife be kind ;
Hoop a leglin, clout a pan,
Or crack a pow wi' ony man ;—
Tell the news in brugh and glen,
Donald Caird's come again.

    Donald Caird's come again !
    Donald Caird's come again !
    Tell the news in brugh and glen,
    Donald Caird's come again.

Donald Caird can wire a maukin,
Kens the wiles o' dun-deer staukin',
Leisters kipper, makes a shift
To shoot a muir-fowl in the drift ;
Water-bailiffs, rangers, keepers,—
He can wauk when they are sleepers ;
Not for bountith or rewaird
Dare ye mell wi' Donald Caird.

    Donald Caird's come again !
    Donald Caird's come again !
    Gar the bagpipes hum amain,
    Donald Caird's come again.

Donald Caird can drink a gill
Fast as hostler-wife can fill ;
Ilka ane that sells gude liquor
Kens how Donald bends a bicker ;

When he's fou he's stout and saucy,
Keeps the cantle o' the causey;
Hieland chief and Lawland laird
Maun gie room to Donald Caird!

Donald Caird's come again!
Donald Caird's come again!
Tell the news in brugh and glen,
Donald Caird's come again.

Steek the amrie, lock the kist,
Else some gear may weel be mis't;
Donald Caird finds orra things
Where Allan Gregor fand the tings[1];
Dunts of kebbuck, taits o' woo,
Whiles a hen and whiles a sow,
Webs or duds frae hedge or yaird—
'Ware the wuddie[2], Donald Caird!

Donald Caird's come again!
Donald Caird's come again!
Dinna let the Shirra ken
Donald Caird's come again.

On Donald Caird the doom was stern,
Craig to tether, legs to airn;
But Donald Caird, wi' mickle study,
Caught the gift to cheat the wuddie;
Rings of airn, and bolts of steel,
Fell like ice frae hand and heel!
Watch the sheep in fauld and glen,
Donald Caird's come again!

Donald Caird's come again!
Donald Caird's come again!
Dinna let the Justice ken,
Donald Caird's come again.

—•◦•—

EPITAPH ON MRS. ERSKINE.

(1819.)

Plain, as her native dignity of mind,
Arise the tomb of her we have resign'd;
Unflaw'd and stainless be the marble
    scroll,
Emblem of lovely form and candid
    soul.

{ [1] At the fireside.]   [2] Hangman's rope.]

But, oh! what symbol may avail to tell
The kindness, wit, and sense, we
    loved so well!
What sculpture show the broken ties
    of life,
Here buried with the parent, friend,
    and wife!
Or on the tablet stamp each title dear,
By which thine urn, Euphemia, claims
    the tear!
Yet taught, by thy meek sufferance,
    to assume
Patience in anguish, hope beyond the
    tomb,
Resign'd, though sad, this votive verse
    shall flow,
And brief, alas! as thy brief span below.

—•◦•—

LIFE IN THE FOREST.

(1822.)

On Ettrick Forest's mountains dun
'Tis blithe to hear the sportsman's gun,
And seek the heath-frequenting brood
Far through the noonday solitude;
By many a cairn and trenched mound,
Where chiefs of yore sleep lone and
    sound,
And springs, where grey-hair'd shep-
    herds tell,
That still the fairies love to dwell.

Along the silver streams of Tweed
'Tis blithe the mimic fly to lead,
When to the hook the salmon springs,
And the line whistles through the rings;
The boiling eddy see him try,
Then dashing from the current high,
Till watchful eye and cautious hand
Have led his wasted strength to land.

'Tis blithe along the midnight tide
With stalwart arm the boat to guide;
On high the dazzling blaze to rear,
And heedful plunge the barbed spear;

Rock, wood, and scaur, emerging
bright,
Fling on the stream their ruddy light,
And from the bank our band appears
Like Genii, arm'd with fiery spears.

'Tis blithe at eve to tell the tale,
How we succeed, and how we fail,
Whether at Alwyn's lordly meal,
Or lowlier board of Ashestiel;
While the gay tapers cheerly shine,
Bickers the fire, and flows the wine—
Days free from thought, and nights
from care,
My blessing on the Forest fair!

—◆◆—

FAREWELL TO THE MUSE.

(1822.)

ENCHANTRESS, farewell, who so oft
hast decoy'd me,
At the close of the evening through
woodlands to roam,
Where the forester, 'lated, with
wonder espied me
Explore the wild scenes he was
quitting for home.
Farewell, and take with thee thy
numbers wild speaking
The language alternate of rapture
and woe:
Oh! none but some lover, whose
heartstrings are breaking,
The pang that I feel at our parting
can know.

Each joy thou couldst double, and
when there came sorrow,
Or pale disappointment to darken
my way,
What voice was like thine, that could
sing of to-morrow,
Till forgot in the strain was the
grief of to-day!

But when friends drop around us in
life's weary waning,
The grief, Queen of Numbers, thou
canst not assuage;
Nor the gradual estrangement of those
yet remaining,
The languor of pain, and the chill-
ness of age.

'Twas thou that once taught me, in
accents bewailing,
To sing how a warrior[1] lay stretch'd
on the plain,
And a maiden hung o'er him with aid
unavailing,
And held to his lips the cold goblet
in vain;
As vain thy enchantments, O Queen
of wild Numbers,
To a bard when the reign of his
fancy is o'er,
And the quick pulse of feeling in
apathy slumbers—
Farewell, then, Enchantress! I meet
thee no more!

—◆◆—

THE MAID OF ISLA.

(1822.)

OH, Maid of Isla, from the cliff
That looks on troubled wave and sky,
Dost thou not see yon little skiff
Contend with ocean gallantly?
Now beating 'gainst the breeze and
surge,
And steep'd her leeward deck in
foam,
Why does she war unequal urge?—
Oh, Isla's maid, she seeks her home.

Oh, Isla's maid, yon sea-bird mark,
Her white wing gleams through
mist and spray,
Against the storm-cloud, lowering
dark,
As to the rock she wheels away;—

[1 Marmion.]

Where clouds are dark and billows
    rave,
  Why to the shelter should she come
Of cliff, exposed to wind and wave?—
  Oh, maid of Isla, 'tis her home!

As breeze and tide to yonder skiff,
  Thou'rt adverse to the suit I bring,
And cold as is yon wintry cliff,
  Where sea-birds close their wearied
    wing.
Yet cold as rock, unkind as wave,
  Still, Isla's maid, to thee I come;
For in thy love, or in his grave,
  Must Allan Vourich find his home.

—*—

CARLE, NOW THE KING'S COME;

BEING NEW WORDS TO AN AULD
SPRING.

*(On the occasion of George IV's visit
to Scotland, August, 1822.)*

THE news has flown frae mouth to
    mouth,
The North for ance has bang'd the
    South;
The deil a Scotsman's die o' drouth,
  Carle, now the King's come!

CHORUS.

  Carle, now the King's come!
  Carle, now the King's come!
Thou shalt dance, and I will sing,
  Carle, now the King's come!

Auld England held him lang and fast;
And Ireland had a joyfu' cast;
But Scotland's turn is come at last—
  Carle, now the King's come!

Auld Reekie, in her rokelay grey,
Thought never to have seen the day;
He's been a weary time away—
  But, Carle, now the King's come!

She's skirling frae the Castle-hill;
The Carline's voice is grown sae shrill
Ye'll hear her at the Canon-mill—
  Carle, now the King's come!

'Up, bairns!' she cries, 'baith grit and
    sma',
And busk ye for the weapon-shaw!
Stand by me, and we'll bang them a'—
  Carle, now the King's come!

'Come from Newbattle's ancient spires,
Bauld Lothian, with your knights and
    squires,
And match the mettle of your sires—
  Carle, now the King's come!

'You're welcome hame, my Montagu[1]!
Bring in your hand the young Buc-
    cleuch;
I'm missing some that I may rue—
  Carle, now the King's come!

'Come, Haddington[2], the kind and gay,
You've graced my causeway mony a
    day;
I'll weep the cause if you should stay—
  Carle, now the King's come!

'Come, premier Duke[3], and carry doun
Frae yonder craig his ancient croun;
It's had a lang sleep and a soun'—
  But, Carle, now the King's come!

'Come, Athole, from the hill and
    wood,
Bring down your clansmen like a clud;
Come, Morton, show the Douglas'
    blood,—
  Carle, now the King's come!

[1] Lord Montagu, uncle and guardian to the young Duke of Buccleuch, placed his Grace's residence of Dalkeith at his Majesty's disposal during his visit to Scotland.
[2] Charles, the tenth Earl of Haddington, died in 1828.
[3] The Duke of Hamilton, as Earl of Angus, carried the ancient royal crown of Scotland on horseback in King George's procession, from Holyrood to the Castle.

'Come, Tweeddale, true as sword to
   sheath;
Come, Hopetoun, fear'd on fields of
   death;
Come, Clerk[1], and give your bugle
   breath;
   Carle, now the King's come!

'Come, Wemyss, who modest merit
   aids;
Come, Rosebery, from Dalmeny
   shades;
Breadalbane, bring your belted plaids;
   Carle, now the King's come!

'Come, stately Niddrie, auld and true,
Girt with the sword that Minden knew;
We have o'er few such lairds as you—
   Carle, now the King's come!

'King Arthur's grown a common crier,
He's heard in Fife and far Cantire,—
"Fie, lads, behold my crest of fire!"
   Carle, now the King's come!

'Saint Abb roars out, "I see him pass,
Between Tantallon and the Bass!"
Calton, get out your keeking-glass—
   Carle, now the King's come!'

The Carline stopp'd; and, sure I am,
For very glee had ta'en a dwam,
But Oman[2] help'd her to a dram.—
   Cogie, now the King's come!

   Cogie, now the King's come!
   Cogie, now the King's come!
   I'se be fou' and ye's be toom,
   Cogie, now the King's come!

PART SECOND.

A HAWICK gill of mountain dew,
Heised up Auld Reekie's heart, I trow,
It minded her of Waterloo—
   Carle, now the King's come!

Again I heard her summons swell,
For, sic a dirdum and a yell,
It drown'd Saint Giles's jowing bell—
   Carle, now the King's come!

'My trusty Provost, tried and tight,
Stand forward for the Good Town's
   right,
There's waur than you been made a
   knight—
   Carle, now the King's come!

'My reverend Clergy, look ye say
The best of thanksgivings ye ha'e,
And warstle for a sunny day—
   Carle, now the King's come!

'My Doctors, look that you agree,
Cure a' the town without a fee;
My Lawyers, dinna pike a plea—
   Carle, now the King's come!

'Come forth each sturdy Burgher's
   bairn,
That dints on wood or clanks on airn,
That fires the o'en, or winds the pirn—
   Carle, now the King's come!

'Come forward with the Blanket Blue[3],
Your sires were loyal men and true,
As Scotland's foemen oft might rue—
   Carle, now the King's come!

'Scots downa loup, and rin, and rave,
We're steady folks and something
   grave,
We'll keep the causeway firm and
   brave—
   Carle, now the King's come!

'Sir Thomas[4] thunder from your rock,
Till Pentland dinnles wi' the shock,
And lace wi' fire my snood o' smoke—
   Carle, now the King's come!

---

[1] Clerk of Pennycuik, bound by his tenure, when the King came to Edinburgh, to receive him at the Harestone with three blasts on a horn.
[2] Landlord of the Waterloo Hotel.

[3] The Blue Blanket is the standard of the incorporated trades of Edinburgh.
[4] Sir Thomas Bradford, then commander of the forces in Scotland.

'Melville, bring out your bands of blue,
A' Louden lads, baith stout and true,
With Elcho, Hope, and Cockburn
    too [1]—
    Carle, now the King's come!

'And you, who on yon bluidy braes
Compell'd the vanquish'd Despot's
    praise,
Rank out—rank out—my gallant
    Greys [2]—
    Carle, now the King's come!

'Cock o' the North, my Huntly braw,
Where are you with the Forty-twa [3]?
Ah! wae's my heart that ye're awa'—
    Carle, now the King's come!

'But yonder come my canty Celts,
With durk and pistols at their belts,
Thank God, we've still some plaids
    and kilts—
    Carle, now the King's come!

'Lord, how the pibrochs groan and
    yell!
Macdonnell's [4] ta'en the field himsell,
Macleod comes branking o'er the fell—
    Carle, now the King's come!

'Bend up your bow each Archer spark,
For you're to guard him light and
    dark;
Faith, lads, for ance ye've hit the
    mark—
    Carle, now the King's come!

Young Errol [5], take the sword of state,
The sceptre, Panie-Morarchate [6];

1 Lord Melville was Colonel of the Mid-Lothian
Yeomanry Cavalry; Sir John Hope of Pinkie, Major;
and Robert Cockburn, Esq., and Lord Elcho, were
captains in the same corps.
2 The Scots Greys, under General Sir James Stewart
of Coltness, were on duty at Edinburgh during the
King's visit. Bonaparte's exclamation at Waterloo
was, ' Ces beaux chevaux gris, comme ils travaillent!
3 Marquis of Huntly, Colonel of the 42nd Regiment.
4 Colonel Ronaldson Macdonnell of Glengarry.
5 The Earl of Errol is hereditary Lord High-
Constable of Scotland.
6 A corruption of the Gaelic *Banamhorar-Chat,*
or the Great Lady (literally *Female Lord of the
Chatte*); the Celtic title of the Countess of Sutherland.

Knight Mareschal, see ye clear the
    gate—
    Carle, now the King's come!

'Kind cummer, Leith, ye've been
    mis-set,
But dinna be upon the fret—
Ye'se hae the handsel of him yet,
    Carle, now the King's come!

'My daughters, come with een sae
    blue,
Your garlands weave, your blossoms
    strew;
He ne'er saw fairer flowers than you—
    Carle, now the King's come!

'What shall we do for the propine—
We used to offer something fine,
But ne'er a groat's in pouch of mine—
    Carle, now the King's come!

'Deil care—for that I'se never start,
We'll welcome him with Highland
    heart;
Whate'er we have he's get a part—
    Carle, now the King's come!

'I'll show him mason-work this day—
Nane of your bricks of Babel clay,
But towers shall stand till Time's
    away—
    Carle, now the King's come!

'I'll show him wit, I'll show him lair,
And gallant lads and lasses fair,
And what wad kind heart wish for
    mair?
    Carle, now the King's come!

'Step out, Sir John [1], of projects rife,
Come win the thanks of an auld wife,
And bring him health and length of
    life—
    Carle, now the King's come!'

[1 Sir John Sinclair,' patron and projector of national
and patriotic plans,' says Lockhart.'

ONE VOLUME MORE.

(1823.)

(Written for the Bannatyne Club.)

Assist me, ye friends of Old Books
    and Old Wine,
To sing in the praises of sage Ban-
    natyne,
Who left such a treasure of old
    Scottish lore
As enables each age to print one
    volume more.

> One volume more, my friends,
>   one volume more,
> We'll ransack old Banny for one
>   volume more.

And first, Allan Ramsay was eager
    to glean
From Bannatyne's *Hortus* his bright
    Evergreen;
Two light little volumes (intended for
    four)
Still leave us the task to print one
    volume more.

> One volume more, &c.

His ways were not ours, for he cared
    not a pin
How much he left out, or how much
    he put in;
The truth of the reading he thought
    was a bore,
So this accurate age calls for one
    volume more.

> One volume more, &c.

Correct and sagacious, then came my
    Lord Hailes,
And weigh'd every letter in critical
    scales,
But left out some brief words, which
    the prudish abhor,
And castrated Banny in one volume
    more.

> One volume more, my friends,
>   one volume more;
> We'll restore Banny's manhood
>   in one volume more.

John Pinkerton next, and I'm truly
    concern'd
I can't call that worthy so candid as
    learn'd;
He rail'd at the plaid and blasphemed
    the claymore,
And set Scots by the ears in his one
    volume more.

> One volume more, my friends,
>   one volume more,
> Celt and Goth shall be pleased
>   with one volume more.

As bitter as gall, and as sharp as a razor,
And feeding on herbs as a Nebu-
    chadnezzar,
His diet too acid, his temper too sour,
Little Ritson came out with his two
    volumes more.

> But one volume, my friends, one
>   volume more,
> We'll dine on roast-beef and print
>   one volume more.

The stout Gothic yeditur[1], next on the
    roll,
With his beard like a brush and as
    black as a coal,
And honest Greysteel[2] that was true to
    the core,
Lent their hearts and their hands each
    to one volume more.

> One volume more, &c.

Since by these single champions what
    wonders were done,
What may not be achieved by our
    Thirty and One?
Law, Gospel, and Commerce we
    count in our corps,
And the Trade and the Press join for
    one volume more.

> One volume more, &c.

---

[1] James Sibbald.   [2] David Herd.

Ancient libels and contraband books,
    I assure ye,
We'll print as secure from Exchequer
    or Jury ;
Then hear your Committee and let
    them count o'er
The Chiels they intend in their
    three volumes more.

    Three volumes more, &c.

They'll produce your King Jamie, the
    sapient and Sext,
And the Bob of Dumblane and her
    Bishops come next;
One tome miscellaneous they'll add to
    your store,
Resolving next year to print four
    volumes more.

    Four volumes more, my friends,
        four volumes more;
    Pay down your subscriptions for
        four volumes more.

—◆—

EPISTLE

TO HIS SON-IN-LAW, JOHN GIBSON LOCK-
HART, ON THE COMPOSITION OF
MAIDA'S EPITAPH.

(1824.)

'Maidae marmorea dormis sub imagine Maida !
Ad januam domini sit tibi terra levis.

'DEAR JOHN,—I some time ago wrote
    to inform his
Fat worship of *jaces*, misprinted for
    dormis;
But that several Southrons assured
    me the *januam*
Was a twitch to both ears of Ass
    Priscian's cranium.
You, perhaps, may observe that one
    Lionel Berguer,
In defence of our blunder appears
    a stout arguer:
But at length I have settled, I hope,
    all these clatters,

By a *rowt* in the papers—fine place
    for such matters.
I have, therefore, to make it for once
    my command, sir,
That my gudeson shall leave the
    whole thing in my hand, sir,
And by no means accomplish what
    James says you threaten,
Some banter in Blackwood [1] to claim
    your dog-Latin.
I have various reasons of weight,
    on my word, sir,
For pronouncing a step of this sort
    were absurd, sir.
Firstly, erudite sir, 'twas against
    your advising
I adopted the lines this monstrosity
    lies in ;
For you modestly hinted my English
    translation
Would become better far such a
    dignified station.
Second—how, in God's name, would
    my bacon be saved,
By not having writ what I clearly
    engraved ?
On the contrary, I, on the whole,
    think it better
To be whipped as the thief, than his
    lousy resetter.
Thirdly—don't you perceive that I
    don't care a boddle
Although fifty false metres were flung
    at my noddle,
For my back is as broad and as hard
    as Benlomon''s,
And I treat as I please both the
    Greeks and the Romans ;
Whereas the said heathens might
    rather look serious
At a kick on their drum from the
    scribe of Valerius [2].
And, fourthly and lastly—it is my
    good pleasure
To remain the sole source of that
    murderous measure.

1 Blackwood's Magazine.   2 Lockhart's novel.

So *stet pro ratione voluntas* — be tractile,
Invade not, I say, my own dear little
dactyl ;
If you do, you 'll occasion a breach
in our intercourse.
To-morrow will see me in town for
the winter-course,
But not at your door, at the usual
hour, sir,
My own pye-house (*pious!*) daughter's
good prog to devour, sir.
Ergo—peace !—on your duty, your
squeamishness throttle,
And we 'll soothe Priscian's spleen
with a canny third bottle.
A fig for all dactyls, a fig for all
spondees,
A fig for all dunces and dominie
Grundys ;
A fig for dry thrapples, south, north,
east, and west, sir,
Speates and raxes[1] ere five for a
famishing guest, sir ;
And as Fatsman[2] and I have some
topics for haver, he 'll
Be invited, I hope, to meet me and
Dame Peveril,
Upon whom, to say nothing of Oury
and Anne, you a
Dog shall be deemed if you fasten
your *janua*.

—••—

LINES

ADDRESSED TO MONSIEUR ALEXANDRE,
THE CELEBRATED VENTRILOQUIST.

(1824.)

OF yore, in old England, it was not
thought good
To carry two visages under one hood ;
What should folk say to *you* ? who
have faces such plenty,
That, from under one hood, last
night show'd us twenty !

Stand forth, arch deceiver, and tell us
in truth,
Are you handsome or ugly, in age
or in youth ?
Man, woman, or child—a dog or
a mouse ?
Or are you, at once, each live thing
in the house ?
Each live thing, did I ask ?—each dead
implement, too,
A workshop in your person,—saw,
chisel, and screw !
Above all, are you one individual?
I know
You must be at least Alexandre and Co.
But I think you 're a troop—an assem-
blage—a mob,
And that I, as the Sheriff, should take
up the job ;
And instead of rehearsing your wonders
in verse,
Must read you the Riot Act, and
bid you disperse.

ABBOTSFORD, *23rd April.*

—••—

EPILOGUE

TO THE DRAMA FOUNDED ON 'SAINT
RONAN'S WELL.'

(1824.)

Enter MEG DODDS, *encircled by a crowd
of unruly boys, whom a town's-officer
is driving off.*

THAT 's right, friend—drive the gait-
lings[1] back,
And lend·yon muckle ane a whack ;
Your Embro' bairns are grown a pack,
    Sae proud and saucy,
They scarce will let an auld wife
walk
    Upon your causey.

---

[1] Spits and ranges.   [2] James Ballantyne.

[1 Children.]

I've seen the day they would been
    scaur'd,
Wi' the Tolbooth, or wi' the Guard,
Or maybe wud hae some regard
      For Jamie Laing—
The Water-hole was right weel wared
      On sic a gang.

But whar's the gude Tolbooth gane
    now?
Whar's the auld Claught[1], wi' red and
    blue?
Whar's Jamie Laing[2]? and whar's
    John Doo[3]?
      And whar's the Weigh-
      house?
Deil hae't I see but what is new,
      Except the Playhouse!

Yoursells are changed frae head to
    heel,
There's some that gar the causeway
    reel
With clashing hufe and rattling wheel,
      And horses canterin',
Wha's fathers daunder'd hame as
    weel
      Wi' lass and lantern.

Mysell being in the public line,
I look for howfs I kenn'd lang syne,
Whar gentles used to drink gude wine,
      And eat cheap dinners;
But deil a soul gangs there to dine,
      Of saints or sinners!

Fortune's[4] and Hunter's[4] gane, alace!
And Bayle's[4] is lost in empty space;
And now if folk would splice a brace,
    Or crack a bottle,
They gang to a new fangled place
      They ca' a Hottle.

The deevil hottle them for Meg!
They are sae greedy and sae gleg,
That if ye're served but wi' an egg,
      (And that's puir pickin',)
In comes a chiel and makes a leg,
      And charges chicken!

'And wha may ye be,' gin ye speer,
'That brings your auld-warld clavers
    here?'
Troth, if there's onybody near
      That kens the roads,
I'll haud ye Burgundy to beer,
      He kens Meg Dodds.

I came a piece frae west o' Currie[5];
And, since I see you're in a hurry,
Your patience I'll nae langer worry,
      But be sae crouse
As speak a word for ane Will Murray[6],
      That keeps this house.

Plays are auld-fashion'd things, in truth,
And ye've seen wonders mair un-
    couth;
Yet actors shouldna suffer drouth,
      Or want of dramock[7],
Although they speak but wi' their
    mouth,
      Not with their stamock.

But ye tak care of a' folk's pantry;
And surely to hae stooden sentry
Ower this big house (that's far frae
    rent-free),
      For a lone sister,
Is claims as gude's to be a ventri—
      How'st ca'd—loquister.

Weel, sirs, gude'en, and have a care
The bairns mak fun o' Meg nae mair;
For gin they do, she tells you fair,
      And without failzie,
As sure as ever ye sit there,
      She'll tell the Bailie.

[1 The Town Guard, or city police; *the Clutchers.*]
[2 An influential police official.]
[3 One of the Town Guard.]
[4 All noted taverns.]

[5 Village near Edinburgh.]
[6 Lessee of the Theatre.]
[7 Food; meal and water.]

EPILOGUE.

(1824.)

THE sages—for authority, pray look
Seneca's morals, or the copy-book—
The sages to disparage woman's
    power,
Say, beauty is a fair, but fading
    flower;—
I cannot tell—I've small philosophy—
Yet, if it fades, it does not surely die,
But, like the violet, when decay'd
    in bloom,
Survives through many a year in rich
    perfume.
Witness our theme to-night, two ages
    gone,
A third wanes fast, since Mary fill'd
    the throne.
Brief was her bloom, with scarce one
    sunny day,
'Twixt Pinkie's field and fatal Fother-
    ingay:
But when, while Scottish hearts and
    blood you boast,
Shall sympathy with Mary's woes
    be lost?
O'er Mary's memory the learnèd
    quarrel,
By Mary's grave the poet plants his
    laurel;
Time's echo, old tradition, makes her
    name
The constant burden of his falt'ring
    theme;
In each old hall his grey-hair'd heralds
    tell
Of Mary's picture, and of Mary's cell,
And show—my fingers tingle at the
    thought—
The loads of tapestry which that poor
    Queen wrought.
In vain did fate bestow a double
    dower
Of ev'ry ill that waits on rank and
    pow'r,
Of ev'ry ill on beauty that attends—
False ministers, false lovers, and false
    friends.
Spite of three wedlocks so completely
    curst,
They rose in ill from bad to worse,
    and worst;
In spite of errors—I dare not say more.
For Duncan Targe lays hand on his
    claymore.—
In spite of all, however humours
    vary,
There is a talisman in that word Mary,
That unto Scottish bosoms all and
    some
Is found the genuine *open sesamum!*
In history, ballad, poetry, or novel,
It charms alike the castle and the hovel,
Even you—forgive me—who, demure
    and shy,
Gorge not each bait, nor stir at every
    fly,
Must rise to this, else in her ancient
    reign
The Rose of Scotland has survived
    in vain.

—◆◆—

ON THE MATERIALS NECESSARY FOR HIS 'LIFE OF NAPOLEON.'

(June, 1825.)

WHEN with Poetry dealing,
Room enough in a shieling:
Neither cabin nor hovel
Too small for a novel:
Though my back I should rub
On Diogenes' tub,
How my fancy could prance
In a dance of romance!
But my house I must swap
With some Brobdingnag chap,
Ere I grapple, God bless me! with
    Emperor Nap.

LINES

TO SIR CUTHBERT SHARP, SUNDERLAND,
TO ASSURE HIM THAT HE WAS NOT
FORGOTTEN.

(1827.)

FORGET thee? No! my worthy fere!
Forget blithe mirth and gallant cheer?
Death sooner stretch me on my bier!
  Forget thee! No.

Forget the universal shout
When 'canny Sunderland' spoke out—
A truth which knaves affect to doubt—
  Forget thee? No.

Forget you? No—though nowaday
I've heard your knowing people say,
Disown the debt you cannot pay,
You'll find it far the thriftiest way—
  But I?—O no.

Forget your kindness found for all
  room,
In what, though large, seem'd still
  a small room,
Forget my *Surtees* in a ball-room—
  Forget you? No.

Forget your sprightly dumpty-diddles,
And beauty tripping to the fiddles,
Forget my lovely friends the *Liddells*—
  Forget you? No.

—◆◆—

THE DEATH OF KEELDAR.

(1828.)

(*Suggested by Cooper's painting.*)

UP rose the sun, o'er moor and mead;
Up with the sun rose Percy Rede;
Brave Keeldar, from his couples freed,
  Career'd along the lea;
The palfrey sprung with sprightly
  bound,
As if to match the gamesome hound;
His horn the gallant huntsman wound;
  They were a jovial three!

Man, hound, or horse, of higher fame,
To wake the wild deer never came,
Since Alnwick's Earl pursued the game
  On Cheviot's rueful day;
Keeldar was matchless in his speed,
Than Tarras, ne'er was stancher steed,
A peerless archer, Percy Rede:
  And right dear friends were they.

The chase engross'd their joys and
  woes,
Together at the dawn they rose,
Together shared the noon's repose,
  By fountain or by stream;
And oft, when evening skies were red
The heather was their common bed,
Where each, as wildering fancy led,
  Still hunted in his dream.

Now is the thrilling moment near,
Of sylvan hope and sylvan fear,
Yon thicket holds the harbour'd deer,
  The signs the hunters know;—
With eyes of flame, and quivering ears
The brake sagacious Keeldar nears;
The restless palfrey paws and rears;
  The archer strings his bow.

The game's afoot!—Halloo! Halloo!
Hunter, and horse, and hound pur-
  sue;—
But woe the shaft that erring flew,—
  That e'er it left the string!
And ill betide the faithless yew!
The stag bounds scatheless o'er the
  dew,
And gallant Keeldar's life-blood true
  Has drench'd the grey-goose
  wing.

The noble hound—he dies, he dies,
Death, death has glazed his fixed eyes,
Stiff on the bloody heath he lies,
  Without a groan or quiver.
Now day may break and bugle sound,
And whoop and hollow ring around,
And o'er his couch the stag may bound,
  But Keeldar sleeps for ever.

Dilated nostrils, staring eyes,
Mark the poor palfrey's mute surprise;
He knows not that his comrade dies,
    Nor what is death—but still
His aspect hath expression drear
Of grief and wonder, mix'd with fear,
Like startled children when they hear
    Some mystic tale of ill.

But he that bent the fatal bow,
Can well the sum of evil know,
And o'er his favourite, bending low,
    In speechless grief recline;
Can think he hears the senseless clay,
In unreproachful accents say,
'The hand that took my life away,
    Dear master, was it thine?

' And if it be, the shaft be bless'd,
Which sure some erring aim address'd,
Since in your service prized, caress'd
    I in your service die;
And you may have a fleeter hound,
To match the dun-deer's merry bound,
But by your couch will ne'er be found
    So true a guard as I.'

And to his last stout Percy rued
The fatal chance, for when he stood
'Gainst fearful odds in deadly feud,
    And fell amid the fray,
E'en with his dying voice he cried,
' Had Keeldar but been at my side,
Your treacherous ambush had been
    spied—
    I had not died to-day!'

Remembrance of the erring bow
Long since had join'd the tides which
    flow,
Conveying human bliss and woe
    Down dark oblivion's river;
But Art can Time's stern doom arrest,
And snatch his spoil from Lethe's
    breast,
And, in her Cooper's colours drest,
    The scene shall live for ever.

THE FORAY

(1830.)

THE last of our steers on the board
    has been spread,
And the last flask of wine in our
    goblet is red;
Up, up, my brave kinsmen! belt
    swords and begone,
There are dangers to dare, and there's
    spoil to be won.

The eyes, that so lately mix'd glances
    with ours,
For a space must be dim, as they gaze
    from the towers,
And strive to distinguish through
    tempest and gloom
The prance of the steed and the toss
    of the plume.

The rain is descending; the wind
    rises loud;
And the moon her red beacon has
    veil'd with a cloud;
'Tis the better, my mates! for the
    warder's dull eye
Shall in confidence slumber, nor
    dream we are nigh.

Our steeds are impatient! I hear my
    blithe Grey!
There is life in his hoof-clang, and
    hope in his neigh;
Like the flash of a meteor, the glance
    of his mane
Shall marshal your march through
    the darkness and rain.

The drawbridge has dropp'd, the bugle
    has blown;
One pledge is to quaff yet—then
    mount and begone!—
To their honour and peace, that shall
    rest with the slain;
To their health and their glee, that
    see Teviot again!

INSCRIPTION

FOR THE MONUMENT OF THE
REV. GEORGE SCOTT.

(1830.)

To youth, to age, alike, this tablet pale
Tells the brief moral of its tragic tale.
Art thou a parent? Reverence this bier,
The parents' fondest hopes lie buried
    here.
Art thou a youth, prepared on life to
    start,
With opening talents and a generous
    heart,
Fair hopes and flattering prospects all
    thine own?
Lo! here their end—a monumental
    stone.
But let submission tame each sorrow-
    ing thought,
Heaven crown'd its champion ere the
    fight was fought.

LINES ON FORTUNE, A SKILFUL MECHANIST.

(1831.)

Fortune, my Foe, why dost thou
    frown on me?
And will my Fortune never better
    be?
Wilt thou, I say, for ever breed my
    pain?
And wilt thou ne'er return my joys
    again?

(*No! let my ditty be henceforth —*)

Fortune, my Friend, how well thou
    favourest me!
A kinder Fortune man did never
    see!
Thou propp'st my thigh, thou ridd'st
    my knee of pain,
I'll walk, I'll mount—I'll be a man
    again.

END OF THE MISCELLANEOUS POEMS.

Notes to Miscellaneous Poems.

WAR-SONG OF THE ROYAL EDIN-BURGH LIGHT DRAGOONS.

P. 701.

'*Nennius.* Is not peace the end of arms?
  Caratach. Not where the cause implies a general
    conquest.
Had we a difference with some petty isle,
Or with our neighbours, Britons, for our landmarks,
The taking in of some rebellious lord,
Or making head against a slight commotion,
After a day of blood, peace might be argued:
But where we grapple for the land we live on,
The liberty we hold more dear than life,
The gods we worship, and, next these, our honours,
And, with those, swords that know no end of battle—
Those men, beside themselves, allow no neighbour:
Those minds, that, where the day is, claim inherit-
    ance,
And, where the sun makes ripe the fruit, their harvest,
And, where they march, but measure out more ground
To add to Rome—
It must not be—No! as they are our foes,
Let 's use the peace of honour—that 's fair dealing;
But in our hands our swords. The hardy Roman,
That thinks to graft himself into my stock,
Must first begin his kindred under ground,
And be allied in ashes.'

                            Bonduca.

This War-Song was written during the apprehension of an invasion[1]. The corps of volunteers to which it was addressed was raised in 1797, consisting of gentlemen, mounted and armed at their own expense. It still subsists, as the Right Troop of the Royal Mid-Lothian Light Cavalry, commanded by the Honourable Lieutenant-Colonel Dundas[2]. The noble and constitutional measure of arming freemen in defence of their own rights was nowhere more successful than in Edinburgh, which furnished a force of 3000 armed and disciplined volunteers, including a regiment of cavalry, from the city and county, and two corps of artillery, each capable of serving twelve guns. To such a force, above all others, might, in similar circumstances, be applied the exhortation of our ancient Galgacus: '*Proinde itur: in aciem, et majores vestros et Posteros cogitate.*' 1812.

---

[1] The song originally appeared in the Scots Magazine for 1802.—LOCKHART.
[2] Now Viscount Melville (1831).

FAREWELL TO MACKENZIE.

P. 722.

The original verses are arranged to a beautiful Gaelic air, of which the chorus is adapted to the double pull upon the oars of a galley, and which is therefore distinct from the ordinary jorrams, or boat-songs. They were composed by the Family Bard upon the departure of the Earl of Seaforth, who was obliged to take refuge in Spain, after an unsuccessful effort at insurrection in favour of the Stuart family, in the year 1718.

PIBROCH OF DONUIL DHU.

P. 731.

This is a very ancient pibroch belonging to Clan MacDonald, and supposed to refer to the expedition of Donald Balloch, who, in 1431, launched from the Isles with a considerable force, invaded Lochaber, and at Inverlochy defeated and put to flight the Earls of Mar and Caithness, though at the head of an army superior to his own. The words of the set, theme, or melody, to which the pipe variations are applied, run thus in Gaelic:—

'Piobaireachd Dhonuil Dhuidh, piobaireachd Dhonuil;
Piobaireachd Dhonuil Dhuidh, piobaireachd Dhonuil;
Piobaireachd Dhonuil Dhuidh, piobaireachd Dhonuil;
Piob agus bratach air faiche Inverlochi.'

'The pipe-summons of Donald the Black,
The pipe-summons of Donald the Black,
The war-pipe and the pennon are on the gathering-
    place at Inverlochy.'

MACKRIMMON'S LAMENT.

P. 744.

Mackrimmon, hereditary piper to the Laird of Macleod, is said to have composed this Lament when the Clan was about to depart upon a distant and dangerous expedition. The Minstrel was impressed with a belief, which the event verified, that he was to be slain in the approaching feud; and hence the Gaelic words, 'Cha till mi tuille; ged thillis Macleod, cha till Mackrimmon,' 'I shall never return; although Macleod returns, yet Mackrimmon shall never return!' The piece is but too well known, from its being the strain with which the emigrants from the West Highlands and Isles usually take leave of their native shore.

Poetry and Verse from the Waverley Novels.

I.

FROM WAVERLEY.

BRIDAL SONG.

AND did ye not hear of a mirth befel
The morrow after a wedding day,
And carrying a bride at home to dwell?
And away to Tewin, away, away?

The quintain was set, and the garlands
were made,
'Tis pity old customs should ever
decay;
And woe be to him that was horsed on
a jade,
For he carried no credit away, away.

We met a concert of fiddle-de-dees;
We set them a cockhorse, and made
them play
The winning of Bullen, and Upsey-
frees,
And away to Tewin, away, away!

There was ne'er a lad in all the parish
That would go to the plough that
day;

But on his fore-horse his wench he
carries,
And away to Tewin, away, away!

The butler was quick, and the ale he
did tap,
The maidens did make the chamber
full gay;
The servants did give me a fuddling cup,
And I did carry 't away, away.

The smith of the town his liquor so
took,
That he was persuaded that the
ground look'd blue;
And I dare boldly be sworn on a
book,
Such smiths as he there 's but a few.

A posset was made, and the women
did sip,
And simpering said, they could eat
no more;
Full many a maiden was laid on the
lip,—
I 'll say no more, but give o'er, (give
o'er).

(APPENDIX TO GENERAL PREFACE—
apud QUEENHOO HALL.)

2 B

LINES BY CAPTAIN WAVERLEY

ON RECEIVING HIS COMMISSION IN COLONEL GARDINER'S REGIMENT.

LATE, when the autumn evening fell
On Mirkwood-Mere's romantic dell,
The lake return'd, in chasten'd gleam,
The purple cloud, the golden beam:
Reflected in the crystal pool,
Headland and bank lay fair and cool;
The weather-tinted rock and tower,
Each drooping tree, each fairy flower,
So true, so soft, the mirror gave,
As if there lay beneath the wave,
Secure from trouble, toil, and care,
A world than earthly world more fair.

But distant winds began to wake,
And roused the Genius of the Lake!
He heard the groaning of the oak,
And donn'd at once his sable cloak,
As warrior, at the battle cry,
Invests him with his panoply:
Then, as the whirlwind nearer press'd,
He 'gan to shake his foamy crest
O'er furrow'd brow and blacken'd cheek,
And bade his surge in thunder speak.
In wild and broken eddies whirl'd,
Flitted that fond ideal world;
And, to the shore in tumult tost,
The realms of fairy bliss were lost.

Yet, with a stern delight and strange,
I saw the spirit-stirring change.
As warr'd the wind with wave and wood,
Upon the ruin'd tower I stood,
And felt my heart more strongly bound,
Responsive to the lofty sound,
While, joying in the mighty roar,
I mourn'd that tranquil scene no more.

So, on the idle dreams of youth
Breaks the loud trumpet-call of truth,
Bids each fair vision pass away,
Like landscape on the lake that lay,
As fair, as flitting, and as frail,
As that which fled the autumn gale—
For ever dead to fancy's eye
Be each gay form that glided by,
While dreams of love and lady's charms
Give place to honour and to arms!
  Chap. v.

——◆◆——

DAVIE GELLATLEY *sings:*—

FALSE love, and hast thou play'd me this
    In summer among the flowers?
I will repay thee back again
    In winter among the showers.
Unless again, again, my love,
    Unless you turn again;
As you with other maidens rove,
    I'll smile on other men.

——

THE Knight's to the mountain
    His bugle to wind;
The Lady's to greenwood
    Her garland to bind.
The bower of Burd Ellen
    Has moss on the floor,
That the step of Lord William
    Be silent and sure.
  Chap. IX.

——◆——

SCENE—*Luckie Macleary's Tavern.*

BARON BRADWARDINE *sings:*—

MON cœur volage, dit-elle,
    N'est pas pour vous, garçon;
Mais pour un homme de guerre,
    Qui a barbe au menton.
        Lon, Lon, Laridon.

Qui porte chapeau à plume,
    Soulier à rouge talon,
Qui joue de la flûte,
    Aussi du violon.
        Lon, Lon, Laridon.

BALMAWHAPPLE *sings* :—

It 's up Glenbarchan's braes I gaed,
And o'er the bent of Killiebraid,
And mony a weary cast I made,
  To cuittle the moor-fowl's tail.

If up a bonny black-cock should spring,
To whistle him down wi' a slug in his
  wing,
And strap him on to my lunzie string,
  Right seldom would I fail.

Chap. xi.

—+◆+—

GELLATLEY'S SONG TO THE DEERHOUNDS.

Hie away, hie away,
Over bank and over brae,
Where the copsewood is the greenest,
Where the fountains glisten sheenest,
Where the lady-fern grows strongest,
Where the morning dew lies longest,
Where the black-cock sweetest sips it,
Where the fairy latest trips it :
Hie to haunts right seldom seen,
Lovely, lonesome, cool, and green,
Over bank and over brae,
Hie away, hie away.

Chap. xii.

—+◆+—

ST. SWITHIN'S CHAIR.

On Hallow-Mass Eve, ere you boune
  ye to rest,
Ever beware that your couch be
  bless'd ;
Sign it with cross, and sain it with bead,
Sing the Ave, and say the Creed.

For on Hallow-Mass Eve the Night-
  Hag will ride,
And all her nine-fold sweeping on by
  her side,
Whether the wind sing lowly or loud,
Sailing through moonshine or swath'd
  in the cloud.

The Lady she sate in Saint Swithin's
  Chair,
The dew of the night has damp'd her
  hair :
Her cheek was pale—but resolved and
  high
Was the word of her lip and the glance
  of her eye.

She mutter'd the spell of Swithin
  bold,
When his naked foot traced the midnight wold,
When he stopp'd the Hag as she rode
  the night,
And bade her descend, and her promise
  plight.

He that dare sit on Saint Swithin's
  Chair,
When the Night-Hag wings the
  troubled air,
Questions three, when he speaks the
  spell,
He may ask, and she must tell.

The Baron has been with King Robert
  his liege,
These three long years, in battle and
  siege ;
News are there none of his weal or
  his woe,
And fain the Lady his fate would
  know.

She shudders and stops as the charm
  she speaks ;—
Is it the moody owl that shrieks ?
Or is that sound, betwixt laughter and
  scream,
The voice of the Demon who haunts
  the stream ?

The moan of the wind sunk silent and
  low,
And the roaring torrent had ceased to
  flow ;

The calm was more dreadful than raging storm,
When the cold grey mist brought the ghastly form !

. . . . . .

Chap. XIII.

—+—

GELLATLEY *sings :—*

YOUNG men will love thee more fair and more fast ;
Heard ye so merry the little bird sing?
Old men's love the longest will last,
And the throstle-cock's head is under his wing.

The young man's wrath is like light straw on fire ;
Heard ye so merry the little bird sing?
But like red-hot steel is the old man's ire,
And the throstle-cock's head is under his wing.

The young man will brawl at the evening board ;
Heard ye so merry the little bird sing?
But the old man will draw at the dawning the sword,
And the throstle-cock's head is under his wing.

Chap. XIV.

—+—

FLORA MACIVOR'S SONG.

THERE is mist on the mountain, and night on the vale,
But more dark is the sleep of the sons of the Gael.
A stranger commanded—it sunk on the land,
It has frozen each heart, and benumb'd every hand !

The dirk and the target lie sordid with dust,
The bloodless claymore is but redden'd with rust ;
On the hill or the glen if a gun should appear,
It is only to war with the heath-cock or deer.

The deeds of our sires if our bards should rehearse,
Let a blush or a blow be the meed of their verse !
Be mute every string, and be hush'd every tone,
That shall bid us remember the fame that is flown.

But the dark hours of night and of slumber are past,
The morn on our mountains is dawning at last ;
Glenaladale's[1] peaks are illumed with the rays,
And the streams of Glenfinnan[2] leap bright in the blaze.

O high-minded Moray![2]—the exiled—the dear !—
In the blush of the dawning the STANDARD uprear !
Wide, wide on the winds of the north let it fly,
Like the sun's latest flash when the tempest is nigh !

Ye sons of the strong, when that dawning shall break,
Need the harp of the aged remind you to wake ?
That dawn never beam'd on your forefathers' eye,
But it roused each high chieftain to vanquish or die.

[1 In Moidart, where Prince Charlie landed in 1745.
[2 Where he displayed his standard.]
[3 Brother of the Marquis of Tullibardine, long a Jacobite exile.]

O, sprung from the kings who in
    Islay kept state,
Proud chiefs of Clan-Ranald, Glen-
    garry, and Sleat!
Combine like three streams from one
    mountain of snow,
And resistless in union rush down on
    the foe.

True son of Sir Evan, undaunted
    Lochiel,
Place thy targe on thy shoulder and
    burnish thy steel!
Rough Keppoch, give breath to thy
    bugle's bold swell,
Till far Coryarrick resound to the knell!

Stern son of Lord Kenneth, high chief
    of Kintail,
Let the stag in thy standard bound
    wild in the gale!
May the race of Clan-Gillean, the
    fearless and free,
Remember Glenlivat, Harlaw, and
    Dundee!

Let the clan of grey Fingon, whose
    offspring has given
Such heroes to earth, and such
    martyrs to heaven,
Unite with the race of renown'd
    Rorri More,
To launch the long galley, and stretch
    to the oar!

How Mac-Shimei will joy when their
    chief shall display
The yew-crested bonnet o'er tresses
    of grey!
How the race of wrong'd Alpine and
    murder'd Glencoe
Shall shout for revenge when they
    pour on the foe!

Ye sons of brown Dermid, who slew
    the wild boar,
Resume the pure faith of the great
    Callum-More!

Mac-Niel of the Islands, and Moy of
    the Lake,
For honour, for freedom, for ven-
    geance awake!

Awake on your hills, on your islands
    awake,
Brave sons of the mountain, the frith,
    and the lake!
'Tis the bugle—but not for the chase
    is the call;
'Tis the pibroch's shrill summons—
    but not to the hall.

'Tis the summons of heroes for con-
    quest or death,
When the banners are blazing on
    mountain and heath;
They call to the dirk, the claymore,
    and the targe,
To the march and the muster, the
    line and the charge.

Be the brand of each chieftain like
    Fin's in his ire!
May the blood through his veins flow
    like currents of fire!
Burst the base foreign yoke as your
    sires did of yore!
Or die, like your sires, and endure
    it no more!

    Chap. XXII.

—◆—

FERGUS *sings*:—

O LADY of the desert, hail!
That lovest the harping of the Gael,
Through fair and fertile regions borne,
Where never yet grew grass or corn.

    And again:—

O vous, qui buvez à tasse pleine,
    A cette heureuse fontaine,
Où on ne voit sur le rivage
    Que quelques vilains troupeaux,
Suivis de nymphes de village,
    Qui les escortent sans sabots ——

    Chap. XXIII.

TO AN OAK TREE

IN THE CHURCHYARD OF ———, IN THE
HIGHLANDS OF SCOTLAND, SAID TO
MARK THE GRAVE OF CAPTAIN WOGAN,
KILLED IN 1649.

EMBLEM of England's ancient faith,
   Full proudly may thy branches
      wave,
Where loyalty lies low in death,
   And valour fills a timeless grave.

And thou, brave tenant of the tomb!
   Repine not if our clime deny,
Above thine honour'd sod to bloom,
   The flowrets of a milder sky.

These owe their birth to genial May;
   Beneath a fiercer sun they pine,
Before the winter storm decay—
   And can their worth be type of
      thine?

No! for, 'mid storms of Fate opposing,
   Still higher swell'd thy dauntless
      heart,
And, while Despair the scene was
      closing,
   Commenced thy brief but brilliant
      part.

'Twas then thou sought'st on Albyn's
      hill
   (When England's sons the strife
      resign'd)
A rugged race, resisting still,
   And unsubdued, though unrefined.

Thy death's hour heard no kindred
      wail,
   No holy knell thy requiem rung;
Thy mourners were the plaided Gael,
   Thy dirge the clamorous pibroch
      sung.

Yet who, in Fortune's summer-shine
   To waste life's longest term away,
Would change that glorious dawn of
      thine,
   Though darken'd ere its noontide
      day?

Be thine the Tree whose dauntless
      boughs
   Brave summer's drought and
      winter's gloom!
Rome bound with oak her patriots'
      brows,
   As Albyn shadows Wogan's tomb.

Chap. XXIX.

———✦———

GELLATLEY *sings:*—

[THEY came upon us in the night,
And brake my bower and slew my
      knight;
My servants a' for life did flee
And left us in extremitie.

They slew my knight to me sae dear;
They slew my knight, and drave his
      gear;]
The moon may set, the sun may rise,
But a deadly sleep has closed his eyes.

.   .   .   .   .

But follow, follow me,
While glowworms light the lea,
I'll show ye where the dead should
      be—
   Each in his shroud,
   While winds pipe loud,
And the red moon peeps dim through
      the cloud.

Follow, follow me;
Brave should he be
That treads by night the dead man's lea.

Chap. LXIII.

II.

FROM GUY MANNERING.

THE NATIVITY CHANT.

(By Meg Merrilies.)

Canny moment, lucky fit;
Is the lady lighter yet?
Be it lad, or be it lass,
Sign wi' cross, and sain wi' mass.

Trefoil, vervain, John's-wort, dill,
Hinders witches of their will;
Weel is them, that weel may
Fast upon Saint Andrew's day.

Saint Bride and her brat,
Saint Colme and his cat,
Saint Michael and his spear,
Keep the house frae reif and wear.

Chap. III.

THE SPINDLE SONG.

(By Meg Merrilies.)

Twist ye, twine ye! even so
Mingle shades of joy and woe,
Hope, and fear, and peace, and strife,
In the thread of human life.

While the mystic twist is spinning,
And the infant's life beginning,
Dimly seen through twilight bending,
Lo, what varied shapes attending!

Passions wild, and follies vain,
Pleasures soon exchanged for pain;
Doubt, and jealousy, and fear,
In the magic dance appear.

Now they wax, and now they dwindle,
Whirling with the whirling spindle.
Twist ye, twine ye! even so
Mingle human bliss and woe.

Chap. III.

THE GIPSY'S DIRGE.

(By Meg Merrilies.)

Wasted, weary, wherefore stay,
Wrestling thus with earth and clay?
From the body pass away;—
    Hark! the mass is singing.

From thee doff thy mortal weed,
Mary Mother be thy speed,
Saints to help thee at thy need;—
    Hark! the knell is ringing.

Fear not snowdrift driving fast,
Sleet, or hail, or levin blast;
Soon the shroud shall lap thee fast,
And the sleep be on thee cast
    That shall ne'er know waking.

Haste thee, haste thee, to be gone,
Earth flits fast, and time draws on,—
Gasp thy gasp, and groan thy groan,
    Day is near the breaking.

    Open locks, end strife,
    Come death, and pass life.

Chap. XXVII.

THE PROPHECY.

(By Meg Merrilies.)

The dark shall be light,
And the wrong made right,
When Bertram's right and Bertram's might
Shall meet on Ellangowan's height.

Chap. XLI.

Glossin *sings:*—

Gin by pailfuls, wine in rivers,
Dash the window-glass to shivers,
For three wild lads were we, brave boys,
And three wild lads were we;
Thou on the land, and I on the sand,
And Jack on the gallows-tree!

Chap. XXXIV.

III.

FROM THE ANTIQUARY.

THE AGED CARLE.

'Why sit'st thou by that ruin'd hall,
 Thou aged carle so stern and grey?
Dost thou its former pride recall,
 Or ponder how it pass'd away?'—

'Know'st thou not me?' the Deep
 Voice cried;
'So long enjoy'd, so oft misused—
Alternate, in thy fickle pride,
 Desired, neglected, and accused!

'Before my breath, like blazing flax,
 Man and his marvels pass away!
And changing empires wane and wax,
 Are founded, flourish, and decay.

'Redeem mine hours—the space is
 brief—
While in my glass the sand-grains
 shiver,
And measureless thy joy or grief
 When TIME and thou shall part for
 ever!'

Chap. x.

——+——

AN EPITAPH.

HEIR lyeth John o' ye Girnell;
Erth has ye nit and heuen ye kirnell.
In hys tyme ilk wyfe's hennis clokit,
Ilk gud mannis herth wi' bairnis was
 stokit.
He deled a boll o' bear in firlottis fyve,
Four for ye halie kirke and ane for
 pure mennis wyvis.

Chap. xi.

——+——

OLD ELSPETH *sings*:—

'THE herring loves the merry moon-
 light,
 The mackerel loves the wind,
But the oyster loves the dredging sang,
 For they come of a gentle kind.'

. . . . . .

Now haud your tongue, baith wife
 and carle,
 And listen, great and sma',
And I will sing of Glenallan's Earl
 That fought on the red Harlaw.

The cronach 's cried on Bennachie,
 And doun the Don and a',
And hieland and lawland may mourn-
 fu' be
 For the sair field of Harlaw.

They saddled a hundred milk-white
 steeds,
 They hae bridled a hundred black,
With a chafron of steel on each
 horse's head,
 And a good knight upon his back.

They hadna ridden a mile, a mile,
 A mile, but barely ten,
When Donald came branking down
 the brae
 Wi' twenty thousand men.

Their tartans they were waving wide,
 Their glaives were glancing clear,
The pibrochs rung frae side to side,
 Would deafen ye to hear.

The great Earl in his stirrups stood,
 That Highland host to see;
Now here a knight that's stout and
 good
 May prove a jeopardie:

'What would'st thou do, my squire
 so gay,
 That rides beside my reyne,
Were ye Glenallan's Earl the day,
 And I were Roland Cheyne?

'To turn the rein were sin and shame,
    To fight were wond'rous peril ;
What would ye do now, Roland
    Cheyne,
    Were ye Glenallan's Earl ?'

'Were I Glenallan's Earl this tide,
    And ye were Roland Cheyne,
The spur should be in my horse's side,
    And the bridle upon his mane.

If they hae twenty thousand blades,
    And we twice ten times ten,
Yet they hae but their tartan plaids,
    And we are mail-clad men.

'My horse shall ride through ranks
    sae rude,
As through the moorland fern,—
Then ne'er let the gentle Norman blude
    Grow cauld for Highland kerne.'

.   .   .   .   .   .

He turn'd him right and round again,
    Said—Scorn na at my mither ;
Light loves I may get mony a ane,
    But minnie ne'er anither.

Chap. XL.

——◆——

MOTTOES.

I KNEW Anselmo. He was shrewd and
    prudent,
Wisdom and cunning had their shares
    of him ;
But he was shrewish as a wayward
    child,
And pleased again by toys which
    childhood please ;
As—book of fables graced with print
    of wood,
Or else the jingling of a rusty medal,
Or the rare melody of some old
    ditty,
That first was sung to please King
    Pepin's cradle.

On Title-page.

'Be brave,' she cried, 'you yet may
    be our guest.
Our haunted room was ever held the
    best :
If, then, your valour can the fight
    sustain
Of rustling curtains, and the clinking
    chain ;
If your courageous tongue have
    powers to talk
When round your bed the horrid
    ghost shall walk ;
If you dare ask it why it leaves its
    tomb,
I 'll see your sheets well air'd, and
    show the room.'

True Story.
Chap. IX.

HERE has been such a stormy encounter
Betwixt my cousin Captain, and this
    soldier,
About I know not what !—nothing,
    indeed ;
Competitions, degrees, and compara-
    tives
Of soldiership !

? A Faire Quarrel.
Chap. XIX.

If you fail honour here,
Never presume to serve her any more ;
Bid farewell to the integrity of arms,
And the honourable name of soldier
Fall from you, like a shiver'd wreath
    of laurel
By thunder struck from a desertlesse
    forehead.

? A Faire Quarrel.
Chap. XX.

The Lord Abbot had a soul
Subtile and quick, and searching as
    the fire :
By magic stairs he went as deep as hell,

And if in devils' possession gold be
    kept,
He brought some sure from thence—
    'tis hid in caves,
Known, save to me, to none.

? The Wonder of a Kingdome.

Chap. xxi.

Who is he?—One that for the lack of
    land
Shall fight upon the water—he hath
    challenged
Formerly the grand whale; and by
    his titles
Of Leviathan, Behemoth, and so forth.
He tilted with a sword-fish—Marry,
    sir,
Th' aquatic had the best—the argument
Still galls our champion's breech.

Old Play.

Chap. xxx.

Tell me not of it, friend—when the
    young weep,
Their tears are lukewarm brine;—
    from our old eyes
Sorrow falls down like hail-drops of
    the North,
Chilling the furrows of our wither'd
    cheeks,
Cold as our hopes, and harden'd as
    our feeling:
Theirs, as they fall, sink sightless—
    ours recoil,
Heap the fair plain, and bleaken all
    before us.

Old Play.

Chap. xxxi.

Remorse—she ne'er forsakes us!—
A bloodhound stanch—she tracks our
    rapid step
Through the wild labyrinth of youthful
    frenzy,
Unheard, perchance, until old age
    hath tamed us;

Then in our lair, when Time hath
    chill'd our joints,
And maim'd our hope of combat, or
    of flight,
We hear her deep-mouth'd bay,
    announcing all,
Of wrath, and woe, and punishment,
    that bides us.

Old Play.

Chap. xxxiii.

Still in his dead hand clench'd remain
    the strings
That thrill his father's heart—e'en as
    the limb,
Lopp'd off and laid in grave, retains,
    they tell us,
Strange commerce with the mutilated
    stump,
Whose nerves are twingeing still in
    maim'd existence.

Old Play.

Chap. xxxiv.

Life, with you,
Glows in the brain and dances in the
    arteries;
'Tis like the wine some joyous guest
    hath quaff'd,
That glads the heart and elevates the
    fancy:
Mine is the poor residuum of the
    cup,
Vapid, and dull, and tasteless, only
    soiling
With its base dregs the vessel that
    contains it.

Old Play.

Chap. xxxv.

Yes! I love Justice well—as well as
    you do—
But, since the good dame's blind, she
    shall excuse me
If, time and reason fitting, I prove
    dumb;—

The breath I utter now shall be no means
To take away from me my breath in future.

Old Play.

Chap. XXXVII.

WELL, well, at worst, 'tis neither theft nor coinage,
Granting I knew all that you charge me with.
What tho' the tomb hath born a second birth,
And given the wealth to one that knew not on't,
Yet fair exchange was never robbery,
Far less pure bounty.

Old Play.

Chap. XXXVIII.

LIFE ebbs from such old age, unmark'd and silent,
As the slow neap-tide leaves yon stranded galley.
Late she rock'd merrily at the least impulse
That wind or wave could give; but now her keel
Is settling on the sand, her mast has ta'en
An angle with the sky, from which it shifts not.
Each wave receding shakes her less and less,
Till, bedded on the strand, she shall remain
Useless as motionless.

Old Play.

Chap. XL.

So, while the Goose, of whom the fable told,
Incumbent, brooded o'er her eggs of gold,

With hand outstretch'd, impatient to destroy,
Stole on her secret nest the cruel Boy,
Whose gripe rapacious changed her splendid dream,
For wings vain fluttering, and for dying scream.

The Loves of the Sea-Weeds.

Chap. XLI.

LET those go see who will—I like it not—
For, say he was a slave to rank and pomp,
And all the nothings he is now divorced from
By the hard doom of stern necessity;
Yet it is sad to mark his alter'd brow,
Where Vanity adjusts her flimsy veil
O'er the deep wrinkles of repentant anguish.

Old Play.

Chap. XLII.

FORTUNE, you say, flies from us; she but circles
Like the fleet sea-bird round the fowler's skiff,—
Lost in the mist one moment, and the next
Brushing the white sail with her whiter wing,
As if to court the aim.—Experience watches,
And has her on the wheel.

Old Play.

Chap. XLIII.

NAY, if she love me not, I care not for her:
Shall I look pale because the maiden blooms?
Or sigh because she smiles—and smiles on others?
Not I, by Heaven!—I hold my peace too dear,

To let it, like the plume upon her cap,
Shake at each nod that her caprice
    shall dictate.
Old Play.

    Chap. XLIV.

IV.

FROM THE BLACK DWARF.

WHEN the devil was sick, the devil
    a monk would be,
When the devil was well, the devil
    a monk was he.

    Chap. VI.

—♦♦—

MOTTOES.

So spak the knicht ; the geaunt sed—
' Lead forth with thé the sely maid,
    And mak me quite of thé and sche ;
For glaunsing ee, or brow so brent,
    Or cheek with rose and lilye blent,
Me-lists not fecht with thé.

    Chap. IX.

I LEFT my ladye's bower last night,
    It was clad in wreaths of snaw ;
I 'll seek it when the sun is bright
    And sweet the roses blaw.
Old Ballad.

    Chap. X.

      'TWAS time and griefs
That framed him thus : Time, with
    his fairer hand,
Offering the fortunes of his former days,
The former man may make him : bring
    us to him,
And chance it as it may.
Old Play.

    Chap. XVI.

V.

FROM OLD MORTALITY.

MAJOR BELLENDEN *sings :—*

AND what though winter will pinch
    severe
Through locks of grey and a cloak
    that 's old,
Yet keep up thy heart, bold cavalier,
    For a cup of sack shall fence the cold.

For time will rust the brightest blade,
    And years will break the strongest
    bow ;
Was never wight so starkly made,
    But time and years would overthrow.

    Chap. XVIII.

—♦♦—

THE VERSES FOUND IN BOTH-WELL'S POCKET-BOOK.

THY hue, dear pledge, is pure and
    bright,
As in that well-remember'd night
When first thy mystic braid was wove,
And first my Agnes whisper'd love.

    Since then how often hast thou
    press'd
The torrid zone of this wild breast,
Whose wrath and hate have sworn
    to dwell
With the first sin which peopled hell,
A breast whose blood 's a troubled
    ocean,
Each throb the earthquake's wild
    commotion !—
O, if such clime thou canst endure,
Yet keep thy hue unstain'd and pure,
What conquest o'er each erring thought
Of that fierce realm had Agnes
    wrought !
I had not wander'd wild and wide,
With such an angel for my guide ;

Nor heaven nor earth could then
　　reprove me,
If she had lived, and lived to love me.

Not then this world's wild joys had
　　been
To me one savage hunting scene,
My sole delight the headlong race,
And frantic hurry of the chase ;
To start, pursue, and bring to bay,
Rush in, drag down, and rend my
　　prey,
Then—from the carcass turn away !
Mine ireful mood had sweetness tamed,
And soothed each wound which pride
　　inflamed !
Yes, God and man might now approve
　　me,
If thou hadst lived, and lived to love me.

Chap. XXII.

—◆◆—

MOTTOES.

AROUSE thee, youth !—it is no common
　　call,—
God's Church is leaguer'd—haste to
　　man the wall ;
Haste where the Red-cross banners
　　wave on high,
Signals of honour'd death or victory.

? James Duff.

Chap. IV.

[MY hounds may a' rin masterless,
　　My hawks may fly frae tree to tree,]
My lord may grip my vassal lands,
　　For there again maun I never be !

Old Ballad.

Chap. XIII.

SOUND, sound the clarion, fill the fife !
　　To all the sensual world proclaim,
One crowded hour of glorious life
　　Is worth an age without a name.

Anonymous.

Chap. XXXIII.

WHERE's the jolly host
You told me of? 'T has been my cus-
　　tom ever
To parley with mine host.

Lover's Progress.

Chap. XL.

————

VI.

FROM ROB ROY.

**FRANCIS OSBALDISTONE'S LINES
TO THE MEMORY OF EDWARD
THE BLACK PRINCE.**

O FOR the voice of that wild horn,
On Fontarabian echoes borne,
　　The dying hero's call,
That told imperial Charlemagne
How Paynim sons of swarthy Spain
　　Had wrought his champion's fall.

Sad over earth and ocean sounding,
And England's distant cliffs astound-
　　ing,
　　Such are the notes should say
How Britain's hope, and France's fear,
Victor of Cressy and Poitier,
　　In Bordeaux dying lay.

' Raise my faint head, my squires,' he
　　said,
' And let the casement be display'd,
　　That I may see once more
The splendour of the setting sun
Gleam on thy mirror'd wave, Garonne,
　　And Blay's empurpled shore.

' Like me, he sinks to Glory's sleep,
His fall the dews of evening steep,
　　As if in sorrow shed.
So soft shall fall the trickling tear,
When England's maids and matrons
　　hear
　　Of their Black Edward dead.

'And though my sun of glory set,
Nor France nor England shall forget
    The terror of my name;
And oft shall Britain's heroes rise,
New planets in these southern skies,
    Through clouds of blood and
        flame.'

Chap. ii.

—+—

FRAGMENT FROM ARIOSTO.

LADIES, and knights, and arms, and
    love's fair flame,
    Deeds of emprise and courtesy, I
        sing;
What time the Moors from sultry
    Africk came,
    Led on by Agramant, their youthful
        king—
Him whom revenge and hasty ire did
    bring
    O'er the broad wave, in France to
        waste and war;
Such ills from old Trojano's death did
    spring,
    Which to avenge he came from
        realms afar,
And menaced Christian Charles, the
    Roman Emperor.

Of dauntless Roland, too, my strain
    shall sound,
    In import never known in prose or
        rhyme,
How he, the chief of judgment deem'd
    profound,
    For luckless love was crazed upon
        a time——

Chap. xvi.

—+—

MOTTOES.

IN the wide pile, by others heeded not,
Hers was one sacred solitary spot,
Whose gloomy aisles and bending
    shelves contain,
For moral hunger food, and cures for
    moral pain.
            Anonymous.
Chap. x.

DIRE was his thought, who first in
    poison steep'd
The weapon form'd for slaughter—
    direr his,
And worthier of damnation, who in-
        still'd
The mortal venom in the social cup,
To fill the veins with death instead of
    life.
            Anonymous.
Chap. xiii.

YON lamp its line of quivering light
    Shoots from my lady's bower;
But why should Beauty's lamp be bright
At midnight's lonely hour?
            Old Ballad.
Chap. xiv.

LOOK round thee, young Astolpho:
    Here's the place
Which men (for being poor) are sent
    to starve in,—
Rude remedy, I trow, for sore disease.
Within these walls, stifled by damp
    and stench,
Doth Hope's fair torch expire; and at
    the snuff,
Ere yet 'tis quite extinct, rude, wild,
    and wayward,
The desperate revelries of wild de-
    pair,
Kindling their hell-born cressets, light
    to deeds
That the poor captive would have died
    ere practised,
Till bondage sunk his soul to his con-
    dition.
            The Prison, Act i. Sc. iii.
Chap. xxii.

Far as the eye could reach no tree was
seen,
Earth, clad in russet, scorn'd the lively
green ;
No birds, except as birds of passage,
flew ;
No bee was heard to hum, no dove to
coo ;
No streams, as amber smooth, as
amber clear,
Were seen to glide, or heard to warble
here.
Prophecy of Famine.
Chap. xxvii.

'Woe to the vanquish'd !' was stern
Brenno's word,
When sunk proud Rome beneath the
Gallic sword—
'Woe to the vanquish'd !' when his
massive blade
Bore down the scale against her ransom
weigh'd,
And on the field of foughten battle still,
Who knows no limit save the victor's
will.
The Gaulliad.
Chap. xxxi.

And be he safe restored ere evening
set,
Or, if there's vengeance in an injured
heart,
And power to wreak it in an armèd
hand,
Your land shall ache for 't.
Old Play.
Chap. xxxii.

Farewell to the land where the clouds
love to rest,
Like the shroud of the dead on the
mountain's cold breast ;

To the cataract's roar where the eagles
reply,
And the lake her lone bosom expands
to the sky.

Chap. xxxvi.

VII.

FROM THE HEART OF MIDLOTHIAN.

Madge Wildfire *sings :—*

When the glede's in the blue cloud,
The lavrock lies still ;
When the hound's in the greenwood
The hind keeps the hill.

O sleep ye sound, Sir James, she said,
When ye suld rise and ride !
There's twenty men, wi' bow and blade,
Are seeking where ye hide.

I glance like the wildfire through
country and town ;
I'm seen on the causeway—I'm seen
on the down ;
The lightning that flashes so bright
and so free,
Is scarcely so blithe or so bonny as me.

What did ye wi' the bridal ring, bridal
ring, bridal ring ?
What did ye wi' your wedding ring,
ye little cutty quean, O ?
I gied it till a sodger, a sodger, a
sodger,
I gied it till a sodger, an auld true love
o' mine, O.

Good even, good fair moon, good even
    to thee ;
I prithee, dear moon, now show to me
The form and the features, the speech
    and degree,
Of the man that true lover of mine
    shall be.

———

It is the bonny butcher lad
    That wears the sleeves of blue,
He sells the flesh on Saturday,
    On Friday that he slew.

———

There's a bloodhound ranging Tin-
    wald Wood,
There's harness glancing sheen ;
There's a maiden sits on Tinwald brae,
And she sings loud between.

———

In the bonnie cells of Bedlam,
    Ere I was ane and twenty,
I had hempen bracelets strong,
And merry whips, ding-dong,
    And prayer and fasting plenty.

———

My banes are buried in yon kirk-yard
Sae far ayont the sea,
And it is but my blithesome ghaist
That's speaking now to thee.

———

I'm Madge of the country, I'm Madge
    of the town,
And I'm Madge of the lad I am
    blithest to own—
The Lady of Beever in diamonds may
    shine,
But has not a heart half so lightsome
    as mine.

I am Queen of the Wake, and I'm
    Lady of May,
And I lead the blithe ring round the
    May-pole to-day ;
The wild-fire that flashes so fair and so
    free
Was never so bright, or so bonnie as me.

———

Our work is over—over now,
The goodman wipes his weary brow,
The last long wain wends slow away,
And we are free to sport and play.

The night comes on when sets the sun,
And labour ends when day is done.
When Autumn's gone, and Winter's
    come,
We hold our jovial harvest-home.

———

When the fight of grace is fought,
When the marriage vest is wrought,
When Faith has chased cold Doubt
    away,
And Hope but sickens at delay,
When Charity, imprisoned here,
Longs for a more expanded sphere,—
Doff thy robes of sin and clay,
Christian, rise, and come away.

———

Cauld is my bed, Lord Archibald,
    And sad my sleep of sorrow :
But thine sall be as sad and cauld,
    My fause true-love ! to-morrow.

And weep ye not, my maidens free,
    Though death your mistress borrow;
For he for whom I die to-day,
    Shall die for me to-morrow.

———

Proud Maisie is in the wood,
    Walking so early ;
Sweet Robin sits on the bush,
    Singing so rarely.

'Tell me, thou bonny bird,
  When shall I marry me?'
'When six braw gentlemen
  Kirkward shall carry ye.'

'Who makes the bridal bed,
  Birdie, say truly?'
'The grey-headed sexton
  That delves the grave duly.

'The glow-worm o'er grave and stone
  Shall light thee steady.
The owl from the steeple sing,
  "Welcome, proud lady."'

Chaps. XIV—XXXIX.

———•◆•———

MOTTOES.

LAW, take thy victim!—May she find
    the mercy
In yon mild heaven which this hard
    world denies her!

Chap. XXIII.

AND Need and Misery, Vice and
    Danger, bind
In sad alliance, each degraded mind.

Chap. XXVIII.

I BESEECH you,
These tears beseech you, and these
    chaste hands woo you,
That never yet were heaved but to
    things holy—
Things like yourself. You are a God
    above us;
Be as a God, then, full of saving mercy!
            The Bloody Brother.

Chap. XXXVI.

———————

VIII.

FROM THE BRIDE OF LAMMERMOOR.

LUCY ASHTON *sings:*—

LOOK not thou on beauty's charming,
Sit thou still when kings are arming,
Taste not when the wine-cup glistens,
Speak not when the people listens,
Stop thine ear against the singer,
From the red gold keep thy finger;
Vacant heart and hand and eye,
Easy live and quiet die.

Chap. II.

———•◆•———

THE FORESTER *sings:*—

THE monk must arise when the matins
    ring,
  The abbot may sleep to their chime;
But the yeoman must start when the
    bugles sing,
  'Tis time, my hearts, 'tis time.

There's bucks and raes on Billhope
    braes,
  There's a herd on Shortwood Shaw;
But a lily-white doe in the garden goes,
  She's fairly worth them a'.

Chap. II.

———•◆•———

THE PROPHECY.

WHEN the last Laird of Ravenswood
    to Ravenswood shall ride,
And woo a dead maiden to be his
    bride,
He shall stable his steed in the Kelpie's
    flow,
And his name shall be lost for evermoe!

Chap. XVII.

MOTTOES.

Ay, and when huntsmen wind the
   merry horn,
And from its covert starts the fearful
   prey,
Who, warm'd with youth's blood in
   his swelling veins,
Would, like a lifeless clod, outstretchèd
   lie,
Shut out from all the fair creation offers?

Ethwald, Act I. Sc. i.

Chap. VIII.

Let them have meat enough, woman
   —half a hen!
There be old rotten pilchards—put
   them off too!
'Tis but a little new anointing of them,
And a strong onion that confounds
   the savour.

Love's Pilgrimage.

Chap. X.

Should I take aught of you? 'tis true
   I begg'd now;
And, what is worse than that, I stole
   a kindness;
And, what is worst of all, I lost my
   way in 't.

Wit without Money.

Chap. XII.

As, to the Autumn breeze's bugle-
   sound,
Various and vague the dry leaves
   dance their round;
Or, from the garner-door, on ether
   borne,
The chaff flies devious from the
   winnow'd corn;
So vague, so devious, at the breath
   of heaven,
From their fix'd aim are mortal
   counsels driven.

Anonymous.

Chap. XIII.

Here is a father now
Will truck his daughter for a foreign
   venture,
Make her the stop-gap to some
   canker'd feud,
Or fling her o'er, like Jonah, to the
   fishes,
To appease the sea at highest.

Anonymous.

Chap. XVI.

Sir, stay at home and take an old
   man's counsel:
Seek not to bask you by a stranger's
   hearth;
Our own blue smoke is warmer than
   their fire.
Domestic food is wholesome, though
   'tis homely,
And foreign dainties poisonous, though
   tasteful.

The French Courtezan.

Chap. XVII.

I do too ill in this,
And must not think but that a parent's
   plaint
Will move the heavens to pour forth
   misery
Upon the head of disobediency.
Yet reason tells us parents are o'erseen
When with too strict a rein they do
   hold in
Their child's affection, and control
   that love
Which the High Powers Divine inspire
   them with.

The Hog hath lost his Pearl.

Chap. XVIII.

And soon they spied the merry-men
   green,
And eke the coach-and-four.

Duke upon Duke.

Chap. XXI.

Why, now I have Dame Fortune
 by the forelock,
And if she 'scapes my grasp, the fault
 is mine;
He that hath buffeted with stern
 adversity
Best knows to shape his course to
 favouring breezes.
                        Old Play.

Chap. XXVI.

IX.

FROM THE LEGEND OF MONTROSE.

From the Gaelic:—

Woe! woe! son of the Lowlander,
Why wilt thou leave thine own bonny
 Border?
Why comest thou hither, disturbing
 the Highlander,
Wasting the glen that was once in fair
 order?

INTRODUCTION.

SONG OF THE DAWN.

Annot Lyle *sings:—*

Birds of omen dark and foul,
Night-crow, raven, bat, and owl,
Leave the sick man to his dream—
All night long he heard your scream.
Haste to cave and ruin'd tower,
Ivy tod, or dingled-bower,
There to wink and mope, for, hark!
In the mild air sings the lark.

Hie to moorish gills and rocks,
Prowling wolf and wily fox;
Hie ye fast, nor turn your view,
Though the lamb bleats to the ewe.

Couch your trains, and speed your
 flight,
Safety parts with parting night;
And on distant echo borne,
Comes the hunter's early horn.

The moon's wan crescent scarcely
 gleams,
Ghost-like she fades in morning beams:
Hie hence, each peevish imp and fay
That scare the pilgrim on his way.
Quench, kelpie! quench, in bog and fen,
Thy torch, that cheats benighted men;
Thy dance is o'er, thy reign is done,
For Ben-y-glow hath seen the sun.

Wild thoughts that, sinful, dark, and
 deep,
O'erpower the passive mind in sleep,
Pass from the slumberer's soul away,
Like night-mists from the brow of day:
Foul hag, whose blasted visage grim
Smothers the pulse, unnerves the limb,
Spur thy dark palfrey, and begone!
Thou dar'st not face the godlike sun.

Chap. VI.

LADY ANNE.

Annot Lyle *sings:—*

November's hail-cloud drifts away,
 November's sunbeam wan
Looks coldly on the castle grey,
 When forth comes Lady Anne.

The orphan by the oak was set,
 Her arms, her feet, were bare;
The hail drops had not melted yet,
 Amid her raven hair.

'And, dame,' she said, 'by all the ties
 That child and mother know,
Aid one who never knew these joys,
 Relieve an orphan's woe.'

The lady said, 'An orphan's state
  Is hard and sad to bear;
Yet worse the widow'd mother's fate,
  Who mourns both lord and heir.

'Twelve times the rolling year has sped,
  Since, when from vengeance wild
Of fierce Strathallan's Chief I fled,
  Forth's eddies whelm'd my child.'

'Twelve times the year its course has
    borne,'
  The wandering maid replied;
'Since fishers on Saint Bridget's morn
  Drew nets on Campsie side.

'Saint Bridget sent no scaly spoil;
  An infant, wellnigh dead,
They saved, and rear'd in want and toil,
  To beg from you her bread.'

That orphan maid the lady kiss'd,—
  'My husband's looks you bear;
Saint Bridget and her morn be bless'd!
  You are his widow's heir.

They've robed that maid, so poor and
    pale,
  In silk and sandals rare;
And pearls, for drops of frozen hail,
  Are glistening in her hair.

    Chap. IX.

—◆—

MOTTOES.

DARK on their journey lour'd the
  gloomy day,
Wild were the hills, and doubtful
  grew the way;
More dark, more gloomy, and more
  doubtful, show'd
The mansion which received them
  from the road.
    The Travellers, a Romance.

    Chap. X.

Is this thy castle Baldwin? Melancholy
Displays her sable banner from the
  donjon,
Dark'ning the foam of the whole surge
  beneath.
Were I a habitant, to see this gloom
Pollute the face of nature, and to hear
The ceaseless sound of wave and sea-
  bird's scream,
I'd wish me in the hut that poorest
  peasant
E'er framed to give him temporary
  shelter.
             ? Brown.
    Chap. XI.

THIS was the entry, then, these stairs
    —but whither after?
Yet he that's sure to perish on the land
May quit the nicety of card and com-
  pass,
And trust the open sea without a pilot.
    Tragedy of Brennovalt.
    Chap. XIV.

SUCH mountains steep, such craggy
    hills,
  His army on one side enclose:
The other side, great griesly gills
  Did fence with fenny mire and moss.

Which when the Earl understood,
  He counsel craved of captains all,
Who bade set forth with mournful
  mood
  And take such fortune as would fall.
    Flodden Field, an Ancient Poem.
    Chap. XVI.

X.

FROM IVANHOE.

THE CRUSADER.

HIGH deeds achieved of knightly fame,
From Palestine the champion came;

The cross upon his shoulders borne,
Battle and blast had dimm'd and torn.
Each dint upon his batter'd shield
Was token of a foughten field ;
And thus, beneath his lady's bower,
He sung, as fell the twilight hour :

' Joy to the fair !—thy knight behold,
Return'd from yonder land of gold ;
No wealth he brings, nor wealth can
    need,
Save his good arms and battle-steed ;
His spurs to dash against a foe,
His lance and sword to lay him low ;
Such all the trophies of his toil,
Such—and the hope of Tekla's smile!

' Joy to the fair ! whose constant knight
Her favour fired to feats of might !
Unnoted shall she not remain
Where meet the bright and noble train ;
Minstrel shall sing, and herald tell —
' Mark yonder maid of beauty well,
'Tis she for whose bright eyes was won
The listed field of Ascalon !

' " Note well her smile !—it edged the
    blade
Which fifty wives to widows made,
When, vain his strength and Mahound's
    spell,
Iconium's turban'd Soldan fell.
See'st thou her locks, whose sunny
    glow
Half shows, half shades, her neck of
    snow ?
Twines not of them one golden thread,
But for its sake a Paynim bled."

' Joy to the fair !—my name unknown,
Each deed, and all its praise, thine own ;
Then, oh ! unbar this churlish gate,
The night-dew falls, the hour is late.
Inured to Syria's glowing breath,
I feel the north breeze chill as death ;
Let grateful love quell maiden shame,
And grant him bliss who brings thee
    fame.'
        Chap. XVII.

THE BAREFOOTED FRIAR.

I 'LL give thee, good fellow, a twelve-
    month or twain,
To search Europe through from By-
    zantium to Spain ;
But ne'er shall you find, should you
    search till you tire,
So happy a man as the Barefooted
    Friar.

Your knight for his lady pricks forth
    in career,
And is brought home at even-song
    prick'd through with a spear ;
I confess him in haste—for his lady
    desires
No comfort on earth save the Bare-
    footed Friar's.

Your monarch ?—Pshaw ! many a
    prince has been known
To barter his robes for our cowl and
    our gown ;
But which of us e'er felt the idle desire
To exchange for a crown the grey
    hood of a Friar ?

The Friar has walk'd out, and where'er
    he has gone,
The land and its fatness is mark'd for
    his own ;
He can roam where he lists, he can
    stop when he tires,
For every man's house is the Bare-
    footed Friar's.

He 's expected at noon, and no wight,
    till he comes,
May profane the great chair, or the
    porridge of plums ;
For the best of the cheer, and the
    seat by the fire,
Is the undenied right of the Barefooted
    Friar.

He's expected at night, and the pasty's
    made hot,
They broach the brown ale, and they
    fill the black pot;
And the goodwife would wish the
    goodman in the mire,
Ere he lack'd a soft pillow, the
    Barefooted Friar.

Long flourish the sandal, the cord,
    and the cope,
The dread of the devil and trust of
    the Pope!
For to gather life's roses, unscathed
    by the brier,
Is granted alone to the Barefooted
    Friar.

    Chap. XVII.

—▸◂—

NORMAN saw on English oak,
On English neck a Norman yoke,
Norman spoon in English dish,
And England ruled as Normans wish;
Blithe world in England never will be
    more,
Till England's rid of all the four.
    Chap. XXVII.

—▸◂—

    ULRICA *sings :—*

WHET the bright steel,
Sons of the White Dragon!
Kindle the torch,
Daughter of Hengist!
The steel glimmers not for the carving
    of the banquet,
It is hard, broad, and sharply pointed;
The torch goeth not to the bridal
    chamber,
It steams and glitters blue with sulphur.
Whet the steel, the raven croaks!
Light the torch, Zernebock is yelling!
Whet the steel, sons of the Dragon!
Kindle the torch, daughter of Hengist!

The black clouds are low over the
    thane's castle :
The eagle screams—he rides on their
    bosom.
Scream not, grey rider of the sable
    cloud,
Thy banquet is prepared!
The maidens of Valhalla look forth,
The race of Hengist will send them
    guests.
Shake your black tresses, maidens of
    Valhalla!
And strike your loud timbrels for
    joy!
Many a haughty step bends to your
    halls,
Many a helmed head.

Dark sits the evening upon the thane's
    castle,
The black clouds gather round;
Soon shall they be red as the blood of
    the valiant!
The destroyer of forests shall shake
    his red crest against them;
He, the bright consumer of palaces,
Broad waves he his blazing banner,
Red, wide, and dusky,
Over the strife of the valiant;
His joy is in the clashing swords and
    broken bucklers;
He loves to lick the hissing blood as
    it bursts warm from the wound!

All must perish!
The sword cleaveth the helmet;
The strong armour is pierced by the
    lance :
Fire devoureth the dwelling of princes,
Engines break down the fences of the
    battle.
All must perish!
The race of Hengist is gone—
The name of Horsa is no more !
Shrink not then from your doom, sons
    of the sword!

Let your blades drink blood like wine;
Feast ye in the banquet of slaughter,
By the light of the blazing halls!
Strong be your swords while your
 blood is warm,
And spare neither for pity nor fear,
For vengeance hath but an hour;
Strong hate itself shall expire!
I also must perish.

Chap. xxxii.

—+—

REBECCA'S HYMN.

When Israel, of the Lord beloved,
 Out from the land of bondage came,
Her fathers' God before her moved,
 An awful guide in smoke and flame.
By day, along the astonish'd lands
 The cloudy pillar glided slow;
By night, Arabia's crimson'd sands
 Return'd the fiery column's glow.

There rose the choral hymn of praise,
 And trump and timbrel answer'd
 keen,
And Zion's daughters pour'd their lays,
 With priest's and warrior's voice
 between.
No portents now our foes amaze,
 Forsaken Israel wanders lone:
Our fathers would not know Thy ways,
 And Thou hast left them to their own.

But present still, though now unseen!
 When brightly shines the prosper-
 ous day,
Be thoughts of Thee a cloudy screen
 To temper the deceitful ray.
And oh, when stoops on Judah's path
 In shade and storm the frequent
 night,
Be Thou, long-suffering, slow to wrath,
 A burning and a shining light!

Our harps we left by Babel's streams,
 The tyrant's jest, the Gentile's scorn;
No censer round our altar beams,
 And mute are timbrel, harp, and horn.
But Thou hast said, The blood of goat,
 The flesh of rams I will not prize;
A contrite heart, a humble thought,
 Are mine accepted sacrifice.

Chap. xxxix.

—+—

A VIRELAI.

The Black Knight *sings:*—

Anna-Marie, love, up is the sun,
Anna-Marie, love, morn is begun,
Mists are dispersing, love, birds sing-
 ing free,
Up in the morning, love, Anna-Marie.
Anna-Marie, love, up in the morn,
The hunter is winding blithe sounds
 on his horn,
The echo rings merry from rock and
 from tree,
'Tis time to arouse thee, love, Anna-
 Marie.

The Jester *responds:*—

O Tybalt, love, Tybalt, awake me not
 yet,
Around my soft pillow while softer
 dreams flit;
For what are the joys that in waking
 we prove,
Compared with these visions, O Tybalt!
 my love?
Let the birds to the rise of the mist
 carol shrill,
Let the hunter blow out his loud horn
 on the hill,
Softer sounds, softer pleasures, in
 slumber I prove,
But think not I dream'd of thee,
 Tybalt, my love.

Chap. xl.

A DUET.

The Knight and Wamba.

(*Both.*)

There came three merry men from
    south, west, and north,
  Ever more sing the roundelay;
To win the Widow of Wycombe forth,
  And where was the widow might
    say them nay?

The first was a knight, and from Tyne-
    dale he came,
  Ever more sing the roundelay;
And his fathers, God save us, were
    men of great fame,
  And where was the widow might
    say him nay?

Of his father the laird, of his uncle the
    squire,
  He boasted in rhyme and in rounde-
    lay;
She bade him go bask by his sea-coal
    fire,
  For she was the widow would say
    him nay.

(*Wamba alone.*)

The next that came forth, swore by
    blood and by nails,
  Merrily sing the roundelay;
Hur's a gentleman, God wot, and hur's
    lineage was of Wales,
  And where was the widow might say
    him nay?

Sir David ap Morgan ap Griffith ap
    Hugh
  Ap Tudor ap Rhice, quoth his
    roundelay;
She said that one widow for so many
    was too few,
  And she bade the Welshman wend
    his way.

But then next came a yeoman, a yeo-
    man of Kent,
  Jollily singing his roundelay;
He spoke to the widow of living and
    rent,
  And where was the widow could
    say him nay?

(*Both.*)

So the knight and the squire were
    both left in the mire,
  There for to sing their roundelay;
For a yeoman of Kent, with his yearly
    rent,
  There ne'er was a widow could say
    him nay.

Chap. XL.

—◆—

DIRGE FOR ATHELSTANE.

Dust into dust,
To this all must;
  The tenant hath resign'd
The faded form
To waste and worm—
  Corruption claims her kind.

Through paths unknown
Thy soul hath flown,
  To seek the realms of woe,
Where fiery pain
Shall purge the stain
  Of actions done below.

In that sad place,
By Mary's grace,
  Brief may thy dwelling be!
Till prayers and alms,
And holy psalms,
  Shall set the captive free.

Chap. XLII.

MOTTOES.

Away! our journey lies through dell
  and dingle,
Where the blithe fawn trips by its
  timid mother,
Where the broad oak, with inter-
  cepting boughs,
Chequers the sunbeam in the green-
  sward alley—
Up and away!—for lovely paths are
  these
To tread, when the glad sun is on his
  throne:
Less pleasant, and less safe, when
  Cynthia's lamp
With doubtful glimmer lights the
  dreary forest.
               Ettrick Forest.
  Chap. xviii.

A train of armèd men, some noble dame
Escorting (so their scatter'd words
  discover'd,
As unperceiv'd I hung upon their
  rear),
Are close at hand, and mean to pass
  the night
Within the castle.
          Orra, a Tragedy.
  Chap. xix.

When autumn nights were long and
  drear,
  And forest walks were dark and dim,
How sweetly on the pilgrim's ear
  Was wont to steal the hermit's
    hymn!

Devotion borrows Music's tone,
  And Music took Devotion's wing,
And, like the bird that hails the sun,
  They soar to heaven, and soaring
    sing.
  The Hermit of St. Clement's Well.
  Chap. xx.

Alas! ·how many hours and years
  have pass'd
Since human forms have round this
  table sate,
Or lamp or taper on its surface
  gleam'd!
Methinks I hear the sound of time
  long past
Still murmuring o'er us in the lofty
  void
Of these dark arches, like the ling'ring
  voices
Of those who long within their graves
  have slept.
           Orra, a Tragedy.
  Chap. xxi.

The hottest horse will oft be cool,
  The dullest will show fire;
The friar will often play the fool,
  The fool will play the friar.
               Old Song.
  Chap. xxvi.

This wandering race, sever'd from
  other men,
Boast yet their intercourse with human
  arts;
The seas, the woods, the deserts which
  they haunt,
Find them acquainted with their secret
  treasures;
And unregarded herbs, and flowers,
  and blossoms,
Display undream'd-of powers when
  gather'd by them.
               The Jew.
  Chap. xxviii.

Approach the chamber, look upon his
  bed.
His is the passing of no peaceful ghost,
Which, as the lark arises to the sky,
'Mid morning's sweetest breeze and
  softest dew,
Is wing'd to heaven by good men's
  sighs and tears!
Anselm parts otherwise.
              Old Play.
  Chap. xxx.

TRUST me, each state must have its
  policies :
Kingdoms have edicts, cities have
  their charters ;
Even the wild outlaw, in his forest-
  walk,
Keeps yet some touch of civil discipline.
For not since Adam wore his verdant
  apron
Hath man with man in social union
  dwelt,
But laws were made to draw that
  union closer.   *Old Play.*

  Chap. XXXII.

AROUSE the tiger of Hyrcanian deserts,
Strive with the half-starved lion for
  his prey ;
Lesser the risk, than rouse the slum-
  bering fire
Of wild Fanaticism.   *Anonymous.*

  Chap. XXXV.

SAY not my art is fraud—all live by
  seeming.
The beggar begs with it, and the gay
  courtier
Gains land and title, rank and rule, by
  seeming :
The clergy scorn it not, and the bold
  soldier
Will eke with it his service. All
  admit it,
All practise it ; and he who is content
With showing what he is, shall have
  small credit
In church, or camp, or state. So wags
  the world.   *Old Play.*

  Chap. XXXVI.

STERN was the law which bade its
  vot'ries leave
At human woes with human hearts to
  grieve ;
Stern was the law, which at the
  winning wile

Of frank and harmless mirth forbade
  to smile ;
But sterner still, when high the iron
  rod
Of tyrant power she shook, and call'd
  that power of God.
              The Middle Ages.
  Chap. XXXVII.

XI.

FROM THE MONASTERY.

'Ne sit ancillae, &c.'

  TAKE thou no scorn
    Of fiction born,
Fair fiction's muse to woo ;
    Old Homer's theme
    Was but a dream,
Himself a fiction too.
Answer to the Introductory Epistle (of
  Captain Clutterbuck).

—◆◆—

'MERRILY SWIM WE.'

THE WHITE LADY *sings :—*

MERRILY swim we, the moon shines
  bright,
Both current and ripple are dancing
  in light :
We have roused the night raven, I
  heard him croak
As we plashed along beneath the oak
That flings its broad branches so far
  and so wide,
Their shadows are dancing in midst
  of the tide.
'Who wakens my nestlings ?' the
  raven he said,
'My beak shall ere morn in his blood
  be red !
For a blue swollen corpse is a dainty
  meal,
And I'll have my share with the pike
  and the eel.'

Merrily swim we, the moon shines
    bright,
There's a golden gleam on the distant
    height:
There's a silver shower on the alders
    dank,
And the drooping willows that wave
    on the bank.
I see the Abbey, both turret and tower,
It is all astir for the vesper hour;
The monks for the chapel are leaving
    each cell,
But where's Father Philip should toll
    the bell?

Merrily swim we, the moon shines
    bright,
Downward we drift through shadow
    and light;
Under yon rock the eddies sleep,
Calm and silent, dark and deep.
The Kelpy has risen from the fathom-
    less pool,
He has lighted his candle of death and
    of dool:
Look, Father, look, and you'll laugh
    to see
How he gapes and glares with his eyes
    on thee!

Good luck to your fishing, whom watch
    ye to-night?
A man of mean or a man of might?
Is it layman or priest that must float
    in your cove,
Or lover who crosses to visit his love?
Hark! heard ye the Kelpy reply as
    we pass'd,—
'God's blessing on the warder, he
    lock'd the bridge fast!
All that come to my cove are sunk,
Priest or layman, lover or monk.'

Landed—landed! the black book hath
    won,
Else had you seen Berwick with
    morning sun!

Sain ye, and save ye, and blithe mot
    ye be,
For seldom they land that go swimming
    with me.
    Chap. v.

THE MONK'S WARNING.

THE WHITE LADY *sings:*—

GOOD evening, Sir Priest, and so late
    as you ride,
With your mule so fair, and your
    mantle so wide;
But ride you through valley, or ride
    you o'er hill,
There is one that has warrant to wait
    on you still.
    Back, back,
    The volume black!
I have a warrant to carry it back.

What, ho! Sub-Prior, and came you
    but here
To conjure a book from a dead woman's
    bier?
Sain you, and save you, be wary and
    wise,
Ride back with the book, or you'll pay
    for your prize.
    Back, back,
    There's death in the track!
In the name of my master, I bid thee
    bear back.

That which is neither ill nor well,
That which belongs not to heaven nor
    to hell,
A wreath of the mist, a bubble of the
    stream,
'Twixt a waking thought and a sleeping
    dream;
    A form that men spy
    With the half-shut eye
In the beams of the setting sun,
    am I.

Vainly, Sir Prior, wouldst thou bar me
    my right!
Like the star when it shoots, I can
    dart through the night;
I can dance on the torrent, and ride
    on the air,
And travel the world with the bonny
    night-mare.
    Again, again,
    At the crook of the glen,
Where bickers the burnie, I'll meet
    thee again.

Men of good are bold as sackless [1],
Men of rude are wild and reckless.
    Lie thou still
    In the nook of the hill,
For those be before thee that wish
    thee ill.

    Chap. XI.

—•◆•—

THE WHITE LADY *sings :—*

    THANK the holly-bush
      That nods on thy brow;
    Or with this slender rush
      I had strangled thee now.

    Chap. X.

—•◆•—

TO THE WHITE LADY.

HALBERT *invokes :—*

    THRICE to the holly brake,
      Thrice to the well—
    I bid thee awake,
      White Maid of Avenel!

    Noon gleams on the lake,
      Noon glows on the fell,—
    Wake thee, O wake,
      White Maid of Avenel.

    Chap. XI.

---

[1] *Sackless*—Innocent.

TO HALBERT.

THE WHITE LADY *sings or speaks :—*

YOUTH of the dark eye, wherefore
    didst thou call me?
Wherefore art thou here, if terrors
    can appal thee?
He that seeks to deal with us must
    know no fear nor failing;
To coward and churl our speech is
    dark, our gifts are unavailing.
The breeze that brought me hither now
    must sweep Egyptian ground,
The fleecy cloud on which I ride for
    Araby is bound;
The fleecy cloud is drifting by, the
    breeze sighs for my stay,
For I must sail a thousand miles before
    the close of day.

———

WHAT I am I must not show—
What I am thou couldst not know—
Something betwixt heaven and hell—
Something that neither stood nor fell—
Something that through thy wit or will
May work thee good—may work
    thee ill.
Neither substance quite, nor shadow,
Haunting lonely moor and meadow,
Dancing by the haunted spring,
Riding on the whirlwind's wing;
Aping in fantastic fashion
Every change of human passion,
While o'er our frozen minds they pass
Like shadows from the mirror'd glass.
Wayward, fickle, is our mood,
Hovering betwixt bad and good,
Happier than brief-dated man,
Living twenty times his span;
Far less happy, for we have
Help nor hope beyond the grave!
Man awakes to joy or sorrow;
Ours the sleep that knows no morrow.
This is all that I can show—
This is all that thou may'st know.

———

Ay! and I taught thee the word and the spell,
To waken me here by the Fairies' Well:
But thou hast loved the heron and hawk,
More than to seek my haunted walk;
And thou hast loved the lance and the sword,
More than good text and holy word;
And thou hast loved the deer to track,
More than the lines and the letters black;
And thou art a ranger of moss and of wood,
And scornest the nurture of gentle blood.

———

Thy craven fear my truth accused;
Thine idlehood my trust abused;
He that draws to harbour late,
Must sleep without, or burst the gate.
There is a star for thee which burn'd,
Its influence wanes, its course is turn'd;
Valour and constancy alone
Can bring thee back the chance that's flown.

———

Within that awful volume lies
The mystery of mysteries!
Happiest they of human race,
To whom God has granted grace
To read, to fear, to hope, to pray,
To lift the latch, and force the way;
And better had they ne'er been born,
Who read to doubt, or read to scorn.

———

Many a fathom dark and deep
I have laid the book to sleep;
Ethereal fires around it glowing—
Ethereal music ever flowing—
  The sacred pledge of Heav'n
    All things revere,
    Each in his sphere,
  Save man for whom 'twas giv'n:

Lend thy hand, and thou shalt spy
Things ne'er seen by mortal eye.

———

Fear'st thou to go with me?
Still it is free to thee
  A peasant to dwell;
Thou may'st drive the dull steer,
And chase the king's deer,
But never more come near
  This haunted well.

———

Here lies the volume thou boldly hast sought;
Touch it, and take it,—'twill dearly be bought.

———

  Rash thy deed,
  Mortal weed
To immortal flames applying;
  Rasher trust
  Has thing of dust,
On his own weak worth relying:
Strip thee of such fences vain,
Strip, and prove thy luck again.

———

Mortal warp and mortal woof
Cannot brook this charmed roof;
All that mortal art hath wrought
In our cell returns to nought.
The molten gold returns to clay,
The polish'd diamond melts away;
All is altered, all is flown,
Nought stands fast but truth alone.
Not for that thy quest give o'er:
Courage! prove thy chance once more.

———

Alas! alas!
Not ours the grace
These holy characters to trace:
  Idle forms of painted air,
  Not to us is given to share
The boon bestow'd on Adam's race.

With patience bide,
Heaven will provide
The fitting time, the fitting guide.

Chap. XII.

———

THIS is the day when the fairy kind
  Sit weeping alone for their hope-
    less lot,
And the wood-maiden sighs to the
    sighing wind,
  And the mermaiden weeps in her
    crystal grot ;
For this is the day that a deed was
    wrought,
  In which we have neither part nor
    share,
For the children of clay was salvation
    bought,
  But not for the forms of sea or air !
And ever the mortal is most forlorn,
Who meeteth our race on the Friday
    morn.

———

DARING youth ! for thee it is well,
Here calling me in haunted dell,
That thy heart has not quail'd,
Nor thy courage fail'd,
And that thou couldst brook
The angry look
Of Her of Avenel.
Did one limb shiver,
Or an eyelid quiver,
Thou wert lost for ever.
Though I am form'd from the ether blue,
And my blood is of the unfallen dew,
And thou art framed of mud and dust,
'Tis thine to speak, reply I must.

———

A MIGHTIER wizard far than I
  Wields o'er the universe his power ;
Him owns the eagle in the sky,
  The turtle in the bower.

Changeful in shape, yet mightiest still,
He wields the heart of man at will,
From ill to good, from good to ill,
  In cot and castle-tower.

———

ASK thy heart, whose secret cell
Is fill'd with Mary Avenel !
Ask thy pride, why scornful look
In Mary's view it will not brook ?
Ask it, why thou seek'st to rise
Among the mighty and the wise ?
Why thou spurn'st thy lowly lot ?
Why thy pastimes are forgot ?
Why thou wouldst in bloody strife
Mend thy luck or lose thy life ?
Ask thy heart, and it shall tell,
Sighing from its secret cell,
'Tis for Mary Avenel.

———

Do not ask me ;
On doubts like these thou canst not
    task me.
We only see the passing show
Of human passion's ebb and flow ;
And view the pageant's idle glance
As mortals eye the northern dance,
When thousand streamers, flashing
    bright,
Career it o'er the brow of night,
And gazers mark their changeful
    gleams,
But feel no influence from their beams.

———

BY ties mysterious link'd, our fated
    race
Holds strange connexion with the
    sons of men.
The star that rose upon the House of
    Avenel,
When Norman Ulric first assumed
    the name,
That star, when culminating in its
    orbit,
Shot from its sphere a drop of diamond
    dew,

And this bright font received it—and
    a Spirit
Rose from the fountain, and her date
    of life
Hath co-existence with the House of
    Avenel,
And with the star that rules it.

———

Look on my girdle—on this thread of
    gold—
'Tis fine as web of lightest gossamer,
And, but there is a spell on 't, would
    not bind,
Light as they are, the folds of my
    thin robe.
But when 'twas donn'd, it was a
    massive chain,
Such as might bind the champion of
    the Jews,
Even when his locks were longest:
    it hath dwindled,
Hath 'minish'd in its substance and its
    strength,
As sunk the greatness of the House
    of Avenel.
When this frail thread gives way, I
    to the elements
Resign the principles of life they lent
    me.
Ask me no more of this!—the stars
    forbid it.

———

Dim burns the once bright star of
    Avenel,
Dim as the beacon when the morn is
    nigh,
And the o'er-wearied warder leaves
    the light-house;
There is an influence sorrowful and
    fearful,
That dogs its downward course. Disastrous passion,
Fierce hate and rivalry, are in the
    aspect
That lowers upon its fortunes.

———

Complain not on me, child of clay,
If to thy harm I yield the way.
We, who soar thy sphere above,
Know not aught of hate or love;
As will or wisdom rules thy mood,
My gifts to evil turn or good.

———

When Piercie Shafton boasteth high,
Let this token meet his eye.
The sun is westering from the dell,
Thy wish is granted—fare thee well!

    Chap. xvii.

—•—

Sir Piercie Shafton *sings* :—

What tongue can her perfections tell,
On whose each part all pens may
    dwell.

(Etcetera, *to the extent of about five
hundred verses, ending thus* : —)
Of whose high praise and praiseful
    bliss,
Goodness the pen, Heaven paper is;
The ink immortal fame doth send:
As I began so I must end.

—•—

The White Lady *chants or recites* :—

He whose heart for vengeance sued
Must not shrink from shedding blood;
The knot that thou hast tied with
    word,
Thou must loose by edge of sword.

———

You have summon'd me once, you
    have summon'd me twice,
And without e'er a summons I come
    to you thrice;
Unask'd for, unsued for, you come to
    my glen;
Unsued and unask'd, I am with you
    agen.

    Chap. xx.

BORDER MARCH.

MARCH, march, Ettrick and Teviot-
dale,
 Why the deil dinna ye march
  forward in order?
March, march, Eskdale and Liddesdale,
 All the Blue Bonnets are bound
  for the Border.
   Many a banner spread,
   Flutters above your head,
 Many a crest that is famous in story.
   Mount and make ready then,
   Sons of the mountain glen,
 Fight for the Queen and the old
  Scottish glory.

Come from the hills where your
 hirsels are grazing,
 Come from the glen of the buck and
  the roe;
Come to the crag where the beacon
 is blazing,
 Come with the buckler, the lance,
  and the bow.
   Trumpets are sounding,
   War-steeds are bounding,
 Stand to your arms then, and
  march in good order;
   England shall many a day
   Tell of the bloody fray,
 When the Blue Bonnets came
  over the Border.

Chap. xxv.

—◆—

THE WHITE LADY TO MARY AVENEL.

MAIDEN, whose sorrows wail the
 living dead,
 Whose eyes shall commune with
  the dead alive,
Maiden, attend! Beneath my foot lies
 hid
 The word, the law, the path which
  thou dost strive

To find, and canst not find. Could
 Spirits shed
Tears for their lot, it were my lot
 to weep,
Showing the road which I shall never
 tread,
Though my foot points it. Sleep,
 eternal sleep,
Dark, long, and cold forgetfulness my
 lot!
 But do not thou at human ills repine;
Secure there lies full guerdon in this
 spot
 For all the woes that wait frail
  Adam's line;
Stoop then and make it yours—I may
 not make it mine!

Chap. xxx.

—◆—

THE WHITE LADY TO EDWARD.

THOU who seek'st my fountain lone,
With thoughts and hopes thou dar'st
 not own;
Whose heart within leap'd wildly glad,
When most his brow seem'd dark and
 sad;
Hie thee back, thou find'st not here
Corpse or coffin, grave or bier;
The dead alive is gone and fled—
Go thou, and join the living dead!

The living dead, whose sober brow
Oft shrouds such thoughts as thou
 hast now,
Whose hearts within are seldom cured
Of passions by their vows abjured;
Where, under sad and solemn show,
Vain hopes are nursed, wild wishes
 glow.
Seek the convent's vaulted room,
Prayer and vigil be thy doom;
Doff the green, and don the grey,
To the cloister hence away!

Chap. xxxii.

THE WHITE LADY'S FAREWELL.

Fare thee well, thou Holly green!
Thou shalt seldom now be seen,
With all thy glittering garlands bending,
As to greet my slow descending,
Startling the bewilder'd hind,
Who sees thee wave without a wind.

Farewell, Fountain! now not long
Shalt thou murmur to my song,
While thy crystal bubbles glancing,
Keep the time in mystic dancing,
Rise and swell, are burst and lost,
Like mortal schemes by fortune cross'd.

The knot of fate at length is tied,
The Churl is Lord, the Maid is Bride!
Vainly did my magic sleight
Send the lover from her sight;
Wither bush, and perish well,
Fall'n is lofty Avenel!

Chap. xxxvii.

—+—

MOTTOES.

O ay! the Monks, the Monks, they
 did the mischief!
Theirs all the grossness, all the
 superstition
Of a most gross and superstitious age.
May He be praised that sent the
 healthful tempest,
And scatter'd all these pestilential
 vapours;
But that we owed them *all* to yonder
 Harlot
Throned on the seven hills with her
 cup of gold,
I will as soon believe, with kind Sir
 Roger,

That old Moll White took wing with
 cat and broomstick,
And raised the last night's thunder.
      Old Play.
Chap. i.

In yon lone vale his early youth was
 bred,
Not solitary then—the bugle-horn
Of fell Alecto often waked its windings,
From where the brook joins the
 majestic river,
To the wild northern bog, the curlew's
 haunt,
Where oozes forth its first and feeble
 streamlet.
      Old Play.
Chap. ii.

A priest, ye cry, a priest!—lame
 shepherds they,
How shall they gather in the straggling
 flock?
Dumb dogs which bark not, how shall
 they compel
The loitering vagrants to the Master's
 fold?
Fitter to bask before the blazing fire,
And snuff the mess neat-handed
 Phillis dresses,
Than on the snow-wreath battle with
 the wolf.
     The Reformation.
Chap. v.

Now let us sit in conclave. That
 these weeds
Be rooted from the vineyard of the
 Church,
That these foul tares be sever'd from
 the wheat,
We are, I trust, agreed. Yet how
 to do this,
Nor hurt the wholesome crop and
 tender vine-plants,
Craves good advisement.
     The Reformation.
Chap. vi.

2 C

Nay, dally not with time, the wise man's treasure,
Though fools are lavish on 't; the fatal Fisher
Hooks souls, while we waste moments.

Old Play.

Chap. VIII.

You call this education, do you not?
Why, 'tis the forced march of a herd of bullocks
Before a shouting drover. The glad van
Move on at ease, and pause a while to snatch
A passing morsel from the dewy green-sward,
While all the blows, the oaths, the indignation,
Fall on the croupe of the ill-fated laggard
That cripples in the rear.

Old Play.

Chap. XI.

There's something in that ancient superstition,
Which, erring as it is, our fancy loves.
The spring that, with its thousand crystal bubbles,
Bursts from the bosom of some desert rock
In secret solitude, may well be deem'd
The haunt of something purer, more refined,
And mightier than ourselves.

Old Play.

Chap. XII.

Nay, let me have the friends who eat my victuals
As various as my dishes. The feast's naught,
Where one huge plate predominates.
John Plaintext,

He shall be mighty beef, our English staple;
The worthy Alderman, a butter'd dumpling;
Yon pair of whisker'd Cornets, ruffs and rees;
Their friend the Dandy, a green goose in sippets.
And so the board is spread at once and fill'd
On the same principle—Variety.

New Play.

Chap. XIV.

He strikes no coin, 'tis true, but coins new phrases,
And vends them forth as knaves vend gilded counters,
Which wise men scorn, and fools accept in payment.

Old Play.

Chap. XV.

Now choose thee, gallant, betwixt wealth and honour;
There lies the pelf, in sum to bear thee through
The dance of youth, and the turmoil of manhood,
Yet leave enough for age's chimney-corner;
But an thou grasp to it, farewell Ambition!
Farewell each hope of bettering thy condition,
And raising thy low rank above the churls
That till the earth for bread!

Old Play.

Chap. XIX.

I hope you 'll give me cause to think you noble,
And do me right with your sword, sir, as becomes
One gentleman of honour to another;

All this is fair, sir—let us make no days on 't,
I 'll lead your way.

Love's Pilgrimage.

Chap. xx.

INDIFFERENT, but indifferent—pshaw !
he doth it not
Like one who is his craft's master—
ne'ertheless
I have seen a clown confer a bloody
coxcomb
On one who was a master of defence.

Old Play.

Chap. xxi.

YES, life hath left him ; every busy thought,
Each fiery passion, every strong affection,
The sense of outward ill and inward sorrow,
Are fled at once from the pale trunk before me ;
And I have given that which spoke and moved,
Thought, acted, suffer'd, as a living man,
To be a ghastly form of bloody clay,
Soon the foul food for reptiles.

Old Play.

Chap. xxii.

'TIS when the wound is stiffening with the cold,
The warrior first feels pain ; 'tis when the heat
And fiery fever of his soul is past,
The sinner feels remorse.

Old Play.

Chap. xxiii.

I 'LL walk on tiptoe ; arm my eye with caution,
My heart with courage, and my hand with weapon
Like him who ventures on a lion's den.

Old Play.

Chap. xxiv.

Now, by Our Lady, Sheriff, 'tis hard reckoning,
That I, with every odds of birth and barony,
Should be detain'd here for the casual death
Of a wild forester, whose utmost having
Is but the brazen buckle of the belt
In which he sticks his hedge-knife.

Old Play.

Chap. xxvii.

YOU call it an ill angel—it may be so ;
But sure I am, among the ranks which fell,
'Tis the first fiend ere counsell'd man to rise,
And win the bliss the sprite himself had forfeited.

Old Play.

Chap. xxx.

AT school I knew him—a sharp-witted youth,
Grave, thoughtful, and reserved amongst his mates,
Turning the hours of sport and food to labour,
Starving his body to inform his mind.

Old Play.

Chap. xxxi.

THEN in my gown of sober gray,
Along the mountain-path I 'll wander,
And wind my solitary way
To the sad shrine that courts me yonder.

There in the calm monastic shade,
All injuries may be forgiven ;
And there for thee, obdurate maid,
My orisons shall rise to heaven.

The Cruel Lady of the Mountains.

Chap. xxxii.

Now on my faith this gear is all
    entangled,
Like to the yarn-clew of the drowsy
    knitter,
Dragg'd by the frolic kitten through
    the cabin,
While the good dame sits nodding
    o'er the fire.
Masters, attend; 'twill crave some
    skill to clear it.
Old Play.

   Chap. xxxiii.

It is not texts will do it: Church
    artillery
Are silenced soon by real ordnance,
And canons are but vain opposed to
    cannon.
Go, coin your crosier, melt your
    church plate down,
Bid the starved soldier banquet in
    your halls,
And quaff your long-saved hogsheads;
    turn them out
Thus primed with your good cheer,
    to guard your wall,
And they will venture for 't.
Old Play.

   Chap. xxxiv.

XII.

FROM THE ABBOT.

The Pardoner *speaks :—*

Listneth, gode people, everiche one,
For in the londe of Babylone,
Far eastward I wot it lyeth,
And is the first londe the sonne espieth,
Ther, as he cometh fro out the sé ;
In this ilk londe, as thinketh me,
Right as holie legendes tell,
Snottreth from a roke a well,
And falleth into ane bath of ston,

Wher chast Susanne in times long gon,
Was wont to wash her bodie and lim—
Mickle vertue hath that streme,
As ye shall se er that ye pas,
Ensample by this little glas—
Through nightés cold and dayés hote,
Hiderward I have it brought ;
Hath a wife made slip or slide,
Or a maiden stepp'd aside ;
Putteth this water under her nese,
Wold she nold she, she shall snese.

   Chap. xxvii.

—◆◆—

MOTTOES.

In the wild storm,
The seaman hews his mast down,
    and the merchant
Heaves to the billows wares he once
    deem'd precious :
So prince and peer, 'mid popular con-
    tentions,
Cast off their favourites.
Old Play.

   Chap. v.

Thou hast each secret of the house-
    hold, Francis.
I dare be sworn thou hast been in
    the buttery
Steeping thy curious humour in fat ale,
And in the butler's tattle—ay, or
    chatting
With the glib waiting-woman o'er
    her comfits :
These bear the key to each domestic
    mystery.
Old Play.

   Chap. vi.

The sacred tapers' lights are gone,
Grey moss has clad the altar stone,
The holy image is o'erthrown,
    The bell has ceased to toll.

The long ribb'd aisles are burst and
    shrunk,
The holy shrines to ruin sunk,
Departed is the pious monk,—
    God's blessing on his soul!
                     Rediviva.
  Chap. VIII.

KNEEL with me, swear it! 'Tis not in
    words I trust,
Save when they're fenced with an
    appeal to Heaven.
                    Old Play.
  Chap. IX.

LIFE hath its May, and all is mirthful
    then:
The woods are vocal, and the flowers
    all odour;
Its very blast has mirth in't,—and
    the maidens,
The while they don their cloaks to
    screen their kirtles,
Laugh at the rain that wets them.
                    Old Play.
  Chap. XI.

NAY, hear me, brother; I am elder,
    wiser,
And holier than thou; and age, and
    wisdom,
And holiness, have peremptory claims,
And will be listen'd to.
                    Old Play.
  Chap. XII.

WHAT! Dagon up again? I thought we
    had hurled him
Down on the threshold never more to
    rise.
Bring wedge and axe; and, neigh-
    bours, lend your hands,
And rive the idol into winter fagots!
  Athelstane, or the Converted Dane.
  Chap. XIII.

NOT the wild billow, when it breaks
    its barrier—
Not the wild wind, escaping from
    its cavern—
Not the wild fiend, that mingles both
    together,
And pours their rage upon the ripen-
    ing harvest,
Can match the wild freaks of this
    mirthful meeting—
Comic, yet fearful, droll, and yet
    destructive.
             The Conspiracy.
  Chap. XIV.

YOUTH! thou wear'st to manhood now
Darker lip and darker brow,
Statelier step, more pensive mien,
In thy face and gait are seen:
Thou must now brook midnight
    watches,
Take thy food and sport by snatches!
For the gambol and the jest,
Thou wert wont to love the best,
Graver follies must thou follow,
But as senseless, false, and hollow.
            Life, a Poem.
  Chap. XVI.

  THE sky is clouded, Gaspard,
And the vexed ocean sleeps a troubled
    sleep
Beneath a lurid gleam of parting sun-
    shine.
Such slumber hangs o'er discontented
    lands,
While factions doubt, as yet, if they
    have strength
To front the open battle.
            Albion, a Poem.
  Chap. XVIII.

IT is and is not; 'tis the thing I sought
    for,
Have kneel'd for, pray'd for, risk'd
    my life and fame for;

And yet it is not—no more than the shadow
Upon the hard, cold, flat, and polish'd mirror,
Is the warm, graceful, rounded, living substance
Which it presents in form and lineament.

Old Play.

Chap. xix.

Now have you reft me from my staff, my guide,
Who taught my youth, as men teach untamed falcons,
To use my strength discreetly: I am reft
Of comrade and of counsel.

Old Play.

Chap. xx.

Give me a morsel on the greensward rather,
Coarse as you will the cooking; let the fresh spring
Bubble beside my napkin, and the free birds,
Twittering and chirping, hop from bough to bough,
To claim the crumbs I leave for perquisites:
Your prison-feasts I like not.

The Woodsman, a Drama.

Chap. xxiii.

'Tis a weary life this—
Vaults overhead, and grates and bars around me,
And my sad hours spent with as sad companions,
Whose thoughts are brooding o'er their own mischances,
Far, far too deeply to take part in mine.

The Woodsman.

Chap. xxiv.

And when Love's torch hath set the heart in flame,
Comes Signor Reason, with his saws and cautions,
Giving such aid as the old grey-beard Sexton,
Who from the church-vault drags his crazy engine,
To ply its dribbling ineffectual streamlet
Against a conflagration.

Old Play.

Chap. xxv.

Yes, it is she whose eyes look'd on thy childhood,
And watch'd with trembling hope thy dawn of youth,
That now, with these same eye-balls, dimm'd with age,
And dimmer yet with tears, sees thy dishonour.

Old Play.

Chap. xxviii.

In some breasts passion lies conceal'd and silent,
Like war's swart powder in a castle vault,
Until occasion, like the linstock, lights it;
Then comes at once the lightning and the thunder,
And distant echoes tell that all is rent asunder.

Old Play.

Chap. xxx.

Death distant?—No, alas! he's ever with us,
And shakes the dart at us in all our actings:
He lurks within our cup while we're in health;
Sits by our sick-bed, mocks our medicines;

We cannot walk, or sit, or ride, or
    travel,
But Death is by to seize us when
    he lists.
                The Spanish Father.

Chap. XXXIII.

Ay, Pedro? Come you here with
    mask and lantern,
Ladder of ropes, and other moonshine
    tools?
Why, youngster, thou may'st cheat
    the old Duenna,
Flatter the waiting-woman, bribe the
    valet;
But know, that I her father play the
    Gryphon,
Tameless and sleepless, proof to fraud
    or bribe,
And guard the hidden treasure of
    her beauty.
                The Spanish Father.

Chap. XXXIV.

It is a time of danger, not of revel,
When churchmen turn to masquers.
                The Spanish Father.

Chap. XXXV.

Ay, sir—our ancient crown, in these
    wild times,
Oft stood upon a cast; the gamester's
    ducat,
So often staked, and lost, and then
    regain'd,
Scarce knew so many hazards.
                The Spanish Father.

Chap. XXXVII.

XIII.

FROM KENILWORTH.

THE OWL SONG.

Of all the birds on bush or tree,
    Commend me to the owl,
Since he may best ensample be
    To those the cup that trowl.
For when the sun hath left the west,
He chooses the tree that he loves the
    best,
And he whoops out his song, and
    he laughs at his jest.
Then, though hours be late, and
    weather foul,
We'll drink to the health of the
    bonny, bonny owl.

The lark is but a bumpkin fowl,
    He sleeps in his nest till morn;
But my blessing upon the jolly owl,
    That all night blows his horn.
Then up with your cup till you stagger
    in speech,
And match me this catch, till you
    swagger and screech,
And drink till you wink, my merry
    men each;
For, though hours be late, and weather
    be foul,
We'll drink to the health of the
    bonny, bonny owl.

Chap. II.

—•◦•—

THE WARDER'S WELCOME TO
KENILWORTH.

(In imitation of Gascoigne.)

What stir, what turmoil, have we for
    the nones?
Stand back, my masters, or beware
    your bones!

Sirs, I'm a warder, and no man
of straw ;
My voice keeps order, and my club
gives law.

Yet soft ! nay stay—what vision have
we here ?
What dainty darling's this ? what
peerless peer ?
What loveliest face, that lovely ranks
enfold,
Like brightest diamond chased in
purest gold ?

Dazzled and blind, mine office I forsake,
My club, my key, my knee, my
homage take.
Bright paragon, pass on in joy and
bliss ;
Beshrew the gate that opes not wide
at such a sight as this !

Chap. xxx.

—+—

MOTTOES.

NAY, I'll hold touch ; the game shall
be play'd out ;
It ne'er shall stop for me, this merry
wager :
That which I say when gamesome, I'll
avouch
In my most sober mood—ne'er trust
me else.
The Hazard-Table.
Chap. iii.

Not serve two masters ?—Here's a
youth will try it,
Would fain serve God, yet give the
devil his due ;
Says grace before he doth a deed
of villany,
And returns his thanks devoutly when
'tis acted.
Old Play.
Chap. iv.

HE was a man
Versed in the world as pilot in his
compass.
The needle pointed ever to that interest
Which was his loadstar, and he spread
his sails
With vantage to the gale of others'
passion.

The Deceiver, a Tragedy.
Chap. v.

THIS is He
Who rides on the court-gale ; controls
its tides ;
Knows all their secret shoals and
fatal eddies ;
Whose frown abases, and whose smile
exalts.
He shines like any rainbow—and,
perchance,
His colours are as transient.
Old Play.
Chap. vii.

THIS is rare news thou tell'st me,
my good fellow ;
There are two bulls fierce battling
on the green
For one fair heifer—if the one goes
down,
The dale will be more peaceful, and
the herd,
Which have small interest in their
brulziement,
May pasture there in peace.
Old Play.
Chap. xiv.

WELL, then, our course is chosen :
spread the sail,—
Heave oft the lead, and mark the
soundings well ;
Look to the helm, good master ; many
a shoal

Marks this stern coast, and rocks
   where sits the siren,
Who, like ambition, lures men to their
   ruin.
              The Shipwreck.

Chap. xvii.

           Now God
Be good to me in this wild pilgrimage!
All hope in human aid I cast behind me.
Oh, who would be a woman? who
   that fool,
A weeping, pining, faithful, loving
   woman?
She hath hard measure still where
   she hopes kindest,
And all her bounties only make her
   ingrates.
          Love's Pilgrimage.

Chap. xxiii.

HARK! the bells summon, and the
   bugle calls,
But she the fairest answers not; the tide
Of nobles and of ladies throngs the
   halls,
But she the loveliest must in secret
   hide.
What eyes were thine, proud Prince,
   which in the gleam
Of yon gay meteors lost that better
   sense,
That o'er the glow-worm doth the
   star esteem,
And merit's modest blush o'er courtly
   insolence?
          The Glass Slipper.

Chap. xxv.

WHAT, man! ne'er lack a draught
   when the full can
Stands at thine elbow, and craves
   emptying! —
Nay, fear not me, for I have no delight
To watch men's vices, since I have
   myself

Of virtue nought to boast of. I 'm
   a striker,
Would have the world strike with
   me, pell-mell all.
          Pandaemonium.

Chap. xxviii.

Now fare thee well, my master! if
   true service
Be guerdon'd with hard looks, e'en
   cut the tow-line,
And let our barks across the pathless
   flood
Hold different courses.
          Shipwreck.

Chap. xxix.

Now bid the steeple rock—she comes,
   she comes!
Speak for us, bells! speak for us,
   shrill-tongued tuckets!
Stand to the linstock, gunner; let thy
   cannon
Play such a peal, as if a Paynim foe
Came stretch'd in turban'd ranks to
   storm the ramparts.
We will have pageants too; but that
   craves wit,
And I 'm a rough-hewn soldier.
   The Virgin-Queen, a Tragi-Comedy.

Chap. xxx.

THE wisest sovereigns err like private
   men,
And royal hand has sometimes laid
   the sword
Of chivalry upon a worthless shoulder,
Which better had been branded by the
   hangman.
What then? Kings do their best,—and
   they and we
Must answer for the intent, and not
   the event.
          Old Play.

Chap. xxxii.

HERE stands the victim—there the proud betrayer,
E'en as the hind pull'd down by strangling dogs
Lies at the hunter's feet, who courteous proffers
To some high dame, the Dian of the chase,
To whom he looks for guerdon, his sharp blade,
To gash the sobbing throat.

The Woodsman.

Chap. XXXIII.

HIGH o'er the eastern steep the sun is beaming,
And darkness flies with her deceitful shadows;
So truth prevails o'er falsehood.

Old Play.

Chap. XL.

XIV.

FROM THE PIRATE.

THE SONG OF THE REIM-KENNAR.

STERN eagle of the far north-west,
Thou that bearest in thy grasp the thunderbolt,
Thou whose rushing pinions stir ocean to madness,
Thou the destroyer of herds, thou the scatterer of navies,
Amidst the scream of thy rage,
Amidst the rushing of thy onward wings,
Though thy scream be loud as the cry of a perishing nation,
Though the rushing of thy wings be like the roar of ten thousand waves,
Yet hear, in thine ire and thy haste,
Hear thou the voice of the Reim-kennar.

Thou hast met the pine-trees of Drontheim,
Their dark-green heads lie prostrate beside their up-rooted stems;
Thou hast met the rider of the ocean,
The tall, the strong bark of the fearless rover,
And she has struck to thee the topsail
That she had not veil'd to a royal armada.
Thou hast met the tower that bears its crest among the clouds,
The battled massive tower of the Jarl of former days,
And the cope-stone of the turret
Is lying upon its hospitable hearth;
But thou too shalt stoop, proud compeller of clouds,
When thou hearest the voice of the Reim-kennar.

There are verses that can stop the stag in the forest,
Ay, and when the dark-colour'd dog is opening on his track;
There are verses can make the wild hawk pause on the wing,
Like the falcon that wears the hood and the jesses,
And who knows the shrill whistle of the fowler.
Thou who canst mock at the scream of the drowning mariner,
And the crash of the ravaged forest,
And the groan of the overwhelmed crowds,
When the church hath fallen in the moment of prayer;
There are sounds which thou also must list,
When they are chanted by the voice of the Reim-kennar.

Enough of woe hast thou wrought on the ocean.
The widows wring their hands on the beach;

Enough of woe hast thou wrought on
the land,
The husbandman folds his arms in
despair;
Cease thou the waving of thy pinions,
Let the ocean repose in her dark
strength;
Cease thou the flashing of thine eye,
Let the thunderbolt sleep in the ar-
moury of Odin;
Be thou still at my bidding, viewless
racer of the north-western
heaven,—
Sleep thou at the voice of Norna the
Reim-kennar.

Eagle of the far north-western waters,
Thou hast heard the voice of the Reim-
kennar,
Thou hast closed thy wide sails at her
bidding,
And folded them in peace by thy side.
My blessing be on thy retiring path;
When thou stoopest from thy place on
high,
Soft be thy slumbers in the caverns of
the unknown ocean,
Rest till destiny shall again awaken
thee;
Eagle of the north-west, thou hast
heard the voice of the Reim-
kennar.

Chap. VI.

—+∗+—

A LAST FAREWELL.

CLAUD HALCRO *sings :*—

FAREWELL to Northmaven,
Grey Hillswicke, farewell!
To the calms of thy haven,
The storms on thy fell,
To each breeze that can vary
The mood of thy main,
And to thee, bonny Mary!
We meet not again!

Farewell the wild ferry,
Which Hacon could brave,
When the peaks of the Skerry
Were white in the wave.
There's a maid may look over
These wild waves in vain,—
For the skiff of her lover—
He comes not again!

The vows thou hast broke,
On the wild currents fling them;
On the quicksand and rock
Let the mermaidens sing them;
New sweetness they'll give her
Bewildering strain;
But there's one who will never
Believe them again.

O were there an island,
Though ever so wild,
Where woman could smile, and
No man be beguiled—
Too tempting a snare
To poor mortals were given;
And the hope would fix there,
That should anchor in heaven.

Chap. XII.

—+∗+—

HAROLD HARFAGER.

THE sun is rising dimly red,
The wind is wailing low and dread;
From his cliff the eagle sallies,
Leaves the wolf his darksome valleys,
In the mist the ravens hover,
Peep the wild dogs from the cover,
Screaming, croaking, baying, yelling,
Each in his wild accents telling,
'Soon we feast on dead and dying,
Fair-hair'd Harold's flag is flying.'

Many a crest on air is streaming,
Many a helmet darkly gleaming,
Many an arm the axe uprears,
Doom'd to hew the wood of spears.

All along the crowded ranks
Horses neigh and armour clanks ;
Chiefs are shouting, clarions ringing,
Louder still the bard is singing,
'Gather footmen, gather horsemen,
To the field, ye valiant Norsemen !

'Halt ye not for food or slumber,
View not vantage, count not number :
Jolly reapers, forward still ;
Grow the crop on vale or hill,
Thick or scatter'd, stiff or lithe,
It shall down before the scythe.
Forward with your sickles bright,
Reap the harvest of the fight ;
Onward footmen, onward horsemen,
To the charge ye gallant Norsemen !

'Fatal Choosers of the Slaughter,
O'er you hovers Odin's daughter ;
Hear the choice she spreads before
ye,—
Victory, and wealth, and glory ;
Or old Valhalla's roaring hail,
Her ever-circling mead and ale,
Where for eternity unite
The joys of wassail and of fight.
Headlong forward, foot and horse-
men,
Charge and fight, and die like Norse-
men !'

Chap. xv.

—◆◆—

THE MEETING OF THE MER-
MAIDS AND MERMEN.

MERMAID.

FATHOMS deep beneath the wave,
Stringing beads of glistering pearl,
Singing the achievements brave
Of many an old Norwegian earl ;
Dwelling where the tempest's raving,
Falls as light upon our ear,

As the sigh of lover, craving
Pity from his lady dear,
Children of wild Thule, we,
From the deep caves of the sea,
As the lark springs from the lea,
Hither come, to share your glee.

MERMAN.

From reining of the water-horse,
That bounded till the waves were
foaming,
Watching the infant tempest's course,
Chasing the sea-snake in his roam-
ing ;
From winding charge-notes on the
shell,
When the huge whale and sword-
fish duel,
Or tolling shroudless seamen's knell,
When the winds and waves are
cruel ;
Children of wild Thule, we
Have plough'd such furrows on the
sea,
As the steer draws on the lea,
And hither we come to share your
glee.

MERMAIDS AND MERMEN.

We heard you in our twilight caves,
A hundred fathom deep below,
For notes of joy can pierce the waves,
That drown each sound of war and
woe.

Those who dwell beneath the sea
Love the sons of Thule well ;
Thus, to aid your mirth, bring we
Dance, and song, and sounding
shell.
Children of dark Thule, know,
Those who dwell by haaf and voe,
Where your daring shallops row,
Come to share the festal show.

Chap. xvi.

NORNA *sings :—*

FOR leagues along the watery way,
    Through gulf and stream my course
      has been ;
The billows know my Runic lay,
    And smooth their crests to silent
      green.

The billows know my Runic lay,—
    The gulf grows smooth, the stream
      is still ;
But human hearts, more wild than
      they,
    Know but the rule of wayward
      will.

One hour is mine, in all the year,
    To tell my woes,—and one alone ;
When gleams this magic lamp, 'tis
    here,—
    When dies the mystic light, 'tis
      gone.

Daughters of northern Magnus, hail !
    The lamp is lit, the flame is clear,—
To you I come to tell my tale,
    Awake, arise, my tale to hear !

NORNA'S INVOCATION.

DWELLERS of the mountain, rise,
Trolld the powerful, Haims the wise !
Ye who taught weak woman's tongue
Words that sway the wise and strong ;
Ye who taught weak woman's hand
How to wield the magic wand,
And wake the gales on Foŭlah's steep
Or lull wild Sumburgh's waves to
    sleep !
Still live ye yet ? Not yours the
    pow'r
Ye knew in Odin's mightier hour.
What are ye now but empty names,
Powerful Trolld, sagacious Haims,
That, lightly spoken, lightly heard,
Float on the air like thistle's beard ?

TROLLD'S REPLY.

A THOUSAND winters dark have flown
Since o'er the threshold of my Stone
A votaress pass'd, my power to own.
    Visitor bold
    Of the mansion of Trolld,
      Maiden, haughty of heart,
      Who hast hither presum'd,—
    Ungifted, undoom'd,
      Thou shalt not depart !
The power thou dost covet
    O'er tempest and wave,
Shall be thine, thou proud maiden!
    By beach and by cave,
By stack and by skerry, by noup [1] and
    by voe [2],
By air [3] and by wick, and by helyer [4]
    and gio [5],
And by every wild shore which the
    northern winds know
And the northern tides lave.
But tho' this shall be given thee, thou
    desperately brave,
I doom thee that never the gift thou
    shalt have
Till thou reave thy life's giver of the
    gift which he gave.

NORNA'S ANSWER.

DARK are thy words, and severe,
    Thou Dweller in the Stone ;
But trembling and fear
    To her are unknown
Who hath sought thee here,
    In thy dwelling lone.

Come what comes soever,
    The worst I can endure :
Life is but a short fever,
    And Death 's the cure.

Chap. XIX.

---

[1] A round-headed eminence.   [2] A creek.
[3] An open sea-beach.   [4] A sea-cave.
[5] A deep ravine admitting the sea.

CLAUD HALCRO AND NORNA.

CLAUD HALCRO.

MOTHER darksome, Mother dread,
Dweller on the Fitful-head,
Thou canst see what deeds are done
Under the never-setting sun.
Look through sleet, and look through
　　frost,
Look to Greenland's caves and coast,—
By the ice-berg is a sail
Chasing of the swarthy whale;
Mother doubtful, Mother dread,
Tell us, has the good ship sped?

NORNA.

The thought of the aged is ever on gear,
On his fishing, his furrow, his flock,
　　and his steer;
But thrive may his fishing, flock,
　　furrow, and herd,
While the aged for anguish shall tear
　　his grey beard.
The ship, well-laden as bark need be,
Lies deep in the furrow of the Iceland
　　sea;
The breeze for Zetland blows fair and
　　soft,
And gaily the garland is fluttering aloft:
Seven good fishes have spouted their
　　last,
And their jaw-bones are hanging to
　　yard and mast;
Two are for Lerwick, and two for
　　Kirkwall,
Three for Burgh Westra, the choicest
　　of all.

CLAUD HALCRO.

Mother doubtful, Mother dread,
Dweller of the Fitful-head,
Thou hast conn'd full many a rhyme,
That lives upon the surge of time:
Tell me, shall my lays be sung,
Like Hacon's of the golden tongue,
Long after Halcro's dead and gone?
Or, shall Hialtland's minstrel own
One note to rival glorious John?

NORNA.

The infant loves the rattle's noise;
Age, double childhood, hath its toys;
But different far the descant rings,
As strikes a different hand the strings.
The eagle mounts the polar sky—
The Imber-goose, unskill'd to fly,
Must be content to glide along,
Where seal and sea-dog list his song.

CLAUD HALCRO.

Be mine the Imber-goose to play,
And haunt lone cave and silent bay;
The archer's aim so shall I shun—
So shall I 'scape the levell'd gun—
Content my verses' tuneless jingle,
With Thule's sounding tides to mingle,
While, to the ear of wondering wight,
Upon the distant headland's height,
Soften'd by murmur of the sea,
The rude sounds seem like harmony!

Mother doubtful, Mother dread,
Dweller of the Fitful-head,
A gallant bark from far abroad,
Saint Magnus hath her in his road,
With guns and firelocks not a few—
A silken and a scarlet crew,
Deep stored with precious merchan-
　　dise,
Of gold, and goods of rare device—
What interest hath our comrade bold
In bark and crew, in goods and gold?

NORNA.

Gold is ruddy, fair, and free,
Blood is crimson, and dark to see;
I look'd out on Saint Magnus Bay,
And I saw a falcon that struck her
　　prey,—
A gobbet of flesh in her beak she
　　bore,
And talons and singles are dripping
　　with gore;
Let him that asks after them look on
　　his hand,
And if there is blood on 't, he 's one
　　of their band.

CLAUD HALCRO.

Mother doubtful, Mother dread,
Dweller of the Fitful-head,
Well thou know'st it is thy task
To tell what Beauty will not ask;
Then steep thy words in wine and
    milk,
And weave a doom of gold and silk,—
For we would know, shall Brenda
    prove
In love, and happy in her love?

NORNA.

Untouch'd by love, the maiden's breast
Is like the snow on Rona's crest,
High seated in the middle sky,
In bright and barren purity;
But by the sunbeam gently kiss'd,
Scarce by the gazing eye 'tis miss'd,
Ere, down the lonely valley stealing,
Fresh grass and growth its course
    revealing,
It cheers the flock, revives the flower,
And decks some happy shepherd's
    bower.

MAGNUS TROIL.

Mother speak, and do not tarry,
Here's a maiden fain would marry.
Shall she marry, ay or not?
If she marry, what's her lot?

NORNA.

Untouch'd by love, the maiden's breast
Is like the snow on Rona's crest;
So pure, so free from earthy dye,
It seems, whilst leaning on the sky,
Part of the heaven to which 'tis nigh;
But passion, like the wild March rain,
May soil the wreath with many a stain.
We gaze—the lovely vision's gone—
A torrent fills the bed of stone,
That hurrying to destruction's shock,
Leaps headlong from the lofty rock.

Chap. XXI.

SONG OF THE SHETLAND FISHERS.

FAREWELL, merry maidens, to song,
    and to laugh,
For the brave lads of Westra are
    bound to the Haaf;
And we must have labour, and hunger,
    and pain,
Ere we dance with the maids of
    Dunrossness again.

For now, in our trim boats of Noroway
    deal,
We must dance on the waves, with
    the porpoise and seal;
The breeze it shall pipe, so it pipe not
    too high,
And the gull be our songstress when-
    e'er she flits by.

Sing on, my brave bird, while we
    follow, like thee,
By bank, shoal, and quicksand, the
    swarms of the sea;
And when twenty-score fishes are
    straining our line,
Sing louder, brave bird, for their spoils
    shall be thine.

We'll sing while we bait, and we'll
    sing while we haul
For the deeps of the Haaf have enough
    for us all:
There is torsk for the gentle, and
    skate for the carle,
And there's wealth for bold Magnus,
    the son of the earl.

Huzza! my brave comrades, give way
    for the Haaf,
We shall sooner come back to the
    dance and the laugh;
For life without mirth is a lamp
    without oil;
Then, mirth and long life to the bold
    Magnus Troil!

Chap. XXII.

CLEVELAND *sings :—*

Love wakes and weeps
While Beauty sleeps!
O for Music's softest numbers,
To prompt a theme,
For Beauty's dream,
Soft as the pillow of her slumbers!

Through groves of palm
Sigh gales of balm,
Fire-flies on the air are wheeling;
While through the gloom
Comes soft perfume,
The distant beds of flowers revealing.

O wake and live!
No dream can give
A shadow'd bliss, the real excelling;
No longer sleep,
From lattice peep,
And list the tale that Love is telling.

———

Farewell! Farewell! the voice you hear
Has left its last soft tone with you;
Its next must join the seaward cheer,
And shout among the shouting crew.

The accents which I scarce could form
Beneath your frown's controlling check,
Must give the word, above the storm,
To cut the mast, and clear the wreck.

The timid eye I dared not raise,
The hand, that shook when press'd to thine,
Must point the guns upon the chase—
Must bid the deadly cutlass shine.

To all I love, or hope, or fear,
Honour, or own, a long adieu!
To all that life has soft and dear,
Farewell! save memory of you!

CLAUD HALCRO *sings or recites :—*

And you shall deal the funeral dole;
Ay, deal it, mother mine,
To weary body, and to heavy soul,
The white bread and the wine.

And you shall deal my horses of pride;
Ay, deal them, mother mine;
And you shall deal my lands so wide,
And deal my castles nine.

But deal not vengeance for the deed,
And deal not for the crime;
The body to its place, and the soul to Heaven's grace,
And the rest in God's own time.

———

Saint Magnus control thee, that martyr of treason;
Saint Ronan rebuke thee, with rhyme and with reason;
By the mass of Saint Martin, the might of Saint Mary,
Be thou gone, or thy weird shall be worse if thou tarry!
If of good, go hence and hallow thee;—
If of ill, let the earth swallow thee;—
If thou 'rt of air, let the grey mist fold thee;—
If of earth, let the swart mine hold thee;—
If a Pixie, seek thy ring;—
If a Nixie, seek thy spring;—
If on middle earth thou 'st been
Slave of sorrow, shame, and sin,
Hast eat the bread of toil and strife,
And dree'd the lot which men call life;
Begone to thy stone! for thy coffin is scant of thee,
The worm, thy play-fellow, wails for the want of thee:
Hence, houseless ghost! let the earth hide thee,
Till Michael shall blow the blast, see that there thou bide thee!—

Phantom, fly hence! take the Cross
for a token,
Hence pass till Hallowmass!—my
spell is spoken.

———

WHERE corpse-light
Dances bright,
Be it by day or night,
Be it by light or dark,
There shall corpse lie stiff and stark.

———

MENSEFUL maiden ne'er should rise,
Till the first beam tinge the skies;
Silk-fringed eyelids still should close,
Till the sun has kiss'd the rose;
Maiden's foot we should not view,
Mark'd with tiny print on dew,
Till the opening flowerets spread
Carpet meet for beauty's tread.

Chap. XXIII.

—+—

NORNA *sings or recites :—*

CHAMPION, famed for warlike toil,
Art thou silent, Ribolt Troil?
Sand, and dust, and pebbly stones,
Are leaving bare thy giant bones.
Who dared touch the wild bear's skin
Ye slumber'd on, while life was in?
A woman now, or babe, may come
And cast the covering from thy tomb.

Yet be not wrathful, Chief, nor blight
Mine eyes or ears with sound or sight!
I come not, with unhallow'd tread,
To wake the slumbers of the dead,
Or lay thy giant reliques bare;
But what I seek thou well canst spare.
Be it to my hand allow'd
To shear a merk's weight from thy
shroud;
Yet leave thee sheeted lead enough
To shield thy bones from weather
rough.

See, I draw my magic knife:
Never, while thou wert in life,
Lay'st thou still for sloth or fear,
When point and edge were glittering
near;
See, the cerements now I sever—
Waken now, or sleep for ever!
Thou wilt not wake—the deed is done!
The prize I sought is fairly won.

Thanks, Ribolt, thanks; for this the
sea
Shall smooth its ruffled crest for thee,
And while afar its billows foam,
Subside to peace near Ribolt's tomb.
Thanks, Ribolt, thanks; for this the
might
Of wild winds raging at their height,
When to thy place of slumber nigh,
Shall soften to a lullaby.

She, the dame of doubt and dread,
Norna of the Fitful-head,
Mighty in her own despite,
Miserable in her might,
In despair and frenzy great,
In her greatness desolate,
Wisest, wickedest who lives,—
Well can keep the word she gives.

Chap. XXV.

—+—

NORNA *recites :—*

THOU, so needful, yet so dread,
With cloudy crest, and wing of red;
Thou, without whose genial breath
The North would sleep the sleep of
death;
Who deign'st to warm the cottage
hearth,
Yet hurls proud palaces to earth,—
Brightest, keenest of the Powers,
Which form and rule this world of
ours,
With my rhyme of Runic, I
Thank thee for thy agency

Old Reimkennar, to thy art
Mother Hertha sends her part;
She, whose gracious bounty gives
Needful food for all that lives.
From the deep mine of the North
Came the mystic metal forth,
Doom'd amidst disjointed stones,
Long to cere a champion's bones,
Disinhumed my charms to aid—
Mother Earth, my thanks are paid.

Girdle of our islands dear,
Element of Water, hear!
Thou whose power can overwhelm
Broken mounds and ruin'd realm
On the lowly Belgian strand;
All thy fiercest rage can never
Of our soil a furlong sever
From our rock-defended land;
Play then gently thou thy part,
To assist old Norna's art.

Elements, each other greeting,
Gifts and power attend your meeting.

Thou, that over billows dark
Safely send'st the fisher's bark,
Giving him a path and motion
Through the wilderness of ocean;
Thou, that when the billows brave ye,
O'er the shelves canst drive the navy,—
Didst thou chafe as one neglected,
While thy brethren were respected?
To appease thee, see, I tear
This full grasp of grizzled hair;
Oft thy breath hath through it sung,
Softening to my magic tongue;
Now, 'tis thine to bid it fly
Through the wide expanse of sky,
'Mid the countless swarms to sail
Of wild-fowl wheeling on thy gale;
Take thy portion and rejoice,—
Spirit, thou hast heard my voice!

She who sits by haunted well,
Is subject to the Nixie's spell;

She who walks on lonely beach,
To the Mermaid's charmèd speech;
She who walks round ring of green,
Offends the peevish Fairy Queen;
And she who takes rest in the Dwar-
fie's cave,
A weary weird of woe shall have.

By ring, by spring, by cave, by shore,
Minna Troil has braved all this and
more;
And yet hath the root of her sorrow
and ill,
A source that's more deep and more
mystical still.

Thou art within a demon's hold,
More wise than Heims, more strong
than Trolld;
No siren sings so sweet as he,
No fay springs lighter on the lea;
No elfin power hath half the art
To soothe, to move, to wring the
heart,—
Life-blood from the cheek to drain,
Drench the eye, and dry the vein.
Maiden, ere we farther go,
Dost thou note me, ay or no!

MINNA.

I mark thee, my mother, both word,
look, and sign;
Speak on with thy riddle — to read it
be mine.

NORNA.

Mark me! for the word I speak
Shall bring the colour to thy cheek.
This leaden heart, so light of cost,
The symbol of a treasure lost,
Thou shalt wear in hope and in peace,
That the cause of thy sickness and
sorrow may cease,
When crimson foot meets crimson
hand
In the Martyr's Aisle, and in Orkney
land.

Be patient, be patient; for Patience
    hath power
To ward us in danger, like mantle in
    shower;
A fairy gift you best may hold
In a chain of fairy gold;
The chain and the gift are each a true
    token,
That not without warrant old Norna
    hath spoken;
But thy nearest and dearest must never
    behold them,
Till time shall accomplish the truths
    I have told them.

    Chap. XXVIII.

—+—

THE PEDLAR *sings his wares :—*

Poor sinners whom the snake deceives,
Are fain to cover them with leaves.
Zetland hath no leaves, 'tis true,
Because that trees are none, or few;
But we have flax and taits of woo',
For linen cloth and wadmaal blue;
And we have many foreign knacks
Of finer waft, than woo' or flax.
Ye gallant Lambmas lads appear,
And bring your Lambmas sisters here,
Bryce Snailsfoot spares not cost or
    care,
To pleasure every gentle pair.

    Chap. XXXII.

—+—

MOTTOES.

'TIS not alone the scene; the man,
    Anselmo,
The man finds sympathies in these
    wild wastes,
And roughly tumbling seas, which
    fairer views
And smoother waves deny him.

        Ancient Drama.
Chap. II.

THIS is no pilgrim's morning: yon
    grey mist
Lies upon hill and dale, and field and
    forest,
Like the dun wimple of a new-made
    widow.
And, by my faith, although my heart
    be soft,
I'd rather hear that widow weep and
    sigh,
And tell the virtues of the dear departed,
Than, when the tempest sends his
    voice abroad,
Be subject to its fury.

        The Double Nuptials.
    Chap. IV.

SHE does no work by halves, yon
    raving ocean;
Engulphing those she strangles, her
    wild womb
Affords the mariners whom she hath
    dealt on,
Their death at once, and sepulchre.

        Old Play.
    Chap. VII.

THIS is a gentle trader, and a prudent.
He's no Autolycus, to blear your eye,
With quips of worldly gauds and
    gamesomeness;
But seasons all his glittering mer-
    chandise
With wholesome doctrine suited to
    the use,
As men sauce goose with sage and
    rosemary.

        Old Play.
    Chap. IX.

    ALL your ancient customs,
And long-descended usages, I'll
    change.
Ye shall not eat, nor drink, nor speak,
    nor move,

Think, look, or walk, as ye were
    wont to do;
Even your marriage-beds shall know
    mutation;
The bride shall have the stock, the
    groom the wall;
For all old practice will I turn and
    change,
And call it reformation—marry, will I!
         'Tis Even that we're at Odds.
   Chap. XI.

WE'LL keep our customs—what is
    law itself,
But old establish'd custom! What
    religion,
(I mean, with one-half of the men
    that use it,)
Save the good use and wont that
    carries them
To worship how and where their
    fathers worshipp'd?
All things resolve in custom—we'll
    keep ours.
         Old Play.
   Chap. XIV.

SEE yonder woman, whom our swains
    revere,
And dread in secret, while they take
    her counsel
When sweetheart shall be kind, or
    when cross dame shall die;
Where lurks the thief who stole the
    silver tankard,
And how the pestilent murrain may
    be cured;—
This sage adviser's mad, stark mad,
    my friend;
Yet, in her madness, hath the art and
    cunning
To wring fools' secrets from their
    inmost bosoms,
And pay inquirers with the coin they
    gave her.   *Old Play.*
   Chap. XXIX.

WHAT ho, my jovial mates! come on!
    we'll frolic it
Like fairies frisking in the merry
    moonshine,
Seen by the curtal friar, who, from
    some christening,
Or some blithe bridal, hies belated
    cell-ward;—
He starts, and changes his bold bottle
    swagger
To churchman's pace professional, and,
    ransacking
His treacherous memory for some
    holy hymn,
Finds but the roundel of the midnight
    catch.
         Old Play.
   Chap. XXX.

I STRIVE like to the vessel in the tideway,
Which, lacking favouring breeze, hath
    not the power
To stem the powerful current. Even
    so,
Resolving daily to forsake my vices,
Habit, strong circumstance, renew'd
    temptation,
Sweep me to sea again. O heavenly
    breath,
Fill thou my sails, and aid the feeble
    vessel,
Which ne'er can reach the blessed
    port without thee!
         'Tis Odds when Evens meet.
   Chap. XXXII.

PARENTAL love, my friend, has power
    o'er wisdom,
And is the charm, which, like the
    falconer's lure,
Can bring from heaven the highest
    soaring spirits.
So, when famed Prosper doff'd his
    magic robe,
It was Miranda pluck'd it from his
    shoulders.   *Old Play.*
   Chap. XXXIII.

Hark to the insult loud, the bitter sneer,
The fierce threat answering to the
   brutal jeer ;
Oaths fly like pistol-shots, and vengeful
   words
Clash with each other like conflicting
   swords.
The robber's quarrel by such sounds
   is shown,
And true men have some chance to
   gain their own.

Captivity, a Poem.

Chap. xxxiv.

XV.

FROM THE FORTUNES OF NIGEL.

MOTTOES.

Now Scot and English are agreed,
And Saunders hastes to cross the
   Tweed,
Where, such the splendours that
   attend him,
His very mother scarce had ken'd
   him.
His metamorphosis behold,
From Glasgow frieze to cloth of gold ;
His back-sword, with the iron hilt,
To rapier, fairly hatch'd and gilt ;
Was ever seen a gallant braver !
His very bonnet's grown a beaver.

The Reformation.

Chap. i.

This, sir, is one among the Seignory,
Has wealth at will, and will to use
   his wealth,
And wit to increase it.   Marry, his
   worst folly
Lies in a thriftless sort of charity,

That goes a-gadding sometimes after
   objects,
Which wise men will not see when
   thrust upon them.

The Old Couple.

Chap. ii.

Ay, sir, the clouted shoe hath ofttimes
   craft in 't,
As says the rustic proverb ; and your
   citizen,
In 's grogram suit, gold chain, and
   well-black'd shoes,
Bears under his flat cap ofttimes a
   brain
Wiser than burns beneath the cap
   and feather,
Or seethes within the statesman's
   velvet nightcap.

Read me my Riddle.

Chap. iv.

Wherefore come ye not to court ?
Certain 'tis the rarest sport ;
There are silks and jewels glistening,
Prattling fools and wise men listening,
Bullies among brave men justling,
Beggars amongst nobles bustling ;
Low-breath'd talkers, minion lispers,
Cutting honest throats by whispers ;
Wherefore come ye not to court ?
Skelton swears 'tis glorious sport.

Skelton Skeltonizeth.

Chap. v.

O, I do know him ; 'tis the mouldy
   lemon
Which our court wits will wet their
   lips withal,
When they would sauce their honied
   conversation
With somewhat sharper flavour.
   Marry, sir,
That virtue 's wellnigh left him ; all
   the juice

That was so sharp and poignant, is
    squeezed out ;
While the poor rind, although as
    sour as ever,
Must season soon the draff we give
    our grunters,
For two-legg'd things are weary on 't.

        The Chamberlain—A Comedy.

Chap. VI.

THINGS needful we have thought on ;
    but the thing
Of all most needful—that which
    Scripture terms,
As if alone it merited regard,
The ONE thing needful—that's yet
    unconsider'd.

        The Chamberlain.

Chap. VII.

AH ! mark the matron well—and
    laugh not, Harry,
At her old steeple-hat and velvet
    guard—
I 've call'd her like the ear of Dionysius;
I mean that ear-form'd vault, built
    o'er the dungeon,
To catch the groans and discontented
    murmurs
Of his poor bondsmen. Even so doth
    Martha
Drink up, for her own purpose, all
    that passes,
Or is supposed to pass, in this wide
    city ;
She can retail it too, if that her profit
Shall call on her to do so ; and retail it
For your advantage, so that you can
    make
Your profit jump with hers.

        The Conspiracy.

Chap. VIII.

BID not thy fortune troll upon the
    whirls
Of yonder dancing cubes of mottled
    bone ;

And drown it not, like Egypt's royal
    harlot,
Dissolving her rich pearl in the
    brimm'd wine-cup.
'These are the arts, Lothario, which
    shrink acres
Into brief yards—bring sterling pounds
    to farthings,
Credit to infamy ; and the poor
    gull,
Who might have lived an honour'd,
    easy life,
To ruin, and an unregarded grave.

        The Changes.

Chap. X.

    THIS is the very barn-yard,
Where muster daily the prime cocks
    o' the game,
Ruffle their pinions, crow till they
    are hoarse,
And spar about a barleycorn. Here,
    too, chickens,
The callow, unfledged brood of
    forward folly,
Learn first to rear the crest, and aim
    the spur,
And tune their note like full-plumed
    Chanticleer.

        The Bear Garden.

Chap. XII.

LET the proud salmon gorge the
    feather'd hook,
Then strike, and then you have him.
    He will wince ;
Spin out your line that it shall whistle
    from you
Some twenty yards or so, yet you
    shall have him.
Marry ! you must have patience ; the
    stout rock
Which is his trust, hath edges some-
    thing sharp ;

And the deep pool hath ooze and
    sludge enough
To mar your fishing—'less you are
    more careful.
       Albion or the Double Kings.
  Chap. XIII.

GIVE way! give way! I must and
    will have justice;
And tell me not of privilege and place;
Where I am injured, there I'll sue
    redress.
Look to it, every one who bars my
    access;
I have a heart to feel the injury,
A hand to right myself, and, by my
    honour,
That hand shall grasp what grey-
    beard Law denies me.
       The Chamberlain.
  Chap. XVI.

COME hither, young one. Mark me!
    Thou art now
'Mongst men o' the sword, that live
    by reputation
More than by constant income.
    Single-suited
They are, I grant you; yet each single
    suit
Maintains, on the rough guess, a
    thousand followers;
And they be men, who, hazarding
    their all,
Needful apparel, necessary income,
And human body, and immortal soul,
Do in the very deed but hazard
    nothing—
So strictly is that ALL bound in re-
    version;
Clothes to the broker, income to the
    usurer,
And body to disease, and soul to
    the foul fiend;

Who laughs to see Soldadoes and
    fooladoes,
Play better than himself his game
    on earth.
       The Mohocks.
  Chap. XVII.

Mother. What! dazzled by a flash
    of Cupid's mirror
With which the boy, as mortal urchins
    wont,
Flings back the sunbeam in the eye of
    passengers,
Then laughs to see them stumble!
  Daughter.   Mother! no;
It was a lightning-flash which dazzled
    me,
And never shall these eyes see true
    again.
       Beef and Pudding,
       An Old English Comedy.
  Chap. XVIII.

By this good light, a wench of match-
    less mettle!
This were a leaguer-lass to love a sol-
    dier,
To bind his wounds, and kiss his bloody
    brow,
And sing a roundel as she help'd to
    arm him,
Though the rough foeman's drums
    were beat so nigh,
They seem'd to bear the burden.
       Old Play.
  Chap. XIX.

CREDIT me, friend, it hath been ever
    thus,
Since the ark rested on Mount Ararat.
False man hath sworn, and woman
    hath believed—
Repented and reproach'd, and then
    believed once more.
       The New World.
  Chap. XX.

Rove not from pole to pole—the man
    lives here
Whose razor's only equall'd by his
    beer ;
And where, in either sense, the cock-
    ney-put
May, if he pleases, get confounded *cut*.

    *For the Sign of an Alehouse kept
        by a Barber.*

   Chap. xxi.

Chance will not do the work, Chance
    sends the breeze ;
But if the pilot slumber at the helm,
The very wind that wafts us towards
    the port
May dash us on the shelves. The
    steersman's part is vigilance,
Blow it or rough or smooth.

                 Old Play.
   Chap. xxii.

This is the time : Heaven's maiden-
    sentinel
Hath quitted her high watch ; the lesser
    spangles
Are paling one by one ; give me the
    ladder
And the short lever ; bid Antony
Keep with his carabine the wicket-
    gate ;
And do thou bare thy knife and follow
    me,
For we will in and do it. Darkness
    like this
Is dawning of our fortunes.

                 Old Play.
   Chap. xxiv.

Death finds us 'mid our playthings—
    snatches us,
As a cross nurse might do a wayward
    child,
From all our toys and baubles. His
    rough call

Unlooses all our favourite ties on earth ;
And well if they are such as may be
    answer'd
In yonder world, where all is judged
    of truly.

                 Old Play.
   Chap. xxv.

Give us good voyage, gentle stream ;
    we stun not
Thy sober ear with sounds of revelry,
Wake not the slumbering echoes of
    thy banks
With voice of flute and horn ; we do
    but seek
On the broad pathway of thy swelling
    bosom
To glide in silent safety.

           The Double Bridal.
   Chap. xxvi.

This way lie safety and a sure
    retreat ;
Yonder lie danger, shame, and
    punishment.
Most welcome danger then—nay, let
    me say,
Though spoke with swelling heart—
    welcome e'en shame ;
And welcome punishment—for, call
    me guilty,
I do but pay the tax that's due to
    justice ;
And call me guiltless, then that punish-
    ment
Is shame to those alone who do in-
    flict it.

             The Tribunal.
   Chap. xxvii.

How fares the man on whom good
    men would look
With eyes where scorn and censure
    combated,
But that kind Christian love hath
    taught the lesson—

That they who merit most contempt
and hate,
Do most deserve our pity.
Old Play.

Chap. xxix.

Marry, come up, sir, with your gentle
blood!
Here's a red stream beneath this coarse
blue doublet,
That warms the heart as kindly as if
drawn
From the far source of old Assyrian
kings,
Who first made mankind subject to
their sway.
Old Play.

Chap. xxxi.

We are not worse at once: the course
of evil
Begins so slowly, and from such slight
source,
An infant's hand might stem its breach
with clay;
But let the stream get deeper, and
philosophy—
Ay, and religion too,—shall strive in
vain
To turn the headlong torrent.
Old Play.

Chap. xxxv.

XVI.

FROM PEVERIL OF THE PEAK.

MOTTOES.

Why then, we will have bellowing of
beeves,
Broaching of barrels, brandishing of
spigots;

Blood shall flow freely, but it shall be
gore
Of herds and flocks, and venison and
poultry,
Join'd to the brave heart's-blood of
John-a-Barleycorn!
Old Play.

Chap. ii.

Here's neither want of appetites nor
mouths;
Pray Heaven we be not scant of meat
or mirth!
Old Play.

Chap. iii.

No, sir, I will not pledge: I'm one of
those
Who think good wine needs neither
bush nor preface
To make it welcome. If you doubt my
word,
Fill the quart-cup, and see if I will
choke on 't.
Old Play.

Chap. iv.

Ascasto. Can she not speak?
Oswald. If speech be only in ac-
cented sounds,
Framed by the tongue and lips, the
maiden's dumb;
But if by quick and apprehensive look,
By motion, sign, and glance, to give
each meaning,
Express as clothed in language, be
term'd speech,
She hath that wondrous faculty; for
her eyes,
Like the bright stars of heaven, can
hold discourse,
Though it be mute and soundless.
Old Play.

Chap. xvi.

This is a love meeting! See the maiden
mourns,
And the sad suitor bends his looks on
earth.

There's more hath pass'd between
    them than belongs
To Love's sweet sorrows.

Old Play.

Chap. xvii.

Now, hoist the anchor, mates ; and
    let the sails
Give their broad bosom to the buxom
    wind,
Like lass that wooes a lover.

Anonymous.

Chap. xix.

He was a fellow in a peasant's garb ;
Yet one could censure you a wood-
    cock's carving,
Like any courtier at the ordinary.

The Ordinary.

Chap. xxii.

We meet, as men see phantoms in a
    dream,
Which glide and sigh, and sign, and
    move their lips,
But make no sound ; or, if they utter
    voice,
'Tis but a low and undistinguish'd
    moaning,
Which has nor word nor sense of
    utter'd sound.

The Chieftain.

Chap. xxiv.

The course of human life is changeful
    still
As is the fickle wind and wandering
    rill ;
Or, like the light dance which the wild
    breeze weaves
Amidst the faded race of fallen leaves ;
Which now its breath bears down,
    now tosses high,
Beats to the earth, or wafts to middle
    sky.

Such, and so varied, the precarious
    play
Of fate with man, frail tenant of
    a day !

Anonymous.

Chap. xxv.

Necessity, thou best of peacemakers,
As well as surest prompter of inven-
    tion—
Help us to composition !

Anonymous.

Chap. xxvi.

This is some creature of the elements
Most like your sea-gull. He can
    wheel and whistle
His screaming song, e'en when the
    storm is loudest ;
Take for his sheeted couch the restless
    foam
Of the wild wave-crest ; slumber in
    the calm,
And dally with the storm. Yet 'tis a
    gull,
An arrant gull, with all this.

The Chieftain.

Chap. xxvii.

I fear the devil worst when gown and
    cassock,
Or, in the lack of them, old Calvin's
    cloak,
Conceals his cloven hoof.

Anonymous.

Chap. xxxi

'Tis the black ban-dog of our jail.
    Pray look on him,
But at a wary distance ; rouse him
    not—
He bays not till he worries.

The Black Dog of Newgate.

Chap. xxxiii.

'Speak not of niceness, when there's
    chance of wreck,'
The captain said, as ladies writhed
    their neck
To see the dying dolphin flap the
    deck :
'If we go down, on us these gentry
    sup ;
We dine upon them, if we haul them
    up.
Wise men applaud us when we eat
    the eaters,
As the devil laughs when keen folks
    cheat the cheaters.'
                    The Sea Voyage.
    Chap. XXXVIII.

CONTENTIONS fierce,
Ardent, and dire, spring from no petty
    cause.
                            Albion.
    Chap. XL.

HE came amongst them like a new-
    raised spirit,
To speak of dreadful judgments that
    impend,
And of the wrath to come.
                    The Reformer.
    Chap. XLIII.

AND some for safety took the dreadful
    leap ;
Some for the voice of Heaven seem'd
    calling them ;
Some for advancement, or for lucre's
    sake—
I leap'd in frolic.
                        The Dream.
    Chap. XLIV.

HIGH feasting was there there ; the
    gilded roofs
Rung to the wassail-health ; the
    dancer's step
Sprung to the chord responsive ; the
    gay gamester

To fate's disposal flung his heap of gold,
And laugh'd alike when it increased
    or lessen'd :
Such virtue hath court-air to teach us
    patience
Which schoolmen preach in vain.
            Why come ye not to Court ?
    Chap. XLV.

HERE stand I tight and trim,
Quick of eye, though little of limb ;
He who denieth the word I have
    spoken,
Betwixt him and me shall lances be
    broken.
    Lay of the Little John de Saintré.
    Chap. XLVI.

XVII.

FROM QUENTIN DURWARD.

COUNTY GUY.

AH ! County Guy, the hour is nigh,
    The sun has left the lea,
The orange flower perfumes the bower,
    The breeze is on the sea.
The lark, his lay who thrill'd all day,
    Sits hush'd his partner nigh ;
Breeze, bird, and flower, confess the
    hour,
    But where is County Guy?

The village maid steals through the
    shade,
    Her shepherd's suit to hear ;
To beauty shy, by lattice high,
    Sings high-born Cavalier.
The star of Love, all stars above,
    Now reigns o'er earth and sky ;
And high and low the influence know—
    But where is County Guy ?
    Chap. IV.

MOTTOES.

FULL in the midst a mighty pile arose
Where iron-grated gates their strength
　oppose
To each invading step; and strong
　and steep
The 'battled walls rose up, the fosse
　sunk deep.
Slow round the fortress rolled the
　sluggish stream,
And high in middle air the warder's
　turrets gleam.
　　　　　　　　　　　Anonymous.
　Chap. III.

PAINTERS show Cupid blind. Hath
　Hymen eyes?
Or is his sight warp'd by those spec-
　tacles
Which parents, guardians, and ad-
　visers lend him,
That he may look through them on
　lands and mansions,
On jewels, gold, and all such rich
　donations,
And see their value ten times
　magnified?—
Methinks 'twill brook a question.
　　The Miseries of Enforced Marriage.
　Chap. XI.

THIS is a lecturer so skill'd in policy,
That (no disparagement to Satan's
　cunning)
He well might read a lesson to the
　devil,
And teach the old seducer new
　temptations.
　　　　　　　　　　　Old Play.
　Chap. XII.

TALK not of kings—I scorn the poor
　comparison:
I am a sage, and can command the
　elements;

At least men think I can; and on that
　thought
I found unbounded empire.
　　　　　　　　　　Albumazar.
　Chap. XIII.

I SEE thee yet, fair France—thou
　favour'd land
Of art and nature—thou art still before
　me;
Thy sons, to whom their labour is a
　sport,
So well thy grateful soil returns its
　tribute;
Thy sun-burnt daughters, with their
　laughing eyes
And glossy raven-locks. But, favour'd
　France,
Thou hast had many a tale of woe to tell,
In ancient times as now.
　　　　　　　　　　　Anonymous.
　Chap. XIV.

HE was a son of Egypt, as he told me,
And one descended from those dread
　magicians,
Who waged rash war, when Israel
　dwelt in Goshen,
With Israel and her Prophet—match-
　ing rod
With his the sons of Levi's—and
　encountering
Jehovah's miracles with incantations,
Till upon Egypt came the avenging
　Angel,
And those proud sages wept for their
　first-born,
As wept the unletter'd peasant.
　　　　　　　　　　　Anonymous.
　Chap. XV.

RESCUE or none, Sir Knight, I am
　your captive;
Deal with me what your nobleness
　suggests—

Thinking the chance of war may one
    day place you
Where I must now be reckon'd—i' the
    roll
Of melancholy prisoners.

          Anonymous.

  Chap. XXIV.

No human quality is so well wove
In warp and woof, but there's some
    flaw in it;
I've known a brave man fly a shep-
    herd's cur,
A wise man so demean him, drivelling
    idiocy
Had wellnigh been ashamed on't.
    For your crafty,
Your worldly-wise man, he, above
    the rest,
Weaves his own snares so fine, he's
    often caught in them.

          Old Play.

  Chap. XXV.

WHEN princes meet, astrologers may
    mark it
An ominous conjunction, full of
    boding,
Like that of Mars with Saturn.

          Old Play.

  Chap. XXVI.

THY time is not yet out—the devil thou
    servest
Has not as yet deserted thee. He aids
The friends who drudge for him, as the
    blind man
Was aided by the guide, who lent his
    shoulder
O'er rough and smooth, until he
    reach'd the brink
Of the fell precipice—then hurl'd him
    downward.

          Old Play.

  Chap. XXIX.

OUR counsels waver like the unsteady
    bark,
That reels amid the strife of meeting
    currents.

          Old Play.

  Chap. XXX.

HOLD fast thy truth, young soldier.—
    Gentle maiden,
Keep you your promise plight—leave
    age its subtleties,
And grey-hair'd policy its maze of
    falsehood;
But be you candid as the morning sky,
Ere the high sun sucks vapours up to
    stain it.

          The Trial.

  Chap. XXXI.

'TIS brave for Beauty when the best
    blade wins her.

        The Count Palatine.

  Chap. XXXV.

XVIII.

FROM ST. RONAN'S WELL.

MOTTOES.

Quis novus hic hospes?

CH'M-MAID!—The Gemman in the
    front parlour!

BOOTS's *free Translation of the Aeneid.*

  Chap. II.

             THERE must
Be government in all society;
Bees have their Queen, and stag-herds
    have their leader;
Rome had her Consuls, Athens had
    her Archons,
And we, sir, have our Managing Com-
    mittee.

      The Album of St. Ronan's.

  Chap. III.

Come, let me have thy counsel, for I
    need it ;
Thou art of those, who better help
    their friends
With sage advice, than usurers with
    gold,
Or brawlers with their swords. I 'll
    trust to thee,
For I ask only from thee words, not
    deeds.

The Devil hath met his Match.

Chap. x.

Nearest of blood should still be next
    in love ;
And when I see these happy children
    playing,
While William gathers flowers for
    Ellen's ringlets,
And Ellen dresses flies for William's
    angle,
I scarce can think, that in advancing
    life,
Coldness, unkindness, interest, or
    suspicion,
Will e'er divide that unity so sacred
Which Nature bound at birth.

Anonymous.

Chap. xi.

Oh ! you would be a vestal maid, I
    warrant,
The bride of Heaven ? Come ! we may
    shake your purpose :
For here I bring in hand a jolly
    suitor
Hath ta'en degrees in the seven
    sciences
That ladies love best—he is young
    and noble,
Handsome and valiant, gay and rich,
    and liberal.

The Nun.

Chap. xxiii.

Thou bear'st a precious burden, gentle
    post,—
Nitre and sulphur ; see that it explode
    not.

Old Play.

Chap. xxvii.

As shakes the bough of trembling leaf,
    When sudden whirlwinds rise ;
As stands aghast the warrior chief,
    When his base army flies——

Chap. xxviii.

It comes—it wrings me in my parting
    hour,
The long-hid crime, the well-dis-
    guised guilt.
Bring me some holy priest to lay the
    spectre !

Old Play.

Chap. xxxii.

On the lee-beam lies the land, boys,
    See all clear to reef each course ;
Let the fore-sheet go—don't mind,
    boys,
    Tho' the weather should be worse.

The Storm.

Chap. xxxiii.

Sedet post equitem atra cura.

Still though the headlong cavalier,
O'er rough and smooth, in wild career,
    Seems racing with the wind,
His sad companion, ghastly pale,
And darksome as a widow's veil,
    Care—keeps her seat behind.

Horace.

Chap. xxxv.

What sheeted ghost is wandering
    through the storm ?
For never did a maid of middle earth
Choose such a time or spot to vent
    her sorrows.

Old Play.

Chap. xxxviii.

Here come we to our close,—for that
    which follows
Is but the tale of dull, unvaried misery.
Steep crags and headlong linns may
    court the pencil,
Like sudden haps, dark plots, and
    strange adventures;
But who would paint the dull and fog-
    wrapt moor,
In its long tract of sterile desolation?

Old Play.

Chap. xxxix.

XIX.

FROM REDGAUNTLET.

HOPE.

As lords their labourers' hire delay,
    Fate quits our toil with hopes to
    come,
Which, if far short of present pay,
    Still owns a debt and names a sum.

Quit not the pledge, frail sufferer, then,
    Although a distant date be given;
Despair is treason towards men,
    And blasphemy to Heaven.

Chap. x.

XX.

FROM THE BETROTHED.

REVEILLÉ.

Soldier, wake! the day is peeping;
Honour ne'er was won in sleeping,
Never when the sunbeams still
Lay unreflected on the hill:
'Tis when they are glinted back
From axe and armour, spear and jack,
That they promise future story,
Many a page of deathless glory.
Shields that are the foeman's terror,
Ever are the morning's mirror.

Arm and up! the morning beam
Hath call'd the rustic to his team,
Hath call'd the falc'ner to the lake,
Hath call'd the huntsman to the brake;
The early student ponders o'er
His dusty tomes of ancient lore.
Soldier, wake! thy harvest, fame;
Thy study, conquest; war, thy game.
Shield, that would be foeman's terror,
Still should gleam the morning's mirror.

Poor hire repays the rustic's pain;
More paltry still the sportsman's gain;
Vainest of all, the student's theme
Ends in some metaphysic dream:
Yet each is up, and each has toil'd
Since first the peep of dawn has smiled;
And each is eagerer in his aim
Than he who barters life for fame.
Up, up, and arm thee, son of terror!
Be thy bright shield the morning's
    mirror.

Chap. xix.

WOMAN'S FAITH.

Woman's faith, and woman's trust—
Write the characters in dust;
Stamp them on the running stream,
Print them on the moon's pale beam,
And each evanescent letter
Shall be clearer, firmer, better,
And more permanent, I ween,
Than the thing those letters mean.

I have strain'd the spider's thread
'Gainst the promise of a maid;
I have weigh'd a grain of sand
'Gainst her plight of heart and hand;
I told my true love of the token,
How her faith proved light, and her
    word was broken:
Again her word and truth she plight,
And I believed them again ere night.

Chap. xx.

VERSES IN THE STYLE OF THE DRUIDS.

I ASK'D of my harp, 'Who hath injured
    thy chords?'
And she replied, 'The crooked finger,
    which I mocked in my tune.'
A blade of silver may be bended—a
    blade of steel abideth:
Kindness fadeth away, but vengeance
    endureth.

The sweet taste of mead passeth from
    the lips,
But they are long corroded by the
    juice of wormwood;
The lamb is brought to the shambles, but
    the wolf rangeth the mountain;
Kindness fadeth away, but vengeance
    endureth.

I asked the red-hot iron, when it
    glimmer'd on the anvil,
'Wherefore glowest thou longer than
    the firebrand?'
'I was born in the dark mine, and the
    brand in the pleasant green-
    wood.'
Kindness fadeth away, but vengeance
    endureth.

I ask'd the green oak of the assembly
    wherefore its boughs were dry
    and sear'd like the horns of the
    stag:
And it show'd me that a small worm
    had gnaw'd its roots.
The boy who remembered the scourge
    undid the wicket of the castle
    at midnight.
Kindness fadeth away, but vengeance
    endureth.

Lightning destroyeth temples, though
    their spires pierce the clouds;
Storms destroy armadas, though their
    sails intercept the gale.

He that is in his glory falleth, and that
    by a contemptible enemy.
Kindness fadeth away, but vengeance
    endureth.

Chap. XXXI.

———

MOTTOES.

IN Madoc's tent the clarion sounds,
    With rapid clangour hurried far;
Each hill and dale the note rebounds,
    But when return the sons of war?
Thou, born of stern Necessity,
Dull Peace! the valley yields to thee,
    And owns thy melancholy sway.
                        Welsh Poem.
Chap. II.

O, SADLY shines the morning sun
    On leaguer'd castle wall,
When bastion, tower, and battlement,
    Seem nodding to their fall.
                        Old Ballad.
Chap. VII.

Now all ye ladies of fair Scotlánd,
    And ladies of England that happy
        would prove,
Marry never for houses, nor marry
        for land,
    Nor marry for nothing but only
        love.
                    Family Quarrels.
Chap. XII.

Too much rest is rust,
    There 's ever cheer in changing;
We tyne by too much trust,
    So we 'll be up and ranging.
                        Old Song.
Chap. XIII.

RING out the merry bells, the bride
    approaches,
The blush upon her cheek has shamed
    the morning,
For that is dawning palely. Grant,
    good saints,
These clouds betoken nought of evil
    omen!
                  Old Play.
  Chap. XVII.

Julia.   GENTLE sir,
You are our captive,—but we'll use
    you so,
That you shall think your prison joys
    may match
Whate'er your liberty hath known of
    pleasure.
  Roderick. No, fairest, we have trifled
    here too long;
And, lingering to see your roses
    blossom,
I've let my laurels wither.
                  Old Play.
  Chap. XXVII.

XXI.

FROM THE TALISMAN.

AHRIMAN.

DARK Ahriman, whom Irak still
Holds origin of woe and ill!
  When, bending at thy shrine,
We view the world with troubled eye
Where see we 'neath the extended sky,
  An empire matching thine?

If the Benigner Power can yield
A fountain in the desert field,
  Where weary pilgrims drink;
Thine are the waves that lash the rock,
Thine the tornado's deadly shock,
  Where countless navies sink!

Or if He bid the soil dispense
Balsams to cheer the sinking sense,
  How few can they deliver
From lingering pains, or pang intense,
Red Fever, spotted Pestilence,
  The arrows of thy quiver!

Chief in Man's bosom sits thy sway,
And frequent, while in words we pray
  Before another throne,
Whate'er of specious form be there,
The secret meaning of the prayer
  Is, Ahriman, thine own.

Say, hast thou feeling, sense, and form,
Thunder thy voice, thy garments storm,
  As Eastern Magi say;
With sentient soul of hate and wrath,
And wings to sweep thy deadly path,
  And fangs to tear thy prey?

Or art thou mix'd in Nature's source,
An ever-operating force,
  Converting good to ill;
An evil principle innate,
Contending with our better fate,
  And oh! victorious still?

Howe'er it be, dispute is vain,
On all without thou hold'st thy reign,
  Nor less on all within;
Each mortal passion's fierce career,
Love, hate, ambition, joy, and fear,
  Thou goadest into sin.

Whene'er a sunny gleam appears,
To brighten up our vale of tears,
  Thou art not distant far;
'Mid such brief solace of our lives,
Thou whett'st our very banquet-knives,
  To tools of death and war.

Thus, from the moment of our birth,
Long as we linger on the earth,
  Thou rul'st the fate of men;

2 D

Thine are the pangs of life's last hour,
And—who dare answer?—is thy
  power,
Dark Spirit! ended THEN?
Chap. III.

—◆—

A MINSTREL *sings :—*

WHAT brave chief shall head the forces
  Where the red-cross legions gather?
Best of horsemen, best of horses,
  Highest head and fairest feather.

Ask not Austria, why 'mid princes
  Still her banner rises highest;
Ask as well the strong-wing'd eagle
  Why to heaven he soars the nighest.
Chap. XI.

—◆—

THE LAY OF THE BLOODY VEST.

BLONDEL *sings :—*

FYTTE FIRST.

'TWAS near the fair city of Benevent,
When the sun was setting on bough
  and bent,
And knights were preparing in bower
  and tent,
On the eve of the Baptist's tournament;
When in Lincoln green a stripling
  gent,
Well seeming a page by a princess
  sent,
Wander'd the camp, and, still as he
  went,
Enquired for the Englishman, Thomas
  à Kent.

Far hath he fared, and farther must
  fare,
Till he finds his pavilion nor stately
  nor rare,—
Little save iron and steel was there;
And, as lacking the coin to pay
  armourer's care,
With his sinewy arms to the shoulders
  bare,
The good knight with hammer and
  file did repair
The mail that to-morrow must see
  him wear,
For the honour of Saint John and his
  lady fair.

'Thus speaks my lady,' the page said
  he,
And the knight bent lowly both head
  and knee,
' She is Benevent's Princess so high
  in degree,
And thou art as lowly as knight may
  well be—
He that would climb so lofty a tree,
Or spring such a gulf as divides her
  from thee,
Must dare some high deed, by which
  all men may see
His ambition is back'd by his high
  chivalrie.

' Therefore thus speaks my lady,' the
  fair page he said,
And the knight lowly louted with
  hand and with head,
' Fling aside the good armour in which
  thou art clad,
And don thou this weed of her night-
  gear instead,
For a hauberk of steel, a kirtle of thread:
And charge, thus attired, in the tournament dread,
And fight as thy wont is where most
  blood is shed,
And bring honour away, or remain
  with the dead.'

Untroubled in his look, and untroubled
    in his breast,
The knight the weed hath taken, and
    reverently hath kiss'd :
' Now blessed be the moment, the
    messenger be blest !
Much honour'd do I hold me in my
    lady's high behest ;
And say unto my lady, in this dear
    night-weed dress'd,
To the best armed champion I will not
    vail my crest ;
But if I live and bear me well 'tis her
    turn to take the test.'
Here, gentles, ends the foremost fytte
    of the Lay of the Bloody Vest.

FYTTE SECOND.

The Baptist's fair morrow beheld
    gallant feats —
There was winning of honour, and
    losing of seats—
There was hewing with falchions, and
    splintering of staves,
The victors won glory, the vanquish'd
    won graves.
O, many a knight there fought bravely
    and well,
Yet one was accounted his peers to
    excel,
And 'twas he whose sole armour on
    body and breast,
Seem'd the weed of a damsel when
    boune for her rest.

There were some dealt him wounds
    that were bloody and sore,
But others respected his plight, and
    forbore.
' It is some oath of honour,' they said,
    ' and I trow
'Twere unknightly to slay him achiev-
    ing his vow.'
Then the Prince, for his sake, bade
    the tournament cease,
He flung down his warder, the trum-
    pets sung peace ;

And the judges declare, and competi-
    tors yield,
That the Knight of the Night-gear,
    was first in the field.

The feast it was nigh, and the mass it
    was nigher,
When before the fair Princess low
    louted a squire,
And deliver'd a garment unseemly to
    view,
With sword-cut and spear-thrust all
    hack'd and pierced through ;
All rent and all tatter'd, all clotted
    with blood,
With foam of the horses, with dust,
    and with mud,
Not the point of that lady's small
    finger, I ween,
Could have rested on spot was un-
    sullied and clean.

' This token my master, Sir Thomas
    à Kent,
Restores to the Princess of fair Bene-
    vent ;
He that climbs the tall tree has won
    right to the fruit,
He that leaps the wide gulf should
    prevail in his suit ;
Through life's utmost peril the prize
    I have won,
And now must the faith of my mistress
    be shown :
For she who prompts knights on such
    danger to run,
Must avouch his true service in front
    of the sun.

' " I restore," says my master, " the
    garment I've worn,
And I claim of the Princess to don it
    in turn ;
For its stains and its rents she should
    prize it the more,
Since by shame 'tis unsullied, though
    crimson'd with gore," '

Then deep blush'd the Princess—yet
    kiss'd she and press'd
The blood-spotted robes to her lips
    and her breast.
'Go tell my true knight, church and
    chamber shall show,
If I value the blood on this garment or
    no.'

And when it was time for the nobles
    to pass,
In solemn procession to minster and
    mass,
The first walk'd the Princess in purple
    and pall,
But the blood-besmear'd night-robe she
    wore over all ;
And eke, in the hall, where they all
    sat at dine,
When she knelt to her father and
    proffer'd the wine,
Over all her rich robes and state jewels
    she wore
That wimple unseemly bedabbled with
    gore.

Then lords whisper'd ladies, as well
    you may think,
And ladies replied with nod, titter,
    and wink ;
And the Prince, who in anger and
    shame had look'd down,
Turn'd at length to his daughter, and
    spoke with a frown :
'Now since thou hast publish'd thy
    folly and guilt,
E'en atone with thy hand for the blood
    thou hast spilt ;
Yet sore for your boldness you both
    will repent,
When you wander as exiles from fair
    Benevent.'

Then out spoke stout Thomas, in hall
    where he stood,
Exhausted and feeble, but dauntless
    of mood :

'The blood that I lost for this daughter
    of thine,
I pour'd forth as freely as flask gives
    its wine ;
And if for my sake she brooks penance
    and blame,
Do not doubt I will save her from
    suffering and shame ;
And light will she reck of thy prince-
    dom and rent,
When I hail her, in England, the
    Countess of Kent.'

Chap. XXVII.

—◆◆—

MOTTOES.

Now change the scene—and let the
    trumpets sound,
For we must rouse the lion in his lair.
           Old Play.
Chap. VI.

THIS is the Prince of Leeches ; fever,
    plague,
Cold rheum, and hot podagra do but
    look on him,
And quit their grasp upon the tortured
    sinews.
           Anonymous.
Chap. IX.

ONE thing is certain in our Northern
    land :
Allow that birth, or valour, wealth, or
    wit,
Give each precedence to their pos-
    sessor,
Envy, that follows on such eminence,
As comes the lyme-hound on the roe-
    buck's trace,
Shall pull them down each one.
    Sir David Lindsay (sic).
Chap. XI.

You talk of Gaiety and Innocence!
The moment when the fatal fruit was
    eaten,
They parted ne'er to meet again; and
    Malice
Has ever since been playmate to light
    Gaiety,
From the first moment when the
    smiling infant
Destroys the flower or butterfly he
    toys with,
To the last chuckle of the dying miser,
Who on his deathbed laughs his last
    to hear
His wealthy neighbour has become a
    bankrupt.
                            Old Play.
    Chap. xiii.

'Tis not her sense—for sure, in that
    There's nothing more than common;
And all her wit is only chat,
    Like any other woman.
                            Song.
    Chap. xvi.

Were every hair upon his head a life,
And every life were to be supplicated
By numbers equal to those hairs quad-
    rupled,
Life after life should out like waning
    stars
Before the daybreak—or as festive
    lamps,
Which have lent lustre to the midnight
    revel,
Each after each are quench'd when
    guests depart!
                            Old Play.
    Chap. xvii.

This work desires a planet'ry in-
    tell'gence
Of Jupiter and Sol; and those great
    spirits
Are proud, fantastical. It asks great
    charges
To entice them from the guiding of
    their spheres
To wait on mortals.
                        Albumazar.
    Chap. xviii.

Must we then sheathe our still vic-
    torious sword;
Turn back our forward step, which
    ever trode
O'er foemen's necks the onward path
    of glory;
Unclasp the mail, which with a solemn
    vow,
In God's own house we hung upon
    our shoulders;
That vow, as unaccomplish'd as the
    promise
Which village nurses make to still their
    children,
And after think no more of?
                    The Crusade, a Tragedy.
    Chap. xix.

When beauty leads the lion in her
    toils,
Such are her charms, he dare not raise
    his mane,
Far less expand the terror of his fangs,
So great Alcides made his club a
    distaff,
And spun to please fair Omphale.
                            Anonymous.
    Chap. xx.

'Mid these wild scenes Enchantment
    waves her hand,
To change the face of the mysterious
    land;
Till the bewildering scenes around us
    seem
The vain productions of a feverish
    dream.
                    Astolpho, a Romance.
    Chap. xxiii.

A GRAIN of dust
Soiling our cup, will make our sense
    reject
Fastidiously the draught which we
    did thirst for ;
A rusted nail, placed near the faithful
    compass,
Will sway it from the truth, and wreck
    the argosy.
Even this small cause of anger and
    disgust
Will break the bonds of amity 'mongst
    princes,
And wreck their noblest purposes.
The Crusade.
  Chap. xxiv.

[THE tears I shed must ever fall !
  I weep not for an absent swain,
For time may happier hours recall,
  And parted lovers meet again.

I weep not for the silent dead,
  Their pains are past, their sorrows
    o'er,
And those that loved their steps must
    tread,
  When death shall join to part no
    more.]

But worse than absence, worse than
    death,
  She wept her lover's sullied fame,
And, fired with all the pride of birth,
  She wept a soldier's injured name [1].
Ballad.
  Chap. xxvi.

WE heard the tecbir,—so the Arabs
    call
Their shout of onset, when with loud
    acclaim
They challenge Heaven to give them
    victory.
Siege of Damascus.
  Chap. xxvii.

---

[1] Only the last stanza is Scott's.

XXII.

FROM WOODSTOCK.

A CONJURATION.

By pathless march, by greenwood tree,
It is thy weird to follow me ;
To follow me thro' the ghostly moon-
    light,
To follow me thro' the shadows of
    night,
To follow me, comrade, still art thou
    bound :
I conjure thee by the unstanch'd
    wound,
I conjure thee by the last words I
    spoke,
When the body slept and the spirit
    awoke,
In the very last pangs of the deadly
    stroke.
  Chap. xiv.

—⧓—

AN HOUR WITH THEE.

AN hour with thee ! When earliest day
Dapples with gold the eastern grey,
Oh, what can frame my mind to bear
The toil and turmoil, cark and care,
New griefs, which coming hours un-
    fold,
And sad remembrance of the old ?
        One hour with thee.

One hour with thee ! When burning
    June
Waves his red flag at pitch of noon ;
What shall repay the faithful swain,
His labour on the sultry plain ;
And, more than cave or sheltering
    bough,
Cool feverish blood and throbbing
    brow ?
        One hour with thee.

One hour with thee ! When sun is set,
Oh, what can teach me to forget
The thankless labours of the day;
The hopes, the wishes, flung away;
The increasing wants, and lessening
    gains,
The master's pride, who scorns my
    pains ?
                One hour with thee.

Chap. xxvi.

——◆——

MOTTOES.

Come forth, old man! Thy daughter's
    side
Is now the fitting place for thee :
When Time hath quell'd the oak's bold
    pride,
The youthful tendril yet may hide
The ruins of the parent tree.

Chap. ii.

Now, ye wild blades, that make loose
    inns your stage,
To vapour forth the acts of this sad
    age,
Stout Edgehill fight, the Newberys
    and the West,
And northern clashes, where you still
    fought best :
Your strange escapes, your dangers
    void of fear,
When bullets flew between the head
    and ear,
Whether you fought by Damme or the
    Spirit,
Of you I speak.

Legend of Captain Jones.

Chap. iii.

        Yon path of greensward
Winds round by sparry grot and gay
    pavilion ;
There is no flint to gall thy tender foot,

There 's ready shelter from each
    breeze, or shower.
But Duty guides not that way : see
    her stand,
With wand entwined with amaranth,
    near yon cliffs.
Oft where she leads thy blood must
    mark thy footsteps,
Oft where she leads thy head must
    bear the storm,
And thy shrunk form endure heat,
    cold, and hunger ;
But she will guide thee up to noble
    heights,
Which he who gains seems native of
    the sky ;
While earthly things lie stretch'd
    beneath his feet,
Diminish'd, shrunk, and valueless.

                Anonymous.

Chap. iv.

My tongue pads slowly under this new
    language,
And starts and stumbles at these
    uncouth phrases.
They may be great in worth and
    weight, but hang
Upon the native glibness of my lan-
    guage
Like Saul's plate-armour on the shep-
    herd boy,
Encumbering and not arming him.

                ? J. B.

Chap. v.

        Here we have one head
Upon two bodies : your two-headed
    bullock
Is but an ass to such a prodigy.
These two have but one meaning,
    thought, and counsel ;
And when the single noddle has spoke
    out,
The four legs scrape assent to it.

                Old Play.

Chap. x.

DEEDS are done on earth,
Which have their punishment ere the
    earth closes
Upon the perpetrators. Be it the
    working
Of the remorse-stirr'd fancy, or the
    vision,
Distinct and real, of unearthly being,
All ages witness that beside the couch
Of the fell homicide oft stalks the
    ghost
Of him he slew, and shows the
    shadowy wound.
                            Old Play.
    Chap. XIV.

WE do that in our zeal,
Our calmer moments are afraid to
    answer.
                        Anonymous.
    Chap. XVII.

THE deadliest snakes are those which,
    twined 'mongst flowers,
Blend their bright colouring with the
    varied blossoms,
Their fierce eyes glittering like the
    spangled dew-drop ;
In all so like what nature has most
    harmless,
That sportive innocence, which dreads
    no danger,
Is poison'd unawares.
                            Old Play.
    Chap. XXIV.

XXIII.

FROM CHRONICLES OF THE CANONGATE.

MR. CROFTANGRY *asketh :—*

WHAT ails me, I may not, as well as
    they,
Rake up some threadbare tales that
    mouid'ring lay

In chimney corners, wont by Christ-
    mas fires
To read and rock to sleep our ancient
    sires ?
No man his threshold better knows
    than I
Brute's first arrival and first victory,
Saint George's sorrel and his cross of
    blood,
Arthur's round board, and Caledonian
    wood.
    Chap. V.

MOTTOES.

(*From* THE TWO DROVERS.)

WERE ever such two loving friends !—
    How could they disagree ?
O thus it was he loved him dear,
    And thought how to requite him,
And having no friend left but he,
    He did resolve to fight him.
                        Duke upon Duke.
    Chap. II.

(*From* MY AUNT MARGARET'S
    MIRROR.)
                        THERE are times
When Fancy plays her gambols, in
    despite
Even of our watchful senses, when
    in sooth
Substance seems shadow, shadow
    substance seems,
When the broad, palpable, and marked
    partition,
'Twixt that which is and is not, seems
    dissolved,
As if the mental eye gain'd power to
    gaze
Beyond the limits of the existing world.
Such hours of shadowy dreams I better
    love
Than all the gross realities of life.
                        Anonymous

XXIV.

FROM THE FAIR MAID OF PERTH.

THE GLEE MAIDEN.

Ah, poor Louise! the livelong day
She roams from cot to castle gay;
And still her voice and viol say,
Ah, maids, beware the woodland way,
　　　　Think on Louise.

Ah, poor Louise! The sun was high,
It smirch'd her cheek, it dimm'd her eye,
The woodland walk was cool and nigh,
Where birds with chiming streamlets
　　vie
　　　　To cheer Louise.

Ah, poor Louise! The savage bear
Made ne'er that lovely grove his lair;
The wolves molest not paths so fair—
But better far had such been there
　　　　For poor Louise.

Ah, poor Louise! In woody wold
She met a huntsman fair and bold;
His baldric was of silk and gold,
And many a witching tale he told
　　　　To poor Louise.

Ah, poor Louise! Small cause to pine
Hadst thou for treasures of the mine;
For peace of mind that gift divine,
And spotless innocence, were thine,
　　　　Ah, poor Louise!

Ah, poor Louise! Thy treasure's reft!
I know not if by force or theft,
Or part by violence, part by gift;
But misery is all that's left
　　　　To poor Louise.

Let poor Louise some succour have!
She will not long your bounty crave,
Or tire the gay with warning stave—
For Heaven has grace, and earth a
　　grave
　　　　For poor Louise.
Chap. x.

THE BLOOD ORDEAL.

Viewless Essence, thin and bare,
Wellnigh melted into air;
Still with fondness hovering near
The earthly form thou once didst wear;

Pause upon thy pinion's flight,
Be thy course to left or right;
Be thou doom'd to soar or sink,
Pause upon the awful brink.

To avenge the deed expelling
Thee untimely from thy dwelling,
Mystic force thou shalt retain
O'er the blood and o'er the brain.

When the form thou shalt espy
That darken'd on thy closing eye;
When the footstep thou shalt hear,
That thrill'd upon thy dying ear;

Then strange sympathies shall wake,
The flesh shall thrill, the nerves shall
　　quake;
The wounds renew their clotter'd flood,
And every drop cry blood for blood.

　　Chap. xxii.

—◆◆—

A MELANCHOLY DIRGE.

Louise *sings to the Prince :—*

　　Yes, thou mayst sigh,
And look once more at all around,
At stream and bank, and sky and
　　ground.
Thy life its final course has found,
　　And thou must die.

　　Yes, lay thee down,
And while thy struggling pulses flutter,
Bid the grey monk his soul-mass
　　mutter,
And the deep bell its death-tone
　　utter—
　　Thy life is gone.

Be not afraid.
'Tis but a pang, and then a thrill,
A fever fit, and then a chill;
And then an end of human ill,
    For thou art dead.

Chap. xxx.

—◆—

BOLD AND TRUE.

OH, bold and true,
In bonnet blue,
That fear or falsehood never knew;
Whose heart was loyal to his word,
Whose hand was faithful to his sword:
Seek Europe wide from sea to sea,
But bonnie Blue-cap still for me!

I 've seen Almayn's proud champions
    prance;
I've seen the gallant knights of France,
Unrivalled with the sword and lance;
I 've seen the sons of England true
Wield the brown bill and bend the yew;
Search France the fair and England
    free—
But bonnie Blue-cap still for me!

Chap. xxxi.

—◆—

MOTTOES.

THE ashes here of murder'd Kings
    Beneath my footsteps sleep;
And yonder lies the scene of death,
    Where Mary learn'd to weep
            Captain Marjoribanks.

INTRODUCTORY.

' BEHOLD the Tiber!' the vain Roman
    cried,
Viewing the ample Tay from Baiglie's[1]
    side;
But where's the Scot that would the
    vaunt repay,
And hail the puny Tiber for the Tay?
            Anonymous.

Chap. i.

---

[1] [A pass of the Ochils above Glenfarg.]

FAIR is the damsel, passing fair,
    Sunny at distance gleams her smile!
Approach—the cloud of woeful care
    Hangs trembling in her eye the
        while.
            Lucinda, a Ballad.

Chap. xi.

THEN up and spak the auld gudewife,
    And, wow! but she was grim,—
' Had e'er your father done the like,
    It had been ill for him.'
            Lucky Trumbull.

Chap. xii.

O FOR a draught of power to steep
The soul of agony in sleep!
            Bertha.

Chap. xv.

A WOMAN wails for justice at the gate,
A widow'd woman, wan and desolate.
            Bertha.

Chap. xx.

LO! where he lies embalm'd in gore,
    His wound to Heaven cries;
The floodgates of his blood implore
    For vengeance from the skies.
            Uranus and Psyche.

Chap. xxiii.

THE hour is nigh; now hearts beat
        high;
    Each sword is sharpen'd well;
And who dares die, who stoops to fly,
    To-morrow's light shall tell.
            Sir Edwald.

Chap. xxxiii.

———

XXV.

FROM ANNE OF GEIERSTEIN.

THE SECRET TRIBUNAL.

'MEASURERS of good and evil,
Bring the square, the line, the level,—
Rear the altar, dig the trench,
Blood both stone and ditch shall drench;
Cubits six, from end to end,
Must the fatal bench extend—
Cubits six, from side to side,
Judge and culprit must divide.
On the east the Court assembles,
On the west the Accused trembles:
Answer, brethren, all and one,
Is the ritual rightly done?'

'On life and soul, on blood and bone,
One for all, and all for one,
We warrant this is rightly done.'

'How wears the night? Doth morning
    shine
In early radiance on the Rhine?
What music floats upon his tide?
Do birds the tardy morning chide?
Brethren, look out from hill and height,
And answer true, how wears the night?'

'The night is old; on Rhine's broad
    breast
Glance drowsy stars which long to rest,
  No beams are twinkling in the east.
There is a voice upon the flood,
The stern still call of blood for blood;
'Tis time we listen the behest.'

'Up, then, up! When day's at rest,
  'Tis time that such as we are
    watchers;
Rise to judgment, brethren, rise!
Vengeance knows not sleepy eyes,
  He and night are matchers.'

Chap. xx.

MOTTOES.

Away with me!
The clouds grow thicker; there! now
    lean on me;
Place your foot here; here, take this
    staff, and cling
A moment to that shrub; now give me
    your hand.
The chalet will be gained in half-an-
    hour.

Chap. ii.

I was one
Who loved the greenwood bank and
    lowing herd,
The russet guise, the lowly peasant's
    life,
Season'd with sweet content, more
    than the halls
Where revellers feast to fever-height.
    Believe me,
There ne'er was poison mix'd in
    maple bowl.

Anonymous.

Chap. v.

When we two meet, we meet like
    rushing torrents;
Like warring winds, like flames from
    various points,
That mate each other's fury. There is
    nought
Of elemental strife, were fiends to
    guide it,
Can match the wrath of man.

Frenaud.

Chap. vi.

They saw that city, welcoming the
    Rhine,
As from his mountain heritage he
    bursts,
As purposed proud Orgetorix of yore,
Leaving the desert region of the hills
To lord it o'er the fertile plains of Gaul.

Helvetia.

Chap. viii.

WE know not when we sleep nor when we wake.
Visions distinct and perfect cross our eye,
Which to the slumberer seem realities;
And while they waked, some men have seen such sights
As set at nought the evidence of sense,
And left them well persuaded they were dreaming.

Anonymous.

Chap. IX.

THESE be the adept's doctrines—every element
Is peopled with its separate race of spirits:
The airy Sylphs on the blue ether float;
Deep in the earthy cavern skulks the Gnome;
The sea-green Naiad skims the ocean-billow;
And the fierce fire is yet a friendly home
To its peculiar sprite, the Sala-mander.

Anonymous.

Chap. X.

TELL me not of it: I could ne'er abide
The mummery of all that forced civility.
'Pray, seat yourself, my lord,'—with cringeing hams
The speech is spoken; and with bended knee,
Heard by the smiling courtier.—
'Before you, sir?'
It must be on the earth then.' Hang it all!
The pride which cloaks itself in such poor fashion
Is scarcely fit to swell a beggar's bosom.

Old Play.

Chap. XXI.

A MIRTHFUL man he was; the snows of age
Fell, but they did not chill him. Gaiety,
Even in life's closing, touch'd his teeming brain
With such wild visions as the setting sun
Raises in front of some hoar glacier,
Painting the bleak ice with a thousand hues.

Old Play.

Chap. XXVIII.

AY, this is he who wears the wreath of bays
Wove by Apollo and the Sisters Nine,
Which Jove's dread lightning scathes not. He hath doft
The cumbrous helm of steel, and flung aside
The yet more galling diadem of gold;
And, with a leafy circlet round his brows,
He reigns the King of lovers and of poets.

Chap. XXIX.

WANT you a man
Experienced in the world and its affairs?
Here he is for your purpose. He's a monk:
He hath forsworn the world and all its work,
The rather that he knows it passing well,—
'Special the worst of it, for he's a monk.

Old Play.

Chap. XXX.

TOLL, toll the bell!
Greatness is o'er;
The heart has broke,
To ache no more;
An unsubstantial pageant all—
Drop o'er the scene the funeral pall.

Old Poem.

Chap. XXXII.

Here's a weapon now,
Shall shake a conquering general in
his tent,
A monarch on his throne, or reach a
prelate,
However holy be his offices,
E'en while he serves the altar.

Old Play.

Chap. xxxiv.

XXVI.

FROM COUNT ROBERT OF PARIS.

MOTTOES.

Othus.   This superb successor
Of the earth's mistress, as thou vainly
speakest,
Stands 'midst these ages as, on the
wide ocean,
The last spared fragment of a spacious
land
That in some grand and awful minis-
tration
Of mighty nature has engulfèd been,
Doth lift aloft its dark and rocky cliffs
O'er the wild waste around, and sadly
frowns
In lonely majesty.

Constantine Paleologus, Scene I.

Chap. ii.

Here, youth, thy foot unbrace,
Here, youth, thy brow unbraid ; ·
Each tribute that may grace
The threshold here be paid.
Walk with the stealthy pace
Which Nature teaches deer,
When, echoing in the chase,
The hunter's horn they hear.

The Court.

Chap. iii.

The storm increases : 'tis no sunny
shower,
Foster'd in the moist breast of March
or April,
Or such as parched Summer cools his
lip with ;
Heaven's windows are flung wide ;
the inmost deeps
Call in hoarse greeting one upon
another ;
On comes the flood in all its foaming
horrors,
And where's the dike shall stop it !

The Deluge, a Poem.

Chap. v.

Vain man ! thou mayst esteem thy
love as fair
As fond hyperboles suffice to raise.
She may be all that's matchless in
her person,
And all-divine in soul to match her
body ;
But take this from me—thou shalt
never call her
Superior to her sex while *one* survives,
And I am her true votary.

Old Play.

Chap. vi.

Between the foaming jaws of the
white torrent
The skilful artist draws a sudden
mound ;
By level long he subdivides their
strength,
Stealing the waters from their rocky
bed,
First to diminish what he means to
conquer ;
Then, for the residue he forms a road,
Easy to keep, and painful to desert,
And guiding to the end the planner
aim'd at.

The Engineer.

Chap. ix.

THOSE were wild times—the antipodes
    of ours :
Ladies were then who oftener saw
    themselves
In the broad lustre of a foeman's
    shield
Than in a mirror, and who rather
    sought
To match themselves in battle, than
    in dalliance
To meet a lover's onset. But though
    Nature
Was outraged thus she was not over-
    come.

    Chap. x.   *Feudal Times.*

WITHOUT—a ruin, broken, tangled,
    cumbrous ;
Within— it was a little paradise,
Where Taste had made her dwelling ;
    Statuary,
First-born of human art, moulded her
    images,
And bade men mark and worship.

                Anonymous.
    Chap. xi.

THE parties met. The wily, wordy
    Greek,
Weighing each word, and canvassing
    each syllable,
Evading, arguing, equivocating.
And the stern Frank came with two-
    handed sword,
Watching to see which way the balance
    sway'd,
That he might throw it in, and turn the
    scales.

    Chap. xii.   *Palestine.*

STRANGE ape of man ! who loathes thee
    while he scorns thee ;
Half a reproach to us and half a jest.

What fancies can be ours ere we have
    pleasure
In viewing our own form, our pride
    and passions,
Reflected in a shape grotesque as
    thine !

                Anonymous.
    Chap. xvi.

'TIS strange that, in the dark sul-
    phureous mine,
Where wild ambition piles its ripening
    stores
Of slumbering thunder, Love will
    interpose
His tiny torch, and cause the stern
    explosion
To burst, when the deviser's least
    aware.

                Anonymous.
    Chap. xvii.

ALL is prepared—the chambers of the
    mine
Are cramm'd with the combustible,
    which, harmless
While yet unkindled as the sable sand,
Needs but a spark to change its nature
    so
That he who wakes it from its
    slumbrous mood,
Dreads scarce the explosion less than
    he who knows
That 'tis his towers which meet its fury.

                Anonymous.
    Chap. xxiv.

HEAVEN knows its time ; the bullet
    has its billet,
Arrow and javelin each its destined
    purpose ;
The fated beasts of Nature's lower
    strain
Have each their separate task.

                Old Play.
    Chap. xxv.

XXVII.

FROM CASTLE DANGEROUS.

MOTTOES.

A TALE of sorrow, for your eyes may
    weep;
A tale of horror, for your flesh may
    tingle;
A tale of wonder, for the eyebrows
    arch
And the blood curdles if you read it
    rightly.
                 Old Play.
  Chap. v.

BEWARE, beware of the Black Friar:
  He still retains his sway,
For he's yet by right the Church's heir
  Whoever may be the lay.
Amundeville is lord by day,
  But the monk is lord by night;
Nor wine nor wassail could raise
  a vassal
  To question that Friar's right.
      Don Juan, Canto XVII (sic).
  Chap. IX.

WHERE is he? Has the deep earth
  swallow'd him?
Or hath he melted like some airy
  phantom
That shuns the approach of morn and
  the young sun?
Or hath he wrapt him in Cimmerian
  darkness,
And pass'd beyond the circuit of the
  sight
With things of the night's shadows?
            Anonymous.
  Chap. XI.

THE way is long, my children, long
  and rough,
The moors are dreary, and the woods
  are dark;
But he that creeps from cradle on to
  grave,
Unskill'd save in the velvet course of
  fortune,
Hath miss'd the discipline of noble
  hearts.
                Old Play.
  Chap. XIV.

HIS talk was of another world; his
  bodements
Strange, doubtful, and mysterious:
  those who heard him
Listen'd as to a man in feverish dreams,
Who speaks of other objects than the
  present,
And mutters like to him who sees a
  vision.
              Old Play.
  Chap. XVIII.

CRY the wild war-note, let the
  champions pass;
Do bravely each, and God defend the
  right.
Upon Saint Andrew thrice can they
  thus cry,
  And thrice they shout on height,
And then match'd them on the
  Englishmen,
  As I have told you right.
Saint George the bright, our ladies'
  knight,
  To name they were full fain;
Our Englishmen they cried on height,
  And thrice they shout again.
              Old Ballad.
  Chap. XX.

END OF POETRY AND VERSE FROM THE WAVERLEY NOVELS.

𝔇ramatic 𝔓ieces.

—◆◆—

HALIDON HILL:

𝔄 𝔐etrical 𝔇rama in 𝔗wo 𝔄cts.

—◆◆—

DRAMATIS PERSONAE.

SCOTTISH.

THE REGENT OF SCOTLAND.
GORDON,
SWINTON,
LENNOX,
SUTHERLAND, } *Scottish Chiefs and*
ROSS, *Nobles.*
MAXWELL,
JOHNSTONE,
LINDESAY,
SYMON DE VIPONT, *a Knight Templar.*

THE PRIOR OF MAISON-DIEU.
REYNALD, *Swinton's Squire.*
HOB HATTELY, *a Border Moss-Trooper.*
Heralds.

ENGLISH.

KING EDWARD III.
CHANDOS,
PERCY, } *English and Norman*
RIBAUMONT, *Nobles.*
THE ABBOT OF WALTHAMSTOW.

ACT I.

SCENE I.

The northern side of the eminence of Halidon. The back scene represents the summit of the ascent, occupied by the rearguard of the Scottish army. Bodies of armed men appear as advancing from different points to join the main body.

Enter DE VIPONT *and the* PRIOR OF MAISON-DIEU.

VIP. No farther, Father—here I need no guidance;

I have already brought your peaceful step
Too near the verge of battle.
  PRI. Fain would I see you join some Baron's banner
Before I say farewell. The honour'd sword,
That fought so well in Syria, should not wave
Amid the ignoble crowd.
  VIP. Each spot is noble in a pitched field,
So that a man has room to fight and fall on 't.
But I shall find out friends. 'Tis scarce twelve years

Since I left Scotland for the wars of
  Palestine,
And then the flower of all the Scottish
  nobles
Were known to me; and I, in my
  degree,
Not all unknown to them.
   PRI. Alas! there have been changes
  since that time.
The Royal Bruce, with Randolph,
  Douglas, Grahame,
Then shook in field the banners which
  now moulder
Over their graves i' the chancel.
   VIP.   And thence comes it,
That while I look'd on many a well-
  known crest
And blazon'd shield, as hitherward we
  came,
The faces of the Barons who displayed
  them
Were all unknown to me. Brave
  youths they seem'd;
Yet, surely, fitter to adorn the tilt-
  yard
Than to be leaders of a war. Their
  followers,
Young like themselves, seem like
  themselves unpractised:
Look at their battle-rank.
   PRI. I cannot gaze on 't with un-
  dazzled eye,
So thick the rays dart back from shield
  and helmet,
And sword and battle-axe, and spear
  and pennon.
Sure 'tis a gallant show! The Bruce
  himself
Hath often conquer'd at the head of
  fewer
And worse appointed followers.
   VIP. Ay, but 'twas Bruce that led
  them. Reverend Father,
'Tis not the falchion's weight decides
  a combat;
It is the strong and skilful hand that
  wields it.

Ill fate, that we should lack the noble
  King
And all his champions now! Time
  call'd them not,
For when I parted hence for Pales-
  tine
The brows of most were free from
  grizzled hair.
   PRI. Too true, alas! But well you
  know, in Scotland
Few hairs are silver'd underneath the
  helmet;
'Tis cowls like mine which hide them.
  'Mongst the laity
War's the rash reaper, who thrusts
  in his sickle
Before the grain is white. In three-
  score years
And ten, which I have seen, I have
  outlived
Wellnigh two generations of our
  nobles.
The race which holds yon summit is
  the third.
   VIP. Thou mayst outlive them also.
   PRI.   Heaven forfend!
My prayer shall be, that Heaven will
  close my eyes,
Before they look upon the wrath to
  come.
   VIP. Retire, retire, good Father!
  Pray for Scotland—
Think not on me. Here comes an
  ancient friend,
Brother in arms, with whom to-day
  I'll join me.
Back to your choir, assemble all your
  brotherhood,
And weary Heaven with prayers for
  victory.
   PRI. Heaven's blessing rest with
  thee, Champion of Heaven,
And of thy suffering country!

   [*Exit* PRIOR. VIPONT *draws a
  little aside and lets down the
  beaver of his helmet.*

Enter SWINTON, *followed by* REYNALD *and others, to whom he speaks as he enters.*

SWIN. Halt here, and plant my pennon, till the Regent
Assign our band its station in the host.

REY. That must be by the Standard. We have had
That right since good Saint David's reign at least.
Fain would I see the Marcher would dispute it.

SWIN. Peace, Reynald! Where the general plants the soldier,
There is his place of honour, and there only
His valour can win worship. Thou'rt of those
Who would have war's deep art bear the wild semblance
Of some disorder'd hunting, where, pell-mell,
Each trusting to the swiftness of his horse,
Gallants press on to see the quarry fall.
Yon steel-clad Southrons, Reynald, are no deer;
And England's Edward is no stag at bay.

VIP. (*advancing.*) There needed not, to blazon forth the Swinton,
His ancient burgonet, the sable Boar
Chain'd to the gnarl'd oak,—nor his proud step,
Nor giant stature, nor the ponderous mace,
Which only he, of Scotland's realm, can wield:
His discipline and wisdom mark the leader,
As doth his frame the champion. Hail, brave Swinton!

SWIN. Brave Templar, thanks! Such your cross'd shoulder speaks you;
But the closed visor, which conceals your features,
Forbids more knowledge. Umfraville, perhaps—

VIP. (*unclosing his helmet*). No; one less worthy of our sacred Order.
Yet, unless Syrian suns have scorch'd my features
Swart as my sable visor, Alan Swinton
Will welcome Symon Vipont.

SWIN. (*embracing him*). As the blithe reaper
Welcomes a practised mate, when the ripe harvest
Lies deep before him, and the sun is high!
Thou'lt follow yon old pennon, wilt thou not?
'Tis tatter'd since thou saw'st it, and the Boar-heads
Look as if brought from off some Christmas board
Where knives had notch'd them deeply.

VIP. Have with them, ne'ertheless. The Stuart's Chequer,
The Bloody Heart of Douglas, Ross's Lymphads,
Sutherland's Wild-cats, nor the royal Lion,
Rampant in golden tressure, wins me from them.
We'll back the Boar-heads bravely. I see round them
A chosen band of lances—some well known to me.
Where's the main body of thy followers?

SWIN. Symon de Vipont, thou dost see them all
That Swinton's bugle-horn can call to battle,
However loud it rings. There's not a boy
Left in my halls whose arm has strength enough
To bear a sword—there's not a man behind,
However old, who moves without a staff.

Striplings and greybeards, every one
  is here,
And here all should be—Scotland
  needs them all;
And more and better men, were each
  a Hercules,
And yonder handful centupled.
    VIP. A thousand followers—such,
    with friends and kinsmen,
Allies and vassals, thou wert wont to
  lead—
A thousand followers shrunk to sixty
  lances
In twelve years' space?—And thy
  brave sons, Sir Alan?
Alas! I fear to ask.
    SWIN. All slain, De Vipont. In my
    empty home
A puny babe lisps to a widow'd
  mother,
'Where is my grandsire! wherefore
  do you weep?'
But for that prattler, Lyulph's house
  is heirless.
I'm an old oak, from which the
  foresters
Have hew'd four goodly boughs, and
  left beside me
Only a sapling, which the fawn may
  crush
As he springs over it.
    VIP.   All slain?—alas!
    SWIN. Ay, all, De Vipont. And
    their attributes,
John with the Long Spear—Archibald
  with the Axe—
Richard the Ready—and my youngest
  darling,
My Fair-hair'd William—do but now
  survive
In measures which the grey-hair'd
  minstrels sing,
When they make maidens weep.
    VIP. These wars with England! they
    have rooted out
The flowers of Christendom. Knights,
  who might win

The sepulchre of Christ from the rude
  heathen,
Fall in unholy warfare!
    SWIN. Unholy warfare? ay, well
    hast thou named it;
But not with England—would her
  cloth-yard shafts
Had bored their cuirasses! their
  lives had been
Lost like their grandsire's, in the bold
  defence
Of their dear country; but in private
  feud
With the proud Gordon, fell my Long-
  spear'd John,
He with the Axe, and he men call'd
  the Ready,
Ay, and my Fair-hair'd Will: the
  Gordon's wrath
Devour'd my gallant issue.
    VIP. Since thou dost weep, their
    death is unavenged?
    SWIN. Templar, what think'st thou
    me? See yonder rock
From which the fountain gushes; is it
  less
Compact of adamant, though waters
  flow from it?
Firm hearts have moister eyes. They
  are avenged;
I wept not till they were—till the
  proud Gordon
Had with his life-blood dyed my
  father's sword,
In guerdon that he thinn'd my father's
  lineage;
And then I wept my sons. And, as the
  Gordon
Lay at my feet, there was a tear for him
Which mingled with the rest: we
  had been friends,
Had shared the banquet and the chase
  together,
Fought side by side; and our first
  cause of strife,
Woe to the pride of both! was but a
  light one.

VIP. You are at feud, then, with the mighty Gordon?

SWIN. At deadly feud. Here in this Border-land,
Where the sire's quarrels descend upon the son,
As due a part of his inheritance
As the strong castle and the ancient blazon;
Where private Vengeance holds the scales of justice,
Weighing each drop of blood as scrupulously
As Jews or Lombards balance silver pence;
Not in this land, 'twixt Solway and Saint Abb's,
Rages a bitterer feud than mine and his,
The Swinton and the Gordon

VIP. You, with some threescore lances, and the Gordon
Leading a thousand followers?

SWIN. You rate him far too low. Since you sought Palestine
He hath had grants of baronies and lordships
In the far-distant North. A thousand horse
His southern friends and vassals always number'd.
Add Badenoch kerne, and horse from Dee and Spey,
He'll count a thousand more. And now, De Vipont,
If the Boar-heads seem in your eyes less worthy
For lack of followers, seek yonder standard,
The bounding Stag, with a brave host around it;
There the young Gordon makes his earliest field,
And pants to win his spurs. His father's friend,
As well as mine, thou wert: go, join his pennon,
And grace him with thy presence.

VIP. When you were friends, I was the friend of both,
And now I can be enemy to neither.
But my poor person, though but slight the aid,
Joins on this field the banner of the two
Which hath the smaller following.

SWIN. Spoke like the generous Knight who gave up all,
Leading and lordship, in a heathen land
To fight a Christian soldier. Yet, in earnest,
I pray, De Vipont, you would join the Gordon
In this high battle. 'Tis a noble youth—
So fame doth vouch him—amorous, quick, and valiant;
Takes knighthood, too, this day, and well may use
His spurs too rashly in the wish to win them.
A friend like thee beside him in the fight
Were worth a hundred spears, to rein his valour
And temper it with prudence. 'Tis the aged eagle
Teaches his brood to gaze upon the sun
With eye undazzled.

VIP. Alas! brave Swinton, would'st thou train the hunter
That soon must bring thee to the bay? Your custom,
Your most unchristian, savage, fiend-like custom,
Binds Gordon to avenge his father's death.

SWIN. Why, be it so! I look for nothing else:
My part was acted when I slew his father,
Avenging my four sons; young Gordon's sword,

If it should find my heart, can ne'er
    inflict there
A pang so poignant as his father's did.
But I would perish by a noble hand,
And such will his be if he bear him
    nobly,
Nobly and wisely, on this field of
    Halidon.

Enter a PURSUIVANT.

PUR. Sir Knights, to council!—
    'tis the Regent's order
That knights and men of leading meet
    him instantly
Before the Royal Standard. Edward's
    army
Is seen from the hill-summit.
    SWIN. Say to the Regent, we obey
    his orders.   [*Exit* PURSUIVANT.
(*To* REYNALD.) Hold thou my casque,
    and furl my pennon up
Close to the staff. I will not show
    my crest,
Nor standard, till the common foe
    shall challenge them.
I'll wake no civil strife, nor tempt the
    Gordon
With aught that's like defiance.
    VIP. Will he not know your
    features?
    SWIN. He never saw me. In the
    distant North,
Against his will, 'tis said, his friends
    detain'd him
During his nurture—caring not, be-
    like,
To trust a pledge so precious near the
    Boar-tusks.
It was a natural but needless caution:
I wage no war with children, for I
    think
Too deeply on mine own.
    VIP. I have thought on it, and will
    see the Gordon
As we go hence to council. I do bear
A cross, which binds me to be Chris-
    tian priest

As well as Christian champion. God
    may grant
That I, at once his father's friend and
    yours,
May make some peace betwixt you.
    SWIN. When that your priestly zeal,
    and knightly valour,
Shall force the grave to render up the
    dead.   [*Exeunt severally.*

SCENE II.

*The summit of Halidon Hill, before the
Regent's Tent. The Royal Standard of
Scotland is seen in the background,
with the Pennons and Banners of
the principal Nobles around it.*

Council of Scottish Nobles and Chiefs.
SUTHERLAND, ROSS, LENNOX, MAX-
WELL, *and other Nobles of the highest
rank, are close to the* REGENT'S *person,
and in the act of keen debate.* VIPONT
with GORDON *and others remain
grouped at some distance on the right
hand of the Stage. On the left, standing also apart, is* SWINTON, *alone
and bare-headed. The Nobles are
dressed in Highland or Lowland
habits, as historical costume requires.
Trumpets, Heralds, &c. are in attendance.*

LEN. Nay, Lordings, put no shame
    upon my counsels.
I did but say, if we retired a little,
We should have fairer field and better
    vantage.
I've seen King Robert, ay, The
    Bruce himself,
Retreat six leagues in length, and
    think no shame on't.
    REG. Ay, but King Edward sent a
    haughty message,
Defying us to battle on this field,
This very hill of Halidon; if we
    leave it

Unfought withal, it squares not with
  our honour.

SWIN. (*apart*). A perilous honour
  that allows the enemy,
And such an enemy as this same
  Edward,
To choose our field of battle! He
  knows how
To make our Scottish pride betray its
  master
Into the pitfall.

[*During this speech the debate
  among the Nobles is continued.*

SUTH. (*aloud*). We will not back
  one furlong—not one yard,
No, nor one inch; where'er we find
  the foe,
Or where the foe finds us, there will
  we fight him.
Retreat will dull the spirit of our
  followers,
Who now stand prompt for battle.

ROSS. My Lords, methinks great
  Morarchat[1] has doubts
That, if his Northern clans once turn
  the seam
Of their check'd hose behind, it will
  be hard
To halt and rally them.

SUTH. Say'st thou, MacDonnell?
  Add another falsehood,
And name when Morarchat was
  coward or traitor?
Thine island race, as chronicles can tell,
Were oft affianced to the Southron
  cause,
Loving the weight and temper of their
  gold
More than the weight and temper of
  their steel.

REG. Peace, my Lords, ho!

ROSS (*throwing down his glove*).
  MacDonnell will not peace! There
  lies my pledge,
Proud Morarchat, to witness thee a liar.

MAX. Brought I all Nithsdale from
  the Western Border,
Left I my towers exposed to foraying
  England
And thieving Annandale, to see such
  misrule?

JOHN. Who speaks of Annandale?
  Dare Maxwell slander
The gentle House of Lochwood[2]?

REG. Peace, Lordings, once again.
  We represent
The Majesty of Scotland: in our
  presence
Brawling is treason.

SUTH. Were it in presence of the
  King himself,
What should prevent my saying ——

Enter LINDESAY.

LIN. You must determine quickly.
  Scarce a mile
Parts our vanguard from Edward's,
  On the plain
Bright gleams of armour flash through
  clouds of dust,
Like stars through frost-mist; steeds
  neigh and weapons clash;
And arrows soon will whistle—the
  worst sound
That waits on English war. You
  must determine.

REG. We are determined. We will
  spare proud Edward
Half of the ground that parts us.
  Onward, Lords;
Saint Andrew strike for Scotland!
  We will lead
The middle ward ourselves, the Royal
  Standard
Display'd beside us; and beneath its
  shadow
Shall the young gallants, whom we
  knight this day,
Fight for their golden spurs. Lennox,
  thou 'rt wise,

---

[1] Morarchate is the ancient Gaelic description of the
Earls of Sutherland.

[2] Lochwood Castle was the ancient seat of the
Johnstones, Lords of Annandale.

And wilt obey command ; lead thou
the rear.

LEN. The rear ! why I the rear ?
The van were fitter

For him who fought abreast with
Robert Bruce.

SWIN. (*apart*). Discretion hath forsaken Lennox too !

The wisdom he was forty years in
gathering

Has left him in an instant. 'Tis
contagious

Even to witness frenzy.

SUTH. The Regent hath determined
well ; the rear

Suits him the best who counsell'd
our retreat.

LEN. Proud Northern Thane, the
van were soon the rear

Were thy disorder'd followers planted
there.

SUTH. Then, for that very word,
I make a vow,

By my broad Earldom, and my father's
soul,

That, if I have not leading of the
van,

I will not fight to-day !

Ross. Morarchat ! thou the leading
of the van ?

Not whilst MacDonnell lives.

SWIN. (*apart*). Nay, then a stone
would speak.

(*Addresses the* REGENT.) May 't please
your Grace,

And you, great Lords, to hear an old
man's counsel,

That hath seen fights enow. These
open bickerings

Dishearten all our host. If that your
Grace

With these great Earls and Lords
must needs debate,

Let the closed tent conceal your disagreement ;

Else 'twill be said, ill fares it with
the flock

If shepherds wrangle when the wolf
is nigh.

REG. The old Knight counsels well.
Let every Lord

Or Chief, who leads five hundred
men or more,

Follow to council ; others are excluded—

We 'll have no vulgar censurers of
our conduct.

[*Looking at* SWINTON.

Young Gordon, your high rank and
numerous following

Give you a seat with us, though yet
unknighted.

GORDON. I pray you, pardon me.
My youth 's unfit

To sit in council, when that Knight's
grey hairs

And wisdom wait without.

REG. Do as you will ; we deign not
bid you twice.

[*The* REGENT, ROSS, SUTHERLAND,
LENNOX, MAXWELL, *&c., enter
the Tent. The rest remain grouped
about the Stage.*

GOR. (*observing* SWIN.) That helmet-
less old Knight, his giant stature,

His awful accents of rebuke and
wisdom,

Have caught my fancy strangely. He
doth seem

Like to some vision'd form which
I have dream'd of,

But never saw with waking eyes till
now.

I will accost him.

VIP. Pray you, do not so ;
Anon I 'll give you reason why you
should not.

There 's other work in hand.

GOR. I will but ask his name. There 's
in his presence

Something that works upon me like
a spell,

Or like the feeling made my childish
ear

Dote upon tales of superstitious
  dread,
Attracting while they chill'd my heart
  with fear.
Now, born the Gordon, I do feel right
  well
I'm bound to fear nought earthly;
  and I fear nought.
I'll know who this man is.

  [*Accosts* SWINTON.

Sir Knight, I pray you, of your gentle
  courtesy,
To tell your honour'd name. I am
  ashamed,
Being unknown in arms, to say that
  mine
Is Adam Gordon.

  SWIN. (*shows emotion, but instantly
  subdues it*). It is a name that
  soundeth in my ear
Like to a death-knell, ay, and like
  the call
Of the shrill trumpet to the mortal
  lists;
Yet 'tis a name which ne'er hath been
  dishonour'd,
And never will, I trust; most surely
  never
By such a youth as thou.

  GOR. There's a mysterious courtesy
  in this,
And yet it yields no answer to my
  question.
I trust you hold the Gordon not unworthy
To know the name he asks?

  SWIN. Worthy of all that openness
  and honour
May show to friend or foe; but, for
  my name,
Vipont will show it you, and, if it
  sound
Harsh in your ear, remember that it
  knells there
But at your own request. This day,
  at least,

Though seldom wont to keep it in
  concealment,
As there's no cause I should, *you* had
  not heard it.

  GOR. This strange——
  VIP. The mystery is needful. Fol-
  low me.
    [*They retire behind the side scene.*
  SWIN. (*looking after them*). 'Tis a
  brave youth. How blush'd his
  noble cheek,
While youthful modesty, and the em-
  barrassment
Of curiosity, combined with wonder,
And half suspicion of some slight in-
  tended,
All mingled in the flush; but soon
  'twill deepen
Into revenge's glow. How slow is
  Vipont!
I wait the issue as I've seen spec-
  tators
Suspend the motion even of the eye-
  lids
When the slow gunner, with his
  lighted match,
Approach'd the chargèd cannon, in
  the act
To waken its dread slumbers.—Now
  'tis out;
He draws his sword, and rushes
  towards me,
Who will nor seek nor shun him.

  Enter GORDON, *withheld by* VIPONT.

  VIP. Hold, for the sake of Heaven!
  O, for the sake
Of your dear country, hold! Has
  Swinton slain your father,
And must you, therefore, be yourself
  a parricide,
And stand recorded as the selfish
  traitor
Who in her hour of need his country's
  cause
Deserts, that he may wreak a private
  wrong?

Look to yon banner—that is Scotland's
   standard;
Look to the Regent—he is Scotland's
   general;
Look to the English—they are Scot-
   land's foemen!
Bethink thee, then, thou art a son of
   Scotland,
And think on nought beside.

   GOR. He hath come here to brave
   me! Off! unhand me!
Thou canst not be my father's ancient
   friend,
That stand'st 'twixt me and him who
   slew my father.
   VIP. You know not Swinton.
   Scarce one passing thought
Of his high mind was with you; now,
   his soul
Is fix'd on this day's battle. You
   might slay him
At unawares before he saw your blade
   drawn.
Stand still, and watch him close.

Enter MAXWELL *from the tent.*

   SWIN. How go our councils,
   Maxwell, may I ask?
   MAX. As wild as if the very wind
   and sea
With every breeze and every billow
   battled
For their precedence.
   SWI. Most sure they are possess'd!
   Some evil spirit,
To mock their valour, robs them of
   discretion.
Fie, fie, upon 't! Oh, that Dunferm-
   line's tomb
Could render up The Bruce! that
   Spain's red shore
Could give us back the good Lord
   James of Douglas!
Or that fierce Randolph, with his
   voice of terror,
Were here to awe these brawlers to
   submission!

   VIP. (*to* GOR.) Thou hast perused
   him at more leisure now.
   GOR. I see the giant form which all
   men speak of,
The stately port, but not the sullen
   eye,
Not the bloodthirsty look that should
   belong
To him that made me orphan. I shall
   need
To name my father twice ere I can
   strike
At such grey hairs, and face of such
   command;
Yet my hand clenches on my falchion
   hilt,
In token he shall die.
   VIP. Need I again remind you that
   the place
Permits not private quarrel?
   GOR. I'm calm. I will not seek—
   nay, I will shun it;
And yet methinks that such debate's
   the fashion.
You've heard how taunts, reproaches,
   and the lie,
The lie itself, have flown from mouth
   to mouth;
As if a band of peasants were disputing
About a football match, rather than
   chiefs
Were ordering a battle. I am young,
And lack experience: tell me, brave
   De Vipont,
Is such the fashion of your wars in
   Palestine?
   VIP. Such it at times hath been;
   and then the Cross
Hath sunk before the Crescent.
   Heaven's cause
Won us not victory where wisdom
   was not.
Behold yon English host come slowly
   on
With equal front, rank marshall'd
   upon rank,
As if one spirit ruled one moving body;

The leaders in their places, each
    prepared
To charge, support, and rally, as the
    fortune
Of changeful battle needs : then look
    on ours,
Broken, disjointed, as the tumbling
    surges
Which the winds wake at random.
    Look on both,
And dread the issue ; yet there might
    be succour.

    Gor. We 're fearfully o'ermatch'd
    in discipline ;
So even my inexperienced eye can
    judge.
What succour save in Heaven ?

    Vip. Heaven acts by human means.
    The artist's skill
Supplies in war, as in mechanic crafts,
Deficiency of tools. There 's courage,
    wisdom,
And skill enough, live in one leader
    here,
As, flung into the balance, might avail
To counterpoise the odds 'twixt that
    ruled host
And our wild multitude. I must not
    name him.

    Gor. I guess, but dare not ask.
    What band is yonder,
Arranged so closely as the English
    discipline
Hath marshall'd their best files ?

    Vip. Know'st thou not the pennon?
One day, perhaps, thou 'lt see it all
    too closely ;
It is Sir Alan Swinton's.

    Gor. These, then, are his, the
    relics of his power ;
Yet worth an host of ordinary men.
And I must slay my country's sagest
    leader,
And crush by numbers that determined
    handful,
When most my country needs their
    practised aid,

Or men will say, ' There goes de-
    generate Gordon ;
His father's blood is on the Swinton's
    sword,
And his is in his scabbard !' [Muses.

    Vip. (apart). High blood and mettle,
    mix'd with early wisdom,
Sparkle in this brave youth. If he
    survive
This evil-omen'd day, I pawn my word
That, in the ruin which I now forbode,
Scotland has treasure left. How close
    he eyes
Each look and step of Swinton! Is it
    hate,
Or is it admiration, or are both
Commingled strangely in that steady
    gaze ?

    [Swinton and Maxwell return from
        the bottom of the stage.

    Max. The storm is laid at length
    amongst these counsellors ;
See, they come forth.

    Swin. And it is more than time ;
For I can mark the vanguard archery
Handling their quivers, bending up
    their bows.

Enter the Regent *and Scottish Lords.*

    Reg. Thus shall it be, then, since
    we may no better ;
And, since no Lord will yield one jot
    of way
To this high urgency, or give the
    vanguard
Up to another's guidance, we will
    abide them
Even on this bent ; and as our troops
    are rank'd,
So shall they meet the foe Chief,
    nor Thane,
Nor Noble, can complain of the
    precedence
Which chance has thus assign'd him.

    Swin. (apart). O sage discipline,
That leaves to chance the marshalling
    of a battle !

Gor. Move him to speech, De
Vipont.

Vip. Move *him!* Move whom?

Gor. Even him, whom, but brief
space since,

My hand did burn to put to utter silence.

Vip. I'll move him to it. Swinton,
speak to them;

They lack thy counsel sorely.

Swin. Had I the thousand spears
which once I led

I had not thus been silent. But men's
wisdom

Is rated by their means. From the
poor leader

Of sixty lances, who seeks words of
weight?

Gor. (*stepping forward*). Swinton,
there's that of wisdom on thy brow,

And valour in thine eye, and that of
peril

In this most urgent hour, that bids
me say—

Bids me, thy mortal foe, say—
Swinton, speak

For King and Country's sake!

Swin. Nay, if that voice commands
me, speak I will;

It sounds as if the dead laid charge
on me.

Reg. (*to* Lennox, *with whom he
has been consulting*). 'Tis better
than you think. This broad hill-
side

Affords fair compass for our power's
display,

Rank above rank rising in seemly
tiers;

So that the rearward stands as fair
and open ——

Swin. As e'er stood mark before an
English archer.

Reg. Who dares to say so? Who
is 't dare impeach

Our rule of discipline?

Swin. A poor Knight of these
Marches, good my Lord;

Alan of Swinton, who hath kept a
house here,

He and his ancestry, since the old days
Of Malcolm, called the Maiden.

Reg. You have brought here, even
to this pitched field,

In which the Royal Banner is display'd,

I think some sixty spears, Sir Knight
of Swinton;

Our musters name no more.

Swin. I brought each man I had;
and Chief, or Earl,

Thane, Duke, or dignitary, brings no
more:

And with them brought I what may
here be useful

An aged eye; which, what with England, Scotland,

Spain, France, and Flanders, hath
seen fifty battles,

And ta'en some judgment of them; a
stark hand too,

Which plays as with a straw with
this same mace,—

Which if a young arm here can wield
more lightly,

I never more will offer word of counsel.

Len. Hear him, my Lord; it is the
noble Swinton:

He hath had high experience.

Max.   He is noted
The wisest warrior 'twixt the Tweed
and Solway:

I do beseech you, hear him.

John. Ay, hear the Swinton; hear
stout old Sir Alan;

Maxwell and Johnstone both agree
for once.

Reg. Where 's your impatience
now?

Late you were all for battle, would
not hear

Ourself pronounce a word; and now
you gaze

On yon old warrior in his antique
armour,

As if he were arisen from the dead
To bring us Bruce's counsel for the battle.

Swin. 'Tis a proud word to speak; but he who fought
Long under Robert Bruce may something guess,
Without communication with the dead,
At what he would have counsell'd. Bruce had bidden ye
Review your battle-order, marshall'd broadly
Here on the bare hillside, and bidden you mark
Yon clouds of Southron archers, bearing down
To the green meadow-lands which stretch beneath;
The Bruce had warn'd you not a shaft to-day
But shall find mark within a Scottish bosom,
If thus our field be order'd. The callow boys,
Who draw but four-foot bows, shall gall our front,
While on our mainward, and upon the rear,
The cloth-yard shafts shall fall like death's own darts,
And, though blind men discharge them, find a mark.
Thus shall we die the death of slaughter'd deer,
Which, driven into the toils, are shot at ease
By boys and women, while they toss aloft
All idly and in vain their branchy horns,
As we shall shake our unavailing spears.

Reg. Tush, tell not me! If their shot fall like hail,
Our men have Milan coats to bear it out.

Swin. Never did armourer temper steel on stithy
That made sure fence against an English arrow.
A cobweb gossamer were guard as good
Against a wasp-sting.

Reg. Who fears a wasp-sting?

Swin. I, my Lord, fear none;
Yet should a wise man brush the insect off,
Or he may smart for it.

Reg. We'll keep the hill; it is the vantage-ground
When the main battle joins.

Swin. It ne'er will join, while their light archery
Can foil our spearmen and our barbèd horse.
To hope Plantagenet would seek close combat
When he can conquer riskless, is to deem
Sagacious Edward simpler than a babe
In battle knowledge. Keep the hill, my Lord,
With the main body, if it is your pleasure;
But let a body of your chosen horse
Make execution on yon waspish archers.
I've done such work before, and love it well;
If 'tis your pleasure to give me the leading,
The dames of Sherwood, Inglewood, and Weardale,
Shall sit in widowhood and long for venison,
And long in vain. Whoe'er remembers Bannockburn,—
And when shall Scotsman, till the last loud trumpet,
Forget that stirring word?—knows *that* great battle
Even thus was fought and won.

Len. This is the shortest road to bandy blows;
For when the bills step forth and bows go back,

Then is the moment that our hardy
    spearmen,
With their strong bodies, and their
    stubborn hearts,
And limbs well knit by mountain
    exercise,
At the close tug shall foil the short-
    breath'd Southron.

Swin. I do not say the field will thus
    be won;
The English host is numerous, brave,
    and loyal ;
Their Monarch most accomplish'd in
    war's art,
Skill'd, resolute, and wary ——

Reg. And if your scheme secure
    not victory,
What does it promise us ?

Swin.   This much at least,—
Darkling we shall not die : the
    peasant's shaft,
Loosen'd perchance without an aim
    or purpose,
Shall not drink up the lifeblood we
    derive
From those famed ancestors who
    made their breasts
This frontier's barrier for a thousand
    years.
We 'll meet these Southron bravely
    hand to hand,
And eye to eye, and weapon against
    weapon ;
Each man who falls shall see the foe
    who strikes him.
While our good blades are faithful to
    the hilts,
And our good hands to these good
    blades are faithful,
Blow shall meet blow, and none fall
    unavenged ;
We shall not bleed alone.

Reg.   And this is all
Your wisdom hath devised ?

Swin. Not all ; for I would pray you,
    noble Lords,

(If one, among the guilty guiltiest,
    might),
For this one day to charm to ten
    hours' rest
The never-dying worm of deadly feud
That gnaws our vexèd hearts ; think
    no one foe
Save Edward and his host. Days
    will remain,
Ay, days by far too many will remain,
To avenge old feuds or struggles for
    precedence ;
Let this one day be Scotland's. For
    myself,
If there is any here may claim from
    me
(As well may chance) a debt of blood
    and hatred,
My life is his to-morrow unresisting,
So he to-day will let me do the best
That my old arm may achieve for the
    dear country
That 's mother to us both.
        [Gordon *shows much emotion
        during this and the preceding
        speech of* Swinton.
Reg. It is a dream—a vision ! If
    one troop
Rush down upon the archers, all will
    follow,
And order is destroy'd : we 'll keep
    the battle-rank
Our fathers wont to do. No more
    on 't. Ho !
Where be those youths seek knight-
    hood from our sword ?
    Her. Here are the Gordon, Somer-
    ville, and Hay,
And Hepburn, with a score of gallants
    more.
    Reg. Gordon, stand forth.
    Gor. I pray your Grace, forgive me.
    Reg. How ! seek you not for knight-
    hood ?
Gor.   I do thirst for 't.
But, pardon me ! 'tis from another
    sword.

REG. It is your Sovereign's ; seek
　　you for a worthier ?
GOR. Who would drink purely
　　seeks the secret fountain,
How small soever, not the general
　　stream,
Though it be deep and wide. My
　　Lord, I seek
The boon of knighthood from the
　　honour'd weapon
Of the best knight and of the sagest
　　leader
That ever graced a ring of chivalry.
Therefore I beg the boon on bended
　　knee,
Even from Sir Alan Swinton. [*Kneels.*
REG. Degenerate boy, abject at
　　once and insolent !
See, Lords, he kneels to him that
　　slew his father !
GOR. (*starting up*). Shame be on him
　　who speaks such shameful word !
Shame be on him, whose tongue
　　would sow dissension
When most the time demands that
　　native Scotsmen
Forget each private wrong !
SWIN. (*interrupting him*). Youth,
　　since you crave me
To be your sire in chivalry, I remind
　　you
War has its duties, Office has its
　　reverence ;
Who governs in the Sovereign's name
　　is Sovereign :
Crave the Lord Regent's pardon.
GOR. You task me justly, and I
　　crave his pardon,
　　　　　[*Bows to the* REGENT.
His and these noble Lords'; and pray
　　them all
Bear witness to my words. Ye
　　noble presence,
Here I remit unto the Knight of
　　Swinton
All bitter memory of my father's
　　slaughter,

All thoughts of malice, hatred, and
　　revenge ;
By no base fear or composition moved,
But by the thought, that in our
　　country's battle
All hearts should be as one. I do
　　forgive him
As freely as I pray to be forgiven,
And once more kneel to him to sue
　　for knighthood.
SWIN. (*affected, and drawing his sword*).
Alas ! brave youth, 'tis I should kneel
　　to you,
And, tendering thee the hilt of the
　　fell sword
That made thee fatherless, bid thee
　　use the point
After thine own discretion. For thy
　　boon—
Trumpets be ready—In the Holiest
　　name,
And in Our Lady's and Saint Andrew's
　　name,
　　　　[*Touching his shoulder with his
　　　　sword.*
I dub thee Knight ! Arise, Sir Adam
　　Gordon !
Be faithful, brave, and O be fortunate,
Should this ill hour permit !
　　　　[*The trumpets sound ; the Heralds
　　　　cry* 'Largesse,' *and the Atten-
　　　　dants shout* 'A Gordon ! A
　　　　Gordon !'
REG. Beggars and flatterers ! Peace,
　　peace, I say !
We'll to the Standard ; knights shall
　　there be made
Who will with better reason crave
　　your clamour.
LEN. What of Swinton's counsel ?
Here's Maxwell and myself think it
　　worth noting.
REG. (*with concentrated indignation*).
Let the best knight, and let the sagest
　　leader,—
So Gordon quotes the man who slew
　　his father,—

With his old pedigree and heavy mace,
Essay the adventure, if it pleases him,
With his fair threescore horse. As
    for ourselves,
We will not peril aught upon the
    measure.
    GOR. Lord Regent, you mistake;
    for if Sir Alan
Shall venture such attack, each man
    who calls
The Gordon chief, and hopes or fears
    from him
Or good or evil, follows Swinton's
    banner
In this achievement.
    REG. Why, God ha' mercy! this
    is of a piece.
Let young and old e'en follow their
    own counsel,
Since none will list to mine.
    ROSS. The Border cockerel fain
    would be on horseback;
'Tis safe to be prepared for fight or flight:
And this comes of it to give Northern
    lands
To the false Norman blood.
    GOR. Hearken, proud Chief of Isles!
    Within my stalls
I have two hundred horse; two
    hundred riders
Mount guard upon my castle, who
    would tread
Into the dust a thousand of your
    Redshanks,
Nor count it a day's service.
    SWIN. Hear I this
From thee, young man, and on the
    day of battle?
And to the brave MacDonnell?
    GOR. 'Twas he that urged me; but
    I am rebuked.
    REG. He crouches like a leash-hound
    to his master!
    SWIN. Each hound must do so that
    would head the deer;
'Tis mongrel curs that snatch at mate
    or master.

    REG. Too much of this. Sirs, to
    the Royal Standard!
I bid you, in the name of good King
    David.
Sound trumpets! sound for Scotland
    and King David.

    [*The* REGENT *and the rest go off,*
    and the Scene closes. Manent
    GORDON SWINTON, *and* VIPONT,
    with REYNALD *and followers.*
    LENNOX *follows the* REGENT*; but*
    returns, and addresses SWINTON.

    LEN. O were my western horse-
    men but come up;
I would take part with you!
    SWIN. Better that you remain.
They lack discretion; such grey head
    as yours
May best supply that want.
Lennox, mine ancient friend and
    honour'd lord,
Farewell, I think, for ever!
    LEN. Farewell, brave friend! and
    farewell, noble Gordon,
Whose sun will be eclipsed even as
    it rises!
The Regent will not aid you.
    SWIN. We will so bear us that as
    soon the blood-hound
Shall halt, and take no part, what
    time his comrade
Is grappling with the deer, as he
    stand still
And see us overmatch'd.
    LEN. Alas! thou dost not know
    how mean his pride is,
How strong his envy.
    SWIN. Then we will die, and leave
    the shame with him.
                [*Exit* LENNOX.
    VIP. (*to* GORDON). What ails thee,
    noble youth? What means this
    pause?
Thou dost not rue thy generosity?
    GOR. I have been hurried on by
    strong impulse,

Like to a bark that scuds before the
storm,
Till driven upon some strange and
distant coast,
Which never pilot dream'd of.
Have I not forgiven?
And am I not still fatherless?
Swin.   Gordon, no;
For while we live I am a father to thee.
Gor. Thou, Swinton? No! that
cannot, cannot be.
  Swin. Then change the phrase, and
say that while we live
Gordon shall be my son. If thou art
fatherless,
Am I not childless too? Bethink thee,
Gordon,
Our death-feud was not like the
household fire,
Which the poor peasant hides among
its embers,
To smoulder on, and wait a time for
waking.
Ours was the conflagration of the forest,
Which, in its fury, spares nor sprout
nor stem,
Hoar oak nor sapling, not to be
extinguish'd
Till Heaven in mercy sends down
all her waters;
But, once subdued, its flame is
quench'd for ever;
And spring shall hide the tract of
devastation
With foliage and with flowers. Give
me thy hand.
  Gor. My hand and heart! – And
freely now to fight!
  Vip. How will you act? (*To*
Swinton.) The Gordon's band
and thine
Are in the rearward left, I think, in
scorn:
Ill post for them who wish to charge
the foremost!
  Swin. We'll turn that scorn to
vantage, and descend

Sidelong the hill; some winding path
there must be.
O, for a well-skill'd guide!
    [Hob Hattely *starts up from
a thicket.*
  Hob. So here he stands. An
ancient friend, Sir Alan,—
Hob Hattely, or, if you like it better,
Hob of the Heron Plume, here stands
your guide.
  Swin. An ancient friend?—a most
notorious knave,
Whose throat I've destined to the
dodder'd oak
Before my castle, these ten months
and more.
Was it not you who drove from
Simprim-mains,
And Swinton-quarter, sixty head of
cattle?
  Hob. What then, if now I lead your
sixty lances
Upon the English flank, where they'll
find spoil
Is worth six hundred beeves?
  Swin. Why, thou canst do it, knave.
I would not trust thee
With one poor bullock; yet would
risk my life,
And all my followers, on thine honest
guidance.
  Hob. There is a dingle, and a most
discreet one
(I've trod each step by starlight),
that sweeps round
The rearward of this hill, and opens
secretly
Upon the archers' flank. Will not
that serve
Your present turn, Sir Alan?
  Swin.   Bravely, bravely!
  Gor. Mount, sirs, and cry my slogan.
Let all who love the Gordon follow me!
  Swin. Ay, let all follow; but in
silence follow.
Scare not the hare that's couchant
on her form;

The cushat from her nest; brush not,
if possible,
The dewdrop from the spray;
Let no one whisper, until I cry
'Havoc!'
Then shout as loud 's ye will. On,
on, brave Hob;
On, thou false thief, but yet most
faithful Scotsman!   [*Exeunt.*

—◦—

ACT II.

Scene I.

*A rising ground immediately in front
of the position of the English main
body.* Percy, Chandos, Ribaumont, *and other English and Norman
Nobles, are grouped on the Stage.*

Per. The Scots still keep the hill;
the sun grows high.
Would that the charge would sound.
Chan. Thou scent'st the slaughter,
Percy. Who comes here?

Enter the Abbot of Walthamstow.

Now, by my life, the holy priest of
Walthamstow,
Like to a lamb among a herd of wolves!
See, he's about to bleat.
Ab. The King, methinks, delays the
onset long.
Chan. Your general, Father, like
your rat-catcher,
Pauses to bait his traps, and set his
snares.
Ab. The metaphor is decent.
Chan.   Reverend sir,
I will uphold it just. Our good King
Edward
Will presently come to this battlefield,
And speak to you of the last tilting
match,
Or of some feat he did a twenty years
since;

But not a word of the day's work
before him.
Even as the artist, sir, whose name
offends you,
Sits prosing o'er his can, until the
trap fall,
Announcing that the vermin are se-
cured,
And then 'tis up, and on them.
Per. Chandos, you give your tongue
too bold a license.
Chan. Percy, I am a necessary evil.
King Edward would not want me, if
he could;
And could not, if he would. I know
my value.
My heavy hand excuses my light
tongue.
So men wear weighty swords in their
defence,
Although they may offend the tender
shin
When the steel-boot is doff'd.
Ab.   My Lord of Chandos,
This is but idle speech on brink of battle,
When Christian men should think
upon their sins;
For as the tree falls so the trunk must lie,
Be it for good or evil. Lord, bethink
thee,
Thou hast withheld from our most
reverend house
The tithes of Everingham and Settle-
ton;
Wilt thou make satisfaction to the
Church
Before her thunders strike thee? I do
warn thee
In most paternal sort.
Chan. I thank you, Father, filially.
Though but a truant son of Holy
Church,
I would not choose to undergo her
censures
When Scottish blades are waving at
my throat.
I'll make fair composition.

AB. No composition; I 'll have all, or none.

CHAN. None, then! 'tis soonest spoke. I 'll take my chance,
And trust my sinful soul to Heaven's mercy,
Rather than risk my worldly goods with thee.
My hour may not be come.

AB. Impious—impenitent—

PER. Hush! the King—the King!

Enter KING EDWARD, *attended by* BALIOL *and others.*

K. ED. (*apart to* CHANDOS). Hark hither, Chandos! Have the York-shire archers
Yet join'd the vanguard?

CHAN. They are marching thither.

K. ED. Bid them make haste, for shame; send a quick rider.
The loitering knaves! were it to steal my venison,
Their steps were light enough. How now, Sir Abbot?
Say, is your reverence come to study with us
The princely art of war?

AB. I 've had a lecture from my Lord of Chandos,
In which he term'd your Grace a rat-catcher.

K. ED. Chandos, how 's this?

CHAN. O, I will prove it, sir! These skipping Scots
Have changed a dozen times 'twixt Bruce and Baliol,
Quitting each House when it began to totter;
They 're fierce and cunning, treacher-ous, too, as rats,
And we, as such, will smoke them in their fastnesses.

K. ED. These rats have seen your back, my Lord of Chandos,
And noble Percy's too.

PER. Ay; but the mass which now lies weltering
On yon hillside, like a Leviathan
That 's stranded on the shallows, then had soul in 't,
Order and discipline, and power of action.
Now 'tis a headless corpse, which only shows
By wild convulsions that some life remains in 't.

K. ED. True, they had once a head; and 'twas a wise,
Although a rebel head.

AB. (*bowing to the* KING). Would he were here; we should find one to match him.

K. ED. There 's something in that wish which wakes an echo
Within my bosom. Yet it is as well,
Or better, that The Bruce is in his grave;
We have enough of powerful foes on earth:
No need to summon them from other worlds.

PER. Your Grace ne'er met The Bruce?

K. ED. Never himself; but in my earliest field
I did encounter with his famous cap-tains,
Douglas and Randolph. Faith! they press'd me hard.

AB. My Liege, if I might urge you with a question,
Will the Scots fight to-day?

K. ED. (*sharply*). Go look your bre-viary.

CHAN. (*apart*). The Abbot has it—
Edward will not answer
On that nice point. We must observe his humour.

[*Addresses the* KING.]

Your first campaign, my Liege? That was in Weardale,
When Douglas gave our camp yon midnight ruffle,
And turn'd men's beds to biers?

K. Ed. Ay, by Saint Edward! I
escaped right nearly.
I was a soldier then for holidays,
And slept not in mine armour: my
safe rest
Was startled by the cry of 'Douglas!
Douglas!'
And by my couch, a grisly chamberlain,
Stood Alan Swinton, with his bloody
mace.
It was a churchman saved me; my
stout chaplain,
Heaven quit his spirit! caught a
weapon up,
And grappled with the giant. How
now, Louis?

*Enter an Officer, who whispers
the* King.

K. Ed. Say to him,—thus—and
thus —— [*Whispers.*
Ab. That Swinton's dead. A monk
of ours reported,
Bound homeward from Saint Ninian's
pilgrimage,
The Lord of Gordon slew him.
Per. Father, and if your house
stood on our borders
You might have cause to know that
Swinton lives,
And is on horseback yet.
Chan. He slew the Gordon;
That's all the difference, a very trifle.
Ab. Trifling to those who wage a
war more noble
Than with the arm of flesh.
Chan. (*apart*). The Abbot's vex'd,
I'll rub the sore for him.
(*Aloud.*) I have seen priests that used
that arm of flesh,
And used it sturdily. Most reverend
Father,
What say you to the chaplain's deed
of arms
In the King's tent at Weardale?
Ab. It was most sinful, being against
the canon

Prohibiting all churchmen to bear
weapons;
And as he fell in that unseemly guise,
Perchance his soul may rue it.
K. Ed. (*overhearing the last words*).
Who may rue?
And what is to be rued?
Chan. (*apart*). I'll match his rever-
ence for the tithes of Everingham.
The Abbot says, my Liege, the deed
was sinful,
By which your chaplain, wielding
secular weapons,
Secured your Grace's life and liberty,
And that he suffers for 't in purga-
tory.
K. Ed. (*to the* Abbot). Say'st thou
my chaplain is in purgatory?
Ab. It is the canon speaks it, good
my Liege.
K. Ed. In purgatory! thou shalt
pray him out on 't,
Or I will make thee wish thyself
beside him.
Ab. My Lord, perchance his soul
is past the aid
Of all the Church may do; there is
a place
From which there's no redemption.
K. Ed. And if I thought my faithful
chaplain there,
Thou shouldst there join him, priest!
Go watch, fast, pray,
And let me have such prayers as will
storm Heaven;
None of your maim'd and mutter'd
hunting masses.
Ab. (*apart to* Chandos). For God's
sake take him off.
Chan. Wilt thou compound, then,
The tithes of Everingham?
K. Ed. I tell thee, if thou bear'st
the keys of Heaven,
Abbot, thou shalt not turn a bolt with
them
'Gainst any well-deserving English
subject.

AB. (*to* CHANDOS). We will compound and grant thee, too, a share
I' the next indulgence. Thou dost need it much,
And greatly 'twill avail thee.

CHAN. Enough! we're friends; and when occasion serves,
I will strike in.

[*Looks as if towards the Scottish Army.*

K. ED. Answer, proud Abbot; is my chaplain's soul,
If thou knowest aught on 't, in the evil place?

CHAN. My Liege, the Yorkshire men have gain'd the meadow.
I see the pennon green of merry Sherwood.

K. ED. Then give the signal instant! We have lost
But too much time already.

AB. My Liege, your holy chaplain's blessed soul—

K. ED. To hell with it and thee! Is this a time
To speak of monks and chaplains?

[*Flourish of Trumpets, answered by a distant sound of Bugles.*

See, Chandos! Percy! Ha, Saint George! Saint Edward!
See it descending now, the fatal hail-shower,
The storm of England's wrath, sure, swift, resistless,
Which no mail-coat can brook. Brave English hearts!
How close they shoot together! as one eye
Had aim'd five thousand shafts, as if one hand
Had loosed five thousand bow-strings!

PER. The thick volley
Darkens the air, and hides the sun from us.

K. ED. It falls on those shall see the sun no more.

The wingèd, the resistless plague is with them;
How their vex'd host is reeling to and fro;
Like the chafed whale with fifty lances in him,
They do not see, and cannot shun the wound.
The storm is viewless as death's sable wing,
Unerring as his scythe.

PER. Horses and riders are going down together.
'Tis almost pity to see nobles fall,
And by a peasant's arrow.

BAL. I could weep them,
Although they are my rebels.

CHAN. (*aside to* PERCY). His conquerors, he means, who cast him out
From his usurpèd kingdom. (*Aloud*)
'Tis the worst of it,
That knights can claim small honour in the field
Which archers win, unaided by our lances.

K. ED. The battle is not ended.

[*Looks towards the field.*

Not ended? scarce begun! What horse are these,
Rush from the thicket underneath the hill?

PER. They're Hainaulters, the followers of Queen Isabel.

K. ED. (*hastily*). Hainaulters! thou art blind; wear Hainaulters
Saint Andrew's silver cross? or would they charge
Full on our archers, and make havoc of them?
Bruce is alive again! ho, rescue! rescue!
Who was 't survey'd the ground?

RIBAU. Most royal Liege—

K. ED. A rose hath fallen from thy chaplet, Ribaumont.

RIBAU. I'll win it back, or lay my head beside it. [*Exit.*

K. Ed. Saint George! Saint Edward! Gentlemen, to horse,
And to the rescue! Percy, lead the bill-men;
Chandos, do thou bring up the men-at-arms.
If yonder numerous host should now bear down
Bold as their vanguard, [*to the Abbot*] thou mayst pray for us;
We may need good men's prayers. To the rescue,
Lords, to the rescue! ha, Saint George! Saint Edward! [*Exeunt.*

Scene II.

A part of the field of battle betwixt the two main armies. Tumults behind the scenes; alarums, and cries of 'Gordon, a Gordon,' 'Swinton,' &c.

Enter, as victorious over the English vanguard, Vipont, Reynald, *and others.*

Vip. 'Tis sweet to hear these war-cries sound together,—
Gordon and Swinton.
Rey. 'Tis passing pleasant, yet 'tis strange withal.
Faith, when at first I heard the Gordon's slogan
Sounded so near me, I had nigh struck down
The knave who cried it.

Enter Swinton *and* Gordon.

Swin. Pitch down my pennon in yon holly bush.
Gor. Mine in the thorn beside it; let them wave,
As fought this morn their masters, side by side.
Swin. Let the men rally, and restore their ranks
Here in this vantage-ground: disorder'd chase

Leads to disorder'd flight; we have done our part,
And if we 're succour'd now, Plantagenet
Must turn his bridle southward.
Reynald, spur to the Regent with the basnet
Of stout De Grey, the leader of their vanguard;
Say, that in battle-front the Gordon slew him,
And by that token bid him send us succour.
Gor. And tell him that when Selby's headlong charge
Had wellnigh borne me down, Sir Alan smote him.
I cannot send his helmet; never nut-shell
Went to so many shivers. Hark ye, grooms!
[*To those behind the scenes.*
Why do you let my noble steed stand stiffening
After so hot a course?
Swin. Ay, breathe your horses, they 'll have work anon,
For Edward's men-at-arms will soon be on us,
The flower of England, Gascony, and Flanders;
But with swift succour we will bide them bravely.
De Vipont, thou look'st sad?
Vip. It is because I hold a Templar's sword
Wet to the crossèd hilt with Christian blood.
Swin. The blood of English archers, what can gild
A Scottish blade more bravely?
Vip. Even therefore grieve I for those gallant yeomen,
England's peculiar and appropriate sons,
Known in no other land. Each boasts his hearth

And field as free as the best lord his
barony,
Owing subjection to no human vassal-
age,
Save to their King and law. Hence
are they resolute.
Leading the van on every day of battle,
As men who know the blessings they
defend ;
Hence are they frank and generous
in peace,
As men who have their portion in its
plenty :
No other kingdom shows such worth
and happiness
Veil'd in such low estate. Therefore
I mourn them.

SWIN. I 'll keep my sorrow for our
native Scots,
Who, spite of hardship, poverty,
oppression,
Still follow to the field their Chieftain's
banner,
And die in the defence on 't.

GOR. And if I live and see my halls
again
They shall have portion in the good
they fight for :
Each hardy follower shall have his field,
His household hearth and sod-built
home, as free
As ever Southron had. They shall
be happy !
And my Elizabeth shall smile to see it!
I have betray'd myself.

SWIN.   Do not believe it.
Vipont, do thou look out from yonder
height,
And see what motion in the Scottish
host,
And in King Edward's. [*Exit* VIPONT.
           Now will I counsel thee ;
The Templar's ear is for no tale of love,
Being wedded to his Order. But
I tell thee,
The brave young knight that hath no
lady-love

Is like a lamp unlighted ; his brave
deeds,
And its rich painting, do seem then
most glorious
When the pure ray gleams through
them.
Hath thy Elizabeth no other name ?

GOR. Must I then speak of her to
you, Sir Alan ?
The thought of thee, and of thy
matchless strength,
Hath conjured phantoms up amongst
her dreams.
The name of Swinton hath been spell
sufficient
To chase the rich blood from her
lovely cheek,
And wouldst thou now know hers ?

SWIN.   I would, nay must.
Thy father in the paths of chivalry,
Should know the load-star thou dost
rule thy course by.

GOR. Nay, then, her name is—
hark——   [*Whispers.*

SWIN. I know it well, that ancient
northern house.

GOR. O, thou shalt see its fairest
grace and honour
In my Elizabeth. And if music touch
thee ——

SWIN. It did, before disasters had
untuned me.

GOR. O, her notes
Shall hush each sad remembrance to
oblivion,
Or melt them to such gentleness of
feeling,
That grief shall have its sweetness.
Who, but she,
Knows the wild harpings of our native
land ?
Whether they lull the shepherd on his
hill,
Or wake the knight to battle ; rouse
to merriment,
Or soothe to sadness ; she can touch
each mood.

Princes and statesmen, chiefs re-
nown'd in arms,
And grey-hair'd bards, contend which
shall the first
And choicest homage render to the
enchantress.
SWIN. You speak her talent bravely.
GOR.   Though you smile,
I do not speak it half. Her gift
creative,
New measures adds to every air she
wakes;
Varying and gracing it with liquid
sweetness,
Like the wild modulation of the lark;
Now leaving, now returning to the
strain!
To listen to her, is to seem to wander
In some enchanted labyrinth of
romance,
Whence nothing but the lovely fairy's
will,
Who wove the spell, can extricate the
wanderer.
Methinks I hear her now!
SWIN.   Bless'd privilege
Of youth! There's scarce three
minutes to decide
'Twixt death and life, 'twixt triumph
and defeat,
Yet all his thoughts are in his lady's
bower,
List'ning her harping!
                    Enter VIPONT.
        Where are thine, De Vipont?
VIP. On death, on judgment, on
eternity!
For time is over with us.
SWIN. There moves not, then, one
pennon to our aid,
Of all that flutter yonder!
VIP. From the main English host
come rushing forward
Pennons enow, ay, and their Royal
Standard;
But ours stand rooted, as for crows to
roost on.

SWIN. (*to himself*). I'll rescue him at
least —Young Lord of Gordon,
Spur to the Regent; show the instant
need —
GOR. I penetrate thy purpose; but
I go not.
SWIN. Not at my bidding? I, thy
sire in chivalry,
Thy leader in the battle? I command
thee.
GOR. No, thou wilt not command
me seek my safety—
For such is thy kind meaning—at the
expense
Of the last hope which Heaven re-
serves for Scotland.
While I abide, no follower of mine
Will turn his rein for life; but were
I gone,
What power can stay them? and, our
band dispersed,
What swords shall for an instant stem
yon host,
And save the latest chance for victory?
VIP. The noble youth speaks truth;
and were he gone,
There will not twenty spears be left
with us.
GOR. No. bravely as we have begun
the field,
So let us fight it out. The Regent's
eyes,
More certain than a thousand messages,
Shall see us stand, the barrier of his
host
Against yon bursting storm. If not
for honour,
If not for warlike rule, for shame at
least
He must bear down to aid us.
SWIN.   Must it be so?
And am I forced to yield the sad
consent,
Devoting thy young life? O, Gordon,
Gordon!
I do it as the patriarch doom'd his
issue;

I at my country's, he at Heaven's
command ;
But I seek vainly some atoning sacrifice,
Rather than such a victim ! (*Trumpets.*) Hark, they come !
That music sounds not like thy lady's
lute.

Gor. Yet shall my lady's name mix
with it gaily.
Mount, vassals, couch your lances, and
cry ' Gordon !
Gordon for Scotland and Elizabeth !'
[*Exeunt. Loud Alarums.*

Scene III.

*Another part of the field of battle, ad-
jacent to the former Scene.*

Alarums. Enter Swinton, *followed
by* Hob Hattely.

Swi. Stand to it yet ! The man who
flies to-day,
May bastards warm them at his household hearth !

Hob. That ne'er shall be my curse.
My Magdalen
Is trusty as my broadsword.

Swi. Ha, thou knave,
Art thou dismounted too ?

Hob. I know, Sir Allan,
You want no homeward guide ; so
threw my reins
Upon my palfrey's neck, and let him
loose.
Within an hour he stands before my
gate ;
And Magdalen will need no other
token
To bid the Melrose monks say masses
for me.

Swi. Thou art resolved to cheat
the halter, then ?

Hob. It is my purpose,

Having lived a thief, to die a brave
man's death ;
And never had I a more glorious
chance for 't.

Swin. Here lies the way to it,
knave. Make in, make in,
And aid young Gordon !

[*Exeunt. Loud and long alarums.
After which the back Scene rises,
and discovers* Swinton *on the
ground,* Gordon *supporting
him ; both much wounded.*

Swin. All are cut down ; the reapers
have pass'd o'er us,
And hie to distant harvest. My toil 's
over ;
There lies my sickle (*dropping his
sword*). Hand of mine again
Shall never, never wield it !

Gor. O valiant leader, is thy light
extinguish'd ?
That only beacon-flame which promised safety
In this day's deadly wrack !

Swin. My lamp hath long been dim !
But thine, young Gordon,
Just kindled, to be quench'd so
suddenly,
Ere Scotland saw its splendour !

Gor. Five thousand horse hung
idly on yon hill,
Saw us o'erpower'd, and no one
stirr'd to aid us !

Swin. It was the Regent's envy.
Out !—alas !
Why blame I him ? It was our civil
discord,
Our selfish vanity, our jealous hatred,
Which framed this day of dole for our
poor country.
Had thy brave father held yon leading
staff,
As well his rank and valour might
have claim'd it,
We had not fall'n unaided. How,
O how

Is he to answer it, whose deed prevented——

GOR. Alas! alas! the author of the
death-feud,
He has his reckoning too! for had
your sons
And num'rous vassals lived, we had
lack'd no aid.

SWIN. May God assoil the dead, and
him who follows!
We've drank the poison'd beverage
which we brew'd:
Have sown the wind, and reap'd the
tenfold whirlwind!
But thou, brave youth, whose nobleness of heart
Pour'd oil upon the wounds our hate
inflicted;
Thou, who hast done no wrong,
need'st no forgiveness,
Why should'st thou share our punishment!

GOR. All need forgiveness. (*Distant alarum.*) Hark, in yonder
shout
Did the main battles counter!

SWIN. Look on the field, brave
Gordon, if thou canst,
And tell me how the day goes. But
I guess,
Too surely do I guess.

GOR. All's lost! all's lost! Of
the main Scottish host,
Some wildly fly, and some rush wildly
forward;
And some there are who seem to
turn their spears
Against their countrymen.

SWIN. Rashness, and cowardice, and
secret treason,
Combine to ruin us; and our hot
valour,
Devoid of discipline, is madmen's
strength,
More fatal unto friends than enemies!
I'm glad that these dim eyes shall
see no more on 't.

Let thy hands close them, Gordon;
I will dream
My fair-hair'd William renders me
that office!   [*Dies.*

GOR. And, Swinton, I will think
I do that duty
To my dead father.

Enter DE VIPONT.

VIP. Fly, fly, brave youth! A
handful of thy followers,
The scatter'd gleaning of this desperate
day,
Still hover yonder to essay thy
rescue.
O linger not! I'll be your guide to
them.

GOR. Look there, and bid me fly!
The oak has fall'n;
And the young ivy bush, which
learn'd to climb
By its support, must needs partake its
fall.

VIP. Swinton? Alas! the best, the
bravest, strongest,
And sagest of our Scottish chivalry!
Forgive one moment, if to save the
living,
My tongue should wrong the dead.
Gordon, bethink thee,
Thou dost but stay to perish with
the corpse
Of him who slew thy father.

GOR. Ay, but he was my sire in
chivalry:
He taught my youth to soar above
the promptings
Of mean and selfish vengeance;
gave my youth
A name that shall not die even on
this death-spot.
Records shall tell this field had not
been lost,
Had all men fought like Swinton and
like Gordon.   [*Trumpets.*
Save thee, De Vipont. Hark! the
Southron trumpets.

VIP. Nay, without thee I stir not.

Enter EDWARD, CHANDOS, PERCY,
BALIOL, *&c.*

GOR. Ay, they come on, the Tyrant
and the Traitor,
Workman and tool, Plantagenet and
Baliol.
O for a moment's strength in this
poor arm,
To do one glorious deed !

[*He rushes on the English, but is
made prisoner with* VIPONT.

K. ED. Disarm them—harm them
not ; though it was they
Made havoc on the archers of our
vanguard,
They and that bulky champion.
Where is he ?
CHAN. Here lies the giant ! Stay !
his name, young Knight ?
GOR. Let it suffice, he was a man
this morning.
CHAN. I question'd thee in sport.
I do not need
Thy information, youth. Who that
has fought
Through all these Scottish wars, but
knows his crest,
The sable boar chain'd to the leafy oak,
And that huge mace still seen where
war was wildest !
K. ED. 'Tis Alan Swinton !
Grim chamberlain, who in my tent at
Weardale,
Stood by my startled couch with
torch and mace,
When the Black Douglas' war-cry
waked my camp.
GOR. (*sinking down*). If thus thou
know'st him,
Thou wilt respect his corpse.
K. ED. As belted Knight and
crowned King, I will.
GOR. And let mine

Sleep at his side, in token that our death
Ended the feud of Swinton and of
Gordon.
K. ED. It is the Gordon ! Is there
aught beside
Edward can do to honour bravery,
Even in an enemy ?
GOR. Nothing but this ;
Let not base Baliol, with his touch
or look,
Profane my corpse or Swinton's. I've
some breath still,
Enough to say—Scotland—Elizabeth !
CHAN. Baliol, I would not brook
such dying looks,
To buy the crown you aim at.
K. ED. (*to* VIPONT). Vipont, thy
crossèd shield shows ill in warfare
Against a Christian king.
VIP. That Christian king is warring
upon Scotland ;
I was a Scotsman ere I was a Templar,
Sworn to my country ere I knew my
Order.
K. ED. I will but know thee as a
Christian champion,
And set thee free unransom'd.

Enter ABBOT OF WALTHAMSTOW.

AB. Heaven grant your Majesty
Many such glorious days as this has
been !
K. ED. It is a day of much and high
advantage ;
Glorious it might have been, had all
our foes
Fought like these two brave cham-
pions. Strike the drums,
Sound trumpets, and pursue the
fugitives,
Till the Tweed's eddies 'whelm them,
Berwick's render'd ;
These wars, I trust, will soon find
lasting close.

MACDUFF'S CROSS.

A Dramatic Sketch.

—◆◆—

DRAMATIS PERSONAE.

NINIAN,
WALDHAVE, } *Monks of Lindores.*   LINDESAY,
MAURICE BERKELEY, } *Scottish Barons.*

TO

MRS. JOANNA BAILLIE,

AUTHORESS OF

'THE PLAYS ON THE PASSIONS.'

———

PRELUDE.

NAY, smile not, Lady, when I speak
    of witchcraft,
And say that still there lurks amongst
    our glens
Some touch of strange enchantment.
    Mark that fragment,
I mean that rough-hewn block of
    massive stone,
Placed on the summit of this mountain-
    pass,
Commanding prospect wide o'er field
    and fell,
And peopled village and extended
    moorland,
And the wide ocean and majestic Tay,
To the far distant Grampians. Do not
    deem it
A loosen'd portion of the neighbouring
    rock,
Detach'd by storm and thunder,—
    'twas the pedestal

On which, in ancient times, a Cross
    was rear'd,
Carved o'er with words which foil'd
    philologists;
And the events it did commemorate
Were dark, remote, and undistin-
    guishable
As were the mystic characters it bore.
But, mark,—a wizard, born on Avon's
    bank,
Tuned but his harp to this wild
    northern theme,
And, lo! the scene is hallow'd. None
    shall pass,
Now, or in after days, beside that stone,
But he shall have strange visions;
    thoughts and words,
That shake, or rouse, or thrill the
    human heart,
Shall rush upon his memory when
    he hears
The spirit-stirring name of this rude
    symbol;
Oblivious ages, at that simple spell,
Shall render back their terrors with
    their woes,
Alas! and with their crimes; and the
    proud phantoms
Shall move with step familiar to his eye,

And accents which, once heard, the ear forgets not,
Though ne'er again to list them. Siddons, thine,
Thou matchless Siddons! thrill upon our ear ;
And on our eye thy lofty Brother's form
Rises as Scotland's monarch. But, to thee,
Joanna, why to thee speak of such visions ?
Thine own wild wand can raise them.

Yet since thou wilt an idle tale of mine,
Take one which scarcely is of worth enough
To give or to withhold. Our time creeps on,
Fancy grows colder as the silvery hair
Tells the advancing winter of our life.
But if it be of worth enough to please,
That worth it owes to her who set the task ;
If otherwise, the fault rests with the author.

SCENE I.

The summit of a Rocky Pass near to Newburgh, about two miles from the ancient Abbey of Lindores, in Fife. In the centre is MacDuff's Cross, an antique monument; and, at a small distance, on one side, a Chapel, with a lamp burning.

Enter, as having ascended the Pass, NINIAN *and* WALDHAVE, *Monks of Lindores.* NINIAN *crosses himself, and seems to recite his devotions.* WALDHAVE *stands gazing on the prospect, as if in deep contemplation.*

NIN. Here stands the Cross, good brother, consecrated
By the bold Thane unto his patron saint,
Magridius, once a brother of our house.

Canst thou not spare an ave or a creed ?
Or hath the steep ascent exhausted you ?
You trode it stoutly, though 'twas rough and toilsome.
    WAL. I have trode a rougher.
    NIN.   On the Highland hills—
Scarcely within our sea-girt province here,
Unless upon the Lomonds or Benarty.
    WAL. I spoke not of the literal path, good father,
But of the road of life which I have travell'd,
Ere I assumed this habit; it was bounded,
Hedged in, and limited by earthly prospects,
As ours beneath was closed by dell and thicket.
Here we see wide and far, and the broad sky,
With wide horizon, opens full around,
While earthly objects dwindle. Brother Ninian,
Fain would I hope that mental elevation
Could raise me equally o'er worldly thoughts,
And place me nearer heaven.
    NIN. 'Tis good morality. But yet forget not,
That though we look on heaven from this high eminence,
Yet doth the Prince of all the airy space,
Arch foe of man, possess the realms between.
    WAL. Most true, good brother; and men may be farther
From the bright heaven they aim at, even because
They deem themselves secure on 't.
    NIN. (*after a pause*. You do gaze—
Strangers are wont to do so—on the prospect.
Yon is the Tay roll'd down from Highland hills,

That rests his waves, after so rude a race,
In the fair plains of Gowrie; further westward
Proud Stirling rises; yonder to the east,
Dundee, the gift of God; and fair Montrose,
And still more northward lie the ancient towers ——
WAL. Of Edzell.
NIN. How? know you the towers of Edzell?
WAL. I've heard of them.
NIN. Then have you heard a tale,
Which when he tells, the peasant shakes his head,
And shuns the mouldering and deserted walls.
WAL. Why, and by whom, deserted?
NIN. Long the tale.
Enough to say that the last Lord of Edzell,
Bold Louis Lindesay, had a wife, and found
WAL. Enough is said, indeed,—since a weak woman,
Ay, and a tempting fiend, lost Paradise,
When man was innocent.
NIN. They fell at strife,
Men say, on slight occasion; that fierce Lindesay
Did bend his sword against De Berkeley's breast,
And that the lady threw herself between;
That then De Berkeley dealt the Baron's death-wound.
Enough, that from that time De Berkeley bore
A spear in foreign wars. But, it is said,
He hath return'd of late; and, therefore, brother,
The Prior hath ordain'd our vigil here,
To watch the privilege of the sanctuary,
And rights of Clan MacDuff.

WAL. What rights are these?
NIN. Most true! you are but newly come from Rome,
And do not know our ancient usages.
Know then, when fell Macbeth beneath the arm
Of the predestined knight, unborn of woman,
Three boons the victor ask'd, and thrice did Malcolm,
Stooping the sceptre by the Thane restored,
Assent to his request. And hence the rule,
That first when Scotland's King assumes the crown,
MacDuff's descendant rings his brow with it;
And hence, when Scotland's King calls forth his host,
MacDuff's descendant leads the van in battle;
And last, in guerdon of the crown restored,
Red with the blood of the usurping tyrant,
The right was granted in succeeding time,
That if a kinsman of the Thane of Fife
Commit a slaughter on a sudden impulse,
And fly for refuge to this Cross MacDuff,
For the Thane's sake he shall find sanctuary;
For here must the avenger's step be staid,
And here the panting homicide find safety.
WAL. And here a brother of your order watches,
To see the custom of the place observed?
NIN. Even so;—such is our convent's holy right,
Since Saint Magridius—blessed be his memory!—

Did by a vision warn the Abbot
Eadmir.
And chief we watch when there is
bickering
Among the neighbouring nobles, now
most likely
From this return of Berkeley from
abroad,
Having the Lindesay's blood upon
his hand.

WAL. The Lindesay, then, was
loved among his friends?

NIN. Honour'd and fear'd he was
—but little loved ;
For even his bounty bore a show of
sternness ;
And when his passions waked, he
was a Sathan
Of wrath and injury.

WAL. How now, Sir Priest!
(*fiercely*)—forgive me (*recol-
lecting himself* —I was dreaming
Of an old baron, who did bear about
him
Some touch of your Lord Reynold.

NIN. Lindesay's name, my brother,
Indeed was Reynold ;—and methinks,
moreover,
That, as you spoke even now, he
would have spoken.
I brought him a petition from our
convent :
He granted straight, but in such tone
and manner,
By my good saint! I thought myself
scarce safe
Till Tay roll'd broad between us.
I must now
Unto the chapel—meanwhile the
watch is thine ;
And, at thy word, the hurrying fugitive,
Should such arrive, must here find
sanctuary ;
And, at thy word, the fiery-paced
avenger
Must stop his bloody course, e'en as
swoln Jordan

Controll'd his waves soon as they
touch'd the feet
Of those who bore the ark.

WAL.   Is this my charge?

NIN. Even so ; and I am near,
should chance require me.
At midnight I relieve you on your
watch,
When we may taste together some
refreshment :
I have cared for it ; and for a flask of
wine—
There is no sin, so that we drink it
not
Until the midnight hour, when lauds
have toll'd.
Farewell a while, and peaceful watch
be with you !

[*Exit towards the Chapel.*

WAL. It is not with me, and alas!
alas !
I know not where to seek it. This
monk's mind
Is with his cloister match'd, nor lacks
more room.
Its petty duties, formal ritual,
Its humble pleasures and its paltry
troubles,
Fill up his round of life ; even as
some reptiles,
They say, are moulded to the very
shape,
And all the angles of the rocky
crevice,
In which they live and die. But for
myself,
Retired in passion to the narrow cell,
Couching my tirèd limbs in its recesses,
So ill-adapted am I to its limits,
That every attitude is agony.
How now ! what brings him back?

Re-enter NINIAN.

NIN. Look to your watch, my
brother ; horsemen come :
I heard their tread when kneeling in
the chapel.

WAL. (*looking to a distance*). My thoughts have rapt me more than thy devotion,
Else had I heard the tread of distant horses
Farther than thou couldst hear the sacring bell;
But now in truth they come : flight and pursuit
Are sights I 've been long strange to.
NIN. See how they gallop down the opposing hill!
Yon grey steed bounding down the headlong path,
As on the level meadow ; while the black,
Urged by the rider with his naked sword,
Stoops on his prey, as I have seen the falcon
Dashing upon the heron. Thou dost frown
And clench thy hand, as if it grasp'd a weapon !
WAL. 'Tis but for shame to see a man fly thus
While only one pursues him. Coward, turn !
Turn thee, I say! thou art as stout as he,
And well mayst match thy single sword with his !
Shame, that a man should rein a steed like thee,
Yet fear to turn his front against a foe !
I am ashamed to look on them.
NIN. Yet look again ; they quit their horses now,
Unfit for the rough path : the fugitive
Keeps the advantage still. They strain towards us.
WAL. I 'll not believe that ever the bold Thane
Rear'd up his Cross to be a sanctuary
To the base coward, who shunn'd an equal combat.
How's this ?—that look—that mien—mine eyes grow dizzy !

NIN. He comes ! Thou art a novice on this watch, —
Brother, I 'll take the word and speak to him.
Pluck down thy cowl ; know that we spiritual champions
Have honour to maintain, and must not seem
To quail before the laity.
    [WALDHAVE *lets down his cowl,
    and steps back.*

Enter MAURICE BERKELEY.

NIN. Who art thou, stranger? speak thy name and purpose.
BER. I claim the privilege of Clan MacDuff.
My name is Maurice Berkeley, and my lineage
Allies me nearly with the Thane of Fife.
NIN. Give us to know the cause of sanctuary?
BER. Let him show it
Against whose violence I claim the privilege.

Enter LINDESAY, *with his sword drawn. He rushes at* BERKELEY; NINIAN *interposes.*
NIN. Peace, in the name of Saint Magridius !
Peace, in our Prior's name, and in the name
Of that dear symbol, which did purchase peace
And goodwill towards man ! I do command thee
To sheathe thy sword, and stir no contest here.
LIN. One charm I 'll try first,
To lure the craven from the enchanted circle
Which he hath harbour'd in. Hear you, De Berkeley !
This is my brother's sword ; the hand it arms

Is weapon'd to avenge a brother's
  death;
If thou hast heart to step a furlong off,
And change three blows—even for
  so short a space
As these good men may say an ave-
  marie—
So Heaven be good to me! I will
  forgive thee
Thy deed and all its consequences.

    BER. Were not my right hand
  fetter'd by the thought
That slaying thee were but a double
  guilt
In which to steep my soul, no bridegroom ever
Stepp'd forth to trip a measure with
  his bride
More joyfully than I, young man,
  would rush
To meet thy challenge.

    LIN. He quails, and shuns to look
  upon my weapon,
Yet boasts himself a Berkeley!

    BER. Lindesay, and if there were
  no deeper cause
For shunning thee than terror of thy
  weapon,
That rock-hewn Cross as soon should
  start and stir
Because a shepherd-boy blew horn
  beneath it,
As I for brag of thine.

    NIN. I charge you both, and in the
  name of Heaven,
Breathe no defiance on this sacred spot,
Where Christian men must bear them
  peacefully,
On pain of the Church thunders.
  Calmly tell
Your cause of difference; and, Lord
  Lindesay, thou
Be first to speak them.

    LIN. Ask the blue welkin, ask the
  silver Tay,
The northern Grampians—all things
  know my wrongs:

But ask not me to tell them, while
  the villain
Who wrought them stands and listens
  with a smile.

    NIN. It is said—
Since you refer us thus to general
  fame—
That Berkeley slew thy brother, the
  Lord Louis,
In his own halls at Edzell ——

    LIN.   Ay, in his halls—
In his own halls, good father; that's
  the word!
In his own halls he slew him, while
  the wine
Pass'd on the board between! The
  gallant Thane,
Who wreak'd Macbeth's inhospitable
  murder,
Rear'd not yon Cross to sanction
  deeds like these.

    BER. Thou say'st I came a guest!
  I came a victim,
A destined victim, train'd on to the
  doom
His frantic jealousy prepared for me.
He fix'd a quarrel on me, and we fought.
Can I forget the form that came
  between us
And perish'd by his sword? 'Twas
  then I fought
For vengeance; until then I guarded
  life;
But then I sought to take it, and
  prevail'd.

    LIN. Wretch! thou didst first dis-
  honour to thy victim,
And then didst slay him!

    BER. There is a busy fiend tugs at
  my heart,
But I will struggle with it! Youthful
  knight,
My heart is sick of war, my hand of
  slaughter;
I come not to my lordships, or my land,
But just to seek a spot in some cold
  cloister

Which I may kneel on living, and, when dead,
Which may suffice to cover me.
Forgive me that I caused your brother's death ;
And I forgive thee the injurious terms
With which thou taxest me.

LIN. Take worse and blacker ! Murderer, adulterer !—
Art thou not moved yet ?

BER.   Do not press me further.
The hunted stag, even when he seeks the thicket,
Compell'd to stand at bay, grows dangerous !
Most true thy brother perish'd by my hand,
And if you term it murder—I must bear it.
Thus far my patience can ; but if thou brand
The purity of yonder martyr'd saint,
Whom then my sword but poorly did avenge,
With one injurious word, come to the valley,
And I will show thee how it shall be answer'd !

NIN. This heat, Lord Berkeley, doth but ill accord
With thy late pious patience.

BER. Father, forgive, and let me stand excused
To Heaven and thee, if patience brooks no more.
I loved this lady fondly—truly loved—
Loved her, and was beloved, ere yet her father
Conferr'd her on another. While she lived,
Each thought of her was to my soul as hallow'd
As those I send to heaven ; and on her grave,
Her bloody, early grave, while this poor hand

Can hold a sword, shall no one cast a scorn.

LIN. Follow me.   Thou shalt hear me call the adulteress
By her right name.   I'm glad there's yet a spur
Can rouse thy sluggard mettle.

BER. Make then obeisance to the blessed Cross,
For it shall be on earth thy last devotion.   [*They are going off.*
WAL. (*rushing forward*). Madmen, stand !
Stay but one second—answer but one question.
There, Maurice Berkeley, can'st thou look upon
That blessed sign, and swear thou 'st spoken truth ?

BER. I swear by Heaven,
And by the memory of that murder'd innocent,
Each seeming charge against her was as false
As our bless'd Lady 's spotless. Hear, each saint !
Hear me, thou holy rood ! hear me from Heaven,
Thou martyr'd excellence !   Hear me from penal fire
(For sure not yet thy guilt is expiated!)
Stern ghost of her destroyer !

WAL. (*throws back his cowl*).   He hears ! he hears ! Thy spell hath raised the dead.

LIN. My brother ! and alive !

WAL. Alive,—but yet, my Richard, dead to thee ;
No tie of kindred binds me to the world ;
All were renounced, when, with reviving life,
Came the desire to seek the sacred cloister.
Alas, in vain ! for to that last retreat,
Like to a pack of bloodhounds in full chase,

My passion and my wrongs have
  follow'd me,
Wrath and remorse; and, to fill up
  the cry,
Thou hast brought vengeance hither.
  LIN.   I but sought
To do the act and duty of a brother.
  WAL. I ceased to be so when I left
  the world;
But if he can forgive as I forgive,
God sends me here a brother in mine
  enemy,
To pray for me and with me. If thou
  canst,

De Berkeley, give thine hand.
    BER. (*gives his hand*). It is the will
Of Heaven, made manifest in thy
  preservation,
To inhibit farther bloodshed; for
  De Berkeley,—
The votary Maurice lays the title down.
Go to his halls, Lord Richard, where
  a maiden,
Kin to his blood, and daughter in
  affection,
Heirs his broad lands:—if thou canst
  love her, Lindesay,
Woo her, and be successful.

THE DOOM OF DEVORGOIL.

—◆◆—

DRAMATIS PERSONAE.

OSWALD OF DEVORGOIL, *a decayed Scottish Baron.*
LEONARD, *a Ranger.*
DURWARD, *a Palmer.*
LANCELOT BLACKTHORN, *a Companion of Leonard, in love with Katleen.*
GULLCRAMMER, *a conceited Student.*
OWLSPIEGLE *and* COCKLEDEMOY, } *Maskers, represented by Blackthorn and Katleen.*

SPIRIT OF LORD ERICK OF DEVORGOIL.

Peasants, Shepherds, and Vassals of inferior rank.

ELEANOR, *Wife of Oswald, descended of obscure parentage*
FLORA, *Daughter of Oswald.*
KATLEEN, *Niece of Eleanor.*

ACT I.

SCENE I.

The Scene represents a wild and hilly, but not a mountainous country, in a frontier district of Scotland. The flat Scene exhibits the Castle of Devorgoil, decayed and partly ruinous, situated upon a Lake, and connected with the land by a drawbridge, which is lowered. Time—Sunset.

FLORA *enters from the Castle, looks timidly around, then comes forward and speaks.*

FLO. He is not here —those pleasures
  are not ours
Which placid evening brings to all
  things else.

SONG.

The sun upon the lake is low,
  The wild birds hush their song,
The hills have evening's deepest glow,
  Yet Leonard tarries long.
Now all whom varied toil and care
  From home and love divide,
In the calm sunset may repair
  Each to the loved one's side.

The noble dame, on turret high,
　Who waits her gallant knight,
Looks to the western beam to spy
　The flash of armour bright.
The village maid, with hand on
　brow,
　The level ray to shade,
Upon the footpath watches now
　For Colin's darkening plaid.

Now to their mates the wild swans
　row,
　By day they swam apart;
And to the thicket wanders slow
　The hind beside the hart.
The woodlark at his partner's side,
　Twitters his closing song;
All meet whom day and care divide,
　But Leonard tarries long.

[KATLEEN *has come out of the Castle
while* FLORA *was singing, and
speaks when the song is ended.*

KAT. Ah, my dear coz!—if that
　your mother's niece
May so presume to call your father's
　daughter—
All these fond things have got some
　home of comfort
To tempt their rovers back: the lady's
　bower,
The shepherdess's hut, the wild
　swan's couch
Among the rushes, even the lark's low
　nest
Has that of promise which lures home
　a lover,—
But we have nought of this.
　FLO. How call you, then, this castle
　of my sire,
The towers of Devorgoil?
　KAT. Dungeons for men, and
　palaces for owls;
Yet no wise owl would change a
　farmer's barn
For yonder hungry hall. Our latest
　mouse,

Our last of mice, I tell you, has been
　found
Starved in the pantry; and the rever-
　end spider,
Sole living tenant of the Baron's halls,
Who, train'd to abstinence, lived a
　whole summer
Upon a single fly, he's famish'd too;
The cat is in the kitchen-chimney
　seated
Upon our last of fagots, destined soon
To dress our last of suppers, and, poor
　soul,
Is starved with cold, and mewling
　mad with hunger.
　FLO. D'ye mock our misery,
　Katleen?
　KAT. No, but I am hysteric on the
　subject,
So I must laugh or cry, and laughing's
　lightest.
　FLO. Why stay you with us, then,
　my merry cousin?
From you my sire can ask no filial duty.
　KAT. No, thanks to Heaven!
No noble in wide Scotland, rich or
　poor,
Can claim an interest in the vulgar
　blood
That dances in my veins; and I might
　wed
A forester to-morrow, nothing fearing
The wrath of high-born kindred, and
　far less
That the dry bones of lead-lapp'd an-
　cestors
Would clatter in their cerements at
　the tidings.
　FLO. My mother, too, would gladly
　see you placed
Beyond the verge of our unhappiness,
Which, like a witch's circle, blights
　and taints
Whatever comes within it.
　KAT. 　　　Ah! my good aunt!
She is a careful kinswoman and
　prudent,

In all but marrying a ruin'd baron,
When she could take her choice of
   honest yeomen ;
And now, to balance this ambitious
   error,
She presses on her daughter's love
   the suit
Of one who hath no touch of noble-
   ness,
In manners, birth, or mind, to recom-
   mend him,—
Sage Master Gullcrammer, the new-
   dubb'd preacher.
   Flo. Do not name him, Katleen !
   Kat. Ay, but I must, and with
   some gratitude.
I said but now, I saw our last of fagots
Destined to dress our last of meals,
   but said not
That the repast consisted of choice
   dainties
Sent to our larder by that liberal suitor,
The kind Melchisedek.
   Flo.   Were famishing the word,
I'd famish ere I tasted them—the
   fop,
The fool, the low-born, low-bred,
   pedant coxcomb !
   Kat. There spoke the blood of
   long-descended sires !
My cottage wisdom ought to echo
   back—
O the snug parsonage ! the well-paid
   stipend !
The yew-hedged garden ! beehives,
   pigs, and poultry !
But, to speak honestly, the peasant
   Katleen,
Valuing these good things justly, still
   would scorn
To wed, for such, the paltry Gull-
   crammer,
As much as Lady Flora.
   Flo. Mock me not with a title,
   gentle cousin,
Which poverty has made ridiculous.
                [*Trumpets far off.*

Hark ! they have broken up the
   weapon-shawing ;
The vassals are dismiss'd, and march-
   ing homeward.
   Kat. Comes your sire back to-
   night ?
   Flo.   He did purpose
To tarry for the banquet. This day
   only,
Summon'd as a king's tenant, he re-
   sumes
The right of rank his birth assigns to
   him,
And mingles with the proudest.
   Kat.   To return
To his domestic wretchedness to-
   morrow !
I envy not the privilege. Let us go
To yonder height, and see the marks-
   men practise :
They shoot their match down in the
   dale beyond,
Betwixt the Lowland and the Forest
   district,
By ancient custom, for a tun of wine.
Let us go see which wins.
   Flo.   That were too forward.
   Kat. Why, you may drop the
   screen before your face,
Which some chance breeze may haply
   blow aside
Just when a youth of special note
   takes aim.
It chanced even so that memorable
   morning
When, nutting in the woods, we met
   young Leonard.
And in good time here comes his
   sturdy comrade,
The rough Lance Blackthorn.

Enter Lancelot Blackthorn, *a
Forester, with the carcass of a deer
on his back, and a gun in his hand.*

   Bla.   Save you, damsels !
   Kat. Godden, good yeoman. Come
   you from the Weaponshaw ?

BLA. Not I, indeed; there lies the mark I shot at.

[*Lays down the deer.*

The time has been I had not miss'd the sport,
Although Lord Nithsdale's self had wanted venison ;
But this same mate of mine, young Leonard Dacre,
Makes me do what he lists. He'll win the prize, though :
The Forest district will not lose its honour,
And that is all I care for—[*some shots are heard.*] Hark! they're at it.
I'll go see the issue.

FLO. Leave not here
The produce of your hunting.

BLA. But I must, though.
This is his lair to-night, for Leonard Dacre
Charged me to leave the stag at Devorgoil ;
Then show me quickly where to stow the quarry,
And let me to the sports—[*more shots*] come, hasten, damsels!

FLO. It is impossible—we dare not take it.

BLA. There let it lie, then, and I'll wind my bugle,
That all within these tottering walls may know
That here lies venison, whoso likes to lift it. [*About to blow.*

KAT. (*to* FLORA). He will alarm your mother ; and, besides,
Our Forest proverb teaches, that no question
Should ask where venison comes from.
Your careful mother, with her wonted prudence,
Will hold its presence plead its own apology.
Come, Blackthorn, I will show you where to stow it.

[*Exeunt* KATLEEN *and* BLACK-THORN *into the Castle. More shooting—then a distant shout. Stragglers, armed in different ways, pass over the Stage, as if from the Weaponshaw.*

FLO. The prize is won ; that general shout proclaim'd it.
The marksmen and the vassals are dispersing. [*She draws back.*

FIRST VASSAL (*a peasant*). Ay, ay, 'tis lost and won,—the Forest have it.
'Tis they have all the luck on 't.

SECOND VAS. (*a shepherd*). Luck, sayst thou, man ? 'Tis practice, skill, and cunning.

THIRD VAS. 'Tis no such thing. I had hit the mark precisely
But for this cursed flint ; and, as I fired,
A swallow cross'd mine eye too. Will you tell me
That that was but a chance, mine honest shepherd ?

FIRST VAS. Ay, and last year, when Lancelot Blackthorn won it,
Because my powder happen'd to be damp,
Was there no luck in that? The worse luck mine.

SECOND VAS. Still I say 'twas not chance ; it might be witchcraft.

FIRST VAS. Faith, not unlikely, neighbours ; for these foresters
Do often haunt about this ruin'd castle.
I've seen myself this spark, young Leonard Dacre,
Come stealing like a ghost ere break of day,
And after sunset too, along this path ;
And well you know the haunted towers of Devorgoil
Have no good reputation in the land.

SHEP. That have they not. I've heard my father say

Ghosts dance as lightly in its moon-
light halls
As ever maiden did at Midsummer
Upon the village green.

    First Vas. Those that frequent
    such spirit-haunted ruins
Must needs know more than simple
Christians do.
See, Lance this blessed moment
leaves the castle,
And comes to triumph o'er us.

Blackthorn *enters from the Castle,
and comes forward while they speak.*

    Third Vas. A mighty triumph!
    What is 't, after all,
Except the driving of a piece of
lead—
As learnèd Master Gullcrammer
defined it—
Just through the middle of a painted
board.

    Black. And if he so define it, by
    your leave,
Your learnèd Master Gullcrammer's
an ass.

    Third Vas. (*angrily*). He is a
    preacher, huntsman, under fa-
    vour.

    Second Vas. No quarrelling, neigh-
    bours—you may both be right.

Enter a Fourth Vassal, *with a gallon
stoup of wine.*

    Fourth Vas. Why stand you brawl-
    ing here? Young Leonard Dacre
Has set abroach the tun of wine he
gain'd,
That all may drink who list. Blackthorn, I sought you;
Your comrade prays you will bestow
this flagon
Where you have left the deer you
kill'd this morning.

    Black. And that I will; but first
    we will take toll
To see if it's worth carriage. Shepherd, thy horn.

There must be due allowance made
for leakage,
And that will come about a draught a-
piece.
Skink it about, and, when our throats
are liquor'd,
We'll merrily trowl our song of
weaponshaw.

    [*They drink about out of the* Shep-
    herd's *horn, and then sing.*

SONG.

We love the shrill trumpet, we love
the drum's rattle,
They call us to sport, and they call
us to battle;
And old Scotland shall laugh at the
threats of a stranger
While our comrades in pastime are
comrades in danger.

If there's mirth in our house, 'tis
our neighbour that shares it;
If peril approach, 'tis our neighbour
that dares it;
And when we lead off to the pipe and
the tabor,
The fair hand we press is the hand
of a neighbour.

Then close your ranks, comrades, the
bands that combine them,
Faith, friendship, and brotherhood,
join'd to entwine them;
And we'll laugh at the threats of each
insolent stranger,
While our comrades in sport are our
comrades in danger.

    Black. Well, I must do mine er-
    rand. Master flagon [*Shaking it.*
Is too consumptive for another bleeding.

    Shep. I must to my fold.

    Third Vas. I'll to the butt of wine,
And see if that has given up the ghost
yet.

    First Vas. Have with you, neigh-
    bour.

[BLACKTHORN *enters the Castle, the rest exeunt severally.* MELCHISEDEK GULLCRAMMER *watches them off the stage, and then enters from the side-scene. His costume is a Geneva cloak and band, with a high-crowned hat; the rest of his dress in the fashion of James the First's time. He looks to the windows of the Castle, then draws back as if to escape observation, while he brushes his cloak, drives the white threads from his waistcoat with his wetted thumb, and dusts his shoes, all with the air of one who would not willingly be observed engaged in these offices. He then adjusts his collar and band, comes forward and speaks.*

GULL. Right comely is thy garb, Melchisedek;
As well beseemeth one, whom good Saint Mungo,
The patron of our land and university,
Hath graced with license both to teach and preach.
Who dare opine thou hither plod'st on foot?
Trim sits thy cloak, unruffled is thy band,
And not a speck upon thine outward man
Bewrays the labours of thy weary sole.
   [*Touches his shoe, and smiles complacently.*
Quaint was that jest and pleasant! Now will I
Approach and hail the dwellers of this fort;
But specially sweet Flora Devorgoil,
Ere her proud sire return. He loves me not,
Mocketh my lineage, flouts at mine advancement—
Sour as the fruit the crab-tree furnishes,

And hard as is the cudgel it supplies;
But Flora—she's a lily on the lake,
And I must reach her, though I risk a ducking.

   [*As* GULLCRAMMER *moves towards the drawbridge,* BAULDIE DURWARD *enters, and interposes himself betwixt him and the Castle.* GULLCRAMMER *stops and speaks.*

Whom have we here? that ancient fortune-teller,
Papist and sorcerer, and sturdy beggar,
Old Bauldie Durward! Would I were well past him!

   [DURWARD *advances, partly in the dress of a palmer, partly in that of an old Scottish mendicant, having coarse blue cloak and badge, white beard, &c.*

DUR. The blessing of the evening on your worship,
And on your taff'ty doublet. Much I marvel
Your wisdom chooseth such trim garb, when tempests
Are gathering to the bursting.
   GULLCRAMMER (*looks to his dress, and then to the sky, with some apprehension*). Surely, Bauldie,
Thou dost belie the evening—in the west
The light sinks down as lovely as this band
Drops o'er this mantle. Tush, man! 'twill be fair.
DUR. Ay, but the storm I bode is big with blows,
Horsewhips for hailstones, clubs for thunderbolts;
And for the wailing of the midnight wind,
The unpitied howling of a cudgell'd coxcomb.
Come, come, I know thou seek'st fair Flora Devorgoil.

GUL. And if I did, I do the damsel grace.
Her mother thinks so, and she has accepted
At these poor hands gifts of some consequence,
And curious dainties for the evening cheer,
To which I am invited. She respects me.

DUR. But not so doth her father, haughty Oswald.
Bethink thee, he's a baron ——

GUL. And a bare one;
Construe me that, old man! The crofts of Mucklewhame—
Destined for mine so soon as heaven and earth
Have shared my uncle's soul and bones between them—
The crofts of Mucklewhame, old man, which nourish
Three scores of sheep, three cows, with each her follower,
A female palfrey eke—I will be candid,
She is of that meek tribe whom, in derision,
Our wealthy southern neighbours nick-name donkeys ——

DUR. She hath her follower too,— when thou art there.

GUL. I say to thee, these crofts of Mucklewhame,
In the mere tithing of their stock and produce,
Outvie whatever patch of land remains
To this old rugged castle and its owner.
Well, therefore, may Melchisedek Gullcrammer,
Younger of Mucklewhame, for such I write me,
Master of Arts, by grace of good Saint Andrew,
Preacher, in brief expectance of a kirk
Endow'd with ten score Scottish pounds per annum,
Being eight pounds seventeen eight in sterling coin—
Well then, I say, may this Melchisedek,
Thus highly graced by fortune, and by nature
E'en gifted as thou seest, aspire to woo
The daughter of the beggar'd Devorgoil

DUR. Credit an old man's word, kind Master Gullcrammer,
You will not find it so. Come, sir, I've known
The hospitality of Mucklewhame;
It reach'd not to profuseness, yet, in gratitude
For the pure water of its living well,
And for the barley loaves of its fair fields,
Wherein chopp'd straw contended with the grain
Which best should satisfy the appetite,
I would not see the hopeful heir of Mucklewhame
Thus fling himself on danger.

GUL. Danger! what danger!
Know'st thou not, old Oswald
This day attends the muster of the shire,
Where the crown vassals meet to show their arms
And their best horse of service?
'Twas good sport
(An if a man had dared but laugh at it)
To see old Oswald with his rusty morion,
And huge two-handed sword, that might have seen
The field of Bannockburn or Chevy-Chase,
Without a squire or vassal, page or groom,
Or e'en a single pikeman at his heels,
Mix with the proudest nobles of the county,
And claim precedence for his tatter'd person
O'er armours double gilt and ostrich plumage.

DUR. Ay! 'twas the jest at which fools laugh the loudest,
The downfall of our old nobility—
Which may forerun the ruin of a kingdom.
I 've seen an idiot clap his hands, and shout
To see a tower like yon [*points to a part of the Castle*] stoop to its base
In headlong ruin; while the wise look'd round,
And fearful sought a distant stance to watch
What fragment of the fabric next should follow;
For when the turrets fall, the walls are tottering.
GUL. (*after pondering*). If that means aught, it means thou saw'st old Oswald
Expell'd from the assembly.
DUR.   Thy sharp wit
Hath glanced unwittingly right nigh the truth.
Expell'd he was not, but, his claim denied
At some contested point of ceremony,
He left the weaponshaw in high displeasure,
And hither comes—his wonted bitter temper
Scarce sweeten'd by the chances of the day.
'Twere much like rashness should you wait his coming,
And thither tends my counsel.
GUL.   And I 'll take it;
Good Bauldie Durward, I will take thy counsel,
And will requite it with this minted farthing,
That bears our sovereign's head in purest copper.
DUR. Thanks to thy bounty! Haste thee, good young master;
Oswald, besides the old two-handed sword,

Bears in his hand a staff of potency,
To charm intruders from his castle purlieus.
GUL. I do abhor all charms, nor will abide
To hear or see, far less to feel their use.
Behold, I have departed. [*Exit hastily.*

Manent DURWARD.

DUR. Thus do I play the idle part of one
Who seeks to save the moth from scorching him
In the bright taper's flame; and Flora's beauty
Must, not unlike that taper, waste away,
Gilding the rugged walls that saw it kindled.
This was a shard-born beetle, heavy, drossy,
Though boasting his dull drone and gilded wing.
Here comes a flutterer of another stamp,
Whom the same ray is charming to his ruin.

Enter LEONARD, *dressed as a huntsman; he pauses before the Tower, and whistles a note or two at intervals—drawing back, as if fearful of observation—yet waiting, as if expecting some reply.* DURWARD, *whom he had not observed, moves round, so as to front* LEONARD *unexpectedly.*

LEON. I am too late—it was no easy task
To rid myself from yonder noisy revellers.
Flora!—I fear she 's angry—Flora! Flora!
SONG.

Admire not that I gain'd the prize
   From all the village crew;
How could I fail with hand or eyes,
   When heart and faith were true!

And when in floods of rosy wine
  My comrades drown'd their cares,
I thought but that thy heart was mine,
  My own leapt light as theirs.

My brief delay then do not blame,
  Nor deem your swain untrue;
My form but linger'd at the game,
  My soul was still with you.

She hears not!

Dur. But a friend hath heard—
  Leonard, I pity thee.

Leon. (*starts, but recovers himself*).
  Pity, good father, is for those in
  want,
In age, in sorrow, in distress of mind,
Or agony of body. I'm in health—
Can match my limbs against the stag
  in chase,
Have means enough to meet my
  simple wants,
And am so free of soul that I can carol
To woodland and to wild in notes as
  lively
As are my jolly bugle's.

Dur. Even therefore dost thou
  need my pity, Leonard,
And therefore I bestow it, praying
  thee,
Before thou feel'st the need, my mite
  of pity.
Leonard, thou lovest; and in that
  little word
There lies enough to claim the
  sympathy
Of men who wear such hoary locks
  as mine,
And know what misplaced love is
  sure to end in.

Leon. Good father, thou art old,
  and even thy youth,
As thou hast told me, spent in cloister'd
  cells,
Fits thee but ill to judge the passions
Which are the joy and charm of social
  life.

Press me no farther, then, nor waste
  those moments
Whose worth thou canst not estimate.
        [*As turning from him.*

Dur. (*detains him*). Stay, young
  man!
'Tis seldom that a beggar claims a debt;
Yet I bethink me of a gay young
  stripling
That owes to these white locks and
  hoary beard
Something of reverence and of grati-
  tude
More than he wills to pay.

Leon. Forgive me, father. Often
  hast thou told me,
That in the ruin of my father's house
You saved the orphan Leonard in his
  cradle;
And well I know, that to thy care
  alone—
Care seconded by means beyond thy
  seeming—
I owe whate'er of nurture I can boast.

Dur. Then for thy life preserved,
And for the means of knowledge
  I have furnish'd
(Which lacking, man is levell'd with
  the brutes),
Grant me this boon—Avoid these
  fatal walls!
A curse is on them, bitter, deep, and
  heavy,
Of power to split the massiest tower
  they boast
From pinnacle to dungeon vault. It
  rose
Upon the gay horizon of proud
  Devorgoil,
As unregarded as the fleecy cloud,
The first forerunner of the hurricane,
Scarce seen amid the welkin's shade-
  less blue.
Dark grew it, and more dark, and still
  the fortunes
Of this doom'd family have darken'd
  with it.

It hid their sovereign's favour, and
   obscured
The lustre of their service, gender'd
   hate
Betwixt them and the mighty of the
   land ;
Till by degrees the waxing tempest
   rose,
And stripp'd the goodly tree of fruit
   and flowers,
And buds, and boughs, and branches.
   There remains
A rugged trunk, dismember'd and un-
   sightly,
Waiting the bursting of the final bolt
To splinter it to shivers. Now, go
   pluck
Its single tendril to enwreath thy brow,
And rest beneath its shade—to share
   the ruin !
  LEON. This anathema,
Whence should it come? How merited ?
   and when ?
  DUR. 'Twas in the days
Of Oswald's grandsire,—'mid Gal-
   wegian chiefs
The fellest foe, the fiercest champion.
His blood-red pennons scared the
   Cumbrian coasts,
And wasted towns and manors mark'd
   his progress.
His galleys stored with treasure, and
   their decks
Crowded with English captives, who
   beheld,
With weeping eyes, their native shores
   retire,
He bore him homeward ; but a tempest
   rose ———
  LEON. So far I 've heard the tale,
And spare thee the recital. The grim
   chief,
Marking his vessels labour on the sea,
And loth to lose his treasure, gave
   command
To plunge his captives in the raging
   deep.

  DUR. There sunk the lineage of a
   noble name,
And the wild waves boom'd over sire
   and son,
Mother and nursling, of the House of
   Aglionby,
Leaving but one frail tendril. Hence
   the fate
That hovers o'er these turrets ; hence
   the peasant,
Belated, hying homewards, dreads to
   cast
A glance upon that portal, lest he see
The unshrouded spectres of the mur-
   der'd dead ;
Or the avenging Angel, with his sword,
Waving destruction ; or the grisly
   phantom
Of that fell Chief, the doer of the deed,
Which still, they say, roams through
   his empty halls,
And mourns their wasteness and their
   lonelihood.
  LEON. Such is the dotage
Of superstition, father, ay, and the cant
Of hoodwink'd prejudice. Not for
   atonement
Of some foul deed done in the ancient
   warfare,
When war was butchery, and men
   were wolves,
Doth Heaven consign the innocent to
   suffering.
I tell thee, Flora's virtues might atone
For all the massacres her sires have
   done,
Since first the Pictish race their stainèd
   limbs
Array'd in wolf's skin.
  DUR. Leonard, ere yet this beggar's
   scrip and cloak
Supplied the place of mitre and of
   crosier,
Which in these alter'd lands must not
   be worn,
I was superior of a brotherhood
Of holy men,—the Prior of Lanercost.

Nobles then sought my footstool many a league,
There to unload their sins ; questions of conscience
Of deepest import were not deem'd too nice
For my decision, youth. But not even then,
With mitre on my brow, and all the voice
Which Rome gives to a father of her church,
Dared I pronounce so boldly on the ways
Of hidden Providence, as thou, young man,
Whose chiefest knowledge is to track a stag,
Or wind a bugle, hast presumed to do.
LEON. Nay, I pray forgive me,
Father ; thou know'st I meant not to presume——
DUR. Can I refuse thee pardon ? Thou art all
That war and change have left to the poor Durward.
Thy father, too, who lost his life and fortune
Defending Lanercost, when its fair aisles
Were spoil'd by sacrilege—I bless'd his banner,
And yet it prosper'd not. But—all I could—
Thee from the wreck I saved, and for thy sake
Have still dragg'd on my life of pilgrimage
And penitence upon the hated shores
I else had left for ever. Come with me,
And I will teach thee there is healing in
The wounds which friendship gives.
[*Exeunt.*

SCENE II.

The Scene changes to the interior of the Castle. An apartment is discovered, in which there is much appearance of present poverty, mixed with some relics of former grandeur On the wall hangs, amongst other things, a suit of ancient armour; by the table is a covered basket; behind, and concealed by it, the carcass of a roe-deer. There is a small latticed window, which, appearing to perforate a wall of great thickness, is supposed to look out towards the drawbridge. It is in the shape of a loop-hole for musketry; and, as is not unusual in old buildings, is placed so high up in the wall, that it is only approached by five or six narrow stone steps.

ELEANOR, *the wife of* OSWALD *of* DEVORGOIL, FLORA *and* KATLEEN, *her Daughter and Niece, are discovered at work. The former spins, the latter are embroidering.* ELEANOR *quits her own labour to examine the manner in which* FLORA *is executing her task, and shakes her head as if dissatisfied.*

ELE. Fy on it, Flora; this botch'd work of thine
Shows that thy mind is distant from thy task.
The finest tracery of our old cathedral
Had not a richer, freer, bolder pattern
Than Flora once could trace. Thy thoughts are wandering.
FLO. They're with my father. Broad upon the lake
The evening sun sunk down ; huge piles of clouds,
Crimson and sable, rose upon his disk,
And quench'd him ere his setting, like some champion
In his last conflict losing all his glory.
Sure signals those of storm. And if my father

Be on his homeward road ——
ELE. But that he will not.
Baron of Devorgoil, this day at least
He banquets with the nobles, who
the next
Would scarce vouchsafe an alms to
save his household
From want or famine. Thanks to a
kind friend,
For one brief space we shall not need
their aid.
FLO. (*joyfully*). What! knew you
then his gift?
How silly I that would, yet durst not
tell it!
I fear my father will condemn us both,
That easily accepted such a present.
KAT. Now, here's the game a by-
stander sees better
Than those who play it. My good
aunt is pondering
On the good cheer which Gullcrammer
has sent us,
And Flora thinks upon the forest
venison.   [*Aside.*
ELE. (*to* FLORA). Thy father need not
know on't; 'tis a boon
Comes timely, when frugality, nay,
abstinence,
Might scarce avail us longer. I had
hoped
Ere now a visit from the youthful donor,
That we might thank his bounty; and
perhaps
My Flora thought the same, when
Sunday's kerchief
And the best kirtle were sought out,
and donn'd
To grace a work-day evening.
FLO. Nay, mother, that is judging
all too close!
My work-day gown was torn, my
kerchief sullied,
And thus—but, think you, will the
gallant come?
ELE. He will, for with these dainties
came a message

From gentle Master Gullcrammer, to
intimate——
FLO. (*greatly disappointed*). Gull-
crammer?
KAT. There burst the bubble—down
fell house of cards,
And cousin's like to cry for't! [*Aside.*
ELE. Gullcrammer? ay, Gullcram-
mer; thou scorn'st not at him?
'Twere something short of wisdom in
a maiden,
Who, like the poor bat in the Grecian
fable,
Hovers betwixt two classes in the
world,
And is disclaim'd by both the mouse
and bird.
KAT. (*aside*). I am the poor mouse,
And may go creep into what hole I
list,
And no one heed me; yet I'll waste
a word
Of counsel on my betters.—Kind my
aunt,
And you, my gentle cousin, were't
not better
We thought of dressing this same
gear for supper,
Than quarrelling about the worthless
donor?
ELE. Peace, minx!
FLO Thou hast no feeling, cousin
Katleen.
KAT. Soh! I have brought them
both on my poor shoulders;
So meddling peace-makers are still
rewarded:
E'en let them to't again, and fight it out.
FLO. Mother, were I disclaim'd of
every class,
I would not therefore so disclaim
myself,
As even a passing thought of scorn to
waste
On cloddish Gullcrammer.
ELE. List to me, love, and let
adversity

Incline thine ear to wisdom. Look
    around thee ;
Of the gay youths who boast a noble
    name,
Which will incline to wed a dowerless
    damsel ?
And of the yeomanry, who, think'st
    thou, Flora,
Would ask to share the labours of his
    farm
An high-born beggar ? This young
    man is modest ——

    Flo. Silly, good mother ; sheepish,
    if you will it.

    Ele. E'en call it what you list ; the
    softer temper,
The fitter to endure the bitter sallies
Of one whose wit is all too sharp for
    mine.

    Flo. Mother, you cannot mean it as
    you say ;
You cannot bid me prize conceited
    folly ?

    Ele. Content thee, child ; each lot
    has its own blessings.
This youth, with his plain-dealing
    honest suit,
Proffers thee quiet, peace, and com-
    petence,
Redemption from a home, o'er which
    fell Fate
Stoops like a falcon. O, if thou
    couldst choose
(As no such choice is given) 'twixt
    such a mate
And some proud noble ! Who, in
    sober judgment,
Would like to navigate the heady
    river,
Dashing in fury from its parent
    mountain,
More than the waters of the quiet lake?

    Kat. Now can I hold no longer !
    Lake, good aunt ?
Nay, in the name of truth, say mill-
    pond, horse-pond ;
Or if there be a pond more miry,

More sluggish, mean-derived, and
    base than either,
Be such Gullcrammer's emblem—and
    his portion !

    Flo. I would that he or I were in
    our grave,
Rather than thus his suit should goad
    me ! Mother,
Flora of Devorgoil, though low in
    fortunes,
Is still too high in mind to join her
    name
With such a base-born churl as Gull-
    crammer.

    Ele. You are trim maidens both !
(*To* Flora.)   Have you forgotten,
Or did you mean to call to *my* remem-
    brance
Thy father chose a wife of peasant
    blood ?

    Flo. Will you speak thus to me,
    or think the stream
Can mock the fountain it derives its
    source from ?
My venerated mother, in that name
Lies all on earth a child should chiefest
    honour ;
And with that name to mix reproach
    or taunt,
Were only short of blasphemy to
    Heaven.

    Ele. Then listen, Flora, to that
    mother's counsel,
Or rather profit by that mother's fate.
Your father's fortunes were but bent,
    not broken,
Until he listen'd to his rash affection.
Means were afforded to redeem his
    house,
Ample and large : the hand of a rich
    heiress
Awaited, almost courted, his accept-
    ance.
He saw my beauty—such it then was
    call'd,
Or such at least he thought it ; the
    wither'd bush,

Whate'er it now may seem, had
    blossoms then,—
And he forsook the proud and wealthy
    heiress,
To wed with me and ruin.
    KAT. (*aside*).   The more fool,
Say I, apart, the peasant maiden then,
Who might have chose a mate from
    her own hamlet.
    ELE. Friends fell off,
And to his own resources, his own
    counsels,
Abandon'd, as they said, the thought-
    less prodigal,
Who had exchanged rank, riches,
    pomp, and honour,
For the mean beauties of a cottage
    maid.
    FLO. It was done like my father,
Who scorn'd to sell what wealth can
    never buy—
True love and free affections. And
    he loves you!
If you have suffer'd in a weary world,
Your sorrows have been jointly borne,
    and love
Has made the load sit lighter.
    ELE. Ay, but a misplaced match
    hath that deep curse in 't,
That can embitter e'en the purest
    streams
Of true affection. Thou hast seen me
    seek,
With the strict caution early habits
    taught me,
To match our wants and means; hast
    seen thy father
With aristocracy's high brow of scorn,
Spurn at economy, the cottage virtue,
As best befitting her whose sires were
    peasants:
Nor can I, when I see my lineage
    scorn'd,
Always conceal in what contempt I
    hold
The fancied claims of rank he clings
    to fondly.

    FLO. Why will you do so? Well
    you know it chafes him.
    ELE. Flora, thy mother is but mortal
    woman,
Nor can at all times check an eager
    tongue.
    KAT. (*aside*). That's no new tidings
    to her niece and daughter.
    ELE. O mayst thou never know the
    spited feelings
That gender discord in adversity
Betwixt the dearest friends and truest
    lovers!
In the chill damping gale of poverty,
If Love's lamp go not out, it gleams
    but palely,
And twinkles in the socket.
    FLO. But tenderness can screen it
    with her veil,
Till it revive again. By gentleness,
    good mother,
How oft I've seen you soothe my
    father's mood!
    KAT. Now there speak youthful hope
    and fantasy!   [*Aside.*
    ELE. That is an easier task in youth
    than age;
Our temper hardens, and our charms
    decay,
And both are needed in that art of
    soothing.
    KAT. And there speaks sad experi-
    ence.   [*Aside.*
    ELE. Besides, since that our state
    was utter desperate,
Darker his brow, more dangerous
    grow his words;
Fain would I snatch thee from the
    woe and wrath
Which darken'd long my life, and
    soon must end it.

    [*A knocking without;* ELEANOR
    shows alarm.

It was thy father's knock, haste to
    the gate.

    [*Exeunt* FLORA *and* KATLEEN.

What can have happ'd? he thought
    to stay the night.
This gear must not be seen.

    [*As she is about to remove the
    basket, she sees the body of the
    roe-deer.*

What have we here? a roe-deer!
    As I fear it,
This was the gift of which poor Flora
    thought.
The young and handsome hunter—
    but time presses.

    [*She removes the basket and the
    roe into a closet. As she has
    done—*

Enter OSWALD *of* DEVORGOIL, FLORA,
    and KATLEEN.

    [*He is dressed in a scarlet cloak,
    which should seem worn and
    old — a headpiece, and old-
    fashioned sword—the rest of his
    dress that of a peasant. His
    countenance and manner should
    express the moody and irritable
    haughtiness of a proud man
    involved in calamity, and who
    has been exposed to recent in-
    sult.*

OSW. (*addressing his wife*). The sun
    hath set ; why is the drawbridge
    lower'd?
ELE. The counterpoise has fail'd,
    and Flora's strength,
Katleen's, and mine united, could not
    raise it.
OSW. Flora and thou! A goodly
    garrison
To hold a castle, which, if fame say
    true,
Once foil'd the King of Norse and all
    his rovers.
ELE. It might be so in ancient
    times, but now ——
OSW. A herd of deer might storm
    proud Devorgoil.

KAT. (*aside to* FLORA). You, Flora,
    know full well one deer already
Has enter'd at the breach; and, what
    is worse,
The escort is not yet march'd off, for
    Blackthorn
Is still within the castle.
    FLO. In Heaven's name, rid him out
    on 't, ere my father
Discovers he is here ! Why went he
    not
Before?
    KAT. Because I staid him on **some**
    little business ;
I had a plan to scare poor **paltry**
    Gullcrammer
Out of his paltry wits.
    FLO.   Well, haste ye now,
And try to get him off.
    KAT.   I will not promise that.
I would not turn an honest hunter's
    dog,
So well I love the woodcraft, out of
    shelter
In such a night as this; far less his
    master:
But I'll do this, I'll try to hide him
    for you.
    OSW. (*whom his wife has assisted to
    take off his cloak and feathered cap*).
    Ay, take them off, and bring my
    peasant's bonnet
And peasant's plaid : I'll noble it no
    farther.
Let them erase my name from
    honour's lists,
And drag my scutcheon at their
    horses' heels ;
I have deserved it all, for I am poor,
And poverty hath neither right of birth,
Nor rank, relation, claim, nor privilege,
To match a new-coin'd viscount,
    whose good grandsire,
The Lord be with him ! was a careful
    skipper,
And steer'd his paltry skiff 'twixt
    Leith and Campvere—

Marry, sir, he could buy Geneva cheap,
And knew the coast by moonlight.

FLO. Mean you the Viscount Ellondale, my father?
What strife has been between you?

OSW.   O, a trifle!
Not worth a wise man's thinking twice about —
Precedence is a toy—a superstition
About a table's end, joint-stool, and trencher.
Something was once thought due to long descent,
And something to Galwegia's oldest baron;
But let that pass—a dream of the old time.

ELE. It is indeed a dream.

OSW. (*turning upon her rather quickly*). Ha! said ye? let me hear these words more plain.

ELE. Alas! they are but echoes of your own.
Match'd with the real woes that hover o'er us,
What are the idle visions of precedence,
But, as you term them, dreams, and toys, and trifles,
Not worth a wise man's thinking twice upon?

OSW. Ay, 'twas for you I framed that consolation,
The true philosophy of clouted shoe
And linsey-woolsey kirtle. I know that minds
Of nobler stamp receive no dearer motive
Than what is link'd with honour. Ribands, tassels,
Which are but shreds of silk and spangled tinsel;
The right of place, which in itself is momentary;
A word, which is but air—may in themselves,

And to the nobler file, be steep'd so richly
In that elixir, honour, that the lack
Of things so very trivial in themselves
Shall be misfortune. One shall seek for them
O'er the wild waves, one in the deadly breach
And battle's headlong front, one in the paths
Of midnight study; and, in gaining these
Emblems of honour, each will hold himself
Repaid for all his labours, deeds, and dangers.
What then should he think, knowing them his own,
Who sees what warriors and what sages toil for,
The formal and establish'd marks of honour
Usurp'd from him by upstart insolence?

ELE. (*who has listened to the last speech with some impatience*). This is but empty declamation, Oswald.
The fragments left at yonder full-spread banquet,
Nay, even the poorest crust swept from the table,
Ought to be far more precious to a father,
Whose family lacks food, than the vain boast,
He sate at the board-head.

OSW. Thou'lt drive me frantic! I will tell thee, woman—
Yet why to thee? There is another ear
Which that tale better suits, and he shall hear it.

[*Looks at his sword, which he has unbuckled, and addresses the rest of the speech to it.*

Yes, trusty friend, my father knew thy worth,
And often proved it—often told me of it.

2 F

Though thou and I be now held
    lightly of,
And want the gilded hatchments of
    the time,
I think we both may prove true metal
    still.
'Tis thou shalt tell this story, right
    this wrong:
Rest thou till time is fitting.   [*Hangs
    up the sword.*

    [*The Women look at each other
    with anxiety during this speech,
    which they partly overhear.
    They both approach* OSWALD.

  ELE. Oswald, my dearest husband!
  FLO.   My dear father!
  Osw. Peace, both! we speak no
    more of this. I go
To heave the drawbridge up.   [*Exit.*
  [KATLEEN *mounts the steps towards
  the loop-hole, and looks out.*
  KAT. The storm is gathering fast;
    broad, heavy drops
Fall plashing on the bosom of the lake,
And dash its inky surface into circles;
The distant hills are hid in wreaths of
    darkness.
'Twill be a fearful night.
  OSWALD *re-enters, and throws him-
  self into a seat.*
  ELE.   More dark and dreadful
Than is our destiny, it cannot be.
  Osw. (*to* FLORA). Such is Heaven's
    will; it is our part to bear it.
We 're warranted, my child, from
    ancient story
And blessed writ, to say that song
    assuages
The gloomy cares that prey upon our
    reason,
And wake a strife betwixt our better
    feelings
And the fierce dictates of the headlong
    passions.
Sing, then, my love; for if a voice
    have influence

To mediate peace betwixt me and my
    destiny,
Flora, it must be thine.
  FLO.   My best to please you!

        SONG.

WHEN the tempest 's at the loudest,
  On its gale the eagle rides;
When the ocean rolls the proudest,
  Through the foam the sea-bird
    glides—
All the rage of wind and sea
Is subdued by constancy.

Gnawing want and sickness pining,
  All the ills that men endure;
Each their various pangs combining,
  Constancy can find a cure—
Pain, and Fear, and Poverty,
Are subdued by constancy.

Bar me from each wonted pleasure,
  Make me abject, mean, and poor;
Heap on insults without measure,
  Chain me to a dungeon floor—
I 'll be happy, rich, and free,
If endow'd with constancy.

—◆◆—

        ACT II.

        SCENE I.

*Chamber in a distant part of the Castle.
A large Window in the flat scene,
supposed to look on the Lake, which
is occasionally illuminated by lightning. There is a Couch-bed in the
Room, and an antique Cabinet.*

Enter KATLEEN, *introducing* BLACK-
        THORN.

  KAT. This was the destined scene
    of action, Blackthorn,
And here our properties. But all in vain,
For of Gullcrammer we 'll see nought
    to-night,

Except the dainties that I told you of.

BLA. O, if he's left that same hog's
  face and sausages,
He will try back upon them, never
  fear it.
The cur will open on the trail of
  bacon,
Like my old brach-hound.

KAT. And should that hap, we'll
  play our comedy,
Shall we not, Blackthorn? Thou shalt
  be Owlspiegle——

BLA. And who may that hard-
  named person be?

KAT. I've told you nine times over.

BLA. Yes, pretty Katleen, but my
  eyes were busy
In looking at you all the time you
  were talking;
And so I lost the tale.

KAT. Then shut your eyes, and let
  your goodly ears
Do their good office.

BLA. That were too hard penance.
Tell but thy tale once more, and I will
  hearken
As if I were thrown out, and listening
  for
My bloodhound's distant bay.

KAT.   A civil simile!
Then, for the tenth time, and the last,
  be told
Owlspiegle was of old the wicked
  barber
To Erick, wicked Lord of Devorgoil.

BLA. The chief who drown'd his
  captives in the Solway:
We all have heard of him.

KAT. A hermit hoar, a venerable
  man
(So goes the legend) came to wake
  repentance
In the fierce lord, and tax'd him with
  his guilt;
But he, heart-harden'd, turn'd into
  derision
The man of heaven, and, as his dignity

Consisted much in a long reverend
  beard,
Which reach'd his girdle, Erick caused
  his barber
This same Owlspiegle, violate its
  honours
With sacrilegious razor, and clip his hair
After the fashion of a roguish fool.

BLA. This was reversing of our
  ancient proverb,
And shaving for the devil's, not for
  God s sake.

KAT. True, most grave Blackthorn;
  and in punishment
Of this foul act of scorn, the barber's
  ghost
Is said to have no resting after death,
But haunts these halls, and chiefly
  this same chamber,
Where the profanity was acted, trim-
  ming
And clipping all such guests as sleep
  within it.
Such is at least the tale our elders tell,
With many others, of this haunted
  castle.

BLA. And you would have me take
  this shape of Owlspiegle,
And trim the wise Melchisedek!
  I wonnot.

KAT. You will not?

BLA. No—unless you bear a part.

KAT. What! can you not alone
  play such a farce?

BLA. Not I, I'm dull. Besides,
  we foresters
Still hunt our game in couples. Look
  you, Katleen,
We danced at Shrovetide—then you
  were my partner;
We sung at Christmas—you kept time
  with me;
And if we go a mumming in this
  business,
By heaven, you must be one, or
  Master Gullcrammer
Is like to rest unshaven.

KAT.   Why, you fool,
What end can this serve?

BLA.   Nay, I know not, I.
But if we keep this wont of being
    partners,
Why, use makes perfect : who knows
    what may happen?

KAT. Thou art a foolish patch. But
    sing our carol,
As I have alter'd it, with some few words
To suit the characters, and I will
    bear   [*Gives a paper.*

BLA. Part in the gambol. I'll go
    study quickly.
Is there no other ghost, then, haunts
    the castle,
But this same barber shave-a-penny
    goblin?
I thought they glanced in every beam
    of moonshine,
As frequent as the bat.

KAT. I've heard my aunt's high
    husband tell of prophecies,
And fates impending o'er the house
    of Devorgoil;
Legends first coin'd by ancient super-
    stition,
And render'd current by credulity
And pride of lineage. Five years have
    I dwelt,
And ne'er saw any thing more mis-
    chievous
Than what I am myself.

BLA. And that is quite enough,
    I warrant you.
But, stay, where shall I find a dress
To play this—what d'ye call him—
    Owlspiegle?

KAT. (*taking dresses out of the cabinet*).
    Why, there are his own clothes,
Preserved with other trumpery of the
    sort,
For we have kept nought but what is
    good for nought.

    [*She drops a cap as she draws out
       the clothes. Blackthorn lifts it,
       and gives it to her.*

Nay, keep it for thy pains, it is a
    coxcomb;
So call'd in ancient times, in ours
    a fool's cap;
For you must know they kept a Fool
    at Devorgoil
In former days; but now are well
    contented
To play the fool themselves, to save
    expenses;
Yet give it me, I'll find a worthy use
    for 't.
I'll take this page's dress, to play the
    page
Cockledemoy, who waits on ghostly
    Owlspiegle;
And yet 'tis needless, too, for Gull-
    crammer
Will scarce be here to-night.

BLA. I tell you that he will; I will
    uphold
His plighted faith and true allegiance
Unto a sous'd sow's face and sau-
    sages,
And such the dainties that you say
    he sent you,
Against all other likings whatsoever,
Except a certain sneaking of affec-
    tion,
Which makes some folks I know of
    play the fool,
To please some other folks.

KAT. Well, I do hope he'll come :
    there's first a chance
He will be cudgell'd by my noble
    uncle—
I cry his mercy! by my good aunt's
    husband,
Who did vow vengeance, knowing
    nought of him
But by report, and by a limping sonnet
Which he had fashion'd to my cousin's
    glory,
And forwarded by blind Tom Long
    the carrier;
So there's the chance, first of a hearty
    beating,

Which failing, we 've this after-plot of vengeance.

Bla. Kind damsel, how considerate and merciful!

But how shall we get off, our parts being play'd?

Kat. For that we are well fitted. Here 's a trap-door
Sinks with a counterpoise; you shall go that way.
I 'll make my exit yonder; 'neath the window,
A balcony communicates with the tower
That overhangs the lake.

Bla. 'Twere a rare place, this house of Devorgoil,
To play at hide-and-seek in: shall we try,
One day, my pretty Katleen?

Kat. Hands off, rude ranger! I 'm no managed hawk
To stoop to lure of yours. But bear you gallantly;
This Gullcrammer hath vex'd my cousin much,
I fain would have some vengeance.

Bla. I 'll bear my part with glee;— he spoke irreverently
Of practice at a mark!

Kat.　That cries for vengeance.
But I must go; I hear my aunt's shrill voice!
My cousin and her father will scream next.

Ele. (at a distance). Katleen! Katleen!

Bla.　Hark to old Sweetlips!
Away with you before the full cry open—
But stay, what have you there?

Kat. (with a bundle she has taken from the wardrobe). My dress, my page's dress—let it alone.

Bla. Your tiring-room is not, I hope, far distant;

You 're inexperienced in these new habiliments—
I am most ready to assist your toilet.

Kat. Out, you great ass! was ever such a fool!　　[Runs off.

Bla. (sings).

O, Robin Hood was a bowman good,
　And a bowman good was he,
And he met with a maiden in merry Sherwood,
　All under the greenwood tree.

Now give me a kiss, quoth bold Robin Hood,
　Now give me a kiss, said he,
For there never came maid into merry Sherwood,
　But she paid the forester's fee.

I 've coursed this twelvemonth this sly puss, young Katleen,
And she has dodged me, turn'd beneath my nose,
And flung me out a score of yards at once;
If this same gear fadge right, I 'll cote and mouth her,
And then! whoop! dead! dead! dead!—She is the metal
To make a woodsman's wife of!
　　　　　　[Pauses a moment.

Well, I can find a hare upon her form
With any man in Nithsdale, stalk a deer,
Run Reynard to the earth for all his doubles,
Reclaim a haggard hawk that 's wild and wayward,
Can bait a wild-cat: sure the devil 's in 't
But I can match a woman! I 'll to study.

　　[Sits down on the couch to examine the paper.

―――――

Scene II.

*Scene changes to the inhabited apart-
ment of the Castle, as in the last
Scene of the preceding Act. A fire
is kindled, by which* Oswald *sits in
an attitude of deep and melancholy
thought, without paying attention to
what passes around him.* Eleanor *is busy in covering a table;*
Flora *goes out and re-enters, as if
busied in the kitchen. There should
be some by-play—the women whispering together, and watching the state
of* Oswald; *then separating, and
seeking to avoid his observation, when
he casually raises his head, and
drops it again. This must be left to
taste and management. The Women,
in the first part of the scene, talk apart,
and as if fearful of being overheard;
the by-play of stopping occasionally,
and attending to* Oswald's *movements, will give liveliness to the
Scene.*

Ele. Is all prepared?

Flo.   Ay; but I doubt the issue
Will give my sire less pleasure than
    you hope for.

Ele. Tush, maid; I know thy
    father's humour better.
He was high-bred in gentle luxuries;
And when our griefs began, I've
    wept apart,
While lordly cheer and high-fill'd
    cups of wine
Were blinding him against the woe
    to come.
He has turn'd his back upon a princely
    banquet:
We will not spread his board this
    night at least,
Since chance hath better furnish'd,
    with dry bread,
And water from the well.

Enter Katleen, *and hears the last
speech.*

Kat. (*aside*). Considerate aunt! she
    deems that a good supper
Were not a thing indifferent even
    to him
Who is to hang to-morrow. Since
    she thinks so,
We must take care the venison has
    due honour.
So much I owe the sturdy knave,
    Lance Blackthorn.

Flo. Mother, alas! when Grief
    turns reveller,
Despair is cup-bearer. What shall
    hap to-morrow?

Ele. I have learn'd carelessness
    from fruitless care.
Too long I've watch'd to-morrow;
    let it come
And cater for itself. Thou hear'st the
    thunder.

[*Low and distant thunder.*

This is a gloomy night—within, alas!

[*Looking at her husband.*

Still gloomier and more threatening.
    Let us use
Whatever means we have to drive
    it o'er,
And leave to Heaven to-morrow.
    Trust me, Flora,
'Tis the philosophy of desperate want
To match itself but with the present
    evil,
And face one grief at once.
Away, I wish thine aid and not thy
    counsel.

[*As* Flora *is about to go off,*
Gullcrammer's *voice is heard
behind the flat scene, as if from
the drawbridge.*

Gul. (*behind*). Hillo—hillo—hilloa
    —hoa—hoa!

[Oswald *raises himself and listens:*
Eleanor *goes up the steps, and*

opens the window at the loophole;
GULLCRAMMER'S *voice is then
heard more distinctly.*

GUL. Kind Lady Devorgoil! sweet
Mistress Flora!
The night grows fearful, I have lost
my way,
And wander'd till the road turn'd
round with me,
And brought me back! For Heaven's
sake, give me shelter!
KAT. *(aside).* Now, as I live, the
voice of Gullcrammer!
Now shall our gambol be play'd off
with spirit;
I'll swear I am the only one to whom
That screech-owl whoop was e'er
acceptable.
OSW. What bawling knave is this
that takes our dwelling
For some hedge-inn, the haunt of
lated drunkards?
ELE. What shall I say? Go, Katleen,
speak to him.
KAT. *(aside).* The game is in my
hands! I will say something
Will fret the Baron's pride; and then
he enters.
(She speaks from the window.) Good
sir, be patient!
We are poor folks; it is but six
Scotch miles
To the next borough town, where
your Reverence
May be accommodated to your wants;
We are poor folks, an't please your
Reverence,
And keep a narrow household; there's
no track
To lead your steps astray——
GUL. Nor none to lead them right.
You kill me, lady,
If you deny me harbour. To budge
from hence,
And in my weary plight, were sudden
death,

Interment, funeral-sermon, tombstone,
epitaph.
OSW. Who's he that is thus clamor-
ous without?
(To ELEANOR.) Thou know'st him?
ELE. *(confused).* I know him? no
—yes—'tis a worthy clergyman,
Benighted on his way; but think not
of him.
KAT. The morn will rise when that
the tempest's past,
And if he miss the marsh, and can avoid
The crags upon the left, the road is
plain.
OSW. Then this is all your piety?
to leave
One whom the holy duties of his office
Have summon'd over moor and wilder-
ness,
To pray beside some dying wretch's
bed,
Who (erring mortal) still would cleave
to life,
Or wake some stubborn sinner to
repentance,—
To leave him, after offices like these,
To choose his way in darkness 'twixt
the marsh
And dizzy precipice?
ELE. What can I do?
OSW. Do what thou canst—the
wealthiest do no more;
And if so much, 'tis well. These
crumbling walls,
While yet they bear a roof, shall now,
as ever,
Give shelter to the wanderer. Have
we food?
He shall partake it. Have we none?
the fast
Shall be accounted with the good
man's merits
And our misfortunes.
*[He goes to the loop-hole while he
speaks, and places himself there
in room of his Wife, who comes
down with reluctance.*

GUL. (*without*). Hillo—hoa—hoa!
By my good faith, I cannot plod it
    farther;
The attempt were death.

    Osw. (*speaking from the window*).
    Patience, my friend, I come to
    lower the drawbridge.

            [*Descends, and exit.*

    ELE. O, that the screaming bittern
    had his couch
Where he deserves it, in the deepest
    marsh!

    KAT. I would not give this sport
    for all the rent
Of Devorgoil, when Devorgoil was
    richest!
(*To* ELEANOR.) But now you chided
    me, my dearest aunt,
For wishing him a horse-pond for his
    portion?

    ELE. Yes, saucy girl; but, an it
    please you, then
He was not fretting me; if he had
    sense enough,
And skill to bear him as some casual
    stranger,—
But he is dull as earth, and every hint
Is lost on him, as hail-shot on the
    cormorant,
Whose hide is proof except to musket-
    bullets!

    FLO. (*apart*). And yet to such a one
    would my kind mother,
Whose chiefest fault is loving me too
    fondly,
Wed her poor daughter!

Enter GULLCRAMMER *his dress damaged
    by the storm;* ELEANOR *runs to meet
    him, in order to explain to him that
    she wished him to behave as a stranger*
    GULLCRAMMER, *mistaking her ap-
    proach for an invitation to familiarity,
    advances with the air of pedantic
    conceit belonging to his character, when*
    OSWALD *enters,—*ELEANOR *recovers
    herself, and assumes an air of dis-*

*tance—*GULLCRAMMER *is confounded,
    and does not know what to make
    of it.*

    Osw. The counterpoise has clean
    given way; the bridge
Must e'en remain unraised, and leave
    us open,
For this night's course at least, to
    passing visitants.
What have we here? is this the
    reverend man?

        [*He takes up the candle, and surveys*
        GULLCRAMMER, *who strives to
        sustain the inspection with con-
        fidence, while fear obviously con-
        tends with conceit and desire to
        show himself to the best advan-
        tage.*

    GUL. Kind sir—or, good my lord
    —my band is ruffled,
But yet 'twas fresh this morning.
    This fell shower
Hath somewhat smirch'd my cloak,
    but you may note
It rates five marks per yard; my
    doublet
Hath fairly 'scaped; 'tis three-piled
    taffeta.

        [*Opens his cloak, and displays his
        doublet.*

    Osw. A goodly inventory. Art thou
    a preacher?

    GUL. Yea; I laud Heaven and good
    Saint Mungo for it.

    Osw. 'Tis the time's plague, when
    those that should weed follies
Out of the common field, have their
    own minds
O'errun with foppery. Envoys 'twixt
    heaven and earth,
Example should with precept join, to
    show us
How we may scorn the world with
    all its vanities.

    GUL. Nay, the high heavens fore-
    fend that I were vain!

When our learn'd Principal such
    sounding laud
Gave to mine Essay on the hidden
    qualities
Of the sulphuric mineral, I disclaim'd
All self-exaltment. And (*turning to
    the women*) when at the dance,
The lovely Saccharissa Kirkencroft,
Daughter to Kirkencroft of Kirken-
    croft,
Graced me with her soft hand, credit
    me, ladies,
That still I felt myself a mortal man,
Though beauty smiled on me.
    Osw. Come, sir, enough of this.
That you 're our guest to-night, thank
    the rough heavens,
And all our worser fortunes; be con-
    formable
Unto my rules; these are no Saccha-
    rissas
To gild with compliments. There 's
    in your profession,
As the best grain will have its piles
    of chaff,
A certain whiffler, who hath dared to
    bait
A noble maiden with love tales and
    sonnets;
And if I meet him, his Geneva cap
May scarce be proof to save his ass's
    ears.
    Kat. (*aside*). Umph! I am strongly
    tempted
And yet I think I will be generous,
And give his brains a chance to save
    his bones.
Then there 's more humour in our
    goblin plot,
Than in a simple drubbing.
    Ele. (*apart to* Flora). What shall
    we do? If he discover him,
He 'll fling him out at window.
    Flo. My father's hint to keep
    himself unknown
Is all too broad, I think, to be neg-
    lected.

    Ele. But yet the fool, if we produce
    his bounty,
May claim the merit of presenting it;
And then we 're but lost women for
    accepting
A gift our needs made timely.
    Kat.   Do not produce them.
E'en let the fop go supperless to
    bed,
And keep his bones whole.
    Osw. (*to his Wife*).   Hast thou
    aught
To place before him ere he seek
    repose?
    Ele. Alas! too well you know our
    needful fare
Is of the narrowest now, and knows
    no surplus.
    Osw. Shame us not with thy nig-
    gard housekeeping;
He is a stranger: were it our last
    crust,
And he the veriest coxcomb e'er wore
    taffeta,
A pitch he 's little short of, he must
    share it,
Though all should want to-morrow.
    Gul. (*partly overhearing what passes
    between them*). Nay, I am no lover
    of your sauced dainties:
Plain food and plenty is my motto
    still.
Your mountain air is bleak, and brings
    an appetite:
A soused sow's face, now, to my
    modest thinking,
Has ne'er a fellow. What think
    these fair ladies
Of a sow's face and sausages?

        [*Makes signs to* Eleanor.

    Flo. Plague on the vulgar hind,
    and on his courtesies,
The whole truth will come out! [*Aside.*
    Osw. What should they think, but
    that you 're like to lack

Your favourite dishes, sir, unless perchance
You bring such dainties with you.

Gul. No, not *with* me; not, indeed,
Directly *with* me; but—aha! fair ladies!   [*Makes signs again.*

Kat. He'll draw the beating down—
Were that the worst,
Heaven's will be done!   [*Aside.*

Osw. (*apart*). What can he mean?
This is the veriest dog-whelp;
Still he's a stranger, and the latest act
Of hospitality in this old mansion
Shall not be sullied.

Gul. Troth, sir, I think, under the ladies' favour,
Without pretending skill in second sight,
Those of my cloth being seldom conjurers——

Osw. I'll take my Bible-oath that thou art none.   [*Aside.*

Gul. I do opine, still with the ladies' favour,
That I could guess the nature of our supper:
I do not say in such and such precedence
The dishes will be placed; housewives, as you know,
On such forms have their fancies; but, I say still,
That a sow's face and sausages——

Osw.   Peace, sir!
O'er-driven jests (if this be one) are insolent.

Flo. (*apart, seeing her mother uneasy*).
The old saw still holds true—a churl's benefits,
Sauced with his lack of feeling, sense, and courtesy,
Savour like injuries.

    [*A horn is winded without; then a loud knocking at the gate.*

Leo. (*without*). Ope, for the sake of love and charity!
    [*Oswald goes to the loop-hole.*

Gul. Heaven's mercy! should there come another stranger,
And he half starved with wandering on the wolds,
The sow's face boasts no substance, nor the sausages,
To stand our reinforced attack! I judge, too,
By this starved Baron's language, there's no hope
Of a reserve of victuals.

Flo. Go to the casement, cousin.

Kat.   Go yourself,
And bid the gallant who that bugle winded
Sleep in the storm-swept waste; as meet for him
As for Lance Blackthorn. Come, I'll not distress you,
I'll get admittance for this second suitor,
And we'll play out this gambol at cross purposes.
But see, your father has prevented me.

Osw. (*seems to have spoken with those without, and answers*) Well, I will ope the door; one guest already,
Driven by the storm, has claim'd my hospitality,
And you, if you were fiends, were scarce less welcome
To this my mouldering roof, than empty ignorance
And rank conceit: I hasten to admit you.   [*Exit.*

Ele. (*to* Flo). The tempest thickens. By that winded bugle,
I guess the guest that next will honour us.
Little deceiver, that didst mock my troubles,
'Tis now thy turn to fear!

FLO. Mother, if I knew less or more
of this
Unthought of and most perilous visit-
ation,
I would your wishes were fulfill'd on
me,
And I were wedded to a thing like yon.
GUL. (*approaching*). Come, ladies,
now you see the jest is threadbare,
And you must own that same sow's
face and sausages ——

Re-enter OSWALD *with* LEONARD, *supporting* BAULDIE DURWARD. *OS-
WALD takes a view of them, as formerly of* GULLCRAMMER, *then speaks.*

Osw. (*to* LEON.) By thy green cas-
sock, hunting-spear and bugle,
I guess thou art a huntsman?
LEON. (*bowing with respect*). A ranger
of the neighbouring royal forest,
Under the good Lord Nithsdale;
huntsman, therefore,
In time of peace, and when the land
has war,
To my best powers a soldier.
Osw. Welcome, as either. I have
loved the chase,
And was a soldier once. This aged
man,
What may he be?
DUR. (*recovering his breath*). Is but
a beggar, sir, an humble mendicant,
Who feels it passing strange, that from
this roof,
Above all others, he should now crave
shelter.
Osw. Why so? You're welcome
both—only the word
Warrants more courtesy than our
present means
Permit us to bestow. A huntsman
and a soldier
May be a prince's comrade, much
more mine;
And for a beggar—friend, there little
lacks,

Save that blue gown and badge, and
clouted pouches,
To make us comrades too; then
welcome both,
And to a beggar's feast. I fear brown
bread,
And water from the spring, will be
the best on 't;
For we had cast to wend abroad this
evening,
And left our larder empty.
GUL. Yet, if some kindly fairy,
In our behalf, would search its hid
recesses,—
(*Apart.*) We'll not go supperless now
—we're three to one.—
Still do I say, that a sous'd face and
sausages ——
Osw. (*looks sternly at him, then at his
wife*). There's something under
this, but that the present
Is not a time to question. (*To* ELE.)
Wife, my mood
Is at such height of tide, that a turn'd
feather
Would make me frantic now, with
mirth or fury!
Tempt me no more; but if thou hast
the things
This carrion crow so croaks for, bring
them forth;
For, by my father's beard, if I stand
caterer,
'Twill be a fearful banquet!
ELE. Your pleasure be obey'd. Come,
aid me, Flora. [*Exeunt.*
[*During the following speeches the
Women place dishes on the table.*
Osw. (*to* DUR.) How did you lose
your path?
DUR. E'en when we thought to find
it, a wild meteor
Danced in the moss, and led our feet
astray.—
I give small credence to the tales of old,
Of Friar's-lantern told, and Will-o'-
Wisp,

Else would I say, that some malicious
demon
Guided us in a round ; for to the
moat,
Which we had pass'd two hours since,
were we led,
And there the gleam flicker'd and
disappear'd
Even on your drawbridge. I was so
worn down,
So broke with labouring through
marsh and moor,
That, wold I nold I, here my young
conductor
Would needs implore for entrance;
else, believe me,
I had not troubled you.
    Osw. And why not, father? Have
you e'er heard aught,
Or of my house or me, that wanderers,
Whom or their roving trade or sudden
circumstance
Oblige to seek a shelter, should avoid
The House of Devorgoil?
    Dur.   Sir, I am English born,
Native of Cumberland. Enough is said
Why I should shun those bowers,
whose lords were hostile
To English blood, and unto Cumber-
land
Most hostile and most fatal.
    Osw. Ay, father. Once my grand-
sire plough'd, and harrow'd,
And sow'd with salt, the streets of
your fair towns ;
And what of that?—you have the
'vantage now.
    Dur. True, Lord of Devorgoil, and
well believe I
That not in vain we sought these
towers to-night,
So strangely guided, to behold their
state.
    Osw. Ay, thou wouldst say, 'twas
fit a Cumbrian beggar
Should sit an equal guest in his proud
halls,

Whose fathers beggar'd Cumberland.
Greybeard, let it be so,
I 'll not dispute it with thee.
    (*To* Leonard *who was speaking to*
    Flora, *but, on being surprised,*
    occupied himself with the suit of
    armour.)
What makest thou there, young man ?
    Leon. I marvell'd at this harness ;
it is larger
Than arms of modern days. How
richly carved
With gold inlaid on steel—how close
the rivets—
How justly fit the joints ! I think the
gauntlet
Would swallow twice my hand.
    [*He is about to take down some*
    part of the Armour; Oswald
    interferes.
    Osw.   Do not displace it.
My grandsire, Erick, doubled human
strength,
And almost human size—and human
knowledge,
And human vice, and human virtue
also,
As storm or sunshine chanced to occupy
His mental hemisphere. After a fatal
deed,
He hung his armour on the wall, for-
bidding
It e'er should be ta'en down. There
is a prophecy,
That of itself 'twill fall, upon the night
When, in the fiftieth year from his
decease,
Devorgoil's feast is full. This is the era ;
But, as too well you see, no meet
occasion
Will do the downfall of the armour
justice,
Or grace it with a feast. There let it
bide,
Trying its strength with the old walls
it hangs on
Which shall fall soonest.

Dur. (*looking at the trophy with a mixture of feeling*). Then there stern Erick's harness hangs untouch'd,

Since his last fatal raid on Cumberland!

Osw. Ay, waste and want, and recklessness—a comrade

Still yoked with waste and want— have stripp'd these walls

Of every other trophy. Antler'd skulls,

Whose branches vouch'd the tales old vassals told

Of desperate chases; partisans and spears;

Knights' barred helms and shields; the shafts and bows,

Axes and breastplates, of the hardy yeomanry;

The banners of the vanquish'd – signs these arms

Were not assumed in vain—have disappear'd.

Yes, one by one they all have disappear'd;

And now Lord Erick's harness hangs alone,

'Midst implements of vulgar husbandry

And mean economy; as some old warrior,

Whom want hath made an inmate of an alms-house,

Shows, 'mid the beggar'd spendthrifts, base mechanics,

And bankrupt pedlars, with whom fate has mix'd him.

Dur. Or rather like a pirate, whom the prison-house,

Prime leveller next the grave, hath for the first time

Mingled with peaceful captives, low in fortunes,

But fair in innocence.

Osw. (*looking at* Dur. *with surprise*). Friend, thou art bitter!

Dur. Plain truth, sir, like the vulgar copper coinage,

Despised amongst the gentry, still finds value

And currency with beggars.

Osw.   Be it so.

I will not trench on the immunities

I soon may claim to share. Thy features, too,

Though weather-beaten, and thy strain of language,

Relish of better days. Come hither, friend,   [*They speak apart.*

And let me ask thee of thine occupation.

[Leonard *looks round, and, seeing* Oswald *engaged with* Durward, *and* Gullcrammer *with* Eleanor, *approaches towards* Flora, *who must give him an opportunity of doing so, with obvious attention on her part to give it the air of chance. The by-play here will rest with the Lady, who must engage the attention of the audience by playing off a little female hypocrisy and simple coquetry.*

Leon. Flora —

Flo. Ay, gallant huntsman, may she deign to question

Why Leonard came not at the appointed hour;

Or why he came at midnight?

Leon. Love has no certain loadstar, gentle Flora,

And oft gives up the helm to wayward pilotage.

To say the sooth, a beggar forced me hence,

And Will-o'-Wisp did guide us back again.

Flo. Ay. ay, your beggar was the faded spectre

Of Poverty, that sits upon the threshold

Of these our ruin'd walls. I 've been unwise,

Leonard, to let you speak so oft with me;

And you a fool to say what you have
  said.
E'en let us here break short; and,
  wise at length,
Hold each our separate way through
  life's wide ocean.

  LEON. Nay, let us rather join our
  course together,
And share the breeze or tempest,
  doubling joys,
Relieving sorrows, warding evils off
With mutual effort, or enduring them
With mutual patience.

  FLO. This is but flattering counsel,
  sweet and baneful;
But mine had wholesome bitter in 't.

  KAT. Ay, ay; but like the sly
  apothecary,
You'll be the last to take the bitter
  drug
That you prescribe to others.

  [*They whisper.* ELEANOR *advances
  to interrupt them, followed by*
  GULLCRAMMER.

  ELE. What, maid, no household
  cares? Leave to your elders
The task of filling passing strangers'
  ears
With the due notes of welcome.

  GUL.   Be it thine,
O Mistress Flora, the more useful
  talent
Of filling strangers' stomachs with
  substantials;
That is to say—for learn'd commentators
Do so expound substantials in some
  places—
With a sous'd bacon-face and sausages.

  FLO. (*apart*). Would thou wert
  sous'd, intolerable pedant,
Base, greedy, perverse, interrupting
  coxcomb!

  KAT. Hush, coz, for we 'll be well
  avenged on him,

And ere this night goes o'er, else
  woman's wit
Cannot o'ertake her wishes.

  [*She proceeds to arrange seats.*
  OSWALD *and* DURWARD *come
  forward in conversation.*

  OSW. I like thine humour well.
  So all men beg——

  DUR. Yes; I can make it good by
  proof. Your soldier
Begs for a leaf of laurel, and a line
In the Gazette; he brandishes his
  sword
To back his suit, and is a sturdy beggar.
The courtier begs a riband or a star,
And, like our gentler mumpers, is
  provided
With false certificates of health and
  fortune
Lost in the public service. For your
  lover,
Who begs a sigh, a smile, a lock of
  hair,
A buskin-point, he maunds upon the
  pad,
With the true cant of pure mendicity,
'The smallest trifle to relieve a
  Christian,
And if it like your Ladyship!'

                  [*In a begging tone.*
  KAT. (*apart*). This is a cunning
  knave, and feeds the humour
Of my aunt's husband, for I must not
  say
Mine honour'd uncle. I will try a
  question.
Your man of merit though, who serves
  the commonwealth,
Nor asks for a requital?

                  [*To* DURWARD.
  DUR.   Is a dumb beggar,
And lets his actions speak like signs
  for him,
Challenging double guerdon. Now,
  I 'll show
How your true beggar has the **fair**
  advantage

O'er all the tribes of cloak'd men-
dicity
I have told over to you. The soldier's
laurel,
The statesman's riband, and the lady's
favour,
Once won and gain'd, are not held
worth a farthing
By such as longest, loudest, canted
for them ;
Whereas your charitable halfpenny,
Which is the scope of a true beggar's
suit,
Is worth *two* farthings, and, in times
of plenty,
Will buy a crust of bread.

    FLO. (*interrupting him, and address-
ing her father*). Sir, let me be
a beggar with the time,
And pray you come to supper.

    ELE. (*to* OSWALD, *apart*). Must *he*
sit with us ?
        [*Looking at* DURWARD.

    OSW. Ay, ay, what else ? since we
are beggars all !
When cloaks are ragged, sure their
worth is equal,
Whether at first they were of silk or
woollen.

    ELE. Thou art scarce consistent.
This day thou didst refuse a princely
banquet,
Because a new-made lord was placed
above thee ;
And now——

    OSW. Wife, I have seen, at public
executions,
A wretch, who could not brook the
hand of violence
Should push him from the scaffold,
pluck up courage,
And, with a desperate sort of cheer-
fulness,
Take the fell plunge himself.
Welcome then, beggars, to a beggar's
feast.

    GUL. (*who has in the meanwhile
seated himself*). But this is more.——
A better countenance,——
Fair fall the hands that sous'd it !——
than this hog's,
Or prettier provender than these same
sausages
(By what good friend sent hither,
shall be nameless,
Doubtless some youth whom love hath
made profuse),
    [*Smiling significantly at* ELEANOR
and FLORA
No prince need wish to peck it. Long,
I ween,
Since that the nostrils of this house
(by metaphor,
I mean the chimneys) smell'd a steam
so grateful—
By your good leave I cannot dally
longer.   [*Helps himself.*

    OSW. (*placing* DURWARD *above* GULL-
CRAMMER). Meanwhile, sir,
Please it your faithful learning to give
place
To grey hairs and to wisdom ; and,
moreover,
If you had tarried for the benedic-
tion——

    GUL. (*somewhat abashed*). I said
grace to myself.

    OSW. (*not minding him*).—and
waited for the company of others,
It had been better fashion. Time has
been,
I should have told a guest at Devorgoil,
Bearing himself thus forward, he was
saucy.

    [*He seats himself, and helps the
company and himself in dumb-
show. There should be a contrast betwixt the precision of
his aristocratic civility, and the
rude under-breeding of* GULL-
CRAMMER.

Osw. (*having tasted the dish next him*). Why, this is venison, Eleanor!

Gul. Eh? What? Let's see!

[*Pushes across* Oswald *and helps himself.*

It may be venison;
I'm sure 'tis not beef, veal, mutton, lamb, or pork.
Eke am I sure, that be it what it will,
It is not half so good as sausages,
Or as a sow's face sous'd.

Osw. Eleanor, whence all this?

Ele. Wait till to-morrow,
You shall know all. It was a happy chance
That furnish'd us to meet so many guests. [*Fills wine.*
Try if your cup be not as richly garnish'd
As is your trencher.[1]

Kat. (*apart*). My aunt adheres to the good cautious maxim
Of—'Eat your pudding, friend, and hold your tongue.'

Osw. (*tasting the wine*). It is the grape of Bordeaux.
Such dainties, once familiar to my board,
Have been estranged from 't long.

[*He again fills his glass, and continues to speak as he holds it up.*

Fill round, my friends—here is a treacherous friend now
Smiles in your face, yet seeks to steal the jewel,
Which is distinction between man and brute—
I mean our reason—this he does, and smiles.
But are not all friends treacherous? one shall cross you

---

[1] Wooden trenchers should be used, and the quaigh, a Scottish drinking-cup.

Even in your dearest interests; one shall slander you;
This steal your daughter, that defraud your purse:
But this gay flask of Bordeaux will but borrow
Your sense of mortal sorrows for a season,
And leave, instead, a gay delirium.
Methinks my brain, unused to such gay visitants,
The influence feels already! we will revel!
Our banquet shall be loud! it is our last.
Katleen, thy song.

Kat. Not now, my lord; I mean to sing to-night
For this same moderate, grave, and reverend clergyman;
I'll keep my voice till then.

Ele. Your round refusal shows but cottage breeding.

Kat. Ay, my good aunt, for I was cottage-nurtured,
And taught, I think, to prize my own wild will
Above all sacrifice to compliment.
Here is a huntsman—in his eyes I read it,
He sings the martial song my uncle loves,
What time fierce Claver'se with his Cavaliers,
Abjuring the new change of government,
Forcing his fearless way through timorous friends,
And enemies as timorous, left the capital
To rouse in James's cause the distant Highlands.
Have you ne'er heard the song, my noble uncle?

Osw. Have I not heard, wench? It was I rode next him,
'Tis thirty summers since—rode by his rein;

We marched on through the alarm'd
  city,
As sweeps the osprey through a flock
  of gulls,
Who scream and flutter, but dare no
  resistance
Against the bold sea-empress. They
  did murmur,
The crowds before us, in their sullen
  wrath,
And those whom we had pass'd,
  gathering fresh courage,
Cried havoc in the rear: we minded
  them
E'en as the brave bark minds the
  bursting billows,
Which, yielding to her bows, burst on
  her sides,
And ripple in her wake. Sing me
  that strain,   [*To* LEONARD.
And thou shalt have a meed I seldom
  tender,
Because they're all I have to give—
  my thanks.

  LEON. Nay, if you'll bear with what
    I cannot help,
A voice that's rough with hollowing
  to the hounds,
I'll sing the song even as old Rowland
  taught me.

SONG.

To the Lords of Convention 'twas
  Claver'se who spoke,
'Ere the King's crown shall fall there
  are crowns to be broke ;
So let each Cavalier who loves honour
  and me,
Come follow the bonnet of Bonny
  Dundee.

  'Come fill up my cup, come fill up
    my can,
    Come saddle your horses, and call
      up your men ;

Come open the West Port, and let
  me gang free,
  And it's room for the bonnets of
    Bonny Dundee !'

Dundee he is mounted, he rides up
  the street,
The bells are rung backward, the
  drums they are beat ;
But the Provost, douce man, said,
  'Just e'en let him be,
The Gude Town is weel quit of that
  Deil of Dundee.'

  Come fill up my cup, &c.

As he rode down the sanctified bends
  of the Bow,
Ilk carline was flyting and shaking her
  pow ;
But the young plants of grace they
  look'd couthie and slee,
Thinking, 'Luck to thy bonnet, thou
  Bonny Dundee !'

  Come fill up my cup, &c.

With sour-featured Whigs the Grass-
  market was cramm'd
As if half the West had set tryst to
  be hang'd ;
There was spite in each look, there
  was fear in each e'e,
As they watch'd for the bonnets of
  Bonny Dundee.

  Come fill up my cup, &c.

These cowls of Kilmarnock had spits
  and had spears,
And lang-hafted gullies to kill Cavaliers;
But they shrunk to close-heads, and
  the causeway was free,
At the toss of the bonnet of Bonny
  Dundee.

  Come fill up my cup, &c.

He spurr'd to the foot of the proud
  Castle rock,
And with the gay Gordon he gallantly
  spoke ;

'Let Mons Meg and her marrows
    speak twa words or three,
For the love of the bonnet of Bonny
    Dundee.'

    Come fill up my cup, &c.

The Gordon demands of him which
    way he goes—
'Where'er shall direct me the shade
    of Montrose!
Your Grace in short space shall hear
    tidings of me,
Or that low lies the bonnet of Bonny
    Dundee.

    Come fill up my cup, &c.

'There are hills beyond Pentland, and
    lands beyond Forth,
If there's lords in the Lowlands,
    there's chiefs in the North;
There are wild Duniewassals, three
    thousand times three,
Will cry *hoigh!* for the bonnet of
    Bonny Dundee.

    Come fill up my cup, &c.

'There's brass on the target of
    barken'd bull-hide;
There's steel in the scabbard that
    dangles beside;
The brass shall be burnish'd, the steel
    shall flash free,
At a toss of the bonnet of Bonny
    Dundee.

    Come fill up my cup, &c.

'Away to the hills, to the caves, to
    the rocks—
Ere I own an usurper, I'll couch with
    the fox;
And tremble, false Whigs, in the
    midst of your glee,
You have not seen the last of my
    bonnet and me!'

    Come fill up my cup, &c.

He waved his proud hand, and the
    trumpets were blown,
The kettle-drums clash'd, and the
    horsemen rode on,
Till on Ravelston's cliffs and on
    Clermiston's lee,
Died away the wild war-notes of
    Bonny Dundee.

    Come fill up my cup, come fill up
      my can,
    Come saddle the horses and call up
      the men,
    Come open your gates, and let me
      gae free,
    For it's up with the bonnets of
      Bonny Dundee!

Ele. Katleen, do thou sing now.
    Thy uncle's cheerful;
We must not let his humour ebb
    again.
Kat. But I'll do better, aunt, than
    if I sung,
For Flora can sing blithe; so can this
    huntsman,
As he has shown e'en now; let them
    duet it.
Osw. Well, huntsman, we must
    give to freakish maiden
The freedom of her fancy. Raise the
    carol,
And Flora, if she can, will join the
    measure.

SONG.

When friends are met o'er merry cheer,
And lovely eyes are laughing near,
And in the goblet's bosom clear
    The cares of day are drown'd;
When puns are made, and bumpers
    quaff'd,
And wild Wit shoots his roving shaft,
And Mirth his jovial laugh has laugh'd,
    Then is our banquet crown'd,
      Ah gay,
    Then is our banquet crown'd.

When glees are sung, and catches
    troll'd,
And bashfulness grows bright and bold,
And beauty is no longer cold,
    And age no longer dull;
When chimes are brief, and cocks do
    crow,
To tell us it is time to go,
Yet how to part we do not know,
    Then is our feast at full,
        Ah gay,
    Then is our feast at full.

    Osw. (*rises with the cup in his hand*).
Devorgoil's feast is full—
Drink to the pledge !

> [*A tremendous burst of thunder
> follows these words of the Song ;
> and the Lightning should seem
> to strike the suit of black Armour,
> which falls with a crash.[1] All
> rise in surprise and fear except
> GULLCRAMMER, who tumbles
> over backwards, and lies still.*

    Osw. That sounded like the judg-
ment-peal : the roof
Still trembles with the volley.
    Dur.   Happy those
Who are prepared to meet such fearful
    summons.
Leonard, what dost thou there ?
    Leon. (*supporting* Flora). The duty
of a man—
Supporting innocence. Were it the
    final call,
I were not misemploy'd.
    Osw. The armour of my grandsire
hath fall'n down,
And old saws have spoke truth.
    (*Musing.*) The fiftieth year—
Devorgoil's feast at fullest ! What to
    think of it——
    Leon. (*lifting a scroll which had fallen
with the armour*). This may in-
form us.

---

[1] I should think this may be contrived, by having
a transparent zig-zag in the flat-scene, immediately
above the armour, suddenly and very strongly
illuminated.

> [*Attempts to read the manuscript,
> shakes his head, and gives it to
> Oswald.*

But not to eyes unlearn'd it tells its
    tidings.
    Osw. Hawks, hounds, and revelling
    consumed the hours
I should have given to study.

> [*Looks at the manuscript.*

These characters I spell not more
    than thou.
They are not of our day, and, as I think,
Not of our language. Where's our
    scholar now,
So forward at the banquet ? Is he
    laggard
Upon a point of learning ?
    Leon. Here is the man of letter'd
    dignity,
E'en in a piteous case.

> [*Drags* GULLCRAMMER *forward.*

    Osw. Art waking, craven ? canst
    thou read this scroll ?
Or art thou only learn'd in sousing
    swine's flesh,
And prompt in eating it ?
    Gul. Eh — ah ! — oh — ho !—Have
    you no better time
To tax a man with riddles, than the
    moment
When he scarce knows whether he's
    dead or living ?
    Osw. Confound the pedant ?—Can
    you read the scroll,
Or can you not, sir ? If you *can*,
    pronounce
Its meaning speedily.
    Gul.   *Can* I read it, quotha !
When at our learned University,
I gain'd first premium for Hebrew
    learning,—
Which was a pound of high-dried
    Scottish snuff,
And half a peck of onions, with a bushel
Of curious oatmeal ; our learn'd Prin-
    cipal

Did say 'Melchisedek, thou canst do
    any thing!'
Now comes he with his paltry scroll
    of parchment,
And '*Can* you read it?'—After such
    affront,
The point is, if I *will*.
    Osw.   A point soon solved,
Unless you choose to sleep among
    the frogs ;
For look you, sir, there is the chamber
    window,
Beneath it lies the lake.
    Ele. Kind master Gullcrammer,
      beware my husband,
He brooks no contradiction—'tis his
    fault,
And in his wrath he's dangerous.
    Gul. (*looks at the scroll, and mutters
      as if reading*)
Hashgaboth hotch-potch—
A simple matter this to make a rout of—
*Ten rashers en bacon, mish-mash venison,
Sausagian soused-face*—'tis a simple
    catalogue
Of our small supper—made by the
    grave sage
Whose prescience knew this night
    that we should feast
On venison, hash'd sow's face, and
    sausages,
And hung his steel-coat for a supper
    bell.
E'en let us to our provender again,
For it is written we shall finish it,
And bless our stars the lightning left
    it us.
    Osw. This must be impudence or
    ignorance !
The spirit of rough Erick stirs within
    me,
And I will knock thy brains out if
    thou palterest !
Expound the scroll to me !
    Gul.   You're over hasty ;
And yet you may be right too. 'Tis
    Samaritan,

Now I look closer on't, and I did
    take it
For simple Hebrew.
    Dur. 'Tis Hebrew to a simpleton,
That we see plainly, friend. Give me
    the scroll.
    Gul. Alas, good friend ! what
    would you do with it ?
    Dur. (*takes it from him*). My best
    to read it, sir. The character is
Saxon,
Used at no distant date within this
    district ;
And thus the tenor runs—nor in
    Samaritan,
Nor simple Hebrew, but in wholesome
    English :—

Devorgoil, thy bright moon waneth,
And the rust thy harness staineth ;
Servile guests the banquet soil
Of the once proud Devorgoil.
But should Black Erick's armour fall,
Look for guests shall scare you all !
They shall come ere peep of day,—
Wake and watch, and hope and pray.

    Kat. (*to* Flora). Here is fine foolery !
    An old wall shakes
At a loud thunder-clap—down comes
    a suit
Of ancient armour, when its wasted
    braces
Were all too rotten to sustain its
    weight—
A beggar cries out, Miracle ! and
    your father,
Weighing the importance of his name
    and lineage,
Must needs believe the dotard !
    Flo. Mock not, I pray you ; this
    may be too serious.
    Kat. And if I live till morning, I
    will have
The power to tell a better tale of
    wonder
Wrought on wise Gullcrammer. I'll
    go prepare me.   [*Exit.*

FLO. I have not Katleen's spirit,
　　yet I hate
This Gullcrammer too heartily, to stop
Any disgrace that's hasting towards
　　him.
　　Osw. (*to whom the Beggar has been
　　　　again reading the scroll*). 'Tis a
strange prophecy! The silver moon,
Now waning sorely, is our ancient
　　bearing—
Strange and unfitting guests ——
　　GUL. (*interrupting him*). Ay, ay,
　　　　the matter
Is, as you say, all moonshine in the
　　water.
　　Osw. How mean you, sir? (*threaten-
　　　　ing.*)
　　GUL. 　　To show that I can rhyme
With yonder bluegown. Give me
　　breath and time,
I will maintain, in spite of his pretence,
Mine exposition had the better sense :
It spoke good victuals and increase of
　　cheer ;
And his, more guests to eat what we
　　have here—
An increment right needless.
　　Osw. 　　　　　Get thee gone ;
To kennel, hound !
　　GUL. The hound will have his bone.
　　[*Takes up the platter of meat, and
　　　　a flask.*
　　Osw. Flora, show him his chamber
　　　　—take him hence,
Or, by the name I bear, I'll see his
　　brains !
　　GUL. Ladies, good night ! I spare
　　　　you, sir, the pains.
　　[*Exit, lighted by* FLORA *with a lamp.*
　　Osw. The owl is fled —I'll not to
　　　　bed to-night ;
There is some change impending o'er
　　this house,
For good or ill. I would some holy man
Were here, to counsel us what we
　　should do !

Yon witless thin-faced gull is but
　　a cassock,
Stuff'd out with chaff and straw.
　　DUR. (*assuming an air of dignity*).
　　I have been wont,
In other days, to point to erring mor-
　　tals
The rock which they should anchor on.
　　[*He holds up a Cross ; the rest take
　　　　a posture of devotion, and the
　　　　Scene closes.*

—◆—

ACT III.

SCENE I.

*A ruinous Anteroom in the castle.
Enter* KATLEEN, *fantastically dressed
to play the character of* COCKLEDEMOY,
with the visor in her hand.

　　KAT. I've scarce had time to glance
　　　　at my sweet person,
Yet this much could I see, with half
　　a glance,
My elfish dress becomes me—I'll not
　　mask me
Till I have seen Lance Blackthorn.
　　Lance ! I say— 　　　　[*Calls.*
Blackthorn, make haste !

Enter BLACKTHORN, *half dressed as*
OWLSPIEGLE.

　　BLA. Here am I — Blackthorn in the
　　　　upper half,
Much at your service ; but my nether
　　parts
Are goblinised and Owlspiegled I
　　had much ado
To get these trankums on. I judge
　　Lord Erick
Kept no good house, and starved his
　　quondam barber.
　　KAT. Peace, ass, and hide you—
　　　　Gullcrammer is coming ;

He left the hall before, but then took
　fright,
And e'en sneak'd back.　The Lady
　Flora lights him—
Trim occupation for her ladyship!
Had you seen Leonard, when she left
　the hall
On such fine errand!
　　Bla. This Gullcrammer shall have
　　　a bob extraordinary
For my good comrade's sake.—But
　tell me, Katleen,
What dress is this of yours?
　　Kat. A page's, fool!
　　Bla.　　　I'm accounted no great
　　　scholar,
But 'tis a page that I would fain pe-
　ruse
A little closer.　　[Approaches her.
　　Kat.　　Put on your spectacles,
And try if you can read it at this dis-
　tance,
For you shall come no nearer.
　　Bla. But is there nothing, then,
　　　save rank imposture,
In all these tales of goblinry at Devor-
　goil?
　　Kat. My aunt's grave lord thinks
　　　otherwise, supposing
That his great name so interests the
　Heavens,
That miracles must needs bespeak its
　fall.
I would that I were in a lowly cottage
Beneath the greenwood, on its walls
　no armour
To court the levin-bolt——
　　Bla. And a kind husband, Katleen,
To ward such dangers as must needs
　come nigh.
My father's cottage stands so low and
　lone,
That you would think it solitude itself;
The greenwood shields it from the
　northern blast,
And, in the woodbine round its latticed
　casement

The linnet's sure to build the earliest
　nest
In all the forest.
　　Kat.　Peace, you fool, they come.
　　[Flora lights Gullcrammer
　　　across the Stage.
　　Kat. (when they have passed). Away
　　　with you!
On with your cloak—be ready at the
　signal.
　　Bla. And shall we talk of that same
　　　cottage, Katleen,
At better leisure? I have much to say
In favour of my cottage.
　　Kat.　　　　If you will be talking,
You know I can't prevent you.
　　Bla.　　　　　　That's enough.
(Aside.) I shall have leave, I see, to
　spell the page
A little closer, when the due time
　comes.

────────

Scene II.

Scene changes to Gullcrammer's
Sleeping Apartment.　He enters,
ushered in by Flora. who sets on
the table a flask, with the lamp.

　　Flo. A flask. in case your Rever-
　　　ence be athirsty;
A light, in case your Reverence be
　afear'd;—
And so sweet slumber to your
　Reverence.
　　Gul.　Kind Mistress Flora, will
　　　you?—eh! eh! eh!
　　Flo. Will I what?
　　Gul. Tarry a little?
　　Flo. (smiling). Kind Master Gull-
　　　crammer,
How can you ask me aught so un-
　becoming?
　　Gul. Oh, fie, fie, fie!　Believe me,
　　　Mistress Flora,
'Tis not for that—but being guided
　through

Such dreary galleries, stairs, and
suites of rooms,
To this same cubicle, I'm somewhat
loth
To bid adieu to pleasant company.

FLO. A flattering compliment! In
plain truth you are frighten'd.

GUL. What! frighten'd!—I—I—am
not timorous.

FLO. Perhaps you 've heard this is
our haunted chamber?
But then it is our best. Your Reverence knows,
That in all tales which turn upon
a ghost,
Your traveller belated has the luck
To enjoy the haunted room—it is
a rule:
To some it were a hardship, but to
you,
Who are a scholar, and not timorous ——

GUL. I did not say I was not timor-
ous,
I said I was not temerarious.
I 'll to the hall again.

FLO. You'll do your pleasure,
But you have somehow moved my
father's anger,
And you had better meet our playful
Owlspiegle—
So is our goblin call'd—than face
Lord Oswald.

GUL. Owlspiegle?
It is an uncouth and outlandish name,
And in mine ear sounds fiendish.

FLO. Hush, hush, hush!
Perhaps he hears us now—(in an
undertone). A merry spirit;
None of your elves that pinch folks
black and blue,
For lack of cleanliness.

GUL. As for that Mistress Flora,
My taffeta doublet hath been duly
brush'd,
My shirt hebdomadal put on this
morning.

FLO. Why, you need fear no goblins.
But this Owlspiegle
Is of another class;—yet has his
frolics;
Cuts hair, trims beards, and plays
amid his antics
The office of a sinful mortal barber.
Such is at least the rumour.

GUL. He will not cut my clothes,
or scar my face,
Or draw my blood?

FLO. Enormities like these
Were never charged against him.

GUL. And, Mistress Flora, would
you smile on me,
If, prick'd by the fond hope of your
approval,
I should endure this venture?

FLO. I do hope
I shall have cause to smile.

GUL. Well! in that hope
I will embrace the achievement for
thy sake. [She is going.
Yet, stay, stay, stay!—on second
thoughts I will not!
I 've thought on it, and will the mortal
cudgel
Rather endure than face the ghostly
razor!
Your crab-tree 's tough but blunt,—
your razor 's polish'd,
But, as the proverb goes, 'tis cruel
sharp
I 'll to thy father, and unto his plea-
sure
Submit these destined shoulders.

FLO. But you shall not,
Believe me, sir, you shall not; he is
desperate,
And better far be trimm'd by ghost or
goblin,
Than by my sire in anger; there are
stores
Of hidden treasure, too, and Heaven
knows what,
Buried among these ruins: you shall
stay.

(*Apart.*) And if indeed there be such
    sprite as Owlspiegle,
And, lacking him, that thy fear plague
    thee not
Worse than a goblin, I have miss'd
    my purpose,
Which else stands good in either
    case. (*Aloud*) Good-night, sir.

    [*Exit, and double-locks the door.*

  GUL. Nay, hold ye, hold! Nay,
    gentle Mistress Flora,
Wherefore this ceremony? She has
    lock'd me in,
And left me to the goblin! (*Listen-
    ing.*)   So, so, so!
I hear her light foot trip to such a
    distance,
That I believe the castle's breadth
    divides me
From human company.   I'm ill at
    ease ;
But if this citadel (*Laying his hand on
    his stomach*) were better victual'd,
It would be better mann'd.

    [*Sits down and drinks.*

She has a footstep light, and taper
    ankle.   [*Chuckles.*
Aha! that ankle! yet, confound it too,
But for those charms Melchisedek
    had been
Snug in his bed at Mucklewhame.   I
    say,
Confound her footstep, and her instep
    too,
To use a cobbler's phrase.   There I
    was quaint.
Now, what to do in this vile circum-
    stance,
To watch or go to bed, I can't
    determine ;
Were I a-bed, the ghost might catch
    me napping,
And if I watch, my terrors will
    increase
As ghostly hours approach.   I'll to
    my bed

E'en in my taffeta doublet, shrink my
    head
Beneath the clothes, leave the lamp
    burning there,
    [*Sets it on the table.*
And trust to fate the issue.

    [*He lays aside his cloak, and
    brushes it, as from habit, start-
    ing at every moment ; ties a nap-
    kin over his head ; then shrinks
    beneath the bed-clothes. He starts
    once or twice, and at length
    seems to go to sleep.   A bell
    tolls* ONE.   *He leaps up in his
    bed.*

  GUL.   I had just coax'd myself to
    sweet forgetfulness,
And that confounded bell—I hate all
    bells,
Except a dinner bell—and yet I lie,
    too,—
I love the bell that soon shall tell the
    parish
Of Gabblegoose Melchisedek's in-
    cumbent.
And shall the future minister of
    Gabblegoose,
Whom his parishioners will soon
    require
To exorcise their ghosts, detect their
    witches,
Lie shivering in his bed for a pert
    goblin,
Whom, be he switch'd or cocktail'd,
    horn'd or poll'd,
A few tight Hebrew words will soon
    send packing?
Tush! I will rouse the parson up
    within me,
And bid defiance —— (*A distant noise.*)
    In the name of Heaven,
What sounds are these! O Lord!
    this comes of rashness !

    [*Draws his head down under the
    bed-clothes.*

Duet without, between OWLSPIEGLE *and* COCKLEDEMOY.

OWLSPIEGLE.

Cockledemoy!
My boy, my boy——

COCKLEDEMOY.

Here, father, here.

OWLSPIEGLE.

Now the pole-star's red and burning,
And the witch's spindle turning,
　　　　Appear, appear!

GUL. (*who has again raised himself, and listened with great terror to the Duet*). I have heard of the devil's dam before,
But never of his child. Now, Heaven deliver me!
The Papists have the better of us there,—
They have their Latin prayers, cut and dried,
And pat for such occasion: I can think
On nought but the vernacular.

OWLSPIEGLE.

Cockledemoy!
My boy, my boy,
　　We'll sport us here;

COCKLEDEMOY.

Our gambols play,
Like elve and fay;

OWLSPIEGLE.

And domineer,

BOTH.

Laugh, frolic, and frisk, till the morning appear.

COCKLEDEMOY.

Lift latch, open clasp,
Shoot bolt, and burst hasp!

[*The door opens with violence. Enter* BLACKTHORN *as* OWL-SPIEGLE, *fantastically dressed as* a Spanish Barber, *tall, thin, emaciated, and ghostly;* KAT-LEEN, *as* COCKLEDEMOY, *attends as his Page. All their manners, tones, and motions, are fantastic, as those of Goblins. They make two or three times the circuit of the room, without seeming to see* GULLCRAMMER. *They then resume their Chant, or Recitative.*

OWLSPIEGLE.

Cockledemoy!
My boy, my boy,
What wilt thou do that will give thee joy?
Wilt thou ride on the midnight owl?

COCKLEDEMOY.

No; for the weather is stormy and foul.

OWLSPIEGLE.

Cockledemoy!
My boy, my boy,
What wilt thou do that can give thee joy?
With a needle for a sword, and a thimble for a hat,
Wilt thou fight a traverse with the castle cat?

COCKLEDEMOY.

Oh, no! she has claws, and I like not that.

GUL. I see the devil is a doting father,
And spoils his children; 'tis the surest way
To make cursed imps of them. They see me not.
What will they think on next? It must be own'd,
They have a dainty choice of occupations.

OWLSPIEGLE.

Cockledemoy!
My boy, my boy,
What shall we do that can give thee joy?
Shall we go seek for a cuckoo's nest?

COCKLEDEMOY.

That's best, that's best!

BOTH.

About, about,
Like an elvish scout,
The cuckoo's a gull, and we'll soon
    find him out.

[*They search the room with mops
    and mows. At length* COCKLE-
    DEMOY *jumps on the bed.* GULL-
    CRAMMER *raises himself half up,
    supporting himself by his hands.*
    COCKLEDEMOY *does the same,
    and grins at him, then skips from
    the bed, and runs to* OWLSPIEGLE.

COCKLEDEMOY.

I've found the nest,
    And in it a guest,
With a sable cloak and a taffeta vest;
He must be wash'd, and trimm'd, and
    dress'd,
To please the eyes he loves the best.

OWLSPIEGLE.

That's best, that's best.

BOTH.

He must be shaved, and trimm'd, and
    dress'd,
To please the eyes he loves the best.

[*They arrange shaving things on
    the table, and sing as they pre-
    pare them.*

BOTH.

Know that all of the humbug, the bite,
    and the buz,
Of the make-believe world, becomes
    forfeit to us.

OWLSPIEGLE (*sharpening his razor*).

The sword this is made of was lost
    in a fray
By a fop, who first bullied and then
    ran away;

And the strap, from the hide of a
    lame racer, sold
By Lord Match, to his friend, for
    some hundreds in gold.

BOTH.

For all of the humbug, the bite, and
    the buz,
Of the make-believe world, becomes
    forfeit to us.

COCKLEDEMOY (*placing the napkin*).

And this cambric napkin, so white
    and so fair,
At an usurer's funeral I stole from
    the heir.

[*Drops something from a vial, as
    going to make suds.*

This dewdrop I caught from one eye
    of his mother,
Which wept while she ogled the
    parson with t' other.

BOTH.

For all of the humbug, the bite, and
    the buz,
Of the make-believe world, becomes
    forfeit to us.

OWLSPIEGLE (*arranging the lather and
    the basin*).

My soap-ball is of the mild alkali
    made,
Which the soft dedicator employs in
    his trade;
And it froths with the pith of a promise,
    that's sworn
By a lover at night, and forgot on the
    morn.

BOTH.

For all of the humbug, the bite, and
    the buz,
Of the make-believe world, becomes
    forfeit to us.
        Halloo, halloo,
        The blackcock crew,

Thrice shriek'd hath the owl, thrice
croak'd hath the raven,
Here, ho! Master Gullcrammer, rise
and be shaven!

Da capo.

GUL. (*who has been observing them*).
I'll pluck a spirit up; they're merry
goblins,
And will deal mildly. I will soothe
their humour;
Besides, my beard lacks trimming.

[*He rises from his bed, and advances with great symptoms of
trepidation, but affecting an air
of composure. The Goblins receive him with fantastic ceremony.*

Gentlemen, 'tis your will I should be
trimm'd—
E'en do your pleasure. [*They point
to a seat—he sits.*]
Think, howsoe'er,
Of me as one who hates to see his
blood;
Therefore I do beseech you, signior,
Be gentle in your craft. I know those
barbers,—
One would have harrows driven across
his visnomy
Rather than they should touch it with
a razor.

OWLSPIEGLE *shaves* GULLCRAMMER,
while COCKLEDEMOY *sings.*

Father never started hair,
Shaved too close, or left too bare;
Father's razor slips as glib
As from courtly tongue a fib.
Whiskers, mustache, he can trim in
Fashion meet to please the women;
Sharp's his blade, perfumed his lather—
Happy those are trimm'd by father!

GUL. That's a good boy. I love to
hear a child
Stand for his father, if he were the
devil,—

[*He motions to rise.*

Craving your pardon, sir. What! sit
again?
My hair lacks not your scissors.

[OWLSPIEGLE *insists on his sitting.*

Nay, if you're peremptory, I'll ne'er
dispute it,
Nor eat the cow and choke upon the
tail:
E'en trim me to your fashion.

[OWLSPIEGLE *cuts his hair, and
shaves his head, ridiculously.*

COCKLEDEMOY (*sings as before*).

Hairbreadth 'scapes, and hairbreadth
snares,
Harebrain'd follies, ventures, cares,
Part when father clips your hairs.
If there is a hero frantic,
Or a lover too romantic;
If threescore seeks second spouse,
Or fourteen lists lover's vows,—
Bring them here: for a Scotch boddle,
Owlspiegle shall trim their noddle.

[*They take the napkin from about
GULLCRAMMER's neck. He makes
bows of acknowledgment, which
they return fantastically, and sing.*

Thrice crow'd hath the blackcock,
thrice croak'd hath the raven,
And Master Melchisedek Gullcrammer's shaven!

GUL. My friends, you are too musical
for me;
But though I cannot cope with you
in song
I would, in humble prose, inquire of
you,
If that you will permit me to acquit
Even with the barber's pence the
barber's service?

[*They shake their heads.*

Or if there is aught else that I can do
for you,
Sweet Master Owlspiegle, or your
loving child,
The hopeful Cockle'moy?

COCKLEDEMOY.

Sir, you have been trimm'd of late,
Smooth's your chin and bald your pate;
Lest cold rheums should work you
    harm,
Here's a cap to keep you warm.

GUL. Welcome, as Fortunatus'
    wishing-cap,
For 'twas a cap that I was wishing for.
(There I was quaint in spite of mortal
    terror.)

[*As he puts on the cap, a pair of
    ass's ears disengage themselves.*

Upon my faith, it is a dainty head-dress,
And might become an alderman!
Thanks, sweet Monsieur,
Thou 'rt a considerate youth.

[*Both Goblins bow with ceremony
to* GULLCRAMMER, *who returns
their salutation.* OWLSPIEGLE
descends by the trap-door. COCK-
LEDEMOY *springs out at window.*

SONG (*without*).

OWLSPIEGLE.

Cockledemoy, my hope, my care,
Where art thou now, O tell me where?

COCKLEDEMOY.

Up in the sky
On the bonny dragonfly;
Come, father, come you too;
She has four wings and strength enow,
And her long body has room for two.

GUL. Cockledemoy now is a naughty
    brat,
Would have the poor old stiff-rump'd
    devil, his father,
Peril his fiendish neck. All boys are
    thoughtless.

SONG.

OWLSPIEGLE.

Which way didst thou take?

COCKLEDEMOY.

I have fall'n in the lake—
Help, father, for Beëlzebub's sake!

GUL. The imp is drown'd—a strange
    death for a devil,—
O, may all boys take warning, and be
    civil;
Respect their loving sires, endure a
    chiding,
Nor roam by night on dragonflies a-
    riding!

COCKLEDEMOY (*sings*).

Now merrily, merrily, row I to shore,
My bark is a bean-shell, a straw for
    an oar.

OWLSPIEGLE (*sings*).

My life, my joy,
My Cockledemoy!

GUL. I can bear this no longer;
    thus children are spoil'd.

[*Strikes into the tune.*

Master Owlspiegle, hoy!
He deserves to be whipp'd, little
    Cockledemoy!

[*Their voices are heard, as if
    dying away.*

GUL. They're gone! Now, am I
    scared, or am I not?
I think the very desperate ecstasy
Of fear has given me courage. This
    is strange, now:
When they were here I was not half
    so frighten'd
As now they're gone: they were
    a sort of company.
What a strange thing is use! A horn,
    a claw,
The tip of a fiend's tail, was wont to
    scare me:
Now am I with the devil hand and
    glove;
His soap has lather'd, and his razor
    shaved me;
I've joined him in a catch, kept time
    and tune,
Could dine with him, nor ask for
    a long spoon;

And if I keep not better company,
What will become of me when I shall
  die?   *[Exit.*

SCENE III.

*A Gothic Hall, waste and ruinous.
The moonlight is at times seen
through the shafted windows*[1]. *Enter*
KATLEEN *and* BLACKTHORN. *They
have thrown off the more ludicrous
parts of their disguise.*

KAT. This way, this way; was
 ever fool so gull'd!

BLA. I play'd the barber better than
 I thought for.
Well, I've an occupation in reserve,
When the long-bow and merry musket
 fail me.
But, hark ye, pretty Katleen.

KAT. What should I hearken to?

BLA. Art thou not afraid,
In these wild halls while playing
 feignèd goblins,
That we may meet with real ones?

KAT.   Not a jot.
My spirit is too light, my heart too
 bold,
To fear a visit from the other world.

BLA. But is not this the place, the
 very hall
In which men say that Oswald's
 grandfather,
The black Lord Erick, walks his
 penance round?
Credit me, Katleen, these half-
 moulder'd columns
Have in their ruin something very
 fiendish,
And, if you'll take an honest friend's
 advice,
The sooner that you change their
 shatter'd splendour
For the snug cottage that I told you of,

---

[1] I have a notion that this can be managed so as to
represent imperfect, or flitting moonlight, upon the
plan of the Fidophusikon.

Believe me, it will prove the blither
 dwelling.

KAT. If I e'er see that cottage,
 honest Blackthorn,
Believe me, it shall be from other
 motive
Than fear of Erick's spectre.
    [A rustling sound is heard.

BLA. I heard a rustling sound—
Upon my life, there's something in
 the hall,
Katleen, besides us two!

KAT.   A yeoman thou,
A forester, and frighten'd! I am sorry
I gave the fool's-cap to poor Gull-
 crammer,
And let thy head go bare.
 [The same rushing sound is repeated.

BLA. Why, are you mad, or hear
 you not the sound?

KAT. And if I do, I take small heed
 of it.
Will you allow a maiden to be bolder
Than you, with beard on chin and
 sword at girdle?

BLA. Nay, if I had my sword,
 I would not care;
Though I ne'er heard of master of
 defence
So active at his weapon as to brave
The devil, or a ghost—See! see! see
 yonder!
  *[A Figure is imperfectly seen
  between two of the pillars.*

KAT. There's something moves,
 that's certain, and the moonlight,
Chased by the flitting gale, is too
 imperfect
To show its form; but, in the name of
 God,
I'll venture on it boldly.

BLA.   Wilt thou so?
Were I alone, now, I were strongly
 tempted
To trust my heels for safety; but with
 thee,

Be it fiend or fairy, I'll take risk to
  meet it.
  KAT. It stands full in our path, and
  we must pass it,
Or tarry here all night.
  BLA.   In its vile company?

  [*As they advance towards the
  Figure, it is more plainly distinguished, which might, I think,
  be contrived by raising successive
  screens of crape. The Figure is
  wrapped in a long robe, like the
  mantle of a Hermit, or Palmer.*

  PAL. Ho! ye who thread by night
  these wildering scenes,
In garb of those who long have slept
  in death,
Fear ye the company of those you
  imitate?
  BLA. This is the devil, Katleen, let
  us fly!   [*Runs off.*
  KAT. I will not fly; why should
  I? My nerves shake
To look on this strange vision, but
  my heart
Partakes not the alarm. If thou dost
  come in Heaven's name,
In Heaven's name art thou welcome!
  PAL. I come, by Heaven permitted.
  Quit this castle:
There is a fate on't; if for good or
  evil,
Brief space shall soon determine. In
  that fate,
If good, by lineage thou canst nothing
  claim;
If evil, much may'st suffer. Leave
  these precincts.
  KAT. Whate'er thou art, be answer'd!
  Know, I will not
Desert the kinswoman who train'd
  my youth;
Know that I will not quit my friend,
  my Flora;
Know that I will not leave the agèd
  man

Whose roof has shelter'd me. This
  is my resolve:
If evil come, I aid my friends to bear it;
If good, my part shall be to see them
  prosper,—
A portion in their happiness from which
No fiend can bar me.
  PAL.   Maid, before thy courage,
Firm built on innocence, even beings
  of nature
More powerful far than thine give
  place and way;
Take then this key, and wait the event
  with courage.

  [*He drops the key. He disappears
  gradually, the moonlight failing at the same time.*

  KAT. (*after a pause*). Whate'er it
  was, 'tis gone! My head turns
  round
The blood that lately fortified my heart
Now eddies in full torrent to my brain,
And makes wild work with reason.
  I will haste,
To living company. What if I meet it
Again in the long aisle, or vaulted
  passage?
And if I do, the strong support that
  bore me
Through this appalling interview,
  again
Shall strengthen and uphold me.

  [*As she steps forward she stumbles
  over the key.*

What's this? The key?—there may
  be mystery in't.
I'll to my kinswoman, when this
  dizzy fit
Will give me leave to choose my way
  aright. [*She sits down exhausted.*

Re-enter BLACKTHORN, *with a drawn
  sword and torch.*

  BLA. Katleen! What, Katleen!
  What a wretch was I

To leave her! Katleen, I am wea-
pon'd now,
And fear nor dog nor devil. She
replies not!
Beast that I was! nay, worse than
beast; the stag,
As timorous as he is, fights for his
hind.
What's to be done? I'll search this
cursed castle
From dungeon to the battlements; if
I find her not
I'll fling me from the highest pin-
nacle——

KATLEEN (*who has somewhat
gathered her spirits, in consequence
of his entrance, comes behind and
touches him; he starts*). Brave sir!
I'll spare you that rash leap. You're
a bold woodsman!
Surely I hope that from this night
henceforward
You'll never kill a hare, since you're
akin to them;
O, I could laugh, but that my head's
so dizzy.

BLA Lean on me, Katleen. By my
honest word,
I thought you close behind; I was
surprised,
Not a jot frighten'd.

KAT. Thou art a fool to ask me to
thy cottage,
And then to show me at what slight
expense
Of manhood I might master thee and it.

BLA. I'll take the risk of that.
This goblin business
Came rather unexpected; the best
horse
Will start at sudden sights. Try me
again,
And if I prove not true to bonny
Katleen,
Hang me in mine own bowstring.
[*Exeunt.*

SCENE IV.

*The Scene returns to the Apartment
at the beginning of Act II.* OSWALD
and DURWARD *are discovered with*
ELEANOR, FLORA, *and* LEONARD.
DURWARD *shuts a Prayer-book, which
he seems to have been reading.*

DUR. 'Tis true; the difference
betwixt the churches,
Which zealots love to dwell on, to
the wise
Of either flock are of far less im-
portance
Than those great truths to which all
Christian men
Subscribe with equal reverence.

Osw. We thank thee, father, for
the holy office,
Still best perform'd when the pastor's
tongue
Is echo to his breast; of jarring
creeds
It ill beseems a layman's tongue to
speak.
Where have you stow'd yon prater?
[*To* FLORA.

FLO. Safe in the goblin-chamber.

ELE. The goblin-chamber!
Maiden, wert thou frantic? If his
Reverence
Have suffer'd harm by waspish
Owlspiegle
Be sure thou shalt abye it.

FLO. Here he comes; he
Can answer for himself!

Enter GULLCRAMMER, *in the fashion in
which* OWLSPIEGLE *had put him:
having the fool's-cap on his head, and
towel about his neck, &c. His
manner through the scene is wild and
extravagant, as if the fright had a
little affected his brain.*

DUR. A goodly spectacle! Is
there such a goblin?

(*To* Oswald.) Or has sheer terror
     made him such a figure?
    Osw. There is a sort of wavering
     tradition
Of a malicious imp who teazed all
    strangers;
My father wont to call him Owl-
    spiegle.
    Gul. Who talks of Owlspiegle?
He is an honest fellow for a devil,
So is his son, the hopeful Cockle'moy.

(*Sings.*)

    My hope, my joy,
    My Cockledemoy!

    Leon. The fool's bewitch'd; the
    goblin hath furnish'd him
A cap which well befits his reverend
    wisdom.
    Flo. If I could think he had lost
    his slender wits,
I should be sorry for the trick they
    play'd him.
    Leon. O fear him not; it were a foul
    reflection
On any fiend of sense and repu-
    tation
To filch such petty wares as his poor
    brains.
    Dur. What saw'st thou, sir?
    What heard'st thou?
    Gul. What was't I saw and heard?
That which old greybeards,
Who conjure Hebrew into Anglo-
    Saxon
To cheat starved barons with, can
    little guess at.
    Flo. If he begin so roundly with
    my father
His madness is not like to save his
    bones.
    Gul. Sirs, midnight came, and
    with it came the goblin.
I had reposed me after some brief
    study;
But as the soldier sleeping in the trench

Keeps sword and musket by him, so
    I had
My little Hebrew manual prompt for
    service.
    Flo. *Sausagian sous'd-face*—that
    much of your Hebrew
Even I can bear in memory.
    Gul.   We 'counter'd,
The goblin and myself, even in mid-
    chamber,
And each stepp'd back a pace, as
    'twere to study
The foe he had to deal with! I be-
    thought me,
Ghosts ne'er have the first word, and
    so I took it,
And fired a volley of round Greek at
    him.
He stood his ground, and answer'd
    in the Syriac;
I flank'd my Greek with Hebrew, and
    compell'd him— [*A noise heard.*
    Osw. Peace, idle prater! Hark—
    what sounds are these?
Amid the growling of the storm with-
    out
I hear strange notes of music, and
    the clash
Of coursers' trampling feet.

       voices (*without*).

We come, dark riders of the night,
And flit before the dawning light;
Hill and valley, far aloof,
Shake to hear our chargers' hoof;
But not a foot-stamp on the green
At morn shall show where we have
    been.

    Osw. These must be revellers be-
    lated.
Let them pass on; the ruin'd halls
    of Devorgoil
Open to no such guests.

    [*Flourish of trumpets at a distance,
    then nearer.*

         They sound a summons;

What can they lack at this dead hour
  of night ?
Look out, and see their number and
  their bearing.
  LEON. (*goes up to the window*). 'Tis
    strange ! One single shadowy
    form alone
Is hovering on the drawbridge ; far
  apart
Flit through the tempest banners,
  horse, and riders,
In darkness lost, or dimly seen by
  lightning.
Hither the figure moves ; the bolts
  revolve,
The gate uncloses to him.
  ELE.   Heaven protect us !

The PALMER *enters.* GULLCRAMMER
    runs off.

  Osw. Whence and what art thou ?
    for what end come hither ?
  PAL. I come from a far land, where
    the storm howls not
And the sun sets not, to pronounce to
  thee,
Oswald of Devorgoil, thy house's
  fate.
  DUR. I charge thee, in the name
    we late have kneel'd to ——
  PAL. Abbot of Lanercost, I bid thee
    peace !
Uninterrupted let me do mine er-
  rand :
Baron of Devorgoil, son of the bold,
  the proud,
The warlike and the mighty, where-
  fore wear'st thou
The habit of a peasant ? Tell me
  wherefore
Are thy fair halls thus waste, thy
  chambers bare ;
Where are the tapestries, where the
  conquer'd banners,
Trophies, and gilded arms, that deck'd
  the walls
Of once proud Devorgoil ?

*[He advances, and places himself
  where the Armour hung, so as
  to be nearly in the centre of the
  scene.*

  DUR. Whoe'er thou art, if thou
    dost know so much,
Needs must thou know ——
  Osw. Peace ! I will answer here ;
    to me he spoke.
Mysterious stranger, briefly I reply :
A peasant's dress befits a peasant's
  fortune ;
And 'twere vain mockery to array
  these walls
In trophies, of whose memory nought
  remains,
Save that the cruelty outvied the
  valour
Of those who wore them.
  PAL.   Degenerate as thou art,
Know'st thou to whom thou say'st
  this ?

*[He drops his mantle, and is dis-
  covered armed as nearly as may
  be to the suit which hung on the
  wall ; all express terror.*

  Osw. It is himself—the spirit of
    mine Ancestor !
  ERI. Tremble not, son. but hear
    me !

*[He strikes the wall ; it opens, and
  discovers the Treasure-Chamber.*

               There lies piled
The wealth I brought from wasted
  Cumberland,
Enough to reinstate thy ruin'd for-
  tunes.
Cast from thine high-born brows that
  peasant bonnet,
Throw from thy noble grasp the
  peasant's staff ;
O'er all, withdraw thine hand from
  that mean mate
Whom in an hour of reckless des-
  peration
                    2 C

Thy fortunes cast thee on. This do,
And be as great as ere was Devorgoil
When Devorgoil was richest!

Dur. Lord Oswald, thou art
tempted by a fiend,
Who doth assail thee on thy weakest
side,—
Thy pride of lineage, and thy love of
grandeur.
Stand fast, resist, contemn his fatal
offers!

Ele. Urge him not, father; if the
sacrifice
Of such a wasted woe-worn wretch
as I am
Can save him from the abyss of misery,
Upon whose verge he's tottering, let
me wander
An unacknowledged outcast from his
castle,
Even to the humble cottage I was
born in.

Osw. No, Ellen, no! It is not thus
they part
Whose hearts and souls, disasters
borne in common
Have knit together, close as summer
saplings
Are twined in union by the eddying
tempest.
Spirit of Erick, while thou bear'st his
shape
I'll answer with no ruder conjuration
Thy impious counsel other than with
these words—
Depart, and tempt me not!

Eri. Then fate will have her course.
Fall, massive grate,
Yield them the tempting view of these
rich treasures,
But bar them from possession!

[*A portcullis falls before the door
of the Treasure-Chamber.*

Mortals, hear!
No hand may ope that grate except
the Heir

Of plunder'd Aglionby, whose mighty
wealth,
Ravish'd in evil hour, lies yonder
piled;
And not his hand prevails without
the key
Of Black Lord Erick; brief space
is given
To save proud Devorgoil. So wills
high Heaven.

[*Thunder; he disappears.*

Dur. Gaze not so wildly; you have
stood the trial
That his commission bore, and Heaven
designs,
If I may spell his will, to rescue
Devorgoil
Even by the Heir of Aglionby. Behold
him
In that young forester, unto whose
hand
Those bars shall yield the treasures of
his house,
Destined to ransom yours. Advance,
young Leonard,
And prove the adventure.

Leon. (*advances and attempts the
grate*).   It is fast
As is the tower, rock-seated.

Osw. We will fetch other means,
and prove its strength,
Nor starve in poverty with wealth
before us.

Dur. Think what the vision spoke;
The key—the fated key ——

Enter Gullcrammer.

Gul. A key? I say a quay is what
we want,
Thus by the learn'd orthographized—
Q, u, a, y.
The lake is overflow'd! A quay,
a boat,
Oars, punt, or sculler, is all one to
me!
We shall be drown'd, good people!

Enter KATLEEN *and* BLACKTHORN.

KAT.   Deliver us!
Haste, save yourselves—the lake is
   rising fast.
   BLA. 'T has risen my bow's height
   in the last five minutes,
And still is swelling strangely.
   GUL. (*who has stood astonished upon
   seeing them*).
We shall be drown'd without your
   kind assistance.
SweetMaster Owlspiegle,your dragon-
   fly!
Your straw, your beanstalk, gentle
   Cockle'moy!
   LEON. (*looking from the shot-hole*).
'Tis true, by all that's fearful! The
   proud lake
Peers, like ambitious tyrant, o'er his
   bounds,
And soon will whelm the castle; even
   the drawbridge
Is under water now.
   KAT. Let us escape! Why stand
   you gazing there?
   DUR. Upon the opening of that
   fatal grate
Depends the fearful spell that now
   entraps us.
The key of Black Lord Erick—ere we
   find it
The castle will be whelm'd beneath
   the waves,
And we shall perish in it!
   KAT. (*giving the key*). Here, prove
   this;
A chance most strange and fearful
   gave it me.
      [OSWALD *puts it into the lock, and
      attempts to turn it; a loud clap
      of thunder.*
   FLO. The lake still rises faster.
   Leonard, Leonard,
Canst thou not save us?
      [LEONARD *tries the lock; it opens
      with a violent noise, and the*

*Portcullis rises. A loud strain
of wild music. There may be
a Chorus here.*

      [OSWALD *enters the apartment, and
      brings out a scroll.*

   LEON. The lake is ebbing with as
   wondrous haste
As late it rose; the drawbridge is left
   dry!
   OSW. This may explain the
   cause.
[GULLCRAMMER *offers to take it.*] But
   soft you, sir,
We 'll not disturb your learning for
   the matter;
Yet, since you 've borne a part in this
   strange drama,
You shall not go unguerdon'd. Wise
   or learn'd,
Modest or gentle, Heaven alone can
   make thee,
Being so much otherwise; but from
   this abundance
Thou shalt have that shall gild thine
   ignorance,
Exalt thy base descent, make thy
   presumption
Seem modest confidence, and find
   thee hundreds
Ready to swear that same fool's-cap
   of thine
Is reverend as a mitre.
   GUL. Thanks, mighty baron, now
   no more a bare one!
I will be quaint with him, for all
   his quips.   [*Aside.*
   OSW. Nor shall kind Katleen lack
Her portion in our happiness.
   KAT. Thanks, my good lord, but
   Katleen's fate is fix'd:
There is a certain valiant forester,
Too much afear'd of ghosts to sleep
   anights
In his lone cottage, without one to
   guard him.

LEON. If I forget my comrade's faithful friendship,
May I be lost to fortune, hope, and
love!
DUR. Peace, all! and hear the
blessing which this scroll
Speaks unto faith, and constancy, and
virtue.

No more this castle's troubled guest,
Dark Erick's spirit hath found rest.
The storms of angry Fate are past,
For Constancy defies their blast.
Of Devorgoil the daughter free
Shall wed the Heir of Aglionby;
Nor ever more dishonour soil
The rescued house of Devorgoil!

AUCHINDRANE, OR THE AYRSHIRE TRAGEDY

DRAMATIS PERSONAE.

JOHN MURE OF AUCHINDRANE, *an Ayrshire Baron. He has been a follower of the Regent, Earl of Morton, during the Civil Wars, and hides an oppressive, ferocious, and unscrupulous disposition under some pretences to strictness of life and doctrine, which, however, never influence his conduct. He is in danger from the law, owing to his having been formerly active in the assassination of the Earl of Cassilis.*

PHILIP MURE, *his son, a wild, debauched profligate, professing and practising a contempt for his father's hypocrisy, while he is as fierce and licentious as Auchindrane himself.*

GIFFORD, *their relation, a Courtier.*

QUENTIN BLANE, *a youth, educated for a Clergyman, but sent by* AUCHINDRANE *to serve in a Band of Auxiliaries in the Wars of the Netherlands, and lately employed as Clerk or Comptroller to the Regiment—disbanded, however, and on his return to his native country. He is of a mild, gentle, and rather feeble character, liable to be influenced by any person of stronger mind who will take the trouble to direct him. He is somewhat of a nervous temperament, varying from sadness to gaiety, accord-*

ing to the impulse of the moment; an amiable hypochondriac.

HILDEBRAND, *a stout old Englishman, who, by feats of courage, has raised himself to the rank of Sergeant-Major (then of greater consequence than at present). He, too, has been disbanded, but cannot bring himself to believe that he has lost his command over his Regiment.*

ABRAHAM,
WILLIAMS,
JENKIN,
And Others, } *Privates dismissed from the same Regiment in which* QUENTIN *and* HILDEBRAND *had served. These are mutinous, and are much disposed to remember former quarrels with their late Officers.*

NIEL MACLELLAN, *Keeper of Auchindrane Forest and Game.*

EARL OF DUNBAR, *commanding an Army as Lieutenant of James I, for execution of Justice on offenders.*

Guards, Attendants, &c. &c.

MARION, *wife of* NIEL MACLELLAN.

ISABEL, *their daughter, a girl of six years old.*

Other Children and Peasant Women.

ACT I.

SCENE I.

A rocky Bay on the coast of Carrick, in Ayrshire, not far from the Point of Turnberry. The sea comes in upon a bold rocky shore. The remains of a small half-ruined Tower are seen on the right hand, overhanging the sea. There is a Vessel at a distance in the offing. A Boat at the bottom of the Stage lands eight or ten persons, dressed like disbanded, and in one or two cases like disabled soldiers. They come straggling forward with their knapsacks and bundles. HILDE-BRAND, *the Sergeant, belonging to the party, a stout elderly man, stands by the boat, as if superintending the disembarkation.* QUENTIN *remains apart.*

ABRAHAM. Farewell the flats of Holland, and right welcome
The cliffs of Scotland! Fare thee well, black beer
And Schiedam gin! and welcome twopenny,
Oatcakes, and usquebaugh!

WILLIAMS (*who wants an arm*).
Farewell, the gallant field, and ' Forward, pikemen!'
For the bridge-end, the suburb, and the lane ;
And ' Bless your honour, noble gentleman,
Remember a poor soldier!'

ABR. My tongue shall never need to smooth itself
To such poor sounds while it can boldly say
' Stand and deliver!'

WIL. Hush, the sergeant hears you !

ABR. And let him hear; he makes a bustle yonder,
And dreams of his authority, forgetting
We are disbanded men, o'er whom his halberd
Has not such influence as the beadle's baton.
We are no soldiers now. but every one
The lord of his own person.

WIL. A wretched lordship, and our freedom such
As that of the old cart-horse, when the owner
Turns him upon the common. I for one
Will still continue to respect the sergeant,
And the comptroller, too,—while the cash lasts.

ABR. I scorn them both. I am too stout a Scotsman
To bear a Southron's rule an instant longer
Than discipline obliges ; and for Quentin,
Quentin the quillman, Quentin the comptroller,
We have no regiment now ; or, if we had,
Quentin's no longer clerk to it.

WIL. For shame! for shame! What! shall old comrades jar thus,
And on the verge of parting, and for ever ?
Nay, keep thy temper, Abraham, though a bad one.
Good Master Quentin, let thy song last night
Give us once more our welcome to old Scotland.

ABR. Ay, they sing light whose task is telling money,
When dollars clink for chorus.

QUE. I've done with counting silver, honest Abraham,
As thou, I fear, with pouching thy small share on 't.
But lend your voices, lads, and I will sing
As blithely yet as if a town were won;

As if upon a field of battle gain'd,
Our banners waved victorious.

[*He sings, and the rest bear chorus.*

SONG.

Hither we come,
Once slaves to the drum,
But no longer we list to its rattle ;
Adieu to the wars,
With their slashes and scars,
The march, and the storm, and the
battle.

There are some of us maim'd,
And some that are lamed,
And some of old aches are complaining ;
But we 'll take up the tools,
Which we flung by like fools,
'Gainst Don Spaniard to go a-cam-
paigning.

Dick Hathorn doth vow
To return to the plough,
Jack Steele to his anvil and hammer ;
The weaver shall find room
At the wight-warping [1] loom,
And your clerk shall teach writing
and grammar.

ABR. And this is all that thou canst
do, gay Quentin ?
To swagger o'er a herd of parish brats,
Cut cheese or dibble onions with thy
poniard,
And turn the sheath into a ferula ?
QUE. I am the prodigal in holy writ ;
I cannot work,—to beg I am ashamed.
Besides, good mates, I care not who
may know it,
I 'm e'en as fairly tired of this same
fighting
As the poor cur that 's worried in the
shambles
By all the mastiff dogs of all the
butchers ;
Wherefore, farewell sword, poniard,
petronel,

---

[1] Nimble-throwing.

And welcome poverty and peaceful
labour.
ABR. Clerk Quentin, if of fighting
thou art tired,
By my good word, thou 'rt quickly
satisfied,
For thou 'st seen but little on 't.
WIL. Thou dost belie him ; I have
seen him fight
Bravely enough for one in his con-
dition.
ABR. What, he ? that counter-cast-
ing, smockfaced boy ?
What was he but the colonel's scrib-
bling drudge,
With men of straw to stuff the regi-
ment roll ;
With cipherings unjust to cheat his
comrades,
And cloak false musters for our noble
captain ?
He bid farewell to sword and petronel !
He should have said, farewell my pen
and standish ;
These, with the rosin used to hide
erasures,
Were the best friends he left in camp
behind him.
QUE. The sword you scoff at is not
far, but scorns
The threats of an unmanner'd mutineer.
SER. (*interposing*). We 'll have no
brawling. Shall it e'er be said,
That being comrades six long years
together,
While gulping down the frowsy fogs
of Holland,
We tilted at each other's throats so
soon
As the first draught of native air
refresh'd them ?
No ! by Saint Dunstan, I forbid the
combat.
You all, methinks, do know this trusty
halberd ;
For I opine, that every back amongst
you

Hath felt the weight of the tough
   ashen staff,
Endlong or overthwart. Who is it
   wishes
A remembrancer now?
       [*Raises his halberd.*

ABR.   Comrades, have you ears
To hear the old man bully? Eyes to see
His staff rear'd o'er your heads, as
   o'er the hounds
The huntsman cracks his whip?
   WIL. Well said! Stout Abraham
   has the right on 't.
I tell thee, sergeant, we do reverence
   thee,
And pardon the rash humours thou
   hast caught,
Like wiser men, from thy authority.
'Tis ended, howsoe'er, and we 'll not
   suffer
A word of sergeantry, or halberd-staff,
Nor the most petty threat of discipline.
If thou wilt lay aside thy pride of
   office,
And drop thy wont of swaggering and
   commanding,
Thou art our comrade still for good
   or evil.
Else take thy course apart, or with
   the clerk there—
A sergeant thou, and he being all thy
   regiment.
   SER. Is 't come to this, false knaves?
   And think you not,
That if you bear a name o'er other
   soldiers,
It was because you follow'd to the
   charge
One that had zeal and skill enough to
   lead you
Where fame was won by danger?
   WIL. We grant thy skill in leading,
   noble sergeant;
Witness some empty boots and sleeves
   amongst us,
Which else had still been tenanted
   with limbs

In the full quantity; and for the argu-
   ments
With which you used to back our
   resolution,
Our shoulders do record them. At
   a word,
Will you conform, or must we part
   our company?
   SER. Conform to you? Base dogs!
   I would not lead you
A bolt-flight farther to be made a
   general.
Mean mutineers! when you swill'd
   off the dregs
Of my poor sea-stores, it was, ' Noble
   Sergeant—
Heaven bless old Hildebrand—we 'll
   follow him,
At least until we safely see him lodged
Within the merry bounds of his own
   England !'
   WIL. Ay, truly, sir; but, mark, the
   ale was mighty,
And the Geneva potent. Such stout
   liquor
Makes violent protestations. Skink
   it round,
If you have any left, to the same
   tune,
And we may find a chorus for it still.
   ABR. We lose our time. Tell us at
   once, old man,
If thou wilt march with us, or stay
   with Quentin ?
   SER. Out, mutineers! Dishonour
   dog your heels !
   ABR. Wilful will have his way.
   Adieu, stout Hildebrand !

   [*The soldiers go off laughing, and
   taking leave, with mockery, of the
   *SERGEANT *and* QUENTIN, *who
   remain on the Stage.*

   SER. (*after a pause*). Fly you not
   with the rest? Fail you to follow
Yon goodly fellowship and fair
   example?

Come, take your wild-goose flight.
I know you Scots,
Like your own sea-fowl, seek your
course together.
   Que. Faith, a poor heron I, who
wing my flight
In loneliness, or with a single partner ;
And right it is that I should seek for
solitude,
Bringing but evil luck on them I herd
with.
   Ser. Thou 'rt thankless. Had we
landed on the coast,
Where our course bore us, thou wert
far from home ;
But the fierce wind that drove us
round the island,
Barring each port and inlet that we
aim'd at,
Hath wafted thee to harbour ; for
I judge
This is thy native land we disembark on.
   Que. True, worthy friend. Each
rock, each stream I look on,
Each bosky wood, and every frowning
tower,
Awakens some young dream of infancy.
Yet such is my hard hap, I might
more safely
Have look'd on Indian cliffs, or Afric's
desert,
Than on my native shores. I 'm like
a babe,
Doom'd to draw poison from my
nurse's bosom.
   Ser. Thou dream'st, young man.
Unreal terrors haunt,
As I have noted, giddy brains like
thine—
Flighty, poetic, and imaginative—
To whom a minstrel whim gives idle
rapture,
And, when it fades, fantastic misery.
   Que. But mine is not fantastic. I
can tell thee,
Since I have known thee still my
faithful friend,

In part at least the dangerous plight
I stand in.
   Ser. And I will hear thee willingly,
the rather
That I would let these vagabonds
march on,
Nor join their troop again. Besides,
good sooth,
I'm wearied with the toil of yesterday,
And revel of last night. And I may
aid thee ;
Yes, I may aid thee, comrade, and
perchance
Thou mayst advantage me.
   Que. May it prove well for both !
But note, my friend,
I can but intimate my mystic story.
Some of it lies so secret, even the
winds
That whistle round us must not know
the whole.
An oath ! an oath !
   Ser. That must be kept, of course ;
I ask but that which thou may'st
freely tell.
   Que. I was an orphan boy, and
first saw light
Not far from where we stand, my
lineage low,
But honest in its poverty. A lord,
The master of the soil for many a mile,
Dreaded and powerful, took a kindly
charge
For my advance in letters, and the
qualities
Of the poor orphan lad drew some
applause.
The knight was proud of me, and in
his halls
I had such kind of welcome as the
great
Give to the humble, whom they love to
point to
As objects not unworthy their pro-
tection,
Whose progress is some honour to
their patron.

A cure was spoken of, which I might serve,
My manners, doctrine, and acquirements fitting.
SER. Hitherto thy luck
Was of the best, good friend. Few lords had cared
If thou couldst read thy grammar or thy psalter.
Thou hadst been valued couldst thou scour a harness,
And dress a steed distinctly.
QUE. My old master
Held different doctrine, at least it seem'd so—
But he was mix'd in many a deadly feud ;
And here my tale grows mystic. I became,
Unwitting and unwilling, the depositary
Of a dread secret, and the knowledge on 't
Has wreck'd my peace for ever. It became
My patron's will that I, as one who knew
More than I should, must leave the realm of Scotland,
And live or die within a distant land.
SER. Ah ! thou hast done a fault in some wild raid,
As you wild Scotsmen call them.
QUE. Comrade, nay ;
Mine was a peaceful part, and happ'd by chance.
I must not tell you more. Enough, my presence
Brought danger to my benefactor's house.
Tower after tower conceal'd me, willing still
To hide my ill-omen'd face with owls and ravens,
And let my patron's safety be the purchase
Of my severe and desolate captivity.

So thought I, when dark Arran, with its walls
Of native rock, enclosed me. There I lurk'd,
A peaceful stranger amid armèd clans,
Without a friend to love or to defend me,
Where all beside were link'd by close alliances.
At length I made my option to take service
In that same legion of auxiliaries
In which we lately served the Belgian.
Our leader, stout Montgomery, hath been kind
Through full six years of warfare, and assign'd me
More peaceful tasks than the rough front of war,
For which my education little suited me.
SER. Ay, therein was Montgomery kind indeed ;
Nay, kinder than you think, my simple Quentin.
The letters which you brought to the Montgomery,
Pointed to thrust thee on some desperate service,
Which should most likely end thee.
QUE. Bore I such letters ? Surely, comrade, no !
Full deeply was the writer bound to aid me.
Perchance he only meant to prove my mettle ;
And it was but a trick of my bad fortune
That gave his letters ill interpretation.
SER. Ay, but thy better angel wrought for good,
Whatever ill thy evil fate designed thee.
Montgomery pitied thee, and changed thy service
In the rough field for labour in the tent,
More fit for thy green years and peaceful habits.
QUE. Even there his well-meant kindness injured me.

My comrades hated, undervalued me,
And whatsoe'er of service I could do
them,
They guerdon'd with ingratitude and
envy.
Such my strange doom, that if I serve
a man
At deepest risk, he is my foe for ever!
   SER. Hast thou worse fate than
others if it were so?
Worse even than me, thy friend, thine
officer,
Whom yon ungrateful slaves have
pitch'd ashore,
As wild waves heap the seaweed on
the beach,
And left him here, as if he had the
pest
Or leprosy, and death were in his
company?
   QUE. They think at least you have
the worst of plagues,
The worst of leprosies,—they think
you poor.
   SER. They think like lying villains
then; I 'm rich,
And they too might have felt it. I 've
a thought—
But stay! what plans your wisdom
for yourself?
   QUE. My thoughts are wellnigh
desperate. But I purpose
Return to my stern patron, there to
tell him
That wars, and winds, and waves,
have cross'd his pleasure,
And cast me on the shore from
whence he banish'd me.
Then let him do his will, and destine
for me
A dungeon or a grave.
   SER. Now, by the rood, thou art
a simple fool!
I can do better for thee. Mark me,
Quentin.
I took my license from the noble
regiment,

Partly that I was worn with age and
warfare,
Partly that an estate of yeomanry,
Of no great purchase, but enough to
live on,
Has call'd me owner since a kinsman's
death.
It lies in merry Yorkshire, where the
wealth
Of fold and furrow, proper to Old
England,
Stretches by streams which walk no
sluggish pace,
But dance as light as yours. Now,
good friend Quentin,
This copyhold can keep two quiet
inmates,
And I am childless. Wilt thou be my
son?
   QUE. Nay, you can only jest, my
worthy friend!
What claim have I to be a burden to you?
   SER. The claim of him that wants,
and is in danger,
On him that has, and can afford pro-
tection:
Thou wouldst not fear a foeman in
my cottage,
Where a stout mastiff slumber'd on
the hearth,
And this good halberd hung above
the chimney?
But come, I have it! thou shalt earn
thy bread
Duly, and honourably, and usefully.
Our village schoolmaster hath left the
parish,
Forsook the ancient schoolhouse with
its yew-trees,
That lurk'd beside a church two cen-
turies older,—
So long devotion took the lead of
knowledge;
And since his little flock are shepherd-
less,
'Tis thou shalt be promoted in his
room;

And rather than thou wantest scholars, man,
Myself will enter pupil. Better late,
Our proverb says, than never to do well.
And look you, on the holydays I'd tell
To all the wondering boors and gap-
    ing children,
Strange tales of what the regiment
    did in Flanders,
And thou shouldst say Amen, and be
    my warrant,
That I speak truth to them.
    QUE. Would I might take thy offer !
        But, alas !
Thou art the hermit who compell'd
    a pilgrim,
In name of Heaven and heavenly
    charity,
To share his roof and meal, but found
    too late
That he had drawn a curse on him
    and his,
By sheltering a wretch foredoom'd
    of heaven !
    SER. Thou talk'st in riddles to me.
    QUE.   If I do,
'Tis that I am a riddle to myself.
Thou know'st I am by nature born
    a friend
To glee and merriment; can make
    wild verses ;
The jest or laugh has never stopp'd
    with me,
When once 'twas set a rolling.
    SER.   I have known thee
A blithe companion still, and wonder
    now
Thou shouldst become thus crest-
    fallen.
    QUE. Does the lark sing her descant
        when the falcon
Scales the blue vault with bolder wing
    than hers,
And meditates a stoop ? The mirth
    thou'st noted
Was all deception, fraud. Hated
    enough

For other causes, I did veil my feelings
Beneath the mask of mirth,—laugh'd,
    sung, and caroll'd,
To gain some interest in my comrades'
    bosoms,
Although mine own was bursting.
    SER.   Thou 'rt a hypocrite
Of a new order.
    QUE. But harmless as the innoxious
        snake,
Which bears the adder's form, lurks
    in his haunts,
Yet neither hath his fang-teeth nor
    his poison.
Look you, kind Hildebrand, I would
    seem merry,
Lest other men should, tiring of my
    sadness,
Expel me from them, as the hunted
    wether
Is driven from the flock.
    SER. Faith, thou hast borne it
        bravely out.
Had I been ask'd to name the merriest
    fellow
Of all our muster-roll, that man wert
    thou.
    QUE. See'st thou, my friend, yon
        brook dance down the valley,
And sing blithe carols over broken rock
And tiny waterfall, kissing each shrub
And each gay flower it nurses in its
    passage,—
Where, think'st thou, is its source,
    the bonny brook ?
It flows from forth a cavern, black and
    gloomy,
Sullen and sunless, like this heart of
    mine,
Which others see in a false glare of
    gaiety,
Which I have laid before you in its
    sadness.
    SER. If such wild fancies dog thee,
        wherefore leave
The trade where thou wert safe 'midst
    others' dangers,

And venture to thy native land, where
    fate
Lies on the watch for thee? Had old
    Montgomery
Been with the regiment, thou hadst
    had no congé.
    QUE. No, 'tis most likely. But I
    had a hope,
A poor vain hope, that I might live
    obscurely
In some far corner of my native
    Scotland,
Which, of all others, splinter'd into
    districts,
Differing in manners, families, even
    language,
Seem'd a safe refuge for the humble
    wretch,
Whose highest hope was to remain
    unheard of.
But fate has baffled me; the winds
    and waves,
With force resistless, have impell'd
    me hither,
Have driven me to the clime most
    dang'rous to me;
And I obey the call, like the hurt deer,
Which seeks instinctively his native
    lair,
Though his heart tells him it is but
    to die there.
    SER. 'Tis false, by Heaven, young
    man! This same despair,
Though showing resignation in its
    banner,
Is but a kind of covert cowardice.
Wise men have said, that though our
    stars incline,
They cannot force us. Wisdom is the
    pilot,
And if he cannot cross, he may evade
    them.
You lend an ear to idle auguries,
The fruits of our last revels—still most
    sad
Under the gloom that follows bois-
    terous mirth,

As earth looks blackest after brilliant
    sunshine.
    QUE. No, by my honest word. I
    join'd the revel,
And aided it with laugh, and song,
    and shout,
But my heart revell'd not; and, when
    the mirth
Was at the loudest, on yon galliot's
    prow
I stood unmark'd, and gazed upon the
    land,
My native land: each cape and cliff
    I knew.
'Behold me now,' I said, 'your
    destined victim!'
So greets the sentenced criminal the
    headsman,
Who slow approaches with his lifted
    axe.
'Hither I come,' I said, 'ye kindred
    hills,
Whose darksome outline in a distant
    land
Haunted my slumbers; here I stand,
    thou ocean,
Whose hoarse voice, murmuring in
    my dreams, required me;
See me now here, ye winds, whose
    plaintive wail,
On yonder distant shores, appear'd to
    call me;
Summon'd, behold me.' And the
    winds and waves,
And the deep echoes of the distant
    mountain,
Made answer—'Come, and die!'
    SER. Fantastic all! Poor boy, thou
    art distracted
With the vain terrors of some feudal
    tyrant,
Whose frown hath been from infancy
    thy bugbear.
Why seek his presence?
    QUE.   Wherefore does the moth
Fly to the scorching taper? Why the
    bird,

Dazzled by lights at midnight, seek the net?
Why does the prey, which feels the fascination
Of the snake's glaring eye, drop in his jaws?

SER. Such wild examples but refute themselves.
Let bird, let moth, let the coil'd adder's prey,
Resist the fascination and be safe.
Thou goest not near this Baron; if thou goest,
I will go with thee.   Known in many a field,
Which he in a whole life of petty feud
Has never dream'd of, I will teach the knight
To rule him in this matter; be thy warrant,
That far from him, and from his petty lordship,
You shall henceforth tread English land, and never
Thy presence shall alarm his conscience more.

QUE. 'Twere desperate risk for both.   I will far rather
Hastily guide thee through this dangerous province,
And seek thy school, thy yew-trees, and thy churchyard ;—
The last, perchance, will be the first I find.

SER. I would rather face him,
Like a bold Englishman that knows his right,
And will stand by his friend.   And yet 'tis folly :
Fancies like these are not to be resisted;
'Tis better to escape them.   Many a presage,
Too rashly braved, becomes its own accomplishment.
Then let us go; but whither? My old head

As little knows where it shall lie to-night,
As yonder mutineers that left their officer,
As reckless of his quarters as these billows,
That leave the withered sea-weed on the beach,
And care not where they pile it.

QUE. Think not for that, good friend.   We are in Scotland,
And if it is not varied from its wont,
Each cot. that sends a curl of smoke to heaven,
Will yield a stranger quarters for the night,
Simply because he needs them.

SER. But are there none within an easy walk
Give lodgings here for hire? for I have left
Some of the Don's piastres (though I kept
The secret from yon gulls) ; and I had rather
Pay the fair reckoning I can well afford,
And my host takes with pleasure, than I'd cumber
Some poor man's roof with me and all my wants,
And tax his charity beyond discretion.

QUE. Some six miles hence there is a town and hostelry ;
But you are wayworn, and it is most likely
Our comrades must have fill'd it.

SER.   Out upon them!
Were there a friendly mastiff who would lend me
Half of his supper, half of his poor kennel,
I would help Honesty to pick his bones,
And share his straw, far rather than I'd sup
On jolly fare with these base varlets!

QUE. We'll manage better ; for our Scottish dogs,
Though stout and trusty, are but ill-instructed
In hospitable rites.—Here is a maiden,
A little maid, will tell us of the country,
And sorely it is changed since I have left it,
If we should fail to find a harbourage.

Enter ISABEL MACLELLAN, *a girl of about six years old, bearing a milk-pail on her head ; she stops on seeing the* SERGEANT *and* QUENTIN.

QUE. There's something in her look that doth remind me—
But 'tis not wonder I find recollections
In all that here I look on. Pretty maid——
SER. You're slow, and hesitate. I will be spokesman.
Good even, my pretty maiden ! Canst thou tell us,
Is there a Christian house would render strangers,
For love or guerdon, a night's meal and lodging ?
ISA. Full surely, sir ; we dwell in yon old house
Upon the cliff—they call it Chapeldonan.   [*Points to the building.*
Our house is large enough, and if our supper
Chance to be scant, you shall have half of mine,
For, as I think, sir, you have been a soldier.
Up yonder lies our house : I'll trip before,
And tell my mother she has guests a-coming ;
The path is something steep, but you shall see
I'll be there first. I must chain up the dogs, too :

Nimrod and Bloodylass are cross to strangers,
But gentle when you know them.
     [*Exit, and is seen partially ascending to the Castle.*

SER.   You have spoke
Your country folk aright, both for the dogs
And for the people. We had luck to light
On one too young for cunning and for selfishness.
He's in a reverie—a deep one sure,
Since the gibe on his country wakes him not.
Bestir thee, Quentın !
QUE.   'Twas a wondrous likeness.
SER. Likeness ! of whom ? I'll warrant thee of one
Whom thou hast loved and lost. Such fantasies
Live long in brains like thine, which fashion visions
Of woe and death when they are cross'd in love,
As most men are or have been.
QUE. Thy guess hath touch'd me, though it is but slightly,
'Mongst other woes : I knew, in former days,
A maid that view'd me with some glance of favour,
But my fate carried me to other shores,
And she has since been wedded. I did think on't
But as a bubble burst, a rainbow vanish'd ;
It adds no deeper shade to the dark gloom
Which chills the springs of hope and life within me.
Our guide hath got a trick of voice and feature
Like to the maid I spoke of ; that is all.

Ser. She bounds before us like
  a gamesome doe,
Or rather as the rock-bred eaglet soars
Up to her nest, as if she rose by will
Without an effort. Now a Nether-
  lander,
One of our Frogland friends, viewing
  the scene,
Would take his oath that tower, and
  rock, and maiden,
Were forms too light and lofty to
  be real,
And only some delusion of the fancy,
Such as men dream at sunset. I my-
  self
Have kept the level ground so many
  years,
I have wellnigh forgot the art to climb,
Unless assisted by thy younger arm.

    [*They go off as if to ascend to the
    Tower, the* Sergeant *leaning
    upon* Quentin.

Scene II.

*Scene changes to the Front of the Old
Tower.* Isabel *comes forward with
her Mother,—*Marion *speaking as
they advance.*

Mar. I blame thee not, my child,
  for bidding wanderers
Come share our food and shelter, if
  thy father
Were here to welcome them; but,
  Isabel,
He waits upon his lord at Auchindrane,
And comes not home to-night.
  Isa.   What then, my mother?
The travellers do not ask to see
  my father;
Food, shelter, rest, is all the poor men
  want,
And we can give them these without
  my father.

Mar. Thou canst not understand,
  nor I explain,
Why a lone female asks not visitants
What time her husband's absent.
  (*Apart.*) My poor child,
And if thou'rt wedded to a jealous
  husband,
Thou'lt know too soon the cause.
  Isa. (*partly overhearing what her
    mother says*). Ay, but I know
    already! Jealousy
Is, when my father chides, and you
  sit weeping.
  Mar. Out, little spy! thy father
    never chides;
Or, if he does, 'tis when his wife
  deserves it.
But to our strangers; they are old
  men, Isabel,
That seek this shelter, are they not?
  Isa.   One is old—
Old as this tower of ours, and worn
  like that,
Bearing deep marks of battles long
  since fought.
  Mar. Some remnant of the wars;
    he's welcome, surely,
Bringing no quality along with him
Which can alarm suspicion. Well,
  the other?
  Isa. A young man, gentle-voiced
    and gentle-eyed,
Who looks and speaks like one the
  world has frown'd on;
But smiles when you smile, seeming
  that he feels
Joy in your joy, though he himself is sad.
Brown hair, and downcast looks.
  Mar. (*alarmed*). 'Tis but an idle
    thought—it cannot be! [*Listens.*
I hear his accents; it is all too
  true—
My terrors were prophetic!
          I'll compose myself,
And then accost him firmly. Thus it
  must be.

    [*She retires hastily into the Tower.*

[*The voices of the* SERGEANT *and* QUENTIN *are heard ascending behind the Scenes.*

QUE. One effort more, we stand upon the level.

I 've seen thee work thee up glacis and cavalier

Steeper than this ascent, when cannon, culverine,

Musket, and hackbut, shower'd their shot upon thee,

And form'd, with ceaseless blaze, a fiery garland

Round the defences of the post you storm'd.

[*They come on the Stage, and at the same time* MARION *re-enters from the Tower.*

SER. Truly thou speak'st. I am the tardier,

That I, in climbing hither, miss the fire,

Which wont to tell me there was death in loitering.

Here stands, methinks, our hostess.

[*He goes forward to address* MARION. QUENTIN, *struck on seeing her, keeps back.*

SER. Kind dame, yon little lass hath brought you strangers,

Willing to be a trouble, not a charge to you.

We are disbanded soldiers, but have means

Ample enough to pay our journey homeward.

MAR. We keep no house of general entertainment,

But know our duty, sir, to locks like yours,

Whiten'd and thinn'd by many a long campaign.

Ill chances that my husband should be absent—

(*Apart*) Courage alone can make me struggle through it—

For in your comrade, though he hath forgot me,

I spy a friend whom I have known in school-days,

And whom I think MacLellan well remembers.

[*She goes up to* QUENTIN.

You see a woman's memory

Is faithfuller than yours; for Quentin Blane

Hath not a greeting left for Marion Harkness.

QUE. (*with effort*). I seek, indeed, my native land, good Marion,

But seek it like a stranger. All is changed,

And thou thyself ——

MAR. You left a giddy maiden,

And find, on your return, a wife and mother.

Thine old acquaintance, Quentin, is my mate—

Stout Niel MacLellan, ranger to our lord,

The Knight of Auchindrane. He 's absent now,

But will rejoice to see his former comrade,

If, as I trust, you tarry his return.

(*Apart.*) Heaven grant he understand my words by contraries !

He must remember Niel and he were rivals ;

He must remember Niel and he were foes ;

He must remember Niel is warm of temper,

And think, instead of welcome, I would blithely

Bid him God speed you. But he is as simple

And void of guile as ever.

QUE. Marion, I gladly rest within your cottage,

And gladly wait return of Niel Mac-
Lellan,
To clasp his hand, and wish him
happiness.
Some rising feelings might perhaps
prevent this ;
But 'tis a peevish part to grudge our
friends
Their share of fortune because we
have miss'd it ;
I can wish others joy and happiness,
Though I must ne'er partake them.

MAR. But if it grieve you——

QUE. No ! do not fear. The brightest gleams of hope
That shine on me are such as are
reflected
From those which shine on others.

[*The* SERGEANT *and* QUENTIN
enter the Tower with the little Girl.

MAR. (*comes forward, and speaks in
agitation*). Even so ! the simple
youth has miss'd my meaning.
I shame to make it plainer, or to say,
In one brief word, Pass on. Heaven
guide the bark,
For we are on the breakers !

[*Exit into the Tower.*

—◆—

ACT II.

SCENE I.

*A withdrawing Apartment in the
Castle of Auchindrane. Servants
place a Table, with a Flask of Wine
and Drinking-Cups.*

Enter MURE *of* AUCHINDRANE, *with*
ALBERT GIFFORD, *his Relation and
Visitor. They place themselves by
the Table after some complimentary
ceremony. At some distance is heard
the noise of revelling.*

AUCH. We're better placed for
confidential talk,

Than in the hall fill'd with disbanded
soldiers,
And fools and fiddlers gather'd on the
highway,—
The worthy guests whom Philip
crowds my hall with,
And with them spends his evening.

GIF. But think you not, my friend,
that your son Philip
Should be participant of these our
councils,
Being so deeply mingled in the
danger—
Your house's only heir—your only
son ?

AUCH. Kind cousin Gifford, if thou
lack'st good counsel
At race, at cockpit, or at gambling
table,
Or any freak by which men cheat
themselves
As well of life, as of the means to live,
Call for assistance upon Philip Mure ;
But in all serious parley spare invoking
him.

GIF. You speak too lightly of my
cousin Philip ;
All name him brave in arms.

AUCH.   A second Bevis ;
But I, my youth bred up in graver
fashions,
Mourn o'er the mode of life in which
he spends,
Or rather dissipates, his time and
substance.
No vagabond escapes his search :
The soldier
Spurn'd from the service, henceforth
to be ruffian
Upon his own account, is Philip's
comrade ;
The fiddler, whose crack'd crowd has
still three strings on't ;
The balladeer, whose voice has still
two notes left ;
Whate'er is roguish and whate'er is
vile,

Are welcome to the board of
Auchindrane,
And Philip will return them shout for
shout,
And pledge for jovial pledge, and
song for song,
Until the shamefaced sun peep at our
windows,
And ask ' What have we here?'
 Gif. You take such revel deeply.
We are Scotsmen,
Far known for rustic hospitality,
That mind not birth or titles in our
guests ;
The harper has his seat beside our
hearth,
The wanderer must find comfort at
our board,
His name unask'd, his pedigree un-
known ;
So did our ancestors, and so must we.
 Auch. All this is freely granted,
worthy kinsman ;
And prithee do not think me churl
enough
To count how many sit beneath my
salt.
I 've wealth enough to fill my father's
hall
Each day at noon, and feed the guests
who crowd it.
I am near mate with those whom men
call Lord,
Though a rude western knight. But
mark me, cousin,
Although I feed wayfaring vagabonds,
I make them not my comrades. Such
as I,
Who have advanced the fortunes of
my line
And swell'd a baron's turret to a palace,
Have oft the curse awaiting on our
thrift,
To see, while yet we live, the things
which must be
At our decease—the downfall of our
family.

The loss of land and lordship, name
and knighthood,
The wreck of the fair fabric we have
built,
By a degenerate heir. Philip has that
Of inborn meanness in him, that he
loves not
The company of betters, nor of equals ;
Never at ease, unless he bears the bell,
And crows the loudest in the company.
He 's mesh'd, too, in the snares of
every female
Who deigns to cast a passing glance
on him—
Licentious, disrespectful, rash, and
profligate.
 Gif. Come, my good coz, think we
too have been young,
And I will swear that in your father's
lifetime
You have yourself been trapp'd by
toys like these.
 Auch. A fool I may have been—
but not a madman ;
I never play'd the rake among my
followers,
Pursuing this man's sister, that man's
wife ;
And therefore never saw I man of
mine,
When summon'd to obey my hest,
grow restive,
Talk of his honour, of his peace
destroy'd,
And, while obeying, mutter threats of
vengeance.
But now the humour of an idle youth,
Disgusting trusted followers, sworn
dependants,
Plays football with his honour and
my safety.
 Gif. I m sorry to find discord in
your house,
For I had hoped, while bringing you
cold news,
To find you arm'd in union 'gainst the
danger.

AUCH. What can man speak that I
would shrink to hear,
And where the danger I would deign
to shun ? [*He rises.*
What should appal a man inured to
perils,
Like the bold climber on the crags of
Ailsa ?
Winds whistle past him, billows rage
below,
The sea-fowl sweep around, with
shriek and clang;—
One single slip, one unadvisèd pace,
One qualm of giddiness—and peace be
with him !
But he whose grasp is sure, whose
step is firm,
Whose brain is constant—he makes
one proud rock
The means to scale another, till he stand
Triumphant on the peak.
GIF. And so I trust
Thou wilt surmount the danger now
approaching,
Which scarcely can I frame my tongue
to tell you,
Though I rode here on purpose.
AUCH. Cousin, I think thy heart was
never coward,
And strange it seems thy tongue should
take such semblance.
I've heard of many a loud-mouth'd,
noisy braggart,
Whose hand gave feeble sanction to
his tongue ;
But thou art one whose heart can think
bold things,
Whose hand can act them, but who
shrinks to speak them !
GIF. And if I speak them not, 'tis
that I shame
To tell thee of the calumnies that load
thee.
Things loudly spoken at the city
Cross,
Things closely whisper'd in our
Sovereign's ear,

Things which the plumed lord and
flat-capp'd citizen
Do circulate amid their different
ranks—
Things false, no doubt ; but, falsehoods
while I deem them,
Still honouring thee, I shun the odious
topic.
AUCH. Shun it not, cousin ; 'tis a
friend's best office
To bring the news we hear unwillingly.
The sentinel, who tells the foe's ap-
proach,
And wakes the sleeping camp, does
but his duty :
Be thou as bold in telling me of danger,
As I shall be in facing danger told of.
GIF. I need not bid thee recollect
the death-feud
That raged so long betwixt thy house
and Cassilis ;
I need not bid thee recollect the league,
When royal James himself stood me-
diator
Between thee and Earl Gilbert.
AUCH. Call you these news ? You
might as well have told me
That old King Coil is dead, and graved
at Kylesfeld.
I'll help thee out : King James com-
manded us
Henceforth to live in peace, made us
clasp hands too.
O, sir, when such an union hath been
made,
In heart and hand conjoining mortal
foes,
Under a monarch's royal mediation,
The league is not forgotten. And
with this
What is there to be told ? The king
commanded—
' Be friends.' No doubt we were so—
who dare doubt it ?
GIF. You speak but half the tale.
AUCH. By good Saint Trimon, but
I'll tell the whole !

There is no terror in the tale for me :
Go speak of ghosts to children ! This
    Earl Gilbert
(God sain him) loved Heaven's peace
    as well as I did,
And we were wondrous friends when-
    e'er we met
At church or market, or in burrows
    town.
'Midst this, our good Lord Gilbert,
    Earl of Cassilis,
Takes purpose he would journey forth
    to Edinburgh.
The King was doling gifts of abbey-
    lands,
Good things that thrifty house was
    wont to fish for.
Our mighty Earl forsakes his sea-
    wash'd castle,
Passes our borders some four miles
    from hence ;
And, holding it unwholesome to be
    fasters
Long after sunrise, lo ! the Earl and
    train
Dismount to rest their nags and eat
    their breakfast.
The morning rose, the small birds
    caroll'd sweetly,
The corks were drawn, the pasty
    brooks incision,
His lordship jests, his train are choked
    with laughter,
When,—wondrous change of cheer,
    and most unlook'd for !
Strange epilogue to bottle and to baked
    meat !—
Flash'd from the greenwood half a
    score of carabines,
And the good Earl of Cassilis, in his
    breakfast,
Had nooning, dinner, supper, all at once,
Even in the morning that he closed
    his journey :
And the grim sexton. for his chamberlain,
Made him the bed which rests the
    head for ever.

GIF. Told with much spirit, cousin.
    Some there are
Would add and in a tone resembling
    triumph.
And would that with these long estab-
    lish'd facts
My tale began and ended ! I must tell
    you
That evil-deeming censures of the
    events,
Both at the time and now, throw
    blame on thee.
Time, place, and circumstance, they
    say, proclaim thee,
Alike, the author of that morning's
    ambush.

AUCH. Ay, 'tis an old belief in
    Carrick here,
Where natives do not always die in
    bed,
That if a Kennedy shall not attain
Methuselah's last span, a Mure has
    slain him.
Such is the general creed of all their
    clan.
Thank Heaven that they 're bound to
    prove the charge
They are so prompt in making. They
    have clamour'd
Enough of this before, to show their
    malice.
But what said these coward pickthanks
    when I came
Before the King, before the Justicers,
Rebutting all their calumnies, and
    daring them
To show that I knew aught of Cassilis'
    journey,
Which way he meant to travel, where
    to halt ?
Without which knowledge I possess'd
    no means
To dress an ambush for him. Did I not
Defy the assembled clan of Kennedys
To show, by proof direct or inferential,
Wherefore they slander'd me with this
    foul charge ?

My gauntlet rung before them in the
court,
And I did dare the best of them to lift it,
And prove such charge a true one.
Did I not?
GIF. I saw your gauntlet lie before
the Kennedys,
Who look'd on it as men do on an adder,
Longing to crush, and yet afraid to
grasp it.
Not an eye sparkled, not a foot
advanced,
No arm was stretch'd to lift the fatal
symbol.
AUCH. Then wherefore do the
hildings murmur now?
Wish they to see again, how one bold
Mure
Can baffle and defy their assembled
valour?
GIF. No; but they speak of evidence
suppress'd.
AUCH. Suppress'd! What evi-
dence?—by whom suppress'd?
What Will-o'-Wisp, what idiot of
a witness,
Is he to whom they trace an empty
voice,
But cannot show his person?
GIF. They pretend.
With the King's leave, to bring it to
a trial;
Averring that a lad, named Quentin
Blane,
Brought thee a letter from the mur-
der'd Earl,
With friendly greetings, telling of his
journey,
The hour which he set forth, the
place he halted at
Affording thee the means to form the
ambush,
Of which your hatred made the
application.
AUCH. A prudent Earl, indeed, if
such his practice,
When dealing with a recent enemy!

And what should he propose by such
strange confidence
In one who sought it not?
GIF. His purposes were kindly, say
the Kennedys—
Desiring you would meet him where
he halted,
Offering to undertake whate'er com-
missions
You listed trust him with, for court
or city :
And, thus apprised of Cassilis' pur-
posed journey,
And of his halting place, you placed
the ambush,
Prepared the homicides ——
AUCH. They're free to say their
pleasure. They are men
Of the new court; and I am but a
fragment
Of stout old Morton's faction. It is
reason
That such as I be rooted from the earth
That they may have full room to
spread their branches.
No doubt, 'tis easy to find strolling
vagrants
To prove whate'er they prompt. This
Quentin Blane—
Did you not call him so?—why comes
he now?
And wherefore not before? This must
be answer'd!
(*Abruptly*.) Where is he now?
GIF. Abroad, they say; kidnapp'd,
By you kidnapp d, that he might die
in Flanders.
But orders have been sent for his dis-
charge,
And his transmission hither.
AUCH. (*assuming an air of com-
posure*). When they produce such
witness, cousin Gifford,
We'll be prepared to meet it. In the
meanwhile,
The King doth ill to throw his royal
sceptre

In the accuser's scale, ere he can know
How justice shall incline it.
    Gif.   Our sage prince
Resents, it may be, less the death of
    Cassilis,
Than he is angry that the feud should
    burn,
After his royal voice had said 'Be
    quench'd' :
Thus urging prosecution less for
    slaughter,
Than that, being done against the
    King's command,
Treason is mix'd with homicide.
    Auch. Ha! ha! most true, my
    cousin.
Why, well consider'd, 'tis a crime so
    great
To slay one's enemy, the King for-
    bidding it,
Like parricide, it should be held
    impossible.
'Tis just as if a wretch retain'd the evil,
When the King's touch had bid the
    sores be heal'd ;
And such a crime merits the stake at
    least.
What! can there be within a Scottish
    bosom
A feud so deadly, that it kept its ground
When the King said Be friends! It
    is not credible.
Were I King James, I never would
    believe it :
I'd rather think the story all a dream,
And that there was no friendship,
    feud, nor journey,
No halt, no ambush, and no Earl of
    Cassilis,
Than dream anointed Majesty has
    wrong!
    Gif. Speak within door, coz.
    Auch. O, true! (*aside*). I shall
    betray myself
Even to this half-bred fool. I must
    have room,
Room for an instant, or I suffocate.

Cousin, I prithee call our Philip
    hither—
Forgive me! 'twere more meet I
    summon'd him
Myself; but then the sight of yonder
    revel
Would chafe my blood, and I have
    need of coolness.
    Gif. I understand thee: I will bring
    him straight.   [*Exit.*
    Auch. And if thou dost, he's lost
    his ancient trick
To fathom, as he wont, his five-pint
    flagons.
This space is mine : O for the power
    to fill it,
Instead of senseless rage and empty
    curses,
With the dark spell which witches
    learn from fiends,
That smites the object of their hate afar,
Nor leaves a token of its mystic action,
Stealing the soul from out the un-
    scathed body,
As lightning melts the blade, nor
    harms the scabbard!
'Tis vain to wish for it! Each curse
    of mine
Falls to the ground as harmless as
    the arrows
Which children shoot at stars! The
    time for thought,
If thought could aught avail me, melts
    away,
Like to a snowball in a schoolboy's
    hand,
That melts the faster the more close
    he grasps it!
If I had time, this Scottish Solomon,
Whom some call son of David the
    Musician [1],
Might find it perilous work to march
    to Carrick.
There's many a feud still slumbering
    in its ashes,

---

[1] The calumnious tale which ascribed the birth of
James VI to an intrigue of Queen Mary with Rizzio.

Whose embers are yet red.   Nobles
   we have,
Stout as old Graysteel, and as hot as
   Bothwell ;
Here too are castles look from crags
   as high
On seas as wide as Logan's.   So the
   King—
Pshaw ! He is here again.

Enter GIFFORD.

GIF.   I heard you name
The King, my kinsman ; know, he
   comes not hither.
   AUCH. (*affecting indifference*). Nay,
   then we need not broach our
   barrels, cousin,
Nor purchase us new jerkins.   Comes
   not Philip ?
   GIF. Yes, sir.   He tarries but to
   drink a service
To his good friends at parting.
   AUCH. Friends for the beadle or
   the sheriff-officer.
Well, let it pass.   Who comes, and
   how attended,
Since James designs not westward ?
   GIF. O you shall have, instead, his
   functionary, fiery
George Home that was, but now
   Dunbar's great Earl ;
He leads a royal host, and comes
   to show you
How he distributes justice on the
   Border,
Where judge and hangman oft reverse
   their office,
And the noose does its work before
   the sentence.
But I have said my tidings best and
   worst.
None but yourself can know what
   course the time
And peril may demand.   To lift your
   banner,
If I might be a judge, were desperate
   game :

Ireland and Galloway offer you convenience
For flight, if flight be thought the
   better remedy ;
To face the court requires the consciousness
And confidence of innocence.   You
   alone
Can judge if you possess these attributes.   [*A noise behind the scenes.*
   AUCH. Philip, I think, has broken
   up his revels ;
His ragged regiment are dispersing
   them,
Well liquor'd, doubtless.   They 're
   disbanded soldiers,
Or some such vagabonds.   Here comes
   the gallant.

Enter PHILIP.   *He has a buff-coat and
head-piece, wears a sword and dagger,
with pistols at his girdle.   He appears
to be affected by liquor, but to be by
no means intoxicated.*

   AUCH. You scarce have been made
   known to one another,
Although you sate together at the
   board.
Son Philip, know and prize our cousin
   Gifford.
   PHI. (*tasting the wine on the table*). If
   you had prized him, sir, you had
   been loth
To have welcomed him in bastard
   Alicant :
I 'll make amends, by pledging his
   good journey
In glorious Burgundy.   The stirrup-
   cup, ho !
And bring my cousin's horses to the
   court.
   AUCH. (*drawing him aside*). The
   stirrup-cup ?   He doth not ride
   to-night !
Shame on such churlish conduct to
   a kinsman !

PHI. (*aside to his father*). I 've news of pressing import.
Send the fool off. Stay, I will start him for you.
(*To* GIF.) Yes, my kind cousin, Burgundy is better,
On a night-ride, to those who thread our moors,
And we may deal it freely to our friends,
For we came freely by it. Yonder ocean
Rolls many a purple cask upon our shore,
Rough with embossèd shells and shaggèd sea-weed,
When the good skipper and his careful crew
Have had their latest earthly draught of brine,
And gone to quench, or to endure their thirst,
Where nectar 's plenty, or even water 's scarce,
And filter'd to the parchèd crew by drops.
    AUCH. Thou 'rt mad, son Philip!— Gifford 's no intruder,
That we should rid him hence by such wild rants:
My kinsman hither rode at his own danger,
To tell us that Dunbar is hasting to us,
With a strong force, and with the King's commission,
To enforce against our house a hateful charge,
With every measure of extremity.
    PHI. And is this all that our good cousin tells us?
I can say more, thanks to the ragged regiment,
With whose good company you have upbraided me ;
On whose authority, I tell thee, cousin,
Dunbar is here already.
    GIF.   Already ?

    PHI. Yes, gentle coz. And you, my sire, be hasty
In what you think to do.
    AUCH. I think thou darest not jest on such a subject.
Where hadst thou these fell tidings?
    PHI. Where you, too, might have heard them, noble father,
Save that your ears, nail'd to our kinsman's lips,
Would list no coarser accents. O, my soldiers,
My merry crew of vagabonds, for ever!
Scum of the Netherlands, and wash'd ashore
Upon this coast like unregarded sea-weed,
They had not been two hours on Scottish land,
When, lo ! they met a military friend,
An ancient fourier, known to them of old,
Who, warm'd by certain stoups of searching wine,
Inform'd his old companions that Dunbar
Left Glasgow yesterday, comes here to-morrow ;
Himself, he said, was sent a spy before,
To view what preparations we were making.
    AUCH. (*to* GIF.) If this be sooth, good kinsman, thou must claim
To take a part with us for life and death,
Or speed from hence, and leave us to our fortune.
    GIF. In such dilemma,
Believe me, friend, I 'd choose upon the instant ;
But I lack harness, and a steed to charge on,
For mine is overtired, and, save my page,
There 's not a man to back me. But I 'll hie
To Kyle, and raise my vassals to your aid,

Phi. 'Twill be when the rats,
That on these tidings fly this house of ours,
Come back to pay their rents. (*Apart.*)
Auch.   Courage, cousin !
Thou goest not hence ill mounted for thy need :
Full forty coursers feed in my wide stalls,
The best of them is yours to speed your journey.
Phi. Stand not on ceremony, good our cousin,
When safety signs, to shorten courtesy.
Gif. (*to* Auch.) Farewell then, cousin, for my tarrying here
Were ruin to myself, small aid to you ;
Yet loving well your name and family,
I 'd fain ——
Phi. Be gone ? that is our object, too ;
Kinsman, adieu.

[*Exit* Gifford. Philip *calls after him.*

        You yeoman of the stable,
Give Master Gifford there my fleetest steed,
Yon cut-tail'd roan that trembles at a spear.

[*Trampling of the horse heard going off.*

Hark ! he departs. How swift the dastard rides,
To shun the neighbourhood of jeopardy !

[*He lays aside the appearance of levity which he has hitherto worn, and says very seriously,*

        And now, my father !
Auch. And now, my son ! thou 'st ta'en a perilous game
Into thine hands, rejecting elder counsel ;
How dost thou mean to play it ?

Phi. Sir, good gamesters play not
Till they review the cards which fate has dealt them,
Computing thus the chances of the game ;
And wofully they seem to weigh against us.
Auch. Exile 's a passing ill, and may be borne ;
And when Dunbar and all his myrmidons
Are eastward turn'd, we 'll seize our own again.
Phi. Would that were all the risk we had to stand to !
But more and worse. A doom of treason. forfeiture,
Death to ourselves, dishonour to our house,
Is what the stern Justiciary menaces ;
And, fatally for us, he hath the means
To make his threatenings good.
Auch. It cannot be. I tell thee, there 's no force
In Scottish law to raze a house like mine,
Coeval with the time the Lords of Galloway
Submitted them unto the Scottish sceptre,
Renouncing rights of Tanistry and Brehon.
Some dreams they have of evidence, some suspicion.
But old Montgomery knows my purpose well,
And long before their mandate reach the camp
To crave the presence of this mighty witness,
He will be fitted with an answer to it.
Phi. Father, what we call great, is often ruin'd
By means so ludicrously dispro-portion'd,
They make me think upon the gunner's linstock,

Which, yielding forth a light about the size
And semblance of the glowworm, yet applied
To powder, blew a palace into atoms,
Sent a young King—a young Queen's mate at least—
Into the air, as high as e'er flew night-hawk,
And made such wild work in the realm of Scotland,
As they can tell who heard; and you were one
Who saw, perhaps, the night-flight which began it.

AUCH. If thou hast nought to speak but drunken folly,
I cannot listen longer.

PHI. I will speak brief and sudden. There is one
Whose tongue to us has the same perilous force
Which Bothwell's powder had to Kirk of Field;
One whose least tones, and those but peasant accents,
Could rend the roof from off our fathers' castle,
Level its tallest turret with its base;
And he that doth possess this wondrous power
Sleeps this same night not five miles distant from us.

AUCH. (who had looked on PHILIP with much appearance of astonishment and doubt, exclaims) Then thou art mad indeed! Ha! ha! I'm glad on't.
I'd purchase an escape from what I dread,
Even by the frenzy of my only son!

PHI. I thank you, but agree not to the bargain.
You rest on what yon civet cat has said:
Yon silken doublet, stuff'd with rotten straw,

Told you but half the truth, and knew no more.
But my good vagrants had a perfect tale:
They told me, little judging the importance,
That Quentin Blane had been discharged with them.
They told me, that a quarrel happ'd at landing,
And that the youngster and an ancient sergeant
Had left their company, and taken refuge
In Chapeldonan, where our ranger dwells;
They saw him scale the cliff on which it stands,
Ere they were out of sight; the old man with him.
And therefore laugh no more at me as mad;
But laugh, if thou hast list for merriment,
To think he stands on the same land with us,
Whose absence thou wouldst deem were cheaply purchased
With thy soul's ransom and thy body's danger.

AUCH. 'Tis then a fatal truth! Thou art no yelper
To open rashly on so wild a scent;
Thou 'rt the young bloodhound, which careers and springs,
Frolics and fawns, as if the friend of man,
But seizes on his victim like a tiger.

PHI. No matter what I am—I'm as you bred me;
So let that pass till there be time to mend me,
And let us speak like men, and to the purpose.
This object of our fear and of our dread,
Since such our pride must own him, sleeps to-night

Within our power:—to-morrow in
Dunbar's,
And we are then his victims.
AUCH. He is in *ours* to-night.
PHI. He is. I'll answer that Mac-
Lellan's trusty.
AUCH. Yet he replied to you to-day
full rudely.
PHI. Yes! The poor knave has
got a handsome wife,
And is gone mad with jealousy.
AUCH. Fool! When we need the
utmost faith, allegiance,
Obedience, and attachment in our
vassals,
Thy wild intrigues pour gall into their
hearts,
And turn their love to hatred!
PHI. Most reverend sire, you talk
of ancient morals,
Preach'd on by Knox. and practised
by Glencairn;[1]
Respectable, indeed, but somewhat
musty
In these our modern nostrils. In our
days,
If a young baron chance to leave his
vassal
The sole possessor of a handsome wife,
'Tis sign he loves his follower; and,
if not,
He loves his follower's wife, which
often proves
The surer bond of patronage. Take
either case:

Favour flows in of course, and vassals
rise.
AUCH. Philip, this is infamous,
And, what is worse, impolitic. Take
example:
Break not God's laws or man's for
each temptation
That youth and blood suggest. I am
a man—
A weak and erring man; full well
thou know'st
That I may hardly term myself a
pattern
Even to my son; yet thus far will I
say,
I never swerved from my integrity,
Save at the voice of strong necessity,
Or such o'erpowering view of high
advantage
As wise men liken to necessity,
In strength and force compulsive.
No one saw me
Exchange my reputation for my
pleasure,
Or do the Devil's work without his
wages.
I practised prudence, and paid tax to
virtue,
By following her behests, save where
strong reason
Compell'd a deviation. Then, if
preachers
At times look'd sour, or elders shook
their heads,
They could not term my walk irre-
gular;
For I stood up still for the worthy
cause,
A pillar, though a flaw'd one, of the
altar,
Kept a strict walk, and led three
hundred horse.
PHI. Ah, these three hundred horse
in such rough times
Were better commendation to a
party
Than all your efforts at hypocrisy,

1 Alexander, fifth Earl of Glencairn, for distinction called 'The Good Earl,' was among the first of the peers of Scotland who concurred in the Reformation, in aid of which he acted a conspicuous part, in the employment both of his sword and pen. In a remonstrance with the Queen Regent, he told her, that 'if she violated the engagements which she had come under to her subjects, they would consider themselves as absolved from their allegiance to her.' He was author of a satirical poem against the Roman Catholics, entitled 'The Hermit of Allareit' (Loretto).—See SIBBALD'S *Chronicle of Scottish Poetry.*—He assisted the Reformers with his sword, when they took arms at Perth, in 1559; had a principal command in the army embodied against Queen Mary, in June 1567; and demolished the altar, broke the images, tore down the pictures, &c., in the Chapel-royal of Holyrood-house, after the Queen was conducted to Lochleven. He died in 1574.

Betray'd so oft by avarice and
  ambition,
And dragg'd to open shame. But,
  righteous father,
When sire and son unite in mutual
  crime,
And join their efforts to the same
  enormity,
It is no time to measure other's faults,
Or fix the amount of each. Most
  moral father,
Think if it be a moment now to weigh
The vices of the Heir of Auchindrane,
Or take precaution that the ancient
  house
Shall have another heir than the sly
  courtier
That's gaping for the forfeiture.
  AUCH. We'll disappoint him,
    Philip,—
We'll disappoint him yet. It is a folly,
A wilful cheat, to cast our eyes behind,
When time, and the fast flitting
  opportunity,
Call loudly, nay, compel us to look
  forward :
Why are we not already at Mac-
  Lellan's,
Since there the victim sleeps ?
  PHI.   Nay, soft, I pray thee.
I had not made your piety my con-
  fessor,
Nor enter'd in debate on these sage
  councils,
Which you're more like to give than
    I to profit by,
Could I have used the time more
  usefully ;
But first an interval must pass between
The fate of Quentin and the little
  artifice
That shall detach him from his comrade,
The stout old soldier that I told you of.
  AUCH. How work a point so
    difficult, so dangerous !
  PHI. 'Tis cared for. Mark, my
    father, the convenience

Arising from mean company. My
  agents
Are at my hand, like a good workman's
  tools,
And if I mean a mischief, ten to one
That they anticipate the deed and
  guilt.
Well knowing this, when first the
  vagrant's tattle
Gave me the hint that Quentin was so
  near us,
Instant I sent MacLellan, with strong
  charges
To stop him for the night, and bring
  me word,
Like an accomplish'd spy, how all
  things stood,
Lulling the enemy into security.
  AUCH. There was a prudent general!
  PHI. MacLellan went and came
    within the hour.
The jealous bee, which buzzes in his
  nightcap,
Had humm'd to him this fellow,
  Quentin Blane,
Had been in schoolboy days an
  humble lover
Of his own pretty wife—
  AUCH. Most fortunate !
The knave will be more prompt to
  serve our purpose.
  PHI. No doubt on't. 'Mid the
    tidings he brought back
Was one of some importance. The
  old man
Is flush of dollars ; this I caused him
  tell
Among his comrades, who became as
  eager
To have him in their company, as e'er
They had been wild to part with him.
    And in brief space,
A letter's framed by an old hand
  amongst them,
Familiar with such feats. It bore the
  name
And character of old Montgomery,

Whom he might well suppose at no
    great distance,
Commanding his old Sergeant Hilde-
    brand,
By all the ties of late authority,
Conjuring him by ancient soldiership,
To hasten to his mansion instantly,
On business of high import, with a
    charge
To come alone.
    AUCH. Well, he sets out, I doubt
    it not : what follows ?
    PHI. I am not curious into others'
    practices ;
So far I 'm an economist in guilt,
As you my sire advise. But on the
    road
To old Montgomery's he meets his
    comrades,
They nourish grudge against him and
    his dollars,
And things may hap, which counsel,
    learn'd in law,
Call robbery and murder. Should
    he live,
He has seen nought that we would
    hide from him.
    AUCH. Who carries the forged
    letter to the veteran ?
    PHI. Why, Niel MacLellan, who
    return'd again
To his own tower, as if to pass the
    night there.
They pass'd on him, or tried to pass,
    a story,
As if they wish'd the sergeant's
    company,
Without the young comptroller's—
    that is Quentin's,
And he became an agent of their
    plot,
That he might better carry on our
    own.
    AUCH. There 's life in it ; yes, there
    is life in 't.
And we will have a mounted party
    ready

To scour the moors in quest of the
    banditti
That kill'd the poor old man ; they
    shall die instantly.
Dunbar shall see us use sharp justice
    here,
As well as he in Teviotdale. You
    are sure
You gave no hint nor impulse to their
    purpose ?
    PHI. It needed not. The whole
    pack oped at once
Upon the scent of dollars. But time
    comes
When I must seek the tower, and act
    with Niel
What farther 's to be done.
    AUCH. Alone with him thou goest
not : he bears grudge.
Thou art my only son, and on a
    night
When such wild passions are so free
    abroad,
When such wild deeds are doing, 'tis
    but natural
I guarantee thy safety. I 'll ride with
    thee.
    PHI. E'en as you will, my lord.
    But, pardon me !
If you will come, let us not have
    a word
Of conscience, and of pity, and for-
    giveness ;
Fine words to-morrow, out of place
    to-night.
Take counsel then, leave all this work
    to me ;
Call up your household, make fit
    preparation,
In love and peace, to welcome this
    Earl Justiciar,
As one that 's free of guilt. Go, deck
    the castle
As for an honour'd guest. Hallow the
    chapel
(If they have power to hallow it) with
    thy prayers.

Let me ride forth alone, and ere the
　　sun
Comes o'er the eastern hill, thou
　　shalt accost him—
' Now do thy worst, thou oft-returning
　　spy,
Here 's nought thou canst discover.'
　　AUCH. Yet goest thou not alone
　　　　with that MacLellan!
He deems thou bearest will to injure
　　him,
And seek'st occasion suiting to such
　　will.
Philip, thou art irreverent, fierce, ill-
　　nurtured,
Stain'd with low vices, which disgust
　　a father ;
Yet ridest thou not alone with yonder
　　man.
Come weal come woe, myself will go
　　with thee.
　　　　[Exit, and calls to horse behind the
　　　　scene.
　　PHIL. (alone). Now would I give
　　　　my fleetest horse to know
What sudden thought roused this
　　paternal care,
And if 'tis on his own account or
　　mine.
'Tis true, he hath the deepest share
　　in all
That 's likely now to hap, or which
　　has happen'd.
Yet strong through Nature's universal
　　reign
The link which binds the parent to
　　the offspring :
The she-wolf knows it, and the tigress
　　owns it.
So that dark man, who, shunning
　　what is vicious,
Ne'er turn'd aside from an atrocity,
Hath still some care left for his
　　hapless offspring.
Therefore 'tis meet, though wayward,
　　light, and stubborn,
That I should do for him all that a son

Can do for sire; and, his dark wisdom
　　join'd
To influence my bold courses, 'twill
　　be hard
To break our mutual purpose.—Horses
　　there !　　　　　　　　　⌊Exit.

—◆—

ACT III.

SCENE I.

*It is moonlight.　The scene is the Beach
beneath the Tower which was exhibited
in the first scene, but the Vessel is gone
from her anchorage.　AUCHINDRANE
and PHILIP, as if dismounted from
their horses, come forward cautiously.*

PHI. The nags are safely stow'd ;
　　their noise might scare him.
Let them be safe, and ready when
　　we need them :
The business is but short.　We 'll call
　　MacLellan,
To wake him, and in quiet bring him
　　forth,
If he be so disposed, for here are
　　waters
Enough to drown, and sand enough
　　to cover him.
But if he hesitate, or fear to meet us,
By heaven I 'll deal on him in Chapel-
　　donan
With my own hand !
　　AUCH. Too furious boy ! alarm or
　　　　noise undoes us ;
Our practice must be silent as 'tis
　　sudden.
Bethink thee that conviction of this
　　slaughter
Confirms the very worst of accusations
Our foes can bring against us.　Where-
　　fore should we,
Who by our birth and fortune mate
　　with nobles,

And are allied with them, take this
    lad's life,
His peasant life, unless to quash his
    evidence,
Taking such pains to rid him from the
    world,
Who would, if spared, have fix'd
    a crime upon us?
PHI. Well, I do own me one of
    those wise folks,
Who think that when a deed of fate
    is plann'd,
The execution cannot be too rapid.
But do we still keep purpose? Is 't
    determined
He sails for Ireland, and without
    a wherry?
Salt water is his passport; is it not so?
    AUCH. I would it could be other-
    wise.
Might he not go there while in
    life and limb,
And breathe his span out in another
    air?
Many seek Ulster never to return;
Why might this wretched youth not
    harbour there?
    PHI. With all my heart.   It is small
    honour to me
To be the agent in a work like this.
Yet this poor caitiff, having thrust
    himself
Into the secrets of a noble house
And twined himself so closely with
    our safety,
That we must perish, or that he must
    die,
I 'll hesitate as little on the action,
As I would do to slay the animal
Whose flesh supplies my dinner.
    'Tis as harmless,
That deer or steer, as is this Quentin
    Blane,
And not more necessary is its death
To our accommodation; so we slay it
Without a moment's pause or hesita-
    tion.

AUCH. 'Tis not, my son, the feeling
    call'd remorse,
That now lies tugging at this heart of
    mine,
Engendering thoughts that stop the
    lifted hand.
Have I not heard John Knox pour
    forth his thunders
Against the oppressor and the man of
    blood,
In accents of a minister of vengeance?
Were not his fiery eyeballs turn'd on
    me,
As if he said expressly 'Thou 'rt the
    man'?
Yet did my solid purpose, as I listen'd,
Remain unshaken as that massive rock.
    PHI. Well, then, I 'll understand
    'tis not remorse,
As 'tis a foible little known to thee,
That interrupts thy purpose.   What,
    then, is it?
Is 't scorn, or is 't compassion? One
    thing 's certain,—
Either the feeling must have free in-
    dulgence,
Or fully be subjected to your reason.
There is no room for these same
    treacherous courses
Which men call moderate measures.
We must confide in Quentin, or must
    slay him.
    AUCH. In Ireland he might live
    afar from us.
    PHI. Among Queen Mary's faithful
    partisans,
Your ancient enemies, the haughty
    Hamiltons,
The stern MacDonnells, the resentful
    Græmes?
With these around him, and with
    Cassilis' death
Exasperating them against you, think,
    my father,
What chance of Quentin's silence.
    AUCH. Too true, too true.   He is
    a silly youth, too,

Who had not wit to shift for his own
    living,
A bashful lover, whom his rivals
    laugh'd at;
Of pliant temper, which companions
    play'd on;
A moonlight waker, and a noontide
    dreamer;
A torturer of phrases into sonnets,
Whom all might lead that chose to
    praise his rhymes.

    Phi. I marvel that your memory
has room
To hold so much on such a worthless
    subject.

    Auch. Base in himself, and yet so
strangely link'd
With me and with my fortunes, that
    I've studied
To read him through and through, as
    I would read
Some paltry rhyme of vulgar prophecy,
Said to contain the fortunes of my
    house;
And, let me speak him truly, he is
    grateful,
Kind, tractable, obedient; a child
Might lead him by a thread. He shall
    not die!

    Phi. Indeed! Then have we had
our midnight ride
To wondrous little purpose.

    Auch.   By the blue heaven,
Thou shalt not murder him, cold selfish
    sensualist!
Yon pure vault speaks it! yonder
    summer moon,
With its ten million sparklers, cries
    Forbear!
The deep earth sighs it forth—Thou
    shalt not murder!
Thou shalt not mar the image of thy
    Maker!
Thou shalt not from thy brother take
    the life,
The precious gift which God alone
    can give!

    Phi. Here is a worthy guerdon
now, for stuffing
His memory with old saws and holy
    sayings!
They come upon him in the very
    crisis,
And when his resolution should be
    firmest,
They shake it like a palsy. Let it be,
He'll end at last by yielding to tempta-
    tion,
Consenting to the thing which must
    be done,
With more remorse the more he
    hesitates.

    [*To his Father, who has stood
fixed after his last speech.*

Well, sir, 'tis fitting you resolve at last,
How the young clerk shall be disposed
    upon;
Unless you would ride home to
    Auchindrane,
And bid them rear the Maiden in the
    court-yard,
That when Dunbar comes, he have
    nought to do
But bid us kiss the cushion and the
    headsman.

    Auch. It is too true; there is no
safety for us,
Consistent with the unhappy wretch's
    life!
In Ireland he is sure to find my
    enemies.
Arran I've proved, the Netherlands
    I've tried,
But wilds and wars return him on my
    hands.

    Phi. Yet fear not, father, we'll
make surer work;
The land has caves, the sea has whirl-
    pools,
Where that which they suck in returns
    no more.

    Auch. I will know nought of it,
hard-hearted boy!

PHI.   Hard-hearted!   Why,   my heart is soft as yours ;

But then they must not feel remorse at once,

We can't afford such wasteful tenderness :

I can mouth forth remorse as well as you.

Be executioner, and I 'll be chaplain,

And say as mild and moving things as you can ;

But one of us must keep his steely temper.

AUCH.   Do thou the deed—I cannot look on it.

PHI.   So be it! walk with me. MacLellan brings him.

The boat lies moor'd within that reach of rock,

And 'twill   require   our   greatest strength combined

To launch it from the beach. Meantime, MacLellan

Brings our man hither. See the twinkling light

That glances in the tower.

AUCH. Let us withdraw ; for should he spy us suddenly,

He may suspect us, and alarm the family.

PHI.   Fear not ; MacLellan has his trust and confidence,

Bought with a few sweet words and welcomes home.

AUCH.   But think you that the Ranger may be trusted ?

PHI.   I 'll answer for him.   Let 's go float the shallop.

[*They go off, and as they leave the Stage,* MACLELLAN *is seen descending from the Tower with* QUENTIN   *The former bears a dark lantern.   They come upon the Stage.*

MAC. (*showing the light*). So—bravely done! That'sthe last ledge of rocks,

And we are on the sands.   I have broke your slumbers

Somewhat untimely.

QUE.   Do not think so, friend.

These six years past I have been used to stir

When the réveillé rung; and that, believe me,

Chooses the hours for rousing me at random,

And, having given its summons, yields no license

To indulge a second slumber. Nay, more, I 'll tell thee,

That, like a pleased child, I was e'en too happy

For sound repose.

MAC.   The greater fool were you.

Men should enjoy the moments given to slumber ;

For who can tell how soon may be the waking,

Or where we shall have leave to sleep again?

QUE. The God of Slumber comes not at command.

Last night the blood danced merry through my veins :

Instead of finding this our land of Carrick

The dreary waste my fears had apprehended,

I saw thy wife, MacLellan, and thy daughter,

And had a brother's welcome ;—saw thee, too,

Renew'd my early friendship with you both,

And felt once more that I had friends and country.

So keen the joy that tingled through my system,

Join'd with the searching powers of yonder wine,

That I am glad to leave my feverish lair,

Although my hostess smooth'd my couch herself,

2 H

To cool my brow upon this moonlight
  beach,
Gaze on the moonlight dancing on the
  waves.
Such scenes are wont to soothe me
  into melancholy ;
But such the hurry of my spirits now,
That every thing I look on makes me
  laugh.
    MAC. I 've seen but few so game-
    some, Master Quentin,
Being roused from sleep so suddenly
  as you were.
    QUE. Why, there 's the jest on 't.
    Your old castle 's haunted.
In vain the host, in vain the lovely
  hostess,
In kind addition to all means of rest,
Add their best wishes for our sound
  repose,
When some hobgoblin brings a press-
  ing message ;
Montgomery presently must see his
  sergeant,
And up gets Hildebrand, and off he
  trudges.
I can't but laugh to think upon the
  grin
With which he doff'd the kerchief he
  had twisted
Around his brows, and put his morion
  on.
Ha ! ha ! ha ! ha !
    MAC. I 'm glad to see you merry,
    Quentin.
    QUE. Why, faith, my spirits are but
    transitory,
And you may live with me a month or
  more,
And never see me smile. Then some
  such trifle
As yonder little maid of yours would
  laugh at,
Will serve me for a theme of merriment.
Even now, I scarce can keep my
  gravity ;

We were so snugly settled in our
  quarters,
With full intent to let the sun be high
Ere we should leave our beds ; and
  first the one
And then the other 's summon'd briefly
  forth,
To the old tune, ' Black Bandsmen,
  up and march ! '
    MAC. Well ! you shall sleep anon,
    rely upon it,
And make up time misspent. Mean-
  time, methinks,
You are so merry on your broken
  slumbers,
You ask'd not why I call'd you.
    QUE.   I can guess,
You lack my aid to search the weir for
  seals,
You lack my company to stalk a deer.
Think you I have forgot your silvan
  tasks,
Which oft you have permitted me to
  share,
Till days that we were rivals ?
    MAC.   You have memory
Of that too ?
    QUE. Like the memory of a dream,
Delusion far too exquisite to last.
    MAC. You guess not then for what
    I call you forth ?
It was to meet a friend.
    QUE. What friend ? Thyself ex-
    cepted,
The good old man who 's gone to see
  Montgomery,
And one to whom I once gave dearer
  title,
I know not in wide Scotland man or
  woman
Whom I could name a friend.
    MAC.   Thou art mistaken,
There is a Baron, and a powerful
  one ——
    QUE. There flies my fit of mirth. You
    have a grave
And alter'd man before you.

MAC. Compose yourself, there is no cause for fear.

He will and must speak with you.

QUE. Spare me the meeting, Niel, I cannot see him.

Say I'm just landed on my native earth;

Say that I will not cumber it a day;

Say that my wretched thread of poor existence

Shall be drawn out in solitude and exile,

Where never memory of so mean a thing

Again shall cross his path; but do not ask me

To see or speak again with that dark man!

MAC. Your fears are now as foolish as your mirth.

What should the powerful Knight of Auchindrane

In common have with such a man as thou?

QUE. No matter what; enough, I will not see him.

MAC. He is thy master, and he claims obedience.

QUE. My master? Ay, my task-master! Ever since

I could write man, his hand hath been upon me;

No step I've made but cumber'd with his chain,

And I am weary on't. I will not see him.

MAC. You must and shall; there is no remedy.

QUE. Take heed that you compel me not to find one.

I've seen the wars since we had strife together;

To put my late experience to the test

Were something dangerous—Ha, I am betray'd!

[*While the latter part of this dialogue is passing,* AUCHINDRANE *and*

PHILIP *enter on the Stage from behind, and suddenly present themselves.*

AUCH. What says the runagate?

QUE. (*laying aside all appearance of resistance*). Nothing, you are my fate;

And in a shape more fearfully resistless,

My evil angel could not stand before me.

AUCH. And so you scruple, slave, at my command,

To meet me when I deign to ask thy presence?

QUE. No, sir; I had forgot I am your bond-slave;

But sure a passing thought of independence,

For which I've seen whole nations doing battle,

Was not, in one who has so long enjoy'd it,

A crime beyond forgiveness.

AUCH.   We shall see:

Thou wert my vassal, born upon my land,

Bred by my bounty; it concern'd me highly,

Thou know'st it did; and yet against my charge

Again I find thy worthlessness in Scotland.

QUE. Alas! the wealthy and the powerful know not

How very dear to those who have least share in't,

Is that sweet word of country! The poor exile

Feels, in each action of the varied day,

His doom of banishment. The very air

Cools not his brow as in his native land;

The scene is strange, the food is loathly to him;

The language, nay, the music jars his ear.

Why should I, guiltless of the slightest crime,

Suffer a punishment which, sparing life,
Deprives that life of all which men
    hold dear?

    AUCH. Hear ye the serf I bred,
      begin to reckon
Upon his rights and pleasure! Who
    am I?
Thou abject, who am I, whose will
    thou thwartest?

    PHI Well spoke, my pious sire!
      There goes remorse!
Let once thy precious pride take fire,
    and then,
MacLellan, you and I may have small
    trouble.

    QUE. Your words are deadly, and
    your power resistless.
I'm in your hands; but, surely, less
    than life
May give you the security you seek,
Without commission of a mortal crime.

    AUCH. Who is't would deign to
    think upon thy life?
I but require of thee to speed to Ireland,
Where thou mayst sojourn for some
    little space,
Having due means of living dealt to
    thee,
And, when it suits the changes of the
    times,
Permission to return.

    QUE.   Noble my lord,
I am too weak to combat with your
    pleasure;
Yet O for mercy's sake, and for the
    sake
Of that dear land which is our common
    mother,
Let me not part in darkness from my
    country!
Pass but an hour or two, and every cape,
Headland, and bay, shall gleam with
    new-born light,
And I'll take boat as gaily as the bird
That soars to meet the morning.
Grant me but this, to show no darker
    thoughts

Are on your heart than those your
    speech expresses!

    PHI. A modest favour, friend, is
    this you ask!
Are we to pace the beach like water-
    men,
Waiting your worship's pleasure to
    take boat?
No, by my faith! you go upon the
    instant.
The boat lies ready, and the ship
    receives you
Near to the point of Turnberry.
    Come, we wait you;
Bestir you!

    QUE. I obey. Then farewell, Scot-
    land
And Heaven forgive my sins, and
    grant that mercy,
Which mortal man deserves not!

    AUCH. (*speaking aside to his Son*).
                    What signal
Shall let me know 'tis done?

    PHI.   When the light is quench'd,
Your fears for Quentin Blane are at
    an end.
(*To* QUE.) Come, comrade, come, we
    must begin our voyage.

    QUE. But when, O when to end it!

    [*He goes off reluctantly with* PHILIP
      and MACLELLAN. AUCHIN-
      DRANE *stands looking after them.*
      The Moon becomes overclouded,
      and the Stage dark. AUCHIN-
      DRANE, *who has gazed fixedly*
      and eagerly after those who have
      left the Stage, becomes animated,
      and speaks.

    AUCH. It is no fallacy! The night
    is dark,
The moon has sunk before the
    deepening clouds;
I cannot on the murky beach dis-
    tinguish
The shallop from the rocks which lie
    beside it;

I cannot see tall Philip's floating plume,
Nor trace the sullen brow of Niel
    MacLellan ;
Yet still that caitiff's visage is before me ;
With chattering teeth, mazed look,
    and bristling hair,
As he stood here this moment ! Have
    I changed
My human eyes for those of some
    night prowler,
The wolf's, the tiger-cat's, or the
    hoarse bird's
That spies its prey at midnight ?
    I can see him —
Yes, I can see him, seeing no one else, —
And well it is I do so. In his absence,
Strange thoughts of pity mingled with
    my purpose,
And moved remorse within me. But
    they vanish'd
Whene'er he stood a living man before
    me ;
Then my antipathy awaked within me,
Seeing its object close within my
    reach,
Till I could scarce forbear him. How
    they linger !
The boat's not yet to sea ! I ask myself,
What has the poor wretch done to
    wake my hatred —
Docile, obedient, and in sufferance
    patient ?
As well demand what evil has the hare
Done to the hound that courses her
    in sport.
Instinct infallible supplies the reason ;
And that must plead my cause. The
    vision's gone !
Their boat now walks the waves ;
    a single gleam,
Now seen, now lost, is all that marks
    her course ;
That soon shall vanish too—then all
    is over !
Would it were o'er, for in this
    moment lies
The agony of ages ! Now, 'tis gone—

And all is acted ! No ! she breasts
    again
The opposing wave, and bears the
    tiny sparkle
Upon her crest — (*A faint cry heard as
    from seaward.*)
        Ah ! there was fatal evidence,
All's over now, indeed ! The light
    is quench'd,
And Quentin, source of all my fear,
    exists not.
The morning tide shall sweep his
    corpse to sea,
And hide all memory of this stern
    night's work.

[*He walks in a slow and deeply
    meditative manner towards the
    side of the Stage, and suddenly
    meets* MARION, *the wife of* MAC-
    LELLAN, *who has descended from
    the Castle.*

Now, how to meet Dunbar — Heaven
    guard my senses !
Stand ! who goes there ? Do spirits
    walk the earth
Ere yet they 've left the body !
MAR.   Is it you,
My lord, on this wild beach at such
    an hour !
    AUCH. It is MacLellan's wife, in
    search of him
Or of her lover, of the murderer,
Or of the murder'd man. Go to,
    Dame Marion,
Men have their hunting-gear to give
    an eye to,
Their snares and trackings for their
    game. But women
Should shun the night air. A young
    wife also,
Still more a handsome one, should
    keep her pillow
Till the sun gives example for her
    wakening.
Come, dame, go back ; back to your
    bed again.

MAR. Hear me, my lord! there have been sights and sounds
That terrified my child and me. Groans, screams,
As if of dying seamen, came from ocean ;
A corpse-light danced upon the crested waves
For several minutes' space, then sunk at once.
When we retired to rest we had two guests,
Besides my husband Niel ; I 'll tell your lordship
Who the men were ———
AUCH. Pshaw, woman, can you think
That I have any interest in your gossips?
Please your own husband ; and that you may please him,
Get thee to bed, and shut up doors, good dame.
Were I MacLellan, I should scarce be satisfied
To find thee wandering here in mist and moonlight,
When silence should be in thy habitation,
And sleep upon thy pillow.
MAR.   Good, my lord,
This is a holiday. By an ancient custom
Our children seek the shore at break of day,
And gather shells, and dance, and play, and sport them
In honour of the Ocean. Old men say
The custom is derived from heathen times. Our Isabel
Is mistress of the feast, and you may think
She is awake already, and impatient
To be the first shall stand upon the beach,
And bid the sun good-morrow.
AUCH.   Ay, indeed?
Linger such dregs of heathendom among you ?

And hath Knox preach'd, and Wishart died, in vain ?
Take notice, I forbid these sinful practices,
And will not have my followers mingle in them.
MAR. If such your honour's pleasure, I must go
And lock the door on Isabel ; she is wilful,
And voice of mine will have small force to keep her
From the amusement she so long has dream'd of.
But I must tell your honour, the old people,
That were survivors of the former race,
Prophesied evil if this day should pass
Without due homage to the mighty Ocean.
AUCH. Folly and Papistry ! Perhaps the ocean
Hath had his morning sacrifice already ;
Or can you think the dreadful element,
Whose frown is death, whose roar the dirge of navies,
Will miss the idle pageant you prepare for ?
I 've business for you, too ; The dawn advances—
I 'd have thee lock thy little child in safety,
And get to Auchindrane before the sun rise ;
Tell them to get a royal banquet ready,
As if a king were coming there to feast him.
MAR. I will obey your pleasure. But my husband——
AUCH. I wait him on the beach, and bring him in
To share the banquet.
MAR.   But he has a friend,

Whom it would ill become him to intrude
Upon your hospitality.

AUCH. Fear not ; his friend shall be
made welcome too,
Should he return with Niel.

MAR. He must, he will return ; he
has no option

AUCH. (apart). Thus rashly do we
deem of others' destiny !
He has indeed no option—but he
comes not.
Begone on thy commission ! I go this
way
To meet thy husband.

[MARION goes to her Tower, and
after entering it, is seen to come
out, lock the door, and leave the
Stage, as if to execute AUCHIN-
DRANE'S commission. He, apparently going off in a different
direction, has watched her from
the side of the Stage, and on her
departure speaks.

AUCH. Fare thee well, fond woman,
Most dangerous of spies; thou pry-
ing, prating,
Spying, and telling woman ! I 've cut
short
Thy   dangerous   testimony—hated
word !
What other evidence have we cut short,
And by what fated means, this dreary
morning !
Bright lances here and helmets ? I
must shift
To join the others.   [Exit.

Enter from the other side the SERGEANT,
accompanied with an officer and
two Pikemen.

SER. 'Twas in good time you came ;
a minute later
The knaves had ta'en my dollars and
my life.

OFF. You fought most stoutly.
Two of them were down,
Ere we came to your aid.

SER.   Gramercy, halberd !
And well it happens, since your leader
seeks
This Quentin Blane, that you have
fall'n on me ;
None else can surely tell you where
he hides,
Being in some fear, and bent to quit
this province.

OFF. 'Twill do our Earl good service.
He has sent
Despatches   into   Holland   for   this
Quentin.

SER. I left him two hours since
in yonder tower,
Under the guard of one who smoothly
spoke,
Although he look'd but roughly ; I
will chide him
For bidding me go forth with yonder
traitor.

OFF. Assure yourself 'twas a con-
certed stratagem.
Montgomery 's been at Holyrood for
months,
And can have sent no letter ; 'twas
a plan
On you and on your dollars, and
a base one,
To which this Ranger was most likely
privy ;
Such men as he hang on our fiercer
barons,
The   ready   agents   of   their   lawless
will ;
Boys of the belt, who aid their master's
pleasures,
And in his moods ne'er scruple his
injunctions.
But haste, for now we must unkennel
Quentin ;
I 've strictest charge concerning him.

SER. Go up, then, to the tower ;
You 've younger limbs than mine.
There shall you find him
Lounging and snoring, like a lazy cur
Before a stable door ; it is his practice.

[*The* OFFICER *goes up to the Tower,
and after knocking without receiving an answer, turns the key
which* MARION *had left in the
lock, and enters;* ISABEL, *dressed
as if for her dance, runs out
and descends to the Stage; the*
OFFICER *follows.*

OFF. There 's no one in the house,
   this little maid
Excepted.

ISA. And for me, I 'm there no longer,
And will not be again for three hours
   good :
I 'm gone to join my playmates on
   the sands.

OFF. (*detaining her*). You shall,
   when you have told to me distinctly
Where are the guests who slept up
   there last night.

ISA. Why, there is the old man, he
   stands beside you,
The merry old man, with the glistening
   hair ;
He left the tower at midnight, for my
   father
Brought him a letter.

SER.   In ill hour I left you,
I wish to Heaven that I had stay'd
   with you ;
There is a nameless horror that comes
   o'er me.
Speak, pretty maiden, tell us what
   chanced next,
And thou shalt have thy freedom.

ISA. After you went last night, my
   father
Grew moody, and refused to doff his
   clothes,
Or go to bed, as sometimes he will do
When there is aught to chafe him.
   Until past midnight,
He wander'd to and fro, then call'd
   the stranger,
The gay young man, that sung such
   merry songs,

Yet ever look'd most sadly whilst he
   sung them,
And forth they went together.

OFF.   And you 've seen
Or heard nought of them since !

ISA. Seen surely nothing, and I
   cannot think
That they have lot or share in what
   I heard.
I heard my mother praying, for the
   corpse-lights
Were dancing on the waves; and at
   one o'clock,
Just as the Abbey steeple toll'd the
   knell,
There was a heavy plunge upon the
   waters,
And some one cried aloud for mercy !
   —mercy !
It was the water-spirit, sure, which
   promised
Mercy to boat and fisherman, if we
Perform'd to-day's rites duly. Let
   me go ;
I am to lead the ring.

OFF. (*to* SER.) Detain her not. She
   cannot tell us more ;
To give her liberty is the sure way
To lure her parents homeward.
   Strahan, take two men,
And should the father or the mother
   come,
Arrest them both, or either. Auchin-
   drane
May come upon the beach; arrest
   him also,
But do not state a cause. I 'll back
   again,
And take directions from my Lord
   Dunbar.
Keep you upon the beach, and have
   an eye
To all that passes there.

            [*Exeunt separately.*

SCENE II.

Scene changes to a remote and rocky part of the Seabeach.

Enter AUCHINDRANE *meeting* PHILIP.

AUCH. The devil's brought his legions to this beach,
That wont to be so lonely; morions, lances,
Show in the morning beam as thick as glowworms
At summer midnight.

PHI. I'm right glad to see them,
Be they whoe'er they may, so they are mortal;
For I've contended with a lifeless foe,
And I have lost the battle. I would give
A thousand crowns to hear a mortal steel
Ring on a mortal harness.

AUCH. How now? Art mad, or hast thou done the turn—
The turn we came for, and must live or die by?

PHI. 'Tis done, if man can do it; but I doubt
If this unhappy wretch have Heaven's permission
To die by mortal hands.

AUCH. Where is he? where's MacLellan?

PHI. In the deep—
Both in the deep, and what's immortal of them
Gone to the judgment-seat, where we must meet them.

AUCH. MacLellan dead, and Quentin too? So be it
To all that menace ill to Auchindrane,
Or have the power to injure him! Thy words
Are full of comfort, but thine eye and look
Have in this pallid gloom a ghastliness,
Which contradicts the tidings of thy tongue.

PHI. Hear me, old man! There *is* a heaven above us,
As you have heard old Knox and Wishart preach,
Though little to your boot. The dreaded witness
Is slain, and silent. But his misused body
Comes right ashore, as if to cry for vengeance;
It rides the waters like a living thing,
Erect, as if he trode the waves which bear him.

AUCH. Thou speakest frenzy, when sense is most required.

PHI. Hear me yet more! I say I did the deed
With all the coolness of a practised hunter
When dealing with a stag. I struck him overboard,
And with MacLellan's aid I held his head
Under the waters, while the Ranger tied
The weights we had provided to his feet.
We cast him loose when life and body parted,
And bid him speed for Ireland. But even then,
As in defiance of the words we spoke,
The body rose upright behind our stern,
One half in ocean, and one half in air,
And tided after as in chase of us.

AUCH. It was enchantment! Did you strike at it?

PHI. Once and again. But blows avail'd no more
Than on a wreath of smoke, where they may break
The column for a moment, which unites
And is entire again. Thus the dead body
Sunk down before my oar, but rose unharm'd,

And dogg'd us closer still, as in
    defiance.
AUCH. 'Twas Hell's own work!
PHI. MacLellan then grew restive
And desperate in his fear, blasphemed
    aloud,
Cursing us both as authors of his ruin.
Myself was wellnigh frantic while
    pursued
By this dead shape, upon whose
    ghastly features
The changeful moonbeam spread a
    grisly light;
And, baited thus, I took the nearest
    way
To ensure his silence, and to quell his
    noise;
I used my dagger, and I flung him
    overboard,
And half expected his dead carcass
    also
Would join the chase; but he sunk
    down at once.
    AUCH. He had enough of mortal
    sin about him,
To sink an argosy.
    PHI. But now resolve you what
    defence to make,
If Quentin's body shall be recognised;
For 'tis ashore already; and he bears
Marks of my handiwork; so does
    MacLellan.
    AUCH. The concourse thickens still.
    Away, away!
We must avoid the multitude.

                    [*They rush out.*

SCENE III.

*Scene changes to another part of the
    Beach. Children are seen dancing,
    and Villagers looking on.* ISABEL
*seems to take the management of the
    Dance.*

VIL. WOM. How well she queens
    it, the brave little maiden!

VIL. Ay, they all queen it from
    their very cradle,
These willing slaves of haughty Auch-
    indrane.
But now I hear the old man's reign is
    ended;
'Tis well! he has been tyrant long
    enough.
    SECOND VIL. Finlay, speak low, you
    interrupt the sports.
    THIRD VIL. Look out to sea—
There's something coming yonder,
Bound for the beach, will scare us
    from our mirth.
    FOURTH VIL. Pshaw, it is but a sea-
    gull on the wing,
Between the wave and sky.
    THIRD VIL.   Thou art a fool,
Standing on solid land; 'tis a dead
    body.
    SECOND VIL. And if it be, he bears
    him like a live one,
Not prone and weltering like a
    drowned corpse,
But bolt erect, as if he trode the waters,
And used them as his path.
    FOURTH VIL.   It is a merman,
And nothing of this earth, alive or dead.

    [*By degrees all the Dancers break
    off from their sport, and stand
    gazing to seaward, while an
    object, imperfectly seen, drifts
    towards the Beach, and at length
    arrives among the rocks which
    border the tide.*

THIRD VIL. Perhaps it is some
    wretch who needs assistance;
Jasper, make in and see.
    SECOND VIL.   Not I, my friend;
E'en take the risk yourself, you'd put
    on others.

    [HILDEBRAND *has entered, and
    heard the two last words.*

SER. What, are you men?
Fear ye to look on what you must be
    one day?

I, who have seen a thousand dead and
dying
Within a flight-shot square, will teach
you how in war
We look upon the corpse when life
has left it.

[*He goes to the back scene, and
seems attempting to turn the
body, which has come ashore
with its face downwards.*

Will none of you come aid to turn
the body?

ISA. You're cowards all.   I'll help
thee, good old man.

[*She goes to aid the* SERGEANT
*with the body, and presently
gives a cry, and faints.* HILDE-
BRAND *comes forward.   All
crowd round him; he speaks
with an expression of horror.*

SER. 'Tis Quentin Blane!   Poor
youth, his gloomy bodings
Have been the prologue to an act of
darkness ;
His feet are manacled, his bosom
stabb'd,
And he is foully murder'd.   The
proud Knight
And his dark Ranger must have done
this deed,
For which no common ruffian could
have motive.

A PEASANT. Caution were best, old
man.   Thou art a stranger,
The Knight is great and powerful.
SER.   Let it be so.
Call'd on by Heaven to stand forth
an avenger,
I will not blench for fear of mortal
man.
Have I not seen that when that inno-
cent
Had placed her hands upon the
murder'd body,
His gaping wounds, that erst were
soak'd with brine,

Burst forth with blood as ruddy as
the cloud
Which now the sun doth rise on ?
PEA. What of that ?
SER. Nothing that can affect the
innocent child,
But murder's guilt attaching to her
father,
Since the blood musters in the victim's
veins
At the approach of what holds lease
from him
Of all that parents can transmit to
children.
And here comes one to whom I'll
vouch the circumstance.

The EARL OF DUNBAR *enters with
Soldiers and others, having* AUCH-
INDRANE *and* PHILIP *prisoners.*

DUN. Fetter the young ruffian and
his trait'rous father !

[*They are made secure.*

AUCH. 'Twas a lord spoke it : I
have known a knight,
Sir George of Home, who had not
dared to say so.
DUN. 'Tis Heaven, not I, decides
upon your guilt.
A harmless youth is traced within
your power,
Sleeps in your Ranger's house—his
friend at midnight
Is spirited away.   Then lights are
seen,
And groans are heard, and corpses
come ashore
Mangled with daggers, while (*to*
PHILIP) your dagger wears
The sanguine livery of recent slaugh-
ter :
Here, too, the body of a murder'd
victim
(Whom none but you had interest to
remove)
Bleeds on a child's approach, because
the daughter

Of one the abettor of the wicked deed.
All this, and other proofs corroborative,
Call on us briefly to pronounce the doom
We have in charge to utter.

AUCH. If my house perish, Heaven's will be done!
I wish not to survive it; but, O Philip,
Would one could pay the ransom for us both!

PHI. Father, 'tis fitter that we both should die,
Leaving no heir behind. The piety
Of a bless'd saint, the morals of an anchorite,
Could not atone thy dark hypocrisy,
Or the wild profligacy I have practised.
Ruin'd our house, and shatter'd be our towers,
And with them end the curse our sins have merited!

END OF THE DRAMATIC PIECES.

𝔑otes to 𝔇ramatic 𝔓ieces.

—◆◆—

I. HALIDON HILL.

NOTE.

THOUGH the Public seldom feel much interest in such communications (nor is there any reason why they should), the Author takes the liberty of stating, that these scenes were commenced with the purpose of contributing to a miscellany projected by a much-esteemed friend. But instead of being confined to a scene or two, as intended, the work gradually swelled to the size of an independent publication. It is designed to illustrate military antiquities, and the manners of chivalry. The drama (if it can be termed one) is, in no particular, either designed or calculated for the stage.

The subject is to be found in Scottish history; but not to overload so slight a publication with antiquarian research, or quotations from obscure chronicles, may be sufficiently illustrated by the following passage from Pinkerton's *History of Scotland*, vol. i. p. 72.

'The Governor (anno 1402) dispatched a considerable force un er Murdac, his eldest son: the Earls of Angus and Moray also joined Douglas, who entered England with an army of ten thousand men, carrying terror and devastation to the walls of Newcastle.

'Henry IV was now engaged in the Welsh war against Owen Glendour; but the Earl of Northumberland, and his son, the Hotspur Percy, with the Earl of March, collected a numerous array, and awaited the return of the Scots, impeded with spoil, near Milfield, in the north part of Northumberland. Douglas had reached Wooler, in his return; and, perceiving the enemy, seized a strong post between the two armies, called Homildon-hill. In this method he rivalled his predecessor at the battle of Otterburn, but not with like success. The English advanced to the assault, and Henry Percy was about to lead them up the hill, when March caught his bridle, and advised him to advance no farther, but to pour the dreadful shower of English arrows into the enemy. This advice was followed by the usual fortune; for in all ages the bow was the English instrument of victory; and though the Scots, and perhaps the French, were superior in the use of the spear, yet this weapon was useless after the distant bow had decided the combat. Robert the Great, sensible of this at the battle of Bannockburn, ordered a prepared detachment of cavalry to rush among the English archers at the commencement, totally to disperse them, and stop the deadly effusion. But Douglas now used no such precaution; and the consequence was, that his people, drawn up on the face of the hill, presented one general mark to the enemy, none of whose arrows descended in vain. The Scots fell without fight, and unrevenged, till a spirited knight, Swinton, exclaimed aloud, 'O my brave countrymen! what fascination has seized you to-day, that you stand like deer to be shot, instead of indulging your ancient courage, and meeting your enemies hand to hand? Let those who will, descend with me, that we may gain victory, or life, or fall like men[1].' This being heard by Adam Gordon, between whom and Swinton there remained an ancient deadly feud, attended with the mutual slaughter of many followers, he instantly fell on his knees before Swinton, begged his pardon, and desired to be dubbed a knight by him whom he must now regard as the wisest and the boldest of that order in Britain. The ceremony performed, Swinton and Gordon descended the hill, accompanied only by one hundred men; and a desperate valour led the whole body to death. Had a similar spirit been shown by the Scottish army, it is probable that the event of the day would have been dif-

[1] 'Miles magnanimus dominus Johannes Swinton, tanquam voce horrida praeconis exclamavit, dicens, O commilitones inclyti! quis vos hodie fascinavit non indulgere solitae probitati, quod nec dextris conseritis, nec ut viri corda erigitis, ad invadendum aemulos, qui vos, tanquam damulos vel hinnulos imparcatos, sagittarum jaculis perdere festinant. Descendant mecum qui velint, et in nomine Domini hostes penetrabimus, ut vel sic vita potiamur, vel saltem ut milites cum honore occumbamus,' &c.—FORDUN, *Scoti-Chronicon*, vol. ii. p. 434.

ferent. Douglas, who was certainly deficient in the most important qualities of a general, seeing his army begin to disperse, at length attempted to descend the hill; but the English archers, retiring a little, sent a flight of arrows so sharp and strong, that no armour could withstand; and the Scottish leader himself, whose panoply was of remarkable temper, fell under five wounds, though not mortal. The English men-of-arms, knights, or squires, did not strike one blow, but remained spectators of the rout, which was now complete. Great numbers of the Scots were slain, and near five hundred perished in the river Tweed upon their flight. Among the illustrious captives was Douglas, whose chief wound deprived him of an eye; Murdac, son of Albany; the Earls of Moray and Angus; and about twenty-four gentlemen of eminent rank and power. The chief slain were, Swinton, Gordon, Livingstone of Calendar, Ramsay of Dalhousie, Walter Sinclair, Roger Gordon, Walter Scott, and others. Such was the issue of the unfortunate battle of Homildon.'

It may be proper to observe, that the scene of action has, in the following pages, been transferred from Homildon to Halidon Hill. For this there was an obvious reason; —for who would again venture to introduce upon the scene the celebrated Hotspur, who commanded the English at the former battle? There are, however, several coincidences which may reconcile even the severer antiquary to the substitution of Halidon Hill for Homildon. A Scottish army was defeated by the English on both occasions, and under nearly the same circumstances of address on the part of the victors, and mismanagement on that of

the vanquished, for the English long-bow decided the day in both cases. In both cases, also, a Gordon was left on the field of battle; and at Halidon, as at Homildon, the Scots were commanded by an ill-fated representative of the great house of Douglas. He of Homildon was surnamed *Tineman,* i.e. *Loseman,* from his repeated defeats and miscarriages; and, with all the personal valour of his race, seems to have enjoyed so small a portion of their sagacity, as to be unable to learn military experience from reiterated calamity. I am far, however, from intimating, that the traits of imbecility and envy attributed to the Regent in the following sketch, are to be historically ascribed either to the elder Douglas of Halidon Hill, or to him called *Tineman,* who seems to have enjoyed the respect of his countrymen, notwithstanding that, like the celebrated Anne de Montmorency, he was either defeated, or wounded, or made prisoner, in every battle which he fought. The Regent of the sketch is a character purely imaginary.

The tradition of the Swinton family, which still survives in a lineal descent, and to which the author has the honour to be related, avers, that the Swinton who fell at Homildon in the manner related in the preceding extract, had slain Gordon's father; which seems sufficient ground for adopting that circumstance into the following dramatic sketch, though it is rendered improbable by other authorities.

If any reader will take the trouble of looking at Froissart, Fordun, or other historians of the period, he will find, that the character of the Lord of Swinton, for strength, courage, and conduct, is by no means exaggerated.

WALTER SCOTT.

ABBOTSFORD, 1822.

II. MACDUFF'S CROSS.

NOTE.

THESE few scenes had the honour to be included in a Miscellany, published in the year 1823, by Mrs. Joanna Baillie, and are here reprinted, to unite them with the trifles of the same kind which owe their birth to the author. The singular history of the Cross and Law of Clan MacDuff is given, at length enough to satisfy the keenest antiquary, in *The Minstrelsy of the Scottish Border.* It is here only necessary to state, that the Cross was a place of refuge to any person related to MacDuff, within the ninth degree, who, having committed homicide in sudden

quarrel, should reach this place, prove his descent from the Thane of Fife, and pay a certain penalty.

The shaft of the Cross was destroyed at the Reformation. The huge block of stone which served for its pedestal is still in existence near the town of Newburgh, on a kind of pass which commands the county of Fife to the southward, and to the north, the windings of the magnificent Tay and fertile country of Angus-shire. The Cross bore an inscription, which is transmitted to us in an unintelligible form by Sir Robert Sibbald.

ABBOTSFORD,
January, 1830

III. THE DOOM OF DEVORGOIL.

NOTE.

THE first of these dramatic pieces was long since written, for the purpose of obliging the late Mr. Terry, then Manager of the Adelphi Theatre, for whom the Author had a particular regard. The manner in which the mimic goblins of Devorgoil are intermixed with the supernatural machinery, was found to be objectionable, and the production had other faults, which rendered it unfit for representation. I have called the piece a Melodrama, for want of a better name ; but, as I learn from the unquestionable authority of Mr. Colman's Random Records, that one species of the drama is termed an *extravaganza*, I am sorry I was not sooner aware of a more appropriate name than that which I had selected for Devorgoil.

The Author's Publishers thought it desirable, that the scenes, long condemned to oblivion, should be united to similar attempts of the same kind ; and as he felt indifferent on the subject, they are printed in the same volume with Halidon Hill and MacDuff's Cross, and thrown off in a separate form, for the convenience of those who possess former editions of the Author's Poetical Works.

The general story of the Doom of Devorgoil is founded on an old Scottish tradition, the scene of which lies in Galloway. The crime supposed to have occasioned the misfortunes of this devoted house, is similar to that of a Lord Herries of Hoddam Castle, who is the principal personage of Mr. Charles Kirkpatrick Sharpe's interesting ballad, in *The Minstrelsy of the Scottish Border*, vol. iv. p. 307. In remorse for his crime, he built the singular monument called the Tower of Repentance. In many cases the Scottish superstitions allude to the fairies, or those who, for sins of a milder description, are permitted to wander with the 'rout that never rest,' as they were termed by Dr. Leyden. They imitate human labour and human amusements, but their toil is useless, and without any advantageous result ; and their gaiety is unsubstantial and hollow. The phantom of Lord Erick is supposed to be a spectre of this character.

The story of the Ghostly Barber is told in many countries ; but the best narrative founded on the passage, is the tale called Stumme Liebe, among the legends of Musaeus. I think it has been introduced upon the English stage in some pantomime, which was one objection to bringing it upon the scene a second time.

ABBOTSFORD,
April, 1830.

IV. AUCHINDRANE, OR THE AYRSHIRE TRAGEDY.

Cur aliquid vidi ? cur noxia lumina feci
Cur imprudenti cognita culpa mihi est ?
OVIDII *Tristium, Liber Secundus.*

NOTE.

THERE is not, perhaps, upon record, a tale of horror which gives us a more perfect picture than is afforded by the present, of the violence of our ancestors, and the complicated crimes into which they were hurried, by what their wise, but ill-enforced, laws termed the heathenish and accursed practice of Deadly Feud. The author has tried to extract some dramatic scenes out of it ; but he is conscious no exertions of his can increase the horror of that which is in itself so iniquitous. Yet, if we look at modern events, we must not too hastily venture to conclude that our own times have so much the superiority over former days as we might at first be tempted to infer. One great object has indeed been obtained. The power of the laws extends over the country universally, and if criminals at present sometimes escape punishment, this can only be by eluding justice,—not, as of old, by defying it.

But the motives which influence modern ruffians to commit actions at which we pause with wonder and horror, arise, in a great measure, from the thirst of gain. For the hope of lucre, we have seen a wretch seduced to his fate, under the pretext that he was to share in amusement and conviviality ; and, for gold, we have seen the meanest of wretches deprived of life, and their miserable remains cheated of the grave.

The loftier, if equally cruel, feelings of

pride, ambition, and love of vengeance, were the idols of our forefathers, while the caitiffs of our day bend to Mammon, the meanest of the spirits who fell. The criminals, therefore, of former times, drew their hellish inspiration from a loftier source than is known to modern villains. The fever of unsated ambition, the frenzy of ungratified revenge, the *perfervidum ingenium Scotorum*, stigmatized by our jurists and our legislators, held life but as passing breath; and such enormities as now sound like the acts of a madman, were then the familiar deeds of every offended noble. With these observations we proceed to our story.

John Muir, or Mure, of Auchindrane, the contriver and executor of the following cruelties, was a gentleman of an ancient family and good estate in the west of Scotland; bold, ambitious, treacherous to the last degree, and utterly unconscientious,—a Richard the Third in private life, inaccessible alike to pity and to remorse. His view was to raise the power, and extend the grandeur, of his own family. This gentleman had married the daughter of Sir Thomas Kennedy of Barganie, who was, excepting the Earl of Cassilis, the most important person in all Carrick, the district of Ayrshire he inhabited, and where the name of Kennedy held so great a sway as to give rise to the popular rhyme,—

'Twixt Wigton and the town of Air,
Portpatrick and the Cruives of Cree,
No man need think for to bide there,
Unless he court Saint Kennedie.'

Now, Mure of Auchindrane, who had promised himself high advancement by means of his father-in-law Barganie, saw, with envy and resentment, that his influence remained second and inferior to the House of Cassilis, chief of all the Kennedys. The Earl was indeed a minor, but his authority was maintained, and his affairs well managed, by his uncle, Sir Thomas Kennedy of Cullayne, the brother of the deceased Earl, and tutor and guardian to the present. This worthy gentleman supported his nephew's dignity and the credit of the house so effectually, that Barganie's consequence was much thrown into the shade, and the ambitious Auchindrane, his son-in-law, saw no better remedy than to remove so formidable a rival as Cullayne by violent means.

For this purpose, in the year of God 1597, he came with a party of followers to the town of Maybole (where Sir Thomas Kennedy of Cullayne then resided) and lay in ambush in an orchard, through which he knew his destined victim was to pass in returning homewards from a house where he was engaged to sup. Sir Thomas Kennedy came alone, and unattended, when he was suddenly fired upon by Auchindrane and his accomplices, who, having missed their aim, drew their swords, and rushed upon him to slay him. But the party thus assailed at disadvantage had the good fortune to hide himself for that time in a ruinous house, where he lay concealed till the inhabitants of the place came to his assistance.

Sir Thomas Kennedy prosecuted Mure for this assault, who, finding himself in danger from the law, made a sort of apology and agreement with the Lord of Cullayne, to whose daughter he united his eldest son, in testimony of the closest friendship in future. This agreement was sincere on the part of Kennedy, who, after it had been entered into, showed himself Auchindrane's friend and assistant on all occasions. But it was most false and treacherous on that of Mure, who continued to nourish the purpose of murdering his new friend and ally on the first opportunity.

Auchindrane's first attempt to effect this was by means of the young Gilbert Kennedy of Barganie (for old Barganie, Auchindrane's father-in-law, was dead), whom he persuaded to brave the Earl of Cassilis, as one who usurped an undue influence over the rest of the name. Accordingly, this hot-headed youth, at the instigation of Auchindrane, rode past the gate of the Earl of Cassilis, without waiting on his chief, or sending him any message of civility. This led to mutual defiance, being regarded by the Earl, according to the ideas of the time, as a personal insult. Both parties took the field with their followers, at the head of about 250 men on each side. The action which ensued was shorter and less bloody than might have been expected. Young Barganie, with the rashness of headlong courage, and Auchindrane, fired by deadly enmity to the House of Cassilis, made a precipitate attack on the Earl, whose men were strongly posted and under cover. They were received by a heavy fire. Barganie was slain. Mure of Auchindrane, severely wounded in the thigh, became unable to sit his horse, and, the leaders thus slain or disabled, their party drew off without continuing the action. It must be particularly observed, that Sir Thomas Kennedy remained neuter in this quarrel, considering his connexion with Auchindrane as too intimate to be broken even by his desire to assist his nephew.

For this temperate and honourable conduct he met a vile reward; for Auchindrane, in resentment of the loss of his relative Barganie, and the downfall of his ambitious hopes, conti ued his practices against the life of Sir Thomas of Cullayne, though totally innocent of contributing to either. Chance favoured his wicked purpose.

The Knight of Cullayne, finding himself obliged to go to Edinburgh on a particular day, sent a message by a servant to Mure, in which he told him, in the most unsuspecting confidence, the purpose of his journey, and named the road which he proposed to take, inviting Mure to meet him at Duppill, to the west of the town of Ayr, a place appointed, for the purpose of giving him any commissions which he might have for Edinburgh, and assuring his treacherous ally he would attend to any business which he might have in the Scottish metropolis as anxiously as to his own. Sir Thomas Kennedy's message was carried to the town of Maybole, where his messenger, for some trivial reason, had the import committed to writing by a schoolmaster in that town, and despatched it to its destination by means of a poor student, named Dalrymple, instead of carrying it to the house of Auchindrane in person.

This suggested to Mure a diabolical plot. Having thus received tidings of Sir Thomas Kennedy's purpose, he conceived the infernal purpose of having the confiding friend who sent the information, waylaid and murdered at the place appointed to meet with him, not only in friendship, but for the purpose of rendering him service. He dismissed the messenger Dalrymple, cautioning the lad to carry back the letter to Maybole, and to say that he had not found him, Auchindrane, in his house. Having taken this precaution, he proceeded to instigate the brother of the slain Gilbert of Barganie, Thomas Kennedy of Drumurghie by name, and Walter Mure of Cloncaird, a kinsman of his own, to take this opportunity of revenging Barganie's death. The fiery young men were easily induced to undertake the crime. They waylaid the unsuspecting Sir Thomas of Cullayne at the place appointed to meet the traitor Auchindrane, and the murderers having in company five or six servants, well mounted and armed, assaulted and cruelly murdered him with many wounds. They then plundered the dead corpse of his purse, containing a thousand merks in gold, cut off the gold buttons which he wore on his coat, and despoiled the body of some valuable rings and jewels.

The revenge due for his uncle's murder was keenly pursued by the Earl of Cassilis. As the murderers fled from trial, they were declared outlaws; which doom, being pronounced by three blasts of a horn, was called 'being put to the horn, and declared the king's rebel.' Mure of Auchindrane was strongly suspected of having been the instigator of the crime. But he conceived there could be no evidence to prove his guilt if he could keep the boy Dalrymple out of the way, who delivered the letter which made him acquainted with Cullayne's journey, and the place at which he meant to halt. On the contrary, he saw, that if the lad could be produced at the trial, it would afford ground of fatal presumption, since it could be then proved that persons so nearly connected with him as Kennedy and Cloncaird had left his house, and committed the murder at the very spot which Cullayne had fixed for their meeting.

To avoid this imminent danger, Mure brought Dalrymple to his house, and detained him there for several weeks. But the youth tiring of this confinement, Mure sent him to reside with a friend, Montgomery of Skellmorly, who maintained him under a borrowed name, amid the desert regions of the then almost savage island of Arran. Being confident in the absence of this material witness, Auchindrane, instead of flying, like his agents Drumurghie and Cloncaird, presented himself boldly at the bar, demanded a fair trial, and offered his person in combat to the death against any of Lord Cassilis's friends who might impugn his innocence. This audacity was successful, and he was dismissed without trial.

Still, however, Mure did not consider himself safe, so long as Dalrymple was within the realm of Scotland; and the danger grew more pressing when he learned that the lad had become impatient of the restraint which he sustained in the island of Arran, and returned to some of his friends in Ayrshire. Mure no sooner heard of this than he again obtained possession of the boy's person, and a second time concealed him at Auchindrane, until he found an opportunity to transport him to the Low Countries, where he contrived to have him enlisted in Buccleuch's regiment; trusting, doubtless, that some one of the numerous chances of war might destroy the poor young man whose life was so dangerous to him.

But after five or six years' uncertain safety, bought at the expense of so much violence and cunning, Auchindrane's fears were exasperated into frenzy when he found this dangerous witness, having escaped from all the perils of climate and battle, had left, or been discharged from, the Legion of Borderers, and had again accomplished his return to Ayrshire. There is ground to suspect that Dalrymple knew the nature of the hold which he possessed over Auchindrane, and was desirous of extorting from his fears some better provision than he had found either in Arran or the Netherlands. But if so, it was a fatal experiment to tamper with the fears of such a man as Auchindrane, who determined to rid himself effectually of this unhappy young man.

Mure now lodged him in a house of his own, called Chapeldonan, tenanted by a vassal and connexion of his called James Bannatyne. This man he commissioned to meet him at ten o'clock at night on the sea-sands near Girvan, and bring with him the unfortunate Dalrymple, the object of his fear and dread. The victim seems to have come with Bannatyne without the least suspicion, though such might have been raised by the time and place appointed for the meeting. When Bannatyne and Dalrymple came to the appointed spot, Auchindrane met them, accompanied by his eldest son, James. Old Auchindrane, having taken Bannatyne aside, imparted his bloody purpose of ridding himself of Dalrymple for ever, by murdering him on the spot. His own life and honour were, he said, endangered by the manner in which this inconvenient witness repeatedly thrust himself back into Ayrshire, and nothing could secure his safety but taking the lad's life, in which action he requested James Bannatyne's assistance. Bannatyne felt some compunction, and remonstrated against the cruel expedient, saying, it would be better to transport Dalrymple to Ireland, and take precautions against his return. While old Auchindrane seemed disposed to listen to this proposal, his son concluded that the time was come for accomplishing the purpose of their meeting; and, without waiting the termination of his father's conference with Bannatyne, he rushed suddenly on Dalrymple, beat him to the ground, and, kneeling down on him, with his father's assistance accomplished the crime, by strangling the unhappy object of their fear and jealousy. Bannatyne, the witness, and partly the accomplice, of the murder, assisted them in their attempt to make a hole in the sand, with a spade which they had brought on purpose, in order to conceal the dead body. But as the tide was coming in, the holes which they made filled with water before they could get the body buried, and the ground seemed, to their terrified consciences, to refuse to be accessory to concealing their crime. Despairing of hiding the corpse in the manner they proposed, the murderers carried it out into the sea as deep as they dared wade, and there abandoned it to the billows, trusting that a wind, which was blowing off the shore, would drive these remains of their crime out to sea, where they would never more be heard of. But the sea, as well as the land, seemed unwilling to conceal their cruelty. After floating for some hours, or days, the dead body was, by the wind and tide, again driven on shore, near the very spot where the murder had been committed.

This attracted general attention, and when the corpse was known to be that of the same William Dalrymple whom Auchindrane had so often spirited out of the country, or concealed when he was in it, a strong and general suspicion arose, that this young person had met with foul play from the bold bad man who had shewn himself so much interested in his absence. It was always said or supposed, that the dead body had bled at the approach of a grandchild of Mure of Auchindrane, a girl who, from curiosity, had come to look at a sight which others crowded to see. The bleeding of a murdered corpse at the touch of the murderer, was a thing at that time so much believed, that it was admitted as a proof of guilt; but I know no case, save that of Auchindrane, in which the phenomenon was supposed to be extended to the approach of the innocent kindred; nor do I think that

the fact itself, though mentioned by ancient lawyers, was ever admitted to proof in the proceedings against Auchindrane.

It is certain, however, that Auchindrane found himself so much the object of suspicion from this new crime, that he resolved to fly from justice, and suffer himself to be declared a rebel and outlaw rather than face a trial. But his conduct in preparing to cover his flight with another motive than the real one, is a curious picture of the men and manners of the times. He knew well that if he were to shun his trial for the murder of Dalrymple, the whole country would consider him as a man guilty of a mean and disgraceful crime in putting to death an obscure lad, against whom he had no personal quarrel. He knew, besides, that his powerful friends, who would have interceded for him had his offence been merely burning a house, or killing a neighbour, would not plead for or stand by him in so pitiful a concern as the slaughter of this wretched wanderer.

Accordingly, Mure sought to provide himself with some ostensible cause for avoiding law, with which the feelings of his kindred and friends might sympathize ; and none occurred to him so natural as an assault upon some friend and adherent of the Earl of Cassilis. Should he kill such a one, it would be indeed an unlawful action, but so far from being infamous, would be accounted the natural consequence of the avowed quarrel between the families. With this purpose, Mure, with the assistance of a relative, of whom he seems always to have had some ready to execute his worst purposes, beset Hugh Kennedy of Garriehorne, a follower of the Earl's, against whom they had especial ill-will, fired their pistols at him, and used other means to put him to death. But Garriehorne, a stout-hearted man, and well armed, defended himself in a very different manner from the unfortunate Knight of Cullayne, and beat off the assailants, wounding young Auchindrane in the right hand, so that he wellnigh lost the use of it.

But though Auchindrane's purpose did not entirely succeed, he availed himself of it to circulate a report, that if he could obtain a pardon for firing upon his feudal enemy with pistols, weapons declared unlawful by act of Parliament, he would willingly stand his trial for the death of Dalrymple, respecting which he protested his total innocence. The King, however, was decidedly of opinion that the Mures, both father and son, were alike guilty of both crimes, and used intercession with the Earl of Abercorn, as a person of power in those western counties, as well as in Ireland, to arrest and transmit them prisoners to Edinburgh. In consequence of the Earl's exertions, old Auchindrane was made prisoner, and lodged in the tolbooth of Edinburgh.

Young Auchindrane no sooner heard that his father was in custody, than he became as apprehensive of Bannatyne, the accomplice in Dalrymple's murder, telling tales, as ever his father had been of Dalrymple. He, therefore, hastened to him, and prevailed on him to pass over for a while to the neighbouring coast of Ireland, finding him money and means to accomplish the voyage, and engaging in the meantime to take care of his affairs in Scotland. Secure, as they thought, in this precaution, old Auchindrane persisted in his innocence, and his son found security to stand his trial. Both appeared with the same confidence at the day appointed, and braved the public justice, hoping to be put to a formal trial, in which Auchindrane reckoned upon an acquittal for want of the evidence which he had removed. The trial was, however, postponed, and Mure the elder was dismissed, under high security to return when called for.

But King James, being convinced of the guilt of the accused, ordered young Auchindrane, instead of being sent to trial, to be examined under the force of torture, in order to compel him to tell whatever he knew of the things charged against him. He was accordingly severely tortured; but the result only served to show that such examinations are as useless as they are cruel. A man of weak resolution, or of a nervous habit, would probably have assented to any confession, however false, rather than have endured the extremity of fear and pain to which Mure was subjected. But young Auchindrane, a strong and determined ruffian, endured the torture with the utmost firmness, and by the constant audacity with which, in spite of the intolerable pain, he continued to assert his innocence, he spread so favourable an opinion of his case, that the detaining him in prison, instead of bringing him to open trial, was censured as severe and oppressive. James, however, remained firmly persuaded of his guilt, and by an exertion of authority quite inconsistent with our present laws, commanded young Auchindrane to be still detained in close custody till further light could be thrown on these dark proceedings. He was detained accordingly by the King's express personal command, and against the opinion even of his privy counsellors. This exertion of authority was much murmured against.

In the meanwhile, old Auchindrane, being, as we have seen, at liberty on pledges, skulked about in the west, feeling how little security he had gained by Dalrymple's murder, and that he had placed himself by that crime in the power of Bannatyne, whose evidence concerning the death of Dalrymple could not be less fatal than what Dalrymple might have told concerning Auchindrane's accession to the conspiracy against Sir Thomas Kennedy of Cullayne. But though the event had shown the error of his wicked policy, Auchindrane could think of no better mode in this case than that which had failed in relation to Dalrymple. When any man's life became inconsistent with his own safety, no idea seems to have occurred to this inveterate ruffian, save to murder the person by whom he might himself be in any way endangered. He therefore attempted the life of James Bannatyne by more agents than one. Nay, he had nearly ripened a plan, by which one Pennycuke was to be employed to slay Bannatyne, while, after the deed was done, it was devised that Mure of Auchnull, a connexion of Bannatyne, should be instigated to slay Pennycuke; and thus close up this train of murders by one, which, flowing in the ordinary course of deadly feud, should have nothing in it so particular as to attract much attention.

But the justice of Heaven would bear this complicated train of iniquity no longer. Bannatyne, knowing with what sort of men he had to deal, kept on his guard, and, by his caution, disconcerted more than one attempt to take his life, while another miscarried by the remorse of Pennycuke, the agent whom Mure employed. At length Bannatyne, tiring of this state of insecurity, and in despair of escaping such repeated plots, and also feeling remorse for the crime to which he had been accessory, resolved rather to submit himself to the severity of the law, than remain the object of the principal criminal's practices. He surrendered himself to the Earl of Abercorn, and was transported to Edinburgh, where he confessed before the King and council all the particulars of the murder of Dalrymple, and the attempt to hide his body by committing it to the sea.

When Bannatyne was confronted with the two Mures before the Privy Council, they denied with vehemence every part of the evidence he had given, and affirmed that the witness had been bribed to destroy them by a false tale. Bannatyne's behaviour seemed sincere and simple, that of Auchindrane more resolute and crafty. The wretched accomplice fell upon his knees, invoking God to witness that all the land in Scotland could not have bribed him to bring a false accusation against a master whom he had served, loved, and followed in so many dangers, and calling upon Auchindrane to honour God by confessing the crime he had committed. Mure the elder, on the other hand, boldly replied, that he hoped God would not so far forsake him as to permit him to confess a crime of which he was innocent, and exhorted Bannatyne in his turn to confess the practices by which he had been induced to devise such falsehoods against him.

The two Mures, father and son, were therefore put upon their solemn trial, along with Bannatyne, in 1611, and, after a great deal of evidence had been brought in support of Bannatyne's confession, all three were found guilty. The elder Auchindrane was convicted of counselling and directing the murder of Sir Thomas Kennedy of Cullayne, and also of the actual murder of the lad Dalrymple. Bannatyne and the younger Mure were found guilty of the latter crime, and all three were sentenced to be beheaded. Bannatyne, however, the accomplice, received the King's pardon, in consequence of his voluntary surrender and confession. The two Mures were both executed. The younger was affected by the remonstrances of the clergy who attended him, and he confessed the guilt of which he was accused. The father, also, was at length brought to avow the fact, but in other respects died as impenitent as he had lived;—and so ended this dark and extraordinary tragedy.

The Lord Advocate of the day, Sir Thomas Hamilton, afterwards successively Earl of Melrose and of Haddington, seems to have busied himself much in drawing up a statement of this foul transaction, for the purpose of vindicating to the people of Scotland the severe course of justice observed by King James VI. He assumes the task in a high tone of prerogative law, and, on the whole, seems at a loss whether to attribute to Providence, or to his most sacred Majesty, the greatest share in bringing to light these mysterious villanies, but rather inclines to the latter opinion. There is, I believe, no printed copy of the intended tract, which seems never to have been published; but the

curious will be enabled to judge of it, as it appears in the next *fasciculus* of Mr. Robert Pitcairn's very interesting publications from the Scottish Criminal Record.

The family of Auchindrane did not become extinct on the death of the two homicides. The last descendant existed in the eighteenth century, a poor and distressed man. The following anecdote shows that he had a strong feeling of his situation.

There was in front of the old castle a huge ash-tree, called the Dule-tree (*mourning tree*) of Auchindrane, probably because it was the place where the Baron executed the criminals who fell under his jurisdiction. It is described as having been the finest tree of the neighbourhood. This last representative of the family of Auchindrane had the misfortune to be arrested for payment of a small debt; and, unable to discharge it, was prepared to accompany the messenger (bailiff) to the jail of Ayr. The servant of the law had compassion for his prisoner, and offered to accept of this remarkable tree as of value adequate to the discharge of the debt. 'What!' said the debtor, 'Sell the Dule-tree of Auchindrane! I will sooner die in the worst dungeon of your prison.' In this luckless character the line of Auchindrane ended. The family, blackened with the crimes of its predecessors, became extinct, and the estate passed into other hands.

Index

Index of First Lines.

[*Mottoes from the* Waverley Novels *are not indexed here*]

PRINTED IN GREAT BRITAIN BY
MORRISON AND GIBB LIMITED, LONDON AND EDINBURGH